W9-CEA-146

FIFTH EDITION

**FIFTH EDITION**

# PSYCHOLOGY

**STEPHEN F. DAVIS**

Texas Wesleyan University

**JOSEPH J. PALLADINO**

University of Southern Indiana

PEARSON

Prentice
Hall

Upper Saddle River, New Jersey 07458

**Library of Congress Cataloging-in-Publication Data**

Davis, Stephen F.
    Psychology / Stephen F. Davis, Joseph J. Palladino.— 5th ed.
      p.  cm.
    Includes bibliographical references and index.
    1. Psychology—Textbooks.  I. Palladino, Joseph J.  II. Title.
    BF121.D35 2006
    150—dc22

                        2005037740

**Editor-in-Chief:** Leah Jewell
**Executive Editor:** Jessica Mosher
**Editorial Assistant:** William Grieco
**Developmental Editor:** Sarah Kravitz
**Senior Marketing Manager:** Jeanette Moyer
**Marketing Assistant:** Alexandra Trum
**Director of Production and Manufacturing:** Barbara Kittle
**Managing Editor (Production):** Joanne Riker
**Assistant Managing Editor:** Maureen Richardson
**Production Liaison:** Randy Pettit
**Production Editor:** Sarvesh Mehrotra, GTS-Techbooks, Inc.
**Permissions Supervisor:** Zachary Boka, ClearPerms, Inc.

**Manufacturing Manager:** Nick Sklitsis
**Manufacturing Buyer:** Sherry Lewis
**Creative Design Director:** Leslie Osher
**Interior and Cover Design:** Laura Gardner
**Director, Image Resource Center:** Melinda Reo
**Manager, Rights and Permissions:** Zina Arabia
**Manager: Visual Research:** Beth Brenzel
**Manager, Cover Visual Research & Permissions:** Karen Sanatar
**Image Permission Coordinator:** Nancy Siese
**Photo Researcher:** Kathy Ringrose
**Composition/Full-Service Project Management:** GTS-Techbooks, Inc.
**Printer/Binder:** Courier Companies, Inc.—Kendallville
**Tyepface:** 10/12 Janson Text

Credits and acknowledgments borrowed from other sources and reproduced, with permission, in this textbook appear on pages 762–765.

Pearson Education LTD.
Pearson Education Singapore, Pte. Ltd
Pearson Education, Canada, Ltd
Pearson Education—Japan

Pearson Education Australia PTY, Limited
Pearson Education North Asia Ltd
Pearson Educación de Mexico, S.A. de C.V.
Pearson Education Malaysia, Pte. Ltd

10 9 8 7 6 5 4 3 2 1
ISBN: 0-13-220840-7

# BRIEF CONTENTS

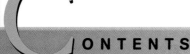

# CONTENTS

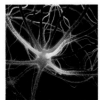

**CHAPTER 8**

Thinking, Language, and
Intelligence   322

**CHAPTER 9**

Development Across the Lifespan   376

**CHAPTER 10**

Sex and Gender   430

**CHAPTER 11**

Personality  476

**CHAPTER 12**

Psychological Disorders  516

**CHAPTER 13**

Therapy  572

**CHAPTER 14**

Health Psychology  612

**CHAPTER** 15

Social Psychology: The Individual in Society  **644**

**CHAPTER** 16

Industrial, Organizational, and Other Applications of Psychology  **688**

Stephen F. Davis is Professor Emeritus of Psychology at Emporia State University in Emporia, Kansas. Currently he serves as Visiting Distinguished Professor of Psychology at Texas Wesleyan University. In 2002–2003 he was the Knapp Distinguished Professor of Arts and Sciences at the University of San Diego. He received his bachelor's and master's degrees in psychology from Southern Methodist University and his Ph.D. in experimental psychology from Texas Christian University. His research, which always includes student assistants, has investigated such diverse topics as academic dishonesty, learning versus grade orientation of students, Type A personality, and the behavioral effects of ingesting toxic metals. He is the author of more than 290 journal articles, 17 books, and more than 850 convention presentations.

Steve's teaching abilities have drawn acclaim on the national level. He has received the National Distinguished Teaching of Psychology Award from the American Psychological Foundation and the Teaching Excellence Award from Division Two (Society for the Teaching of Psychology) of the American Psychological Association. His professional accomplishments also include serving as president of the Southwestern Psychological Association, the Southern Society for Philosophy and Psychology, and Division Two of the American Psychological Association. He also served as the National President of Psi Chi (The National Honor Society in Psychology). He has been elected as a Fellow of the American Psychological Association, the American Psychological Society, and the American Association of Applied and Preventive Psychology.

Joseph J. Palladino is Chair and Professor of Psychology at the University of Southern Indiana in Evansville, Indiana. He received all his academic degrees from Fordham University, including his Ph.D. in general theoretical psychology. His numerous articles and presentations have covered topics such as sleep and dreams, the death penalty, extra-credit opportunities, teaching methods, and techniques to encourage research by undergraduate students.

Joe founded the Mid-America Undergraduate Psychology Research Conference in 1982; it celebrated its 25th anniversary in April 2006. The Mid-America Conference for Teachers of Psychology, which he founded in 1984, became the model for regional teaching conferences. His contribution to the continuing education of teachers was recognized by the Faculty Service Award presented by the National University Continuing Education Association in 1991. In 1990 he received the Teaching Excellence Award from Division Two (Society for the Teaching of Psychology) of the American Psychological Association. He was elected to Fellow status in the American Psychological Association in 1989 and served as the president of Division Two in 1991–1992. He has also served Division Two as a consulting editor and the Methods and Techniques editor of Teaching of Psychology, and as chair of the program committee. In 2000 he received the University of Southern Indiana Alumni Association Faculty Recognition Award. He served as Midwestern Vice President of Psi Chi, The National Honor Society in Psychology (2000–2002). For years he and Mitch Handelsman of the University of Colorado at Denver wrote the column "On the Light Side." The column appeared in the Psi Chi newsletter, Eye on Psi Chi. Patterning Seinfeld, the two of them called it quits after nine years. Currently, Dr. Palladino is the Chair of the Division One (American Psychological Association) Humor Committee. He also enjoys speaking to faculty on "The Humor of Teaching; the Teaching of Humor." In addition, he created a number of the cartoons that accompanied the "On the Light Side" columns; and several of these now appear in this textbook.

# PREFACE

## TO THE INSTRUCTOR

We began the first edition of this text with the premise that introductory psychology may be the only psychology course your students ever take. With that in mind, we set out to write a text that would make the beginning psychology course an engaging, relevant, and interactive experience. We have maintained this philosophy in all five editions of this text.

Between the two of us, we have taught introductory psychology for over 60 years. Our experience has taught us that students would rather be "talked with" than "talked to." We hope that as students read the fifth edition of this book they will have the feeling they are engaging in a conversation with us. We have also attempted to convey the excitement and love of psychology that we hope characterize our own classes.

## OUR OBJECTIVES IN THE FIFTH EDITION

Our objectives for this edition were to make the book as accessible as possible to students, to encourage active learning through the design and features of our text, and to help students apply what they learn in this class to their own lives.

**Accessibility**   As in the first four editions of this text, our first objective is to make our book intellectually and financially accessible to students. We've worked hard to develop a conversational and interactive style of writing that will appeal directly to students. Rather than trying to impress colleagues with our command of the material, our primary interest is always making sure that the student comes away with a clear understanding of key principles. We're also very conscious of the fact that the cost of college tuition and textbooks can put a strain on students' (and parents'!) finances. That's why this book is priced significantly lower than most comprehensive, hardcover introductory psychology texts. We, along with Prentice Hall, are committed to providing students a quality educational package at the lowest possible price.

**Active Learning**   We believe that students learn better when they are actively engaged in the process, so we've built several features into each chapter that are designed to facilitate active learning. Each major section begins with a brief **vignette** that includes questions to spark interest and anticipation for the content to come. Several times within each chapter, **Psychological Detective** features ask students to consider a question about the topic under discussion. The question may deal with issues such as research ethics, how to conduct research, or the importance of a particular research finding. The student is asked to supply an answer to the question before reading further. **Hands-On** questionnaires and exercises bring your students into direct contact with the

material presented in the chapter. Each chapter also includes **Check Your Progress** quizzes after each major section. These allow students to test their mastery of the material they have just read and to prepare for exams.

Helping students succeed is the goal of every instructor; and toward that end we have incorporated two instructional aids in this edition. A "To the Student" study skills section (pp. xxi–xxvii) helps students assess their own learning styles and apply them in the areas of note taking, reading, memory, and test taking. We also have "Study Tips" in the margins of each chapter, which offer students specific strategies on how to master key concepts in the course.

**Applied Knowledge**   Psychology is a dynamic discipline that is constantly seeking new ways to apply knowledge gained from research. Within each chapter, we stress the wide range of practical applications of psychological research. Based on a thorough coverage of research methods and in the interest of making students better consumers of psychological information (see Chapter 1), we present these applied findings throughout to demonstrate the relevance of research to everyday life. Examples deal with sleep problems (Chapter 4), efforts to determine if people are telling the truth (Chapter 6), determining if individuals have problems with alcohol (Chapter 4), improving your memory (Chapter 7), and using personality tests in employment situations (Chapter 16).

## WHAT'S NEW IN THE FIFTH EDITION?

As in prior editions, we believe that the most effective approach is to continue to provide an interactive framework, numerous illustrations, and pedagogical aids designed to help students study and review material as they progress through each chapter. The 16 chapters of this text follow the sequence that has become standard in introductory psychology textbooks, beginning with the nature of psychology and its biological foundations and ending with maladaptive behaviors, therapy, health psychology, social psychology, and industrial/organizational psychology. One chapter not always found in other texts is Chapter 10, Sex and Gender. We believe that this topic is important enough in today's world to warrant an entire chapter.

Although a chapter on sex and gender is not always included in introductory textbooks, we decided to continue to include it for several reasons. First, reviewer input was positive on its coverage and supportive of its continued inclusion. Second, we believe the topics in this chapter (e.g., sex role stereotyping, sexual harassment) are important for understanding both the individual and society. Third, many of the topics in this chapter are not only inherently interesting to students (e.g., sexual behavior), it is very likely that they receive limited attention in other classes.

**New Material in Each Chapter** In preparing the fifth edition, we streamlined our presentation in all chapters, enhanced our coverage of several key topics, updated research examples, and introduced relevant and exciting new material. We also added additional photos and figures throughout to motivate the reader and amplify the exposition. Specific changes to the fifth edition include:

## Chapter 1—Psychology, Research, and You

- Addition of a section on the new and rapidly growing specialty, environmental psychology, with special emphasis on conservation psychology.
- Addition of new material on ethnic minorities in American psychology.
- Updated data on employment and salaries for psychologists.
- Updated data on receipt of psychology Ph.D.s by specialty area.

## Chapter 2—Behavioral Neuroscience

- Expanded coverage of neurotransmitters to include glutamate.
- Added current research that has identified new roles for the cerebellum.
- Material on plasticity of the brain has been greatly expanded and now includes historically significant material (i.e., brains of rats raised in enriched versus impoverished environments) and new data on brain changes that occur following various therapies intended to address problems ranging from stuttering to the motor effects of strokes.
- New, pedagogically effective figures on the autonomic nervous system and reflexes have been added along with talking graphics to enhance understanding of the operation of neurons.

## Chapter 3—Sensation and Perception

- Addition of new material on subliminal exposure.
- Addition of a section on the effects of talking on cell phones while performing complex tasks, such as driving.
- Addition of new material on the effects of sensory and perceptually isolated and confined environments.

## Chapter 4—States of Consciousness

- Updated information on the length of circadian rhythms to reflect current knowledge.
- Added National Sleep Foundation survey results on sleep length and sleep satisfaction.
- New information on the functions of sleep includes discussion of fatal familial insomnia and the cell repair hypothesis.

- Updated and expanded discussions of narcolepsy, sleep apnea, SIDS, and REM sleep behavior disorder; added a table comparing nightmares and night terrors in children.
- Updated all survey data on drug use, expanded discussion of binge drinking and its effects, added new material on meth and marijuana.

## Chapter 5—Basic Principles of Learning

- New figures enhance understanding of classical conditioning and reinforcement.
- Expanded discussion of the classical conditioning of attitudes.
- Added material on Thorndike and the Puzzle Box provides a historical context for discussion of operant conditioning.
- Clarified the difference between positive reinforcer (and negative reinforcer) and the processes of positive reinforcement and negative reinforcement.
- Expanded discussion of shaping, escape conditioning, and punishment.
- Updated and expanded material on observational learning of violence from various media.

## Chapter 6—Motivation and Emotion

- Added new material on cognitive dissonance and smoking.
- Expanded discussion of the prevalence of obesity and added a table of BMI values.
- Expanded discussion of anorexia nervosa and bulimia nervosa and added cross-cultural information on historical and current incidence.
- Added new information on attempts to design lie detection methods; added updates on legal aspects of such efforts.
- Added new information on emotional intelligence, including components that make up emotional intelligence.

## Chapter 7—Memory

- Added updates of information on paired associate learning, including the role of Mary Whiton Calkins.
- Added to the discussion of serial position effect and the curve of forgetting.
- New material on eidetic imagery.
- New information on the cognitive interviews describes ways psychologists have tried to reduce errors in eyewitness reports.
- New material on the pegword technique, and new table on memory illusions along with more memory activities for students.
- Extensive revision of figures to enhance student understanding.

## Chapter 8—Thinking and Intelligence

- Added several new problems for students to solve as they read the material, which enhance active learning.
- Updated material on multiple intelligences.
- Added material on the effects of early intervention programs on intelligence.
- Expanded table of milestones of language development.

## Chapter 9—Development Across the Lifespan

- Addition of new material on gender differences in adjustment to bereavement.
- Addition of new material on the lasting effects of childhood poverty.
- Addition of new material on the psychological and academic consequences of Internet use by low-income children.
- Addition of new material on attachment and culture, and attachment and mating.
- Addition of new material on supporting the functional independence of older adults via home technology.

## Chapter 10—Sex and Gender

- Expanded discussion of sexually transmitted diseases and added a table describing several of them.
- Added new material on the effects of stereotype vulnerability on the math achievement of females.
- Greatly revised, reorganized, and streamlined the discussion of sexual harassment.

## Chapter 11—Personality

- Addition of a new section on perfectionism.
- Addition of new material on Mayer's "Primary Four" alternative to the Big Five.
- Addition of new material on children who are prone to take risks.
- Addition of new material on the effects of acting extraverted.

## Chapter 12—Psychological Disorders

- Added new material and case on conversion disorder; updates of insanity cases discussed in the text.
- Greatly expanded the discussion of suicide with multiple examples and world-wide data.
- Updated discussion of the role of dopamine in the development of schizophrenia.
- Added new data illustrating physiological indicators found among those identified as exhibiting antisocial personality disorder.

## Chapter 13—Therapy

- Addition of a new section on the current status of the mental health system in the United States.

- Addition of a new section on delivering psychological treatment in rural areas.
- Addition of new material on the relation of religiosity/spirituality to treatment effectiveness.
- Addition of new material on mental health treatment in college students.
- Update of material on self-help sites and the Internet.

## Chapter 14—Health Psychology

- Addition of a section on the relation of religiosity/spirituality and health.
- Addition of new material on teens and smoking.
- Addition of new material on adult crying and its effect on health.
- Addition of current material on obesity, the American culture, and health.
- Addition of new material on the relation of anger and anxiety to health.

## Chapter 15—Social Psychology: The Individual in Psychology

- Addition of new material on affiliation.
- Addition of new material on stereotypes, especially "homegrown" stereotypes.
- Addition of new material on heat and violence.
- Addition of new section on terror management theory.

## Chapter 16—Industrial/Organizational and Applied Psychology

- Addition of new section on research methods in I/O psychology.
- Addition of new material on the development of corporate ethics.
- Addition of new material on the cost of alcoholism on production/productivity.

## DESIGN AND PEDAGOGY FOR ACTIVE LEARNING

In keeping with our goals of making this text accessible and encouraging active learning, we have devoted a great deal of attention to the text's design and pedagogical aids. Our experience in the classroom tells us that students tend to skip over material that is boxed or separated from the main narrative, viewing it as less important and not likely to be on the test. We have therefore made a deliberate decision not to include long sections of boxed material. Instead, we offer very brief features within the body of the text that encourage students to read actively, review often, and apply concepts immediately.

***Expanded Focus on Study Skills*** In response to reviewer feedback we have expanded the "To the Student" section at the beginning of the text to help students develop better study skills right from the start. This section includes an assessment tool to help students become aware of their own learning styles, as well as specific strategies for improving their skills in the areas of note taking, reading, memory, and test taking. We have revised and added more brief "Study Tips" in the margins of each chapter which offer specific suggestions for studying key concepts in the text.

*Chapter Outline* Each chapter begins with a detailed chapter outline that lets students know what to expect in that chapter.

*Chapter in Perspective* We open each chapter with a brief discussion of how the material fits with the "big picture." As we progress from the chapters that emphasize basic processes to those that deal with more complex behaviors, we show students how chapters build on one another to create a more complete understanding of behavior.

*Opening Vignettes* Each major section begins with a brief **vignette** that includes questions to spark interest and anticipation for the content to come.

*Psychological Detective* Every chapter includes several **Psychological Detective** features that ask students to consider a question about the topic under discussion. The question may deal with issues such as research ethics, how to conduct research, or the importance of a particular research finding. We ask the student to supply an answer to the question before reading further.

*Hands-On* We include at least one **Hands-On** activity in every chapter that features a questionnaire or similar interactive exercise. These activities bring the students into direct contact with the material presented in the chapter.

*Myth or Science* These brief sections compare the findings of psychological research with widely held popular notions and help students evaluate "pop psychology" claims.

*Margin Definitions* Since so much of the terminology in this course is new to students, we believe it is important to provide instant access to definitions. We therefore include the definition of each key term in the margin on the page where that term is introduced.

*Review Summaries and Check Your Progress Quizzes* Students learn material more effectively when it is presented in smaller "chunks" of information. We have therefore included **Review Summaries** and **Check Your Progress Quizzes** at the end of each major section within chapters. These "intellectual speed bumps" ask students to slow down, review what they have just read, and quiz themselves to determine if they have understood the previous section before moving on to the next. The total number of items contained in the **Check Your Progress** sections has been expanded to provide more comprehensive coverage of the material in each section.

## Print and Media Supplements for the Instructor

*NEW:* **OneKey** *for Psychology,* **Fifth Edition** New to this edition is Prentice Hall's all-inclusive online resource which offers instructors and students all of their resources—all in one place, available 24/7—all organized to accompany this text. With **OneKey,** you will enliven your lectures with more presentation material than you ever imagined. Your students will study smarter with the ebook and diagnostic test that creates a customized study plan designed to help students prepare for—and perform better on—exams. **OneKey** is available for instructors by going to **www.prenhall.com/onekey** and following the instructions on the page. **OneKey** is available in *WebCT, BlackBoard* or *Prentice Hall's Course Compass* formats. See your Prentice Hall representative for further information.

*Live!Psych* **Experiments and Activities** **NEW** to *Psychology, Fifth Edition* are *Live!Psych Experiments*  This series of over a dozen media experiments was developed to offer students an interactive way to master the major concepts presented in Introductory Psychology and to reinforce the scientific nature of the discipline. For each experiment, students are given an introduction to the experiment topic, a history and background for the specific experiment, instructions on how to complete the experiment and several test trials. The student's own individual data from the experiment is gathered, analyzed and compared to published studies to illustrate the significance of the results. Students can print or e-mail the results of their participation to instructors for a grade. The following experiments have been integrated into the text with marginal icons: Hemispheric Specialization, Serial Position Effects, Weber's Law, Memory Span, Depth of Processing, Mere Exposure Effect, Selective Attention, Priming/Ambiguous Figures, Transfer of Emotions, Classical Conditioning, Latent Learning, Mental Rotation, and more! For the development of the *Live!Psych* Experiments, a special thank you goes to Linda Lockwood, Metro State College, the content author, and to the members of our Live!Psych review board.

*Live!Psych* Activities offer over 30 highly interactive media simulations and animations, integrated into the text and developed to teach the key concepts, often the concepts students find most challenging and crucial to understanding psychology. Designed to get students to interact with the material and to appeal to different learning styles, these media activities were created in consultation with psychology instructors and carefully reviewed by a board of experts to ensure accuracy and pedagogical effectiveness.

Both *Live!Psych* Experiments and *Live!Psych* Activities are available in **OneKey** or on a CD-ROM. Contact your local Prentice Hall representative for more information.

*Instructor's Resource Manual* (0-13-220834-2) We believe that you will find a wealth of helpful information and other resources in the Instructor's Manual written by Laura Overstreet (Tarrant County College). The fifth edition IRM includes expanded "Lecture Enhancers" as well as demonstrations, activities, and student assignments. Each chapter describes how students can use resources on the Companion Website, *Live!Psych* and the Video Classics in Psychology CD-ROM as homework assignments or activities. The manual also offers a number of cross-cultural and multicultural resources and teaching ideas for each chapter.

*Test Item File (0-13-220835-0)* The authors' involvement in all aspects of the ancillary program for the fifth edition is clearly illustrated in the Test Item File, which was written by Joe Palladino. Drawing on his experience as a graduate student in Dr. Anne Anastasi's Test Construction class at Fordham University, Joe has carefully reviewed and rewritten the items to improve clarity and coverage of the material and to ensure that the vocabulary level is accessible to students.

The items continue to be coded as either definitional/factual or applied/conceptual. The Test Item File now includes a two-page Total Assessment Guide that lists all of the test items in an easy to reference guide.

*Instructor's CD-ROM (0-13-220831-8)* This valuable, time-saving supplement brings together all of the Davis and Palladino instructor resources in one convenient place. The CD-ROM offers presentation resources, including Power-Point presentations customized for this text. It also includes Word files for the Instructor's Resource Manual and the Test Item File.

*NEW: Prentice Hall's TestGen (0-13-220836-9)* Available on dual-platfom CD-ROM, this test generator program provides instructors with "best in class" features in an easy-to-use program. You can create tests using the TestGen Wizard to select questions and then modify them using the built in Question Editor. You can also create unlimited versions of a single test. The Quiz Master feature allows online test delivery. TestGen comes with an Instructor Gradebook and full technical support.

*PH Color Transparencies for Introductory Psychology 2006 (0-13-188688-6)* This set of over 120 full-color transparencies offers a wealth of illustrations, figures, and graphs from the text, as well as images from a variety of other sources.

*PowerPoint Presentations (on the Instructor's CD-ROM and the PsychologyCentral Website)* Cynthia Reed of Tarrant County College has created PowerPoint presentations for each chapter to give you even greater flexibility in your lectures. The presentations highlight all of the key points in each chapter of the text and include many graphics and tables from the text.

*Classroom Response Systems* Because Pearson Education has formed partnerships with the leading classroom-response systems on the market, instructors who are using a classroom response system with a Pearson textbook are entitled to student and department savings. Whether you are considering a system for the first time or are interested in expanding a program department-wide, Prentice Hall can help you select the best system for your needs. For more information please visit **http://www.prenhall.com/crs**.

## Video Resources for Instructors

Prentice Hall is proud to present you with the following video packages, available exclusively to qualified adopters of *Psychology, Fifth Edition*.

*NEW* **Introductory Psychology Teaching Films Boxed Set** Offering you an easy to use multi-DVD set of videos, organized by chapter topics, to incorporate into your Introductory Psychology course, this resource offers you over 80 short video clips of 5 to 15 minutes in length from many of the most popular video sources for Psychology content, such as ABC News; the *Films for the Humanities* series; PBS, and more! Available to qualified adopters, contact your local Prentice Hall Representative for more information.

*NEW* **Classic Experiments in Psychology from Pennsylvania State Media. Edited by Dennis Thompson, Georgia State University** This five DVD set includes videos for Introductory Psychology, Developmental Psychology, Social Psychology, Clinical Psychology, and Experimental Psychology. Each DVD includes the best-known classic film footage for key concepts and researchers in the field of Psychology. Most clips are from 5 to 15 minutes in length. Available to qualified adopters, contact your local Prentice Hall representative for more information.

*NEW* **Prentice Hall *Lecture Launcher* Video for Introductory Psychology** Adopters can receive this new video that includes short clips covering all major topics in introductory psychology. The videos have been carefully selected from the *Films for Humanities and Sciences* library and edited to provide brief and compelling video content for enhancing your lectures. Contact your local representative for a full list of video clips on this tape.

*The Brain* **Video Series** Qualified adopters can select videos from this series of eight, one-hour programs that blend interviews with world-famous brain scientists and dramatic reenactments of landmark cases in medical history. Programs include The Enlightened Machine, The Two Brains, Vision and Movement, Madness, Rhythms and Drives, States of Mind, Stress and Emotion, and Learning and Memory. Contact your local representative for more details.

**The *Discovering Psychology* Video Series** Qualified adopters can select videos from this series produced in association with the American Psychological Association. The series includes thirteen tapes, each containing two half-hour segments. Contact your local sales representative for a list of videos.

**Films for Humanities and Sciences Video Library** Qualified adopters can select videos on various topics in psychology from the extensive library of *Films for the Humanities and Sciences.* Contact your local sales representative for a list of videos.

### Print and Media Supplements for the Student

**NEW SafariX WebBooks**    This new *Pearson Choice* offers students a subscription to *Psychology, Fifth Edition* online at a 50% savings. With the SafariX WebBook, students can search the text, make notes online, print out reading assignments that incorporate lecture notes, and bookmark important passages. Ask your Prentice Hall representative for details, or visit **www.safarix.com.**

*Study Guide* (0-13-220838-5)    Prepared by Cynthia Smith and Margaret Felton at the University of Southern Indiana. The thoroughly revised study guide encourages students to reinforce their learning by providing chapter reviews and self-tests.

*Companion Website* (www.prenhall.com/davis)    All of the online resources on the Companion Website have been carefully created to reinforce students' understanding of the concepts in the text. Students can take online quizzes and get immediate scoring and feedback. Davis and Palladino's fifth edition Companion Website is found at **www.prenhall. com/davis.**

*Video Classics in Psychology* **CD-ROM**    Using the power of video to clarify key concepts in the text, this CD-ROM offers original footage of some of the best-known classic experiments in psychology, including Milgram's obedience study, Watson's Little Albert, Bandura's Bobo doll, Pavlov's dogs, Harlow's monkeys, and others. In addition, students can see interviews with renowned contributors to the field like B. F. Skinner, Carl Rogers, Erik Erikson, Carl Jung, and others. Each video is preceded by background information on the importance of that experiment or researcher to the field, and is followed by questions that connect the video to concepts presented in the text. The **Video Classics** CD-ROM can be packaged with Davis and Palladino's fifth edition. Contact your local representative for the value-pack ISBN.

*Audio Study Guide: VangoNotes*    Hear it. Get it. You're busy. We get it. With VangoNotes you can study "in between" all the other things you need to get done. VangoNotes gives you the confidence you need to succeed in the classroom. They're **flexible;** just download and go. And, they're **efficient.** Use them in your car, at the gym, walking to class, wherever. Get yours today and start studying. Go to **www.vangonotes.com** to purchase the audio study guide for Davis and Palladino's *Psychology 5e.*

*OneSearch Guide with ResearchNavigator*(™)    This guide gives students a quick introduction to conducting research on the Web and introduces Research Navigator(™). RN helps students find, cite, and conduct research with three exclusive databases: EBSCO's ContentSelect Academic Journal Database; *The New York Times* Search by Subject Archive; and Best of the Web Link Library. Ask your Prentice Hall representative for ordering information.

**Contact your Prentice Hall representative to package any of these supplementary texts with *Psychology, Fifth Edition*:**

*Current Directions in Introductory Psychology: Reading from the American Psychological Society*    This exciting reader includes over 20 articles that have been carefully selected for the undergraduate audience, and take from the very accessible *Current Directions in Psychological Science* journal. These timely, cutting-edge articles allow instructors to bring their students real-world perspective about today's most current and pressing issues in psychology.

*NEW: TIME Special Edition: Psychology*    Prentice Hall and *TIME Magazine* are pleased to offer you and your students a chance to examine today's most current and compelling issues in an exciting and new way. *TIME Special Edition: Psychology* offers a selection of fifteen *TIME* articles on today's most current issues and debates in the field of psychology. It is perfect for discussion groups, in-class debates, or research assignments.

*Forty Studies that Changed Psychology*, **Fifth Edition**    by Roger Hock (Mendocino College). Presenting the seminal research studies that have shaped modern psychological study, this brief supplement provides an overview of the environment that gave rise to each study, its experimental design, its findings, and its impact on current thinking in the discipline.

*The Psychology Major: Careers and Strategies for Success,* **Third Edition**    by R. Eric Landrum (Idaho State University), Stephen Davis (Emporia State University), and Terri Landrum (Idaho State University). This text provides valuable information on career options available to psychology majors, tips for improving academic performance, and a guide to the APA style of research reporting.

*How to Think Like a Psychologist: Critical Thinking in Psychology,* **Second Edition**    by Donald McBurney (University of Pittsburgh). This unique supplementary text uses a question-answer format to explore some of the most common questions students ask about psychology.

## ACKNOWLEDGMENTS

No textbook is the product of the authors' efforts alone. In preparing this fifth edition of *Psychology*, we have benefited from the insights of many colleagues in the discipline. First, we would like to thank the following colleagues who provided expert feedback and detailed suggestions for the fifth edition:

**Nancy Ashton,** *Richard Stockton College*
**LeAnn Binger,** *Richard Bland College*

**Chris Bloom,** *University of Southern Indiana*
**Robin Campbell,** *Brevard Community College*
**Keith Carroll,** *Benedictine University*
**Pamela Cingel,** *St. Thomas University*
**Julie Evey,** *University of Southern Indiana*
**Michael Feiler,** *Merritt College*
**Melissa I. Gebbia,** *Hofstra University*
**Thuy Karafa,** *Ferris State University*
**Susan P. Luek,** *Millersville University*
**Tracy Manning,** *Grossmont Community College*
**Glenn Meyer,** *Trinity University*
**Eleanor Midkiff,** *Palomar College*
**Lakshmi Narayanan,** *Florida Gulf Coast University*
**Cynthia J. Smith,** *University of Southern Indiana*

We would also like to express our thanks to the following individuals who reviewed this and prior editions of our text:

**Lois Attore,** *Orange Coast College*
**Ruth L. Ault,** *Davidson College*
**Ellen C. Banks,** *Daemen College*
**William A. Barnard,** *University of Northern Colorado*
**Jeff Bartel,** *Kansas State University*
**Joe Bean,** *Shorter College*
**Angela Becker,** *Indiana University–Kokomo*
**Barney Beins,** *Ithaca College*
**Daniel Berch,** *University of Cincinnati*
**Joy L. Berrenberg,** *University of Colorado at Denver*
**Amy D. Bertelson,** *Washington University*
**Deborah L. Best,** *Wake Forest University*
**Michael Best,** *Southern Methodist University*
**Jeanine R. Bloyd,** *Spoon River College*
**Charles Brewer,** *Furman University*
**Ross Buck,** *University of Connecticut*
**Stan Bursten,** *Cameron University*
**Joni Caldwell,** *Union College*
**David M. Carkenord,** *Longwood College*
**Peter Carswell,** *Asheville-Buncombe Technical Community College*
**Avi Chaudhuri,** *McGill University*
**Sandy Ciccarelli,** *Gulf Coast Community College*
**Ronald Comer,** *Princeton University*
**Gary Coover,** *Northern Illinois University*
**Catharine L. Cowan,** *Southwest State University*
**Michael Crabtree,** *Washington and Jefferson College*
**W. A. Cronin-Hillix,** *San Diego State University*
**Denys deCatanzaro,** *McMaster University*
**Patricia Decker,** *DeVry Institute of Technology*
**William Domhoff,** *University of California–Santa Cruz*
**Betty Dorr,** *Fort Lewis College*
**Julie Earles,** *Florida Atlantic University*
**Robert Emery,** *University of Virginia*
**Robert Emmons,** *University of California–Davis*
**Julie Evey,** *University of Southern Indiana*
**Roberta A. Eveslage,** *Johnson County Community College*

**Julie Evey,** *University of Southern Indiana*
**Sandra R. Fiske,** *Onondaga Community College*
**Karen E. Ford,** *Mesa State College*
**Grace Galliano,** *Kennesaw State College*
**Tracey Geer,** *University of Arizona*
**Judith Gibbons,** *St. Louis University*
**Peter J. Giordano,** *Belmont University*
**Nuria Giralt,** *University of Arizona*
**John Governale,** *Clark College*
**Richard A. Griggs,** *University of Florida*
**Sid Hall,** *University of Southern Indiana*
**Wayne Hall,** *San Jacinto College Central*
**Bernice B. Harshberger,** *Carteret Community College*
**Diane Herbert,** *SUNY Farmingdale*
**David K. Hogberg,** *Albion College*
**William D. Hopkins,** *Berry College*
**Phyllis A. Hornbuckle,** *Virginia Commonwealth University*
**James Huntermark,** *Missouri Western State College*
**Ted Jaeger,** *Westminster College*
**John Jahnke,** *Miami University*
**George G. Janzen,** *Ferris State University*
**Laurie L. Jensen,** *Northern State University*
**James M. Jones,** *University of Delaware*
**William Kelemen,** *University of Missouri–St. Louis*
**Mark Kelland,** *Lansing Community College*
**Allen Keniston,** *University of Wisconsin–Eau Claire*
**Stephen Klein,** *Mississippi State University*
**Sherry Lantinga,** *Dorot College*
**Patricia Lanzon,** *Henry Ford Community College*
**Randy Larsen,** *University of Michigan*
**Leslie Joy Larson,** *SUNY Farmingdale*
**Lindette Lent,** *Arizona Western College*
**Neil Lutsky,** *Carleton College*
**Salvador Macias III,** *University of South Carolina*
**Harold L. Mansfield,** *Fort Lewis College*
**Tom Marsh,** *Pitt Community College*
**Janet R. Matthews,** *Loyola University*
**Ron Mosher,** *Rock Valley College*
**David Murphy,** *Waubonsee College*
**David E. Neufeldt,** *Hutchinson Community College*
**Michele Paludi,** *Union College*
**Jeffrey Pedroza,** *Lansing Community College*
**Marites Pinon,** *Southwest Texas State*
**Retta E. Poe,** *Western Kentucky University*
**Janet Proctor,** *Purdue University*
**Patricia Puccio,** *College of DuPage*
**Elane Rehr,** *Diablo Valley College*
**Neil Salkind,** *University of Kansas*
**Lauren Scharff,** *Stephen F. Austin State University*
**Connie Schick,** *Bloomsburg University*
**H. R. Schiffman,** *Rutgers University*
**Brian Schrader,** *Emporia State University*
**George Schreer,** *Plymouth State College*
**Alan Schultz,** *Prince Georges Community College*
**Matthew J. Sharps,** *California State University–Fresno*

**Craig A. Smith,** *Vanderbilt University*
**Randolph A. Smith,** *Ouachita Baptist University*
**Steven M. Smith,** *Texas A&M University*
**Susan Nash Spooner,** *McLennan Community College*
**Kimberly Stoker,** *Holmes Community College*
**Chuck Strong,** *Northwest Mississippi Community College*
**Michael J. Strube,** *Washington University*
**Christopher Taylor,** *University of Arizona*
**DeAnna L. Timmerman,** *Roane State Community College*
**Larry R. Vandervert,** *Spokane Falls Community College*
**Eva D. Vaughan,** *University of Pittsburgh*
**Lisa Vogelsang,** *University of Minnesota-Duluth*
**Wilse Webb,** *University of Florida*
**Robert A. Wexler,** *Nassau Community College*
**Gordon Lee Whitman,** *Sandhills Community College*
**Patrick S. Williams,** *University of Houston–Downtown*

**Edie Woods,** *Madonna University*
**Janice Yoder,** *University of Akron*
**Otto Zinser,** *East Tennessee State University*

The editorial team at Prentice Hall deserves special praise.

Finally, we express our deepest appreciation to our own teachers. Among them we count Anne Anastasi, Virginia Chancey, David Landrigan, Wayne Ludvigson, Alvin North, and Jack R. Strange. Special thanks to "The Teacher of Teachers," Bob Daniel.

S.F.D.

J.J.P.

# TO THE STUDENT

## LEARNING STYLES—AN IMPORTANT PART OF SUCCESSFUL STUDYING

It happens in nearly every college course: Students listen to lectures throughout the semester. Each student hears the same words at the same time and completes the same assignments. However, after finals, student experiences will range from fulfillment and high grades to complete disconnection and low grades or withdrawals.

Many causes may be involved in this scenario—different levels of interest and effort, for example, or outside stresses. Another major factor is *learning style* (any of many particular ways to receive and process information). Say, for example, that a group of students is taking a freshman composition class that is often broken up into study groups. Students who are comfortable working with words or happy when engaged in discussion may do well in the course. Students who are more mathematical than verbal, or who prefer to work alone, might not do as well. Learning styles and capacities play a role.

There are many different and equally valuable ways to learn. The way each person learns is a unique blend of styles resulting from distinctive abilities, challenges, experiences, and training. To be a successful learner, you need to maximize your strengths and compensate for your weaknesses.

The assessment in this section, *Multiple Pathways to Learning*, will help you discover what those strengths and weaknesses are. With this information, you can set specific goals for positive change in how you study, manage time, remember material, and much more. The better you know yourself, the better you are able to handle different learning situations and challenges.

## MULTIPLE INTELLIGENCES THEORY

In 1983, Howard Gardner, a Harvard University professor, changed the way people perceive intelligence and learning with his Multiple Intelligences Theory. This theory holds that there are at least eight distinct *intelligences* possessed by all people, and that every person has developed some intelligences more fully than others. (Gardner defines an "intelligence" as an ability to solve problems or fashion products that are useful in a particular cultural setting or community.) According to the Multiple Intelligences Theory, when you find a task or subject easy, you are probably using a more fully developed intelligence; when you have more trouble, you may be using a less developed intelligence.

On the next page are descriptions of each of the intelligences, along with characteristic skills. The *Multiple Pathways to Learning* assessment, based on Gardner's work, will help you determine the levels to which your intelligences are developed. You will find the assessment on p. xxiii. As you complete the assessment, try to answer the questions objectively—in other words, answer the questions to best indicate who you are, not who you want to be (or who your parents or instructors want you to be). Then, enter your scores on p. xxiv. Don't be concerned if some of your scores are low—that is true for almost everyone.

## PUTTING ASSESSMENTS IN PERSPECTIVE

Before you complete the *Multiple Pathways to Learning* assessment, remember: No assessment has the final word on who you are and what you can and cannot do. An intriguing but imperfect tool, its results are affected by your ability to answer objectively, your mood that day, and other factors. Here's how to best use what this assessment, or any other, tells you:

**Use Assessments for Reference** Approach any assessment as a tool with which you can expand your idea of yourself. There are no "right" answers, no "best" set of scores. Think of your responses in the same way you would if you were trying on a new set of eyeglasses to correct blurred vision. The glasses will not create new paths and possibilities, but will help you see more clearly the ones that already exist.

**Use Assessments for Understanding** Understanding the level to which your intelligences seem to be developed will help prevent you from boxing yourself into categories that limit you. Instead of saying "I'm no good in math," someone who is not a natural in math can make the subject easier by using appropriate strategies. For example, a learner who responds to visuals can learn better by drawing diagrams of math problems. The more you know yourself, the more you will be able to assess and adapt to any situation—in school, work, and life.

**Face Challenges Realistically** Any assessment reveals areas of challenge as well as ability. Rather than dwelling on limitations (which may promote a negative self-image) or ignoring them (which may lead to unproductive choices), use what you know from the assessment to look at where you are and set goals that will help you reach where you want to be.

**Explore Strategies in All Areas** Following the assessment, you will see study strategies geared toward the four intelligences most relevant for studying this text. Explore many different strategies, not just the ones that apply to your strengths. Why? Because you have abilities in all areas, though some are more developed than others, you may encounter useful suggestions under any of the headings. Furthermore, your abilities and learning styles change as you learn, so you never know what might work for you. Finally, when you are faced with tasks and academic areas that you find difficult, strategies geared toward your weaker areas may help. For example, if you are not strong in logical-mathematical intelligence and have to take a math-heavy science course, the suggestions geared toward logical-mathematical learners may help you build what skill you have.

## Intelligences and Characteristic Skills

| Intelligence | Description | Characteristic Skills |
|---|---|---|
| Verbal/Linguistic | Ability to communicate with language through listening, reading, writing, speaking. | • Analyzing own use of language<br>• Remembering terms easily<br>• Explaining, teaching, learning, and using humor<br>• Understanding syntax and meaning of words<br>• Convincing someone to do something |
| Logical/Mathematical | Ability to understand logical reasoning and problem solving, particularly in math and science. | • Recognizing abstract patterns and sequences<br>• Reasoning inductively and deductively<br>• Discerning relationships and connections<br>• Performing complex calculations<br>• Reasoning scientifically |
| Visual/Spatial | Ability to understand spatial relationships and to perceive and create images. | • Perceiving and forming objects accurately<br>• Manipulating images for visual art or graphic design<br>• Finding one's way in space (using charts and maps)<br>• Representing something graphically<br>• Recognizing relationships between objects |
| Bodily/Kinesthetic | Ability to use the physical body skillfully and to take in knowledge through bodily sensation. | • Connecting mind and body<br>• Controlling movement<br>• Improving body functions<br>• Working with hands<br>• Expanding body awareness to all senses<br>• Coordinating body movement |
| Intrapersonal | Ability to understand one's own behavior and feelings. | • Evaluating own thinking<br>• Being aware of and expressing feelings<br>• Taking independent action<br>• Understanding self in relationship to others<br>• Thinking and reasoning on higher levels |
| Interpersonal | Ability to relate to others, noticing their moods, motivations, and feelings. | • Seeing things from others' perspective<br>• Cooperating within a group<br>• Achieving goals with a team<br>• Communicating verbally and non-verbally<br>• Creating and maintaining relationships |
| Musical/Rhythmic | Ability to comprehend and create meaningful sound and recognize patterns. | • Sensing tonal qualities<br>• Creating or enjoying melodies and rhythms<br>• Being sensitive to sounds and rhythms<br>• Using "schemas" to hear music<br>• Understanding the structure of music and other patterns |
| Naturalistic | Ability to understand the features of the environment. | • Deep understanding of nature, environmental balance, ecosystem<br>• Appreciation of the delicate balance in nature<br>• Feeling most comfortable when in nature<br>• Ability to use nature to lower stress |

## STUDY STRATEGIES FOR DIFFERENT LEARNING STYLES

Finding what study strategies work best for you can be a long process of trial and error. However, if you explore strategies in the context of learning style, you can give yourself a head start. After having completed the *Multiple Pathways to Learning* assessment, you will be able to look at the following material with a more informed view of what may help you most.

The strategies presented here are linked to four intelligences, selected because they have the most relevance to your study in this course—Verbal/Linguistic, Logical/ Mathematical, Visual/Spatial, and Interpersonal. Although they are written in the context of strength, remember that the strategies can also help you build up an area of weakness. Try

(continued on p. xxiv)

# Multiple Pathways to Learning

Each intelligence has a set of numbered statements. Consider each statement on its own. Then rate how closely it matches who you are right now by writing a number on the line next to the statement. Finally, total each set of six questions.

1 rarely    2 sometimes    3 usually    4 always

1. _____ I enjoy physical activities.
2. _____ I am uncomfortable sitting still.
3. _____ I prefer to learn through doing rather than listening.
4. _____ I tend to move my legs or hands when I'm sitting.
5. _____ I enjoy working with my hands.
6. _____ I like to pace when I'm thinking or studying.
_____ **TOTAL for Bodily-Kinesthetic**

7. _____ I use maps easily.
8. _____ I draw pictures or diagrams when explaining ideas.
9. _____ I can assemble items easily from diagrams.
10. _____ I enjoy drawing or taking photographs.
11. _____ I do not like to read long paragraphs.
12. _____ I prefer a drawn map over written directions.
_____ **TOTAL for Visual-Spatial**

13. _____ I enjoy telling stories.
14. _____ I like to write.
15. _____ I like to read.
16. _____ I express myself clearly.
17. _____ I am good at negotiating.
18. _____ I like to discuss topics that interest me.
_____ **TOTAL for Verbal-Linguistic**

19. _____ I like math.
20. _____ I like science.
21. _____ I problem-solve well.
22. _____ I question why things happen or how things work.
23. _____ I enjoy planning or designing something new.
24. _____ I am able to fix things.
_____ **TOTAL for Logical-Mathematical**

25. _____ I listen to music.
26. _____ I move my fingers or feet when I hear music.
27. _____ I have good rhythm.
28. _____ I like to sing along with music.
29. _____ People have said I have musical talent.
30. _____ I like to express my ideas through music.
_____ **TOTAL for Musical**

31. _____ I like doing a project with other people.
32. _____ People come to me to help them settle conflicts.
33. _____ I like to spend time with friends.
34. _____ I am good at understanding people.
35. _____ I am good at making people feel comfortable.
36. _____ I enjoy helping others.
_____ **TOTAL for Interpersonal**

37. _____ I need quiet time to think.
38. _____ When I need to make a decision, I prefer to think about it before I talk about it.
39. _____ I am interested in self-improvement.
40. _____ I understand my thoughts, feelings, and behavior.
41. _____ I know what I want out of life.
42. _____ I prefer to work on projects alone.
_____ **TOTAL for Intrapersonal**

43. _____ I enjoy being in nature whenever possible.
44. _____ I would enjoy a career involving nature.
45. _____ I enjoy studying plants, animals, forests, or oceans.
46. _____ I prefer to be outside whenever possible.
47. _____ When I was a child I liked bugs, ants, and leaves.
48. _____ When I experience stress I want to be out in nature.
_____ **TOTAL for Naturalist**

## Scoring Grid for *Multiple Pathways to Learning*

For each intelligence, shade the box in the row that corresponds with the range where your score falls. For example, if you scored 17 in Bodily-Kinesthetic intelligence, you would shade the middle box in that row; if you scored a 13 in Visual-Spatial, you would shade the last box in that row. When you have shaded one box for each row, you will see a "map" of your range of development at a glance.

A score of 20–24 indicates a high level of development in that particular type of intelligence, 14–19 a moderate level, and below 14 an underdeveloped intelligence.

| | 20–24 (Highly Developed) | 14–19 (Moderately Developed) | Below 14 (Underdeveloped) |
| --- | --- | --- | --- |
| Bodily-Kinesthetic | | | |
| Visual-Spatial | | | |
| Verbal-Linguistic | | | |
| Logical-Mathematical | | | |
| Musical | | | |
| Interpersonal | | | |
| Intrapersonal | | | |
| Naturalist | | | |

strategies from all different areas and evaluate them. Do the ones that match your strengths work best for you? Do the ones that correspond to your weaker areas help you improve? Does a winning strategy come from an unexpected intelligence area? What might you learn about yourself from examining the strategies that help you?

**Note Taking** Because it is virtually impossible to take notes on everything you hear or read, the act of note taking provides an opportunity for you to evaluate what is worth remembering and write it down. Note taking keeps you actively involved with the material and helps organize your thinking. Knowing how you learn will help decide how to take notes in class and from the textbook.

*Learners with Verbal/Linguistic Strength* Words are your thing, and notes are comprised of words, so you generally take comprehensive notes. In fact you may often overdo it by trying to write down everything that you hear. Your challenge is to be selective, and organized, with what you write.

- Rewrite notes to cut out unnecessary material and focus on the important ideas.
- Summarize the main ideas and supporting points of chapters.
- Avoid writing out every word—use abbreviations and other "personal shorthand."

*Learners with Logical/Mathematical Strength* You prefer organized notes that flow logically. Unfortunately, not all

classes and instructors make it possible for you to take the kind of notes you prefer. You often need time to convert your notes into a more structured format.

- On your own time, rewrite notes and organize the material logically.
- Write outlines of class notes or text material.
- Leave one or more blank spaces between points, in case making your notes more logical requires filling in missing information later.

*Learners with Visual/Spatial Strength* You retain best what is presented in some sort of graphic, visual format. Courses that primarily consist of lectures don't make the most of your abilities. Look for materials that tap into your strength—or create them when none exist.

- Take notes in a visual style—for example, use a "mind map" or "think link" that connects ideas and examples using shapes and lines.
- Use different colors—either during class or after—to organize your notes.
- Color-code your textbook by making notations in colors that you link to different ideas or types of information (for example, in a science text, circle important vocabulary in red and pivotal events in blue).

*Learners with Interpersonal Strength* Material stays with you best when you learn it and review it actively with others.

Some classes give you the opportunity to interact—and some don't. Make your notes come alive by making interaction a part of your note taking experience.

- Go over notes with one or more fellow students, helping one another fill in the gaps.
- Solidify your understanding of your notes by teaching concepts to someone else.
- If you tend to talk with classmates and get distracted, try not to sit with your friends.

**Reading**   Research has shown that it is far more effective to break your reading into several steps than to spend the same amount of time going through the material once. SQ3R is a textbook reading technique that will help you grasp ideas quickly, remember more, and review effectively for tests. The symbols S-Q-3-R stand for *survey, question, read, recite,* and *review.* Following is a brief overview of SQ3R.

**Survey**   *Surveying* refers to the process of previewing, or pre-reading, a book before you actually study it. When you survey, pay attention to frontmatter (table of contents and preface); chapter elements (title, outline or list of objectives, headings, tables and figures, quotes, summary, other features); and backmatter (glossary, index, bibliography).

**Question**   *Questioning* means reading the chapter headings and/or objectives and, on a separate piece of paper or in the margins, writing questions linked to them. If your reading material has no headings, develop questions as you read. These questions focus your attention and increase your interest, helping you build comprehension and relate new ideas to what you already know.

**Read**   Your questions give you a starting point for *reading,* the first R in SQ3R. Learning from textbooks requires that you read *actively*—engaging with the material through questioning, writing, note taking, and other activities. As you read, focus on your Q-stage questions, look for important concepts, and make notations in your textbook (marginal notes, highlighting, circling key ideas). Read in segments and make sure you understand what you read as you go.

**Recite**   Once you finish reading a topic, stop and answer the questions you raised in the Q stage of SQ3R. You may decide to *recite* each answer aloud, silently speak the answers to yourself, tell or teach the answers to another person, or write your ideas and answers in brief notes. Because writing from

memory checks your understanding, it is often the most effective way to solidify what you have read.

**Review**   *Review* soon after you finish a chapter. Reviewing, both immediately and periodically in the days and weeks after you read, strengthens your understanding. Reviewing techniques include rereading, answering study questions, summarizing, group discussion, quizzing yourself, and making flash cards. Reviewing in as many different ways as possible increases the likelihood of retention.

This text has features that fit into the SQ3R steps and reinforce your learning. The table at the bottom of the page shows how you can use specific features as you move through the steps of SQ3R.

Following are some reading tips geared toward the intelligences:

**Learners with Verbal/Linguistic Strength**   You tend to function well as a reader. Set yourself up for success by being as critical as you can be when you read.

- As you read the text, highlight no more than 10%.
- Mark up your text with marginal notes while you read.
- Recite information by rewriting important ideas and examples.

**Learners with Logical/Mathematical Strength**   When reading material is organized and logical, you tend to do well. When it is not, you may run into trouble.

- Look for patterns and systems in your reading material.
- Read material in sequence.
- Think about the logical connections between what you are reading and the world at large.

**Learners with Visual/Spatial Strength**   Textbooks with tables, figures, and other visuals help you to retain the concepts in your reading. You can make your own when there are few or none.

- As you read, take note of all visuals—photos, tables, figures, and other visual aids.
- Reconstruct what you have read using a visual organizer (mind map, timeline, chart).
- Take time out to visualize concepts as you read.

**Learners with Interpersonal Strength**   Since reading is solitary, not your strongest setting, you need to set up situations

| Survey | Question | Read | Recite | Review |
|---|---|---|---|---|
| A **Chapter Outline** begins each chapter | **Questions** appear after each major chapter heading and also in the **Psychological Detective** features | The text is designed to flow, minimizing interruptions to the reader | **Check Your Progress** quizzes appear at the end of each main section of each chapter | **Review Summaries** appear at the end of each main chapter section; **Study Charts** appear in many chapters |

where group interaction can enhance your understanding of what you read.

- Start a study group that discusses assigned class readings.
- Have a joint reading session with a friend and take turns summarizing sections for each other.
- Teach someone else selected concepts from your reading.

**Memory** In one theory, the human memory is compared to a computer, with an encoding stage, a storage stage (with three storage levels—sensory, short-term, and long-term), and a retrieval stage. Taking this view, memory improvement involves rehearsing information in order to move it from short-term to long-term memory. Another theory proposes that there are different levels of processing information that lead to varying degrees of memory. From this perspective, improving your memory requires using increased effort when processing information. You can learn more about some of the following strategies in Chapter 7 of the text.

*Learners with Verbal/Linguistic Strength* Use words to rehearse information.

- Write summaries of your text passages and notes.
- Rewrite notes, working to make them neater, more concise, easier to understand.
- Make up word-based mnemonics, such as acronyms.

*Learners with Logical/Mathematical Strength* Organizing your material will help you remember.

- Impose structure on information—write outlines, use grouping or chunking techniques.
- Put dates and events into timelines.
- Review systematically—for example, for 30 minutes at a particular time every day.

*Learners with Visual/Spatial Strength* Make your material visual.

- Draw mind maps and fill them in with important information.
- Turn information into charts or graphs.
- Use imagery—visualize items as you learn them.

*Learners with Interpersonal Strength* Reviewing with others helps you cement what you learn.

- Discuss material in a group; make quizzes for one another; teach one another.
- Work together to create mnemonic devices.
- Perform songs or poems for others that contain the information you need to remember.

**Test Taking** Test taking is about learning. Tests are designed to show what you have learned and to help you figure out where you need to work harder. The best test takers understand that they train not just for the test but to achieve a solid level of competence. Using a learning styles-based approach to studying for and taking tests will boost your ability—if you learn the material in the way that suits you best, you will best be able to retain it and communicate it in a testing situation as well as in a real-life scenario.

*Learners with Verbal/Linguistic Strength* Put your focus on words to good use.

- Think of and write out questions your instructor may ask on a test—and write answers.
- Pay attention to important words—directions that tell you how to answer, for example, or negatives that sway the meaning of a question ("Which of the following is not . . .").
- For math and science tests, do word problems first—and translate the words into formulas.

*Learners with Logical/Mathematical Strength* Find a sequential system.

- Devise and use a system that you prefer—going through the test in its exact order, for example, or doing all the simple problems first and then coming back to harder ones.
- Outline the key steps involved in topics on which you may be tested.
- If you don't know the right answer to a multiple-choice question, look for patterns that may lead to the right answer. For example, when there are two similar choices, one of them is usually correct.

*Learners with Visual/Spatial Strength* Do what you can to make the test appeal to the visual.

- Underline key words and phrases in the test questions.
- Make drawings to illustrate concepts you are being tested on.
- Create mind maps to organize your thoughts before completing an essay question.

*Learners with Interpersonal Strength* Testing, usually a solitary enterprise, rarely makes use of your strengths. Do what you can to set up preparation situations that provide interaction.

- Study for tests in pairs and groups.
- In your group, write possible test questions and ask each other questions in an oral-exam type format.
- Debrief with others—talk about the test, how you answered questions, what you wish you had done differently, and what you will do differently next time.

## SUMMING UP

Now that you have explored some possibilities of how to apply your learning styles knowledge to your study techniques, you can try out strategies and evaluate what works best for you. As you read the text, watch for "Study Tips" in the text margins that offer specific strategies for mastering key concepts in the text. The "Study Tips" are marked with icons that recall each of the four learning styles, and look like this:

 For Verbal/Linguistic

 For Logical/Mathematical

 For Visual/Spatial

 For Interpersonal

Refer to your study guide for additional material to help you review and prepare for exams. Also, if you have online access, check out the Companion Website to this text at **www.prenhall.com/davis**, where you'll find:

- *Live!Psych* animations that enhance the visual learning aspect of key concepts in almost every chapter.

- Interactive lectures that summarize each section and include graphics.

- Interactive quizzes that give you instant feedback.

- Flashcards to boost your memory of key terms.

Be strategic as you read, study, and learn, and you will find that your self-knowledge and your abilities can move you toward a bright future in college and beyond.

These study tips are from *Keys to Success*, Fifth Edition, © 2005, written by Carol Carter, Joyce Bishop, and Sarah Lyman Kravits, and published by Prentice Hall.

# Psychology, Research, and You

This chapter introduces you to psychology, a field that has grown tremendously over the years. Here we describe the methods psychologists use to gather information about the numerous problems and areas they research, examine the historical development and growth of psychology, and look at the different types of jobs that psychologists currently hold. In addition to introducing you to the broad and exciting field of psychology, we explain how you can become a knowledgeable consumer of psychological research. The results and claims of psychological research fill our daily lives; we need to know how to evaluate them. Once we have put contemporary psychology in perspective in this chapter, we will be ready to examine its special topics in greater detail in subsequent chapters.

Almost every day we encounter events in our lives or in the mass media that involve what we call "psychology." These events cover a wide variety of topics. Consider the following examples.

**EXAMPLE 1.** Patty's friends have convinced her to take one of the many tests they have located on the Internet. Patty has always wanted to know her IQ, so she selects an IQ test with a picture of Albert Einstein at the top.

She answers multiple-choice questions such as "What is the color of the sky at night?" and "The color of the sky is caused by." After she completes the test, she is told her score is 48 and is able to view a list of people who had received high scores on this test. Because her score of 48 is toward the top of the list and more than 162,000 persons had visited this Internet site, Patty is convinced that she has a high IQ. We will have more to say about Patty's IQ test in Chapter 8.

**EXAMPLE 2.** At a university on the other side of town, Keith's psychology instructor begins the class by asking, "How much electric shock, from 0 to 450 volts, would you administer to someone as part of a psychology experiment?" Keith learns that a social psychologist, Stanley Milgram (1974), conducted a study in which people were asked to administer shocks to others as part of what they believed was an investigation of how people learn. Although no shocks were actually delivered, the participants were unaware of this fact. They continued to administer "shocks" even when they believed that the shocks could be harmful. Keith is both surprised and saddened by the results of Milgram's study, which we discuss in more detail in Chapter 15.

# BECOMING A PSYCHOLOGICAL DETECTIVE

Each of these situations poses questions that psychologists might ask and try to answer. Yes, psychologists are very much like detectives; they seek to find the best answers to questions about behavior. A psychologist has earned a doctoral degree and is interested in the behavior of human beings and animals. We define **psychology** as the science of behavior and mental processes. Although this definition emphasizes behavior, it does not exclude the rich inner life that we all experience; it includes dreams, daydreams, and other inner experiences. As a science of behavior and mental processes, psychology provides the tools we need to answer questions about IQ testing, ethics in research, and countless other issues.

**psychology**
Science of behavior and mental processes

Obedience to authority can be incredibly powerful. In 1978 Jim Jones persuaded his followers to give cyanide-laced Kool-Aid to their children and then poison themselves.

To understand each of these situations, you need to be clear about what happened before you can determine why and how each one happened. For example, was Patty's IQ score an accurate indication of her intellectual ability? Will most people administer a 450-volt shock to another person as part of a study of learning? How strong is obedience to authority? Answering such questions helps you understand similar situations and provides the tools you need to answer questions about other situations.

How can you learn to be a psychological detective when every day you are bombarded by information designed to influence your opinion, persuade you to buy products, entertain you, or inform you about the world (McDonald, Nail, & Levy, 2004)? The information flows from newspapers, radio, television, family and friends, and advertisements. Often it takes the form of headlines like the following:

Miracle Happy Pill Banishes the Blues

You'll Read 200% Faster with Better Comprehension

Recovered Memories Point to a History of Abuse

Hidden Messages in Rock Songs Linked to Suicides

Three-Year-Old Psychic Predicts the Future

To evaluate such information, psychologists have found certain techniques to be helpful in thinking critically. We introduce these techniques in the next section, but first, let's consider a common alternative: folk wisdom.

When we try to understand events in the world around us, we sometimes turn to what is known as *folk wisdom*. Table 1-1 contains examples of folk wisdom in the form of proverbs. Read each proverb and decide whether you agree with it.

Such efforts to explain events are usually presented in ways that can never be proved wrong (Davis & Smith, 2005). Look at the list of proverbs again and notice that the proverbs in List B contradict those in List A. Folk wisdom can provide an explanation for every conceivable event—as well as for its exact opposite (Teigen, 1986). Hence folk wisdom provides answers for all situations but explains none. If folk wisdom does not provide helpful guidance in understanding our world, where can we turn?

The answer is to look for insights and explanations through psychological research methods. Psychologists are trained to ask good questions, to gather useful information, to arrive at appropriate conclusions, and to develop and ask further questions based on the information collected. However, there are right and wrong ways to ask questions and arrive at conclusions. Becoming a good psychological detective requires practice. To understand the need to practice the skills of a psychological detective, let's journey back to England in 1920.

**TABLE 1-1**

## Folk Wisdom

This test of folk wisdom includes general principles of behavior. Which ones do you agree with? Why?

| List A | List B |
|---|---|
| 1. Look before you leap. | 1. People who hesitate are lost. |
| 2. You can't teach an old dog new tricks. | 2. It's never too late to learn. |
| 3. Out of sight, out of mind. | 3. Absence makes the heart grow fonder. |
| 4. Two heads are better than one. | 4. If you want something done right, do it yourself. |
| 5. A penny saved is a penny earned. | 5. Nothing ventured, nothing gained. |
| 6. Opposites attract. | 6. Birds of a feather flock together. |

# Arthur Conan Doyle's Belief in Fairies

After World War I, *spiritualism* (a belief in the supernatural) sparked interest on both sides of the Atlantic. Almost every city had several *mediums*—people who claim that they can contact the spirit world and communicate with the dead during a séance (Hines, 1988). The participants in a séance hold hands as they sit around a table in a darkened room. Strange things often seem to happen during a séance: Spirits are heard to speak through floating trumpets, cool breezes and touches are felt, and tables tip over even when no one has touched them.

Sir Arthur Conan Doyle, the creator of the master detective Sherlock Holmes, was deeply interested in spiritualism. His interest started as a hobby but later became the focus of his life because he wished to communicate with his son, who had been killed in World War I. In fact, Doyle believed he had spoken with his son on several occasions (Hanson & Hanson, 1989).

In May 1920, Doyle heard reports that fairies had been photographed; he greeted the reports with enthusiasm because they seemed to confirm his belief in the existence of the spirit world. The photographs had been taken by two young girls who said they had observed the fairies in a nearby field. Doyle dismissed the possibility of fraud because the girls were young and did not know how to use photographic equipment (although one of them had worked in a photography shop). In 1921, he presented the results of his investigation in a book, *The Coming of the Fairies*. Doyle's authoritative statements led many people to believe that the photographs were genuine, and hundreds of people wrote to him describing fairies they had seen in their gardens (Randi, 1987).

Modern technology has shown the fairies to be a hoax. Computer enhancement of the photographs reveals that the supposed fairies were actually cardboard cutouts from a children's book suspended by almost invisible threads.

What lessons can we learn from the story of the fairies? First, although prominent public figures may have great credibility, their statements should not keep us from asking our own questions. Second, we should be aware of the potential for **bias,** or beliefs that interfere with objectivity. Such preconceptions can cloud our observations, influence the questions we ask, determine the methods we use, and influence our interpretation of the data we gather. Before Conan Doyle had seen the photographs of the fairies, he was already convinced of the existence of a spiritual realm. Had Doyle been a good detective, he would have recognized the potential for bias, asked good questions, and arrived at appropriate conclusions.

**The Law of Parsimony.** In studying Doyle's claim that fairies exist, you have applied the **law of parsimony.** Suppose we have two or more explanations for an event or a claim. Which one should we accept? Assume for a moment that all the proposed explanations explain the event or claim. The law of parsimony tells us to adopt the simplest explanation—the one that requires the fewest assumptions.

Doyle was faced with two explanations for the apparent sighting of the fairies by the girls. One explanation was that the girls had actually seen the fairies. The second explanation was that the girls had played an elaborate hoax on Doyle. Which explanation is simpler and involves fewer assumptions? Clearly, the belief in the existence of fairies involves many more complex assumptions than does the view that the girls perpetrated a hoax.

One of our goals in writing this book is to help you become a better psychological detective—capable of asking good questions, collecting useful information, arriving at defensible conclusions, and being aware of your own biases and those of others. The process we discuss can be applied to the story of

**bias**
Beliefs that interfere with objectivity

**law of parsimony**
Principle that simple explanations of phenomena are preferred to complex explanations

Frances Griffiths is shown with some of the cardboard cutouts she used to convince Sir Arthur Conan Doyle that she had contacted the fairies.

Doyle's fairies, to everyday headlines in news stories and advertisements, to this chapter's opening examples of IQ testing and 450-volt shocks, and to countless events you experience during the course of a typical day.

# Guidelines for the Psychological Detective

How do you know what to believe? How do you separate sense from nonsense? Critical thinking, or the reasoning we do in order to determine whether a claim is true (Clifford, Boufal, & Kurtz, 2004), is a cornerstone of psychology. In this book, you will read about many experiments in which psychologists put critical thinking into action to reach conclusions about behavior and experience. You will be encouraged to assess facts intelligently and improve your own reasoning skills. And you will learn how to evaluate critically the information you read and hear in the media and elsewhere. Use the following questions as guidelines in evaluating a statement or claim.

**What Is the Statement or Claim, and Who Is Making It?**    Before accepting a statement or claim, consider the possibility of personal bias. Whenever a person makes what seems like an extraordinary claim, always ask yourself if he or she has anything to gain by making that claim. Salespeople have a personal stake in convincing you to purchase the products they sell. For example, car dealers want new customers to know that past buyers have been satisfied, and to prove their point they often offer the results of surveys. Car manufacturers mail surveys to recent buyers to determine their level of satisfaction. According to *Consumer Reports* ("Selling It," 1991), some car dealers have offered their customers incentives to complete these surveys—but only if they take the survey to a dealer, who is more than happy to help them complete it!

Besides considering the influence of personal bias, we should evaluate the authority of the person making the claim. Authority figures often provide helpful insights, but we should not be blinded by those insights. Remember, credibility does not automatically transfer from one field of expertise to another.

We have focused on the potential for bias among people who make some claim. We must recognize, however, that the very assumptions we hold can themselves create biases that in turn influence our views of claims, questions, or proposed solutions to a problem. The influence of bias is not limited to the experts; we are all subject to its influence and must strive to recognize its sometimes subtle effects. Table 1-2 contains a

**STUDY TIP**

Name a bias that you have seen in people you know or even in yourself. Evaluate the bias: What effects does it have on behavior and belief? What are the results of such behaviors or beliefs, and are the results positive or negative?

## TABLE 1-2

### Simple Questions That May Reveal Some Evidence of Bias

Answer each of the following questions as well as you can. Then compare your answers with those on page 37.

1. Is the sun closer to the Earth or farther from the Earth during the winter months, or is the distance the same in summer and winter?
2. Whose face appears on a penny?
3. Who stole the greatest number of bases in a single season of professional baseball?
4. Can you transform the following figure into a perfect square using just one straight line?

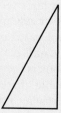

**Source:** Adapted from Beins (1993).

series of seemingly simple questions. Try answering them, and then check to see if your answers are correct.

### Is the Statement or Claim Based on Scientific Observations?

Many people support conclusions about behavior by citing personal experiences or anecdotes. For example, you may think that you succeeded on an exam because you sat in your "lucky seat." Personal experiences are also frequently offered as proof of the quality of particular products, ranging from detergents to cars.

Whenever you come across such a claim, ask whether it is justified. For example, does the fact that one customer is satisfied with a product prove that the product is consistently satisfactory? Critical thinking also requires us to question where the facts came from. Was the information based on scientific research or was it based on casual observation? Later in this chapter we discuss several research methods that psychologists use to collect data for answering questions. Only one of these methods, the experimental method, can provide the basis for cause-and-effect statements.

Popular sources ranging from such tabloids as the *National Enquirer*, the *Star*, and the *National Examiner* to more respected newspapers such as *The New York Times* and the *Philadelphia Inquirer* often print news related to psychology. However, fewer than 50% of these articles specify the research methods on which the claims in these news stories are based. Thus many sources of the claims we read in the print media pay little attention to the process of scientific inquiry, which makes it difficult for us to evaluate these claims. The same cautions hold true for the Internet. Anyone can create a Web page and post information on the Internet. There is no guarantee that the information you find there is accurate.

### What Do Statistics Reveal?

Many students are fearful of statistics in any form, yet we use statistics all the time—although not always wisely. Never hesitate to ask for numbers to support a claim, but be sure you understand them.

Claims are often presented as some type of average (or typical score). An average conveys information about the middle of a distribution, or collection of numbers. There are actually three types of averages, however, and you need to know which type is being presented and whether it is appropriate.

When evaluating claims, we need to know whether the findings could have occurred by chance. Researchers usually report the likelihood that their findings might have resulted from the operation of chance alone. Findings that exceed chance occurrence are said to be *statistically significant*. It is important to remember that you cannot tell if a finding is statistically significant just by looking at the results; a statistical test needs to be performed.

Such tests, and other statistical topics, are covered in Appendix A. We encourage you to read this material at this time; it will improve your ability as a psychological detective.

### Are There Plausible Alternative Explanations for the Statement or Claim?

Researchers frequently report that two variables (behaviors or events) are related. When we deal with an association between two variables, called a *correlation* (see p. 12), we must consider the possibility that the relation is actually due to a third variable. The fact that two events are correlated does not *prove* that one of the events caused the other; however, knowing the relation between two events helps us to make predictions about when events will occur in the future. For example, whenever the moon is full, the police report more crimes and emergency rooms treat more accident victims. Is there a relation between the full moon and these occurrences? Researchers who have examined broader periods have consistently failed to find such a relation (Rotton & Kelly, 1985).

Although all the world's events demand an explanation, some are mere coincidences. Consider the statements in Table 1-3. Did one of the factors cause the other or are there other factors involved?

Among the many claims we encounter every day are ones about drugs and other remedies. Patients may respond to drug treatment even if the treatment contains no active ingredient. Why? If you expect that a drug will give you relief from some ailment, that belief itself may bring about a reduction in the symptoms. This positive response associated with your belief or attitude is termed the **placebo effect**. The claims made

**placebo effect**
In drug research, positive effects associated with a person's beliefs and attitudes about the drug, even when it contains no active ingredients

**TABLE 1-3**

## Cause and Effect

Consider each of the following statements. Does one of the factors in each statement cause the other? If not, what other factors might be involved?

1. The phone always rings when I'm in the shower.
2. I lose my keys only when I'm in a hurry.
3. People always call at the wrong time.
4. It always rains just after I wash the car.
5. An item goes on sale the day after I buy it.
6. The doorbell always rings just as the baby is going to sleep.

**STUDY TIP**

Gather in a group of four. In a current newspaper or magazine article, find a statement or claim. Assign one of the four "Guidelines for the Psychological Detective" to each of the four group members. Then, each student should evaluate the claim using his or her chosen guideline and share this information with the group.

for drugs often sound quite impressive; when judging a drug's effectiveness, however, we need to know how many patients may have improved because of the placebo effect alone. Only when we have obtained this comparative information can we judge the true effectiveness of a drug.

We have presented four guidelines that can be helpful in evaluating a claim:

1. What is the statement or claim, and who is making it?
2. Is the statement or claim based on scientific observations?
3. What do statistics reveal?
4. Are there plausible alternative explanations for the statement or claim?

Using these guidelines does not guarantee that you will always arrive at a complete and accurate understanding of any claim or proposed explanation. Not even a well-conducted scientific experiment can guarantee that you have found the truth. Depending on the specific type of experiment conducted, the culture in which the experiment is conducted, and the personal interpretation of the results, different views of "the truth" may exist. The guidelines do, however, help you avoid certain pitfalls that can easily lead to inaccurate conclusions.

In the next section we examine the methods psychologists use to answer research questions. These techniques truly are the tools of the psychological detective.

## R E V I E W   S U M M A R Y

1. The events of our daily lives pose questions that psychologists can answer. In answering these questions, **psychology** can help us develop the skills needed to evaluate claims critically.

2. The case of Sir Arthur Conan Doyle and the photographs of alleged fairies teaches us the importance of asking good questions and demonstrates the importance of being aware of how **bias** can influence the questions we ask and the conclusions we draw.

3. When there are two (or more) competing explanations for an event or claim, the **law of parsimony** indicates that we should select the one requiring the fewest assumptions.

4. By asking good questions, collecting useful data, and arriving at defensible conclusions, we can become good consumers of psychological research.

5. In evaluating causal or research claims, we need to know exactly what the claim is and who is making it. Authority figures

often have great credibility, but their expertise does not transfer from one field to another, and their pronouncements should not be accepted uncritically.

6. Determining whether claims are based on scientific observations is also important. Even though science does not guarantee that the researcher will find truth, conclusions based on systematic and empirical (objectively quantifiable) observations of large samples are stronger than those based on a few personal testimonials.

7. Understanding and using statistics is a great aid in evaluating claims. Psychologists usually report the likelihood that their findings might have resulted from chance alone.

8. We need to realize that a relation between two events does not prove that one of the events caused the other. We should consider alternative explanations that might account for a particular event or claim.

## ✓ CHECK YOUR PROGRESS

1. What is the *best* definition of the discipline of psychology?

   a. the science of behavior

   b. the science of mental processes

   c. the science of behavior and mental processes

   d. the science of human behavior and mental processes

2. What is the major problem in relying on folk wisdom or proverbs to explain behavior?

   a. Folk wisdom and proverbs cannot be refuted because they can account for any event.

   b. Folk wisdom and proverbs are never correct.

   c. Folk wisdom and proverbs are too vague.

   d. Folk wisdom and proverbs provide no insight into behavior.

3. Which of the following is likely to be characteristic of biased scientific investigation?

   a. Researchers remain objective at all costs.

   b. Researchers allow preconceptions to cloud their observations.

   c. Researchers require more stringent proof than what is normally demanded.

   d. Researchers ask their own questions, regardless of what other people tell them.

4. Read each of the following claims and assess its validity by using the guidelines for the psychological detective presented on pages 6–8.

   a. Students in an introductory psychology course were intrigued by the topic of dreams; they posed questions about dream recall, the meaning of dreams, and the presence of color in dreams. They decided to conduct a survey to answer their question about color in dreams. The students reported whether color appeared in any dream they had had the previous night. Only 2 of the 50 students reported color in their dreams. The class concluded that we rarely dream in color.

   b. A testing firm reported the results of a taste test of two colas under the heading "Fizzy Beats Foamy." The company concluded that "an amazing 60% said Fizzy tastes as good as or better than Foamy."

   c. In the disorder known as *autism*, the affected person tends to avoid human contact and displays little or no ability to speak; many people with this disorder are also mentally retarded. To help autistic persons communicate, researchers developed a technique in which an assistant guided an autistic person's arm to point to letters on a keyboard and thus spell words. With this assistance, people who were previously unable to communicate reportedly learned how to spell correctly, to construct grammatically correct sentences, to write poetry, and to solve math problems. Critics were skeptical, however. They noticed that the autistic persons rarely looked at the keyboard while the assistant guided their arms.

5. Which guideline for the psychological detective is concerned with the question of cause and effect?

   a. What do statistics reveal?

   b. What is the statement or claim, and who is making it?

   c. Is the statement or claim based on scientific observations?

   d. Are there plausible alternative explanations for the statement or claim?

**ANSWERS: 1. c  2. a  3. b  4. a.** The claim of rarely dreaming in color is not based on scientific observation. Moreover, this finding also could be explained by other factors, such as poor recall of one's dreams. **b.** There are several problems with the finding that "an amazing 60% said Fizzy tastes as good as or better than Foamy." We really do not know who participated in the taste test; perhaps they were paid employees of the Fizzy Company. The 60% figure that seems to support the company's claims is misleading at best. What if 90% of this number feel that both brands taste equally good? That leaves only 10% who like Fizzy better than Foamy and 40% who like Foamy better. Much more information is needed. **c.** There is no indication that the autistic individuals had anything to do with the movement of their arms. It is likely that the facilitator was responsible for the results we are considering. **5. d**

# RESEARCH METHODS IN PSYCHOLOGY

Sam and Ann spent Saturday afternoon surfing the Internet and were amazed at the variety of sites they visited. The claims for the superiority of this or that product were almost beyond belief. They found numerous sites where they could order products being advertised by celebrities. They wondered if the products were as good as the celebrities claimed. *How would psychologists answer the kinds of questions that Sam and Ann asked?*

The science of psychology is concerned with events like these and the ones described at the beginning of this chapter. The goals of psychology are to describe such events, to make predictions about the conditions that gave rise to them, and then to use that knowledge to predict and possibly to control events in the future.

**scientific method**
System of investigation in which a person makes careful observations of a phenomenon, proposes theories to explain the phenomenon, makes hypotheses about future behaviors, and then tests these hypotheses through more research and observation

**theory**
Explanation for a phenomenon based on careful and precise observations

**hypothesis**
Prediction about future behaviors that is derived from observation and theories

**case study**
In-depth study of a single person that can often provide suggestions for further research

**naturalistic observation**
Study of behavior in its typical setting, with no attempt to alter it

As we have noted, psychology is the scientific study of behavior and mental processes. What makes psychology a science? Psychologists share a basic assumption with all other sciences: Physical and psychological events have causes that can be uncovered through scientific investigation. Scientists do not rely on guesswork, hunches, or unsystematic collections of personal experiences. Rather, they use a system of investigation known as the **scientific method.** Like all scientists, psychologists begin their work by making very careful and precise observations of different phenomena or events. They then use the information they have obtained to develop explanations for the phenomena they have observed, which we call **theories.** From these theories psychologists develop **hypotheses,** which are predictions about future behaviors. They then test these hypotheses through more research and observation.

How do psychologists collect the data they need to develop theories and test hypotheses? Psychologists use a number of research methods, including case studies, naturalistic observations, and experiments. Each method has strengths and weaknesses; all of them contribute to our knowledge of claims and events. The choice of the specific method used usually is determined by the type of problem being investigated.

## The Case Study

The **case study** (sometimes called a *clinical study*) is an in-depth analysis of one person. This method was popularized by Sigmund Freud (see Chapter 11) as he developed his psychoanalytic theory of personality. A major advantage of the case study is that concentrating on one person (or sometimes a few people) allows researchers to gather a great deal of detailed information. The goal of a case study is to use the information obtained from one person to understand the behaviors of others. The case study is often an excellent source for suggesting research ideas that can be explored with other methods.

One potential disadvantage of the method is that what we learn by studying one person may not necessarily apply to other people. For example, an intensive study of the interpersonal behaviors and personality attributes of the president of the United States may not tell us much about such behaviors and attributes in other American men or women. The president lives in unique circumstances and leads a life that few people can relate to. Findings that have limited applicability are said not to *generalize*.

## Naturalistic Observation

1.1

The goal of **naturalistic observation** is to describe the settings, frequency, and characteristics of certain behaviors in the real world. For example, psychologists interested in the use of seat belts have stationed themselves at the exits of shopping malls to see how many drivers used them. They have also observed whether children riding in the cars used seat belts. When psychologists make naturalistic observations, they observe behaviors as they occur, without intervening or altering the behaviors in any way.

The observers must be careful not to affect the behaviors they observe and record. Observations that interfere with the behavior being studied are termed *reactive*. Have you ever noticed someone in a restaurant watching you while you are eating? If so, you are familiar with a reactive observation. Try to remember if the observer's scrutiny may have changed your behavior in any way. For example, did you check to see if you had food on your clothing or face, or did you make an effort to use your best table manners? Psychologists who make naturalistic observations try to make sure that they themselves are not observed—they try to blend in with the surroundings so that they are not noticed by the persons being observed. Another method is to find some way to gather data without being physically present. For example, Gibson, Smith, and Torres (2000) were interested in whether proximity of a bystander was related to the glancing behavior of a person using an automated teller machine (ATM). From their concealed vantage point, they observed that as bystander distance decreased, glancing behavior by the person using the ATM increased.

By using a one-way mirror, the researcher is concealed and can make naturalistic observations of the children at this day care center.

## Correlational Research

Imagine that it is your senior year in high school and you are faced with all the choices and decisions involved in getting ready to go to college. Before applying to the college of your choice, you likely took an entrance examination, such as the Scholastic Aptitude Test (SAT) or the American College Test (ACT). What purpose do tests such as the SAT and ACT serve? Psychologists have found that the scores on these tests are related to (*correlated with*) your performance as a college student. This means that knowing scores on the SAT or ACT enables educators to *predict* how a student will do during his or her first year in college. Keep in mind, though, that just because two variables are correlated, even highly correlated, one variable does not *cause* the other. In this case, SAT or ACT scores are related to—but do not actually cause—grade point averages.

Figure 1-1 presents two possible **scatterplots**—graphs that illustrate the relation between two variables (in this case, SAT scores and first-year [freshman] grade point average). In these examples, each dot in the scatterplot represents one student.

1.2

**scatterplot**
Graph that depicts the relation between two variables

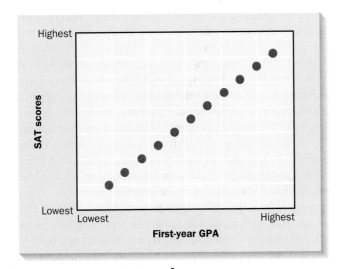

A

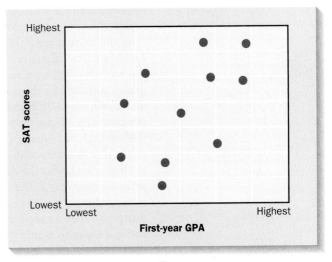

B

**FIGURE 1-1**  Scatterplots indicating (A) a perfect positive relation and (B) a moderate positive relation between SAT scores and first-year grade point average (GPA).

**correlation coefficient**
Number ranging between −1.00 and +1.00 that represents the degree and direction of relation between two variables

The location of the dot is determined by both the student's SAT score (along the vertical axis) and his or her freshman grade point average (along the horizontal axis). If the relation between SAT scores and grades was perfect—that is, if the student with the highest SAT score had the highest grade point average and so on down the line—the dots would fall on a straight line from the lower left to the upper right, as in Figure 1-1A. The collection of dots in Figure 1-1B looks more like a large oval running from the lower left to the upper right of the diagram; the higher the SAT score, the greater the *tendency* to have a higher grade point average. Hence there is some predictability here, but it is not perfect.

Scatterplots tell us whether the values of two variables are *correlated*—whether they tend to occur together. We can summarize the information presented in a scatterplot with a single number, a bit of shorthand that is very helpful when you do not have a scatterplot handy. This number, known as a **correlation coefficient,** is symbolized by the letter *r* (see Appendix A). A correlation coefficient can have a value ranging from −1.00 to +1.00—no higher and no lower. The number tells you the strength of the correlation, and the sign tells you the direction of the relation. What do those numbers mean? First, disregard the sign (− or +) in front of the numbers for a moment. The higher the *r*, the stronger the relation. Thus if *r* is 0.70, the two variables are more strongly associated than they would be if *r* were 0.30. If *r* is 0, the two variables are not related at all.

The sign (− or +) tells us the *direction* of the relation. A plus sign tells us that as the values of one variable (in our example, SAT scores) increase, so do the values of the other (in our example, grade point average). Thus values of both variables are headed in the same direction; they are *positively correlated*. Consequently, if SAT scores are high, grade point averages also tend to be high. Similarly, the number of hours students study for an exam and the grades they earn are positively correlated. By contrast, a minus sign tells us that the values of the two variables travel in opposite directions; they are *negatively correlated*. As the values of one variable increase, the values of the other tend to decrease. For example, students who study a great deal should make fewer errors on an exam. Those who do not study much would probably make more errors. The variables of study time and errors on an exam are negatively correlated.

## Hands On

Here's an opportunity for you to heighten your understanding of correlational research by constructing a scatterplot. Use the time of each of your classes as one variable. Plot each of these times on the vertical axis of your graph. Start with your earliest morning class and work toward your latest afternoon class. Be sure to leave some space between each class time (don't crowd them all at the lower end of the axis). Your grades will be the second variable; you will plot them on the horizontal axis. Start with the lowest grades and increase them in equal units as you move further out on this axis (e.g., 40, 50, 60, 70, 80, 90, 100). It's an easy task to plot your grades as a function of class time. You can plot your grades for each test in all of your classes, or you can plot several tests on the same graph. Now, examine the scatterplot to see if the variables correlate. If the scatterplot flows from the upper left of the graph to the lower right, then your grades are better earlier in the day (this is a negative correlation; as class time gets earlier, the grades get better). If the scatterplot flows from the lower left to the upper right, then your grades get better as class time gets later (this is a positive correlation). What if the scatterplot doesn't seem to flow in either direction? We hope that you are ahead of us and said that this would be a zero (or close to it) correlation. Based on what you find, is time of day a factor for you when it comes to grades?

In addition to being a great hands-on exercise, this activity is an excellent logical-mathematical study tip.

## Psychological Detective

Here is your first opportunity to be a psychological detective. We have embedded several of these psychological detective features in each chapter to help you sharpen your critical thinking skills. Please give these sections some thoughtful attention and generate some answers for each question before reading further.

The two variables in our preceding example were SAT scores and grade point average. Before reading further, make a list of some factors that could be responsible for the association between these variables.

One factor that could explain the association between SAT scores and grades is the possibility that certain students (especially those with higher SAT scores) were raised by families that stressed enrichment and learning activities. These families provided information and experiences that contributed to better study habits—and, consequently, higher grades—and higher SAT scores. We highlight this possibility because a correlation between two variables does not mean that one variable causes the other. The two variables may be related because of the influence of a third variable. Correlations do allow us to make predictions, however; the larger the correlation, the better the prediction.

## Survey Research

Psychologists and other social scientists devised the **survey method** of research to gather data from a sample that represents a larger population. Surveys are often used because they can be efficient ways to collect large amounts of information. They can be conducted in face-to-face interviews, by telephone through written questions, and even by computer.

An interest in understanding violence might lead researchers to ask, "How much violence exists in our society?" We could answer this question by asking every person in the country whether he or she had been the victim of a violent crime (such as robbery or assault) during the past year, but this approach would be extremely expensive and impractical.

Surveys are a means of collecting large amounts of information. Face-to-face interviews allow interviewers to ask for clarification of answers.

## Psychological Detective

Suppose that we decided to answer our question about violence by examining the number of violent crimes reported to the police. Can you think of reasons why this approach might not provide an accurate estimate of the amount of violent crime in our society? What are some ways the type of survey might influence the information that is collected? Write down some reasons before reading further.

The number of violent crimes reported to the police would not reflect the actual amount of violent crime in society because many crimes are never reported. In 1988, the U.S. Department of Justice found that only 37% of all crimes were actually reported to the police; that is, for every 37 crimes reported, 63 were not reported (Jamieson & Flanagan, 1988). To counteract the problem of underreported crimes, the Justice Department collects data on crime victimization in its annual National Crime Victimization Survey. The survey depends on victims' reports; therefore, it cannot assess the frequency of murder, a crime that is typically reported to police or discovered by them. How "violent" crimes are defined also will influence the number of crimes that are reported. Is death or hospitalization included in the definition? Is property damage a requirement? These features of the survey will have a direct influence on the number of violent crimes that are reported.

In another example of survey research, McKinney and McAndrew (2000) sought to determine the tolerance of homosexuality among male and female collegiate athletes

**survey method**
Research method that involves collecting information from a selected group of people who are representative of a larger group

**FIGURE 1-2** Tolerance of homosexuality by athletic status and sex.

**Source:** McKinney BA, McAndrew FT (2000). Sexuality, gender, and sport: Does playing have a price? *Psi Chi Journal of Undergraduate Research*, 5, 152–158.

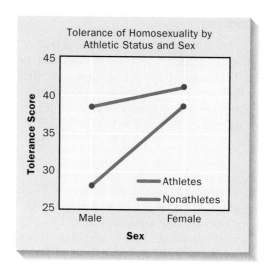

**representative sample**
Sample selected so that it reflects the characteristics of a population of interest to the researcher

**experimental method**
Research method that involves manipulating independent variables to determine how they affect dependent variables

and nonathletes. As you can see in Figure 1-2, their results showed that male athletes were significantly less tolerant of homosexuality than any of the other groups.

When conducting a survey, researchers must obtain a **representative sample**—one that is selected to reflect the characteristics of a larger group (the *population*). The researcher tries to make sure that the sample is a miniature version of the population. You see the survey method applied every November, when news anchors announce election winners based on information from polling researchers, with only 2% of the vote tabulated. How can anyone make a prediction based on 2% (or even less) of the vote? News organizations can make these predictions because their polling experts have identified key areas within the state that represent the entire population from the standpoint of gender, ethnicity, and political preference; thus a small but representative segment of the population can be used to predict the way the entire population is voting.

Obtaining a representative sample is not the only important consideration when conducting surveys. Questions must be carefully worded to elicit meaningful and useful responses. Consider a survey of the number of headaches reported by respondents. When the question was phrased "Do you get headaches frequently, and, if so, how often?" the average number of reported headaches was 2.2 per week. When the word *occasionally* was substituted for the word *frequently*, the average number of headaches reported was only 0.7 per week (Loftus, 1975).

Survey questions are sometimes slanted in ways that invite biased results. For example, in 1993, H. Ross Perot and his United We Stand organization conducted a nationwide survey. Skeptical of the results, *Time* and CNN asked Yankelovich Partners, a professional survey company, to conduct two surveys of random samples of the U.S. population. One sample was given Perot's version of the questions; the second sample was asked similar questions that had been rewritten to reduce the potential for bias. Perot phrased one question this way: "Should laws be passed to eliminate all possibilities of special interests giving huge sums of money to candidates?" The Yankelovich version was "Should laws be passed to prohibit interest groups from contributing to campaigns they support?" The results were eye-opening. To the Perot version, 80% of respondents said yes and 17% said no. In the Yankelovich survey, 40% favored the passing of such laws, whereas 55% supported the right to contribute (Moore & Parker, 1995). As we noted earlier, the nature of a survey and the way a project is conducted can result in different views of the true state of affairs.

## The Experimental Method

The research methods described so far can provide useful leads, strong data, and excellent descriptions. Yet, as we saw with correlational research, those methods cannot provide us with cause-and-effect statements. By contrast, the **experimental method**

1.3

can provide such statements. With this method, researchers manipulate certain *variables*, or factors, to determine how they affect other variables. Therefore it is considered the most powerful research method.

The logic of the experimental method starts with a *hypothesis*, or testable prediction, about which variable or variables cause the behavior under consideration. For example, which variables could conceivably affect violent behavior? Some possibilities are crowding, frustration, and hot weather. Each of these variables could affect the probability that an act of violence might occur. Even though hypotheses guide many experiments, Proctor and Capaldi (2001) caution against relying too heavily on hypotheses to guide psychological research. They believe that research should be guided by observable findings, not just by predictions made by an experimental hypotheses.

In the logic of an experiment, the variables that might cause an effect are called **independent variables.** The psychologist's goal is to manipulate one or more independent variables to determine the effect on a **dependent variable**—a behavior that shows the outcome of an experiment by revealing the effects of an independent variable (Smith & Davis, 2004). In the study of violence, hitting a person could be a dependent variable; the number of hits might change if we manipulated an independent variable that actually affects the probability of violence, such as observing an aggressive model. Researchers are careful to offer clear and precise definitions for both the independent and dependent variables. Such definitions, known as **operational definitions,** allow other researchers to replicate (repeat) an experiment exactly as it was originally done in order to verify the findings. In a simple case, some participants in the experiment are exposed to the independent variable; they constitute the **experimental group.** Other participants are not exposed to the independent variable; they constitute the **control group** that will be compared with the experimental group on the dependent variable. If our independent variable had an effect on violence, the value of the dependent variable (number of hits) exhibited by the control group and the experimental group would be quite different.

Let's consider a classic experiment. In the 1960s, Albert Bandura and colleagues (Bandura, Ross, & Ross, 1963) conducted an experiment to determine whether children learn aggressive behaviors by observing the actions of others. They hypothesized that children who observed an adult behaving aggressively would be more likely than children who observed an adult not behaving aggressively to exhibit aggressive actions. Nursery school children were assigned to two groups; one group observed an aggressive adult model, and the other group observed a nonaggressive model. The independent variable in this experiment was observing an aggressive or a nonaggressive model. Later, all the children were given an opportunity to hit a Bobo doll (see Figure 1-3A); therefore, the dependent variable was the number of blows directed at the Bobo doll. Bandura and colleagues found that children who observed an aggressive model engaged in more aggressive behavior than those who observed a nonaggressive model. The independent variable (observing an aggressive model) led to a higher rate of aggression (hitting a Bobo doll)—the dependent variable (see Figure 1-3B).

Although the research demonstrated that modeling can play a part in causing children to act aggressively, you need to keep some other factors about the experiment in mind. The specific details of the experiment, such as the type of participants, age of the models, sex of the models, measure of aggression, and so forth, may have influenced the results. Possibly other procedures, participants, and measures of aggression would have produced different results. Such considerations clearly point to the need to replicate or repeat research; they also highlight the care that experimenters must take in conducting and interpreting their research.

## Psychological Detective

Suppose that Bandura and colleagues had assigned all of the boys to the group that observed the aggressive model and all of the girls to the group that observed the nonaggressive model. Could they conclude that boys were more aggressive because

**independent variable**
Variable manipulated by a researcher to determine its effects on a dependent variable

**dependent variable**
Variable that shows the outcome of an experiment by revealing the effects of an independent variable

**operational definition**
A careful and precise definition that allows other researchers to repeat an experiment

**experimental group**
The group in an experiment that receives the effect of the independent variable being manipulated

**control group**
A comparison group in an experiment that does not receive the effect of the independent variable being manipulated

A

B

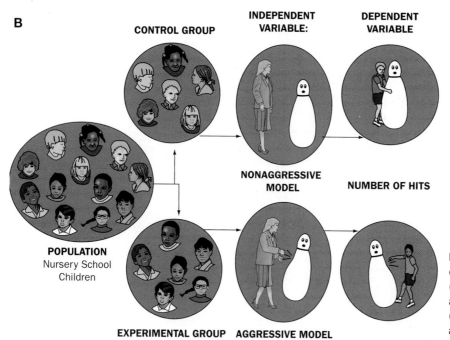

**FIGURE 1-3** (A) Children who observe an adult hitting a Bobo doll (top row) are likely to exhibit similar aggressive behaviors (bottom rows). (B) Design of the Bandura, Ross, and Ross (1963) study of the effects of modeling on aggression.

they observed an aggressive model? Give this question some thought, and write down your response before reading further.

If all the boys had been assigned to the group that observed an aggressive model, we could not conclude that the aggressive model was responsible for their aggression in the second part of the experiment. Boys might be more aggressive than girls no matter what kind of model they observed. The logic of the experimental method requires that the *only* difference between groups be the independent variable (or variables) manipulated by the experimenter—in this case, the type of model observed. If you hold all other variables that could also influence the results of the experiment—known as **extraneous variables**—constant, you may identify the cause of the behavior under consideration. If all of the boys had been assigned to the aggressive-model group, there would be two possible explanations for any increased aggression: being a boy and observing an aggressive model.

In general—and this was also true for the study by Bandura and colleagues—we need to select two groups that are as much alike as possible before an experiment begins. One way to accomplish this objective is to use the procedure called **random assignment,** or assignment of participants to two or more groups on the basis of chance. Random assignment usually results in two groups that are quite similar in many characteristics. In this case, we would probably have about the same numbers of boys and girls in each group (see Figure 1-3B).

However, random assignment does not solve all problems and make all research perfect. For example, psychological researchers originally believed that their clothing, behavior, attitudes, and expectations did not influence the performance/behavior of their research participants. This view has changed drastically. One of the most widely cited studies of the effects of human experimenter expectancy involved the IQ scores of grade-school children (Rosenthal & Jacobson, 1968). At the start of the school year, all children in the classes that were studied took an IQ test. Then several children in each class were *randomly* selected, and their respective teachers were told that these children were "intellectual bloomers." Several months later, when all the children retook the IQ test, the IQ scores of the intellectual bloomers had increased more than those of the other children. Because the intellectual bloomers were randomly selected, it is doubtful that they were intellectually superior. However, they were perceived in this manner and were treated differently by the teachers. In turn, these students responded in accordance with the teachers' expectations. Recent research has shown that the expectation effect "occurs well beyond the confines of the classroom or the laboratory" (Rosenthal, 2003, p. 152). For example, several experiments have investigated the influence of health care workers' expectations on the health outcomes of their patients. One such study, conducted in a nursing home, showed that raising caretakers' expectations for residents' health outcomes led to a reduction in the depression levels of the residents.

In later chapters, you will see these research methods applied to answer questions about a wide range of behaviors. Examining the following Study Chart should help you understand the differences among these research methods. Remember that each

**extraneous variables**
Variables, other than the independent variable, that can influence the outcome of an experiment

**random assignment**
Assignment of experimental participants to two or more groups on the basis of chance

## *Study* CHART

### Research Methods in Psychology

| Method | Description |
| --- | --- |
| Case study | Use of information obtained from one person or a few people to illuminate the behaviors of others and to suggest further research. |
| Naturalistic observation | Observation of behaviors as they occur, without any intervention or alteration. |
| Correlational research | Research in which data on the incidence of two variables are analyzed to determine the extent to which those variables tend to occur together. |
| Survey research | Research in which information is gathered from a representative sample of a larger population, using face-to-face or telephone interviews or written questions. |
| Experimental method | Research technique in which an independent variable (or variables) is manipulated to determine whether it affects a dependent variable—a behavior that is the outcome of an experiment. |

method can make a contribution to our understanding and that the methods are often used in combination.

In this section, we have seen how, through careful design and execution, experimental research can show cause and effect. Once a research project is completed, however, the results must be analyzed before they can be understood and shared with other professionals.

# Statistics and Psychologists

The practice of doing experiments created the need for methods to summarize experimental results before researchers presented them to the scientific community.

### Psychological Detective

Why is it necessary to summarize research data before disseminating them? Jot down some answers to this question before reading further.

**statistics**
Branch of mathematics that involves the collection, analysis, and interpretation of data

**descriptive statistics**
Procedures used to summarize any set of data

**inferential statistics**
Procedures used to analyze data after an experiment is completed; used to determine if the independent variable has a significant effect

**measures of central tendency**
Descriptive measures of a set of data that tell us about a typical score

**measures of variability**
Descriptive measures that tell us about the amount of variability or spread in a set of data

If you are conducting an experiment and a classmate simply hands you a sheet of paper with several hundred scientific observations on it, you are no closer to having an answer to your research question than before you started. You need to make sense of the data that have been collected. Psychologists have turned to a branch of mathematics called *statistics* for assistance. **Statistics** involves the summarization, analysis, and interpretation of data. The two main branches of statistics assist you in making decisions in different ways. **Descriptive statistics** are procedures used to summarize a set of numbers so that you can understand and talk about them more intelligibly. **Inferential statistics** are procedures used to analyze data after an experiment is conducted to determine if an independent variable had a significant effect. Let's see how these two branches of statistics operate.

**Descriptive Statistics.**   Your instructor just returned the test you took Tuesday. The score on your paper is 67. What is your reaction? Because you do not have enough information to know whether your score of 67 is good or bad, a reaction of uncertainty and confusion is understandable and predictable.

### Psychological Detective

What additional information do you require to judge the quality of your work? Give this question some thought and write down your answers before continuing.

Your first response may have been "How did the rest of the class do?" You're on the right track, but let's see if we can be a bit more precise. First, we need to know what the typical score was. When we report the typical score in a set of numbers, we are presenting a **measure of central tendency.** Undoubtedly you are already familiar with one measure of central tendency, the arithmetic average or *mean*, which is calculated by dividing the total of the scores by the number of scores. By itself, however, a measure of central tendency does not provide enough information for you to fully understand your test score of 67; you also need to know about the *variability* or spread of the other scores in the class. **Measures of variability** provide information about the variability or spread of the scores in a set of data. If all of the scores are clustered closely around the *mean* or another measure of central tendency, then you will view the score of 67 differently than if the scores are spread out widely. Measures of central tendency and variability are the primary descriptive statistics used by psychologists; they are described in more detail in Appendix A.

**Inferential Statistics.**    When an experiment is conducted, we hope that the manipulation of our independent variable will have a pronounced effect on the dependent variable. Typically, the effect of the independent variable is evaluated by the difference between the groups in the experiment; the larger the difference, the greater the effect of the independent variable. Not all differences between groups, however, are attributable to the influence of the independent variable. Sometimes the differences are due to chance variation among the participants in the groups. Even though we may select our groups randomly, they will never be perfectly identical. So how does the experimenter distinguish between differences among the experimental participants and differences caused by the independent variable? *Inferential statistics* offer a solution to this dilemma. Conducting an inferential statistical test allows the researcher to mathematically evaluate the difference between the groups in an experiment and decide whether the observed difference occurred frequently or rarely by chance. If the difference occurs *rarely* by chance, then the experimenter concludes that the result is "significant" and that the difference was caused by the independent variable. Further discussion of inferential statistics and a sample inferential statistical test are found in Appendix A.

Research, however, is not conducted or reported in a vacuum; psychologists are obligated to adhere to a code of ethical behavior.

# Research Ethics

Let's return to the Milgram study described at the beginning of this chapter (see p. 3). Imagine being a participant and being asked to administer an electric shock of 450 volts to another person. How would you react if you agreed to administer the shock? Later, you are told that no shocks were actually delivered, but you realize that if they had been delivered, you might have killed someone. Clearly, there is the potential for long-term traumatic effects on the research participants in this experiment. This example highlights a major concern for researchers: how to conduct research in an ethical manner.

The American Psychological Association (2002) has adopted ethical guidelines that prescribe standards of conduct for the professional work of psychologists in their roles as researchers, clinicians, and teachers. These guidelines include several general principles. For example, psychologists must maintain high standards of competence in their work, including recognizing the limitations of their expertise. They also must show respect for the rights and dignity of people, such as rights to privacy and confidentiality.

The ethical guidelines for conducting research require that all research proposals be reviewed to ensure compliance with the guidelines. Each proposal must be approved by an institutional review board (IRB) established by a college, university, or other organization where research is conducted (Smith & Davis, 2004). Moreover, the Association for the Accreditation of Human Research Protection Programs (AAHRPP) was founded in 2001 to certify and oversee human research participant programs, including IRBs (Dingfelder, 2004).

**Protection from Harm.**    What's more, the ethical guidelines state that psychologists who conduct research using human participants must ensure that they are protected from physical and psychological harm. For this reason, the study conducted by Milgram several decades ago would not be permitted today. Although no shocks were actually given, the study required the participants to obey the experimenter despite the moral imperative that they not hurt another person. This type of conflict is certainly unpleasant and could cause psychological harm to some people.

What the researcher considers to be a risky or potentially harmful situation may depend on the type of participants chosen for a project. For example, experiments involving physical exertion, such as testing the effects of exercise on subsequent memory tasks, which pose no risk to healthy participants, may constitute a significant risk for persons in poor health. Likewise, the age of the participant may be a relevant consideration in

**Source:** *Psi Chi Newsletter* 22, no. 1 (Winter 1996). Reprinted with the permission of Psi Chi.

**informed consent**
Written document in which a person who might be involved in a research study agrees to participate after receiving information about the researcher's specific procedures

**debriefing**
Procedure during which a complete explanation of research that has involved deception is provided to a participant

determining potential emotional harm or distress in studies involving the selection of liked and disliked peers.

**Confidentiality.** The ethical guidelines also require that any research records associated with a person's name or identity be kept confidential. For example, psychologists may use code names or numbers for their participants so that information cannot be associated with the actual names of people who have taken part in research.

**Voluntary Participation.** Participants, including college students in introductory courses, must be told that their participation in research is voluntary. They cannot be coerced into participating. College students may be part of a pool from which researchers draw participants for their studies. If a student objects to participating, he or she must be given an opportunity to select other ways to earn the same amount of credit or to complete the course requirement. In other words, no one may be punished for not participating in research. To enable potential participants to make proper judgments about their participation, the researcher must describe the procedures of the experiment and obtain a written agreement to participate, which is called an **informed consent.** This document indicates that the participant knows the nature of the research and what he or she has agreed to do before participating.

**Deception and Intimidation.** Some experiments require the use of deception. For example, researchers would be unable to study the true effectiveness of drug treatments without the use of placebos. Participants who are given placebos are led to believe they are taking the actual drug so that researchers can assess the influence of expectations on the drug's effectiveness. When psychologists use deception in their research, their participants must undergo a **debriefing** session immediately after the study in which they are given a complete explanation of the research that has used deception. During the debriefing, participants are allowed to ask questions and the researcher checks for possible negative aftereffects of the deception. In addition, participants in psychological research have the right to end their participation at any time. Researchers cannot use any form of threat or intimidation to force them to complete tasks in a study.

**STUDY TIP**

Identify visuals—icons or pictures—to assign to each of the principles of research ethics to help you remember them.

**The Ethics of Research with Animals.** As you will see throughout this book, many of psychology's most enduring findings have resulted from research with animals (Domjan & Purdy, 1995). For example, much of our knowledge about the structure and functioning of the brain (Chapter 2), sensation and perception (Chapter 3), motivation and emotion (Chapter 6), basic processes of learning (Chapter 5), developmental processes (Chapter 9), and maladaptive behavior (Chapter 12) is the result of animal research. Even though psychology and biology are often closely linked as a pair of life sciences (Simonton, 2004), the use of animals in biological research is accepted, whereas the use of animals in psychological research has not gone unchallenged (Mukerjee, 1997).

The ongoing debate between advocates of using animals in research and those who deplore such efforts has been heated and emotional at times (Galvin & Herzog, 1992). Animal rights activists view the use of animals in psychological and medical research as cruel and unnecessary. What's more, they note that such research often involves stress, pain, punishment, or social and environmental deprivation (Bowd & Shapiro, 1993; Rollin, 1985). On the other hand, the value of animal research has been defended by arguments that such research has led to improvements in human welfare (Baldwin, 1993; Miller, 1985). Psychological and medical researchers point out that some types of research could not be conducted without using animals. Ethical Standard 8.09 adopted by the American Psychological Association (2002) lists seven areas of concern in the ethical treatment of animals in psychological research.

Dr. Jesse Purdy studies the behavior and learning abilities of fish in his laboratory at Southwestern University.

1. Psychologists acquire, care for, use, and dispose of animals in compliance with current federal, state, and local laws and regulations and with professional standards.

2. Psychologists trained in research methods and experienced in the care of laboratory animals supervise all procedures involving animals and are responsible for ensuring appropriate consideration of their comfort, health, and humane treatment.

3. Psychologists ensure that all individuals under their supervision who are using animals have received instruction in research methods and in the care, maintenance, and handling of the species being used, to the extent appropriate to their role.

4. Psychologists make reasonable efforts to minimize the discomfort, infection, illness, and pain of animal subjects.

5. Psychologists use a procedure subjecting animals to pain, stress, or privation only when an alternative procedure is unavailable and the goal is justified by its prospective scientific, educational, or applied value.

6. Psychologists perform surgical procedures under appropriate anesthesia and follow techniques to avoid infection and minimize pain during and after surgery.

7. When it is appropriate that an animal's life be terminated, psychologists proceed rapidly, with an effort to minimize pain and in accordance with accepted procedures.

Researchers who use animals in their research are subject to a long list of regulations, including local, state, and federal laws. These regulations seek to define under what circumstances it is acceptable to sacrifice animals for research. Moreover, the regulations often mandate certain requirements concerning food, cage space, and veterinary care (Animal Behaviour, 2004).

A number of factors influence individuals' judgments about the ethics of using animals in research. These factors are complex and include the similarity of the animals to humans, their "cuteness," and the perceived importance of the research to alleviating human suffering (Herzog, 1990).

The influence of the animal rights movement is evident. A decline in the number of studies using certain animal species such as cats, dogs, and rabbits may be due, in part, to the attention that the animal rights movement has focused on this issue (Gluck & Bell, 2003). What's more, researchers are now looking for ways to reduce the number of animals used in research. For example, they are investigating alternatives to the use of animals for testing potentially toxic chemicals. The new methods do not involve testing intact higher animals, such as dogs and cats; instead, they rely on bacteria, cultured animal cells, or fertilized chicken eggs (Goldberg & Frazier, 1989). Such methods, however, do not eliminate the need for animals in certain types of research. Opinions on the use of animals in research will no doubt continue to be highly personal, emotional, and strong (Furnham, McManus, & Scott, 2003; Roberts & Krystal, 2003).

Now that we have discussed the need to be a good psychological detective and the methods used by psychologists to conduct and analyze their research, it is time to stand back and get a general overview of the field of psychology before we begin our chapter-by-chapter coverage of specific psychological topics. A brief review of the history of modern psychology and a consideration of the activities of contemporary psychologists should prepare you for this more in-depth coverage.

# REVIEW SUMMARY

**1.** The goals of psychology are to describe, predict, and control behavior. These goals are accomplished by using the **scientific method,** which is systematic and empirical (based on observable events).

**2.** A **case study** is an in-depth analysis of a single person or event. Although the findings of a case study may apply only to the person or event studied, they may provide direction for further study using other methods.

**3.** To study behavior in real-life settings, psychologists often use **naturalistic observation.** This technique also may suggest research projects using more controlled approaches. In using naturalistic observation, the onlooker must be unobtrusive and avoid influencing the behavior being studied.

**4.** **Correlational research** tells whether the values of two variables are related. Although correlational methods do not inform us about causality, they can provide useful insights and help us to make predictions.

**5.** By asking questions of a **representative sample,** researchers using the **survey method** can provide useful information about a much larger population. The wording of the questions can influence participants' responses.

**6.** Because it can generate cause-and-effect statements, many psychologists believe that the **experimental method** is the most powerful research approach. By manipulating an **independent variable** (the cause), the researcher determines whether it influences the **dependent variable** (the effect). Despite these strengths, the results and interpretation of a scientific experiment can be influenced by the specific way the research is conducted, the culture in which the research is conducted, and the experimenter's personal biases.

**7.** **Statistics** involves the collection, analysis, and interpretation of data. **Descriptive statistics** summarize data, whereas **inferential statistics** are used to determine if the results of an experiment are significant.

**8.** **Measures of central tendency** provide information about the typical score in a set of numbers. **Measures of variability** provide information about the variability or spread in a set of data.

**9.** The American Psychological Association has established ethical guidelines for making decisions about research with both human and animal participants.

# ✓ CHECK YOUR PROGRESS

**1.** Which research method focuses on gathering detailed information about one individual?

  **a.** a case study
  **b.** an experiment
  **c.** a correlational study
  **d.** a naturalistic study

**2.** Which aspect of a correlation coefficient tells you the *direction* of the relation between the variables? Why?

**3.** Which goal of psychology is most closely met through naturalistic observation?

  **a.** altering behavior
  **b.** predicting behavior
  **c.** describing behavior
  **d.** controlling behavior

**4.** The variable an experimenter manipulates in order to determine its effects in an experiment is called the

  **a.** dependent variable.
  **b.** extraneous variable.
  **c.** controlled variable.
  **d.** independent variable.

**5.** What kind of statistical procedure is used to analyze data after an experiment is conducted to determine whether the independent variable had a significant effect?

  **a.** descriptive
  **b.** inferential
  **c.** summary
  **d.** biased

**6.** Discuss one of the strengths and one of the weaknesses of naturalistic observation as a research technique. What is a reactive measure? How can it be avoided?

**7.** In each of the following sets of correlation coefficients, which one represents the strongest relation?

  **a.** $+0.25 - 0.30 + 0.10$
  **b.** $+0.65 - 0.88 - 1.00$
  **c.** $-0.20 - 0.05 + 0.33$

**8.** "Correlation does not imply causality." What does this statement mean?

**9.** How do researchers ensure that their groups of participants are equal before they begin an experiment?

  **a.** They randomly assign participants to groups.
  **b.** They measure the dependent variable repeatedly.
  **c.** They use independent variables that are correlated with extraneous variables.
  **d.** They assign participants who have identified themselves as having control of extraneous variables.

**10.** Identify the independent variable and the dependent variable in each of the following situations:

  **a.** A researcher is interested in how fast college students can turn off a buzzer when it sounds. The participants are tested under two conditions: dim light and bright light.
  **b.** The Board of Directors of the National Football League has decided that half of its teams will sell beer until the

end of the game; the other half will stop sales at the end of the third quarter. The board is conducting a study to determine whether the timing of beer sales influences the number of fights and arrests that occur at games.

**c.** An industrial psychologist has developed two possible packages for a new shampoo that will be on the market soon. She is interested in determining which package has the greater sales appeal.

# THE ORIGINS OF MODERN PSYCHOLOGY

In their psychology class this morning, Carol and James heard their professor say that "psychology has a long past but only a short history." *What could their professor have meant?*

Although people have observed and studied human behavior for millennia, scientific psychology is a relatively new discipline. The origins of modern psychology can be traced to the University of Leipzig in Germany, where the first laboratory devoted to the scientific study of psychology was established in 1879.

## Wundt and Structuralism

Wilhelm Wundt (1832–1920) is credited with establishing the first psychology laboratory (Nicholas, Gyselinck, Murray, & Bandomir, 2002). Because the profession of psychology was not a career choice at that time, Wundt was originally trained as a physician. His mission in establishing the laboratory was to describe the contents of the conscious mind. Wundt and his student Edward B. Titchener (1867–1927), who brought Wundt's type of psychology to the United States, wanted to study psychology in the same way that a person would study physics or chemistry. If researchers could break down the contents of the mind into basic units like the basic elements of matter in chemistry, they could identify the structure of conscious experience and describe its major components (for example, feelings, sensations, and images). This approach to psychology became known as **structuralism.**

Titchener's research depended on a method called **introspection,** in which participants gave verbal reports of their conscious experiences. For example, participants given an orange would not describe it as a fruit but would instead describe its color, shape, and texture and other aspects of their own experience of the orange. Across a variety of tasks, however, the participants had difficulty producing similar reports; this fact raised questions about the existence of any common elements of conscious experience. Structuralism was replaced by other approaches, and at times conscious experience was not even considered a legitimate subject of psychological research.

During the past decade or two, psychologists have rediscovered conscious experience and investigated it using more sophisticated techniques than those available to the structuralists at the end of the 19th century (Coon, 1993). Today a rapidly growing area of psychology has broadened the early interests of structuralists; it is called

Wilhelm Wundt is credited with establishing the first psychology laboratory in 1879.

Archives of the History of American Psychology–The University of Akron.

**structuralism**
Earliest approach in modern psychology, founded by Wilhelm Wundt; its goal was to analyze the basic elements of conscious experience

**introspection**
Structural psychologists' major method, in which participants reported the contents of their conscious experience

**cognitive psychology**
Study of higher mental processes, such as thinking, knowing, and deciding

**functionalism**
Approach to psychology that focused on the purposes of consciousness

**Gestalt psychology**
Approach to psychology most noted for emphasizing that our perception of a whole is different from our perception of the individual stimuli

**cognitive psychology.** Cognitive psychologists are not interested in the structure of conscious experience; instead, they study higher mental processes such as thinking, knowing, and deciding. Their research is designed to determine how we store and recall information, solve problems, and make decisions (Bourne, Dominowski, Loftus, & Healy, 1986). We discuss the cognitive perspective in greater detail later in this chapter.

## Functionalism

A new approach to psychology developed in the United States in the late 1800s. **Functionalism** was concerned not with the structure of the mind but with the purposes of consciousness—what the mind does and why. One early proponent of functionalism, William James (1842–1910), was especially interested in what he termed the "stream of consciousness" (Simon, 1996). Because consciousness was like a continually flowing stream, it could not be easily broken down into its elements, as Wundt had hoped. According to James, if it were broken down into elements, it would lose its reality.

Functionalists wanted to see how people use information to adapt to their environment (Leahey, 2001). James and his functionalist colleagues were among the first applied psychologists; they were interested in the practical aspects of psychology, such as creating optimal conditions for learning or selecting the right workers for various jobs. Functionalism reached its peak in 1906 with James Rowland Angell's presidential address to the American Psychological Association. During its influential period, functionalism was associated most strongly with James Rowland Angell at the University of Chicago and Robert S. Woodworth at Columbia University.

## Gestalt Psychology

A group of psychologists who termed their approach **Gestalt psychology,** which was noted for emphasizing that perception of a whole differs from that of the individual stimuli that make up the whole, spearheaded the challenge to the structuralists' notion that conscious experience could be broken down into elements (Ash, 1995). The key members of this group were Max Wertheimer (1880–1943), Wolfgang Köhler (1887–1967), and Kurt Koffka (1886–1941). The Gestalt approach started in Germany in 1912, when Wertheimer (Leahey, 2001) described the visual illusion called *apparent motion*, in which a rapid sequence of stationary images creates the illusion of movement, as in a movie (Rock & Palmer, 1990; see Figure 1-4).

Soon Gestalt psychologists were describing other phenomena that supported their contention that what we perceive (the whole) is different from the sum of its parts (the individual stimuli). We perceive unified forms, rather than bits and pieces. Because the German word *Gestalt* can be translated as "pattern," "shape," or "configuration," it is not surprising that Gestalt psychologists have made their greatest contributions in the area of perception, as we see in Chapter 3.

**FIGURE 1-4** Although a strip of film contains a series of separate images, we perceive those images as continuous when they are projected on a screen. This phenomenon, known as *apparent motion*, gave rise to the Gestalt school of psychology.

# The Behavioral Perspective

The **behavioral perspective,** unlike the approaches we have discussed thus far, focuses on observable behaviors; thus it does not speculate about mental processes such as thinking. Moreover, this perspective emphasizes the importance of learning in understanding how various behaviors occur.

In the early 1900s the Russian physiologist Ivan Pavlov (1849–1936) was studying digestion in dogs when he noticed a curious phenomenon. When the dogs were about to be fed, they began salivating at the sight of the food or the jangling of keys used to unlock the rooms where they were kept. The dogs seemed to have learned an association between certain sounds or sights and being fed. As we see in Chapter 5, this simple observation led to the development of our understanding of how organisms learn to associate events in their environments.

The American psychologist John B. Watson (1878–1958) read about Pavlov's work and saw great promise in it. Watson believed psychology should be concerned not with the mind or consciousness but solely with observable behaviors. He asserted that the application of rigorous scientific principles, as used in Pavlov's laboratory, could lead to major advances (Buckley, 1989). Watson developed and applied his principles in the laboratory under strictly controlled conditions. Laboratory animals made excellent subjects for his research, which he later expanded to human participants.

The behavioral tradition started by Pavlov and continued by Watson found many strong proponents. The most notable was B. F. Skinner (1904–1990), who has been called the "greatest contemporary psychologist" (Fowler, 1990). In some ways, Skinner's approach to psychology was simple: Behavior changes as a result of its consequences (Leahey, 2004). Thus environmental consequences, rather than free will, shape human behavior. The behavioral psychologist's goal is to identify and change the environmental conditions that control behavior (O'Neill, 1995).

Skinner's followers used many of his basic principles to alter human behavior in a variety of settings (Martin & Pear, 1996). Some of Skinner's methods have been used to teach people diagnosed with schizophrenia to speak after years of being mute, to improve safety in manufacturing plants, and to teach basic skills to mentally retarded persons. If you have ever visited an amusement park that features trained dolphins, seals, whales, or other animals, you have seen an application of Skinner's principles (see Chapter 5).

# Sigmund Freud and the Psychodynamic Perspective

Historically, Skinner's approach followed the development of Watson's behaviorism. At about the same time Watson was defining psychology as the study of observable behavior, however, Sigmund Freud (1856–1939), across the Atlantic, was delving deeply beneath observable behaviors (Gelfand & Kerr, 1992). Few people have had such a profound impact on the way we think about ourselves as Freud, and few have been—or continue to be—so controversial (Crews, 1996).

Freud was trained as a neurologist rather than a psychologist. The patients who came to him suffered from a variety of anxieties and other disturbances. Freud and his followers developed the **psychodynamic perspective,** which suggests that both normal and abnormal behaviors are determined primarily by unconscious forces. The term *psychodynamic* is used because these forces are believed to interact with one another. Freud's experiences in treating his patients convinced him that the unconscious mind exerted great control over behavior. Among the observations that led him to this conclusion were "slips of the tongue," in which the patients' true feelings were apparently revealed, and analysis of his patients' dreams. Freud came to believe that the mind often disguises dreams so that the dreamer is not aware of their true meaning (see Chapter 4).

Freud also focused on early childhood experiences as a major influence on personality development. According to Freud, if you want to understand a person's personality, you must examine his or her early experiences, which could have long-lasting effects.

**Ivan Pavlov.** His studies of digestion in dogs led to important observations about how animals associate events in their environment.

**John B. Watson.** The founder of behaviorism declared that psychologists should limit their research to observable behaviors.

**behavioral perspective**
Perspective that focuses on observable behavior and emphasizes the learned nature of behavior

**psychodynamic perspective**
View taken by Sigmund Freud and his followers suggesting that normal and abnormal behaviors are determined primarily by unconscious forces

**B. F. Skinner.** His principles provided the basis for many applications of psychology.

**Sigmund Freud.** His influence can be seen not only in psychology but in many other fields.

**psychoanalytic therapy**
Treatment for maladaptive behavior developed by Sigmund Freud; its goal is to bring unconscious causes of behavior to the conscious level

**humanistic perspective**
Approach to psychology associated with Abraham Maslow and Carl Rogers; emphasizes free will and individuals' control of their own behavior

**physiological perspective**
View that behaviors and mental processes can be understood and explained by studying the underlying physiology

Freud gained great fame and notoriety by suggesting that people (even children) are driven by motives that are sexual in nature.

In treating his patients, Freud first turned to hypnosis (see Chapter 4), but he abandoned it when he determined that not everyone could be hypnotized. The treatment approach for maladaptive behavior that he eventually developed, known as **psychoanalytic therapy,** attempts to bring unconscious causes of distress to the conscious level. According to Freud, once the sources of distress are brought to awareness, they can be changed.

## The Humanistic Perspective

Over time, the psychodynamic and behavioral approaches were questioned. Many psychologists viewed the behavioral approach as cold and unappealing. To these psychologists, the notion that all behavior is controlled by environmental circumstances left no room for personal freedom, and the suggestion that we are doomed to behave in environmentally determined ways was unattractive. These critics believed that behaviorists seemed to avoid the unique and positive qualities of human behavior, such as creativity and love. What's more, the argument went, their views of human nature were either neutral or negative.

To some, the psychodynamic approach was no more appealing because its proponents viewed behavior as resulting from irrational forces that are not even under conscious control. Psychoanalysts studied people suffering from a variety of pathological problems, whereas behaviorists attempted to identify conditions that influence behavior by studying lower animals under controlled laboratory conditions. Critics argued that neither of these perspectives led to a true understanding of human behavior because neither focused on the creative potential and psychological health of human beings. As a result, a new approach to psychology developed. Emphasizing free will and individuals' control of their own behavior, the **humanistic perspective** was characterized by a distinctly positive view of human nature. Humanistic psychologists viewed themselves as a "third force" because they were an alternative to the behavioral and psychodynamic perspectives in psychology (Leahey, 2004).

The proponents of this approach, notably Carl Rogers (1902–1987) and Abraham Maslow (1908–1970), focused on the freedom they believed characterizes human behavior. According to the humanists, people have choices in their lives, and we cannot understand their choices by studying animals in laboratories or people experiencing adjustment problems.

Rather than attempting to develop general principles, Rogers and Maslow sought to understand each person as a unique individual. Humanists believe that each person experiences the world differently. One of the most important humanistic principles is that all human beings have a basic need to grow to their fullest potential. The humanists' major contributions to psychology have been their dramatically different view of human nature and the development of a variety of psychotherapeutic techniques (Barton, 1992).

## The Physiological Perspective

As we discuss in Chapter 2, every behavior of human beings and animals is related to some physiological change within the body. These physiological changes are the focus of psychologists interested in the **physiological perspective.** Physiological psychologists have a special interest in the functioning of the brain and the rest of the nervous system (Kalat, 2001). To assess neurological function, they now use sophisticated equipment that can create images of the brain. These imaging techniques reveal differences in the functioning of various areas of the brain, depending on the task given to a person.

Physiological psychologists also study how our nerve cells, called *neurons*, communicate with one another through special chemical substances called *neurotransmitters*. Scientists have identified a number of different neurotransmitters; each seems to play a special role in a variety of normal and abnormal behaviors. Most drugs influence our emotions and behaviors by altering levels of these neurotransmitters in the body.

In recent years, physiological psychologists have shown a special interest in the influence of heredity on personality characteristics, abilities, and the potential for developing certain abnormal behavior patterns. A number of psychologists are examining the wide range of physiological changes that occur when we are under stress. Their research has determined that illness is not simply a function of the presence of disease-causing viruses or bacteria. More and more, psychologists are investigating how personal factors such as how we deal with stress can influence our health status.

## The Evolutionary Perspective

Determining why a behavior or physical structure developed and how that behavior or structure aids in adaptation to the environment characterizes the **evolutionary perspective.** Charles Darwin (1859), who popularized the theory of evolution, maintained that evolution unfolds according to the principle of *natural selection*, which states that the strongest or most fit organisms are those that have adapted best to their environment. These organisms are more likely to survive and pass on their characteristics (genes) to future generations. Organisms with (or that inherit) different characteristics are less likely to survive. Therefore, researchers who work from an evolutionary perspective consistently ask what role a physiological structure or behavior plays in helping the organism survive and adapt to its environment. Researchers have successfully applied the evolutionary explanation to numerous areas, such as mate selection, aggression, kin selection, care of offspring, and parenting.

Let's see what an evolutionary explanation for a common behavior might look like. Consider a pet cat. What happens when the cat is frightened? The cat's hairs "stand on end." An evolutionary researcher would want to understand how this behavior contributed to the survival of the species. The most plausible explanation is that when the hairs are erected, the animal looks larger and more intimidating to potential predators. Hence, millions of years ago, cats that were able to erect their hairs when they were frightened were more likely to scare off predators and survive to pass their genes on to future generations. Thus, this once-adaptive behavior persisted and continues to be displayed.

Now, let's consider an evolutionary explanation for a human behavior. Likely, we would receive little disagreement that aggression has the potential to aid in adaptation to the environment; aggressive organisms are able to acquire resources and defend their own territories. Now, would we predict a difference between men and women in the total amount of aggression they would display? No, there doesn't seem to be any reason to make such a distinction. How about the type of aggression they would display? Here's where evolutionary theory makes a distinction between men and women. It is predicted that men will display more direct aggression (hitting, kicking), whereas women will display more indirect aggression (gossiping, ostracizing). Why? The evolutionary explanation centers on maternal involvement on the part of women. According to Hagenah, Heaps, Gilden, and Roberts (2001), "high amounts of maternal care given to offspring require that women minimize their risk of physical injury" (p. 128). Indirect aggression minimizes the chances of retaliatory injury compared to direct aggression. Research by Buss and Shackelford (1997) and Hagenah et al. (2001) supports these evolutionary predictions.

In addition to behaviors, evolutionary psychologists are interested in why certain physical structures developed and how they contribute to adaptation. Consider the evolution of the human hand. Why do comparable structures differ among different species? Because such considerations will include an examination and understanding of the functioning of the structure involved, evolutionary psychologists frequently employ a *functional approach* in their research. Often they compare the use of a structure among species; such comparisons use the *comparative approach*.

## The Cognitive Perspective

Because they focused only on observable behaviors, the behaviorists did not study cognitive processes—processes such as thinking, remembering, and determining how material

**Carl Rogers.** His system of humanistic psychology focused on free will and being able to control one's own behavior.

**Candace Pert.** This physiological psychologist discovered the brain receptors for the neurotransmitters called endorphins and enkephalin.

**evolutionary perspective**
Interest in the role a physiological structure or behavior plays in helping an organism adapt to its environment

**cognitive perspective**
View that focuses on the study of how thought occurs, how our memories work, and how information is organized and stored

**Mary Whiton Calkins,** the 14th president of the American Psychological Association, was the first woman to be elected to that position.

**Christine Ladd-Franklin** was a noted researcher who was denied a regular academic position because she was married.

**Beverly Inez Prosser** (1897–1934) was the first African-American woman to receive a doctoral degree in educational psychology.

is organized and stored in the mind—as part of the mainstream of psychological research. Consequently, from the 1920s to the 1960s, psychologists gave little research attention to these processes. Certain psychologists, however, disagreed that observable behavior should be the sole subject matter of psychology. For example, the Gestalt psychologists advocated the study of cognitive processes. Psychologists George Miller and Jerome Bruner established the Center for Cognitive Studies at Harvard University in 1960, and Ulric Neisser published the book *Cognitive Psychology* in 1967. The appearance of a widely read article supporting the study of cognitive processes (Liebman, 1979), combined with the ability of the computer to simulate human thought processes, generated considerable interest and research. Many psychologists have accepted the **cognitive perspective**—where the focus is on how thought occurs, memory processes, and information storage and utilization—and currently conduct research in the area of cognitive processes.

## The Cultural and Diversity Perspective

Attend a major meeting of psychologists and you are likely to be surrounded by dozens of different types of psychologists. Many are employed by colleges and universities, where they may teach, conduct research, or work in a psychological clinic sponsored by the university. The presence of women and minority psychologists provides a vivid contrast to the Caucasian, male-dominated field of only a few years ago. Psychologists are beginning to realize that the culture in which research is conducted; the gender, ethnicity, and personal biases of the researcher; and the gender and ethnicity of the research participants all influence our research results and contribute to our conception of "truth." Psychology is becoming more diverse, but this has not always been the case (Minton, 2000).

In the past, numerous barriers limited access to the field, especially for women and ethnic minorities. For example, Mary Whiton Calkins (1863–1930) completed her work at Harvard University, where she was a student of William James, but the university refused to award the doctoral degree she had earned because it did not grant degrees to women (Furumoto, 1979). Despite this setback, Calkins had a distinguished career in teaching, founded one of the first psychology laboratories in the United States, and was the first woman to be elected president of the American Psychological Association (Madigan & O'Hara, 1992).

In some cases, marital status and family ties hindered the careers of the first female psychologists. For example, the noted researcher Christine Ladd-Franklin "was not considered a suitable candidate for any regular academic position" because she was married (Furumoto, 1992, p. 180). Similarly, the tradition of the eldest daughter taking care of her aging parents cut short the budding career of Milicent Shinn, the first woman to receive a Ph.D. from the University of California at Berkeley in 1898. Shinn established herself as a leading expert on the mental and physical growth of infants and seemed poised for an eminent career in psychology until her parents' illness forced her to return to her family farm (Scarborough & Furumoto, 1987). Her career stopped completely at that point and was never resumed.

A century after Harvard refused to award Calkins a doctoral degree, women are entering the field of psychology in great numbers (see Figure 1-5). Women outnumber men two to one as undergraduate psychology majors and now earn more doctoral degrees in psychology than do men.

The struggle of racial minorities to become recognized professionals parallels that of the early women psychologists. Robert Guthrie (1998) summarized the struggles of African-American psychologists in his influential book *Even the Rat Was White*. For example, he indicates that professional training was not an option for black Americans during the late 1800s and early 1900s. It wasn't until 1920 that Francis C. Sumner (1895–1954) became the first African American to receive a Ph.D. in psychology. Subsequently, Sumner established the psychology program at Howard University and turned it into the major source for doctoral degrees for African-American students during the

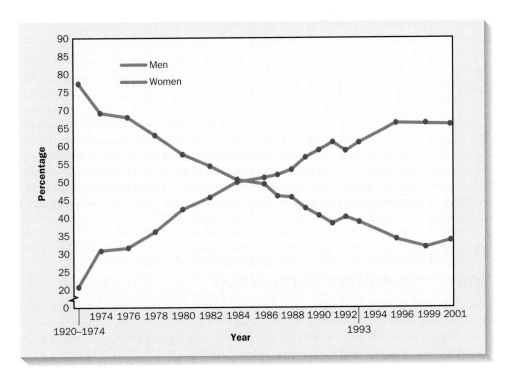

**FIGURE 1-5**  Percentages of doctoral degrees in psychology awarded to men and women.

**Sources:** Bailey (2004); Henderson, Clarke, and Woods (1998).

**Milicent Shinn** was the first woman to receive a Ph.D. from the University of California at Berkeley. She later abandoned her career to care for her aging parents.

first half of the 20th century. Sumner has been followed by a succession of eminent African-American psychologists such as James Arthur Bayton (1912–1990), who achieved national recognition for his marketing research.

Doctoral degrees in psychology were not granted to African-American women until the 1930s. Two women in this group are noteworthy. Inez Beverly Prosser (1897–1934) was the first African-American woman to receive a doctoral degree in educational psychology; she received this degree from the University of Cincinnati in 1933. Her doctoral dissertation research was on "Non-Academic Development of Negro Children in Mixed and Segregated Schools." Unfortunately, her career was cut short by a tragic automobile accident on August 28, 1934; she passed away on September 5, 1934. Ruth Winifred Howard (1900–1997) received her Ph.D. in psychology in 1934 from the University of Minnesota. She was the first person to publish research on triplets.

Until recently, few members of racial minority groups obtained jobs in psychology. Today the number of minority candidates receiving doctoral degrees and finding employment in psychology is increasing (Howard et al., 1986). In fact, in 1970 the American Psychological Association elected an African American, Kenneth B. Clark (1914–2005), as its president. Clark is noted for his research on the harmful effects of segregation, which was cited by the Supreme Court in the landmark 1954 case, *Brown v. Board of Education*. His wife, Mamie Phipps Clark (1917–1983), received her doctoral degree in psychology from Columbia University in 1944 and achieved considerable recognition through her research and publication on such topics as "The Development of Consciousness of Self and Emergence of Racial Identification in Negro Preschool Children," which appeared in a 1939 issue of the *Journal of Social Psychology*.

An Asian American, Richard Suinn, was elected president of the American Psychological Association in 1997. However, attaining prestigious offices in professional associations is not the only visible sign of the influence of culture and diversity.

The impact of different cultures and diversity on psychology is seen in contemporary psychological literature. Studies on diverse groups and topics—such as gender issues, ethnic groups, national cultures, sexual orientation, and persons with disabilities—abound in the psychological journals. It is arguable (Matsumoto, 1998) that there is a revolution afoot in the field of psychology; there is a move toward a cultural psychology where such

**Kenneth B. Clark** was the first African American to serve as president of the American Psychological Association.

**Mamie Phipps Clark** conducted important research on consciousness of self and social identification in African-American preschoolers.

**environmental, population, and conservation perspective**
View that psychologists should be concerned with the interactions among human behavior, the population, and the environment

**eclectic approach**
View of psychology that combines several different approaches

topics are the rule rather than the exception. Psychologist David Matsumoto believes that "the psychological principles we derive about people may be consistent or discrepant across cultures. To the extent that differences do exist, it is important for all of us to appreciate how cultural factors moderate our psychological processes. In gaining such appreciation, we can learn how our own viewpoint, developed within our own cultural framework, can distort our interpretation of others' behaviors." For example, in a cross-cultural study of the intensity of facial expressions of emotion in Americans and Japanese, Matsumoto, Kasri, and Kooken (1999) showed that Americans exaggerated their ratings. Previously, it had been assumed that the difference between the two cultures occurred because Japanese participants suppressed their ratings. At the same time, we need to know what kinds of cross-cultural similarities exist in psychological principles and basic processes. Knowledge about these similarities as well should help us in our endeavors to apply these principles to improve our lives (Matsumoto, 1997, p. 2).

## The Environmental, Population, and Conservation Perspective

The later 20th century witnessed an increasing concern for the effects of overpopulation on the quality of life and the quality of our environment. These concerns are responsible for the development of a new perspective in psychology: the **environmental, population, and conservation perspective.** According to Clay (2001), "whether they're talking about trash, overpopulation or global warming, environmental psychologists agree that human behavior is the cause of environmental degradation. They agree that incentives like bottle deposits encourage people to recycle, that posted reminders get them to turn off their lights and that conveniently placed trash cans keep them from littering" (p. 42).

In short, these psychologists are applying psychological principles to help save the planet. The challenge facing these professionals is the task of increasing proenvironmental behavior. Their task is a daunting but very important one. Those psychologists most directly interested in fostering the practice of conservation have established a listserv that you may be interested in investigating. To subscribe, send an e-mail to conservation-psychology-request@umich.edu with the word SUBSCRIBE as the subject of the message.

These different perspectives are summarized in the following Study Chart.

## PRESENT-DAY PSYCHOLOGY

Psychologists today are interested in a diversity of topics. In fact, there are few endeavors that would not interest at least one of the more than half-million psychologists in the world (Rosenzweig, 1992).

Present-day psychologists do not align themselves strictly with any of the approaches we outlined in our earlier discussion of the origins of psychology. Instead they tend to choose the approach they consider appropriate to each issue under consideration. Because they use several approaches, many psychologists have adopted an **eclectic approach** to psychology.

Most psychology majors who complete their education with a B.A. or B.S. degree are employed by for-profit companies and not-for-profit organizations (Ballie, 2001). Many psychologists earn an advanced degree, usually a doctorate. The majority of psychologists who have earned advanced degrees are either self-employed or work in some type of educational setting (Ballie, 2001). In a number of states, a person cannot assume the title of *psychologist* unless he or she meets certain standards of education and training set by a state board. Psychologists all over the world are working to establish the legal status for their profession. Their purpose is to protect the public by ensuring that people who represent themselves as psychologists have appropriate training and professional experience.

## *Study* CHART

### Major Perspectives in Psychology

| Perspective | Description | Key Figures |
| --- | --- | --- |
| Structuralism | Attempted to identify the basic elements and structure of conscious experience | Wilhelm Wundt (1832–1920) and Edward B. Titchener (1867–1927) |
| Functionalism | Concerned with the purposes of consciousness—what the mind does and why—and how that information could be put to practical use | William James (1842–1910) and James Rowland Angell (1869–1949) |
| Gestalt psychology | Made major contributions to understanding how we perceive the world as different from the sum of its individual elements | Max Wertheimer (1880–1943), Wolfgang Köhler (1887–1967), and Kurt Koffka (1886–1941) |
| Behavioral | Focuses on observable behaviors without speculating about mental processes such as thinking; a major emphasis is that learning plays a key role in controlling and influencing all behaviors | John B. Watson (1878–1958) and B. F. Skinner (1904–1990) |
| Psychodynamic | Based on the belief that the unconscious mind exerts great control over behavior and that early childhood experiences are a major influence on personality development | Sigmund Freud (1856–1939) |
| Humanistic | Focuses on the creative potential and psychological health of human beings while emphasizing the individual's interpretation of events | Carl Rogers (1902–1987) and Abraham Maslow (1908–1970) |
| Physiological | Focuses on the underlying physiology involved in all forms of behavior and mental processes; uses increasingly sophisticated research tools to investigate brain functioning and conduction of nerve impulses; also investigates the role of heredity in normal and abnormal behavior patterns | Karl S. Lashley (1890–1958) |
| Evolutionary | Focuses on why a particular behavior or physical structure developed and how that behavior or structure aids in adaptation to the environment | D. M. Buss |
| Cognitive | Focuses on the processes of thinking, memory, and organizing and storing information | George Miller (b. 1920), Jerome Bruner (b. 1915), and Ulric Neisser (b. 1928) |
| Cultural and diversity | Focuses on the influence that different cultures and diverse individuals have on the research process and the results of that process | Janet Hyde and David Matsumoto |
| Environmental, population, and conservation | Focuses on the interactions between human behavior and population and the environment | Susan Clayton and George Wilmouth |

Although all psychologists share a keen interest in advancing our knowledge of human and animal behavior through research, some psychologists, by choice, engage in little or no research. A rapidly growing number of psychologists have entered what are termed *health service provider* or *direct service specialties* (Howard et al., 1986). These psychologists are interested primarily in the applications of psychology. As you can see from Figure 1-6, the largest specialty in psychology is a direct service one: clinical psychology.

**FIGURE 1-6** Specialties in psychology.

**Note:** Figures are based on a survey of doctoral recipients, 2002.

**Source:** Bailey (2004).

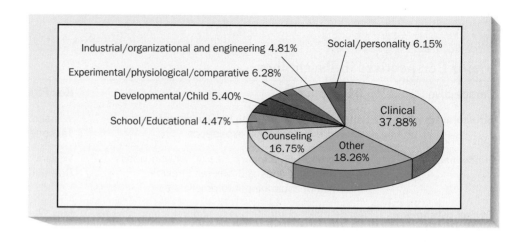

Industrial/organizational and engineering 4.81%

Social/personality 6.15%

Experimental/physiological/comparative 6.28%

Developmental/Child 5.40%

School/Educational 4.47%

Counseling 16.75%

Clinical 37.88%

Other 18.26%

# PSYCHOLOGICAL SPECIALTIES

**Clinical and Counseling Psychology.** Most students who major in psychology are interested in the work done by clinical psychologists. More and more students want to "work with people." Although most psychologists work with people in one way or another, those involved in **clinical psychology** specialize in helping people with behavioral or emotional problems adjust to the demands of life.

Clinical psychologists are frequently confused with psychiatrists (Murstein & Fontaine, 1993). Members of these two professions share an interest in diagnosing and treating people who are experiencing various behavioral and emotional problems. Clinical psychologists and psychiatrists differ, however, in the advanced degrees they obtain and in other aspects of their training. After completing an undergraduate degree, clinical psychologists earn a doctoral degree (Ph.D. or Psy.D.), which usually takes 4 or more years. They then complete an internship of at least 1 year to develop their diagnostic and therapeutic skills; during this time, they are supervised by experienced clinical psychologists.

By contrast, **psychiatrists** are medical doctors; they have earned an M.D. degree. After graduating from medical school, they complete a 3-year residency, often at a major psychiatric hospital. Although some aspects of the training of clinical psychologists and psychiatrists are similar, there are major differences. For example, psychiatrists are trained in the medical assessment of disorders and hence are more likely to view the disorders as caused by medical conditions.

A specialty that has much in common with clinical psychology is **counseling psychology;** counseling psychologists also administer psychological tests and provide therapy. One difference between clinical and counseling psychologists involves the types of clients they see. Counseling psychologists often work with clients who have less serious problems than those of patients seen by clinical psychologists. For example, the counseling psychologist is more likely to deal with people who are having difficulty dealing with everyday problems, such as a physical handicap or a vocational decision.

**Other Specialties.** Many people believe that psychologists are engaged exclusively in providing diagnostic and therapeutic services to sufferers of mental disorders; however, there is a wide range of specialties beyond clinical and counseling psychology. For example, you may hear the term *experimental psychologist* used to describe psychologists who conduct experiments; however, because many different types of psychologists conduct experiments, the term **research psychologist** is more appropriate. Table 1-4 summarizes these research specialties. Often you will find research psychologists dividing their duties between conducting research and teaching at a college or university.

Because modern psychology is identified so highly with the United States, we may have a tendency to view our psychological research as applying to all other cultures. The view that other cultures are an extension of your own is called **ethnocentrism** (Smith &

**clinical psychology**
Specialty of psychology that involves the diagnosis and treatment of psychological disorders

**psychiatrist**
Medical doctor with specialized training in the medical treatment of mental and emotional disorders

**counseling psychology**
Specialty of psychology that deals with less serious problems than those treated by clinical psychologists

**research psychologist**
Psychologist whose primary activity is to conduct and report the results of experiments

**ethnocentrism**
The view that other cultures are an extension of one's own

**TABLE 1-4**

## Research Psychologists and Their Interests

| Area or Specialty | Description of Research Interests |
| --- | --- |
| Animal behavior | Behavior and basic learning processes; comparative studies using different species |
| Biopsychology/ neuropsychology | Physiological mechanisms of learning, memory, and behavior |
| Cognitive processes | Mental processes used to take in, store, and utilize information in thinking, remembering, and making decisions |
| Cross-cultural | Research conducted to determine whether results are universal or culture-specific |
| Developmental | Processes of growth, development, and change throughout the entire life span |
| Educational | Application of psychological findings and principles to the classroom |
| Motivation | Causes and consequences of motivation in animals and humans |
| Personality | Factors that make individuals unique, as well as factors that are shared |
| Psychometrics | Theoretical and practical aspects of psychological testing and measurement |
| Sensation and perception | Process of sensory input and the use and interpretation of sensory information |
| Social | Influence of other people on behavior |

Davis, 2004). **Cross-cultural psychology** is a branch of psychology that seeks to determine if research results are universal (that is, if they can be generalized or applied to other cultures [Matsumoto, 1994]). As psychologists recognize the increasingly diverse nature of their field, the importance of cross-cultural research is clearly highlighted. The understanding of "human" behavior requires that we know which of our findings are universal and which are limited to specific cultures. This approach has aided the development and expansion of the culture and diversity perspective we discussed previously.

### Psychological Detective

How might cultural differences affect the development and conduct of psychological research? Write down some possibilities before reading further.

The different attitudes, values, and behaviors held by different cultures can influence the choice of research problems, the research hypothesis that is developed, the variables that are studied, and even the type of survey or questionnaire that is used. In short, culture has the potential to influence all aspects of psychological research. Hence we must be very cautious in generalizing results from one culture to another. Finally, keep in mind that there are numerous different cultural groups within the United States; their differences must also be considered. Just because a piece of research was conducted in the United States does not guarantee that its results are applicable to all Americans. Clearly, these cross-cultural issues must be the concern of all research psychologists.

**cross-cultural psychology**
Branch of psychology whose goal is to determine if research results can be applied to other cultures

**school psychologist**
Psychologist whose specialty encompasses diagnosing and treating learning disabilities and providing consultation on other problems of school-age children

**industrial and organizational (I/O) psychologist**
Psychologist who applies psychology to problems of businesses and other organizations

**consumer psychology**
Specialty of psychology that studies consumers and the choices they make

**health psychology**
Subfield of psychology that is concerned with how psychological and social variables affect health and illness

**forensic psychologist**
Psychologist who applies psychology to law and legal proceedings

**School psychologists** are employed by school systems as consultants to other educational personnel. Can you imagine a time when "there were no state or national level organizations to serve the interests of school psychologists, no codes of practice, no training or credentialing guidelines, and no accreditation or credentialing" (Fagan, 2000, p. 756)? In the 21st century, with such organizations as the National Association of School Psychologists (NASP) developing standards, accrediting programs, and hosting an annual national convention, and the American Psychological Association having a separate division for school psychologists, such conditions may seem more like a flight into imagination and fancy than based in reality. These conditions were, however, the order of the day in the late 1800s and early 1900s. Currently, a school psychologist may visit several schools in a district during the course of a week to make psychological evaluations, discuss specific students with teachers, and meet with parents.

**Industrial and organizational psychologists** (also known as **I/O psychologists;** see Chapter 16) are concerned with all aspects of work and the structure and function of organizations. Their responsibilities vary with the employer, but they may be asked to design a system for selecting employees or to implement an employee assistance program to deal with alcoholism, drug abuse, and stress both on and off the job. Once new employees are hired, I/O psychologists may assist in designing and evaluating programs to train them for their new jobs. In addition, they may be asked to design methods to measure worker productivity, increase worker motivation, evaluate work schedule efficiency, or design systems for resolving disputes within organizations (Rogelberg, 2002).

Some I/O psychologists are involved in the design of equipment and manufacturing plants. When they design equipment, they take into consideration the relation between the worker and the equipment, as well as the capabilities of the worker. These psychologists are also called *human factors psychologists,* and they work in a specialty called *ergonomics.*

**Consumer psychology** is the scientific study of the behavior of consumers. Although your last purchase of a portable cassette player or a hair dryer may have seemed an unremarkable event, such apparently casual events provide the basis for consumer psychologists' questions. They may want to know how you became aware of the product, how you went about evaluating various brands, or what made you select a particular brand.

A recent addition to the list of psychology's specialties is **health psychology.** This diverse and rapidly growing specialty is concerned with the relations between psychological factors and health. Health psychologists work to promote health and prevent illness; they study the causes and treatments of illness and the ways people cope with their illnesses (see Chapter 14). They also investigate ways to reduce the risk for disease by changing unhealthy or harmful behaviors (Friedman, 2002). For example, they may investigate the effects of exercise on cholesterol levels and subsequent heart attacks, or they may evaluate techniques to encourage the practice of safe sex. Because stress is an ever-present part of our lives, health psychologists also try to increase our understanding of the factors related to stress and to discover ways to alleviate its negative consequences. For example, health psychologist Tom Boll is using psychological tests and other measures to select potential heart transplant patients who are best able to handle the stress of the operation (De Angelis, 1992).

**Emerging Specialties.**    Psychology is not a static science; its proponents continually strive to discover new arenas for research and application. Among the recent additions to the field are forensic (legal) psychology, sport psychology, and neuropsychology.

**Forensic psychologists** work within the legal system; they may work in a prison to evaluate incoming prisoners or assist in selecting a jury for a trial (Porter, 2004). Carefully wording the questions asked of prospective jurors can help identify potentially biased jurors, who can then be excused from service (Goodman, Loftus, & Greene, 1990). Forensic psychologists also provide testimony as expert witnesses (see Chapter 7). For example, psychologist Elizabeth Loftus has testified many times about how stress affects the accuracy of recalled events, how observing violent crimes affects eyewitness identifications, or how police lineups can sometimes lead witnesses to an incorrect identification of a suspect (Hardy & Van Leeuwen, 2004).

**TABLE 1-5**

## Job Titles Held by Psychology Majors with Bachelor's Degrees

### A. Job Titles Directly Related to Psychology

| | | |
|---|---|---|
| Academic advisor | Director of volunteer services | Public information specialist |
| Alcohol/drug abuse counselor | Eligibility worker | Public relations specialist |
| Behavior analyst | Employment counselor | Publications researcher |
| Career counselor | Family services worker | Radio/TV research assistant |
| Career planning and placement | Gerontology aide | Rehabilitation advisor |
| Counselor | Group home coordinator | Residential counselor |
| Case management aide | Housing/student life coordinator | Residential youth counselor |
| Case worker | Life skill counselor | Secondary school teacher |
| Child care worker | Mental health technician | Social service assistant |
| Child protection worker | Mental retardation unit manager | Social services director |
| Community outreach worker | Parole officer | Social work assistant |
| Community support worker | Political campaign worker | Urban planning research assistant |
| Corrections officer | Probation officer | Veteran's advisor |
| Counselor aide | Program manager | |
| Day care center supervisor | Public affairs coordinator | |

### B. Job Titles Not Directly Related to Psychology but Appropriate for Psychology Majors

| | | |
|---|---|---|
| Administrative assistant | Fast food restaurant manager | Newspaper reporter |
| Advertising agent | Film researcher/copywriter | Occupational analyst |
| Advertising trainee | Financial researchers | Park and recreation director |
| Affirmative action representative | Historical research assistant | Personnel worker/administrator |
| Airline reservations clerk | Hospital patient services representative | Public information officer |
| Claims specialist | Human resources recruiter | Public relations |
| College admissions officer | Insurance agent | Sales representative |
| Community recreation worker | Intelligence officer | Small business owner |
| Congressional aide | Job analyst | Staff training and development |
| Customer relations | Law enforcement officer | Statistical assistant |
| Customer service representative | Loan officer | Store manager |
| Director of alumni relations | Lobbying organizer | Technical writer |
| Director of fund raising | Management trainee | Vocational rehabilitation counselor |
| Employee counselor | Marketing representative | Warehouse manager |
| Employee relations assistant | Marketing researcher | |
| Energy researcher | Media buyer | |

**Source:** Adapted from Landrum and Davis (2004).

**sport psychologist**
Psychologist who provides services to athletes and coaches based on psychological principles

**neuropsychologist**
Psychologist trained in the diagnosis and rehabilitation of brain disorders

**Sport psychologists** apply the theories and knowledge of psychology to enhance athletes' performance (Holowchak, 2002). They may consult with coaches about the use of specific coaching techniques or provide supportive therapy and encouragement to players recovering from injuries. They also help athletes improve their performance by using techniques such as relaxation and imagery (Murphy, 1994). Since 1978, sport psychologists have been part of the team of experts who help U.S. athletes prepare for the Olympics.

Given that Congress designated the 1990s as "the decade of the brain," it is not surprising that one of the emerging specialties in psychology is concerned with brain functioning (see Chapter 2). **Neuropsychologists** are trained to diagnose disorders of the brain. Using various tests, they try to identify specific brain areas that may be malfunctioning. They often conduct research to identify early symptoms that predict the development of disorders such as Huntington's disease (Diamond, White, Myers, & Mastromauro, 1992). They also devise rehabilitation programs to help patients regain as much of their abilities as possible after suffering brain damage, strokes, or traumatic brain injury (Diller, 1992).

If you are thinking about a career in psychology after you graduate, there are numerous employment opportunities for psychology majors with a bachelor's degree. In fact, the job possibilities are as diverse as the field of psychology itself. Several job possibilities are shown in Table 1-5.

# REVIEW SUMMARY

1. The history of modern psychology began in 1879, when Wilhelm Wundt established the first psychology laboratory at the University of Leipzig in Germany. The goal of Wundt's school of psychology, known as **structuralism,** was to identify the elements of conscious experience by using the method of **introspection.**

2. Another perspective, which came to be known as **functionalism,** focused on the purposes of consciousness and was especially concerned with the applications of psychology. **Gestalt psychology** is concerned primarily with our perception of our environment. **Cognitive psychology** studies higher mental processes such as thinking, knowing, and deciding.

3. Influenced by the Russian physiologist Ivan Pavlov, John B. Watson was interested in how the environment affects behavior. Because consciousness cannot be observed directly, Watson defined psychology as the study of observable behavior. The **behavioral perspective** was continued by B. F. Skinner, probably the best-known and most influential psychologist of our time.

4. Sigmund Freud's **psychodynamic perspective** focused on unconscious determinants of behavior. Freud also developed a treatment approach known as **psychoanalytic therapy.**

5. Dissatisfaction with both the behavioral and psychodynamic perspectives led psychologists Abraham Maslow and Carl Rogers to develop the **humanistic perspective.** Humanists believe that other perspectives pay too little attention to uniquely human characteristics such as free will and individual control.

6. The **physiological perspective** focuses on the underlying biological bases of all forms of behavior.

7. The **evolutionary perspective** focuses on why a particular behavior or physical structure developed and how that behavior or structure aids in adaptation to the environment.

8. The field of psychology has begun to recognize the contributions made by women and ethnic minorities, and additional contributions from these groups can be expected in the future. The **cultural and diversity perspective** focuses on such research contributions.

9. The **environmental, population, and conservation perspective** emphasizes the interaction among human behavior, population, and the environment.

10. Most psychologists have earned a doctoral degree (Ph.D. or Psy.D.). Although many psychologists teach and engage in research, a growing number provide direct services to clients.

# ✓ CHECK YOUR PROGRESS

1. Who is credited with establishing the first psychological laboratory?
   a. Ivan Pavlov
   b. William James
   c. Max Wertheimer
   d. Wilhelm Wundt

2. An early proponent of functionalism who was interested in the stream of consciousness was
   a. Ivan Pavlov
   b. William James
   c. Wilhelm Wundt
   d. Max Wertheimer

3. Gestalt psychology had its greatest impact in the study of

   a. memory
   b. perception
   c. nerve conduction
   d. abnormal behavior

4. What barrier to becoming a psychologist did Mary Whiton Calkins face in the late 1880s?

   a. As a woman, she could not complete graduate courses at Harvard.
   b. Because she was a woman, Harvard would not award her the doctoral degree she earned.
   c. Women could not establish psychological laboratories in the United States at that time.
   d. She was not allowed to join the American Psychological Association.

5. What is the current gender representation in psychology?

   a. Men earn more doctoral degrees than do women.
   b. Women and men earn approximately equal numbers of doctoral degrees.
   c. Women earn more doctoral degrees than do men.
   d. Psychology does not categorize doctoral degrees by gender.

6. Each of the following descriptions could apply to one of the historical perspectives on psychology discussed in this chapter. Which perspective best fits the description?

   a. believes unconscious forces are the most significant determinants of behavior
   b. is concerned with the biological processes involved in a behavior
   c. is interested in the elements of consciousness
   d. believes the whole is different from the sum of its parts
   e. is interested in studying decision making and problem solving

7. Identify the person who is most likely to have made each of the following statements.

   a. "I never received my Ph.D., although I earned it."
   b. "The study of my patients convinces me that unconscious forces lie beneath many of their disturbances."
   c. "What impresses me about human behavior is the freedom each of us has to make choices."

8. Name the type of psychologist (or specialty) described in each of the following:

   a. was asked to diagnose and treat a 35-year-old man who hears frightening voices every day
   b. helped an out-of-work auto mechanic decide on a new career
   c. designed a survey to determine whether purchasers of a liquid detergent were satisfied with the product
   d. testified as an expert witness on factors that influence the accuracy of eyewitnesses

**ANSWERS: 1.** d  **2.** b  **3.** b  **4.** b  **5.** c  **6. a.** Psychodynamic  **b.** Physiological  **c.** Structuralism  **d.** Gestalt **e.** Cognitive  **7. a.** Mary Whiton Calkins  **b.** Sigmund Freud  **c.** Abraham Maslow or Carl Rogers  **8. a.** Clinical psychologist  **b.** Counseling psychologist  **c.** Consumer psychologist  **d.** Forensic psychologist

---

**ANSWERS** **To Questions in Table 1-2**

1. The answer depends on the hemisphere you are in when you answer the question. For people in the Northern Hemisphere, the Earth is closer to the sun from September to May; for people in the Southern Hemisphere, the Earth is closer to the sun from May to September. The degree of warmth is not associated with distance from the sun; the tilt of the earth as it receives the sun's rays determines warmth.

2. It depends. If the country minting the coin is the United States, the answer is Abraham Lincoln (you may be aware

of the much older and very valuable "Indianhead" pennies). In Canada, the Queen of England appears on a penny.

3. The answer is Sophie Kurys, who played for the Racine Belles in the Women's Professional Baseball League in 1946; she stole 202 bases.

4. The answer is simple, provided that assmptions do not get in your way. Extend the line on the right side downward and you will produce the number 4 (a perfect square).

## CHAPTER 2

# Behavioral Neuroscience

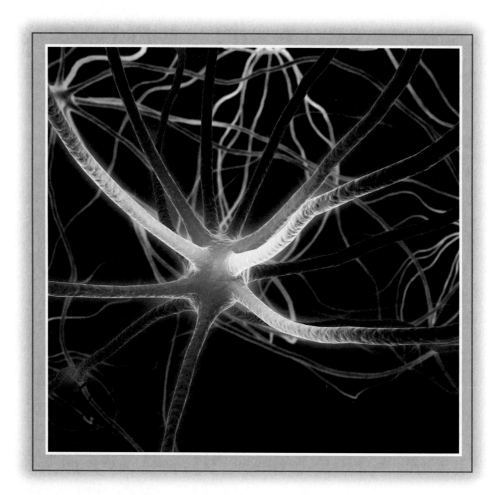

## CHAPTER OUTLINE

Tis chapter begins our in-depth exploration of the various areas of psychology. As you progress through the pages of this book, you will notice that our plan is to move from basic topics to general and broad ones. Notice we did not say that we would progress from the simple to the complex. As you read about the nervous system, the endocrine system, and our basic biological processes in this chapter, we are sure you will agree that these topics are not simple. Sensing, processing, and responding are vital to our ability to adapt to a changing environment. In subsequent chapters we expand our discussion of the biological basis of psychological processes to include such topics as how we receive and process information from the environment (Chapter 3) and the various states of consciousness that we experience (Chapter 4). From time to time throughout the book we will return to a consideration of the biological basis of behaviors to help explain topics such as human development (Chapter 9), the varieties of abnormal behavior (Chapter 12), and some forms of treatment (Chapter 13).

## BIOLOGY AND BEHAVIOR

Thousands of years ago, our ancestors roamed the planet trying as best they could to survive. They faced animals that saw them as prey, and they navigated in darkness that frequently made moving about very dangerous. Some of our ancestors survived and passed on their genes to subsequent generations; others perished. Across thousands of years and numerous generations, the brain and the rest of the human nervous system were evolving. Those persons who survived left us a legacy of emotional reactions such as fear that had survival value, as well as a broad collection of bodily changes that motivated us to fight or to flee. As new ways of coping with the environment developed, the brain encoded these methods, which enabled us to transmit them to new generations for future use. *What is the significance of biology for understanding animal and human behavior?*

The study of the relation between biological and psychological functions is rapidly expanding, complex, and fascinating. Knowing how the human body and brain work helps us to understand many areas of psychology: the nature of personality, the causes of certain abnormal behaviors, our reaction to stressful situations, the effectiveness of some types of therapy with certain patients but not with others, and much more. Recognition of the importance of the relation of the nervous system to behavior led the U.S. Congress to designate the 1990s as "the decade of the brain."

In their efforts to understand the brain and the rest of the nervous system, many researchers have adopted an *evolutionary perspective* (Gaulin & McBurney, 2001; McKee, Poirier, & McGraw, 2005), which focuses on the role a particular physical structure or behavior plays in helping an organism adapt to its environment over time. This perspective began with an around-the-world scientific journey taken by Charles Darwin. The large array of animal and plant species Darwin collected was intriguing; he wondered why nature came in so many varieties. His efforts to answer this question led to "what may be the single most important and far-reaching scientific theory that has ever been formulated" (Gaulin & McBurney, 2001, p. 19). Darwin (1859) maintained that

**natural selection**
According to Charles Darwin, the process by which inherited characteristics that lead to an advantage in adapting to the environment are more likely to be passed on to subsequent generations through genetic material

**behavioral neuroscience**
A general term encompassing a range of disciplines such as neurology, psychology, and psychiatry that focus on the role of the nervous system, especially the brain, in understanding behavior

**stimulus**
Environmental feature that provokes a response from an organism

**receptors**
Specialized cells that are sensitive to specific types of stimulus energy

2.1

evolution unfolds according to the principle of **natural selection:** the process by which inherited characteristics that lead to an advantage in adapting to the environment are more likely to be passed on (through genetic material) to future generations. Over thousands of years of evolution, mutations have occurred in the grand plan for development contained in an organism's genes. Some of these mutations result in changes that increase the chances of survival. For example, the mutation resulting in an eagle's strong talons and sharp beak gave those organisms an advantage in catching and devouring prey compared to eagles without these changes. Consequently, these physical characteristics were passed to future generations. Certain species of moths have spots on their wings that resemble the eyes of the predator owl. How would such a characteristic be advantageous? These spots are generally hidden; however, when a bird approaches, the moth's wings flip open, exposing the eyespots. Birds tend to fly away when they see the spots, keeping the moths relatively safe from predators (Carlson, 2001). Accordingly, researchers who work from an evolutionary perspective ask what role a physical structure or behavior plays in helping an organism survive and adapt to its environment.

In addition to studying the process of natural selection, researchers focus on discovering the actual genetic material responsible for the physical structure or behavior under investigation. We say more about genetics in Chapter 9. Keep the evolutionary perspective in mind as you read this book. See if it helps you understand why a particular behavior or physical structure developed.

The researchers who study the biological basis of animal and human behavior are working in an area called **behavioral neuroscience.** This relatively new term focuses attention on the relation between biological factors and behavior. What's more, the term implies that these scientists represent several disciplines including psychology (especially physiological psychologists), biology, medicine, and others. Why are so many disciplines involved? These researchers are studying the nervous system, which includes the brain—the most complex machine ever constructed. In fact, the brain is infinitely more complex than the most sophisticated computer! Our examination of this very complex machine begins with an overview of how humans relate to their environment.

To survive, human beings must be able to perform three interrelated activities: sensing events, or *stimuli*; processing stimuli; and responding to stimuli. A **stimulus** is a feature in the environment—such as a traffic light, a sign, an alarm, or the smell of smoke—that may provoke a response. **Receptors** are specialized cells of the nervous system that sense stimuli. We discuss several receptors (for example, those located in the

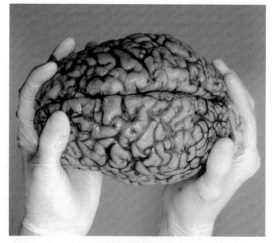

Although the laptop on the left and the human brain on the right are approximately the same size, the computer is the product of the human brain. Despite its size, the human brain has been called the most complex machine ever constructed. Part of its complexity derives from the millions of connections that are possible among its parts. And unlike the computer, the human brain is capable of creativity and can, in some ways, even repair damage to itself.

**A** Sensing

**B** Processing

**C** Responding

**FIGURE 2-1**    An example of the activities of sensing, processing, and responding to stimuli. You are driving down the road and come to a light that is amber, about to turn red. You also notice (Step 1) a sign restricting turns, depending on the time of day. You have a lot of information to process and sort out (Step 2). You decide to stop at the light and quickly recognize that you can make the turn on a red light after stopping. You stop and then proceed to make the turn (Step 3).

eyes and ears) in Chapter 3. For now, remember that we are concerned with a chain of events that typically begins when a stimulus activates a receptor.

The second activity in the chain is interpreting, or *processing*, the information that reaches the receptors. This processing typically takes place in the brain. Once we've processed and understood the sensory input, we may need to respond to it. Therefore, the third activity occurs when the brain sends messages to the muscles to produce a response. As you can see in Figure 2-1, these three activities are involved in events as common as driving a car.

# THE NERVOUS SYSTEM

The activities of sensing, processing, and responding are coordinated and controlled by the nervous system, which has two major divisions (Figure 2-2): the **central nervous system (CNS)** and the **peripheral nervous system (PNS).** The CNS consists of the brain and spinal cord; the PNS connects the outer portions (or periphery) of the body with the CNS.

The brain has two halves (called *hemispheres*), one for the right side of the body and one for the left. The right hemisphere receives input from the left side of the body, and the left hemisphere receives input from the right side of the body. The arrangement whereby each hemisphere receives input from the opposite side of the body is called *contralateral conduction*. The basic cells of the nervous system are **neurons,** and we will say more about them shortly. First, we take a closer look at the PNS and CNS.

## The Peripheral Nervous System

The PNS consists of all the parts of the nervous system that are outside the CNS. If we think of the nervous system as a computer, the PNS would consist of the "peripherals," such as the monitor, keyboard, and printer, which transport information into and out of the central portion of the computer. The two major divisions of the PNS are the somatic nervous system and the autonomic nervous system (see Figure 2-2).

**The Somatic Nervous System.**    The **somatic nervous system** of the PNS makes contact with the environment. It consists of nerves that connect receptors to the spinal cord and brain, as well as nerves that go *to* and *from* the brain and spinal cord to the muscles. Nerves that carry information from receptors to the brain and spinal cord are called

**central nervous system (CNS)**
Division of the nervous system that consists of the brain and spinal cord

**peripheral nervous system (PNS)**
Division of the nervous system that consists of the neural fibers lying outside of the brain and spinal cord

**neurons**
Basic cells of the nervous system

**somatic nervous system**
Division of the peripheral nervous system that consists of nerves coming from the receptors to the brain and spinal cord, as well as nerves that go from the brain and spinal cord to the muscles

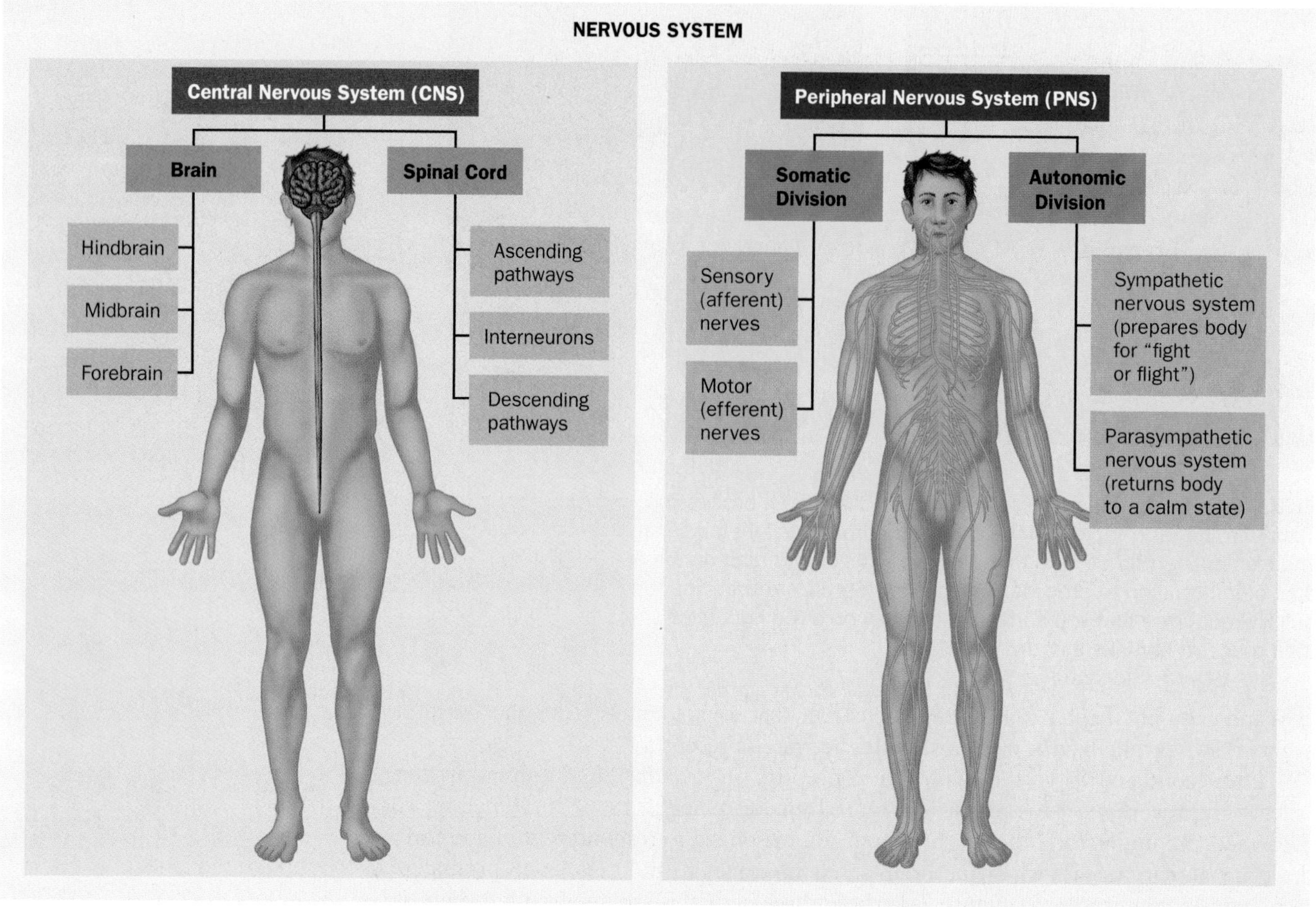

**NERVOUS SYSTEM**

**Central Nervous System (CNS)**

| Brain | | Spinal Cord |
|---|---|---|
| Hindbrain | | Ascending pathways |
| Midbrain | | Interneurons |
| Forebrain | | Descending pathways |

**Peripheral Nervous System (PNS)**

| Somatic Division | | Autonomic Division |
|---|---|---|
| Sensory (afferent) nerves | | Sympathetic nervous system (prepares body for "fight or flight") |
| Motor (efferent) nerves | | Parasympathetic nervous system (returns body to a calm state) |

**FIGURE 2-2** Major divisions of the nervous system: the CNS and the PNS. The CNS consists of the brain and spinal cord. The PNS connects the outer portions of the body with the CNS.

**afferent (sensory) nerves**
Nerves that carry information from the receptors to the spinal cord and brain

**efferent (motor) nerves**
Nerves that carry information from the brain and spinal cord to the muscles

**STUDY TIP**

Make flash cards for the peripheral and central nervous systems, using all of the vocabulary associated with these systems. On one side, write a vocabulary word; on the other side, write the definition and indicate "Peripheral" or "Central." Then, do flash-card drills with a classmate. Drill once to identify whether a vocabulary word or phrase is associated with the peripheral or central nervous system; drill again to define the word or phrase.

**afferent (sensory) nerves;** those that carry information from the brain and spinal cord to the muscles are called **efferent (motor) nerves.** The somatic nervous system is involved in sensing and responding, Steps 1 and 3 of the chain of events described in Figure 2-1. As you are driving, your eyes scan the environment and you pick up the changing traffic light and signs (Step 1). Afferent nerves convey information about the traffic light and signs to the CNS to be processed: Is the light red or is it amber? Do I step on the brake or continue; and, if I continue, may I turn on a red light (Step 2)? Efferent nerves then convey information from the CNS so that you can make a response (Step 3). Because the responses we make are often planned and organized, the somatic division is said to be a *voluntary* system—that is, under our conscious control.

**The Autonomic Nervous System.** The **autonomic nervous system** of the PNS affects our organs and glands in ways that regulate bodily functioning. Because the autonomic nervous system operates without our conscious awareness, it is described as an *automatic,* or *involuntary,* system. The autonomic nervous system has two main components: the sympathetic nervous system and the parasympathetic nervous system.

**The Sympathetic Nervous System.** The **sympathetic nervous system** mobilizes the body in times of stress or danger. In ancient times, this mobilization was especially helpful in dealing with dangerous animals. Our ancestors' bodies were prepared for "fight or flight" when their sympathetic system was activated (see Chapters 6 and 14). Have you ever been scared by a clap of thunder? How did you react when someone suddenly pulled in front of you as you were driving? Did your heart start to race? Did your skin tingle? Did your muscles tense? These indicators of physiological arousal were produced by the sympathetic nervous system.

## Psychological Detective

On a very dark night, you are walking to your car in the mall parking lot. Because of the throngs of holiday shoppers, you were relegated to a parking spot that seems to be miles from the mall. Your arms are filled with bundles, and you struggle to hold on to everything you spent your hard-earned money to buy. Suddenly, a figure dressed in dark clothing and a ski mask rushes at you from between two cars and throws you to the ground. The sympathetic nervous system signals its call to arms. You become prepared for fight or flight—mostly flight, in this case. Imagine yourself in this situation. Which sympathetic processes are in operation? Write down the processes that you would experience and then read further.

**autonomic nervous system**
Division of the peripheral nervous system involved in the control of bodily functioning through organs and glands

**sympathetic nervous system**
Subdivision of the autonomic nervous system that is responsible for mobilizing the body in times of stress, preparing organisms for fight or flight

The reactions that you experience when you were attacked in the parking lot are evidence that the sympathetic nervous system is operating. During these times the body is prepared for action by a series of coordinated changes, including enlargement (dilation) of the pupils of the eyes, acceleration of the heart rate, inhibition of digestive activities, and release of sugar (glucose) to produce the energy for the fight-or-flight response.

Look at Figure 2-3 to see the major sympathetic responses. Are there any that you are not experiencing when you are "scared out of your wits" at a horror movie? Most likely you experience all of them to some degree in this rather stressful situation. Notice that some of these processes involve an increase in a particular bodily function, whereas others involve a decrease in function.

**FIGURE 2-3** The sympathetic and parasympathetic nervous systems of the autonomic nervous system and their functions.

**Source:** Goodenough et al. (2005).

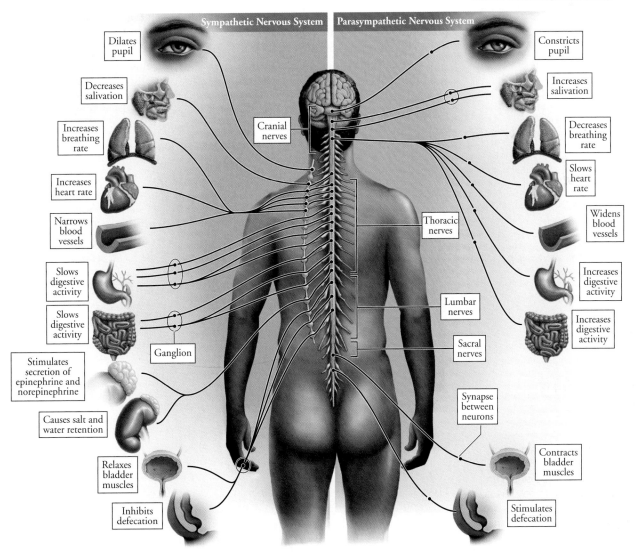

**parasympathetic nervous system**
Subdivision of the autonomic nervous system that is responsible for returning the body to a resting or balanced state

**reflex**
Automatic behavior in response to a specific stimulus

**The Parasympathetic Nervous System.**    The **parasympathetic nervous system** slows the processes that have been accelerated by activation of the sympathetic nervous system. For example, when the parasympathetic nervous system is operating, the pupils of the eye constrict (or close) and your heart rate slows. These effects, and others shown in Figure 2-3, return the body to a more normal or balanced state of functioning characterized by an optimal range of physiological processes called *homeostasis*.

## The Central Nervous System

The other major division of the nervous system, the CNS, consists of the brain and spinal cord (see Figure 2-2). The CNS is analogous to the engine of a car or to the central processing unit (CPU) of a computer. The following section introduces some of the components of the CNS.

**The Spinal Cord.**    The spinal cord is tucked safely into a protective jacket known as the *vertebral column*, which in humans is made up of 24 bones called *vertebrae*. The sensory nerves of the PNS enter the spinal cord and the motor nerves exit the spinal cord between the vertebrae in an orderly manner (see Figure 2-4): Sensory nerves enter the back portion of the spinal cord; motor nerves exit from the front portion. The spinal cord serves as the body's information superhighway. Information that is not processed solely within the spinal cord itself is sent to the brain via ascending pathways; information that is sent back down from the brain follows descending pathways. Within the CNS, *interneurons* connect neurons to each other. They send information either directly to a motor nerve so that a response can be made or send up the spinal cord for further processing by the brain. Figure 2-4 shows interneurons in the spinal cord.

When information provided by the sensory nerves does not have to travel all the way to the brain to produce a response, automatic behaviors known as **reflexes** are produced. The message that brings about a reflex typically takes a shorter journey than

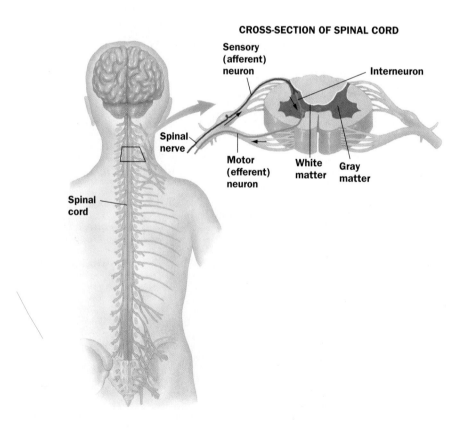

**FIGURE 2-4**  Cross section of the spinal cord. Sensory nerves enter and motor nerves exit in an organized manner. In many cases, the sensory and motor nerves are connected by small interneurons.

the journey all the way to the brain. This shortened distance means faster conduction, which has an evolutionary advantage. Touch a hot stove and your hand withdrawal occurs quickly. Why? The sensory message does not have to go all the way to the brain. Consider Ted, who likes to walk around his house without shoes or socks protecting his feet. He likes the comfort of going shoeless, but sometimes he pays a price because just the other day several glasses broke on the tile floor in the kitchen. As he strolls across the kitchen Ted is not looking for pieces of broken glass, but they find his foot and create a wound. A sensory message (pain) is sent speeding on its way to the spinal cord, where it connects with an interneuron. In turn, a motor neuron sends a message to the appropriate muscle to contract and lift Ted's foot off the glass shards. Reflexes occur *very* rapidly: the reaction to a painful stimulus occurs in approximately 0.8 millisecond (a millisecond is 1/1,000th of a second).

Perhaps the beauty of the nervous system lies in the fact that while the spinal reflex was removing Ted's foot from the glass, a pain message from his foot was also being sent to his brain (see Figure 2-5). This message takes longer to get to the brain than it does to get to the spinal cord because the distance is greater. By the time the pain message reaches his brain, Ted has already withdrawn his foot. Of course, this sensory information will likely form the basis of some decision making initiated by the brain: care for the wound and sweep the floor carefully (Goodenough McGuire, & Wallace, 2005).

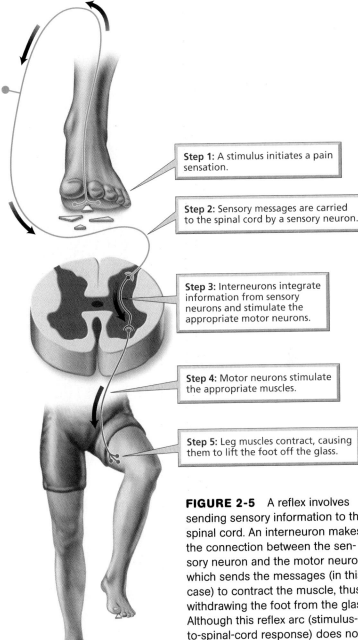

**Step 1:** A stimulus initiates a pain sensation.

**Step 2:** Sensory messages are carried to the spinal cord by a sensory neuron.

**Step 3:** Interneurons integrate information from sensory neurons and stimulate the appropriate motor neurons.

**Step 4:** Motor neurons stimulate the appropriate muscles.

**Step 5:** Leg muscles contract, causing them to lift the foot off the glass.

**FIGURE 2-5**  A reflex involves sending sensory information to the spinal cord. An interneuron makes the connection between the sensory neuron and the motor neuron, which sends the messages (in this case) to contract the muscle, thus withdrawing the foot from the glass. Although this reflex arc (stimulus-to-spinal-cord response) does not involve processing by the brain, the same message (pain) is sent all the way to the brain for further processing.

**Source:** Goodenough et al. (2005).

## THE ENDOCRINE SYSTEM

Besides the nervous system, which is crucial to the activities of sensing, processing, and responding, another system plays a major role in shaping and controlling behavior and mental processes. The **endocrine system** consists of glands that produce and *secrete* (release) chemicals known as **hormones.** When stimulated, endocrine glands secrete hormones into the bloodstream. The blood flow carries hormones throughout the body and, ultimately, to their target, which may be another gland located some distance away. As we discuss the endocrine system, keep in mind that it can, and does, interact with the nervous system.

**endocrine system**
System of glands that produce and secrete chemicals called *hormones* that can have effects some distance from the gland that secreted the hormone

**hormones**
Chemicals produced by the glands of the endocrine system that are carried by the bloodstream to other organs throughout the body

## Major Endocrine Glands

The locations of some of the major endocrine glands are shown in Figure 2-6. A brief description of the function of each gland follows.

**The Pineal Gland.**    The pineal gland, located deep in the center of the brain, produces the hormone *melatonin*, especially at night. Nighttime elevations in circulating

**FIGURE 2-6** Locations and functions of the major endocrine glands.

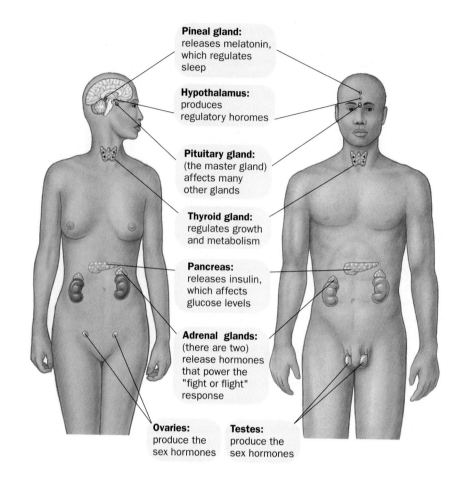

**Pineal gland:** releases melatonin, which regulates sleep

**Hypothalamus:** produces regulatory hormones

**Pituitary gland:** (the master gland) affects many other glands

**Thyroid gland:** regulates growth and metabolism

**Pancreas:** releases insulin, which affects glucose levels

**Adrenal glands:** (there are two) release hormones that power the "fight or flight" response

**Ovaries:** produce the sex hormones

**Testes:** produce the sex hormones

melatonin levels can be explained by the fact that the pineal gland receives input from our visual pathways—from the retina of the eye, to the hypothalamus, to the pineal gland (Goodenough et al., 2005). This hormone is important in regulating our sleep–wake cycle (see Chapter 4). As night approaches and we get closer to our usual bedtime, melatonin levels increase. As daylight approaches and we awaken, melatonin levels decrease.

**The Pancreas.** Located near the stomach and small intestine, the **pancreas** secretes one of the best-known hormones, *insulin*. The cells of our body require insulin to use blood sugar (called *glucose*); without insulin, cells do not receive adequate nourishment from the available glucose. Too little sugar in the blood (hypoglycemia) can lead to perspiration, shallow breathing, anxiety, and even unconsciousness. Sixteen million people in the United States have a hormonal disease called *diabetes*, which affects glucose levels (Mader, 2000). If untreated, diabetes can result in blindness, kidney disease, and circulatory disorders. In *Type I (juvenile-onset) diabetes*, the pancreas does not produce insulin because the body's immune system attacks the cells in the pancreas responsible for insulin production. As a result, insulin injections are needed to replace the hormone the body is not producing on its own. *Type II diabetes* (also known as *non-insulin-dependent diabetes*) was formerly called *adult-onset diabetes* because it usually develops after age 40; however, it has begun to occur in younger people. This type of diabetes accounts for 90 to 95% of all cases of diabetes (Goodenough et al., 2005). In Type II diabetes, insulin is produced but the body's cells are insensitive to it. Obesity and inactivity are factors that increase the risk of this type of diabetes. This form of diabetes can be controlled, to a degree, by a balanced, low-fat diet and exercise.

**pancreas**

An endocrine gland that lies between the stomach and the small intestine; the primary hormone released, insulin, regulates levels of glucose in the body

The pancreas is a good example of the feedback system of the endocrine glands. When you eat a meal and the food is broken down into glucose, the rise in glucose level in your blood signals (feedback) the pancreas to secrete insulin. Then as the blood glucose level drops, the amount of insulin secreted by the pancreas decreases. As we have noted, in diabetic patients the body either does not produce the needed insulin or the cells do not respond to the insulin that is present.

**Hypothalamus.** Located rather deep in the brain, this small gland actually has multiple roles. It is both an endocrine gland and a key center for a wide variety of behaviors related to survival. The **hypothalamus** signals its close neighbor, the pituitary, to release hormones that have a range of effects. It also contains key centers for controlling aggression (fighting), fleeing, sexual activity, and hunger.

**The Pituitary Gland.** The **pituitary gland** is often called the *master gland* because its secretions control many other glands. The *pituitary* is responsible for release of *somatotropin*, a growth hormone that acts directly on bones and muscles to produce the growth spurt that accompanies puberty. The *thyroid-stimulating hormone* stimulates the thyroid gland to regulate the release of its hormone, *thyroxine*. *Adrenocorticotropic hormone (ACTH)*, which has been linked to learning and memory, causes the adrenal glands to secrete *cortisol*, resulting in acceleration of the production of energy-producing glucose during stress. The release of these pituitary hormones reflects the interplay between the nervous system and the endocrine system.

**The Thyroid Gland.** This butterfly-shaped gland is located below the *larynx* (voice box). When activated by the pituitary's *thyroid-stimulating hormone*, the **thyroid gland** secretes thyroxine, which regulates the body's growth and metabolic rate. Undersecretion of thyroxine (*hypothyroidism*) results in a small, dwarflike person. Administration of thyroid hormone can initiate growth; however, treatment must start within 2 months of birth or mental retardation will result. If hypothyroidism occurs in adults, the individual will exhibit lethargy, weight gain, slower pulse rate, and thickening and puffiness of the skin. These conditions can be corrected by administering doses of thyroid hormone (Mader, 2000). Oversecretion of thyroxine results in *hyperthyroidism*. One form of *hyperthyroidism*, Graves' disease, is characterized by protruding eyes, nervousness, hyperactivity, irritability, and a wild stare. Untreated hyperthyroidism can lead to death from heart disease.

**The Gonads.** The **gonads**—**ovaries** in women and **testes** in men—produce sex hormones (*androgens* in men; *estrogens* in women) that activate reproductive organs and structures at puberty. These hormones also affect the appearance of secondary sex characteristics like facial and body hair, change of voice, and breast development (see Chapters 9 and 10). Testosterone levels are also related to aggressiveness (Dabbs & Morris, 1990; Dabbs, Riad, & Chance, 2001); higher levels of testosterone are associated with greater aggressiveness.

Some athletes take *anabolic steroids*, or artificial versions of testosterone, which occurs in both males and females. Taken in pill form or by injection, anabolic steroids build muscle faster (*anabolic* means "growing" or "building"). They also weaken the immune system (thus making people more susceptible to disease) and can lead to liver damage. Anabolic steroids are associated with shrinkage of the testes in males and cessation of menstruation in women; mood changes including severe depression and irritability may also occur.

If a postmenopausal woman is treated with estrogen (estrogen replacement therapy), her brain will behave like the brain of a younger woman in terms of reading and memory (Restak, 2000). Estrogen also seems to increase activation of brain regions responsible for storing the sounds that make up the words we speak. Although some

**hypothalamus**
Gland and brain structure that sends signals to the pituitary gland and contains key centers for fighting, fleeing, sexual activity, and hunger

**pituitary gland**
Called the *master gland* because its secretions control many other glands; this endocrine gland is located in the brain below the thalamus and hypothalamus

**thyroid gland**
Endocrine gland located just below the larynx that releases hormones including thyroxine, which has widespread effects throughout the body via its effects on metabolic rate

**gonads**
General term that refers to sex glands in either males (testes) or females (ovaries); they release hormones that affect sexual development

**ovaries**
Female gonads

**testes**
Male gonads

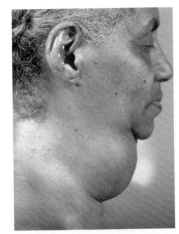

The normal production of thyroid hormones sets the rate of cell metabolism. The body needs iodine (often found in table salt) to manufacture thyroid hormones. In the absence of the needed iodine, the thyroid continues to try to manufacture its hormones, but the result is a swollen and enlarged thyroid gland or *goiter*, as shown here. Although goiter occurs infrequently in the United States, it is a problem in many parts of the world.

**adrenal glands**
Pair of glands located at the top of each of the kidneys; they release a range of hormones including epinephrine and norepinephrine

**STUDY TIP**

From memory and using an informal outline form, list the endocrine glands and write a summary of the function of each.

researchers believe that estrogen reduces the possibility of heart disease, any potential effects on the heart are still a matter of controversy.

**The Adrenal Glands.**     When you experience stress, the **adrenal glands** secrete *epinephrine* and *norepinephrine* (originally called *adrenaline* and *noradrenaline*, respectively), which power sympathetic nervous system activity. These hormones help us respond to stress by producing the fight-or-flight response (see Chapters 6 and 14). As a result, our heart rate, respiratory rate, and blood glucose levels rise. These hormones also reach the brain, where they are responsible for the increased mental alertness needed to either flee or fight (Goodenough et al., 2005). When the adrenal cortex is stimulated by the pituitary hormone ACTH, it secretes *glucocorticoids*, steroid hormones that are involved in the production of glucose.

The endocrine system is an important, if sometimes overlooked, part of the human body. Although it is easy and convenient to talk about the endocrine system and the nervous system as if they were completely independent, they are not. For example, when our body prepares for fight or flight, the nervous system sends the first alarm to activate the sympathetic nervous system, but it is the endocrine system's hormones (especially epinephrine and norepinephrine) that keep the level of arousal up over a longer period of time. When you are under stress, the adrenal glands secrete epinephrine and norepinephrine, preparing you to make a fight-or-flight response. The importance of hormones is also seen in our understanding of various disorders. For example, is a young adult's depression a reaction to recent disturbing life events or does it reflect alteration in one or more of the hormones? Is a young child's hyperactivity an indication of youthful exuberance or a disorder such as attention deficit/hyperactivity disorder? Or might it be the end result of alterations in the hormones produced by the thyroid gland?

So far, we have provided an overview of the entire nervous system along with a more detailed look at the endocrine system. But what is it that makes the entire nervous system operate? In the next section, we will take a closer look at the smallest units of the nervous system—the microscopic cells that make up our nervous system.

# REVIEW SUMMARY

1. The **evolutionary perspective** stresses the role of physiological structures and behaviors in an organism's adaptation to the environment and ultimate survival. The principle of **natural selection** states that the most fit organisms survive because they adapt best to the environment and thus pass on their genes to future generations. The term **behavioral neuroscience** describes the work of scientists from several disciplines who attempt to understand how the nervous system is related to behavior.

2. We use sensing, processing, and responding to interact with the environment. The nervous system, which is divided into the **central nervous system** (CNS—brain and spinal cord) and the **peripheral nervous system** (PNS—all parts of the nervous system outside the CNS), coordinates these three activities.

3. The PNS is composed of the **somatic nervous system** and the **autonomic nervous system.** The somatic nervous system

consists of **afferent (sensory) nerves** that run from the receptors to the spinal cord and brain and **efferent (motor) nerves** that run to the glands and muscles. The autonomic nervous system consists of the **sympathetic nervous system,** which mobilizes the body's resources, and the **parasympathetic nervous system,** which returns the body to a normal state of *homeostasis.*

4. The spinal cord is composed of **sensory** (afferent or ascending) and **motor** (efferent or descending) nerves; interneurons may connect sensory and motor neurons.

5. The endocrine system affects behavior by producing and secreting **hormones,** which are chemicals that regulate body functions. Among the major endocrine glands are the **pineal gland, hypothalamus, pituitary gland, thyroid gland, pancreas, gonads,** and **adrenal glands.**

## ✓ CHECK YOUR PROGRESS

**1.** What is the evolutionary perspective?

**2.** On your way to class you see a $5 bill in the street. Because you want something more than a soda for lunch, you claim the bill as yours. For this situation, describe each of the steps involved in interacting with the environment—sensing, processing, and responding.

**3.** For each of the following activities, indicate whether the sympathetic or parasympathetic nervous system of the autonomic nervous division is involved.

   **a.** A sinking feeling in the pit of your stomach tells you that you are lost in a rundown section of a city at night and do not have a cell phone or money to catch a bus.
   **b.** Getting "psyched up" before a football game, you are ready to devastate the opponents.
   **c.** Soothing music helps calm you after a very frustrating test.

**4.** Which of these are reflexes? Explain why.

   **a.** deciding to see a movie
   **b.** blinking when a puff of air hits your eye
   **c.** a baby's sucking when a pacifier is placed in her mouth
   **d.** jerking your hand out of very hot water

**5.** Which cells detect stimuli?

   **a.** glands
   **b.** effectors
   **c.** receptors
   **d.** sensory tracts

**6.** Which endocrine gland produces insulin?

   **a.** pineal
   **b.** thyroid
   **c.** adrenals
   **d.** pancreas

**7.** Jake caught his hand in a tight space under the seat of his car. The resulting pain signals traveled to the brain via _____ nerves, and the message to pull harder to release his hand was sent from the brain to his hand via _____ nerves.

   **a.** afferent, efferent
   **b.** primary, secondary
   **c.** central, peripheral
   **d.** involuntary, voluntary

**8.** Which of these is the result of sympathetic nervous system activity?

   **a.** Digestion increases.
   **b.** Your heart rate increases.
   **c.** The pupils of your eyes constrict.
   **d.** The rate of release of sugar is decreased.

**9.** Physicians in training use a computer that presents cases and then requests the likely diagnosis and course of treatment. The current patient is 16-year-old Tim, who is very muscular, is depressed, and has testes that have shrunk considerably. Which of these will the future physicians suggest as their course of action?

   **a.** Check for high dopamine levels.
   **b.** Check for possible use of anabolic steroids.
   **c.** Run tests that might reveal the use of substances like marijuana.
   **d.** Run tests that might reveal the presence of a malformed spleen.

**10.** Which endocrine gland is called the *master gland*?

   **a.** pineal
   **b.** thyroid
   **c.** pituitary
   **d.** pancreas

**ANSWERS: 1.** Based on the theory of Charles Darwin, the evolutionary perspective focuses on how and why a particular physical structure developed over time. **2.** *Sensing*—seeing the $5 bill; *processing*—deciding you need the money for lunch; *responding*—picking up the $5 bill. **3. a.** Sympathetic **b.** Sympathetic **c.** Parasympathetic **4. a.** Not a reflex—voluntary behavior **b.** Reflex—involuntary behavior **c.** Reflex—involuntary behavior **d.** Reflex—involuntary behavior **5.** c **6.** d **7.** a **8.** b **9.** b **10.** c

# NEURONS: BASIC CELLS OF THE NERVOUS SYSTEM

Every year students at the local high school get to select from a list of field trips that meet their particular needs and interests. Jackie and several of her friends are thinking of careers in medicine and psychology, so they decide to take the field trip to a major research hospital. When they arrive, they are taken on a tour with several stops. Peering through a very high-power, specialized microscope, one by one they get to see what nerve cells look like. The neuroscientist conducting the tour tells the students that the conduction of a nerve impulse is both electrical and chemical in nature. The students begin to wonder how such a process occurs when the neuroscientist tells them that what is amazing is that the nerve cells don't actually touch each other when they communicate. *How can nerve cells communicate with one another if they never touch?*

As we mentioned earlier, the nervous system is composed of cells called *neurons*. Like other cells in the body, neurons have a nucleus, are enclosed in a membrane, and contain an assortment of smaller structures. Unlike other cells, however, neurons send messages to and receive them from one another. Neurons come in a variety of sizes and shapes. Motor neurons usually have longer distances to travel, so they tend to be large. Interneurons are small, so a large number of them can occupy a given area. The greater the number of neurons in an area, the more complex the interconnections among them.

## Components of the Neuron

Although neurons come in a variety of sizes and shapes, they share some common characteristics. One observer compares neurons to trees in a forest and weaves an intriguing description of this microscopic forest:

> Neurons grow like quaking aspens in the forests of the mind, sprouting from one matrix, a hidden grove. Unlike other cells, they don't move or divide. They assume branching shapes from pyramid to star. Best of all, they talk among themselves, eavesdrop, dash off messages. For that purpose, they have two kinds of limbs, dendrites and axons: the former to listen, the latter to speak. Dangling from a neuron's pouchy trunk, dendrites hear what neighboring neurons signal through their axons. Like elegant ladies air-kissing so as not to muss their makeup, dendrites and axons don't quite touch. The contact happens in less than one thousandth of a second, a spell of microtime powerful as fate. (Ackerman, 2004, pp. 37–38)

The common elements of most neurons are seen in the existence of a cell membrane, dendrites, soma (cell body), an axon, and terminal buttons (see Figure 2-7). We

**FIGURE 2-7** The basic structures of all neurons are the dendrites, soma (cell body), axon, and terminal buttons. In some neurons, the axon may be covered by a myelin sheath, which is white in appearance.

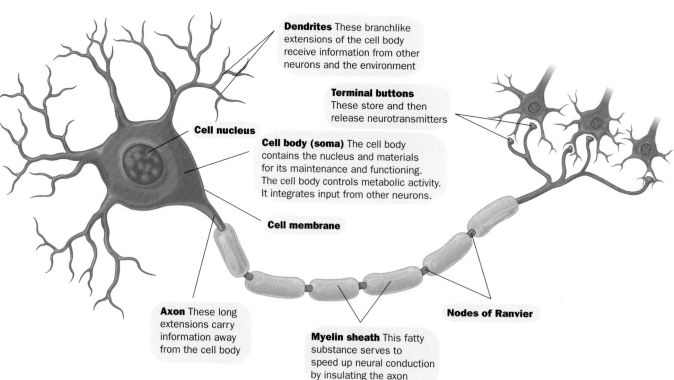

**Dendrites** These branchlike extensions of the cell body receive information from other neurons and the environment

**Terminal buttons** These store and then release neurotransmitters

**Cell nucleus**

**Cell body (soma)** The cell body contains the nucleus and materials for its maintenance and functioning. The cell body controls metabolic activity. It integrates input from other neurons.

**Cell membrane**

**Axon** These long extensions carry information away from the cell body

**Myelin sheath** This fatty substance serves to speed up neural conduction by insulating the axon

**Nodes of Ranvier**

will first look at the common components and what they do; then we will consider the part that makes neurons different—the myelin sheath.

The *cell membrane* is like a fence that surrounds the entire neuron, giving it shape and keeping the cell's internal fluids inside. The cell membrane, however, is *semipermeable*: It allows some—but not all—substances to pass through it. The short, branchlike structures of neurons, called **dendrites,** receive signals or information from the receptors (for example, the eyes, ears, skin) or from other neurons. Most neurons have many (even thousands of) dendrites, just like the braches of a tree. Hence, it is possible for a single neuron to receive signals from many other neurons.

Once a signal has been received by the dendrites, it passes through the **soma** or *cell body*. Like other cells, the soma of the neuron has a nucleus containing genetic material and is involved in the *metabolic* (energy regulation) processes of the cell. The soma relays the neural signal from the dendrites to the axon.

The **axon** is the long part of the neuron that transmits electrical signals to other neurons and to muscles and glands. Only one axon extends from the cell body of each neuron. Whereas most dendrites tend to be rather short, axons can vary greatly in length (but have a constant diameter), depending on the location of the neuron. The axons of some neurons located in the brain are microscopic; others are quite long. For example, the axon of a motor neuron can stretch from your spinal cord all the way to your hand or foot.

Although only one axon leaves the soma (cell body), it may branch several times before it reaches its target. Because the axon branches, the same signal can be sent to several different neurons. Most axons have several small knobs, called **terminal buttons,** at their ends. The terminal buttons store neurotransmitters (in structures called *vesicles*) prior to their release and are directly involved in transmitting a chemical and an electrical signal from one neuron to the next.

**The Myelin Sheath.**    Now that we know the structures common to all neurons, we can examine how neurons differ. One of the major differences among neurons is found in their axons. The axon in Figure 2-7 is surrounded by a **myelin sheath,** which is a fatty protein substance. Myelin is whitish in appearance, which accounts for the whitish appearance of the spinal cord with its long myelin-covered axons. On the other hand, there are fewer myelin-covered axons in the brain, which appears grayish, the color of the rest of the neuron as well as that of unmyelinated axons. The myelin sheath serves as a kind of living electrical tape that insulates the axons, thus preventing short circuits between neurons.

The myelin sheath is composed of **glial cells** (from the Greek word for "glue"), another special type of cell found in the nervous system. Glial cells have several functions: removing waste, occupying vacant space when neurons die, guiding the migration of neurons during brain development, and insulation. If neurons are the stars of the show, then glial cells are the supporting cast members. Just as in the movies, there are scores of supporting players with small, but important, parts to play. Glial cells are considerably smaller but more numerous than neurons; there are about nine glial cells for every neuron (Fields, 2004). The view of glial cells as supporting players is beginning to change, however. Neuroscientists now know that glial cells can communicate with neurons and with one another about the messages that travel among neurons. The glial cells may actually change those signals at the point where neurons communicate with one another, and they may influence the gaps where this communication occurs. As a result of this new information, neuroscientists speculate that glial cells may play a role in learning and forming memories. What's more, they may play a role in repairing damage to neurons. For example, they can clean up spills of glutamate, an important brain chemical that nevertheless can be toxic in excess (Ackerman, 2004).

Consider what happens when you accidentally put your hand on a hot stove. It is imperative that you remove it—immediately! From an evolutionary perspective, the speed of reactions like motor responses is important; escaping from a predator often requires speed. Without that speed, there is a reduced chance of passing on one's genes! Even though a signal is transmitted rapidly down the axon, motor axons are often very

 **2.2**

**dendrite**
Short, branchlike structure of a neuron that receives information from receptors and other neurons

**soma**
Cell body of a neuron, which contains the nucleus

**axon**
Elongated part of a neuron that transmits information to other neurons, muscles, and glands

**terminal buttons**
Component of a neuron located at the ends of the axon where neurotransmitters are stored before being released into the synapse

**myelin sheath**
Whitish, fatty protein substance, composed of glial cells, that covers some axons and increases the speed of neural transmission

**glial cell**
Special type of cell found in the nervous system that forms the myelin sheath, which increases the speed of neural conduction by providing insulation of the axons

long (axons in the spinal cord can be 3 feet or longer); therefore, anything that speeds up transmission will help. Accelerating the transmission of the neural signal is one function of the myelin sheath (Toates, 2001) (see Figure 2-7). Myelin does not cover the entire length of any axon; it is interrupted by what are called *nodes of Ranvier*. A nerve impulse "jumps" successively from one node of Ranvier to the next, resulting in transmission that is up to 100 times faster than neural impulses on unmeylinated axons (Goodenough et al., 2005).

### Psychological Detective

What happens when the myelin sheath degenerates? Review what you have learned about the myelin sheath and give this question some thought. Write down your answer before reading further.

Although many diseases of the nervous system affect the soma or cell body, some destroy the mylein sheath. Among these *demyelinating* diseases are *amyotrophic lateral sclerosis* (Lou Gehrig's disease) and multiple sclerosis (Andreasen, 2001). **Multiple sclerosis (MS)** occurs when the immune system attacks the myelin sheath that covers axons in the CNS (brain and spinal cord). These damaged areas of the myelin become hardened scars called *scleroses* (hence the name of the disease) (Goodenough et al., 2005). The disease usually affects young adults at an average age of 30. For reasons that are not clear, MS occurs two to three times more often in women and is more common in temperate climates (Murray, 2005; Wallin, Page, & Kurtzke, 2004). The most common symptoms of MS are muscle weakness; numbness and tingling in the limbs, trunk, or face; visual disturbances such as blurry vision; and gait/balance problems (Arnett, 2003). Although the disease has little effect on life expectancy, it has a significant effect on a person's quality of life and can also affect memory and visual spatial abilities (Beatty & Aupperle, 2002; Murray, 2005). As the disease progresses, entire myelin sheaths are destroyed. The severity of the disease depends on where the damage occurs. Damage to myelin sheaths in the spinal cord or brain stem is very serious because the myelin does not regenerate; such damage can leave the patient wheelchair-bound (Vertosick, 1996).

## The Synapse and Neurotransmitters

You now know the components of neurons, but how do these special cells work? In this section we explore how neurons are organized and how information is transmitted from one neuron to another.

**The Synapse.** To send messages, neurons must be organized in a particular way. Because a neural signal is sent from one neuron to the next through the terminal buttons of the axons, the most common arrangement is for a neuron's terminal buttons to be near, but *not* touching, the receptive dendrites of neighboring neurons. This arrangement is diagrammed in Figure 2-8. The membrane on the side that sends the message is the *presynaptic* membrane. The membrane on the receiving side of the synapse, the *postsynaptic* membrane, can be viewed as a docking station.

The most common arrangement at the end of an axon consists of a terminal button to send the signal, a dendrite to receive the signal, and the gap between the two, which is the synapse. The **synapse** (Greek for "clasp together") is microscopic—2/100th of a micrometer (a micrometer is 1/1,000th of a millimeter)—yet the neurons *never* touch each other. To give you a better idea of the size of the synapse, it would take more than 12.5 million of them to fill an inch.

**Neurotransmitters.** If there is a gap between the neurons, why doesn't the neural signal simply stop when it arrives at the terminal buttons? The answer involves special chemicals called **neurotransmitters**, which are stored in vesicles of the terminal buttons at the ends of axons. When the electrical signal reaches the terminal buttons, it causes the

---

**multiple sclerosis (MS)**
Disease caused by degeneration of myelin in the central nervous system. Plaques formed in the myelin sheath interfere with neural transmission, resulting in a variety of effects, depending on their location in the body, but most often affecting motor movement

**synapse**
Site where two or more neurons interact but do not touch; neurotransmitters are released into the space in order to continue neural impulses

**neurotransmitters**
Chemical substances that are stored in terminal buttons and released into the synapse between two neurons to carry signals from one neuron to the next

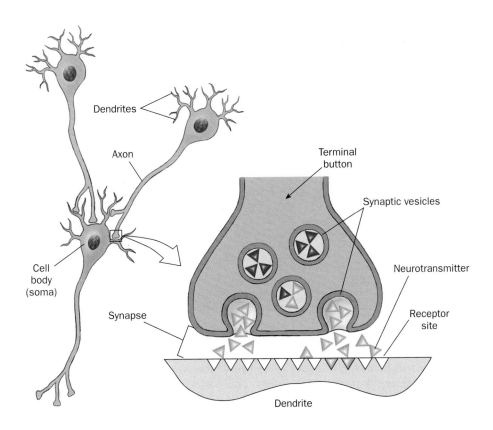

**FIGURE 2-8** Neurons communicate with one another as well as with muscles and glands across microscopic spaces called *synapses*. At the end of the neuron's axon are terminal buttons, where we find synaptic vesicles. The neurotransmitters packaged in these vesicles are released into the synapse, where they carry the neural message to dendrites of the receiving neuron.

vesicles in the terminal button to release a chemical signal in the form of a neurotransmitter into the synapse. As the neurotransmitter enters the synapse, it contacts the postsynaptic membrane (usually the dendrite) of the next neuron. When the molecules of the neurotransmitter contact specially shaped receptor sites located on the postsynaptic membrane, they attach, or bind, to them, thereby allowing the neural signal to be transmitted from one neuron to the next.

When the neurotransmitter occupies the appropriate receptor site, depending on the type of neurotransmitter and the location of the synapse in the nervous system, one of two outcomes is possible. The neuron that is receiving the neurotransmitter may become more likely to transmit the message to subsequent neurons; this process is called *excitation*. In other instances, the neuron that receives the neurotransmitter becomes *less* likely to transmit the message to subsequent neurons; this process is called *inhibition*.

The importance of neurotransmitters in even basic behaviors like moving about is evident in the case of John, a 65-year-old carpenter. Several years ago, John noticed that his fingers felt stiff and that he was beginning to exhibit slight tremors in both hands. Over the course of several months, his condition became progressively worse until he was unable to work.

After a physical examination and a series of diagnostic tests, a neurologist determined that John suffers from *Parkinson's disease*, which usually occurs in people over age 50. Many people are aware of this disease because several well-known individuals are counted among the afflicted: boxer Muhammad Ali, actor Michael J. Fox, and former Attorney General Janet Reno. They have a disease that results from the death of neurons in the brain that release the neurotransmitter dopamine; the loss of these dopamine-releasing neurons makes it difficult to initiate motor movements (MacPhee & Steward, 2001; Stone & Darlington, 2000). People with Parkinson's disease have to bring all their attention to bear on acts as simple as getting out of a chair, holding a coffee cup, or starting to walk. In addition, their muscles become more rigid because they are partially contracted; other symptoms include tremors, slowed movements, and poor balance.

Although we do not know the specific cause of the loss of these dopamine-releasing neurons, there are several possible explanations: brain infections, injury, strokes, tumors, and toxins.

Former heavyweight boxing champion Muhammad Ali once proclaimed that he could "float like a butterfly, sting like a bee." Parkinson's disease robbed him of his athletic ability in the ring. Actor Michael J. Fox was diagnosed with Parkinson's disease in 1991. The Michael J. Fox Foundation for Parkinson's Research is dedicated to ensuring the development of a cure within this decade. Both Muhammad Ali and Michael J. Fox have testified before Congress in support of increased funding of research to find a cure for Parkinson's disease.

## Psychological Detective

If Parkinson's disease results from low dopamine levels, a likely treatment would seem to be administering dopamine to patients. This logical treatment, however, is not successful. Give this situation some thought and think of reasons why the solution to the problems of Parkinson's disease is not administering dopamine.

The brain is a complex and crucial organ that must be protected. Although the skull offers some protection, the environment contains numerous substances that could have toxic effects on the brain. Through thousands of years of evolution, humans developed a *blood-brain barrier* (Pinel, 2006; Toates, 2001), a screenlike element that allows some substances into the brain and keeps out other substances. Sometimes this barrier keeps out potentially helpful substances; for example, dopamine does not cross the blood-brain barrier. As we will see (Chapter 4), this barrier can also let in some potentially harmful substances like alcohol. L-dopa is a chemical *precursor* of dopamine (a building block that certain brain neurons use to manufacture dopamine), and it crosses the blood-brain barrier. Once L-dopa crosses the blood-brain barrier, neurons in the brain use it to manufacture dopamine (Pinel, 2006). The resulting increase in dopamine levels can lead to significant improvement in the motor symptoms of patients suffering from Parkinson's disease: "Patients who may have been virtually immobile with Parkinson's disease, even for several years, suddenly come alive within an hour or so of taking L-dopa" (Stone & Darlington, 2000, p. 120).

This treatment, however, does not cure Parkinson's disease. After several years, patients gradually lose sensitivity to the treatment and the positive effects of L-dopa wear off (Pinel, 2006). The possibility of transplanting fetal tissue into the brains of Parkinson's disease patients to replace damaged dopamine-producing cells may hold promise; however, several failed attempts have added an element of debate and restraint (Olanow, et al., 2003; Pinel, 2006). Surgeons have recently developed an implantable electronic device that stimulates the affected brain areas. This treatment, *deep brain stimulation*, has been used for several movement disorders (Anderson, Burchiel, Hogarth, Favre, & Hammerstand, 2005; Tarsy, 2001).

Here is a closer look at some of the major neurotransmitters:

**Dopamine.** This neurotransmitter controls arousal levels and, as we have discussed, plays a significant role in motor movement. What's more, dopamine is involved in brain pathways that are responsible for reward and punishment. As a result, dopamine seems to play a role in producing dependence on (addiction to) drugs such as amphetamines, cocaine, and morphine (Kuhn, Swartzwelder, & Wilson, 2003). All of these drugs increase the release of dopamine from nerve cells in the brain (Stone & Darlington, 2000).

**Serotonin.**    In the late 1960s, faculty members at a major university were joking with one of their colleagues who had devoted his career to studying serotonin. Why would anyone devote a career to what was then viewed as "sleep juice" and nothing more? How wrong they were! In the 21st century, we now know that serotonin plays a role in weight regulation, sleep, depression, suicide, obsessive–compulsive disorder, aggression, and a wide range of other disorders and behavior problems (Dolan, Anderson, & Deakin, 2001; Mann, Brent, &, Arange, 2001). For example, compared to a control group, people who committed suicide had fewer neurons that used serotonin in the area of the brain just above the eyes. What's more, those who used the most deadly means to commit suicide (that is, took the most pills or jumped from the highest point) had the least serotonin activity in this area of the brain (Ezzell, 2003). Levels of the neurotransmitter, serotonin, are increased by such well-known antidepressant drugs as Celexa, Paxil, Prozac, and Zoloft.

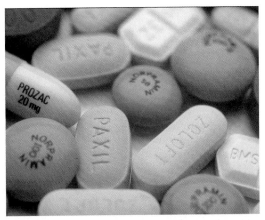

The well-known prescription drugs Celexa, Paxil, Prozac, and Zoloft are classified as antidepressants and affect the neurotransmitter serotonin. They are currently prescribed for a wide range of psychological and medical problems.

**Acetylcholine.**    The neurotransmitter, acetylcholine (ACh), was the first to be discovered; it controls activity in brain areas related to attention, learning, and memory. People with Alzheimer's disease (see Chapter 9) typically have low levels of ACh; drugs that boost its levels *may* improve memory. This devastating disease generally afflicts older people, although some variants may occur in people in their 50s. Alois Alzheimer first described the disease about 100 years ago: A 51-year-old woman exhibited memory deficits and other symptoms that became much worse in a short period of time until she was no longer able to care for herself. Five years later, an autopsy revealed the pathological changes that are the hallmark of the disease: plaques in the brain and tangles (long, knotted filaments) inside neurons (Ingram, 2003).

In industrial countries, Alzheimer's disease is the third leading cause of death after heart disease and cancer. Each year, almost 400,000 new cases are reported in the United States (*Harvard Mental Health Letter*, 2001). People afflicted with Alzheimer's disease exhibit the progressive loss of memory first described by Alois Alzheimer, and as in his original description, they eventually are completely incapable of caring for themselves. The following description gives a glimpse of this disease: "Imagine your brain as a house filled with lights. Now imagine someone turning off the lights one by one. That's what Alzheimer's disease does. It turns off the lights so that the flow of ideas, emotions and memories from one room to the next slows and eventually ceases" (Nash, 2000, p. 51).

ACh also operates at the junction of many of our nerves and skeletal muscles. For hundreds of years, South American Indians have rubbed a poison, *curare*, on the ends of their arrowheads. When the curare enters the victim (animal or human), it takes the place of acetylcholine in synapses. Messages from the brain are carried down the nerves, but when they reach the muscles the messages do not get through, resulting in paralysis and death.

Improperly preserved food may contain the botulin bacterium, which prevents the release of ACh. Without ACh, the muscles we use to breathe are paralyzed, resulting in death from respiratory failure. The venom in a black widow spider's sting stimulates a flood of ACh; the resulting muscle spasms can also cause death.

**Glutamate.**    The most widely distributed excitatory neurotransmitter in the body is *glutamate*. As such, it is called upon quite frequently to keep the lines of communication among neurons open, engage in passing along information, and may well play a role in learning. Yet, this neurotransmitter also seems to have a darker side. Excessive levels of glutamate may cause neurons to become overexcited, and they may die as a consequence. This may account for the loss of neurons that can occur in strokes, head injuries, and some seizure disorders (Bradshaw, 2003). Consequently, researchers are working on methods to keep glutamate levels in check when various insults to brain tissue occur (Molineuvo, Liado, & Rami, 2005).

Charlton Heston was diagnosed with Alzheimer's disease in 2002. During his career he had leading roles in more than 60 movies; he is best known for his roles in "Ben Hur" and "The Ten Commandmants." In a statement he said to reporters, "If you see a little less spring in my step, if your name fails to leap to my lips, you'll know why. And if I tell you a funny story for the second time, please laugh anyway." Heston was a friend of former President Ronald Reagan who announced in 1994 that he had Alzheimer's disease. Shortly before his death in June, 2004 at age 93 Nancy Reagan described her husband's condition in these words, "Ronnie's long journey has finally taken him to a distant place where I can no longer reach him."

**GABA.**   GABA (gamma-aminobutyric acid) is an inhibitory neurotransmitter that is widely distributed throughout the brain and the spinal cord. What purposes do inhibitory neurotransmitters serve? The neurons in the brain are packed tightly, and they are closely interconnected. The general effect of excitatory neurotransmitters on these neurons is to increase the tendency to excite their neighboring neurons, which excite other neurons, and so on down the line. Without the braking action of inhibitory neurotransmitters, neurons could fire uncontrollably, which is what occurs when someone experiences an epileptic seizure. Thus, the damping effect of inhibitory neurotransmitters is necessary to create a balance in the brain.

The importance of inhibitory neurotransmitters is also apparent in the following scenario. Imagine that you have removed a very hot pot from the stove. Although you are using a pot holder, it is not thick enough to provide protection from the searing heat. The pain caused by the heat triggers a withdrawal reflex that would cause you to drop the hot pot, yet you manage to get it to the table without dropping it. How did this happen? In this case, the excitatory neurotransmitter was powering motor neurons to pull away from the pot (and drop it). However, this excitation was counteracted by inhibition from the brain, which recognized the disaster that would occur if you dropped the pot (Carlson, 2001).

**Norepinephrine.**   This primarily excitatory neurotransmitter (which is also a hormone) induces physical and mental arousal and heightens our mood. It is found in the autonomic nervous system and is part of the power behind the fight-or-flight response. Norepinephrine has also been implicated in anxiety disorders such as panic attacks (see Chapter 12).

2.3

Table 2-1 provides a review of the features of the neurotransmitters we just discussed. This table will serve as a helpful review, so refer to it often.

**TABLE 2-1**

## Selected Neurotransmitters: Their Effects, Locations, and Functions

| Neurotransmitters | Effects | Location | Functions |
|---|---|---|---|
| Acetylcholine (ACh) | Excitatory or inhibitory | Brain, spinal cord, synapses of the parasympathetic nervous system | Involved in muscle movement and memory, Alzheimer's disease is associated with low levels |
| Dopamine | Inhibitory or excitatory | Brain (three major circuits: hypothalamus, pituitary, midbrain) | Involved in movement and reward centers; destruction of dopamine-secreting neurons can lead to Parkinson's disease; implicated in the development of schizophrenia |
| Gamma-aminobutyric acid (GABA) | Inhibitory | Local transmission in the CNS | Involved in levels of excitability; drugs used to treat anxiety increase the ability of GABA to bind to postsynaptic sites, which lead to reduced arousal |
| Norepinephrine | Generally excitatory | Brain stem (nerve tracts extend to many areas of the brain and spinal cord) and sympathetic nervous system | Involved in sympathetic nervous system activity; influences arousal, mood, and reward centers; cocaine and amphetamines block reuptake |
| Serotonin | Inhibitory or excitatory | Brain stem (nerve tracts extend to many areas of the brain and spinal cord) | Involved in mood, appetite, sleep, aggression |
| Glutamate | Excitatory | Brain and throughout the CNS | Involved in memory but can also cause damage to neurons if its levels are excessive |

## Hands On

## Orientation, Memory, and Concentration Test

INSTRUCTIONS: Score 1 point for each wrong answer, up to the maximum. Multiply the number of mistakes by the weight. Then add to get the final score.

| Questions | Maximum Number of Errors | Errors × Weight = Score |
|---|---|---|
| 1. What year is it now? | 1 | × 4 = |
| 2. What month is it now? | 1 | × 3 = |
| *Repeat this memory phrase after me:* John Brown, 42 Market Street, Chicago | | |
| 3. About what time is it? (within 1 hour) | 1 | × 3 = |
| 4. Count backwards from 20 to 1. | 2 | × 2 = |
| 5. Say the months in reverse order. | 2 | × 2 = |
| 6. Repeat the memory phrase again. | 5 | × 2 = |

Total score can range from 0 (no mistakes) to 28 (all wrong). A score greater than 10 is usually consistent with dementia. Alzheimer's disease is the most common form of dementia.

**Source:** *Time*, July 17, 2000, p. 56 (from Gerontological Society of America).

**STUDY TIP**

Design and create a visual organizer that illustrates the characteristics of the major neurotransmitters. You can use a mind map or think-link format, different color pens, pictures, or whatever visual strategy works best for you.

**Clearing the Synapse.** How do neurotransmitters get out of the synapse? Think about this question for a moment and you will understand the importance of clearing synapses. It's like your telephone. If you talk to only one person and never hang up, only one message can be sent and received. You must hang up to receive additional calls. Likewise, synapses must be cleared, and cleared rapidly, before additional signals can be transmitted.

The synapse is cleared in one of two ways, depending on the particular neurotransmitter involved (Toates, 2001). In the first method, *breakdown*, the neurotransmitter (for example, ACh) is broken down and removed from the synapse. After ACh affects the next neuron, an enzyme (acetycholinesterase) breaks it down. Once the ACh is broken down and the receptor sites are unoccupied, the postsynaptic membrane can receive another signal. This rapid breakdown is important for producing the rapid motor responses required to play the piano, type, or use a calculator.

The second method for clearing the synapse, *reuptake*, involves taking the neurotransmitter back into the vesicles of the terminal buttons from which it came. Once the neurotransmitter has produced its effect on the postsynaptic membrane, it reenters the vesicles of the terminal buttons, where it is ready to be used again. All neurotransmitters, except ACh, are removed from the synapse by reuptake.

**Neurotransmitters and Drug Action.** Understanding the way neurotransmitters operate has increased our knowledge of how drugs affect the brain and, consequently, our behavior. Most drugs exert their effects by influencing the operation of a neurotransmitter: Some drugs increase the effectiveness of neurotransmitters; other drugs reduce their effectiveness. Regardless of the specific effect that a drug may have, it is very likely that the key biological action takes place in or near the synapse.

**Agonists.** Drugs that promote or enhance the operation of a neurotransmitter are called **agonists**. The effects of neurotransmitters can be enhanced in a number of ways (see Figure 2-9). For example, some agonists eliminate the enzyme that breaks down the neurotransmitter in the synapse. Without the enzyme, the neurotransmitter remains active in the synapse for a longer period, resulting in a more intense response. For example, the drug physostigmine inactivates the acetycholinesterase that breaks down

**agonists**
Drugs that enhance the effects of a particular neurotransmitter

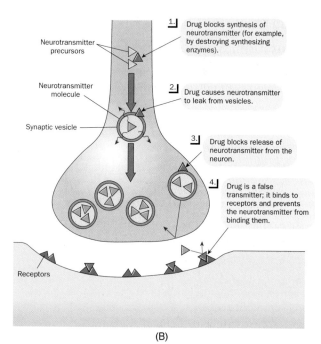

**FIGURE 2-9** (A) Agonists are drugs that increase the effectiveness of a neurotransmitter. (B) Antagonists are drugs that decrease the effectiveness of a neurotransmitter. Both types of drugs can work in a variety of ways.

ACh. Thus the ACh remains active longer. Drugs such as physostigmine produce a range of behavioral effects that may include nightmares and vivid dreaming (see Chapter 4), as well as parasympathetic effects such as decreased heart rate and constriction of the pupils of the eyes.

The class of drugs known as *benzodiazepines* enhances the ease or "tightness" of binding of the neurotransmitter *GABA* (Liska, 2004). Although the name *benzodiazepines* may not be familiar, you may have heard of the trade names Ativan, Librium, Serax, Valium, and Xanax. These drugs are most often prescribed to reduce anxiety, but they also promote sleep, relax the muscles, reduce the symptoms associated with withdrawal from alcohol, and decrease the likelihood of seizures (Griffith, 2004).

Another class of drugs, *selective serotonin reuptake inhibitors (SSRIs)*, is often used to relieve depression, although these drugs are also prescribed for obsessive–compulsive disorder, panic disorder, and social phobias (Griffith, 2004; Liska, 2004). Drugs such as Prozac block the reuptake of the neurotransmitter serotonin into the terminal buttons. When reuptake is blocked, the neurotransmitter remains active in the synapse for a longer time period than usual. Because depression is alleviated when the effective level of serotonin in the synapse is raised, researchers have proposed that depression can occur when levels of this neurotransmitter are abnormally low.

**Antagonists.** Drugs that oppose or inhibit the operation of a neurotransmitter are called **antagonists.** Antagonists can work in a variety of ways to reduce the effectiveness of a given neurotransmitter (see Figure 2-9). For example, they may attach to receptor sites and block the neurotransmitter from attaching there. By stopping the action of the neurotransmitter, they prevent transmission of neural signals. For example, the drug haloperidol (Haldol) attaches to dopamine receptors and blocks them; as a result, less dopamine binds to the receptors on the postsynaptic membrane. As we will see in Chapter 12, researchers believe that some psychological disorders (for example, schizophrenia) result from high levels of dopamine. Drugs such as haloperidol are effective in the treatment of these disorders because they reduce the level of dopamine.

**antagonists**
Drugs that oppose or inhibit the effects of a particular neurotransmitter

Other drugs block the storage of the neurotransmitter. When the vesicles of the terminal buttons empty their contents into the synapse, a reduced amount of the neurotransmitter is released, and the effect on the postsynaptic membrane is less than normal. The blood pressure drug reserpine operates in this manner. Reserpine destroys the membranes of the terminal buttons that contain dopamine. With no membrane to protect it, the dopamine is destroyed by an enzyme inside the terminal button. As a result, less dopamine is released into the synapse.

**Neuromodulators.**    The search for additional neurotransmitters led to the discovery of other chemicals, **neuromodulators,** that can influence the transmission of signals between neurons. The release and action of neurotransmitters are confined to synapses in a specific area; the distribution of neuromodulators is more widespread. For example, neuromodulators can have simultaneous effects on diverse brain regions; their activity may be indirect and longer-lasting. Some neuromodulators produce their effects by facilitating the release of neurotransmitters; others inhibit the release of neurotransmitters.

One of the best-known neuromodulators, morphine, relieves pain. Consider the case of Kevin, who broke his leg while playing football. The injury was so severe that Kevin had to be hospitalized and given morphine injections to reduce the pain. Morphine blocks or inhibits transmission of neural signals that transmit pain signals. Perhaps the body produces a substance that is similar to morphine; otherwise, would it have developed receptors for such substances?

This question led researchers to seek and locate receptors that are sensitive to chemicals like morphine (Pert & Snyder, 1973). They reasoned that these receptors do not exist just to receive external substances like morphine, so they set out to identify the endogenous (internal) chemicals that naturally occupy these receptors and found our body's natural painkilling chemicals (Hughes et al., 1975). The best known of these natural pain killers are the **endorphins,** which are released in response to pain or during vigorous exercise. Endorphins are endogenous opioids, which means they are opium-like chemicals produced from within. They reduce the sensation of pain and induce feelings of relaxation, exhilaration, and even euphoria (Pert, 2002). Even after long runs, some runners experience a "runner's high," which is likely due to the body's production of endorphins. Have you heard of someone who can have dental work (for example, teeth drilled) without injections of a painkiller? One explanation for this phenomenon is that people differ in their levels of endorphins.

Humans have an elaborate and complex system to sense pain and then block it (Fernandez & Turk, 1992). Would it be better if we did not sense pain at all? Consider the case of Miss C., who had been insensitive to pain from birth (Melzack & Wall, 1982):

> The young lady . . . seemed normal in every way except that she had never felt pain. As a child, she had bitten off the tip of her tongue while chewing food and had suffered third-degree burns after kneeling on a radiator to look out of the window. . . . She felt no pain when parts of her body were subjected to strong electric shock, to hot water . . . , or to a prolonged ice-bath. (pp. 16–17)

Miss C. was unusual because she lived into her teens. Most people who cannot sense pain die at an early age. To adapt to and survive in our environment, we must be able to sense occurrences that could lead to injury or illness.

# The Neural Signal

Earlier in this chapter we mentioned that the basic function of the nervous system is to receive information or signals from specialized cells called *receptors.* As demonstrated in the example of figuring out traffic signals and how to respond, a great deal of this information is processed by the brain and then translated into action. We now turn our attention to the neural signals themselves. To understand the signals, we must consider the inside and outside of the neuron at the same time.

Why would the human body contain receptors for a substance similar to morphine? This intriguing question led researchers to discover that nature had prepared us to deal with pain by providing us with our own pain killers—endorphins. Endorphins not only reduce pain, they can also induce relaxation and even euphoria, which is sometimes seen in a "runner's high."

**neuromodulators**
Chemicals that may have a widespread or general effect on the release of neurotransmitters

**endorphins**
Substances produced by the body that block pain; these substances are opium-like chemicals

**resting state**
Electrical charge (270 mV) of
a neuron when it is not firing

**action potential**
Reversal in electrical charge of a
neuron that occurs when the
neuron fires

If you examine the chemicals on the outside of the neuron's semipermeable cell membrane and compare them with the chemicals on the inside of the cell membrane, you will notice a difference in small electrically charged particles called *ions*. The two types of ions, positive (+) and negative (−), resemble the two poles or ends of a battery. The most important negative ion is chloride ($Cl^-$); potassium ($K^+$) and sodium ($Na^+$) are important positive ions.

When a neuron is not sending or receiving a signal, it is in a **resting state,** with more negative ions on the inside than on the outside. Relative to the outside, the inside of the neuron is about 270 millivolts (a millivolt, mV, is 1/1,000th of a volt) when the neuron is in the resting state. Because of this unequal distribution of ions, the neuron is *polarized*, like a battery. This 270-mV difference in electric charge between the inside and outside of a neuron at rest is the *resting potential*.

What happens when a neurotransmitter enters the synapse? One of two reactions may occur. The presence of the neurotransmitter may result either in *depolarization* (the neuron becomes *less* negatively charged) or *hyperpolarization* (the neuron becomes *more* negatively charged). Which reaction occurs is determined by the type of neurotransmitter (excitatory or inhibitory) and the location of the synapse. For example, the presence of ACh at synapses located in skeletal muscles results in depolarization; its presence at synapses located in other parts of the body, such as the heart, results in hyperpolarization.

When excitatory neurotransmitters occupy appropriate receptor sites, they cause the cell membrane to allow positive ions to pass inside (see Figure 2-10). The increase of positive ions on the inside of the neuron causes the resting potential to drop. This change, which brings the potential closer to zero, is depolarization. If enough of the neurotransmitter is present to cause the dendrite and soma to depolarize to between 265 and 260 mV, the neuron generates its own electrical signal. At this threshold (the minimum amount of change required for the neuronal response to occur) the axon membrane suddenly allows large quantities of positive ($Na^+$) ions to rush inside. In less than a millisecond the neuron changes from 260 to 130 mV, completely reversing its electrical nature or polarity. This reversal along the axon is the neural signal we have been talking about. We call it an **action potential,** or *all-or-none response*: When the axon

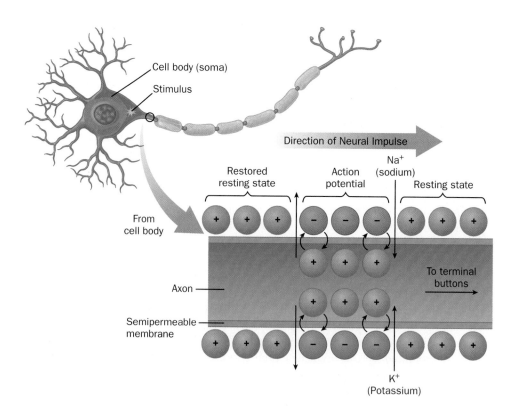

**FIGURE 2-10** The sequence of events that occurs within neurons as the neural signal moves along the length of neurons.

**Source:** Adapted from Morris and Maisto (2002); Worchel and Shebilske (1995).

fires, it does not fire more or less than it did last time. An action potential has the same magnitude each time.

Once the dendrite and soma reach the threshold, the action potential spreads rapidly down the axon until it reaches the terminal buttons, where it causes the release of a neurotransmitter. The action potential, or signal, is nothing more than an exchange of ions. For axons that do not have a myelin sheath, the ion exchange takes place along the entire axon. If a myelin sheath is present, the ion exchange occurs only at the nodes of Ranvier. Hence there is less work to be done, and the action potential arrives at the terminal buttons more rapidly. The large myelinated axons in your legs transmit action potentials as rapidly as 100 meters per second (224 miles per hour); small, unmyelinated axons (such as the ones in your brain) conduct action potentials as slowly as 1 meter per second (2.24 miles per hour).

At the same time that the action potential is being transmitted, the initiating neurotransmitter is being cleared out of the synapse. Removal of the neurotransmitter causes the receiving neuron to return to a resting state and allows it to generate another action potential—that is, to fire again. When the neuron is being reset—called the *refractory period*—the neuron cannot fire again. When the neuron returns to the resting state, it can be fired normally.

The action potential and the refractory period occur within 2 milliseconds. Many messages can be transmitted when neurons fire 500 or more times per second! The rate at which neurons fire is important because stimulus magnitude or intensity is indicated in this manner. Strong stimuli produce a high rate of firing; weaker stimuli produce a lower rate of firing. The pressure from a fly landing on your hand results in a low rate of firing compared with the pressure of a 50-pound weight on your hand.

Not all neurons respond to the presence of a neurotransmitter by depolarizing or generating an action potential; the result may be just the opposite. In these cases the neurotransmitter is inhibitory, and causes additional negative ions to cross the cell membrane and enter the neuron. When inhibition occurs, the neuron becomes more negative than it was during the resting state (hyperpolarized), making an action potential harder, if not impossible, to generate. Some ACh synapses in the parasympathetic system reflect this inhibitory nature. When ACh is released, the neurons hyperpolarize, and the result is a decrease in a parasympathetic activity such as heart rate.

Now that we have discussed the workings of the basic units of the nervous system (neurons) and the operation of neurotransmitters, we are ready to move on to the bigger picture—the brain. We will begin our discussion of the brain by looking at the methods neuroscientists have used to investigate the structure and function of the brain. As you will see, some remarkable advances have occurred, in part, by putting computers to work in studying the brain. Then we will look at the specific structures and functions of the brain itself.

## REVIEW SUMMARY

**1.** The cells that make up the nervous system, **neurons,** are composed of **dendrites** (*receive* signals from adjacent neurons), a **soma** or cell body, an **axon** (*send* signals), and **terminal buttons** (where neurotransmitters are stored in vesicles).

**2. Neurotransmitters** enable the signal from one neuron to be relayed to other neurons across the synapse, a small gap that separates neurons. A **myelin sheath** covers the axons of some neurons to increase the speed of the neural signal.

**3.** Among the key neurotransmitters, *dopamine* has been implicated in the development of Parkinson's disease. *Acetylcholine*

(ACh) seems to play a role in Alzheimer's disease, and serotonin has been implicated in a variety of disorders, including depression and obsessive–compulsive disorder.

**4. Neuromodulators** have more widespread and indirect effects than neurotransmitters and also influence transmission between cells.

**5. Agonists** are drugs that promote the action of a neurotransmitter; **antagonists** are drugs that oppose or inhibit the action of a neurotransmitter.

**6.** Neurotransmitters must be removed from the synapse before another signal can be transmitted. Removal is accomplished either by destroying the neurotransmitter (breakdown) or by taking it back into the terminal buttons (reuptake).

**7.** *Ions* (electrically charged particles) are found on the inside and outside of the neuron's semipermeable cell membrane. When a neuron is in a resting state, more negative ions are on the inside of the cell than on the outside.

**8.** Neurotransmitters stimulate the cell membrane to allow ions to enter the neuron, resulting in either *depolarization* (positive ions move inside the neuron, resulting in excitation) or *hyperpolarization* (additional negative ions move inside, resulting in inhibition).

**9.** If depolarization of the dendrite and soma reaches a threshold level, the axon quickly reverses its electrical charge, and the signal is transmitted to the next neuron. This reversal in electrical charge is known as the **action potential.**

# ✓ CHECK YOUR PROGRESS

**1.** What are the basic building blocks of the nervous system?

   **a.** cones
   **b.** neurons
   **c.** agonists
   **d.** dendrites

**2.** Send is to receive as _____ is to _____.

   **a.** axon, soma
   **b.** myelin, axon
   **c.** soma, dendrite
   **d.** axon, dendrite

**3.** While moving furniture in his apartment, Andy notices the insulation on the wire for a lamp and is reminded of something he learned in class today. If the topic was the structure of the neuron, what part was the focus of Andy's thoughts?

   **a.** soma
   **b.** synapse
   **c.** terminal button
   **d.** myelin sheath

**4.** A teacher tries to make learning the terminology of neurons a visual exercise. She has two students play the role of neurons. At one point, she says that one neuron "spits" a chemical at the other to continue neural conduction. What is the name for the chemical that was spit?

   **a.** myelin
   **b.** hormone
   **c.** endorphin
   **d.** neurotransmitter

**5.** Which individual is most likely to be diagnosed as suffering from MS?

   **a.** Alice, who is 18 and suffers from insomnia and depression
   **b.** Carol, who is 30 and has muscle weakness and blurry vision
   **c.** Daniel, who is 68 and exhibits symptoms of depression as well as a loss of the ability to smell
   **d.** Darla, who is 34 and has difficulty remembering what day it is and believes that people do not like her

**6.** Which of these is the best description of what happens when a neural signal proceeds down an axon?

   **a.** ebb and flow of hydraulic pressure
   **b.** flood of a neurotransmitter under high pressure
   **c.** a rapid exchange of charged particles called *ions*
   **d.** pulling and pushing of tension within the cell body

**7.** Once a neurotransmitter has been released, it must be removed from the synapse before the neuron can fire again. What are the two major ways in which this is accomplished?

   **a.** reduction and retrieval
   **b.** breakdown and reuptake
   **c.** inactivation and innervation
   **d.** condensation and expiration

**8.** As part of a drug company's research project, participants are given a drug described as an *agonist*. Because you are new to your job in the company, you wonder what effect this drug is likely to have. After looking up the term, which of these will you conclude is the likely effect of the drug?

   **a.** The drug will cause genetic mutations.
   **b.** The drug will self-destruct after hitting its target organ.
   **c.** The drug will increase the effectiveness of a particular neurotransmitter.
   **d.** The drug will multiply rapidly in the body, so its effects will be greater than was originally anticipated.

**9.** What is one purpose of the myelin sheath that covers the axons of some neurons?

   **a.** to increase speed of a neural impulse
   **b.** to store neurotransmitters for later use
   **d.** to protect neurons from toxins and viruses
   **d.** to destroy neurotransmitters that are present at excessive levels

**10.** After a physical exam and a series of interviews, Sid's psychiatrist suggested that a trial of Prozac would be the best course of treatment for his presenting problem. Which of the following describes Sid's likely diagnosis and the neurotransmitter targeted by the proposed treatmentt?

   **a.** schizophrenia and ACh
   **b.** depression and serotonin
   **c.** panic attacks and dopamine
   **d.** bipolar disorder and norepinephrine

Winebarger, & Taplin, 2002). These comparisons are made with tests that evaluate sensory abilities (for example, vision and hearing), intelligence, memory, and language. In addition to administering tests to determine which brain areas regulate which processes, neuropsychologists coordinate and direct treatment programs. Not surprisingly, there have been major advances in neuropsychology after wars in which a large number of injuries occurred. Advances in locating key parts of the brain and identifying their functions led to increased attempts to alter those structures when abnormal behaviors were noticed. Various forms of brain surgery (psychosurgery) to alter abnormal behaviors were prominent among these efforts.

**Stereotaxic Surgery.**    In 1904, brain researchers created a device that made studying certain brain structures possible (Valenstein, 1973, 1986). Before the invention of this device, structures that were deep in the brain could be examined only by removing or damaging the tissue that covered them. The *stereotaxic instrument* holds the head in a fixed position and allows an electrode (a fine piece of specially treated wire) to be inserted into a specified area of a patient's brain. The electrode is thin enough that it does not damage tissue as it passes through. The electrode can record electrical brain activity, stimulate brain activity with a mild electric current, or destroy a brain area by lesioning (or destroying) the area by passing a strong electric current through it. These procedures (recording, stimulating, and lesioning) provide information about the functions of various structures and are commonly used to study brain functioning in animals. The stereotaxic instrument is also used to inject chemicals into selected brain areas. These chemicals can be used to stimulate or destroy brain areas (Joyner & Guillemot, 1994), either temporarily or permanently.

Stereotaxic instruments are individually created for each species and have been used on a variety of animals and humans. The stereotaxic instrument depicted in Figure 2-13 is used to study and to treat human brains. The use of this technique raises ethical questions, such as the risk that the operation will cause permanent changes in the patient's abilities or personality (Valenstein, 1986). For this reason, stereotaxic surgery (a form of psychosurgery) on humans is a last resort. When it is used, the purpose is to destroy a brain area believed to be malfunctioning and creating serious behavior problems such as excessive, unprovoked violence (Mark & Ervin, 1970). In another procedure, parts of the brain that are thought to cause especially troubling forms of obsessive–compulsive disorder (see Chapter 12) are destroyed (Jenike, 1998) in an effort to reduce the severity of the symptoms.

**The Electroencephalograph.**    More recently developed techniques have enabled neuroscientists to examine brain functions and anatomy without resorting to autopsy or invasive stereotaxic surgery. In 1929 Hans Berger developed the **electroencephalograph (EEG),** a device that monitors and records the brain's electrical activity. To make an EEG recording, a technician places several round metal discs, called *electrodes*, on a patient's scalp. These electrodes sense brain activity occurring in the region beneath them and transmit this information to the EEG system, which amplifies the signals. These amplified signals activate a pen that records the type of electrical activity (known as *brain waves*) occurring in the region monitored, thus producing an *electroencephalogram*.

Brain waves (identified by Greek letters) are distinguished by their frequency, which is measured in cycles per second (called *hertz* and abbreviated *Hz*), and their amplitude (the height of the wave on the EEG record), which reflects strength. Brain researchers have labeled a number of different types of brain waves; each is generally associated with a particular state of consciousness (see Figure 2-14). In other words, the presence of a particular type of brain waves tells us something about what

Clinical neurophysiologists have developed an array of measures to assess people who have suffered brain damage. These clinical measures not only help identify the specific form of brain damage, they are also useful in devising approaches for rehabilitation. The patient pictured here has suffered a stroke, and his language abilities are being assessed in order to help him communicate better.

**electroencephalograph (EEG)**
Device that monitors and records electrical activity of the brain in the form of a graphic representation of brain waves

**FIGURE 2-13**  The stereotaxic instrument allows researchers to insert a fine piece of wire called an *electrode* into deep brain areas. The electrode can be used to record brain activity, stimulate a brain area, or destroy (lesion) an area. This technique has been used to reduce the symptoms of disorders such as obsessive–compulsive disorder.

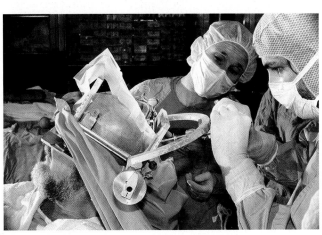

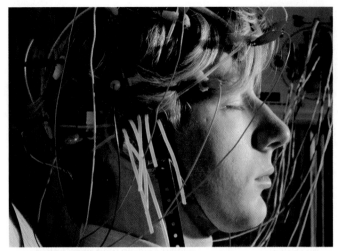

This EEG participant is shown with scalp electrodes in place. Each small electrode senses the electrical signals generated by millions of brain neurons under it.

**FIGURE 2-14** The brain's electrical signals are sensed by electrodes attached to the skull, and then they are amplified and recorded. Several of the commonly observed types of brain waves are illustrated here.

is going on in the brain at the time. Here are some of the most commonly identified brain waves:

**Alpha Waves.** These are fast brain waves (8 to 12 Hz) that are not high in amplitude. The brain generally produces alpha waves when the individual is in a calm, relaxed state and is not concentrating on anything in particular. Close your eyes and relax and your brain is likely to produce alpha waves; open your eyes and pay attention to your surroundings and the alpha waves will disappear.

**Beta Waves.** These are very fast brain waves (13 to 30 Hz) but are not high in amplitude. They are associated with mental activity such as reading this chapter, taking notes in class, or answering test questions. Beta waves may be absent or reduced if there is damage to the brain.

**Theta Waves.** These slow brain waves (3.5 to 7 Hz) are irregular in frequency and low in amplitude. When we are in a light stage of sleep or daydreaming, our brains are likely to produce this type of wave; however, theta waves are normal in waking children up to 13 years of age.

**Delta Waves.** These brain waves are the slowest (below 3.5 Hz) and the highest in amplitude. Delta waves are quite common in infants up to 1 year of age and in the deepest stages of sleep. Brain lesions may be associated with delta wave production either at the site of the lesion or more generally across the brain.

We will have more to say about brain waves and the different states of consciousness with which they are associated in Chapter 4.

The EEG is useful for detecting the abnormal brain waves found in epilepsy, for identifying certain sleep disorders (see the Chapter 4 discussion of narcolepsy), and for providing evidence of the possible presence of brain tumors. The EEG is also used to confirm the state called *brain death* in which a flat EEG tracing indicates that no brain activity is occurring (Afifi & Bergman, 2005). Despite these uses, the EEG has limited usefulness for neuroscientists because it is not precise enough to monitor localized activity in specific brain areas. Because of the general nature of the EEG, more detailed technology has been developed to determine which brain areas are involved with the behavior in question. For example, neuroscientists can now use *magnetoencephalography* (MEG) to measure the brain's magnetic fields and thus determine levels of electrical activity. This method is easier to use and more precise than the traditional EEG procedure (Huettel, Song, & McCarthy, 2004).

The development of new techniques to investigate the brain and the rest of the nervous system has occurred at a rapid pace. In recent years our understanding of neural activity has "jumped a quantum leap" (Gazzaniga, Ivry, & Mangun, 1998, p. 77), including development of methods to record the activity of a single neuron in animals. Neuroscientists no longer have to rely on gross measures such as the EEG, which records and averages the activity of millions of neurons. Using these techniques, scientists have learned that neurons involved in the processing of visual information in primates do not all respond to the same elements of the stimulus. In fact, neurons that are adjacent to one another may or may not respond to characteristics such as stimulus shape or movement.

**Computerized Brain Imaging.** The advent of computers has led to major advances in the study of the brain. With the

| Alpha waves | Alpha waves are characteristic of normal resting adults |
| --- | --- |
| Beta waves | Beta waves typically accompany intense concentration |
| Theta waves | Theta waves are seen in children, in frustrated adults, and in very light sleep |
| Delta waves | Delta waves occur in deep sleep and in certain pathological states |

1 sec

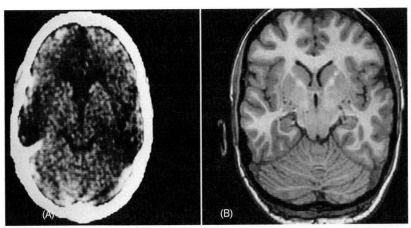

**FIGURE 2-15** The CT or CAT scan on the left (A) was a dramatic improvement over X-rays when it was introduced in the 1970s. Since that time, techniques such as MRI (right) have further improved the clarity of the images. Using MRI, (B) researchers are now able to distinguish brain gray matter, white matter, and cerebrospinal fluid (which appears black). The improved imaging capability has led to major advances in research and also makes it possible to visualize brain injuries and malfunctions that were not visible using earlier techniques.

**Source:** Allen, Bruss, and Damasio (2004).

**positron emission tomography (PET)**
Imaging technique that involves monitoring the metabolic activity of the brain

**computerized axial tomography (CT or CAT)**
Imaging technique that involves the production of a large number of X-rays interpreted by a computer

**magnetic resonance imaging (MRI)**
Imaging technique that involves the use of radio waves and a strong magnetic field to produce a signal that can be interpreted by a computer

newest techniques, a computer uses measures of brain activity to produce a brain image. Some of these brain imaging techniques provide static or single-point-in-time pictures of brain structures that are similar to the way an X-ray provides an image of a bone. These static images are provided by computerized axial tomography (CT or CAT) and magnetic resonance imaging (MRI). In addition, the most recently developed brain imaging techniques provide ongoing or dynamic images of the brain. **Positron emission tomography (PET)** is one example of these dynamic scans; however, these scans tend to be expensive and therefore are not as widely used as the other brain scans.

If you were to undergo a **CT or CAT (computerized axial tomography)** scan, an imaging technique involving computer interpretation of a large number of X-rays, you would find yourself lying on a table with your head positioned inside a large collar-like structure called a *gantry*. An X-ray machine located inside the gantry is completely rotated around the patient's head while numerous X-rays are taken. The patient remains in the CT scanner for approximately 15 to 30 minutes. The X-rays are taken from a variety of angles, and a computer combines the X-rays to produce multiple brain images. Figure 2-15A shows the result of a CT scan.

**Magnetic resonance imaging (MRI)** uses a strong magnetic field and radio waves rather than X-rays (Warach, 1995). With this process, a patient's head is positioned within a strong magnetic field, which causes the hydrogen atoms in brain cells to become aligned—that is, to spin in the same direction. Radio waves directed at the brain cause the spinning hydrogen atoms to emit a signal. The denser or thicker the tissue, the greater the number of hydrogen atoms and, therefore, the stronger the signal. A computer amplifies and analyzes signals from the hydrogen atoms to construct a picture of the brain tissues. The MRI procedure takes about twice as long as a CT scan, but the results are often worth the extra time. For example, MRI can distinguish gray matter, white matter (generally nerve fibers with myelin sheaths), and cerebrospinal fluid that fills spaces within and around the brain (Allen et al., 2004). Compare Figures 2-15A and 2-15B, and you will see that the details produced by MRI are superior to those of CT.

A patient preparing for a CT scan is about to be positioned in the gantry.

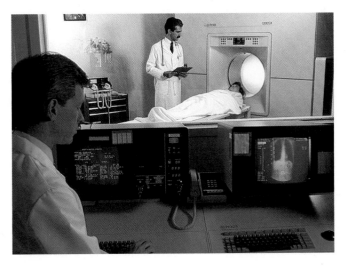

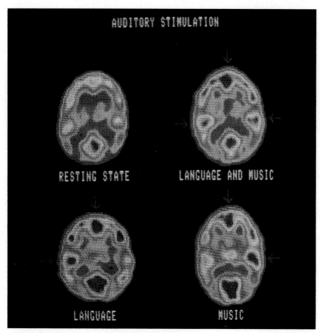

AUDITORY STIMULATION

RESTING STATE          LANGUAGE AND MUSIC

LANGUAGE                MUSIC

**FIGURE 2-16** Photographs of PET scans taken while a person is in a resting state, and while listening to music and language, together and separately. The color of the scan reveals the level of activity in various areas of the brain: Red and yellow indicate a high level of brain activity; green indicates an average level of activity, and blue indicates a below-average level of activity.

PET provides information about the brain's ongoing metabolic activity or energy use. With this procedure, the patient is injected with a radioactive form of glucose (blood sugar). Because active neurons require larger amounts of fuel, the radioactive glucose accumulates in the most active areas of the brain. PET scans the brain and monitors the radioactivity of various brain areas. Figure 2-16 shows patterns of brain activity while a person is resting and listening to language and/or music. Neuroscientists program their computers to illustrate levels of brain activity via color; however, the selection of the particular colors is arbitrary. In general, they use yellow and red to illustrate high glucose utilization (highest activity), green to indicate average activity, and blue to indicate below-average activity. As you can see, there are different levels of activation and in different areas of the brain, depending on whether we are resting, listening to language, or listening to music. Although the PET scan provides useful information, it is time-consuming and requires the patient to be conscious and able to process the stimuli that are presented. Nevertheless, it has proven quite valuable to neuroscientists who have been studying the relation between the nervous system and various mental processes.

MRI will not work well and is potentially dangerous if you have a heart pacemaker or any other metal implant. The magnets in an MRI instrument exert a gravitational pull that is approximately 40,000 times greater than that of the earth (Carter, 1998)! Technicians who forget to take off watches or jewelry have been dragged across a room by the MRI magnet. In 2001, a 6-year-old boy was undergoing a routine MRI scan following surgery to remove a brain tumor. When an oxygen tank was wheeled into the room, the powerful MRI magnets turned the 6.5-pound metal tank into a projectile. Two days later the boy died of the resulting injuries (Archibold, 2001).

Although standard MRI produces excellent structural images, it does not depict *ongoing* (temporal) brain activity. **Functional magnetic resonance imaging (fMRI),** a modified version of standard MRI, provides excellent structural views and temporal changes in brain activity (Huettel et al., 2004). Neuroscientists have used the fMRI to determine the role played by various brain structures in a range of behaviors (Pine et al., 2001; Whalen et al., 2001). For example, dyslexics tend to underuse the more efficient word processing regions of the brain and instead rely on speech production areas. Quickly, now, what is 12 × 11? About how many miles is it from your classroom to the nearest McDonald's? Using fMRI scans, researchers found that college students use different brain areas in answering these types of questions. When doing multiplication tables, students use areas involved with verbal memory; when giving distance estimates, they rely on regions involved with visual and spatial tasks (Murray, 2000). This type of research would not have been possible just a few years ago.

## Psychological Detective

A construction worker suffered a head injury that may have resulted in brain damage. If you were on duty in the emergency room when the patient arrived, what technique would you use to diagnose the extent of any possible brain damage? Your choices include EEG, MEG, a CT scan, a PET scan, and MRI. Think about the situation, and write down the procedure you would recommend. Why did you make this choice?

**functional magnetic resonance imaging (fMRI)**
A modification of the standard MRI procedure that allows both structural and temporal images of the brain to be gathered

Because of the time involved, MRI is not used when quick evaluations are needed. The PET scan and EEG procedure would not be used because they are not designed to detect damaged tissue and the results are not sufficiently precise. Accident victims typically require quicker CT scans. In this section we have discussed the various methods neuroscientists use to study the brain; now we turn our attention to what those methods have revealed about the structures and functioning of the brain.

## Major Components of the Brain

What makes us different from other organisms on this planet? Is it our height? Surely not, for there are taller organisms. How about our speed? What are your chances of winning a race when pitted against a horse? Most people would say it is our brain, but they may be surprised by a few facts. You see, humans do not have the largest brain of any creature on the planet. Here are the humbling facts, which indicate that size is not everything (Restak, 2000):

- A sperm whale has a brain weighing 7,800 grams
- An elephant's brain weighs 6,000 grams
- The bottlenose dolphin's brain weighs 1,500 grams
- An average human brain weighs 1,300 to 1,400 grams (about 3 pounds)

What makes us unique? Consider these facts: Blood flow to the brain accounts for 15 to 20% of the blood leaving the heart. Why? It takes a lot of blood, glucose, and oxygen to run the estimated 100 billion or more neurons in the brain 24 hours a day, 7 days a week. Every thought we have, every breath we take, every emotion we experience, every decision we make involves this approximately 3-pound mass that is "as big as a coconut, the shape of a walnut, the colour of uncooked liver and the consistency of chilled butter" (Carter, 1998, p. 15). Each neuron can make contact with thousands of other neurons, thus creating a network that is not matched anywhere in nature or made by the hands of humans. As noted earlier, the complexity of the human brain cannot be matched by modern computers.

Before we discuss some of the more complicated processes controlled by the brain, let's begin with a review of some behaviors that do not even reach the brain. Recall that some of your behavior consists of reflexes like knee jerks and an attempt to yank your hand out of a car door. As we noted, such behaviors are not processed by the brain; apparently, the time saved by restricting these behaviors to the spinal cord had survival value, and thus they have been passed on. But we live in an ever-changing environment with new challenges that require more than reflexes. What would you do if your hand were stuck below the seat in your car and you couldn't pull it free? Let's follow that information as it is sent up the spinal cord to the brain. (Bear in mind that although it takes us some time to describe this journey, the entire process happens in milliseconds.)

Initially the information travels upward in a group of nerves called a *tract*; its ultimate destination is the brain, which sits on top of the spinal cord. The three main divisions of the brain are the hindbrain, the midbrain, and the forebrain. A cross section of the brain is shown in Figure 2-17. Let's take a closer look.

**The Hindbrain.**   As the information about what has happened to your hand leaves the spinal cord, it passes through structures in the **hindbrain**. The major components of the hindbrain are the medulla, the pons, and the cerebellum. From an evolutionary perspective, these are the oldest parts of the brain, and they have important survival functions. The **medulla** (short for *medulla oblongata*) contains our respiratory center, which keeps us breathing, especially when we are asleep. Obviously, we can breathe voluntarily (take a deep breath now) or involuntarily without thinking about it. If our respiratory center is damaged, however, we cannot breathe automatically because we would have to think about every breath. Thus, if we stopped thinking, we would stop breathing (Vertosick, 1996)! The medulla also controls heart rate, vomiting, swallowing, yawning, and blood circulation (Afifi & Bergman, 2005). When the hand-in-the-door information reaches and activates the medulla, that structure may cause your breathing to increase.

The **pons** (from the Latin for "bridge") connects the two halves of the brain at the hindbrain level; this part of the hindbrain is important for sleep and arousal. The

"Whoa! *That* was a good one! Try it, Hobbs—just poke his brain right where my finger is."

**hindbrain**
Oldest of the three main divisions of the brain; its major structures are the medulla, pons, and cerebellum

**medulla (medulla oblongata)**
Structure located in the hindbrain that regulates automatic responses such as breathing, swallowing, and blood circulation

**pons**
Structure of the hindbrain that connects the two halves of the brain; has nuclei that are important for sleep and arousal

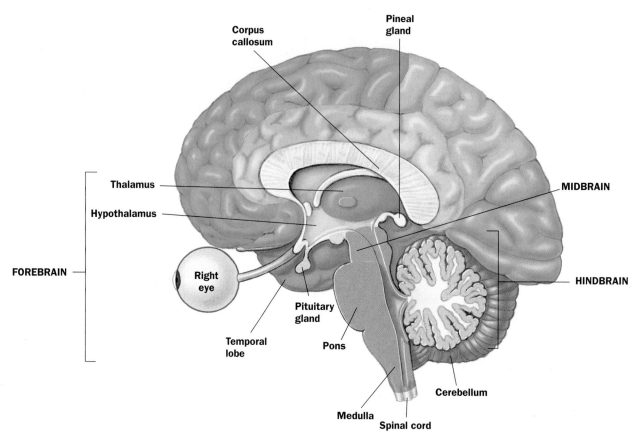

**FIGURE 2-17** A cross section of the brain showing structures at the hindbrain, midbrain, and forebrain levels.

cerebellum coordinates skilled movement sequences that deal with objects in motion. Without the control exerted by the **cerebellum,** we would have great difficulty performing such behaviors as pointing to a moving object. Although it is accurate to say that the cerebellum coordinates motor movements, this description fails to explain how the cerebellum works in conjunction with other brain areas that initiate motor movements (which we will discuss later). The cerebellum fine-tunes the gross motor signals that come from the upper brain; thus, the cerebellum's output is purely inhibitory. Neurons in the cerebellum dampen the activity of other neurons in the brain (Vertosick, 1996); however, it does not take much to disrupt the work of the cerebellum. Even small amounts of alcohol can affect it. Drivers suspected of driving under the influence of alcohol are often asked to complete a series of tests that can indicate if their motor coordination has been affected by alcohol's influence on the cerebellum.

In the past, the focus of attention was on the cerebellum's role in coordinating motor movements. With the array of sophisticated new research tools at their disposal, neuroscientists have begun to reconsider this description. For example, they found that the cerebellum is actually larger than was thought when it was referred to as the *lesser brain*: The cerebellum is approximately equal to the size of one of the cerebral hemispheres. What's more, the cerebellum seems to contain more neurons than the rest of the brain. Here are other intriguing findings:

- Patients with damage to the cerebellum are more error prone when performing certain *verbal* tasks.
- Patients with neurodegenerative diseases that shrink the cerebellum are often less accurate than others in judging fine differences between the pitch of two tones.
- People with damage to the cerebellum are prone to make more errors when asked to detect the presence, speed, and direction of moving objects.

**cerebellum**
Structure of the hindbrain that coordinates muscular movements

Police officers use a variety of tests (called *field sobriety tests*) to determine if a driver has been driving under the influence of alcohol. Among the tests are walking a straight line heel to toe or closing one's eyes and touching the tip of the nose with a finger. The detrimental effects of alcohol on the cerebellum are likely to be seen in the driver's performance on such tests.

These are certainly not findings one would expect from a brain region focused solely on motor coordination. Patients can also recover from injuries to the cerebellum. Although removal of the cerebellum disrupts movement coordination, with time normal function can be regained to a considerable degree. These findings suggest a general and subtle support function in sensory, cognitive, and affective processes that goes well beyond motor movement alone (Bower & Parsons, 2003; Paquier & Marien, 2005).

**The Midbrain.**    Continuing its trip to the higher brain centers, the information about your injured hand passes through the **midbrain.** Together the hindbrain and midbrain are known as the **brain stem** because they form the stem, or stalk, on which the remainder of the brain rests. The midbrain also is composed of nerve pathways that go *to and from* higher brain centers. Psychologists have found that this complex network of fibers, known as the **reticular formation,** is very important in controlling our level of arousal or alertness. Actually, the reticular formation reaches all the way from the hindbrain through the midbrain and into the forebrain.

When you first moved into your new dormitory room or apartment, you probably did not sleep very well for several nights. Every little noise probably sounded like a cannon going off in your bedroom. Now that you are accustomed to your new environment, you can (and do) sleep through everything (except classes). Your reticular formation was involved in this change because it acts like a gatekeeper. When we need to be aware of new and unfamiliar information, such as the sound of an ambulance or a fire engine, the reticular formation allows it to pass on to higher brain centers for processing. Familiar information that is of no immediate consequence, such as the sound of a refrigerator motor or air conditioner, is blocked by the reticular formation, and we do not become aware of it.

**The Forebrain.**    As the injured-hand information leaves the brain stem and moves upward, it enters the **forebrain.** Examination of the forebrain reveals that this part of the brain is divided into two distinct halves with duplicate structures in each half. These two halves or hemispheres are connected by a wide band of fibers known as the **corpus callosum** ("hard body"). The two hemispheres of the forebrain communicate with each other through the corpus callosum. Within the forebrain, the areas that the information about your injured hand encounters first are collectively known as *subcortical structures* because they are located beneath the other main division of the forebrain, the **cerebral cortex** (also known as the *cerebrum*) or outer covering of the brain.

Several of the major subcortical structures are summarized in Table 2-2 and appear in Figure 2-17. Take some time to familiarize yourself with these structures and their functions, and refer to Figure 2-17 so that you know the location of each one.

**midbrain**
Major division of the brain that contains fibers known as the *reticular formation*

**brain stem**
The oldest part of the brain; begins at the top of the spinal cord and contains brain centers responsible for basic survival activities

**reticular formation**
Nerve fibers passing through the midbrain that control arousal

**forebrain**
Major division of the brain that consists of subcortical structures and the cerebral cortex

**corpus callosum**
Wide band of neural fibers that connects the two hemispheres of the brain

**cerebral cortex (cerebrum)**
The convoluted (wrinkled) outer layer of the brain

2.4

**limbic system**
System of interconnected subcortical structures that regulates emotions and motivated behaviors, such as hunger, thirst, aggression, and sexual behavior

**thalamus**
Subcortical structure that relays incoming sensory information to the cerebral cortex and other parts of the brain

---

**TABLE 2-2**

## Selected Subcortical Structures and Their Functions

**Limbic system**
A group of structures involved in the control and direction of emotional behavior. The amygdala is involved in emotional reactivity, aggression, and the processing of odors. The hippocampus is involved in emotional reactivity and the storage of memories.

**Hypothalamus**
Some neurons in the hypothalamus are involved in the control of arousal, emotionality, food and water intake, sexual behavior, and body temperature; considered by some researchers to be part of the limbic system. Other hypothalamic neurons control pituitary hormone production and release.

**Thalamus**
A structure that integrates incoming sensory information and relays it to appropriate areas of the cerebral cortex.

**Basal ganglia**
A group of structures located near the thalamus that are involved in the control of slow voluntary movements, such as standing, sitting, and walking.

---

Deep down in the brain—below the cortex—you will find the *basal ganglia*, a series of interconnected structures that play a significant role in motor movement. These structures are also connected to other parts of the brain that play a role in motor movement. The motor difficulties that occur in Parkinson's disease are the result of loss of neurons in the basal ganglia that produce dopamine.

The **limbic system** (see Figure 2-18) is a group of interrelated subcortical structures that are involved in the regulation of emotions and motivated behaviors such as hunger, thirst, aggression, and sexual behavior (see Table 2-2).

The **thalamus** (from the Greek word for "inner room") is important because it sends sensory information to the cerebral cortex and other parts of the brain. Because so much information comes into and goes out of the thalamus, it is called the brain's "great relay station." A large number of nerve fibers radiate from the thalamus and route information to specific areas of the cerebral cortex (Barth & MacDonald, 1996). For example, some fibers go to your sensory cortex, and others go to your motor cortex. The major structures of the brain are summarized in the Study Chart on page 73.

You may be wondering how sensory information finds its way to the correct location for further processing. Remember that nerve tracts bring sensory information up the spinal cord and then through the brain stem. When these tracts reach the thalamus, each goes to an area that is appropriate for the information it is carrying. There is an area for vision, one for audition (hearing), one for taste, one for touch, and so on for all the other senses, except the sense of smell, which is processed in the olfactory bulb. Information is then relayed from these areas to appropriate areas of the cortex.

Ultimately, the information about your hand caught in the car door reaches the appropriate areas in the cerebral cortex. As you can see in Figure 2-18, the cerebral cortex covers the subcortical structures we have been discussing. As Figure 2-19 shows, the cortex in lower animals such as frogs or cats is smooth and not very thick. The more complex the brain, the rougher the cortex. The human cortex has a very wrinkled and crumpled appearance that

**FIGURE 2-18** Major components of the limbic system. The limbic system has connections to the frontal lobes, as well as other parts of the brain.

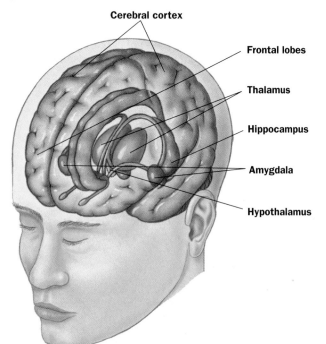

Cerebral cortex

Frontal lobes

Thalamus

Hippocampus

Amygdala

Hypothalamus

## *Study* CHART

### Major Structures of the Brain

| Location | Structure | Function |
|---|---|---|
| Hindbrain | Medulla | Controls autonomic responses such as heart rate breathing, swallowing, and blood circulation |
| | Pons | Serves as a bridge to connect the brain's two halves |
| | Cerebellum | Coordinates muscular movements; may have a general and subtle support function in sensory, cognitive, and affective processes |
| Midbrain | Reticular formation | Controls levels of arousal or alertness |
| Forebrain | Corpus callosum | Allows the forebrain's two hemispheres to communicate |
| | Cerebral cortex (cerebrum) | Handles sensory processing, motor control, memory formation and storage |
| | Limbic system | Regulates emotions and motivated behaviors such as hunger, thirst, aggression, and sexual behavior |
| | Thalamus | Integrates incoming information and relays it to the cerebral cortex |

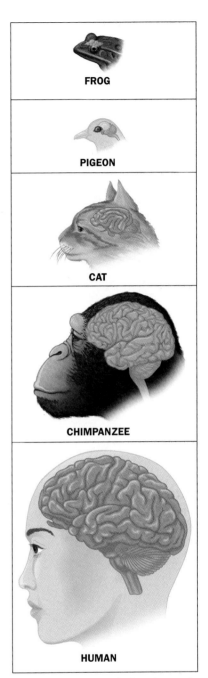

**FROG**

**PIGEON**

**CAT**

**CHIMPANZEE**

**HUMAN**

**FIGURE 2-19** Both the size and the surface of the brain (the cortex) differs across species. In general, more sophisticated and developed organisms have a more wrinkled and crumpled cortex. This wrinkling and crumpling is nature's way of stuffing more cortex into the limited space provided by the skull.

resembles a walnut or cauliflower. In prehistoric times, when the human brain began to develop, a great deal of growth and expansion took place in the cerebral cortex. Because the brain was confined within the bony skull, this growth caused the expanding cortex to wrap around subcortical parts of the brain and take on its characteristic ridges and valleys (called *fissures*). If the cortex for various organisms were unfolded, here is what you would find that:

- A rat's cortex (basically smooth) would be the size of a postage stamp.
- A monkey's cortex would be the size of an envelope.
- A chimp's cortex would be approximately the size of one of the pages in this book.

The human cortex would take up about four pages of this book. This expansion and development of the cerebral cortex sets the human brain apart from the brains of lower animals. In fact, the human cerebral cortex has been described as "the most intricately organized and densely populated expanse of biological real estate in the world" (Restak, 2000, p. 20).

Because the ridges and valleys are similar from one person to the next, they are used as landmarks to locate specific areas of the cortex, called *lobes*. Figure 2-20 shows the locations and functions of each of the four lobes—frontal, temporal, parietal, and occipital lobes—in each hemisphere. (Remember, there are two halves, or hemispheres, of the brain. The cortex of each hemisphere has four lobes.) Each of the lobes seems to have some specialized responsibilities. Here is a closer look at each of them.

**Frontal Lobes.**    As a result of their names, the **frontal lobes** are easy to locate. What's more, they are easy to spot because they are quite large (compared to the other lobes), accounting for almost 50% of the volume of each of the cerebral hemispheres (Restak, 2000). The frontal lobes are frequently referred to as the brain's *executive arm* (Goldberg, 2001) based on their responsibilities: language, movement, reasoning, planning, problem solving, and personality. Figure 2-21 illustrates the amount of the frontal lobes' *primary*

**frontal lobes**
The largest lobes of the cortex; they contain a motor strip, Broca's area (speech), and areas responsible for decision making

**FIGURE 2-20** Locations and functions of the four lobes of the cerebral cortex. *Frontal lobes:* involved in the control of body movement, decision making, and language. *Temporal lobes:* serve a variety of functions, including memory and processing of auditory information. *Parietal lobes:* contain major sensory areas of the cortex. The sensory information, however, is received from the opposite side of the body. Thus, the left parietal lobe receives information from the right side of the body, and vice versa. *Occipital lobes:* contain the primary visual-processing areas of the cortex.

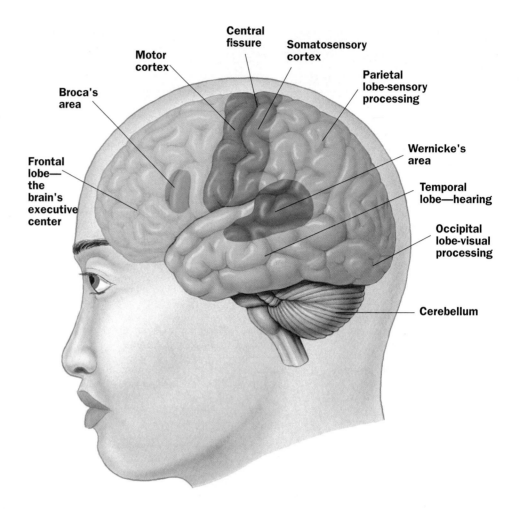

*motor cortex* devoted to various parts of the body. In general, more cortical area is devoted to motor functions that are most important to our survival. Because the use of our hands is so important to survival, large motor areas are devoted to manual dexterity.

The importance of the frontal lobes is clearly revealed in the case of Phineas Gage. As you will recall from our earlier discussion, a tamping iron was blown through Gage's head, yet he lived to tell about it. Miraculously, the tamping iron (1.25 inches in diameter) created a tunnel from just under his left eye through his skull, yet it did not damage any areas necessary for survival. Gage's vision and motor abilities were not affected. The physical results of the accident were evident in the scars, but the damage to his personality seemed extensive to those who knew him best and proclaimed that he was "no longer Gage." His ability to plan and to make good decisions were severely impacted. Formerly an efficient, dependable, and responsible worker, he would never return to the type of work he had enjoyed, and was even relegated to being a side show attraction in the circus. The damage made him susceptible to the kinds of whims that the frontal lobes generally hold at bay via their inhibitory functions. Gage died 11½ years after the accident as a result of severe seizures, which were likely a result of the accident.

**Parietal Lobes.** The **parietal lobes** are located just behind the frontal lobes. Their major responsibility is to process every sensation except smell, which, as we discuss in Chapter 3, has direct connections to the limbic system of the brain. The parietal lobes can also be thought of as a *sensory integrator* because they are responsible for body position as well as our sensory cortex or *somatosensory strip.* Figure 2-21 presents a map of the sensory cortex. Notice how the parts of the body that are most important in dealing effectively with the environment have the largest brain areas. For example, information received from your fingers is more important to your survival than information received

**parietal lobes**
Lobes located behind the frontal lobes and containing the sensory cortex

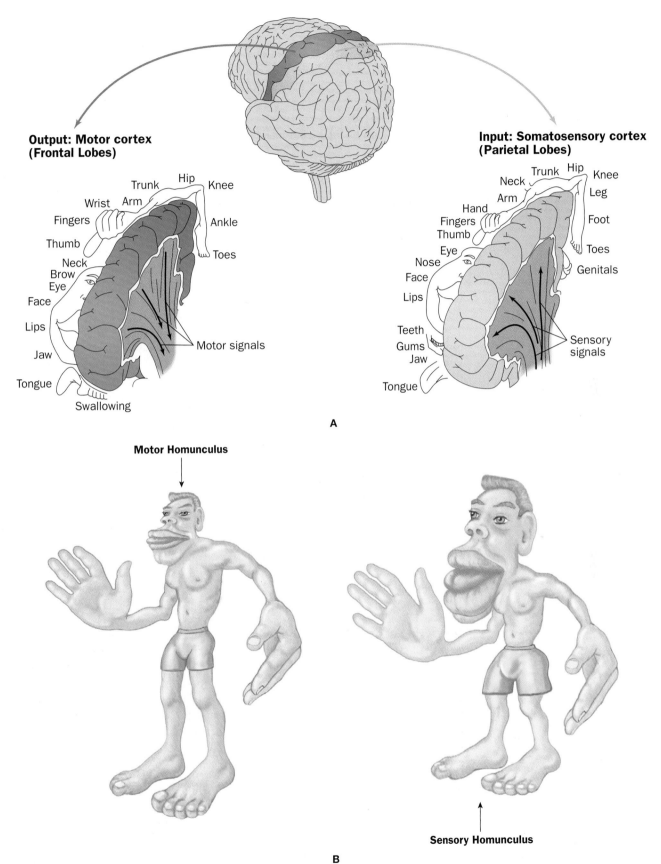

**Output: Motor cortex
(Frontal Lobes)**

**Input: Somatosensory cortex
(Parietal Lobes)**

A

**Motor Homunculus**

**Sensory Homunculus**

B

**FIGURE 2-21**  (A) Map of the primary motor cortex and somatosensory cortex. More important senses occupy larger areas. (B) These odd-looking figures are called *homunculi* (singular, *homunculus*). A homunculus represents how human beings would look if our bodies were in proportion to the amount of brain space devoted to our motor and sensory functions.

from the middle of your back. Therefore, more brain area is devoted to the fingers than to the back.

Damage to the parietal lobes can result in a neurological condition called *neglect syndrome*. If the damage affects the *somatosensory strip*, the patient will fail to acknowledge objects or events in the space opposite the lesion. For example, damage to the right parietal lobe renders a patient unable to perceive or respond to stimuli on the left side. One consequence of this syndrome is that patients may neglect an entire side of their own body and fail to engage in typical behaviors such as grooming.

## Myth or Science

How did neuroscientists map the brain's motor and somatosensory strips? Electrically stimulating parts of the brain provided the information needed to create these maps. Typically, this procedure can occur while patients are fully awake; interestingly, the brain has no pain receptors, so patients do not experience any pain from the electrical simulation. Put an electrode on a spot near the top of the brain in the right frontal lobe's motor strip and a person will move his or her left hand. Keep moving that electrode just a bit and the whole series of motor movements and brain areas responsible for such movements will be revealed.

One of the interesting findings from efforts to map the brain is that stimulating most areas of the brain does not give rise to a motor response or a particular sensory impression. In fact, much of the brain is composed of what are called *association areas* that connect other areas with one another. In many ways, these areas are like highways; in this case, they move memories, thoughts, and impressions, connecting them with other elements such as emotions and future plans. Thus, a very large part of the brain "is employed in the grand saga of making associations among events, ideas, personal experiences, strategies, and people" (Ackerman, 2004, p. 18). Because most of the brain is composed of association areas, many people believe that we use only 10% of our brain. Psychologist Donald McBurney (2002) has called this belief "one of the hardiest weeds in the garden of psychology." Although this notion is appealing and perhaps we would even want it to be true, it is *not* true. Although much of the brain is association area, this does not mean these are unused areas. The results of the brain scans discussed earlier indicate that large areas of the brain are used for various cognitive tasks, and these areas are often different, depending on the task at hand. So, you certainly should give a task your best effort, but don't be fooled into believing that 90% of your brain is not used.

**Temporal Lobes.**   The **temporal lobes** have a several functions, including the processing of auditory information; in most people the left side interprets the meaning of speech (Wernicke's area). These lobes also play a significant role in learning, memory, and emotions. Consequently, damage to the temporal lobes can impact our ability to learn new behaviors or new information. Attacks of anger and rage have been associated with seizures that involve temporal lobes (Drubach, 2000). In part, these various outcomes are related to the temporal lobes' connections to the hippocampus and amygdala, which are important in learning, memory, and emotion.

**Occipital Lobes.**   The back of the brain contains the **occipital lobes,** which may be the simplest of the lobes in terms of responsibilities. The occipital lobes' primary responsibility is to processes visual information. Although we receive sensory visual information through the eyes, we process and understand it via a remarkably complex process that involves highly specialized neurons. For example, some neurons are activated only by vertical lines, others by horizontal lines, and yet others by lines of a certain length. What's more, some neurons respond only to certain colors or to specific shapes. The neurons in the occipital lobes are organized in a hierarchical fashion: The first line of neurons processes simple visual information such as contrast and carries this

**temporal lobes**
Lobes responsible for hearing and understanding speech (Wernicke's area)

**occipital lobes**
Lobes located at the back of the brain that are responsible for processing visual stimuli

information to a second layer of neurons that processes shapes and then on to additional layers of neurons for complete processing of the incoming visual input (Drubach, 2000).

Each of the occipital lobes processes information received from half of the visual field. This contralateral organization means that information from the right visual field is sent to the left occipital lobe and vice versa. Of course, there are numerous connections between the two occipital lobes, so visual information is ultimately processed holistically unless there is some type of damage. Damage to both occipital lobes may cause *cortical blindness,* which means that there is no damage to the eyes but the occipital lobes are unable to process the visual information received. If only one occipital lobe is damaged, the result is blindness in the opposite visual field.

Consider the following case: Dr. P. was a music teacher who had some very peculiar visual problems. He was frequently seen patting parking meters, which he mistook for children (Sacks, 1985). This problem is called *visual agnosia,* the inability to identify objects visually. The problem was the result of a tumor in the visual area of his brain. Despite these problems, Dr. P. was able to continue teaching music until the last days of his life. Researchers concluded that he was suffering from visual agnosia—he did not recognize or remember anything he saw. In fact, he once mistook his wife's head for his hat—he tried to lift it from her body and put it on his head.

Do you remember your first day at school and the first class you attended? Did you scan the students in the class hoping to recognize a familiar face? Recognizing faces is an important function of the nervous system; it forms the basis of our reactions to others as well as our predictions about their behavior. For some people, however, recognizing faces becomes difficult or even impossible. Brain damage, especially to the temporal and/or occipital lobes, can disrupt our ability to recognize faces, although recognition via voice is not affected. This inability to recognize faces, called *prosopagnosia,* is not a result of intellectual deterioration or damage to the eyes. In one particular case, a patient who could not recognize his wife noticed a strange person staring at him. The patient had been staring at himself in a mirror!

**Language and the Brain.**   One of the key differences that sets humans apart from lower animals is the existence of a complex and continually developing language. As a result, it is not surprising that neuroscientists have focused on the brain structures responsible for language as well as the problems that develop when these areas are damaged. As we saw earlier, Broca's area (in most people it is located in the *left* frontal lobe) is the key area involved in language production. Wernicke's area (in most people it is located in the *left* temporal lobe) is the key area involved in understanding language. Damage to either or both areas can have significant effects on a person's language abilities.

The term **aphasia** refers to a loss of the ability to speak or understand written or spoken language. Aphasia is quite common, occurring in approximately 40% of people who have suffered a stroke (Gazzaniga et al., 1998). Damage to Broca's area results in *nonfluent aphasia.* People with this type of aphasia have difficulty producing speech, although they generally understand what others say to them. The speech of people with Broca's aphasia is often slow, effortful, and lacking function words and thus resembles a telegram. Stringing together the appropriate words or combining words to express their thoughts is typically a struggle. Here is an example of the spontaneous speech of a person with Broca's aphasia: "Son . . . university . . . smart . . . boy . . . good . . . good . . .". They may also experience difficulty understanding reversible sentences such as "The boy was hit by the girl. Who hit whom?" Although you would have no difficulty answering this question, damage to Broca's area is likely to lead the person to answer "Boy hit girl" (Gazzaniga et al., 1998, p. 307).

In 1874, the German neurologist Carl Wernicke (1848–1905) identified a second brain area that plays a significant role in language. Damage to Wernicke's area results in language problems called *fluent aphasia.* In contrast to the speech of people with damage to Broca's area, damage to Wernicke's area results in fluent-sounding but meaningless speech. Imagine listening to someone who speaks another language (Dutch, for example). Although you may not understand a word of what is being said, what you hear

**aphasia**
General term for problems in understanding or producing spoken or written language

sounds just fine to your ear. If the speaker has Wernicke's aphasia, however, the following might be a translation of what sounded right to your ear:

> I called my mother on the television and did not understand the door. It was not too breakfast, but they came from far to near. My mother is not too old for me to be young. (Gazzaniga et al., 1998, p. 308)

Although the Dutch version of this translation might have flowed smoothly, the translation indicates it is utterly without meaning and also contains several semantic errors.

Broca's and Wernicke's aphasias are the two most common, but there are other types. For example, *optic aphasia* is the inability to read more than one letter at a time (Buxbaum & Coslett, 1996), whereas a person suffering from *word deafness* cannot understand spoken language despite the presence of normal hearing and reading abilities (Davis, 1993).

**Apraxias** are deficits in nonverbal skills. As you might suspect, apraxias involve damage to the right hemisphere. Depending on the site of the damage, one might observe a *dressing apraxia*, in which a person has trouble putting clothing on one side of the body, or a *constructional apraxia*, in which a person cannot copy a simple drawing.

Oliver Sacks (1985) reported an interesting apraxia that involved the inability to smell odors. After a head injury, a gifted young man suffered complete loss of his sense of smell. This loss was a terrible blow to him: "It was like being struck blind. My whole world was suddenly radically poorer" (Sacks, 1985, p. 159). Some time passed, and he felt he was regaining his ability to smell. Once again he could savor the fine aroma of his favorite pipe. Examination showed that he had not regained any ability to smell, however: His memories of favorite aromas were taking over and making his world more complete. In addition to the scent of his pipe, he could smell a cup of coffee and the aromas of spring.

In addition to apraxias, the right hemisphere controls *prosody*, the ability to express emotion. People suffering from *motor aprosodia* speak in a flat monotone regardless of their real feelings. Such people simply cannot display emotions.

## The Split Brain

Earlier in this chapter we described the two hemispheres of the cerebral cortex, which are connected by the corpus callosum (about the size of a small banana). For years, psychologists wondered what would happen if the corpus callosum was cut, eliminating communication between the two hemispheres. Would there be two independent minds inside one head? In the early 1960s, two neurosurgeons, Philip Vogel and Joseph Bogen, discovered that cutting the corpus callosum reduced seizures in untreatable epileptic patients. Even though we do not know exactly why this operation controls seizures, it is still performed as a last resort in severe cases of epilepsy.

Initially, no other changes were noticed in patients who had this operation; however, research by Nobel Prize winner Roger Sperry (1964) and his colleague Michael Gazzaniga (1967) produced some remarkable findings. They showed that in people with a severed corpus callosum, the two hemispheres appeared to be doing different things. Indeed, it was as if there were two minds in one head! For example, the right hand might unbutton the patient's shirt, while the left hand buttoned it! Such conflicts typically occur shortly after surgery and tend to subside as the separated hemispheres learn to work together (Myers & Sperry, 1985).

Let's look at the logic behind the Sperry and Gazzaniga testing procedure. Figure 2-22 shows the transmission of visual information from the left and right visual fields to the brain. If you trace the pathways, you see that when the corpus callosum is cut and the person focuses on the center of the visual field, information presented to the left visual field of each eye goes only to the right hemisphere, whereas information presented to the right visual field goes only to the left hemisphere. In people with an intact corpus callosum, information presented to only one hemisphere is quickly transmitted to the other. In short, in a person with a severed corpus callosum, the two hemispheres of the brain cannot communicate with each other.

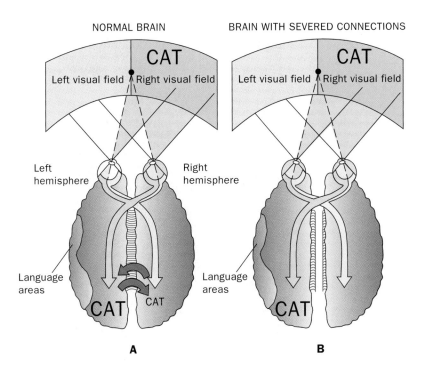

NORMAL BRAIN

BRAIN WITH SEVERED CONNECTIONS

**A**

**B**

**FIGURE 2-22** Transmission of visual information to the brain. All information from the right visual fields goes to the left hemisphere, whereas information from the left visual fields goes to the right hemisphere. In Part A, the image in the right visual field will travel over the corpus callosum to the right hemisphere. In Part B, the corpus callosum is severed, so the image cannot be transferred to the right hemisphere.

## Psychological Detective

Assume that you have undergone this operation. You are seated in the testing apparatus, wearing a special set of glasses that allows a technician to present a visual stimulus separately to either your right or your left visual field. What kinds of responses might you be required to make when an object is presented to you? Will the response you are able to make differ, depending on which hemisphere receives the information? Write down and explain your answers to these questions before reading further.

Suppose that we flash a picture of a baseball in your right visual field and ask you to name the object. If we trace the visual input, we find that it ends in the left hemisphere. Responsibility for naming the object falls on the left hemisphere. If we switched visual fields, the right hemisphere would be involved. Such tasks pose major problems for patients with a severed corpus callosum; they can name an object only when it is presented to the right visual field (and thus making its way to the left hemisphere). If, however, the task is reversed, so that the patient is shown the word *baseball* in the left visual field and told to select what was seen from a group of objects on a table with the left hand, the left visual field–right hemisphere combination can perform the task, whereas the right visual field– left hemisphere combination cannot (see Figure 2-23). Why?

Studies like those just described support the conclusion that the left hemisphere is involved in speech and language production. Thus you can easily identify a baseball or a cup of coffee when it is presented to your right visual field because this information is processed in the left hemisphere. In addition, the left hemisphere operates in a logical, sequential, and analytical manner (Bradshaw & Nettleton, 1981).

Although the right hemisphere has limited language functions (Levy, 1983), it is essential for adding emotional content to our speech (Shapiro & Danly, 1985). It is also important for spatial abilities such as recognizing complex geometric patterns (Clarke, Assal, & deTribolet, 1993) and people's faces and selecting objects. The right hemisphere operates in a more holistic or all-encompassing manner.

We do not want to leave you with the impression that the split-brain operation leaves the patient in an unusual or abnormal state. Other than having some trouble

*Live!* psych    2.5

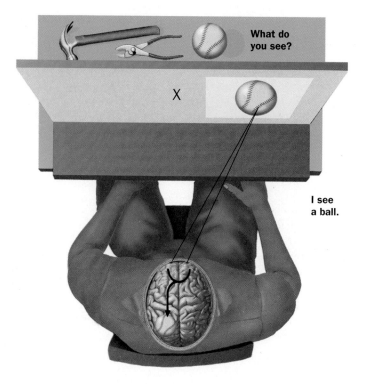

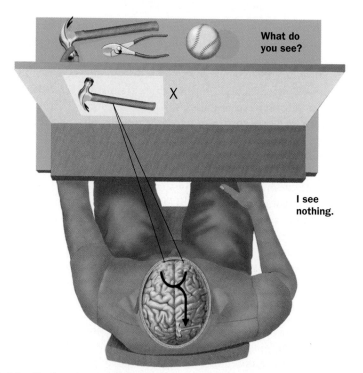

**FIGURE 2-23** Testing the split-brain patient. In the top panel, the image of a baseball is projected on the right side of the screen and transmitted to the patient's left hemisphere. The patient is able to select the object by touch from a group and identify it verbally. When the image of a hammer is projected on the left side of the screen and transmitted to the right hemisphere (bottom panel), the patient is able to locate the object by touch but cannot identify it verbally.

maintaining attention, split-brain patients do not suffer deficits in intelligence or motivation (Hoptman & Davidson, 1994).

## The Plastic Brain

The word *plastic* is not likely one that you would ever consider using with reference to the brain; yet, it is actually an apt description. Plastic can be molded and changed into many forms. It is a pliable material that can take on different forms and even functions. In some ways, the same can be said of the brain, which can change remarkably over time. Consider just a few of the remarkable findings that neuroscientists have presented in recent years.

- Using MRI scans, researchers examined a small structure on the top of the temporal lobe where sound is processed. They compared 25 people who had been deaf from birth and 25 hearing individuals who had been matched on sex and age. The ratio of gray to white matter was higher in the deaf people compared to the hearing controls. The increase was due to a reduction in white matter volume (as gray matter varied little between hearing and deaf individuals). What could account for this anatomical difference? Perhaps the auditory deprivation from birth experienced by those who are deaf may have led to less myelinization, fewer connections among neurons, and a gradual decay of unused axonal fibers. Apparently, exposure to sound had *changed* the anatomy of the brain (Allen et al., 2004; Emmorey, Allen, Bruss, Schenker, & Damasio, 2003).

- Persistent stuttering is a serious problem for many, but treatment techniques are available. Some evidence suggests that stuttering is related to an abnormality in the white matter speech areas of the left hemisphere. Before and after undergoing stuttering therapy, nine men underwent neuroimaging studies. The results indicated that following the therapy, these men exhibited more widespread activation in the frontal speech and language regions and temporal areas. The researchers suggested that the treatment had led to a remodeling of the brain circuitry around the areas that had caused the problem (Neumann et al., 2005).

- The life of a lab rat is probably rather simple: The cage is barren, there are no objects to explore or manipulate, and fellow lab rats are in nearby cages but no closer. Although the rat's basic needs for food and water are satisfied, there is little stimulation. On the other hand, imagine a group of rats in cages with fellow rats and a variety of objects such as slides. Would raising rats in an *impoverished* versus an *enriched* environment make any difference in the brain? The answer appears to be yes. Rats raised in enriched environments had more neuronal connections

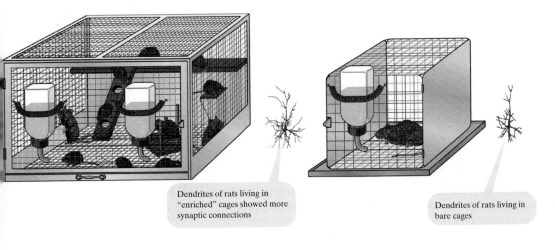

Dendrites of rats living in "enriched" cages showed more synaptic connections

Dendrites of rats living in bare cages

Raising rats in enriched environments (left) compared to an impoverished environment (right) can change the brain. One of the most dramatic effects was the increase in dendritic connections in the brains of rats raised in enriched environments.

**Source:** Rosenzweig, Bennett, and Diamond (1972).

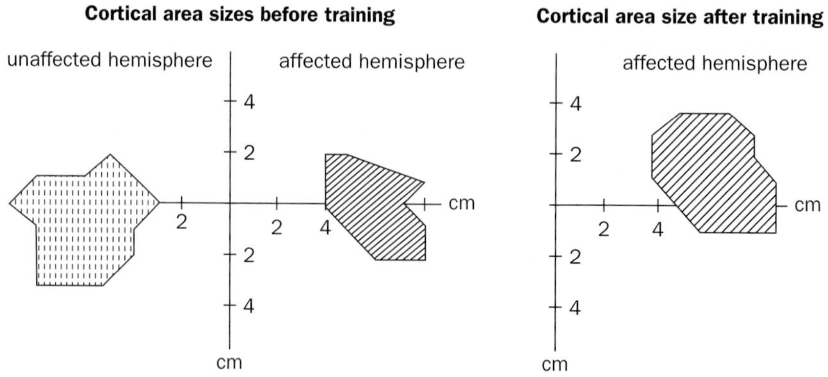

**Cortical area sizes before training** **Cortical area size after training**

unaffected hemisphere | affected hemisphere

affected hemisphere

**FIGURE 2-24** Constraint-induced movement therapy is used to help stroke patients recover some use of their extremities. A patient with an affected arm would have the less affected arm constrained for most of the waking hours, thus forcing the patient to use the more affected arm. This therapy can yield significant improvements in the functioning of the affected limb. These improvements are associated with changes in the CNS. The figures here represent the size of the primary motor cortex that elicits responses in an important muscle of the hand. After therapy, the size of the area had actually increased. In other words, the brain had changed as a result of experience.

**Source:** Taub (2004).

(dendrites) and seemed to perform better on several tests (Kleim, Vij, Ballard, & Greenough, 1997; Rosenzweig, 1984, 1996).

- A stroke changes a person's life, but is the change permanent? Can the motor deficits that often follow a stroke be treated effectively? Edward Taub (2004) found that monkeys that had connections to their forelimb surgically disconnected could recover some of the function. How? Taub used a technique that forced the animals to use the limb that had been surgically damaged. Using what he termed "constraint- induced movement therapy" with human stroke patients, Taub found remarkable evidence of at least a partial recovery. Most impressive are the findings that show actual changes in the motor cortex of humans (see Figure 2-24).

Consider one more case: For the first 3 years of his life, Matthew developed normally, like other children. Just before he turned 4, however, Matthew began to experience seizures that did not respond to drug treatments. The seizures were severe (life-threatening) and frequent (as often as every 3 minutes). The eventual diagnosis was Rasmussen's encephalitis—a frightening name for a rare and incurable condition that includes epilepsy, cognitive and motor decline, and loss of brain cells (Tran, Day, Eskin, Carney, & Maria, 2000). Neurosurgeons proposed an extreme treatment—removal of half of Matthew's brain. The surgery, a *hemispherectomy*, is performed a few dozen times each year in the United States (Pulsifer et al., 2004). Matthew's parents agonized over their difficult choice—a radical surgical procedure or almost certain death. They decided on the surgery, which was performed at Johns Hopkins Hospital in Baltimore (Swerdlow, 1995).

### Psychological Detective

Can people live with only half of their brain? What are the likely consequences of such a drastic surgical intervention? Give these questions some thought, and then write your response before you read further.

After the surgery, Matthew was left with a scar that runs along one ear and disappears under his hair; his face has no lopsidedness. He has no right peripheral vision in either eye, a slight limp, and limited use of his right arm and hand. The space left by removal of the left hemisphere quickly filled with cerebrospinal fluid. The hoped-for elimination of the life-threatening seizures was the most positive outcome, and it occurs in the majority of children who undergo this very serious surgery (Pulsifer et al., 2004).

After discussing all of the parts of the brain and their associated functions, it would seem impossible to survive if half of the brain were surgically removed (or damaged in an accident). The cerebrospinal fluid that filled the space left by removal of Matthew's left hemisphere does not operate like the brain's neurons. It would seem that functions of the lost parts of the brain would be lost forever. Yet, the brain is remarkably adaptable, especially to a change that occurs early in life, as it did for Matthew (Johnston, 2004). After the surgery, Matthew underwent weekly speech therapy. As part of the therapy, the therapist placed cards in front of him. If the card said "fast things," Matthew had to name as many fast things as he could. He did not offer as many examples as other children of his age; however, he made progress in the use of language. As in other children who have undergone this operation, the remaining parts of Matthew's brain took over some of the tasks of the part that was removed. This ability to change is what neuroscientists mean when they say that the brain is *plastic*.

One reason the brain, especially in children, can change in response to experiences (including removal of an entire hemisphere) is that humans do not come into this world with a fully developed, hard-wired brain. In contrast to fish and reptiles, young mammals (including humans) are cared for by adults. "Consequently, the evolutionary process did not have to produce a brain with specialized circuits that performed specialized tasks. Instead, it could simply produce a larger brain with an abundance of neural circuits that could be modified by experience" (Carlson, 2001, p. 18).

For as long as we can remember, teachers have taught and students have believed that it is impossible to grow new neurons in the human brain. Now new data are challenging this longstanding notion in ways that suggest that the brain is even more plastic than we had imagined (Gibbs, 1998).

Although researchers have known for some time that animals such as the rat, opossum, and tree shrew can grow new neurons as adults, this process has, until recently, never been demonstrated in humans. Certainly, the invasive procedures, such as sacrificing the organism to prepare brain sections, used to make such determinations in animals are not applicable to humans. Likewise, because "new" and "old" neurons are indistinguishable (Gibbs, 1998), postmortem examination of the brain did not offer researchers a viable tool for addressing this research question.

A group of researchers devised a simple, yet ingenious, technique (Eriksson et al., 1998) to investigate the development of new brain cells (*neurogenesis*). They located an oncologist (cancer specialist) who was tracking the progress of tumors by injecting patients with a chemical that labeled cells that had divided. Fortunately, this chemical (bromodeoxyuridine) can be seen under a microscope. The researchers obtained five postmortem brain samples from this group of patients (the patients' ages ranged from 57 to 72). Microscopic examination of these samples located the bromodeoxyuridine and indicated that hundreds of new neurons had developed in an area of the hippocampus. As we are learning, the brain is more plastic (changeable) than we had ever imagined.

In this chapter we have examined the biological foundations of psychology: the nervous system—especially the brain—and the endocrine system. We have seen how these systems are involved in sensing, processing, and responding to stimuli in our environment. In the next chapter, we look more closely at these processes. We explore the ways in which specialized receptors in the nervous system sense stimuli and how the resulting sensations are processed to produce the perceptions that are the raw materials of psychological functioning.

**STUDY TIP**

Create a detailed outline of the major components of the brain, including the forebrain, midbrain, hindbrain, and the various lobes.

# REVIEW SUMMARY

**1.** *Phrenology* is a pseudoscience popularized in the 1800s by Franz Joseph Gall, who believed we could determine a person's skills and characteristics by identifying bumps on the skull.

**2.** Early studies of brain functioning involved stimulating or removing portions of the cortex. The **stereotaxic instrument** allowed examination of structures that are deep within the brain.

**3.** The **electroencephalograph (EEG)** provides an investigator with a chart of a person's brain waves. Images of the structures of the brain can be produced by computerized techniques such as **PET (positron emission tomography)**, **CT** or **CAT (computerized axial tomography)**, **MRI (magnetic resonance imaging)**, and **fMRI (functional magnetic resonance imaging)**.

**4.** The brain is divided into the **hindbrain** (which handles survival functions and motor control), the **midbrain** (where the **reticular formation** is located), and the **forebrain** (two hemispheres joined by the **corpus callosum**).

**5.** The cerebral cortex covers the forebrain and is divided into four lobes: **frontal, parietal, temporal,** and **occipital.**

**6.** A group of *subcortical structures* involved in emotion, memory, eating, drinking, and sexual behavior are located beneath the cortex. These structures include the **limbic system, thalamus,** and **hypothalamus.**

**7.** Studying the human brain yields information about **aphasias** (language deficits) and **apraxias** (nonverbal deficits).

**8.** The split-brain operation involves cutting the corpus callosum to help reduce epileptic seizures. The study of split-brain patients provides information about the functions of the two hemispheres. The left hemisphere is responsible primarily for language abilities and speech production, as well as rational and logical thought; the right hemisphere is better suited to dealing with spatial relations and the perception of more holistic concepts.

**9.** The brain has been described as *plastic,* which means that it can change over time and recover to some degree even from removal of an entire hemisphere.

# ✓ CHECK YOUR PROGRESS

**1.** Suppose you are hooked up to an EEG while reading this question. Much later in the day, you are deeply asleep when your brain waves are assessed. Which two brain waves would we find on the EEG records at these two points in time?

**a.** beta and delta
**b.** alpha and beta
**c.** theta and delta
**d.** theta and alpha

**2.** As part of a research project, you agree to undergo a brain scan. According to the informed consent form, you will be injected with a radioactive form of glucose. Which of the following brain scans is being used?

**a.** magnetic resonance imaging (MRI) scan
**b.** computerized axial tomography (CT) scan
**c.** positron emission tomography (PET) scan
**d.** functional magnetic resonance imaging (fMRI) scan

**3.** Why is Phineas Gage so well known to neuroscientists?

**a.** He developed the EEG.
**b.** He suffered a form of epilepsy that was treated with surgery.
**c.** The effects of his brain damage helped us understand brain functioning.
**d.** The development of brain scans was dependent on his willingness to undergo invasive brain surgery.

**4.** Damage to Wernicke's area is likely to have an effect on a person's ability to

**a.** eat a balanced diet.
**b.** maintain fluid balance.

**c.** understand spoken language.
**d.** anticipate the consequences of aggressive behavior.

**5.** Explain how the two hemispheres of the brain can be separated. Why has this operation been performed? What are its consequences?

**6.** If Andy has damage to his occipital lobes, which of the following is most likely to be observed during testing by a neuropsychologist?

**a.** Andy will not know his name.
**b.** Andy will exhibit visual difficulties.
**c.** A slight hand tremor will be noticed.
**d.** A series of violent outbursts will occur.

**7.** Rose suffered a stroke that resulted in what a neurologist and a neuropsychologist described as *nonfluent aphasia.* What is the most likely location of the brain damage caused by the stroke?

**a.** left frontal lobe
**b.** left parietal lobe
**c.** right occipital lobe
**d.** right temporal lobe

**8.** Which part of the brain is responsible for breathing, heart rate, swallowing, and blood circulation?

**a.** pons
**b.** thalamus
**c.** medulla
**d.** reticular formation

**9.** A series of brain scans reveals that Denise has slight damage to the left front lobe of her brain. Neurologists suspect that the damage will develop further over time, so they plan to make careful observations of Denise. Which of these will be most helpful in charting the progress of the damage?

a. levels of hunger and thirst
b. visual acuity in her right eye
c. glucose levels after fasting for 24 hours
d. motor movements on the right side of her body

**10.** A neuroscientist was invited to speak to a class on the issue of whether the brain changes over time. Which of the following is the best title for this presentation?

a. "More Plastic Than We Ever Thought"
b. "The Brain Is Like a Mountain: Ever Moved a Mountain?"
c. "Resisting the Effects of Experience to Protect the Brain"
d. "Our Genes Are Responsible for the Changes in the Brain Over Time"

**ANSWERS: 1.** a  **2.** c  **3.** c  **4.** c  **5.** The two hemispheres can be separated by surgically cutting the corpus callosum. This operation has been done to reduce the symptoms of severe forms of epilepsy.  **6.** b  **7.** a  **8.** c  **9.** d  **10.** a

# Sensation and Perception

## CHAPTER OUTLINE

In Chapter 2 we discussed the importance of our physiological makeup in adapting to the demands of our constantly changing environment. In Chapter 3 we take this discussion a step further. First, we examine the systems that receive sensory information about vision, hearing, taste, smell, body position, and movement. Then we see how we process or perceive this information to bring meaning to it. Keep in mind that this meaning varies according to experience and culture. For example, many people in the United States report seeing the "man in the moon" when they look at the moon on a clear night. Native Americans, however, report seeing a rabbit, and Chinese people see a woman trying to escape from her husband (Samovar & Porter, 1991).

As you read the remainder of this book, keep in mind that the basic building blocks of sensation and perception are crucial to states of consciousness (Chapter 4), emotional behaviors and reactions to stress (Chapters 6 and 14), learned responses (Chapters 5 and 7), maladaptive responses (Chapter 12), and our interactions with other people (Chapter 15). Without adequate sensory input and perceptual processing, these and other more elaborate systems simply would not perform appropriately.

# SENSATION, PERCEPTION, AND PSYCHOPHYSICS

**For some time, you have been planning to have several friends over for dinner—not carry-out pizza, but something you prepare yourself. The big day is here and you've spent the whole afternoon in the kitchen. The aromas filling your apartment suggest that a superb meal is in the making. To be sure that everything tastes as good as it smells, you sample the offerings frequently. The more you sample, however, the less satisfied you are. The spicy sauce tastes bland, and the potato dish does not seem to have any flavor. Some additional spices will cure this problem, you hope.** *Are more spices the solution to your problem?*

The problem just described has to do with how we experience and understand our world—that is, it is concerned with the processes of sensation and perception.

## Sensation and Perception

In Chapter 2 we discussed the sensitivity of specialized cells, called *receptors*, to specific types of environmental stimuli. **Sensation** refers to the activation of these receptors, and sensations can be viewed as the basic building blocks of perception. **Perception** is the process of organizing and attempting to understand the sensory stimulation we receive. When the receptors are stimulated, information can be transmitted to the brain. Transmission of neural impulses to the brain is not enough, however, to give us an understanding and awareness of our surroundings.

If the receptors do not receive stimulation from the environment or are unable to process the information they receive, no information is transmitted to the brain and perception does not occur (Orbach, Mikulincer, Sirota, & Giboa-Schechtman, 2003). For example, people who are color-blind cannot tell from their perception of color

**sensation**
Activation of receptors by stimuli in the environment

**perception**
The process of organizing and making sense of sensory information

The sights, sounds, and odors of a large city provide ample stimuli to activate the sensory receptors (sensation). The brain will interpret these stimuli (perception).

**transduction**
Conversion of stimuli received by the receptors into a form (patterns of neural impulses) that can be used by the nervous system

**adaptation**
Loss of sensitivity to a stimulus by the receptors as a result of continued presentation of that stimulus

when a traffic light is red or when it is green; because they cannot sense color information, they depend on brightness and position cues to determine the color of the signal.

It sounds simple—activate the receptors (sensation) and then transmit the information to the brain to make sense of it (perception). As you will see, however, the process is more complicated than that.

To activate a particular receptor, a specific type of energy must be present—light waves for vision, movement of air molecules for hearing, molecules in a liquid solution for taste, and so forth. If you shine a flashlight in your ear, do not expect to have a visual response; there are no light-sensitive receptors there.

As we saw in Chapter 2, neurons operate on the basis of changes in electrical charge and the release of chemical substances called *neurotransmitters*. Somehow, the physical energies of light and sound waves and those of odor and taste molecules must be changed into electrochemical forms the nervous system can process. This process of converting the stimulation received by the receptors into electrochemical energy that can be used by the nervous system is called **transduction.** When you hear a sound, for example, sound waves cause a number of very fine hairs located in your inner ear to bend. These hairs are your auditory receptors. If they are bent sufficiently, the first neuron in the auditory pathway will fire (display an all-or-none response). Now auditory information can be transmitted to your brain.

Continued presentation of the same stimulus, however, causes the receptors to become less sensitive to that particular stimulus; hence, a stronger stimulus is required to activate the receptors. This process, known as **adaptation,** occurs very rapidly when odors and tastes are involved. In some cases—for example, when a sewer is clogged—adaptation is highly desirable. In other situations, such as when preparing dinner for your friends, adaptation may be disadvantageous. Think back to the cooking scenario at the beginning of this chapter. Are more spices the solution to your tasting problem? Because your repeated tastings have caused your receptors to adapt, a stronger stimulus (in this case, more spices) is now required to activate them. Therefore adding spices may create a bigger problem than the one you think you have. Your guests, whose receptors have not adapted the way yours have, will find the meal very spicy!

## Psychophysics

Before we explore how our sensory systems operate, let's take a look at the methods used by early researchers, known as *psychophysicists*, who studied the relations between the mind and the body. At the same time that Wilhelm Wundt was founding psychology (1879), a group of German psychophysicists were studying the relation between stimuli and the participant's experience. Their basic procedures were clear and straightforward. A stimulus was presented, and the individual was asked to indicate whether the stimulus was perceived (when only one stimulus was presented) or if the stimulus that was presented differed noticeably from a comparison stimulus that was also presented. In short, they studied the relation between the mind and the body.

Ernst Weber (1795–1878) was interested in determining the smallest detectable difference between two stimuli. For example, can you tell that a 105-watt light bulb is brighter than a 100-watt bulb? Would you notice that a 95-watt light bulb is dimmer than a 100-watt bulb? Weber's research indicated that the amount of change required to perceive such a difference could be described by the formula $K = \Delta I / I$. This formula, known as **Weber's law,** indicates that the change in stimulus intensity ($\Delta I$) divided by the comparison intensity ($I$) is equal to a constant ($K$). The constant is relatively the same for all tests of the same sense, but it differs from one sense to another. For example, the constant for identifying noticeable changes in auditory intensity is 5%, whereas the constant for vision is 8%. Thus, you wouldn't reliably be able to differentiate 95 watts and 100 watts, or 100 watts and 105 watts, but you could differentiate 95 watts and 105 watts.

Weber's study of the **just noticeable difference (jnd),** or the smallest difference between two stimuli that is noticeable 50% of the time, gave psychology one of its first laws. By showing that the amount of stimulus increase or decrease required to notice a change, divided by the original stimulation, was a constant, Weber showed how the mind (our perceptions) could be related to the body (the physical stimulation we receive). Even though researchers have treated these psychophysical laws as if they applied to all situations in a general manner, Lockhead (2004) has presented data indicating that psychophysical judgments are made within and influenced by the context (and by memories). Clearly, there is more research to be conducted in the area of psychophysics.

## Thresholds

**Absolute and Differential Thresholds.** How intense does a stimulus need to be in order for it to be noticed by a receptor? Through his study of sensory thresholds, Gustav Fechner (1801–1887) refined and expanded the work Weber had begun. Because of his extensive research on psychophysics, some historians of psychology believe that Fechner deserves to be known as the originator of modern psychology. Fechner studied both the absolute threshold and the differential threshold. To determine the **absolute threshold,** one asks, "What is the smallest amount of stimulus energy that must be present for perception to occur 50% of the time?" As you can see from Table 3-1, the absolute threshold for each of our senses is astonishingly low.

Ernst Weber (1795–1878) studied the smallest detectable difference between two stimuli.

**Weber's law**
The observation that the amount of stimulus increase or decrease required to notice a change, divided by the original stimulation, is a constant

**just noticeable difference (jnd)**
Smallest difference between two stimuli that is noticeable 50% of the time by participants

**absolute threshold**
Minimum amount of energy required for conscious detection of a stimulus 50% of the time by participants

**TABLE 3-1**

### Examples of Absolute Thresholds

| Sense | Threshold |
|---|---|
| Vision | A candle flame at 30 miles on a clear, dark night |
| Audition | The tick of a watch 20 feet away in a quiet room |
| Olfaction | One drop of perfume diffused throughout a small house |
| Gustation | One gram of the bitter substance denatonium saccharide diffused in 1 million grams of water |
| Touch | An insect wing falling on your cheek from a distance of 1 cm |

**differential threshold**
Smallest amount of stimulation that must be added to or subtracted from an existing stimulus for a person to be able to detect a change 50% of the time (see **jnd**)

**signal detection theory**
The contention that the threshold varies with the nature of the stimulus (signal) and with background stimulation (noise)

**subliminal stimuli**
Stimuli that are below the threshold of consciousness

To determine the **differential threshold** or **jnd,** we investigate the amount of stimulus energy that must be added to or subtracted from an existing stimulus for a participant to notice a difference (that is, to produce a *just noticeable difference*) 50% of the time. For example, a psychophysicist studying the differential threshold might be interested in how much the intensity of a light or a tone must be increased (or decreased) for a test participant to notice the change. Think back to the cooking vignette that opened this chapter: When you were trying to decide how much spice should be added, you were dealing with a differential threshold problem.

Although Fechner's research on the absolute and differential thresholds was important, it failed to take into account two factors: (a) the condition under which the stimulus was perceived and (b) the nature of the perceiver. Both factors are important in determining thresholds. For example, the task of determining either the differential or the absolute threshold for a light is much more difficult in a brightly lit room than in a darkened room. In a brightly lit room, distinguishing changes in the target stimulus (*signal*) from the background illumination (*noise*) is more difficult than in a darkened environment. **Signal detection theory,** or the contention that the threshold varies with the nature of the signal and noise, was developed to explain the difficulties one might encounter in distinguishing a certain stimulus from the background or noise (Swets, Tanner, & Birdsall, 1961). Signal detection problems occur frequently in everyday life. How often have you thought you heard (or later learned that you failed to hear) the ringing of your doorbell or telephone (*signal*) while you were watching television or listening to music (background *noise*)?

The importance (or lack of importance) of detecting the signal also influences our detection of it. If your car is in the repair shop and you are waiting for a call telling you that it is ready, detecting the signal (hearing the phone ring) is very important. You can afford to make a few mistakes (for example, picking up the phone only to hear the dial tone), as long as you answer it when the repair shop calls. Such mistakes are called *false positives* because we mistakenly believe that the awaited signal is present. A radar operator who is monitoring for incoming enemy aircraft cannot afford to make any false-positive mistakes; such errors would result in a full-scale alert and the mobilization of many personnel. By the same token, the radar operator cannot afford to overlook any incoming enemy aircraft. Such mistakes are called *false negatives*. Such errors might prove to be costly in terms of loss of life and property. These decisional factors (see Table 3-2) are called *receiver operating characteristics*. Understanding such decisions as indicating that you think a target is there when it isn't, or vice versa, is important to a complete understanding of whether a stimulus is detected.

**Subliminal Perception.**  The study of thresholds raises an interesting question. Can stimuli that are below the threshold for perception have any effect on us? Such events are called **subliminal stimuli** because, even though they do activate our receptors, we are not consciously aware of them. For example, if a persuasive message (see Chapter 15) could arouse our unconscious motives, it might stand a better chance of succeeding because we would not consciously try to resist it. This is the premise behind the use of subliminal perception in advertising. Because *subliminal* stimuli are below the level of conscious awareness, they should have a direct effect on unconscious motivation. To accomplish this goal, visual stimuli may be presented so rapidly that we do not consciously

**TABLE 3-2**

### Receiver Operating Characteristics in Signal Detection Theory

| | Signal Present | Signal Absent |
|---|---|---|
| **Respond "present"** | True positive | False positive |
| **Respond "absent"** | False negative | True negative |

perceive them, or tape recordings may be played during sleep (Ap, 2004). Thus, some researchers believe that both subliminal visual and auditory stimuli may have an effect on our behavior.

The most famous apparent demonstration of the effectiveness of subliminal perception occurred in 1956, when ads for popcorn and soft drinks were supposedly shown at 1/3000-second intervals during a movie. Because this interval is too short for conscious awareness, moviegoers would have been unaware that they had seen the ads. Yet popcorn and soft drink sales supposedly rose dramatically (McConnell, Cutler, & McNeil, 1958). Despite the claim of the success for subliminal perception in that instance, convincing data were never presented. Moreover, more adequately controlled studies have failed to reproduce those results (Trappey, 1996).

Although a limited number of presentations of a subliminal stimulus, as in the popcorn and soft drink example, may not alter our behaviors dramatically and immediately, there is some evidence that repeated subliminal presentations may change our attitudes and opinions (Abrams & Greenwald, 2000). For example, Monahan, Murphy, and Zajonc (2000) reported that participants who had 25 repeated subliminal exposures to novel and ambiguous visual stimuli rated their mood more positively than did participants who had only one subliminal exposure. Thus, it is clear that subliminal stimuli can influence our attitudes. Certainly, this area needs more scientific research.

With this general information about sensation, perception, and the methods of psychophysics in mind, we can now look at several of our sensory systems to see how they operate.

# SENSORY SYSTEMS

**If you spend time watching other people, you will notice that they blink frequently. Although the rate of blinking varies from one person to another, the average rate is about one blink every 4 seconds (Records, 1979). When the air is dry, the blink rate goes up. Why? Because blinking moistens the delicate surface on the front of the eye and keeps it from drying out. *How else is blinking related to our sensory processes?***

Many people would argue that vision is the most important and most highly valued sense. Ask several people which of their senses they would least be willing to lose, and almost all of them would say vision. We fear blindness because we are primarily visual creatures. Why? Our brain has more neurons devoted to vision than to hearing, taste, or smell (Restak, 1994).

What adjustments would you have to make in your lifestyle if you lost your sight? Compare these changes to the adjustments that would be required if you lost your sense of smell. Given the importance of vision and the ease with which the eyes can be studied, it is not surprising that vision is the sense that has been studied most thoroughly.

## Vision

To appreciate our visual abilities, we need to know two things: what we see and the components of our visual system.

### What We See: The Visual Stimulus.
Vision is a process that involves the reception of electromagnetic waves by visual receptor cells. This kind of energy travels in waves that vary greatly in length. For example, gamma waves are very short, whereas some of the waves involved in broadcasting are miles long. We measure **wavelengths,** or the length of waves, in nanometers (nm), which are billionths of a meter. The only light waves that humans can detect have wavelengths between approximately 380 and 760 nm (see Figure 3-1). This limited range of stimuli (the human eye can see only a small

**wavelength**
Physical length of a light wave measured in nanometers

**FIGURE 3-1** The visible spectrum and the three characteristics—wavelength (hue or color), amplitude (intensity or brightness), and saturation (purity)—of the visual stimulus.

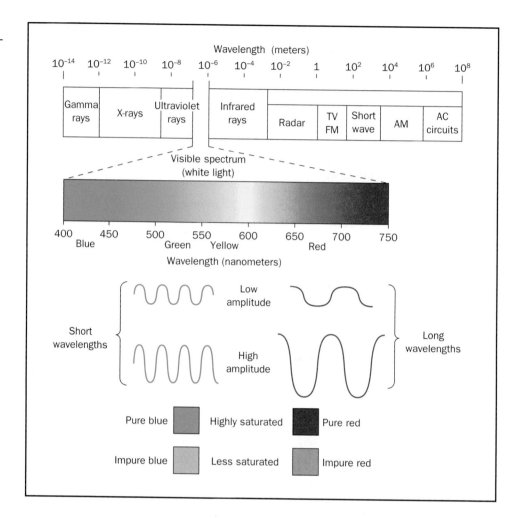

portion of the spectrum) is called the *visible spectrum*. Different light wavelengths are associated with different colors. For example, we see a wavelength of 425 nm as violet and a wavelength of 650 nm as red. Thus the psychological counterpart of wavelength is *hue* or color.

As you can see from Figure 3-1, light waves can differ in two additional ways: amplitude and saturation. **Amplitude** refers to the strength or intensity (brightness) of the light. **Saturation** refers to the "trueness" or purity of the colors we perceive. The more saturated a color seems, the more likely you are to be seeing only one wavelength.

To understand the concept of saturation, we need to distinguish between radiant light and reflected light. With **radiant light,** visible energy is emitted (released) directly by an object. There are only a few sources of radiant energy: the sun, light bulbs, and other hot, energy-releasing objects. If you place a piece of red cellophane in front of a light bulb, you will see a red light because red wavelengths are shown through the red cellophane.

What happens when you simultaneously look at red and green lights? As you can see in Figure 3-2A, you will perceive yellow. If you add a blue light to the red and green mixture, you will see white. Why? Because the three primary wavelengths are added together and are being sensed at the same time. *Adding* the three primary wavelengths results in the perception of white (in other words, no specific wavelength is dominant).

With **reflected light,** by contrast, energy is reflected by objects. Most of the light waves we receive are not radiant; they are reflected from objects in our environment. In other words, the light waves strike an object and bounce off it; we receive the waves that have bounced off the object. You perceive the colors of grass, a rose, and your sweater as a direct result of the reflection of light from those objects.

**amplitude**
Strength or intensity of a stimulus (brightness for visual stimuli; loudness for auditory stimuli)

**saturation**
Trueness or purity of a color

**radiant light**
Visible energy emitted by an object

**reflected light**
Energy that is reflected by objects

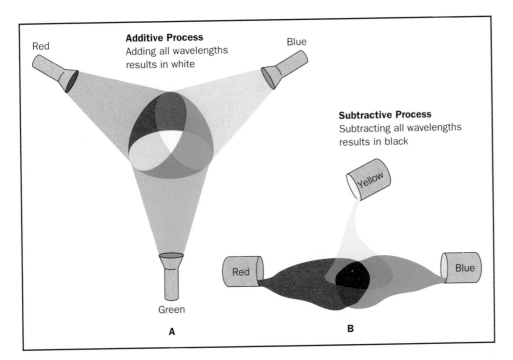

**FIGURE 3-2** The additive and subtractive processes of color mixing. (A) When lights are mixed, wavelengths are added. For example, red and green lights combine to form yellow. (B) When paints are mixed, wavelengths are subtracted. For example, red, yellow, and blue paints combine to form a dark or blackish color.

## Psychological Detective

What is it about reflected light waves that enables us to see different colors (wavelengths)? Spend a few moments thinking about the process that might make the reflection of different wavelengths possible. Here's a hint: When light strikes an object, are all the different wavelengths reflected to your eye? Write down your suggestions before reading further.

Knowing that objects absorb light waves in addition to reflecting them should help you understand the reflection of different colors. If all of the light waves are absorbed, the object or surface appears black; by contrast, if all of the light waves are reflected, the object or surface appears white. We see colors when certain wavelengths are reflected and others are absorbed. As you can see in Figure 3-2B, when red, yellow, and blue

The red car is a source of *reflected light*, whereas the light bulb is a source of *radiant light*.

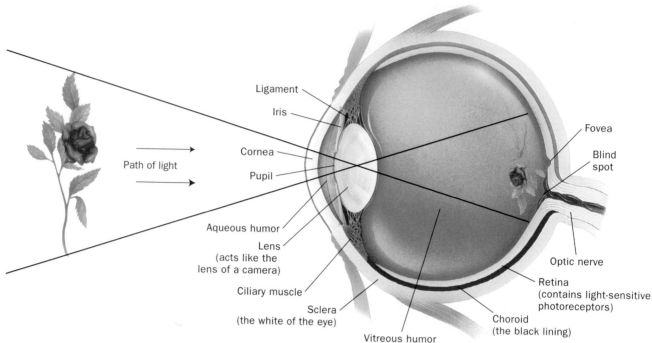

**FIGURE 3-3**  Structures of the eye.

**Source:** Pinel (1993).

**3.1** Live! psych

paints are mixed, all wavelengths are absorbed or subtracted, and the result is black because no hue is reflected.

If a surface reflects only one wavelength, the color you perceive is pure. The degree of purity decreases as the number of different, *reflected* wavelengths increases.

**How We See: The Visual System.**    Vision involves a complex chain of events. The structures of the eye are depicted in Figure 3-3. Familiarize yourself with them as we trace how light waves travel through the eye.

Initially, light waves pass through the protective *cornea*. The cornea is transparent but becomes an opaque, whitish covering, known as the *sclera*, over the rest of the eyeball. In addition to its protective function, the cornea helps focus the light waves.

After striking the cornea, light waves enter an open area called the *anterior chamber*. Here they pass through the *aqueous humor*, a clear watery fluid. This fluid, which is continuously recycled, helps supply nourishment to the eye. Then the light waves are funneled through the small opening known as the *pupil*. The pupil is surrounded by a colored membrane, the *iris*, which changes shape (like the diaphragm of a camera) to regulate the size of the pupil and therefore the amount of light taken in.

Next, the light passes through the *lens*. The lens, which is supported by two powerful *ciliary muscles*, is elastic; it can change shape to focus the visual image. Changing the shape of the lens to focus is known as **accommodation.**

After passing through the lens, the light waves enter a second, larger open space called the *posterior chamber*. Another clear, jellylike fluid, the *vitreous humor*, fills the posterior chamber. The vitreous humor also provides nourishment and helps give shape to the eye. Finally, the light waves strike the **retina,** the light-sensitive tissue at the back of the eye that contains the visual receptors (*rods* and *cones*). The basic sequence to remember is

Cornea → pupil → lens → retina.

Figure 3-4 shows that the retina is made up of several layers: The three major layers are the ganglion cell layer, the bipolar cell layer, and the photoreceptor layer.

This explanation would be much simpler if we could tell you that when the light waves strike the retina, they first stimulate the receptors and then progressively activate

**accommodation**

In focusing, action of the ciliary muscles to change the shape of the lens

**retina**

Tissue that contains the visual receptors, located at the back of the eye

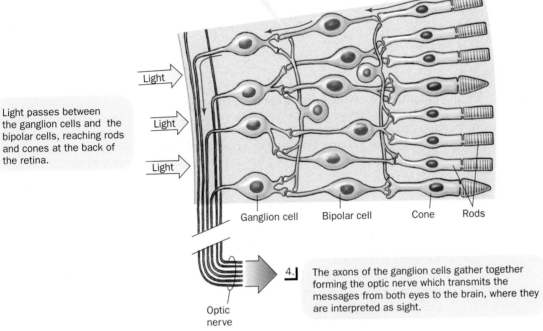

3. Now, the bipolar cells transmit this information to the ganglion cells.

2. The rods and cones, which are sensitive to light, respond by transmitting information to the bipolar cells.

1. Light passes between the ganglion cells and the bipolar cells, reaching rods and cones at the back of the retina.

Light

Light

Light

Ganglion cell    Bipolar cell    Cone    Rods

Optic nerve

4. The axons of the ganglion cells gather together forming the optic nerve which transmits the messages from both eyes to the brain, where they are interpreted as sight.

**FIGURE 3-4**  Layers of cells in the retina.

**Source:** Dowling and Boycott (1966).

layers of cells located toward the back of the retina, with the optic nerve exiting at the very back of the retina and going to the brain. In reality, however, the reverse is true: After light strikes the surface of the retina, it must travel *through* several layers of cells before it activates the visual receptors, which make up the back layer of the retina (see Figure 3-4). Light waves cause the receptors to change their electrical charge. If that change is great enough, the **bipolar cells** fire. If enough bipolar cells fire, the next layer of cells, the **ganglion cells,** fires. The axons of the ganglion cells come together to form the optic nerve, which carries visual information to higher brain centers.

Why are our visual receptors "wired" backwards? The arrangement may seem impractical, but it is the only way the receptors can be positioned close to the blood supply that lies behind the retina to receive the proper nutrients and maintain their correct biochemical status.

At the point where the axons of the ganglion cells come together and leave the eyeball, there are no receptors. This area is known as the **blind spot.** If you follow the directions in Figure 3-5, you will experience your own blind spot.

**bipolar cells**
Cells in the retina that connect the receptors to ganglion cells

**ganglion cells**
Cells in the retina whose axons form the optic nerve

**blind spot**
Location at which the optic nerve leaves the eyeball; contains no receptors

## Psychological Detective

As we suggested at the beginning of this section, blinking may have more to do with sensation than just keeping the eyes moist. When you blink, light does not enter your visual system. Because no light is being processed during a blink, you should experience 15 or more brief visual blackouts each minute. Can you explain why we do not experience such blackouts? Write down some possible reasons before reading further.

**FIGURE 3-5** Hold the book about 20 inches in front of you. Close your left eye and stare at the X with your right eye. Gradually move the book toward you. The bird that is approaching its nest will disappear when its image is focused on the blind spot. As the book continues to move toward your eyes, the image will reappear as it moves off the blind spot. Do you now understand how you may miss things because they were in the blind spot of your eye?

Frances Volkmann, Curnin Riggs, and Robert Moore (1980) proposed that when the brain signals the eyelids to close in a blink, it also stops or inhibits activity in the visual system. When the blink is completed, the visual system returns to its normal functioning. Thus information about visual blackouts simply is not transmitted or processed. Also, because we have a very brief (lasts about one quarter of a second) memory that persists during the blinks—*iconic memory*—for the object we are looking at, we remember the object and do not notice the blinks.

**The Visual Pathway.** The pathway taken by the optic nerve is diagrammed in Figure 3-6. The optic nerves from each eye join at the **optic chiasm,** which is located on the underside of the brain just in front of the pituitary gland. The fibers from the nasal half (closest to the nose) of the retina cross to the opposite hemisphere; those from the peripheral (outlying) half of each retina continue to the hemisphere on the same side of the body. The next stop is an area in the *thalamus*, the relay station in the *forebrain* (see Chapter 2). Ultimately, the visual information is received by the occipital lobes of the cortex, where higher-level visual processing begins (Payne & Cornwell, 2004).

**The Visual Receptors.** Because they are so important to what we see, the visual receptors, the rods and cones, deserve special attention. The **rods** (120 to 125 million per eye) are the most prevalent visual receptors. They have a lower threshold and lower acuity (sharpness of perception) than cones and do not detect color. By contrast, the **cones** (6 to 7 million) are less prevalent, have a higher threshold and higher acuity, and are able to detect color. The rods are slender and cylindrical, whereas the cones are much broader (see Figure 3-4). Most of the cones are found in one area, the **fovea,** an indented spot in the center of the retina (see Figure 3-3). Both the rods and cones contain light-sensitive chemicals called *photopigments*. When light strikes the rods and cones, it causes a chemical reaction in these photopigments. This change *hyperpolarizes* (see Chapter 2) the rods and cones and releases their inhibitory influence on the bipolar cells (Drubach, 2000). With this inhibition removed, the bipolar cells exhibit excitation, and a message is sent to the brain.

Look again at Figure 3-4. Do you see that the cones have a more direct, or one-to-one, hookup with the bipolar cells? Compare this arrangement with that of the rods: Several rods synapse (come close to but do not actually touch; see Chapter 2) on each bipolar cell. Which receptor do you think provides more detailed and precise information? If you are unsure, consider this analogy: Suppose that you are having a one-on-one

**optic chiasm**
Point at which the optic nerve fibers from each eye join; fibers from the nasal half of the retina cross to the opposite hemisphere of the brain

**rods**
Most prevalent visual receptors; have a lower threshold and lower acuity than cones and do not detect color

**cones**
Visual receptors that are less prevalent than rods; have a higher threshold and higher acuity and are able to detect color

**fovea**
Indented spot in the center of the retina that contains only cones

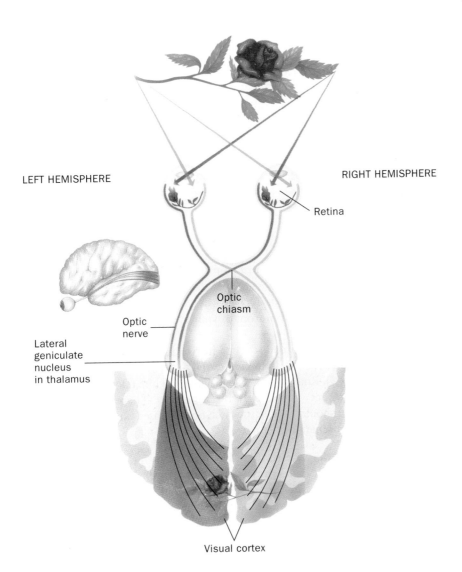

**FIGURE 3-6** Pathway taken by a visual stimulus from the eye to the brain.

LEFT HEMISPHERE

RIGHT HEMISPHERE

Retina

Optic chiasm

Optic nerve

Lateral geniculate nucleus in thalamus

Visual cortex

discussion with a classmate about the next psychology test. Each of you knows exactly what the other is saying. This conversation is like the information sent by the cones to the bipolar cells—it is clear and direct. In comparison, information transmission from the rods to the bipolar cells would be like members of a large psychology class heatedly discussing posttraumatic stress disorder. Because of the size of the class, you often cannot tell exactly who is talking at any given moment.

To experience the difference in the acuity (sharpness), of the rods and cones, hold this book about 12 inches from your face and look straight at it. Focus on a letter in the middle of a word in the middle of a paragraph. Now, *without* moving your eyes, see how many letters to the left and right of your target letter you can read clearly.

### Psychological Detective

The letters to the left and right of your target letter should appear blurred and more difficult to read. Why? Give the situation some thought, and write down some possibilities before reading further.

The letters you are looking at are not focused on the same areas of the retina. Because you are looking straight at the target letter, it is focused on the cone-rich fovea,

**TABLE 3-3**

## Differences Between Rods and Cones

| Rods | Cones |
|---|---|
| 1. Are numerous and found in the peripheral retina | 1. Are concentrated primarily in the fovea |
| 2. Have a lower threshold for activation | 2. Have a higher threshold for activation |
| 3. Have lower acuity | 3. Have higher acuity |
| 4. Do not process color | 4. Process color |

**FIGURE 3-7** Watch the rose turn black! Under high levels of illumination we are using our cones and can see color. As we experience lower levels of illumination, however, we shift to rod vision and cannot see color. To experience this shift, find a room in which the lighting can be decreased gradually with a dimmer switch. Slowly turn the intensity of the lights down, and you will see the rose change from red to black—the point at which you have shifted from cone to rod vision.

**trichromatic theory**
Color vision theory stating that there are three types of color receptors

**opponent-process theory**
Color vision theory stressing the pairing of color experiences; activation of one process can inhibit its partner

whereas the letters to the left and right of your target letter are focused on areas of the retina around the fovea. Rods predominate in these areas. The lowered acuity of the rods causes the image to become blurred. That is why you hold documents with fine print, such as your apartment lease, right in front of your eyes: to focus the print on the cones in the fovea.

We have said that rods and cones differ in two important respects: Rods have a lower threshold than cones, so less light is required to activate them, and cones are used for color vision (Table 3-3). Rod vision is like black-and-white television—you can adjust brightness levels, but you see only black, white, and gray. Therefore, if illumination is decreased gradually, you should be able to watch objects lose their color. Use Figure 3-7 to demonstrate this phenomenon.

**Theories of Color Vision.**    Researchers have long known that the sensation of color is transmitted to the brain by cones in the retina; until recently, however, they have not known exactly how this happens. Two theories, originally proposed in the 1800s, have guided our progress toward understanding this process. The **trichromatic theory** was originally proposed by Thomas Young in 1802 and modified by Hermann von Helmholtz in 1852. Young and Helmholtz believed that there are three types of cones, each maximally responding to one of the three primary colors: red, green, and blue. What about all the different shades of color that we see? According to the trichromatic theory, different shades are created when we receive sensory input in different amounts or proportions from the three types of cones.

There is some support for this theory. In the 1960s, researchers (such as Brown & Wald, 1964) identified three types of cones in the retina, each of which is sensitive to one of the primary colors. These three types of cones are maximally sensitive to wavelengths of either 445, 535, or 570 nm. As you can see by comparing these values with those in Figure 3-1, Young and Helmholtz were a bit off in proposing red, green, and blue wavelengths; blue-violet, green, and yellow-green wavelengths are the maximally sensitive wavelengths (Pick & Reid, 1995).

If the trichromatic theory seems to account for color vision, do we need to discuss the second theory of color vision? For several years after the existence of three types of cones was verified, researchers did not think so. Continued research, however, has provided support for another theory of color vision. When it was originally proposed in 1870 by Ewald Hering, the **opponent-process theory** stated that the cones are arranged in pairs; red is paired with green, whereas blue is paired with yellow. The operation of one member of a pair directly inhibits or opposes the operation of the other member. For example, if a red cone fires, the green cone paired with it is inhibited, and vice versa.

As knowledge of the retina grew, the opponent-process theory was abandoned when the trichromatic theory was verified. By the late 1960s, however, brain researchers (such as De Valois & Jacobs, 1968) who recorded the signals from single neurons

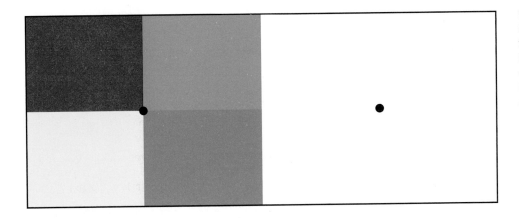

**FIGURE 3-8** Color afterimages. Stare at the dot in the center of the four color patches for 1 minute. Now stare at the dot in the center of the right panel. The color afterimages you see will be the opposites of the first ones you looked at.

discovered that some pairs of cells do respond as Hering had said. These cells are not cones, however, and they are not located exclusively in the retina. These *opponent-process cells* are found in the lateral geniculate nucleus (LGN), an area of the thalamus (see Figure 3-6). Opponent-process cells also exist in the bipolar cell layer of the retina. Therefore the trichromatic theory accounts for color processing by the cones in the retina, whereas the opponent-process theory accounts for color processing by the bipolar cells and the thalamus.

Opponent-process cells may also be responsible for the production of color afterimages. A **color afterimage** is the perception of a color that is not really present; it occurs after viewing the opposite or complementary color. For example, after staring at a red object, you will see a green afterimage when the object is taken away (see Figure 3-8); green is the opposite of, or *complementary* to, red. According to the opponent-process theory, continual viewing of red weakens the ability to inhibit green; adaptation has occurred.

**Color Deficiencies.**    People who suffer deficits in color vision are said to be *color deficient* (Kalat, 2001). In rare instances they can see no color; these people are called **monochromats.** Monochromats possess only one type of cone; as a result, in affected people the brain treats all received light waves as the same, and only shades of gray are perceived.

You can experience what it is like to be a monochromat. Because rods are monochromatic receptors, they process only shades of gray. The next time you are in dim light and cannot see color, you will know how true monochromats perceive the world.

Dichromats are another type of color-deficient people. A **dichromat** has trouble seeing one of the primary colors (red, blue, or green). A person with this deficiency lacks one type of cone and therefore has trouble with the opponent-process function. If the deficiency involves a red or green cone, the person sees only blues and yellows and shades of gray. If the deficiency concerns the blue cones, the person sees only reds and greens and shades of gray. Special tests have been developed to evaluate color deficiencies. One of these test patterns is shown in Figure 3-9. If you do not see a number there, you may have trouble with red–green color vision.

Because there are more male than female dichromats, color deficiencies may have a genetic or hereditary basis (Bollinger, Bialozynski, Nietz, & Nietz, 2001). Factors such as diabetes, a diet lacking in vitamin $B_{12}$, or a change in the lens of the eye, which filters color, can lead to an acquired color deficiency. For example, as we grow older, the lens becomes yellow and loses some of its ability to filter short wavelengths. This change can lead to color confusion, especially between blues and greens. Color confusion may become a life-threatening problem for elderly people who have to deal with colored medicine pills and capsules.

**color afterimage**
Perception of a color that is not really present; occurs after viewing the opposite or complementary color

**monochromat**
Person who sees only shades of gray; caused by a rare form of color deficiency

**dichromat**
Person who has trouble seeing one of the primary colors (red, blue, or green); caused by a form of color deficiency

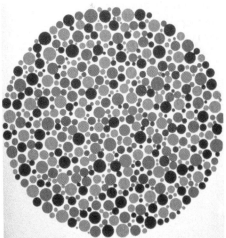

**FIGURE 3-9**  A test for color deficiency. All of the dots in this pattern are of the same brightness. Only the difference in wavelength allows one to see a number. Individuals who do not see the number may have trouble with red–green color vision.

# REVIEW SUMMARY

1. **Sensation** refers to stimulation or activation of the receptors. Sensations are the basic building blocks of **perception,** the process of interpreting or making sense of our sensory input.

2. Receptors for each sensory system respond to only one type of environmental stimulus. **Transduction** is the process by which the receptors change the energy they receive into a form that can be used by the nervous system. **Adaptation** occurs when continued presentation of the same stimulus results in a loss of sensitivity.

3. Psychophysicists, such as Ernst Weber and Gustav Fechner, studied the relationship between the mind and the body. **Weber's law** relates the amount of change in a stimulus and the conscious experience of change in the stimulus. Fechner studied the smallest amount of energy that could be detected 50% of the time (the **absolute threshold**) and the smallest change that could be detected 50% of the time (the **differential threshold** or **just noticeable difference [jnd]**).

4. The visual receptors, the **rods** and **cones,** respond to a limited range of light waves, the visible spectrum. Light waves differ in terms of **wavelength** (hue) or color, **amplitude** (intensity), and **saturation** (purity).

5. The **cones** have greater acuity, respond to color, and have a higher threshold for activation; the **rods** have lower acuity, respond to black and white and shades of gray, and have a lower threshold.

6. The visual receptors are located in the **retina** at the back of the eye. To reach the receptors, light waves pass through several other structures in the eye, as well as several layers of retinal cells.

7. Two theories of color vision have been formulated. The **trichromatic theory** proposes that there are three different types of cones; the **opponent-process theory** argues that color-sensitive cells are arranged in pairs. Both theories are supported by research findings.

8. **Dichromats** lack the ability to see one of the three primary colors. **Monochromats** are unable to see color.

# ✓ CHECK YOUR PROGRESS

1. Sensation refers to
   a. activation of the receptors.
   b. attempting to understand the stimulation we receive.
   c. reduction in sensitivity of receptors to a particular stimulus.
   d. converting stimulation received by receptors into electrochemical energy.

2. Match each term with its characteristic.
   a. Differential threshold
   b. Absolute threshold
   c. Sensation
   d. Rods
   e. Cones
   f. Wavelength

   1. Sensitive to color
   2. Activation of receptors
   3. Minimum amount of energy
   4. Less visual acuity
   5. Minimum change in energy
   6. Hue

3. You push the volume button on your remote control until you can tell that the television's sound is louder. The number of times you pushed the button represents your
   a. perceptual limit.
   b. absolute threshold.
   c. signal detection phase.
   d. just noticeable difference.

4. The process by which receptors become less sensitive to repetitions of the same stimulus is called
   a. adaptation.
   b. transduction.
   c. sensation.
   d. perception.

5. You are watching TV while expecting an important phone call. Periodically you think you hear the phone and pick up the receiver, only to hear a dial tone. According to signal detection theory, what type of decision have you made?
   a. false negative
   b. false positive
   c. true negative
   d. true positive

6. Erin has learned to create a "truly blue" light by focusing on only one wavelength of the visible spectrum. She is most likely to be concerned with which property of light?
   a. amplitude
   b. magnitude
   c. intensity
   d. saturation

7. "We can see only a small portion of the visible spectrum." Explain this statement.

8. What color would you see if a researcher simultaneously passes radiant light through red, yellow, and blue filters?
   a. white
   b. black
   c. dark gray
   d. light gray

9. Which sensory receptors receive information related to color?
   a. rods
   b. cones
   c. sclera
   d. transducers

**10.** Alex's hospital chart has the following notation: "Patient is a monochromat." Assuming that this notation is accurate, what would you conclude about Alex?

   **a.** He sees only bright colors.
   **b.** He cannot distinguish colors.
   **c.** He prefers one color over others.
   **d.** He can pay attention to only one input at a time.

**11.** Opponent-process theory accounts for

   **a.** color blindness.
   **b.** why we need rods and cones.
   **c.** our ability to see in the dark and the light.
   **d.** color processing by the bipolar cells and thalamus.

**ANSWERS: 1.** a **2.** a-5, b-3, c-2, d-4, e-1, f-6 **3.** d **4.** a **5.** b **6.** d **7.** Our visual receptors are sensitive only to wavelengths between 380 and 760 nm. **8.** a **9.** b **10.** b **11.** d

## Audition (Hearing)

Next to vision, the sense of hearing, or **audition,** is our most important link to the environment. Just as we see light waves, we hear sound waves. In this section we explore what we hear (the auditory stimulus) and how we hear (the auditory system).

**What We Hear: The Auditory Stimulus.**   Have you ever stopped to ask, "What is a sound wave?" To understand audition, we need to answer that question. A *sound wave* is essentially moving air. Objects that vibrate cause air molecules to move, and the movements of these molecules make up sound waves. Examples of sound waves are shown in Figure 3-10.

Like light waves, sound waves have three distinct characteristics: wavelength (frequency), amplitude (intensity), and purity (also known as *timbre*). Shorter wavelengths

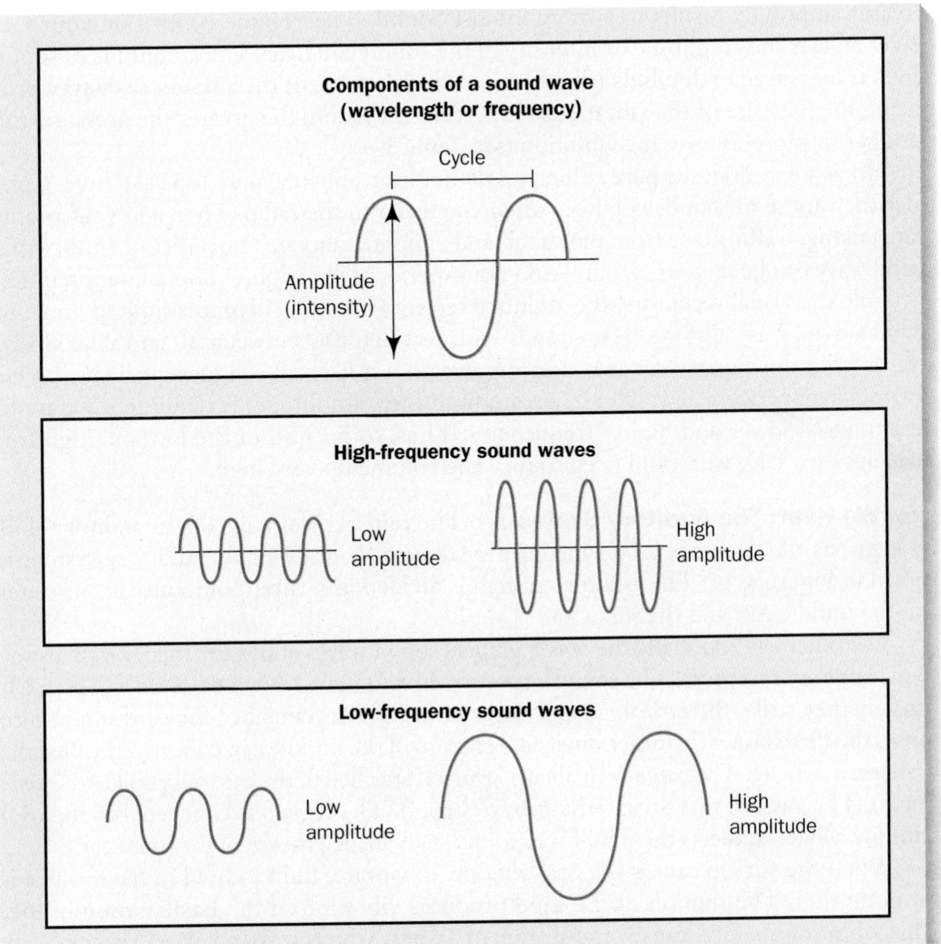

**audition**
Sense of hearing

**FIGURE 3-10** Sound waves are measured in terms of the number of times the wave repeats itself each second. Each repetition is called a *cycle*. Cycles per second are also called *hertz* (Hz). The greater the hertz, the higher the pitch of the sound. Some objects vibrate more strongly than others. This difference in vibration results in varied amplitudes or intensities of the sound waves. The stronger the vibration, the more intense the sound.

**TABLE 3-4**

## Various Sounds, Their Decibel Level, and the Risk of Damage to the Auditory System

| Decibel Level | | Situation Harmful Exposure Time |
|---|---|---|
| 180 | Rocket launch | Immediate permanent hearing loss |
| 150 | Jet plane, shotgun blast | Any exposure dangerous |
| 120 | Rock concert (near speakers) | Immediate danger |
| 100 | Chain saw | Damage in 2 hours |
| 90 | Truck traffic, lawnmower, motorcycle | Damage possible in less than 8 hours |
| 80 | Heavy city traffic | Damage possible after 8 hours |
| 70 | Constant exposure to a noisy restaurant | Critical level—prolonged exposure can result in damage |
| 60 | Normal conversation | No danger |

**hertz (Hz)**
Unit of measure (in cycles per second) of the frequency of a sound wave

**decibel (db)**
Unit of measure of the amount of energy producing the vibrations we perceive as sound

**timbre**
The purity of a sound wave

**ossicles**
Three bones (hammer, anvil, and stirrup) located in the middle ear that conduct sound from the outer to the inner ear

**oval window**
Structure that connects the middle ear with the cochlea of the inner ear; its movement causes fluid in the cochlea to move

**basilar membrane**
Membrane located in the cochlea of the inner ear; movement of cochlear fluid causes it to vibrate

**organ of Corti**
Structure located on the basilar membrane of the inner ear that contains the auditory receptors

**tectorial membrane**
Membrane located above the organ of Corti in the inner ear

occur more frequently; longer wavelengths occur less frequently. Frequency is measured in cycles per second and expressed in **hertz (Hz).** People with longer vocal cords have lower voices (lower frequencies) than people with shorter vocal cords because the longer vocal cords of lower-voiced people do not vibrate as rapidly.

As with light waves, the amplitude, or height, of the sound wave affects its intensity. Greater amplitude results in a more intense sound. The volume control on your CD player adjusts the amplitude or intensity of the sound you hear. The amplitude of sound waves is measured in **decibels (db).** Decibel levels represent the amount of energy producing the pressure of the vibrations we perceive as sound; the greater the pressure, the stronger or more intense the vibration (see Table 3-4).

Just as we seldom see pure colors, we do not hear only one pure tone at a time. Consider the variety of sounds you hear when you listen to the radio. Then add your roommate talking, traffic noise from the street, and a ringing phone. The purity or **timbre** of a sound wave can be measured, but we do not experience many pure tones in our lifetimes.

Like the visual receptors, the auditory receptors are sensitive to a limited range of sound waves. Basically, we hear sounds with wavelengths between 20 and 20,000 Hz. Even within this normal range of hearing, we do not hear all sounds equally well. Our hearing is more acute at 1,000 Hz; greater intensity (amplitude) is required if we are to hear tones at lower and higher frequencies. Thus, to hear all of the low and high frequencies on a CD, we would need to turn the volume up very high.

**How We Hear: The Auditory System.** The remarkable range of our auditory ability suggests the presence of an intricate system. A diagram of the auditory system is shown in Figure 3-11. The auditory system is divided into three components: the outer ear, the middle ear, and the inner ear.

The outer ear, especially the *pinna,* gathers sound waves and starts them on their way to the auditory receptors. The sound waves are then funneled down the *auditory canal.* Ultimately they strike the *eardrum* and cause it to move. Movement of the eardrum in turn causes the three bones (hammer, anvil, and stirrup) of the middle ear, collectively called the **ossicles,** to vibrate. The *hammer* (malleus), which is attached to the eardrum, strikes the *anvil* (incus). The anvil in turn strikes the *stirrup* (stapes). The stirrup is connected to the **oval window,** which connects the middle ear to the snail-shaped *cochlea* of the inner ear.

When the stirrup causes the oval window to vibrate, fluid located in the cochlea is set in motion. The motion of the fluid produces vibration in the **basilar membrane.** This vibration in turn causes the **organ of Corti,** which rests on it, to rise and fall. When the organ of Corti moves upward, the hair cells that project from it brush against the **tectorial membrane** located above it (see Figure 3-11).

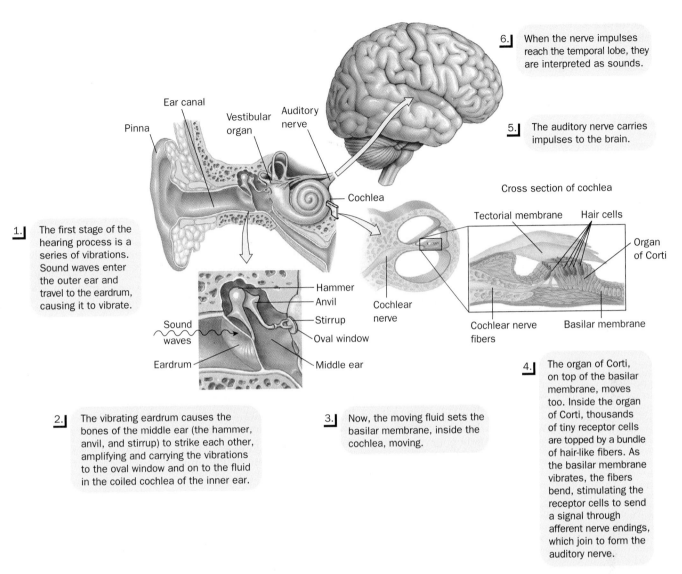

6. When the nerve impulses reach the temporal lobe, they are interpreted as sounds.

5. The auditory nerve carries impulses to the brain.

Cross section of cochlea

Tectorial membrane    Hair cells

Organ of Corti

Cochlear nerve    Basilar membrane
fibers

Cochlear nerve

Ear canal

Pinna

Vestibular organ

Auditory nerve

Cochlea

1. The first stage of the hearing process is a series of vibrations. Sound waves enter the outer ear and travel to the eardrum, causing it to vibrate.

Hammer
Anvil
Stirrup
Oval window
Middle ear

Sound waves

Eardrum

4. The organ of Corti, on top of the basilar membrane, moves too. Inside the organ of Corti, thousands of tiny receptor cells are topped by a bundle of hair-like fibers. As the basilar membrane vibrates, the fibers bend, stimulating the receptor cells to send a signal through afferent nerve endings, which join to form the auditory nerve.

2. The vibrating eardrum causes the bones of the middle ear (the hammer, anvil, and stirrup) to strike each other, amplifying and carrying the vibrations to the oval window and on to the fluid in the coiled cochlea of the inner ear.

3. Now, the moving fluid sets the basilar membrane, inside the cochlea, moving.

**FIGURE 3-11** Sound waves enter the outer ear, activate the hammer, anvil, and stirrup in the middle ear, and then cause activation of the auditory receptors in the inner ear.

The hair cells are the auditory receptors where transduction occurs. Contact with the tectorial membrane causes them to bend; when they bend, they depolarize (Kalat, 2001). Sufficient depolarization of the auditory receptors causes the neurons that synapse with them to fire. The axons of these neurons come together before they leave the cochlea to form the *auditory nerve*, which transmits auditory information to higher brain centers. From the cochlea, the auditory nerve travels to the medulla, where some fibers cross to the opposite hemisphere. The remaining fibers do not cross. The next stop is the thalamus. Ultimately the information reaches the temporal lobe of the cortex for processing.

At present, there are two theories to explain how we hear different tones or pitches. The older **place theory,** proposed by Hermann von Helmholtz in 1863, says that hair cells located at different places on the organ of Corti transmit information about different pitches. For example, bending hair cells located near the oval window results in the perception of higher frequencies, whereas bending those located farther away results in the perception of lower frequencies. The place theory says that what you hear depends on which hair cells are activated. For this theory to be correct, the basilar membrane has to vibrate in an uneven manner, which is exactly what happens with frequencies above 1,000 Hz. This uneven vibration, known as a *traveling wave*, is caused by the differential thickness of the basilar membrane. The 1961 Nobel Prize winner Georg von Bekesy

**3.2**

**place theory**
Theory stating that the basilar membrane vibrates at different places to create the perception of different pitches

**frequency theory**
Theory stating that the basilar membrane vibrates at different rates to create the perception of different pitches

(1899–1972; Evans, 2003) demonstrated that the basilar membrane is thinnest near the oval window and becomes progressively thicker (von Bekesy, 1956).

What about frequencies below 1,000 Hz? Here the **frequency theory** of Ernest Rutherford applies. In 1886, Rutherford suggested that we perceive pitch according to how rapidly the basilar membrane vibrates. The faster the vibration, the higher the pitch, and vice versa. The frequency theory works fine with frequencies up to 100 Hz; typically, however, neurons do not fire more than 100 times per second. How do we get from 100 to 1,000 Hz, where the place theory begins? The *volley principle* (Rose, Brugge, Anderson, & Hind, 1967) suggests a likely possibility. According to this view, at frequencies above 100 Hz auditory neurons do not all fire at once; instead they fire in rotation or in volleys. For example, for a 300 Hz tone, one group would fire at 100 Hz, to be followed by a second group that also fired at the next 100 Hz interval, and then by a third group that fired at the next 100 Hz interval. The activation of these three groups of neurons would tell the nervous system that you had heard a tone of 300 Hz.

Certainly the ability to discriminate among various pitches is an important attribute. Equally important is our ability to locate sound in space. Think of how confusing our world would be if we could not tell where sounds were coming from. Driving would be a nightmare, we could not tell which people were talking to us unless we saw their lips moving, and it would be impossible to find a lost child by hearing a call for help.

Two mechanisms help us locate the source of a sound. The first is blockage of certain sounds by the head. Because the head partially blocks sound waves coming from the opposite side of the body, those sounds are a bit weaker and are perceived as farther away. For example, if someone on your right side is talking to you, the sounds of his or her speech enter your right ear unblocked. Your head, however, partially blocks these sounds before they enter your left ear. In this way, the sounds entering your right ear are a bit stronger than those entering your left ear, and you are aware that the person is on your right. Similarly, your pinnas (outer ears) help block sounds coming from directly behind you.

The second mechanism is time delay in neural processing. The brain processes the difference in time when a sound enters one ear and when it enters the other ear to enable you to locate sounds in space. If a sound is presented on your right, it enters your right ear first, then enters your left ear. Even though the time difference may be only a few milliseconds, it is enough time for your brain to process and help you locate objects in space.

The characteristics of both light and sound waves are summarized in the Study Chart. Spend a few minutes reviewing facts about the frequency, amplitude, and saturation of light and sound waves.

## *Study* CHART

### Characteristics of Light and Sound Waves

| Characteristic | Description | Unit of Measurement | Visible/Audible Range |
|---|---|---|---|
| **Wavelength (frequency)** | Length of the wave, represented by the distance between the crests of successive waves | Light: nanometers (1 nm one billionth of a meter) Sound: hertz (Hz; cycles per second) | Light: 380–760 nm Sound: 20–20,000 Hz |
| **Amplitude** | Strength or intensity of the wave, represented by its height | Sound: decibels (db; amount of energy producing the wave) Light: foot-candles (ft-c; usually measured with a light meter) | Sound: 0–180 db Light: varies according to reception; rods are more sensitive than cones |
| **Saturation** | "Trueness" of the color/sound percentage | Presence of wavelengths other than the target wavelength | Depends on percentages of other wavelengths |

**Hearing Disorders.** For a number of years, reports in the media have warned that loud noises such as those from rock concerts, jet planes, sirens, and air hammers can cause hearing damage. If you are like most people, you probably want to know if these claims are true. Some damage-risk comparisons are presented in Table 3-4. Extended exposure to sounds with intensities of 70 db or more can result in hearing loss. As the decibel level increases, the exposure time needed to produce damage decreases. In other words, the louder the sound, the shorter the exposure time before your hearing is damaged. The loud noise from a car stereo that has an added bass box to increase the power, or standing near the speakers in a club or at a concert, can also produce other problems. For example, British doctors are seeing a significant increase in *pneumothorax* (collapsed lungs). One doctor has linked this increase in pneumothorax to boosted car stereo power and the loud sounds of rock concerts and clubs.

Are you doomed to suffer from hearing loss? Contemporary living involves potentially dangerous sounds; however, the extent of exposure to them is often within your control.

Many people have hearing problems. Three such problems have been studied extensively: conduction deafness, sensorineural deafness, and central deafness. The first two may be caused by exposure to very loud noises. **Conduction deafness** refers to problems associated with conducting or transmitting sounds through the outer and middle ears. In addition to excessive exposure to loud noises that can cause the eardrum to burst, common causes of conduction deafness are excessive ear wax or damage to the hammer, anvil, or stirrup. **Sensorineural deafness** is caused by damage to the inner ear, especially the hair cells. Noise that is sufficiently loud to cause the hair cells to break can cause this type of deafness. **Central deafness** is caused by disease and tumors in the auditory pathways and auditory cortex of the brain. Although sensorineural and central deafness can be inherited (Kral, Hartman, Tillein, Heid, & Klinke, 2002), they can also develop from exposure to measles and other contagious diseases before birth, an inadequate oxygen supply during birth, and childhood diseases such as meningitis.

Conduction deafness can be treated; hearing aids are often used to offset hearing loss resulting from damage to the bones of the middle ear. Sensorineural and central deafness are treatable only with cochlear implants, which stimulate the auditory nerve, or surgery of the auditory portion of the central nervous system. However, in many cases, there is no way to restore hearing when there is sensorineural or central deafness.

**conduction deafness**
Deafness caused by problems associated with transmitting sounds through the outer and middle ears

**sensorineural deafness**
Deafness caused by damage to the inner ear, especially the hair cells

**central deafness**
Deafness resulting from disease and tumors in the auditory pathways or auditory cortex of the brain

**gustation**
Sense of taste

# The Chemical Senses: Taste and Smell

Unlike humans, many animal species rely heavily on the chemical senses (taste and smell); hence these are sometimes called *primitive senses*. Taste involves the mixing of molecules in a liquid, and smell involves the mixing of molecules in the air.

**Taste (Gustation).** Few people would disagree that **gustation** (the technical term for taste) is a meaningful and often enjoyable link with our environment. As one researcher has described it, "The tongue is like a kingdom divided into principalities according to sensory talent. It would be as if all those who could see lived to the east, those who could hear lived to the west, those who could taste lived to the south, and those who could touch lived to the north. A flavor traveling through this kingdom is not recognized in the same way in any two places" (Ackerman, 1990, p. 139). Because taste receptors adapt so quickly and because tasting typically does not occur without smelling and other sensory input (Stillman, 2002), our knowledge of the sense of taste is not as complete or as accurate as it could be.

**What We Taste: The Gustatory Stimulus.** The stimuli for taste are molecules dissolved in a liquid. But how do we account for the distinctive tastes of dry foods? If you think of the saliva that is produced when you eat dry foods, you know the source of the liquid. Have you ever eaten dry cereal as a snack? The first few bites are likely to be bland and dry, but when your saliva starts flowing, the full flavor of the food comes through.

**FIGURE 3-12** (A) The large, round tastebuds are clearly visible in this photograph. (B) Pathway of the gustatory nerve.

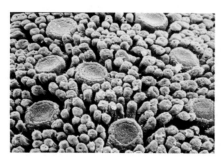

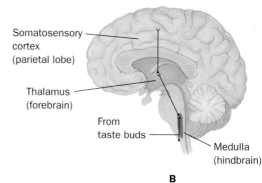

Somatosensory cortex (parietal lobe)

Thalamus (forebrain)

From taste buds

Medulla (hindbrain)

A

B

**taste buds**
Structures that contain the taste receptors

**papillae**
Bumps or protrusions distributed on the tongue and throat that are lined with taste buds

**microvilli**
Hairs that project from taste receptors

**How We Taste: The Gustatory System.** Once molecules are in solution, they can come into contact with the taste receptor cells, which are located in structures known as **taste buds** (see Figure 3-12A). Each taste bud contains between 50 and 100 taste receptors (Smith & Margolskee, 2001). The taste buds line the walls of small bumps on the tongue and throat called **papillae** (Latin for "bumps"). Although the primary locations of the taste buds are the tip, back, and sides of the tongue, some taste buds are located in the back of your throat, on the roof of your mouth, and inside your cheeks. The number of papillae differs from person to person. People who have only a few papillae may be somewhat deficient in their ability to taste, whereas people who have a large number of papillae are termed *supertasters* (Beckman, 2004). However, being a supertaster may have some drawbacks as well as benefits. On the down side, supertasters do not like strong-flavored foods and beverages. Hence, they avoid barbecue, spicy Italian and Mexican food, rich desserts, and even some vegetables. On the positive side, supertasters have better cholesterol profiles and tend to be slimmer than normal tasters. Certainly, research in this area will continue.

Individual taste receptor cells do not last forever; with a life expectancy of only 10 days to 2 weeks, the cells within a taste bud are continually being replaced (McLaughlin & Margolskee, 1994). The number of taste buds increases during childhood to a maximum of about 10,000. At approximately age 40 the trend reverses, and our sense of taste declines (Schiffman, 1983).

How do the taste receptors work? Although researchers are not absolutely sure, the most credible theories advanced to date suggest that molecules in the solution attach to or fit into receptor sites. The actual taste receptor sites are located on microscopic hairs, known as **microvilli,** that project from the tips of the taste receptor cells. The receptor sites have different geometric shapes or different types of ion channels (Gilbertson & Boughter, 2003), so the shape of the molecule determines whether it fits into a specific receptor site.

For nearly a century, researchers have agreed with the proposal that we are sensitive to at least four primary tastes: sweet, sour, bitter, and salty (Henning, 1916). In the late 1990s, receptor sites for a fifth taste, *umam* (savory or meaty), were identified; however, researchers are not in complete agreement that umami really is a separate taste (Smith & Margolskee, 2001). Hence it is reasonable to suppose that there are at least four different types (shapes) of receptor sites. The arrangement is like a key fitting into a lock. In this case, the key is the molecule and the lock is the receptor site. Once the sites are occupied, depolarization occurs and information is transmitted through the gustatory nerve to the brain (see Figure 3-12B). A number of molecules can occupy a receptor site: The better the fit, the greater the depolarization (McLaughlin & Margolskee, 1994). Keep in mind, however, that the lock-and-key theory is not absolute. Even though a receptor signals a certain taste more than others, it can also contribute to the perception of other tastes (Erickson, DiLorenzo, & Woodbury, 1994).

## Psychological Detective

This four-taste, lock-and-key theory sounds reasonable, but has it occurred to you that we experience more than four tastes? With only four proposed types of receptor sites, how do you explain the wide variety of tastes that we are able to experience? Write down some possible answers before reading further.

The explanation of our ability to experience a variety of tastes despite the existence of only four types of receptor sites appears to lie in the *pattern* or *combination* of neural activity the gustatory nerve sends to the brain (Pfaffmann, 1955). For example, one taste could be represented by considerable activity from all receptors except the salty ones, whereas a second taste could be represented by high activity levels of only two types of receptors.

As Figure 3-12B shows, the gustatory nerve goes from the taste buds to the medulla in the hindbrain (see Chapter 2), where they synapse. From there the information travels to the thalamus and is then relayed to the somatosensory cortex in the forebrain. At this point you are able to determine the nature of the taste you have experienced. The nature and amount of this brain activity can have a pronounced effect on how sophisticated our taste experience is. For example, professional wine tasters (sommeliers) show a burst of electrical activity in brain areas that deal with memory encoding (see Chapter 7) and emotional responses (see Chapter 6) that normal people do not display. Hence, the sommeliers are likely to have a more elaborate and satisfying experience when tasting wine.

Throughout the world, humans have learned to like many tastes. Because various food sources are more plentiful in different locations and countries, cultural and ethnic differences in tastes have developed. As Diane Ackerman (1990) points out, "Many people eat rodents, grasshoppers, snakes, flightless birds, kangaroos, lobsters, snails, and bats. Unlike most other animals, which fill a small yet ample niche in the large web of life on earth, humans are omnivorous. Diversity is our delight" (p. 133).

**Smell (Olfaction).**     Unlike animals that rely on their sense of smell for survival (Ru & Makosso, 2001), humans typically do not pay much attention to odors unless they are unusually bad (like 3-week-old perishable garbage) or unusually pleasant (like a freshly baked pizza). **Olfaction,** the ability to sense odors, is not crucial to our survival, but certain odors—such as those of leaking gas, spoiled food, or smoke—are important. Even if olfaction is not essential for survival, consider how bland our world would seem if we could smell nothing. Humans can recognize approximately 10,000 scents; many animals, such as bloodhounds, can detect and discriminate among many more.

**What We Smell: The Olfactory Stimulus.**     Odors are produced by molecules in the air. The more easily a substance's molecules mix with the air, the easier it is for us to smell it. Gasoline molecules mix with air quite easily and are readily detected; glass molecules do not mix well. Can you describe the smell of glass? Although no one can describe the smell of glass, some people cannot even describe the smell of common odors. More than 2 million Americans have a significant loss in the ability to smell. This condition, called *anosmia*, can result from genetic defects, aging, viruses, allergies, or certain prescription drugs. The most common cause, however, is head trauma, which can shear off axons that run from the olfactory nerves to the brain (deKruijk et al., 2003). Moreover, researchers have found that specific olfactory deficits may be characteristic of specific disorders (Dingfelder, 2004). For example, people suffering from schizophrenia (see Chapter 12) often cannot identify the odors of cheese and bananas, whereas people suffering from Parkinson's disease have trouble identifying the odors of pizza, clove, and wintergreen.

**How We Smell: The Olfactory System.**     Olfaction is not considered a major sensory system in humans and therefore has not received as much research attention as vision

**olfaction**
Sense of smell

**FIGURE 3-13** The location of the olfactory receptors makes them very difficult to study.

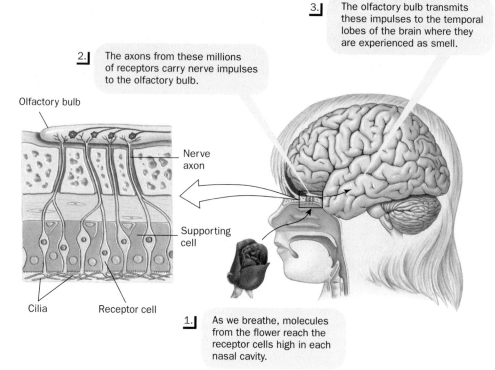

**2.** The axons from these millions of receptors carry nerve impulses to the olfactory bulb.

**3.** The olfactory bulb transmits these impulses to the temporal lobes of the brain where they are experienced as smell.

Olfactory bulb

Nerve axon

Supporting cell

Cilia

Receptor cell

**1.** As we breathe, molecules from the flower reach the receptor cells high in each nasal cavity.

and hearing. What's more, the location of the olfactory receptors makes it difficult to examine them directly. You may be surprised by that statement until you realize that the nose does not contain the olfactory receptors; its function is to collect and filter the air we breathe. As you can see in Figure 3-13, the olfactory receptors are located in an area of tissue of about 2.5 cm (1 in.) square in each nasal cavity (Breer & Boekhoff, 1992).

We have about 10 million olfactory receptors, each of which has 6 to 12 hairlike projections called *cilia*. Like taste receptors, olfactory receptors are continually dying and being replaced (Wang, Wysocki, & Gold, 1993). The life span of an olfactory receptor is about 5 to 8 weeks.

In 1991, Linda Buck and Richard Axel identified several specific olfactory receptor sites. Other researchers (Raming et al., 1993) have since identified additional ones. In fact, there may be as many as 1,000 different types of olfactory receptor sites. Although researchers do not know a great deal about how they work, the olfactory receptors appear to operate under the same type of lock-and-key/pattern recognition (Malnic, Hirono, & Buck, 1999) principle as the taste receptors (Amoore, 1970). When air molecules of a certain shape fit into a receptor site, the receptor depolarizes and a message is sent to the brain. The olfactory nerve takes a somewhat different route to the brain from the other senses we have discussed. The first step is a synapse in the *olfactory bulb*, which is located near the optic chiasm on the underside of the brain. From there, some of the olfactory nerve fibers go to the amygdala, which, as noted in Chapter 2, is part of the limbic system. From the amygdala the olfactory nerve travels to the thalamus and hypothalamus and then on to the cerebral cortex for higher-level processing.

The link between odors and memories is familiar to everyone. Charles Dickens claimed that a mere whiff of the type of paste used to fasten labels to bottles brought back all the anguish of his earliest years, when bankruptcy had driven his father to abandon him in a hellish warehouse where such bottles were made. Do you ever find that the smell of gasoline, pizza, fresh-baked bread, after-shave lotion, sweat, perfume, or pine trees evokes memories? Likewise, many travelers also comment that different countries and cultures have their own unique smells. How old are these memories? How vividly do you recall them? Are there emotions attached to them?

For most people, a number of odors are associated with very emotional memories (Pierce, Cohen, & Ulrich, 2004). This relation is a natural consequence of the fact that the *limbic system*, the emotional center of the brain, is involved in the processing of odors and memories. Diane Ackerman (1990) described the memories that are triggered by odors in the following manner: "Smells detonate softly in our memory like poignant land mines, hidden under the weedy mass of many years and experiences. Hit a tripwire of smell and memories explode all at once. A complex vision leaps out of the undergrowth" (p. 5). Manufacturers of cologne and perfume have long taken advantage of their knowledge of the involvement of the limbic system in processing odors.

## Myth or Science

Sometimes the outlandish claims that characterize much popular psychology actually lead to scientifically sound experiments and meaningful discoveries. For example, in the early 1980s, most people scoffed at the proposal that spraying a fragrance in the air would improve productivity, dismissing it as just another advertising gimmick. Research, however, has actually supported this claim. For example, certain psychologists (Warm, Dember, & Parasuraman, 1991) found that men and women who smelled a pleasant peppermint odor performed significantly better on a boring computer task than comparable participants who breathed only unscented air. Another researcher (Griffin, 1992) reported similar results in a large commercial firm in Tokyo and in New York subway cars.

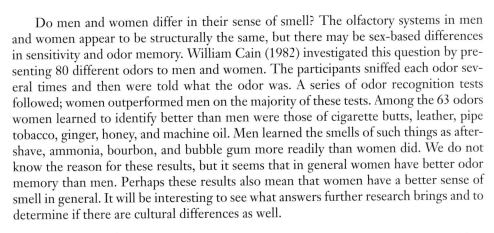

Do men and women differ in their sense of smell? The olfactory systems in men and women appear to be structurally the same, but there may be sex-based differences in sensitivity and odor memory. William Cain (1982) investigated this question by presenting 80 different odors to men and women. The participants sniffed each odor several times and then were told what the odor was. A series of odor recognition tests followed; women outperformed men on the majority of these tests. Among the 63 odors women learned to identify better than men were those of cigarette butts, leather, pipe tobacco, ginger, honey, and machine oil. Men learned the smells of such things as aftershave, ammonia, bourbon, and bubble gum more readily than women did. We do not know the reason for these results, but it seems that in general women have better odor memory than men. Perhaps these results also mean that women have a better sense of smell in general. It will be interesting to see what answers further research brings and to determine if there are cultural differences as well.

**The Interaction of Smell and Taste.** So far we have treated smell and taste as if they were independent; however, these two sensations interact quite dramatically to determine flavor—remember how your food tasted the last time you had a head cold? One set of researchers (Mozel, Smith, Smith, Sullivan, & Swender, 1969) reported the results of an experiment that proved the interdependence of smell and taste in experiencing a flavor. In this study they placed a drop of a certain flavor on a participant's tongue and asked the person to identify the taste. When participants could smell normally, they were correct on most tries; when the experimenter prevented them from smelling, however, they were often unable to identify it. For example, when participants could taste and smell coffee, its flavor was identified correctly nearly 90% of the time. When they were permitted only to taste, its flavor was identified correctly less than 5% of the time.

You can demonstrate this phenomenon yourself. Cut an apple and a potato into small pieces. Close your eyes, hold your nose, and have a friend put a piece of apple (or potato) into your mouth. Can you tell whether you were given an apple or a potato? When we must rely on taste alone, we often confuse various flavors (Mozel et al., 1969). Thus, odor is an important cue to what food we are eating and how it should taste.

The interaction of taste and smell does not end with the demonstration that odors and odor memories influence our perception of taste. When an odor component is added to a taste, the sensation of taste—not that of odor—is amplified (Murphy, Cain, & Bartoshuk, 1977). Prove it for yourself: Start eating with your fingers pinching your nostrils closed, then add the odor component by releasing your fingers to open your nostrils. The flavor will seem to come alive in your mouth because chewing releases chemicals into the nasal passages.

## Somatosensory Processes

Vision, hearing, taste, and smell are important senses; however, they are not our only ones. If you have ever ridden a roller coaster at an amusement park, ridden in a fast-moving subway train that stopped suddenly, worn a piece of clothing that was too small, or put your hand into a pan of scalding water, you are well aware of your other senses. In this section we discuss the somatosensory processes: the vestibular sense, the kinesthetic sense, and the cutaneous senses.

**Vestibular Sense.**   The **vestibular sense,** which originates in the inner ear (see Figure 3-11), provides information about the body's orientation and movement (Wade, 2003). The vestibular system consists of the three semicircular canals in the inner ear and the utricle. The **semicircular canals** are located at right angles to each other to provide information about movement in all directions. Each semicircular canal is filled with a jellylike fluid that moves as the head moves. Movement of the fluid in the canal causes hair cells located in the canal to bend. Bending the hair cells sends information about movement to the brain.

   The **utricle,** a fluid-filled chamber also located in the inner ear, operates on the same principle as the semicircular canals and serves as a gravity detector. To experience the vestibular system, move your head and continue reading. You should have no problem. Now try moving the book while you are reading. The act of reading should be noticeably harder. Why? Because our head movement activates our vestibular system. When we sense movements of our eyes, head, and body, we can make adjustments to keep our world in some perspective. This perspective helps us to orient ourselves to our environment.

**Kinesthetic Sense.**   Have you ever sat on one leg or kept an arm in an awkward position until it tingled or "went to sleep"? Remember how difficult it was to walk or move your arm under those circumstances? The reason for the difficulty is that when this tingling sensation occurs, you no longer have adequate information to determine the location of your leg or arm. Such information about our muscles and joints constitutes our **kinesthetic sense.** Sense receptors located in the joints and muscles send information to the brain concerning muscle tension and joint position. The brain combines this information with other sensory input, such as vision and audition, to help you determine the location of your limbs. Even though we seldom think about or are consciously aware of the muscular adjustments and receptors that are involved in adapting to our environment, these processes are crucial for effective, efficient adaptation to our environment.

   Carello and Turvey (2004) highlight the importance of this sensory system:

> The sensory disorder of peripheral neuropathy, a disconnection between these muscle receptors and the brain, provides a good example of the muscle sense's subtle functioning. The neuropathic individual finds standing, walking, reaching, and manipulating objects extremely challenging and often impossible. These activities can be accomplished only with considerable concentration and intellectual effort. Vision must substitute, however imperfectly, for the loss of feeling. Walking, for example, requires watching each leg, in turn, as it swings stiffly forward in order to decide explicitly when and where that forward movement should be stopped. (p. 147)

**The Cutaneous Senses.**   The **cutaneous senses** involve several kinds of information that are sensed by receptors in the skin (Augurelle, Smith, Lejeune, & Thonnard, 2003). A microscopic view of the skin yields an amazing picture (see Figure 3-14).

The vestibular sense is active during this Olympic skater's performance.

**vestibular sense**
System located in the inner ear that allows us to make adjustments to bodily movements and postures

**semicircular canals**
Fluid-filled passages in the inner ear that detect movement of the head

**utricle**
Fluid-filled chamber in the inner ear that detects changes in gravity

**kinesthetic sense**
System of receptors located in the muscles and joints that provides information about the location of the extremities

**cutaneous senses**
System of receptors located in the skin that provides information about touch, pressure, pain, and temperature

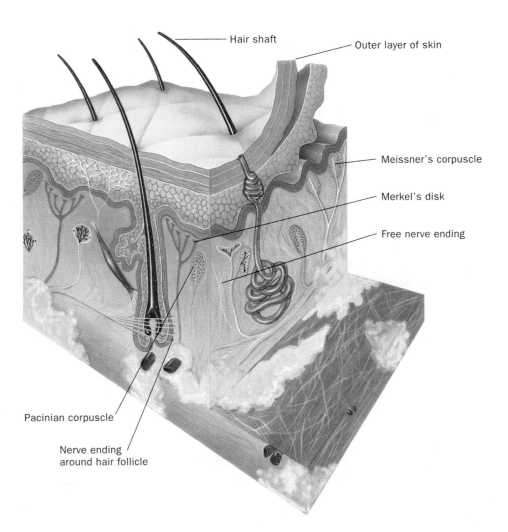

Hair shaft

Outer layer of skin

Meissner's corpuscle

Merkel's disk

Free nerve ending

Pacinian corpuscle

Nerve ending
around hair follicle

**FIGURE 3-14** Cross section of the skin showing several of the receptors located there.

**Source:** Shaver and Tarpy (1993).

Some sections of our skin are packed with a variety of receptors that respond to some form of cutaneous information—touch or pressure, pain, and temperature. The wide variety of skin receptors for touch or pressure are called *mechanoreceptors*; the receptors for temperature are called *thermoreceptors*.

**Pain.** The sensation of pain is caused by a harmful stimulus such as extreme heat or cold, toxic chemicals, or breaking or invasion of the skin. The general term for receptors that respond to painful stimuli is *nocioreceptors*. Think of the different types of pain you have experienced. A bright, sharp pain can be caused by pinprick, whereas a dull, chronic pain can result from physical overexertion. Because pain warns us of impending injury, it helps us adapt to the environment.

One theory of pain, the **gate control theory** (Melzack & Wall, 1965; Sufka & Price, 2002), has greatly influenced our understanding of pain. According to this theory, pain impulses are transmitted from the *receptors* (free nerve endings) to the spinal cord. The axons of the pain neurons release substance P (see Chapter 2) in the spinal cord (Piercey et al., 1981). In turn, substance P causes neurons in the spinal cord to send information about pain to the brain for processing and perception.

Thus the painful stimulus, in conjunction with substance P, opens the pain gate. How is the gate closed? Neurons that descend from the brain to the spinal cord release opioid peptides (see Chapter 2) called *endorphins*. In turn, the endorphins block the release of substance P (Reichling, Kwait, & Basbaum, 1988), and the pain gate is closed. Pain and stressful or thrilling situations are among the conditions that elicit the release of endorphins.

**gate control theory**
Theory of pain stating that the release of substance P in the spinal cord produces the sensation of pain

**STUDY TIP**

In a group of five, assign each student one of the five senses. Each student should prepare a short oral report on the basic facts of his or her sense and deliver it to the group.

**cutaneous receptors**
Receptors in the skin that provide sensory information

Is pain perceived similarly by all people? Evidently not. For example, Hall and Davies (1991) found that varsity female athletes had higher pain thresholds than female nonathletes. Likewise, cultural differences in the response to pain have been reported. For example, Nepalese research participants have higher pain thresholds than Western research participants (Clark & Clark, 1980).

The **cutaneous receptors** work together to provide comprehensive information concerning the types of objects we encounter. Once the cutaneous information has been sensed, the sensory nerves travel up the spinal cord and synapse in the thalamus. The sensory information is then relayed to the somatosensory cortex, which is located in the parietal lobe (see Chapter 2), for higher-level processing. As you saw in the map of the sensory cortex (Figure 2-21), the areas of the skin with the most receptors send information to larger areas of the cortex.

The following Study Chart summarizes the properties and operation of the five major senses.

## *Study* CHART

### The Five Senses

| Sense Experience | Receptors | Objective Stimulus | Subjective |
|---|---|---|---|
| The ability to detect stimuli | Specialized cells that allow us to experience this sense | Energy or chemicals that cause these receptors to fire | What we experience when these receptors fire |
| **Vision** | *Rods and cones* in the retina | Electromagnetic waves between 380 and 760 nm | LIGHT |
| **Hearing (Audition)** | *Hair cells* in the basilar membrane | Molecules that vibrate between 20 and 20,000 Hz | SOUNDS |
| **Taste (Gustation)** | *Microvilli* on the tongue | Molecules of substances dissolved in a liquid | TASTES |
| **Smell (Olfaction)** | *Olfactory cells* in the walls of the passageway between the nose and the throat | Molecules of substances in the air | ODORS |
| **Touch (Cutaneous)** | *Mechanoreceptors* in the skin that respond to skin deformation | Skin indentation, vibrations, and hair movements; changes in temperature; and mechanical or thermal stimuli that begin near levels that can produce tissue damage | PRESSURE |
| | *Thermoreceptors* in the skin that respond to changes in temperature | | TEMPERATURE |
| | *Nocioreceptors* in the skin that respond to painful stimuli | | PAIN |

## REVIEW SUMMARY

**1. Audition,** the sense of hearing, is initiated by the movement of molecules in the air. Vibration of the eardrum starts a chain reaction that results in movement of fluid in the inner ear and the bending of specialized hair cells, which are the receptors for hearing.

**2.** The pitch or frequency of a sound wave is determined by the location of the hairs that are activated **(place theory)** and the rapidity with which the basilar membrane vibrates **(frequency theory).**

**3.** Hearing disorders can result from damage to the bones of the middle ear **(conduction deafness),** the inner ear, especially

the hair cells **(sensorineural deafness),** or the auditory nerve and auditory cortex **(central deafness).**

**4.** The chemical senses include the sense of taste **(gustation)** and the sense of smell **(olfaction).**

**5.** Molecules in solution stimulate taste. Hairs, located on structures known as **taste buds,** serve as the receptors. Although receptors may respond to several tastes, each one is maximally sensitive to one of four tastes: sweet, sour, bitter, or salty.

**6.** Molecules in the air stimulate the sense of smell. Hairs located in the nasal cavity serve as the receptors. Olfaction has a direct connection to the limbic system; as a result, many of our memories involving odors are highly emotional.

**7.** The **vestibular sense** enables us to adjust to different bodily movements. The **kinesthetic sense** allows us to determine the position of our extremities. **Cutaneous receptors** for pressure, pain, and temperature are located in the skin.

## ✓ CHECK YOUR PROGRESS

**1.** Describe what causes a sound wave. How are sound waves measured?

**2.** Match each term with a term closely associated with it.

| | |
|---|---|
| **a.** Hertz (Hz) | **1.** Taste receptors |
| **b.** Pacinian corpuscle | **2.** Vestibular sense |
| **c.** Decibels (db) | **3.** Somatosensory processing |
| **d.** Microvilli | **4.** Position of arms and legs |
| **e.** Semicircular canals | **5.** Pain |
| **f.** Substance P | **6.** Frequency |
| **g.** Kinesthesis | **7.** Intensity |

**3.** What is the basic function of the outer ear?

**a.** to protect the eardrum
**b.** to gather and guide sound waves to the eardrum
**c.** to amplify low-intensity sounds so that they can be heard
**d.** to reduce high-intensity sounds to tolerable levels

**4.** What theory proposes that above 100 Hz auditory neurons do not fire all at once but in rotation?

**a.** place theory
**b.** volley principle
**c.** frequency theory
**d.** rotational theory

**5.** We can locate sounds around us through

**a.** the volume of sound and the timbre of sound.
**b.** the volley principle and the volume of sound.
**c.** the timbre of sound and the differences in time for sound to reach each ear.
**d.** the volume of sound and the differences in time for sound to reach each ear.

**6.** What are papillae?

**a.** gustatory receptors
**b.** protrusions that contain taste buds
**c.** the most sensitive portion of the taste bud
**d.** taste buds located at the back of the throat

**7.** Herman has been having a difficult time smelling the baker's hot apple pie. He may be suffering from

**a.** anosmia.
**b.** anoxic syndrome.
**c.** olfactory decline.
**d.** gustatory seclusion.

**8.** Distinguish between the stimuli for taste and smell.

**9.** Why has research on the olfactory system not progressed at a rapid rate?

**10.** Feedback about our balance and bodily position is provided by movement of fluid in the

**a.** cochlea.
**b.** nasal cavities.
**c.** semicircular canals.
**d.** Meissner corpuscles.

**ANSWERS: 1.** Movement of air molecules causes a sound wave. Sound waves are measured in decibels. **2.** a-6, b-3, c-7, d-1, e-2, f-5, g-4 **3.** b **4.** b **5.** d **6.** b **7.** a **8.** Gustatory (taste) stimuli are molecules in a liquid solution, whereas olfactory stimuli are molecules in the air. **9.** Research in olfaction has not progressed at a rapid rate because olfaction is not considered one of the major senses and because the olfactory receptors are rather inaccessible and difficult to study. **10.** c

# PERCEPTION

**Spring break is over, and you are driving back to school. Having savored every minute of your leisure time, you get a late start and skip lunch and dinner. Now it's 9 P.M., and you have become painfully aware of every sign on the highway that mentions food. The other signs are a blur; in fact, you aren't even sure that there have been any other signs. At last you reach the exit for the fast-food place you've been reading about for the past 25 miles. You pull off; after a burger, fries, and a shake, you're back on the road.** *Why did you fail to perceive the other billboards?*

As we discussed at the beginning of this chapter, perception is the process of organizing and making sense of the stimuli in our environment. Because we rely so heavily on the visual sense, much of our knowledge about perception has been learned through research on vision. Thus, to understand perceptual processes, we focus on visual perception. Many of the processes that we discuss also apply to other senses, however; as you read this section, try to use these principles to describe the perception of sounds, tastes, and odors as well as pressure, pain, and temperature.

Like so many areas in psychology, perception is not a simple and straightforward matter. Because our motives (needs, drives, and even prejudices) may distort or determine what we perceive, our discussion of perception begins with a description of how attention is influenced by motivation and attention.

## Motivation and Attention

We do not perceive everything in our environment; our motives greatly influence our perceptions. Similarly, certain stimuli are more likely than others to attract our attention.

**Motivational Influences.**   Think back to our opening vignette—to the part about noticing only those billboards advertising food. In this scenario, why did you fail to perceive the other billboards? Those other billboards certainly activated your receptors (sensation), but you did not perceive them because they were not related to hunger, your dominant motive at the time. Now that your need for food has been satisfied, you begin to notice other things. You glance at your instrument panel and panic—the gas gauge reads "empty"! Now you become aware of an entirely different set of billboards—those advertising gas stations.

**Attention.**   We cannot possibly attend to and process all of the stimuli received by our sensory systems at any one moment; some of them must be filtered out. Have you ever tried to listen to two friends talk to you at the same time? This is an example of the need to filter information.

### Hands On

You can re-create such a situation by conducting a *dichotic listening* exercise (Goodwin, 1988). In dichotic listening experiments, a different message is presented to each of a participant's ears, and the participant is asked to recall both messages. These experiments usually involve the use of a tape recorder and special headphones. However, three people, minus this equipment, can accomplish the same goal. The procedure is as follows: Place three chairs side by side. You, the participant, sit in the middle chair. Have a person seated on your right and a person seated on your left read different passages at the same time. After a fixed amount of time, such as 20 or 30 seconds, try either to repeat verbally or write down whatever you can recall. You can create interesting variations of this basic procedure, such as a male voice in one ear and a female voice in the other ear or fast reading in one ear and slow reading in the other. When you try to listen to both messages, you will probably find yourself switching back and forth between them and becoming quite confused.

**divided attention**

The ability to process more than one source of stimulation at the same time

Dichotic listening tasks are designed to study **divided attention**, the ability to attend to more than one message or type of information at the same time. Research in this area has uncovered some intriguing information about human perception. For example, we hear (and understand) much more than the information of which we are consciously aware. This fact is demonstrated by the famous "cocktail-party phenomenon" (Cherry & Bowles, 1960). With this phenomenon, the scene is a typical weekend party—lots of people doing lots of talking. You are having a conversation with five or six friends when suddenly you hear your name mentioned in a conversation on the other side of the room. Your name was not shouted, and you are not aware of anything else that was said—only your name. Clearly, you have been listening to and processing other conversations during your conversation with your friends. Only when the content included something important, like your name, did the conversation enter your consciousness and sharpen your awareness or perception.

The *cocktail-party phenomenon* demonstrates that attention can be divided to some extent. The ability to listen to two messages at once might be very beneficial. Can you do anything to make this task easier or more effective? The answer is to practice. The more you practice at processing two separate messages simultaneously, the more skilled you will become at it. And, you will find that it is easier to divide your attention when you are processing different *types* of information. For example, most of us have little difficulty listening to a CD while driving. We divide our attention between the visual stimuli involved in driving and the auditory stimuli produced by the CD. We do not want to leave you with the impression that trying to divide your attention is always a good objective. The numerous traffic accidents that have resulted from people trying to talk on cell phones while they are driving is a good example of a potentially hazardous situation.

The cocktail-party phenomenon. You can hear something that is very important to you, such as your name, even though it is said in a normal voice across a noisy room.

In addition to needs, motives, and prejudices, certain aspects of stimuli determine which ones get our attention. For example, people generally pay more attention to stimuli that are larger, louder, or more colorful than others. You can watch television commercials any night of the week to see how advertisers exploit this phenomenon. What's more, your attention is attracted to stimuli that stand out from or contrast with the objects around them.

When something happens unexpectedly, our attention is attracted very quickly. When contrast and surprise combine, our attention is commanded even more quickly. If your instructor wore pajamas to class, for example, this unusual occurrence would catch your attention immediately.

Although motivation and attention are important aspects of perception, they do not provide the complete picture. Once a stimulus has attracted our attention, there are basic perceptual abilities that we use to respond to it.

## Basic Perceptual Abilities: Patterns and Constancies

We perceive objects in our environment as having features such as pattern, constancy, depth, and movement. Our perception of these objects and their features is so automatic that we often take them for granted. However, they are crucial components of perception. In this section we describe them in detail.

**Pattern Perception.**   Among the most basic perceptual abilities is the ability to perceive patterns. To survive in modern society, we must be able to perceive a staggering number of shapes and figures. A few of the patterns we deal with every day are the letters of the alphabet, traffic signs, friends' facial features, food items in the grocery store, the buildings in an apartment complex, and the automobiles in a parking lot. Psychologists refer to the ability to discriminate among different shapes and figures as **pattern perception**. Although some cortical cells appear to function as *feature detectors* that are sensitive to specific shapes, such as lines, bars, or edges, we still need to translate these features into a perception of our environment (Hughes, Nozawa, & Kitterle, 1996). There are several theories concerning the process of pattern perception.

The **feature analysis theory** of pattern perception (Lindsay & Norman, 1977) states that we perceive basic elements of an object and mentally assemble them to create a complete object. As when a house is built, various pieces are put together until the structure is completed. In short, we start from the bottom and work up to a completed and recognizable building. Once the object has been assembled, it is matched against

**pattern perception**
The ability to discriminate among different figures and shapes

**feature analysis theory**
Theory of pattern perception stating that we perceive basic elements of an object and assemble them mentally to create the complete object

**perceptual constancy**
The tendency to perceive the size and shape of an object as constant even though its retinal image changes

**shape constancy**
The tendency to perceive the shape of an object as constant despite changes in its retinal image

**size constancy**
The tendency to perceive the size of an object as constant despite changes in its retinal image

items stored in memory. If there is a match, we are able to identify the item. If there is no match, we probably search for the memory that resembles it most closely.

In terms of perceptual processes, your perceptual experience starts with receptor activity and works toward progressively higher brain centers. This process of starting with basic elements and working toward a more complex perception is known as a *bottom-up model*. If, however, we look at the task of recognizing words, this bottom-up model of feature analysis runs into problems. Several studies (such as those by Johnston & McClelland, 1973, 1974) have shown that we can recognize an entire word better than we recognize individual letters. These results suggest that, at least in some instances, we use a *top-down approach* in which the whole object is recognized before its component parts are identified. But top-down processing results in mistakes when the word is not perceived correctly, such as reading the word *house* for the word *horse*.

**Perceptual Constancies.** You do not have to treat every perceptual change as if your environment had changed completely. Once you have identified an object, you continue to recognize it even if its location and distance from you change, thereby casting a different image on your retina. A change in the retinal image does not signal a change in the object. This tendency to perceive the size and shape of objects as relatively stable despite retinal changes is called **perceptual constancy.** The importance of perceptual constancies should be obvious; they allow us to deal with our environment as relatively stable and unchanging.

**Shape Constancy.** **Shape constancy** means that your perception of the shape of an object as viewed from different angles does not change even though the image projected on your retina does so. In other words, the shape of an object is perceived independently of the image it casts on the retina. This phenomenon is easy to demonstrate. Look at this book from a number of angles. You see nothing but a book being held in different positions. The same could be said for the opening and closing of a door or the image of a car making a left turn in front of you. The image on your retina changes dramatically, yet the object you perceive does not. Almost any moving object displays the principle of shape constancy. For the perception of shape constancy to occur, however, the object must be familiar and must be seen in an identifiable context. If there is no context or background to which the object can be related, it appears to float in space, and you cannot judge its correct orientation; shape constancy disappears.

**Size Constancy.** **Size constancy** also helps us to maintain consistency in our perceptual environment. As objects move toward us, their retinal images enlarge; as they move farther away, their retinal images diminish. We do not perceive the size of those objects as changing, however; instead, we perceive the objects as moving toward or away from us. Size constancy depends on our familiarity with the object and on our ability to judge distance. When we are dealing with familiar objects and can easily judge distances, we are more likely to perceive the size of the objects as being constant. When we are dealing with unfamiliar objects and our ability to estimate distance is poor, the objects may appear to change size.

To understand this point, consider a classic example. C. M. Turnbull (1961), an anthropologist, was studying the BaMbuti Pygmies in the dense forest of the Belgian Congo. During his studies, Turnbull traveled from one group of Pygmies to another. On one trip, which took him across the plains, he was accompanied by a youngster, Kenge, who had spent his entire life in the dense forest. Having never been on the plains, Kenge was unable to judge distances and determine the size of unfamiliar objects. A distant herd of buffalo presented a major problem; Kenge "tried to liken the distant buffalo to the various beetles and ants with which he was familiar" (Turnbull, 1961, p. 305). Imagine Kenge's surprise when, as they drove closer to the buffalo, he thought he saw the animals grow steadily larger. Clearly, our culture and experiences influence our perceptions of real life and of pictures.

Can you tell the size of this object? When we can't rely on cues for distance or the size of other objects, size constancy is not good. See the end of the chapter for another photo that gives you a better idea as to the size of this object.

Because they are automatic processes, size and shape constancy may seem rather simple; however, these constancies involve much processing. We are using familiar background objects for purposes of comparison (size constancy) and to anchor our perceptions (shape constancy). If the background objects are eliminated and we are confronted with an unfamiliar object, however, we have difficulty perceiving its correct size and distance. As in the story of Kenge, without distance cues and other objects with which to make comparisons, we cannot judge size well. Similarly, without a background to anchor our perceptions, moving objects may appear to change shape rather than simply to move in space.

Auditory constancies are another important aspect of perception. We perceive words as the same when they are spoken by many people with very different voices. Likewise, a melody is recognizable even when it is played on different instruments and in different keys.

**Depth Perception.**   In addition to a world of constancies, we experience a third dimension, **depth perception.** For decades, psychologists have been puzzled by the question of how we are able to perceive depth or distance. The surface of the retina is two-dimensional (top to bottom, side to side), yet we are able to judge distances and locate objects in space (three-dimensionally) quite well. Two main types of cues, binocular and monocular, are used to create our perception of depth. **Binocular cues** require the integrated use of both eyes, whereas **monocular cues** are effectively processed using information from only one eye.

**Binocular Cues.**   Two binocular cues are adjustments of the eye muscles (a weak/nonprecise cue) and binocular disparity. Let's consider eye muscle adjustments first. Our eyes are supported by muscles that move the eyeball to allow us the best possible view. They also provide feedback for judging distance. When objects are near, the eyes rotate toward a center point. You can feel the muscle tension when you look at objects that are very close. To experience this sensation, focus on this sentence and gradually move the book closer to your eyes. The closer the book gets, the more eye muscle strain you feel; the farther away the book is, the less eye muscle strain you experience. Binocular disparity provides more precise depth cues than eye muscle adjustments.

If you open and close one eye and then the other, it is obvious that you do not see exactly the same thing with each eye. The closer the object, the greater the difference between what the two eyes see. This difference occurs because each eye sees from a different angle, a phenomenon known as **binocular disparity.** When the images from both eyes merge in the brain, a sense of depth is created. The random-dot stereogram (Burgess, Rehman, & Williams, 2003) relies completely on binocular disparity cues (there are no monocular cues present) to create the perception of depth. If you are having difficulty seeing the three-dimensional image, don't despair; many people have a hard time seeing the image because of the abnormal focusing (focusing *behind* the picture, not on the picture itself) that is required. What's more, at least 2 to 3% of the population cannot see the image because they have weak or slightly misaligned eyes that keep them from detecting binocular disparity cues.

Researchers have identified cortical cells that respond to binocular disparity (Gonzalez, Justo, Bermudez, & Perez, 2003), assuming that the activity of these cells is a primary cue for depth. You can easily demonstrate binocular disparity by closing one eye and aligning your two index fingers. Now switch eyes. Are the fingers still aligned? This misalignment is even greater when the fingers are closer to the face compared with when they are at arm's length.

**Monocular Cues.**   Monocular cues, which can be perceived by either eye alone, also help determine depth (Ciuffreda & Engber, 2002). For example, when the ciliary muscles change the shape of the lens in accommodation, the muscle adjustments are sensed and are used to help determine distance.

**depth perception**
The ability to perceive our world three-dimensionally

**binocular cues**
Cues for depth perception that involve the use of both eyes

**monocular cues**
Cues for depth perception that involve the use of only one eye

**binocular disparity**
The difference between the images seen by the two eyes

3.3

**FIGURE 3-15** Monocular cues for depth perception: interposition and brightness (left); texture gradient and linear perspective (center); and texture, linear perspective, and interposition (right).

Artists use numerous monocular cues—including interposition (near objects partially obscure more distant objects), *texture gradient* (the texture of a surface becomes smoother with increasing distance), *linear perspective* (parallel lines appear to converge as they recede into the distance), and *relative brightness* (brighter objects appear closer than duller-appearing ones)—to create the illusion of depth. These cues also operate in our day-to-day environment, as you can see in Figure 3-15. After you have studied the three photographs, look around the room you are in and identify other examples of these cues.

**FIGURE 3-16** The visual cliff. Will the child perceive depth or move onto the glass that covers the deep side of the visual cliff?

In addition to demonstrating the importance of binocular and monocular cues for depth perception, psychologists have investigated whether this perceptual ability is innate or learned. For example, Eleanor Gibson (1910–2002; Gibson & Walk, 1960) has successfully used the visual cliff (see Figure 3-16) to test depth-perception ability in human infants and children as well as in a variety of animals. The visual cliff consists of a two-sided chamber; the bottom of one side of the chamber is shallow and within easy reach, whereas the bottom of the other side is deep. Both sides of the chamber are covered by glass. A test participant is placed on a small platform in the center of the visual cliff and must choose between crawling to the shallow or deep side. Human infants avoid the deep side from the time they are mobile. Although humans perceive depth from about 6 months of age, when placed over the visual cliff, they can perceive that something is different much earlier. Infants as young as 2 to 4 months old had a significantly higher heart rate when placed on the deep side of the visual cliff. Gibson's research on perception is so significant that she was awarded the National Medal of Science by President George Bush in 1992, the highest honor that can be bestowed on a scientist by the president of the United States.

## Gestalt Principles of Perceptual Organization

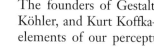

**3.4**

The founders of Gestalt psychology (see Chapter 1)—Max Wertheimer, Wolfgang Köhler, and Kurt Koffka—proposed that we are born with the ability to organize the elements of our perceptual world in very predictable ways (Sharps & Wertheimer,

"Osgood wondered, 'Is line A actually longer than line B, or
is it just the merciless sun and the shifting desert sands
playing havoc with a man's senses?'"

**FIGURE 3-17** Example of figure–ground relations.

2000). The goal of these automatic organizing processes is to produce the best or most complete perception of our environment. Among the most familiar of these processes are figure–ground distinctions and the grouping of elements.

**Figure and Ground.** The Gestalt psychologists emphasized that one of the ways in which we organize our perceptual world is by sorting stimuli into figure and background (or ground) (Humphreys & Mueller, 2000). The figure is the focus of our attention; the ground constitutes the remainder of our perception. An example of a **figure–ground relation** is shown in Figure 3-17. Notice that what we focus on—the figure—tends to be smaller, more colorful, or brighter than the background.

Sometimes these automatic processes can trick us. Look at Figure 3-18 and decide what is figure and what is ground in each example. In each instance, the figure–ground relation is unclear or ambiguous, and the task is much more difficult than that in Figure 3-17. When we are confronted with ambiguous figures like those in Figure 3-18, we are able to organize the material in at least two ways. Which do you see first? That may depend on top-down influences created by reading the caption (Did it say "young woman" or "old woman" first?) or on the features that first attracted your attention. Once you have seen both figures in an ambiguous drawing, you can easily reverse the figure–ground relation.

**figure–ground relation**
Organization of perceptual elements into a figure (the focus of attention) and a background

A   Letters or objects?

B   Vase or faces?

C   Young woman or old woman?

D   Rabbit or duck?

**FIGURE 3-18** Examples of ambiguous or unclear figure–ground relations. Which object do you see first in each picture? Does it make seeing the other figure more difficult?

**proximity**
Gestalt principle stating that perceptual elements that are close together are seen as a group

**similarity**
Gestalt principle stating that perceptual elements that are similar are seen as a group

**good continuation**
Gestalt principle stating that smooth, flowing lines are more readily perceived than choppy, broken lines

**closure**
Gestalt principle stating that organizing perceptions into whole objects is easier than perceiving separate parts independently

**apparent motion**
Illusion of movement in a stationary object

How often do you encounter figure–ground problems in your day-to-day activities? For example, while driving, have you ever stopped next to a large truck at a traffic light? Suddenly you feel yourself moving backward! Have your brakes failed? Your foot is on the brake, and you push it harder. Nothing happens, however—the backward motion continues. Only then do you realize that the truck—not your car—is moving.

Unconsciously you perceived your car as the figure and the larger truck as the ground. Because figures normally move across a background, you perceived yourself, rather than the truck, as the moving object. Can you think of other examples of how your perceptions have been fooled by unusual figure–ground relations?

**Principles of Grouping.** In addition to showing that we perceive figure–ground relationships, the Gestalt psychologists demonstrated that we organize our perceptions by grouping elements (King, 2001). The way we group perceptual elements is extremely important. Think of how much trouble you would have if you had to deal with every perceptual element independently. The letters you are reading fall into groups we call words. What would reading be like if you had to think about every single letter? What would it be like to listen to someone speak if you couldn't group the sounds into words? We function more effectively and efficiently when we organize perceptual elements into groups.

Several conditions promote the grouping of perceptual elements. Although we discuss these conditions separately, keep in mind that more than one of them can operate at a time. See how many of these conditions you notice in your day-to-day life.

With **proximity,** one of the most elementary Gestalt grouping principles, items that are close to each other are perceived as a group. The words strung together on this page are an example of proximity. According to the Gestalt principle of **similarity,** items that are alike are grouped together: XXXOOO, perceived as three Xs and three Os. These two principles are illustrated in Figure 3-19. Do they operate effectively with senses other than vision? Think about musical melodies or spoken words. What would they be like if you had to pay attention to each separate note or sound?

The Gestalt principle of **good continuation** says that we perceive continuous, flowing lines more easily than choppy or broken lines. What do you see in the fourth panel of Figure 3-19? It should be easier to see a continuous flowing figure rather than two separate lines, as predicted by the Gestalt psychologists.

Now examine the third panel in Figure 3-19. What do you see? It's a bicycle, of course, but is the drawing complete? To complete the picture and identify the object, you had to create the missing pieces perceptually. This process illustrates the Gestalt principle of **closure,** which says that organizing our perceptions into complete objects is easier than perceiving each part separately.

## Perception of Movement

Suppose you are on your way to your next class when you notice a message on an electronic sign. It is one of those signs, like a theater marquee, that has letters and words that appear to move across it. Our perception of separate words is created because of the proximity of the letters that make up each group (word) and the spaces between successive groups of letters. Unlike the letters you are reading in this book, the letters on the electronic sign are made up of separate, unconnected points—and we connect them using the principle of closure.

This sign, however, adds another dimension to our consideration of perception. Although the words do not really move across the sign, they appear to do so. **Apparent motion** is the illusion of movement in a stationary object. In the electronic sign, it is created by turning the lights on and off in a particular sequence. How prevalent is apparent motion? Consider movies, television, videocassettes, and DVDs. All of these forms of entertainment rely on the brain's ability to create the perception of motion from a series of still pictures.

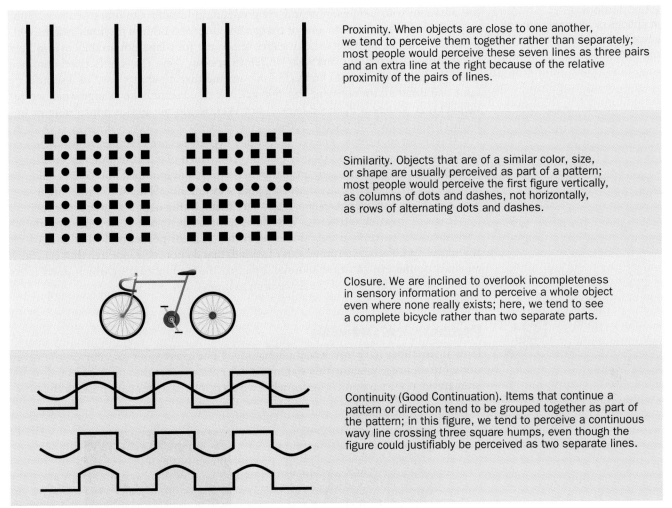

Proximity. When objects are close to one another, we tend to perceive them together rather than separately; most people would perceive these seven lines as three pairs and an extra line at the right because of the relative proximity of the pairs of lines.

Similarity. Objects that are of a similar color, size, or shape are usually perceived as part of a pattern; most people would perceive the first figure vertically, as columns of dots and dashes, not horizontally, as rows of alternating dots and dashes.

Closure. We are inclined to overlook incompleteness in sensory information and to perceive a whole object even where none really exists; here, we tend to see a complete bicycle rather than two separate parts.

Continuity (Good Continuation). Items that continue a pattern or direction tend to be grouped together as part of the pattern; in this figure, we tend to perceive a continuous wavy line crossing three square humps, even though the figure could justifiably be perceived as two separate lines.

**FIGURE 3-19**  Examples of the Gestalt principles of grouping. The grouping of perceptual elements allows us to deal more effectively with our environment.

## Hands On

Motion is so important that your brain creates the illusion of movement even when there is none (Suzuki & Peterson, 2000). This phenomenon, known as the *autokinetic effect*, keeps the visual receptors from adapting. If your receptors adapted, vision would cease. To demonstrate the autokinetic effect, you will need a small flashlight, some string, and a very dark room. Hang the flashlight, pointed down, from a light fixture or ceiling fan. Turn the flashlight on and all the other lights in the room off. Sit on the floor and stare at the flashlight. Within a minute or less the light should appear to move, usually in an elliptical (egg-shaped) pattern. This effect is due to small, involuntary eye movements that the brain doesn't track, so it perceives object motion.

# Perceptual Hypotheses and Illusions

We have said that perception involves the brain's attempt to interpret and make sense of the stimuli we receive from our environment. Constancy, figure–ground relations, and grouping processes help us develop educated guesses, or inferences, about the nature of those stimuli. Such inferences are called **perceptual hypotheses,** and they routinely shape our perceptual experience. For example, your perceptual hypothesis may be that

**perceptual hypothesis**
Inference about the nature of stimuli received from the environment

**perceptual illusions**
Misperceptions or interpretations of stimuli that do not correspond to the sensations received

the events in your perceptual world are constant and stable. On other occasions your perceptual hypothesis will be one of change and diversity. Both hypotheses and the ability to discriminate between them are very important for adaptation to the environment (Wasserman, Young, & Cook, 2004). Before you say "yes, that's only good common sense that everyone already knows," don't assume that it's always easy to discriminate same and different (or constant and change). We can discriminate change when we anticipate that change is likely or logical; however, we do not notice improbable or unlikely changes very well (Greer, 2004).

If you stop and think about it, perceptual hypotheses are examples of *top-down processing* that we discussed previously (see p. 116). Much of the time our perceptual hypotheses are accurate, but sometimes they are wrong. For example, how often could you have sworn that your professor said a paper was due next Thursday rather than next Tuesday? Have you ever been absolutely sure that a traffic light was green, not red?

It is easy to trick our senses into developing an incorrect perceptual hypothesis. Such incorrect perceptual hypotheses form the basis for **perceptual illusions,** which are misperceptions or interpretations of stimuli that do not correspond to the sensations received by the eye or other senses (Toppino, 2003). The case in which grass looks greener on the other side of the fence is an example.

## Psychological Detective

How many times have you heard people say, "The grass looks greener on the other side of the fence"? Usually this statement refers to the fact that most of us fail to appreciate what we have and long for what we do not have. Does real grass on the other

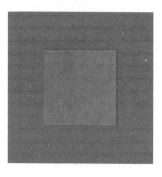
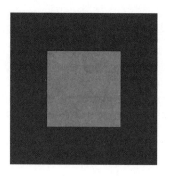

**A**

**FIGURE 3-20** The type of stimulus and the context in which you view that stimulus can trick your visual sense. (A) The gray in the orange square looks darker than the gray in the blue square even though they are exactly the same. (B) Even though this pattern is regular and uniform, when you look at it your eyes create patterns and movement within the larger pattern. (C) When you do not look directly at the intersections of the white rows and colums, you should see gray spots. If you look directly at these intersections, the spots will disappear.

**B**

**C**

side of a real fence actually appear greener? Give this question some thought. Write down your answer, and the reasons for it, before reading further.

The answer to the greener-grass question is yes, and there is an explanation. When you look directly down at the grass in your yard, you see both green grass and the dark brown soil in which it is growing. These colors blend together. When you look at the grass across the fence, however, you are not looking straight down, and therefore you do not see the brown soil. Hence you perceive the grass on the other side of the fence as being a purer shade of green. Your senses are tricked into believing that the grass really is greener on the other side of the fence. Figure 3-20 shows how your visual sense may be tricked by the perceptual stimulus.

The development of incorrect perceptual hypotheses is at the heart of perceptual illusions. Some of our favorites are shown in Figure 3-21. Look at each and decide what

 **3.5**

**STUDY TIP**

Draw your own original pictures for each of the principles of grouping.

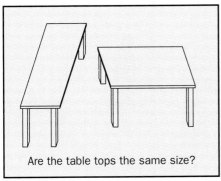

Are the table tops the same size?

**A**

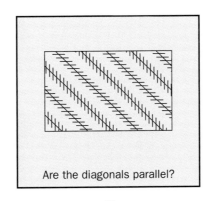

Are the diagonals parallel?

**B**

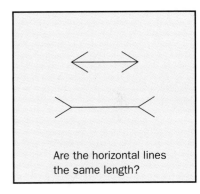

Are the horizontal lines the same length?

**C**

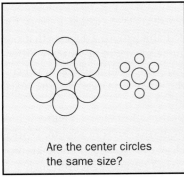

Are the center circles the same size?

**D**

How many legs does the elephant have?

**E**

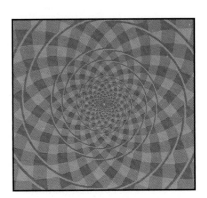

**F**

**FIGURE 3-21** Perceptual hypotheses may be the cause of many illusions. (A) Because it is narrow, the table on the left is perceived as being longer than the table on the right is wide; it is not. (B) The short crossing lines (some people call them *feathers*) help create the perception that the longer lines are not parallel; they are. (C) The <> symbols or "wings" at the ends of the top lines and the >< symbols at the ends of the bottom line create the illusion that the top line is shorter than the bottom line. The amount of error in judging the Muller-Lyer illusion depends on a number of factors (Wraga, Creem, & Proffitt, 2000), such as the angle and length of the wings. (D) Because it is surrounded by several larger circles, the center circle on the left is perceived as smaller than the center circle on the right (Ebbinghaus illusion). The two circles are exactly the same size. (E) Even though we know that an elephant has only four legs, the additional leg shapes are compelling cues. Are the elephant's real legs dark or light in color? (F) Fraser's spiral creates the illusion of a spiral. If you check carefully, there is no spiral, just a series of concentric circles.

**FIGURE 3-22** If you assume that the Ames room is a regularly shaped room with a normal ceiling height, then the person in the right corner appears much larger than she should be.

**Source:** Seaman and Kenrick (1994).

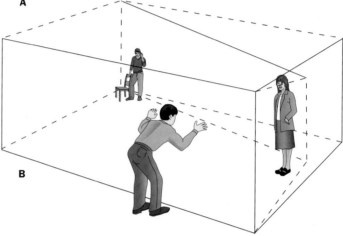

**STUDY TIP**

Create an outline summary of the basic perceptual abilities (patterns and constancies).

perceptual hypothesis you have developed for it. Figure 3-21D, which depicts the Ebbinghaus illusion (Franz, Gegenfurtner, Bulthoff, & Fahle, 2000), suggests that our perceptual hypotheses are influenced by contrast or the tendency to accentuate differences. In this illusion, big circles make a central circle appear small, whereas small circles make a central circle look larger. What aspects of the other drawings trick the visual system causing us to develop incorrect perceptual hypotheses?

One of the most fascinating perceptual illusions is the Ames room. Figure 3-22A shows the view that you would have if you were looking into the Ames room. Notice how much bigger the woman on the right appears. How can this be? People are not supposed to vary this much in height. The explanation is in Figure 3-22B. Although you assume that the room is perfectly square, it is not square. The floors you thought were level are not level. The woman is actually closer to you and casts a larger image on your retina. Without information to tell you that one person is closer and on a floor that slants upward, you conclude that this person is abnormally large.

## Contemporary Issues and Findings in Perception Research

**Parallel Processing, Visual Search, Cell Phones, and the Application of Basic Perceptual Research.** During "the decade of the brain" (the 1990s), research on perceptual processes progressed rapidly. According to Woods and Krantz

(2001), recent advances in the study of brain functioning promise to change our conception of sensory processes and perception. For example, studies of the human visual cortex (Zeki, 1993) indicate that sensory processing does not occur in a strictly sequential manner where one part of the brain performs an activity and then passes the modified sensation on to another brain area for additional processing. The picture that emerges is of a *parallel processing system* (Dosher, Han, & Lu, 2004) in which information simultaneously flows both from lower to higher levels and from higher to lower levels in the brain.

For example, exciting breakthroughs also are occurring in the study of higher-level, more cognitive processes, such as visual search (Geisler & Chou, 1995). **Visual search** is the process of identifying the presence or absence of a target stimulus among a group of distractor items. Research on this topic shows that when stimuli have high *salience* (that is, when they are relevant, meaningful, or distinctive), visual search is done efficiently, rapidly, and in a parallel manner. Indeed, such high-salience stimuli seem to "pop out" from the distractors. Such features as color, motion, brightness (McCarley, Kramer, Colcombe, & Scialfa, 2004) and prior experience with the target (Lubow & Kaplan, 1997) help create the pop-out effect. The combination of these features (for example, color and form [D'Zmura, Lennie, & Tiana, 1997]), however, can result in a more lengthy and difficult visual search. There are several notable applications of visual search research to real-life situations in which target stimuli must be detected from distractors. These include controlling air traffic (McCarley, Kramer, Wickens, Vidoni, & Boot, 2004), driving an automobile (Lajunen, Hakkarainen, & Summala, 1996), and monitoring visual displays (Liu, 1996).

Basic perception research also is playing an important role in our understanding of the family of learning problems known as *dyslexia* (Savage, 2004). For example, Stein and Walsh (1997) provided data showing that dyslexia is linked to abnormal neural development. Moreover, children with the most common form of dyslexia, *specific reading disability* (Colangelo, Buchanan, & Westbury, 2004), have been shown to have a number of perceptual difficulties. The specific nature of the problem faced by dyslexic people was unveiled by Ballew, Brooks, and Annacelli (2001), who studied the effect of contrast on reading ability. They found that as the contrast between individual letters and the background was reduced, the reading performance of dyslexic children decreased *significantly* more than the reading performance of normal children. Woods and Oross (1998) reported that special stimuli and conditions were not needed to produce these conditions. Clearly, perception research has the potential to offer easily implemented solutions, such as maintaining high letter–background contrast, that can aid the dyslexic individual. What's more, perception researcher Lauren Scharff and her colleagues (Scharff & Ahumada, 2001; Scharff, Hill, & Ahumada, 2000) have shown that the type of background texture can affect text readability for normal individuals. This area of applied perception research is paying rich dividends for a wide range of individuals.

If you own a flat-screen computer monitor or television, scanner, color printer, or digital camera, contemporary perception research has impacted your life. According to Woods and Krantz (2001), the development of high-tech displays for these applications and "for harsh visual environments such as the airplane cockpit" is one of the prime areas of perception research. For example, someone has to make sure that the colors on these devices are accurate; that's the task of the perception researcher.

Basic perception research also has the potential to have an impact on a major recent phenomenon—the use of cell phones while driving an automobile. Research has shown that engaging in cognitive tasks, such as complex conversations, results in a reduction of drivers' attention (Adelson, 2003). Moreover, Strayer, Drews, and Johnston (2003) found that when participants engaged in *hands-free* cell phone conversations under simulated driving conditions, their short-term memory for billboards and signs was impaired. This reduced attention to billboards and signs resulted in impaired reactions to other vehicles that braked (see also Recarte & Nunes, 2003).

**visual search**
Identifying the presence of a target stimulus among a group of other, distractor items

Without question, basic perception research has provided important information and promises to yield additional real-life applications in the future. It also has the potential to tell us about social processes.

**Perception Is Affected by Social Context.**   Because most stimuli have physical properties that can be described precisely, it is easy to get the impression that perception is a rather automatic and mechanical process. In fact, some psychologists have held this view for years. The view is changing rather dramatically, however. Researchers are showing that even basic perceptual phenomena can be influenced by social context. Consider an intriguing research project from the University of Amsterdam, Holland (Stapel & Koomen, 1997).

Do you remember the Ebbinghaus illusion (see Figure 3-21D)? In this illusion, the perceived size of the center circle is influenced by the size of the circles that surround it: When the surrounding circles are large, the center circle is seen as smaller, and vice versa. Stapel and Koomen wondered if this effect could be obtained with stimuli other than geometric figures. If the effect could be obtained with nongeometric figures, they then wondered if other factors influenced it. To answer these questions, they conducted two experiments. In both experiments, college students estimated the size of a human face that was surrounded by faces or other objects.

In the first experiment the target stimulus (a face) was surrounded by (a) identical faces, (b) same-gender faces, (c) different-gender faces, or (d) nonperson objects (trucks or handbags). The magnitude of the illusion was greatest when the target stimulus was surrounded by identical stimuli. Thus the target face was perceived as largest when it was surrounded by small, identical faces. As you can see in Figure 3-23, same-gender faces produced the next largest contrast, followed by different-gender faces, and nonperson stimuli. Clearly, the type of stimulus that surrounds the target has a significant effect on perception of the target: not all stimuli are perceptually equal.

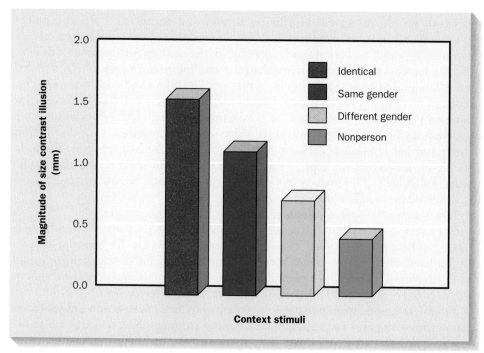

**FIGURE 3-23**   Results from Stapel and Koomen's Experiment 1, showing the magnitude of the size contrast illusion as a function of physical appearance of context stimuli. *Illusion magnitude* is defined as the difference between the targets in two types of stimulus configurations: the target stimulus surrounded by small context stimuli versus the same target stimulus surrounded by large context stimuli.

**Source:** Stapel and Koomen (1997).

### Psychological Detective

The results of this experiment suggest the operation of a general underlying principle. Spend a few minutes reviewing the results of this study, making sure to consult Figure 3-23. Collect your thoughts and then write down your impression of the general principle.

The results of Experiment 1 indicate that the greater the similarity between the target in the center and the surrounding stimuli, the more pronounced the illusion (the greater the perceived contrast). Stapel and Koomen refer to this effect as "similarity breeds comparability"—that is, the more similar the target and the surrounding objects, the more likely you are to compare them and experience the illusion. This general principle was given an interesting and important twist in Experiment 2.

The stimuli from Experiment 1 were used in Experiment 2. Some participants, however, were given a social description of the target and surrounding faces before they judged the size of the target. For example, one group was told that the faces were *all* of students. These social descriptions tend to increase perceived similarity of the target and surrounding stimuli. Thus, comparability of the stimuli was greater and the magnitude of the illusion also was increased. For example, even though the target face was female and the surrounding faces were male, when participants were told they were all students (or lawyers), the size of the illusion increased and did not differ from the illusion that occurred when the faces were identical. Thus, nonphysical (social) factors can—and do—influence our basic perception of human and nonhuman objects. We encounter the influence of social context again when we discuss social psychology (Chapter 15).

Now that we have examined both standard and contemporary perceptual phenomena, we turn our attention to an area that always receives considerable media attention—paranormal phenomena.

# PARANORMAL PHENOMENA

**Thousands of handbills were distributed, posters were displayed, and newspaper advertisements were placed to announce the first public appearance of a famous psychic who had spent years being tested in laboratories around the world. Extra chairs were brought in to accommodate the huge crowd that wanted to see and hear the lecture and demonstration. The psychic began by showing plants perceiving animosity or affection from people. Next, he drew some geometric figures that matched those drawn by a member of the audience. Finally, from about 20 feet away and using only the power of his mind, he caused a large heavy rocking chair to move back and forth (Gordon, 1987).** *What do people believe is the cause of such phenomena?*

According to a 1990 survey (Gallup & Newport, 1991) of more than 1,000 adult Americans, 93% believe in at least one *paranormal* (literally, "beyond normal") or psychic phenomenon, and almost half believe in five or more. Belief in such phenomena is widespread among college students. One-third of them express belief in reincarnation; a similar number believe that communication with the dead is possible. Over half believe that their dreams predict events such as the death of a family member or a natural disaster (Messer & Griggs, 1989).

Undoubtedly you have heard about **extrasensory perception (ESP),** which refers to experiences or behaviors that occur without sensory contact—in other words, without the use of our sensory receptors. The term *ESP* is reserved for paranormal phenomena that do not involve the senses. The most frequently mentioned examples of ESP are clairvoyance, telepathy, and precognition. *Clairvoyance* (from the French for

**extrasensory perception (ESP)**
Behaviors or experiences that cannot be explained by information received by the senses

"clear seeing") is the claimed ability to "see" information from objects or events without direct contact with the senses. If you could tell us what was in a closed box that you had never seen, you might be demonstrating clairvoyance. *Telepathy* is the claimed ability to perceive the thoughts or emotions of others without the use of recognized senses. *Precognition* is knowledge of a future event or circumstance obtained by paranormal means. *Psychokinesis* (once known as *telekinesis*) is the claimed power of the mind to influence matter directly. Because psychokinesis does not involve perception, some researchers do not consider it an example of ESP. The term *parapsychology* is often used to refer to "the study of paranormal phenomena, which are considered to be well outside the bounds of established science" (Hines, 1988, p. 7).

## Skeptical Scientists

The study of paranormal phenomena dates from the late 1800s, when there were numerous investigations of *spirit mediums*—people who claimed that they could receive messages from the dead. Modern research on paranormal phenomena began with Joseph Banks Rhine (1895–1980), who coined the term *extrasensory perception* in 1934 and established a laboratory at Duke University.

Many of Rhine's experiments used a deck of Zener cards, which consists of five each of the following designs: circle, cross, rectangle, star, and wavy lines. In a typical study, the participant's task was to guess the design on each card as an experimenter selected it from the deck. Using statistical procedures, Rhine compared each person's success with the success rate expected on the basis of chance—which is 20%, or one in five correct. A number of participants did better than chance and seemed to defy those odds. Unfortunately, some of the best performers may have had an opportunity to cheat. What's more, success rates exceeding chance may also have been due to irregularities in the cards that participants could use as clues. For example, with the right light it was sometimes possible to read the symbol through the back of a worn card.

The claims offered by supporters of ESP are sometimes presented in ways that make designing a definitive test difficult, if not impossible. (Recall the guidelines for evaluating claims presented in Chapter 1.) For example, when participants have done worse than expected on the basis of chance, parapsychologists have taken it as evidence of what has been termed *psi-missing*, or purposely giving the wrong answer. Such claims put critics in the position of playing a game of "heads I win, tails you lose." On the basis of such findings, James Alcock (1989) concluded that parapsychology has failed to produce scientific evidence of its validity. It is not surprising that parapsychology has been termed a "controversial science" (Broughton, 1991).

Most scientists agree that allegedly paranormal phenomena can be explained without resort to nonnormal evidence. Paranormal explanations would require that we rewrite well-established scientific principles to account for them. The law of parsimony (see Chapter 1) suggests that we look for explanations that require fewer assumptions, provided that they can explain the phenomenon in question.

## A Believing Public

"Evidence for paranormal claims comes in many guises," one researcher observes. "The overwhelming bulk of the evidence comes from personal experience, anecdotes, and

Examples of Zener cards that are used in parapsychological research.

folklore. Although psychologists and other scientists realize that such evidence is unreliable, almost every believer has become convinced because of such evidence" (Hyman, 1989, p. 15). According to Wayne Messer and Richard Griggs (1989), over 40% of college students reported having experienced dreams that predict the future (precognitive dreams). The accuracy of these dreams can be checked by keeping a written dream diary. Even people who claim that their dreams "always come true" find that this is not the case when they use a dream diary to check their accuracy.

The surveys cited earlier indicate that many people believe in psychic phenomena. Why? The answer is simple: Many people have psychic experiences, or at least experiences they interpret as such (Wiseman, Greening, & Smith, 2003). Psychologists suggest that paranormal experiences are an inevitable consequence of the way we perceive and remember information (Blackmore, 1992). Explanations that rely on some proposed "will to believe" do not enhance our understanding.

We can be fooled by our experiences in much the same way we are fooled by the visual illusions described earlier in the chapter. One illusion that encourages belief in paranormal phenomena such as ESP occurs when we consider coincidences, such as dreams that come true, as evidence of a connection. We have all had an experience similar to this: "He called me today after we hadn't heard from each other in 15 years. I had been thinking about him just a few hours earlier. I know it's not a coincidence—it must be ESP." No doubt the experience is real, but its origins lie in our internal processing, not in the external world. Coincidences do happen!

Imagine sitting in front of a computer designed to generate heads or tails in a coin-tossing game. Your task is to guess whether a head or a tail will appear on the screen. How many correct guesses (called *hits*) do you think you will achieve in 20 trials? ESP believers guessed that they would average 7.0 hits; nonbelievers guessed an average of 9.6 hits (Blackmore & Troscianko, 1985). Moreover, the believers were more likely to decide that they had influenced the computer, even when the computer was generating a random series of heads and tails. Why? As mentioned earlier, believers underestimate the number of correct guesses achieved by chance alone. People who consistently underestimate chance occurrences may look elsewhere for explanations, and paranormal explanations may look attractive. Underestimating chance underlies the tendency to interpret ordinary coincidence as psychic events and thus strengthens belief in such phenomena.

The media also affect belief in the paranormal, although they may reflect rather than cause the beliefs. Simply stated, paranormal phenomena sell—whether they be ghosts, reincarnation, or spoon bending. Newspaper stories of alleged paranormal phenomena are often reported as facts, with extensive coverage of the proponents' views and less attention to the skeptics' views (Klare, 1990).

**A Final Word.** There is a wide variety of paranormal phenomena, and many people report personal experience with some of them. Scientists and believers disagree about what constitutes proof of such phenomena. Believers present anecdotes and point to laboratory research (Hergovich, 2004). Skeptics point to flaws in the laboratory research, and psychologists offer explanations for many of these personal experiences. Because psychologists can point to reasons that such phenomena may not occur, they cannot disprove them; the burden of proof for such extraordinary claims rests with the people making the claim.

Although the methods of studying paranormal phenomena have improved, "the goal of a conclusively convincing demonstration or a repeatable experiment has not been achieved" (Blackmore, 1994). At the beginning of the twentieth century, the magician Harry Houdini challenged mediums to produce phenomena he could not duplicate. No one succeeded. Since 1964, the magician James Randi has offered a substantial reward (currently $1 million) to anyone who could demonstrate paranormal power under satisfactory observing conditions (see Randi's Web site for complete details: http://www.randi.org). Again, no one has succeeded. Should we therefore dismiss even the possibility of paranormal phenomena? Before we do, let's consider an important history lesson: Some phenomena that in the past were considered to be paranormal, impossible, or even fraudulent have since been verified to be real.

"The Amazing Randi." Magician James Randi has offered $1 million to anyone who can demonstrate paranormal power under satisfactory observing conditions.

As late as the 1700s, most people believed that the notion of rocks falling from the sky was ridiculous. Anyone suggesting the possibility was met with jeers that might be similar to the reception often given to present-day reports of unidentified flying objects. Despite these reactions, what was once believed to be impossible is indeed possible: Meteorites do fall from the sky. Perhaps the lesson of history is twofold: First, a certain amount of humility in what we believe becomes us; second, we can be open-minded without neglecting the need for empirical evidence.

# REVIEW SUMMARY

1. **Perception** is the process of organizing and making sense of the stimuli in our environment. Our motives help determine which stimuli we perceive.

2. We engage in *selective attention* because we cannot process all of the stimuli we encounter. Dichotic listening experiments study **divided attention.** With practice we can learn how to divide our attention effectively.

3. To attract our attention, stimuli should be more colorful, larger, and louder than other stimuli in our environment.

4. The ability to discriminate among shapes and figures is known as **pattern perception.** The **feature analysis theory** states that we perceive the elements of an object and then combine them to produce our perception of the object (bottom-up processing). Other research has shown that we perceive the object before we perceive its elements (top-down processing).

5. We experience **perceptual constancies** when our perception of an object does not change, even though the retinal image changes. **Size constancy** and **shape constancy** depend on the presence of a background and our ability to judge distance.

6. The Gestalt psychologists demonstrated that we actively organize our perceptual world into meaningful groups or wholes.

The **figure–ground relation** is one of the most basic perceptual organizations. Additional principles for the grouping of stimulus elements are **proximity, similarity, good continuation,** and **closure.**

7. **Perceptual hypotheses** are inferences about the nature of the stimuli we sense. **Perceptual illusions** and ambiguous figures may cause us to develop incorrect perceptual hypotheses.

8. Parallel, as opposed to sequential, processing appears to characterize much of our perceptual activity. Parallel processing is seen in **visual search,** in which a target stimulus must be distinguished among a group of distractors.

9. Perception may be influenced by the social context. For example, the Ebbinghaus illusion is influenced by the type of social stimuli used.

10. **Extrasensory perception (ESP)** refers to the occurrence of experiences or behaviors in the absence of an adequate stimulus. Such occurrences are considered to be paranormal, or beyond our normal sensory abilities. Clairvoyance, telepathy, precognition, and psychokinesis are examples of paranormal phenomena.

# ✓ CHECK YOUR PROGRESS

1. What is selective attention? Why is it an important feature of the perceptual process?

2. Which of the following illustrates that we hear and understand much more information than actually enters conscious awareness?

   a. focused attention
   b. cocktail-party phenomenon
   c. dichotic listening experiments
   d. motivational effects on perception

3. According to feature analysis theory, how do we identify objects that we perceive?

4. Under what circumstances can divided attention occur most easily?

   a. when you are under stress
   b. when attention to small details is critical
   c. when you are performing two tasks that are highly related
   d. when you are performing tasks that are simple and well practiced

5. What is meant by perceptual constancy? Give examples of shape and size constancy.

6. Convergence and binocular disparity are important cues for the perception of

   a. depth.
   b. patterns.
   c. constancy.
   d. thresholds.

7. What is a figure–ground relationship? What features characterize figures?

8. Which Gestalt principle helps our perception of
WWW XXX?
   a. similarity
   b. figure–ground
   c. inclusiveness
   d. good continuation

9. Your mother claims that she was able to read your mind and knew you would try to sneak some food before dinner. What form of ESP might she claim she was using?

a. telepathy
b. clairvoyance
c. precognition
d. psychokinesis

10. What law argues that we should search for explanations of paranormal phenomena that fit within well-established scientific principles?

a. law of parsimony
b. law of simplicity
c. law of common sense
d. law of irreproducible results

**ANSWERS: 1.** Selective attention involves attending to some stimuli and not others. It is important in helping organisms concentrate on the stimuli that are most relevant at the time. **2. b 3.** We identify the elements or features of the object in question; then we assemble these features to create the complete, identifiable object—that is, bottom-up processing. **4. d 5.** Perceptual constancy involves the perception of a stable object despite a changing retinal image. An example of shape constancy would be the perception that an airplane does not change shape as it rises into the sky and the retinal image of the plane changes. The fact that the same plane is seen as moving farther away, and not physically changing shape, is an example of size constancy. **6. a 7.** The figure–ground relationship is the organization of the perceptual stimuli we receive into a figure and a background. Figures typically are smaller, brighter or colorful, and display motion. **8. a 9. a 10. a**

**ANSWER** **To Photo Question on Page 116**

With the appropriate cues to distance and size, the object you saw on p. 116 may be much larger than you thought it was.

# States of Consciousness

Our journey toward understanding behavior has led us to the study of fundamental processes—the functioning of the brain and the nervous system, and sensing and perceiving our environment. Our focus on fundamental processes continues as we investigate changes in our awareness. The term *consciousness* is difficult to define. As you read these words, you are conscious, but how does brain tissue make a person conscious?

In this chapter we learn that ongoing bodily changes called *biological rhythms* can influence our ability to sense and perceive stimuli. Changes in our awareness can also be brought on artificially—through drugs or perhaps through induction of a hypnotic state. Our discussion will include evidence that social factors can also affect our awareness.

Like the ocean tides, most of our internal biological processes follow a rhythm of alternating high and low levels. Some biological processes are accompanied by changes in our awareness or level of consciousness. For example, the rhythm of sleep and wakefulness is accompanied by the change in consciousness we call *dreaming*. For centuries people have found ways to alter their consciousness through such means as drug use or hypnosis. These are just some of the topics we encounter in this chapter.

## WHAT IS CONSCIOUSNESS?

**To fulfill a requirement in a psychology course, Amy agrees to participate in several research projects. For the first one, she must carry a beeper with her throughout the day. The device sounds at irregular intervals to alert her to write down whatever is running through her mind at the time. When her participation in the project is completed, the researcher tells her that the topic of the research was consciousness. *How do psychologists define consciousness?***

To be conscious is to be aware, but aware of what? Psychologists define **consciousness** as personal awareness of feelings, sensations, and thoughts. Driving through an unfamiliar city would provide ample opportunities to understand changes in your level of consciousness. You are aware of an increased feeling of tension; you grip the steering wheel tightly. Your mouth has gone dry; beads of sweat cascade down your face. You see cars weaving in and out of traffic as if they were performing a high-speed ballet. You scan your rear-view mirror and see a big truck behind you, or is it in your trunk? You start thinking that you shouldn't be driving in this city during rush hour. Finally, you reach the outskirts of the city and enter the suburbs. You see a snazzy sports car speed past you and picture yourself behind the wheel. Wait a minute! You just passed your exit!

As we noted in Chapter 1, William James described consciousness as a stream. Like a stream, consciousness is continuous, can change, and has depth. But the stream of consciousness is personal; it is very much your own. Let's return to your drive through an unfamiliar city. Throughout the drive, your awareness of external stimuli—such as other cars—and internal stimuli—such as the seat belt against your body—probably changed. What's more, as you left the city, you daydreamed about a sports car. During this fantasy, your attention was directed inward and away from external sources of stimulation. To drive through the city, you had to focus your attention on the events around you; it was no time for consciousness to wander. But once you left the city, your attention could

**consciousness**
A person's awareness of feelings, sensations, and thoughts at a given moment

The "lost in my thoughts" look may be a clue that this person is engaged in the altered state of consciousness called *daydreaming*. Daydreaming is so common that we might not even realize that it has occurred. There is a good chance that you will daydream several times today, perhaps while driving, watching television, or attending class.

stray, and you missed your exit. We often engage in everyday behaviors without being completely aware of them—that is, they can occur outside of consciousness.

This form of consciousness involving fantasy, occurring while you are awake, is called **daydreaming.** Almost all people daydream, although the frequency drops as we get older (Giambra, 1999–2000). Most daydreams are spontaneous images or thoughts that pop into our mind for a brief time and are then forgotten. We can, however, become adept at using daydreams to solve problems, to rehearse a sequence of events, or to find new ideas. Some daydreams are deliberate attempts to deal with situations like a boring job by providing internal stimulation. Nevertheless, most daydreams are related to such everyday events as paying bills or selecting clothes to wear. About two-thirds of daydreams are related to the daydreamer's immediate situation. Contrary to popular belief, only a small proportion of daydreams involve sexual content (Klinger, 1990). Yet, approximately 95% of men and women report having had sexual daydreams at some time (Leitenberg & Henning, 1995).

Psychologists have devised ingenious ways to investigate changes in our consciousness, particularly daydreaming. For example, they have equipped people with beepers that sound at random intervals to signal them to report their thoughts in writing (Klinger, 1990). These beepers are one of the methods used to study daydreaming. The advantage of this method is that it does not rely on memory.

The experience of daydreaming is different from normal waking consciousness, and for that reason it is called an *altered state of consciousness*. In fact, using an electroencephalogram (EEG), brain researchers have found that daydreaming is associated with changes in the ratio of several different brain waves (Cunningham, Scerbo, & Freeman, 2000). During the course of a day, our consciousness can change even more dramatically than during daydreaming. For example, the use of alcohol or other drugs often leads to major changes in consciousness and observable behavior. As we discuss later, some researchers consider hypnosis to be an altered state of consciousness. Likewise, the rhythmic changes of sleeping and dreaming dramatically alter personal awareness. We discuss the study of sleep and dreams as we investigate both consciousness and the biological rhythms of life.

## THE RHYTHMS OF LIFE

**A jet flying from Taiwan to Los Angeles lost power in one engine and fell about 6 miles, resulting in injuries to two passengers and structural damage to the aircraft. Although the power loss was an accident, the pilot may have failed to monitor the instruments carefully. Investigators determined that the accident occurred 5 hours beyond the time when the pilot was accustomed to going to sleep (Lauber & Kayten, 1988). Tim, a worker in a nuclear power plant, read a newspaper account of the accident and wondered whether working the night shift might affect his ability to monitor instruments and make critical decisions. *What are the effects of shift work on alertness and decision making?***

All living organisms exhibit built-in rhythms or cycles of internal biological activity called *biological rhythms*. Biological rhythms such as the heartbeat that are shorter than 24 hours are called *ultradian* rhythms. Longer rhythms, such as the menstrual cycle, are known as *infradian* rhythms. Some of the most important biological rhythms, however, occur on a daily schedule.

## Circadian Rhythms

Internal biological changes that occur on a daily schedule are called **circadian rhythms** (*circa*, "about"; *dies*, "day") and have been found in nearly all species (Czeisler, Buxton, & Khalsa, 2005). Most of us have a single sleep period every 24 hours. The sleep–wake

**daydreaming**
A form of consciousness involving fantasies, usually spontaneous, that occurs while a person is awake

**circadian rhythms**
Internal biological changes that occur on a daily schedule

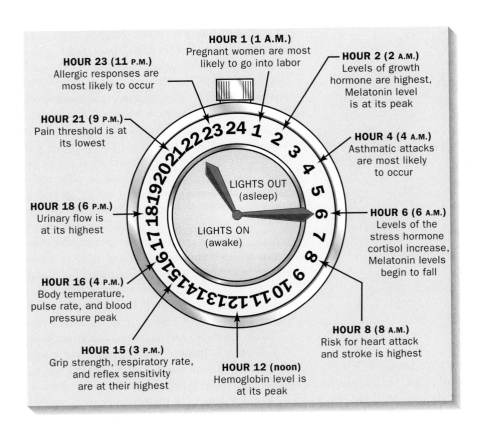

**HOUR 1 (1 A.M.)**
Pregnant women are most
likely to go into labor

**HOUR 2 (2 A.M.)**
Levels of growth
hormone are highest,
Melatonin level
is at its peak

**HOUR 23 (11 P.M.)**
Allergic responses are
most likely to occur

**HOUR 21 (9 P.M.)**
Pain threshold is at
its lowest

**HOUR 4 (4 A.M.)**
Asthmatic attacks
are most likely
to occur

**HOUR 18 (6 P.M.)**
Urinary flow is
at its highest

LIGHTS OUT
(asleep)

LIGHTS ON
(awake)

**HOUR 6 (6 A.M.)**
Levels of the
stress hormone
cortisol increase,
Melatonin levels
begin to fall

**HOUR 16 (4 P.M.)**
Body temperature,
pulse rate, and blood
pressure peak

**HOUR 8 (8 A.M.)**
Risk for heart attack
and stroke is highest

**HOUR 15 (3 P.M.)**
Grip strength, respiratory rate,
and reflex sensitivity
are at their highest

**HOUR 12 (noon)**
Hemoglobin level is
at its peak

**FIGURE 4-1** Biological
processes that follow a circadian
rhythm. Researchers and
physicians are becoming more
aware of the effects of circadian
rhythms on biological and
psychological processes.

**Source:** Young (2000).

cycle is just one of our circadian rhythms; scientists can detect peaks and valleys in body temperature, heart rate, and hormone levels during a 24-hour period (Foster & Kreitzman, 2004). For example, levels of the stress hormone cortisol are negligible an hour or two before sleep, begin increasing before we awaken, and reach a peak at or near awakening (Moore-Ede, Sulzman, & Fuller, 1982). Circadian rhythms are also important in detecting diseases and in planning drug treatments (Lamberg, 1994). The results of medical tests can depend on when the test is given; drugs that help at one time of day may harm at another. A common practice in testing the toxicity of drugs and additives is to administer these to rats and mice; however, their nocturnal existence may yield results that are misleading when these drugs are used on humans (Foster & Kreitzman, 2004). One researcher has identified over 100 drugs, including a number used to treat cancer, that vary significantly in their effects as a consequence of when they are given in a 24-hour period (Bjarnason, Jordan, & Sothern, 1999). The peak times for a number of indicators of health and disease are shown in Figure 4-1.

**The Sleep–Wake Cycle.**  *Chronobiology* is the branch of science that investigates and applies information about biological rhythms. To determine what controls our biological rhythms, researchers have observed volunteers who were isolated from all time cues—no watches, television, radio, or newspapers—in caves or special apartments. In order to check the accuracy of our internal clock, researchers recorded the daily rhythms of hormones and body temperature in 24 healthy young and old men and women for 1-month. They found that our internal clock is quite accurate: The daily cycles averaged 24 hours and 11 minutes (Czeisler et al., 1999; Honma, Hashimoto, Nakao, & Honma, 2003).

Where is this internal clock? The answer is in the *suprachiasmatic nucleus* (SCN), a pinhead-sized collection of neurons located in the hypothalamus (see Chapter 2), just above the

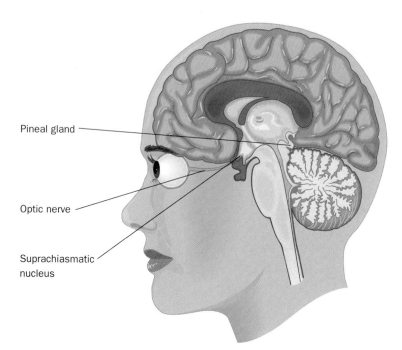

Pineal gland

Optic nerve

Suprachiasmatic
nucleus

**FIGURE 4-2** The SCN has connections to the visual pathways, which provide information used in regulating circadian rhythms, including release of melatonin by the pineal gland.

**Source:** Young (2000).

optic chiasm (Young, 2000; Zisapel, 2001). These neurons receive information about light and dark from the eyes and their nerve pathways (Moore-Ede, 1993). The SCN serves as a central internal clock that exerts indirect control over neurons throughout the body (see Figure 4-2); however, there appear to be peripheral clocks located throughout the body (Czeisler et al., 2005).

Exactly how the biological clock operates is still under investigation. Researchers suspect that the hormone melatonin, produced by the *pineal gland* (see Chapter 2), is involved (Young, 2000). Bright light suppresses melatonin production; darkness triggers secretion of the hormone. In fact, the concentration of melatonin in the blood is 10 to 15 times higher at its peak (about 2 hours before bedtime) than during daylight, which suggests that it may be the final trigger for sleep (Pelayo, Chen, Monzon, & Guilleminault, 2004). Because of its effects on our circadian rhythms, melatonin is sometimes referred to as "nature's sleeping pill." Health food stores sell synthetic forms of this hormone, which the public has embraced. Most researchers, however, are more cautious in their assessments of this hormone that has been touted as a "wonder drug" for insomnia, cancer, high blood pressure, Alzheimer's disease, AIDS, and heart disease (Foster & Kreitzman, 2004). The National Institutes of Health State-of the-Science conference on insomnia (2005) recently concluded that there is little evidence for the efficacy of melatonin in treating insomnia. An additional reason for caution lies in the fact that as a diet supplement melatonin does not fall under the Food and Drug Administration's regulations for safety, purity, and efficacy. What's more, it cannot be patented, so there is little incentive for companies to fund investigations into its long-term safety (Foster & Kreitzman, 2004). If you are considering using melatonin, the best advice for now may be to "sleep on it" until its effectiveness and long-term safety have been clearly established.

**Body Temperature.** You might be surprised to find that your body temperature is not a constant 98.6 °F; rather, it fluctuates 2 to 3 degrees over the course of a day (see Figure 4-3). The 24-hour (circadian) rhythm of body temperature is controlled by the SCN (Coleman, 1995).

### Psychological Detective

At some time most students have "pulled an all-nighter." If you are one of these students, you may have noticed something unusual while you worked against the rapidly approaching morning deadline. At some point you may have felt a bit of a chill. Did the room temperature drop or is there another explanation? Think about this question, and write down your answer before reading further.

Body temperature is related to our level of alertness and our sleep–wake cycle. In fact, observations of circadian cycles without time cues show that sleep is associated more with our body temperature at bedtime than with the number of hours we have been awake (Czeisler, Weitzman, Moore-Ede, Zimmerman, & Knauser, 1980). Higher temperature (but not at fever levels) typically corresponds to elevated levels of alertness; low temperature generally corresponds to reduced alertness and motivation. Body temperature generally reaches its lowest point during the second half of our nighttime sleep

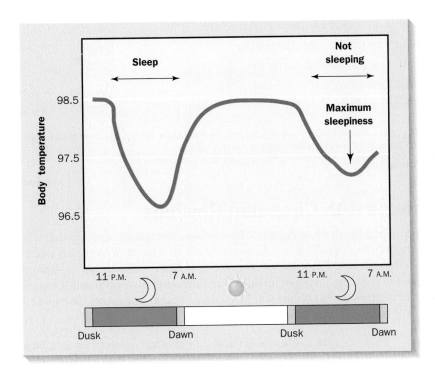

**FIGURE 4-3** The circadian rhythm of body core temperature. If you have ever "pulled an all-nighter," you probably felt chilly in the middle of the night. Even if the temperature of the room remained the same, your core body temperature fell, and you found it increasingly difficult to concentrate.

**Source:** Moore-Ede (1993).

episode (Czeisler et al., 2005). If you are awake in the middle of the night, you are likely to feel a chill as your temperature reaches its lowest point. Core body temperature rises after we wake up and usually peaks in the afternoon. For most people the body is primed for high levels of efficiency in the afternoon.

The sleep–wake and body temperature cycles are typically synchronized. When we are deprived of time cues or when we travel through time zones or change work shifts, however, these cycles can become uncoupled and cause problems such as fatigue and sleepiness.

Have you heard the terms *night owls* and *early birds* (or *larks*) applied to people with different sleep habits? Early birds or larks (*morning type*) get up easily and are more alert and active in the morning than in the evening; they find it difficult to sleep late and fall asleep quickly in the evening. The lark's peak temperature occurs early in the day, around 8 A.M. By contrast, night owls (*evening type*) are able to sleep late in the morning, do not really get going until the afternoon, and take a long time to fall asleep at night. The night owl's temperature peaks later in the day, around 8 P.M. or later. You can complete the questionnaire on this page to determine whether you tend to be an owl or a lark. These differences reflect differing sleep–wake and temperature cycles (Duffy, Rimmer, & Czeisler, 2001), which seem to be influenced by genetic factors (Foster & Kreitzman, 2004; Hur, Bouchard, & Lykken, 1998). These physiological differences can influence preferred study times, interpersonal activity, health, and other aspects of a person's life.

## Hands On

### Are You an Owl or a Lark?

Indicate your response to each of the following by checking the circle next to either day or night?

1. I am most alert during the                               Day ○      Night ○
2. I feel I have the most energy during the              Day ○      Night ○
3. I prefer to take classes during the                   Day ○      Night ○
4. I prefer to study during the                           Day ○      Night ○
5. I prefer to work during the                            Day ○      Night ○

| | | |
|---|---|---|
| 6. I come up with the best ideas during the | Day ○ | Night ○ |
| 7. I enjoy recreation most during the | Day ○ | Night ○ |
| 8. I am most productive during the | Day ○ | Night ○ |
| 9. I feel I am most intelligent during the | Day ○ | Night ○ |
| 10. When I graduate, I prefer to find a job during the | Day ○ | Night ○ |

**Note:** Eight or more answers of either Day or Night indicate that you are either a lark or an owl. In-between scores indicate that you are neither clearly an owl or a lark.

**Source:** Wallace (1993).

## Problems with Circadian Rhythms

If you travel in a jet plane across a few time zones, you will understand that it is not so easy to alter our biology (Foster & Kreitzman, 2004). The modern era has stretched the body's ability to adapt. For example, the ability to travel great distances through many time zones in little time has given rise to the phenomenon known as **jet lag,** the temporary maladjustment that occurs when a change of time zone causes biological rhythms to be out of step with local time.

**Jet Lag.**    Hop on a jet in New York, and 2 hours later you can be in Chicago; the change of one time zone requires only a minor adjustment of your internal clock. A trip from New York to London takes about 7 hours via a jet traveling through five time zones. You might be in London at 8 A.M., but your body thinks it is the middle of the night (3 A.M. in New York). Your circadian rhythms are not synchronized with your surroundings; as a result, you are likely to experience the symptoms of jet lag: fatigue, irritability, difficulty concentrating, inability to fall asleep, body aches, and disorientation, along with digestive and appetite problems (Foster & Kreitzman, 2004).

### Psychological Detective

Your travel plans call for several long-distance trips by jet that take you across the country and around the world. Which direction of travel would be easier to adjust to: *east to west* or *west to east*? Why? What could you do to adjust to the time changes brought about by your travel?

Jet lag has little to do with the length of your flight; the key is the number of time zones you cross. Increase the number of time zones you cross, and you increase the need for adjustment. If you travel from New York to Lima, Peru—*directly* south through the same time zone—you do not need to reset your internal clock. But a trip from Los Angeles to Hong Kong takes you through several time zones, requiring a major adjustment. The direction of travel influences the speed with which the body adapts. A westward trip—say, from New York to San Francisco—is equivalent to delaying your sleep by 3 hours and is called a *phase delay*. Of course, you can stay at home and have a similar experience. If you typically go to sleep at midnight, try delaying your sleep 3 hours until 3 A.M. and you will experience a phase delay. If you travel east from San Francisco to New York, you shorten the day to 21 hours, which is known as a *phase advance*. Once again, stay at home and try to move up your sleep 3 hours. If you typically go to sleep at midnight, try to sleep at 9 P.M. Generally, delaying sleep (phase delays or east–west travel) tends to be easier than moving up our bedtime (phase advances or west–east travel).

If you travel great distances and expect to experience jet lag, here is some advice. During short stays, eat and sleep on your home time so that you don't need to reset your internal clock. For longer stays, start adjusting before you leave by eating meals according to the time of your destination. When you arrive at your destination, use the most powerful time cue—sunlight—to reset your internal clock to local time (Czeisler et al., 1986). Note that the timing of your exposure to strong light is a key factor (Foster & Kreitzman, 2004;

**jet lag**

Temporary maladjustment that occurs when a change of time zones causes biological rhythms to be out of step with local time

Young, 2000). Our biological clock interprets exposure to bright light near the end of the usual sleep period (for example, 4 A.M.) as a dawn signal (a new day is starting) that advances the internal clock and initiates a period of activity. By contrast, exposure to bright light near the end of the normal active period (awake hours) delays the clock and makes people want to go to sleep later than their normal time.

**Shift Work.**   Consumers need and want products, protection, and entertainment around the clock. Rotating work shifts fulfill the demand for 24-hour-a-day staffing of stores, manufacturing plants, hospitals, and recreational facilities. However, there are problems associated with shift work.

At the beginning of this section you met Tim, who was concerned that rotating shift work might affect his alertness and decision-making capacity in his job at a nuclear power plant. Tim is not alone: More than 25 million Americans (27% of full-time workers) work a shift other than the day shift (Golden & Jorgensen, 2001). Many of them report symptoms like those of jet lag, health effects, and social and family problems (Kimball, 2000).

Let's take a closer look at Tim's rotating schedule. At the end of a day shift, he heads home and retires for the night at 11 P.M. After 1 week on the day shift, he rotates to the night shift, working from 11 P.M. until 7 A.M. Trying to sleep at 2:00 in the afternoon is almost impossible because his body is not ready for sleep. It is, however, ready for sleep when he arrives at work! "The shift worker may wish to sleep, but the circadian rhythms may be preventing it" (Foster & Kreitzman, 2004, p. 206).

Shift work often leads to a cumulative sleep loss. As many as 75% of night shift workers experience sleepiness on every night shift, and 20% report having fallen asleep on the job (Akerstedt, 1991). The sleepiness resulting from shift rotation doesn't make it difficult to walk, see, or hear. But people who don't get enough sleep can't think, can't make appropriate judgments, and can't maintain long attention spans. On-the-job errors peak during the night shift, which can adversely affect work performance and even compromise public safety (Scott, 1994). The sleepiness resulting from rotating shift work can interfere with a person's ability to administer drugs to patients, to navigate a plane, or to operate a nuclear power plant. Sleepiness was a factor in serious accidents at two nuclear power plants (Chernobyl in the Ukraine and Three Mile Island in Pennsylvania), the explosion at the Union Carbide plant in Bhopal, India, and the *Exxon Valdez* oil spill in Alaska. What's more, an investigation of the 1986 explosion of the space shuttle *Challenger* cited errors in judgment that were related to sleep loss and rotating shift work during the early morning hours (*Report of the Presidential Commission on the Space Shuttle Challenger Accident*, 1986). Sleep deprivation and sleep disorders contribute to accidents, reduced productivity, and higher medical costs (Fritz, 1993; National Commission on Sleep Disorders Research, 1992).

Although the human body was designed to sleep at night and be alert and active during the day, we now live in a 24/7 society. To meet demands for services and products, employers are increasing the number of workers assigned to rotating and nonday shifts.

**Improving Shift Work.** A typical rotation schedule calls for a week each on the day, night, and evening shifts, in that order. Although a week on a shift is not enough time for workers to adjust to their new schedule, they often shift again at the end of the week. This rotating schedule is the equivalent of working successive weeks in Denver, Paris, and Tokyo. Typical rotating shifts do not provide enough time for workers' circadian rhythms to adjust before they are required to rotate again (Kimball, 2000).

Researchers have some advice for people who schedule or work rotating shifts (Akerstedt, 1991; Czeisler, Moore-Ede, & Coleman, 1982). Workers should rotate in a "clockwise" direction (from days to evenings to nights) so that the changes are phase delays, not phase advances. If you work from 7 A.M. to 4 P.M. and go to sleep at 10 P.M., it would not be difficult for you to delay your sleep until after the evening shift ends at 11 P.M. When shifts rotate in a "counterclockwise" direction (from days to nights to evenings), workers must try to sleep during the time they had been working. The advantages of rotating in a clockwise direction can be enhanced by allowing workers to spend more than 1 week on a shift so that they have more time to reset their internal clocks. Rotating shifts in a clockwise direction has been shown to improve the satisfaction of both workers and their families, increase productivity, and lead to fewer accidents.

# REVIEW SUMMARY

1. **Consciousness** is personal awareness of feelings, sensations, and thoughts. Changes from normal consciousness are known as *altered states of consciousness.* One common change in consciousness is **daydreaming.**

2. A number of biological processes follow regular rhythms or cycles that vary in length. The study of biological rhythms, *chronobiology,* includes research on the effects of such cycles on the diagnosis and treatment of diseases.

3. **Circadian rhythms** are biological changes that occur on a daily schedule, including the sleep–wake cycle and the body temperature cycle.

4. Circadian rhythms are controlled by the *suprachiasmatic nucleus (SCN),* which is located in the hypothalamus and acts as

an internal clock. Levels of *melatonin,* a hormone secreted by the pineal gland are affected by light and darkness; thus melatonin may play a role in controlling biological rhythms. By isolating volunteers in an environment without time cues, researchers have found that our circadian rhythms are very close to 24 hours.

5. Jet travel and shift work can disrupt the sleep–wake cycle. The symptoms of **jet lag** result from the difference between our internal clock and the time in our environment. It is easier to adapt to phase delays (east–west travel) than to phase advances (west–east travel). Rotating shifts can be improved by using a clockwise rotation (days to evenings to nights), which involves a series of phase delays.

 **CHECK YOUR PROGRESS**

1. What do psychologists mean when they use the word - *consciousness?*

2. According to researchers, which of the following is a common daydream?

   a. winning a Nobel Prize
   b. writing the "world's greatest novel"
   c. dealing with an everyday situation
   d. punishing oneself for thinking about sex

3. Dave is experiencing insomnia and decides to research the available treatments. One of the treatments, melatonin, is intriguing because it is a naturally occurring hormone. After he finishes his research, what conclusion is he likely to arrive at concerning the effectiveness of melatonin?

   a. Melatonin does not cross the blood-brain barrier.
   b. Melatonin increases the length of sleep only in the elderly.

   c. The dosage that can induce sleep is also likely to induce a coma.
   d. There is no evidence for the efficacy of melatonin as a treatment for insomnia.

4. Where in the brain is our internal clock located?

   a. pons
   b. cerebellum
   c. thyroid gland
   d. hypothalamus

5. Dave has volunteered to take part in research designed to investigate a substance believed to influence sleep. The researchers will tell him what the substance is at the end of a 2-month trial. After 2 months, Dave is likely to find that he was taking

   a. thyroxin.
   b. dopamine.

   c. melatonin.
   d. norepinephrine.

**6.** Which *one* of the following journeys would be classified as a phase advance of your sleep–wake cycle?

   a. Paris to Detroit
   b. Rome to Denver
   c. Chicago to London
   d. New York to Miami

**7.** As part of a course on Sleep and Dreams, Alicia has the opportunity to sleep in a sleep laboratory where her sleep and hormone levels are monitored. If she is a typical sleeper and neither a night owl nor a lark, when would her level of melatonin begin to fall?

   a. 2 A.M.
   b. 4 A.M.
   c. 6 A.M.
   d. midnight

**8.** Dana and her roommate Barbara have been described as a *lark* and a *night owl,* respectively. To a researcher, the use of these terms suggests that these roommates differ primarily in what aspect of their behavior?

   a. total amount they sleep per week
   b. timing of the peak body temperature during the day
   c. levels of GABA circulating in their bodies across the day
   d. total amount of time they spend tossing and turning during the night

**9.** The Mega-Store in town will be open 24 hours. The manager hired a consultant to design the best possible rotating shifts for full-time employees. Which of the following schedules would the consultant recommend?

   a. 2 shifts of days, then 2 on evenings, and 2 on nights
   b. 1 week on days, 1 week on nights, and 1 week on evenings
   c. 2 weeks on days, 2 weeks on evenings, and 2 weeks on nights
   d. 2 weeks on night shift, 1 week on days, and 2 weeks on evening

**10.** One of the main problems with rotating shifts is that the typical shifts are _____, whereas the body is most able to adapt to shifts that are _____.

   a. circadian, infradian
   b. ultradian, infradian
   c. clockwise, counterclockwise
   d. counterclockwise, clockwise

# THE STUDY OF SLEEP

Sara and Jim are fascinated by their infant daughter. They frequently tiptoe into her room at night to check on her. At times they notice that her body is completely still, yet her eyes dart quickly back and forth. They had not realized that it is possible to see someone's eyes move beneath closed eyelids. They wonder what those eye movements mean. *What is the significance of the eye movements that occur while we sleep?*

Much of what we know about sleep derives from research conducted in sleep laboratories since World War II. Researchers representing several disciplines—including neurology, psychiatry, and psychology—have probed thousands of people in search of solutions to the mysteries of sleep and dreams.

Hans Berger's invention of the *electroencephalograph* (*EEG*) in 1929 made it possible to study the living brain without entering it (see Chapter 2). Although the EEG was a significant advance, *the* major breakthrough in studying sleep was the observation of the eyes of sleeping people. One research team attached electrodes next to the eyes of sleeping people to provide a continuous record of periods during which the eyes moved back and forth (Aserinsky & Kleitman, 1953). Researchers coined the term *rapid eye movement* (*REM*) to describe this phenomenon.

At the beginning of this section you met Sara and Jim, who were curious about their daughter's eye movements during sleep. We now know they were observing REM sleep. What is the significance of the eye movements? When awakened from REM sleep, people are very likely to report dreams (Dement, 1978; Dement & Wolpert, 1958; Martin, 2004). Although REM sleep has been equated with dreaming, dreams are not restricted to REM sleep (Cavallero, Cicogna, Natale, & Occhionero, 1992; Foulkes, 1962). As we will see, sleep researchers have identified a number of physiological changes that characterize REM sleep.

The one-third of our lives we spend asleep has been full of mysteries, which researchers are beginning to unravel. Changes in sleep across the lifespan are one of the clues researchers use in studying sleep.

**STUDY TIP**

Identify your general sleeping and waking times. Using the sleep stage graph (Figure 4-6) as a guide, graph your own sleep stages, noting the times at which you would, on average, be in a REM or NREM stage.

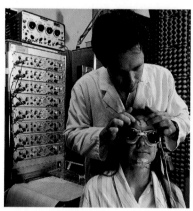

A polysomnograph amplifies and records signals associated with physiological changes that occur during a night in a sleep laboratory. Although a wide variety of measurements may be taken, the most typical measures include brain waves, muscle tension, eye movements, and heart rate.

**polysomnograph**
Instrument that amplifies and records signals associated with biological changes taken during a night in a sleep laboratory

**non-REM (NREM) sleep**
Sleep Stages 1, 2, 3, and 4; NREM sleep consists primarily of Stages 3 and 4 (deep sleep) early in the night and Stage 2 later on

**slow-wave sleep**
Deep sleep of NREM Stages 3 and 4, characterized by delta waves

**FIGURE 4-4** Although the rituals that sometimes precede sleep may lead us to believe that sleep is a gradual process, the tale of the EEG record tells a different story. As this figure illustrates, one moment you are awake and the next you are asleep. Sleep embraces us in an instant.

**Source:** Dement and Vaughan (1999).

# A Night in a Sleep Lab

A posted request for sleep study volunteers catches your attention. Imagine being paid for sleeping! You call the researcher, who tells you she is interested in the sleep patterns of college students with part-time jobs. You arrive 2 hours before your usual bedtime. A technician attaches several dime-sized electrodes to different parts of your body. The electrodes detect physiological changes that occur during the night. The information is fed to a **polysomnograph** (*poly*, "many"; *somni*, "sleep"; *graph*, "written or drawn"), an instrument that amplifies signals associated with the physiological changes and produces a record of them on paper, computer disk, or tape.

The technician attaches several electrodes to your scalp to measure brain waves. Two more electrodes, one near each eye, provide data for the *electro-oculograph* (*EOG*), which detects eye movements. An electrode under your chin measures muscle activity; your heart rate is monitored by an electrocardiograph (EKG). When other devices that measure breathing, hormone levels, oxygen in the blood, and temperature are added, you look and feel like a robot.

You are ushered into a soundproof room, where every movement and sound you make will be recorded. Apprehensive about possible equipment malfunction, you find fearful thoughts running through your mind. The *first-night effect* is likely to make your sleep unlike that of a night at home; for example, you are likely to have a delay in the onset of sleep (Hirshkowitz, 2002). As a consequence, researchers usually discard the first night's data. The next night, having adapted to your new surroundings, you sleep comfortably.

# The Stages of Sleep

Although it seems that sleep is a gradual process, the EEG tells a different tale. One second you are awake, and a second later you are asleep (see Figure 4-4). During a typical night you pass through five stages of sleep: REM sleep and four other stages of sleep known as Stages 1, 2, 3, and 4. During each stage of sleep, a distinctive "signature" of brain waves appears on the EEG record (Carskadon & Dement, 2005) (see Figure 4-5). Let's take a closer look at these stages.

**NREM Sleep.** You begin sleep with Stage 1 and then progress to Stages 2, 3, and 4 (Carskadon & Dement, 2005). At each step the task of being roused from sleep becomes more difficult. These four stages are known collectively as **non-REM (NREM)** sleep. You typically spend a few minutes in Stage 1 (see Figure 4-6), a transitional phase between wakefulness and sleep; Stage 2 sleep occupies about 50% of an adult's sleep. The EEG heralds the arrival of Stage 2 with the appearance of *sleep spindles*, bursts of activity on the EEG record, and *K complexes*. These large deflections in the waveform occur about every 2 minutes, apparently serving as built-in vigilance that keeps us poised to awaken if necessary. What is it that leads to a K complex? The answer is certain sounds or other external or internal stimuli. For example, whisper your friend's name during Stage 2 sleep and K complexes appear on the EEG record (Harvard Medical School, 2001) (see Figure 4-5). Finally, you descend to Stages 3 and 4, which together are known as **slow-wave sleep** or *delta sleep*. Waking someone from slow-wave sleep is quite difficult; people awakened from this deep sleep are likely to be disoriented and groggy. During deep sleep, your breathing becomes more regular, your blood pressure falls, and

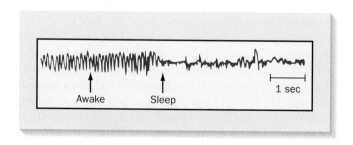

Awake    Sleep    1 sec

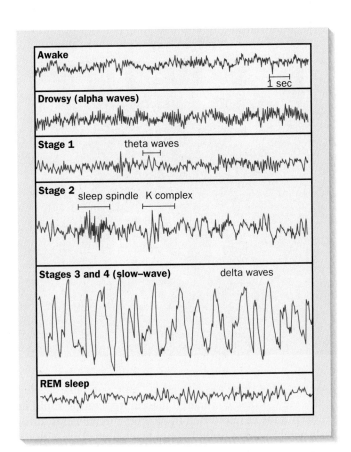

**FIGURE 4-5** EEG markings from a recording made in a sleep laboratory. Each stage of sleep has its own identifying marks on the EEG record.

**Source:** Havri (1992).

your pulse rate slows to about 20 to 30% of its waking rate (Harvard Medical School, 2001). Delta waves first appear in Stage 3, in which they account for 20 to 50% of the brain waves. By Stage 4 sleep, delta waves make up more than 50% of the brain waves. Sleep patterns may vary from one person to another but generally progress as outlined in Figure 4-6 (Carskadon & Dement, 2005). As you can see, from the deep sleep of Stages 3 and 4 a person ascends through lighter NREM stages and then enters a dramatically different stage of sleep called *REM*.

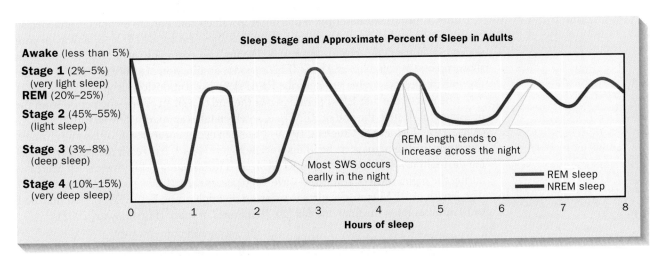

**FIGURE 4-6** The stages of sleep throughout the night. The cycle of sleep follows a rather consistent pattern throughout the night and from person to person. Each sleep cycle lasts approximately 90 to 100 minutes and consists of a series of NREM stages followed by REM sleep. Most slow-wave sleep occurs during the early part of the night; most REM sleep occurs later. REM periods generally become longer as sleep time increases.

**FIGURE 4-7** PET scans of the brain during REM sleep (left), NREM sleep (right), and waking hours (bottom). The colors red and yellow indicate higher levels of metabolic activity. Note the similarity in the level of activity during REM sleep and waking hours.

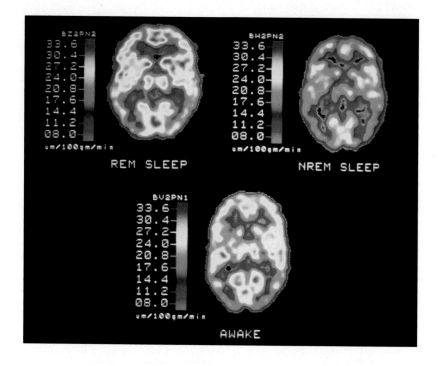

**rapid eye movement (REM) sleep**
Sleep stage characterized by rapid eye movements, dreams, high levels of brain activity, and muscle paralysis

**REM Sleep.** At one time sleep was viewed as "time out," like turning off your car's motor; however, this view is now considered inaccurate. During **rapid eye movement (REM) sleep**—a sleep stage characterized by rapid eye movements, dreams, high brain activity, and muscle paralysis—the brain is more like a parked car with its motor racing. Signs of activity are obvious: Heart rate and respiration are more variable than they are during NREM stages; brain temperature is elevated (Martin, 2002). The sympathetic nervous system is twice as active during REM sleep as when you are awake (Harvard Medical School, 2001). Men have penile erections; women experience increased blood flow in the genital area, and their nipples are erect (Martin, 2002). These indications of sexual arousal are not related to erotic dreams, however. The EEG record of a person in REM sleep resembles that of an awake person (review Figure 4-5). Intense activity of neurons throughout the brain make a PET scan (see Chapter 2) look like a lit Christmas tree; brain temperature increases as more blood flows to the brain (see Figure 4-7). As we saw in Figure 4-6, adults spend 20 to 25% of the night in this supercharged stage of sleep.

Let's return to our description of a night in a sleep lab. The lab technician attached an electrode to your chin to detect muscle activity. Why? During REM sleep, activity in your skeletal (voluntary) muscles is suppressed, leaving you essentially paralyzed; this paralysis shows up first in your chin and neck. This curious combination of an active brain with inactive muscles led researchers to describe REM sleep as "paradoxical sleep" (Martin, 2002).

The end of the first REM period marks the end of a sleep cycle—the period from the beginning of sleep to the end of REM sleep—which takes approximately 90 to 100 minutes (Allen, 1997; Dement & Vaughan, 1999). The sleep cycle repeats itself, with some changes, four to six times a night in most adults (review Figure 4-6). Changes in the sleep cycle during the night involve slow-wave and REM sleep. The amount of slow-wave sleep decreases during the night; most of your slow-wave sleep occurs early (Carskadon & Dement, 2005). The length of REM episodes increases during the night: The first REM period may be 5 to 10 minutes long; the final one can last 30 minutes or more (Hirshkowitz, 2002).

## Differences in Individual Sleep Patterns

As you can see in Figure 4-8, the amount of time people sleep varies with age. During the first week of life, most infants sleep about 16 hours a day; some newborns, however, sleep as little as 11 hours and others more than 20. These large differences are likely due to genetic factors; sleep length is more similar in identical twins than in fraternal twins (Heath, Kendler, Eaves, & Martin, 1990).

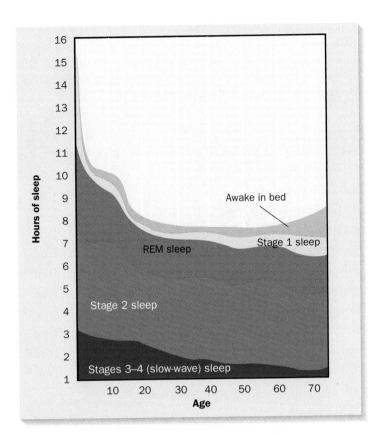

**FIGURE 4-8** Sleep length over the lifespan. Sleep length drops rapidly from infancy to adolescence and then changes at a much slower rate.

**Source:** American Medical Association (1984).

Sleep length decreases with age through adolescence, but it does not change much from early adulthood to the 70s. Should you worry if you don't sleep for 7 or 8 hours, as the average adult does? When it comes to sleep, one size does not fit all. How do you assess your own need for sleep? The key question to ask is, "Are you refreshed after you awaken?" For an increasing number of people, the answer is no.

The *multiple sleep latency test* is a sensitive indicator of a person's level of sleepiness. With this technique, you try to fall asleep every 2 hours during normal waking hours. If you fall asleep, a researcher will wake you and repeat the request later. Falling asleep easily is a sign that your daily amount of sleep does not satisfy your need. Numerous such observations have convinced some sleep experts that "most people no longer know what it feels like to be fully alert" (Coleman, 1995, p. 67). Consider the following: Prior to Thomas Edison's invention of the light bulb, most adults slept 10 hours each night. During the course of the next century, the average hours of sleep per night decreased to approximately 8 (National Commission on Sleep Disorders Research, 1993). The National Sleep Foundation (2005c) survey of sleep length reveals that sleep length continues to decline: 40% of adults reported that they slept less than 7 hours per night on weekdays. On weekends, 25% got fewer than 7 hours of sleep (see Figure 4-9). What's more, many adolescents are not getting an adequate amount of sleep, which has been implicated as one factor in the increased rate of car accidents among young people (Carskadon, 2002).

Sleep researcher James Maas (1998) sees serious problems in this declining sleep length. "The third of your life that you should spend sleeping has profound effects on the other two-thirds of your life, in terms of alertness,

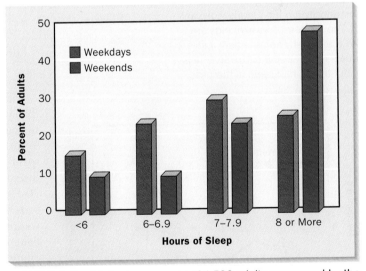

**FIGURE 4-9** A telephone survey of 1,506 adults sponsored by the National Sleep Foundation indicates that the amount of sleep adults have on weekdays and weekends differs. The increased sleep on weekends suggests that we are attempting to overcome the "sleep debt" that occurs primarily during weekdays.

**Source:** National Sleep Foundation (2005c).

energy, mood, body weight, perception, memory, thinking, reaction time, productivity, performance, communication skills, creativity, safety, and good health" (p. 6). There is a growing recognition that an epidemic of sleepiness is affecting us (Brink, 2000; Dement, 1999; Maas, 1998). You can assess you own level of continuing sleep deprivation by completing the following questionnaire in the Hands On activity.

## Hands On

Here is a chance to assess your level of sleep deprivation. Please indicate true or false for the following statements:

| | | | |
|---|---|---|---|
| 1. I often fall asleep watching TV. | | True ○ | False ○ |
| 2. I often feel drowsy while driving. | | True ○ | False ○ |
| 3. I have dark circles around my eyes. | | True ○ | False ○ |
| 4. I often need a nap to get through the day. | | True ○ | False ○ |
| 5. I often fall asleep while relaxing after dinner. | | True ○ | False ○ |
| 6. I often sleep extra hours on weekend mornings. | | True ○ | False ○ |
| 7. I have trouble concentrating and remembering. | | True ○ | False ○ |
| 8. It's a struggle for me to get out of bed in the morning. | | True ○ | False ○ |
| 9. I feel tired, irritable, and stressed out during the week. | | True ○ | False ○ |
| 10. I often fall asleep within five minutes of getting into bed. | | True ○ | False ○ |
| 11. I often fall asleep in boring meetings or lectures in warm rooms. | | True ○ | False ○ |
| 12. I often fall asleep after heavy meals or after a low dose of alcohol. | | True ○ | False ○ |
| 13. I need an alarm clock in order to wake up at the appropriate time. | | True ○ | False ○ |
| 14. I feel slow with critical thinking, problem solving, and being creative. | | True ○ | False ○ |
| 15. Weekday mornings I hit the snooze button several times to get more sleep. | | True ○ | False ○ |

If you answered true to 3 or more of these 15 items, you are probably not getting enough sleep.

**Source:** Maas (1998).

**FIGURE 4-10** Number of awakenings during the night. The number of awakenings increases dramatically among elderly individuals. The numerous awakenings are one reason why some elderly individuals report that their sleep is less restful than it had been in the past.

**Source:** Hartmann (1987).

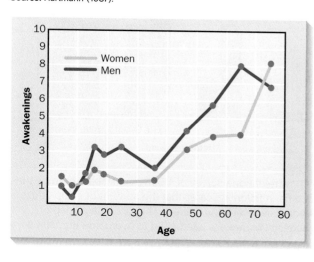

Contrary to common belief, older people do not need less sleep than younger adults. They do, however, awaken more often during the night; consequently, their sleep is more fragmented (see Figure 4-10). The *sleep efficiency index*—the proportion of bedtime actually spent sleeping—reveals what happens to sleep as we grow older. Sleep efficiency is above 95% for men and women through their 30s. It drops to about 80% among people in their 70s for two reasons. First, the deep sleep of Stage 4 is either markedly reduced or completely absent. Second, elderly people spend more time in the lighter stages of sleep, which makes them more susceptible to awakening. Most adults have just one period of sleep every 24 hours; babies have six to eight sleep periods per day. The next time you hear someone say that he or she "slept like a baby," point out that a baby's sleep consists of several short episodes of sleep. Over time those short episodes join together (see Figure 4-11); by 6 months of age, about 80% of babies sleep through the night (Webb, 1992).

Toddlers are likely to have two episodes of sleep per day (night sleep and an afternoon nap). Most children stop napping when they attend elementary school, yet as many as 50% of college students take naps either every day or occasionally to compensate for lost nighttime sleep. In addition to college students, many other healthy adults nap; the frequency of napping increases with age in adults. Many adults nap once or more per week—most often when their night sleep is inadequate, as is often the case when one works night or rotating shifts (Ohayon & Zulley, 1999). Although some nappers experience *sleep inertia*, a temporary feeling of impairment that follows awakening, naps typically improve mood and performance (Hayashi, Watanabe, & Hori, 1999). One caution: Naps of approximately 20 minutes seem best; when the nap reaches 45 minutes or more, you are likely to reach the deeper stages of sleep and can wake up feeling rather groggy.

One type of nap, the *siesta*—a 1- to 2-hour nap, usually taken in the afternoon following a noon meal—is, in part, a culturally determined sleep practice. The practice developed as a way to avoid the hottest part of the day in tropical climates such as the Mediterranean countries of Spain and Italy, as well as parts of Central and South America. After a siesta, people return to work during the cooler hours of the day. Most people who take a siesta reduce their amount of nighttime sleep; thus the combination of nighttime sleep and a siesta is within the average range. An added advantage of siestas is that they counteract the body's normal postlunch dip in alertness (Foster & Kreitzman, 2004). The increasing rate of worldwide industrialization, however, has reduced the frequency of this practice (Kribbs, 1993).

## The Functions of Sleep

If you live to be 75 years old, you will have spent one-third of your life (about 220,000 hours) sleeping. But why do we sleep? Attempts to answer this question have yielded results that are controversial, so the answer remains elusive (Rechtschaffen, 1998). Common sense tells us that we sleep to restore our fatigued bodies; however, this notion is difficult to reconcile with certain facts. If you spend most of the day in bed, you will still sleep that night even though your energy expenditure and the "wear and tear" on your body have been kept to a minimum. Sleeping after spending the entire day in bed reflects the operation of the built-in circadian sleep–wake cycle, which causes sleepiness at about the same time every day. Starvation, surgery, and other physical demands, however, sometimes lead to increases in slow-wave sleep. This deep sleep is the stage during which rest and repair are likely to occur.

A common approach to answering the question "Why do we sleep?" is to deprive organisms of sleep and see what happens. The results are sometimes dramatic: Sleep deprivation leads to death in rats (Siegel, 2003). These animals lose weight despite increases in food consumption, which suggests that they are experiencing excessive heat loss. Some humans suffer from a rare degenerative brain disease called *fatal familial insomnia*, which leads to death after several months. However, it is not clear if these deaths are due to the brain damage or to sleep deprivation.

Efforts to sleep deprive humans have been undertaken with caution, yet they have yielded interesting and perhaps surprising results. In January 1959, a 32-year-old disc jockey named Peter Tripp decided to go without sleep for 200 hours as a publicity stunt to raise money for charity. Undaunted by experts who warned of the risk of death, Tripp persevered. When he found it extremely difficult to stay awake after 135 hours, he turned to stimulants (amphetamines) that altered his perceptions: Specks of dust became insects; a bureau drawer burst into flames. Yet he hosted his show, "Your Hits of the Week," between 5 and 8 P.M. each day without giving any hint of what he was enduring. After 201 hours without sleep, he slept for 13 hours; the only symptom he experienced as a result of his ordeal was a slight depression that lasted for a few months.

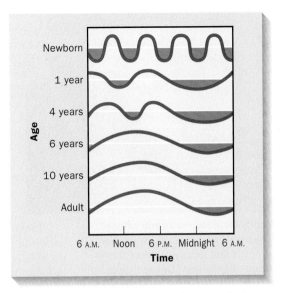

**FIGURE 4-11**  Sleep periods (shaded time periods) at different ages. As most parents know, newborns have several periods of sleep that are spread across the 24-hour day, with no differentiation between night and day. These sleep periods quickly consolidate into one long period, primarily at night, plus a nap. Most adults have a single long period of sleep, usually during the night; however, some adults nap (not shown in this figure), thus exhibiting a pattern that is common at a younger age.

**Source:** Moorcroft (1993).

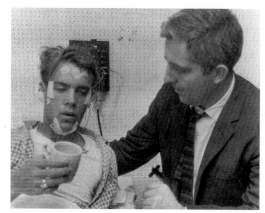

Randy Gardner, who went without sleep for 264 hours, is shown here after his first recovery sleep. Sleep researcher William Dement, who monitored Gardner's sleep deprivation, looks on. Despite going for 11 days without sleep, Randy slept only 15 hours on the first night after his then record-setting period of sleep deprivation.

In 1964, Randy Gardner, a 17-year-old California high school student, along with two of his friends, submitted an entry on sleep deprivation to a high school science fair. The goal was for Randy to go without sleep for 264 hours. Gardner used no stimulants—not even coffee—during his 11 days without sleep (Gulevich, Dement, & Johnson, 1966). Going without sleep for such a lengthy time was not easy. On the second day, Randy had difficulty focusing his eyes, and as a result he had to stop watching television. On subsequent nights he experienced memory lapses, difficulty concentrating, slurred speech, hallucinations, and delusions. On the ninth day, his eyes drifted independently from side to side! On the first night, after setting what was then a world record for sleep deprivation, he slept less than 15 hours, and, as was widely reported, he suffered no long-term physical problems (Coren, 1996).

Peter Tripp and Randy Gardner extended the limits of sleep deprivation without suffering any apparent serious *long-term* consequences. In fact, "systematic studies of total sleep deprivation in humans revealed no permanent effects and few profound deficits" (Anch, Browman, Mitler, & Walsh, 1988, p. 9). Although Tripp and Gardner *appeared* to go without sleep for several days, we now know that total sleep deprivation is almost impossible except in rare neurological disorders such as fatal familial insomnia, mentioned previously. Sleep deprivation does lead to lapses of attention, forgetfulness, and impaired performance. Why? The answer seems to be *microsleeps,* which are brief episodes of sleep (up to 30 seconds) that intrude on wakefulness. As the period of sleep deprivation gets longer, microsleeps become longer and more frequent; thus, *total* sleep deprivation does not occur for very long in humans. Although microsleeps do not compensate for all of the lost sleep, they reveal how powerful the urge to sleep can be when we try to deny it for extended periods.

Sleep may have developed in different species in ways that increased their chances of survival (Webb, 1992). We know that all species sleep, although some may postpone it for long periods of time. In some species, such as marine mammals, sleep occurs in one hemisphere of the brain at a time (one hemisphere sleeps while the other is awake) (Zepelin, Siegel, & Tobler, 2005). The range of sleep needs among all species is impressive: An opossum sleeps 18 hours a day; an elephant can get by on 3 hours. Whether a species adapts best by sleeping a lot or a little may depend on two factors: the animal's vulnerability to predators and its need for food. Animals that are at great risk from predators must be alert because periods of inactivity put them in grave danger (Webb, 1988). Lions sleep for 2 or 3 days after consuming a meal of gazelle or antelope, possibly because they have so few enemies (Hobson, 1989).

Another factor in sleep length is an organism's size. Bigger animals (elephants, giraffes, large primates such as humans) sleep less than smaller organisms. In general, smaller animals have higher metabolic rates and higher brain and body temperatures. Higher metabolism generates *free radicals*—chemicals that can damage and even kill cells. The damage can be dealt with by replacing damaged cells with new ones, but most brain regions do not produce significant numbers of new brain cells after birth. Lower metabolic rates and lower brain temperature in NREM sleep may provide an opportunity to deal with any damage done during waking. This *cell-repair hypothesis* could explain NREM sleep but not REM sleep. Why? The brain cannot repair itself when it is very active, as it is during REM sleep (Siegel, 2003).

Researchers have also deprived people of REM sleep by waking them whenever they entered this stage. When REM-deprived people were allowed to sleep without interruption on subsequent nights, they exhibited an increased percentage of REM sleep, a phenomenon known as the **REM rebound.** The body apparently needs REM sleep because it attempts to recapture some if it is lost. But demonstrating a need does not tell us what purpose it serves. "The mystery exposed by the discovery of REM sleep remains. We do not know the biologic need that initiates REM sleep" (Siegel, 2005, p. 131).

The release of neurotransmitters called *monoamines* (norepinephrine, serotonin, and histamine) ceases during REM sleep (Siegel, 2003). Brain cells that make monoamines get a heavy-duty workout during the day. If these neurotransmitters were active all of the

**REM rebound**
An increase in the typical amount of REM sleep following reduction of REM sleep owing to sleep deprivation or the use of certain drugs that reduce REM sleep

time, receptors for them could become desensitized. Cessation of monoamine release during REM sleep allows these receptor systems to rest and regain full sensitivity.

## Myth or Science

Evidence suggesting that memories may be consolidated during REM sleep leads us to ask this question: "Can we learn new material while asleep?" The popular press has heralded sleep learning as an easy way to learn. Imagine playing a tape of course material while you sleep and waking the next morning with the material in your memory. Unfortunately, laboratory evidence reveals that although we may process some sensory information during sleep, as when we awaken to the sound of a fire alarm or a crying baby, we do not retain information for later recall. Some people who appeared to retain information from their sleep were actually awake, based on EEG records, during the playing of the tape. Thus sleep learning appears to be a myth born of wishful thinking (Badia, 1993).

Another possibility is that REM sleep might play a role in memory consolidation; however, the evidence for this function is weak and contradictory (Siegel, 2003). For example, people who have brain damage that prevents REM sleep have normal or even improved memory. Many drugs used to treat depression reduce or eliminate REM sleep, yet there are no reports of memory deficits attributable to such treatments (Siegel, 2005). Although sleep deprivation affects concentration and performance, REM deprivation after alert learning does not appear to affect retention of new information. In fact, learning ability across species is unrelated to REM duration. In humans, there is no relation between REM and IQ or school performance.

One additional possibility is that REM sleep may serve to provide external stimulation that leads to neuronal development, especially in animals that have delayed sensory development. There is a clue in the fact that half of a newborn's 16 hours of sleep per day is spent in REM sleep; premature babies spend even more than half of their sleep in REM sleep (Roffwarg, Muzio, & Dement, 1966). Why do babies spend so much time in REM sleep? REM sleep—a period of high activity in the brain—may provide babies with the stimulation they cannot provide for themselves. This stimulation may be necessary for brain development.

# Sleep Problems

The increase in the number of clinics that diagnose and treat sleep disorders attests to the fact that sleep is not always peaceful and restful. According to the National Sleep Foundation's (2005b) *Sleep in America* poll, 26% of adults said they experienced "a good night's sleep" only a few nights a month, rarely, or never. Twenty-four percent of the respondents said they had a good night's sleep a few nights a week. Sleep disorders range from annoying to life-threatening and can be divided into three categories: insomnia, hypersomnias, and parasomnias.

**Insomnia.** "I couldn't sleep at all last night; I was tossing and turning." If this condition sounds familiar, you are not alone. **Insomnia** (*in*, "no," *somnus*, "sleep"), the most common sleep complaint, is defined as inadequate or poor-quality sleep characterized by one or more of the following: difficulty initiating sleep (called *sleep-onset insomnia*), difficulty maintaining sleep, or waking too early in the morning (National Institutes of Health, 2005). Sleep specialists also classify insomnia as either *acute* or *chronic*. Short-term or acute insomnia lasts up to a month and is usually due to temporary situations such as life stress, disruption of circadian rhythms owing to jet lag or nighttime work, job loss, or relationship problems. Most people fall asleep within 15 minutes after their head hits the pillow (Hirshkowitz, 2002); others toss and turn. This type of insomnia is usually associated with stressful events and often disappears when those events end. For example, you may toss and turn the night before an important test or interview, but the next night you probably will have no trouble sleeping. Long-term or chronic insomnia lasts for a month or longer and

**insomnia**
Complaints of difficulty falling asleep, staying asleep, frequent awakenings, or poor-quality sleep

WHEN HE WAS A CHILD, BOB'S PARENTS REPEATEDLY TOLD HIM TO "TRY HARDER" TO FALL ASLEEP. AT AGE 50, HE FINALLY REALIZES THAT WAS NOT VERY GOOD ADVICE.

**Source:** From *Eye on Psi Chi Newsletter* 2, no. 3 (Spring 1998). Reprinted with permission.

can be secondary to medical, physical, or psychological conditions, another sleep disorder, or substances (such as too much caffeine) and medications (National Sleep Foundation, 2005a).

Over-the-counter (nonprescription) sleep aids such as Nytol and Sominex are frequently used to treat insomnia. Most of these drugs contain an antihistamine that causes drowsiness, which can extend into waking hours and affect our ability to drive. What's more, sleep expert William Dement notes, "Most over-the-counter 'sleep aids' have no proven efficacy" (Dement & Vaughan, 1999, p. 163).

A number of prescription drugs are available to treat insomnia. Although sleeping pills do not cure insomnia, they do provide relief from the symptoms. The use of sedative or hypnotic drugs to treat insomnia has declined, however, as a result of growing recognition of their side effects and other problems. For example, if you use them every night, they may lose their effectiveness in a few weeks as your body adjusts to them. Sleeping pills that reduce REM sleep can cause a REM rebound when you stop taking them. During succeeding nights, insomnia may return along with nightmares produced by the additional REM sleep. More recently developed drugs such as Ambien (Zolipidem) have advantages over other drugs used to treat insomnia. Ambien works quickly (often after 30 minutes), leaves the body typically within 5 hours (Harvard Medical School, 2001), and has little or no potential to become addictive (Dement & Vaughan, 1999).

Psychological treatments such as relaxation and stimulus control are quite effective in reducing sleep latency (the amount of time required to fall asleep) and increasing sleep time (Murtagh & Greenwood, 1995). The *stimulus control method*—used for sleep-onset insomnia—is a set of rules designed to establish better sleeping habits. People with sleep-onset insomnia are instructed to lie down to sleep only when sleepy, not to use the bed for anything except sleep and sex, and to get out of bed if unable to sleep (Bootzin, Epstein, & Wood, 1991). These suggestions are also elements of good sleep hygiene; in fact, the best way to deal with insomnia is to practice good sleep hygiene. For example, maintain a regular sleep schedule and avoid caffeine. Table 4-1 lists several suggestions to help you sleep better.

## TABLE 4-1

### Suggestions for Good Sleep

1. Maintain regular sleep and waking times (even on weekends) to establish a consistent circadian rhythm.
2. Avoid extreme temperatures and noise. Reduce the amount of light entering the room.
3. Take time to "wind down" before you head off to sleep; establish relaxing presleep rituals such as soft music or a warm bath.
4. If you are unable to fall asleep within 15 to 20 minutes, get up and go to another room. Stay up as long as 30 minutes, then return to the bedroom to sleep. If you still cannot fall asleep, get up again. The goal is to associate the bed with falling asleep quickly.
5. Don't take your worries to bed. If you must worry, set aside some time earlier in the day. Don't make the bed the place to agonize over your problems.
6. Avoid alcohol, caffeine, and nicotine. Large doses of alcohol disrupt sleep. Caffeine and nicotine are stimulants, which cause arousal rather than sleep. What's more, chronic use of sleeping pills can be ineffective and even detrimental to good sleep.
7. Eat light snacks that may help you sleep, especially if they contain L-tryptophan, which is found in milk, cheese, and other foods.
8. Exercise during the day promotes slow-wave sleep, but do not exercise within 3 hours of bedtime because its arousing effect can delay sleep.

**Hypersomnias.**    Although our culture does not recognize excessive daytime sleepiness as a serious complaint, it can be a symptom of a serious medical disorder. **Hypersomnias** are sleep disorders characterized by excessive daytime sleepiness. They include narcolepsy and sleep apnea.

**Narcolepsy.**    Imagine that you feel sleepy every day. Your eyes droop as you struggle to remain awake, but sleep wins and your head plunges to your chest. Excessive daytime sleepiness, regardless of the amount of nighttime sleep, is one of the symptoms of **narcolepsy** (*narce*, "numbing"; *lepsis*, "attack"), a lifelong sleep disorder that afflicts .05% of the population, or 1 in every 2,000 people (Dement & Vaughan, 1999). Daytime sleepiness can be caused by many factors, so diagnosis in a sleep disorders clinic is needed to determine its cause. Narcolepsy usually begins in adolescence or early adulthood; however, 10 to 15 years may elapse before a correct diagnosis is made (National Institute of Neurological Disorders and Stroke, 2005).

Now imagine a friend who suddenly collapses to the floor while telling you a joke. Your friend has just experienced one of the symptoms of narcolepsy—*cataplexy* (*cata*, "down"; *plexis*, "strike"), a sudden loss of muscle tone often triggered by a strong emotion such as anger or even laughter. Attacks of cataplexy range from partial muscle weakness to an almost complete loss of muscle tone that lasts for a few seconds to a minute. One victim continually fell asleep while in high school and college. Repeated bouts of sleep led to 15 automobile accidents by age 25; fortunately, no one was seriously injured (Fritz, 1993). Two other symptoms of narcolepsy are *hypnagogic hallucinations*—intense, vivid dreams that occur at the beginning of sleep—and paralysis at the beginning of sleep or upon awakening.

### Psychological Detective

The symptoms of narcolepsy share a common connection. Use what you have learned about sleep to suggest what is wrong with the sleep of people who have narcolepsy that could cause these symptoms. You need to analyze each of the symptoms to find the connection. Write down your answer before reading further.

Sleep researchers have found that narcolepsy occurs when REM sleep intrudes into wakefulness. A review of the symptoms reveals how they are related to REM sleep. For example, the loss of muscle tone in cataplexy is consistent with the paralysis of skeletal muscles that occurs during REM sleep. The exact mechanism that causes REM sleep to spill over into waking time is not yet understood, although new research suggests that the medial medulla in the hindbrain may play a key role in this disorder because it suppresses muscle activity during REM sleep. In a study of narcoleptic dogs, the medial medulla was found to fire at high rates during waking. Thus, "a group of neurons that is supposed to be active only during REM sleep to suppress muscle tone and protect us from the elaborate motor programs that accompany our dreams is being triggered during waking" (Siegel, 2000, p. 78). One marker for the development of narcolepsy seems to be a brain chemical called *hypocretin*. Most cases of narcolepsy are caused by the loss of neurons (in the hypothalamus) that produce hypocretin, a peptide that plays a role in promoting wakefulness (Mignot, 2005; Siegel, 2005). Although there is no cure for narcolepsy, stimulant drugs are used to reduce the sleepiness. The FDA has approved a drug, *modafinil* (Provigil), for sleepiness, which is also prescribed for sleep problems related to shift work. In addition, antidepressant drugs can control the cataplexy (National Institute of Neurological Disorders and Stroke, 2005). Scheduled naps may reduce the severity of the symptoms of narcolepsy, especially the sleepiness (Littner et al., 2001; Rogers, Aldrich, & Lin, 2001).

**Sleep Apnea.**    For years, Reverend Allen lacked energy and slept so poorly that he rarely awakened feeling refreshed. After retiring from the ministry he hoped to get

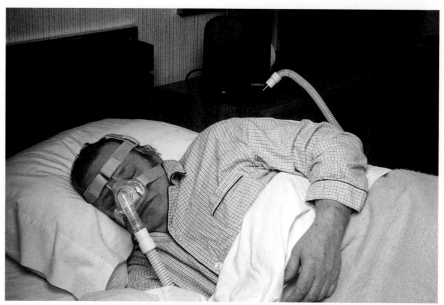

Sleep apnea can be treated with continuous positive airway pressure (CPAP). The mask over the sufferer's face is connected to a compressor that maintains a steady flow of air to keep the airway from collapsing.

**sleep apnea**
Sleep disorder characterized by pauses in breathing during sleep; most prevalent in older overweight men

**parasomnias**
Sleep disorders, other than insomnia and hypersomnia, which occur more frequently in children and often disappear without treatment

plenty of rest and feel better, but this was not to be. He began to lose his coordination and found that walking and writing were difficult. Although he had been treated for heart problems and other symptoms, no definitive cause had been identified. One day his wife was reading a magazine article that described symptoms of sleep apnea; they seemed to fit her husband perfectly, and he agreed. They spent the next few months in a futile search for help until someone put them in touch with a sleep disorders clinic in another city. By this time, his symptoms had become more serious; he hoped he could make it to one more Christmas. His clinic appointment was set for a few days before Christmas, but he was so frail that his wife thought about canceling because she was afraid he might die on the trip to the clinic. He was determined to keep the appointment. The sleep specialist immediately suspected severe sleep apnea and rearranged his schedule so that Reverend Allen could be tested that evening. The testing revealed sleep apnea. With treatment he experienced a new beginning. A man who had been near death and was barely able to shuffle across his living room was now walking three-quarters of a mile every day (Pascualy & Soest, 2000).

**Sleep apnea** (from the Greek word for "absence of breathing") is a serious, potentially life-threatening condition in which the flow of air to the lungs stops for at least 10 seconds and may not start again for a minute or longer. Estimates of the number of people who have sleep apnea run as high as 20 to 25 million (Pascualy & Soest, 2000). The risk of developing sleep apnea is higher among men and obese people (Brock & Shucard, 1994). Even mild cases are associated with an increased risk of cardiovascular disease (Meoli et al., 2001). Apnea victims may awaken hundreds of times a night, and although they become accustomed to this pattern, the repeated awakenings leave them extremely tired and often complaining of insomnia. Consequently, excessive daytime sleepiness is one of the key symptoms that can suggest a diagnosis (National Institute of Neurological Disorders and Stroke, 2005). Despite the serious health consequences associated with sleep apnea, at least 80% of all cases are probably unrecognized (Young, Evans, Finn, & Palta, 1997).

There are two forms of sleep apnea: *central* and *obstructive*. Central sleep apnea (the less common form) occurs when the brain fails to send the appropriate signals to the muscles for breathing. Obstructive sleep apnea (which Reverend Allen experienced) is far more common and occurs when air cannot flow into or out of the person's nose or mouth despite continued efforts to breathe. After going without oxygen for as long as 90 seconds, the brain signals an emergency wake-up to fill the lungs with air.

Some cases of sleep apnea respond to changes in sleep position or weight loss; in other cases, tongue-retaining devices or jaw retainers may be used to keep the airway free of obstruction. A very effective treatment for apnea is *continuous positive airway pressure* (*CPAP*, pronounced "see-pap"). At night a mask placed over the patient's nose is connected by a tube to a compressor that maintains a flow of pressured air to the lungs to prevent airway collapse. In other cases, surgical methods, including laser procedures, are used; for example, soft tissue at the back of the throat may be shrunk or removed to enlarge the breathing passage.

**Parasomnias.** The **parasomnias** are undesirable and/or distressing sleep behaviors other than insomnia and hypersomnia that occur exclusively during sleep or that are worsened by sleep. This diverse group of disorders ranges from bedwetting to nightmares. They occur more frequently in children than in adults, perhaps reflecting the immaturity of a child's nervous system. Although many parasomnias disappear over time without treatment, some are potentially dangerous and even deadly.

**Sleepwalking.** As many as 20% of the population have experienced one or more episodes of **sleepwalking.** Most episodes occur in children, and a susceptibility to sleepwalking runs in families (Hobson & Silvestri, 1999). Although sleepwalkers walk about with their arms stretched out in front of them in the movies, a typical real-life episode may involve merely sitting up in bed. When a sleepwalker does get out of bed, he or she may stumble about in a disoriented state and turn on lights, eat cat food sandwiches, or walk through open doors or windows. The eyes are likely to be open, but the mind is at least partly closed for the moment: The person's EEG shows an unusual mixture of the brain waves associated with deep sleep and relaxed wakefulness. Sleepwalkers generally return to normal sleep in their own bed with no recall the next morning.

Here is some helpful advice for parents of sleepwalkers: Remove any electrical cords that might cause tripping; locate the sleepwalker's bedroom on the first floor; and lock windows and doors. In most cases, sleepwalking occurs for a few years and then disappears without treatment.

## Psychological Detective

Sleepwalkers can engage in some odd behaviors if they ramble about the house. Does this mean they are acting out a dream? Give this question some thought, and write down an answer before reading further.

Because the skeletal muscles are paralyzed during REM sleep, sleepwalkers do not act out their dreams. Instead, sleepwalking occurs during Stage 4 sleep and hence is more likely to occur during the first third of the night (Keefauver & Guilleminault, 1994; review Figure 4-6).

Sleepwalking is closely associated with slow-wave sleep, but another sleep disorder that resembles sleepwalking occurs during REM sleep. *REM sleep behavior disorder (RBD)* is a syndrome of injurious or disruptive behavior that emerges during REM sleep. The paralysis of muscles that normally occurs during REM sleep does not occur in people with this disorder; consequently, they are capable of "acting out their dreams." RBD occurs primarily in older men, with an average age of onset in the 50s (Mahowald & Schenck, 2003; Schenck, Hurwitz, & Mahowald, 1993). The behavior may consist of sitting up, jumping out of bed, yelling, running, and punching, which frequently results in injuries to the victim and spouse. Approximately 85% of people with this disorder hurt themselves, and about half injure their bed partner (Harvard Medical School, 2001). One suspected cause of RBD is subtle age-related changes in the brain that affect the mechanism that usually suppresses voluntary muscle activity during REM sleep. Although the symptoms of RBD can be treated effectively with mild tranquilizers, accumulating evidence suggests that the disorder is often a forerunner of degenerative neurological conditions such as Parkinson's disease and several other forms of dementia (Hirshkowitz, 2002; Mahowald & Schenck, 2003).

**Enuresis.** Sleep specialists do not consider **enuresis** (bedwetting) a disorder unless the child is at least 5 years old (Friman & Warzak, 1990). It is viewed as a disorder of arousal: The child has an elevated arousal threshold, which means it is difficult to awaken after the bedwetting episode. Like other childhood sleep disorders, enuresis probably reflects an immature nervous system that could run in families but is expected to improve with maturation of the CNS. Most bedwetting occurs in the first half of the night during NREM sleep; it has no relation to any particular NREM stages (Bandla & Splaingard, 2004). Drug treatments can pose health risks and are often ineffective (Friman &

**sleepwalking**
A parasomnia that occurs during Stage 4 sleep, usually in children; most often consists of sitting up in bed

**enuresis**
Bedwetting, a sleep disorder that occurs primarily in children and is considered a disorder of arousal that is likely to improve with maturation of the CNS

Warzak, 1990; Toren et al., 2001). Other approaches to dealing with enuresis include waking the child periodically throughout the night and rewarding the child for sleeping through the night without wetting the bed. A common treatment is the "pad and buzzer," or urine alarm (Houts, 1991). A urine sensor, either placed under the bedsheets or sewn into the child's underpants, is connected to a buzzer that sounds when the first drops of urine fall on it. The resultant awakenings make the child aware of bladder pressure. Once children have gained this awareness, they awaken spontaneously before beginning to urinate. Most children outgrow enuresis, as they do sleep terrors and sleepwalking, which suggests that all three are related to delayed maturation.

**Sleep Terrors and Nightmares.**    **Sleep terrors** (also called *night terrors*) are intensely frightening experiences that begin during Stage 4 sleep. About 5% of children between ages 2 and 5 experience sleep terrors; the disorder usually disappears as the child matures. The first sign of a sleep terror is often a blood-curdling scream, usually followed by sitting up in bed. The accompanying physiological arousal is remarkable: The heart rate can triple in a minute, breathing is labored, and the sleeper becomes soaked with perspiration. Children are usually unable to recall the experience, which often terrifies their parents. By contrast, adult victims of night terrors (who have the experience very rarely) tend to recall the event in detail.

**Nightmares** are frightening dreams that occur during REM sleep (Zadra & Donderi, 2000); however, they are mild compared with sleep terrors (see Table 4-2). Children are most susceptible to nightmares because they spend so much time in REM sleep; the rate of occurrence may be as high as 50% in children ages 3 to 6 (Hobson & Silvestri, 1999). In some cases, the anxiety associated with nightmares may be so strong that it leads to a form of insomnia called *REM sleep interruption insomnia* (Hobson & Silvestri, 1999).

### Psychological Detective

Suppose you are the only technician working in a sleep laboratory. Two people are scheduled to spend a night in the laboratory in separate rooms; one suffers from sleep terrors and the other suffers from nightmares. You want to be present to observe each

**sleep terror**
Partial awakening from Stage 4 sleep characterized by loud screams and extreme physiological arousal

**nightmare**
Frightening dream that usually awakens a sleeper from REM sleep; occurs most often in children ages 3 to 6

### TABLE 4-2

## A Comparison of Sleep Terrors and Nightmares (with a Focus on Children)

### In a sleep terror, the child is likely to

resist parental interventions
be confused upon awakening
have a brief and rapid return to sleep
be in non-REM (slow-wave sleep)
have poor to absent recall of the event
exhibit intense autonomic nervous system discharges
experience the episode during the first third to first half of the night

### In a nightmare the child is likely to

be alert upon awakening
have a prolonged return to sleep
be easily comforted by parents
experience the event during REM (dream sleep)
have clear recall of the dream/detailed story
experience mild autonomic nervous system activity
experience the event during the second half to last third of the sleep period

**Source:** Sheldon (2004).

of the disorders, but you can't be in two places at once. If both people begin sleeping at the same time, can you accomplish your objective? Give this question some thought, and write down an answer, with reasons, before reading further.

Sleep terrors are a Stage 4 sleep disorder; they occur early in the night, usually within 2 hours after the person has fallen asleep. Nightmares take place during REM sleep, so they are likely to occur closer to the time of awakening, when REM episodes are longer. Even though you are the only technician on duty, you should be able to observe both the sleep terror and the nightmare.

**SIDS.** Each year, approximately 3,000 apparently healthy infants are found dead in their cribs after a night's sleep or a midday nap (National Institute of Child Health and Human Development, 2001). **Sudden infant death syndrome (SIDS)** is the sudden death of an apparently healthy infant under 1 year of age that is not explained by an autopsy and investigation of the child's history and death scene. SIDS is the leading cause of death between the ages of 1 month and 1 year; most cases occur between 2 and 4 months of age. We do not know what causes SIDS, but we do know that several factors increase the risk: sleeping in the prone position (on the belly), a recent illness, sleeping on a soft mattress, and elevated room temperature. The specific means by which these factors contribute to SIDS is not yet known. One possibility is that soft bedding material obstructs the air passage. Another possibility is that soft mattresses reduce air movement, which can increase the likelihood that the baby will rebreathe the carbon dioxide that was just exhaled (Ponsonby, Dwyer, Gibbons, Cochrane, & Wang, 1993). Infants who have died of SIDS have a deficiency in the binding of the neurotransmitter acetylcholine in the medulla—the part of the brain that controls breathing (see Chapter 2). This deficiency seems to render these infants less able to respond with protective reflexes that ensure proper breathing when their oxygen level drops (Kinney et al., 1995).

The "Back to Sleep" program has been successful in reducing the incidence of SIDS in the United States and other countries. Pediatricians and other health care providers are using materials such as these to convey this simple, potentially life-saving advice. Racial and ethnic factors seem to play a part in the risk of SIDS: It is approximately twice as high among African Americans as among Caucasians.

A public health campaign, using the slogan "Back to Sleep," has encouraged caregivers to place infants to sleep on their side or back. In several countries these campaigns have led to decreases of approximately 40 to 50% in the SIDS death rate (National Institute of Child Health and Human Development, 2001). In addition, some caregivers now use electronic monitors that track an infant's breathing and sound an alarm if it stops.

## Dreams: Nighttime Theater

A **dream** is "a succession of images, predominantly visual in quality, which are experienced during sleep" (Hall, 1966, p. 3). Opinions vary about the importance we should attach to this succession of images, but psychologist Calvin Hall believes that interpreting our dreams can enhance our self-knowledge.

As typically defined, dreams occur during REM sleep; however, do not let the association between REM and dream reports lead you to conclude that NREM sleep is a mental wasteland. When awakened from NREM sleep, people are likely to report some mental content. There are, however, qualitative differences between REM and NREM reports. REM dream reports are more vivid, more visual, more dramatic, more emotional, and more active. NREM reports tend to be just the opposite; they

**sudden infant death syndrome (SIDS)**
The unexpected death of an apparently healthy infant up to age 1 that is not explained by autopsy, medical case information, or an investigation of the death scene

**dream**
A succession of predominantly visual images experienced during sleep

## *Study* CHART

### Common Sleep Disorders

| Disorder | Description |
|---|---|
| Insomnia | Inadequate or poor-quality sleep characterized by one or more of the following: difficulty initiating sleep (sleep-onset insomnia), difficulty maintaining sleep, waking too early in the morning, or staying asleep. Has been treated with over-the-counter sleep aids that contain an antihistamine, sedative or hypnotic drugs, or a number of psychological treatments such as relaxation and stimulus control. |
| Narcolepsy | A potentially serious disorder consisting of excessive daytime sleepiness and symptoms related to the intrusion of REM sleep into the waking hours, including cataplexy (sudden muscle weakness related to strong emotions). Treatment consists of stimulant drugs and antidepressant drugs; naps may be helpful. |
| Sleep apnea | Frequent pauses in breathing, especially in overweight men, causing hundreds of brief awakenings during sleep. Treatments include CPAP, changes in sleep position, weight loss, tongue-retaining devices, and surgery. |
| Sudden infant death syndrome (SIDS) | The leading cause of death in infants between 1 month and 1 year of age. Placing the infant on the side or back to sleep may reduce the incidence of SIDS. |
| Sleepwalking | A parasomnia that occurs during Stage 4 sleep, especially in children, and may reflect the immaturity of the nervous system. Preventive measures such as locking windows and doors can reduce the chance of injury. |
| Enuresis | Bedwetting that can be treated with the urine alarm (pad and buzzer); may reflect a delay in the maturation of the CNS. |
| Sleep terror | Partial awakening from Stage 4 sleep accompanied by a high level of physiological arousal; may occur simultaneously with sleepwalking. Children typically do not recall any of the terror. |
| Nightmare | A frightening dream that occurs during REM and therefore is likely to occur near the end of sleep. |
| Restless legs syndrome | Unpleasant crawling, prickling, or tingling sensations in the legs and feet with constant leg movement during the day and insomnia at night. Although this syndrome may develop at any age, it is more common in the elderly. |
| Bruxism | Clenching or grinding of the teeth (which also occurs during non-sleep) often resulting in disorders of the jaw, jaw pain and soreness, headaches, earaches, damaged teeth, and other problems. Typical treatments are the use of mouth guards or appliances called *splints*, which help protect the teeth from the pressure of the clenching. |

often resemble thoughts and are more concerned with current problems than are REM dreams.

**Why We Forget Our Dreams.** Dream recall varies from one person to another; some people recall a dream every morning, whereas others rarely recall any dreams. Sigmund Freud proposed that the primary reason for forgetting dreams is repression—a process that pushes anxiety-arousing material deep into our unconscious. In order to shed some light on this issue, psychologist David Cohen randomly divided college students into two groups and asked both groups to write down their dreams upon awakening (Cohen & Wolfe, 1973). Students in the experimental group called the weather information number and recorded the weather prediction before writing down their dreams. Those in the control group spent about 90 seconds (the time required to call for the weather report) lying in bed before writing. Obtaining the weather report had a dramatic effect on dream recall: 33% of the students who called for the weather report recalled a dream compared to 63% of those who did not call. Cohen and Wolfe concluded that engaging in various activities after we awaken interferes with our ability to remember our dreams. Interference, not repression, is apparently the major reason we forget dreams.

**Culture and Dreams.** It doesn't matter where you live or who you are; fall asleep, and at some point you will dream. Although some people claim they never dream, when awakened during the night in a sleep laboratory they inevitably report dreams. Whether a person remembers a dream upon awakening in the morning depends, in part, on factors such as interference but also on how one's culture views dreams. Different cultures place varying emphases on dreams and support different beliefs concerning dreams. For example, many people in the United States view dreams as irrelevant fantasy with no connection to everyday life. By contrast, people in other cultures view dreams as key sources of information about the future, the spiritual world, and the dreamer. Such cultural views can influence the probability of dream recall. In many modern Western cultures, people rarely remember their dreams upon awakening. The Parintintin of South America, however, typically remember several dreams every night (Kracke, 1993), and the Senoi of Malaysia discuss their dreams with family members in the morning (Hennager, 1993).

Some cultures view dreams as real acts or channels of communication. A story of a missionary in one such culture illustrates the point: The missionary was amazed by the frequency of reports of adultery confessed by his converts. Later he discovered they were confessing sins they had carried out during their dreams. Among the Parintintin people, having an erotic dream may mean that the other person is thinking about the dreamer with desire. The Arapesh people of New Guinea believe that dreaming of someone else in an erotic manner is equivalent to actual intimate contact (Kracke, 1993). Similarly, the Senoi view dreams as a "co-reality" with waking life; to them, the dream world exists along with the waking world. If something occurs in one, it also occurs in the other. The Senoi believe that dreams reflect ongoing life events, and thus view them as an important guiding force in their lives. What's more, Senoi children are encouraged to report dreams and to use them to manipulate reality (Hennager, 1993).

A method of analyzing dreams proposed by Calvin Hall (called *content analysis* of dreams) has been used to study dreams in a number of cultures. The results reveal both consistencies and differences that may reflect cultural emphasis on dreaming as well as differing cultural experiences. For example, the dreams of college students in the Netherlands contain fewer examples of physical aggression than the dreams of Americans. Perhaps this difference in dream content reflects the fact that the United States is the most violent industrialized nation, whereas the Netherlands is one of the least violent (Domhoff, 1996). The dreams of Japanese college students have fewer animals than the dreams of Americans. One possibility for this finding is that dreams reflect the primarily urban settings and the relative absence of pets in Japan. The dreams of Japanese students also contain more familiar than unfamiliar people compared with the dreams of Americans.

**Interpreting Dreams.** According to Sigmund Freud (1900– 1965), the dream you remember in the morning is the **manifest content.** If you told someone the dream you had last night, you would be reporting its manifest content. Freud believed, however, that we must probe beneath the obvious content for the deeper underlying meaning— that is, we must seek the **latent content.** The latent content is transformed into the manifest content by a process called *dream work*. Analysis of the manifest content would reveal attempts to fulfill wishes, especially of a sexual or aggressive nature, of which the dreamer was not consciously aware. These wishes are expressed in a symbolic form, which is the manifest content of our dreams.

Despite Freud's focus on dreams as a form of wish fulfillment, decades of research have produced little to suggest that dreams serve this purpose (Fisher & Greenberg, 1977, 1996). Thus, Freud's notion that dreams somehow fulfill our sexual and aggressive desires suffered the same fate as his idea that repression causes us to forget our dreams: Neither withstood the scrutiny of scientific research.

**manifest content**
According to Freud, the dream as reported by the dreamer

**latent content**
According to Freud, the deeper underlying meaning of a dream, connected by symbols to the manifest content

**Source:** Reprinted with special permission of Psi Chi.

**activation-synthesis hypothesis**
Explanation of dreams that suggests that they result when the cortex seeks to explain the high level of neuronal activity occurring during REM sleep

Does this mean that dreams are useless, that they should never be considered? Might the symbols that Freud thought filled our dreams have some meaning nonetheless, even if they were not in the form of wish fulfillment? Symbols in dreams could explain rather than disguise or distort meaning (Hall, 1966). For example, although a number of dream symbols can represent sex organs (sticks or knives may represent the male sex organ; ovens or chests may represent the female sex organ), most people understand the symbols; thus they do not hide meaning. There are also a number of common elements in dreams. For example, most dreams include about two characters besides the dreamer, men dream about men more than about women, women dream about men and women equally, unpleasant emotions outnumber pleasant emotions, and hostile acts outnumber friendly acts.

Brain researchers J. Allan Hobson and Robert McCarley (1977) offer a different approach to explaining dreams. Their **activation-synthesis hypothesis** begins with the different ways brain cells turn on and off during waking as well as during both REM and NREM sleep (Hobson, 2005). As we have seen, the brain is very active during REM sleep. Hobson and McCarley believe that dreams arise during REM sleep from random bursts of activity from nerve cells in the brain stem. The cortex of the brain then tries to make sense of these haphazard signals. Nevertheless, dreams can be disjointed and jumbled because they begin as random signals. Hobson and McCarley also draw parallels between brain activity and the characteristics of our dreams. For example, the brain centers responsible for motor activity fire furiously during REM sleep, but motor movement is blocked in the spinal cord and brain stem. Rapid firing of neurons also occurs in the brain centers responsible for the sense of balance, which may account for dream reports of flying. Remember, the eyes are moving rapidly, so it is not surprising that dreams are characterized by vivid visual imagery. Although this theory offers a physiological basis for dreams, it does not explain why certain themes may consistently appear in a person's dreams. This consistency is hard to explain if dreams are the result of random signals (Cartwright & Lamberg, 1992).

In sum, there are a number of approaches to the study and interpretation of dreams. For theorists who emphasize the personal meaning of dreams, dream interpretation involves symbols that may not be difficult to understand. By contrast, the activation-synthesis hypothesis states that the cortex creates dreams to explain elevated levels of brain activity during REM sleep. No one explanation of dreams is likely to satisfy everyone.

## REVIEW SUMMARY

**1.** The major breakthrough in the study of sleep was the observation of rapid eye movements (REM). Measures of physiological processes such as the electroencephalograph (EEG) also aid sleep research.

**2.** A sleep cycle lasts approximately 90–100 minutes and starts with **non-REM (NREM) sleep.** We descend through NREM Stages 1 to 4 and then ascend through them to **rapid eye movement (REM) sleep.** The average adult repeats this cycle about four to six times each night.

**3.** Sleep decreases from about 16 hours at birth to about 7 to 8 hours in young adulthood, with little change thereafter. Observations of sleeping people suggest that many people are not getting enough sleep. Sleep efficiency (time in bed actually asleep) is lower among elderly people, who experience less slow-wave sleep and spend increased time in the lighter stages of sleep. Naps are more common than many people believe.

**4.** Sleep-deprived persons experience *microsleeps,* which can cause poor performance on tasks that require attention. REM sleep deprivation leads to the **REM rebound,** an increase in the amount of REM sleep. Cessation of monoamine release during REM allows these receptor systems to rest. Infants spend about 50% of their sleep in REM sleep, perhaps to provide stimulation needed for brain development. Sleep may have evolved to fill time, but the amount of sleep in each species depends on vulnerability to predators and the need to find food.

**5.** Most cases of **insomnia** are of short duration. Sleeping pills have limited usefulness and should be used with care. The *stimulus control* method is an effective treatment for sleep-onset insomnia.

**6. Hypersomnias** are sleep disorders marked by excessive daytime sleepiness. **Narcolepsy** is characterized by daytime sleepiness, cataplexy, and other symptoms consistent with the intrusion of REM sleep into waking hours. Overweight middle-aged men are susceptible to **sleep apnea,** which consists of frequent pauses in breathing during the night.

**7. Parasomnias** are sleep disturbances other than insomnia and hypersomnias. **Enuresis** (bedwetting) is a common disorder in childhood that can be treated with the urine alarm. **Sleepwalking** and **sleep terrors** are associated with Stage 4 sleep, tend to occur in children, and usually disappear without treatment. *REM sleep behavior disorder* occurs in older men and consists of aggressive actions during REM sleep. **Nightmares** are bad dreams that occur during REM sleep. **Sudden infant death syndrome (SIDS)** is the leading cause of death among infants between 1 month and 1 year of age. Placing infants to sleep on the back may reduce the incidence of SIDS.

**8.** As typically defined, dreams are associated with REM sleep, although NREM sleep is not a mental void. Freud suggested that dreams serve to fulfill sexual and aggressive wishes and that we forget dreams due to repression. Analysis of the **manifest content** of a dream yields the dream's **latent content,** or supposed true meaning. Research has not supported Freud's views on dreams. For example, forgetting dreams seems better explained by waking activities that interfere with dream recall than by repression. Dreams often reflect cultural characteristics such as a focus on relationships and levels of aggression in a culture.

**9.** The **activation-synthesis hypothesis** suggests that dreams result from attempts by the brain to make sense of high levels of neuronal activity.

# ✓ CHECK YOUR PROGRESS

**1.** People observed in a sleep laboratory have several measuring devices attached to them. Name the device used to measure each of the following:

   **a.** heart rate
   **b.** brain waves
   **c.** eye movements

**2.** If awakened at random, who is most likely to be in REM sleep?

   **a.** a 1-year-old child
   **b.** a 12-year-old adolescent
   **c.** a 32-year-old adult
   **d.** a 72-year-old adult

**3.** If you awaken a 27-year-old person at a randomly selected point of sleep, which of the following stages is most likely to be observed on the EEG?

   **a.** Stage 1
   **b.** Stage 2
   **c.** Stage 3
   **d.** REM sleep

**4.** You have been invited to spend the night observing in the university sleep lab. A technician shows you how the various devices are connected, and then you spend most of the night watching the EEG results from a volunteer. Which of the following would be the best description of the record?

   **a.** REM, Stage 1, Stage 2, Stage 3, Stage 4
   **b.** Stage 1, Stage 2, REM, Stage 3, Stage 4
   **c.** REM, NREM stages, REM, NREM stages
   **d.** NREM stages, REM, NREM stages, REM

**5.** Jim, a sleep laboratory volunteer, goes to sleep at around midnight and spends 8 hours asleep. If you want to wake Jim from slow-wave sleep, when should you try to awaken him?

   **a.** close to 6 A.M.
   **b.** about 45 minutes after he has fallen asleep
   **c.** approximately 4 hours into the sleep period
   **d.** as close to the time he normally wakes as possible

**6.** Give two reasons why the sleep of older people is less efficient than that of younger people.

**7.** Researchers have not found a complete answer to the question "Why do we sleep?". One intriguing possibility is that the sleep time of various species is designed to provide a period of immobilization. Their length of sleep, in turn, depends on several factors; name two.

**8.** Your roommate has had a terrible time over the past 6 weeks; every night is a struggle to get some sleep. She seeks some relief in sleeping pills but asks your advice. What should you tell her about the over-the-counter medication she has selected?

   **a.** These drugs are habit-forming.
   **b.** These medications can make you drowsy in the morning.
   **c.** These drugs are safe but only if taken at half of the recommended dosage.
   **d.** The sleep induced by such drugs is likely to be associated with nightmares.

**9.** Identify the sleep disorder that is most likely afflicting each of these people:

   **a.** Nathan experiences extreme daytime sleepiness and collapses to the floor after he tells a joke.
   **b.** Sixty-year-old Mel loves his wife very much, so he is puzzled to learn that he has attacked her during the night.
   **c.** A newspaper article described the death of 4-month-old Jessica from what was described as "the leading cause of death in children between the ages of 1 month and 1 year."
   **d.** Several times during the past month, 3-year-old Daniel has screamed loudly while asleep. When his parents rush to him, they find that his heart appears to be racing and he is soaked in perspiration.

e. Because Jason has felt sleepy every day for several years, his physician recommended that he be examined at a sleep disorder clinic, where they find that he awakens hundreds of times each night.

f. For the past few weeks, Janice has awakened and found herself quite anxious about the dream she just had.

**10.** Your psychology instructor assigns every student to portray a famous figure in the history of psychology. You are to portray Sigmund Freud and his views on dreaming. If you are required to give a title for your presentation, which of these would be most appropriate?

a. "Using Dreams to Tell the Future"
b. "Satisfying Our Desires in Fantasy"
c. "Dreams: Just So Much Neurological Nonsense"
d. "Remembering Past Lives Through Dream Themes"

**ANSWERS: 1. a.** EKG **b.** EEG **c.** EOG **2. a** **3. b** **4. d** **5. b** **6.** Compared to younger people, older individuals spend less time in the deep sleep of Stage 4 and more time in the light sleep of Stage 1. Consequently, they are more easily awakened. **7.** vulnerability to predators and need for food **8. b** **9. a.** narcolepsy **b.** REM sleep behavior disorder **c.** sudden infant death syndrome **d.** sleep terror **e.** sleep apnea **f.** nightmare **10. b**

# HYPNOSIS

Last week Beth and Jason attended a stage hypnotist's performance. The audience eagerly anticipated the show, and they were not disappointed. During the course of the show, an audience member was hypnotized and asked to stretch his body across two chairs—head and shoulders on one chair and feet on the other. Then the hypnotist stood atop this "human plank" to show that a hypnotized person can support the hypnotist's entire weight. *Does hypnotism explain the human plank demonstration?*

You may have seen performances by stage hypnotists or read advertisements claiming that hypnosis can help us lose weight, stop smoking, or study more effectively. The power attributed to hypnosis has intrigued and challenged practitioners, researchers, and theorists for more than a century.

## The History of Hypnosis

In the 18th century, hypnosis was called *mesmerism*, after the Austrian physician Franz Anton Mesmer (1734–1815). Mesmer captured the imagination of many residents of Paris by claiming that he could cure everything from toothaches to paralysis. He believed that the atmosphere was filled with an invisible magnetic force that he could accumulate in his body and transfer to the bodies of sick people. Patients who hoped to be healed sat around a tub filled with water, iron filings, and ground glass. Then Mesmer made a grand entrance and passed iron rods over the patients or touched them with a wand. The patients started shaking; their arms and legs moved involuntarily; some fainted. Mesmer assured them that several treatments would reestablish their bodies' magnetic equilibrium and cure their ailments. Countless testimonials attested to the healing power of the magnetic fluid.

The medical and scientific communities viewed Mesmer's treatments with skepticism and petitioned for an investigation. In 1784, a commission chaired by Benjamin Franklin concluded that the patients' reactions were due to imagination, not magnetism. Mesmer was discredited, but his technique survived to be used by others. In 1843, James Braid, a Scottish surgeon, changed its name to *hypnosis*.

## Hypnotic Induction

**Hypnosis** has been defined as "a social interaction in which one person, designated the subject, responds to suggestions offered by another person, designated the hypnotist, for experiences involving alterations in perception, memory, and voluntary action" (Kihlstrom, 1985, p. 385). Some theorists view hypnosis as an altered state of consciousness, called the

Franz Anton Mesmer developed an unorthodox method of treating illnesses. He believed that a fluidlike substance occurred in nature and that magnetic forces could alter this substance, thus leading to cures. Eventually, Mesmer concluded that magnets were not necessary; passing hands over the body was sufficient to create the necessary magnetic forces, or so he thought. The techniques he developed, often called *mesmerism,* evolved into hypnosis.

**hypnosis**
State of heightened susceptibility to suggestions

*hypnotic trance*; others claim that hypnotized people behave in accordance with their expectations about hypnosis. To understand why these different views persist, we need to take a closer look at the phenomenon of hypnosis and how it is produced.

Human responses to hypnotists' communications led researchers to the concept of *suggestibility*, or "hypnotizability." People clearly differ in suggestibility—that is, in how readily they follow a hypnotist's suggestions. A hypnotist needs to create a situation in which people are especially likely to follow suggestions, instructions, or requests. This process is known as *hypnotic induction*. Traditional hypnotic induction involves having the individual gaze at an object, inducing relaxation, fostering imagination, and encouraging drowsiness.

Suppose you have agreed to be hypnotized. The hypnotist may tell you to "relax and concentrate" on an object such as a watch. "You are becoming more relaxed. Your eyelids are becoming heavier. You are becoming sleepy." Although the word *hypnosis* is derived from the Greek word for "sleep," hypnosis is not sleep. The EEG of a hypnotized person indicates relaxation, not sleep.

After a brief induction such as the one just described, the hypnotist uses a number of tests to judge your degree of susceptibility to hypnosis. The most widely used measure is the *Stanford Hypnotic Susceptibility Scales*, which were developed in the late 1950s. This measure of responsiveness to hypnosis consists of 12 activities that test the depth of the hypnotic state. You may be asked to "lock the fingers of both hands together so tightly that they cannot be separated." Can you separate your fingers? Or you may be told that you have no sense of smell before a vial of ammonia is waved under your nose (Nash, 2001). Such tests allow hypnotists to determine whether you are susceptible to hypnosis. Scores on such tests occur in a normal distribution, which means that most people fall in the middle, with fewer at the extremes (Patterson, 2004). If you are highly susceptible today, you are likely to be highly hypnotizable 25 years from now because susceptibility to hypnosis appears to be quite stable over time (Nash, 2001; Piccione, Hilgard, & Zimbardo, 1989).

## Hypnotic Phenomena

A hypnotist *cannot* make you do anything you would not do otherwise. Hypnosis does not endow you with superhuman strength; you will not be able to lift a car while hypnotized unless you can lift it while not hypnotized! Hypnosis depends on establishing a positive relationship between the hypnotist and the hypnotized person.

In this section we examine some of the claims made for hypnosis. We begin with some of the more dramatic claims—those dealing with pain reduction and medical treatment.

**Pain Reduction and Medical Treatment.** Since the 1800s, numerous researchers have described the use of hypnosis to reduce the pain of surgery, childbirth, burns, cancer, and dental procedures. The lack of proper experimental controls in the reported cases should make us skeptical, but it does not preclude the possibility that some people benefit from such treatment.

### Psychological Detective

An advertisement for pain-free dentistry attracts your attention, but you have some questions about the treatment. A friend tells you he has had several dental procedures done under hypnosis and has felt no pain. What components of hypnosis might be helpful in reducing pain or alleviating certain medical problems?

Several elements of hypnotic induction could help reduce pain. First, relaxation, which is typically included in the induction, can help reduce pain. Second, the hypnotist's encouragement may help patients who are experiencing pain. Third, in helping people withstand pain, repeated presentations of the hypnotic induction are more effective than a single presentation (Price & Barber, 1987). The multiple presentations may serve as relaxation reminders or may distract the person from the experience of pain.

In addition to alleviating pain, hypnosis has been used to combat common medical problems. A review of the effectiveness of hypnosis in treating medical conditions such as asthma and behavior problems such as smoking revealed few differences between treatments with or without hypnosis (Spanos, 1991). The benefits that did occur were likely due to the patients' attitudes and expectations rather than to any intrinsic effect of hypnosis. On the other hand, a review of 18 studies led to the conclusion that hypnosis provided pain relief for 75% of the people who were studied (Montgomery, DuHamel, & Redd, 2000). Hypnosis may have different effects on acute (short-term) versus chronic (long-term) pain. Chronic pain (primarily headaches) was reduced by hypnosis, but the effects were generally equivalent to those of relaxation training (Patterson & Jensen, 2003), which recalls some of the points made by researchers who find that hypnosis may have effects that are due to factors other than the hypnotism itself.

Hypnosis can be made more effective by matching the treatment to the specific pain. Research reveals that pain has both an emotional component (for example "this pain is awful") and a sensory component (that is, pain intensity on a 0 to 10 scale). If patients undergoing hypnotic treatment for pain are told they will suffer less of the emotional component of pain, their brains will reveal activation in different areas compared to patients who are told they will experience less intense pain (Patterson, 2004). Such findings suggest ways for clinicians to modify their hypnotic suggestions for the greatest benefit to their patients.

**Memory Effects.**    After a hypnotic session, some hypnotized people may report that they cannot remember events that occurred during the session. Perhaps these lost memories can be recovered when the hypnotist gives a particular signal. Hypnosis has been proposed as an aid to memory, which would be a major benefit to the police. Witnesses or victims of crimes do not have photographic memories, and the stress associated with traumatic events like observing a murder or suffering an assault makes it difficult to remember the event accurately.

The use of testimony that has been hypnotically refreshed but not confirmed by physical evidence has, however, aroused serious concern (Giannelli, 1995). When people undergo hypnosis to refresh their memories, their recall often contains distortions and false memories, which may have been inadvertently implanted during the hypnotic sessions. Nevertheless, these people tend to be more confident of the accuracy of their memories than people who have not undergone hypnosis (Spiegel & Scheflin, 1994; Steblay, Mehrkens, & Bothwell, 1994). As one expert observed, "Researchers in the field of hypnosis have known for well over a century that false memories can be implanted in individuals through the use of formal hypnotic procedures or even through simple suggestion" (Yapko, 1994, p. 96). Currently almost all hypnotically elicited testimony is excluded from the court system because the questions that have been raised about use of the technique pose risks to defendants in criminal cases (Newman & Thompson, 2001).

**Perception.**    Positive and negative hallucinations are among the various perceptual effects reported by people who have been hypnotized. *Positive hallucinations* are reports of seeing an object that is not really present. For example, a hypnotized person may report petting an imaginary cat. With *negative hallucinations*, a hypnotized person fails to perceive an object that is present. For example, he or she may walk into a chair in the middle of a room.

A clever approach to testing the validity of hypnotically induced perceptual changes is to give a hypnotic suggestion of deafness and ask a hypnotized person to read aloud. His (or her) words are played back to him (or her) a half second after they are spoken; this delay is confusing for the average hearing person. If hypnotic deafness had been induced, the delayed feedback would have no effect; however, studies have found that it has as great an effect on hypnotized people as it does on those who have not been hypnotized (Baker, 1990).

**Age Regression.**    In the phenomenon of *age regression*, hypnotized people are given suggestions that allegedly lead them to relive events that occurred when they were younger—often during childhood—and to feel and act like a child of that age. The changes observed in adults who have responded to such suggestions can be dramatic and seem to offer convincing evidence that age regression has occurred.

Are the changes attributed to hypnotic age regression different from those that could occur in someone who has not been hypnotized? In one study, 92% of hypnotized people who had regressed to their 10th birthday correctly identified the day of the week on which the event took place, and 84% of those who had regressed to their 4th birthday did the same (True, 1949).

## Psychological Detective

These findings are impressive, but are you convinced that the participants recalled the day of the week of their 4th or 10th birthday? Can you recall the day of the week of your last birthday? Subsequent researchers found a major flaw in this study that explained the high rates of recall. Can you think of a research flaw that might account for these results? Write it down before reading further.

The hypnotist-experimenter who conducted this study had a perpetual calendar on his desk. As he questioned the participants, he could have subtly cued the correct answer when asking such questions as "Was it Wednesday?" When other investigators corrected this methodological flaw, they could not replicate the finding.

Hypnotic regression has been used to take people on even more impressive journeys—journeys to previous lives. In hypnotic *past-life regression*, people are said to report prior lives as well as events from earlier times. Such reports, however, depend in part on suggestions by the hypnotist. If the hypnotist expresses little belief in past-life regression, participants report few such experiences (Spanos, Menary, Gabora, Du Breuil, & Dewhirst, 1991). These past-life reports are also sprinkled with errors of historical fact that people from the relevant historical period would be unlikely to make. For example, one person claimed to be Julius Caesar, emperor of Rome, in 50 B.C. Do you see the problem? The designations B.C. and A.D. were not used until centuries later (Spanos, 1987–1988).

## Explanations of Hypnosis

As noted earlier, researchers are divided in their explanations for hypnosis. According to the *cognitive-social view*, the phenomena we label *hypnotic* occur when someone enacts the role of a hypnotized person. This view suggests that hypnosis is not an altered state of consciousness.

One of the problems in viewing hypnosis as an altered state of consciousness is that it is difficult to know when a person is hypnotized. Veteran hypnosis researcher Ernest Hilgard (1991) admitted that "it would be more comfortable for the investigator if there were some precise indicator of the establishment of a hypnotic condition, but so far that has eluded investigators" (p. 39). What's more, some of the feats attributed to hypnosis can also be accomplished by people who have not undergone hypnotic induction.

At the beginning of this section we met Beth and Jason, who attended a stage hypnotist's performance. They were amazed when a hypnotized person who was stretched across two chairs was able to hold the weight of the hypnotist on his chest. Do we need the concept of hypnosis to explain this human plank demonstration? The photograph on this page shows two people, neither of whom is hypnotized, performing the human plank feat. The demonstration works if the hypnotist is not very heavy and does not remain in position for long. If Beth and Jason had known what you now know, they would not have been so amazed.

If the shoulders and feet are properly supported, the weight of a person standing on the chest of the human plank can be supported. The weight is carried by the strong muscles of the shoulders, back, buttocks, and legs. If, however, these muscles are weak or if the chairs slide, serious injury can result.

## Psychological Detective

The cognitive-social perspective views hypnotized people as behaving the way they believe hypnotized people behave. If you were participating in an experiment on hypnosis, how would you behave as a hypnotized person? Give this question some thought, examining your expectations about hypnosis, and write down your answer before reading further.

**STUDY TIP**

Reread the section on hypnosis. In addition to the definitions in the margin, find at least five additional terms that you either did not know before this reading or want to solidify in your memory. Write down each term and define it in the context of your reading.

**dissociation**
Splitting of conscious awareness that is believed to play a role in hypnotic pain reduction

In one study (Baker, 1990) the researcher asked several students to undergo hypnotic induction before making an instructional videotape. When he found that he needed more volunteers, he asked studio personnel to fill in, although they were not hypnotized. They behaved so similarly that the audience could not distinguish the fill-ins from those who had undergone hypnotic induction. All participants sat with their eyes closed, looked sleepy, and complied with requests to lower and raise their hands. When told that their chairs were burning hot, everyone got up. This demonstration reveals that people easily conform to their perceptions of what hypnotized people do, which is to respond automatically to suggestions (Lynn, Rhue, & Weekes, 1989).

Earlier in this chapter we mentioned pain reduction as a claim made for hypnosis. Among the most striking demonstrations of pain reduction through hypnosis are those occurring during dental procedures or childbirth. Ernest Hilgard (1904–2001) proposed an explanation of hypnotic phenomena that originated in studies of people experiencing painful stimuli. Hilgard (1991) suggests that hypnosis involves a **dissociation,** or splitting of conscious awareness. Examples of dissociation can occur in ordinary activities. Have you ever been reading a book, only to find that you had no idea what you had read for the past several minutes? Your eyes were following the text, but your mind was daydreaming; the act of reading and the memory of what you read were dissociated from the experience of daydreaming.

Hilgard proposes that some people, when facing painful stimuli, can dissociate the experience so successfully that one part of the mind is aware of the pain while another is unaware of it. The two parts of the mind are separated and have no knowledge of each other. But what type of person is capable of dissociating consciousness in this way? An excellent predictor of hypnotizability is a tendency to become heavily involved in imaginative activities and to have exceptionally vivid images that occur without much deliberate effort (Wilson & Barber, 1983). These fantasy-prone people spend about half of their time absorbed in fantasy. In fact, their sexual fantasies are so powerful that they claim to be capable of achieving orgasm without physical stimulation. Their very vivid imaginations can serve a useful function by enabling them to alter their consciousness in ways that are adaptive—for example, by using dissociation to deal with pain.

There are competing explanations for hypnosis; in fact, experts disagree as to whether hypnosis is a phenomenon that even needs explanation.

## REVIEW SUMMARY

**1. Hypnosis,** a heightened state of suggestibility, can be traced to the 18th century, when Franz Anton Mesmer claimed he had the power to induce magnetic equilibrium in the bodies of his patients. In contrast to the popular view that hypnosis is an altered state of consciousness, evidence suggests that it does not differ from a state of relaxation.

**2.** Hypnosis has been used to reduce pain in various kinds of medical treatments. It is not clear, however, what aspect of hypnosis may be responsible for pain reduction; relaxation, distraction, and expectations seem to play significant roles.

**3.** Hypnosis has been used to improve recall; however, hypnotically refreshed memories tend to contain distortions and false reports.

**4.** In hypnotic *age regression,* a hypnotized person appears to return to childhood or perhaps even to past lives. Research indicates that age regression results in the reporting of fantasies or memories suggested by the hypnotist.

**5.** The cognitive-social explanation suggests that the observed phenomena can be explained by the relation between the hypnotist and the hypnotized person, as well as by widely shared expectations about the procedure. Another explanation, offered by Ernest Hilgard, suggests that **dissociation,** or a splitting of consciousness, may be at work in hypnosis.

## ✓ CHECK YOUR PROGRESS

**1.** What force did Mesmer claim to harness in his efforts to cure various ailments?

**a.** the soul

**b.** sleep juice

**c.** magnetism

**d.** "virtual essence"

**2.** A student agrees to take part in research on hypnosis. As part of the informed consent, the researcher tells the student that the Stanford Hypnotic Susceptibility Scale will be administered. What is the student likely to be asked to do during administration of this test?

a. The student will be asked to count back from 100.

b. After being told that she cannot smell, she will have a vial of ammonia waved in front of her.

c. After being told that she is a weight lifter, she will be asked to try to lift an automobile.

d. The student will be asked to report her thoughts at random intervals across the next 24 hours.

3. A researcher administers a measure of hypnotizability to college students. Twenty years later, the same individuals are contacted and administered the same measure. Which correlation coefficient most likely describes the relation between the two sets of scores?

a. .00

b. +.75

c. +.20

d. −.65

4. A person is hypnotized and is given the posthypnotic suggestion that she is deaf. How would a researcher test the validity of the suggestion for deafness?

a Play the hypnotized person's favorite music.

b. Check the level of delta waves in the brain.

c. Feed back her reading with a delay of about a half second.

d. Watch her body movements to detect any hint that she can hear.

5. Which of the following seem to be key elements of hypnotic induction?

a. Relaxation, concentration, and listening to the hypnotist's commands

b. Changes in brain waves, relinquishing control, and extensive memory

c. High levels of creativity, willingness to "let go," and a desire to experience new levels of consciousness

d. Belief in an afterlife, obedience to authority figures, and willingness to dispense with cherished beliefs

6. There is controversy concerning whether hypnosis can reduce pain or cure medical problems. Which elements of hypnosis may be responsible for reports of pain reduction in hypnotized patients?

a. distraction and relaxation

b. increased concentration and placebo effects

c. daydreaming during hypnosis and placebo effects

d. visual and auditory hallucinations and an altered state of consciousness

7. Early research on the effects of age regression through hypnosis seemed to suggest that hypnosis could bring back memories of an earlier time. What serious flaw was identified in this research?

a. A calendar on the desk probably led the researcher to cue the answers.

b. The participants were all highly hypnotizable individuals who were recruited by proponents of hypnosis.

c. A combination of hypnosis and truth serum was used rather than the usual hypnotic induction.

d. The participants were recruited from the ranks of actors who enjoyed reenacting historical battles and thus were knowledgeable of historical facts.

8. A witness is hypnotized to help refresh the memory of a crime she witnessed. The prosecutor would like to admit the testimony, but the judge wants to hear from experts on hypnotically refreshed testimony. What will the experts say is the likely effect of hypnosis on memory?

a. Hypnosis tends to cause widespread repression of anxiety-related memories.

b. The witness will believe she is recalling more information, but some of her memories may have been suggested during the interview.

c. Hypnosis will tend to enhance memory for minor details, but it will have little effect on memory for the major elements of the crime.

d. The witness will remember many more concrete details as a result of the reduction in anxiety induced by the hypnotic trance.

9. What does Hilgard mean by *dissociation,* and how does he use this concept to explain hypnotic phenomena, especially pain reduction?

**ANSWERS: 1.** c **2.** b **3.** b **4.** c **5.** a **6.** a **7.** a **8.** b **9.** Dissociation is a splitting of consciousness. Hilgard proposes that some people can dissociate the experience of painful stimuli so that one part of the mind is aware of the pain and another is unaware of it. These parts are separated and have no awareness of each other.

# ALTERING CONSCIOUSNESS WITH DRUGS

Two middle-aged couples having dinner at an upscale restaurant were talking about drugs, politics, and taxes. They agreed that they would never use any drugs that could affect their minds. Halfway through the meal, they asked the waitress to bring them another bottle of wine. Later, they had several cups of coffee with their chocolate pie. After dinner, they went for a walk and smoked a few cigarettes. *Are illicit drugs the only substances that can affect consciousness, perception, mood, and behavior?*

**TABLE 4-3**

# The Effects of Major Drugs

| Drug | Source | Common or Slang Names | Means of Administration | Typical Reactions |
|------|--------|----------------------|-------------------------|-------------------|
| **DEPRESSANTS** | | | | |
| **Alcohol** | Fermenting sugar and yeast | Booze, juice, sauce, brew hooch, porter | Taken orally | Tension reduction, reduced inhibitions, relief from anxiety, drowsiness |
| **Barbiturates** | Synthetically derived | Barbs, blues, yellow jackets, jellies, luds, quads | Taken orally, injected | Tension reduction, reduced inhibitions, relief from anxiety, drowsiness |
| **Benzodiazepines** | Synthetically derived | Roofies, tranqs, valums, gofers, jellies, vallies | Taken orally | Tension reduction, reduced inhibitions, relief from anxiety, drowsiness |
| **STIMULANTS** | | | | |
| **Amphetamines** | Synthetically derived | Uppers, speed, crank, beanies, dominoes | Taken orally, injected | Increased alertness, elevated mood, reduced fatigue, increased motor activity |
| **Cocaine** | Coca plant | Coke, rock, blow, snow Paradise white, snow cones | Taken orally (chewed), injected, snorted, smoked | Increased alertness, elevated mood, reduced fatigue, increased motor activity |
| **OPIATES** | | | | |
| **Morphine** | Opium poppy | White stuff, M, morf, dreamer | Taken orally, injected | Relaxed euphoria, sedation, reduced apprehension |
| **Heroin** | Morphine | Junk, china white, smack, hero | Inserted rectally, injected, smoked | Relaxed euphoria, sedation, reduced apprehension |
| **HALLUCINOGENS** | | | | |
| **Lysergic acid diethylamide (LSD)** | Ergot fungus on rye and other grains | Acid, LSD-25, blotter acid, microdot | Taken orally | Illusions, hallucinations, distortions in time, anxiety, enhanced sensory experience |
| **Marijuana** | *Cannabis sativa* (hemp) plant | Pot, grass, weed, reefer astro turf, Don Juan, yellow submarine, Aunt Mary | Taken orally, smoked | Euphoria, relaxed inhibitions, increased sense of well-being |

**psychoactive substances**
Chemicals that affect consciousness, perception, mood, and behavior

Many people use the term *drug* to refer to illegal, possibly addicting, substances as opposed to the medical agents taken to cure illnesses. Actually, the term refers to both legal and illegal substances; a drug is any chemical that modifies physiological functioning. **Psychoactive substances,** which include many illegal or illicit drugs, are chemicals that can alter consciousness, perception, mood, and behavior.

The two couples just described claimed they would never use any drugs that could affect their minds. Yet within a few hours, they used three legal psychoactive substances: alcohol (in wine), caffeine (in coffee and chocolate pie), and nicotine (in cigarettes).

| Consequence of an Overdose | Medical Uses | Effects on Neurotransmitters |
| --- | --- | --- |
| Disorientation, loss of consciousness, lack of coordination; at very high levels, death may occur as a result of cessation of respiration | Antiseptic | Enhances the activity of GABA, decreases the activity of glutamate and acetylcholine, augments the action of dopamine; alters the processes of neuronal membranes |
| Impaired motor and intellectual performance; coma and death at high doses when mixed with alcohol | Sedative, sleeping pill, anesthetic, prevents seizures and convulsions | Enhances the activity of GABA |
| Impaired motor and intellectual performance, although generally these effects are not as dangerous as those of barbiturates because these drugs do not produce significant depression of respiration | Sedative, sleeping pill, anxiety reduction, prevents seizures and convulsions | Enhances the activity of GABA |
| Anxiety, suspiciousness, paranoia, hallucinations | Treatment of attention-deficit hyperactivity disorder, narcolepsy, diet aid in weight-loss programs | Blocks the reuptake of dopamine and norepinephrine |
| Anxiety, suspiciousness, paranoia, hallucinations | Local anesthetic for eye, ear, and throat surgeries | Blocks the reuptake of dopamine and norepinephrine |
| Possible death owing to depression of the respiratory system | Painkiller, cough suppressant | Inhibits the release of substance P and increases the release of dopamine |
| Possible death owing to depression of the respiratory system | – | Inhibits the release of substance P and increases the release of dopamine |
| "Bad trip," characterized by anxiety, panic attacks, or serious psychotic reactions | – | Interferes with the normal action of serotonin, which in turn triggers responses that involve several other neurotransmitters |
| Impaired learning and coordination, dizziness, paranoia, hallucinations | Reduction of nausea and vomiting associated with chemotherapy for cancer | Affects specific brain receptors, which are structurally similar to opiate receptors |

When they said they would never use drugs, they meant illegal, mind-altering drugs; they were assuming that the legal substances they were using would not affect their minds. But as we will see shortly, they were mistaken. The most common psychoactive substances can be divided into four categories on the basis of their effects: depressants, stimulants, opiates, and hallucinogens (see Table 4-3).

The National Household Survey on Drug Use and Health estimates that 19.1 million people (aged 12 or older) in the United States used an illicit drug in the 30 days prior to the survey. This number represents 7.9% of the population aged 12 or older.

**FIGURE 4-12** Percent of 12th graders who have used any illicit drug, several specific illicit drugs, or alcohol in the 30 days prior to being surveyed for the University of Michigan's Monitoring the Future study.

**Source:** Johnson, O'Malley, Bachman, and Schulenberg (2005).

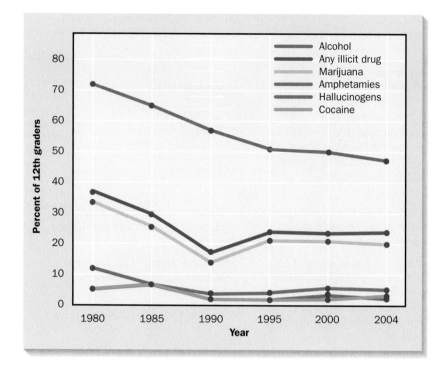

**STUDY TIP**

Gather in a group of four. Each student should study one of the four classes of drugs as described in Table 4-3 (The Effects of Major Drugs) and present a description to the group. The presenting student should ask the listening students to volunteer examples of each drug category.

**substance abuse**
Pattern of substance use that has detrimental effects on a person's health and safety, as well as on social and occupational roles

**substance dependence**
More serious pattern of substance use than that found in substance abuse; popularly called *addiction* and often characterized by drug tolerance and withdrawal symptoms when use of the drug is stopped

**tolerance**
Need for increasing dosages of a drug to achieve the same effect as earlier, smaller doses

**withdrawal**
Changes in behavior, cognition, and physiology that occur when stopping or reducing the heavy and prolonged use of a psychoactive substance

Marijuana, the most commonly used illicit drug, was used by 14.6 million, which is 76% of current illicit drug users. There were 2.0 million current cocaine users and 1.0 million users of hallucinogens (Substance Abuse and Mental Health Services Administration, 2004). Every year, surveys of high school seniors provide statistics on the percentage that use various drugs. Figure 4-12 shows the percentage of high school seniors who are current users of several drugs (used the drug in the 30 days prior to the survey) across a number of years.

The effects of most psychoactive substances can be explained by the changes they cause in the action of neurotransmitters (see Chapter 2), especially in the brain. Thus, most psychoactive substances can have wide-ranging effects. The regular and excessive use of drugs can lead to a pattern of maladaptive behavior known as a *substance use disorder* that includes substance abuse and substance dependence (American Psychiatric Association, 2000). **Substance abuse** occurs when use of a substance disrupts family and social relationships, interferes with work, and/or creates health and safety hazards for the abuser.

People who display **substance dependence,** a more serious disorder that is popularly called *addiction*, develop a physical dependence on the substance in addition to a pattern of abuse. Physical dependence is evident in the phenomenon of **tolerance,** which occurs when a person needs increasing doses of a substance to achieve the effect formerly obtained from a smaller dose. **Withdrawal,** characterized by changes in behavior, cognition, and physiology, may then occur if the person stops taking the substance or reduces the amount taken. The symptoms of withdrawal range from irritability to a craving for the substance that can begin within hours of taking the last dose.

A common denominator in drugs of abuse (cocaine, alcohol, opiates, amphetamine) is that they stimulate release of dopamine in the brain's reward circuitry, which projects from the base of the brain (an area called the *nucleus accumbens*) to the hippocampus and amygdala. When we do something that provides a reward (such as ingesting a substance), the hippocampus lays down a memory of this rapid sense of satisfaction, and the amygdala creates a learned response to cues associated with taking the substance (*Harvard Mental Health Letter*, 2004). Thus, stimulation of this pathway reinforces behavior that sets up a vicious cycle leading to increased craving for the drug (addiction) at the same time that the negative effects of the drug on health are increasing. This system is so powerful that researchers have seen the brain light up on PET scans when cocaine addicts were offered a snort (Nestler & Malenka, 2004). What's more, twin and adoption studies show that about 50% of the variation in susceptibility to addiction is hereditary (*Harvard Mental Health Letter*, 2004).

In the remainder of this section, we take a closer look at each of the major categories of psychoactive substances.

## Depressants

**Depressants** are drugs that slow functioning of the CNS. Among the depressants are alcohol, barbiturates, and the benzo-diazepines (Liska, 2004; Stevens & Smith, 2001). **Alcohol** is one of the most widely used psychoactive substances in the United States and throughout the world. Barbiturates are less common but are still readily available. Benzodiazepines are often called *minor tranquilizers*.

**Alcohol.**    Along with nicotine and caffeine, alcohol might be called an unrecognized drug. We are so accustomed to consuming alcohol that "to drink" often means to drink alcoholic beverages unless otherwise specified. The following are some significant facts about alcohol use in the United States:

- Alcohol contributes to 100,000 deaths per year and an economic cost of $185 billion (Harwood, 2000); approximately 40% of traffic fatalities are alcohol-related (National Highway Transportation Administration, 2005). By contrast, the number of deaths attributed to all illegal drugs (178 drugs are illegal in the United States) is 8,000 (Gahlinger, 2004).

- A survey of college students found that 50% of men and 39% of women engaged in *binge drinking* (drinking five or more drinks in a row for men or four or more for women during the 2 weeks prior to the survey). Frequent binge drinkers account for 23% of all students, but they consume 73% of the alcohol college students drink. As you will see in Figure 4-13, binge drinking is associated with a range of health and other problems such as property damage (Wechsler, Davenport, Dowdall, Moeykens, & Castillo, 1994; Wechsler & Wuethrich, 2002). Binge drinking during the college years can have an impact well beyond college. A 10-year follow-up of college students indicated that compared to nonbinge drinkers, binge drinkers had higher rates of academic attrition, early departure from college, did worse in their jobs, and had higher rates of alcohol dependence and abuse (Jennison, 2004).

- In 2004, 33% of high school seniors had been drunk in the 30 days prior to completing a survey on drug use; high school seniors had a 2.8% rate of daily use of alcohol; 77% had used alcohol at some time during their lives (Johnson, O'Malley, Bachman, & Schulenberg, 2005).

The use of alcohol is associated with a range of medical and mental health problems. Heavy alcohol use is linked to several forms of cancer, antisocial personality disorder (see Chapter 12), and heart damage (O'Connor & Schottenfeld, 1998). *Moderate* consumption of alcohol, however, is associated with a lower risk of heart disease; the exact mechanism by which this occurs is not known, although alcohol seems to reduce cholesterol levels (Klatsky, 2003; Zakhari, 1997). Given the well-known risks associated with alcohol, health professionals are exercising caution in making any recommendation to consume alcohol lest it be misunderstood. Many of us adhere to the philosophy that anything that is good for us is even better if consumed in larger amounts! Alcohol is the primary contributor to cirrhosis, a disease of the liver that is the ninth leading cause of death in the United States (Census Bureau, 2005). It is important to identify

**depressants**
Drugs such as alcohol and barbiturates that slow the activity of the CNS

**alcohol**
Depressant psychoactive substance, also known as *ethanol* or *ethyl alcohol*

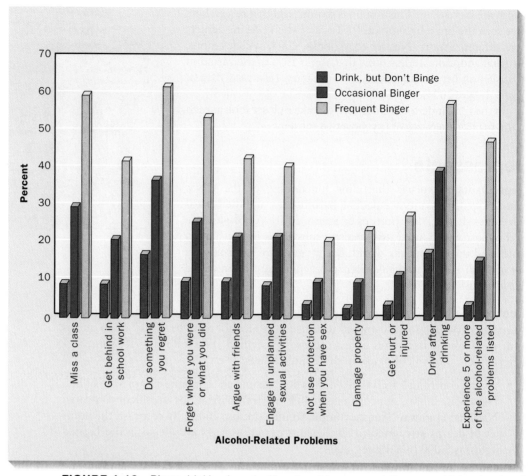

**FIGURE 4-13** Binge drinking is a significant problem, especially among high school and college populations. The frequency of a wide range of problems rises with the level of binge drinking.

**Source:** Wechsler and Wuethrich (2002).

and treat alcohol abuse or dependence as early as possible. The questionnaire in Table 4-4 is designed to help people determine whether they have a problem with alcohol.

**Effects of Alcohol.**    The alcohol in beer, distilled liquor, and wine is ethyl alcohol, or ethanol. This colorless liquid contains a high number of calories (210 calories in 1 ounce of pure alcohol) that provides energy but no nutrients to nourish the body (Stevens & Smith, 2001). Drinking alcoholic beverages adds calories to your diet at the same time that it slows the rate at which you burn fat. The fat that is not broken down is likely to be deposited on your hips, thighs, and stomach (Suter, Schutz, & Jequier, 1992).

Alcohol content varies with the beverage: Beer is 3% to 6% alcohol, wine is 8% to 20%, and distilled beverages are 40% to 50%. Typical or standard servings of these beverages contain similar amounts of alcohol: A 12-ounce beer contains .60 ounce of alcohol, or about the same amount of alcohol contained in a 5-ounce serving of wine or a 1.5-ounce serving of a distilled beverage. Thus, the effects of alcohol do not depend so much on what you drink as on how much you drink.

Your body can break down alcohol before it affects you if you consume it slowly, but few people consume it slowly enough (the liver can break down the alcohol in one standard serving per hour). The amount of alcohol in the blood depends in part on how long it takes the stomach to empty its contents into the small intestine, where most of the alcohol enters the bloodstream (McKim, 2000). If you slow the stomach's emptying time, you slow (but do not stop) the release of alcohol into the blood. One reason to eat

## TABLE 4-4

## Alcohol Use Disorders Identification Test (AUDIT) Core Questionnaire

The World Health Organization developed this self-report questionnaire as a measure of alcohol consumption, symptoms of dependence, and personal and social harm owing to drinking, especially in the past year. The AUDIT is effective in detecting hazardous or harmful drinking as well as confirming cases of alcohol dependence.

1. How often do you have a drink containing alcohol?

    (0) Never
    (1) Monthly or less
    (2) 2 to 4 times a month
    (3) 2 to 3 times a week
    (4) 4 or more times a week

2. How many drinks containing alcohol do you have on a typical day when you are drinking?

    (0) 1 or 2
    (1) 3 or 4
    (2) 5 or 6
    (3) 7 to 9
    (4) 10 or more standard drinks

3. How often do you have six or more drinks on one occasion?

    (0) Never
    (1) Less than monthly
    (2) Monthly
    (3) Weekly
    (4) Daily or almost daily

4. How often during the last year have you found that you were not able to stop drinking once you had started?

    (0) Never
    (1) Less than monthly
    (2) Monthly
    (3) Weekly
    (4) Daily or almost daily

5. How often during the last year have you failed to do what was normally expected from you because of drinking?

    (0) Never
    (1) Less than monthly

    (2) Monthly
    (3) Weekly
    (4) Daily or almost daily

6. How often during the last year have you needed a first drink in the morning to get yourself going after a heavy drinking session?

    (0) Never
    (1) Less than monthly
    (2) Monthly
    (3) Weekly
    (4) Daily or almost daily

7. How often during the last year have you had a feeling of guilt or remorse after drinking?

    (0) Never
    (1) Less than monthly
    (2) Monthly
    (3) Weekly
    (4) Daily or almost daily

8. How often during the last year have you been unable to remember what happened the night before because you had been drinking?

    (0) Never
    (1) Less than monthly
    (2) Monthly
    (3) Weekly
    (4) Daily or almost daily

9. Have you or someone else been injured as a result of your drinking?

    (0) No
    (2) Yes, but not in the last year
    (4) Yes, during the last year

10. Has a relative, friend, doctor, or other health worker been concerned about your drinking or suggested you cut down?

    (0) No
    (2) Yes, but not in the last year
    (4) Yes, during the last year

Scores of 8 or above are associated with hazardous or harmful alcohol use.

**Source:** Bohn, Babor, and Kranzler (1995); Saunders, Aasland, Babor, de la Fuente, & Grant, (1993).

food while drinking alcoholic beverages is that the presence of food in your stomach slows the emptying process.

*Blood alcohol concentration (BAC)* is the percentage of alcohol in the blood; a BAC of .05% is 5 parts of alcohol per 1,000 parts of blood. Forty-six states and the District of Columbia use a BAC of .08 as the legal definition of intoxication. In these states a driver who tests at or above a BAC of .08 is deemed to be "per se intoxicated," and thus no additional proof of driving impairment is required (Findlaw, 2005). All states

**FIGURE 4-14** BAC levels. The concentration of alcohol in the blood is related to body weight and the number of drinks consumed. The BAC levels in this chart assume that the drinks have been consumed in 1 hour. At the same weight and after consuming identical amounts of alcohol, women will typically have a slightly higher BAC than men. The shaded areas represent BAC levels that would meet the new .08 standard for defining driving under the influence.

**Source:** Pennsylvania Liquor Control Board (1995).

### Approximate Blood Alcohol Percentage: Men
Body Weight in Pounds

| Drinks | 100 | 120 | 140 | 160 | 180 | 200 | 220 | 240 |
|---|---|---|---|---|---|---|---|---|
| 0 | .00 | .00 | .00 | .00 | .00 | .00 | .00 | .00 |
| 1 | .04 | .03 | .03 | .02 | .02 | .02 | .02 | .02 |
| 2 | .08 | .06 | .05 | .05 | .04 | .04 | .03 | .03 |
| 3 | .11 | .09 | .08 | .07 | .06 | .06 | .05 | .05 |
| 4 | .15 | .12 | .11 | .09 | .08 | .08 | .07 | .06 |
| 5 | .19 | .16 | .13 | .12 | .11 | .09 | .09 | .08 |
| 6 | .23 | .19 | .16 | .14 | .13 | .11 | .10 | .09 |
| 7 | .26 | .22 | .19 | .16 | .15 | .13 | .12 | .11 |
| 8 | .30 | .25 | .21 | .19 | .17 | .15 | .14 | .13 |
| 9 | .34 | .28 | .24 | .21 | .19 | .17 | .15 | .14 |
| 10 | .38 | .31 | .27 | .23 | .21 | .19 | .17 | .16 |

### Approximate Blood Alcohol Percentage: Women
Body Weight in Pounds

| Drinks | 90 | 100 | 120 | 140 | 160 | 180 | 200 | 220 | 240 |
|---|---|---|---|---|---|---|---|---|---|
| 0 | .00 | .00 | .00 | .00 | .00 | .00 | .00 | .00 | .00 |
| 1 | .05 | .05 | .04 | .03 | .03 | .03 | .02 | .02 | .02 |
| 2 | .10 | .09 | .08 | .07 | .06 | .05 | .04 | .04 | .04 |
| 3 | .15 | .14 | .11 | .10 | .09 | .08 | .07 | .06 | .06 |
| 4 | .20 | .18 | .15 | .13 | .11 | .10 | .09 | .08 | .08 |
| 5 | .25 | .23 | .19 | .16 | .14 | .13 | .11 | .10 | .09 |
| 6 | .30 | .27 | .23 | .19 | .17 | .15 | .14 | .12 | .11 |
| 7 | .35 | .32 | .27 | .23 | .20 | .18 | .16 | .14 | .13 |
| 8 | .40 | .36 | .30 | .26 | .23 | .20 | .18 | .17 | .15 |
| 9 | .45 | .41 | .34 | .29 | .26 | .23 | .20 | .19 | .17 |
| 10 | .51 | .45 | .38 | .32 | .28 | .25 | .23 | .21 | .19 |

Your body can get rid of one drink per hour.
One drink is 1.5 oz. of 80 proof liquor, 12 oz. of beer, or 5 oz. of table wine.

The National Institute on Alcohol Abuse and Alcoholism has targeted the college-age population for programs designed to reduce alcohol-related problems.

## Alcohol Myths

**1 MYTH:** I can drink and still be in control.
**FACT:** Drinking impairs your judgment, which increases the likelihood that you will do something you'll later regret such as having unprotected sex, being involved in date rape, damaging property, or being victimized by others.

**2 MYTH:** Drinking isn't all that dangerous.
**FACT:** One in three 18- to 24-year-olds admitted to emergency rooms for serious injuries is intoxicated. And alcohol is also associated with homicides, suicides, and drownings.

**3 MYTH:** I can sober up quickly if I have to.
**FACT:** It takes about 3 hours to eliminate the alcohol content of two drinks, depending on your weight. Nothing can speed up this process—not even coffee or cold showers.

**4 MYTH:** It's OK for me to drink to keep up with my boyfriend.
**FACT:** Women process alcohol differently. No matter how much he drinks, if you drink the same amount as your boyfriend, you will be more intoxicated and more impaired.

**5 MYTH:** I can manage to drive well enough after a few drinks.
**FACT:** About one-half of all fatal traffic crashes among 18- to 24-year-olds involve alcohol. If you are under 21, driving after drinking any alcohol is illegal and you could lose your license. The risk of a fatal crash for drivers with positive BACs compared with other drivers (i.e., the relative risk) increases with increasing BAC, and the risks increase more steeply for drivers younger than age 21 than for older drivers.

**6 MYTH:** I'd be better off if I learn to "hold my liquor."
**FACT:** If you have to drink increasingly larger amounts of alcohol to get a "buzz" or get "high," you are developing tolerance. Tolerance is actually a warning sign that you're developing more serious problems with alcohol.

**7 MYTH:** Beer doesn't have as much alcohol as hard liquor.
**FACT:** A 12-ounce bottle of beer has the same amount of alcohol as a standard shot of 80-proof liquor (either straight or in a mixed drink) or 5 ounces of wine.

National Institute on Alcohol Abuse and Alcoholism

National Institutes of Health

Questions? Visit your campus health center or NIAAA at http://www.niaaa.nih.gov

use a stricter standard (called *zero tolerance*) for drivers younger than 21; a BAC of up to .02 (depending on the state) defines driving under the influence (DUI). As you can see in Figure 4-14, your BAC depends primarily on your weight and the number of drinks you have consumed. A person who weighs 120 pounds will have a much higher BAC than one who weighs 240 pounds if they both consume the same number of drinks during the same period of time. A woman who weighs the same as a man and consumes the same amount of alcohol will have a slightly higher BAC level. This sex difference in BAC levels may be due to differences in the level or the efficiency of an enzyme (alcohol dehydrogenase) that breaks down alcohol. For reasons that are not yet understood, the enzyme is not as efficient in women as it is in men (Braun, 1996). With a BAC of about .32, you could endure surgery without awareness; BAC levels of .40 and higher can paralyze the part of the brain (the medulla) that controls breathing and thus cause death (Wechsler & Wuethrich, 2002).

Alcohol affects virtually all organs of the body, especially the brain. Did you ever wonder why some of your friends behave in outrageous ways at parties after having consumed alcohol? Alcohol depresses brain areas that inhibit behavior, thereby allowing the person to engage in behaviors that might not otherwise occur. Even at low levels, alcohol quickly affects vision, reaction time, muscle coordination, and judgment.

One reason people drink alcohol is the expectation of positive effects (Jung, 2001): They believe alcohol helps them feel better, overcome a gloomy mood, or fall asleep more easily. The "feel-good" effects of alcohol are often immediate, whereas negative consequences are often delayed, sometimes by minutes (loss of coordination) or years (loss of liver function) (Martinic & Leigh, 2004). In low doses, alcohol reduces anxiety in nervous or shy persons, but in higher doses, it interferes with sexual performance (Crowe & George, 1989). Shakespeare summarized the effects of alcohol on sexual arousal in these words from *Macbeth* (Act 2, Scene 1): "It provokes the desire but takes away the performance."

People who have been drinking alcoholic beverages may end up in a sexual or driving situation that seems to contradict their usual attitudes and intentions. Why? Alcohol leads to an altered state of consciousness characterized by a decreased capacity to attend to information. In one study, sober and intoxicated college students expressed equally negative attitudes when they were asked general questions about drinking and driving. When asked more specific questions, however, such as "Would you drink and drive only a short distance?" intoxicated students were less likely than sober ones to say no (MacDonald, Zanna, & Fong, 1995). Thus, intoxicated persons may attend only to the most salient cues at the moment, such as the desire to get home as quickly as possible. This *alcohol myopia* (Steele & Josephs, 1990) may account for a number of instances in which intoxicated drinkers engage in behaviors that contradict attitudes they express while sober.

Among the factors responsible for drinking are social pressures and the expectation of positive effects of alcohol.

There appears to be a relation between alcohol and aggression. For example, approximately 42% of the violent crimes reported to police yearly involved alcohol, and estimates for specific crimes are even higher (National Institute on Alcohol Abuse and Alcoholism, 1997). Recent laboratory research has clarified our understanding of the association between alcohol and aggression. At low BAC levels, expectations seem to play a significant role in the effects of alcohol; at higher levels, the biological effect of alcohol on the brain is probably the prime determinant of its influence. Violence is more likely to occur at higher BAC levels (Chermack & Taylor, 1995). The specific mechanism that accounts for increased aggression after ingestion of high doses of alcohol is not known. Alcohol has a wide range of effects that may play a role. For example, high doses of alcohol reduce fear, which may diminish the concern about potential harm resulting from aggressive actions.

MRI images of the brains of two men, one with and one without a history of heavy alcohol consumption. The dark areas reveal enlarged ventricles (fluid-filled spaces) resulting from a loss of brain tissue. Changes such as this one are common in persons who have consumed large amounts of alcohol for many years.

One serious consequence of long-term heavy consumption of alcohol is a form of withdrawal called *delirium tremens* (*DTs*). The symptoms include severe anxiety, a fast pulse, and even death. Vivid hallucinations, especially of small, quickly moving insects or animals, also occur and can heighten anxiety. The hallucinations may result from the REM rebound, because alcohol suppresses REM; when alcohol is withdrawn, a great deal of REM returns.

Another long-term consequence of alcohol use is *Korsakoff's syndrome*, a severe brain impairment characterized by forgetting incidents of one's daily life as soon as they occur. Consequently, people with this syndrome virtually live in the past. For example, a person who developed this condition in the 1960s might believe that the president of the United States today is John F. Kennedy (Oscar-Berman, Shagrin, Evert, & Epstein, 1997). An alcoholic's diet often lacks certain vitamins; a deficiency in thiamine (a B vitamin) plays a crucial role in the development of Korsakoff's syndrome. Extensive use of alcohol can damage brain areas that are important to memory, such as the hippocampus (Sullivan & Marsh, 2003).

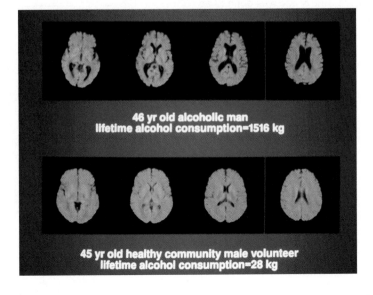

46 yr old alcoholic man
lifetime alcohol consumption=1516 kg

45 yr old healthy community male volunteer
lifetime alcohol consumption=28 kg

Although the number and percentage of highway deaths that are alcohol-related dropped over the past decade, approximately 40% of highway deaths are related to the use and abuse of alcohol. The Vermont state trooper shown here is reviewing what remains of a car involved in an accident that killed four teenagers after a night of heavy drinking.

**STUDY TIP**

After reading the section on alcohol, write a short summary describing what you believe to be the most significant patterns of alcohol use. Support your opinion with descriptions of the consequences of these patterns.

**Factors That Influence Alcohol Use.**     Drinking patterns vary among different populations within our society. For example, men are more likely to drink alcohol and more likely to drink greater amounts (see Figure 4-15). According to the National Household Survey on Drug Abuse and Health (Substance Abuse and Mental Health Services Administration, 2004), 57.3% of males aged 12 or older were current drinkers compared to 43.2% of females (that is, had consumed at least one drink in the 30 days prior to the survey). Among males aged 12 and over, there were 35.5 million (30.9%) who had engaged in binge drinking in the 30 days prior to the survey; among females there were 18.2 million binge drinkers, or 14.8%.

In the United States the 1-year prevalence of alcohol abuse and dependence (commonly called *alcoholism*) is approximately 7% of people over age 18, a total of about 14 million people. The rates of alcohol abuse and dependence vary according to a number of factors, especially the person's sex (Grant et al., 2004). The rates of alcohol abuse and dependence are higher for men than for women. Age is also a factor: The 1-year

**FIGURE 4-15** Heavy alcohol use. Heavy use was defined as consuming five or more drinks on the same occasion on at least 5 different days in the past 30 days. The rates for men are significantly higher than those for women. This patterns hold for each ethnic group.

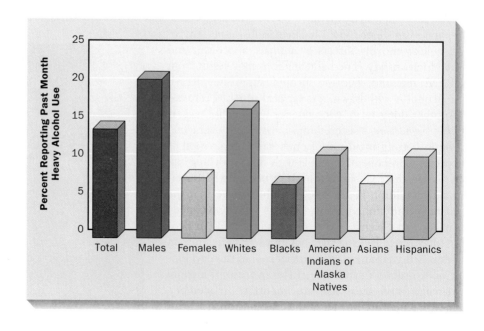

prevalence of problem drinking is much higher among persons aged 18 to 29 than at other ages (Grant et al., 1994).

Both physiological and social factors play important roles in alcohol consumption. About 50% of East Asians have a deficiency in the enzyme that breaks down alcohol in the body. As a result, they may experience *flushing* when they consume as little as one drink. This reaction involves a reddening of the face and neck that may be accompanied by headaches, nausea, and other symptoms (Liska, 2004). Therefore, Asians are often thought to be unlikely to become problem drinkers. Asian Americans report lower levels of alcohol drinking than Caucasians, which may be due to this reaction (Akutsu, Sue, Zane, & Nakamura, 1989). Surveys of drinking among men in Korea and Japan, however, have revealed alcohol abuse and dependence to be at least as high as it is in the United States (Helzer et al., 1990; Yamamoto & Lin, 1995). By contrast, Chinese people in Taiwan drink significantly less than Koreans and Japanese do, and they are less likely to develop alcohol abuse and dependence. Korean and Japanese men often feel social pressures to drink, even though their capacity to handle alcohol is limited. By contrast, Chinese culture advocates moderation in the use of alcohol (Yamamoto & Lin, 1995).

**Barbiturates and Benzodiazepines.**   **Barbiturates** are commonly called "downers" because they depress the functioning of the CNS. Depending on the dosage, their effects range from mild sedation to coma (Julien, 2001; Kuhn, Swartzwelder, & Wilson, 2003). At very high doses, barbiturates can lead to serious withdrawal symptoms, including life-threatening convulsions. Barbiturates have a very narrow therapeutic ratio, which means that the amount needed for a therapeutic effect is close to the amount that can be dangerous or even lethal (Gahlinger, 2004). These drugs interfere with the oxygen-using and energy-producing systems in the body, which induces sleep but can lead to death and coma (Liska, 2004).

Because most barbiturates cause drowsiness, in the past they were used to treat insomnia. This use has declined dramatically, however, as physicians have recognized that barbiturates do not induce natural sleep; rather, they suppress REM and Stage 4 sleep. What's more, it is easy to take a lethal overdose of barbiturates. A person with a sleep problem might seek a prescription for a barbiturate and then either knowingly or unknowingly also consume some alcohol. The combination of these two drugs dramatically reduces CNS activity, sometimes leading to death. In fact, many of the effects of barbiturates are indistinguishable from those of alcohol.

Because barbiturates have been used to induce sleep, they have been called *sedative-hypnotics*. Their use as sleep-inducing drugs has generally been taken over by the benzodiazepines (see Chapters 2 and 13), which are considered safer than barbiturates (Gahlinger, 2004; Kuhn et al., 2003). Both barbiturates and benzodiazepines (also called *minor tranquilizers*) work by increasing the binding of the inhibitory neurotransmitter GABA (see Chapter 2). In addition to their use in treating sleep-related difficulties, benzodiazepines are used in the treatment of anxiety and agitation and to relax muscles (Griffith, 2004; McKim, 2000). Among the common benzodiazepines are diazepam (Valium), alprazolam (Xanax), and flurazepam (Dalmane). One of the other benzodiazepines, Rohypnol, is known on the street as "rophies," Mexican Valium, and Roach. Its detrimental effects on memory and its quick action as a sedative that can last for 8 hours have led to its nickname, the "forget pill" or "forget-me pill." The pill has been slipped into drinks of unsuspecting women who have been raped.

# Stimulants

**Stimulants** are drugs that speed up the activity of the CNS. Among the most common stimulants are a group of synthetic drugs called *amphetamines* such as *Benzedrine* and *Dexedrine* (McKim, 2000). Also known as "uppers" or "speed," these drugs stimulate the release of the neurotransmitters dopamine and norepinephrine. In low to moderate doses, amphetamines increase alertness, elevate mood, reduce appetite and the need for

**barbiturates**
Depressant drugs that are used to induce sleep but can be deadly when combined with alcohol

**stimulants**
Drugs that increase the activity of the CNS

During the 1800s, cocaine was an ingredient (often in trace amounts) in thousands of patent medicines. Until 1903 Coca-Cola contained cocaine and was marketed as a cure for headaches and other ills.

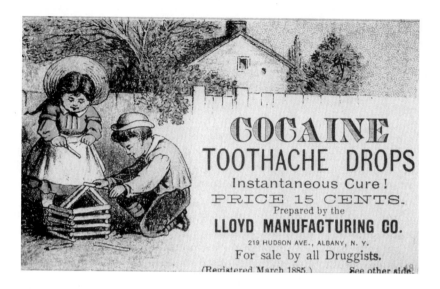

sleep, and induce euphoria. Larger doses of amphetamines cause irritability and anxiety or bring on a serious reaction that is indistinguishable from paranoid schizophrenia (see Chapter 12).

**Amphetamines** have a wide range of effects that mimic the body's reaction to stress: increasing blood pressure, increasing respiration rate, diverting blood from internal organs to skeletal muscle, and suppressing appetite (Liska, 2004). They were formerly used in weight-loss programs because they increase metabolism, but they are rarely used for that purpose today because their rapid tolerance can lead to serious physical and psychological effects. Among the few appropriate medical uses of amphetamines are the treatment of narcolepsy and *attention-deficit hyperactivity disorder* (*ADHD*) (Greenhill, 2005), which is diagnosed in 3 to 5% of school-age children (Daw, 2001). Children with this disorder exhibit high levels of activity and are inattentive and impulsive. The drug allows them to focus their attention, which, in turn, calms them down. *Ritalin*, an amphetamine-like drug, is the most frequently prescribed drug for the treatment of ADHD in children.

Another stimulant, *cocaine*, is extracted from the leaves of the coca plant that grows primarily in Peru and Bolivia. For centuries, inhabitants of the Andes Mountains have chewed coca leaves to counteract fatigue (McKim, 2000). Popular views of cocaine have changed dramatically over the years. In the 1800s, cocaine was hailed as a wonder drug and even used in cold remedies. Sigmund Freud proposed it as a cure for depression, fatigue, and alcohol problems (Julien, 2001). Until 1903 it was an ingredient in Coca-Cola. During the 1960s and 1970s, cocaine use was often associated with glamorous industries and lifestyles, such as show business and professional sports. Current surveys indicate that 2.5% (5.9 million) of the population used cocaine in the past year, and .80% (2 million) reported its use in the 30 days prior to the survey. About 15% of Americans aged 12 and older (34.1 million) have used cocaine at least once (Substance Abuse and Mental Health Services Administration, 2004).

Cocaine is the most potent stimulant of natural origin. Street dealers generally dilute it with inert substances such as cornstarch, talcum powder, and/or sugar, or with active drugs such as amphetamines. It can be eaten, injected into the veins, smoked, or inhaled through the nose (snorted). When cocaine is snorted, it reaches the brain in 1 to 3 minutes and produces a high that lasts for half an hour. When smoked, it produces an effect in 10 seconds that peaks in 3 to 5 minutes and lasts for about 15 minutes. Because the high produced by smoked cocaine is so short and intense, it is especially addictive (Gahlinger, 2004). When it is injected, its potency is increased greatly, making this practice very dangerous and potentially lethal. *Crack* is a purified form of cocaine that is very potent when smoked. The term *crack* derives from the crackling sound heard when the drug is mixed with chemicals and heated. The use of crack leads to a high in

**amphetamines**
Stimulants that are used to treat attention-deficit hyperactivity disorder and narcolepsy

The use of methamphetamine is a serious and growing problem. Although there are restrictions on the sale of ingredients, these restrictions have not had much impact. The ingredients are widely available, useful products such as over-the-counter cold tablets. When meth labs are discovered, officials must carefully dispose of the mixture of ingredients as it poses a danger to those who live nearby.

less than 10 seconds. All forms of cocaine increase the release and block the reuptake of dopamine and norepinephrine in the brain. A rapid and powerful high is followed by a dramatic low that creates a craving for more of the drug. Laboratory animals have been observed to self-administer cocaine until they died (Siegel, 1989). Cocaine increases heart rate and blood pressure, raises mental awareness, and reduces fatigue. These effects are similar to those of amphetamines, although they do not last as long.

Methamphetamine is a stimulant that has been called "America's most dangerous drug" (Jefferson, 2005); it can be snorted, smoked, or injected. In 2003, over 1 million Americans aged 12 and over were current users of *meth*, *crystal*, *speed*, or *ice* (Substance Abuse and Mental Health Services Administration, 2004). Methamphetamine is less expensive and possibly more addictive than cocaine or heroin (Miller, 2005). It was used by Japanese kamikaze pilots during World War II; today it is Japan's most popular illicit drug. Its popularity is attributed to its ability to boost energy, induce euphoria, and suppress appetite. Its use in the United States began in rural areas and on the West Coast, but it has spread rapidly across the entire country (Jefferson, 2005). It floods the brain's reward system with dopamine, so much so that the system becomes worn out. The long-term consequences can be chronic apathy and inability to experience any pleasure at all. Too much of a "good" thing can be just that in the case of meth.

Methamphetamine is typically made in small home operations called "meth labs." The ingredients are found in readily available products, including the ephedrine or pseudoephedrine found in over-the-counter cold and allergy tablets as well as chemicals found in brake cleaner, drain cleaner, and camera batteries. The federal and state governments have been trying to limit the quantities of such products that can be sold in order to reduce the amount of methamphetamine that is manufactured and distributed (Gahlinger, 2004).

*Methylenedioxymethamphetamine (MDMA)* is a synthetic substance that can be manufactured from readily available materials (Stevens & Smith, 2001). MDMA or *ecstasy* is also known as *XTC, Adam, MDM, hug, beans,* and *love drug.* In 2004, 11 million people aged 12 or older used ecstasy at least once; 450,000 of them were current users (defined as having used the drug within the 30 days prior to the survey [Substance Abuse and Mental Health Services Administration, 2004]. MDMA is frequently used in combination with other drugs, including caffeine, methamphetamine, cocaine, ephedrine (a stimulant), and ketamine (an anesthetic used by veterinarians, although it also has uses in humans). Although it is typically taken orally in the form of tablets or capsules, it can also be snorted or injected in the form of pure powder dissolved in water; its effects last for 4 to 6 hours (Kuhn et al., 2003).

MDMA is chemically similar to the stimulant methamphetamine and the hallucinogen mescaline (National Institute on Drug Abuse, 2005), yet its effects are unique. For example, its resemblance to stimulants has a notable exception: MDMA users experience a warm state of "empathy" and good feelings for all around them (Kuhn et al., 2003). MDMA is used at "raves" or all-night underground dance parties. In high doses,

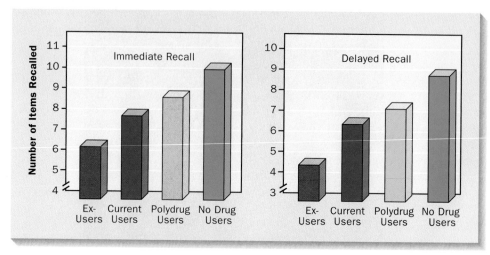

**FIGURE 4-16** There is growing evidence that the drug ecstasy (MDMA) can have dramatic effects on an individual's memory and attention. These changes may not be reversible.

**Source:** National Institute of Drug Abuse (2001).

**opiates**
A group of naturally occurring or synthetic drugs that have properties similar to those of opium and thus reduce pain

The seedpod (top) of the poppy plant is the source of opium, which can be processed into morphine and codeine. Opium poppies have several petals, which last for 2 to 4 days and then drop off, revealing a small, round, green fruit or pod. The opium is collected from these pods by scratching or scoring them, which allows the opium to ooze out. The collected opium can then be processed into morphine, codeine, and heroin. Possession of this plant was declared illegal by the Opium Poppy Control Act of 1942.

it can interfere with the body's ability to regulate temperature (National Institute on Drug Abuse, 2005). Using ecstasy at rave parties tends to increase the risks of exhaustion and dehydration, and deaths due to heat stroke have been reported (Jung, 2001; Kuhn et al., 2003). Like amphetamines, MDMA increases dopamine and norepinephrine levels, typically to levels that are higher than those that occur with the use of cocaine. Unlike amphetamines, MDMA also increases serotonin levels; in fact, it is better at releasing serotonin into synapses than the other neurotransmitters (Kuhn et al., 2003). Some evidence suggests that people who take MDMA, even just a few times, may risk developing permanent problems with learning and memory (see Figure 4-16), possibly as a result of damage to neurons that use serotonin (Stevens & Smith, 2001).

Although it is not generally considered a drug and certainly does not require a prescription, *caffeine* is a widely available and frequently used stimulant. Caffeine is found in a variety of foods and drinks, including coffee, tea, chocolate, soft drinks, and some nonprescription drugs. Heavy and continuous use of food products that contain caffeine is responsible for many cases of insomnia. The effects of caffeine are not as severe as those of other stimulants because large amounts of caffeine would be necessary to cause similar symptoms.

Also included in the category of stimulants is *nicotine*, a potent substance that activates the brain, heart, and nervous system. Next to caffeine, nicotine is the most widely used stimulant in our society. Found in tobacco products, it increases blood pressure and heart rate, and it stimulates the body's fight-or-flight response. There are at least 1,200 toxic chemicals in tobacco smoke, many of which cause cancer. Cigarette smoke contains tar; a number of gases, including carbon monoxide; and, of course, nicotine. More than a decade ago the Surgeon General of the United States (U.S. Department of Health and Human Services, 1988) cited cigarette smoking as the largest single preventable cause of premature death in the United States. Nevertheless, millions of Americans continue to smoke: In 2004 more than 70 million people (aged 12 and over) were current users of cigarettes or other tobacco products (Substance Abuse and Mental Health Services Administration, 2004). We discuss the health problems associated with smoking in more detail in Chapter 14.

## Opiates

The term **opiates** or *opioids* refers to a group of naturally occurring or synthetic drugs (see the discussion of endorphins in Chapter 2) that have properties similar to those of opium.

This family of drugs is also called *narcotic analgesics* (or just *narcotics*) because they produce analgesia (loss of sensitivity to pain) and make a person sleepy (McKim, 2000). Opium is derived from the unripe seedpod of the poppy plant. Although the poppy had its origins in Asia (including Afghanistan), it is now grown in countries with similar climates throughout the world, including Mexico and South America, which are major sources of U.S. heroin (Liska, 2004; McKim, 2000). When the poppy is scratched, it oozes a sap, which is scraped off a day later and formed into cakes of opium. Two of the drugs derived from this *opium* are *morphine* and *codeine* (Liska, 2004); of the two, morphine is the more powerful painkiller. Also included in the opiate category is *heroin*, a semisynthetic compound that is produced from morphine. Its many street names include *horse, junk, Big H,* and *antifreeze.* Heroin gets to the brain faster and in higher concentrations than morphine. In recent years there has been an increase in heroin use and a shift from injecting it to smoking or sniffing heroin with improved purity levels. People who use opiates at first experience a sleepy, pleasant euphoria and relief from anxiety and stress. Continued use, however, leads to tolerance that makes it impossible to feel any pleasurable effects.

Opiates are highly addictive and potentially dangerous. Depending on the dosage, the method of administration, and the user's tolerance level, their effects can range from mild sedation and relaxation to paralysis and death. Opiates are also associated with powerful withdrawal effects. Withdrawal from opiates produces *agitated dysphoria,* a condition characterized by symptoms including pain throughout the body, sweating, and stomach upset that may be mistaken for flu symptoms. Today the primary medical uses of opiates are pain relief (analgesia), relief of coughing, and treatment of diarrhea (Griffith, 2004).

## Hallucinogens

**Hallucinogens** are drugs that can change a person's perception, thinking, emotions, and self-awareness. They have been used for thousands of years in magical, mystical, and religious ceremonies. This class of drugs, sometimes called *psychedelic drugs,* includes compounds that are natural in origin as well as a growing number of drugs produced in laboratories. Hallucinogens can produce hallucinations, time and space distortions, and symptoms similar to those found in severe psychological disorders.

**Lysergic acid diethylamide (LSD)** is a colorless, odorless, and slightly bitter to tasteless drug derived from ergot, a fungus that grows on rye and other grains. Usually taken by mouth, LSD is rapidly absorbed by the body, and a small amount finds its way to the cortex. LSD is often added to absorbent paper such as blotter paper and divided into small decorated squares. The effects of LSD depend on the amount taken; the user's personality, mood, and expectations; and the surroundings in which the drug is used. Physical effects include sweating, dilated pupils, elevated body temperature, and increased heart rate and blood pressure. Changes in sensations and emotions, however, are much more dramatic than the physical signs. A user may feel several emotions at once or swing rapidly from one emotion to another. Larger doses can produce delusions and hallucinations such as changing colors and shapes. Another reaction to the use of LSD, the *flashback,* is most likely to occur in people who are chronic users of hallucinogens. Without having taken the drug again, the person can suddenly experience a recurrence of aspects of an earlier drug experience, complete with feelings of paranoia and perceptual distortions.

**Phencyclidine piperidine (PCP)** can have depressant, stimulant, hallucinogenic, or analgesic effects, depending on the dosage. This white crystalline powder with a bitter taste can be eaten, smoked, or inhaled through the nose (snorted). Among its common or slang names are *angel dust* (when mixed with mint leaves, parsley, or low-grade marijuana), *ozone, rocket fuel,* and *killer joints* (when combined with marijuana). Because it is frequently mixed with other illicit drugs, it is difficult to obtain accurate reports of the extent of PCP use.

The varied effects of PCP include euphoria, very unpleasant feelings, dizziness, seizures, distorted sensations, hallucinations, coma, and even a tendency to commit violent acts. A particularly dangerous effect of PCP is a type of *dissociation* in which

**hallucinogens**
Drugs that can cause changes in thinking, emotion, self-awareness, and perceptions; these changes are often expressed in hallucinations

**lysergic acid diethylamide (LSD)**
Powerful hallucinogen derived from ergot, a fungus found on rye and other grains

**phencyclidine piperidine (PCP)**
Powerful hallucinogen that can have unpredictable depressant, stimulant, hallucinogenic, or analgesic effects

The term *marijuana* refers to the leaves and flowers of the cannabis plant, which is dried into a tobacco-like substance. The potency of marijuana varies, depending on the source and selection of plant materials, although the marijuana available today has higher levels of THC than the marijuana that was available during the 1960s and 1970s.

**Source:** J. J. Palladino.

**marijuana**
Substance derived from the *Cannabis sativa* plant

sensory inputs are so distorted that the user experiences no pain. In this condition a user might incur serious physical injury without realizing it. For example, one user was so disoriented that she jumped into a swimming pool and tried to exit from the bottom (Liska, 2004).

**Marijuana** is the most commonly used illicit drug in the United States (Substance Abuse and Mental Health Services Administration, 2004). It consists of the dried leaves and flowers of the *Cannabis sativa* (hemp) plant, which can be smoked, eaten, or drunk. Most often, it is smoked as a cigarette (a joint or a nail) or in a pipe (a bong). It is also mixed with food or used to brew tea. Hashish, or *hash*, is a more potent form of marijuana made by pressing resin from the leaves or flowers of the cannabis plant. Almost 97 million Americans (46%) aged 12 and older have used marijuana at least once in their lives and 14.6 million are current users (6.2%). In 2003, there were 2.6 million new marijuana users, which means each day an average of 7,000 Americans tried marijuana for the first time (Substance Abuse and Mental Health Services Administration, 2004).

Of the more than 400 compounds found in marijuana (Grinspoon & Bakalar, 1993), one is an important psychoactive ingredient—*delta-9-tetrahydrocannabinol* (*THC*). By-products of THC can be detected for days or weeks following even brief use of marijuana. This compound is rapidly absorbed into blood and tissue throughout the body, including the brain. It stimulates nerve receptors in the cortex and hippocampus, which are areas responsible for motor activity, concentration, and memory (Figure 4-17). Marijuana is known to be able to disrupt attention, short-term memory, and coordination (Cowley, 1997; Ilan, Smith, & Gevins, 2004; Lane, Cherek, Lieving, & Tcheremissine, 2005). The subjective experience of the marijuana high is influenced by the person's expectations about how he or she will feel, the amount of the drug taken, and its potency. Small to moderate doses of THC usually lead to feelings of well-being and euphoria and an intense hunger known as the *munchies*. Large doses can cause paranoia and hallucinations. The most common effects of THC, however, are an increase in heart rate and bloodshot eyes (McKim, 2000).

In Chapter 2 we described the story of researchers who wondered why the brain would have receptors for opiate-like substances; their search led them to find endorphins

**FIGURE 4-17** Marijuana can have a range of effects from its impact on memory, to a reduction in anxiety, to its ability to suppress vomiting and enhance appetite. These effects can be traced to the widespread locations of brain receptors that respond to the active ingredients in marijuana.

**Source:** Nicoll and Alger (2004).

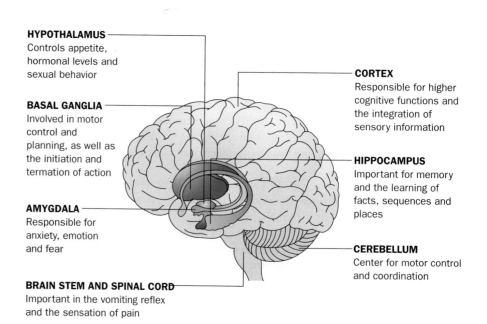

**HYPOTHALAMUS**
Controls appetite, hormonal levels and sexual behavior

**BASAL GANGLIA**
Involved in motor control and planning, as well as the initiation and termation of action

**AMYGDALA**
Responsible for anxiety, emotion and fear

**BRAIN STEM AND SPINAL CORD**
Important in the vomiting reflex and the sensation of pain

**CORTEX**
Responsible for higher cognitive functions and the integration of sensory information

**HIPPOCAMPUS**
Important for memory and the learning of facts, sequences and places

**CEREBELLUM**
Center for motor control and coordination

or endogenous opiates. Similarly, researchers wondered why the brain would have receptors for THC. Their search led them to discover nerve receptors in the brain that are specific for cannabinoids, which suggests that the brain manufactures its own marijuana (a family of brain substances called *endocannabinoids*). The first cannabinoid to be discovered was named *anandamide* from *ananda*, a Sanskrit word meaning "bliss." The greatest concentrations of cannabinoid receptors are found in the cerebellum, basal ganglia, and hippocampus, thus accounting for marijuana's wide range of actions (Gahlinger, 2004). These substances act in a rather peculiar way—they are pseudoneurotransmitters that can reduce the effectiveness of the inhibitory neurotransmitter GABA, thus increasing the transmission occurring at certain synapses (Nicoll & Alger, 2004).

At one time marijuana was portrayed as a "killer weed" that drove people to insanity and violence. Nevertheless, it became widely used during the 1960s and 1970s. Currently, opinions on the potential harm and the medical uses of marijuana are sharply divided. On the one hand, marijuana abuse is perceived to lead to a number of detrimental health effects (Substance Abuse and Mental Health Services Administration, 2002). On the other hand, some evidence suggests that marijuana can alleviate pain and anxiety, suppress vomiting, and enhance appetite, which are important for patients suffering the side effects of chemotherapy for cancer (Nicoll & Alger, 2004; Piomelli, 2004). In recent years, an ongoing debate has focused on the potential medical benefits of marijuana. One side sees marijuana as a "wonder drug," whereas the other side considers it "inherently evil" (Brownlee, 2003). In the late 1990s, voters in several states approved the use of marijuana for such medical reasons. The White House Office of National Drug Control Policy commissioned the Institute of Medicine to review the scientific literature on the benefits and problems associated with marijuana use (Joy, Watson, & Benson, 1999). After reviewing the available evidence, they arrived at the following conclusions: "Although marijuana smoke delivers THC and other cannabinoids to the body, it also delivers harmful substances, including most of those found in tobacco smoke. In addition, plants contain a variable mixture of biologically active compounds and cannot be expected to provide a precisely defined drug effect. For those reasons there is little future in smoked marijuana as a medically approved medication" (p. 178).

In 2001, the U.S. Supreme Court ruled that marijuana had no medical benefit worthy of exception to existing laws on approval of drugs for medical use. In 2005, the Supreme Court decided that the federal government had the authority to enforce its laws banning the use of marijuana even if state law allowed such use. The suit was brought by two California women who were using marijuana for serious and debilitating disorders. Their use of marijuana was consistent with California's Compassionate Use Act, which allows patients to use small quantities of marijuana if it is recommended by a physician. Nine other states have similar laws. The Supreme Court ruling led John Walaters, the Director of National Drug Control Policy to declare the "end of medical marijuana as a political issue." Whether Walaters is correct or not will be known in the coming years. At the very least, it seems prudent to suggest that the court did not put an end to all marijuana use. Patients still have access to a synthetic form of marijuana called dronabinol marketed under the brand name Marinol.

## REVIEW SUMMARY

**1. Psychoactive substances** are drugs that affect consciousness, perception, mood, and behavior. Regular and excessive use can lead to **substance abuse** or **substance dependence**.

**2. Alcohol** use is associated with a range of medical and psychological consequences. One major effect is on parts of the brain responsible for inhibiting behavior.

**3.** The effects of alcohol are related to *blood alcohol concentration (BAC)*, an indication of the amount of alcohol in the blood. Your BAC is determined by how much you drink, the time you take to drink it, your weight, and whether you have consumed food before or while drinking.

**4.** Expectations about the effects of alcohol can influence drinking patterns. The relation of alcohol to violence, however, seems to be due to its biological effects, not to expectations. The rate of alcohol abuse and dependence is higher in men than in women.

**5.** Like alcohol, **barbiturates** and benzodiazepines are depressants that slow the activity of the CNS.

**6. Stimulants** such as **amphetamines** speed up the activity of the nervous system. One of the most widely used stimulants is *caffeine,* which is found in foods such as chocolate and beverages such as coffee. *Nicotine,* a major component of tobacco smoke, is associated with preventable diseases such as heart disease. *Cocaine* can get to the brain quickly and cause a powerful high followed by a dramatic low. Methamphetamine is a stimulant that is manufactured in small labs using readily available

ingredients. *MDMA* or *ecstasy* is similar to the stimulant methamphetamine and the hallucinogen mescaline, yet it induces a state of empathy.

**7. Opiates,** such as *morphine* and *codeine,* are derived from the seedpod of the poppy plant; their primary medical use is to reduce pain. *Heroin* is a semisynthetic compound derived from morphine.

**8. Hallucinogens** can cause changes in perception, including hallucinations. Among the best-known hallucinogens are **lysergic acid diethylamide (LSD)** and **phencyclidine piperidine (PCP) Marijuana** consists of dried leaves and flowers from the *Cannabis sativa* plant. The active psychoactive ingredient in marijuana is *delta-9-tetrahydrocannabinol (THC).*

## ✓ CHECK YOUR PROGRESS

1. Indicate whether each of the following is a depressant, a stimulant, an opiate, or a hallucinogen: ethyl alcohol, cocaine, caffeine, morphine, PCP, nicotine.

2. What processes or disorders are being described in the following examples?

   a. Despite regulations prohibiting alcohol use by pilots for 8 hours before a flight, Ted consumed 10 beers before piloting a plane. He said that 10 beers in him is not the same as 10 beers in someone who has not been drinking as long as he has. On what concept is his argument based?

   b. After taking barbiturates for 3 years, Jack wants to stop. When he tries to do so, however, he experiences disturbing physical and psychological symptoms. What is the name of the syndrome Jack is experiencing?

3. Which individual is engaged in a pattern called *binge drinking*?

   a. Sal frequently will consume five or more drinks at a single sitting.

   b. When she drinks, Alice will consume wine, beer, or a distilled beverage.

   c. Each time Tim goes out for a leisurely dinner he consumes enough alcohol to bring his BAC to .10.

   d. While "out on the town," Jean often switches back and forth from beer to wine and then to some distilled drink across several hours.

4. What BAC defines intoxication in most of the states?

   a. .05
   b. .08
   c. .12
   d. .15

5. A patient at the local hospital has been diagnosed with delirium tremens. Based on this diagnosis, which of the following is most likely to have occurred before his hospitalization?

   a. He consumed a combination of cocaine and heroin.
   b. He stopped consuming alcohol after years of heavy use.

   c. After years of smoking marijuana he suddenly switched to PCP.
   d. After consuming beer for years, he decided to try some distilled liquor.

6. Seven-year-old Andy has been diagnosed with attention-deficit hyperactivity disorder. Which of the following drug categories would be prescribed for this disorder?

   a. opiates
   b. stimulants
   c. depressants
   d. hallucinogens

7. Which drug is someone taking if its primary effects are to increase dopamine and norepinephrine levels in the brain?

   a. PCP
   b. heroin
   c. cocaine
   d. a benzodiazepine

8. Which individual is most likely experiencing withdrawal from opiates?

   a. Juan, who has been sleeping for 20 hours straight and has a rapid pulse
   b. Cara, who reports pain throughout her body and other symptoms that resemble the flu
   c. Ed, who has tremors and tics and cannot sit still for more than a few minutes at a time
   d. Debra, who has been consuming large amounts of carbohydrate-rich foods and has an elevated blood pressure

9. Studies of brain receptors that respond to the active ingredients in marijuana indicate that certain areas have an abundance of such receptors. Which brain areas are among those the have a large number of such receptor neurons?

   a. hippocampus, hypothalamus, cerebellum
   b. parietal lobes, pons, corpus callosum

c. hypothalamus, occipital lobes, thalamus
d. basal ganglia, temporal lobes, septum

**10.** You read a newspaper article on "The Most Commonly Used Illicit Drug" and recognize that the article must be focused on

a. heroin.
b. cocaine.
c. Ecstasy.
d. marijuana.

**ANSWERS: 1.** Ethyl alcohol is a depressant; cocaine is a stimulant; caffeine is a stimulant; morphine is an opiate; PCP is a hallucinogen; nicotine is a stimulant. **2. a.** tolerance **b.** withdrawal **3. a 4. b 5. b 6. b 7. c 8. b 9. a 10. d**

# Learning

## CHAPTER OUTLINE

Nearly every organism must learn to survive in its environment. Indeed, the ability to adapt to the environment is often a key to determining which organisms survive long enough to pass on their genes to future generations. According to the evolutionary perspective, learning is an adaptive behavior that supports *natural selection*. We have already examined the physical structures (Chapter 2) and sensory and perceptual processes (Chapter 3) we use to interact with our environment. In some cases our responses to environmental stimuli, such as reflexively blinking in response to a puff of air, are routine, very brief in duration, and do not even enter consciousness. In other instances our awareness is critical when it comes to responding to and interacting with our environment. For example, we need to remember how to call 911 to summon help when we arrive at the scene of a serious car accident; we need to know how to format our computer so that we can type the 10-page paper that is due next Wednesday; and we need to know how to turn off the water when we discover a leak in the bathroom that could cause significant damage to our belongings and to those of people in surrounding apartments. Similarly, once a field rat has found a way into a farmer's corn crib, it is helpful for the rat to remember how to return to this food source in the future. These longer-lasting effects of interacting with the environment are the focus of this chapter and the next. In short, they are what we mean when we speak of *learning*. In this chapter we discuss several basic forms of learning.

## WHAT IS LEARNING?

**For a person who has grown up in a small Nebraska town, driving in big-city traffic can be an anxiety-provoking experience. The furious pace and the large number of vehicles on the road can be overwhelming at first; with cars to the left, to the right, and almost in the trunk, there is little sanity in sight! After several months of driving to and from work during the height of rush hour in Chicago, however, Linda, who grew up in a small town, has become a real pro at driving in big-city traffic. *Why would Linda's improved driving ability be considered an example of learning?***

Psychologists define **learning** as a relatively permanent change in behavior or the potential to make a response that occurs as a result of experience (Hergenhahn & Olson, 2001; Mazur, 2006). This definition distinguishes learned behaviors from those that occur automatically in response to external events, like shivering in a cold wind or sweating when it is hot. By including the concept of experience in the definition, we distinguish between learned behaviors and behaviors that become possible as our physical capabilities develop—that is, *maturation*. For example, when you were 6 months old, it is unlikely that you were able to walk. Around the time of your first birthday (or shortly after), the ability to walk emerged. Did it occur as a result of learning? As we will see, the answer is no. When you were 2 years old, you did not have the strength to lift a 5-pound weight. By the time you were 10, however, lifting 5 pounds was easy. You did not have to learn anything to be able to walk or to pick up the 5-pound weight. As a result of the process of *maturation* (see Chapter 10), your muscles and nerves had developed to the point where you were able to walk and to lift the weight.

**learning**
A relatively permanent change in behavior or the potential to make a response that occurs as a result of experience

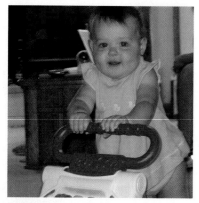

Eleven-month-old Victoria Marie is very close to walking but is not quite there yet. Ten days after this photograph was taken she took her first steps without the aid of a table, chair, or other object to steady her. Was her walking the result of learning? The answer is no. Her nerves and muscles had developed via a process called *maturation* to the point where this ability unfolded.

To return to our question, why would Linda's improved driving ability in Chicago be considered an example of learning? Unless Linda was very young at the time she began big-city driving, we can rule out maturation as a cause for the change in her behavior. Likewise, the change in Linda's driving behavior is not an automatic response, like shivering in a cold wind or blinking when a puff of air is directed toward your eyes. Rather, the repeated experience of rush-hour city driving has brought about a change in her behavior; she has *learned*.

In this chapter we first discuss two of the three basic types of learning, *classical* (or respondent) *conditioning* and *operant* (or instrumental) *conditioning*. Later in the chapter we will explore more cognitively oriented perspectives on learning along with the third basic type of learning, *observational* learning or modeling. Keep in mind that the word *conditioning* refers to the fact that the learner forms an association, usually between a stimulus and a response or between two stimuli.

## CLASSICAL CONDITIONING

A psychology instructor passes a can of powdered lemonade mix around the classroom; each student puts a spoonful of the powder on a sheet of paper. Once all students have their own lemonade powder, they are instructed to wet one of their fingers. When the instructor says "now," each student puts a small amount of lemonade powder on his or her tongue with the moistened finger. The effect of putting lemonade powder on the tongue is predictable: The mouth puckers, and saliva begins to flow. The instructor has the students repeat this procedure several times during the class period until all the lemonade powder is gone. Before the class period ends, the instructor says "now" without warning. The students' mouths pucker, and saliva flows. *What is the purpose of this class demonstration?*

This demonstration is an example of classical conditioning, which has become so closely associated with the Russian scientist Ivan Pavlov (1849–1936) that it is often called *Pavlovian conditioning*. Pavlov was a physiologist who had earned a medical degree; his work was so well respected that he received a Nobel Prize in Medicine in 1904 for his research on digestion.

Ivan Pavlov's research on digestion was so well regarded that he was awarded the Nobel Prize in 1904. In the course of his research, he surgically brought the opening of the salivary gland to the outside of the dog's skin so that the secretion of saliva could be seen and measured. Over time, Pavlov and his research team noticed that the dogs began salivating to stimuli other than food. The precision of the laboratory provided Pavlov with the setting in which he could investigate the components of what became known as *Pavlovian conditioning* or *classical conditioning*.

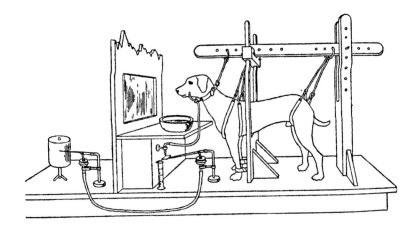

**FIGURE 5-1** Ivan Pavlov's research on digestion led to the awarding of the Nobel Prize in Medicine. What piqued Pavlov's interest was the tendency for the dogs to begin to salivate to stimuli such as the experimenter's footsteps. As a result, many researchers followed his lead and developed equipment like that shown here in order to investigate the principles of classical conditioning.

**Source:** Mazur (2006).

As part of his study of digestion, Pavlov surgically inserted a tube into dogs' mouths in order to collect and measure the amount of saliva the dogs produced (see Figure 5-1). He found that the dogs tended to salivate before food was placed in their mouths. In fact, they salivated at the sight of the dish for the food, the sight of the food itself, and the sound of the researcher's footsteps. Pavlov coined the term "psychic secretions" to describe what he observed, which he first viewed as an obstacle to his research on digestion. Consequently, he set out to get rid of these secretions but soon found that he was on to something much bigger than psychic secretions. The dogs had formed associations between a variety of stimuli (sight of the food dish, the food itself, and footsteps) and the meat powder, which brought forth the salivation he had observed. These various stimuli had become signals indicating that meat powder would soon be delivered into the dog's mouth. In short, they had learned.

Although Pavlov conducted much of his research with dogs, examples of classical conditioning can be found in many human behaviors. **Classical conditioning** is a form of learning that occurs when two stimuli—a neutral stimulus and an unconditioned stimulus—that are paired (presented together) become associated with each other. For example, the sight of McDonald's golden arches and the smell and taste of a juicy burger have occurred together, and as a result, many people associate the golden arches with tasty fast food.

## The Basic Elements of Classical Conditioning

The procedure for establishing classical conditioning is to present two events—called *stimuli*—so that the pairing of these two events causes a human participant or animal to make an *association* between them. At the start of conditioning, the first event, which in a laboratory setting may be the presentation of a light, a tone, or a word, is neutral—that is, not currently associated with the response to be established. What was the neutral stimulus in the lemonade example at the start of this section? Keep reading and you will find out. When this **neutral stimulus (NS)** is presented, the participant may notice that it is there, but it does not cause any particular reaction. By presenting the second event, called an **unconditioned stimulus (UCS),** after the NS, however, we transform the NS into a **conditioned stimulus (CS).** The NS becomes a CS because it is repeatedly paired with a UCS. This pairing eventually causes the participant to establish an association between the two events; the CS comes to *predict* or signal the occurrence of the UCS. In the lemonade powder example the word *now* was the NS; it became a CS after it was paired with the lemonade powder.

As the term suggests, the UCS automatically produces a reaction; the participant does not have to be trained to react to it. The UCS never fails to produce the same reaction. Food in your mouth causes you to salivate; touching a hot stove causes you to jerk your hand away; a puff of air to your eye causes you to blink; a loud noise causes you to react with the startle response. In psychological terms, the UCS *elicits*, or calls forth,

**classical conditioning**
Learning that occurs when two stimuli—a conditioned stimulus (originally a neutral stimulus) and an unconditioned stimulus—are paired and become associated with each other

**neutral stimulus (NS)**
Stimulus that, before conditioning, does not elicit a particular response

**unconditioned stimulus (UCS)**
Stimulus that automatically produces a response without any previous training

**conditioned stimulus (CS)**
Neutral stimulus that acquires the ability to elicit a conditioned response after being paired with an unconditioned stimulus

**unconditioned response (UCR)**
Reaction that is automatically produced when an unconditioned stimulus is presented

**conditioned response (CR)**
Response elicited by a conditioned stimulus that has been paired with an unconditioned stimulus; is similar to the unconditioned response

a response. The reaction that is elicited by the UCS is called the **unconditioned response (UCR).** If you have a feeling that we have already discussed this type of response, you are correct. These UCRs are reflexes, like those we described in Chapter 2. You do not have to learn a UCR; all organisms come equipped by nature with these built-in responses, which generally have survival value. For example, you do not learn to jerk your hand away when you touch a hot stove; you pull it away automatically. It is a built-in (unconditioned) response that may serve to protect you from further harm. As part of a routine physical examination, a physician may use a small rubber hammer to hit an area just below your knee. When your lower leg kicks up, the physician knows that particular reflex (called *knee flexion*) is working properly (see Chapter 2). Now, what is the UCR in the lemonade powder example?

When a participant associates the NS (for example, a light or a tone) with the UCS, the NS is transformed into a CS that can elicit a response similar to the UCR (for example, a little less saliva). The response caused by the CS is known as the **conditioned response (CR).** When the CS elicits the CR, we say that classical conditioning has occurred. Pavlov (1927) used food as the UCS in his pioneering studies. While a metronome was ticking (CS), he placed a small amount of meat powder (UCS) into a hungry dog's mouth. The meat powder caused the dog to begin salivating (UCR). Later, when just the sound of the ticking metronome was presented, the dog salivated (CR).

Let's return to the earlier demonstration in which lemonade powder was associated with the word "now" (Cogan & Cogan, 1984) so that you can experience classical conditioning firsthand. Consider what occurred naturally (UCS–UCR) and what was learned (CS–CR) and complete the blanks in this sentence to see if you can apply the terminology just described to the demonstration. "The CS, _____, paired with the UCS, _____, results in the UCR, _____." The CS is the word "now." The lemonade powder is the UCS; it automatically elicits the UCR of puckering and salivating. Initially the word "now" is a neutral stimulus. After it is paired with the lemonade powder several times, however, it becomes a CS and now elicits the CR of puckering and salivating.

Let's put these elements together in another example. Suppose that your younger brother is just tall enough to reach a hot skillet on the stove. He grabs it and immediately drops it. His pain is obvious and intense, and you try to comfort him. Finally, his tears stop, and you put the incident out of your mind. Three days later, however, the same skillet is again on the stove. Your brother enters the kitchen, sees the skillet, and begins to cry. Clearly, the skillet has taken on a new meaning for him, demonstrating that some stimuli are so memorable that they produce learning without the need for repeated pairings.

In classical conditioning terms, initially the skillet was an NS (did not cause any particular response); after conditioning, it became the CS. The intense heat was the UCS, which always elicits pain and an avoidance response. Those responses—the pain and jerking the hand away or dropping the skillet—constitute the UCR. Remember that the classical conditioning sequence involves first presenting the NS and then following it with the UCS. If these two events are associated, the NS becomes a CS that signals that the UCS is on its way.

After a conditioning experience of this type, when the CS is encountered alone, it produces a response—the CR—that is very similar to the UCR. In our example, the sight of the skillet reminds your brother of the pain he experienced. The classical conditioning sequences for this situation and for Pavlov's dogs are presented in diagrammatic form in Figure 5-2.

UCSs do not have to be painful events like pain, electric shock or hitting your finger with a hammer (Capaldi & Sheffer, 1992; Owens, Capaldi, & Sheffer, 1993). A variety of stimuli can serve as a UCS; their associated responses are reflexes that are often crucial for biological functioning, survival, and reproduction (Baldwin & Baldwin, 2001). For example, a bite of your favorite food when you are hungry automatically causes you to salivate. Food in your mouth is the UCS; salivation is the UCR. The positive feelings you experience when you receive a kiss or a hug are also examples of a UCS. Table 5-1 lists common UCSs and UCRs; these stimuli and

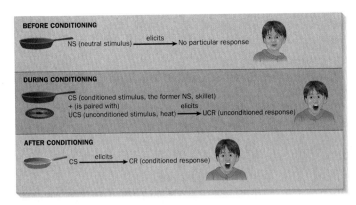

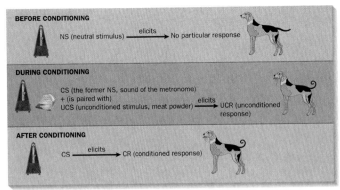

A                                                                   B

**FIGURE 5-2** Two examples of classical conditioning. Using our symbols, we can describe classical conditioning in the following manner: *Before Conditioning*: The NS originally does not elicit a specific response. *During Conditioning*: The NS (now called the CS) is presented just before the UCS. The UCS automatically elicits a UCR. *After Conditioning*: Later, when the CS is presented by itself, a CR, which is similar to the UCR, occurs. In short, a new response, the CR, has been conditioned to the CS because the CS has been paired with the UCS.

---

**TABLE 5-1**

## Common Unconditioned Stimuli (UCSs) and Their Associated Unconditioned Responses (UCRs)

The associations between these stimuli and responses are built in or innate. Each of the responses can be elicited from the organism by using the appropriate stimulus.

| UCS | UCR |
|---|---|
| **Voluntary muscles** | |
| sharp or hot stimuli | jerk away and cry |
| blows, shock, burns | withdrawal |
| object touches lip | sucking |
| **Circulatory system** | |
| high temperature | sweating, flushing |
| sudden loud noise | blanching, pounding heart |
| **Digestive system** | |
| good food | salivation |
| bad food | sickness, nausea, vomiting |
| **Respiratory system** | |
| irritation in nose | sneeze |
| throat clogged | cough |
| allergens | asthma attack |
| **Emotional system** | |
| painful blow | fear |
| sexual stimulation | erotic feeling |
| **Reproductive system** | |
| genital stimulation | vaginal lubrication, penile erection, orgasm |
| nipple stimulation | milk release (in lactating women) |

**Source:** Baldwin and Baldwin (2001).

their associated responses are found throughout our bodily systems. What is important about classical conditioning is that organisms learn to respond not only to the original UCS, they learn to respond to other CSs that become *associated* with our reflexes (Baldwin & Baldwin, 2001).

Obviously, psychologists do not hide in restaurants waiting to present a tone while you are eating, nor do most instructors take lemonade powder to class with them. Yet people become classically conditioned in much the same way that Pavlov's dogs did. For example, the sights and sounds that accompany meals can become CSs. For many people, the unique decor of a restaurant, an advertisement, or a menu may act as a CS. Have you ever found yourself salivating as you looked at the tempting pictures in an advertisement or browsed up and down the aisles of a grocery store? Numerous examples of classical conditioning of CRs exist in everyday life. Is there a particular song (CS) that prompts you to recall a happy moment (CR)? Do you know someone who purchases cars only of a certain color because that color was associated in the past with a favorite car?

## Hands On

## Conditioning Your Friends

The ease with which classical conditioning is demonstrated in class can be duplicated in real life. This demonstration rests on the premise that most people have been conditioned to flinch (the startle response) when they see someone stick a balloon with a pin. (The pin is the CS, the bang is the UCS, and the startle response is the UCR.) Use the following procedure to surprise your friends and observe classical conditioning at the same time.

You will need about 20 good-quality balloons and a needle. Any sharp sewing needle will do, but for especially dramatic effect, a foot-long needle is best. Blow up 15 to 20 balloons. Then have a friend pop five or six of them with the needle. Next, have your friends watch you use the needle to pop five or six more balloons. Once you have popped several of them, stick the needle into an area of the balloon where there is less tension (the nipple or around the knot). Because there is less tension at these points, the rubber is relatively thick, and the balloon does not pop when it is stuck with the needle. Your friends will still flinch, however. Why? They have been *conditioned* to expect a loud bang. If you use a foot-long needle, you can make the effect even more dramatic by passing the needle completely through the balloon (enter at the nipple and exit at the knot; see the accompanying photographs).

Dr. Edie McClellan of Ohio University Eastern prepares to demonstrate that a needle can be put through a balloon and not pop it. When the needle approaches the balloon (A), many students flinch—a conditioned response based on past experiences of hearing the noise as a pin was pushed into a balloon. Sticking the needle through the thick part of the balloon allows the needle to be passed entirely through the balloon without popping it (B).

**A**

**B**

## Psychological Detective

Think of your own examples of classical conditioning. You will probably find it easiest to start with the UCS, then decide what the UCR is, and finally determine what CSs might readily occur in the presence of the UCS. Think of a food smell that makes you remember a pleasant childhood memory—perhaps cookies baking or the cinnamon smell of hot apple pie. Do you think of a particular event, and does your mouth water? The food you enjoy is the UCS. What is the UCR? The CS? The CR? (See some possible answers at the end of the chapter.)

# Classical Conditioning Processes

Ivan Pavlov's research revealed several important processes of classical conditioning besides those discussed so far. These findings fall into two general categories: *acquisition*, or how we develop CRs, and *extinction*, or how we eliminate those responses.

**Acquisition.** Acquisition is the training stage during which a particular response (for example, salivating or blinking) is learned (occurs after a CS is presented). Several factors influence the acquisition of CRs. Among them are the order in which the CS and UCS are presented, the intensity of the UCS, and the number of times the CS and UCS are paired (Barker, 2001). We now take a closer look at each of these factors.

**Sequence of CS–UCS Presentation.** The sequence in which the CS and UCS are presented influences the strength of conditioning. The optimum sequence is for the CS to precede the UCS (by about .50 second). For example, Pavlov sounded the tone before putting meat powder in the dogs' mouths. This sequence is often called *forward conditioning*. Other sequences, such as the UCS preceding the CS (that is, *backward conditioning*), produce weaker conditioning if it produces any conditioning at all. Why? If the CS occurs after the UCS, it cannot serve as a signal of what is about to occur. The tone (CS) must precede presentation of the meat powder (UCS); reversing the sequence does not provide meaningful information to the organism.

**Strength of the UCS.** The stronger the UCS, the stronger the conditioning (Holloway & Domjan, 1993). When Pavlov gave his dogs a small amount of meat powder, they did not salivate as much as they did when he gave them larger amounts of meat powder. The hot skillet your younger brother grabbed on the stove was a painful and salient stimulus. Stronger UCSs elicit stronger UCRs; weaker UCSs elicit weaker UCRs.

**Number of CS–UCS Pairings.** The more times the CS and UCS are presented together, the stronger the CR becomes. It is easy to conduct research on the relation between the CS and the UCS when we can use a laboratory setup such as Pavlov's. Under such conditions, the number of times the CS and UCS are presented can be determined precisely. What's more, the laboratory environment allowed Pavlov to eliminate extraneous stimuli (such as footsteps) and to deliver the stimuli of interest in specific amounts at specified times; consequently, he focused his research on the stimuli of greatest interest (such as

**Source:** Psi Chi Newsletter. Reprinted with the permission of Psi Chi.

5.1

**FIGURE 5-3** Acquisition patterns in classical conditioning when the UCS is presented at different percentages on trials (a series of presentations of stimuli). Within a given trial, the CS and UCS were paired 25% to 100% of the time. Some participants received the CS and UCS on every presentation during a trial; in other cases, the UCS was presented with the CS only 25% of the time. Across trials, greater pairing of the UCS with the CS led to stronger conditioning, that is, more frequent occurrence of the CR.

**Source:** Hartman and Grant (1960).

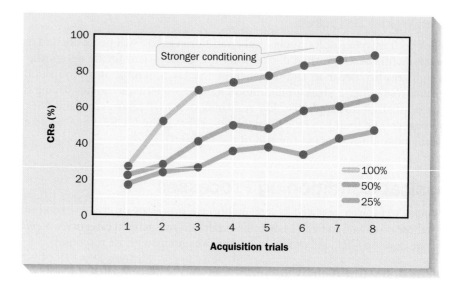

the sound of the metronome). The effects of varying numbers of CS–UCS pairings, however, can also be demonstrated in real life. If your little brother grabs the hot skillet more than once, chances are good that his CR to the skillet will be stronger. If you have eaten at an exceptionally fine restaurant several times, your CRs to the sight of the restaurant and its menu will be stronger than they would be if you had eaten there only once before. Figure 5-3 displays several patterns of classical conditioning acquisition; as you can see, as the percentage of pairings increases, acquisition of the CR becomes stronger.

**Extinction.** Once a CR has been acquired, what can be done to extinguish or eliminate that response? The easiest procedure is to present the CS without the UCS (CS alone) and record how strong the CR is and how many times or how long we can present the CS alone before the CR disappears (extinguishes). The number of times the CS is presented without the UCS is a very important factor in eliminating the CR. When Pavlov repeatedly sounded the tone (CS) without giving the dogs any meat powder (UCS), the number of drops of saliva produced gradually decreased each time the tone was sounded. Similarly, if your brother grabs the skillet several times when it is cold, his fear will decrease a little each time.

*Extinction* is a general term for a reduction and eventual disappearance of a behavior; in the case of classical conditioning, extinction occurs when repeated presentation of the CS alone leads to a decrease in the strength of the CR (Schreurs, 1993). The stronger the CR, the longer extinction takes. What takes place during acquisition influences the process of extinction. For example, the stronger the UCS and the more frequently it is presented during acquisition, the longer it will take to extinguish the CR.

**Spontaneous Recovery.** At times, classical conditioning participants seem to forget that extinction has occurred. Consider Pavlov's dog once again. Only the CS (a bell in this case) has been presented to the dog several times during its daily extinction session. The CR (salivation) has decreased until it appears that the dog is not salivating at all after the bell is presented. When the dog is returned to its cage, we might conclude that the extinction process is complete. When the CS is presented on the following day, however, the dog begins to salivate once more. Pavlov (1927) called this phenomenon **spontaneous recovery** because the CR recovers some of the strength it lost during previous extinction sessions. This process is diagrammed in Figure 5-4. The amount of spontaneous recovery decreases from day to day until the CR finally does not occur at the start of a session. At this point, extinction of the response is probably complete. One of the reasons spontaneous recovery occurs is that extinction is rarely complete. When extinction trials (the CS presented alone) take place, the organism reduces its tendency to respond but that tendency is not eliminated in most cases.

**spontaneous recovery**
Reappearance of an extinguished CR after the passage of time

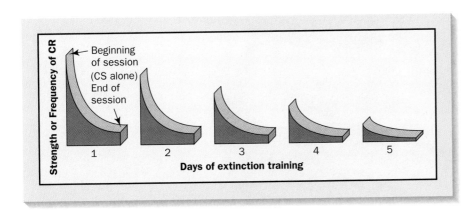

**FIGURE 5-4** Extinction occurs when the tone (CS) is presented without meat powder (UCS). By the end of each daily extinction session, the CR is quite weak. It regains some strength, however, by the start of the next session, a phenomenon known as *spontaneous recovery*. By the end of extinction, the CR is quite low, and the amount of spontaneous recovery may be undetectable.

Spontaneous recovery is not limited to laboratory experiments; it occurs in real-life situations as well. Suppose you went skiing last winter and on the second day you experienced a very bad fall. After summoning as much courage and determination as possible, you put your skis on and went back out on the slopes for the next 2 days. Thankfully, there were no additional spills, and your fear seemed to be extinguished. But is it completely extinguished, never to return again? Now, a full year later, you return to the ski resort. You experience a degree of apprehension as you pull on your ski boots. You thought the fear had disappeared—that it had been extinguished—by the time you were finished skiing last year, but a bit seems to have returned (spontaneous recovery) this year.

People who are the age of your middle-aged authors played with a variety of toys and games as children several decades ago. We didn't have DVDs, computers, video games, or other modern playthings. Red wagons, dolls, and bicycles brought hours of joy to these young children. Some of these playthings may have been stored in attics where they remained undisturbed and unseen for decades. A visit to the attic and the sight of one of these playthings will likely bring back the joy of many years ago. This example illustrates that spontaneous recovery can occur across years and even decades, and it is as likely to occur for a pleasant CS as for an unpleasant CS.

Figure 5-5 illustrates the relations among acquisition, extinction, and spontaneous recovery. Consult this figure as you read this section to provide you with the "big picture" of the elements and processes involved in classical conditioning.

**Generalization and Discrimination.**   Suppose that several days after your little brother made the mistake of grabbing the hot skillet, the two of you are walking through the housewares section of a department store when he starts crying and refuses to walk any farther. He acts as if his feet were set in concrete; "Not one more foot" he says with determination. You note where he is looking—at a display of skillets. Is he afraid of them also? Yes, he is, and the more those skillets resemble the one at home, the greater is his fear.

When a response occurs to stimuli that are similar to a CS, **generalization** has taken place. The effects of classical conditioning may be applied (generalized) to other stimuli that are similar to the original CS; they "spread" from the original stimulus to others. For example, although Pavlov's dogs were conditioned to salivate in response to a specific tone (CS), they also salivated when other, similar tones were presented (see Figure 5-6). Someone who has acquired a fear of snakes might react with fear when seeing a piece of rope lying on the ground a few feet away. The similarity of the snake to the rope elicits the fear response (CR), which generalized from the snake. Suppose your favorite color is red, and whenever you see it you

**generalization**
Occurrence of responses to stimuli that are similar to a CS

**FIGURE 5-5** The basic phases of classical conditioning. In the acquisition or training phase, the CS and UCS are paired together and lead to the UCR. This pairing eventually leads to production of the CR following the CS. Repeated presentation of the CS alone leads to extinction. Following the passage of time, presentation of the CS alone may lead to spontaneous recovery of the CR.

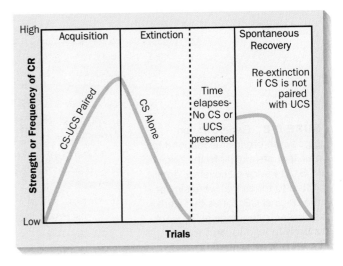

A bad fall on a ski slope can result in a classically conditioned fear. Getting up and "hitting the slopes" immediately after such a fall is one of the best ways to extinguish the fear. The extinction may be "forgotten" over the summer, resulting in spontaneous recovery of the fear response when you hit the slopes once again the following year.

**discrimination**
Occurrence of responses only to a specific CS

feel warm and cozy all over. You might have a similar, perhaps muted, reaction to pink and perhaps even to orange.

It is easy to see how generalization occurs. If you have ever been stung by a wasp, you probably have a healthy respect for all flying insects, especially those that resemble wasps. Your response has generalized from one stimulus to others. But if you are not stung every time you encounter a flying insect, many of these generalized responses will be extinguished. As children we quickly discover that butterflies and moths do not sting, whereas hornets and bees do. We therefore come to fear the stinging insects but not the others. In other words, we learn to distinguish or discriminate between CSs that accurately predict the occurrence of the UCS and those that do not (Bouton & Brooks, 1993; Nakajima, 1993). Through this process of **discrimination,** we have extinguished our fear of insects that do not sting but have retained our fear of insects that do. Generalization and discrimination work in opposite ways. Whereas generalization makes you more likely to respond to similar stimuli, discrimination narrows your response to the appropriate stimulus and no other. Discrimination thus requires stimuli that are clearly distinguishable. For example, if you could not easily distinguish between insects that sting and those that do not, imagine how apprehensive you would be whenever you went outdoors.

Almost every day, one of your authors takes a power walk through the neighborhood for exercise and weight control. One walk left him facing a large, long-haired, black dog, which apparently saw him as lunch and took a small but painful bite out of his leg. From that point on, this author has feared not only that dog but dogs that are similar (generalization) in size and color. On the other hand, this fear is not elicited by small

**FIGURE 5-6** Generalization occurs when organisms respond to stimuli that are similar to the original CS. As Pavlov discovered, dogs salivated to tones that were similar to the original CS. Tones that were less similar to the original CS were less likely to lead to the CR of salivation.

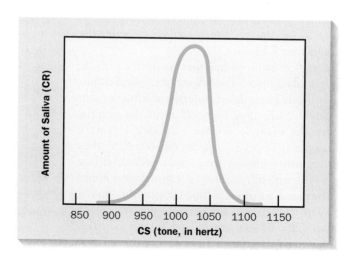

dogs of other colors (discrimination). One way to remember discrimination and generalization is to consider the following: Generalization widens or increases the range of stimuli that call forth a CR; discrimination narrows or decreases the range of stimuli that call forth a CR.

Pavlov (1928) understood this principle and investigated it. He trained a group of dogs to discriminate between a circle and an ellipse; the circle was always associated with food. Once this association was established, Pavlov changed the ellipse over a series of presentations until it was indistinguishable from the circle.

### Psychological Detective

What behavior(s) did Pavlov's dogs show when confronted by these two indistinguishable stimuli? Write down your answer before reading further.

Because the dogs were unable to discriminate between the two stimuli, they salivated to both of them. They displayed other behaviors that did not occur when they were able to discriminate between the two stimuli. They whined and yelped, became agitated, and tried to escape from their harnesses. These behaviors continued outside the experimental room. Pavlov called these inappropriate behaviors *experimental neuroses* and believed they occur when an animal or human attempts to solve a discrimination task that cannot be solved. This analysis provides a clue concerning a possible origin of some abnormal behaviors in humans (see Chapter 12; Baumrind, 1983). As the next section shows, such agitation and apprehension can influence our behavior.

## Applications of Classical Conditioning: Phobias and Beyond

In 1913, John B. Watson, a proponent of *behaviorism*, proclaimed that psychologists should study only directly observable behaviors (see Chapter 1). According to behaviorists, the primary business of psychology is to study observable behaviors such as jogging in the park, running through an airport to catch a flight, and even the observable components of emotion. Anything having to do with thinking, feeling, or consciousness was not considered an appropriate subject of psychological study because such "mentalistic" processes, if they existed at all, could not be observed directly. The behaviorists' goal was to discover which observable stimuli elicit which responses (observable behaviors). In pursuit of this goal, John Watson and his assistant, Rosalie Rayner, classically conditioned 11-month-old "Little Albert" to fear a white rat (Watson & Rayner, 1920). At first, Albert showed no fear of the rat and even allowed it to crawl on him. While Little Albert was playing with the rat, Watson hit a steel rod with a hammer, making a sudden, deafening noise. Not surprisingly, Albert was startled. Each time the loud noise was paired with the presence of the rat, Albert cried in fear. After several pairings of the two stimuli, Albert started crying at the sight of the rat, even when there was no noise, and he eventually came to fear any object that resembled a rat, such as a white rabbit and even the white whiskers on a Santa Claus mask. Albert developed a phobia for rats and rat like objects. Unfortunately, no one followed Albert throughout his life; hence we do not know how long these phobias plagued him, nor do we know if Albert ever overcame his fear of rats and similar stimuli.

Let's analyze the elements of Little Albert's fear. What UCS was used? What was the UCR? What were the CS and the CR? While you think about these questions, remember that the rat was also exposed to a frightening situation. For both Little Albert and the rat, the UCS was the loud noise created by hitting a steel bar with a hammer. The UCR was the state of being startled and scared. For Albert, the CS was the rat; for the rat, the CS was Albert. The CR for both of them was fear of an object that signaled that a loud noise might follow. These relations are diagrammed in Figure 5-7.

John B. Watson (left), his research assistant Rosalie Rayner (right), and Little Albert were part of one of the most well-known research efforts in psychology. The findings showed how classical conditioning could be responsible for the development of phobias. This research, however, raised many ethical questions; it could not be conducted under the ethics code in place today.

 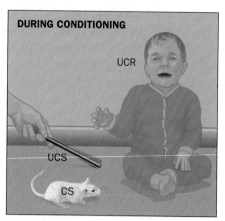 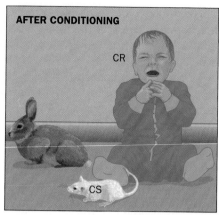

**FIGURE 5-7** Conditioning Little Albert to fear a white rat. *Before Conditioning*: Originally, Little Albert has no fear of the white rat (the NS for Little Albert); the rat has no fear of Little Albert (the NS for the rat). *During Conditioning*: While Little Albert is playing with the rat, John Watson strikes a steel bar. The loud noise (UCS) elicits a startle and fear response (UCR). The white rat (now the CS) is associated with the loud noise for Little Albert. Little Albert (now the CS) is associated with the loud noise for the rat. *After Conditioning*: Later, the white rat elicits fear in Little Albert. Other objects, such as a rabbit, that are similar to the white rat now elicit fear in Little Albert, and the boy, in turn, elicits fear in the rat.

Many UCRs have an emotional component that is either pleasurable or aversive. When a reflex is elicited, it often brings up emotional responses, as was the case with Little Albert. As we have seen, some of these emotional reactions are pleasurable (for example, involving food and sex), whereas others are aversive (for example, painful stimuli). These pleasure and pain components of our reflexes can be traced to our basic biological survival functions (Keltner & Haidt, 1999; Levenson, 1999).

### Psychological Detective

The Watson and Rayner study is important because it was one of the first efforts to show that an emotional reaction like fear could be classically conditioned (resulting in a *conditioned fear response*); however, it raises questions about the ethics of psychological research (see Chapter 1). Was it acceptable for Watson and Rayner purposely to frighten Little Albert so intensely? Would you allow such research to be conducted with your child? Would such a procedure be acceptable if the child's parents authorized it? Write down your responses and the reasons for them before reading further.

*The Ethical Principles of Psychologists and Code of Conduct*, published by the American Psychological Association (2002), would probably say "no" to these questions. If Watson and Rayner were to conduct their research with Little Albert in the 21st century, they would have difficulty meeting the ethical standards you read about in Chapter 1.

Despite the questionable ethics exhibited in the Little Albert research, classical conditioning has been a focus of attention in our efforts to understand phobias since the 1920s. Consider the case of Scott, who was 3 years old when playmates locked him in an abandoned refrigerator, where he nearly died of suffocation. Ever since then, he has avoided closed spaces. Now, 25 years later, he is still deathly afraid of closed spaces and anything that reminds him of them. He cannot stand to ride in an elevator and always takes the stairs, even in high-rise buildings. Even seeing a picture of a refrigerator makes him break out in a cold sweat. If you were unaware of Scott's background, his intense fear of closed spaces, such as elevators, compact cars, and small rooms, might seem strange to you. Although you may not fear closed spaces to the same degree as Scott, chances are good that you are afraid of some objects or situations that most people do not fear. How do we acquire these apparently unrealistic, irrational fears?

Many of our fears and anxieties may have been classically conditioned, as in the case of Scott's fear of closed spaces. Because he was locked in an abandoned refrigerator when he was a child and nearly died, Scott now fears anything that remotely resembles a closed space. He has a condition known as a *phobia*; more specifically, he is suffering from *claustrophobia* (*claustrop*, "enclosed place"; *phobos*, "fear"). A **phobia** is an irrational fear of an activity, object, or situation that is out of proportion to the actual danger it poses. Phobias can create so much anxiety that they interfere with normal functioning; consequently, they are classified as *anxiety disorders* (see Chapter 12). Other people with phobias may not be able to recall a specific event that is the cause of the phobia. Thus many phobias exert their influence in a seemingly mysterious and potentially detrimental way.

Phobias can interfere with a person's daily activities. For example, a salesperson suffering from *glossophobia* (fear of speaking) would not do very well in the business world, where meeting and greeting clients are the order of the day. A paramedic or a nurse with *hemophobia* (fear of blood) would find it difficult to get through a normal day that could be filled with medical emergencies that require dealing with blood. A psychiatrist, Joseph Wolpe (1915–1997), developed a treatment, known as *systematic desensitization*, to help eliminate phobias (Martin & Pear, 2003; Rachman, 2000). Systematic desensitization involves classically conditioning a desired response, relaxation, to the phobic stimuli; it has been quite successful in treating a range of phobias (Powell, 2004; Schneider & Nevid, 1993; Ventis, Higbee, & Murdock, 2001). For example, using this procedure, a person with claustrophobia, like Scott, is conditioned to relax in enclosed spaces. We discuss systematic desensitization in greater detail in Chapter 13.

### Classical Conditioning of Our Attitudes.

How do you feel when you see an American flag being burned? How do you feel about the use of steroids by professional athletes? Does the thought of eating snails cause you to become upset? For each of these situations, you probably have a general reaction ranging from very positive to very negative, which psychologists call an *attitude*. Although the topic of attitudes is of special interest to social psychologists (see Chapter 15), it is also of interest to psychologists who focus on learning. One way learning theorists believe attitudes develop is via classical conditioning.

If a potential attitude object (CS) such as a particular make of car is repeatedly paired with a UCS that is either positive or negative, an attitude is likely to form. This process is the basis of attitude formation that can occur with regard to racial prejudice, brand preferences, and a wide range of objects and situations we encounter every day. To expand our knowledge of attitude formation, undergraduates took part in what was described as research on video surveillance and vigilance (Olson & Fazio, 2001). These students were told that hundreds of images would be presented randomly on a computer

**phobia**
Irrational fear of an activity, object, or situation that is out of proportion to the actual danger posed

Classical conditioning of our attitudes. By associating images of Pokemon cartoon characters with either positive words or images or negative words or images, researchers found they could induce positive or negative attitudes in college students. This demonstration reveals how advertising can use classical conditioning to influence our attitudes toward a wide range of products and services.

**learned motives**
Motives that are learned or acquired, usually through classical conditioning

**learned goals (incentives)**
Goals or incentives that are learned, usually through classical conditioning

screen. Each image was paired with either a positive word (such as *excellent* or *awesome*) or image (such as puppies or a hot-fudge sundae) or a negative word (such as *terrible* or *awful*) or image (such as a cockroach or a man wielding a knife). The target images (CS) were Pokemon cartoon characters. The researchers found that participants reported positive evaluations of the Pokemon images paired with positive words or images and negative evaluations of those that had been paired with negative words or images.

What was especially interesting was the fact that participants did not recognize the connection between the cartoon characters they came to like (positive attitudes) and the fact that they had been associated with positive words or images. In other words, attitudes can develop without awareness of the classical conditioning process that is occurring. You probably realize that every day you are subjected to similar real-life "experiments" when advertisers bombard you with words and images of attractive people, beautiful scenes of nature, and indications of wealth and good fortune that they wish to associate with their products. Sometimes the associations do not make sense, but they can nevertheless be effective. For many years, cigarettes were associated with the great outdoors and adventure. Never mind that using the product is likely to make you less likely to enjoy the benefits of the outdoors. Advertisers are hoping that such images and words rub off on you, influence your evaluations of their products, and entice you to make a purchase.

**Classical Conditioning and Our Motives.** As the discussion of Little Albert and the development of phobias reveals, classical conditioning has a lot more to say about human and animal behavior than you might think based on its origins in research on salivation. As a result of his conditioning, Little Albert was motivated to avoid rats and other furry animals. As we will see next, classical conditioning can lead organisms to develop a range of other behaviors that can have long-lasting influences. Even though Jim did not have cats as pets when he was a child, his friends persuaded him to adopt the cute stray kitten he found last week. Jim is now convinced that this was a very bad idea. Each evening, when Jim has settled into his favorite chair to watch the evening news, the kitten launches a sneak attack. After a week of this behavior, Jim becomes tense as soon as he sits in his favorite chair, whether the kitten is in the room or not. The sound of the evening news increases his anxiety. When Jim leaves the room, he immediately feels better.

What is the relation among the kitten's attacks, Jim's tension and anxiety, and motivation? Parts of the story about Jim and his cat may sound familiar. Can we describe the cat's sneak attack in psychological terms you have learned? Would certain responses automatically follow such an attack? Yes, pain, fear, or anxiety would follow. What kind of stimuli automatically elicits a response? Remember, UCSs elicit UCRs. What about Jim's favorite chair and the evening news program? What role do they serve? After these stimuli have been associated with cat attacks several times, they cause Jim to become tense and anxious. These are CSs, and the tension and anxiety they produce are CRs.

How is Jim's conditioned anxiety related to motivation? Through the process of classical conditioning, Jim's favorite chair and the evening news have become CSs that elicit anxiety and tension. These feelings of anxiety and tension are unpleasant, so he is motivated to reduce them when they occur by leaving the room. Motives that are acquired through the process of classical conditioning are called **learned motives.** Many other motives are acquired in this manner. Phobias are excellent examples of learned motives. If you have a phobia of an object or situation, you are motivated to avoid that object or situation; if you find yourself facing the phobic object, you are motivated to put distance between you and the object. Classical conditioning appears to be at the core of many of these unusual fears.

The same procedure and logic can be applied to the learning of goals and incentives. Many of the goals and incentives that motivate our behavior are learned through classical conditioning; hence they are termed **learned goals (incentives).** Consider money, diamonds, gold, and concert tickets. An infant's response to these objects should convince you that they do not possess intrinsic value; we must learn their value before they can affect our behavior.

# Classical Conditioning After Pavlov

Our conception of classical conditioning has changed since Pavlov's time. We now know that conditioning is not an automatic process that simply links CSs and UCSs. Today, psychologists place more emphasis on what information the CS seems to tell or convey to the participant.

**Contingency Theory.** One principle that has emerged from this continued research is that the better the CS predicts the occurrence of the UCS, the stronger the conditioning will be (Bolles, 1979; Rescorla, 1968). We encountered the importance of predictability when we discussed the sequence of CS–UCS presentation on page 191. A study of classical conditioning in two groups of rats illustrates this point (Rescorla, 1968). For the first group, the CS (tone) was always *followed by* the UCS (a shock). The animals in this group were called the *contingent group* because the occurrence of shock always followed (was contingent on) the tone. The animals in the second group heard the tone *before* or *after* the shock was presented. These animals were called the *noncontingent group* because the occurrence of shock did not always follow (was not contingent on) the tone. Because the tone perfectly predicted the UCS for the *contingent* animals, classical conditioning was strong. For the *noncontingent* animals, classical conditioning was weaker because the CS did not always precede the UCS.

This relation should not be surprising. As we have seen, a strong and predictable CS is the goal of the acquisition or training process during which an association between the CS and UCS is formed. A particular CS predicts that a particular UCS is about to occur. For example, the sound of the ticking metronome reliably predicted delivery of meat powder for Pavlov's dogs. Conversely, when we undertake extinction, we try to *convince* the participant that the CS will no longer be followed by—will no longer predict—the UCS (Delemater, 1995). The more reliable the CS is in predicting the UCS, the harder it will be to extinguish the CR. As the next section shows, however, CSs do not automatically become associated with UCSs, even if they are predictable.

**Blocking.** If classical conditioning simply involves the pairing of a CS and a UCS, the time at which the pairing occurs should not make any difference. But the timing of the pairing does matter. Consider the following research. One group of rats was classically conditioned by presenting a tone (CS) and following it with an electric shock (UCS) (Kamin, 1969). Once a response to the tone was conditioned, a second CS (a light) was also presented before the shock. A second group of animals received only pairings of the light and the shock. The researcher then tested the strength of conditioning to the light. This experimental arrangement is shown in Figure 5-8.

**FIGURE 5-8** Research on blocking has convincingly demonstrated that the pairing of the CS and UCS is not the only factor involved in classical conditioning. The timing of the pairing can lead to results in which prior pairings can *block* the effect of a particular CS.

**Source:** Kamin (1969).

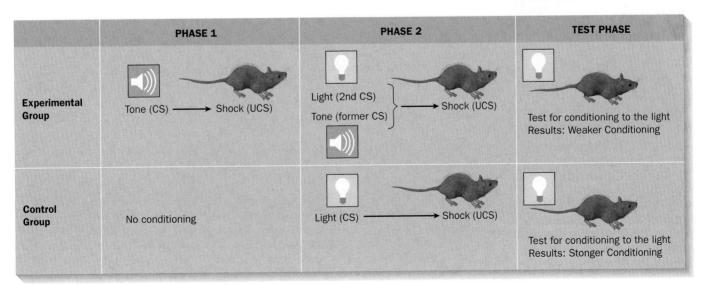

**blocking**
Situation in which the conditionability of a CS is weakened when it is paired with a UCS that has previously been paired with another CS

**taste-aversion learning**
Development of a dislike or aversion to a flavor or food that has been paired with illness

Conditioning was weaker for the animals that received tone–shock pairings before tone and light were paired with shock. The animals that received only the light–shock pairing demonstrated stronger conditioning. The conditioning of the tone before presenting the light had *blocked* or reduced the conditioning of the light.

If you consider predictability again, the results of this experiment make sense. If the tone had already been established as a predictable CS, another predictable CS was not needed (Williams, 1994). For the animals that had already received tone–shock pairings, the result was **blocking** of the light–shock association. Because light was the only CS presented to the other group of animals, it was conditioned strongly.

## Evolution and Classical Conditioning: Taste-Aversion Learning and Preparedness

Suppose that you have just moved to a large metropolitan area, which is quite different from the small town you left behind. For example, the variety of restaurants is amazing. Last night, friends took you to a seafood restaurant where you ate coconut shrimp for the first time. The décor and atmosphere of the restaurant were delightful; the taste of the food was extraordinary and unlike any you had ever had. Unfortunately, however, during the night you came down with the stomach flu that had been going around. For the rest of the night you were nauseated and even worse! These events may not seem to involve learning, but classical conditioning took place: You were conditioned to avoid coconut shrimp. Why? As it turns out, "the brain is not equally sensitive to all types of stimuli. Some types of stimuli are much more important for survival than others, and evolutionary processes have prepared the brain to locate some types of causal correlations more easily than others" (Baldwin & Baldwin, 2001, p. 24).

**Taste Aversion.**    Does becoming nauseated after eating a food that is unusual to you have anything to do with learning? The notion of *predictability* is again helpful. Whenever a person or animal becomes ill after consuming a food with a novel taste (taste aversion), that taste (CS) may become a predictor of illness.

**Taste-aversion learning** involves the development of an aversion to (dislike of) a flavor that has been associated with illness (Batsell & Best, 1992, 1993). In the mid-1960s, John Garcia and his colleagues demonstrated that when a novel flavor was used as the CS and illness or nausea was the UCR, rats developed an intense aversion to the flavor, which has become known as the *Garcia effect*. Classical conditioning of a tone and food occurs best when the tone is sounded just 0.50 second before the food is presented, but strong taste aversions can be conditioned when illness occurs more than an hour (or more) after the taste is experienced (Garcia, Ervin, & Koelling, 1966). When Garcia et al.'s research was first reported, it was greeted with much skepticism because it did not seem to follow established principles of classical conditioning. The significant amount of time between the presentation of the CS and the UCS was at odds with what researchers had learned from decades of laboratory research. As a result, Garcia's research was refused publication in the major journal devoted to animal behavior. It is a credit to Garcia's persistence that his work was not only ultimately accepted, it is considered a classic in demonstrating that "an animal's evolutionary inheritance places limits on what it can learn" (Leahey, 2001, p. 288).

There are two points of interest in these taste-aversion studies. First, the flavor had to be novel for it to become associated with the illness. If you have eaten steak for years, it is not likely to be associated with illness: A flavor that has been consumed many times does not predict illness, but the taste of something you have not consumed before (coconut shrimp) does. Second, the time between the onset of the CS (taste) and the onset of the UCS (illness) can be quite lengthy, yet strong conditioning still occurs.

Humans form taste aversions quite readily. Think of the times you have been nauseated after eating. In most of these cases, had you just consumed a *novel* food or beverage? In fact, such experiences are surprisingly common. In one survey of undergraduates,

John Garcia. For many decades, researchers were convinced that classical conditioning could occur only if the timing between the CS and UCS was very brief. John Garcia's research dramatically changed this view, and showed us how an organism's evolutionary history could influence what it could learn.

65% of students reported having at least one food aversion. Most food aversions develop several hours after eating food associated with sickness (Logue, Ophir, & Strauss, 1981). What's more, such aversions do not extinguish easily; they can last for 50 years or more (Garb & Stunkard, 1974). Taste aversions can occur in situations when we know that the illness was caused by something like the flu. The more highly developed part of our brain that "knows" this information apparently is no match for the more primitive wiring that makes it easier to associate illness with some food, even if we are wrong. Thousands of years of evolution have created a brain that, on the one hand, knows better but, on the other hand, relies on the wisdom of our evolutionary heritage. In many ways, it is not nice to fool mother nature when she tells us that it is best to stay away from a novel food because the odds are that it is what caused our illness.

Sometimes taste aversions have serious detrimental effects. For example, children undergoing chemotherapy for cancer can develop food aversions that can affect their ability to consume a normal diet. Psychologists have applied their knowledge of taste aversions to this problem (Bernstein, 1978; Bernstein & Webster, 1980, 1982). Children were allowed to eat an unusually flavored ice cream (called "Mapletof") shortly before receiving nausea-producing chemotherapy treatment for cancer. Later, these children ate less Mapletof ice cream than did a second group of patients whose treatment consisted of surgery rather than chemotherapy. The second group of children had also eaten some Mapletof ice cream before treatment. Their treatment did not produce nausea, so they did not associate the ice cream flavor with illness. Clearly the taste–illness pairing is crucial for the development of taste aversion.

Subsequent research demonstrated that consumption of the Mapletof ice cream *before* chemotherapy reduced the patients' reluctance to consume their normal diet. After chemotherapy, patients who had previously eaten the Mapletof ice cream and had formed a taste aversion to this flavor were more willing to consume their normal diet than were patients who had not eaten any Mapletof ice cream. The formation of a taste aversion to the Mapletof ice cream tended to *block* the formation of taste aversions to other foods and thus helped the patients maintain their normal diet without becoming nauseated.

**Preparedness.** As we have seen, certain stimuli, such as flavors, can be associated with certain UCRs, such as illness, more easily than they can be associated with other UCRs, such as electric shock. Animals seem to be biologically ready or **prepared** to associate certain CSs with certain UCSs (Seligman, 1970). Some events seem to go together naturally, whereas others do not. For humans and many animal species, taste and illness form one such natural pairing; presenting a tone or light CS with an electric shock is another natural pair. If instead we try to pair the tone or light CS with illness or the taste CS with an electric shock, we get only weak conditioning (Garcia & Koelling, 1966). Other pairings also are learned quite easily. For example, humans, as well as many household pets, seem prepared to associate the sight of lightning (CS) with the sound of thunder. Preparedness occurs when some species are more biologically ready to form certain associations; it may explain why some phobias are learned so easily (see Chapter 12). We do not seem prepared, however, to associate loud noises with nausea or illness.

Consider the following research: Investigators presented blue, sour-tasting water (CS) to quail and then made the birds ill temporarily by giving them a nausea-producing drug (Wilcoxin, Dragoin, & Kral, 1971). After becoming ill, these birds had a strong aversion to the blue color but not to the sour taste. These findings suggest that the quail were unprepared—or *contraprepared*—to make the taste–illness association. Preparedness theory suggests one important means by which animals adapt to their environments: They learn to avoid potentially dangerous stimuli that had made them ill on a previous occasion. Avoiding such substances increases their chances of survival. With their keen eyesight, birds are more likely to discriminate stimuli on the basis of color, whereas rats and mice, whose eyesight is poor, are likely to discriminate on the basis of taste. Preparedness theory is an excellent example of the evolutionary perspective at work. Animals are prepared to make associations that help them adapt to the environments they inhabit.

**STUDY TIP**

After reading the section on the elements of classical conditioning, brainstorm in a group of three or four. Think of at least three additional examples, not mentioned in the text, of ways in which human behavior is conditioned. Discuss each behavior and how the conditioning occurred.

**preparedness**
Theory that organisms are biologically ready or prepared to associate certain CSs with certain UCSs

# REVIEW SUMMARY

**1. Learning** occurs when experience produces a relatively permanent change in behavior, which distinguishes learning from behavior changes resulting from maturation.

**2. Classical conditioning** involves pairing an **unconditioned stimulus (UCS)**, which automatically elicits an **unconditioned response (UCR)**, with a **conditioned stimulus (CS)**, which is neutral at the start of conditioning. Several pairings during an acquisition phase lead to a situation in which the CS presented by itself elicits a **conditioned response (CR)**.

**3.** When the UCS is intense and presented more frequently, stronger classical conditioning is produced. The classically conditioned response is eliminated or extinguished when the UCS (for example, meat powder) is removed or not presented; this process is called *extinction*. **Spontaneous recovery** of the CR occurs when time is allowed to pass between extinction sessions. **Generalization** occurs when CRs are elicited by stimuli that are similar to the CS. The opposing process of **discrimination** involves responding only to the appropriate CS. Thus, generalization and discrimination are opposing processes.

**4.** John Watson and Rosalie Rayner demonstrated that emotions can be learned by classically conditioning 11-month-old Little Albert to fear a white rat. This child exhibited a **phobia**, which is a fear of certain activities, objects, or situations. The research conducted by Watson and Rayner would not be considered ethical by present-day standards for conducting research. Attitudes toward products and other objects can be induced via classical conditioning; advertisers make use of this finding by trying to associate positive feelings with their products. **Learned motives** and **learned goals** (or **incentives**) are acquired through classical conditioning.

**5.** Current understanding of classical conditioning suggests that although the association of a CS with a UCS is important in establishing conditioning, the real key is the degree to which the CS predicts occurrence of the UCS. Previous trials of a CS–UCS pairing can **block** the effectiveness of a second CS.

**6.** For many species, the pairing of a novel taste with the experience of illness can result in **taste-aversion learning**, which occurs readily in humans. **Preparedness** is evident when some species are more likely to form certain associations than others.

# ✓ CHECK YOUR PROGRESS

**1.** Have you ever found yourself salivating while walking through the bakery section of a supermarket? What was the UCS? The CS? The CR?

**2.** Complete the following:
   **a.** Before conditioning, the _____ is automatically elicited by the _____.
   **b.** The CR is strengthened if the _____ and _____ are paired frequently.
   **c.** Extinction of a classically conditioned response involves presentation of only the _____. In other words, the _____ is removed.
   **d.** Extinction causes the _____ to grow gradually _____.

**3.** State which aspect of classical conditioning is illustrated by each of the following situations:
   **a.** A tone sounds; half a second later, a puff of air is delivered to your eye and you blink. Once the conditioned eye blink has been established, the puff of air is discontinued and the tone is presented by itself a number of times.
   **b.** As a child you had the misfortune of being stung by a bee. In addition to the pain of the sting, your breathing became difficult and you were rushed to the hospital for treatment. Twenty years later, you have a fear of bees and other flying insects.
   **c.** Your roommate went to a new restaurant for dinner and developed a severe case of intestinal flu later that night. The lemon shrimp he had eaten caused the restaurant to lose a customer.
   **d.** Children who play with large plastic bags sometimes become trapped inside the bag and nearly suffocate.

If they are fortunate enough to be rescued, they will probably have a conditioned fear of closed spaces.

**4.** What was the CS in the case of Little Albert?
   **a.** rat
   **b.** hammer
   **c.** small toy
   **d.** loud noise

**5.** Sara is taking an Experimental Psychology course, which requires her to demonstrate classical conditioning. She decides to play the first words of a country song before she squirts lemon juice into a participant's mouth. After several trials, the participant reacts with a facial expression that seems to indicate that she anticipates the sour-tasting lemon juice. Before the participant leaves the lab, however, Sara must extinguish this response. What is the *best* way for her to accomplish this goal?
   **a.** She should play the country song several times without squirting lemon juice.
   **b.** She should randomly squirt small amounts of lemon juice into the participant's mouth for about 15 minutes.
   **c.** After playing a rock-and-roll song as loud as the original song, she should squirt water into the participant's mouth.
   **d.** After playing a rock-and-roll song at half the volume of the original song, she should squirt a mixture of water and lemon juice into the participant's mouth.

**6.** For the past few months, Sara has been using a perfume called Passion. Her boyfriend, Jim, really likes the perfume. In fact, on several occasions, he has passed women who were wearing Passion and had the same reaction: his heart rate increased. In this example, the perfume is the _____ and Jim's increased heart rate is the _____.

    a. CS, UCS
    b. CS, CR
    c. UCS, UCR
    d. UCS, UR

7. Taste aversions seem to be specific examples of what type of learning?

    a. insight learning
    b. vicarious learning
    c. operant conditioning
    d. classical conditioning

8. Last week Jason saw a movie that vividly depicted a serial killer's gruesome murders. When school began, Jason had an uncomfortable feeling when one of his teachers walked into class. After class, he realized that the teacher had a striking resemblance to the serial killer. Ted's reaction to the teacher is an example of

    a. extinction.
    b. acquisition.

    c. discrimination.
    d. generalization.

9. Why is Little Albert such a well-known individual in the history of psychology?

    a. He outlined key elements of classical conditioning based on his research with dogs.
    b. A serious bout of the flu led him to discover the major principles of taste-aversion learning.
    c. He was the subject of research that illustrated how classical conditioning can explain the development of phobias.
    d. After he developed a strong aversion to needles, pins, and injections, he found a way to use hypnosis to overcome such reactions.

10. Which of these illustrates a UCR?

    a. A large ice cream sundae
    b. Your favorite ice cream shop
    c. Salivation when you taste an ice cream sundae
    d. Salivation when you see your favorite ice cream shop

**ANSWERS: 1.** UCS—the taste of the bakery goods you've eaten before CS—the sight and smell of the bakery goods CR—salivation **2. a.** UCR, UCS **b.** CS, UCS **c.** CS, UCS **d.** CR, weaker **3. a.** extinction **b.** generalization **c.** taste aversion **d.** conditioned fear response or phobia **4. a 5. a 6. b 7. d 8. d 9. c 10. c**

# OPERANT CONDITIONING

Bob's roommate, Greg, is a complete slob. In Bob's view, the condition of Greg's room is Greg's business, but the condition of the bathroom they share is another matter. Almost every week they argue about cleaning the bathroom, and Bob ends up doing the cleaning. When the unfairness of the situation is more than Bob can stand, he tries a new approach. Whenever Greg does anything to help clean the apartment, Bob praises him: "Good job, Greg; the apartment looks great." Gradually Greg begins helping on a more regular basis, and one week he even offers to clean the bathroom. *What technique did Bob use to get Greg to help clean the apartment?*

We now turn our discussion to the second basic type of learning, operant conditioning. In **operant conditioning**, also known as *instrumental conditioning*, an organism operates on its environment to produce a change (Leahey & Harris, 2001; Mazur, 2006). In other words, the organism's behavior is *instrumental*—it results in a change in the environment. As you will see, the type of change that is produced is a critical element of this type of learning.

## Reinforcers: The Basic Concept of Operant Conditioning

In the early 1900s, educator Edward Lee Thorndike (1874–1949) developed an influential theory of learning based on his study of hungry animals (1898, 1911, 1927). Thorndike placed the experimental animal (such as a cat or dog) in a small chamber that he had dubbed the *puzzle box* (see Figure 5-9A). If the animal performed the appropriate

**operant conditioning**
Learning that occurs when the participant must make a response to produce a change in the environment

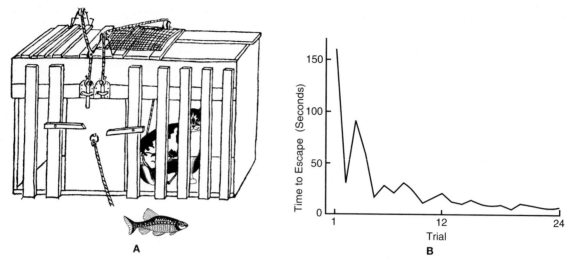

**FIGURE 5-9** Thorndike's research set the stage for the development of operant conditioning. Using the puzzle box (A), he showed that behaviors that he described as satisfiers tended to be stamped into the organism. Initially, the animal made random responses in an attempt to get out of the puzzle and get the fish (a satisfier), but soon it hit upon behaviors that led to its successful escape and to the food outside the puzzle box (B).

**law of effect**
Thorndike's view that reinforcers promote learning, whereas punishers lead to the unlearning of responses

behavior, the puzzle box door opened, and the animal could exit and eat some food that had been placed just outside the door. In some cases, getting out of the puzzle box required a simple response such as pressing a lever or stepping on a platform. In other cases, the required response was more difficult. For example, the animal might have to make three separate responses: pulling a string (which lifted one bolt), stepping on a platform (which lifted the other bolt), and reaching through the bars and turning one of two latches in front of the door. When Thorndike first placed an animal in the puzzle box (either the simple or complex version), it usually took a long time to escape. The animal typically moved around in the puzzle box and explored various parts of the chamber, apparently in a random manner. Eventually, the animal performed the response or responses that opened the door. Thorndike returned the animal to the puzzle box many times and recorded the amount of time it took to escape. Typical results of this procedure can be seen in Figure 5-9B. Thorndike believed that the animal's first successful response was most likely an accidental one. Over time animals took less time to escape, thus becoming more proficient at performing the appropriate response (or responses). This observation led to what Thorndike called the **law of effect** (Thorndike, 1911): Presenting a "satisfier" leads to the strengthening or learning of new responses, whereas presenting an "annoyer" leads to the weakening or unlearning of responses. In this case, the satisfier (getting out and obtaining food) seems to have been stamped into the animal's repertoire, whereas unsuccessful attempts seem to have been stamped out of the repertoire of behaviors.

Thorndike's work set the stage for the development of operant conditioning. The specific terminology would change, but the basic ideas had their roots in Thorndike's puzzle box. Probably no one has been associated more closely with operant conditioning than the late Harvard psychologist B. F. Skinner (1904–1990), who has been described as the most famous psychologist who has ever lived (Fowler, 1990). Skinner was strongly influenced by Edward Thorndike, as well as by John B. Watson's behavioral view of psychology (see page 195). As we have seen, Watson believed that if we could understand how to predict and control behavior, we would know all there was to know about psychology. Skinner therefore began to look for the stimuli that control behavior. To isolate those effects, he developed a special testing environment called an *operant conditioning chamber*, which is usually referred to as a *Skinner box* (see Figure 5-10). Although Skinner relied on the use of animals such as rats and pigeons, his ideas can be and have been applied to human behavior. The advantage of the Skinner box and laboratory studies is that they allow researchers to exert a great deal of control in their research, and thus the researchers are in a better position to identify the actual influences on behavior.

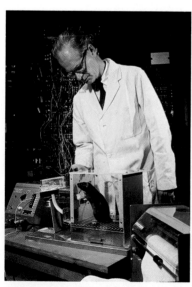

B. F. Skinner training a rat in a Skinner box.

**FIGURE 5-10** (A) An operant conditioning chamber, or Skinner box. Pecking the circular disk or "key" is the target response that delivers a food reinforcer for the pigeon. (B) The cumulative recorder automatically logs the participant's responses.

Disk (Key)

Grain delivery system

Direction of recorder's movement over time

Direction of pen movement with responses

**Skinner Box (Operant conditioning chamber) A**

**Cumulative recorder B**

Let's take a moment to return to the question we posed earlier: How did Bob convince Greg to help clean their apartment? The answer is that he praised his behavior, thus using what Skinner called a **reinforcer** (or *satisfier* in Thorndike's terminology). In some cases, operant behavior may result in the delivery of a stimulus or an event. Using the term *reinforcer* avoids use of terms such as *satisfier*, which was too mentalistic and imprecise for Skinner. When you insert money into a soda machine, for example, you receive a cold drink. When Greg cleaned the apartment, he received praise. In other instances, the operant behavior may result in the elimination of a stimulus or an event. For example, you have probably learned the quickest way to eliminate the sound your alarm clock makes early in the morning. Such events, or reinforcers, are at the heart of operant conditioning. Thus we can define a reinforcer as an event or a stimulus that makes the behavior it follows more likely to occur again (Skinner, 1938). For example, obtaining a cold drink from the soda machine and eliminating the annoying sound of your alarm clock are both reinforcers. The behavior that a reinforcer follows can be thought of as the *target response*—it is the behavior that we want to strengthen or increase. Reinforcers can be either positive or negative; in either instance, they can serve to increase the occurrence of the target response.

**reinforcer**
Event or stimulus that increases the frequency of the response that it follows

**positive reinforcer**
Event or stimulus presented after the target response that increases the likelihood that this response will occur again

**Positive and Negative Reinforcers.** **Positive reinforcers** are events or stimuli such as food, water, money, and praise that are *presented* after the target response occurs.

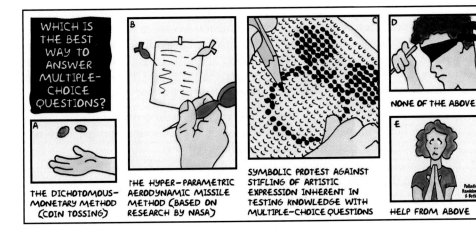

WHICH IS THE BEST WAY TO ANSWER MULTIPLE-CHOICE QUESTIONS?

A
THE DICHOTOMOUS-MONETARY METHOD (COIN TOSSING)

B
THE HYPER-PARAMETRIC AERODYNAMIC MISSILE METHOD (BASED ON RESEARCH BY NASA)

C
SYMBOLIC PROTEST AGAINST STIFLING OF ARTISTIC EXPRESSION INHERENT IN TESTING KNOWLEDGE WITH MULTIPLE-CHOICE QUESTIONS

D
NONE OF THE ABOVE

E
HELP FROM ABOVE

**Source:** Psi Chi Newsletter. Reprinted with the permission of Psi Chi.

**negative reinforcer**
Event or stimulus removed after the target response, thereby increasing the likelihood that this response will occur again

**primary reinforcer**
Stimulus that has innate reinforcing properties

**secondary reinforcer**
Stimulus that acquires reinforcing properties by being associated with a primary reinforcer

**positive reinforcement**
Increase in the frequency of a target behavior (response) that occurs when a behavior is followed by presentation of a positive reinforcer

**Source:** Psi Chi Newsletter. Reprinted with the permission of Psi Chi.

They are generally considered desirable and pleasant, and are therefore sought by people and animals alike. For example, a real estate agent earns a commission for each house she sells; the commissions reinforce her efforts to sell as many houses as possible. Your little brother is allowed to watch cartoons on Saturday mornings after he has cleaned his room; as a result, he cleans his room every Saturday. We hope that you have been praised for receiving good grades on psychology tests; the praise should encourage you to study even harder in the future.

**Negative reinforcers** are events or stimuli that are removed because a response has occurred. Examples of negative reinforcers include playing music to reduce boredom, cleaning your room so that your roommate will stop complaining that you're a slob, and taking medication to reduce the pain of a recent hernia repair. In these situations something stopped (boredom), was removed (criticism) or was reduced (pain) because you performed a target response.

**Primary and Secondary (Conditioned) Reinforcers.** A **primary reinforcer** is an event or stimulus that has innate (that is, biological) reinforcing properties; you do not have to learn that such stimuli are reinforcers. For a hungry person, food is a primary reinforcer. Water is another primary reinforcer, especially on a very hot day; and the rest provided by sleep, which is welcome, refreshing, and too often insufficient for our needs, is a third example of a primary reinforcer. Needless to say, not all events or stimuli that might follow a behavior will necessarily satisfy some biological need such as hunger, thirst, or sleep. A **secondary reinforcer** is a stimulus that acquires reinforcing properties by being associated with a primary reinforcer. Because you must learn that such stimuli are reinforcers, they are also called *conditioned reinforcers*. Money is probably the single best example of a secondary reinforcer. By itself, money has no intrinsic value; children learn that money can be exchanged for primary reinforcers such as ice cream, soda, popcorn, or candy. We also use money to purchase other foods, beverages, and a place to catch up on our sleep, whether it is our apartment, a house, or a hotel room.

# Contingencies and Behavior

Skinner coined the term *operant conditioning* because the behaviors we emit voluntarily (as opposed to behaviors that are elicited or "pulled" from the organism) *operate* on the environment around us in some way. The resulting changes in the environment determine what happens to a given target behavior (response). If a behavior is followed by a positive reinforcer—as when a student answers a question and the professor says "Excellent!"—the behavior tends to increase in the future. Skinner noted that a contingency is established between the behavior and the outcomes: Contingencies take the form of "If _____ then _____" relations. *If* a student gives a good answer, *then* the professor will say "Excellent (see Figure 5-11)." In other cases, such as punishment, the contingency is different: *If* a child runs into the street, *then* his parents will spank him, which to leads to a decrease in the behavior (running into the street) in the future.

**Positive Reinforcement.** Positive reinforcement is an easy concept to grasp because there are so many examples in everyday life. **Positive reinforcement** occurs when a target behavior (response) is followed by presentation of a positive reinforcer, which has the effect of making the behavior more likely to occur in the future. Here are examples of positive reinforcement from everyday life presented in the form of contingencies:

- *If* 5-year old Agnes picks up all the toys from the bedroom floor (target behavior), *then* her mom will give her more dessert at dinner time (presentation of a positive reinforcer resulting in positive reinforcement).
- *If* 16-year-old Jason cuts the lawn (target behavior), *then* his parents will give him the keys to the family car on Saturday night (presentation of a positive reinforcer resulting in positive reinforcement).

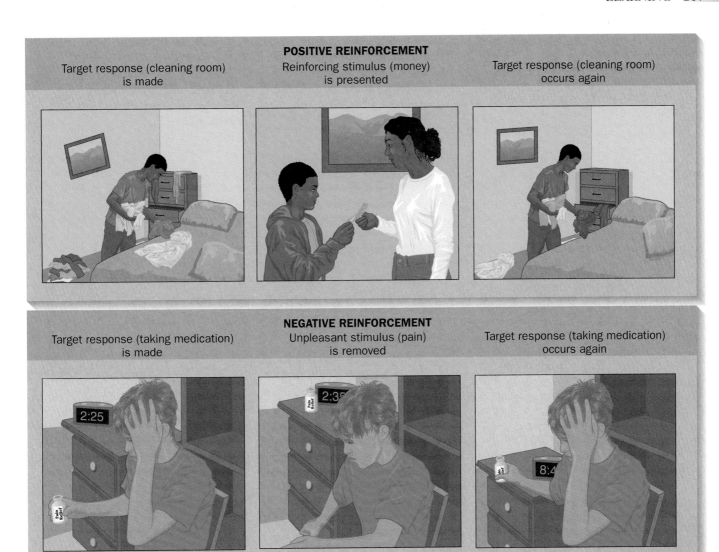

## POSITIVE REINFORCEMENT

| Target response (cleaning room) is made | Reinforcing stimulus (money) is presented | Target response (cleaning room) occurs again |

## NEGATIVE REINFORCEMENT

| Target response (taking medication) is made | Unpleasant stimulus (pain) is removed | Target response (taking medication) occurs again |

**FIGURE 5-11**   Diagram of the operation of positive and negative reinforcers. In the top panel, the target response of cleaning the room is reinforced with money (a positive reinforcer), resulting in *positive reinforcement* (increase in the target response). In the bottom panel, the target response (taking medication for a painful headache) removes the pain (a negative reinforcer), resulting in *negative reinforcement* (an increase in use of the medication). Note that both positive and negative reinforcement lead to increases in the frequency of target responses.

- *If* a salesperson for a medical billing company signs up two new customers (target behavior), *then* the company president will give the salesperson a bonus of $500 (presentation of a positive reinforcer resulting in positive reinforcement).
- *If* a paramedic makes an accurate assessment of a patient's breathing problem and administers life-saving treatment (target behavior), *then* the supervisor will praise her assessment and treatment decisions (presentation of a positive reinforcer resulting in positive reinforcement).

Although these examples may lead you to believe that positive reinforcement increases behaviors that are praiseworthy and desirable, as you will see this is not always the case. Suppose a student consults a concealed cheat sheet during a test or passes answers to a friend. The target responses here are the acts of cheating. The reinforcer is receiving a high (or passing) grade. Because the grade is given (presented), it is a

When rates of detection and punishment are very low, cheating rates may be very high.

**shaping**
A form of operant conditioning in which a desired response is taught by reinforcement of successive responses that more closely resemble the target response

positive reinforcer, which results in positive reinforcement of cheating behavior. Do threats of punishment counteract this behavior? The answer appears to be no; the number of students who admit to having cheated on examinations is quite high: As many as 40 to 95% of college students surveyed have reported having cheated at some time (Burnett, Rudolph, & Clifford, 1998; Davis & Ludvigson, 1995; Jensen, Arnett, Feldman, & Cauffman, 2002); consequently, cheating is a serious concern on many college campuses (McCabe, Trevino, & Butterfield, 2001; Whitley & Keith-Spiegel, 2002).

### Psychological Detective

Can a positive reinforcer encourage unethical behavior? Consider the problem of cheating. Children are taught that cheating is wrong, but this behavior persists in most segments of our society. Why? Take a few moments to analyze the behavior of cheating in operant conditioning terms. Be sure to write down the target response and the reinforcers.

There is growing concern that the current expansion of distance learning formats may make it even easier for students to cheat (Kennedy, Nowak, Raghuraman, Thomas, & Davis, 2000; Underwood & Szabo, 2003). What's more, detection rates are very low—frequently less than 2% (Haines, Diekhoff, LaBeff, & Clark, 1986). Thus a very small number of cheaters are caught, and even fewer are punished. The prospect of achieving an easy grade, coupled with a relatively low chance of getting caught, can be a powerful reinforcer of cheating on tests.

**5.2**

**Shaping.**　Take a moment to think about everyday behaviors that you observe in your environment. As you think about these behaviors, you may realize that the final behavior does not always occur from the start. For example, it is not likely that you learned to drive after just one ride around the block. How does Skinner explain how we develop complex behaviors, which may not exist before training begins?

When you start training a rat in a Skinner box (see page 205), don't expect much from the rat. The rat will not begin pressing the lever or bar as soon as it enters this new environment. You may have to help it learn to press the lever or bar to receive food. The technique you will use is a form of operant conditioning called **shaping.** Shaping involves reinforcing successive responses that more closely resemble the desired target response; in other words, you are using the method of *successive approximations*. When using this method, you generally withhold reinforcement until the animal engages in a behavior that comes closer to the desired target response. Although the concept of shaping is reasonably clear, actually doing the job may be difficult. The timing of reinforcement presentation is crucial; if reinforcers are not presented at exactly the right moment, an inappropriate response may be shaped.

For a rat learning to press a lever for food, the sequence of events might go as follows: When the rat is near the food dish, you drop a piece of food into it. Eating the food reinforces the behavior of approaching the dish. Once the rat has learned where the food is, you begin offering reinforcers only when the rat goes near the response lever. Gradually you make your response requirements more demanding until the rat must actually touch the lever to receive the reinforcement. Once the rat has started touching the lever, you can require that the lever be pressed before the reinforcement is given. In this way you have gradually made the response that produces reinforcement more closely resemble (*successively approximate*) the target response of pressing the lever. In short, you have *shaped* the rat's response.

One of the best-known cases of shaping involves a patient who was admitted to a mental hospital at the age of 21 with the diagnosis of schizophrenia (see Chapter 12); he had been "completely mute almost immediately upon commitment" (Isaacs, Thomas, & Goldiamond, 1960). No one had been able to coax a single word out of him for 19 years! He lived day in and day out without uttering a word, staring ahead with a fixed gaze. One

Rats can learn to play basketball. Students at DeKalb High School under the direction of their teacher, Dr. Jim Divine, used shaping techniques to teach rats to play basketball. They rats were excellent at dunking (as shown here), although they struggled from the three-point line!

day, a psychologist accidentally dropped a pack of chewing gum. The patient's eyes turned to focus on the gum and then returned to their fixed gaze. Finally, there was a small sign of responsiveness. Could gum be used as a reinforcer? For the next 2 weeks the psychologist held up the gum in front of the patient, waiting for some visual contact. Once this response occurred, the patient was given some gum. Then the psychologist withheld gum until the patient responded with *both* visual contact and lip movement. A painstaking process of shaping eventually led to the patient saying "Gum, please"—his first words in 19 years.

Shaping has a wide range of applications and is an especially effective tool derived from operant conditioning principles. If teachers find that their students are not able to provide correct answers to questions posed in class, they can praise partial answers and even effort. Gradually, they can raise expectations so that students have to give more complete responses to earn praise (Eggen & Kauchak, 2001). If you have ever seen bears roller skating, seals catching balls, dolphins "flying" through hoops, or pigeons playing ping pong, you have been entertained by the results of a long series of steps that *shaped* these behaviors (Coren, 1999). When you stop to think about the range of behaviors we engage in every day, especially the more complex ones, you can see how important shaping can be. Driving a car, tying shoes, playing the piano, and typing are all behaviors that we probably learned through shaping.

### Psychological Detective

Whether or not we realize it, shaping techniques have been used to help us acquire many new behaviors. Think about behaviors such as talking, writing, and driving a car. These behaviors were gradually shaped through the appropriate delivery of reinforcers. Remember when you learned to drive? How were your driving skills when you first started driving? How are they now? In which ways were those skills shaped? Recall these behaviors and events and relate them to our discussion of operant conditioning before you read further.

Most of the behaviors of animals we see in shows and theme parks do not occur in their natural habitats. Animal trainers use operant conditioning methods, especially shaping, to train raccoons, seals, whales, dolphins, and other creatures. The key to shaping is to break down complex behaviors into smaller and easier behaviors and then to reinforce successive approximations to the ultimate, more complex behavior.

The first time you sat behind the wheel, you were probably unable to drive around the block or parallel park like an experienced driver. To drive around the block, you had to become accustomed to the rear-view mirrors, use the turn signals, apply the brakes, and perhaps shift gears. Then there was parallel parking, which required much practice. Your instructor reinforced good driving techniques with phrases like "Good job," "Excellent," and "Way to go." Gradually your skills improved until you could maneuver your car into a small space without any difficulty.

Now recall the case of the roommates Bob and Greg, who had trouble keeping their apartment clean. Bob was shaping Greg's behavior. At first he praised anything Greg did to help keep the apartment clean. Gradually he reserved his praise for greater efforts, until finally Greg was cleaning the apartment on a regular basis.

**The Premack Principle.** Imagine that you are a music teacher in a middle school where your students love to play modern jazz–rock compositions. Unfortunately, they are less than enthusiastic when it comes to playing the standard works of music that are part of the required curriculum (Eggen & Kauchak, 2001). How would you use the principles of operant conditioning to deal with this problem? One clever way of addressing this problem involves use of the *Premack Principle*, named after the psychologist David Premack (1965). Premack determined that the opportunity to participate in a preferred activity (playing jazz-rock in this case) could reinforce less preferred activities (playing the standard music pieces). What Premack described in operant conditioning terms has been known for some time as "Grandma's Rule" ("First eat your vegetables, and then you can have dessert").

**negative reinforcement**
Increase in the frequency of a target behavior (response) that occurs when a negative reinforcer is removed or terminated; escape conditioning and avoidance conditioning are examples

The Premack Principle was used in a potentially life-threatening situation—that of a 7-year-old boy who refused to eat all but very specific foods. When his parents offered him other foods, he became aggressive and difficult to handle. His parents were concerned that his self-imposed diet restriction posed serious health risks. They sought the assistance of a therapist who devised a treatment program based on the Premack Principle. At mealtime, the parents told the boy that if he ate a small amount of a *new* food, he could then eat one of his favorite foods. If he did not eat this new food, he was given one of his less preferred foods so that he would not go hungry. Over time, the boy began to eat a wider variety of foods and was calmer when presented with new foods (Brown, Spencer, & Stella, 2002).

There are numerous other examples of the Premack Principle, including these:

- Completion of homework (less preferred activity) is reinforced by the opportunity to play (preferred activity).
- Football players get to run new plays (preferred activity) after they have run their required laps (less preferred activity).
- Raking and bagging leaves on Saturday morning (less preferred activity) is reinforced by the opportunity to play a video game on Saturday afternoon (preferred activity).

**Negative Reinforcement.**     Negative reinforcement has always seemed to be a more difficult concept than positive reinforcement for students to grasp. When students see the word *negative*, they often assume that a behavior decreases. Don't get caught up in this misconception, which has been called one of the major mistakes made by students of psychology (Leahey & Harris, 2001; McConnell, 1990). Both positive and negative reinforcers can make the target behavior or response more likely to occur. If a negative reinforcer has been effective, the target response that terminated it is likely to occur again. **Negative reinforcement** occurs when a target behavior (response) is followed by removal or reduction of a negative reinforcer, which leads to an increase in the frequency of the target behavior (see Figure 5-11 on p. 207). Consider the following examples of negative reinforcement presented in the form of contingencies:

- *If* Ann gets into her car and hears the annoying "ding" of the seat belt alarm, *then* she buckles her seat belt (target response) and the annoying sound disappears (removal of a negative reinforcer leading to negative reinforcement).
- *If* Jason puts on sunburn treatment lotion (target behavior), *then* his pain seems to vanish (removal of a negative reinforcer resulting in negative reinforcement).
- *If* Joe becomes anxious when he spots a large, black, long-haired dog about 200 yards away and turns in the direction opposite of the dog (target behavior), *then* his anxiety level drops with every step he takes away from that dog (removal of a negative reinforcer resulting in negative reinforcement).
- *If* Warren is working at home today and the temperature rises to an uncomfortable level, *then* he walks to the thermostat and lowers the temperature to a more comfortable level (target behavior). He finds that the uncomfortable heat is removed (removal of a negative reinforcer resulting in negative reinforcement).

Consider the following case: Jason, an attendant at a state hospital, was considered a model employee; he was hardworking, punctual, and well liked by the patients. There was just one problem: Jason had a tendency to slouch while he worked. Although slouching is not a major problem, it presents an inappropriate role model for patients. Several psychologists designed a shoulder harness that held an elastic cord across Jason's back. In turn, the cord was wired to a small tone generator and a clicker. The harness was not visible when Jason wore a shirt and sweater over it. When he slouched, the elastic cord stretched and caused a clicking sound. Three seconds later, a loud aversive tone sounded and remained on until Jason stopped slouching. When Jason exhibited good posture, he could *escape* the sound of the tone. And if he continued to display good posture, he could *avoid* the loud tone altogether. Before Jason wore the apparatus, he slouched about 60% of the time. After wearing the apparatus, he slouched only 1% of the time (Martin & Pear, 2003).

*Escape conditioning* occurs when certain stimuli whose removal immediately after the occurrence of a response increase the likelihood of that response. Thus, escape conditioning is an example of negative reinforcement. Examples of escape conditioning abound in everyday life. For example, when a room is too cold, we escape the chill by putting on an extra sweater. If a street repair crew is working outside our home, we might close the window to escape the noise. One disadvantage of escape conditioning is that the aversive stimulus must be presented for the desired response to occur. In the escape conditioning procedure used with Jason, the loud tone was on before Jason showed good posture. Therefore, escape conditioning is generally not a final contingency for maintaining behavior but is preparatory for *avoidance conditioning*. Avoidance conditioning occurs when a behavior increases in frequency if it prevents an aversive stimulus from occurring. During the avoidance procedure used with Jason, good posture *prevented* the tone from occurring.

**Extinction.**    Just as with classical conditioning, behaviors (responses) can be extinguished. **Extinction** is a process that leads to elimination of behaviors (responses). As we saw when we discussed classical conditioning, extinction of classically conditioned responses involves presenting the CS without the UCS. In operant conditioning, extinction involves following the target behavior with no reinforcers. To put extinction in terms of the contingencies: If Johnny screams while his parents are shopping, his parents will ignore his behavior. Unfortunately, in real life, parents with the best of intentions often reinforce the screaming. Parents often are so upset and embarrassed that they are likely to reinforce their child's screaming by giving the child a piece of candy or some other goodie (a positive reinforcer).

We pointed out earlier that reinforcement does not increase only desirable behaviors. What's more, parents (and others) can unwittingly reinforce the very behaviors they seek to extinguish. Consider the following example: When he was born, Raymond suffered severe oxygen deprivation, which resulted in brain damage and mental retardation. When he was 2 years old, he began to hit his head hard against the wall. His horrified parents would run to him, hold him, and kiss him each time he hit his head against the wall. To their dismay, the head banging not only continued, it *increased*. Concerned about their child's safety and well-being, they turned to a psychologist, who agreed to come to their house and observe (naturalistic observation). The next day, the psychologist called with a plan to eliminate the head banging, but it was not what Raymond's parents expected to hear. The psychologist said their attention was reinforcing Raymond's head banging. In terms of contingencies, the situation can be described as follows:

- *If* Johnny hits his head against the wall, *then* his parents will shower him with attention.

The plan to eliminate the head banging involved extinction, which means that his parents had to remain passive and not respond to the head banging. The psychologist pointed out a problem called the *extinction burst* (Mazur, 2006), which means that a behavior often increases once extinction begins before it is finally eliminated. In this case, an increase in an already high rate of head banging could be very dangerous; therefore, the psychologist arranged to have a protective head cover (similar to a football helmet) put on Raymond. The first few days were extremely difficult for his parents, but with encouragement from the psychologist they adhered to the plan and remained passive. Eventually, the head banging was extinguished; its frequency dropped to zero.

**Operant Conditioning and Stimulus Control.**    Bringing a behavior under stimulus control means that a particular stimulus or signal tells the participant that its responses will be reinforced. In an operant conditioning chamber, for example, a green light or a tone can be a signal to a rat that pressing the lever will be reinforced. Such a signal is called a **discriminative stimulus.** When the light or tone is present, lever presses are reinforced under the schedule of reinforcement that the rat has experienced during training. When the discriminative stimulus is absent, the responses are not reinforced, and extinction occurs.

**extinction**
A general term for the reduction and elimination of behaviors; in classical conditioning, extinction occurs when repeated presentation of the CS alone leads to a reduction in the strength of the CR; in operant conditioning, extinction occurs when a behavior is no longer followed by a reinforcer

**discriminative stimulus**
Stimulus or signal telling the participant that responding will be reinforced

Using extinction to eliminate head banging. When extinction procedures are used (ignoring an undesirable behavior), the behavior sometimes actually increases initially. This increase can be dangerous in cases of head banging, consequently, the child is often given a protective head cover as shown here.

The "open" sign is a discriminative stimulus signaling that the response of pulling the door handle will be reinforced by being able to enter Mother Myrick's for an afternoon snack.

A vast number of discriminative stimuli are found in the real world. The "Open" sign in a store window is a discriminative stimulus signaling that the response of reaching for the door handle will be reinforced by being able to enter the store and shop. The color of the traffic light at an intersection signals that the response of stopping your car (red) or proceeding through the intersection (green) will be reinforced by safe arrival at your destination. Your friend's mood serves as a signal that a response such as telling a joke or making a sympathetic remark will be appreciated.

# Schedules of Reinforcement

In an operant conditioning chamber, the experimenter can deliver reinforcers, such as a food pellet for a hungry rat or pigeon, according to a preset pattern. Figure 5-10 (p. 205) shows an instrument, known as a *cumulative recorder*, that logs the participant's responses. The results sheet, known as a **cumulative record,** shows the rate of responding in a series of operant conditioning trials; the steeper the line, the higher the rate of responding. Keep in mind that a cumulative recorder keeps track of the accumulation of target responses over time, hence the term *cumulative*.

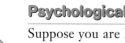

### Psychological Detective

Suppose you are looking at the cumulative record of a rat that is being trained in a Skinner box. As you hold the rat in your hand, you scan the record and note something interesting. Across several days, the record shows a straight horizontal line. What happened to the rat's target response?

This rat has stopped performing the target behavior. The fact that you are holding it, of course, indicates that the animal is still alive. The researcher put this rat on a schedule that led to the reduction and elimination of the behavior (extinction).

A preset pattern or plan for delivering reinforcement, a **schedule of reinforcement,** is an important determinant of behavior (Mazur, 2006; Shull & Lawrence, 1998). Once a target response has been shaped, the experimenter can arrange to have the reinforcer delivered according to a specific schedule. Most plans or schedules for delivering reinforcers fall into two major categories: *continuous* and *intermittent* (partial) reinforcement. What this means is that reinforcement will follow every target behavior or it will follow the target behavior every now and then.

**Continuous Reinforcement.** The most basic schedule of reinforcement is **continuous reinforcement,** in which the participant is given a reinforcer after each target response occurs. For example, a rat in a Skinner box receives a food pellet for each bar press; a soda machine delivers a cold drink each time you put money in it. A continuous schedule of reinforcement produces a reasonably high rate of responding. Once the reinforcer loses its effectiveness, however, the response rate drops quickly. Food pellets reinforce responding in a hungry rat, but they are not effective after the rat has eaten a large number of them.

**Intermittent (Partial) Reinforcement.** In schedules of reinforcement that do not involve the use of continuous reinforcement, some responses are *not* reinforced. The term **intermittent (or partial) reinforcement** describes these noncontinuous patterns of delivering reinforcement. There are two main types of intermittent schedules: *ratio* and *interval*.

**Ratio Schedules.** When a **ratio schedule** is in effect, the number of responses determines whether the participant receives reinforcement. In some cases the exact number of responses that must be made to receive a reinforcer is specified. For example, a pigeon may be required to peck a disk (key) five times before grain (a positive reinforcer) is presented. When the number of responses required to produce a reinforcer is specified, the arrangement is known as a *fixed-ratio (FR) schedule*. Requiring a pigeon to peck five times to receive reinforcement is designated as a *fixed-ratio 5 (FR-5)* schedule. We can think of a continuous reinforcement schedule as a *fixed-ratio 1 (FR-1)* schedule.

**cumulative record**
Results of a series of operant conditioning trials, shown as rate of responding

**schedule of reinforcement**
Preset pattern for delivering reinforcement

**continuous reinforcement**
Reinforcement that follows every target response

**intermittent (or partial) reinforcement**
Reinforcement that does not follow every target response

**ratio schedule**
Reinforcement schedule in which reinforcement is based on the number of responses; the number may be set (FR schedule) or may vary from one reinforcement to the next (VR schedule)

"*Actually, he's easy to train, everytime I press the buzzer, he brings me food.*"

On other occasions we may not want to specify the exact number of responses. Sometimes the reinforcer will be delivered after 15 responses, sometimes after 35 responses, sometimes after 10 responses, and so forth. Because the exact number of responses required for a reinforcer is not specified, this arrangement is called a *variable-ratio (VR) schedule.* We use the average number of responses to indicate the specific type of VR schedule. In our example, in which the values 15, 35, and 10 were used, the average number of responses would be 20 [(15 + 35 + 10)/3 = 20]. This particular schedule would be designated as a *variable-ratio 20 (VR-20)* schedule.

Participants usually make many responses on VR and FR schedules. Frequent responding makes good sense in these situations: The more responses that are made, the more frequently participants receive reinforcers. Although both FR and VR schedules produce many responses, VR schedules tend to produce higher rates of responding. These differences in rates of responding are shown in Figure 5-12.

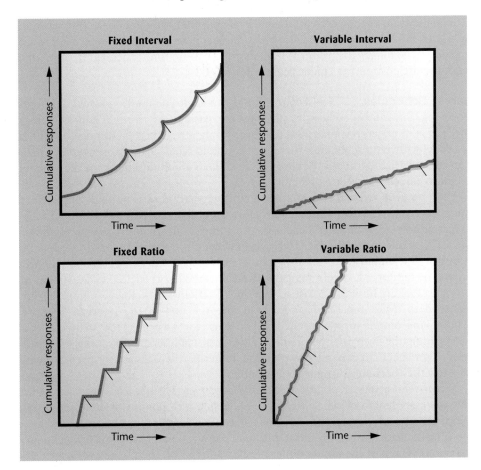

**FIGURE 5-12** Examples of partial schedules of reinforcement. The steeper the slope of the line, the higher the rate of responding. Note that the responding ceases (flat line) for a brief period after reinforcement has been delivered under a demanding FR schedule. This pause does not occur when the VR schedule is in effect. On a fixed-interval (FI) schedule, most responses are made toward the end of the interval, when a response will be reinforced. Once the reinforcer has been delivered and the interval begins again, the rate of responding decreases drastically. Under a variable-interval (VI) schedule, the participant cannot predict the end of the interval and therefore cannot judge when to respond. A low, steady rate of responding is maintained.

**Source:** Morris and Maisto (2006).

**interval schedule**
Reinforcement schedule based on the passage of time and in which a single response at the end of the designated interval is reinforced; intervals may be set (FI schedule) or may vary from one reinforcement to the next (VI schedule)

Last year Barbara and her friends spent spring break in Las Vegas. The slot machines proved to be her downfall. Sometimes the jackpot bell rang and she collected a potful of quarters, which encouraged her to continue playing. Before she knew it, she had been putting quarters into the "one-armed bandit" for 6 hours. When she counted her winnings and losses, she had spent $250 just to win $33. Slot machines "pay off" on a VR schedule. As Barbara put quarter after quarter into the machine, she was probably thinking, "Next time the bell will ring, and I'll get the jackpot." She knew that she would receive a reward (hitting the jackpot) at some point, but because slot machines operate on a VR schedule, she could not predict when she would be rewarded. If you have ever become "hooked" on playing the lottery, you can understand this process. The VR schedules of reinforcement can lead to high rates of responding in a Skinner box or in front of a one-armed bandit in Las Vegas.

When an FR schedule is in effect, participants may pause for a brief period after the reinforcement has been delivered. This *postreinforcement pause* typically does not occur when a VR schedule is used. When an FR schedule is used, the reinforcer seems to serve as a signal to take a short break. If you were responding on an FR schedule, you might be thinking, "Five more responses until I get the reinforcer; then I'll rest for a bit before I start responding again." Psychologist James Mazur describes the operation of an FR schedule of reinforcement and its associated postreinforcement pause:

> When I was an undergraduate, I worked in a factory for several summers, and I had the opportunity to observe workers who were paid by the piecework system. . . . Once a worker started up the machine, he almost always worked steadily and rapidly until the counter on the machine indicated that 100 pieces had been made. At this point, the worker would record the number completed on a work card and then take a break. . . . After this pause, the worker would turn on the machine and produce another 100 hinges. These workers needed very little supervision from their boss. The boss did not have to prod them to work faster or chastise them for taking excessively long breaks. (Mazur, 2006, p. 147)

The duration of the postreinforcement pause is not the same for all FR schedules; the higher the schedule (the greater the number of responses required to produce a reinforcer), the longer the pause. What's more, the more time expended in responding, the longer the postreinforcement pause will be.

**Interval Schedules.** The second type of intermittent (partial) schedule of reinforcement, the interval schedule, involves the passage of time. When an **interval schedule** is in effect, responses are reinforced only after a certain interval of time has passed. As with ratio schedules, there are two basic types of interval schedules, fixed-interval and variable-interval. Table 5-2 lists some common examples of the schedules of reinforcement that we are discussing.

Under a *fixed-interval (FI) schedule*, a constant period of time must pass before a response is reinforced. Responses made before the end of that period are not reinforced. No matter how many times you check your mailbox, you will not receive mail until it is time for the daily mail delivery. Under an FI schedule, participants try to estimate the passage of time and make most of their responses toward the end of the interval, when they will be reinforced. If your mail always is delivered between 3:00 and 3:30 P.M., you won't start looking for it until close to that time. Participants (humans or animals), however, tend to make *anticipatory responses* before the end of the interval. Suppose a Thanksgiving dinner turkey is scheduled to roast for 4 hours. How many of us can resist opening the oven door before the 4 hours, especially as the end of the 4-hour time period approaches? In general, however, the longer participants stay on an FI schedule, the better they become at timing their responses.

When reinforcement occurs on a *variable-interval (VI) schedule*, participants never know the exact length of time that must pass before a response is reinforced; the time interval changes after every reinforcement. Because a response can be reinforced at any time, it makes sense for participants to maintain a steady—but not especially high—rate of responding. Think of the times you have called a friend on the phone only to get voice

## TABLE 5-2

## Reinforcement Schedules and Examples

| Continuous | 1. A teacher "walks students through" the steps for solving simultaneous equations. They are liberally praised at each step as they first learn the solution.<br>2. Several times every day, the driver of a large delivery van puts the key into the ignition and each time the engine turns over, allowing her to drive to the next stop on her delivery route.<br>3. A student deposits several coins into a soda vending machine. Every time she does this, she receives a bottle of soda. |
|---|---|
| Fixed-ratio | 1. A salesperson receives a bonus for selling cars. After he has sold 10 cars, he receives $500 that is added to his regular salary. FR-10<br>2. The algebra teacher announces, "As soon as you've done three problems in a row correctly, you may start on your homework assignments so that you'll be able to finish by the end of class." FR-3<br>3. An assembly-line worker has to put together several components to build the brake housing for new cars. For every 12 brake housings completed, the worker receives $5. FR-12 |
| Variable-ratio | 1. Students volunteer to answer questions by raising their hands and are called on at random.<br>2. Door-to-door salespeople have to make a lot of calls before being able to sell magazine subscriptions. Over time, they figure that they need to make about 10 calls to sign one subscription; sometimes they have to make more and sometimes fewer. VR-10<br>3. A group of friends decides to spend some vacation time together in Las Vegas. Many of them are excited about the opportunity to play the slot machines. Several of them spend hours feeding quarters into the machines. They are told that 1 quarter in 250 turns out to be a winner. VR-250 |
| Variable-interval | 1. Students are given unannounced quizzes; consequently, they have been studying at a fairly even rate across the semester.<br>2. A group of students decide to hitchhike across the United States during the summer. The amount of time they spend walking along the highway waiting for a ride varies a great deal. Sometimes, they get a ride after just a few minutes; at other times, they have to wait several hours for a ride.<br>3. Andy is a college freshman who relies on his parents to deposit money into his account. The exact date they send the money varies quite a bit, but on average they deposit money into Andy's account about every 2 weeks (sometimes it is 1 week, sometimes 3, and sometimes more). VI-2 |
| Fixed interval | 1. Students are given a quiz every Friday.<br>2. The chefs at a local restaurant known for great roasts set the timer for 3 hours in order to cook the roasts to perfection. FI-3<br>3. Every 2 weeks on Friday, all the employees of the medical billing company receive their pay in the form of a check. |

mail. You probably did not start redialing at a frantic pace. Most likely you initially called back a few minutes later, and then a few minutes after that if you were not successful, and so on. You did not know if your friend was having several short conversations or a lengthy one—that is, you did not know when your dialing would be reinforced by the sound of a ringing telephone. Only time would tell. At some point your friend hung up, and you were able to get through. As time passed, your chances of getting through got better and better.

The average amount of time that must elapse before a response produces reinforcement under a VI schedule influences the rate of responding; the longer the interval, the lower the rate of responding. For example, pigeons reinforced on a VI 2-minute schedule responded between 60 and 100 times per minute, whereas pigeons reinforced on a VI 7-minute schedule responded 20 to 70 times per minute (Catania & Reynolds, 1968). The characteristic response patterns for FI and VI schedules are shown in Figure 5-12.

A classic example of an interval schedule of reinforcement is a course in which students take only a midterm exam and a final exam (equally spaced throughout the semester). On this system, many students will devote their time to studying near the end of the fixed interval (right before the midterm and then right before the final), when they cram as much as they can for the upcoming exam. (As we will see in Chapter 7, cramming is not an especially effective approach to studying, especially if students are concerned about long-term recall of the material). Perhaps a more effective approach would be to put the class on a variable interval schedule. If this schedule were used, it

## Study CHART

### Comparison of Classical and Operant Conditioning

| Basic Process | Classical Conditioning | Operant Conditioning |
|---|---|---|
| | A UCS causes a UCR; after a CS is paired with the UCS several times, the CS comes to elicit a CR. | Reinforcement (positive and negative) is used to shape a target response; once the response is established, a schedule of reinforcement (fixed or variable, interval or ratio) may be implemented to maintain it. |
| **Training**—acquisition of a new response. | The CS and UCS are paired; after several pairings the CS comes to elicit a CR. | Because the target response is followed by a reinforcer, its probability or rate increases. |
| **Extinction**—probability or frequency of a conditioned response is decreased. | The CS is presented alone, and a decrease in the CR is observed. | Reinforcement is discontinued, and the rate of responding gradually decreases. |
| **Generalization**—responses are made to stimuli other than those used in training. | Stimuli similar to the CS elicit the CR. | Responding occurs when stimuli similar to the discriminative stimulus are presented. |
| **Discrimination**—responses are made only to stimuli used in training. | Stimuli that are similar to the CS do not elicit a CR. | Only the discriminative stimulus results in responding. |

would likely lead to steady study behavior across the semester as opposed to last-minute cramming. Why? A variable interval schedule means that students do not know when the next exam (or quiz) is coming, so it would be best to be prepared all of the time. Of course, we also recognize that most students would probably object to such an exam/quiz schedule. Anticipating just such a response, most faculty members shy away from such an approach, despite its apparent benefits in terms of study behavior.

The Study Chart above compares classical and operant conditioning. Check your understanding of these basic forms of learning before reading further.

**The Partial Reinforcement Effect.**   Every day you look in your mailbox for a letter from a friend. After 3 months of looking, you are finally convinced that your friend is not going to write; no letters have come, and there is no reason to expect any. Completely removing the reinforcer—in this case, your friend's letters—from the operant conditioning situation eventually results in extinction, or elimination, of the operantly conditioned response. There are some basic similarities between the way extinction is produced in classical conditioning (omit the UCS, CS alone) and the way it is produced in operant conditioning (removing the reinforcer).

As you saw earlier in this chapter, intermittent or partial reinforcement schedules can produce high rates of responding. This outcome is especially true of ratio schedules, in which the harder the participants work, the more reinforcement they receive. Because partial reinforcement schedules involve making a number of responses that are not reinforced, it may be difficult to tell when reinforcement has been discontinued completely and when it has merely been delayed. Because Barbara cannot tell whether the slot machine is broken or whether it will pay off the next time she puts in a quarter, she continues to play. Many players stop only when all their money is gone. Gambling is not the only behavior occurring on a partial schedule of reinforcement. Do you know a friend who has a lucky seat in class? Do you know someone who carries a rabbit's foot for luck? Do you own a lucky hat that you must wear to the big game? These are all examples of behaviors that could be described as superstitious. A critical thinker might collect data to determine that any supposed relation between the lucky seat and grades does not hold up to scrutiny, but few of us check the data. Superstitious behaviors are generally reinforced on partial schedules of reinforcement just like slot machines, and they are difficult to stop (Vyse, 1997).

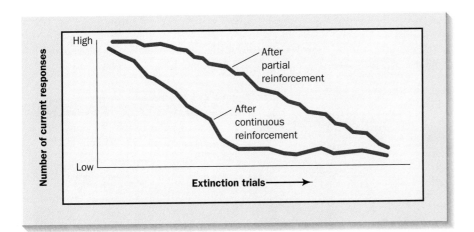

**FIGURE 5-13** Extinction of a bar-press response after continuous and partial reinforcement training in a Skinner box.

Do you see a general pattern concerning extinction and operant conditioning? If reinforcement is delivered in a predictable manner, it should be easier to tell when it has been discontinued and when extinction has begun. Hence extinction should occur more rapidly following FR training than following VR training. Likewise, extinction should occur more rapidly following FI training than following VI training. What's more, it should be even easier to extinguish responding that has been conditioned through the use of continuous reinforcement than responding that has been conditioned through any partial or intermittent schedule.

These facts have been verified experimentally. The **partial reinforcement effect** states that extinction of operant behavior is more difficult after partial or intermittent reinforcement than after continuous reinforcement. Have you ever taken pity on a hungry stray cat and put out some food for it? Sometimes when it comes to your door you feed it, and at other times you don't. When you finally decide you are never going to feed the cat again, you find it will not go away. The cat has been reinforced on an intermittent or partial schedule of reinforcement. It will return again and again for quite some time. Figure 5-13 shows differences in extinction after continuous and partial reinforcement training in a Skinner box.

Knowledge of the effects of various schedules of reinforcement and the workings of the partial reinforcement effect can be helpful when devising behavior modification programs in a wide range of settings. Consider the following situation: Eleven-year-old Alice was a fifth-grade student of average intelligence. During math classes, she spent much of the time off-task (that is, not paying attention); consequently, she made numerous errors on the arithmetic problems she was to complete. Alice's teacher, who was knowledgeable in the use of operant conditioning, devised a plan to keep Alice focused on the problems and completing them successfully. Every day during the math class, a teaching assistant worked with Alice. During the first 2 days, the assistant would say "Good work" or "Excellent job" when Alice solved a problem. During the next 2 days, the teacher raised the number of problems that needed to be solved before the reinforcer was presented to four. Thus, the assistant moved the schedule of reinforcement from FR-2 to FR-4. A few days later, the number of problems that needed to be solved was raised again, this time to 8 and then to 16. Alice's rate of successful problem solving tripled; the highest work rate occurred at the end of the study, when she was praised for solving 16 problems. In addition, Alice was attending to the task 100% of the time (adapted from Martin & Pear, 2003).

## Punishment: The Opposite of Reinforcement

We have seen that the effect of a reinforcer (either positive or negative) is to increase the likelihood of a target response. A **punisher** has the opposite effect: to decrease the likelihood or rate of responding of a target response.

Everyone seems to have an opinion about the usefulness and desirability of punishment. Thorndike concluded that punishment might not be effective, but he may have

**partial reinforcement effect**
Phenomenon in which extinction of an operant response following partial or intermittent reinforcement takes longer than extinction following continuous reinforcement

**punisher**
Stimulus that produces a decrease in responding; may take the form of presentation of a stimulus or termination of a stimulus

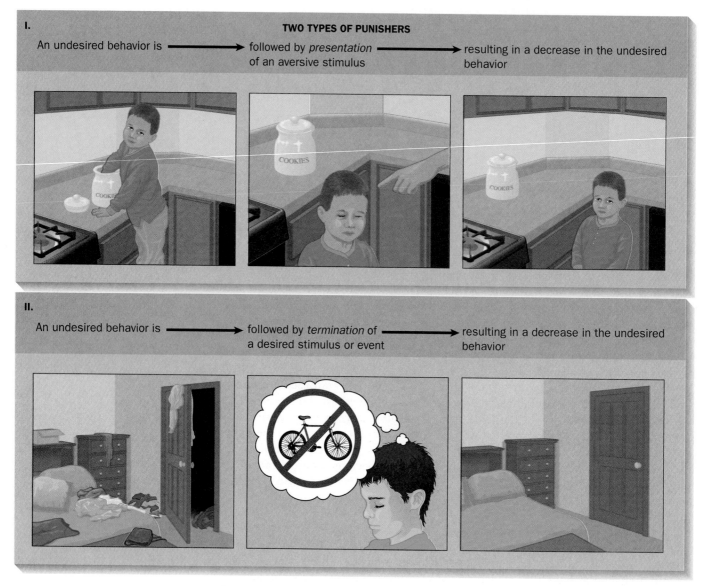

**FIGURE 5-14** Diagram of the operation of punishers. There are two types of punishers: (A) presenting an aversive stimulus (negative reinforcer) such as scolding, and (B) removing a desired stimulus (positive reinforcer) such as use of a bicycle. In both cases, the end result is punishment or a decrease in the response rate of the behavior.

been premature in dismissing its influence. We now turn our attention to different types of punishers as well as some guidelines for using punishment effectively.

Punishers may be (1) aversive stimuli or events that are presented or (2) pleasant stimuli or events that are removed (see Figure 5-14). Remember that reinforcement (positive or negative) *increases* the rate of responding, whereas **punishment** *decreases* the rate of responding. For example, if a rat in an operant conditioning chamber receives an electric shock after pressing a bar, its rate of bar pressing decreases. If a child is scolded for playing in the street, that behavior is likely to occur less often. These are examples of punishment. Other examples of punishment include taking away a child's allowance, grounding a teenager, or swatting your cat for scratching the furniture. Note that punishment decreases or *suppresses* behavior; it rarely eliminates behavior, as is the case in extinction. In fact, punishment is not an especially effective means of altering behavior. Just think of a class clown in grade school. How effective was punishment in reducing his or her performances? In most cases the answer is probably "not very effective." As we will see shortly, several factors influence the effectiveness of punishment, and most of these factors do not occur in the case of the class clown. For example, punishment tends to be more effective when each

**punishment**
The process of using a punisher to decrease the response rate

instance of the undesirable behavior is punished. It is unlikely that any teacher is able to catch and punish each of the class clown's performances, which therefore are reinforced by the typical response of other students. On a larger scale, the ineffectiveness of punishment can be seen in a wide variety of behaviors that society seeks to influence by using punishment. How many of you have exceeded the posted speed limit in the past 24 hours? We would not be surprised to find that the vast majority fall into the category of speeders whose behavior is not affected by punishment when the probability of being ticketed is low. What's more, in the United States we seek to reduce the incidence of murder by imposing the death penalty. No matter which side of this highly emotional issue you happen to be on, the fact remains that we have one of the highest rates of murder in the world.

Class clown. Efforts to use punishment to reduce a class clown's antics are often unsuccessful. Teachers rarely are able to punish each incident.

One common example of the use of punishment is spanking or corporal punishment. A surprising number of U.S. parents believe spanking is an acceptable, important, and desirable element of child rearing. In fact, almost half of mothers with children less than 4 years old and almost 20% of mothers with children 1 year of age or younger believe it is appropriate to spank a child under 1 year of age (Springen, 2000; Straus, Gelles, & Steinmetz, 2003). Opinions on spanking vary dramatically from country to country and culture to culture. For example, Austria, Germany, and Sweden have banned spanking, whereas the prevailing view in the United States embraces the practice, as described in the commonly heard advice "Spare the rod and spoil the child" (Durant, 1999; Gershoff, 2002). Our culture values individual freedom; consequently, decisions concerning the use of physical punishment of children are viewed as private family matters, which are outside the prying eyes of government regulators. Advocates of punishment readily point out that punishment does indeed suppress undesirable behaviors, often immediately. On the other hand, evidence suggests that it also creates a number of problems. For example, children who were spanked tend to have lower-quality parent–child relationships, higher levels of delinquency, and more antisocial behavior; are more likely to have psychological problems; and are more likely to abuse their own spouses and children when they become adults (Gershoff, 2002; Kazdin & Benjet, 2003). The last finding is often cited as an example of the *cycle of violence* phenomenon in which abused children grow up to be abusers themselves.

## Psychological Detective

We have examined how to present reinforcers to obtain a high rate of responding. How can punishment be administered in order to maximize its effects? Select a behavior that you or society find undesirable and that you would like to see decreased. Then formulate specific answers to this question and write them down before reading further.

If punishment is to be used effectively, there are several procedures that should be followed (Axelrod & Apsche, 1983; Azrin & Holz, 1966):

1. The punisher should be delivered (positive) or taken away (negative) *immediately after the response that is to be eliminated.* Slapping your cat for digging up your African violets while you were out will have no effect except perhaps to make you feel better. Why not? The cat will not see any connection between the earlier undesirable behavior and the current punishment.

2. The punisher should be *strong enough to make a real difference.* Being grounded for 2 days may not matter very much, but being grounded for 2 months is a different story. Most people consider the use of extremely strong punishers, particularly those involving physical or violent punishment, unacceptable, if not ethically wrong. We do not want to inflict so much punishment that real damage results.

3. The punishment should be administered *after each and every undesired target response.* Punishment is less effective when you do not punish all of the undesired responses; it must be administered consistently. Thus, if you want to stop a child from using offensive language, you should punish the child every time he or she uses it. Permitting even one episode of the undesired behavior to occur after previous punishment greatly decreases the effectiveness of the punishment.

**4.** There should be *no unauthorized escape from the punisher*. If the punishment is not applied uniformly, its effects will be weakened. Rats are very clever; frequently they learn how to hang upside down from the top of a cage to avoid an electric shock to their feet.

**5.** If you use punishment, be prepared for the possibility of *aggressive responding*. Rats do not like to be shocked, children do not like to have their television privileges taken away, and spankings can elicit behaviors other than crying. Children who are spanked may retaliate by kicking and biting. Note that aggressive responding may be directed toward a person, an animal, or an object that cannot retaliate, such as a pet dog or cat; such behavior is called *displaced aggression*. Nor does aggressive behavior always end when the punishment ends. As a child, did you ever try to "get even" with your parents after being punished? In short, punishment can teach a child to use force or other violence against people.

**6.** Provide an *alternative desired behavior* that can gain a reinforcer for the person. Giving a child a spanking for playing in the street may not be especially effective if there is nowhere else to play. Clearly, it is very difficult to use punishment effectively. Perhaps the best solution is to reinforce an alternate desired behavior. The use of *redirecting* as a disciplinary technique in child-care settings provides an example. When a child engages in an inappropriate behavior, the child is removed from the scene and given another, appropriate activity to engage in. Praising the child for success in this appropriate activity is reinforcement of an alternate, desired behavior.

The accompanying Study Chart summarizes the difference between reinforcement and punishment.

**STUDY TIP**

Create an outline summarizing the basic points of the material on the Skinner box, shaping, and schedules of reinforcement.

## Study CHART

### Positive and Negative Reinforcement Compared with Punishment

| Reinforcement | Results in an increase in responding |
|---|---|
| POSITIVE | A stimulus is presented after a target response; an increase in responding occurs (for example, receiving good grades increases the amount of time one studies). |
| NEGATIVE | A stimulus is removed after a target response; an increase in responding occurs (for example, if playing music reduces boredom, the frequency of playing music increases). |
| **Punishment** | **Results in a decrease in responding** |
| POSITIVE | A stimulus is presented after a target response; a decrease in responding occurs (for example, washing a child's mouth out with soap for cursing reduces the number of curse words the child says). |
| NEGATIVE | A stimulus is removed after a target response; a decrease in responding occurs (for example, Saturday morning cartoon privileges are taken away because the child's chores have not been completed). |

## REVIEW SUMMARY

**1. Operant conditioning** occurs when an organism performs a target response that is followed by a reinforcer, which affects the probability that the behavior (target response) will occur again.

**2.** All reinforcers increase the frequency of the response they follow. **Positive reinforcers** are presented after the target response has been made; **negative reinforcers** are withdrawn or taken away after the target response has been made. **Primary reinforcers** (for example, food) satisfy basic biological needs; **secondary (conditioned) reinforcers** (for example, money) acquire their power to reinforce behavior by being associated with primary reinforcers.

**3.** Complex responses may be acquired gradually through the process of **shaping** (*successive approximations*). Psychologists can keep track of the rate of responding by using a **cumulative record**, which keeps track of all target responses made by an organism across time. A **discriminative stimulus** signals that responses will be reinforced. Behavior is said to be under stimulus control when responding occurs only when the discriminative stimulus is present.

4. Once a behavior has been acquired, it may be reinforced according to a particular **schedule of reinforcement.** When a **ratio schedule** is in effect, the number of responses is important. *Fixed-ratio (FR) schedules* require that a set number of responses be made before a reinforcer is delivered; *variable-ratio (VR) schedules* require that the participant perform differing numbers of responses to obtain a reinforcer. With an **interval schedule,** a certain amount of time must pass before a response is

reinforced. With a *fixed-interval (FI) schedule,* the time interval is constant; the time interval changes after each reinforcer is delivered when a *variable-interval (VI) schedule* is used. Operant responses that are on an intermittent schedule of reinforcement during training take longer to extinguish than responses that have received continuous reinforcement. This phenomenon is known as **intermittent** (or **partial**) **reinforcement.**

5. The opposite of reinforcement, **punishment,** involves presentation or withdrawal of stimuli called **punishers,** which results in suppression of the target behavior.

## ✓ CHECK YOUR PROGRESS

1. For each of the following situations, find the response that is being reinforced, identify the reinforcer, and determine which schedule of reinforcement is being used.

   a. Playing the lottery has become so popular that people line up to buy lottery tickets. Sometimes they win, and sometimes they lose.

   b. A friend has a part-time job making telephone calls to convince people to sign up for a credit card. For every 25 new customers who sign up, your friend receives a bonus.

   c. Each morning, rain or shine, your dog, McDuff, comes to the back door to wait for his breakfast, which he receives every morning.

   d. Every time Alan experiences a headache, he takes the medication that his physician prescribed and the pain is relieved enough that he can go about his daily routine without any problems.

2. For each of the following situations, indicate whether a positive or negative reinforcer is being used.

   a. A rat presses a bar to turn off an electric foot shock.
   b. A child digs through a new box of cereal to get a prize.
   c. A teenager pretends to be sick in order to receive extra attention.
   d. A student pretends to be sick in order to avoid having to make a presentation in class.

3. For each of the following, indicate whether partial reinforcement is involved. If it is, indicate the likely schedule of reinforcement.

   a. receiving praise for each good grade you make
   b. sometimes getting caught for speeding
   c. having never been caught for cheating in high school
   d. occasionally finding money on the ground as you walk to class
   e. playing basketball on a team that won 3 out of 15 games last year
   f. driving around and around a full parking lot until someone leaves and you can park your car

4. Explain why learning to play the piano is an example of shaping. What would the reinforcer or reinforcers be in this situation?

5. In which type of conditioning is the learner's behavior important in bringing about the learning?

   a. backward conditioning
   b. classical conditioning
   c. operant conditioning
   d. Pavlovian conditioning

6. When the teacher returned yesterday's arithmetic exam with a grade of 100, Alicia smiled. Several hours later she handed the report card to her parents, who took her for her favorite ice cream sundae. When they arrived home, they told Alicia that she did not have to put the dishes away—a job that Alicia does not like. Alicia's mom is taking an Introduction to Psychology course, in which she is required to describe examples of operant conditioning from her own experience or the experiences of family members. When she writes her report, it is sure to contain which of the following?

   a. two examples of the Premack Principle and one example of shaping
   b. two examples of positive reinforcement and one example of extinction
   c. one example of positive reinforcement and two examples of negative reinforcement
   d. two examples of positive reinforcement and one example of negative reinforcement

7. What is the graph that shows the pattern of a rat's responding in a Skinner box?

   a. shaping record
   b. response pattern
   c. cumulative record
   d. reinforcement pattern

8. The effect of _____ is to decrease the likelihood or rate of a target response.

   a. punishment
   b. positive reinforcement
   c. negative reinforcement
   d. intermittent reinforcement

**9.** What is the partial reinforcement effect?
  **a.** Extinction after continuous reinforcement is more difficult.
  **b.** Extinction after partial reinforcement is more difficult.
  **c.** Learning under continuous reinforcement is more difficult.
  **d.** Learning under partial reinforcement is more difficult.

**10.** What two opposing processes are involved in creating discriminative stimuli?
  **a.** cognition and shaping
  **b.** discrimination and generalization
  **c.** negative and positive reinforcement
  **d.** modeling and observational learning

# COGNITIVE AND SOCIAL PERSPECTIVES ON LEARNING

The door to the garage was ajar and Mary became frightened; she was afraid that someone might be trying to rob the house. Trembling, she peeked into the garage to discover that her 3-year-old son was in the driver's seat of the family van, fiddling with the key. Suddenly the engine started to run, and Mary made a dash to the car to prevent an accident. At a family gathering several weeks after this event, Mary was discussing what had happened; family members seemed quite surprised that a 3-year-old could start the car. One of Mary's cousins, Amy, is a psychology major who had some ideas concerning what happened that day. *How would psychologists explain how this 3-year-old managed to start the van?*

We encountered contingency theory and blocking in our study of classical conditioning (see page 199). These processes suggest that classical conditioning is not a simple mechanical process; rather, mental activity or thought processes (cognition) are involved to some degree. The relation of cognition to basic learning processes, such as insight learning and latent learning, has been studied for many decades.

## The Role of Cognition

Two of the most compelling examples of how cognitive factors are involved in learning are insight learning and latent learning. At several points we discussed elements of learning that had distinctly cognitive components. For example, the ability of a CS to predict the occurrence of the UCS suggests that organisms assess this element of the learning situation. The effects of various schedules of reinforcement on responding also suggest an element of active processing rather than having behaviors stamped in mechanically. For example, human participants on FR schedules of reinforcement become very good at assessing where they are in terms of the likelihood of receiving reinforcement. These and other examples suggest that organisms are much more active than early learning theorists might have imagined.

**insight learning**
Sudden grasp of a concept or the solution to a problem that results from perceptual restructuring; typically characterized by an immediate change in behavior

**Insight Learning.** The importance of cognition to operant conditioning can be seen in the process known as insight learning. **Insight learning** is a form of operant conditioning in which we restructure our perceptual stimuli (we see things in a different way), make an instrumental (operant) response, and generalize this behavior to other situations.

In short, it is not blind, trial-and-error learning that develops gradually but a type of learning that occurs suddenly and relies on cognitive processes. It is the "aha!" experience we have when we suddenly solve a problem.

Research by the Gestalt psychologist (see Chapter 1) Wolfgang Köhler (1927) exemplifies insight learning. Using chimpanzees as his test animals, Köhler gave them the following problem: A bunch of bananas was suspended out of reach of the chimps. To reach the bananas, the chimps had to stack three boxes on top of one another and then put together the pieces of a jointed pole to form a single longer pole. After several unsuccessful attempts at jumping and trying to reach the bananas, Köhler's star pupil, Sultan, appeared to survey the situation (mentally rearrange the stimulus elements that were present) and solve the problem in the prescribed manner. Köhler believed that Sultan had achieved insight into the correct solution of the problem.

Consider the solution of a particularly difficult math problem. You struggle and struggle to solve the problem, without success. In frustration you set the problem aside and turn to another assignment. All of a sudden you understand what is required to work the math problem successfully; you've had an "aha!" experience. How you perceive the situation has changed; insight has occurred. Once this problem has been solved, you are able to solve others like it. Similarly, one of your authors works on word puzzles almost every day. Sometimes he struggles to rearrange the mixed-up letters (anagrams) to form words, and sometimes the answers appear almost instantly. Quite often (especially after he takes a brief break from the puzzle), an answer seems to occur quickly, as insight has been achieved.

Thus cognitive processes are important in helping us to adapt to our environment. As we shall see, other organisms—even rats—may use cognitive processes as they go about their daily activities.

**Latent Learning.** Psychologist Edward C. Tolman presented persuasive evidence for the use of cognitive processes in basic learning in his study of maze learning by rats (Tolman & Honzik, 1930). Tolman is associated most often with his study of **latent learning,** which occurs when learning has taken place but is not demonstrated. In one of Tolman's most famous studies, three groups of rats learned a complex maze that had many choices and dead ends. One group of rats was always reinforced with food for successfully completing the maze. These animals gradually made fewer and fewer errors until, after 11 days of training, their performance was nearly perfect. A second group was never reinforced; the rats continued to make numerous errors. The third (latent-learning) group of animals did not receive reinforcement for the first 10 days of training. On the 11th day, reinforcement was provided. The behavior of these animals on the 12th day is of crucial importance. If learning occurs in a gradual trial-and-error manner, the rats' performance on the 12th day should not have differed much from their performance on the 11th day. If, however, the rats used cognitive processes to learn to navigate the maze, they would exhibit dramatic behavior changes.

In fact, on the 12th day these rats learned to solve the maze as quickly as the rats that had been continually reinforced (see Figure 5-15). How did these rats learn so

**latent learning**
Learning that has occurred but is not demonstrated

**STUDY TIP**

Create a visual organizer that shows behaviors with cognitive requirements (insight learning, latent learning, etc.) and their most important elements.

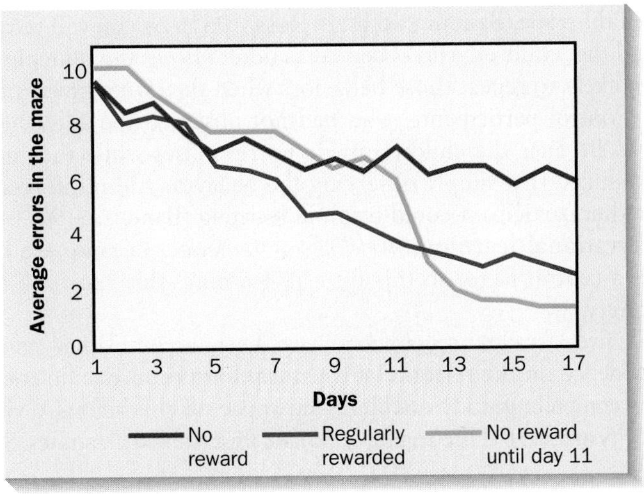

**FIGURE 5-15** Results of Tolman and Honzik's maze-running experiment are not easily explained by operant conditioning concepts. This research was a significant contributor to the development of more cognitively oriented views of how organisms learn.

**Source:** Tolman and Honzik (1930).

New York Yankees and Hall of Fame baseball player, Yogi Berra, once said "You can learn a lot by watching." There is growing concern that many young people are modeling the violence they see in movies and video games. Today's video games are realistic, attractive, exciting, and captivating. The challenge in the future may be to design games that are as equally attractive and exciting yet provide opportunities to model prosocial and non-violent forms of behavior.

**observational learning (modeling)**
Learning that occurs through watching and imitating the behaviors of others

quickly? Tolman argued that by wandering through the maze for 10 days before the introduction of reinforcement, these animals had formed a *cognitive* map of the maze. In other words, they had learned to solve the maze, but this knowledge had remained latent (unused) until reinforcement was introduced on the 11th day. Then, on the 12th day, these rats demonstrated that they knew how to get to the location of the reinforcement. Their latent learning had manifested itself. The implications of this finding are clear: It is possible to learn a behavior, yet that learning may not be directly observed.

## Observational Learning

As the previous discussion suggests, our behavior and the behavior of other animals is not just mechanically stamped in or out. A degree of cognitive activity or processing of information is involved when we learn. Consider the following example. Imagine that you have given permission for your 6-year-old son and 8-year-old daughter to participate in a psychological experiment at the local university. During the experiment, each child watches an adult play with a large inflatable doll that can double as a punching bag. Because the doll's base contains sand, the doll bounces back when it is punched and then is ready for more punches. The adult delivers a merciless beating to the doll; then each child is given an opportunity to play with the doll. What can this experiment tell us about learning?

For many years psychologists believed that a participant must actually perform an operant response for learning to occur. In the early 1960s, Albert Bandura and his colleagues changed this view (Bandura, Ross, & Ross, 1963). As you will recall from Chapter 1, they found that children who observed an adult *hitting* and punching an inflatable Bobo doll were likely to repeat those behaviors when they were given a chance to play with the doll. Control participants, who had not observed the adult model, behaved less aggressively. Because the children made no responses while they were watching, researchers concluded that simply observing the behavior and reinforcement (or punishment) of another participant could result in learning (Bandura, 1977). Such learning is termed **observational learning**, *modeling*, or *imitation*. Because the observation of other people is a central factor in this form of learning, this approach is often called *social learning theory*.

For almost five decades, researchers have been accumulating correlational and experimental evidence on the relation between exposure to media violence and real-life aggression. One compelling study examined the impact of children's TV viewing at age 8 on criminal activity at age 30 (Huesmann, 1986). As Figure 5-16 illustrates, 8-year-old boys

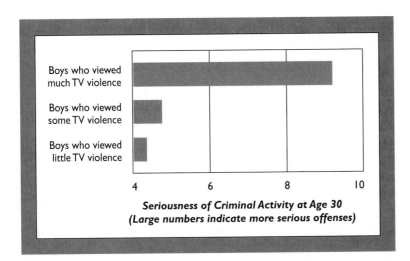

**FIGURE 5-16** Researchers have found an association between the levels of exposure to television violence among boys and the seriousness of criminal activity at age 30.

**Source:** Huesmann (1986).

who watched large doses of TV violence had the most extensive criminal records as 30-year olds. This finding was true for both males and females, even though females had lower overall levels of criminal activity The general conclusion from the accumulated evidence is: Violent media is causally related to short-term and long-term expressions of aggression.

Albert Bandura's research was important when it was first reported, but its implications seem to grow in importance as media dominate our lives, especially those of young people. A few facts derived from surveys of families will give us an idea of the potential impact that media can have for good or bad (Rideout, Vandewater, & Wartella, 2003; Roberts, Foehr, Rideout, & Vrodie, 1999; Woodward, 2000). Walk into the typical family home and you are likely to find at least one television set, but this is only the beginning of the potential for exposure to violence via media because new forms of media are created all the time. For example, most families have at least one VCR or DVD, and the majority (approximately three in four) subscribe to cable or satellite television. You will find a video game system in the homes of 7 of every 10 families; a similar percentage own at least one computer. The majority of children have a television in their bedroom (including 30% of children between ages 0 and 3)! The current generation of children has grown up on television and other media. In fact, children spend more time watching television than engaging in any other activity except going to school and sleeping (Liebert & Sprafkin, 1988; Roberts et al., 1999).

Sixty-one percent of all television programs contain some violence, but only 4% present any antiviolence messages (Wilson et al., 1997). What's more, nearly 70% of TV programs targeted to children contain acts of physical aggression (Wilson, 2002). In nearly 75% of the violent scenes, there is no immediate punishment or condemnation of the violence. Much of the violence is sanitized: 51% of violent interactions on TV feature no pain and 47% feature no harm. Of all the violent scenes on television, 86% feature no blood or gore (Wilson et al., 1998).

One of the consequences of this exposure to media violence is *desensitization*, which is a reduction in distress-related physiological reactivity to observations or thoughts of violence. People who watch a lot of media violence experience less physiological arousal. Why is this important? That physiological arousal tends to inhibit violence, emotional behavior, and thoughts of violence. Simply put, watching media violence can make people cease to respond to violence as they once did, thus making it more likely that they may engage in violence (Huesmann et al., 2003).

A recent concern focuses on video games, which can be extremely violent. Craig Anderson and Karen Dill (2000) found that playing violent video games was positively correlated with aggressive behavior and delinquency in children. The cautions we raised concerning correlational evidence in Chapter 1 should lead you to wonder if there is a *causal* relation here. In a second study, these researchers found that exposing a random sample of children to a graphically violent video game had a direct and immediate impact on their aggressive thoughts and behavior. What's more, a review of the literature on

The graphic and extensive nature of violence on television and in computer games is a growing concern, especially as more and more children have access to such material. In this screen shot from the Mortal Kombat website, a character is shown slashing another's character's head off with swords growing out of his forearm.

the effects of video game violence led researchers (Anderson & Bushman, 2001) to the following conclusion:

> The results clearly support the hypothesis that exposure to violent video games poses a public-health threat to children and youth, including college-age individuals. Exposure is positively associated with heightened levels of aggression in young adults and children, in experimental and nonexperimental designs, and in males and females. Exposure is negatively associated with prosocial behavior. (p. 358)

Although there are major differences between songs and visual media such as television, research has established that aggressive words can prime aggressive thoughts, perceptions, and behavior, hence the concern for the potential effects of violent lyrics on songs. Craig Anderson and his colleagues (2003) investigated the effects of songs and violent lyrics (control participants heard similar but nonviolent songs) on aggressive thoughts and hostile feelings in five separate experiments using college students as participants. The general trend of the results was clear. "The increase in aggressive thoughts was shown in three different ways. Violent songs led to more aggressive interpretations of ambiguously aggressive words, increased the relative speed with which people read aggressive (versus nonaggressvie) words, and increased the proportion of aggressive words completions." One especially interesting finding was that the violent song effects did not interact with trait hostility or with gender. The consistency of the results across five experiments was impressive. Of course, the effects of violent song lyrics might be limited in time, especially if some positive event follows the violent lyrics.

At this point, research on the effects of violent lyrics is still in its infancy. Nevertheless, there are sound theoretical and empirical reasons for researchers to expect the effects of song lyrics on aggressive behavior to be similar to the well-established effects of exposure to TV and movie violence, as well as the recently determined effects of violent video games.

In a report entitled "The Influence of Media Violence on Youth," Craig Anderson and his colleagues concluded that the existing "research literature clearly reveals that exposure to violent media plays an important causal role in violence in modern society" (Anderson et al., 2003, p. 105). Does this mean that media violence is the necessary or sufficient cause of aggression? The answer is no. Many young children and adolescents will have a history of exposure to violent media and will never kill anyone. Similarly, there will be 45-year-olds who smoke two packs of cigarettes a day and do not have lung cancer. Their personal experiences lead both to reject the causal argument because it does not apply to the facts of their situation, but they are wrong. Violence in media increases the propensity for violence, just as cigarette smoking increases the likelihood of developing cancer.

If you stop to think about it, observational learning is the main way we learn about our culture and its customs and traditions. Let's return to the vignette that opened this section. Observational learning is most likely how Mary's 3-year-old son learned to start the car. He has probably observed his mother and father put the key in the ignition and turn it hundreds if not thousands of times.

One of the keys to observational learning appears to be that the participant identifies with the person being observed. If we put ourselves in the other person's place for a moment, we are better able to imagine the effects of the reinforcer or punisher. This phenomenon is called *vicarious reinforcement* or *vicarious punishment*. Table 5-3 describes the major effects of vicarious (through another) consequences and their implications for learning.

Observational learning is a widespread phenomenon that is even found among a number of animals. For example, rats that observed the extinction behavior of other rats subsequently stopped responding more rapidly than did rats that did not observe extinction performance (Heyes, Jaldow, & Dawson, 1993). In another experiment, monkeys reared in a laboratory didn't fear snakes. After watching another group of monkeys

**TABLE 5-3**

## Major Effects of Vicarious Consequences

| Vicarious Reinforcement | Vicarious Punishment |
|---|---|
| Conveys information about which behaviors are appropriate in which settings | Conveys information about which behaviors are inappropriate in which settings |
| Arousal of the emotional responses of pleasure and satisfaction in the observer | Tends to exert restraining influence on imitation of modeled behavior |
| After repeated reinforcements, incentive-motivational effects are generated; behavior acquires functional value | Tends to devalue the model's status because the behavior did not lead to a reinforcement |

**Source:** Adapted from Gredler (2001).

react fearfully to snakes, however, the nonfearful monkeys developed a pronounced fear of snakes (Cook, Mineka, Wolkenstein, & Laitsch, 1985).

Attempts to influence behavior through observational learning occur every day (along with efforts based on classical conditioning). Turn on the television and you are bombarded with commercials, which often have elements of observational learning. If you drive this kind of car, wear these clothes, use this brand of perfume, shower with this soap, use this shampoo, and eat this kind of breakfast, you will be rich, famous, powerful, sexy, and so forth, just like the models in the commercials.

According to the social learning theory proposed by Albert Bandura (1986), for observational learning to be effective, the following conditions must be present:

**1.** You must pay attention to what the other person is doing and what happens to him or her.

**2.** You probably will not make the modeled response immediately, so you need to store a memory of the situation you have observed. For example, catchy advertising jingles that run through our heads continuously help us remember a particular commercial and its message (see Chapter 7).

**3.** You must be able to repeat or reproduce the behavior you observed. It might be wonderful to dream of owning a Porsche, but most of us will never be able to reproduce the behaviors needed to obtain one, regardless of how often we watch the commercial.

**4.** Your motivational state must be appropriate to the behavior you have learned through observation. Watching numerous commercials of people drinking a particular soft drink will not normally cause you to purchase one if you are not thirsty.

**5.** You must pay attention to discriminative stimuli. Sometimes we do not choose the best time and place to imitate someone else's behavior. For example, it would not be wise for teenagers to model some of their peers' behaviors at the dinner table.

Observational learning has also been used to reduce or eliminate phobias. For example, adults with an intense fear of snakes were shown live models handling live snakes (Bandura, Blanchard, & Ritter, 1969). These individuals were then encouraged to handle the snakes themselves. A final test indicated that they had less fear of snakes than those people who had watched a film of people handling snakes and a control group who had received no treatment.

We have presented this chapter's various concepts and principles separately to make your learning and understanding easier. In reality, classical conditioning, operant conditioning, observational learning, and punishment are not mutually exclusive. They can, and do, occur simultaneously.

**Source:** Psi Chi Newsletter. Reprinted with the permission of Psi Chi.

**STUDY TIP**

Rewrite in your own words, providing two examples to illustrate, the conditions necessary for effective observational learning.

# REVIEW SUMMARY

**1. Insight learning** involves restructuring our perceptual stimuli to achieve the solution to a problem. Such perceptual restructuring and solutions typically occur rapidly.

**2. Latent learning** occurs when learning has taken place but is not demonstrated until a later time.

**3. Observational learning** takes place when we observe and identify with the behaviors of others. Advertisements and television commercials appeal to this process. Televised violence may result in observational learning and lead to an increase in violent behaviors.

# ✓ CHECK YOUR PROGRESS

**1.** Which situation(s) involve(s) observational learning?

a. Learning to drive by taking a driver education course that emphasizes behind-the-wheel experience

b. Pushing the remote control to change channels on the television

c. Using a video to learn how to play golf

d. Seeing friends go by on their motorcycles, saying to yourself, "I bet I can do that," and trying it

e. Salivating every time you pass your favorite restaurant

**2.** Concern has been raised about violence in television and films because of research evidence about

a. modeling.

b. classical conditioning.

c. operant conditioning.

d. negative reinforcement.

**3.** Which of the following is the best summary of the evidence on the relation between video game violence and aggression?

a. To date, only correlational research has been reported.

b. There is little relation between the two; extreme cases are highlighted in the media.

c. Although the correlational research finds an association, no laboratory research supports any conclusion beyond an association.

d. Both correlational and laboratory-based research support the existence of a relation between the two.

**4.** When Tolman ran rats through mazes, what phenomenon did he discover that has influenced conceptions of learning?

a. The rats relied far more on smell than on any other sense in navigating tbe mazes.

b. There was evidence that the rats had formed a cognitive map of the mazes that yielded evidence of learning when they were reinforced.

c. The rats were more likely to learn to navigate the mazes if they were reinforced on a VI schedule than on any other schedule of reinforcement.

d. There was evidence that even rats could demonstrate a particular form of observational learning because rats that merely watched other rats learned the mazes very quickly.

**5.** Which of these is another common name for the approach that Albert Bandura described in his famous research involving Bobo dolls?

a. modeling

b. latent learning

c. cognitive imagery

d. respondent conditioning

**6.** Evidence offered by Wolfgang Köhler supported the existence of

a. insight learning.

b. operant conditioning.

c. respondent conditioning

d. vicarious conditioning

**7.** A news report focuses on *desensitization* of violence, which is a new term for you. Consequently, you look it up and are intrigued by the potential for research. Which of the following experiments would be the best example of an effort to investigate the effects of desensitization?

a. an analysis of the amount of violence found in children's programs on Saturday morning

b. a correlational analysis to determine the relation between family size and propensity toward violence

c. an analysis of physiological changes that occur among frequent versus nonfrequent viewers of media violence

d. an experiment to determine how prosocial messages are received and processed by children as they watch TV

**8.** You are given the assignment of writing a paper on the work of Wolfgang Köhler, Edward Tolman, and Albert Bandura. Which of the following would be the best summary of the main points you will make in your paper?

a. Reinforcers are important in all forms of learning.

b. Learning is the result of either operant or classical conditioning.

c. Some cognitive processing of information occurs when we learn.

d. The primary ways in which we learn can be traced to our reflex actions.

**ANSWERS: 1. a.** Not observational learning **b.** Not observational learning **c.** Observational learning **d.** Observational learning **e.** Not observational learning **2.** a **3.** d **4.** b **5.** a **6.** a **7.** c **8.** c

## ANSWERS    To Psychological Detective Example of Classical Conditioning

**PAGE 191**

For the food example, the UCS is the food in your mouth, and the UCR is salivation that occurs when the food is in your mouth. The CS is the name of the food that is spoken to you, and the CR is the salivation that occurs when you hear the name of your favorite food. In the example of Scott's fear of closed spaces, the UCS is being locked in the abandoned refrigerator and the UCR is nearly suffocating. Anything that resembles a closed space is the CS, and his fear of closed spaces is the CR.

# Motivation and Emotion

## CHAPTER OUTLINE

So far we have described the methods psychologists use to answer questions they pose and how you can become educated consumers of information. We have seen how we receive and process information from the environment, and we have examined states of consciousness. Our knowledge of how humans and animals learn adds to our understanding of behavior. Now we consider two related topics, motivation and emotion, which together will help us further understand complex behaviors.

The term *motivation* is derived from the Latin word *movere*, meaning "to move." Motivation is concerned with the causes of behavior—that is, what "moves" organisms to behave. We begin the chapter with a discussion of theories of motivation and then focus on three specific motives. Next, we turn to an element of our behavior that has some significant evolutionary advantages—emotions. Think of times you have experienced positive or negative emotions. How do such experiences impart advantages? As we explore this topic, you will see that the brain plays a key role in regulating emotions. Because culture also affects behavior, we explore global similarities and differences in emotional expression. In the last part of this chapter we see how the cognitive evaluation (appraisal) of situations affects our emotional responses.

## WHAT IS MOTIVATION?

**After 2 hours of hiking, Dan and Dana stop for a drink to quench their thirst. Later in the day they stop to eat some of the food they brought along. While sitting and relaxing, they talk about what they will do the next day and decide to climb a mountain because "it is there." They also decide to add to their rock collection by picking up some specimens as they hike.** *Why were these behaviors performed? What caused them?*

These questions are the core of the study of motivation, which has three aspects: (1) the factor or motivational state that prompts behavior, (2) the goal(s) toward which the behavior is directed, and (3) the reasons for differences in the intensity of the behavior. Some examples are easier to explain than others. We understand why Dan and Dana drank water and why they ate. When it comes to climbing the mountain and collecting rocks, however, the explanations are not quite as straightforward.

Combining the three aspects, we define **motivation** as physiological and psychological factors that account for the arousal (energizing), direction, and persistence of behavior. Note that motivation is a hypothetical state. We cannot directly see or touch it; we must infer it from observable behaviors. Consider two rats that have learned to press a lever to receive food in a Skinner box. Once this behavior has been learned, what causes it to be performed again? Perhaps the sight of the cage or the lever elicits the lever-press response. Although these stimuli may influence the rats' behavior, there is another equally important factor—hunger. If the rats are hungry (a motivational state), they press the lever to obtain food (the goal).

Why does one rat make twice as many responses (and receive twice as many food pellets) as another rat? If the first rat has not been fed for 12 hours, whereas the second rat was fed 6 hours earlier, we conclude that differences in motivational state influenced

**motivation**
Physiological and psychological factors that account for the arousal, direction, and persistence of behavior

the behavior. In other words, the first rat is hungrier. These three aspects fit together this way: The hungry rat presses the lever (behavior) to obtain food (goal); the hungrier the rat (level of motivation), the more frequent the lever presses.

# THEORIES OF MOTIVATION

Our opening vignette tells us something else about motivation: It can be complex. Why do people climb mountains or collect rocks? To understand this complexity, researchers have proposed several theories. One group of theories focuses on biological factors, as evident in hunger; a second group focuses on cognitive processes. Abraham Maslow's theory combines biological and cognitive factors. The following sections examine these approaches to motivation.

## Biological Theories

Biological theories focus on biological or physiological processes that determine behavior. Among these processes are unlearned behaviors that are part of an organism's repertoire from birth. When such unlearned behaviors are more complex than simple reflexes, such as the eye blink, they are called **instincts**. These involuntary, unlearned, species-specific behaviors are triggered by specific environmental events called *releasing stimuli*. For example, bats locate objects like moths through the use of sonar waves, which are similar to radar. The sound of sonar waves serves as a releasing stimulus for moths, triggering erratic flights to safety in patches of grass.

**FIGURE 6-1** The male stickle-back on the right has assumed the head-down threat posture because of the intruding male on the left.

**Source:** Tinbergen (1951).

**instincts**

Unlearned species-specific behaviors that are more complex than reflexes and triggered by environmental events called *releasing stimuli*

**Ethology.**  *Ethology* is the scientific study of animal behavior under natural conditions. The ethologist Niko Tinbergen (1951) was interested in studying reproductive and aggressive behavior in the stickleback, a species of fish. During the spring, physiological changes cause male sticklebacks to develop a red spot on their belly. Tinbergen determined that the red spot is a releasing stimulus. Male sticklebacks establish territories and build tunnel-like nests. When another male swims into one of these territories, the presence of the intruding male releases a characteristic threat display by the territory's owner (see Figure 6-1).

Do instincts also direct human behavior? Robert Ardrey (1966) makes a case for a human instinct to establish and defend territories. He notes a "parallel between human marriage and animal pairing" and "between human desire for a place that is one's own and the animal instinct to stake out such a private domain" (p. 101). People sometimes discuss a "maternal instinct" and an "aggressive instinct." Although such behaviors may be instincts in some lower animals, there is no convincing proof of it in humans. Why? It is difficult to rule out the influence of learning in such situations. Although attempts to explain human behavior by using the concept of instincts failed, psychologists continued their interest in the influence of biological factors on behavior.

**Frank and Ernest**

**Source:** Copyright © Thaves. Reprinted with permission.

**Internal States, Drives, and Drive Reduction.** When John B. Watson founded behaviorism, his goal was to understand the relations between environmental stimuli and responses. Understanding those relations would allow us to make accurate predictions about which behavior would occur when a certain stimulus was present, or so he thought. Although behaviorists believed that an unchanging situation or stimulus would evoke the same response every time, this was not the case.

When environmental stimuli remain constant, behavior does not always follow suit. For example, Curt Richter (1922) found that the activity level of female rats peaked every fifth day, even though they were tested in the same apparatus. This increase in activity coincided with the *estrus*, or sexual receptivity, cycle. The estrus cycle created an internal motivational state that influenced the rat's behavior.

An internal motivational state that is created by a physiological need is a **drive.** Drives can activate more than one response. If food is not freely available, a hungry rat may try other responses that allowed it to secure food in the past. What would you do if you had no money to buy lunch? You might search your car for change, ask a friend for a loan, or check vending machines for change that people have forgotten. Motivated behavior is goal directed; the internal motivational state of hunger prompts or drives your behaviors toward the goal of obtaining food.

Clark Hull (1943, 1952) used the concept of drives to link physiological processes and behavior. Figure 6-2 illustrates how drives operate. A drive is created by a physiological need, such as lack of water. Once created, the drive can activate several responses, including learned ones such as lever pressing. The goal of these responses is to do or secure something that reduces the drive (leading to drive reduction), thereby returning the body to a more normal or balanced state of physiological functioning called *homeostasis.*

Let's return to our opening scenario. Because Dan and Dana were thirsty, they drank some water; later they were hungry, so they ate. In both cases they were returning their bodies to the more balanced state of physiological functioning that existed before they were in a thirsty or hungry state. The **drive-reduction theory** views motivated behavior as designed to reduce a physiological imbalance and return the organism to homeostasis.

Drive reduction signals the organism that a particular need has been reduced and that behaviors designed to reduce other current drives can be engaged. Some theorists view drive reduction as necessary for learning; behaviors that result in drive reduction are learned. Each time a behavior results in drive reduction, the strength of the habit (or tendency) to perform that behavior increases slightly. When a behavior

According to the drive-reduction theory, the strength of a particular drive determines our behavior. Following a storm, people are especially concerned with reaching shelter.

**drive**
Internal motivational state created by a physiological need

**drive-reduction theory**
Theory that views motivated behavior as directed toward the reduction of a physiological need

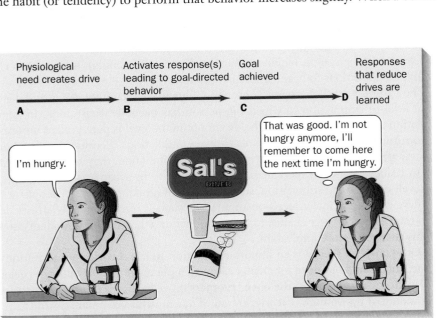

**FIGURE 6-2** Drive-reduction model. A drive is created by a physiological need (A). This drive activates responses (B). These responses are directed toward achieving a goal that reduces the drive by satisfying the need (C). Responses that reduce drives are learned (D).

These monkeys spent hours just opening and closing latches. Some researchers suggest that their curiosity drive is high.

has been followed by drive reduction many times, the habit strength, or tendency to perform under similar situations, is very high. When you are hungry at noon, what behavior are you most likely to perform?

**Optimum-Level Theories.** Why would monkeys press a lever for the opportunity to watch a toy electric train (Butler & Harlow, 1954) or work for hours on a complicated lock that provided no reward other than opening it (Harlow, Harlow, & Meyer, 1950)? Why do humans spend hours trying to solve crossword puzzles? Drive theory might explain these behaviors in terms of the reduction of a *stimulus drive*, such as curiosity or exploration. Ask yourself what you would do under the following conditions: (a) a helicopter hovers nearby, and (b) while in an art museum you see a sign that says "Do Not Touch." When a stimulus drive is sufficiently strong, it elicits behaviors such as looking up at the helicopter or touching the work of art. Successful completion of these behaviors reduces the drive; consequently, the frequency of these behaviors should increase in the future.

Although this analysis is reasonable, the definition and measurement of a stimulus drive such as curiosity are not as straightforward as the definition and measurement of hunger. We can restrict food intake to create hunger, but what do we restrict to activate the curiosity drive?

Is there another way to view the behaviors just described? Consider an experiment (Haber, 1958) in which human volunteers were first adapted (became accustomed) to water at 68°F. Later they rated water that was slightly above or slightly below 68°F as pleasant, whereas they rated much cooler and much warmer water as unpleasant or aversive.

### Psychological Detective

Stop for a moment and think about the results of this study. What information does it provide about motivated behavior? How would the drive-reduction theory explain the results? Write down some possible answers before reading further.

These results suggest that we do not always seek to reduce stimulation as the drive-reduction theory predicts; rather, experiencing change in stimulation is important. The 68°F water was boring; a change in stimulation was pleasant. If, however, the change in temperature was too great, it was perceived as unpleasant. Other instances in which stimulation may be sought include riding a roller coaster, singing in the shower, and changing radio stations to hear something different.

The optimum level of arousal or change differs from person to person and depends on the level of stimulation to which the person has become accustomed. In general, stimulation that is too far above or below an optimum level is perceived as unpleasant. This **optimum-level theory** allows us to make predictions. Because people in urban and rural areas have adapted to different levels of stimulation, they should react differently to reduced sensory experiences. (People who live in urban areas have adapted to high levels of noise and stimulation, such as incessant honking in traffic; people in rural areas have adapted to lower levels of stimulation, such as birds singing.) Sensory deprivation represents a greater change for urban individuals than for rural residents, so they rate this change as more unpleasant.

Optimum-level theory is an important addition to the theories of motivation that helps us understand our need for change. Some people move to the country to get away from the hectic pace of life in the big city; others move to the exciting big city to escape the boredom of the country. Clearly, not all of our motives are innate (instinct theory) or designed to reduce needs (drive-reduction model).

**optimum-level theory**
Theory that the body functions best at a specific level of arousal, which varies from one individual to another

# Cognitive Theories

Cognitive theories of motivation focus on how we process and understand information. When you are hungry, you do not always eat just to reduce a drive. You make decisions about what and where you will eat. Cognitive theories view individuals as thinking about, planning, and exercising control over their behavior. The most prominent cognitive theories are cognitive-consistency theories and Maslow's hierarchy of needs.

**Cognitive-Consistency Theories.**    According to cognitive-consistency theories, we are motivated to achieve a psychological state in which our beliefs and behaviors are consistent because inconsistency between beliefs and behaviors is unpleasant (Elliot & Devine, 1994). Students who think about studying but never get around to it need to achieve consistency between their thoughts and actions. They may achieve consistency by deciding they are too tired to study. Think of this motive as a need to achieve *psychological* homeostasis.

A psychological state known as **cognitive dissonance** (see Chapter 15) occurs when a person has two inconsistent or incompatible thoughts or cognitions (Aronson, Wilson, & Akert, 2002; Festinger, 1957). Because cognitive dissonance produces discomfort, it motivates us to reduce the discomfort in ways that are similar to how hunger and thirst motivate us to reduce discomfort (Aronson et al., 2002). In this case, we seek to reduce the discomfort by creating *cognitive consonance*—the state in which our cognitions are compatible with one another.

An example of a situation that could lead to cognitive dissonance is shown in Figure 6-3. Suppose you were instructed to select one of two gifts. Before picking a gift, you rate the desirability of the items. If you chose between a highly desirable gift and a less desirable gift, the decision is easy. The decision is more difficult when the choice is between two very desirable gifts.

Choosing one gift means rejecting the second. When the second gift is less desirable, the decision is easy. But choosing between equally desirable gifts creates conflict. Once such a difficult decision has been made, many people wonder whether they made the right decision. This *postdecisional dissonance* is reduced by raising one's evaluation of the chosen item and decreasing the evaluation of the rejected item. After the decision has been made, the two items are no longer rated as equally desirable, thus reducing cognitive dissonance.

Dissonance can occur in situations other than choosing between two desirable items: exposure to information that contradicts one's beliefs and challenges to one's opinions. Imagine being required to convince others that a boring task (such as adding columns of numbers) is exciting. Your appraisal of the boring task is likely to improve, and dissonance is reduced. If we are exposed to information that contradicts our beliefs,

**cognitive dissonance**
Aversive state produced when an individual holds two incompatible thoughts or cognitions

**FIGURE 6-3** In research on cognitive dissonance, participants were instructed to select which of two gifts they would like to receive. When one gift was low in desirability and the other was high in desirability, the choice was easy and cognitive dissonance was low or absent. On the other hand, when both gifts were high in desirability, the choice was more difficult. After participants made their choice, the chosen gift was rated more positively, whereas the rejected gift was rated more negatively. These differences in ratings reflect the operation of cognitive dissonance.

**hierarchy of needs**
Maslow's view that basic needs must be satisfied before higher-level needs can be satisfied

**self-actualization**
Need to develop one's full potential; the highest level of Maslow's hierarchy

**STUDY TIP**

From memory, list the five needs in Maslow's hierarchy of needs, leaving space between each. Then, in the space below each need, write down as many examples of the need as you can.

Based on Maslow's hierarchy of needs, we might predict that prisoners in Nazi concentration camps would be motivated by their basic survival needs. In contrast to this prediction, some prisoners in Nazi concentration camps, such as one at Mittlebau Dora in Nordhausen, Germany (1945), put the survival of others before their own and offered food, clothing, and, at times, even their own lives.

dissonance is aroused, and we are likely to seek additional information that supports our belief. For example, smokers have been bombarded by reports of the dangers of smoking. They may search for reports that support their smoking behavior and may focus on people who have smoked for decades with no apparent ill effects. In fact, an observational study of men who regularly spent time at a cigar shop engaged in conversation on a variety of topics supports this view of cognitive dissonance. None of their discussions were as passionate as those concerning the health risks of cigar smoking. They crafted arguments to refute the medical research findings and to insulate themselves from the impact of antismoking messages, thus reducing their cognitive dissonance when they lit up (Desantis, 2003). Dissonance is also created when our opinions are challenged. Consider your reaction when your political beliefs are challenged. The agreement of others who hold opinions similar to yours reduces the dissonance. Although psychologists have focused on cognitive dissonance from an individual perspective, the phenomenon occurs in group settings also. When individuals find that their opinions are at odds with those of the group, thus causing cognitive dissonance, they are likely to try to reach a consensus by persuading others, changing their own positions to match those of the group, or joining a group with attitudes that are consistent with their own (Matz & Wood, 2005).

**Incentive Theories.**   We cannot explain all motives as instincts, drive reduction, or the resolution of cognitive dissonance. Have you ever daydreamed of owning a new red convertible? You save money, and you are driving it. What motives are involved? How would a drive-reduction theory of motivation explain your desire for the convertible? It is difficult to imagine any physiological drive that has been reduced by your car-buying behavior. Nor is it likely that the car is a releasing stimulus for instinctive behavior. Because drive-reduction and instinct theories do not explain behaviors like car buying, some theorists focus on incentives or goals in motivating our behaviors.

Drive-reduction theories say that our biological drives push us toward goals. By contrast, incentive theories see motivated behavior as being pulled by the incentive or goal; the larger or more powerful the incentive, the stronger the pull. It is more compelling to argue that we are pulled by the lure of our dream car than to suggest that we have a car-buying drive.

**Maslow's Hierarchy of Needs.**   Abraham Maslow's (1970) **hierarchy of needs** combines biological and psychological aspects of motivation (see Chapter 11). According to Maslow, five categories of motivated behavior can be ordered in a hierarchical fashion along two dimensions: (a) the *type* of motivation (from innate physiological motives to more psychological learned motives) and (b) the *strength* of the motivation (from strongest to weakest). This arrangement of motives is shown in Figure 6-4. The strongest and most physiologically based motives involve satisfying basic or survival needs such as hunger and thirst.

According to Maslow, we attempt to satisfy stronger motives before trying to satisfy motives that are higher in the hierarchy. Thus *physiological* needs (such as hunger) must be met before safety needs (security) can be satisfied. Safety needs are satisfied by a stable job, insurance, and financial reserves for emergencies. For the few people who successfully satisfy their physiological, safety, belongingness, and esteem needs, yet another need, *self-actualization*, emerges. **Self-actualization** comes from developing one's unique potential to its fullest extent. Each of us strives to become the very best (carpenter, truck driver, and so on) that our potential allows us to become. Because our struggle to satisfy needs that are lower in the hierarchy is a continuing one, only a small number of people achieve self-actualization.

Maslow's theory is often characterized as a *growth theory of motivation* because people strive to satisfy successively higher needs. As we satisfy needs at progressively higher levels of the hierarchy, we grow as individuals; this growth influences how we behave when we are later forced to confront lower-level needs again. Although we might expect

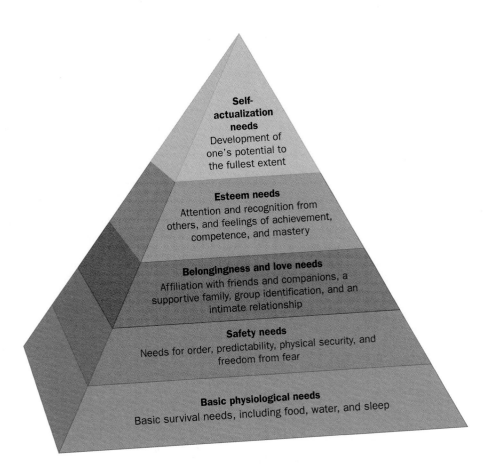

**Self-actualization needs**
Development of one's potential to the fullest extent

**Esteem needs**
Attention and recognition from others, and feelings of achievement, competence, and mastery

**Belongingness and love needs**
Affiliation with friends and companions, a supportive family, group identification, and an intimate relationship

**Safety needs**
Needs for order, predictability, physical security, and freedom from fear

**Basic physiological needs**
Basic survival needs, including food, water, and sleep

prisoners of war to be concerned only with their survival, many prisoners in Nazi concentration camps gave their food, clothing, and even their lives for others.

Critics note that not everyone proceeds through the hierarchy as Maslow outlined. What's more, in some societies people have difficulty meeting basic needs, yet they may be able to satisfy higher needs, as when a couple struggles to establish a family and to make ends meet while growing closer to each other as a result of their struggle.

**Motives and Conflict.** Both drive-reduction theory and Maslow's hierarchy of needs may make you think that people deal with only one motive at a time. A moment of reflection will convince you that this is not the way the real world operates. We are frequently confronted by several motives. There are four situations involving multiple motives: *approach-approach, avoidance-avoidance, approach-avoidance, and multiple approach-avoidance*.

Some conflicts, especially approach-approach, are relatively easy to resolve. Other conflicts, like approach-avoidance, can be difficult to resolve. Among the most difficult conflicts are those involving multiple approach-avoidance, where several goals have both good and bad features. Suppose you need a new computer and have decided to shop around. As you weigh the pros and cons of various brands, you are overwhelmed by indecision. Which one will you buy? Each set has good and bad features. You are caught in a multiple approach-avoidance situation.

Multiple approach-avoidance conflicts are similar to many daily experiences in which we are attracted to and repulsed by a variety of goals. By continuing to evaluate the features of the various brands, costs, and dealer reputation, you can resolve the computer conflict. When such conflicts occur over interpersonal relationships that have several positive and negative factors, such as marriage or divorce, they can have serious long-lasting effects.

A climb up a steep mountain is an example of approach (conquering the mountain) and avoidance (fear of falling) conflict.

# REVIEW SUMMARY

1. **Motivation** refers to physiological or psychological factors that account for the arousal, direction, and persistence of behavior. The aspects of motivation are (a) a motivational state that prompts the behavior, (b) the goal toward which the behavior is directed, and (c) reasons for variability in the intensity of the behavior.

2. Biological theories of motivation focus on the importance of biological processes in determining motivated behavior. **Instincts** are unlearned, species-specific behaviors that are more complex than reflexes and triggered by environmental events called *releasing stimuli*.

3. Internal motivational states or **drives** are created by physiological needs, such as the need for food. Drives produce motivated behavior. Because drives are aversive, the goal of motivated behavior is drive reduction.

4. Unlike **drive-reduction theories, optimum-level theories** propose that there is a level of arousal at which organisms function best. To reach this level, the organism may seek added stimulation or arousal.

5. Cognitive theories of motivation focus on the active processing of information. Cognitive-consistency theories stress the need to achieve a psychological state in which one's thoughts are consistent. **Cognitive dissonance** occurs when incompatible thoughts create an aversive state that the organism is motivated to reduce. Incentive theories of motivation stress the goals toward which the organism is pulled.

6. According to Maslow's theory, motivational needs are arranged **hierarchically** from basic physiological needs to **self-actualization.**

7. The existence of multiple motives often results in conflicts. The most common conflicts are approach-approach, avoidance-avoidance, approach-avoidance, and multiple approach-avoidance.

## ✓ CHECK YOUR PROGRESS

1. Describe the three general aspects of motivation.

2. Indicate which theory of motivation (instinct, drive reduction, cognitive dissonance, incentive) is exemplified by each of the following behaviors:

   a. Birds build nests in the spring.
   b. You stay up late to finish reading an exciting novel.
   c. Although you don't like chicken, you eat your roommate's chicken leftovers because there is nothing else in the house and you haven't eaten anything the entire day.

3. You have only $100 remaining from your paycheck. This amount is just enough to do only two of the following:

   a. Pay your electric bill.
   b. Go to a new play that you want to see.
   c. Buy next week's groceries.

   According to Maslow, which two will you choose? Why?

4. Which of the following is an example of a need on Maslow's hierarchy?

   a. creativity
   b. daydreaming
   c. self-esteem
   d. responsibility

5. On a field trip for a biology class, the instructor points out the behavior of moths that suddenly take flight as if possessed by an "inner force." Later, the instructor tells the students that they observed what was probably instinctive flight that occurred following a

   a. releasing stimulus.
   b. drive reducer.
   c. stimulus drive.
   d. dissonant event.

6. Alan needs to buy a car. He prefers sports cars but they are expensive, so he settles on a family car. How might Alan resolve the cognitive dissonance that occurred when he made his purchase?

   a. He will read the owner's manual and follow the instructions.
   b. He will double payments on the car loan to pay it off in a shorter period of time.
   c. He will realize that the car he purchased has certain advantages over the sports car.
   d. He will spend a great deal of time daydreaming about the car that he preferred to purchase.

7. What do we call unlearned behaviors that are more complex than an eye blink and are part of an organism's repertoire from birth?

   a. drives
   b. instincts
   c. releasing behaviors
   d. universal behaviors

8. When a person has two inconsistent or incompatible thoughts or motives, this situation creates cognitive

   a. need.
   b. consonance.
   c. dissonance.
   d. consistency.

9. Andrew has not eaten since breakfast, and it is almost 8 P.M. On his way home from work, he stops at his favorite

restaurant for a juicy steak with all the trimmings. Although he says he is "stuffed," he orders a slice of apple pie, which he devours. Which two theories of motivation would be most helpful in explaining Andrew's behavior?

a. instinct and drive reduction
b. drive reduction and incentive
c. optimum level of arousal and instinct
d. self-actualization and cognitive consistency

10. Drives serve to activate responses that are aimed at reducing the drive, thereby returning the body to a more normal state called

a. stability.
b. equilibrium.
c. homeostasis.
d. physiological balance.

# SPECIFIC MOTIVES

As part of a project for a class on advertising, Scott and Jane are collecting information on the motives that advertisers use to attract people to purchase products. They conclude that many advertisers gear their advertisements toward arousing sexual motives, even in cases when the product has little to do with sexual behavior. *Why do advertisers use sexual motives to sell their products?*

Up to this point we have concentrated on a theoretical overview of motivated behavior. These theories try to provide insight into all motivated behavior without focusing on any given motive. Psychologists are interested in specific motives, as well as the big picture of theoretical overviews. Here we will focus on three specific motives: hunger, sex, and achievement.

## Hunger

Drive theories of motivation view hunger as a physiological need that pushes us to behave in particular ways: We eat because we must do so to survive. Incentive theories stress the attractive properties of the food we plan to consume and where we plan to eat. According to drive theories, we eat to live; according to incentive theories, we live to eat. Regardless of which motivational theory you espouse, questions about hunger need to be answered. What are the physical signals for hunger? Where are these signals processed and translated into action?

An early explanation for hunger proposed that blood glucose (blood sugar) is an important hunger signal. When our supply of glucose is high and the cells of the body are able to use it, hunger is low. As the blood sugar supply decreases, hunger increases.

The amount of stored body fat also serves as a hunger signal. When a person's weight falls, fat is withdrawn from the fat cells and a hunger signal is sent to the brain. When fat cells are full, no signal is sent. The hypothalamus is the brain structure that receives hunger signals. Surgically removing (lesioning) two areas of the hypothalamus in rats yielded different results. Lesions in the lateral (side) hypothalamus reduced food intake; lesions in the ventromedial (front center) hypothalamus increased food intake. Lateral hypothalamic lesions may result in starvation and death, yet removing the ventromedial hypothalamus does not create an animal that overeats until it dies. These animals become quite obese, but their weight eventually stabilizes at a new, higher level. These areas of the hypothalamus are important in determining eating behavior, but they are part of a very complex system. For example, a bundle of nerve fibers that passes close to the lateral hypothalamus is also important in regulating hunger, and insulin regulates how much glucose is burned. Cholecystokinin, a

**STUDY TIP**

In magazines and/or newspapers, find two examples for each of how the hunger motive, the sex motive, and the achievement motive are used by advertisers to attract the reader's attention.

Supersizing. For years, the average serving size has increased for a wide variety of products. As a result, a serving now contains far more calories. In the case of Coca-Cola, a single serve bottle is approximately three times larger today than it was in 1894 (6.5 oz. compared to 20 oz.), and it has more than 3 times as many calories (79 calories compared to 250 calories).

**Source:** Spake (2002).

Although heredity plays a major role in determining how much we weigh, obese people experience discrimination and a lack of acceptance. Increasingly, they are organizing to encourage greater acceptance and understanding.

hormone active in the small intestine, appears to be another stop-eating signal (Klein, 2000). More recently, researchers have found that the hormone leptin produced by fat cells in the stomach suppresses appetite and stimulates energy expenditure, and thus is involved in regulating body fat (Holtkamp et al., 2003). What has become clear is that regulation of hunger and body fat is more complex than was originally believed (Nash, 2002).

**Nutrition and Eating.** Several decades ago, the major dietary problem Americans faced was obtaining sufficient amounts of vitamins and nutrients. Today the major problems are excesses and imbalances in the food we consume. Dietary factors contribute substantially to the burden of preventable illnesses and premature deaths in the United States. According to the Surgeon General of the United States (U.S. Department of Health and Human Services, 2001), 300,000 deaths per year are attributable to overweight and obesity and the risk of death rises with increasing weight. Obesity is a significant risk factor for heart disease, high blood pressure (twice as common in adults who are obese), and diabetes (over 80% of people with diabetes are overweight or obese). Obesity and overweight are associated with several types of cancer (colon, gallbladder, prostate, and kidney) (U.S. Department of Health and Human Services, 2001; World Health Organization, 2005). A prospective study of more than 900,000 people first studied in 1982 and followed up for 16 years revealed that of all the deaths from cancer, 14% of those among men and 20% of those among women could be attributed to overweight and obesity (Calle, Rodriquez, Walker-Thurmond, & Thun, 2003). In fact, overweight and obesity have been implicated in 4 of the top 10 causes of death in the United States (National Center for Health Statistics, 2004). The estimated cost associated with overweight and obesity in the United States in 2000 was $117 billion in medical expenses and lost productivity (U.S. Department of Health and Human Services, 2001). Overweight and obesity are also problems across the globe: There are more than 1 billion overweight people worldwide, and at least 300 million of them are obese. An estimated 22 million children under age 5 are estimated to be overweight worldwide (World Health Organization, 2005).

Imagine men and women hundreds or even thousands of years ago. They struggled to survive, never knowing where, or if, the next meal was coming. Would the hunt be successful? Would they be able to find a tree filled with edible berries over the next hill? Not only was food scarce, but getting it required a great deal of physical energy. Consequently, evolution favored those who ate as many calories as they could to protect against famine and thus have the energy to survive and pass on their genes to the next generation. But times have changed. University of Colorado nutrition researcher James Hill says, "Our physiology tells us to eat whenever food is available. And now, food is always available" (quoted in Spake, 2002, p. 41). Today, food is so abundant in the United States that we have 3,800 calories available per person per day, yet we need only half of this amount. Between 1984 and 2000 we increased our daily intake of calories by 500 per day. What's more, we tend to eat out more often, and much of what we consume has more fat, less fiber, more cholesterol, and more calories than homemade meals (Spake, 2002). And lest we forget, we live in the era of supersizing our meals; for pennies more, we can add hundreds of calories. In fact, simply increasing the size of portions (as occurs in supersizing) increases the amount of food we consume (Rolls, Roe, Kral, Meengs, & Wall, 2004). While we are consuming more calories, we are engaging in less activity to burn those calories. Modern conveniences have reduced our energy expenditure dramatically: According to *Healthy People 2010*, 40% of adults aged 18 and older engaged in *no* leisure-time physical activity (U.S. Department of Health and Human Services, 2000). When was the last time you got up from a chair to change a television channel? Excess calories that are not burned can turn into added pounds quickly.

**How Does My Weight Compare?**    Am I overweight? Am I obese? And just what is the difference? How much should I weigh?

### Psychological Detective

Like most people, you probably wonder how your weight compares with that of other people. How can you collect information to make those comparisons, and how can you be sure that such comparisons are meaningful? Write down your answer before reading further.

A common way to find our desirable weight was to look it up in tables first published by the Metropolitan Life Insurance Company in 1959. Insurance companies had found that weight levels were related to death rates. People were classified as *overweight* if their weight exceeded the range in the table by 10% to 20%. If it exceeded the range by more than 20%, they were classified as **obese.** The insurance company tables of desirable weights (for example, 126 pounds for a woman who stands 5 feet 4 inches and 154 for a man of 5 feet 10 inches) are considered lean; about 80% of Americans would exceed those standards today (Wickelgren, 1998).

Although insurance company tables are the common method of assessing our weight, they are not ideal for several reasons. These tables typically are based on a sample of people who can afford insurance—usually middle- or upper-class and young or middle-aged. What's more, these tables do not accurately represent the entire population. Furthermore, as people grow older, they tend to weigh more as a result of metabolic and other factors; this increase in weight may be greater than the tables suggest because people over 55 are not well represented in the samples used to establish the tables.

**The Body Mass Index (BMI).**    For decades we checked insurance charts to determine where we stand in the battle of the bulge, but now a new tape measure is in use. In 1998, the National Heart, Lung, and Blood Institute (NHLBI) announced new guidelines (intended for the identification and treatment of those who are overweight or obese) based on **body mass index (BMI)** (Shapiro, 1998)—a ratio of weight to height squared. This single number represents your height and weight without regard to gender; it correlates with body fat. Elevated BMI is associated with increased risks for hypertension, cardiovascular disease, Type II (adult-onset) diabetes, and sleep apnea. The degree of health risk is evident in a longitudinal study of almost 6,000 men and women: Each increase of 1 in BMI raised the risk of heart failure 5% in men and 7% in women (Kenchaiah et al., 2002). What's more, BMI is a better predictor of disease risk than body weight alone. On the other hand, BMI is not a suitable measure for everyone: Competitive athletes and body builders often have a high BMI as a result of their large amount of muscle tissue, which weighs more than fat tissue. Consequently, their BMI overestimates their disease risk. In addition, the following individuals should not use the BMI: women who are pregnant or lactating, children, and frail and sedentary individuals. You can find your BMI by looking at the cross section of your height and weight in Table 6-1. Although the exact cutoffs that trigger recommendations to lose weight are still debated (Strawbridge, Wallhagen, & Sheman, 2000), the NHLBI guidelines are: overweight, 25–29.9; obese, 30 or greater. Surveys of the general population yield relatively high rates of overweight and obesity among adults as well as children. What's more, these problems have become more pronounced in just a few decades (see Figures 6-5 and 6-6 on p. 243).

**The Biology of Obesity.**    To understand efforts to control weight, we need to know about calories. A *calorie* (shorthand for *kilocalorie*) is a measure of energy: One calorie is the amount of heat needed to raise the temperature of 1 kilogram of water 1°C. A pound

**obesity**
Body weight of 20% or more in excess of desirable body weight

**body mass index (BMI)**
A numerical index calculated from a person's height and weight that is used to indicate health status and disease risk

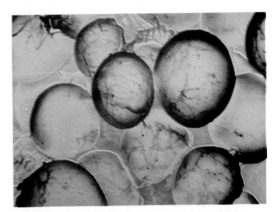

Fat cells expand easily, and they are easy to maintain once they have expanded. It is difficult to lose weight because the body interprets efforts to lose pounds as the equivalent of famine. To conserve energy, the body lowers its resting metabolic rate, thus burning fewer calories.

## TABLE 6-1

**Body Mass Index (BMI). Locate Your Height in the Column on the Left, Then Find Your Weight to the Right. Your BMI Can be Found in Boldface Above Your Weight.**

| BMI | 19 | 20 | 21 | 22 | 23 | 24 | 25 | 26 | 27 | 28 | 29 | 30 | 31 | 32 | 33 | 34 | 35 | 36 | 37 | 38 | 39 | 40 | 41 | 42 | 43 | 44 | 45 | 46 | 47 | 48 | 49 | 50 |
|---|---|---|---|---|---|---|---|---|---|---|---|---|---|---|---|---|---|---|---|---|---|---|---|---|---|---|---|---|---|---|---|---|
| | Normal | | | | | | Overweight | | | | | Obese | | | | | | | | | | Extreme Obesity | | | | | | | | | | |
| **Height (inches)** | | | | | | | | | | | | Body Weight (pounds) | | | | | | | | | | | | | | | | | | | | |
| 58 | 91 | 96 | 100 | 105 | 110 | 115 | 119 | 124 | 129 | 134 | 138 | 143 | 148 | 153 | 158 | 162 | 167 | 172 | 177 | 181 | 186 | 191 | 196 | 201 | 205 | 210 | 215 | 220 | 224 | 229 | 234 | 239 |
| 60 | 97 | 102 | 107 | 112 | 118 | 123 | 128 | 133 | 138 | 143 | 148 | 153 | 158 | 163 | 168 | 174 | 179 | 184 | 189 | 194 | 199 | 204 | 209 | 215 | 220 | 225 | 230 | 235 | 240 | 245 | 250 | 255 |
| 62 | 104 | 109 | 115 | 120 | 126 | 131 | 136 | 142 | 147 | 153 | 158 | 164 | 169 | 175 | 180 | 186 | 191 | 196 | 202 | 207 | 213 | 218 | 224 | 229 | 235 | 240 | 246 | 251 | 256 | 262 | 267 | 273 |
| 64 | 110 | 116 | 122 | 128 | 134 | 140 | 145 | 151 | 157 | 163 | 169 | 174 | 180 | 186 | 192 | 197 | 204 | 209 | 215 | 221 | 227 | 232 | 238 | 244 | 250 | 256 | 262 | 267 | 273 | 279 | 285 | 291 |
| 66 | 118 | 124 | 130 | 136 | 142 | 148 | 155 | 161 | 167 | 173 | 179 | 186 | 192 | 198 | 204 | 210 | 216 | 223 | 229 | 235 | 241 | 247 | 253 | 260 | 266 | 272 | 278 | 284 | 291 | 297 | 303 | 309 |
| 68 | 125 | 131 | 138 | 144 | 151 | 158 | 164 | 171 | 177 | 184 | 190 | 197 | 203 | 210 | 216 | 223 | 230 | 236 | 243 | 249 | 256 | 262 | 269 | 276 | 282 | 289 | 295 | 302 | 308 | 315 | 322 | 328 |
| 70 | 132 | 139 | 146 | 153 | 160 | 167 | 174 | 181 | 188 | 195 | 202 | 209 | 216 | 222 | 229 | 236 | 243 | 250 | 257 | 264 | 271 | 278 | 285 | 292 | 299 | 306 | 313 | 320 | 327 | 334 | 341 | 348 |
| 72 | 140 | 147 | 154 | 162 | 169 | 177 | 184 | 191 | 199 | 206 | 213 | 221 | 228 | 235 | 242 | 250 | 258 | 265 | 272 | 279 | 287 | 294 | 302 | 309 | 316 | 324 | 331 | 338 | 346 | 353 | 361 | 368 |
| 74 | 148 | 155 | 163 | 171 | 179 | 186 | 194 | 202 | 210 | 218 | 225 | 233 | 241 | 249 | 256 | 264 | 272 | 280 | 287 | 295 | 303 | 311 | 319 | 326 | 334 | 342 | 350 | 358 | 365 | 373 | 381 | 389 |
| 76 | 156 | 164 | 172 | 180 | 189 | 197 | 205 | 213 | 221 | 230 | 238 | 246 | 254 | 263 | 271 | 279 | 287 | 295 | 304 | 312 | 320 | 328 | 336 | 344 | 353 | 361 | 369 | 377 | 385 | 394 | 402 | 410 |

**Source:** *Adapted from Clinical Guidelines in the Identification, Evaluation, and Treatment of Overweight and Obesity in Adults: The Evidence Report.*

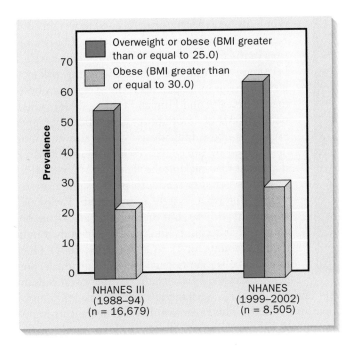

**FIGURE 6-5** Prevalence of overweight and obesity among adults in the United States. Results from the 1988–1994 and 1999–2002 National Health and Nutrition Examination Surveys indicate that a majority of adults are overweight (BMI of 25 to 29.9) or obese (BMI of 30 and above).

**Source:** Centers for Disease Control, National Center for Health Statistics (2004a).

of fat contains 3,500 calories, so to lose a pound a week, we would have to reduce calorie consumption by 500 calories a day (Goodenough, McGuire, & Wallace, 2005)!

Have you ever heard people say that they were "born to be fat" or that they inherited their weight problem from their parents? There is considerable evidence to support such statements. Only about 5% of cases of obesity result from physical causes such as endocrine dysfunctions or damage to the hypothalamus (Bray, 2004; Grilo & Pogue-Geile, 1991). What about the other cases? The correlations between the weights of adult twins who had been raised apart were 0.70 for men and 0.66 for women. These correlations were only slightly lower than those for twins who had been reared together (Stunkard Harris, Pedersen, & McClearn, 1990). The evidence suggests that the influence of genetics on weight is substantial no matter whether we use pounds, waist circumference,

**Source:** Copyright © 2000 Ziggy and friends, Inc. Reprinted courtesy of Universal Press Syndicate.

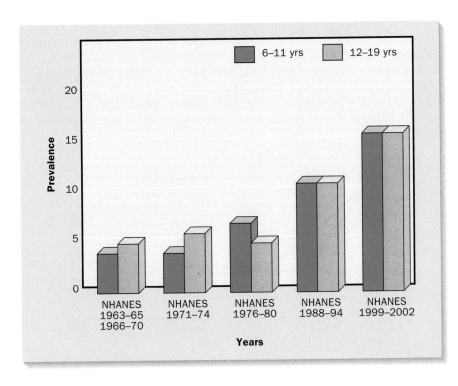

**FIGURE 6-6** Prevalence of overweight among children and adolescents in the United States. Results from the 1999–2002 National Health and Nutrition Examination Survey indicate that 16% of children and adolescents ages 6–19 are overweight. The trend since 1963 has been upward. Among children ages 6–11, the percentage that are overweight is now four times higher.

**Source:** Centers for Disease Control, National Center for Health Statistics (2004b).

To illustrate the delicate balance of calorie intake, energy expenditure, and weight, consider the following: An adult who eats approximately 10 additional calories per day (assuming no other changes in his or her energy expenditure) would add a pound of weight in a year. In an era of supersizing, very few of us are adding a mere 10 calories per day, so the weight gain is likely to be far more significant.

skin folds, or other measures related to weight (Bulik, Sullivan, & Kendler, 2003; Schousboe et al., 2004). The risk of obesity clearly runs in the family. Overweight adolescents have a 70% chance of becoming overweight or obese adults; this risk factor increases to 80% if one or more parents is overweight or obese (U.S. Department of Health and Human Services, 2001). The risk of extreme obesity (BMI of 45 or above) is significantly higher in families of extremely obese individuals. "Body size and weight are highly determined by our genes. Picking the right parents is far more important than picking the right diet" (Rodin, 1992, p. 175).

Thus heredity seems to play a significant role in what we weigh. But what exactly is inherited? Everyone has a certain amount of body fat, but the amount varies from one individual to another. Fat accounts for 20 to 25% of body weight in women; in men it accounts for 15 to 18% (Hales, 2001). Obese people have more fat cells than normal-weight individuals, possibly owing to genetic factors. As adults, the number of fat cells in our body does not change except under unusual circumstances, such as liposuction, in which fat is surgically scooped out of the body. This operation has become surprisingly common: It is the most common cosmetic procedure performed on adults and the sixth most common among adolescents (Sarver, 2001). Fat cells can, however, swell (become larger). When cells swell to hold additional fat, they require little energy to maintain themselves.

Heredity may also influence what we weight by affecting our *basal metabolic rate* (*BMR*), the minimum energy needed to keep an awake, resting body alive. Generally, BMR represents 60 to 75% of the body's energy needs. Males usually have a higher BMR than females because they tend to have more muscle and less fat than females (see Figure 6-7). Muscle uses more energy than does fat. As we get older, we lose muscle mass and our BMR declines. This age-related change can easily add extra pounds each year after age 35 (Goodenough et al., 2005).

**Social and Cultural Factors in Weight.**    Accumulating research suggests that biological factors alone do not fully explain obesity; thus, we should also consider social and cultural factors (Sobal & Stunkard, 1989). According to *Healthy People 2010* (U.S. Department of Health and Human Services, 2000), 23% of U.S. adults ages 20 years and older were obese (defined as a BMI of 30 or more) and 11% of children and adolescents (ages 6 to 19) were overweight or obese; however, the problem does not occur evenly across the population. Among women, obesity is related to social class. For example, 35% of women living in poverty are obese. Rates of obesity are higher among people in the lower socioeconomic classes than among those in the middle and upper socioeconomic classes (Bray, 2004). The relation between obesity and social class is inconsistent for men and for children (Sobal & Stunkard, 1989). Rates of obesity vary greatly from

**FIGURE 6-7**  Basal (resting) metabolic rates. The rate at which the body burns energy for basic survival needs (for example, beating of the heart and breathing) is different for men and women and changes as we grow older. As a result, it becomes more difficult to lose weight as we grow older.

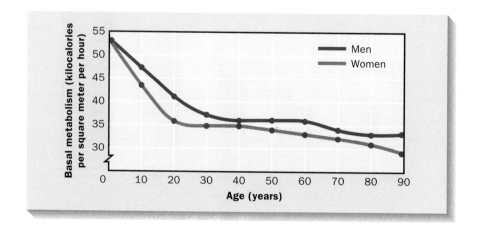

country to country, which suggests that culture plays a role. For example, in China, Japan, and certain African countries the rates of obesity are below 5%, whereas in urban Samoa the rate of obesity is 75% (World Health Organization, 2005).

**Dieting.** Our culture has an insatiable desire for books, devices, drugs, and programs to make us fitter, healthier, and slimmer. What's more, the diets often offer conflicting guidance on what we should and should not consume (Christensen, 2003). There is a high rate of dieting, even among children and adolescents (Thompson & Smolak, 2001), which seems to reflect dissatisfaction with one's body. When considering diets, it is important to note that the body does not treat all calories alike (Rodin, 1992). One gram of carbohydrates or protein contains 4 calories, whereas 1 gram of fat contains 9 calories (Bernard & Krupat, 1994). What's more, high-fat diets require fewer calories for digestion than high-carbohydrate diets. Once the fat is deposited in the body, few calories are needed to maintain it, so it is difficult to remove.

Keep in mind that weight loss early in any diet is due primarily to loss of water and a drastic reduction in calories. This drastic calorie reduction is unlikely to be sustained, and weight is likely to return. As you change your behaviors (increase exercise, reduce fat intake, etc.), sustained weight loss may occur, but the body adjusts its metabolism to accommodate the reduction in calories. Why? This adjustment may well reflect our evolutionary heritage as an attempt to conserve energy by reducing the rate at which calories are consumed by the body. Such a change would help people prepare for what in the past would be an inevitable famine. Subsequent weight loss may become more difficult. Losing a pound of fat is a very slow process. A 100-pound person would have to jump rope for 7 hours; a 150-person would have spend 15 hours walking at 3 miles per hours to lose 1 pound (American Heart Association, 2005). We do not burn as many calories per minute of physical activity as perhaps some of us believe (see Table 6-2). Losing weight, therefore, involves patience and the commitment to significant lifestyle changes. If you are having trouble shedding pounds, do not be discouraged. Be realistic, however, about the amount of weight you can lose and your chances of keeping it off. Table 6-3 lists some helpful suggestions.

| TABLE 6-2 | | | |
|---|---|---|---|
| **Approximate Number of Calories Spent per Hour by a 100-, 150-, and 200-Pound Person While Engaged in a Particular Physical Activity** | | | |
| **Activity** | **100 lb** | **150 lb** | **200 lb** |
| Bicycling, 6 mph | 160 | 240 | 312 |
| Bicycling, 12 mph | 270 | 410 | 534 |
| Jogging, 7 mph | 610 | 920 | 1,230 |
| Jumping rope | 500 | 750 | 1,000 |
| Running 5.5 mph | 440 | 660 | 962 |
| Running 10 mph | 850 | 1,280 | 1,664 |
| Swimming, 25 yds/min | 185 | 275 | 358 |
| Swimming, 50 yds/min | 325 | 500 | 650 |
| Tennis singles | 265 | 400 | 535 |
| Walking, 2 mph | 160 | 240 | 312 |
| Walking, 3 mph | 210 | 320 | 416 |
| Walking, 4.5 mph | 295 | 440 | 572 |

**Source:** American Heart Association (2005).

**TABLE 6-3**

## Behaviors That Contribute to Weight Reduction

- Engage in physical activity, which enhances long-term weight loss because it burns calories.

- Recognize that weight control demands permanent lifestyle change and not a temporary diet.

- Eat more slowly. Discover exactly how food tastes and thus allow the body's signals (for example, a feeling of fullness) more time to work.

- Reduce the percentage of calories derived from fat. Even if you replace those calories with carbohydrates, your body uses more calories to break down carbohydrates than it does to break down fat.

- Reduce cues that tempt you to eat. Store food out of sight; do not shop on an empty stomach. Eat more low-calorie foods like carrots and popcorn (limit the butter) that provide bulk and thus make you feel full.

- Set realistic goals. Few of us are going to look like the models in magazine advertisements. Positive physical and psychological benefits of weight loss often occur at levels above a proposed ideal weight.

- Enhance the taste of reduced-fat meals by adding spices and thus boost the effectiveness of diets without boosting the calories. Why? Most diets fail because they take the pleasure out of eating. The fat in most foods makes them more flavorful, creamy, and juicy.

- Enlist the support of family members and friends. Tell them that you want to lose weight and that it is important to you. Ask them to refrain from offering you an extra piece of pie or a second serving of pork chops. Friends and relatives can also provide emotional support when needed.

- Eat a piece of fruit to decrease your appetite. Contrary to folklore, not all sugars are bad for us. The fructose found in fruits and honey tends to make us feel full. We tend to consume more calories after a glucose snack (glucose is a common form of sugar found in many foods) than after a fructose snack with equal calories.

**anorexia nervosa**

A potentially life-threatening eating disorder occurring primarily in adolescent and young adult females; an intense fear of becoming fat leads to self-starvation and weight loss accompanied by a strong belief that one is fat despite objective evidence to the contrary

**bulimia nervosa**

Eating disorder in which a victim alternatively consumes large amounts of food (gorging) and then empties the stomach (purging), usually by induced vomiting

Caraline, 28 years old, told a reporter, "I'm not telling you how much I weigh because I'm ashamed I don't weight less." She later died of complications due to anorexia nervosa.

**Source:** Oltmanns and Emery (2001).

**Eating Disorders.** Two eating disorders are so serious that they are potentially life-threatening: **anorexia nervosa** (anorexia) and **bulimia nervosa** (bulimia). A high rate of dissatisfaction with one's body, especially in Western countries, has led many people, especially women, to begin dieting in order to control their weight, often in response to social and cultural pressure to be thin (Thompson & Smolak, 2001; Yanovski & Stunkard, 2004). Some of them develop the two disorders we will focus on here.

The literal meaning of *anorexia nervosa*—"nervous loss of appetite"—is misleading; people with this disorder are hungry, yet they deny their hunger due to an intense fear of becoming fat or gaining weight (Keel, 2005). "For them, food is an enemy—a threat to their sense of self, identity, and autonomy" (Hales, 2001, p. 258). Their self-starvation is not caused by any known physical disease. By definition they maintain a body weight that is less than 85% of their expected weight, often by exercising compulsively; the average victim of anorexia nervosa loses a substantial amount of weight, typically 25 to 30% of normal body weight (Hsu, 1990). This weight loss is associated with numerous medical complications. If the victim is young enough, her sexual development may be arrested ("Anorexia Nervosa—Part I," 2003); if she is older, she may experience *amenorrhea* (absence of at least three consecutive menstrual cycles) (Keel, 2005). In men, testosterone levels drop (Hales, 2001). People with anorexia may also suffer abdominal pain, anemia, cold intolerance, constipation, hypotension (low blood pressure), and lethargy. A lack of nutrients causes the body to compensate; for example, calcium extracted from the bones may lead to stress fractures that may occur while simply walking (American Psychiatric Association, 2000; Yanovski & Stunkard, 2004). Altered potassium and sodium levels can lead to cardiac arrest or kidney failure. What's more, anorexia is associated with depression, low self-esteem, bulimia nervosa, and obsessive–compulsive disorder (American Psychiatric Association, 2000). Yet, after they lose so much weight that bones protrude, their body image is so distorted that they continue to believe they weigh too much. Tragically, an estimated 5% of victims literally starve themselves to death (Stuart & Laraia, 2005).

Anorexia nervosa occurs most often in young women, usually between the ages of 13 and 20, with a mean age of onset of 17 (American Psychiatric Association, 2000). The disorder affects between .50% and 1% of the female population (Stuart & Laraia, 2005); men have less than 10% of all cases of the disorder (Keel, 2005). The number of cases of anorexia nervosa increased over the 20th century. Although it was once thought to occur only in Western cultures, recent research suggests that it is found in non-Western countries also (Keel, 2005; Keel & Klump, 2003). The first treatment objective is resumption of normal eating and weight gain (Hill & Pomeroy, 2001). Approximately 50% of patients with anorexia can be treated as outpatients; the remaining patients require hospitalization. Individuals who suffer from anorexia must develop insight into their negative feelings about their bodies and the behaviors that accompany those feelings. Without this insight, any weight gain will probably be temporary, and the patient will revert to anorectic habits. Cognitive therapy, which helps patients understand the thoughts and feelings associated with the disorder, and behavior therapy, which helps change patients' undesirable behavior, are effective treatments (Yanovski & Stunkard, 2004).

*Bulimia nervosa* (literally, "continuous nervous hunger") is an urge to eat huge quantities of food (as much as 20,000 calories) in a short span of time; it often develops during adolescence or early adulthood (American Psychiatric Association, 2000). Like anorexia, bulimia is most common among young women (typical age of onset is 15 to 18). The estimated lifetime prevalence is 1 to 4% of females (Stuart & Laraia, 2005); the prevalence increased in the second half of the 20th century (Keel & Klump, 2003). A feeling of lack of control over eating is common during an episode. Depression and guilt often set in afterward and lead to purging through self-induced vomiting, excessive use of laxatives (as many as 200 laxatives a week) or diuretics (purging type), or extreme exercise (nonpurging type). Vomiting brings stomach acid in contact with the teeth, which can corrode the enamel and lead to tooth decay. There are a number of medical complications: alteration of the gag reflex so that it is triggered too easily or unintentionally; enlargement of the salivary glands (leading victims to have a "chipmunk" cheek appearance); imbalances in potassium, sodium, and calcium; irregular heartbeat; osteoporosis; and seizures. Victims of bulimia may also have scars and abrasions on their hands from the self-induced vomiting (Hales, 2001; Yanovski & Stunkard, 2004). In addition to a range of physical health problems, bulimia nervosa is associated with an increased risk of anxiety disorders, mood disorders, and diabetes. Unlike anorectic women, however, bulimic women are not underweight and they are less likely to need hospitalization (Hill & Pomeroy, 2001). Their weight is usually normal or just above the normal range. For this reason, bulimia is easier to hide than anorexia, and hence it is more difficult to calculate the number of people who suffer from this disorder.

In sum, people with bulimia have a very distorted and negative image of their bodies. They face continuous self-imposed pressure to do something about their weight. If only the weight would come off, they believe, happiness and popularity will follow. That situation never materializes; therefore, bulimic individuals can never be satisfied with their appetite.

# Sex

A glance at television, magazine, and newspaper advertising will convince you that sex is a powerful motive. Although sex is usually categorized as a biological motive, it differs from other biological motives such as hunger and thirst. Sexual behavior is required for

*"Trust me—sex sells."*

survival of the species, but sexual deprivation does not lead to a person's death, as does food and water deprivation. Hunger and thirst are aversive states that we seek to reduce; by contrast, sexual arousal is a pleasurable state. In this section we examine the influence of various mechanisms on sexual behavior.

An individual's potential to respond sexually to persons of the same sex, the opposite sex, or both is called **sexual orientation.** The most common cultural norm is *heterosexuality* (from the Greek word *hetero*, meaning "the other of two"), which means that a person is sexually attracted to someone of the opposite biological sex. *Homosexuality* (from the Greek word *homo*, for "the same") means that a person is sexually attracted to someone of the same biological sex. Homosexuals have adopted the term *gay* to put their sexual orientation in a more positive light than other terms. In common usage, this term refers to males and sometimes to females; the term *lesbian* is reserved exclusively for women who are sexually attracted to other women (Friedman & Downey, 1994). The sexual orientation known as *bisexuality* refers to attraction to people of both sexes. Many surveys of sexual orientation and practices overlook the category of bisexuality by classifying people with any same-sex behavior as homosexual.

In some cases, people born with the genitals of one sex feel that they are of the other sex and are trapped in the wrong body; this condition is called *transsexualism*. Some of these people choose to change their sexual identity by having surgery. (We say more about transsexualism in Chapter 12.)

Growing evidence suggests that biological factors play an important role in the development of sexual orientation. A tiny portion of the hypothalamus is twice as large in men as in women and two to three times larger in heterosexual than in homosexual men (Le Vay & Hamer, 1994). The growth of neurons in this region may be related to the level of testosterone: The higher the level of testosterone, the greater the number of surviving neurons and hence the larger the region. Thus, testosterone levels may be unusually low in the fetuses of males who become gay and unusually high in the fetuses of females who become lesbian.

Twin research also suggests a genetic component for homosexuality: Among males, when an identical twin is homosexual, the other twin is also homosexual in 57% of the cases. Among fraternal twins, in 24% of the cases both twins are homosexual. Among women, approximately 50% of identical twins, 16% of fraternal twins, and 13% of sisters of lesbians are also lesbians (LeVay & Hamer, 1994). These data are consistent with a genetic influence that a recent review estimated to be in the range of 50 to 60% (Rahman & Wilson, 2003), but they do not exclude possible environmental influences. Because all genetically identical individuals do not share the same sexual orientation, environmental influences are likely to have some effect (Yoder, 2003).

**sexual orientation**

Tendency for a person to be attracted to individuals of the same sex, the opposite sex, or both

**External Factors.**    Sexual behavior in animals is controlled by genetically programmed factors, especially hormone levels (see Chapter 2). As a result, female animals are receptive to sexual overtures only at certain biologically determined times, when they are "in heat" (in estrus).

### Psychological Detective

In what ways is sexual arousal in human beings different from sexual arousal in animals? What are the consequences of these differences in arousal? Give these questions some thought, and write down your answers before reading further.

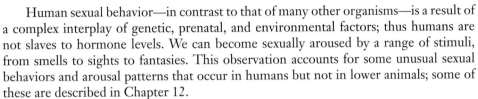

Human sexual behavior—in contrast to that of many other organisms—is a result of a complex interplay of genetic, prenatal, and environmental factors; thus humans are not slaves to hormone levels. We can become sexually aroused by a range of stimuli, from smells to sights to fantasies. This observation accounts for some unusual sexual behaviors and arousal patterns that occur in humans but not in lower animals; some of these are described in Chapter 12.

In many species, male sexual responsiveness is linked to external cues. The odor emitted by a female dog when she ovulates is an external cue for sexual advances by male dogs. Such odors, called **pheromones,** are created by chemicals that elicit a particular response in a species (Sam et al., 2001). Although the existence of human pheromones has not been convincingly demonstrated, there is interesting speculation on the subject. The menstrual cycles of college women living in the same dormitory became synchronized during the first 4 months of dorm life. Similar menstrual synchrony has been found among lesbian couples (Weller & Weller, 1992). The convergence of the menstrual cycles of women who live in close proximity to one another might be caused by an as yet unidentified pheromone transmitted from one woman to another (McClintock, 1971), which are examples of so-called primers that influence long-term changes in hormone levels. Although researchers have been searching for quicker-acting substances (called *releasers*), the general trend seems to be excitement following a discovery of a supposed substance and then a series of failures to replicate its supposed effects on humans. Nevertheless, commercially available products are sold with the claim that they act as pheromones. The best advice seems to be "Buyer beware" because there is no convincing evidence that they work as advertised (Benson, 2002).

Although the importance of external sexual stimuli cannot be disputed, internal factors such as hormones and brain mechanisms are also important determinants of sexual behavior.

**Hormones.**    As we described in Chapter 2, there are two major sex hormones: testosterone and estrogen. Although many people believe that men and women have entirely different sex hormones, both genders have measurable quantities of estrogen and testosterone. The amounts of these hormones differ in men and women: testosterone dominates in men, estrogen in women.

Sex hormones are highly significant in directing sexual behavior in lower animals; however, their role in directing human sexual behavior is less clear. Although testosterone levels are related to sexual activity (Dabbs & Dabbs, 2000) and castration may result in a decline in sexual desire in men (Money, 1980), it does not end sexual activity. On the other hand, studies relating estrogen level and sexual interest have failed to detect a consistently strong relationship between hormone level and sexual interest or activity (Miracle, Miracle, & Baumeister, 2003).

**Brain Mechanisms.**    In addition to its involvement in determining hunger and thirst, the hypothalamus regulates sexual behavior. External signals (such as odors, visual signals, and sounds) and internal stimuli (such as the rise and fall of estrogen levels in females) stimulate the hypothalamus to release chemicals known as *releasing factors*

**pheromones**
Chemical odors emitted by some animals that appear to influence the behavior of members of the same species

that cause other glands to release their hormones. In turn, these releasing factors stimulate the pituitary gland to secrete follicle-stimulating hormone (FSH) and luteinizing hormone (LH) into the bloodstream. FSH stimulates ovulation in the female and sperm production in the male, whereas LH stimulates the ovaries to secrete estrogen and the testes to secrete testosterone. As the female's estrogen level declines at ovulation, stimulation of the hypothalamus to secrete the releasing factor is reduced. A reduction in sexually arousing external stimuli results in a decrease in the production of hypothalamic releasing factors in men and women.

Although the factors controlling sexual behavior are complex, male sex drive is related, in part, to testosterone levels. Therefore, attempts to alter aggressive, inappropriate sexual behavior such as the urge to engage in sex with children (*pedophilia*) have focused on medications. The drug *medroxyprogesterone acetate* (MPA, or Provera) has been prescribed for aggressive sexual deviations because it lowers testosterone levels (Maletzky & Field, 2003). After being injected into muscle tissue, it is slowly released into the bloodstream.

**The Sexual Response.**   Alfred Kinsey and colleagues (Kinsey, Pomeroy, & Martin, 1948, 1953) conducted pioneering research on sexual behavior. Among other things, they found that the incidence of premarital intercourse, masturbation, and homosexuality was higher than had previously been believed.

One criticism of the Kinsey surveys was that the participants were not randomly selected. A more recent survey updated and expanded the Kinsey surveys of several decades ago. The University of Chicago's National Opinion Research Center conducted a survey of more than 3,000 randomly selected American men and women between ages 18 and 59 (Laumann, Gagnon, & Michaels, 1994). The survey participation rate was quite high—80% of individuals contacted agreed to answer questions concerning their sexual behavior. This survey provided a great deal of information about sexual behavior (see Figure 6-8). One interesting finding is that the most common sexual practice is monogamy, which perhaps stands in contrast to what media outlets seem to suggest.

Laboratory research conducted by William Masters and Virginia Johnson (1966) led them to describe four phases of the sexual response during intercourse: *excitement, plateau, orgasm,* and *resolution.* Each phase is characterized by specific physiological and

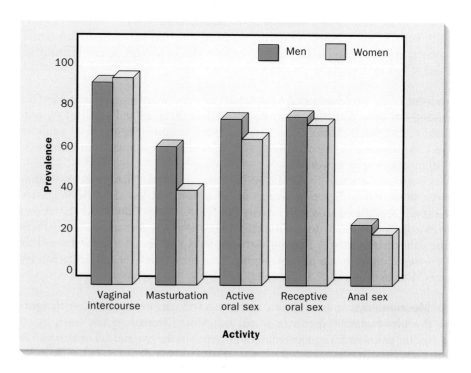

**FIGURE 6-8**   Results of the National Opinion Research Center survey of sexual practices. The percentages refer to the number of respondents who found sexual activity to be "very appealing."

**Source:** Laumann et al. (1994).

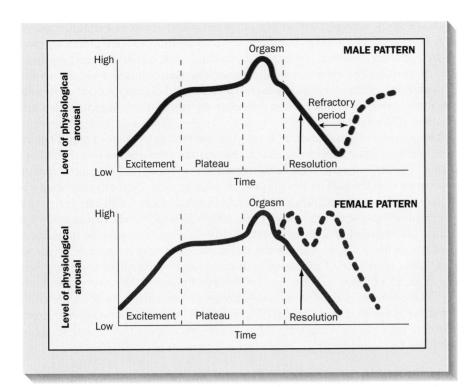

**FIGURE 6-9** The four stages of the human sexual response cycle. Although men and women share the basic response cycle (excitement, plateau, orgasm, resolution), there are some differences. Following resolution, men enter a refractory period during which they are not sexually excitable. On the other hand, women may experience several orgasms before entering resolution.

**Source:** Adapted from Masters and Johnson (1966).

behavioral changes (see Figure 6-9); this pattern varies, however, from person to person and in any individual at different times and under different circumstances (Masters, Johnson, & Kolodny, 1994). For example, physiological responses can be sluggish as a result of high levels of alcohol, fatigue, or recuperation from illness.

The sexual response is not just a genital event; many body systems are involved (Masters et al., 1994). For example, during sexual arousal our sensory awareness changes dramatically. Our sense of touch can become magnified as sexual involvement heightens. The senses of vision and hearing are often diminished when sexual arousal is very high. These changes in sensory awareness at high levels of sexual arousal may explain why some people may be surprised to discover that they have been scratched or bitten during sexual activity.

During the excitement phase, sexual arousal increases rapidly; heart rate, blood pressure, and respiration rise. Arousal continues to build, but at a slower rate, during the plateau phase. Orgasm occurs when sexual arousal reaches maximum intensity, with respiration, heart rate, and blood pressure increasing even further at this stage. Women are capable of multiple orgasms, but men rarely experience more than one orgasm during an episode of sexual intercourse.

During the resolution phase, physiological changes associated with sexual arousal gradually decline. If orgasm has not been experienced, however, the resolution phase is extended. Men become much less responsive to stimulation after orgasm; this unresponsiveness is called the *refractory period*. Some scholars have revised the model to account for the role of intimacy needs, the relational context of arousal, and the cognitive interpretation of sexual stimuli in women's sexual arousal (Basson, 2001, 2002).

In addition to describing the human sexual response, Masters and Johnson investigated *sexual dysfunctions*, which leave people unable to function normally in their sexual response (see Chapter 10). It is not unusual for most people to experience an occasional lack of interest in sexual activity, difficulty becoming aroused, or problems related to orgasm. A diagnosis of sexual dysfunction is reserved for those cases in which the difficulties in sexual functioning occur persistently, causing significant distress or problems for the individual or couple (American Psychiatric Association, 2000; Bach, Wincze, & Barlow, 2001). Sexual dysfunction is more common in women (43%) than men (31%), and is more likely among those with poor physical and emotional health (Laumann, Paik, & Rosen, 1999). Among the common sexual dysfunctions are *premature ejaculation*—the tendency to reach orgasm and ejaculate with minimal sexual stimulation before, or shortly after, penetration and before the man wants it to occur. In *female orgasmic disorder*, a woman repeatedly experiences delayed orgasm or none at all following a normal sexual excitement phase and adequate stimulation (American Psychiatric Association, 2000; Bach et al., 2001).

Although their original research focused on the physical aspects of sexual behavior, Masters and Johnson found that many sexual dysfunctions respond to psychological treatment. In fact, current treatments emphasize a cognitive-behavioral approach, which may serve as the sole treatment or as an adjunct to medical or surgical interventions; most professionals acknowledge that both psychological and biological factors play a role in sexual dysfunctions (Bach et al., 2001). Therapists believe that couples, not individuals, have sexual problems; therefore they emphasize treating both partners in cases of sexual dysfunction. Among the techniques that may be used is *sensate focus*, which is based on the belief that sexually dysfunctional couples have lost the ability to think and feel in a sensual way as a result of stress and pressure they associate with intercourse. The couple may need to be reacquainted with the pleasures of tactile contact. Each partner learns that being touched is pleasurable, and that exploring and caressing the partner's body can be stimulating. During the early stages of treatment, intercourse is prohibited because requiring it might increase tension.

## Achievement

Most people are sure that they understand what achievement is and can provide examples of achievement-related behavior, but it is difficult to define achievement precisely: "Achievement behaviors are those behaviors concerned with manipulating the environment according to rules and standards" (Hoyenga & Hoyenga, 1984, p. 374). **Achievement** consists of three components: (a) behaviors that manipulate the environment in some manner, (b) rules for performing those behaviors, and (c) accepted performance standards against which people compete and compare their performance. Studying hard to earn good grades is an example of achievement behavior; the grades are the achievement toward which the behavior is aimed.

Achievement and competition permeate society. The prevalence of achievement-oriented behaviors has prompted theorists to propose the existence of an achievement

**achievement**
Manipulation of the environment according to established rules to attain a desired goal

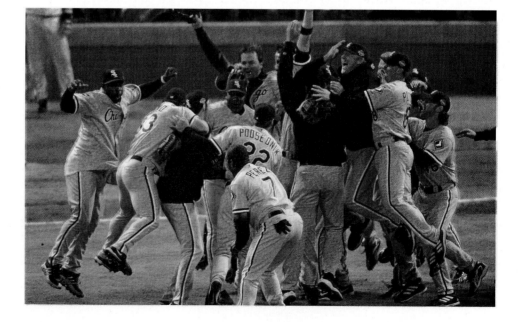

Numerous examples of achievement-oriented behaviors occur every day. These behaviors include academic achievements such as "acing a test" and sports achievements. Some achievements result in recognition in the form of praise, plaques, or ribbons; for many forms of achievement, personal satisfaction is all that matters to the participants.

motive. Because achievement behaviors are directed toward attaining a pleasurable award/goal or avoiding an aversive event, incentive theories are often used to explain achievement behaviors.

The Thematic Apperception Test (TAT) has been used to measure levels of achievement motivation (Atkinson, 1974; McClelland, 1958, 1985). When you take the TAT, you are asked to create a story about a series of pictures that depict people in ambiguous situations. Participants are believed to attribute their own motives to the figures in the ambiguous pictures. Participants whose stories have a great deal of achievement content are considered high in the achievement motive; participants whose stories contain little achievement content are considered low in this motive.

Some theorists stress the need to succeed; others stress the need to avoid failure. The difference between the two needs can be illustrated by two students who earn As in the same course but for different reasons. One student is motivated to earn the A because of the pride that comes from mastering the material. The other student earns the A to avoid the shame associated with failing or making a lower grade.

Consider an example. Kurt volunteered to take part in a psychological experiment. The first task he was asked to complete was to make up a story about each of a series of pictures (TAT). After relating the stories, he was given a stack of cards with a figure (see Figure 6-10) printed on each.

His task was to trace around the figure without retracing a line or lifting his pencil. He was told that "the probability of success on this task is 70%." Thus the chances of succeeding were more than two times greater than the chances of failing. After trying to trace the same diagram on several cards, however, Kurt decided that he did not want to experience any more failures, so he quit. He wondered how many cards were traced by the experiment's other participants.

What does this experiment tell us about the need to achieve? Before we go any further, we should point out that the pattern used in this research, the Euler diagram, is *not* solvable. You cannot trace around the entire figure without retracing a line or lifting your pencil.

How was Kurt's need to achieve evaluated? The content of the stories provides a measure of achievement motivation. Is achievement the only motive TAT stories measure? No, the motive to avoid failure can also be measured. Recall that Kurt wondered how other participants were doing. What if there were two groups—one composed of participants high in the need to achieve and the other of participants high in the need to avoid failure? Would you predict that the response of these two groups to this unsolvable task would differ? What about after several failures? Achievement-motivated participants would be energized to continue responding in order to achieve. The participants who were motivated to avoid failure would stop tracing sooner in order to avoid further failure. When such an experiment was conducted, these were exactly the results that were obtained (Feather, 1961). Participants with a high need for achievement attempted more tracings than participants with a strong desire to avoid failure. The need to achieve is a powerful motive that influences the behavior of both children and adults, but it is more complex than many of us believe.

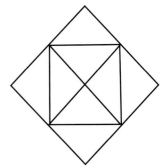

**FIGURE 6-10** The Euler diagram. Participants were asked to trace around the figure without retracing a line or lifting the pencil.

# REVIEW SUMMARY

**1.** One factor in hunger regulation is blood sugar (glucose) levels. Low blood sugar levels signal hunger, and high blood sugar levels signal that the organism is full. In addition, levels of fat are also used by the body in regulating hunger.

**2. Obesity** is associated with several physical illnesses. The **body mass index (BMI)**, a single number derived from a person's height and weight, is a better predictor of disease risk than insurance company tables of desirable weights.

**3.** Genetic factors play a key role in determining a person's weight. The *basal metabolic rate* is the rate at which a person burns calories to keep the body functioning. Our metabolic rate declines with age and is lower in females than in males.

4. A person with **anorexia nervosa** will lose a significant amount of weight. A person with **bulimia nervosa** engages in a gorging-purging cycle, which involves taking in large amounts of food and then vomiting.

5. Although sex is classified as a biological motive, it is different from other biological motives in important ways. **Sexual orientation** is a person's tendency to be sexually attracted to one sex or the other or both. Sexual behavior is influenced by external factors, brain mechanisms, and hormones. **Pheromones** are chemicals that elicit a response in members of the same species. The display of sexual behavior in lower organisms is tied to hormone levels in the blood. Human sexual behavior

results from a complex interplay of genetic, hormonal, and psychological factors. Masters and Johnson outlined the stages of sexual arousal: excitement, plateau, orgasm, and resolution. They also developed techniques to treat sexual dysfunctions.

6. **Achievement** consists of behaviors that manipulate the environment, rules for those behaviors, and standards for judging performance. The need to achieve can be measured by responses to the Thematic Apperception Test (TAT).

# ✓ CHECK YOUR PROGRESS

1. What is the best description of BMI?
   a. a measure of the rate at which the body uses energy
   b. a single number used to assess health status
   c. an indication of the amount of fat that cells can hold
   d. an indicator of cardiovascular health and fitness

2. Which person has a BMI that places him or her just above the NHBLI cutoff for obesity?
   a. Mai, whose BMI is 20
   b. Jennifer, whose BMI is 24
   c. Danny, whose BMI is 31
   d. Justin, whose BMI is 36

3. Damage to which of the following areas of the brain is most likely to affect an animal's hunger?
   a. frontal lobes
   b. hypothalamus
   c. hippocampus
   d. parietal lobes

4. Which drug is used to reduce testosterone levels?
   a. dopamine
   b. pheromone
   c. Provera
   d. Valium

5. What stage of the Masters and Johnson sexual response cycle occurs when sexual arousal increases rapidly and heart rate, blood pressure, and respiration increase?
   a. excitement
   b. plateau
   c. orgasm
   d. resolution

6. After years of blaming each other for their sexual problems, a couple seeks therapy. The therapist recommends sensate focus. How will the therapist explain this treatment?
   a. "Let's analyze the primary cause of your problems."

   b. "Here are changes in your diets that can increase hormone levels."
   c. "I want the two of you to spend time caressing and exploring each other's bodies and experiencing the pleasure of touch."
   d. "I want you to daydream about each other and then engage in sexual intercourse each night for at least one week."

7. Describe the three components of achievement behavior. Why is each a necessary ingredient of achievement?

8. What is one major reason for our tendency to gain weight as we grow older?
   a. Metabolic rates slow as we age.
   b. As we grow older, we consume more calories.
   c. Activity levels increase in order to maintain vigor.
   d. As we grow older our diets contain higher percentages of dietary fat.

9. How many calories are there in one pound of fat?
   a. 3500
   b. 2000
   c. 1500
   d. 750

10. What are common medical complications associated with bulimia nervosa?
   a. acne, cold sweat, and insomnia
   b. slowed blood clotting, skin rashes, and seizures
   c. difficulty breathing, frequent colds, and high fevers
   d. tooth decay, irregular heartbeat, imbalances in potassium levels

**ANSWERS: 1.** b **2.** c **3.** b **4.** c **5.** a **6.** c **7.** Behaviors that manipulate the environment, rules for performing these behaviors, and accepted performance standards against which performance is evaluated/compared. These three components are needed to explain the full range of achievement-motivated behaviors. **8.** a **9.** a **10.** d

# THE WHAT AND THE WHY OF EMOTION

**Tim stands in front of the microphone to deliver a presentation. The room is not really hot; it only seems that way to Tim. As he begins to speak, a strange sensation grips his throat. He tries to clear his throat, hoping the words will pass his cotton-dry lips. His viselike grip on the podium causes an aching sensation in his hands and forearms. The growing restlessness of the audience is not a real threat, yet Tim acts as if it were. His heart seems to be "off to the races." Tim hopes no one sees the ocean of perspiration that is soaking his body. The rational part of his being tells him that his imagination has gotten the better of him, yet he cannot shake the dread that has taken hold of his body. *What does Tim's experience tell us about the study of emotion?***

Imagine life without emotion: There is no joy associated with great art. A vicious crime elicits no anger or disgust. Watching our favorite sports team never leads to "the thrill of victory or the agony of defeat." Sadness does not follow the death of a loved one because we do not experience love. Without emotion, life would be listless and colorless, like a meal in need of seasoning. But emotions do more than provide color and spice; they can actually help us survive.

Not long ago, many scientists considered emotion trivial, not worthy of study. Let poets and philosophers analyze emotions, they argued. Scientists should focus on the rational part of human nature. Emotions, they argued, represent the animal, irrational side of human nature capable of disrupting rational thought. This disregard of the emotional part of human nature has changed; an expanding body of research has focused on the what, why, and how of emotions.

The common term for what Tim experienced is *stage fright*, an extreme example of emotion. Significant increases in heart rate, feelings of distress, and elevated levels of hormones related to stress occur during stage fright (Fredrikson & Gunnarsson, 1992). Tim's experience echoes what happens when we face real threats such as losing control of a car on an ice-covered road or being mugged. This phenomenon tells us how the study of emotions connects our present with the past.

Your heart pounds, your mouth is dry, and the pupils of your eyes are dilated. These physiological changes are the result of the activity of the sympathetic branch of the autonomic nervous system (see Chapter 2), which prepares us for fight or flight. We burn energy at a higher rate than normal in this state of heightened arousal, so we perspire to cool down. After this "call to arms," the parasympathetic branch of the autonomic nervous system takes control to calm the body and return all systems to normal resting levels. Spending extended periods of time in the aroused state that accompanies some emotions can have devastating effects on the body and on our health (see Chapter 14).

But what is emotion? Like many terms we use each day, *emotion* is not easy to define. This difficulty is reflected in the more than 90 definitions that were offered during the 20th century (Plutchik, 2001). Try describing what you know about the term. You decide that emotion is different from rational thought; it is not the same as information acquired through our senses or stored in memory. Emotions do not last long (Edwards, 1998; Ekman, 1992). When the subjective feelings associated with emotions last for an extended period of time, we call them *moods*.

The word *emotion* is derived from the Latin word meaning "to move"; the prefix *e-* means "away." As the preceding vignette reveals, emotion can be described as a state of awareness that has several components. Thus our definition of **emotion** encompasses physiological indices such as changes in heart rate, overt behaviors such as facial expressions and tightly grabbing the podium, and elicitors of emotion such as concern about giving a talk. But a key question remains: What is the purpose of our emotions?

**emotion**
Physiological changes and conscious feelings of pleasantness or unpleasantness, aroused by external and internal stimuli, that lead to behavioral reactions

## Relating Emotions and Behavior: The Evolutionary Perspective

In his book *The Expression of Emotions in Man and Animals*, Charles Darwin (1872/1965) suggested that emotional expressions have a biological basis. According to Darwin, animals and humans share similar facial and postural expressions that have common origins and functions. For example, both humans and higher primates seem to frown; most animals bare their teeth during anger or rage. Later we will see that the facial expressions humans display during emotional reactions are quite similar across cultures.

But why would such expressions be passed down from species to species and across generations? Darwin suggested that these expressions communicate information about events that help organisms adapt. For example, the ability to communicate fear of a predator is important to prey animals; emotions can also communicate a willingness to fight an enemy.

Emotions can increase the chances of survival by providing a readiness for actions such as fighting predators that have helped us survive throughout our evolutionary history (Plutchik, 1993, 2001). Take anger as an example: It "intimidates, influences others to do something you wish them to do, energizes an individual for attack or defense and spaces the participants in a conflict" (Plutchik, 2001, p. 348). Fear quickly drives blood to the large muscles, making it easier to run; surprise raises our eyebrows so that the eyes widen to collect more information. Some gestures associated with emotional reactions may have descended from our human ancestors who did not have a well-developed spoken language; perhaps they relied on nonverbal communication to promote survival. In summary, emotions warn us of danger, guide us to what is desirable and satisfying, and convey our intentions to others.

## THE PHYSIOLOGICAL COMPONENTS OF EMOTION

**One Saturday night, 16-year-old Matilda Crabtree planned to go to her friend's house to spend the night; her parents would go to visit their friends. When her parents returned at about 1 A.M., they heard noises and suspected they had caught a burglar in the act. They did not know Matilda and her friend had returned home and were making noises as they hid in a closet ready to spring a practical joke. Bobby Crabtree picked up his pistol and walked cautiously toward Matilda's bedroom. As he entered the room, Matilda jumped out of the closet and yelled, "Boo!" A shot rang out; a bullet lodged in Matilda's neck. Her last words to her father were "I love you, Daddy." She died about 12 hours later. In an instant, fear had mobilized Bobby Crabtree toward actions meant to protect himself and his family. Thousands of years of evolution had prepared him for a rapid response. In the split second he will remember for the rest of his life, he did not have time to recognize his daughter's voice (Nossiter, 1994). *What brain circuits are involved when we react instantly to events such as the suspicion that a burglar might be in the house?***

Matilda Crabtree was shot by her father, who mistook her for a burglar. Her father's action was an instantaneous reaction to a perceived threat that left him no time to determine that the person he was shooting was his own daughter.

If asked to provide a definition of emotion, many people offer examples of physiological activity. Why? Our body's generalized arousal is often the most perceptible sign of emotion to the person as well as to observers. You can imagine what was happening in Bobby Crabtree's body as he made his way to confront a suspected burglar. That arousal motivates us toward a course of action that may help us survive. At times, however, emotions can be disruptive, as any student who has suffered test anxiety knows.

# Early Theories of Emotions

Given the prominence of the physiological components of emotion, it is not surprising that the first theoretical explanations of emotion focused on this component. We will turn to these explanations next.

**The James-Lange Theory.** In 1884, William James (1842–1910) proposed a theory that was independently proposed in 1885 by a Danish physiologist, Carl Lange (1836–1900); it is referred to as the **James-Lange theory** of emotion.

Before the James-Lange theory, it was assumed that an internal or external stimulus triggers an emotion and the emotion, in turn, produces physiological changes. The sequence stimulus → emotion → physiological changes is called the **commonsense view of emotions**. The James-Lange theory reversed the commonsense notion that perception of an emotional event caused a physiological state that we label as emotion.

James believed the order of the last two events should be reversed: stimulus → physiological changes → emotion. Thus the James-Lange theory states that physiological changes occur *before* the emotion and actually create the feelings we label as an emotion. For example, the feelings you experience while listening to "The Star-Spangled Banner" are a result of physiological changes. The sounds of the music are received by the sensory cortex, which activates the sympathetic branch of the autonomic nervous system. Then impulses from the sympathetic division are sent to the cortex to create the appropriate emotional feeling. In other words, the physiological changes precede and produce the emotion: We feel sorry because we cry, afraid because we tremble, and *not* the other way around.

Today scientists know a lot more than James and Lange did about the physiological changes associated with emotion. As a result, they have several criticisms of the James-Lange theory. For example, sometimes we experience emotion before the body's systems have had time to react, as the case of Bobby Crabtree reveals. Furthermore, if emotion is equivalent to general physiological arousal, how do we sort out differences between fear and love, excitement and joy, and so on? There is no doubt that physiological arousal plays a part in emotion, but it does not necessarily cause emotion.

**The Cannon-Bard Theory.** The James-Lange theory was criticized by Walter Cannon and his colleague Philip Bard, who argued that the physiological changes that occur during emotional episodes are not diverse or complex enough to account for the range of emotions we experience. What's more, Cannon (1927) believed that many physiological changes, especially those involving hormones, are too slow to serve as the basis of emotions. The fear you feel when an airplane pilot announces "a problem with our engines" is instantaneous and precedes physiological changes such as the release and influence of epinephrine (adrenaline). This sequence of reactions contradicts the James-Lange theory.

Cannon and Bard created a theory of emotions that focuses on the thalamus, a relay point for sensory information traveling to the cerebral cortex. According to the **Cannon-Bard theory,** information from incoming emotional stimuli is relayed simultaneously to the cortex and to the internal organs of the sympathetic system. Thus our emotional feelings do not depend on the occurrence of bodily changes (James-Lange theory), nor do the bodily changes result from a prior emotional feeling (commonsense view). The feeling and physiological components of an emotion occur simultaneously.

The Cannon-Bard theory may reconcile differences between the commonsense view and the James-Lange theory, but it is not perfect. Karl Lashley (1938) noted that the Cannon-Bard theory places heavy responsibility on the thalamus. For this theory to be correct, the thalamus must be capable of interpreting and relaying the full range of both physiological and emotional reactions. It is doubtful that the thalamus is this versatile. Although the thalamus does relay information, it appears that other areas of the brain are required to interpret this information fully.

**James-Lange theory**
Theory that physiological changes precede and cause emotions

**commonsense view of emotions**
View that emotions precede and cause bodily changes

**Cannon-Bard theory**
Theory that the thalamus relays information simultaneously to the cortex and to the sympathetic nervous system, causing emotional feelings and physiological changes to occur at the same time

**STUDY TIP**

Compare the James-Lange theory of emotion to the Cannon-Bard theory. How are they similar and different? Which seems to make more sense, and why?

# Physiological Differences among Emotions

Although it may be difficult to distinguish one emotion from another solely on the basis of physiological changes, some differences offer important cues. People cry when they are sad, sometimes when they are happy, but almost never when they are angry or disgusted (Scherer & Wallbott, 1994). When researchers asked almost 3,000 students from 37 countries to describe various emotional experiences, they found widespread agreement about the primary physiological sensations that occurred (Scherer & Wallbott, 1994; see Table 6-4).

Establishing the physiological specificity of emotions does not require that every emotion have a unique physiological signature, only that some emotions differ from others in consistent ways. Finding such evidence has not been easy because emotions generally last for only a few seconds (Edwards, 1998). What's more, researchers must find a way to elicit an emotion before it can be studied. In one method (Ekman, Levenson, & Friesen, 1983; Levenson, Ekman, & Friesen, 1990), students and actors followed instructions to create facial expressions. Look in the mirror and follow these instructions: "Pull your eyebrows down and together. Raise your upper eyelid. Push your lower lip up and press your lips together" (Levenson et al., 1990, p. 365). You have just portrayed anger. The researchers coached participants to help them comply with the instructions; then they recorded autonomic nervous system indices while participants held the expressions.

Evidence based on this type of research suggests that there are several differences among emotions. One consistent finding is that anger tends to be associated with cardiovascular changes (Cacioppo, Klein, Berntson, & Hatfield, 1993). Heart rate increases with anger, fear, and sadness; it decreases with disgust (see Figure 6-11). Compared with anger, fear is associated with lower blood pressure, cooler surface temperature, and less blood flow to the body's periphery (Levenson, 1992, 1994). Our language reflects some physiological differences: We use phrases such as "blood boiling" and "hot under the collar" when we talk about anger but not when talking about disgust or happiness. The description "white with fear" reflects the cooler skin temperature associated with this emotion.

**TABLE 6-4**

## Percentage of Participants Reporting Physiological Changes with Specific Emotions

| Emotion | Change Reported | Percentage of Participants |
|---|---|---|
| Anger | Faster heartbeat | 50 |
| | Tensed muscles | 43 |
| | Faster breathing | 37 |
| Fear | Faster heartbeat | 65 |
| | Tensed muscles | 52 |
| | Faster breathing | 47 |
| Joy | Increased temperature | 63 |
| | Faster heartbeat | 40 |
| | Decreased muscle tension | 10 |
| Sadness | Crying/sobbing | 55 |
| | Faster heartbeat | 27 |
| | Tensed muscles | 27 |
| Shame | Increased temperature | 40 |
| | Faster heartbeat | 35 |
| | Lump in throat | 24 |

**Source:** Scherer and Wallbott (1994).

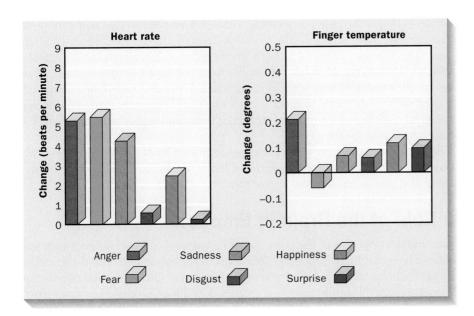

**FIGURE 6-11** Physiological (autonomic nervous system) differences in emotions. Heart rate increases with anger, fear, sadness, and happiness; finger temperature increases with anger and decreases with fear.

**Source:** Levenson, Ekman, and Friesen (1990).

Robert Levenson and his colleagues (1992) traveled to western Sumatra, in Indonesia, to study the Minangkabau, an agrarian society with a female-oriented socioeconomic organization. This society emphasizes external aspects of emotion and has a strong prohibition against public displays of anger. Levenson and his colleagues found evidence of similarities and differences between the Minangkabau and Americans. Young male participants who posed the facial expressions of emotions had the same physiological distinctions found among Americans. This finding suggests that the posed faces cause autonomic changes that are prewired and largely culture-free. The sensory signals from facial muscles did not, however, produce the same subjective feelings that they did in Americans.

We can observe physiological patterns in certain emotions such as embarrassment, which can lead to blushing. Imagine this scenario: You are seated in a room with several other people waiting to listen to an audiotape of *your* singing. As the first tones come over the sound system, capillaries in your cheeks, ears, neck, and upper chest (the "blush region") fill with blood, raising the temperature and making your skin hot (Shearn, Bergman, Hill, & Abel, 1990). Blushing in darker-skinned people can appear as a further darkening of the skin, or it may not be observable by others at all (Leary, Britt, Cutlip, & Templeton, 1992).

Although Darwin (1872/1965) thought this peculiar human expression served no function, blushing may communicate the message that the person values the positive regard of others. Almost all people have blushed, although those who are especially concerned with how others evaluate them are more prone to blush (Leary & Meadows, 1991; Leary et al., 1992). Threats to one's public image, such as being made to look incompetent, are strong elicitors of blushing; simply being the center of attention, however, may be sufficient to cause some people to blush. Blushing can also occur when we are praised or told that we appear to be blushing.

We know that particular physiological changes occur with certain emotions in people everywhere, from the streets of Baltimore to the rain forests of Borneo, from the deserts of the southwestern United States to river towns in the Mekong Delta (Mesquita & Fridja, 1992). But some differences in physiological reactions may result from cultural influences. For example, in the United States and other countries that encourage individuality, emotional expressions tend to last longer and are more intense (see the discussion of individualism and collectivism in Chapter 11). On the other hand, researchers failed to find differences between Chinese Americans and Mexican Americans in physiological aspects of their emotional responses to an acoustic startle of sufficient magnitude (115 db) to produce a strong defensive response. The two groups were selected because they were thought to differ dramatically in their views concerning emotion. The Chinese culture has been portrayed as valuing emotional control and moderation, whereas the Mexican culture has been portrayed as valuing free and open expression of emotion. Whether the noise presented was anticipated, unanticipated, or anticipated with instructions to modify one's emotional response made no difference; physiological responses were similar across conditions and across cultural groups (Soto, Levenson, & Ebling, 2005).

The importance of physiological aspects of emotion leads to questions about which parts of the nervous system are significant. Clearly, the brain has a key role to play in emotions, as it does in most of our behaviors.

## The Role of the Brain in Emotion

The size and development of the cortex separates more developed animals such as primates from lower animals. The *cortex* (often called the rational part of the brain) grew from what could be called the emotional part of the brain. Our sophisticated cortex provides more options following emotional arousal. A rabbit being chased by a predator has few responses to its deathly fear—either it runs faster than ever, or it loses the race and its life. By contrast, the highly evolved human cortex offers several options: run, fight, dial 911, and so on (Goleman, 1995).

Of all the parts of the brain, the limbic system is probably the most important in a discussion of emotion. This network of structures located beneath the cortex includes the *amygdala*, the *hippocampus*, and the *hypothalamus*. The primary role of the hippocampus appears to be in processing memories. The amygdala—a small almond-shaped structure—receives sensory inputs and is essential in evaluating the emotional meaning of stimuli. Research has substantiated the importance of the amygdala to emotions; for example, animals whose amygdala is removed lack fear and rage responses.

Joseph LeDoux (1996) has found that the amygdala reacts instantly to sensory inputs and can trigger the fight-or-flight response while the cortex is evaluating inputs and making decisions. This sequence of brain activity helps us understand Bobby Crabtree's rapid response in firing his gun. LeDoux focused on fear because it occurs across cultures and in many species and plays a key role in some psychological disorders (see Chapter 12). Using rats as his experimental animals, LeDoux played a tone and applied a brief electric shock to the rats' feet.

### Psychological Detective

Think of yourself as one of LeDoux's rats. Each time you hear a tone, you also receive a mild electric shock to your foot. How would this experience change your behavior? Write down your answer before reading further.

Later, when the tone was sounded again (without the accompanying shock), the animals froze and their blood pressure and heart rates increased. The rats seemed to have learned to fear the tone. LeDoux used electrodes to trace nerve impulses that carried information about the sound from the ear to the thalamus. From the thalamus, the information sped to the cortex, where it was evaluated; then the impulse went to the amygdala. The pathway from the thalamus to the sensory cortex to the amygdala involves several neural links that add time to the process.

The signal about the tone followed a second route—from ear to thalamus to amygdala (see Figure 6-12). But why would two routes, one cortical and one subcortical, carry the same information? The shorter (subcortical) route conserves time, which permits emotional responses to begin in the amygdala before we completely recognize what we are reacting to or what we are feeling. As LeDoux explains, "Failing to respond to danger is more costly than responding inappropriately to a benign stimulus" (LeDoux, 1994, p. 56).

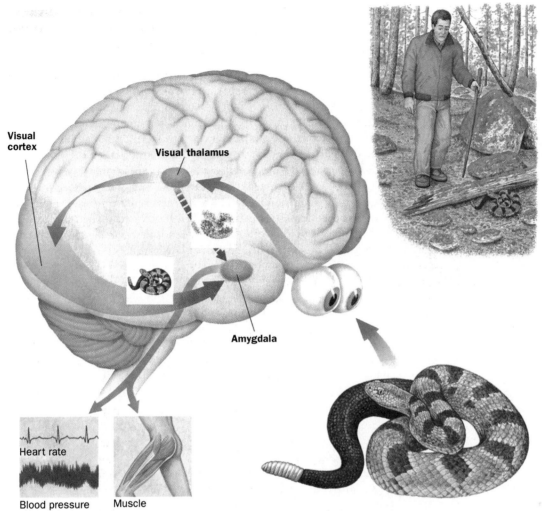

**FIGURE 6-12** Cortical and subcortical paths of information related to potentially fear-inducing stimuli. Information about a visual stimulus first travels to the thalamus, which passes the information directly to the amygdala (red). This rapid transmission provides a quick response to potential danger (green). The thalamus also sends the information to the visual cortex, where greater perceptual sophistication and added time lead to a determination that there is a snake on the path (blue). Relaying this determination to the amygdala leads to increases in heart rate and blood pressure and to muscle contraction. If, however, the cortex had determined that the object is not a snake, the message to the amygdala would reduce the fear response.

**Source:** LeDoux (1994).

Researchers continue to discover additional information on the amygdala's role in emotions. For example, human participants who were taught to associate a visual cue with shock exhibited increased blood flow to the amygdala when they saw the cue later. In other research, patients with a damaged amygdala rated faces with negative expressions to be as trustworthy as faces with positive expressions (Mlot, 1998). Functional magnetic resonance images of the brain (see Chapter 2) reveal evidence of activation of the amygdala when people view facial expressions of fear and anger (Whalen et al., 2001). Although different regions of the amygdala were especially active with each of these emotions, there is little doubt that the amygdala plays an important role in emotions. The range of emotions for which the amygdale plays a role seems to expand at a rapid rate; recent research indicates that the amygdala is activated while viewing pictures portraying sadness (Wang, McCarthy, Song, & LaBar, 2005).

**The Brain's Hemispheres and Emotions.**    Clearly, subcortical areas are involved in fear, but the entire brain plays a role in emotion. Physicians, clinical neuropsychologists, and relatives of people who have suffered brain damage have noted that right-hemisphere damage often leaves victims emotionally indifferent. These observations are consistent with research on brain activity during emotional expressions. Stroke patients with right-hemisphere damage have trouble expressing emotion and perceiving emotional signals from others. These people may understand the statement "I am angry" but fail to detect the speaker's tone of voice or angry facial expression. Patients with right-hemisphere disease or damage have more difficulty than patients with left-hemisphere damage in processing facial expressions or emotionally charged speech. The right hemisphere appears to be specialized for perceiving emotion from facial expressions.

When normal people report negative emotions such as fear or disgust, there is increased activity in their right hemisphere; the left hemisphere is more active during positive emotions such as happiness (Davidson, 1993; Ekman, Davidson, & Friesen, 1990). The frontal regions of the left and right hemispheres may be specialized for approach and withdrawal processes, respectively (Davidson, 1993).

**Lack of Emotion.**    Although we think that all humans share and express emotions, some people have difficulty expressing their emotions and understanding the emotions of others (McDonald & Prkachin, 1990). As a result, these people find it difficult to maintain relationships, and their lack of emotional responsiveness often infuriates their partners. This emotional difficulty, called *alexithymia*, is derived from Latin: *a* ("without"), *lex* ("word"), and *thymia* ("feeling"). Thus, the word refers to a deficiency characterized by having no words to describe feelings (Linden, Wen, & Paulhus, 1995). Consider the following case:

> Gary, a successful 35-year-old surgeon, is articulate and reflective when discussing art and science. By contrast, he has difficulty speaking about his emotions and is unresponsive to the emotions exhibited by others. After he married Ellen, she was often angry with him, although he rarely understood why. She urged him to begin psychotherapy. During a group therapy session, he said, "I don't naturally express my emotions" and was relieved to hear that others had similar problems. When someone described him as too intellectual, he smiled in agreement. He described his difficulty with emotion in these words: "I have no strong feelings, either positive or negative." (Swiller, 1988)

People with alexithymia lack self-awareness; they rarely cry, are described as colorless and bland, and are not able to discriminate among different emotions. They are often unaware of what others around them feel. They do not differ from others in the number or type of words used to describe their dreams; however, their dreams are rated as less fantastic (Parker, Bauermann, & Smith, 2000). People with alexithymia tend to be men who come from families that provided little positive communication and few models for expressing emotions (Berenbaum & James, 1994). Their characteristics tend to be stable across time (Honkalampi et al., 2001).

Twin studies indicate that facets of alexithymia are probably caused by either shared environmental factors or genetic factors; in other words, a clear case has not been made for either environmental or genetic factors (Valera & Berenbaum, 2001). Although alexithymia is not an officially recognized psychiatric or psychological diagnosis, interest in this condition has grown because it is associated with physical symptoms, drug problems, depression, and stress-related disorders (Honkalampi, Hintikka, Laukkanen, Lehtonen, & Viinamaki, 2001; Saarijaervi, Salminen, & Toikka, 2001).

## Evaluating the Lie Detector

What a boost it would be to police if they could attach electrodes to a suspect, ask questions, monitor physiological indices, and determine if the person was deceptive. The

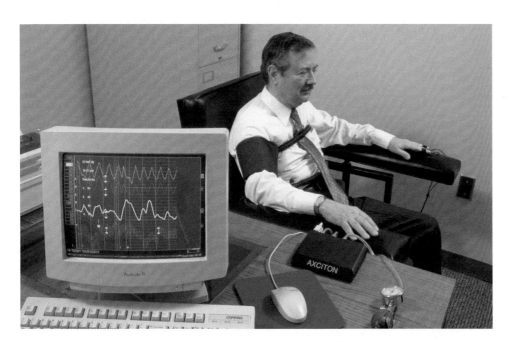

Administration of a polygraph test typically involves the use of electrodes to measure several physiological indicators thought to be related to deception.

premise of lie detection is simple: A specific physiological change tells us that a person has been deceptive. You may be surprised to learn that the device we call a *lie detector* does not actually detect lies (Vrij, 2001). What we call a lie detector is really a **polygraph** (literally, "many writings"). This electronic device was conceived by psychologist William Marston in 1915; it simultaneously senses and makes records of several physiological indices, including blood pressure, heart rate, respiration, and galvanic skin response (GSR)—changes in the skin's ability to conduct electrical current that are associated with levels of perspiration. Computerized scoring systems have been developed to interpret results (Olsen, Harris, Capps, & Ansley, 1997).

Although most state and federal courts prohibit testimony based on lie detectors (Knight, 2004; Saxe, 1994), police often use them to clear suspects, to verify witness' statements, or to find new leads. In the past, polygraphs were used frequently in preemployment screenings and to uncover employee theft; however, the *Employee Polygraph Protection Act of 1988* prohibits most employment-related uses. Elsewhere, the Supreme Court of Canada ruled that polygraph evidence could not be admitted in court, and a court ruling in Australia is likely to put an end to the use of polygraphs in court proceedings there (Freckelton, 2004).

One method of administering a polygraph test—*the guilty knowledge test (GKT)*—was designed to reveal whether a person has specific information relevant to a crime (Rosenfeld, 1995). Questions focus on pertinent details of the crime that only the guilty party and the police know. Thus only the guilty person is expected to react strongly to relevant details of the crime. A second common method of administering the polygraph is the *Control Question Test* (also called the *Relevant/Irrelevant Test*). With this method, examiners compare physiological responses to control or irrelevant questions (for example, "Is your name Dan?") that are not expected to create arousal to the arousal associated with answers to questions about the crime (for example, "Did you take that computer?") (see Figure 6-13).

Because polygraph tests measure physiological responses, efforts to modify these responses can affect test accuracy. The methods used to alter physiological responses—called *countermeasures*—include drugs, physical methods (such as biting the tongue), and *mental methods* (such as counting backward by sevens) (Vrij, 2001). In one study, half of the guilty people defeated the polygraph test (were judged innocent) by using countermeasures (Honts & Kircher, 1994). The use of countermeasures is a serious—perhaps insurmountable—problem for examiners because it is difficult to detect.

**polygraph**
An electronic device (often called a *lie detector*) that senses and records changes in several physiological indices including blood pressure, heart rate, respiration, and galvanic skin response

**FIGURE 6-13** A record of a polygraph test. Most polygraph methods involve comparing an individual's physiological arousal to different questions. For example, a participant would not be expected to exhibit a great deal of physiological arousal when asked "Is your name John Donald?" If the person had stolen an expensive camera, polygraph examiners expect to see physiological arousal to a question such as "Did you steal a camera?"

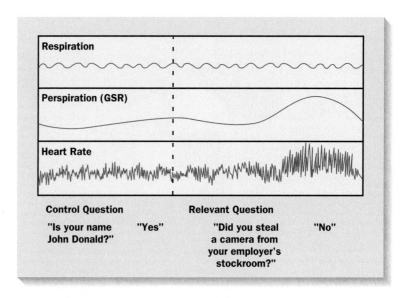

## Psychological Detective

Imagine that you have been "hooked up" to a polygraph. An examiner walks into the room and requests that you answer all questions truthfully. What physiological changes might occur as you answer the questions? Why do you think these changes would occur?

Polygraph tests have been viewed as an invasion of privacy and criticized on ethical, legal, and scientific grounds (National Research Council, 2003). Perhaps the most compelling criticism is that the basic premise is faulty: "If there were a specific lie response, then modern psychophysiological techniques would probably allow us to detect it and the dream of a genuine lie detector would be a reality" (Lykken, 1981, p. 51). The physiological changes thought to reveal deception could, however, result from anxiety about being interrogated, anger at being asked to take the test, or fear from pondering the consequences of "failing" the test. You might react in any of these ways if you were hooked up to a polygraph (Knight, 2004). We cannot measure deception directly (Iacono & Lykken, 1997), and when we attempt to do so, errors can result.

The most common error in using a polygraph is identifying an innocent person as not telling the truth, called a *false positive* (Vrij, 2001). Classification of a guilty person as innocent is called a *false negative*. Although some research indicates that polygraphs can have a high degree of accuracy, critics note that quite often examiners had access to information beyond the polygraph, which could improve accuracy. Regardless, it seems that efforts to identify guilty persons will identify some honest people as deceptive (Lykken, 1998), and some critics describe the number of errors as "substantial" (Vrij, 2001). What's more, some individuals identified as possessing psychopathic traits (see Chapter 12) seem especially able to avoid detection by polygraph examinations, in part as a result of their reduced GSR (Verschuere, Crombez, De Clercq, & Koster, 2005).

The hope that we can find a method to identify deception continues. The growing concern about national security has intensified the search for technology to identify those who try to deceive (Knight, 2004). For example, using functional magnetic resonance imaging (fMRI), researchers found significantly increased activity in brain areas associated with attention as well as areas that initiate voluntary movement. Thermal imaging technology is used to identify facial changes, such as warming around the eyes, that are hypothesized to accompany deception (Slotnick, 2002). Another approach avoids the polygraph altogether, relying instead on reaction time, which can be measured electronically (Seymour, Seifert, Shafto, & Mosmann, 2000). College students who were asked to commit a bogus crime (logging on to a university computer and sending another suspect a message) were identified by longer reaction times to key words relevant to the crime. When asked to avoid detection of critical knowledge, participants were not able to do so; 95% of participants were correctly classified as guilty or not guilty. Additional research will further test this idea, especially on populations other than college students.

Lawrence Farwell uses a technique that he describes as *brain fingerprinting*, which uses technology to determine whether specific information is stored in a person's brain (Knight, 2004). This technique relies on examining brain waves in search of event-related potentials (ERPs), a well-documented phenomenon in brain research. The examiner looks for the P300 brain wave, so called because it appears about 300 milliseconds after a stimulus that holds some special significance for the person. As soon as a new technology is developed, however, evidence suggests that it is subject to some of the same countermeasures that have defeated traditional polygraphs (Rosenfeld, Soskins, Bosh, & Ryan, 2004).

We have seen that physiological components of emotion are important in describing our own emotions and the emotional reactions we perceive in others. Unfortunately, the focus on physiological components has led to the controversial lie detector. As we will see, we must consider other components of emotions to develop a more complete picture.

# REVIEW SUMMARY

1. **Emotion** is the awareness of a feeling elicited in response to an environmental stimulus, accompanied by physiological changes and certain overt behaviors such as facial expressions.

2. Darwin proposed that emotions may be innate behaviors, passed on genetically, that help organisms adapt to their environments.

3. The **commonsense view of emotions** states the sequence of events in emotional responding as emotional stimulus → emotion → physiological changes.

4. The **James-Lange theory** states that physiological changes precede and actually create emotions. The sequence of events in emotional responding is emotional stimulus → physiological changes → emotion.

5. The **Cannon-Bard theory** stresses the role of the thalamus in simultaneously relaying emotional input to the cortex and the sympathetic nervous system.

6. There are some physiological differences among the emotions such as increased heart rate in anger. *Blushing* is elicited by a number of circumstances that usually involve concern about how others evaluate the person.

7. *Alexithymia* is a marked inability to experience and express emotions.

8. The **polygraph** records physiological measurements thought to indicate deception. Physiological changes can, however, result from anxiety, anger, or fear. Failure to recognize possible causes of arousal can incorrectly identify people as being deceptive (false positives).

# ✓ CHECK YOUR PROGRESS

1. What is Darwin's view on the functions of emotions in animals and human beings?

2. What evidence did Darwin use to support his view of the functions of emotion?

3. You are walking in the forest and see a bear. What happens at this point according to the James-Lange theory?

   a. physiological changes followed by fear
   b. fear followed by physiological changes
   c. physiological changes and fear simultaneously
   d. physiological changes and context appraisal followed by fear

4. According to Joseph LeDoux's research, which part of the brain plays an especially important role in learning a fear reaction?

   a. amygdala
   b. cerebellum
   c. hypothalamus
   d. corpus callosum

5. How do researchers elicit emotional reactions in research designed to study physiological changes associated with different emotions?

**6.** When a person is experiencing happiness, we are likely to see evidence of elevated activation in the

   **a.** cerebellum.
   **b.** hippocampus.
   **c.** left hemisphere.
   **d.** right hemisphere.

**7.** Which of these is most characteristic of a person who exhibits alexithymia?

   **a.** in a constant state of fear
   **b.** can decode emotions from voice only
   **c.** has difficulty finding words to discuss emotions
   **d.** reacts very strongly with anger to any provocation

**8.** What is the *literal* meaning of the word polygraph?

   **a.** lie detector
   **b.** many writings
   **c.** deception recorder
   **d.** physiological detector

**9.** Your grandfather recently suffered a brain injury. You notice that he has difficulty recognizing faces and interpreting emotion from tone of voice. Based on these observations, you suspect that the damage occurred in the

   **a.** hippocampus.
   **b.** hypothalamus.
   **c.** left hemisphere.
   **d.** right hemisphere.

**10.** A convict wants to "cut a deal" with the prosecutor to reduce his sentence. The prosecutor asks the convict to agree to testify in another case and take a polygraph examination to ensure that the testimony is truthful. The convict intends to lie during the polygraph examination and in court by using countermeasures. How might he try to keep his lies from being discovered?

   **a.** He will answer all questions with one-word answers.
   **b.** He will count back from 100 by sevens during the examination.
   **c.** He will take his cues from the examiner's tone of voice during the examination.
   **d.** He will ask difficult questions to be repeated so that he can collect himself and lie more effectively.

**ANSWERS: 1.** According to Darwin, emotions involve expressions that communicate information about present or future events that help organisms adapt to their environments. **2.** Darwin pointed to animals' baring their teeth during anger to support his view on emotion. **3.** a **4.** a **5.** One method of eliciting emotions in order to study physiological differences is to ask research participants to follow muscle-by-muscle instructions to create facial expressions associated with different emotions. **6.** c **7.** c **8.** b **9.** d **10.** b

# THE EXPRESSIVE COMPONENTS OF EMOTIONS

For a research project, you are asked to look at photographs of facial expressions and select the emotion exhibited from a list. The task is easy, and you finish quickly. As you leave, you ask the researcher about the purpose of the research. She says that you participated in a study of the universality of emotional expressions. *Are the same emotional expressions recognized around the world?*

The face is a like a bulletin board. How would you know that a friend is afraid, angry, or happy? Consistent with evolutionary theory, the face plays a key role in communicating emotion, so it is not surprising that a great deal of research has focused on two related questions: Are the same emotions recognized around the world? and How many emotions exist?

## Universal Elements in the Facial Expression of Emotion

Evidence for the universal occurrence of facial expressions of emotion comes from several sources. Observations of the emotional expressions of infants show that even infants born blind and deaf display the same facial expressions in similar situations (Galati, Scherer, & Ricci-Bitti, 1997). For example, one emotion observed in babies is disgust. This expression may have evolved from sensory experiences that kept animals from eating spoiled food (identified from an offensive smell). Eventually disgust came under

**TABLE 6-5**

## Percent Agreement across Cultures in Recognizing Basic Emotions

| | Happiness | Surprise | Sadness | Fear | Disgust | Anger |
|---|---|---|---|---|---|---|
| Germany | 93 | 87 | 83 | 86 | 61 | 71 |
| Italy | 97 | 92 | 81 | 82 | 89 | 72 |
| Japan | 90 | 94 | 87 | 65 | 60 | 67 |
| Sumatra | 69 | 78 | 91 | 70 | 70 | 70 |
| Turkey | 87 | 90 | 76 | 76 | 74 | 79 |
| United States | 95 | 92 | 92 | 84 | 86 | 81 |

**Source:** Ekman et al. (1987).

some voluntary control; facial expressions of disgust now occur as responses to circumstances that have less to do with the taste of foods and a lot to do with reactions to moral offenses, foul language, or poor hygiene (Rozin, Lowery, & Ebert, 1994).

Paul Ekman (2003) and his associates (1987) asked thousands of people around the world to play a game of "name that emotion" (see Table 6-5). They concluded that people from Western and Eastern literate cultures, including Japan and the United States, associate similar emotions with certain facial expressions. In fact, even people from an isolated preliterate culture in New Guinea readily identified photographs of various emotions, although they exhibited some difficulty distinguishing fear from surprise (Ekman, 1994; Izard, 1994). These people could not have learned the meanings of facial expressions through the media. The researchers reversed the study design and found that the people of New Guinea posed facial expressions that were understandable to Western observers. More recent research involving people from the United States, India, and Japan reveals that although emotions tend to be recognized across the globe, it is easier for people to recognize emotions when they view people from their own culture (Elfenbein, Mandal, Ambady, Harizuka, & Kumar, 2002).

As we will see later, the rest of the body is often involved in communicating emotions, yet much of the research has focused on the face. What's more, research described thus far has used static photographs rather than dynamic portrayals of emotions. In an intriguing study, researchers used videotaped expressions of emotions (for example, anger and sadness) that were described in the literature of Hindu people of India some 2,000 years ago (Hejmadi, Davidson, & Rozin, 2000). These dynamic portrayals involved the face and body, especially the hands. College students from the United States and India identified the emotions at levels that were well above chance. Thus the evidence demonstrates that there are universal emotions that are commonly presented and recognized across the globe.

To date, no one has found people who smile when they are disgusted or frown when overjoyed. These findings support the notion that humans have innate, genetically wired templates for expressing different emotions. "It makes sense that there should be similarities across cultures. Human beings belong to the same species: our brains, our bodies, our autonomic nervous systems, our hormones, and our sense organs are similarly constructed" (Ellsworth, 1994, p. 25).

 6.1

**How Many Emotions Are There?**   The negative emotions—including anger, disgust, and fear—seem to have distinctive facial signals. By contrast, the facial expressions of positive emotions are more blurred. Why? From an evolutionary perspective, it is probably sufficient to know that an emotion is positive without knowing the specific emotion.

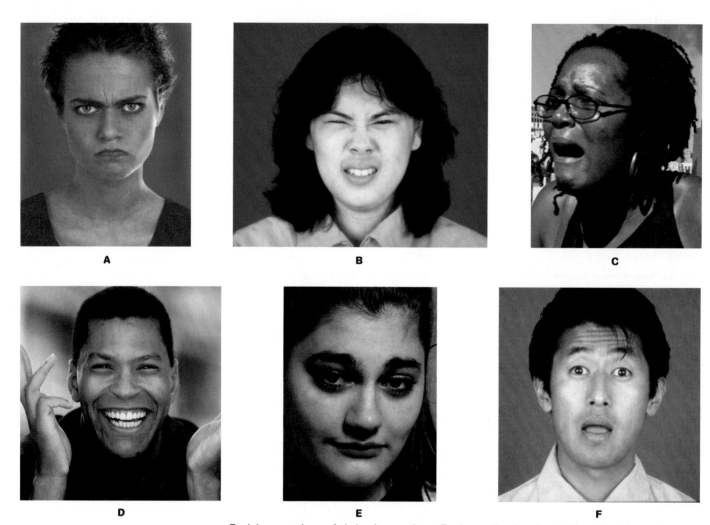

Facial expressions of six basic emotions. Each emotion involves a blueprint of movements of several sets of muscles: the brow and forehead; eyes, eyelids, and the nose; and the lower face.
A. Anger: Eyes have a penetrating stare; vertical crease in the brow; lids are tensed; lips are pressed together or opened and pushed forward.
B. Disgust: Raised cheeks, wrinkled nose; lower lip either pulled up or lowered and slightly protruding; upper lip is raised; lower eyelid is pushed up, and brows are lowered.
C. Fear: Eyebrows are raised and drawn together; wrinkles in the middle of the forehead; eyes are open and tense; mouth is open; lips may be drawn back tightly.
D. Happiness: Raised cheeks; raised corners of the mouth and crow's feet (wrinkles from the outer corner of the eyes); teeth sometimes are exposed.
E. Sadness: Uplifted inner corner of the eyebrows; lowered upper eyelids; raised corners of the upper eyelid; downturned lips.
F. Surprise: Raised brow; the eyes are open wide; dropped jaw; wrinkled forehead; open mouth.

There are at least six emotions recognized everywhere: anger, disgust, fear, happiness, sadness, and surprise. Agreement is highest for facial expressions of happiness (Elfenbein & Ambady, 2002). There is some disagreement about the universality of other emotions such as contempt, guilt, interest, and shame (Ekman, 1992; Matsumoto, 1992), and as we will see later, some models of emotion suggest that there are more than six primary emotions. Recently, researchers reported a high degree of reliability in identifying the emotion of pride, which participants distinguished from related emotions such as happiness. The expression of pride consists of a small smile, head tilted slightly back, visible expanded posture, and arms raised above the head or hands on hips. An

Source: Reprinted with the permission of Psi Chi.

"HERE ARE THE SIX PRIMARY EMOTIONS RECOGNIZED AROUND THE WORLD."

"RESEARCHERS HAVE RECENTLY DISCOVERED A NEW EMOTION...."

interesting finding was that this recognition was reduced when the expression was restricted to the head and shoulders, and it was not greater than chance when the expression was restricted to the face (Tracy & Robins, 2004).

The labels we use to describe emotions are a shorthand for a number of processes and responses that occur during an emotion: physiological changes, facial expressions, appraisal of the preceding event, memories, and expectations. What's more, emotions shade into one another, making it difficult to agree on the specific label for an emotion. When does impatience become anger? Within each of the basic emotions, the related facial expressions share certain core properties; thus they can be viewed as variations within a family reflecting the level of intensity (level of arousal) of an emotion, whether the emotion is controlled, whether it is simulated or spontaneous, and the specifics of events that provoked the emotion (Ekman, 1993). For example, there is a questioning surprise, a dumbfounded surprise, and a dazed surprise. The intensity of anger is conveyed in 60 facial expressions, which range from minor annoyance to uncontrollable rage.

Robert Plutchik (1980, 2001) has developed a visual vocabulary that allows him to talk about and compare emotions. He proposes eight basic emotions: joy, trust, fear, surprise, sadness, disgust, anger, and anticipation. These primary emotions can be viewed as four pairs of polar opposites, and each emotion exists in varying degrees of intensity. These primary emotions are building blocks that can be combined to create more complex emotions, just as primary colors are combined to form different hues. The result is a three-dimensional structure consisting of eight groupings of primary emotions arranged in tiers representing degrees of intensity and purity.

Each color in Figure 6-14 represents a different emotion; anger is presented as red, terror as green. Each color is brightest at the top of the figure; the brighter the color, the more intense the emotion. If you are so angry that you are throwing things against the wall and screaming, you are in a rage, which is at the top of the anger section. If someone just cut in front of you in line at the supermarket and you are not in a hurry, you might be merely annoyed. The emotions at the top level exist in pure form; those at lower levels can be combined to create other feelings. For example, combining fear and surprise yields awe; hostility is a blend of anger and disgust. Opposites such as fear and anger may not blend at all; a person experiencing both may feel pulled in two directions at once.

**The Facial Feedback Hypothesis.** Recall the emphasis Darwin placed on facial expressions of emotions. The **facial feedback hypothesis** is an extension of Darwin's (1872/1965) view that the intensity of an emotion is strengthened when it is accompanied by muscular activity and weakened when it is not accompanied by such activity (Cacioppo, Bush, & Tassinary, 1992; Izard, 1990). The facial feedback hypothesis states that feedback from facial expression affects emotional expression and behavior.

Darwin based his views on speculation and conjecture. How could a researcher demonstrate that facial features can influence our emotions?

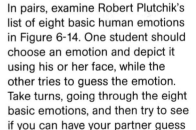

**STUDY TIP**

In pairs, examine Robert Plutchik's list of eight basic human emotions in Figure 6-14. One student should choose an emotion and depict it using his or her face, while the other tries to guess the emotion. Take turns, going through the eight basic emotions, and then try to see if you can have your partner guess some of the modified emotions listed as "changes in intensity."

**facial feedback hypothesis**
Hypothesis that making a certain facial expression will produce the corresponding emotion

**FIGURE 6-14** The eight basic human emotions and some combinations, according to Robert Plutchik.

**Source:** Plutchik (2001).

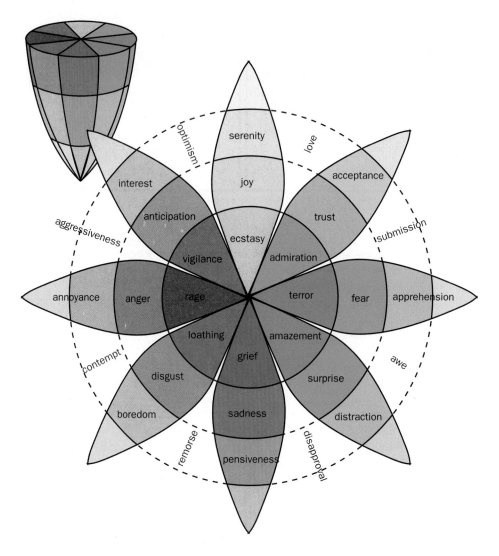

## Psychological Detective

Suppose you have volunteered to be a participant in an experiment on motor activity. You are sitting with a pencil clenched between your teeth. A few minutes ago, your task was to cross out some letters. Now you are judging the humor in a series of cartoons. This task does not seem related to motor ability; humor is more of an emotional response. How does holding a pencil in your teeth relate to the facial feedback hypothesis? Think about this question, analyze the situation, and write down some answers before reading further.

College students were told that they were going to participate in a study of psychomotor ability "using parts of their body that they would normally not use for such tasks" (Strack, Martin, & Stepper, 1988, p. 770). The students held pencils in their mouths and then engaged in tasks that required writing. One group held their pencils with their lips, which prevented use of the muscles involved in smiling. Another group held the pencils in their teeth, which allowed them to use those muscles.

The dependent variable (see Chapter 1) was students' ratings of the funniness of a series of *Far Side* cartoons. If the facial feedback hypothesis is correct, students who held pencils in their teeth and could smile should have rated the cartoons as funnier than those who held pencils in their lips and could not smile. The results confirmed this prediction: The cartoons were rated as funnier by the participants who held the pencils with their teeth than by those who held the pencils with their lips.

A second study confirmed and extended this finding (Martin, Harlow, & Strack, 1992). Participants who held their faces in an expression of happiness while they read a story rated the story more positively than those who had angry faces while reading the story. The level of arousal also influenced the intensity of the emotion: Participants who had exercised for 90 seconds before reading the story had stronger emotions than participants who had not exercised. A recent extension and replication of this research lends further credence to the findings. People who were asked to hold a pencil in their mouths to facilitate smiling not only reported more positive affect, they also exhibited greater physiological arousal compared to those who held a pencil in ways that inhibited smiling (Soussignan, 2002). There are two versions of this theory. One says that manipulating facial muscles brings forth emotional experiences in all of its aspects; the other says that feedback from the facial muscles affects the emotion's intensity.

**Display Rules: The Effects of Culture.** Even if certain emotions are universal, culture can influence their expression. Some differences in emotional expression can be accounted for by **display rules**—cultural norms that tell us which emotions to display, to whom, and when (Ekman, 1993). Which emotions we display depend on the situation and who is present. For example, only the really brave or independently wealthy fail to smile when the boss tells a joke. These requirements or expectations can lead us to exhibit emotions we may not actually feel or fail to exhibit emotions we do feel.

Paul Ekman showed a stress-inducing film of surgery to male college students in Tokyo, Japan, and Berkeley, California (Ekman & Friesen, 1971). At first, the participants watched the film while alone; later, a scientist (dressed in a lab coat) entered the room and sat down while the participants watched the film. Videotapes recorded by a hidden camera revealed that students of both countries exhibited similar distressed expressions when they were alone. In addition, they reported similar feelings and had similar physiological responses. When talking to the researcher, however, the Japanese students remained composed, whereas the American students openly displayed their feelings. Why did the two groups behave differently? Compared with Americans, the Japanese are more sensitive to status differences (Barnlund, 1989); their display rules discourage them from displaying negative emotions in the presence of individuals of higher status. Thus they expressed the same emotions as the Americans when they were alone, but they did not exhibit those emotions when the scientist was present.

Other examples of display rules abound. For example, the Utku Eskimos strongly condemn the feeling of anger, whereas certain Arab groups view a man's failure to respond with anger as dishonorable (Ellsworth, 1994). Display rules also influence the perceptions of emotions in others. For example, compared with Americans, Japanese people perceive less intense emotions whether viewing faces of Americans or Japanese (Matsumoto & Ekman, 1989).

**Smiling.** Smiling is a social act; we rarely smile when we are alone (Provine, 1997, 2000). It is such a prominent social signal that we can recognize a smile 300 feet away (Blum, 1998). Smiles can reflect enjoyment resulting from amusement, pleasure, praise, or relief. We also smile, however, when we are not experiencing true enjoyment: A "false smile" is made deliberately to convince another that enjoyment is occurring; a "masking smile" conceals negative emotion; a "miserable smile" acknowledges a willingness to tolerate unpleasant circumstances (Ekman, Davidson, & Friesen, 1990). Thus at times the universal facial expression of happiness can be deceiving.

## Psychological Detective

Think of a time you have smiled when you were not experiencing enjoyment. How might that smile differ from a smile of true enjoyment? Give this question some thought, and write down your answer before you read further.

**display rules**
Culturally specific rules for which emotions to display, to whom, and when

**FIGURE 6-15** Two major muscle groups are involved in a smile. The genuine or Duchenne smile of enjoyment involves the orbicularis oculi muscles, which wrap around the eyes and crinkle the outer corner of the eyes. The zygomatic muscles run from the cheekbone to the corner of the mouth and pull the lips up.

**Source:** Martini and Bartholomew (2000).

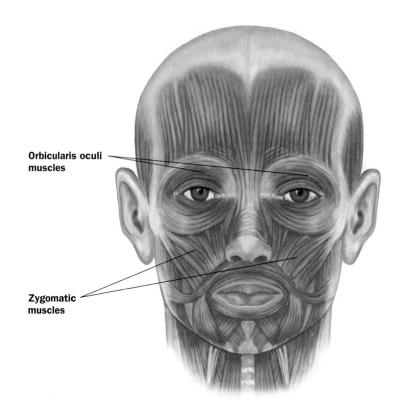

Orbicularis oculi muscles

Zygomatic muscles

A French physician, Guillaume Duchenne de Boulogne (1806–1875), suggested that genuine smiles of enjoyment result from contraction of two facial muscle groups (see Figure 6-15): the *zygomatic muscles* and the *orbicularis oculi muscles*. Although at least 18 different smiles can be identified (for example, cruel, false, and polite smiles), only the *Duchenne smile* reveals true enjoyment. Duchenne noticed that when people put on a phony smile, they smile with their cheeks, not their eyes. Why? The orbicularis oculi (which wraps around the eye) is not under voluntary control, so smiles of faked enjoyment do not activate this muscle. Now you understand why you have difficulty smiling naturally when photographers ask you to "Say cheese" (Damasio, 1994). The zygomatic muscles pull up the lip corners toward the cheekbone. The orbicularis oculi muscles pull skin above and below the eye toward the eyeball, resulting in these changes in appearance (see Figure 6-16): The cheeks are pulled up, the skin below the eye may bag

**FIGURE 6-16** Paul Ekman demonstrates the difference between a faked smile and a genuine (Duchenne) smile of enjoyment. Can you tell the difference? One key to differentiating a genuine smile from a faked smile is to observe the area near the eyes. Crow's feet appear with a genuine smile (right).

**Source:** Michael Klauseman/NYT Pictures.

or bulge, the lower eyelid moves up, and wrinkles known as *crow's feet* may appear at the outer corner of the eye socket (Frank & Ekman, 1993). Duchenne smiles last longer than faked smiles; their occurrence is related to ratings of enjoyment, whereas the occurrence of other smiles is not (Ekman, Friesen, & O'Sullivan, 1988).

Smiling provides another example of the operation of display rules. If you walk into a store anywhere in the United States, you expect a smile from the clerk. That smile is a greeting that says "You are welcome to shop in this establishment and we want your business." But a smile is not the cultural norm in this situation in Korea. Consequently, Korean business owners in the United States who fail to smile (following their culture's display rules) are often perceived as hostile, although that surely is not their intent (Lindsey & Beach, 2004).

## Nonverbal Communication

Imagine spending an hour among people who speak another language. You might be surprised that you can learn a lot about people even if you do not speak their language. You would find it almost impossible not to communicate. For example, your quizzical facial expression right now sends a message that you are experiencing doubt. When we communicate, intentionally or unintentionally, by using body movements, gestures, facial expressions, eye contact, personal space, and touching rather than words, we are using **nonverbal communication** (Knapp & Hall, 1997; Lindzey & Beach, 2004).

Tone of voice and posture can convey information that is different from what we verbalize. Someone who claims to be fine but is sobbing is viewed differently from when he or she is smiling. Consider the word *no*. It can be a simple, unemotional response to a question. If it is uttered while you are stomping your foot and pounding the table, however, the meaning becomes "Absolutely not!" Add a rising inflection, and it is converted into a question. A crooked smile and a slight hand wave alters the meaning to disbelief (Ruchlis, 1990). Thus nonverbal cues can overshadow the literal meaning of our words (Archer & Akert, 1984).

**Body Language.** In addition to facial expressions, we communicate messages about our feelings through gaze, gestures, posture, and gait. The following examples can convey emotion: the "high five," handshakes, and putting a hand on a person's shoulder. We will briefly discuss several types of body language: emblems, illustrators, regulators, and adaptors.

*Emblems* are nonverbal gestures and movements that have well-understood definitions (Archer, 1997); they are also called *symbolic gestures* (see Figure 6-17). We use emblems intentionally to communicate a specific meaning (Richmond & McCroskey, 1995). Nod your head and most people know you mean "yes." There is general agreement on emblems for "I warn you" and "It's cold" (Kleinke, 1986), although emblems may not have the same meaning across cultures (Ekman, Friesen, & Bear, 1984).

Ask a restaurant server in southern Italy for something not on the menu and the likely response is not a side-to-side head shake but a quick upward head toss often accompanied by a "tsskk" sound. Winston Churchill, prime minister of Great Britain during World War II, used the "V for victory" (palm-forward) sign. Change the gesture to the palm-back position, and it becomes a gross insult (Morris, 1994).

*Illustrators* are nonverbal gestures or movements made while speaking that accent or emphasize words. Unlike emblems, however, they do not communicate specific meanings. Illustrators such as waving your arms or pounding a table may enhance your words, but they do not stand alone (Ekman et al., 1984). Illustrators clarify verbal statements or a position by drawing a picture or pointing. They also communicate intensity of emotion: Active gestures indicate strong intensity, whereas gestures such as shrugging indicate weak emotional involvement.

*Regulators* are actions such as eye contact and head nods that coordinate the flow of communication among two or more people. They are used to begin conversations and to signal when a listener is ready to speak and a speaker is ready to listen. The most common regulator for initiating an interaction is the handshake.

Nonverbal cues like the stance and expression of this police officer can arouse specific emotions.

**nonverbal communication**
Communication that involves movements, gestures, facial expressions, eye contact, use of personal space, and touching

Former British Prime Minister Winston Churchill's famous "V for victory" sign can take on very different meanings if the position of the palm is reversed.

**FIGURE 6-17** Gestures that have specific meanings are called *emblems;* the meaning of these gestures may vary from culture to culture.

**Sources:** Aronson et al. (2002); Ekman et al. (1984); Morris (1994).

**"I am impatient."** Frequently occurs when we have been kept waiting or when we are impatient because something is not happening. Considered a symbolic form of "running away," this emblem might be associated with the urge to get up and go. In evolutionary terms, our hands were once our front feet. Rhythmic tapping of the foot has the same meaning. The use of these gestures is widespread.

**"Shame on you!"** One forefinger is rubbed up and down the other, which symbolizes friction. Used in North America.

**"Everything is fine", or "good."** The ring gesture displayed with the thumb and forefinger tips has been known for 2,000 years. It is used throughout North America and Europe. In Germany, Greece, Turkey, the Middle East, and parts of South America, it symbolizes an orifice and can be a sneering insult. In Belgium and France, the ring symbolizes a zero, indicating that an individual or an object is worthless. In parts of southern Italy, it is a vulgar expression for rectum. In Japan, the ring is a symbol for a coin, and the gesture is usually asking for money or commenting on the cost of something.

**"No good."** The thumb is jerked downward several times or may be held in an inverted position. Originated in ancient Rome to represent the stabbing of a defeated gladiator. When the audience wanted the man to be killed, they thrust their thumbs downward as if plunging a sword into his body. Its use is widespread.

**The "hand-purse" gesture:** This gesture is formed by straightening the fingers and thumb of one hand and bringing them together so the tips touch, pointing upwards. This gesture has no clear meaning in American culture. However, in Italy, it means "What are you trying to say?"; in Spain, it means "good"; in Tunisia, it means "Slow down"; and in Malta, it means "You may seem good, but you are really bad."

*Adaptors* (or *manipulators*) are movements or objects manipulated for a purpose; we use these when we find ourselves in a particular mood or situation. They include what we do with our bodies (scratching, grooming) or with objects (doodling, fiddling with a pencil or pen). Adaptors have no specific meaning, although they generally increase when people become uncomfortable (Ekman et al., 1984).

**Paralanguage.** A great deal of nonverbal communication occurs by way of vocal expression such as tone of voice, rate of speech, pauses, sighs, loudness, emphasis, and even silence. Silence, for example, frequently accompanies sadness, shame, guilt, fear, and disgust (Scherer & Wallbott, 1994). **Paralanguage** involves communication above and beyond the specific spoken words. "It is not what you say, it is how you say it. And the *how* is conveyed by paralanguage" (Weaver, 1993, p. 269).

Emotions are often associated with shifts in tone of voice. The frequency (pitch; see Chapter 3) of vocalizations increases in many emotions. Although emotions presented at similar levels of arousal (intensity) cannot be distinguished from one another, utterances associated with various emotions are usually presented at different intensity levels. These differences allow us to recognize different emotions from the voice alone at better than chance levels. Sadness and anger are the easiest emotions to recognize, followed by fear (Pittam & Scherer, 1993).

**paralanguage**
Communication that involves aspects of speech such as rate of talking and tone of voice, but not the words used

## Gender Effects

A frequently asked question about emotion is, Do men and women differ in their emotional reactions or their ability to detect (decode) emotions in others? One approach to answering this question involves use of the *Interpersonal Perception Test (IPT),* which consists of 30 brief videotaped scenes used to evaluate and teach forms of communication. For example, one scene shows a man telling two versions of his life: a true version and a fabricated one. Viewers are asked to determine which version is the lie and which the truth (Costanzo & Archer, 1989, 1991). Across ages, cultures, and stimulus persons, women are more accurate than men in decoding emotion from nonverbal cues offered by the face, body, and voice (Hall, 1984). Objective observations support the common stereotype that, compared with men, women exhibit a greater degree of facial expressivity of positive and negative emotions except anger (Brody & Hall, 1993; Grossman & Wood, 1993; Kring & Gordon, 1998; Wang, McCarthy, Song, & LaBar, 2005).

In one study, researchers asked men and women to generate verbal descriptions of their anticipated feelings and those of another person for each of 20 scenarios (Barrett, Lane, Sechrest, & Schwartz, 2000). The responses were scored for the degree to which discrete emotion terms were used in describing self and others. "Women displayed more emotional awareness than did men . . . women used emotion language to represent their own and others' emotional experience with more differentiation and complexity" (p. 1031). What's more, the results were not due to any differences in verbal ability between men and women.

One possible explanation for these differences is that women are expected to be nurturing and are often the primary caregivers in the family and workplace (for example, a nurse or teacher). These roles and occupations require sensitivity to others' needs and emotional expressions; men's typical roles are less likely to emphasize emotional responsiveness (Brody & Hall, 1993; Grossman & Wood, 1993). There are also differences in infancy and preschool years: A greater variety of emotions are displayed to, and discussed with, infant and preschool girls than boys (Brody & Hall, 1993).

Researchers have also examined facial muscle differences in men and women exposed to slides of positive and negative stimuli. Women exhibit a higher level of facial muscle movement than men, which suggests that the self-reports on emotional responsiveness are accurate. These differences occurred when the participants were given no clear instructions concerning the appropriate emotional response; thus participants probably relied on their knowledge of the typical roles that men and women engage in. When participants were given instructions that associated either an increase or a decrease in emotional responsiveness with psychological adjustment, there were no differences between men and women.

Neuroscientists have also investigated possible differences between men and women in judging emotions from facial expressions (Gur et al., 1995). Volunteers judged whether the face of a man or a woman showed happiness or sadness. Men and women were almost infallible when judging facial expressions of happiness. The results were different, however, when they judged sad faces. Women correctly identified a sad face 90% of the time whether presented by a man or a woman; in contrast, men recognized sadness on the faces of men 90% of the time (same as the women) but were only 70% correct when judging sadness on women's faces. The findings make sense in evolutionary terms; men would need to be especially vigilant about men's faces, lest they miss early hints that they were about to be attacked (Begley, 1995).

## REVIEW SUMMARY

**1.** There is strong evidence for universal recognition of at least six basic emotions: anger, disgust, fear, happiness, sadness, and surprise.

**2.** Robert Plutchik has offered a model of how emotions can be combined to yield blends that differ in intensity.

**3.** The **facial feedback hypothesis** contends that feedback from facial muscles affects our experience of emotion.

**4. Display rules** are culturally specific prescriptions that tell us which emotions to display, to whom, and when. Such rules account for some cross-cultural differences in the expression of emotion.

**5.** A real smile of enjoyment, the *Duchenne smile,* involves activation of muscles that are not activated during faked smiles.

**6. Nonverbal communication** involves communication through body language, movements, and gestures. There are four major categories of body language: emblems, illustrators, regulators, and adaptors. The meaning of certain gestures varies with the culture.

7. **Paralanguage** involves communication through tone of voice, rate of speech, pauses, sighs, and loudness.

8. Compared with men, women report more emotional experiences and greater comfort with emotions. One possible explanation is that women's roles and occupations tend to require greater sensitivity to emotional expressions in others.

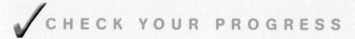

## ✓ CHECK YOUR PROGRESS

1. Which emotion is recognized most easily across cultures?
   a. fear
   b. anger
   c. disgust
   d. happiness

2. Describe the key elements of Plutchik's model of emotions.

3. Which of the following is the best indication that a person who is smiling is experiencing true enjoyment?
   a. crow's feet
   b. raised eyebrows
   c. right-hemisphere activation
   d. increased blood flow to the amygdala

4. You are taking part in an enjoyable experiment—watching comedy movies. In which condition will you find the movies funniest?
   a. You hold a pencil in your lips.
   b. You hold a pencil in your teeth.
   c. You wrinkle your nose while watching the movies.
   d. You wrinkle your forehead while watching the movies.

5. Give an example of each category of body language: emblems, regulators, adaptors, and illustrators.

6. How do emotion researchers explain the universality of facial expressions?
   a. Anthropologists have passed these expressions from culture to culture.
   b. Facial expressions are learned via the same methods around the world.
   c. These facial expressions help people adapt by communicating information.

   d. Exposure to media, especially cable television, has spread these expressions around the world.

7. Which emotion does Plutchik include among his proposed eight basic emotions?
   a. fury
   b. responsibility
   c. anticipation
   d. disappointment

8. Which statement reflects a core idea of the facial feedback hypothesis?
   a. Men do not express emotion via the face.
   b. Emotional facial expressions are similar all over the world.
   c. Information from facial muscles intensifies emotional experiences.
   d. When one facial expression occurs, we quickly register its opposite on the face.

9. If you do not know whether you should cry at the movies while visiting friends in Japan, you may be confused about
   a. display rules in Japan.
   b. paralanguage in Japan.
   c. the use of doublespeak in Japan.
   d. unconscious communication in Japan.

10. What type of nonverbal communication are you using if you look away after you are done speaking?
   a. emblem
   b. adaptor
   c. regulator
   d. illustrator

**ANSWERS: 1.** d **2.** Plutchik proposed that eight basic emotions can be viewed as polar opposites; each emotion exists in varying degrees of intensity. These primary emotions are building blocks that can be combined into more complex emotions. **3.** a **4.** b **5.** Emblems—nodding your head to indicate "yes"; Regulators—eye contact and head nods that coordinate the flow of communication in a conversation; Adaptors—doodling, fiddling with a pen or pencil; Illustrators—waving your arms or pounding a table to enhance your words. **6.** c **7.** c **8.** c **9.** a **10.** c

# THE COGNITIVE COMPONENTS OF EMOTION

Being a parent is a tough job. Make no mistake: Marie and Joe's teenager is well behaved, respectful, and earns good grades. In their state a person can obtain a driver's license at age 16, which Marie and Joe insist is too young. On a typical summer night, their daughter is out with friends. Marie and Joe hold a vigil for her safe return. As the family curfew approaches, they pace as several thoughts run through their minds. They are not sure what they are feeling. Is it anger or is it fear? When their teenager arrives home safely, they feel relief. Does that mean that they were anxious, fearful, or what? *How do we determine which emotions we are experiencing?*

Among the situations that can elicit emotional responses are interpersonal actions and natural events such as thunder. But does the event itself lead to emotional responses? Does our language play a role in emotion? And how does our interpretation of an event influence our emotions? These are some of the topics we explore as we continue our study of emotions.

## The Language of Emotion

The words we use to describe our experiences are important. In fact, cultures and languages vary in the number of terms they use to describe emotion. English has a larger word pool than other languages. More than 2,000 English words describe emotions, compared with 1,500 words in Dutch, 230 in Malay, and 7 among the Chewong, a society of hunter-gatherers living in the rain forest of Malaysia (Russell, 1991).

Some differences in the words used to describe emotions are especially worthy of note. For example, the Japanese translation for the English word *depression*, *yuutsu*, does not capture the English meaning. How do researchers know this? They asked people in different cultures to provide free associations to the words under investigation (Russell & Sato, 1995).

Some English words describe categories of emotion that have no equivalents in other languages; other languages have emotion words with no equivalents in English. For example, in English we distinguish apprehension, dread, horror, and terror as degrees of fear. The Australian aboriginal language uses one word, *gurakadj* (Russell, 1991). The English language distinction between shame and embarrassment is not made in Japanese. Although the Tahitians have 46 words for types of anger (English has *annoyance*, *rage*, *irritation*, and so forth), they have no concept of sadness. Of course, the fact that a language has no word for an emotion does not mean that the emotion does not occur in that culture, only that the emotion is not represented by a single term (Ekman, 1993).

There is no English word for certain emotions found elsewhere; the German word *schadenfreude* (literally, "harm joy") refers to the pleasurable feelings one person derives from another person's misfortune. The Japanese word *ijirashii* refers to feelings associated with seeing someone praiseworthy overcoming an obstacle (Russell, 1991). The Japanese word *amae* literally means "sweet dependency," and specifies an interdependent relationship involving the expectation of acceptance and care by others (Matsumoto, 1996). The importance of amae in Japan exemplifies how emotional life is shaped by culture. In community-oriented cultures like Japan, emotions focus not on the individual's needs and abilities but on feelings that emphasize links among people.

**The Schachter and Singer Appraisal Model.**    These language differences suggest that how we think about events may affect emotional experiences. Along similar lines, Stanley Schachter (1922–1997) and Jerome Singer (1962, 2001) proposed a theory that stresses physiological processes and the evaluation of context as determinants of emotion. According to Schachter and Singer, physiological arousal is an *undifferentiated* state that can be given a number of labels. The labels we use to describe our emotions depend on our immediate environment and what is on our mind at the particular moment.

How could you test this theory's predictions? Creating a context in which a specific emotion is experienced seems easy enough. People could interact with a confederate of the experimenter who pretends to be experiencing a particular emotion such as euphoria (happiness). The confederate's behavior creates a context that suggests an interpretation of the events. We need to find some way to create the physiological changes in each test participant.

The emotion this person is feeling is probably clear; however, we are not sure what led to this particular emotional reaction. If the same situation occurred to another person, the response could be quite different, depending on how the situation was appraised.

Injections of epinephrine (adrenaline), a substance that increases heart rate and creates generalized arousal (sympathetic activation), were used to create physiological changes similar to those experienced during a genuine emotional reaction. To disguise the drug's effects, participants in the experimental groups were told that they were receiving a vitamin supplement called Suproxin, which would produce no noticeable effects. Then each participant was put in a room with a confederate who acted either euphoric or very angry. The control participants who were told what physiological effects would occur did not experience these emotions.

Because the participants in the experimental group could not attribute their physiological arousal to any external causes, they attributed it to the presence of an emotional reaction. When asked what type of emotion they were experiencing, the individuals who had interacted with the happy confederate said they were happy; those who interacted with the angry confederate reported being angry. Thus the context in which an emotion is experienced plays a role in deciding which emotion is felt.

**Other Appraisal Theories of Emotion.**    In the 1960s, several psychologists developed similar theories to suggest that emotions result from the way we interpret or appraise our environment (Ellsworth, 1994; Roseman, Dhawan, Rettek, Naidu, & Thapa, 1995). These appraisal theories elaborate Schachter and Singer's claim that differences in emotion result from differences in how perceivers interpret their environment. If people interpret their environment differently, they will experience different emotions. For example, a specific situation does not produce shame; a person's interpretation of an event produces shame (Lewis, 1993a). Sorrow is different from anger because people see the situation differently. What separates appraisal theories from Schachter and Singer's efforts is that these theories attempt to define the kinds of interpretation that contribute to different emotions (Ellsworth, 1994; Lazarus, 1994).

Similar emotions appear in most cultures because events that occur are similar, as are appraisals of those events (Lazarus, 1994). Observers distinguish which emotion someone is experiencing not so much from the expression as from knowledge of which emotions are likely to occur in a given situation. Different cultures emphasize or deemphasize certain emotions, however. Suppose two people from different cultures have experienced a failure in school. In one culture, it is not desirable to blame failure on lack of effort. In the other culture, it is not desirable to blame failure on lack of ability. In the first case, to suggest that failure is due to lack of effort can lead to shame or anger. In the second case, such an explanation has little or no emotional spinoff; lack of effort might even provide a socially acceptable excuse for failure. Thus cultural values that define what is offensive or threatening shape the appraisal of events and the emotions experienced (Lazarus, 1994).

Psychologist Robert Zajonc (1980) has argued, in contrast, that emotion does not even require prior cognition; the two are basically separate. This approach makes some sense from an evolutionary perspective because emotions preceded a cognitive response in evolution; therefore we do not need cognitive appraisal in order to experience some emotional reactions. One of the best examples of emotion without cognition is the rapid fear response that we discussed earlier in this chapter.

# The Development of Emotion

Emotions in infancy range from general distress to pleasure. Joyful expression emerges as infants smile and appear to show excitement and happiness when confronted with familiar events such as the faces of people they know. Sadness emerges at about 3 months in connection with the withdrawal of positive stimulus events (Lewis, 1993a).

Early on, children learn that emotional expression is more than making faces and sounds; it requires timing, an understanding of context, and knowledge of the audience receiving the communication. By the age of 2, most toddlers have begun to work this out. For example, a child who is hurt while playing and begins to cry may stop and look around to find someone to hear the cries. Determined to find an audience for the emotional expression, the child walks closer to the house, spots Mom or Dad within earshot, and begins to cry in earnest.

Emotional expressions that resemble those seen in adults are observed in children under 1 year of age. Which emotions do you believe these children are expressing?

At approximately 3 years of age, the emotions a child experiences become highly differentiated (Lewis, 1993a). What accounts for this major change? The answer is that the child develops some fairly sophisticated cognitive abilities that set the stage for a new set of emotions. The child has acquired a sense of self-awareness, a set of standards, an understanding of what constitutes success or failure, and the ability to evaluate his or her behavior compared to the standards. These abilities are the basis for the self-conscious emotions—the negative emotions of shame and guilt and the positive emotion of pride (Lewis, 1993b, 1995). These emotions are also intimately connected and can lead to other emotions such as anger and sadness. Shame results when an individual senses having failed to live up to his or her standards (Lewis, 1992). The shamed person wishes to hide, disappear, or die. This intensely negative and painful emotion can disrupt behavior, confuse thinking, and render the person speechless (Lewis, 1993b). In fact, physical abuse appears to have long-lasting effects on the ability to perceive emotions in facial expressions. Children between the ages of 8 and 10 were shown digitally morphed faces ranging from happy to fearful or angry to sad. Abused children were more likely to categorize a face as angry even when it showed only a slight amount of anger. What's more, compared to nonabused children, abused children exhibited more brain activity when viewing an angry face, suggesting that the abuse shaped their ability to recognize facial expressions (Pollak & Tolley-Schell, 2003).

Guilt (or regret) is produced when a person evaluates his or her behavior as a failure and focuses on the specific features of the self or actions that led to the failure. These people are pained by the evaluation of the failure, but they direct the pain to the cause of the failure or the object of the harm. Guilt is associated with some corrective action taken to repair the failure and prevent it from happening again. Therefore guilt is not as intensely negative as shame, and does not lead to confusion and loss of action.

Pride and shame are quite different from happiness and sadness. If you win a lottery, you will probably feel quite happy about the money, but you would not feel pride, because winning is not viewed as having anything to do with your behavior. You might feel sad if you were not able to do something, but if it was not your fault, you would not feel shame or guilt.

**Emotional Intelligence.** The term *emotional intelligence* describes four qualities: (a) the ability perceive emotions in others, (b) the ability to facilitate thought, (c) understanding emotions, and (d) managing emotions (Grewal & Salovey, 2005). This concept recognizes the fact that brain power, as measured by tests of intelligence and standardized achievement tests, is not necessarily as important for success as the qualities outlined here, which have gone unrecognized (Cooper & Sawaf, 1997; Goleman, 1995). In fact, emotional intelligence seems unrelated to measures of general intelligence (Derksen, Kramer, & Katzko, 2002). Psychologists have been developing the concept as well as working on various ways to assess emotional intelligence (Schutte et al., 1998). One popular way of assessing emotional intelligence is to use paper-and-pencil measures such as the *Self-Report Emotional Intelligence Test (SREIT)*. Another common technique is to ask people who interact with each other to rate one another's degree of emotional intelligence (Grewal & Salovey, 2005).

The term *emotional intelligence* encompasses at least four skills; the ability to perceive emotions accurately, the ability to use emotions to facilitate thinking and reasoning, the ability to understand emotions, and the ability to manage emotions in oneself and in others. These skills can significantly impact a person's functioning at home, school, work, and in relationships with others.

**Source:** Grewal and Salovey (2005).

Use of these various measures of emotional intelligence has yielded some interesting and intriguing results. For example, couples completed a paper-and-pencil measure of emotional intelligence along with several questionnaires designed to tap aspects of their relationships. Happiness was correlated with high scores on emotional intelligence for both partners; when one partner had a high score and the other had a low score, satisfaction tended to fall in an intermediate range (Brackett & Mayer, 2003). In another study, supervisors and workers rated each other on items thought to tap aspects of emotional intelligence (such as "This person handles stress without getting too tense"). Employees who scored high on emotional intelligence received more positive ratings from both peers and supervisors. What's more, their peers reported that they had fewer conflicts with them and perceived them as creating a positive atmosphere at work (Lopes et al., 2004).

Some people do not even recognize which emotion they are experiencing. For example, they may not realize that they are actually angry at a person for dying. Or consider a parent who yells at a child who has just run into the street. Is the parent expressing anger at the act of disobedience or fear at what could have happened? Recognizing which emotions we are feeling is a key element of emotional intelligence because it helps individuals understand how their thinking can be affected by the emotions they are experiencing.

Some impulses appear easier to control than others; anger is one of the hardest to control, perhaps because of its evolutionary value in priming people to action. Dwelling on anger actually increases its power. To control anger, the body needs a chance to use up the adrenaline through exercise, relaxation techniques, or the well-known admonition to count to 10. Understanding how anger can affect our behavior is an excellent example of emotional intelligence in action (Goleman, 1995). In fact, education involves incorporating training in self-awareness, self-control, and empathy—and the arts of listening, resolving conflicts, and cooperation. To those who argue that schools have too much to teach students already without adding instruction in emotional intelligence, proponents of such instruction suggest that it would be easier to teach students who can maintain their emotional equilibrium in the face of a wide variety of stressors at home and in the community (Sleek, 1997).

# REVIEW SUMMARY

**1.** Languages and cultures differ in the number of words that describe categories of emotion. Some words refer to emotions that are not described in all cultures or languages.

**2.** Schachter and Singer proposed a theory that described emotion as beginning with undifferentiated arousal. The specific emotion label we use to describe the arousal depends on our interpretation of the context.

**3.** Appraisal theories of emotion propose that the way we make judgments about events leads to emotional reactions. Cultural values can influence people's emotions.

**4.** A key cognitive ability is evaluating one's behavior in relation to internal or external standards. This ability is the basis of the self-conscious emotions such as shame, guilt, and pride.

**5.** The concept of *emotional intelligence* includes such abilities as understanding emotions and managing emotions.

# ✓ CHECK YOUR PROGRESS

**1.** Give examples of words from other cultures that describe categories of emotion that do not have counterparts in English.

**2.** You are walking in the forest and see a bear. According to Schachter and Singer, what happens at that point?
   **a.** physiological changes, followed by fear
   **b.** fear, followed by physiological changes
   **c.** physiological changes and fear simultaneously
   **d.** physiological changes and context appraisal, followed by fear

**3.** How did Schachter and Singer create physiological arousal similar to that experienced during emotional reactions in their experimental participants?
   **a.** Participants were given epinephrine injections.
   **b.** They had participants exercise before entering the laboratory.
   **c.** Participants watched a frightening movie before the experiment began.
   **d.** They told the participants that a dangerous chemical was leaking from an adjacent laboratory.

**4.** Which of these is a self-conscious emotion?
   **a.** fear
   **b.** shame
   **c.** disgust
   **d.** happiness

**5.** Define the term *emotional intelligence*.

**6.** Which child is most likely to experience a self-conscious emotion?
   **a.** a child who takes her first step
   **b.** a child who is able to eat by himself
   **c.** a child who spills food all over a new dress
   **d.** a child who uses the telephone without any help

**7.** The theory proposed by Stanley Schachter and Jerome Singer stressed that the physiological process and _____ are important determinants of emotion.
   **a.** context
   **b.** stimuli
   **c.** intensity
   **d.** the unconscious

**8.** What element of the Schachter and Singer experiment would likely be considered unethical today?
   **a.** interacting with an angry confederate
   **b.** giving participants an injection of adrenaline
   **c.** interacting with a confederate who is euphoric
   **d.** misleading participants about the effects of adrenaline injections.

**9.** What is the general finding from cross-cultural studies of words used to describe emotions?
   **a.** Some cultures have words for unique emotions.
   **b.** The same words for emotions are used in all cultures.
   **c.** A word must exist before an emotion can be experienced.
   **d.** Compared to other cultures, English-language cultures have relatively few words for emotions.

**10.** What is the significance of the word *amae* in Japanese culture?
   **a.** The word, which means "sweet dependency," shows how emotions can be shaped by culture.
   **b.** The word, which means "love," illustrates the importance Japanese culture places on the elderly.
   **c.** The word is used as a reminder to Japanese people to be restrained in showing emotions to others.
   **d.** The word, which means "depression," illustrates that even a psychological disorder can have positive aspects.

**ANSWERS: 1.** The German word *schadenfreude* means "harm joy," and the Japanese word *ijirashii* refers to feelings associated with seeing someone praiseworthy overcoming an obstacle. **2.** d **3.** a **4.** b **5.** Emotional intelligence is the ability to perceive emotion, facilitate thought, understand emotion, and manage emotion. **6.** c **7.** a **8.** d **9.** a **10.** a

CHAPTER 7

# Memory

## CHAPTER OUTLINE

I n Chapter 5 we examined the basic learning processes, especially classical conditioning and operant (instrumental) conditioning, that are characteristic of a wide variety of organisms. In this chapter we highlight some uniquely human aspects of learning and memory. We begin with early studies of memory, giving special attention to the pioneering work of Hermann Ebbinghaus. We then examine the phenomenon of memory in detail and discuss several recent developments in the study of memory. After a look at some techniques for improving your memory, we explore the physiological basis of learning and memory.

In addition to helping us adapt more effectively to our environment, the processes covered in this chapter clear the way for improved communication and the storage of knowledge. As you might have sensed, we are beginning to focus on the processes that define what makes us human and the way we function as individuals and as members of groups.

Before we begin an in-depth examination of memory, let's define our topic. This task may be more difficult than you think; memory is one of those abilities we take for granted. Certainly memory is related to learning. If we did not learn or acquire new knowledge, we would have nothing to store in our memories. In many instances, memories last an incredibly long time. Putting these ideas together, we can tentatively define **memory** as a system or process by which the products or results of learning are stored for future use.

## INITIAL STUDIES

**When Sue graduated from high school, she enrolled in a college several hundred miles from her home. After completing college, she accepted a job as a YMCA program director in a large metropolitan area. Because her trips back home were infrequent, she lost contact with her high school classmates. She has not seen most of them in years. Her 25th high school reunion is approaching, and Sue wonders how good her memory is. How many of her former classmates will she recognize?** *How good is our memory for faces after a long interval of time?*

The scientific study of human memory is almost as old as scientific psychology itself. The pioneer in this area was Hermann Ebbinghaus, a patient and thorough German psychologist who conducted his studies of memory in the late 1800s and early 1900s (Ebbinghaus, 1885). Ebbinghaus asked questions such as "What conditions are favorable (or unfavorable) for linking or associating the words, sounds, and visual stimuli that make up our store of learned knowledge?"

Because everyday words already have meanings and associations attached to them (that is, some learning has already taken place), Ebbinghaus used other stimuli in many of his experiments. A focus of his research was on **nonsense syllables**, which are usually composed of three letters arranged in a consonant-vowel-consonant sequence. For example, *gok, taf, keb,* and *tup* are nonsense syllables. Because nonsense syllables were supposed to have no meaning, Ebbinghaus believed he could study how associations between these stimuli are formed without any other factors, such as previous learning, complicating the results.

**memory**
System or process by which the products or results of learning are stored for future use

**nonsense syllables**
Stimuli used to study memory; typically composed of a consonant-vowel-consonant sequence

Armed with these new stimuli, Ebbinghaus began his studies with only one research participant: himself. In most instances the task consisted of memorizing lists of nonsense syllables. Before you start questioning the importance of studying how one learns a sequence of nonsense syllables, think about all the lists or sequences that we learn (Curran & Keele, 1993). As grade school children, we learn the alphabet, the names of the presidents, and the multiplication tables. As we grow up, we learn telephone numbers, ZIP codes, addresses, and lock combinations. Ebbinghaus's studies of lists were actually quite relevant.

### Psychological Detective

Ebbinghaus's next step was to devise a way to measure memory. Now, if someone says that all you have to do to measure memory is to ask a participant what he or she has learned, you might be skeptical. Measuring memory is more complicated than that. Before you read further, write down some ideas about how you might measure memory when a participant is learning a list of nonsense syllables. Be sure to identify the specific response you are measuring.

Ebbinghaus's method for measuring memory of lists of nonsense syllables was called **serial learning** (also known as *ordered recall*). As a participant, you are given a set of items to remember and asked to reproduce the sequence in the exact order in which it was presented (Marshuetz, 2005). This technique reveals whether you have mastered the correct sequence of the syllables or other stimuli like numbers (Baddeley, Papagno, & Andrade, 1993). For example, if you dial or key in 343-7355 on the telephone instead of 343-3755 (the number that was supposed to be learned), serial learning is not perfect.

A second method, **paired-associate learning,** was developed by Mary Whiton Calkins (1863–1930), the first woman to serve as president of the American Psychological Association (see Chapter 1; Madigan & O'Hara, 1992). In this task you associate an unfamiliar word or nonsense syllable with a familiar word. This technique is often used to learn the vocabulary for a foreign language—remember the flash cards you used to learn Spanish or French? The test consists of presenting the familiar word and then producing the foreign word associated with it.

A third method of measuring memory is **free recall.** Here the task is to remember as many items as possible, regardless of the sequence (Baddeley, 2004). Naming the major parts of a neuron (see Chapter 2), the major sleep disorders (see Chapter 4), or the components of classical conditioning (see Chapter 5) are examples of free recall. Free recall is now the preferred method of measuring learning. You can experience this method right now. Cover each word in Table 7-1 with a card and then read one word at a time at a comfortable pace. When you get to the bottom of the list, you will find the instruction to "Recall" the words. Write down as many of the words as you can remember.

One of the most interesting findings from studies of free recall is that the position or order of the material to be recalled affects the chances that it will be remembered. For example, items near the beginning of the list are typically recalled well (the *primacy effect*); items near the end of the list are also recalled well (the *recency effect*). Items in the middle of the list tend to be recalled less well than items at the beginning or end of the list. This phenomenon, called the **serial position effect** (Baddeley, 2004), was discovered by Mary Whiton Calkins (Madigan & O'Hara, 1992; see Figure 7-1).

## The Curve of Forgetting

One of the most important findings of Ebbinghaus's research is the curve of forgetting. Ebbinghaus found that memory for learned material is best right after the learning session. As time passes, we forget more and more. This basic finding has been replicated (reproduced) numerous times since Ebbinghaus discovered it. As you can see from Figure 7-2, Jenkins and Dallenbach (1924) found that participants recalled the most when they were tested immediately after learning. The participants learned a list of 10

Hermann Ebbinghaus (1850–1909) was a pioneer in the study of human memory.

**serial learning**
Learning procedure in which material that has been learned must be repeated in the order in which it was presented; also known as *ordered recall*

**paired-associate learning**
Learning procedure in which items to be recalled are learned in pairs. During recall, one member of the pair is presented and the other is to be recalled

**free recall**
Learning procedure in which material that has been learned may be repeated in any order

**serial position effect**
Tendency for items at the beginning and end of a list to be learned better than items in the middle

**TABLE 7-1**

## Free Recall

*Instructions:* Try to remember the words in this list. Place a card over the list and then reveal one word at a time. When you get to the bottom of the list, close the book and write down as many of the words as you can remember.

Hospital

Lawn

Doorbell

Laundry

Street

Mouse

Radio

Wood

Sofa

Garage

**\*Recall\***

nonsense syllables and then were asked to recall the list 1/2 hour and 2, 4, and 8 hours later. One-half hour after the initial training session, the participants were able to recall only half of the list; their performance continued to deteriorate with the passage of time. The importance of these results is clear: You can expect your best recall shortly after a learning session. Another important finding from the Ebbinghaus laboratory involves what is called *distributed practice*. Simply put, it is better to distribute learning trials across a period of time than to mass them in a single block of learning. "When it comes to learning, a little every day is the optimal way" (Baddeley, 2004, p. 70). Of course, distributed practice is exactly the opposite of what students do when they cram for exams. Students who cram are relying on the high rate of recall immediately after learning trials. They often ignore the high rate of *forgetting* that occurs even immediately after learning. Most students cram because they don't properly plan their study time. There

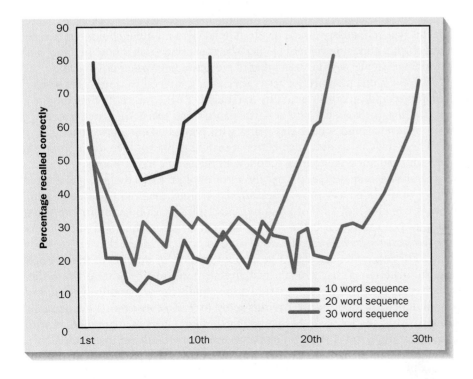

**FIGURE 7-1** The tendency for items at the beginning of a list or at the end of a list to be recalled more easily than items in the middle of a list is called the *serial position effect*. As you can see, this phenomenon occurs with lists of various sizes.

**Source:** Baddeley (2004).

**FIGURE 7-2** Number of nonsense syllables recalled at various intervals following learning for two participants. Recall dropped dramatically with time, but it was higher if they slept after learning. In agreement with Ebbinghaus's research, the greatest decrease in recall occurred very shortly after learning had taken place.

**Source:** Jenkins and Dallenbach (1924).

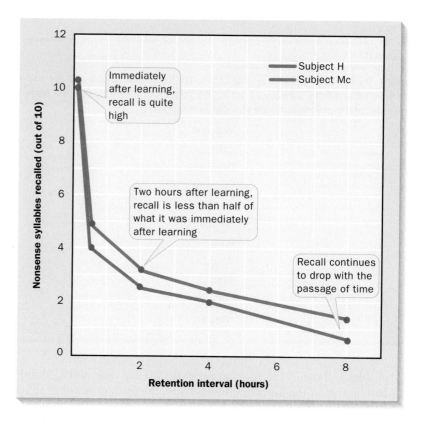

**7.1**

are effective techniques that you can use to improve the way you study. You will find several suggestions for improving your studying in the section on Techniques for Improving Memory later in this chapter.

## Recognition and Relearning

Two additional procedures for measuring memory, the recognition test and the relearning test, supplement the three methods just described. In the **recognition test,** participants pick out items to which they were previously exposed from a longer list that also contains unfamiliar items (Haist, Shimamura, & Squire, 1992; Yonelinas, Hockley, & Murdock, 1992). This type of memory task is involved in taking a multiple-choice test. Recall Sue from this chapter's opening vignette. When she attends her high school reunion, Sue will be performing a similar task in attempting to recognize her former classmates.

How good is our memory for faces after a long interval of time? The results of a research project indicate that our ability to remember faces for a long time is quite good (Bruck, Cavanagh, & Ceci, 1991). Participants were asked to match current photographs of former high school classmates with photos taken approximately 25 years earlier. Those individuals did much better at matching photos than did a group of participants who had not gone to high school with the people in the photos.

A **relearning test** is exactly what the term implies. After the passage of a certain amount of time (called a *retention interval*), the original material is learned again. For example, you might study a list of 15 nonsense syllables on Monday afternoon. You study the list until you can repeat it three times without an error; this level of performance, your *performance criterion*, is established by the researcher. One week later you study the same list. The researcher calculates the amount of time, or number of trials, it takes to relearn the material so that you can match your performance criterion, and the two scores are compared. If learning occurred more rapidly the second time you studied the list, this difference is reported as a **savings score** (or *relearning score*). A good example of relearning is studying for a comprehensive final exam. Chances are good that, with the right concentration, it will take you less time and effort to relearn the material.

**recognition test**
Test in which retention is measured by the ability to pick out previously learned items from a list that also contains unfamiliar items

**relearning test**
Test of retention that compares the time or trials required to learn material a second time with the time or trials required to learn the material the first time

**savings score**
Difference between the time or trials originally required to learn material and the time or trials required to relearn the material; also known as *relearning score*

Although the work of Ebbinghaus and other early psychologists provided a basic understanding of human memory, much more has been discovered since then. Today few psychologists study how people learn lists of nonsense syllables; they are more interested in examining the processes by which memories are formed, stored, retrieved, and used. This shift in interest occurred because most psychologists abandoned the mechanical association-based model of memory in which items were simply linked to other items. A new view of the mind began to emerge—one suggesting that the mind is an active agent with many other organizational properties. This developing view prompted different questions. How do we store items in memory? Once memories are stored, how do we retrieve them?

**encoding**
First stage of the memory process; in it information is transformed or coded (a transduction process) into a form that can be processed further and stored

# MODELS OF MEMORY

**Ann is phenomenal! She knows every client by name and can recall the details of particular accounts with ease. She always makes the right decision, often under extreme pressure, and never seems ruffled or disturbed. Business appointments with her are a pleasure. Her friends have frequently commented that her memory is "like a computer."** *In what ways might a computer and human memory be alike?*

## Human Memory as an Information Processing System

Like the computer, researchers have characterized human memory as an information processing system that has three separate stages: an *input* or *encoding stage*, a *storage stage*, and a *retrieval stage* during which an already stored memory is called into consciousness (see Figure 7-3). Let's take a closer look at each of these stages.

**7.2**

**Encoding.**    In the **encoding** stage, sensory information is received and coded, and then transformed into neural impulses that can be processed further or stored for later use. Just as the computer changes keyboard entries into usable electronic symbols that may be stored on a computer disk, sensory information is *transduced*, or converted, into neural impulses (see Chapter 3) that can be used and stored by the brain. In addition to transduction, a great deal of the encoding process appears to be devoted to rehearsing (practicing or repeating) the input, organizing it into groups, and relating the groups to already stored information. Encoding may even involve giving this information a special name or label.

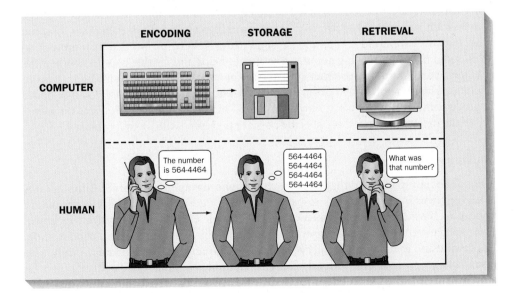

**FIGURE 7-3**  Because it has separate encoding, storage, and retrieval stages, human memory is similar to an information processing system like the computer.

What memories does this grade school science class help you retrieve?

Suppose that as you drive to school, you listen to a new song on the radio. The sounds are transduced into neural impulses, which are then recognized as making up a song. You remember hearing similar songs and classify the one you are listening to as belonging to that group—for example, "smooth jazz" or "oldie." This procedure is very much like installing a computer program; information is encoded in the central processing unit, and the user gives it a name and file path that helps relate it to similar programs.

**Storage.**    The second stage of memory processing is **storage.** Like the computer program, the encoded information must be stored in the memory system if we plan to retain it for any length of time or use it more than once. Although some bits of information are stored briefly, used only once, and then discarded, others, like certain telephone numbers, are used frequently and are therefore stored on a more permanent basis.

**Retrieval.**    Once a computer program has been named and stored, we can "call it up" by its name and use it again. Human memory works in much the same way. When we recall or bring a memory into consciousness, we have retrieved it. This recall process is known as memory **retrieval.**

We do not store information in memory randomly. The information is organized and related to already stored information in ways that allow us to use certain cues to retrieve it.

### Psychological Detective

To see how the retrieval process works, write down the name of your fourth-grade teacher. After you have done so, describe the process that led you to that particular name.

**storage**
Second stage of the memory process; in it information is placed in the memory system. This stage may involve either brief or long-term storage of memories

**retrieval**
Third stage of the memory process; in it stored memories are brought into consciousness

**eidetic imagery**
A form of memory, often called *photographic memory,* which consists of especially vivid visual recollections of material

The words *fourth-grade teacher* are the stimuli that activated your memories of the fourth grade. As you retrieve these memories while searching for the name of your teacher, you may recall your school building, your fourth-grade classroom, the ride to school on the bus, and the names of your classmates. In turn, each of these memories could serve as a stimulus to retrieve related memories. There are probably many stimuli that could help you retrieve the name of your fourth-grade teacher.

In some instances, the network of related memories is small and only a few specific cues will successfully retrieve a certain memory. For example, suppose you are in the supermarket trying to choose a brand of detergent when an apparent stranger begins a conversation with you. The "stranger" is talking as if you have known each other for some time, but you have no idea what this person's name is. Why do we find it so difficult to recall some names? Knowing about retrieval cues helps answer this question. When the stranger reminds you that you met last Saturday at a party, it is as though a light goes on. Suddenly you remember who this person is and where you met. Because you met under special circumstances, the party, only cues related to that situation will retrieve the memory of the meeting. When those specific cues are presented, the memory returns.

### Myth or Science

How often have you heard that someone has a "photographic memory"? Although it is likely that this comment refers to people with very good memories, some people do appear to have photographic memory. People with **eidetic imagery** (the technical term for photographic memory) say that they can look at a written page, person, slide, or drawing and then later mentally see that image (Guenther, 1998; Haber, 1969). The visual image persists after stimulation (for example, a slide is turned off), can be scanned like a photograph, and offers relatively accurate detail. In fact, it appears as if these people take photographs and store them in their minds for future use. For example, when you need information from a page in a book, you retrieve that page from memory and read it. Leonardo da Vinci and Napoleon Bonaparte are two famous people who had photographic memory. Leonardo could draw detailed portraits of people after meeting them only once. Napoleon could glance at a map briefly and later recall the location of every stream, town, and hill. Eidetic imagery appears to be relatively rare, however. Estimates of the percentage of the population with eidetic imagery are often in single digits (Haber & Haber, 1964). Would this ability be great at test time? Perhaps. It seems, however, that once the image has faded (such images last for up to 4 minutes), the memory seems no better than the memories of those who do not possess eidetic imagery (Haber, 1969; Haber & Haber, 1964).

## The Stages-of-Memory Model

Our encoding-storage-retrieval model of memory would serve our purpose quite well if we had only one type of memory to store. We have, however, at least three well-defined types of memory: sensory memory, short-term memory, and long-term memory. So the information processing model must be modified to read as follows:

Encoding → "type" of storage → retrieval

The rest of this section describes the three types of memory and the ways they are used in our daily lives. The stages-of-memory model (also called the *traditional model*) that we discuss is shown in Figure 7-4, it was developed by Richard Atkinson and Richard Shiffrin (1968).

**Sensory Memory.**    As the name implies, **sensory memory** is a memory or storage of sensory events such as sights, sounds, and tastes, with no further processing or interpretation. Because sensory memory provides us with a fleeting image of the stimuli present at a particular moment, it has the potential to be huge. Because many stimuli are received all the time, sensory memory appears to last only briefly, about 0.5 to 1.0 second, depending on which sensory system is involved.

Sensory information that is not selected for further processing by higher brain centers decays and is replaced by incoming stimuli. As you saw in Chapter 3, we cannot attend to and process all the stimuli we receive; some of them must be filtered out. Stimuli that we attend to are those that are selected from sensory memory for further processing; other stimuli are lost.

After a moment's reflection, you might ask, "If sensory memories last such a short time, how can you demonstrate that they really exist?" In a compelling set of experiments,

**sensory memory**
Very brief (0.5 to 1.0 second for visual stimuli and 2 to 3 seconds for auditory stimuli) but extensive memory for sensory events

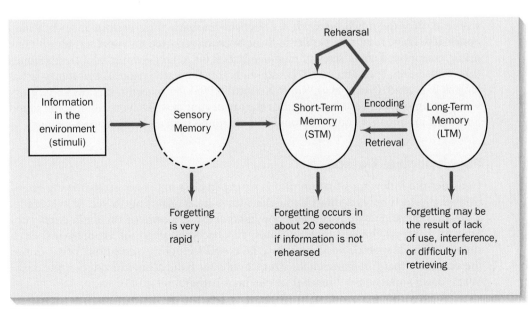

**FIGURE 7-4** The stages-of-memory model.

researchers presented a display of 12 letters to participants (Sperling, 1960). The pattern might look like this:

| | | | | |
|---|---|---|---|---|
| D | C | R | M | ← High tone |
| Y | N | S | V | ← Medium tone |
| I | E | G | Z | ← Low tone |

The entire pattern was flashed for only 1/20th of a second. The participants then recalled and wrote down as many letters as possible. Typically, they were able to identify only 4 or 5 of the 12 letters. That does not seem like good evidence for any kind of memory! Some changes made in later experiments, however, produced dramatic improvement. One modification involved assigning a different audible tone to each row of the stimulus pattern: a high tone to the top row, a medium tone to the middle row, and a low tone to the bottom row. As before, the entire pattern of 12 letters was flashed for 1/20th of a second. Immediately afterward, one of the three tones was sounded, and the participants were asked to write down the letters in the row designated by the tone. When tones accompanied the presentation of the letters, participants correctly identified three or four letters in a row, regardless of which row was signaled. Clearly, much more information was potentially available in memory than the original experiment had indicated. Because they did not know in advance which row would be signaled, the participants had to have a memory of all the letters when one of the tones was sounded. Timing is important, however; when the tone was sounded a second after the letters were presented, participants could remember only one or two letters in the designated row. Thus a significant amount of information is lost from sensory memory very quickly after the stimuli are presented.

The amount of information lost from sensory memory is not a fixed quantity. Rather, it depends on the amount of processing effort that is expended in the next stage of memory. We can either process a few items very thoroughly and lose a great deal from sensory memory or we can process a larger number of items less thoroughly and retain more from sensory memory.

Because it is important and easy to study, we have been talking exclusively about visual sensory memory. Do we have brief sensory memories for our other senses? Although less research has been done on this topic, the answer appears to be yes. Ulric Neisser (1967) proposed the existence of an *auditory* or *echoic sensory memory*. His proposal was supported by a study in which participants heard simultaneous lists of letters from three loudspeakers in different locations (Darwin, Turvey, & Crowder, 1972). If students tried to report the letters from all three loudspeakers, they did poorly; if they were asked to repeat the letters from a specific speaker immediately after the list was read, they did much better. If a delay was imposed, their performance decreased noticeably. These results are similar to those Sperling reported for visual stimuli with one major exception. Echoic sensory memory lasts a bit longer—closer to 2 to 3 seconds (Lu, Williamson, & Kaufman, 1992), although, some research suggests that it may last as long as 10 seconds (Sams, Hari, Rif, & Knuutila, 1993). You can also experience auditory sensory memory. Hit your hands against the top of your desk. Do you still hear the sound for a brief instant after you have stopped? This sound is an auditory sensory memory.

### Psychological Detective

Consider the following situation. Jim is sitting in class but is not really paying attention to the lecture. His mind is on the movie he is planning to see that evening. Without realizing it, he is rubbing one hand along the edge of the desk. After rubbing his hand on the desk several times, Jim becomes aware of his behavior. Each time his hand leaves the desk, he is sure he is still feeling the sensation. What causes the sensation that Jim experiences after he rubs his hand along the edge of the desk? Write down some possibilities before reading further.

Sensory memory appears to be involved in the sensation Jim is experiencing. Try it yourself. Rub your hand quickly along the edge of your desk or a table—heel first, fingertips last. For a brief instant after your hand leaves the desk, you will have the sensation that you are still touching it. You have just experienced an example of *tactile (touch) sensory memory*.

According to the stages-of-memory model, what happens to the information that is selected from sensory memory and not lost? To answer this question, we need to continue our exploration of the various types of memory.

**Short-Term Memory.** Once information has been attended to or selected from sensory memory, it is transferred to conscious awareness (Engle, Cantor, & Carullo, 1993; Laming, 1992). According to the stages-of-memory view, information must be processed in **short-term memory (STM)** before it can be transferred to more permanent storage in long-term memory. What is this STM? As the name implies, STM lasts for only a short period—perhaps several seconds. Although researchers have not determined exactly how long such memories endure, it appears that items are lost from STM in about 10 to 20 seconds.

For example, research in which participants recalled a three-letter stimulus found that recall fell from 90% correct immediately after presentation of the stimulus to 10% correct after 18 seconds (Brown, 1958; Peterson & Peterson, 1959). Why? Two processes appear to be at work: (a) Unless memories are practiced or rehearsed, they become weaker and fade away; and (b) to make room for new incoming information, some of the memories in STM are pushed out or displaced. In the Brown and Peterson and Peterson studies, the participants counted backward by threes to prevent practice after learning the three-letter stimulus. Their results indicated that much of this displaced information is simply lost, but some is transferred to long-term memory.

## Psychological Detective

Study the following phone numbers for 15 seconds:

316-343-5800

401-246-4531

912-692-3423

Now write them on a piece of paper without looking at this page. You probably found this task difficult. You would be able to handle two phone numbers better. Why? Write down some possible answers before reading further.

Exercises like this one, coupled with extensive research, prompted psychologist George Miller (1956) to propose that we can hold approximately seven items (plus or minus two) in STM (often called the "magic number") at any one time. After a moment's reflection, you might be sure that this 7 +/− 2 proposal is incorrect. When we remember two telephone numbers, we are dealing with more than nine items (7 +/− 2). That would be true if we counted each digit separately. Most people remember telephone numbers (with area code) not as 10 separate digits but as three *chunks*. Think of a chunk as a meaningful unit of information (Gobet et al., 2001). Try this: Say the first telephone number aloud, and you can "hear" the chunks. When you said the telephone number aloud, you probably said 316 (pause), 343 (pause), 5800. A chunk is like a pail into which we pour several individual items that can then be recalled together from memory. With two phone numbers, each having an area code, you have only six chunks to remember.

What Miller demonstrated with the principle of grouping or chunking is that although STM may be limited to five to nine items (7 +/− 2), each item may consist of a chunk or group of items. In this way the capacity of STM can be increased significantly.

**short-term memory (STM)**
Memory stage in which information is held in consciousness for 10 to 20 seconds

George Miller, former president of the American Psychological Association, proposed that we can hold 7 +/− 2 items in STM at any one time.

Without rehearsal, STM does not last very long.

## Psychological Detective

What would you do if you wanted to remember the following list? Study it for 15 seconds; then close your book and write down as many of the items as possible.

| | | | |
|---|---|---|---|
| telephone | Ford | pine | Toyota |
| poplar | fax | Chevrolet | cherry |
| oak | compact disk | walnut | radio |
| Buick | Mazda | television | DVD |
| cedar | mail | audiocassette | Pontiac |
| Saturn | maple | elm | Honda |

There are 24 items in this list, considerably more than the magic number 7 +/− 2. Hence it will be difficult for you to remember each word by itself. If, however, you set up three categories (trees, automobiles, and communication devices) and put each item into the appropriate category, you should have no trouble remembering all 24 items (see Figure 7-5).

The original concept of STM posed a major problem: It was too short. Although 10 or 20 seconds was sufficient to input and store new information, it did not allow time for processing information (Ashcraft, 2006). The initial 10- to 20-second STM period often leads to a second phase, **working memory**, during which attention and conscious effort are brought to bear on the material at hand. Working memory is like a mental workbench or a place where mental effort is applied (Baddeley, 2004; Nairne, 2003). If you attempt to solve the following problem, you will probably find that you held the intermediate answer in memory while computing the next part, then held the updated intermediate value, and so forth:

$$\frac{2 \times 5/6 + 4}{\frac{1}{2} \times (6 + 3)}$$

What's more, comprehension of sentences can sometimes tax our immediate memory processes. Try to understand the following:

I know that you are not unaware of my inability to speak German.

While you are trying to make sense of this sentence you learn it piece by piece, then put the pieces together (Ashcraft, 2006). When we retrieve words from long-term memory and put them together in a sentence, the process of putting words together occurs in working memory. For example, let's say that you are listening to a lecture in which your instructor makes an interesting but very complicated point. While you hold the sentence in STM, you retrieve word meanings from long-term memory. Then, in light of what you already know (retrieval from long-term memory), you use working memory to make sense of the new sentences you've just heard. Using brain-imaging techniques (see Chapter 2), researchers have begun to isolate brain regions that are active when we use

**working memory**
Second stage of short-term memory; in it attention and conscious effort are brought to bear on material

**FIGURE 7-5** Chunking helps us create categories that increase the amount of information we can hold in STM.

working memory. For example, order and item memory are separable, and different brain regions seem to be involved (Marshuetz, 2005). Other research reveals that "human spatial working memory is partly mediated by regions in the parietal and prefrontal cortex" (Smith, 2000, p. 45). Future research using brain imaging techniques will define these and other brain regions involved in working memory more precisely.

**Long-Term Memory.**    What would your interactions with your environment be like if STM was the only type of memory you had? Because you lacked any capacity for permanent memory storage, you would have to learn the same things *over* and *over* again. (We describe a person who has only STM later in this chapter.) It is critical to be able to transfer information from STM to more permanent storage in **long-term memory (LTM).** The stages-of-memory model stresses the importance of rehearsal or practice in this transfer. Items that are rehearsed seem more likely to be transferred than unrehearsed items. For example, you will remember your friend's new telephone number better if you repeat (rehearse) it several times rather than repeating it just once.

There are different types of rehearsal; some types aid in transferring information to LTM, and others do not. One researcher conducted a series of studies of a phenomenon known as *directed forgetting* (Björk, 1975). In these experiments two groups of participants were asked to learn several lists of items, such as nonsense syllables or telephone

**long-term memory (LTM)**
Memory stage that has a very large capacity and the capability to store information relatively permanently

**FIGURE 7-6** Design of a directed-forgetting experiment.

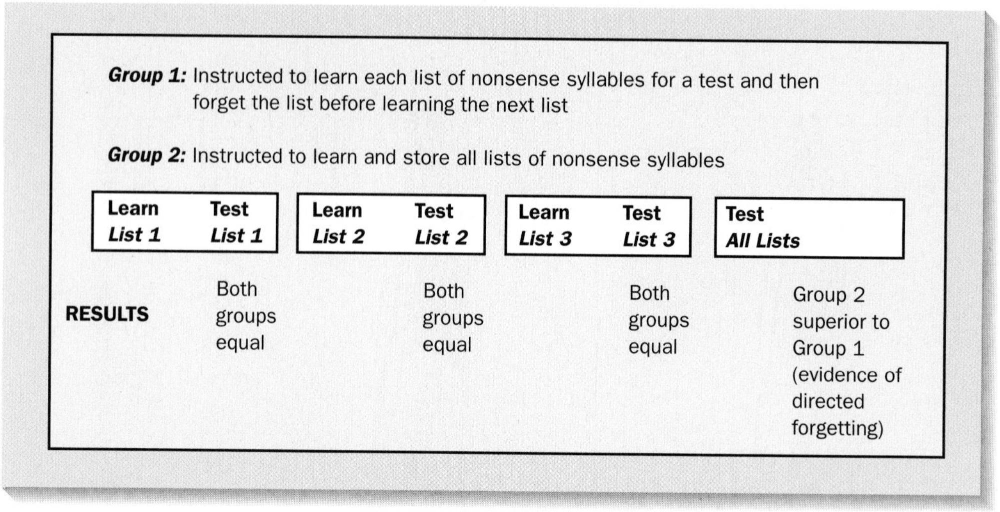

**Group 1:** Instructed to learn each list of nonsense syllables for a test and then forget the list before learning the next list

**Group 2:** Instructed to learn and store all lists of nonsense syllables

| Learn<br>List 1 | Test<br>List 1 | Learn<br>List 2 | Test<br>List 2 | Learn<br>List 3 | Test<br>List 3 | Test<br>All Lists |
|---|---|---|---|---|---|---|

**RESULTS** — Both groups equal | Both groups equal | Both groups equal | Group 2 superior to Group 1 (evidence of directed forgetting)

**maintenance rehearsal**
Rehearsal used when we want to save or maintain a memory for a specified period of time

**elaborative rehearsal**
Rehearsal in which meaning is added to the material to be remembered

**proactive interference**
Situation in which previously learned information hinders the recall of information learned more recently

7.3

numbers. Both groups were given the same amount of time to rehearse each list after it was presented. A retention test was given before presentation of the next list. Before beginning the experiment, one group was told to forget all the items from a given list immediately after the retention test. The second group was told to remember all the lists. A typical directed-forgetting experiment (see Fleck, Berch, Shear, & Strakowski, 2001) is diagrammed in Figure 7-6.

Although no differences were found between the groups in retention of individual lists of nonsense syllables, large differences were apparent on a retention test given after all the lists had been presented. The participants who had been directed to forget did much worse than those who had been directed to remember. These differences appear to be caused by different types of rehearsal.

Two types of rehearsal—maintenance and elaborative—have been studied. We use **maintenance rehearsal** when we want to save or maintain a memory for a short period. Examples of maintenance rehearsal include the telephone number for the pizza restaurant you have just looked up or the material you tried to cram for a test. Maintenance rehearsal ensures that the memory remains until it has been used and is then discarded; research participants who are directed to forget a list as soon as they have learned and repeated it use this type of rehearsal. Participants who are instructed to remember a list use **elaborative rehearsal,** which adds meaning to material that we want to remember. For example, you increase your chances of remembering someone's name if meaningful elements are present when you are introduced. Where does the person work or live? What are his or her hobbies? An introduction such as "I would like you to meet my friend Jason Downey. Jason works as the chief parole officer for the state. He is an avid sky diver" provides several elements that are useful to memory. Earlier we saw that the more meaningful material is, the better it is learned. Elaborative rehearsal is an example of this process at work; it results in a more permanent memory and promotes the transfer of information to LTM (Bartlett, 1932; Best, 1999). Unlike STM, LTM has a very large, if not unlimited, capacity.

**Forgetting.** Once a memory has been transferred from STM to LTM, it is supposed to be there on a *permanent* basis. If that is true, why do we forget? Some memory loss may be due to the fading or *decay* of memories (Dosher & Ma, 1998), but much loss appears to be caused by *interference*. Old memories that are already stored may be recalled instead of the specific memory we are seeking. This effect is called **proactive interference.** Proactive interference occurs when old information hinders our memory of the new information. When you move to a new house or apartment, you have a new address and telephone number. How often do you find yourself using the old address or phone number? Sometimes this problem lasts for years. Another example of proactive interference can be seen every January, when millions of people continue to write the previous year on their bank checks.

Similarly, information that was learned *after* the material we want to remember may hinder the recall of the earlier learned material. This process is called **retroactive interference.** Sometimes it is important to remember old addresses and phone numbers, but try as we might, new addresses and phone numbers are the only ones that come to mind. The other information may be stored in LTM, but we simply cannot retrieve it. Proactive and retroactive interference are diagrammed in Figure 7-7.

**retroactive interference**
Situation in which information learned more recently hinders the recall of information learned previously

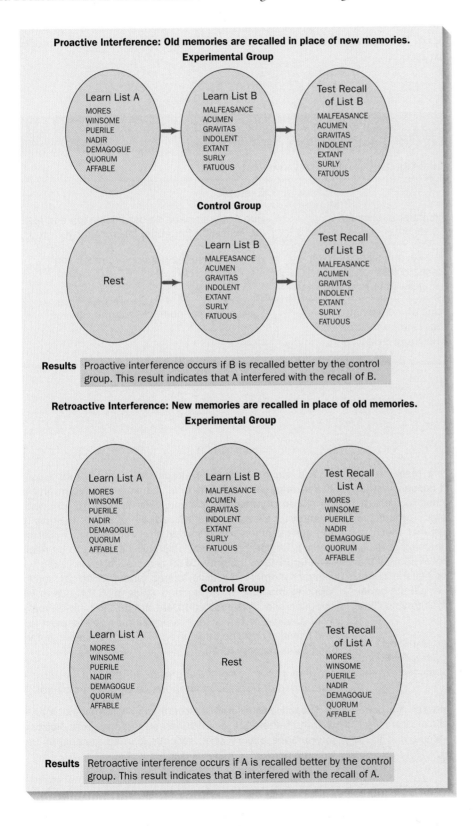

**FIGURE 7-7** Research designed to test proactive and retroactive interference.

What happens when we retrieve a memory from LTM? As we saw in Figure 7-3, the stages-of-memory model suggests that when a memory is recalled from LTM and enters consciousness, it is placed directly into STM. There it may be combined with new information that has been received, creating a new memory. If this new memory is properly rehearsed, it may be transferred to LTM for more permanent storage. The following Study Chart summarizes the main components of the stages-of-memory model.

The stages-of-memory approach is not the only model of memory that has been developed. We explore a second influential model, the levels-of-processing model, in the next section.

## *Study* CHART

### Types of Memory According to the Stages-of-Memory Model

| Type | Description | Example |
|------|-------------|---------|
| Sensory | Storage of a large number of sensory events for 0.5 to 1.0 second. | Rubbing your hand across a table top and feeling the sensation for a brief instant after you stop. |
| Short-term (STM) | Working memory is a second stage of STM. Lasts for a few seconds unless rehearsal takes place. Conscious awareness is involved. | Remembering the name of a person you just met. |
| Long-term (LTM) | More permanent form of memory storage. Rehearsal or practice is important for transferring memories from STM to LTM. | Your telephone number or home address. |

## REVIEW SUMMARY

1. Hermann Ebbinghaus conducted pioneering research on **memory** in the late 1800s. Ebbinghaus devised nonsense syllables, which he believed had no meaning attached to them, to study how associations between stimuli are formed. Through the use of **serial learning,** Ebbinghaus determined that much of what we learn is forgotten very shortly after a learning session. When we try to recall a list of items, we tend to recall items at the beginning (primacy effect) and the end (recency effect) better than items in the middle. This phenomenon is called the **serial position effect.** Other methods of studying memory include **paired-associate learning** and **free recall.**

2. These basic methods were developed and expanded by incorporating additional tasks, such as the **recognition test** and the **relearning test.** The **savings score** is produced by the relearning method.

3. Some investigators have drawn a parallel between the computer and human memory. Computers and human memory have (a) an input or **encoding** stage, (b) a **storage** stage, and (c) a **retrieval** stage.

4. The stages-of-memory (traditional) model proposes that there are three types of memory: sensory, short-term, and long-term. **Sensory memory** is a very brief (lasting 0.5 to 1 second) memory for a large array of (visual) stimuli. **Eidetic imagery** (photographic memory) occurs when after stimulation a visual image persists longer than normal. This ability appears to be relatively rare. **Short-term memory (STM)** is more limited in capacity than sensory memory but lasts longer (about 10 to 20 seconds). **Working memory** is the second stage of STM, during which attention and conscious effort are brought to bear on material. With practice or rehearsal, memories may persist even longer and ultimately may be transferred to more permanent storage in **long-term memory (LTM).**

5. Memories may not be retrievable from LTM because they have faded or because of interference by other memories.

6. **Proactive interference** occurs when old material interferes with the retrieval of material learned more recently. **Retroactive interference** occurs when recently learned material interferes with the retrieval of material learned earlier.

## ✓ CHECK YOUR PROGRESS

1. Kevin and Sharin are participants in a memory experiment. Their task is to learn a list of items such as *bok* and *gex*. What are these items called? Why are they used in the study of memory?

2. Explain the statement "Human memory is like an information processing system."

3. Indicate whether each of the following statements describes sensory memory, STM, or LTM.

   a. very large capacity
   b. capacity of 7 +/− 2 items
   c. "permanent" storage
   d. lasts only .5 to 1.0 second
   e. lasts 10 to 20 seconds

4. Describe working memory. How does it differ from STM?

5. You attempt to remember a phone number by repeating it over and over to yourself. What type of rehearsal are you using?

   a. condensed
   b. permanent
   c. elaborative
   d. maintenance

6. Much memory loss appears to be due to

   a. fading.
   b. disuse.
   c. interference.
   d. poor encoding.

7. Your final exam was a nightmare. All you could remember was the material you had just learned; the older material seemed to have vanished from your memory. This type of memory failure is an example of what kind of interference?

8. Once he has learned the list of items, Kevin's task is to reproduce them in the order in which they were presented. What term do psychologists use for this procedure for measuring memory?

   a. recognition
   b. free recall
   c. serial learning
   d. paired-associate

9. Ted recently moved from New York to Denver, and now he has a new telephone number. When people ask him for his new telephone number, the number he recalls is the old number. What psychological phenomenon is occurring here?

   a. savings
   b. recognition
   c. interference
   d. repression

10. Picking a suspect out of a police lineup is an example of

   a. recall.
   b. recognition.
   c. relearning.
   d. paired-associate learning.

**ANSWERS: 1.** Nonsense syllables. Nonsense syllables are used to avoid the influence of previous associations on learning. **2.** There is an encoding stage, a storage stage and a retrieval stage in both the information system and human memory. **3. a.** Sensory memory or LTM. **b.** STM. **c.** LTM. **d.** Visual sensory memory. **e.** STM. **4.** Working memory follows the initial 10 to 20 seconds of STM. During working memory, attention and conscious effort are brought to bear on the material. **5. d. 6. c. 7.** Retroactive **8. c. 9. c. 10. b.**

# OTHER APPROACHES TO MEMORY

Myra volunteered to participate in an experiment involving memory. Her initial task was to read an article in a psychological journal. After reading the article, she was instructed to prepare a brief presentation about the article from the perspective of its author. Finally, Myra took a test that dealt with the content of the article. *What did these procedures have to do with memory?*

Although the stages-of-memory or traditional model makes good sense and has generated a large amount of research activity, it is not the only account of how memory works. In this section we examine several other models of the memory process.

## The Levels-of-Processing Model

The **levels-of-processing model** proposed by Fergus Craik and Robert Lockhart (1972) represents a radical departure from the stages-of-memory model (Challis, 1993; Challis & Brodbeck, 1992). Craik and Lockhart proposed that there is only one type of

**levels-of-processing model**
Theory stating that deeper processing of information increases the likelihood that the information will be recalled

**FIGURE 7-8** The levels-of-processing model of memory.

memory store and that its capacity is enormous, if not unlimited. Once memories have entered this store, they may be retained there for extremely long periods.

You may be thinking, "One large memory store in which memories last for long periods—that seems simple enough. If that's the way our memory is set up, however, why do we forget some things faster than others?" That question gets to the heart of Craik and Lockhart's view of memory: What really matters is the way we process information. Rehearsal is important, but how we rehearse is even more important. As you can see in Figure 7-8, Craik and Lockhart believe that we can engage in several levels of rehearsal or processing. The maintenance and elaborative rehearsal techniques discussed earlier are only two examples.

A very shallow or simple level might involve processing only the physical characteristics of an object. Thus we might characterize the object in Figure 7-8 as red and rectangular. At a deeper or more complex level of processing, we consider additional characteristics such as the fact that the object has pages. This addition is a form of elaborative rehearsal. Now we are dealing with a red, rectangular book. Adding even more *meaning*—that is, moving to an even deeper level of processing—we now consider what type of book this is and whether it will help us in any of our courses this semester. This last type of processing requires that we examine the book and compare it with other books and with information already stored in memory. Which courses are we taking? Which books are being used in those courses? Will this book help?

We do not automatically progress from one level to another simply because we spend more time processing. If all of our processing time is spent at a very shallow level, our memory will be stored only in terms of shallow cues such as color, shape, or sound. When we want to retrieve this memory, only those shallow cues will be able to access and retrieve it. For example, if we listened only to the sound of a person's name, we might not be able to retrieve it later. The person's physical features, occupation, personality, address, and so forth would be of no help because those cues were not rehearsed when the memory was stored. The sound of the person's name is the only cue that will access the memory of the name. These physical cues are less meaningful; therefore, they do not remain in our memory store as long as more meaningful cues that are rehearsed at deeper levels of processing. In other words, the deeper the level of processing, the greater the likelihood that the information will be stored. Time of processing is not as important as depth of processing.

The instructions given to research participants can have a dramatic effect on what is learned. In one classic study (Hyde & Jenkins, 1969), researchers demonstrated the effects that different types of processing can produce. They instructed four groups of participants to study the same list of words. The specific instructions differed for each group, as shown in Table 7-2. A recall test was then given to all four groups. The test was a surprise for Groups 1, 2, and 3 but not for Group 4.

**STUDY TIP**

Compare and contrast the stages-of-memory model and levels-of-processing theory. Indicate which makes more sense to you as a model of memory, and why. If your ideal model contains elements of both, describe it.

**TABLE 7-2**

## Instructions Given to Participants in the Hyde and Jenkins (1969) Experiment

| | |
|---|---|
| Group 1 | Count the letters in each word. |
| Group 2 | Mark all the *e*'s in each word. |
| Group 3 | Rate the pleasantness of each word. |
| Group 4 | Memorize the words for a later recall test. |

The results (see Figure 7-9) indicated that the participants in Groups 1 and 2 remembered significantly *fewer* words than did the participants in Groups 3 and 4. Because Groups 3 and 4 did not differ, we can conclude that the surprise value of the test did not produce these results. The groups differed in terms of the level of processing in which they engaged. Groups 1 and 2 never dealt with the words themselves—they just counted letters (Group 1) or marked *e*'s (Group 2). Hence Groups 1 and 2 processed the information at a very shallow level. Because they had to take the words into account, the participants in Group 3 (who rated the pleasantness of the words) and Group 4 (who memorized the words for a test) processed the information at deeper levels and therefore remembered it better.

Consider the memory experiment described at the beginning of this section. What did these procedures have to do with memory? The experiment in which Myra participated was concerned with levels of processing. Unknown to Myra, other participants were required only to read the journal article; they were not required to prepare the brief presentation. When researchers designed the study, they hypothesized that preparing the presentation would require a deeper level of processing and result in better comprehension (Kixmiller, Wann, Weaver, Grover, & Davis, 1987). This prediction was borne out by the experiment's results.

Although many studies have produced results indicating that depth or level of processing influences our memories, this theory has not gone unchallenged. Critics assert that the exact meaning of the term *level of processing* has not been specified (Baddeley, 1998, 2004). Without a clear definition of what a level is or how to measure it objectively, it is difficult to know how many levels there are. Such criticism has encouraged some researchers to view different levels of processing in terms of the amount of cognitive or mental effort expended. In their view, the greater the effort, the deeper the level of processing.

In support of this proposition, several studies have been interpreted as showing that better retention is linked to greater effort. For example, imagine that you are part of an experiment in which the task is to learn words that rhyme. You are presented with a word,

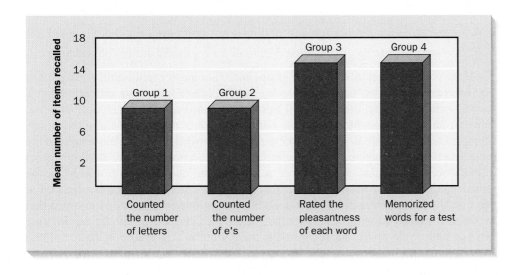

**FIGURE 7-9** Mean correct responses on a recall test. Only the participants in Group 4 knew they would be tested. Processing at a deeper level (Group 3) improved memory.

**Source:** Adapted from Hyde and Jenkins (1969).

Remembering how to rollerblade is an example of procedural memory.

such as *cat*, and asked to generate a word, such as *bat*, that rhymes with it. Your task is to memorize the rhyming words that you have generated. Will you remember your rhyming words better than people who were asked only to memorize rhyming words that were presented to them? Because your effort in generating and memorizing the words was greater than their effort in merely memorizing them, the answer is yes.

Finally, the levels-of-processing model assumes that processing occurs through a succession of independent stages; this assumption has yet to be verified. Because of such issues, other approaches have been developed.

## Different Types of Long-Term Memory

Recent research has demonstrated that there is more than one type of LTM. We do not just place a memory into LTM (the stages-of-memory model) or simply process at a deeper level (the Craik-Lockhart model). The type of information being processed influences the nature of the stored memory. Four major categories or types of LTM have been proposed: *procedural, semantic, episodic,* and *priming* (or *implicit*). In addition, current research has improved our understanding of encoding, processing, and retrieval strategies. We examine some of these current approaches in the following sections.

**Procedural Memory.**    **Procedural memories** are the memories we use in making responses and performing skilled actions (Anderson & Fincham, 1994). Remembering how to rollerblade is an example of procedural memory. Procedural memories are often used at the same time as other types of memory. For example, remembering how to drive a car involves procedural memory. Remembering the traffic laws, however, does not involve the use of motor skills; it involves the memory of general principles. Memory for general principles is known as *semantic memory*.

**Semantic Memory.**    Our fund of general knowledge is stored in **semantic memory**. Because we are dealing with general knowledge, specific dates and times that pertain to people are not included in our semantic memories. You will find these items in episodic memory. Semantic memory includes concepts, the meanings of words, and facts (Lesch & Pollatsek, 1993; Rohrer, Wixted, Salmon, & Butters, 1995). The following are some examples of items that might be stored in semantic memory:

1. Oil is one of the main ingredients in asphalt.
2. The three branches of government are the executive, legislative, and judicial.
3. In a tennis match, the winner of six games generally wins a set unless the players are tied.
4. Interstate highways that run east and west are given even-number designations.
5. In intercollegiate sports, Division 3 schools do not award athletic scholarships.

Have you ever been asked a question you could not answer immediately, yet you felt the correct response was "on the tip of your tongue"? Such a question produces what is known as the **tip-of-the-tongue (TOT) phenomenon** (Brown & McNeill, 1966). You know the answer is there, but you cannot retrieve it. In fact, many people who are experiencing TOT may be able to report the first letter of the word, they may know some of the other letters in the word, how many syllables are in the word, and are likely to report related words. The degree of information available during the experience of TOT can be remarkable, especially when you consider that the person cannot report the word itself. For example, the Italian language designates as either masculine or feminine even words that would have no such designations in most languages, including English. In Italian there are two words for stone: *sasso* is masculine and *pietra* is feminine (Caramazza & Miozzo, 1997;

**procedural memory**
Memory for making responses and performing skilled actions

**semantic memory**
Memory for general knowledge

**tip-of-the-tongue (TOT) phenomenon**
Condition of being almost, but not quite, able to remember something; used to investigate the nature of semantic memory

Vigliocco, Antonini, & Garrett, 1997). When caught in the TOT dilemma, Italian speakers are often able to report whether the blocked word is masculine or feminine.

## Psychological Detective

Let's test your semantic memory. Write down the answer to each of the following questions before reading further.

1. Which ocean is adjacent to California?
2. Which term do we use to describe a car that runs on both gasoline and battery power?
3. What substance found in many foods can lead to clogged arteries?
4. What does a bear do in the winter?
5. Which river separates Indiana from Kentucky?

How many of these questions produced a TOT response? Were you able to search your stored memories and find the correct answer? (The answers can be found at the end of the chapter.) Because most TOT experiences seem to involve semantic memory, they have been studied thoroughly by psychologists who want to learn more about this type of memory and how it is retrieved. Apparently, we are systematic and organized when we search our semantic memories (Reason & Mycielska, 1982). By observing how people search their stored knowledge, we can learn more about the vast network of semantic memories.

## Hands On

## TOT Phenomenon and Memory

To get a better idea of how the TOT phenomenon is relevant to the study of memory, take the following test. Using strips of cardboard, cover both columns of the letters that follow and write down as many state capitals as you can. Then uncover the columns and see if these alphabetical cues aid your recall for those that were on the tip of your tongue. The answers can be found at the end of the chapter.

| State | First Letter of Capital | State | First Letter of Capital |
|---|---|---|---|
| Alabama | M | Maryland | A |
| Connecticut | H | Massachusetts | B |
| Florida | T | Mississippi | J |
| Georgia | A | Nebraska | L |
| Idaho | B | New Jersey | T |
| Iowa | D | Oregon | S |
| Kentucky | F | Texas | A |
| Louisiana | B | Wyoming | C |

**Episodic Memory.** Our personal experiences are stored in **episodic memory.** These memories involve events that occurred at certain times with specific people, places, and things (Goldringer, 1996; Levy et al., 1995; Nyberg & Tulving, 1996). The following are some examples of your authors' episodic memories. What episodic memories do you have?

**1.** Being in Dallas, Texas, the day President John F. Kennedy was assassinated
**2.** Seeing tornadoes devastate Nashville, Tennessee, in the spring of 1998
**3.** Watching television coverage of hurricane Katrina in 2005

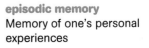

**episodic memory**
Memory of one's personal experiences

**flashbulb memory**
Very detailed memory of an arousing, surprising, or emotional situation

**4.** Arriving on campus for the first day of college

**5.** Watching baseball pitcher Nolan Ryan strike out his 5,000th batter in 1989 and win his 300th major league game in 1990

Just as the TOT phenomenon has been studied to help us learn more about semantic memory, flashbulb memories have been examined to provide information about episodic memory. **Flashbulb memories** are detailed memories of situations that are very arousing, surprising, or emotional. Our memories of such events are often more detailed than our memories of more usual, everyday episodes. For example, Danish people who lived through the Nazi occupation and ultimate liberation had very vivid memories of events from World War II. In fact, their memories for factual questions (such as the weather) were checked against objective records. What's more, members of the resistance movement had more vivid, detailed, and accurate memories than did persons without such participation (Berntsen & Thomsen, 2005). You might think of flashbulb memories as similar to photos taken with a digital camera. Push the button, and in a few seconds you have a perfect re-creation of the scene that you can look at whenever you want. In your mind, the situation is illuminated just as it occurred. Because more effort is expended in the formation of flashbulb memories, such highlighting of details might lead to deeper levels of processing as well as provide more cues for retrieval.

Because flashbulb memories are tied to specific dates, places, and times, it is difficult to give examples that everyone can immediately identify. Some people vividly remember where they were when President Kennedy was assassinated in 1963, but others do not. Other flashbulb memories are the explosion of the space shuttle *Challenger* in 1986, the tearing down of the Berlin Wall in 1989, and the death of Princess Diana in 1997 (Hornstein, Brown, & Mulligan, 2003). The terrorist attacks on the World Trade Center in New York and the Pentagon in Washington, DC, in 2001 are currently flashbulb memories for many people. As new generations grow up, they will not have these flashbulb memories. The strong emotional reactions to events such as those described above seem to provide fertile ground to establish long-lasting memories. On the other hand, evidence indicates that the memories may not be as accurate or consistent as they were once believed to be (Talarico & Rubin, 2003). The emotional component of the memory may lead us to discuss the memory over and over; such repeated rehearsal can at times have the effect of altering the memory, although confidence in the memory often remains quite high.

Where were you on September 11, 2001? These images reflect flashbulb memories for many people worldwide.

**Priming or Implicit Memory.** The recent addition of **priming or implicit memory** to the list of memory types may be one of the most important advances in the study of memory (Poldrack & Cohen, 1998; Schachter & Badgaiyan, 2001). "Priming is a nonconscious form of human memory, which is concerned with perceptual identification of words and objects and which has only recently been recognized as separate from other forms of memory or memory systems" (Tulving & Schachter, 1990, p. 301).

Because priming or implicit memory does not operate on a conscious level, it is difficult to detect and study. The first evidence for priming came from studies of *amnesia*, or memory loss (Warrington & Weiskrantz, 1968). Even though the patients with amnesia had extremely poor memory for recent events, allowing them to study a group of words helped them later when they had to learn those same words. The earlier study period primed or sensitized them to the words they were to learn in the later session. Even though they had no *memory* of the first study session, the *primed* patients with amnesia performed better than other patients with amnesia and normal individuals who had not studied the items earlier. Somehow the earlier study session prepared (primed) the amnesiac patients to recognize the objects they were to learn. Subsequent studies (Schweinberger, 1996) of nonamnesiac individuals examined the timing and production of brain waves to study priming. Priming effects are revealed when appropriate brain waves are shown earlier in primed participants.

Although we still have a great deal to learn, priming appears to facilitate procedural and semantic memory processes by improving our ability to identify perceptual stimuli or objects we encounter (Rajaram & Roediger, 1993). At an unconscious level, priming memory alerts us that we have encountered a particular object previously (Musen & Squire, 1993). This priming effect is better when deeper levels of processing are involved (Hamann & Squire, 1996). The different types of LTM are summarized in the following study chart. Spend a few minutes reviewing it before reading further.

**priming or implicit memory**
Unconscious memory processing in which prior exposure to stimulus items may aid subsequent learning

**STUDY TIP**

In a group of four, each student should briefly study and then describe to the group one of the four types of long-term memory. After a student describes a type, the rest of the group should brainstorm examples of that type.

## Retrieval

Last year during spring break, Jennifer paid a surprise visit to her former first-grade teacher. Even though the teacher had not seen Jennifer in 10 years, she immediately said, "Well, Jennifer, how are you? Do you still have Buffy, your pet boa constrictor?" At times we are able to retain and retrieve some remarkable memories. Conversely, sometimes things we should remember seem to be gone forever. For example, are you among the large number of people who seem unable to remember their license plate and telephone numbers?

## *Study* CHART

### Types of Long-Term Memory

| Type | Description | Examples |
|---|---|---|
| Procedural | Memories used in making responses and skilled actions. | Remembering how to ride a bicycle, play tennis, or drive a car. |
| Semantic | Our store of general knowledge. | Water freezes at 32°F; Texas is the largest of the continental states; metabolism decreases when animals hibernate. |
| Episodic | Memories of personal events. | Your high school graduation, your first day at college, getting your driver's license. |
| Implicit (priming) | Nonconscious form of LTM that is related to identification of words and objects. | Allowing amnesia patients to study an object and later finding that learning is enhanced even though they do not remember seeing the object. |

**Source:** GEECH. Reprinted by permission of United Features Syndicate, Inc.

**Retrieval from STM.**   As mentioned earlier, retrieval is the process by which we locate a memory that has been stored and then bring it into consciousness. Because most people have both extremely good and extremely poor memories, psychologists are interested in studying retrieval.

## Psychological Detective

When you read the heading "Retrieval from STM," the following question may have occurred to you: "If the information in STM is already in our consciousness, why would we talk about retrieving it?" Give this question some thought, and write down some possible reasons before reading further.

A series of studies by S. Sternberg (1966, 1975) suggested that retrieval from STM is not instantaneous; we *do* have to scan our STM, locate an item, and process it. Sternberg asked participants to hold a series of letters (such as B, Q, R, D, T, and P) in STM for later recall. But instead of being given the recall test they expected, they were presented with a letter, such as B, and were asked whether it was in the list they were holding in STM. If retrieval was not involved, the participants should have responded almost instantaneously. As it turned out, they did not. What's more, as additional letters were added to the list held in STM, the participants took longer to answer. They were scanning the entire list in STM to match the test letter with those they had stored. The longer the list in STM, the longer the search process required to make a match.

**Retrieval from LTM.**   The process of scanning items in STM to retrieve a specific memory is rather straightforward, but retrieval of long-term memories is a different story. Depending on the situation, various processes may be involved. For example, we have to distinguish between retrieval of memories in recognition tasks and retrieval of memories in recall tasks.

Which type of test would you rather take—a short-answer or essay test in which you have to produce all of the answers, or a multiple-choice test in which you have to recognize the correct answer? Most people prefer the multiple-choice test because it is easier; all you have to do is choose the right answer. Consider the following questions on material from Chapter 4. Which question is easier?

1. Which sleep disorder is characterized by extreme sleepiness, cataplexy, and sleep paralysis?
   a. enuresis
   b. narcolepsy
   c. sleep apnea
   d. somnambulism

2. Which sleep disorder is characterized by extreme sleepiness, cataplexy, and sleep paralysis?

If recognition tasks are easier, perhaps they do not require the same amount or type of retrieval processing. It may be simpler to retrieve memories through recognition.

Many researchers supported this view until Tulving and his colleagues demonstrated that in some situations, recall memory is actually superior to recognition memory!

Although one type of memory task is not always easier than the other, perhaps the process of retrieval is the same for both. John Anderson and Gordon Bower (1974) have proposed that recognition and recall use the same retrieval process. Both recall and recognition retrieval have an initial stage during which we search stored memories. This search leads us to a large number of *related* words and phrases. In short, we do not store information as separate bits and pieces; much of it is stored as a semantic network of related items.

**Semantic networks** are formed by related concepts (called *nodes*) that are linked together (Collins & Loftus, 1975; Collins & Quillian, 1972). For example, mentioning the concept "newspaper" might activate the semantic network shown in Figure 7-10. The process of activating a network constitutes the retrieval process. The length of the lines (called *links*) that connect the various concepts in the newspaper network reflects the strength of the association; shorter links imply stronger associations. For example, the association between "newspaper" and "reporter" is stronger (shorter link) than the association between "newspaper" and "rain" (longer link). Note that in the semantic network every concept is related to the core concept—in this case, "newspaper." In some instances, the relation is direct; in others, it is indirect.

Not all of our stored memories are arranged in semantic networks in which one concept triggers a network of related items. There are numerous occasions when we are required to use a grouping or cluster of knowledge about a sequence of events or an object. Such clusters of knowledge or typical ways of thinking about things are called **schemas** (Ahn, Brewer, & Mooney, 1992; Dopkins, Pollatsek, & Nordlie, 1994). For example, suppose that a friend asked you to tell her about the concert you went to last weekend. Because you have been to several concerts during the past year, you have an organized cluster of knowledge (a schema) about going to concerts. Thus your recall of last weekend's concert will be influenced by your schema for concerts and the specific events that occurred at the concert in question. Similarly, you have schemas for a visit to a doctor, the first day of class, a wedding ceremony, negotiations to buy a new car, and so on.

To get a better idea of the nature of semantic networks and schemas, let's say you have learned a list of words that included the word *horse*. Later in the day you take a recognition test in which you are given a longer list of words and are asked to pick out

**semantic network**
Network of related concepts that are linked together

**schema**
Grouping or cluster of knowledge about an object or sequence of events

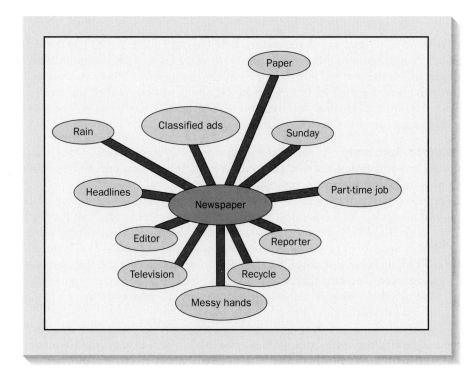

**FIGURE 7-10** A semantic network for the concept "newspaper." Longer lines depict weaker associations (links); shorter lines depict stronger links.

**encoding specificity**
Theory stating that the effectiveness of memory retrieval is directly related to the similarity of the cues present when the memory was encoded and when the memory is retrieved

the ones you have learned. You come to the word *horse*, which serves as a retrieval cue for the semantic network that contains your horse-related memories. Now your job is to determine whether the word *horse* was on the list you learned earlier. Sorting through all of your horse memories could be a rather imposing and confusing task, especially if there are many strong links. On the other hand, the word *aardvark* should be easier to recognize as one of the words you learned because it should activate fewer links than *horse*.

The same process is involved when we retrieve memories under recall conditions. For example, an essay question on your psychology test might ask you to name the four lobes of the cortex. You start scanning your semantic network for items related to the concept "lobes of the cortex." You find a network of related information that includes subcortical structures, stereotaxic surgery, and a group of items that includes the terms *frontal, temporal, parietal,* and *occipital*—the four cortical lobes you've been looking for.

Consider the next question on the test: "Explain the contributions of Ivan Pavlov". In this case, you need to recall more than just names to answer the question; you need to activate an organized cluster of knowledge, a schema. Your schema for Pavlov contains the information the instructor wants. In fact, it contains even more than you need to recall. Could there be some way to retrieve only the desired memory?

**Encoding Specificity.**    The **encoding specificity** hypothesis states that the effectiveness of memory retrieval is directly related to the similarity of the cues present when the memory was originally encoded to the cues present when the memory is retrieved (Gerrig & McKoon, 2001; Tulving, 1983). In short, specific cues are encoded, and these cues, or very similar ones, should be present when retrieval is attempted.

Have you ever had difficulty recalling material you have studied? Part of the problem may be that the studying took place in one location and the testing occurred in a very different place. Most of the effective retrieval cues (those in the room where you studied) were missing in the classroom where you took the test. Hence it was difficult for you to retrieve the needed information.

### Psychological Detective

How can you solve this recall problem? Give this issue some thought and write down some possibilities before reading further.

Try to do some studying in the room where the test will be given. The cues in the room will be among those that can help you retrieve the memory. If you cannot study in the room where the test will be given, try varying the locations where you study. This variety will prevent a single set of cues from becoming associated with the memory of the material you are learning. As a result, retrieval of your memories will be tied less directly to a specific set of environmental cues.

**Eyewitness Testimony.**    One of the most intriguing applications of the encoding specificity hypothesis has been in the area of eyewitness testimony. Such testimony often plays an important part in jury trials.

The possibility that eyewitness reports may be inaccurate has stimulated a large amount of research. One of the most startling findings concerns what can happen to a memory once it has been retrieved. Earlier we saw that when a memory is retrieved from LTM, it appears to be placed in STM for conscious processing. While this memory is in STM, however, it is possible to add new information to it and then *reencode* the modified memory. The next time you retrieve the new memory, your report may not correspond exactly to what actually happened because the new memory now contains the additional information.

This effect was tested in several ingenious experiments conducted by Elizabeth Loftus and her colleagues (Loftus, 1979; Loftus, Miller, & Burns, 1978). The design of

One group saw the red sports car approaching a *stop* sign.

**EXPERIMENTAL DESIGN**

| STEP 1 | STEP 2 | STEP 3 | RESULTS |
|---|---|---|---|
| See slides of red sports car approaching a *stop* sign. | Answer questions about what they had seen. *Consistent* participants had questions about stop signs. *Inconsistent* participants had questions about yield signs. | View slides and pick those that were seen in Step 1. | Participants who were asked consistent questions in Step 2 were significantly more accurate in picking the slides they had seen than were the inconsistent participants. |

The other group saw the red sports car approach a *yield* sign.

**EXPERIMENTAL DESIGN**

| STEP 1 | STEP 2 | STEP 3 | RESULTS |
|---|---|---|---|
| See slides of red sports car approaching a *yield* sign. | Answer questions about what they had seen. *Consistent participants* had questions about yield signs. *Inconsistent participants* had questions about stop signs. | View slides and pick those that were seen in Step 1. | Participants who were asked consistent questions in Step 2 were significantly more accurate in picking the slides they had seen than were the inconsistent participants. |

**FIGURE 7-11** Diagram of the Loftus (1979) experiment on eyewitness accuracy.

**Source:** Loftus (1979).

one of those experiments is diagrammed in Figure 7-11. In this experiment, two groups of people watched a series of slides that showed an impending collision between a red sports car and another automobile. One group saw the sports car approach a stop sign at an intersection. The second group saw the sports car approach a yield sign at the intersection. After the slide presentation was completed, the participants were asked a series of questions about what they had seen. For half of the participants in each group, the questions were consistent with what they had seen. In other words, if they had seen a stop sign, the questions referred to a stop sign, and if they had seen a yield sign, the questions referred to a yield sign. For the remaining participants in each group, the questions were inconsistent—if they had seen a stop sign, the questions referred to a yield sign, and vice versa. Finally, all participants were shown pairs of slides and asked to pick the one they had actually seen (a recognition test).

As you would expect, a large number (75%) of the participants who were asked consistent questions after seeing the slides picked the slide they had seen. When they were asked inconsistent questions, however, only 40% were able to select the slide they had actually seen. The inconsistent questions altered their memory of the incident. Later, when they retrieved this memory, many participants reported an incorrect memory because they had encoded inaccurate information in their memory after being asked questions that were inconsistent (Ayers & Reder, 1998; Garry & Polaschek, 2000; Porter, Birt, Yuille, & Lehman, 2000). The results of this type of research have significant implications for how police interrogate eyewitnesses. They must be careful in how they formulate questions because suggestive questioning may alter witnesses' memories of an incident (Schacter, 2001).

In addition to demonstrating the memory-altering effects of questions, research has shown that (a) participants have trouble distinguishing between individuals of other races and (b) violence interferes with memory retrieval (Loftus, 1984). What's more, the correlation between confidence and eyewitness identification accuracy is low, although it can rise and fall as a function of such things as viewing conditions (Loftus, 1984; Wells et al., 2000). Moreover, the false memory effect is exceptionally strong and does not dissipate easily or quickly (Carpenter, 2000). The problems and concerns that such results create for the credibility of eyewitness testimony are obvious.

Eyewitnesses cannot be relied on to provide accurate information. Memory for events can be influenced by many factors, including the questions that are asked after an incident.

What you say you saw may not be what actually happened: our memories can be changed. These changes may not be intentional, but the potential for altering eyewitness reports must be recognized and addressed.

**State-Dependent Learning.** For a number of years, psychologists have known that if you learn material under certain special conditions, your retrieval of that material will be successful under the same conditions. For example, Randi drank a lot of coffee while she was studying for her last psychology test. Coffee contains a generous amount of caffeine, a central nervous system stimulant, so Randi was quite alert during her study session. Her physiological state became one of the stimuli that were present when the memories of the material she was studying were encoded. The implication from the encoding specificity hypothesis should be clear: Randi's retrieval will be best when she is tested after drinking a considerable amount of coffee. In other words, material learned in a particular physiological state is recalled best in the same physiological state, a phenomenon known as **state-dependent learning.**

Gordon Bower (1981) extended this finding to include mood states, such as being happy or sad. His logic was simple. If you learn material while you are happy (or sad), you should retrieve that material more easily when you are happy (or sad). If the mood state that was present during learning differs from the one present during testing, retrieval should be more difficult (Weaver & McNeill, 1992).

As we saw in Chapter 3, odors can be linked to both emotions and memories. The link between odor and memory has been tested experimentally (Schab, 1990). Students smelled an odor both while they were generating antonyms (opposites) to a set of stimulus words such as *large* and *beautiful* and while they were recalling those antonyms later. These students recalled more antonyms than other students who had smelled an odor only during the learning session or only during the test session. Three very different odors (chocolate, apple-cinnamon scent, and mothball) were used separately to demonstrate that this memory effect was not limited to one specific odor. The results indicated that regardless of the odor type, participants who smelled the same odor during both training and testing remembered antonyms better than participants who smelled an odor only during training or only during testing.

The phenomenon of state-dependent learning indicates that memories acquired under a specific set of circumstances may be difficult to retrieve at another time or under different circumstances. Perhaps we have memories of events that occurred years ago waiting to be triggered.

If you drink a stimulant, such as coffee, while studying, the state-dependent learning phenomenon predicts that you will be better able to retrieve your memories of the material you studied if you drink a stimulant beforehand.

**state-dependent learning**
Theory stating that when we learn something while in a specific physiological state, our recall of that information will be better when we are in the same physiological state

## The Repressed/Recovered Memory Controversy

One of the most dramatic and significant controversies in recent years involves reports of the sudden recall of repressed memories of childhood sexual abuse. For example, a newspaper article carried the headline "Eyewitness Errors Can Doom Innocent" (Associated Press, 2000). Retrieval of such memories has been reported to occur decades after the abuse. The significance of this issue is evident in the fact that the American Psychological Association and the British Psychological Association asked groups of experts to study the issue and write policy statements (Lindsay & Read, 1993). This issue attracted so much professional attention that in 1997 an entire issue of *Current Directions in Psychological Science* was devoted to it. The following cases illustrate the basis for the controversy.

**Case 1.** While Melody was in the hospital for treatment of depression, her therapist repeatedly suggested that her depression resulted from incest during childhood. After a few sessions, Melody reported that her father had raped her when she was 4 years old. When pressed for details, she wrote pages of her emerging repressed memories, including being molested by her father when she was 1 year old. She confronted her parents and consulted a lawyer about filing charges against her father. After leaving the hospital and consulting new therapists, Melody concluded that the abuse never occurred. She now says that the memories were "a figment of my imagination encouraged by my therapists and the pop psychology books I was reading" (Wartik, 1993, p. 64).

**Case 2.** Claudia lost more than 100 pounds in a hospital program for treatment of obesity. While in the hospital, she had flashbacks of sexual abuse committed by her brother. After she joined a therapy group for incest survivors, the memories of abuse flooded back. Her brother had died in the Vietnam War more than 15 years before her memories surfaced. Claudia's parents had left his room untouched since his death. She searched his room and found pornographic materials, handcuffs, and a diary in which he had described sexual "experiments" with his sister (Bower, 1993).

**Case 3.** Nadean Cool, a nurse's aid, sought therapy in 1986 to help her cope with her reaction to a traumatic event experienced by her daughter. Using a variety of techniques, including, hypnosis, a psychiatrist "uncovered evidence" that Cool had repressed memories of having been in a satanic cult, of eating babies, of being raped, and of having sex with animals. What's more, she came to believe she had 120 different personalities as a result of the sexual and physical abuse she had experienced. Eventually, Cool realized that false memories had been implanted, and she sued the psychiatrist. In 1997, her case was settled out of court for $2.4 million (Loftus, 1997).

About half of the states in the United States have extended the statute of limitations, allowing people who retrieve memories of abuse to sue alleged perpetrators within 3 to 6 years of the time the memories emerge. A growing number of victims have used these revised laws to file civil and criminal actions.

Kelly Michaels worked at the Wee Care Day Nursery in Maplewood, New Jersey. As his temperature was being taken at a doctor's office one child said his teacher did the same thing. The accusations against her soon snowballed. Based on repeated interviews with highly suggestive and leading questions, the children said Kelly licked peanut butter off their genitals, forced them to drink urine and eat feces, and assaulted them with objects ranging from silverware to Lego blocks. Despite the absence of forensic evidence to support these accusations, she was convicted of 15 charges and sentenced to 47 years. The case against her was eventually overturned due to a lack of evidence; prosecutors decided that they would not take her to trial again.

How are repressed memories retrieved? Psychotherapy (see Chapter 13) is the most common vehicle for the retrieval of memories of childhood abuse (generally incest). Typically, a person (usually a 20- to 30-year-old woman) seeks therapy for any of several problems. Many therapists believe that childhood sexual abuse is associated with a range of problems. Consistent with this belief, some of them ask about the existence of childhood abuse in the first therapy session, and some even insist that such abuse occurred, despite the client's denials.

Many therapists rely on memory-recovery techniques they believe help their patients remember repressed memories of abuse. For example, 83% of a sample of therapists agreed with the statement "Hypnosis seems to counteract the defense mechanism of repression, lifting repressed material into conscious awareness" (Yapko, 1994, p. 57). Unfortunately, memory-recovery techniques (like hypnosis, imagery, dream interpretation, and journal writing) can also help people create compelling illusory memories (Ceci & Loftus, 1994; Schacter, 2001; Yapko, 1994). Although there have been impressive successes in using hypnosis to aid recall, the technique is likely to elicit inaccurate reports. Hypnosis tends to increase confidence in the memories but has little positive influence on the accuracy of recall. What's more, it may be instrumental in implanting false memories "in individuals through the use of formal hypnotic procedures or even through simple suggestions, without formal hypnosis" (Yapko, 1994, p. 96).

What is the evidence for repression? The theory that memories can be repressed is a cornerstone of the debate (Arrigo & Pezdek, 1997). Yet, after 70 years of looking, researchers have not found evidence that the process actually exists (Holmes, 1994). In a typical evaluation of repression, participants learn groups of words. Then half of the participants are stressed by being told that they failed a test or that they have some personality defect; the other participants are either told that they passed the test or they are given neutral personality comments. When asked to recall the words, participants exposed to stress recall fewer words. This result seems consistent with the notion that they had been repressing memories associated with stress. Later, when the stressed individuals are told that they had passed a difficult test or that the earlier test results had been false, they remember the words as well as the control participants did. Researchers have found that the participants were concentrating on the experience of the stressful event instead of shutting it out, as repression suggests. Thus participants recalled the words poorly because of the distraction created by concentrating on the stressful event rather than because of repression. Critics argue, however, that laboratory studies of repression are not relevant to the kinds of real-life traumas that have been associated with repressed memories.

It seems possible that we can lose contact with memories for long periods of time; however, repression is an overused explanation of such memory failures. The more likely explanations are normal forgetting, deliberate avoidance, and *infantile amnesia*, or the inability to form memories early in life (Ceci & Loftus, 1994). Recall from the first year of life is highly unlikely because the hippocampus is not sufficiently developed to establish long-lasting memories (Loftus, 1997).

There is no evidence that people who report memories of abuse are involved in deliberate deception (Yapko, 1994). On the contrary, it is possible to create false memories of a childhood event (for example, being lost in a shopping mall) that never happened (Loftus, 1997; Loftus & Ketcham, 1994). Twenty-four adults read a booklet containing three one-paragraph true stories of events that had actually happened to them; these events had been recounted by a parent, an older sibling, or another close relative. A fourth story (the lost-in-the-mall story) was not true but had believable elements: lost for an extended period of time, crying, receiving aid and comfort from an elderly woman, and reunion with the family. After reading the stories, participants wrote what they remembered about the events. If they did not remember an event, they were told to write that they did not remember. Two subsequent interviews examined how much detail they could remember and how their memories compared to those of their relative. On follow-up interviews, 25% of the participants claimed to remember the fictitious event. The creation of false memories is not limited to "memories" of events from childhood. Saul Kassin and his colleagues found that college students who were falsely accused of having damaged a computer by pressing the wrong key often came to believe and confess to such an act. A confederate who claimed to have seen the student engage in the act seemed to lead many participants to confess (Kassin & Kiechel, 1996).

Perhaps the major problem in evaluating memories of childhood sexual abuse is that there is no way to distinguish true repressed memories from false ones (Lindsay & Read, 1993; Loftus, 1993, 1997). Ceci and Loftus (1994) write, "The point is not that suggestive memory techniques unalterably lead to false memory, but merely that they may do so" (p. 359). There is a risk of uncritical acceptance of allegations made by patients: "These activities are bound to lead to an increased likelihood that society in general will disbelieve the genuine cases of childhood sexual abuse that truly deserve our sustained attention" (Loftus, 1993, p. 534).

The problems associated with both hypnosis and the use of suggestive questions (discussed earlier) led researchers to develop new procedures to increase retrieval of accurate information. Listening to numerous tape recordings of police interviews provided researchers with information on traditional police interviews. Typically, the interviewer asked many questions (which often elicited brief responses), usually asked closed-ended questions, and frequently interrupted, thus interfering with the flow of information and making it difficult to establish rapport. One of the most effective new approaches, the *cognitive interview*, is designed to avoid use of suggestive or leading questions and to establish rapport that is likely to elicit narrative descriptions of an incident (Fisher, 1995; Fisher & Geiselman, 1992). In contrast to the traditional interview, the interviewer using the cognitive approach asks fewer questions that are generally open-ended. The interviewee is given plenty of time to respond, so he or she is providing a narrative rather than responding to a series of rapid-fire, closed-ended questions.

The interview begins by asking the person to report everything about a relevant incident (for example, a question is likely to be phrased as "Describe the incident" rather than "What color was the car?"). A second component of the interview requires witnesses to reinstate mentally the context or setting in which the incident occurred. Such reinstatement can enhance memory retrieval. Next, the witness is asked to try to recall events in different temporal orders (beginning to end, end to beginning, and so on). Finally, the witness is asked to take different perspectives on an event such as mentally viewing the event from the perspective of the perpetrator or the victim. Research shows that this technique increases witness recall; generally, there is an increase of 35 to 75% in the amount of information gathered compared to typical police interviews. Although there may be inaccurate information, it tends to be small (Brock, Fisher, & Cutler, 1999; Clifford & Gwyer, 1999; Colwell, Hiscock, & Memon, 2002; Kebell, Milne, & Wagstaff, 1999; Kohnken, Milne, Memom, & Bull, 1999; Memom & Higham, 1999).

## Memory Illusions

Clearly, the false-memory research and the repressed-memory controversy have stimulated considerable research. Indeed, a new view of memory may be emerging from this research: "memory is fallible, quirky, and essentially reconstructive in nature" (Lynn & Payne, 1997, p. 55).

Because false memories "occur in many different contexts and can be quite compelling" (Payne, Neuschatz, Lampinen, & Lynn, 1997, p. 56), several investigators view such occurrences as *memory illusions*. (Do you remember some of the visual illusions from Chapter 3? With visual illusions, we see things that don't exist.) In the case of memory illusions, we may remember things that never happened (see Table 7-3).

**TABLE 7-3**

## Memory Illusions

**Cryptoamnesia:** A special type of plagiarism in which we inadvertently forget the actual source of information we read and use the material as if it were our own.

**Déjà vu:** This term, derived from the French, means "already seen." Déjà vu is the unusual feeling or illusion or having already seen or experienced something that is actually experienced for the first time. The term is widely quoted in the words of former baseball player Yogi Berra, who said, "It's déjà vu all over again."

**Paramnesia:** A condition in which the proper meaning of words cannot be remembered.

**Jamais vu:** Essentially the opposite of déjà vu, this condition occurs when a person experiences a scene or situation that is generally part of everyday life yet believes it to be unfamiliar.

The strength and believability of memory illusions are shown in studies in which lists of words were learned (Payne, Elie, Blackwell, & Neuschatz, 1996). In these studies, participants claimed that they remembered exactly who said the critical but nonexistent words. What's more, some participants refused to believe that the nonexistent words were not part of the original list, even when they heard a playback of the original tape. Other research clearly indicates that memory illusions are created for very complex situations, such as being hospitalized at a young age (see, for example, Loftus, 1997). Memory illusions are often very strong and believable, and they seem to operate much in the same manner as other normal memory processes.

Even though memory illusions appear to operate similarly to other normal memory processes, there are some differences between them and true memories. Perhaps the most apparent difference concerns the amount of detail that is recalled: Greater detail is recalled with true memories (Mather, Henkel, & Johnson, 1997; Norman & Schachter, 1997).

What part of the brain is involved in creating memory illusions? Daniel Schachter and his colleagues reported data suggesting that the right frontal lobe plays an important role (Schachter, 1997; Schachter, Curran, Galluccio, Milberg, & Bates, 1996). For example, a patient with damage to the right frontal lobe displayed significantly more memory illusions than did people without frontal lobe damage.

Memory illusions are also relevant to eyewitness testimony. However, research has progressed far beyond demonstrating the fallibility of eyewitness testimony to examining specific factors, other than adding misleading questions and planting pieces of misinformation, that can create such memory illusions. For example, Maggie Bruck and Stephen Ceci (1997) demonstrated that interviewer bias is one of the factors leading to memory illusions. Likewise, research on the accuracy of memory recall under hypnosis indicates that such memories are no more accurate than those recalled under nonhypnotized conditions (Erdelyi, 1994). In fact, highly hypnotizable individuals report more memory illusions than do nonhypnotized persons (Lynn, Lock, Myers, & Payne, 1997; Lynn, Myers, & Malinoski, 2000). Although warning people of the possibility of suggestibility before hypnosis reduces the number of memory illusions, it does not eliminate them (Green, Lynn, & Malinoski, 1998).

Clearly, memory illusions are very real and very prevalent. It will be interesting to see what future research will uncover.

# TECHNIQUES FOR IMPROVING MEMORY

Brad is an art major who is having difficulty in his U.S. history course. He cannot remember such facts as the major battles of the Civil War. They have no meaning for him. His friends' advice has not helped. Brad is very frustrated

**TABLE 7-4**

## Factors That Influence Human Learning and Memory

| Factor | Effect |
| --- | --- |
| Number of study sessions | The greater the number of study (learning) sessions, the better the learning and memory. |
| Distribution of study sessions | Study sessions should be spread out. Spaced practice is more effective than massed practice. |
| Meaningfulness of material | Material that is meaningful will be learned better and remembered longer. |
| Similarity of items | A group of items of the same general type will be learned better than a group of dissimilar items. |
| Serial position | Items at the beginning and end of a study session or list will be learned better than items in the middle. |

and is thinking of dropping the course. Yet he must pass this required course to complete his degree. *What can Brad do to improve his memory?*

## Influential Factors

Psychologists have been trying to answer this question for a long time (Higbee, 1993). As you can see from Table 7-4, they have found several factors that influence learning and memory. Among those factors are number of study sessions, distribution of study sessions, meaningfulness of material, similarity of items, and serial position.

Assuming that Brad really has tried to study, the key to remembering the history assignment is finding some meaning in the material. As long as U.S. history has little meaning or relevance to him, he will have difficulty learning it.

Understanding the factors presented in Table 7-4 also helps us to answer the question "What is the best way to study for a test?" Brad now knows he will do better on his tests if he studies as often as possible (increases the number of sessions) but takes several breaks between study sessions (improves the distribution of sessions). For the best learning to occur, the material he is studying should be meaningful (Moravcsik & Healey, 1995), and he should not try to study several different topics during the same session (maintain similarity of items). Finally, the *serial position effect* indicates that he should give a little extra attention to material he studies during the middle portion of a study session (Baddeley, 2004; Gershberg & Shimamura, 1994; Madigan & O'Hara, 1992). You might want to try these procedures yourself; they could help raise your grades.

## Processing Strategies

Now that you understand how to arrange your study sessions and the type of material that should be studied, you want to know more. Why do some people remember better than others? Do they have special secrets or tricks? This section describes memory techniques that have been shown to work. These active learning devices or methods are called **mnemonic devices;** they are useful because they associate new information with previously stored memories (Ashcraft, 2006). Thus they are forms of elaborative

**7.4**

rehearsal and result in deeper processing. To remember new material, you first recall previously learned (familiar) information and then recall the new information that has been associated with it. You can decide whether mnemonic devices really work. As with anything else, some practice is required to learn to use them effectively. Among the most common techniques are imagery, the method of loci, the pegword technique, grouping, and coding.

**Imagery.**     If you create and use mental pictures or images of the items you are studying, you will remember better (Dewhurst & Conway, 1994; Paivio, 1971). Repeating items over and over again is not an especially effective method to help you remember them; however, visualizing them as you are learning can dramatically increase recall. When we try to remember by using both the words and the images, we have a *dual system* for coding the information, which increases the chances that it will be remembered (Sadoski & Paivio, 2001). For example, if you are learning the components of classical conditioning (see Chapter 5), you should not simply think "CS," "UCS," "UCR," and "CR"; rather, visualize a concrete example of each. The CS might be a noisy buzzer, the UCS a delicious apple pie, and so forth. This process of visualizing items as they are being learned is known as *imagery*.

Beyond this general finding, two more specific techniques for mental imagery have been developed. They are known as the *method of loci* and the *pegword technique*.

**Method of Loci.**     The method of loci can be traced back to the days of ancient Greek orators who used visual imagery and memorized locations to help them remember speeches or entire epics. *Loci* is the Latin word for "places;" the already stored cues for the **method of loci** are familiar specific places. When using this mnemonic device, you start with a set of familiar locations. For example, if you live on campus, you could list (in order) the major landmarks you see every time you walk from your dormitory room to the student union. Such landmarks could include the door to your room, the staircase to the first floor, the outside door, a tree, a statue, the science hall, and so forth, until you enter the front door of the student union. Then you would assign to each location an item that you want to learn. So if you were trying to learn the parts of the brain, you could pair the medulla with your door, the cerebellum with the staircase to the first floor, and so on. You could imagine an animated medulla hanging on your door. The cerebellum could become the staircase. Some people believe that more bizarre images have a greater effect on improving memory (Hirshman, Whelley, & Palij, 1989). To recall the parts of the brain in order, you would call up the mental image of the things you encounter on the way to the student union and remember the part of the brain associated with each location. This procedure may sound a bit complex, but it has been found to be highly effective.

### Psychological Detective

Don, the rock-and-roll expert, can name in order all of the songs on each of the most popular "oldies" rock CDs. Tonight Don is studying for a psychology test. During this study session, he listens to some of his favorite songs. Don hopes that rather than interfering with his studying, listening to music will help him to score higher on the test. He plays one type of music for each section of material he is studying. He studies the first section while Beatles music is playing; during the next section he listens to some Billy Joel, and so it goes for the rest of the evening. How will Don's unusual study session assist him when he takes the test? Write down an answer to this question before reading further.

**method of loci**
Use of familiar locations as cues to recall items that have been associated with them

**pegword technique**
Use of familiar words or names as cues to recall items that have been associated with them

**Pegword Technique.**     In the **pegword technique**, which is similar to the method of loci, you start with a list of items that you already know quite well (see Table 7-5). For Don to learn a set of items, all he has to do is assign one item to each song on a particular CD. When he is ready to recall the new information, he simply remembers the song titles and the item associated with each. Don is using the pegword technique to help him remember material for his psychology test. For example, basic learning terms (see Chapter 5) such as *CS, UCS, UCR, CR, reinforcement,* and *extinction* may be associated with the titles on the Beatles CD. Items having to do with states of consciousness (Chapter 4)

## TABLE 7-5

### The Pegword Mnemonic Technique

| Numbered Pegs | Words to Be Learned | Image | |
|---|---|---|---|
| One is bun | Cup | | Hamburger bun with a smashed cup |
| Two is a shoe | Flag | | Running shoes with flag |
| Three is a tree | Horse | | Horse stranded in top of tree |
| Four is a door | Dollar | | Dollar bill tacked to front door |
| Five is a hive | Brush | | Queen bee brushing her hair |
| Six is sticks | Pan | | Boiling a pan full of cinnamon sticks |
| Seven is heaven | Clock | | St. Peter checking the clocks at the gates of heaven |
| Eight is a gate | Pen | | A picket fence gate with ballpoint pens as pickets |
| Nine is a vine | Paper | | Honeysuckle vine with newspapers instead of blossoms |
| Ten is a hen | Shirt | | A baked hen in the platter wearing a flannel shirt |

**Source:** Ashcraft (2006).

might be associated with titles on the Billy Joel CD. The main difference between the pegword technique and the method of loci is that in the method of loci you visualize specific *locations*, whereas in the pegword technique you think of an already established list of items.

**Grouping (Chunking).** What is your telephone number? You will answer with a group of numbers, such as 316-555-5800. Since the time of the first experiment on grouping (Bousfield, 1953), psychologists have consistently found that we tend to group or *chunk* items when we recall them. If you must learn material in a certain order, you can group together the first three or four items, the next three or four, and so forth. We use this method of grouping when we learn telephone numbers. If the material does not have to be remembered in a particular order, the possibilities for grouping increase greatly. You can group items according to their type, their ending, their length, or any other way in which they are similar. How would you remember the following words?

dolphin, green bean, Mickey Mouse, beet, Goofy, carrot,
minnow, squash, bass, Minnie Mouse, spinach, trout,
Pluto, salmon, celery, perch, Donald Duck

Study this list for 1 minute; then close the book and write down as many of the words as you can. Did you group the items into three familiar categories—fish, vegetables, and Walt Disney characters? If you did not use those three categories, did you use others? If so, how did they differ from the categories we proposed? Chunking seems to be used most frequently and effectively with STM tasks, such as remembering a phone number or a list of words.

**Coding.** Items that are not very meaningful or relevant to the learner are not learned as well or as easily as more meaningful or relevant items. Some people create special

**acronym**

A word formed by the initial letter(s) of the items to be remembered

**acrostic**

A verse or saying in which the first letter(s) of each word stands for a bit of information

**STUDY TIP**

Make a set of flash cards with the names of the different processing strategies on one side and their definitions on the other. When you are studying material from this or another class, choose a card at random, test yourself on the definition, and then try out that particular strategy with the material you are studying.

codes to help them learn material that lacks relevance. They code the less relevant material in a meaningful form and then remember the coded items. It is important, however, to be able to decode the items once they have been learned. For example, the nonsense syllables *cib, xos,* and *gip* would be difficult to remember because they do not have high levels of meaning. What if we were to code each by printing it backward? In that case *cib* becomes *bic, xos* becomes *sox,* and *gip* becomes *pig.* These coded syllables are high in meaning and therefore are much easier to remember. When we want to recall the coded stimuli, all we have to do is reverse the order of the letters after the familiar words have been recalled.

**Acronyms and Acrostics.**   Acronyms and acrostics are two popular coding techniques. An **acronym** is a word formed by the initial letter(s) of the items to be remembered. To remember the desired information you recall the acronym and then decode it. For example, to help remember the names of the Great Lakes, all you need to do is recall the acronym HOMES and then decode it: H (Lake Huron), O (Lake Ontario), M (Lake Michigan), E (Lake Erie), and S (Lake Superior).

An **acrostic** is a verse or saying (often unusual or humorous) in which the first letter(s) of each word stands for a bit of information. For example, let's say you are assigned the task of remembering the names of the first seven presidents of the United States in order. One approach would be to use rote memorization. On the other hand, you might do better, spend less time, and have more fun if you made up a little phrase such as this: "**W**ashington **a**nd **J**efferson **m**ade **m**any **a** **j**oke." The first letter of each word in this saying stands for the last name of a president: George **W**ashington, John **A**dams, Thomas **J**efferson, James **M**adison, James **M**onroe, John Quincy **A**dams, and Andrew **J**ackson. Students frequently create acronyms and acrostics when they study for tests.

Evaluating techniques for improving memory naturally led psychologists to look for the physiological basis of memory. We consider their findings next.

# REVIEW SUMMARY

**1.** Craik and Lockhart proposed only one type of memory. The **level of processing** may determine the permanence of the storage of this memory.

**2.** There are at least four types of LTM: **procedural, semantic, episodic,** and **priming** (or **implicit**) **memory.** Each serves to store a different kind of information.

**3.** The **tip-of-the-tongue (TOT) phenomenon** has been used to study the network of semantic memories, whereas the study of **flashbulb memories** has provided information about episodic memory.

**4.** Research on the retrieval of memories has shown that we scan both STM and LTM to locate an item we wish to recall.

**5. Encoding specificity** has a great deal to do with the ease with which a memory is retrieved. If the cues that were present when a memory was encoded or stored are not present during retrieval, it is difficult to retrieve that memory. Encoding specificity appears to be at work in **state-dependent learning,** which states that we recall information better when we learn and are tested in the same physiological/psychological state. **Schemas** are clusters of knowledge or typical ways of thinking about

things. As such, they not only reflect how we store information, they can also influence how we retrieve information from memory.

**6.** It has been suggested that memories of childhood sexual abuse may be repressed and recalled during adulthood. Many of these repressed memories appear to have been induced during therapy sessions by suggestions made by the therapist. Psychologists have developed a number of techniques, including the cognitive interview, in order to assist in collecting information from eyewitnesses.

**7.** The number of sessions, distribution of practice, meaningfulness of items, similarity of items, and *serial position* of items influence human learning. Our memory can be improved by using a **mnemonic device** such as imagery. The **method of loci** and the **pegword technique** are two popular mnemonic devices.

**8.** Grouping and coding are two other techniques that can be used as memory aids. **Acronyms,** words formed by the first letter(s) of the items to be remembered, and **acrostics,** a verse or saying in which the first letter(s) of each word stands for a bit of information, are two popular forms of coding.

## ✓ CHECK YOUR PROGRESS

**1.** If your strategy in studying for a test is to memorize all the material, you may not do as well as someone else who relates the course material to real-life events. Why?

**2.** What is the main problem with the levels-of-processing approach to the study of memory?

**3.** How does the Craik-Lockhart model of memory differ from the traditional model of memory?

   **a.** The second model hypothesizes only one type of LTM.

   **b.** The second model assumes that retrieval is not an active process in STM.

   **c.** The first model hypothesizes only one type of memory but different levels of information processing.

   **d.** The first model uses semantic networking as a core concept in determining what is retained in working memory.

**4.** What is the most important question for Craik and Lockhart's view of memory?

   **a.** How long do memories last?

   **b.** How do we process information?

   **c.** How are visual memories stored?

   **d.** How much can we store in memory?

**5.** Which aspect of golf involves procedural memory?

   **a.** recalling how to swing the golf club

   **b.** recalling the time you made a hole-in-one

   **c.** recalling what type of golf ball you're using

   **d.** recalling that golf was first played in Scotland

**6.** The tip-of-the-tongue (TOT) phenomenon is to semantic memory as flashbulb memories are to

   **a.** implicit memory.

   **b.** semantic memory.

   **c.** episodic memory.

   **d.** procedural memory.

**7.** Which of the following illustrates a schema?

   **a.** the definition of the word *mild*

   **b.** the grocery list you just memorized

   **c.** your knowledge about going to a play

   **d.** your memory of a time you played basketball

**8.** How were psychologists able to implant false memories of a childhood experience of being lost in a mall?

   **a.** They used hypnosis followed by repeated suggestions that such an event had indeed occurred.

   **b.** Using specifically created newspaper clippings, they interspersed the reports with other clippings from the same time period.

   **c.** They collected real memories from family members and asked individuals for their memories of the true memories along with the memory they sought to implant.

   **d.** Combining sodium amytal treatment with dream imagery, they created an altered state of consciousness that made participants susceptible to suggestive scenes that they were asked to imagine.

**9.** Psychologists who speak of working memory are referring to a second stage of

   **a.** STM.

   **b.** LTM.

   **c.** episodic memory.

   **d.** primary memory.

**10.** What technique did ancient Greek orators use to remember speeches?

   **a.** coding

   **b.** transfer

   **c.** method of loci

   **d.** state dependence

**ANSWERS: 1.** You are processing at a very shallow level. The person who relates the material to real-life events is processing at a much deeper level. **2.** The term *level of processing* has never been clearly defined. **3.** c **4.** b **5.** a **6.** c **7.** c **8.** c **9.** a **10.** c

# THE PHYSIOLOGICAL BASIS OF LEARNING AND MEMORY

When H.M. was 7 years old, he was struck by a bicycle, fell, and injured his head. Although there appeared to be only minimal damage, several years later he began experiencing minor but intense brain seizures. A major seizure occurred when he was 16. By the time he was 27, the frequency and intensity of the seizures warranted surgery to remove large portions of his hippocampus and amygdala (see Chapter 2). The operation took place in 1953. *What can an operation to control seizures tell us about memory?*

In addition to identifying and studying the processes that occur during learning and memory, psychologists have attempted to isolate the physical changes that accompany those processes. In other words, they have attempted to pinpoint and describe the physiological basis of learning and memory. Their research has focused on patients who suffer memory loss as a result of head injuries or operations like the one just described.

# Amnesias

After experiencing a physical or psychological trauma, a person can lose his or her memory of people, places, and things. Such memory losses are called **amnesias.** We discuss amnesias caused by psychological traumas in Chapter 12. The study of amnesias resulting from physical trauma provides insight into the nature of memory. Two types of amnesias have been identified: *anterograde* and *retrograde.*

**Anterograde Amnesia and the Hippocampus.** The inability to store new information after a traumatic physical event is known as **anterograde amnesia.** The case of H.M. is a well-known example of anterograde amnesia (Scoville & Milner, 1957). What can this case tell us about memory?

As it turned out, H.M.'s operation, in which large portions of the hippocampus were removed, provided information about the nature of memory. After the operation, H.M. was unable to form new memories; his entire world consisted of memories formed before 1953. He did not remember the names of people he had just met, what he ate for lunch, what was on television last night, or what year it is. In short, his daily experience consisted exclusively of STM, of living from moment to moment, except for his pre-1953 memories.

### Psychological Detective

On the basis of this case, you should be able to reach two tentative conclusions. One has to do with the stages-of-memory processing discussed earlier; the second concerns the physiological basis of memory. Spend a few moments reviewing this information; then write down the two conclusions.

If you believe that H.M.'s problem has to do with the memory-storage process, you are correct. For H.M., new information is not reaching long-term storage. Thus we are led to the second conclusion: The hippocampus is involved in the process of storing new memories. Notice we said that this structure is *involved in the process* of storing new memories, not that new memories are stored in this structure. If memories were stored in the hippocampus, H.M.'s operation would have erased memories stored before 1953.

The conclusion that the hippocampus is involved in storing memories is supported by animal research. When the hippocampus is removed from both hemispheres of the brain in laboratory animals, the animals have difficulty holding information about a learning task they have just mastered in STM (Baddeley, 1988).

**Retrograde Amnesia and the Consolidation Hypothesis.** Physical trauma may also result in the loss of memory of events that occurred before the trauma. In such cases we are dealing with **retrograde amnesia.** The fact that the greatest memory loss is for events that occurred just before the trauma suggests an interesting and testable hypothesis. Based on the notion that memories must "set" or "consolidate" to be stored in LTM, the **consolidation hypothesis** predicts that memories that are interfered with before they have consolidated will not be stored. This process is analogous to baking a cake: If the oven door is opened, the cake will fall. The blow on the head that produces retrograde amnesia has interrupted the consolidation process for recent memories.

**amnesia**
Loss of memory that occurs as a result of physical or psychological trauma

**anterograde amnesia**
Inability to store new memories after a traumatic event

**retrograde amnesia**
Loss of memories that were stored before a traumatic event

**consolidation hypothesis**
Hypothesis that memories must be consolidated or set before they can be stored

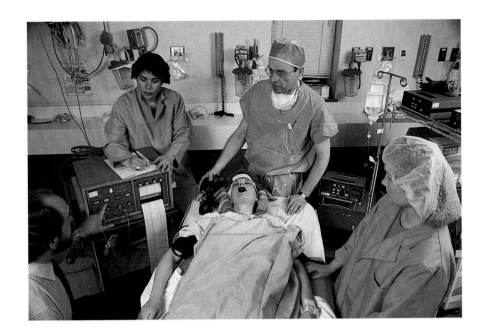

A human patient undergoing ECT may suffer from retrograde amnesia. According to the consolidation hypothesis, this loss of memory occurs because consolidation and transfer to LTM do not take place.

Both human and animal studies have provided evidence to support the consolidation hypothesis. For example, in some cases of severe depression, *electroconvulsive therapy* (*ECT*), also known as *electroshock therapy*, may be used (see Chapter 13). This procedure involves passing an electric current through the patient's brain. In addition to reducing the depression, ECT produces strong retrograde amnesia. Early studies found that the application of electroconvulsive shock (ECS) to animals shortly after a learning task also produced retrograde amnesia, suggesting that it interferes with the formation of a memory. What's more, the longer the delay between completion of the task and the application of ECS, the less the effect of ECS. In the longer delay conditions, we assumed that the memory had more time to consolidate and therefore ECS did not interfere with it as much.

In one study of the effects of ECS (Chorover & Schiller, 1965), rats were placed on small platforms. The normal response of a rat in this situation is to step down from the platform. When the rats stepped down, however, they received an electric shock to their feet. The rats' task was to learn to stay on the platform to avoid a foot shock. Five groups of rats were tested. These groups received ECS (by passing a mild electric current through the brain) either 3, 5, 7, 10, or 30 seconds after stepping off the platform and receiving a foot shock. Figure 7-12 shows that the longer the interval between the learning task and the delivery of ECS, the greater the percentage of animals that stayed on

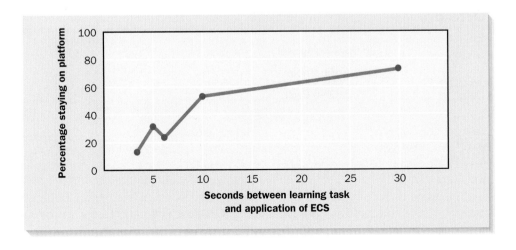

**FIGURE 7-12** The longer the delay between original learning and an ECS, the greater the percentage of animals who avoided foot shock by staying on the platform.

**Source:** Chorover and Schiller (1965).

the platform on the next trial. Thus it appears that the memory of receiving the foot shock after stepping off the platform was consolidated more strongly when ECS was applied either 10 or 30 seconds after a foot shock. Although not all animal studies have supported the consolidation hypothesis as well (Maki, 1986), there is no doubt that ECS impairs memory storage.

## REVIEW SUMMARY

1. Physical trauma may result in a loss of memory known as **amnesia. Anterograde amnesia** occurs when new information cannot be stored, although old memories remain intact. It can result from damage to the hippocampus. **Retrograde amnesia** occurs when memories for events that happened before the traumatic event are lost. It may occur when memories are not allowed to **consolidate** or set.

## ✓ CHECK YOUR PROGRESS

1. Loss of memory owing to a physical trauma is known as
   a. amnesia.
   b. habituation.
   c. consolidation.
   d. long-term potentiation.

2. After a serious car accident, John cannot remember driving in the rain. Nor can he recall skidding and plowing into a truck. This deficit is an example of
   a. retrograde amnesia.
   b. anterograde amnesia.
   c. encoding specificity.
   d. state-dependent learning.

3. What notion is supported by the fact that ECT disrupts memories?

   a. neural circuits
   b. consolidation hypothesis
   c. synaptic changes and memory
   d. protein synthesis and memory

4. Which kind of amnesia results from damage to the hippocampus? Why?

5. Laboratory rats prefer to be in dark places; hence they move readily from a brightly lit chamber to a dark one. Assume that a foot shock is administered when the rats enter the dark compartment. What should the rats learn from this experience? What will happen if they receive an ECS 3 seconds after receiving a foot shock in the dark compartment? What would happen if an ECS was administered 1 hour after the rats received a foot shock in the dark compartment?

**ANSWERS: 1.** a **2.** a **3.** b **4.** Anterograde amnesia. Damage to the hippocampus results in the inability to form new memories. **5.** The rats should learn not to enter the dark compartment. If an ECS is administered 3 seconds after the shock in the dark compartment, there may be considerable disruption of consolidation. If an ECS is administered 1 hour after the shock in the dark compartment, the memory will have set and an ECS will have no effect.

---

**ANSWERS** | To Psychological Detective

**PAGE–301**

1. Pacific Ocean

2. Hybrid

3. Cholesterol

4. Hibernate

5. Ohio River

## ANSWERS   To Hands-On Exercise

### PAGE 301

How many capitals were on the tip of your tongue the first time you went through the list of states? Did the first letter help you recall any additional names?

| State | Capital |
|-------|---------|
| Alabama | Montgomery |
| Connecticut | Hartford |
| Florida | Tallahassee |
| Georgia | Atlanta |
| Idaho | Boise |
| Iowa | Des Moines |

| State | Capital |
|-------|---------|
| Kentucky | Frankfort |
| Louisiana | Baton Rouge |
| Maryland | Annapolis |
| Massachusetts | Boston |
| Mississippi | Jackson |
| Nebraska | Lincoln |
| New Jersey | Trenton |
| Oregon | Salem |
| Texas | Austin |
| Wyoming | Cheyenne |

## CHAPTER 8

# Thinking, Language, and Intelligence

## CHAPTER OUTLINE

The brain plays a key role in basic processes such as sensing and perceiving the environment, emotional reactions, and states of consciousness. Most of the basic processes we have discussed thus far are also found in lower animals, so we may wonder what separates lower animals from human beings.

The human brain endows us with remarkable abilities to solve problems and to make decisions. In this chapter we explore some of humans' remarkable abilities. As we explore these abilities, we also find that humans can be misled by some of the methods we use to solve problems and make decisions. One of the most remarkable human achievements—the development of complex language—sets us apart from other species. One way to view the intellectual achievements of human beings is to consider this fact: Only human beings are capable of creating methods to measure their intellectual achievements. One of the more contentious issues we discuss is the measurement of intelligence. Our analysis of this topic shows us how the study of a topic changes over time and how new ways of conceptualizing intelligence are offered.

## THINKING

**After agreeing to take part in an experiment, Sandy was asked to sit in front of a computer screen and view a series of geometric figures that were presented in pairs (see Figure 8-1). Her task was simple: Determine whether the paired figures are the same or different. In some cases she quickly made the determination; in others the process took longer. Although she guessed that the experiment was designed to study thinking, she wondered how psychologists could study such an unseen process. *How do psychologists study thinking?***

In Chapter 1 we described how John B. Watson, the founder of behaviorism, redirected psychology to focus on the observation of external events. Because conscious experience could not be observed directly, he concluded that it was not worthy of scientific investigation. Terms such as *thinking* or *thoughts* were not precise, so Watson turned to the study of the muscle movements of subvocal speech as the basis of what we call thinking. Does Watson's proposal to study the muscle movements related to speech seem far-fetched? Ask someone a question (preferably one requiring some deliberation) and watch the person's lips as he or she considers how to respond. Do the person's lips move? As part of his effort to make psychology more objective, Watson claimed that psychologists could study thinking if it consisted of observable muscle movements like those that occur when we speak silently to ourselves.

If thinking consists of barely detectable motor movements, it would be impossible to think if all of our motor muscles were paralyzed. To test this notion, Scott Smith injected himself with curare (see Chapter 2), a poison that blocks conduction in motor neurons and therefore causes paralysis (Smith, Brown, Toman, & Goodman, 1947). Had he not been connected to a respirator that could breathe for him, he would have died. While he was paralyzed, his colleagues asked him questions and gave him problems to solve. After the effects of the curare wore off, Smith told his colleagues what he had been *thinking* while he was paralyzed. His courageous efforts demonstrated that thinking consists of more than just muscle movements.

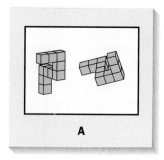

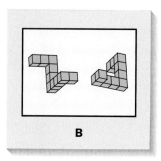

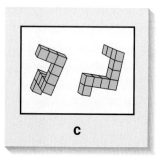

**FIGURE 8-1** Pictures of three-dimensional objects shown to participants by Shepard and Metzler (1971). For each, look at the object on the left and determine whether the object on the right is a rotated view of the same object.

**Source:** Shepard and Metzler (1971).

# Cognitive Psychology

Although the results reported by Smith and his colleagues were striking, behaviorism remained a dominant force in psychology for more than half of the 20th century (Guenther, 1998). Eventually a new perspective, cognitive psychology, gained prominence. **Cognitive psychology** is a branch of psychology that examines *thinking*: how we know and understand the world, solve problems, make decisions, combine information from memory and current experience, use language, and communicate our thoughts to others. **Thinking** is a mental process involving the manipulation of information in the form of images or concepts that is inferred from our behavior. Thinking is evident, for example, when we solve a problem or make a decision.

Cognitive psychologists infer mental processes from the observable behaviors of the people they study. For example, to uncover problem-solving strategies, they may ask people to think aloud as they solve problems (called a *verbal protocol*). In the following discussion we consider one way in which cognitive psychologists draw inferences about thinking—through the study of images.

**Images.**    What route do you follow when you walk from the front door of your apartment to your bedroom? What is the shape and color of a highway "yield" sign? Many people report that they visualize events and objects to answer such questions. Visual imagery, the experience of seeing even though the event or object is not actually viewed, can activate brain areas responsible for visual perception, such as the occipital lobes (see Chapter 2). Images do not have to be visual, however; they can be auditory or even olfactory (involving the sense of smell).

Before the development of sophisticated equipment to study brain activation, two researchers, Roger Shepard and Jacqueline Metzler (1971, 1994), investigated how people answer questions about visually presented material. Look again at Figure 8-1, and examine the paired drawings to determine whether the objects on the right are the same as those on the left. If you rotated the objects on the left, would they be the same as those on the right? The pairs of geometric figures used by Shepard and Metzler differed in orientation to each other between 0 and 180 degrees. Half of the pairs were matches that had been rotated; the other half were mirror images that could not be rotated to match. How would you go about answering questions about these pairs of figures? Would you create a visual image of the objects in your mind?

## Psychological Detective

The study of visual imagery poses some difficulty for researchers: The process of thinking cannot be directly observed. How could researchers draw inferences about the mental processes involved in answering questions about the paired objects in Figure 8-1? Give this question some thought, and write down your answer before reading further.

**cognitive psychology**
The subfield of psychology concerned with the study of higher mental processes such as thinking, knowing, and deciding

**thinking**
Manipulation of information in the form of mental images or concepts

Shepard and Metzler found that people were accurate in judging whether the pairs of figures were the same or different. When the object had been rotated a great deal, however, participants took longer to decide whether it was the same or different. Why? The researchers inferred that the increased time was spent *mentally* rotating the figures. The greater the degree of rotation, the longer people took to rotate the configuration back to the original orientation. To behaviorists, such inferences about unseen mental processes are not a legitimate part of science. In science, however, inference is common: Geologists use the Earth's sediment layers to infer past events, and physicists cannot observe gravity directly, even though they study its effects.

Visual images allow us to scan information stored in memory and answer questions like the ones we asked earlier; they also help us plan a course of action. For example, Albert Einstein's insight into the theory of relativity occurred when he created a visual image of chasing after and matching the speed of a beam of light. Later he turned this visual image into words. The following examples illustrate the value of imagery in our thinking, as well as its potential application in sports.

Suppose we need to describe the size of an acre. How could we convey this information? If we told you that there are 43,560 square feet in an acre, would that help you understand how large an acre is? Perhaps not. If, however, we used a visual image and told you that an acre is about the size of a football field minus the end zones, we would probably make it more understandable.

Words like *book*, *laptop*, and *pencil* readily give rise to visual images and are easier to remember than low-imagery words like *ambition*, *integrity*, and *responsibility* (Paivio, 1971, 1986). Why? High-imagery words offer two pegs on which to hang our memories: visual images and meaning (see Chapter 7). By contrast, low-imagery words must be remembered from their meaning alone.

Sport psychologists have advocated visual imagery as a practice technique to enhance attention and performance in a number of sports as well as an aid in rehabilitating injuries (Calmels, Berthoumieux, & d'Arripe-Longueville, 2004; Nordin & Cumming, 2005; Smith, Holmes, Whitmore, Collins, & Devonport, 2001). A review of evidence on the effects of imagery on sports performance led to the conclusion that imagery has a positive and significant effect on performance (Driskell, Copper, & Moran, 1994). How does visual imagery enhance performance? Measures of blood flow in the brain show that mental practice can activate brain structures without actual physical movement; this activation appears to improve the control and execution of movement (Decety & Ingvar, 1990; Roure et al., 1999).

Although images play an important role in cognition, not all thinking involves imagery. Much of it involves the formation and use of concepts. Next, let's look at the role that concepts play in thinking.

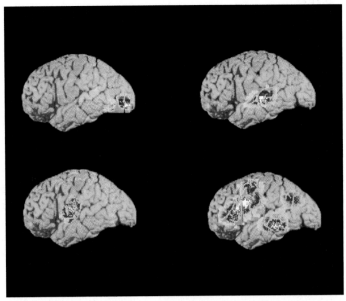

Sight, hearing, speaking, and thinking activate different areas of the brain (indicated in red on this positron emission tomography scan). Visual imagery activates the occipital lobes (top left), which are responsible for processing visual information.

Visualizing a football field (without the end zones) makes it easier to comprehend the size of an acre.

**concepts**
Mental categories that share common characteristics

**Concepts.**  What would life be like if we had to deal separately with each individual animal, object, and person in our environment? How could we learn the names of all of them? We avoid such problems by using **concepts**—mental representations of a class (chairs, dogs, teachers) of things. Cabbage, peppers, and string beans are examples of the concept "vegetables." Concepts reduce the load on memory and enhance our ability to communicate; they also allow us to make predictions about our world.

Imagine sitting behind the wheel of an unfamiliar car. You can predict how the car operates, know the type of fuel needed, understand what happens when you put the key in the ignition, and locate several controls. You can do these things because you understand the concept "car." Much of what we learn in school, especially grade school, involves concepts such as colors, letters, species of living organisms, whole numbers and fractions, time, and distance. The use of such concepts makes communicating a great deal of information possible with relative ease.

One way we classify something as an example of a concept is to use rules that tell us what is and what is not an instance of the concept. Objects that follow the rules and have certain properties are called *positive instances* of the concept; the absence of such properties is the mark of a *negative instance* of the concept. Such rules work well for defining a concept such as a "square" (closed two-dimensional figure with four equal sides connected at 90 degree angles) (Ross & Spalding, 1994).

## Psychological Detective

An example of the rules approach to concepts can be found in Figure 8-2, where we have provided positive and negative instances of a concept. Your job is to figure out the rules we used. The first and fourth examples illustrate the concept (positive instances); the second and third examples do not illustrate the concept (negative instances). Write down the rule (or rules) you believe defines the concept. (The correct answer appears at the end of the chapter.)

One way you might learn this new concept is to use trial-and-error learning: You suggest a preliminary idea of what the concept might be; then you systematically test this idea or hypothesis on new examples. Researchers have used this approach in laboratory studies on concept formation. Were you able to identify the concept illustrated in Figure 8-2? As you thought about this concept, you probably noticed that this laboratory-based example is not like those you encounter in everyday life, which usually are more complicated and not defined by neat sets of rules.

Now try to list the properties that could be used to classify an animal as a dog. You might suggest four legs, some fur, and a tail, but so far the list of properties still includes cats, foxes, and wolves. You can see that listing a set of properties as the rules for

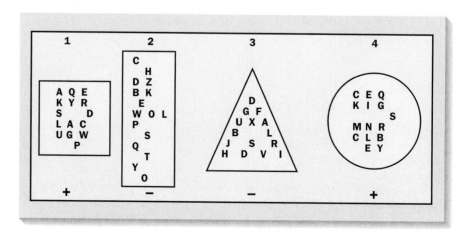

**FIGURE 8-2**  Sample material used in concept formation experiments.

**FIGURE 8-3**   All the animals in the photo on the left can be classified under the concept of "dog." Does the fox pictured on the right also belong to this concept? Why or why not?

defining a concept does not always work well. Why? As the dog example shows us, many concepts have unclear boundaries (see Figure 8-3). It seems that we do not form concepts the way participants in laboratory research do, by creating a list of properties. Instead we often rely on a **prototype,** or best example, of each concept. When we encounter a new object, we compare it to the prototype.

Think of the concept "fruit." What prototype (image or word) do you have in mind right now? Did you think of an orange, a plum, a date? Think of the concept "sports." Which of these best fits your prototype of a sport: car racing, chess, or baseball? Now think of a bird. What do you have in mind? When people rated the degree to which various fruits represented the concept "fruit," they rated orange and apple as the best examples; tomato and avocado were least likely to serve as the prototype of a fruit (Rosch, 1975). When we asked you to think of a bird, did you think of a cardinal, a robin, or a sparrow? You probably did not think of a chicken or a penguin.

We classify new objects according to their similarity to our prototypes. Thus membership in a concept category is not an all-or-nothing matter; rather, there are often degrees of similarity to the prototypes. The concepts we encounter and use every day do not have sharp boundaries and are not based on a specific, concrete set of properties.

What's more, our concepts do not exist independently, isolated one from another; rather, they are organized into a hierarchy. Let's take the concept of furniture, for example, where related concepts organized under it become increasingly specific. At the next lower level, we might have different types of furniture, including one labeled "chair." Below this heading is yet another level that would include "recliner," "rocking chair," "desk chair," and so forth (Ashcraft, 2006; Ross & Spalding, 1994).

As we have seen, concepts reduce the load on our memory because we don't have to remember every instance of objects separately. At times, we rely on memory to help us solve problems that are related to similar ones we have seen before. Even when a problem is not similar to past problems, we can turn to some problem-solving methods that have generally stood the test of time.

## Problem Solving

Every day we encounter a variety of minor problems; occasionally we face major ones. You may find that the wheels of your car spin on the ice, a zipper on your luggage breaks as you board a flight, or your computer crashes at the most inconvenient time. Some problems are easy to solve, others require great effort, and some may be unsolvable.

Problems can differ along several dimensions; for example, some are well defined or structured, and others are ill defined or unstructured (Alexander, 2006). Well-defined problems have three specified characteristics: a clearly specified beginning state

**prototype**
A specific example of a particular concept that is readily brought to mind; viewed as the most typical or best example of a particular concept

**algorithm**
A systematic procedure that is guaranteed to furnish the correct answer to a problem if it is followed correctly because the procedure involves evaluating all possible solutions

(*the starting point*), a set of clearly specified tools or techniques for finding the solution (*the needed operations*), and a clearly specified solution state (*the final product*) (Guenther, 1998; Medin, Ross, & Markman, 2001). A well-defined problem might take the form of "How should I program my word processor to fit a 500-word essay on two pages?" or "If you and a friend can plant three pine trees in 60 minutes, how many pine trees can you and two friends plant in 4 hours?"

Ill-defined problems have a degree of uncertainty or "messiness" about the starting point, needed operations, and final product. Such problems can have numerous acceptable responses, and the criteria for judging the responses are not necessarily simple and straightforward (Alexander, 2006). An ill-defined question might take the form of "What programs could we institute to reduce reliance on nonrenewable sources of energy like oil?" or "What are 10 unusual uses for the Styrofoam popcorn that comes in packing crates?"

**Problem-Solving Methods.**   When you recognize that a problem exists, you can search your memory to determine if you have faced a similar problem in the past; if so, you can retrieve the solution from memory and apply it to the current problem (see Chapter 7). If the problem is new and there is no solution in long-term memory, you can use several strategies to attack the problem. High-speed computers have provided scientists with a model that can be used to understand human thinking. To use the computer as a model of human thought, however, researchers need to know what human beings do when they solve problems. Two general approaches to solving problems can be programmed into a computer: algorithms and heuristics.

**Algorithms.**   One strategy you could use to solve some problems guarantees a correct solution in time (provided that a solution exists). An **algorithm** is a systematic procedure or specified set of steps for solving a problem, which may involve evaluating all possible solutions (Ashcraft, 2006; Medin et al., 2001). One example of an algorithm is the mathematical formula used to determine the area enclosed by a rectangle: Length multiplied by width gives the answer.

### Psychological Detective

Here is an opportunity for you to solve a problem that could involve the use of an algorithm. An *anagram* is a collection of letters that can be rearranged to form one or more words. Consider the following anagram:

O  E  V  S  L

How would you go about finding the word? As you try to solve this problem, pay attention to exactly what you do.

**8.1**

Try your hand at solving these anagrams. *Hint:* Each of them is related to material found in the preceding chapters.

O V P A L V

U R Y V S E

R O N E U N

A I T E N R

O M R E Y M

T E O P A I

Finding the solution to our anagram problem is a bit more complicated than using the formula for the area of a rectangle. Before you start writing all the possible arrangements of these five letters, note that they can be arranged in 120 different ways. Of course, not all such arrangements are words, and few of them are even remotely similar to real words.

Algorithms tell us exactly what to do to reach a solution, but they can be time-consuming. If you spent 1 second on each combination of five letters, you could spend 2 minutes solving this simple anagram. Because most people solve the anagram in considerably less than 2 minutes, they probably use a method other than an algorithm. (The possible answers to the anagram are *solve, loves,* and *voles.*)

Now consider the following examples:

**1.** If you toss a coin, what is the probability of getting a head?

**2.** If you toss a coin, what is the probability of getting heads *two* times in a row?

The answer to the first question is easy—the probability of tossing heads is .50 (50% heads and 50% tails). But the second question poses some difficulty for many students: In a survey of undergraduates 89% got the first question correct, but only 42% were correct on the second. Why? Most students do not know the formula (an algorithm) for calculating the probability of a sequence of independent events: It is the probability of the event (.50 in this case) multiplied by itself once for each event in the sequence, or $.50 \times .50 = .25$. In other words, tossing two coins can yield the following results: TH, HT, HH, TT; thus, the probability of two heads is .25, or 25% (Ashcraft, 2006).

Algorithms do not provide answers when the problems are not clearly specified. No procedures can be set up in advance to guarantee a solution for such problems. What's more, some problems are so vast that algorithms are impractical. For example, chess players do not rely on algorithms because it would take centuries to examine all possible arrangements of the chess pieces.

**Heuristics.** While you were trying to solve the anagram, you may have decided that the vowels O and E should be separated. It might also be a good idea to separate the V and the S because this combination of letters does not occur frequently in English words; on the other hand, SO is a common combination. These rules of thumb are examples of a problem-solving approach known as **heuristics** (derived from the Greek word meaning "to invent or discover"). Heuristics do not guarantee solutions, but they make more efficient use of time. Using heuristics may lead to quick solutions or to no solution at all.

**Obstacles and Aids to Problem Solving.** Researchers have compared the problem solving of experts and nonexperts and have found that experts know more information to use in solving problems. More important, experts know how to collect and organize information and are better at recognizing patterns in the information they gather. We can use the knowledge researchers have gained to improve our own problem-solving capabilities and avoid obstacles.

**Setting Subgoals.** As we have noted, one way to study problem solving is to ask people to think aloud. This procedure enables a researcher to follow a person's problem-solving efforts. Using this technique, psychologists have found that expert problem solvers are adept at breaking problems down into subgoals, which can be attacked and solved one at a time. These intermediate subgoals can make problems more manageable and increase the chance of reaching a solution.

### Psychological Detective

Try this problem. Nine adults and two children want to cross a river, using a raft that will carry either one adult or two children. The raft must be paddled by a person; it cannot be pulled across the river by a rope. How many times must the raft cross the river to accomplish this goal? (A round trip equals two crossings.) Write down your answer before reading further.

This is not an easy problem. Remember that effective problem solvers break down large problems into smaller subgoals; it is difficult to solve such a massive problem in one swipe. First, you need to know how many crossings are required to transport one adult across the river. You find that it takes four crossings to move one adult across the river and return the boat to the original dock. If the two children cross the river, one of the children can return the boat. When the child returns, an adult can cross alone and the other child returns the boat. To move the nine adults across the river, you must repeat that sequence of four trips eight more times; it will take 36 trips to move nine adults. One final trip is needed to move the two children across, for a total of 37 trips.

**heuristics**
Educated guesses or rules of thumb for solving problems that are not guaranteed to yield the correct answer

The keys to solving this problem are (a) to identify the sequence needed to transport one adult across the river and (b) to determine that the sequence can be repeated. Finding the solution requires that you break the problem into manageable intermediate subgoals (one person at a time).

**Approach to Representing Problems.** Information that is not organized effectively can hinder problem solving. At times, we may rely on memory; at other times, external representations of a problem are helpful.

Consider the following problem. There are three boxes of equal size. Inside each box are two smaller boxes. Inside each of the smaller boxes are four even smaller boxes. How many boxes are there all together? The chances of solving this problem improve if it is represented somewhere other than in our heads. Students who were prompted to draw the problem solved it more frequently. (The correct answer is 33 boxes.)

What is 2/3 of 1/2? When you first read this problem, you may be confused and conclude that it is difficult. Now let's represent the problem as 2/3 × 1/2. This shows us that we could represent it as "What is 1/2 of 2/3?" This small change in representation converts a moderately difficult problem into a simple one in which the answer almost jumps off the page. Now try to solve a slightly different kind of problem.

### Psychological Detective

Connect the nine dots in Figure 8-4 with four straight lines without lifting your pencil from the page. Try to solve this problem before reading further.

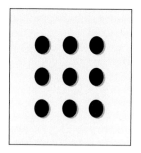

**FIGURE 8-4** The nine-dot problem.

What did you see when you looked at the dots? Your perception of the dots probably followed the Gestalt principles of perceptual organization discussed in Chapter 3. One difficulty many people face in solving this problem is the tendency to see the dots as a boundary enclosing a rectangle. Thus our perception can lead us astray; however, nothing in the problem prevents us from taking our pencil outside the imaginary boundary that our mind creates. Try the problem; then turn to the end of the chapter for some solutions.

Here's another problem to solve. How would you put 27 pigs into four pens with an odd number of pigs in each pen? Most problem solvers try to figure a way to divide 27 into four odd numbers. This approach seems reasonable until you realize that it is not possible. You tried this approach because you perceived the solution to involve four separate and distinct pens. *Hint:* Try looking at the relation among the pens again. Consult the end of the chapter for the answer to this problem.

Now try to solve the problems presented in Figure 8-5.

**FIGURE 8-5** Try your hand at solving three more problems. The key to solving them is to break away from obvious ways of looking at things. Consider other perspectives; otherwise, you will box yourself in, as you did if you treated the nine dots in Figure 8-4 as a rectangle. The answers appear at the end of the chapter.

**Source:** Michalko (1991).

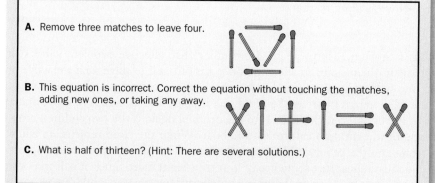

**A.** Remove three matches to leave four.

**B.** This equation is incorrect. Correct the equation without touching the matches, adding new ones, or taking any away.

**C.** What is half of thirteen? (Hint: There are several solutions.)

**FIGURE 8-6** The Maier two-string problem. The two strings hanging from the ceiling are to be tied together, using only the chair and the pliers.

**Source:** Maier (1931).

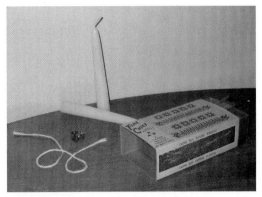

**FIGURE 8-7** The candle problem. Using only the materials pictured, find a way to mount the candle on the wall so that it can be used.

**Source:** Duncker (1945).

**Rigidity.** Using past experience is often helpful in solving problems, but sometimes it can block the path of our problem-solving efforts. *Rigidity* is the tendency to rely too heavily on past experience in solving problems. A specific example of rigidity is the difficulty we experience in using familiar objects and concepts in new ways, which is termed **functional fixedness.** One example of functional fixedness, shown in Figure 8-6, is Maier's classic two-string problem (Maier, 1931). The two strings hanging from the ceiling are to be tied together. Among the objects in the room are a chair and a set of pliers.

The strings are too far apart to allow the person to grasp both of them and tie them together. Not surprisingly, most of the solutions tried by participants in Maier's study involved the chair, although unsuccessfully. What is the solution? Think about it for a while.

The solution to this problem is to tie the pliers to the end of one string, set the string in motion like a pendulum, then catch it and tie it to the other string. The solution may seem obvious now, but only 39% of participants in Maier's experiment solved the problem in the 10 minutes allotted. Why did they experience so much trouble with this problem? They displayed functional fixedness: They did not see that the pliers could be used in an unusual way. Now look at Figure 8-7.

## Psychological Detective

Your task is to solve the problem presented in Figure 8-7. Imagine that you are in a small, nearly empty room. On the floor are the following objects: a box of wooden kitchen matches, a piece of string, a candle, and several thumbtacks. There is no electricity in the room. The task is to use the materials in the figure to mount the candle on the wall (Duncker, 1945). Write down your solution to the problem before reading further.

The solution is presented at the end of the chapter. Many people fail to solve this problem as a result of functional fixedness. Because the matches are shown in the

**functional fixedness**
Inability to see new uses for familiar objects

**TABLE 8-1**

## Luchins Water Jug Problems

The goal is to obtain the desired quantity of water by using the jugs specified.

| Problem | Capacity of Jug A | Capacity of Jug B | Capacity of Jug C | Desired Quantity |
|---|---|---|---|---|
| 1 | 29 | 3 | 0 | 20 |
| 2 | 21 | 127 | 3 | 100 |
| 3 | 14 | 163 | 25 | 99 |
| 4 | 18 | 43 | 10 | 5 |
| 5 | 9 | 42 | 6 | 21 |
| 6 | 20 | 59 | 4 | 31 |
| 7 | 23 | 49 | 3 | 20 |
| 8 | 28 | 59 | 3 | 25 |

**Source:** Luchins (1946).

box, people attempting to solve this problem often fail to see the box as a possible support for the candle.

**Set Effect.** As we have shown, problem solvers can experience difficulty in representing a problem and may also rely only on common uses of objects. Depending on prior experience is another way we restrict ourselves to certain problem-solving approaches even if they are not the most effective. Such a bias is called the **set effect**.

Luchins (1942) presented individuals with the problem outlined in Table 8-1. In this problem, the goal is to obtain the specified amount of water by using the jugs shown. After the first warmup problem, the solution takes the form of B minus A minus 2C: Fill Jug B, then pour enough water to fill Jug A, and fill Jug C twice. This solution works for Problems 2 through 6.

Success in solving the first few water jug problems creates a "set" or tendency to use the same approach for the rest of the problems; after all, that approach worked. Nevertheless, there is an easier way to solve Problems 7 and 8. Those problems can be solved with fewer steps by first filling Jug A and then using it to fill Jug C. You may have failed to see this easier solution as you routinely applied the method that had worked so well for the earlier problems. You can continue to develop your problem-solving skills by trying the problems in Figure 8-8.

The problems we have described here have solutions. In problem solving we search for solutions; however, our thinking does not involve just solving problems. Sometimes we are asked to weigh the advantages and disadvantages of different courses of action. Here there is no problem to be solved, but there is a decision to be made.

## Making Decisions

Each day we make dozens—perhaps hundreds—of decisions. What is the easiest way to get to the family reunion next week? Should I go to the bank today or wait until tomorrow? Some of these decisions are easy; others are more difficult. How do we make such decisions?

The brain enables us to process vast amounts of information quickly and accurately. Heuristics are often helpful and economical and can lead to good decisions; at times, however, they may also lead to bad decisions. The same principles that allow us to make

**STUDY TIP**

In a group of three, discuss the material describing problem solving. Together, create a basic problem-solving plan, label the steps, and note pitfalls to avoid. Then name an ill-defined problem that one member of the group needs to solve, talk through it using your plan, and identify some possible solutions.

**set effect**
Bias toward the use of certain problem-solving approaches because of past experience

## A Hare-Brained Scheme

A farmer buys 9 rabbits but does not know which ones are male and which are female. Until he can find out, he wants to keep them apart. The problem is that the farmer has only one square pen. Show him how he can build two more square pens inside this large pen so that each rabbit will have its own separate area.

## Ten Bowling Pins

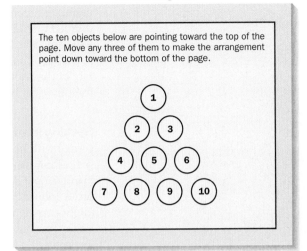

The ten objects below are pointing toward the top of the page. Move any three of them to make the arrangement point down toward the bottom of the page.

## Six Drinking Glasses

By handling and moving only one glass, change the arrangement so that no full glass is next to another full one, and no empty glass is next to another empty one.

1   2   3   4   5   6

## Six Pennies

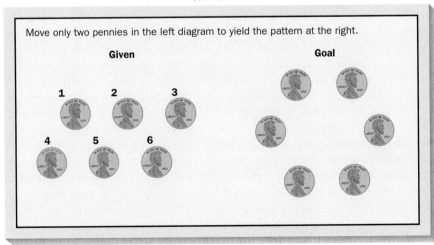

Move only two pennies in the left diagram to yield the pattern at the right.

**Given**

1   2   3
4   5   6

**Goal**

**FIGURE 8-8** Here is an opportunity to try your problem-solving abilities on several different types of problems. Remember our discussion of the obstacles we face when we try to solve problems. Don't let these obstacles impede your efforts. Try each one of these problems before checking the answers at the end of the chapter.

judgments easily and often successfully are also responsible for some of our errors. For example, suppose that you see a red car that was involved in an accident. Have you ever decided that people who drive red cars drive faster and less safely than other drivers? If you were asked to estimate the number of crimes in which people plead "not guilty by reason of insanity," it is likely that you would overestimate the actual number by quite a bit. In this section we look closely at some of the most important heuristics and their usefulness in making decisions.

**Seeking Information to Confirm a Solution.** The series *2, 4, 6* follows a rule concerned with how the numbers relate to one another. Your task is to discover the rule by suggesting other sets of numbers that follow it. Because the numbers increase by *2*, many people suggest a series such as *12, 14, 16*, followed by one like *22, 24, 26*. Both series follow the rule. Buoyed by these two confirmations of the proposed rule, you might confidently announce that the rule requires that the numbers increase by 2; however, you would be wrong. In fact, 79% of participants in a study confidently stated an incorrect rule when given this problem (Wason, 1960).

A common mistake in testing hypotheses is to commit to one hypothesis without adequately testing other possibilities; this is known as **confirmation bias.** In our example, the correct rule is that the series must consist of three positive numbers that increase. If you tried a series like *1, 2, 3*, we would tell you that the series follows the rule and you could modify your initial hypothesis. People who found the correct rule earliest had generated more *negative* instances, which provided information they could use to modify their hypotheses. This example illustrates an important aspect of our problem-solving and decision-making behavior: the tendency to seek instances that confirm our beliefs, solutions, or hypotheses and to avoid instances that disconfirm them.

The following story illustrates the power of the confirmation bias. Several children were playing a game of "20 Questions;" the goal was to find a number between 1 and 10,000. They cheered when the teacher said, "Yes, it is between 5,000 and 10,000" and groaned when the answer was "No, it is not between 0 and 5,000." Although both answers conveyed the same amount of information, confirmation was met with jubilation; a lack of confirmation was greeted with disappointment. As adults we do not outgrow the tendency to seek confirmation.

**Representativeness.** When we use the **representativeness heuristic,** we determine whether an event, an object, or a person resembles (or represents) a prototype. Suppose that Ted, a college graduate, is very careful and concerned about details. He rarely tells jokes and seems to lack creativity. Give him a task, and he will carry it out according to the rules. Is Ted an accountant or a writer? Your conclusion would most likely be based on the similarity you perceive between Ted's characteristics and those you believe are common among accountants and writers; you would be using the representativeness heuristic. In essence you are looking for a match between Ted and the prototype of either an accountant or a writer. Including information about the number of accountants (30%) and writers (70%) in a group did not alter predictions of Ted's occupation (Kahneman & Tversky, 1973, 2000). Participants were swayed by the similarity of Ted's personality characteristics to the common stereotype of an accountant, which is quite different from the stereotype of a writer, who may be perceived as creative, tolerant, and open to experience. Because Ted's profile sounds like one we associate with accountants, it therefore represents our prototype of accountants. In this case the representativeness heuristic—a rule of thumb—leads us to assume that the similarity in the personality profile is a more powerful predictor than the odds of selecting an accountant from a group with a small number of accountants.

Here is a simple exercise that will illustrate the representativeness heuristic. Take a few pennies from your pocket and drop them on the table.

**confirmation bias**
Committing to one hypothesis without adequately testing other possibilities

**representativeness heuristic**
Heuristic in which one determines whether a particular instance represents a certain class or category

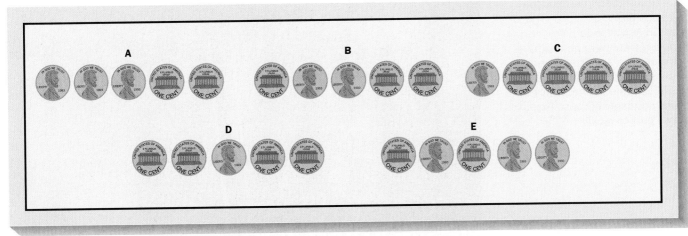

**FIGURE 8-9** Look at each series of coin tosses. In observing these series, many people conclude that some of them are more representative of true randomness than others. In fact, all of these series were generated by a computer.

## Psychological Detective

Suppose that you and a friend are tossing coins. Your friend tosses five heads in a row. It is your turn to bet on the next coin toss. Will it be heads or tails? Write down your choice and your reason for making the choice before reading further.

We expect the number of heads and tails to be approximately equal in the long run and random processes "to look" random (Burns & Corpus, 2004). In fact, research findings and our experiences tell us that fair coins behave this way across many tosses. Although we expect to find this approximate equality in the short run, chance does not operate that way. Betting that the next toss will be tails after your friend has tossed five heads in a row is like saying that the coin "knows" what happened on the previous five tosses and therefore heads is "due." Although a run of five heads does not seem to be representative of a random distribution of heads and tails, the odds on the next coin toss are *still* 50:50. Those prior tosses do not affect the odds. This faulty assumption is called the *gambler's fallacy*—another example of the representativeness heuristic. A series of heads and tails that does not look like chance is taken as evidence that a nonchance process is operating. Surprisingly, consecutive runs of heads and tails in random sequences can appear to be quite ordered. Some of the computer-generated sequences in Figure 8-9 look more random than the others. Some gamblers may misread the series of heads and tails and assume that they have a better chance of predicting the next toss than is actually the case.

**Availability.** The **availability heuristic** involves making judgments of the frequency of events based on how easily examples of the event come to mind. This "ease of retrieval" is what the term *availability* means (Ashcraft, 2006). Consider the following: Are there more words with *r* as the first letter than as the third letter? A quick word inventory leads you to conclude that there are more words that begin with *r*, but you are wrong. Why? Words that begin with *r*—*read*, *rich*, *reward*, and *right*—come to mind more easily than words such as *fare*, *mark*, *street*, and *word*.

We assume that easily recalled items occur more frequently than ones that do not come to mind readily. What's more, we assume that what comes to mind easily is also more likely to occur in the future (Dawes, 1998; Kahneman & Tversky, 2000). Ease of recall often—but not always—*is* correlated with actual data. Who is most likely to be killed in a drunk-driving accident? Most people believe that the answer is an innocent victim. According to the National Highway Traffic Safety Administration (2005a), however, the person most likely to die in a drunk-driving accident is a drunk driver. Why do we give the

The bets placed by gamblers are sometimes influenced by their observations of runs of numbers or colors. They often assume that a run that does not appear to be random (that is, a repeated sequence) will reverse itself in the short run.

**availability heuristic**
Heuristic in which the probability of an event is determined by how readily it comes to mind

Crash investigators examine the wreckage of an Air France flight at Pearson Airport in Toronto. Although there were no deaths in this crash, the extensive coverage given to such accidents leads many to overestimate the frequency of airline accidents because examples are so easy to recall.

wrong answer? It is easier to recall incidents in which an innocent person was the victim of a drunk-driving accident because such events are considered newsworthy. Drunk drivers die on the nation's highways every day, yet few of those accidents receive media attention.

Although the events covered by the media may not affect us directly, they play a role in how we assess our risk of accidents, catastrophes, or diseases. Imagine two of your friends discussing the relative safety of traveling to a vacation destination by either plane or automobile. News coverage of a recent plane crash leads them to decide in favor of travel by car, which they believe is safer. We may be misled because examples of airline accidents are dramatic and thus easy to recall. Yet more people are killed in cars and trucks during a single week than in plane crashes over the course of an entire year. In 2004, 37,142 motorists were killed in traffic crashes (the total rises to 42,636 when nonmotorists such as pedestrians are included). In a typical week 714 people die in traffic crashes involving passenger vehicles, trucks, and motorcycles in the United States (National Highway Traffic Safety Administration, 2005b). During the same period, there were 1,715 deaths in civil aviation accidents; the vast majority of these deaths were in general aviation (private aviators and air taxi operators). The total number of deaths attributed to scheduled commercial air carriers was 13 (National Transportation Safety Board, 2005b).

**Comparison.** We often make decisions by comparing the information we have obtained to some standard. Your standards are constantly changing, and these changes can affect your judgments. For example, a temperature of 68°F seems pleasant in the winter but cool in the summer.

Would you drive 20 minutes to save $5? Your answer may depend on the basis of comparison. If a toaster costs $45 at one store and the same toaster is available for $40 at another, are you likely to drive to the store with the lower price? Would you make the drive to buy a suit priced at $295 instead of $300 (Kahneman & Tversky, 2000; Tversky & Kahneman, 1981)? Most people say they would make the drive for the toaster but not for the suit, yet the amount of money saved would be the same! These choices are examples of the just noticeable difference we discussed in Chapter 3. In short, we tend to see the benefits or gains of a comparison in relative rather than absolute terms.

**Framing.** When we make decisions, we are also influenced by whether our attention is drawn to positive or negative outcomes; psychologists refer to this presentation of an issue as **framing** (Guenther, 1998; Kahneman & Teversky, 2000). When we make decisions, we are generally risk averse; that means we want to stay away from negative outcomes. Unfortunately, this tendency has the potential to mislead us at times, causing us to fail to see that the way identical information is presented can make a difference in

**framing**

The tendency for decision making to be influenced by presentation of negative or positive outcomes; decision making tends to be risk averse

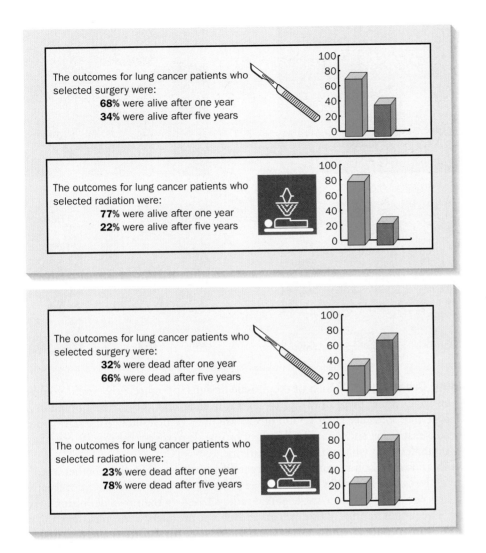

The outcomes for lung cancer patients who selected surgery were:
**68%** were alive after one year
**34%** were alive after five years

The outcomes for lung cancer patients who selected radiation were:
**77%** were alive after one year
**22%** were alive after five years

The outcomes for lung cancer patients who selected surgery were:
**32%** were dead after one year
**66%** were dead after five years

The outcomes for lung cancer patients who selected radiation were:
**23%** were dead after one year
**78%** were dead after five years

**FIGURE 8-10** The way an issue is framed can influence our decision making even on such important issues as medical treatment. In this case, people were presented with survival rates for one of two types of treatment (surgery represented by the scalpel or radiation represented by the patient receiving this treatment). When survival rates for 1 and 5 years were presented, most people selected surgery. When the same information was presented in terms of death rates, only a slight majority opted for surgery. These differences in selecting treatment options occurred despite the fact that the presented information was the same; it simply had been framed differently.

decision making. Imagine that you have lung cancer, and the treatment options are surgery or radiation. To help you make an informed decision, your physician tells you the results for lung cancer patients who selected surgery: 68% are alive after 1 year, and 34% are alive after 5 years. For lung cancer patients who selected radiation, 77% are alive after 1 year, and 22% are alive after 5 years. Given this information, which treatment do you select? The vast majority of peoples would select surgery.

Let's change the framing a bit. Suppose you are given the following information: Among patients who selected surgery, 32% are dead after 1 year and 66% are dead after 5 years. Among patients who selected radiation, 23% are dead after 1 year and 78% are dead after 5 years. Which treatment do you select now? Only a slight majority select surgery. Note that the choices framed in terms of living or dying are identical (see Figure 8-10), yet the framing affects the option selected.

These scenarios did not result from stupidity or a malfunctioning brain: "They illustrate how the mind actually works. Put in evolutionary terms, the mind has evolved to be effective in situations that are most likely to arise" (Restak, 1988, p. 238). We have developed methods of making decisions that work well most—but not all—of the time.

## Creativity

Although we often face difficulties when trying to solve problems or in making decisions, we are capable of impressive and creative solutions and judgments. Yet **creativity,** or the ability to produce work that is both novel and appropriate (Sternberg & Lubart, 1999), is a difficult concept to explain.

**STUDY TIP**

Create icons or pictures to help you remember each of the decision-making heuristics.

creativity
The ability to produce work that is both novel and appropriate

**FIGURE 8-11** Judging creativity. These mosaics were constructed by individuals with different levels of creativity. Which would you judge to be creative?

**Source:** Barron (1958).

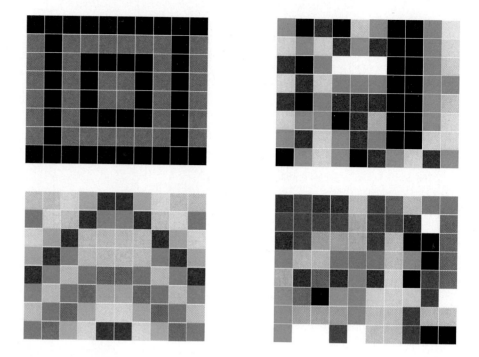

**Defining Creativity.** Which of the mosaic designs in Figure 8-11 would you judge to be creative? Show these drawings to several friends, and ask for their opinions. Do they agree that some are creative and others are not? Which ones? Although you may find a consensus, you and your friends might be unable to report the precise criteria that you used in deciding what constitutes creativity.

If there is no absolute standard for creativity, how can we judge whether a work is creative? Teresa Amabile (1982, 1996) has proposed a *consensual* assessment of creativity. She asked a group of judges to make global ratings based on their own definitions of creativity. The judges' ratings of both verbal and artistic products were consistent and reliable. People seem to agree on what is and is not creative, but we still can't define it. Subsequent research indicates that the consensual assessment of creativity yields at least moderately reliable ratings of creativity of a number of products as well as across cultures (Chen et al., 2002; Hickey, 2001).

**Measuring Creativity.** Intelligence tests were not designed to measure creativity, so it is not surprising that the correlation between measures of creativity and intelligence is weak to moderate (+.10 to +.50) (Lubart, 2003). High intelligence does not guarantee high creativity; low intelligence does not halt creativity. In many cases, "The creative solution is not known beforehand, and there is an immense range of possibility for new developments once we get into a problem. Not only are there no 'right or wrong' answers, there really are no 'answers' at all, until they have been tested in someone else's perception, or by external reality" (Barron, 1988, p. 85). This analysis suggests that many examples of creativity may begin as ill-defined or unstructured problems.

Imagine that thinking is like a line. When all lines of thought converge on one correct answer, we have an example of *convergent thinking*. By contrast, *divergent thinking* takes our thinking in different directions in search of multiple answers to a question. Of the two, divergent thinking is related more closely to creativity.

Creativity typically involves seeing nontypical yet plausible ways of associating items or seeing aspects of an item that are real and useful but not usually the primary focus of our attention. You can gain insight into this process by completing items from the Remote Associates Test in Table 8-2. This test was designed to measure the process of making new associations. Success on the test calls for flexibility in making associations, fluency in the use of language, and originality.

Psychologists have devised other ways to measure creativity. In the Unusual Uses Test, for example, you would be asked to think of unusual uses for common objects such

**TABLE 8-2**

## Sample Items from the Remote Associates Test

In this test you are presented with three words and asked to find a fourth word that is related to the other three. For example, what word do you think is related to these three?

cookies    sixteen    heart

The answer in this case is sweet. Cookies are sweet; sweet is part of the phrase "sweet sixteen" and part of the word "sweetheart." Here is another example:

poke    go    molasses

The answer is slow: slowpoke, go slow, slow as molasses. As you can see, the fourth word may be related to the other three for various reasons. Now try these.

| | | |
|---|---|---|
| 1. flap | tire | beanstalk |
| 2. mountain | up | school |
| 3. package | cardboard | fist |
| 4. surprise | line | birthday |
| 5. madman | acorn | bolt |

**Source:** Mednick and Mednick (1967).

as a brick, a ball, or a paper clip. In another measure of creativity, the Consequences Test, you would offer responses to questions such as "What would happen if people could become invisible at will?" "What would happen if all electrical generating plants closed at noon each day?" "What would happen if everyone could read everyone else's mind?" The responses are judged on the basis of novelty and appropriateness. For example, in response to the first item, you could say, "It would rain for 40 days and 40 nights." Although this response is novel (statistically rare), it is not appropriate in the context of the question. Conversely, if someone replied, "We couldn't see other people," the response would be appropriate but not novel. Thus there are two key elements in the definition of creativity as the ability to produce work that is both novel and appropriate.

**Personal Factors in Creativity.**     Are there other keys to understanding creativity? Several personal characteristics distinguish creative people from less creative people. Creative people are not afraid of hard work; they give it their undivided attention and persevere in the face of obstacles.

Another mark of a creative person is a willingness to take risks and expose oneself to the potential for failure. Choreographer Twyla Tharp (2003) notes that when she tapes a 3-hour improvisional session with a dancer she may find 30 seconds of useful material, which means she rejects 99.7% of her day's work, a process she says is painful but necessary for the creative process to occur. Her work puts her in contact with the world's greatest and most famous dancers. Here is how she describes one of them:

> Some of my favorite dancers at New York City Ballet were the ones who fail the most. I always love watching Mimi Paul: she took big risks onstage and went down often. Her falls reminded you that the dancers were doing super-human things onstage. . . . And hitting the ground seemed to transform Mimi: It was as though the stage absorbed the energy of her fall and injected it back into her with an extra dose of fearlessness. Mimi would bounce up, ignore the fall, and right before my eyes would become superhuman again. (pp. 213–214)

Such people can put their self-esteem on the line for the prospects of rewards greater than others might ever dream about. For example, Thomas Edison conducted more than 2,000 experiments with different possible filaments for a light bulb before finding one that would not burn out quickly. Experts declared Fred Smith's concept for Federal Express to be unworkable. Today Federal Express is a leader in delivering packages (from letters to jet engines) anywhere in the world overnight. What's more, creative people tolerate ambiguity, complexity, or a lack of symmetry. According to one expert, "It is clear that creative persons are especially disposed to admit complexity and even disorder into their perceptions without being made anxious by the resulting chaos. It is not so much that they like disorder per se, but that they prefer the richness of the disordered to the stark barrenness of the simple" (MacKinnon, 1978, p. 62).

**Situational Factors in Creativity.**    Creativity often emerges when we rearrange what is known in new and unusual ways that can yield creative ideas, goods, and services. Humor and playfulness provide fertile ground for forming new associations and arrangements. Mozart recognized this possibility when he wrote, "When I feel well and in a good humor, or when I am taking a drive or walking after a good meal, . . . thoughts crowd into my mind as easily as you could wish" (Ghiselin, 1952, p. 44).

Alice Isen and colleagues asked college students to solve the candle problem presented in Figure 8-7 (Isen, Daubman, & Nowicki, 1987). Before trying to solve the problem, some students watched a comedy film; 75% of them found the solution. Only 13% of students who did not watch a comedy film solved the problem. In another experiment, Isen and her colleagues placed students into three groups. The students in the first group watched a comedy film; those in the second group exercised for 2 minutes; and the third group, the control group, had no special preparation. All the students then tried to solve problems similar to those in the Remote Associates Test in Table 8-2. The first group solved more problems than the other two; Isen and her colleagues concluded that induced positive feelings can facilitate creativity.

In one study, participants were asked to tell a story or make a collage. Some of them completed the work in exchange for a reward; others were not rewarded (Amabile, Hennessey, & Grossman, 1986). Judgments of the creativity exhibited in the stories or collages were lower when the participants had received a reward. This result was consistent with other studies that have found that extrinsic rewards (as opposed to intrinsic rewards) can change the perceptions of activities and also lower interest in them.

Another perspective on the motivation underlying creativity focuses on how the motivator actually affects the person: Does it direct attention toward the task rather than the goal? A *task-focusing* motivator energizes a person to work and keeps the person's attention on the task. By contrast, a *goal-focusing* motivator leads a person to focus attention on rewards such as money to the detriment of the task. Intrinsic motivators tend to be task-focusing because a goal such as personal fulfillment is integrated with the task. Extrinsic motivators tend to be goal-focusing because the rewards are noticeable and distinct from the task. People vary, however, in how they focus. Some people focus on goals, which may distract them from the task; others focus on the task. Thus extrinsic motivators may have either benefits or negative effects, depending on how they influence a person's focus (Lubart, 1994).

Creativity often flourishes with the right mix of intrinsic and extrinsic motivation. Thomas Edison's first invention was an automatic vote recorder for Congress. When he presented it to a member of Congress, he was told that efficiency in lawmaking was the last thing Congress wanted. From that point on, Edison said that the only reason he invented was to make money; he didn't have the time or interest to modify the world to fit his inventions.

**Enhancing Creativity at Work.**    Businesses grow and prosper by adapting and creating new products and developing markets. Consequently, the business community has an interest in developing their employees' creativity. Companies such as Frito-Lay and Texas Instruments have introduced creativity-enhancing methods into their training with outstanding results. There is no magic in enhancing creativity; it takes the right attitude and technology in a work climate that is receptive to creative thinking and new ideas (Van Gundy, 1995). Individual and organizational creativity are closely interlocked. For example, environmental conditions at work—including control over one's work and sufficient time to think—facilitate creativity (Amabile, 1988). Among the other important organizational influences on creativity is encouragement of risk taking, generating ideas, and sharing ideas. One concrete example of the effects of these influences occurred in the development of 3M's Scotchgard. The open communication that was encouraged allowed an idea that originated outside the organization to be developed by scientists in one unit of the company and applied in another research unit (McLean, 2005).

One key to developing creativity is to be alert to potential problems that might be solved with creative solutions. For example, a track coach paid attention when his runners complained that their running shoes were causing blisters. The coach, Bill Browerman, was confident that he could improve the design of existing shoes. He cut patterns for the shoes out of grocery bags and found lightweight materials that improved the cushion and traction. Browerman's shoes are known today by the brand name Nike.

We could also learn from the story of the Swiss inventor George de Mestral. The name may be unfamiliar, but his invention is well known. One day he went hunting with his dog; they accidentally brushed against a bush that left both of them covered with burrs. When he tried to remove them, they clung stubbornly to his clothes. To most of us this would be a minor annoyance, but not to de Mestral. After he got home, he looked at the burrs under a microscope and discovered that hundreds of tiny hooks on each burr had snagged the threads of his pants. The result of this accident was the invention of Velcro fasteners.

We may not all brush up against new ideas as de Mestral did, but we can set the table for creativity. Unfortunately, most people believe that the world is divided into two types of people: creative ones and the rest of us. Yet if you spend some time watching children play, you'll see a great deal of creativity. What happens to diminish creativity as we become adults? Children's imaginations roam freely and are not limited by reality because they are not constrained by adult rules of thinking: "They don't know that they have to color inside the lines" (Wujec, 1995, p. 20). Adults are expected to be serious, yet playfulness and humor can help develop flexible thinking. We need to be open to "fooling around" with ideas to explore new mental connections (Morreall, 1997). Injecting humor and playfulness into the work situation can stimulate a creative mind set (Epstein, 2000), including the use of games and puzzles designed to enhance creativity (see Figure 8-12).

Quite often people fail to develop creative ideas because they do not believe they can be creative (Michalko, 1991). The first step in developing one's creativity is to acknowledge and confront these negative thoughts and replace them with positive thoughts. For example, many workers say to themselves, "I'll never be able to do it." This thought can be altered to the following: "I'll do a little bit at a time to get started. There is no reason that I have to do it all on a crash schedule."

Creativity consultants also aim to inject change into the lives of employees. They encourage employees to break habits by taking a different route to work, listening to a different radio station, or reading different magazines. These minor changes help employees break out of a rut, expose them to new ideas, and get them thinking rather than operating on automatic pilot. Employees are encouraged to look around, to make notes, and to collect lots of ideas.

Although we often associate the word *creativity* with works of art, creativity flourishes in a wide variety of venues including business environments. Many of the new technological gadgets available today reflect creative efforts to develop and apply technology.

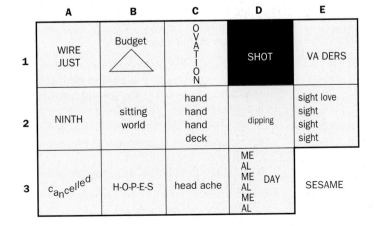

|   | A | B | C | D | E |
|---|---|---|---|---|---|
| 1 | WIRE JUST | Budget △ | OVATION | SHOT | VA DERS |
| 2 | NINTH | sitting world | hand hand hand deck | dipping | sight love sight sight sight |
| 3 | cancelled | H-O-P-E-S | head ache | ME AL ME AL DAY ME AL ME AL | SESAME |

**FIGURE 8-12** Creativity consultants often suggest that their clients do some puzzle-solving exercises to prepare them to be more creative. In this example, each box is a kind of puzzle for familiar words or phrases. For example, Box 1a can be read "Just under the wire." Try to decipher the other boxes. The solutions can be found at the end of the chapter.

**Source:** Wujec (1995).

We also need to recognize that creativity can take many forms. Henry Ford said he invented nothing new; he combined the inventions of others into a car. Ivory soap was run through an ice cream machine to add air that increased the sudsing and allowed the bar to float. Sometimes creativity is remarkably simple: The key to the initial success of Domino's pizza was promising home delivery in 30 minutes or less.

Creative people can look at the same thing as everyone else but see something different (Wujec, 1995). For example, Arthur Fry, a chemist, was working with a glue that was to be used on fixed surfaces like bulletin boards. Unfortunately, it did not work well. One day while singing he had a creative insight: The adhesive could be used on a bookmark that would replace the little pieces of paper he used to mark his hymn book. Fry used the glue to develop Post-It notes.

# REVIEW SUMMARY

1. Behavioral psychologists believed that thinking could be equated with muscle movements of the vocal apparatus; however, research has shown that this is not correct.

2. **Cognitive psychology** is the study of thinking. **Thinking** involves manipulation of information that can take the form of images or concepts. Visual imagery is the experience of seeing without the object or event actually being viewed.

3. **Concepts** are mental representations that facilitate thinking and reduce the number of elements we must consider. Concepts may be defined by their properties; however, we usually identify specific examples as members of a concept by judging their degree of similarity to a **prototype**, or best example, of the concept.

4. An **algorithm** is a method of solving problems that involves systematically exploring all possible solutions until the correct one is reached. Algorithms can be time-consuming and do not work for problems that are not clearly defined.

5. **Heuristics** are educated guesses or rules of thumb that are used to solve problems. Although the use of heuristics does not guarantee a solution, it is more time-efficient than using algorithms.

6. Rigidity is the tendency to rely on past experiences to solve problems. One form of rigidity, **functional fixedness**, is the inability to use familiar objects in new ways. Likewise, **set effect** predicts that we will attempt to use solutions that have been successful in the past, even when they are not the most effective. The **confirmation bias** occurs when we commit to one hypothesis without adequately testing other possibilities.

7. The **representativeness heuristic** predicts that we will base decisions on the similarity of characteristics of the situation to previously established concepts. The **availability heuristic** involves judging the probability of events by the readiness with which they come to mind. The way in which information is presented can dramatically alter our decision making; this effect is called **framing**. We also make decisions by comparing the information we have received to some standard. Heuristics facilitate good decisions but may sometimes result in bad ones.

8. **Creativity** depends on divergent thinking rather than the convergent thinking assessed in tests of intelligence. Creative people have a high capacity for hard work, a willingness to take risks, and a high tolerance for ambiguity and disorder. The business community is interested in enhancing creativity to develop and market products and services. The methods used to enhance creativity include engaging in humorous and playful activities.

# ✓ CHECK YOUR PROGRESS

1. Identify each of the following:
   a. an educated guess based on some rule of thumb to solve a problem
   b. using a mechanical method to generate all possible solutions to a problem
   c. relying too heavily on past experience in solving current problems

2. What is the advantage of creating an external representation when you are solving a problem?

3. You are engaged in a thought game in which your task is to discover the rule by which a series of numbers has been constructed. You are presented with the series *2, 5, 8*. What is the next number? You answer *11*. Which approach to problem solving does your guess illustrate? Why might this approach not be effective?

4. Eve decides to investigate the relation between intelligence and creativity. Through consultation with her teacher, she selects measures of intelligence and creativity. When the data are collected, she correlates the scores for all the participants in her sample. What is the likely outcome of her research?
   a. It is impossible to correlate creativity, so her research will not reveal any results.
   b. The tests of creativity and intelligence will reveal a low to moderate positive correlation.

c. The tests of creativity and intelligence will reveal a high negative correlation.

d. The tests of creativity and intelligence will reveal a low to moderate negative correlation.

5. Which of the following has been found to facilitate creativity?

a. remarkable rote memory
b. a history of childhood rebellion
c. positive feelings induced by humor
d. the presence of the mental disorder schizophrenia

6. Teresa Amabile developed a method of identifying creative works. Which statement could summarize her work?

a. Creativity occurs under conditions that focus on extrinsic motivation.
b. Only experts in a given field can offer legitimate opinions on creativity.
c. People reliably identify what they think is creative even if they fail to offer a precise definition.
d. There is no way to identify creative works; we must rely on the artist to make such judgments lest we inhibit freedom of expression.

7. When asked to name a sports car, Hank says "Mustang" and Sally says "Corvette." A psychologist who is studying thinking might describe these two cars as examples of the _____ used by Hank and Sally.

a. heuristics
b. prototypes

c. representatives
d. confirmations

8. Which of these is the best example of functional fixedness?

a. Sally is unable to use a saw.
b. Darla uses a comb to fix her hair before an interview.
c. Dan fails to realize that he could use his shoe to pound a nail into the wall.
d. Sam decides he is not going to use a steak knife on a hamburger.

9. Researchers called 1,000 people and asked them to estimate the number of defendants who would be found "not guilty by reason of insanity" out of 100. The respondents consistently overestimated the actual number. Which concept is a psychologist likely to use in explaining the survey results?

a. algorithm
b. availability
c. representativeness
d. functional fixedness

10. What concept do psychologists used to explain the greater ease we have in remembering words like *car* and *book* compared to *integrity* and *responsibility*?

a. framing
b. imagery
c. creativity
d. availability

**ANSWERS: 1. a.** heuristic **b.** algorithm **c.** rigidity **2.** Reduces the burden on memory **3.** You have generated a solution to the problem without considering that the sequence does not increase by three. Although you have found a solution that confirms your hypothesis, you have failed to generate other possibilities. **4.** b **5.** c **6.** c **7.** b **8.** c **9.** b **10.** b

# LANGUAGE

You have agreed to take care of your 30-month-old niece while her parents go out for dinner and a movie. You are intrigued by some of the words she uses. For example, she says the word *mouses*, although you are fairly sure that no one has taught her that word. While she is eating dinner she asks for more "chicken on the cob." When you realize that she delights in eating corn on the cob, you conclude that to her a chicken leg looks like a cob! *How do children's speech errors help us understand the way they acquire language?*

The use of language to communicate is basic to the human ability to develop, refine, and exchange ideas; in fact, language is a universal feature of human society. Language acquisition is therefore a critical component of the child's developing cognitive abilities. Both children and adults use language and images to create concepts and solve problems. This section examines the way language develops and how it both reflects and determines our thinking.

## Language Development

Between birth and the beginning of formal schooling, children accomplish a monumental feat: They learn to speak and understand language (Collins & Kuczaj, 1991). *Speech* is what people actually say; *language* is the understanding of the rules of what they

**phoneme**
The smallest units of sound understood as part of a language; there are approximately 200 phonemes in all languages of the world, but each language uses about 20 to 60

**morpheme**
In a language, the smallest unit of sound that conveys meaning

**syntax**
The organization of words into phrases and sentences; thus, an understanding of word order to convey ideas

say. To understand the magnitude of this task, consider this: Apart from stock phrases and remarks such as "Thank you" or "How are you?", almost every sentence we speak or write has never before been spoken or written. Every day we read sentences that we have never encountered before, yet we understand almost every one of them (Ashcraft, 2006; Lederer, 1991).

Acquiring any of the approximately 4,000 languages is a remarkable accomplishment because there is so much to learn. First, a child uses **phonemes** (from the Greek word for "sound"), which are the building blocks of language. Phonemes are unique sounds that can be joined to create words. They include consonant sounds like the sound of *d* in *dog* and *did* and vowel sounds like the *a* in *at* and *ant* (Kail, 2004). Although there are approximately 200 different phonemes in all the spoken languages, most languages use only 20 to 60 phonemes. English has 26 letters but 40 to 46 phonemes because the same letter, alone or in combination, can represent more than one sound. (Experts disagree on whether some sounds are separate phonemes or blends; hence, there is a range of the estimated number of phonemes.) Perhaps you remember feeling confused when you first learned that the same symbol on the printed page—say *c* or *gh*—could be pronounced in more than one way. A similar experience occurs when we learn a foreign language.

Although it is often convenient to think of words as the basic units of meaning in language, many words have more than one part that has meaning. A **morpheme** is the smallest unit of language that has meaning. For example, the word *constructed* has three morphemes: *con*, *struct*, and *ed*, the last of which indicates past tense; *unhappiness* has three. When we learn to organize words into phrases and sentences, we are acquiring what is called **syntax.**

**The Acquisition of Language.** The baby's early cries and other sounds are probably responses to the environment and to internal needs such as hunger. No matter what language their parents speak (and even if the parents are deaf), babies make the same sounds at about the same time. At about 2 months of age, an infant begins *cooing*. These brief, vowel-like utterances (e.g., "ooooooo" and "ahhhhhhh") are sometimes accompanied by consonants and often occur when infants are comfortable or when parents or other caregivers attempt to communicate (Bukatko & Daehler, 2004). At about 6 months of age, infants begin *babbling*, making one-syllable speech-like sounds that usually contain *both* vowels and consonants but have no meaning (Kail, 2004). Toddlers exhibit a pattern of rising or falling pitch called *intonation*. In a declarative sentence, pitch rises then falls toward the end of the sentence. In a question, the pitch is level and then rises toward the end of the question. Both patterns are found in the babbling of infants between ages 8 and 11 months. If a baby is exposed to a language with different intonation patterns, such as French, his or her babbling will reflect the intonation patterns of that language (Kail, 2004).

Toddlers who hear English at home will utter their first word that conveys meaning at about 1 year. Because parents are usually the child's primary caregivers, it is not surprising that the child's first words are usually *mama* or *dada*. By the age of 18 months, the average toddler uses as many as 50 words. Most of these words are used for naming objects, such as *doggie*, but some are action words such as *bye-bye*. At about this age, toddlers combine two or more words to express a single idea, which results in the child's first sentence. Vocabulary development continues at a rapid pace during the preschool years.

Psychologists are especially interested in three characteristics of the infant's language. First, young children often use *telegraphic speech*—they leave words out of sentences, as in a telegraph message (Bukatko & Daehler, 2004). Despite the missing words, the intent of the sentence is usually clear, especially if the nonverbal context helps listeners decipher the child's meaning. For example, Dad knows what his daughter wants when he hears "Daddy juice." Second, children seem to know how to string words together to convey the intended meaning in the correct sequence for their language. If a child sees a car run over a ball, the child might say, "Car hit ball." (The child would not say "Ball

Although children appear to learn many elements of language from adults (as well as from other children), they also abstract rules of language that enable them to generate words that they have never heard spoken by adults.

hit car.") Third, children often overgeneralize grammatical rules, so the plural of *mouse* should be *mouses*! Children also add *ed* at the end of verbs to indicate past tense. For example, young children will say, "Doggie runned away."

According to behaviorists, including B. F. Skinner (1957), language is learned like other behaviors: through imitation, association, and reinforcement (Leahey & Harris, 2001). Children hear others talk and imitate the sounds they hear. For example, parents will point to an object and name it, and children repeat the words. What's more, sounds that resemble words are reinforced; sounds that do not resemble words may be extinguished. For instance, the baby's babbling of *mama* produces reinforcers such as food, a smile, or a hug. The more often this sequence of behaviors and reinforcers is repeated, the more strongly *mama* is associated with the presence of the child's mother. Likewise, the correct sequencing of words to form sentences is reinforced, whereas incorrect sequences may be extinguished. The following is an example of the acquisition of sounds and words as a result of reinforcement (Eggen & Kauchak, 2001):

> A 2-year-old picked up a ball and said, "Baa."
>
> Mom smiled broadly and said, "Good boy! Ball."
>
> The little boy repeated, "Baa."
>
> Mom responded, "Very good."

Although this behavioral theory of language acquisition explains how children can learn words from adults, it fails to explain how they create new and unique words and sentences. Cognitive scientist Steven Pinker (1994) considers it folklore that parents teach children language; parents do not provide explicit grammar lessons. The credit for the acquisition of language should go to the children.

The remarkable ability of children to master the complex rules of language and to use an extensive vocabulary within about 5 years suggests the existence of a built-in brain mechanism that makes this development possible. Except in rare and extreme situations in which access to language samples is denied, the acquisition of language is virtually guaranteed for children up to about age 5 or 6 and becomes more difficult thereafter. There is a critical period during which language develops quite easily, as most college students in foreign language classes know quite well. According to this *nativist* theory of language, children are innately predisposed to acquire language. The major advocate of this position, Noam Chomsky (1972), has called this innate ability our *language acquisition device* (*LAD*). When children hear speech, the LAD programs their brain to analyze what they hear and to extract the rules of grammar. The LAD is responsible for the emergence of babbling and the imitation of speech sounds. Because of these experiences, children are able to apply those rules to their own sentences. Children are not taught grammar explicitly; rather, they construct the rules from the examples they hear. Although parents and others help this process along by providing models of appropriate language use, children are also exposed to inappropriate uses. Consider the following exchange over breakfast between 6-year-old John and his 3-three-old brother Mike as they discussed the relative dangers of forgetting to feed the goldfish versus overfeeding the goldfish:

> *John:* It's worse to forget to feed them.
>
> *Mike:* No, it's badder to feed them too much.
>
> *John:* You don't say badder, you say worser.
>
> *Mike:* But it's baddest to give them too much food.
>
> *John:* No, it's not. It's worst to forget to feed them.

**Source:** Adapted from Bee, 1989, p. 276.

The LAD explains why children in different cultures follow the same (presumably innate) stages of language acquisition (see Table 8-3); it also explains why deaf children pass through stages of language development that are analogous to those exhibited by hearing children. Although the LAD explains how children learn the complex rules of language; it does not explain why children raised by their parents at home show better

**TABLE 8-3**

## The Sequence of Language Development in a Child

| Age (Months) | Language Development |
|---|---|
| 2 | Infants have a social smile with interaction and begin cooing. |
| 3–4 | Babies master reciprocal coos between themselves and others. |
| 4 | They belly laugh and become more interactive. |
| 6 | Babies try monosyllabic vowels (described as "squeals with lots of vowels"). |
| 9 | Babies try consonants such as "ba," "ga," and "da." A baby will utter nonsensical sounds in the sentence structure of speech. At this stage, babies understand much more than they can express, so they can do a simple command such as "Wave bye-bye." |
| 12 | Babies can say their first word (with meaning); it is often "Mama" or "Dada." |
| 15 | Toddlers use about five words. |
| 18 | A child will use 10 to 15 words and can point out and name body parts. This is the fun, picture-book stage. |
| 24 | A child should have a 200-word vocabulary and be able to construct two-word sentences such as "Give me" and "That's mine." A stranger should be able to understand about half of what the child says. |
| 36 | A stranger should recognize about 75 percent of the child's speech. |

**Source:** Cincinnati's Children's Hospital Medical Center (2003).

language development than children raised in institutions. Learning theorists point to the greater availability of reinforcements at home than in institutions. As predicted by learning theory, much of the variety in children's language abilities can be attributed to environmental differences.

Most psychologists favor a combination of learning and nativist theories (Eggen & Kauchak, 2001; Kail, 2004). That is, some of our linguistic abilities seem to be innately determined, and others are acquired through learning. Researchers disagree, however, as to which behaviors belong in which category.

**American Sign Language.** When we think of a language, we often think of an oral-auditory one—that is, one that is heavily dependent on audition. Not all languages fit this category, however. A prominent example is *American Sign Language (ASL)* or *Ameslan*, a manual-visual language developed within the American deaf community that is distinct from oral-auditory languages. ASL is not a signed version of English; it is unique, separate, and distinct from English, with its own grammar and syntax (Grayson, 2003). ASL is used by an estimated 500,000 deaf people in the United States and Canada. People who use ASL communicate rapidly via thousands of manual signs and gestures. Words are assembled from hand shapes, hand motions, and the positions of the hands in front of the body (see Figure 8-13). Contrary to common belief, there is no universal sign language. A person who uses ASL could not communicate with someone who uses British Sign Language. What's more, a deaf signer who learns a second sign language as an adult will sign with a foreign accent (Hickok, Bellugi, & Klima, 2001).

Facial expression and pantomimes of emotions such as lifted eyebrows punctuate and place emphasis in sentences. They may also serve as adverbs; for example, a slight display of the tongue as if in distaste during the sentence "I slept" turns the meaning into

"I slept badly." ASL also intensifies meaning by making the sign more rapidly, so "quickly" becomes "more quickly."

Although they do not involve spoken words, sign languages are highly structured linguistic systems with all of the grammatical complexity (rules and syntax) found in spoken languages (Hickok et al., 2001; Pinker, 1994). In fact, they are produced and processed by the same parts of the brain involved in spoken language (Hickok et al., 2001). What's more, deaf children reared in an environment in which they have no access to spoken language and were not taught sign language have been known to invent their own sign language. Until recently, the education of the deaf population emphasized lip reading and speech training to the exclusion of sign language. Approximately 90% of deaf children are born to hearing parents who are often discouraged from signing to their deaf children because the use of sign language might impede their progress in learning English. In recent years, however, this policy has begun to change as a result of pressure from the deaf community. Today ASL is recognized as a legitimate language, and many deaf people emphasize learning sign language over speech therapy. What's more, thousands of hearing people have learned ASL as a second language, and it is offered as part of the curriculum in schools and colleges, where it sometimes satisfies a foreign language requirement (Grayson, 2003).

**FIGURE 8-13** Examples of hand symbols that indicate words in ASL. In the past, sign language was thought to be a form of pantomime that relied on the similarity of its symbols to the ideas they represent. Some signs, called *iconic*, seem to reflect the object they represent; however, most signs are complex abstract symbols.

**Source:** Grayson (2003).

## Thinking and Language

As we have seen, thinking can involve visual images as well as concepts, which are elements of language. In addition, language can have even more dramatic influences on our thinking. The *linguistic relativity hypothesis* advanced by Benjamin Lee Whorf (1897–1941) suggests that syntax (word order) and vocabulary can mold thinking. Whether syntax and vocabulary actually *mold* our thinking is matter of debate; however, there is little doubt that elements of language can influence how we perceive and remember our world (Boroditsky, 2001). For example, some cultures have number terms for "one-two-many," which make it difficult to understand situations that require other numerical evaluations. Imagine a situation where there are 60 football players and 30 pairs of cleats. English speakers would have no difficulty understanding that some of the football players are going to be without cleats; however, people in a culture that has number terms only for "one-two-many" would find it difficult to describe and understand the situation (Hunt & Agnoli, 1991).

Consider the following: People were shown drawings that could represent either of two objects; the experimenters gave the objects either of two names. As you see in Figure 8-14, the original language labels used by the experimenters influenced the participants' memory for and subsequent drawings of the objects (Carmichael, Hogan, & Walter, 1932).

**Using Language to Limit Thought.** Author George Orwell considered language to be a potential weapon that could be used to exploit, oppress, or manipulate people. Published in 1949, Orwell's novel *Nineteen Eighty-Four* describes how a totalitarian state created an official state language called Newspeak to reduce the range of thought among its citizens. Although Orwell's account of language as a tool for political control was fictional, there are many current examples of the use of language to influence and control thinking.

The use of language by business, educational, and governmental organizations can mislead or control perception and thinking. The term *doublespeak* describes language that is purposely designed to make the bad seem good, to turn a negative into a positive, or to avoid or shift responsibility (see Table 8-4). "Doublespeak is not a slip of the tongue, or

**FIGURE 8-14** Effects of verbal labels on reproduction of drawings. The figures on the left were shown to participants along with one of the two verbal labels. The figures that these individuals drew later were influenced by the verbal labels they had been given.

**Source:** Carmichael, Hogan, and Walter (1932).

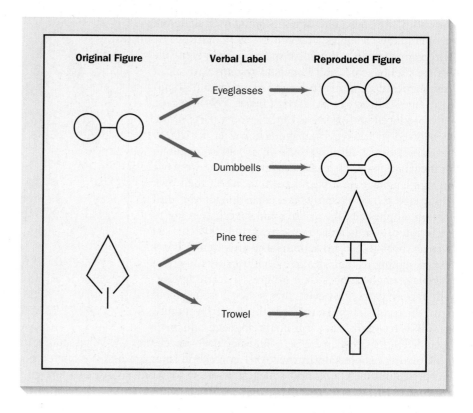

language used out of ignorance, but is instead a very conscious use of language as a weapon or tool by those in power to achieve their ends at our expense" (Lutz, 1990, p. xii).

One form of doublespeak is the *euphemism*, an acceptable or inoffensive word or phrase used in place of an unacceptable or offensive one. We frequently use *passed away* when talking to a bereaved person to demonstrate our sensitivity for that person's feelings. When you excuse yourself from the table at a restaurant, you are likely to say that you are headed to the *restroom* rather than the *bathroom*. No one is misled by these uses of language. But when a Pentagon spokesperson announces that a military unit was "servicing the target," few of us realize that the unit was killing the enemy. Politicians may report that their cities have *pavement deficiencies* rather than potholes. Perhaps some of you work as *part-time scanning professionals*, otherwise known as *grocery checkout clerks*. In sum, although words may not actually determine our thoughts, examples like these indicate that careful selection of words can steer our thoughts in certain directions.

### TABLE 8-4

### Examples of Doublespeak

| Term in Ordinary English | Term in Doublespeak |
|---|---|
| Desks | Pupil stations |
| Dead | Nonviable condition |
| New taxes | Revenue enhancement |
| Bar bouncer | Entertainment coordinator |
| Invasion | Predawn vertical insertion |
| Farm animals | Grain-consuming animal units |
| Fired | Nonpositively terminated or reclassified |
| Lying | Massaging the truth |

**Sources:** Lederer (1991); Lutz (1990).

**Language and Gender.**   Consider the following sentence: "A skilled doctor makes an accurate diagnosis, and then he communicates the information to the patient." What images came to mind when you read this sentence? Now read the following sentences, and pay attention to the images that come to mind:

- A teacher must be careful when he grades exams.
- After a patient takes the prescribed medicine, he needs to rest.
- A business executive must consider all aspects of an issue before he decides on a course of action.

When you read a sentence such as "A skilled doctor makes an accurate diagnosis, and then he communicates the information to the patient," you may not consider the possibility that the doctor is female.

The word *he* may not be intended to convey whether the person is a man or a woman, but most people assume the speaker meant that the person was a man. If the images that came to your mind were primarily men, you are not alone. Most people call up such images when they read sentences like these (Gastil, 1990; Hamilton, 1991; Henley, 1989). Girls and women make up almost 52% of the human race, yet they are systematically left out in daily speech (Paludi, 2002). The words *he*, *his*, and *man* refer to men, but they are often also used to encompass both men and women. These examples demonstrate how the words we use can guide our thinking, perhaps in ways we had not intended or recognized.

Janet Hyde (1984a) asked grade school children to create a story about an individual whose job was that of a "wudgemaker." Groups of children listened to descriptions of a wudgemaker that differed only in the pronouns used: *he*, *she*, *they*, *his*, or *her*. After hearing the story, the children created their own stories. Children who had heard stories with the pronoun *he* put women in their stories only 17% of the time. Apparently, the children understood *he* to refer exclusively to men. What's more, children who heard *he* stories rated women as less competent than men in the job of wudgemaker. Thus the use of a single word can have a significant influence on children's ideas.

## Psychological Detective

Read the following sentences:

- The department *chairman* decided to schedule the course in the later afternoon.
- The chemical company *spokesman* will not answer questions concerning the spill in the river.
- Language separates *mankind* from other creatures.

Rewrite these sentences to avoid the suggestion that the person or people in them must be male. Write down your answers before reading further.

Using the word *he* or words like *chairman* when gender is not relevant to the intended meaning conveys the inaccurate notion that gender is a relevant dimension. Some minor wording changes may reduce the stereotyping that occurs when the words are associated with being male. For example, when the title of *chairman* is changed to *chairperson*, most people report fewer male images in describing this occupation; there is little difference in images associated with *chairman* and *chair*. Thus we could substitute *chairperson*, *spokesperson*, and *human beings* (or *humankind*) for the italicized words in the Psychological Detective exercise. Professional organizations such as the American Psychological Association, commercial publishers, and many newspapers and magazines have developed guidelines for unbiased (gender-inclusive) language. For example, using plural forms and the pronoun *they* and using gender-neutral job titles (*police officers, firefighters*) lets us include all people and thus avoids stereotypes that can perpetuate prejudice (Helgeson, 2005).

Next, we turn our attention to a topic that has a long history in psychology and has proven to be one of the most controversial: intelligence. This broad term is often used to encompass several of the abilities that we have focused on so far in this chapter, such as skills in language and in problem solving.

# REVIEW SUMMARY

**1.** Between birth and the beginning of formal schooling, children learn to speak and understand language. **Phonemes** are the individual sounds of a language; **morphemes** are its smallest meaning-bearing elements. An understanding of the proper order of words in phrases and sentences demonstrates an understanding of **syntax.**

**2.** There are two major theories of language acquisition: the notion that language is a learned response acquired like any other behavior and the view that children are innately predisposed to acquire language through a built-in *language acquisition device* (*LAD*).

**3.** American Sign Language (ASL) relies on hand shapes, hand motions, and the positions of the hand in front of the body.

**4.** The *linguistic relativity* hypothesis suggests that our use of words (and syntax) can influence and even guide thought processes. Although using the male pronoun *he* to refer to both men and women may be convenient, it can lead people to think that only men are being considered. Several organizations have developed guidelines for using language in a gender-neutral manner.

# ✓ CHECK YOUR PROGRESS

**1.** The basic sounds of a language are called _____; the smallest meaning-bearing elements of a language are _____.

  **a.** heuristics; syntax
  **b.** syntax; heuristics
  **c.** morphemes; phonemes
  **d.** phonemes; morphemes

**2.** You are writing a paper on Noam Chomsky's views on language. Which title captures the main points the paper should convey?

  **a.** "Language: Like Any Other Behavior"
  **b.** "Language Is Learned Via Modeling"
  **c.** "The Brain Extracts the Rules of Grammar"
  **d.** "The Genetic Coding of Different Languages Around the World"

**3.** Which of the following is the best summary of the linguistic relativity hypothesis?

  **a.** Each language has a limited number of sounds with which to convey ideas.
  **b.** Languages differ in their degree of complexity as a result of the needs of the society.
  **c.** The order of words and syntax can influence how we perceive and remember our world.
  **d.** The human brain is limited in the number of concepts it can handle; thus the same ideas are expressed across the planet.

**4.** How are people who use ASL able to convey ideas such as "badly" or "poorly?"

  **a.** They rely on their eyebrows to express such ideas.
  **b.** The signs are made at different speeds to express such ideas.
  **c.** ASL does not use adverbs, so it is not as expressive as spoken languages.
  **d.** ASL uses a limited number of simple gestures involving both hands that express such ideas.

**5.** At about what age do most children speak their first understandable word?

  **a.** 6 months
  **b.** 8 months
  **c.** 12 months
  **d.** 15 months

**6.** What is the first stage in the development of language?

  **a.** cooing
  **b.** babbling
  **c.** repetition
  **d.** generalization

**7.** Developmental milestones are helpful in determining if infants have problems that need attention. Which child does not seem to be reaching language milestones at the expected age?

  **a.** At 8 months of age Don started cooing.
  **b.** Diane started babbling at 5 months.
  **c.** Carlos said his first clearly understandable words at 11 months.
  **d.** At the age of 18 months, Carol has used two-word sentences but still babbles on occasion.

**8.** What process is occurring when infants form strings of sound containing *both* vowel and consonant sounds?

  **a.** morphing
  **b.** babbling
  **c.** gurgling
  **d.** sounding

**9.** A young child says, "Mommy go," signifying that her mother is going to the store. What does this example illustrate about language development?

  **a.** babbling speech
  **b.** overgeneralization
  **c.** telegraphic speech
  **d.** autonomous grammar

**10.** Behavioral neuroscientists are using brain scans to identify the parts of the brain involved when people use an oral-auditory language and when they use sign language. What are the brain scans likely to reveal?

    **a.** The same brain areas are involved in both languages.

    **b.** Sign language depends primarily on the right hemisphere.

    **c.** Both languages rely primarily on subcortical areas of the brain.

    **d.** The primary parts of the brain involved in both languages are the occipital lobes.

# INTELLIGENCE

Alex's second-grade teacher gave him a letter to take to his parents. Because Alex is experiencing difficulty in class, the teacher consulted with the school psychologist. They agreed that it would be potentially beneficial to administer an intelligence test and other measures to Alex. They expect that the information obtained from the testing session will help them plan a better educational program to meet Alex's needs. *Why were psychological tests first developed?*

You are familiar with psychological tests because you have taken such tests in school. A psychological test is an objective measure of a *sample* of behavior that is collected according to well-established procedures. Thus psychological tests are like the tests used in other sciences: They are composed of observations made on a small but carefully chosen sample of a person's behavior (Anastasi & Urbina, 1997). Such tests are used for a range of purposes, including measuring differences among people in characteristics such as intelligence and personality (Domino, 2000; Gregory, 2004). The primary purpose of one of the first psychological tests was to identify children with below-average intellectual ability so that they could be given schooling designed to improve that ability.

### Psychological Detective

Think about what makes a person intelligent. What behaviors or characteristics do you expect to observe in someone who is judged to be intelligent? Write down your answer before reading further.

To answer this question, Robert Sternberg and his colleagues (Sternberg, Conway, Ketron, & Bernstein, 1981) asked people in supermarkets, train stations, and a college library to record behaviors and characteristics related to the concept of intelligence. The researchers then gave the resulting list of behaviors and characteristics to other people, who rated the importance of each as an element of intelligence. The laypersons' descriptions of intelligence emphasized practical problem solving ("identifies connections among ideas"), verbal ability ("speaks clearly and articulately"), and social competence ("displays interest in the world at large"). Experts who were asked similar questions viewed intelligence in a comparable fashion, with some differences of emphasis (Snyderman & Rothman, 1987).

## Cultural Views of Intelligence

The descriptions of intelligence offered by people in supermarkets or college libraries were obtained in the United States. How a person defines intelligence depends on whom we ask, and the answers differ across time and place (Sternberg & Kaufman, 1998). Thus,

**intelligence**
The ability to excel at a variety of tasks, especially those related to academic success

what behaviors are perceived as examples of intelligent behavior is influenced in part by culture. Furthermore, culture can influence the processes that underlie intelligent behavior as well as the direction that intellectual development takes (Miller, 1997).

The Japanese place greater emphasis on the process of thinking than people in the United States (Tajima et al., 1991). Japanese people listed several characteristics of intelligence that deal with the process of thinking, such as "good judgment" and "good memory." Americans placed greater importance on external appearances and outcomes when listing characteristics that describe intelligence. The conceptions of intelligence among Taiwanese Chinese included interpersonal intelligence, intrapersonal intelligence, and self-assertion (Sternberg & Kaufman, 1998). Differences such as these suggest that there may be significant differences between Eastern and Western conceptions of intelligence—differences that may be due, in part, to the kinds of skills that cultures value (Srivastava & Misra, 1996).

In Africa, conceptions of intelligence focus on skills that facilitate and maintain harmonious group relations (Ruzgis & Grigorenko, 1994). For example, parents in Kenya emphasize responsible participation in family and social life as important aspects of intelligence (Super & Harkness, 1982). What's more, Kenyan children from a rural village perform better on tests of indigenous intelligence that require them to perform a task that is adaptive for them (recognizing how to use natural herbal medicines to fight illness) than they do on Western-style vocabulary tests (Sternberg et al., 2000). In Zimbabwe the word for "intelligence," *ngware*, means to be prudent and cautious, particularly in social relationships (Sternberg & Kaufman, 1998).

As we continue our exploration of the concept of intelligence, it is important to be aware that the definition used in Western cultures, especially the United States, does not necessarily match definitions used in other parts of the world. What's more, efforts to develop tests to quantify intelligence are primarily a Western phenomenon. Those tests may not be appropriate when translated and used in other cultures because the underlying definition of intelligence may not fit the culture's view.

We can define **intelligence** as the overall ability to excel at a variety of tasks, especially those related to success in schoolwork. Judging from the level of agreement in the United States on the characteristics of an intelligent person, the measurement and understanding of intelligence would not seem controversial. Nevertheless, this topic is one of the most contentious in psychology. The next section explores how psychologists measure intelligence, why these measures were developed, and why the concept of intelligence is controversial.

## The History of Intelligence Testing

We can trace the study of differences in intelligence to an Englishman, Sir Francis Galton (1822–1911), an inventor and explorer whose interests ranged from meteorology to identifying fingerprints. This wealthy man's passion for measurement convinced him that virtually anything could be measured, from beauty, to personality, to how boring lectures might be (Brookes, 2004; Gregory, 2004). What's more, he shared an interest in heredity with his half cousin, Charles Darwin. Galton believed that heredity was responsible for human differences in intelligence and ability (Brookes, 2004). To check this notion, he traced the family trees of approximately 1,000 distinguished artists, judges, military commanders, poets, scientists, and statesmen and found that a large proportion of these eminent people had eminent family members. On the basis of such findings, Galton contended in his book *Hereditary Genius: An Inquiry into Its Laws and Consequences* (1869) that eminence and creativity run in families because they are inherited characteristics; he dismissed the potential influence of environmental factors.

Galton set out to measure differences in degree of eminence and, presumably, in the level of intelligence in his anthropometric ("human measurement") laboratory in London. Beginning in 1884, visitors stopped in to have the keenness of their eyesight and reaction time to stimuli measured. Galton believed that highly successful people

Sir Francis Galton (1822–1911) was interested in measuring "anything and everything," this interest led to his pioneering efforts to investigate the effects of heredity on intelligence.

perceive the world more accurately than less successful people. Thus their eyesight should be keener and their reactions quicker than those of less eminent people. Contrary to Galton's beliefs, the results showed that eminent people did *not* perceive the world any better than others.

Alfred Binet (1857–1911), a French psychologist, spent years considering ways to measure intelligence. Eventually he decided to assess more complex intellectual functions than sensory discrimination, including memory and reasoning. In 1881, the French Ministry of Education decided that all children must attend school. Before that time, the schools were not obligated to teach children with widely varying ability levels because slow learners usually did not attend school. Consequently, the curriculum was geared to average and above-average students. After the decision, teachers had to adapt their methods to teach children with a wider range of abilities. In 1904, a French commission studying the education of children with below-average ability decided that placing slower learners in special classes would be more effective than keeping them with learners performing at grade level or higher. Although teachers could offer judgments concerning their students' abilities, the commission recognized that such judgments might be tainted by factors (such as discipline problems) that were not related to ability. Their search for an objective measure as the basis for class placement decisions concerning the children led them to Binet.

Binet and his colleague, Theophile Simon (1873–1961), collected simple problems that required higher mental processes such as reasoning, memory, and spatial thinking. In 1905, they developed the Binet-Simon scale. Typical items required children to define common words ("What is a pencil?"), name objects seen in pictures, tell how two objects are alike ("How are a cow and a dog alike?"), draw designs from memory, and repeat a string of spoken digits. Completion of some items seemed to represent an ability level that was typical of children of a certain age, whereas completion of other items was associated with those of a different age. On the basis of this observation, Binet and Simon proposed the concept of **mental age.** To determine a child's mental age, they compared the child's performance to that of the average child at each age. For example, a mental age of 6 indicated that a child's performance was similar to the performance of other 6-year-olds. A 6-year-old child with a mental age of 8 performed much better than the average 6-year-old. Binet believed the use of his scale would increase the likelihood that all children would receive an appropriate education. In fact, he expected that attention, memory, and judgment could be improved with practice and appropriate methods.

### The Stanford-Binet Intelligence Scale.

In the United States, Lewis Terman (1877–1957), a Stanford University psychologist, revised the Binet-Simon scale and extended it for use with adults. His Stanford-Binet Intelligence Scale was first published in 1916 and has been modified several times since then; the current version is the Stanford-Binet–Fifth Edition (Roid, 2003).

In 1912, the German psychologist William Stern (1871–1938) devised an index of intelligence by dividing a child's mental age (MA) by his or her chronological age (CA). Terman adopted this idea in the Stanford-Binet test and added one more feature; he multiplied the index by 100 to eliminate decimals. The resulting statistic is the **intelligence quotient (IQ),** calculated, as just explained, as MA/CA 100. Thus one's IQ is a ratio of MA divided by CA, multiplied by 100. For example, a 9-year-old child with a mental age of 9 would have an IQ of 100 ($9/9 \times 100 = 100$). If the same child had a mental age of 6, the calculation of the IQ would be $6/9 \times 100 = 67$. Finally, if the child's mental age was 12, the IQ would be $12/9 \times 100 = 133$. The intelligence quotient made it possible to express a child's intellectual ability relative to that of children of the same age.

The French psychologist Alfred Binet (1857–1911) was responsible for the development of the first intelligence test. The creation of the test was the result of a specific task given to Binet and his colleague, Simon—create a method to identify students who were learning at a slower rate than the majority of students. As a result, most subsequent intelligence tests have been tied to academic achievement.

**mental age**
Measure of intelligence derived by comparing an individual's score on an intelligence test with the average performance of individuals of the same age

**intelligence quotient (IQ)**
Score that indicates how an individual compares with others on an intelligence test

The information from an intelligence test can reveal learning disabilities as well as identify a child's areas of strength. This picture shows a simulated test.

**The Wechsler Scales.** When David Wechsler (1896–1981) was chief psychologist at Bellevue Hospital in New York City, he found it difficult to test adults with the Stanford-Binet Intelligence Scale. Although the Stanford-Binet had been adapted for testing adults by adding more difficult items, time limits on some items handicapped a number of adults. Furthermore, even though the concept of MA could be applied to children, whose intellectual ability changes from year to year, it could not be applied to adults. The pace of change in intelligence slows considerably in the adult years, so the MAs of the average 28- and 29-year-old are not likely to differ. For these reasons, Wechsler developed a new intelligence test for adults. Scores on this test are calculated by comparing a person's score with scores obtained by people of a range of ages rather than a single age. The current version of this test, known as the Wechsler Adult Intelligence Scale-III (WAIS-III, see Figure 8–15), is used to assess people between the ages of 16 and 74 (Wechsler, 1997).

Wechsler's scales have also been adapted to assess intelligence at earlier ages. The Wechsler Intelligence Scale for Children-III (WISC-III) tests children aged 6 to 16, and the Wechsler Preschool and Primary Scales of Intelligence-Revised (WPPSI-R) is used to assess children aged 4 to 61/2 (Wechsler, 1992, 1994). The multiple scores of the Wechsler subtests provide valuable information about individual strengths and weaknesses and can be helpful in identifying learning disabilities in children.

The Stanford-Binet Intelligence Scale and the Wechsler intelligence tests are individual tests (one person is tested at a time) that must be administered by a qualified examiner. Administering one of these tests takes between 1 and 2 hours. Individual intelligence tests offer several advantages compared with group tests. The examiner can directly observe the examinee's reactions, put him or her at ease before the test, and determine whether the examinee understands the instructions. When large numbers of people must be tested, however, these measures of intelligence are time-consuming.

**STUDY TIP**

Create a timeline illustrating the history of intelligence testing, including names of significant figures and brief descriptions of important events.

## Principles of Psychological Tests

A psychological test is like a three-legged stool: If one leg is missing or broken, the stool collapses. Like that stool, psychological tests have three legs representing the essential elements for their effective and appropriate use: reliability, validity, and standardization. These principles apply to all psychological tests, whether they are designed to measure intelligence or personality (see Chapter 11).

| SUBTEST (VERBAL) | DESCRIPTION | SAMPLE ITEMS |
|---|---|---|
| Information | Orally presented questions that tap knowledge of common events, objects, places, and people. | How many wings does a bird have? How many nickels make a dime? |
| Similarities | Examinee is asked to explain the similarity in pairs of words that are presented orally. | In what way are a lion and tiger alike? In what way are a saw and a hammer alike? |
| Arithmetic | A series of arithmetic questions are to be solved without use of pencil and paper or calculator. | Three women divided eighteen golf balls equally among themselves. How may golf balls did each person receive? |
| Vocabulary | Examinee must provide definitions for a series of orally presented words. | What does **near** mean? What does **slander** mean? |
| Comprehension | A series of orally presented questions that require the examinee to give solutions to everyday problems or to demonstrate understanding of social rules and concepts. | What should you do if you see someone forgot his book when he leaves a restaurant? What is the advantage of keeping money in the bank? |
| Digit Span | Number sequences are presented orally, and the examinee is asked to repeat them verbatim or in reverse order. | I am going to say some numbers. Listen carefully, and when I am through you say them right after me: 2, 4, 7. Repeat these numbers backward: 4, 6, 1, 7, 5. |
| SUBTEST (PERFORMANCE) Picture Completion | The examinee is asked to identify the important part that is missing in each of a set of colorful pictures of common objects and themes. | Look at this picture. What important part is missing? |
| Digit Symbol-Coding | Each of a series of shapes or numbers is paired with a simple symbol; based on a key, the examinee draws the symbol under the corresponding number. | Look carefully at the key that matches numbers with symbols. Then write the number that goes with each symbol in the space below it. 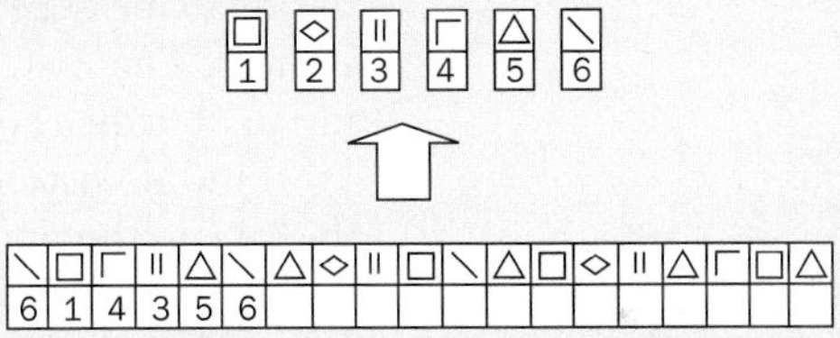 |
| Picture Arrangement | A set of colorful pictures is presented out of order, and the examinee rearranges them into a logical story sequence. | Arrange the pictures on these cards so they tell a story that makes sense.  |
| Block Design | The examinee uses two-color blocks to replicate a design from a model or a picture. | Arrange the blocks so they look like the design in the picture. 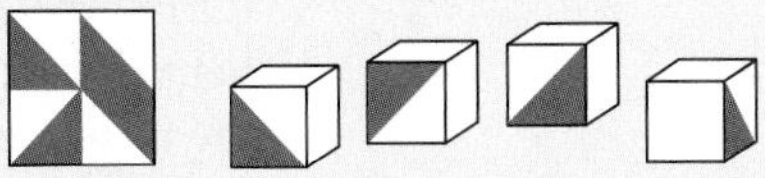 |
| Symbol Search | The examinee scans two groups of symbols (a target composed of two symbols) and a search group of 5 symbols and indicates whether either target symbol matches any symbols in the search group. | 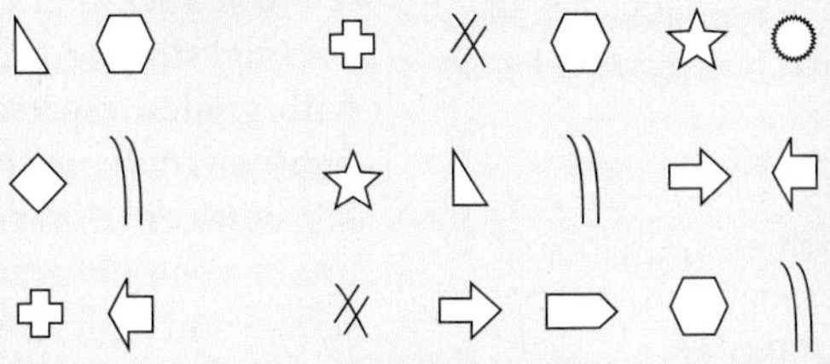 |

**FIGURE 8-15** The WAIS-III is an individually administered intelligence test; its subtests consist of verbal and performance items.

**Source:** Sample items from the Wechsler Adult Intelligence Scale (WAIS–III) 3rd edition. © The Psychological Corporation. Reproduced by permission. All rights reserved.

*"You can't build a hut. You don't know how to find edible roots and you know nothing about predicting the weather. In other words, you do terribly on our I.Q. test."*

**Source:** Reprinted by permission of Sidney Harris.

**Reliability.** To stand up to scrutiny, a psychological test must demonstrate **reliability;** that is, it must yield relatively consistent or repeatable results (Gregory, 2004). Like other measuring devices, a psychological test is of little value if it provides inconsistent results. For example, you might be delighted to find that your bathroom scale reads 138 pounds, indicating that you lost the 12 pounds you wanted to shed. But when you step on the scale again to double-check the weight, the digits flash 154! Your scale is of little value because it is not reliable; it is time to buy a new one. If the scale were a psychological test, it would be time to look for a new measure.

Psychologists use several approaches to determine whether a test is reliable. They can administer a test twice to a group of people, separating the two administrations by a short time period (a few days or a week). Using a correlation coefficient, they can measure the similarity in the scores obtained on the two occasions (see Chapter 1). If the scores are similar, they have established *test-retest reliability*. In another approach, known as the *alternate-forms method*, two different but equivalent forms of a test are administered to the same group of people. If the individuals' scores on the two forms are comparable, the test is reliable.

A psychological test has good reliability if the correlation coefficient that describes the similarity in pairs of scores is .80 or higher. The reliability of the Stanford-Binet and Wechsler intelligence tests is generally .90 or higher (Domino, 2000; Gregory, 2004). Even if a test provides reliable scores, however, we need to know whether the test is valid before we are ready to use it.

**Validity.** A psychological test can be reliable, but it is of little value unless it is valid as well. On the other hand, an unreliable test cannot be valid. **Validity** tells us whether the test actually measures what its developers intended it to measure. Suppose that we decide to measure anxiety levels by asking people to write down the names of the Seven Dwarfs. The written reports might be very reliable, yet those reports would have nothing to do with anxiety. Thus, reliability does not guarantee validity.

How do psychologists establish test validity? The information they use varies with the type of test and the purpose for which it was designed. For example, for most of the tests you take in college, validity can be established by demonstrating that the test reflects the course content. Students who complain to professors that tests cover only a small part of the material or do not reflect the course material at all are questioning the *content validity* of the test. When a test is used to predict whether examinees will succeed in a particular task or job, the test should have high *predictive validity*.

Another way psychologists establish test validity is by demonstrating relations between test scores and other measures or behaviors that should in theory be related to the test. For example, we would expect a valid test of anxiety while delivering a speech in front of a class to be related to physiological responses (for example, how much you perspire), amount of uncertainty in a speech (for example, the number of "ums" and "ahs" during the speech), ability to maintain eye contact with the audience, and several other behaviors. The relations between the test and these various responses is an indication of the test's *construct validity*.

For a number of reasons, establishing the validity of measures of intelligence is not a straightforward task. Traditionally, psychologists have correlated intelligence scores with grades, especially in elementary school and high school. In general, correlations between measures of school achievement such as grades and teacher ratings of students fall between .40 and .60 (Neisser et al., 1996; Wechsler, 1991). Correlations between intelligence and grades in college and graduate school are lower than those for elementary school and high school. What's more, everyday problems often have little relation to the knowledge or skills acquired in school. For this reason, intelligence tests are often controversial. As we will see later, this controversy has spurred psychologists to look at the concept of intelligence in new and expanded ways that take the concept beyond its traditional connection with grades in school.

**Standardization.** The third crucial element of a well-developed psychological test is **standardization,** meaning that the test is administered the same way every time it is

**reliability**
Degree to which repeated administrations of a psychological test yield consistent scores

**validity**
Degree to which a psychological test measures what its developers intended it to measure

**standardization**
The development of procedures for administering psychological tests and the collection of norms that provide a frame of reference for interpreting test scores

## *Study* CHART

### Principles of Psychological Tests

**Reliability**: Does the test yield consistent results?

- If a test is administered on Monday to a group of fourth through eighth graders, will they obtain similar scores when the same test is readministered the following week?

- There are two forms of a test designed to measure test anxiety in college students; they are designated Form A and B. Will students' scores on Form A be similar to their scores on Form B?

**Validity**: Does the test measure what it was intended to measure?

- If a test is designed to measure spatial ability needed in the job of an airplane pilot, will the scores on the test predict which persons will make the best pilots?

- Are scores on tests of intelligence related to the grades students receive in various elementary and high school classes?

- Are persons who receive high scores on a test that seeks to identify characteristics related to depression likely to be diagnosed as depressed when they are interviewed by clinical psychologists and psychiatrists?

**Standardization and norms**: Does the test have guidelines that specify the instructions, time limits, and scoring procedures? Are there norms to use in interpreting the scores?

- Does the test administrator know when to stop administering items on a particular subscale of an intelligence test, depending on the number of items failed in a row?

- Are the scores obtained on a test of general knowledge of public events different, depending on the age of the people who take the test?

used. The instructions, time limits (if any), and scoring procedures must remain identical from one use to the next.

The development of norms is another important aspect of test standardization. At the beginning of Chapter 1 we met Patty, who completed an IQ test on the Internet. She wondered what her obtained score meant; perhaps she asked a friend, "What did you get?" If so, she was searching for information to help her interpret her score by comparing it to those obtained by others. **Norms** are scores obtained by a relatively large sample of similar people on the same test. They provide the frame of reference we need to interpret scores on a given test (see Study Chart).

The scores that describe many physical and psychological characteristics, including height, weight, anxiety, and intelligence, are distributed in the population in a certain way. Most people obtain scores near the middle of the distribution of test scores or physical measurements. The number of people obtaining a given score decreases as we move from the middle to the tails of the distribution (see Figure 8-16). For example, the height of an average adult American is 66.5 inches (McDowell, Fryar, Hirsch, & Ogden, 2005). The heights of most adults tend to be close to this average; few adults are 46 inches or 86 inches tall. This commonly encountered distribution of scores is called the **normal curve** (or *distribution;* see Appendix A). Measures of intelligence fit this distribution, with the average (mean and median) score set at 100. This bell-shaped curve is widely used because many biological and psychological variables are distributed in the population as described by this curve. About two-thirds of Americans have IQs between 85 and 115, in the large middle section of the bell-shaped curve.

## Extremes of Intelligence

Intelligence test scores below 70 or above 130 occur in less than 5% of the population (see Figure 8-16); people with such statistically rare scores are designated as *exceptional*. Those with scores below 70 *may* be diagnosed as mentally retarded if they also exhibit significant deficits in everyday adaptive behaviors, such as self-care, social skills, or communication

**norms**
Distribution of scores obtained by a large sample of people who have taken a particular psychological test

**normal curve**
Symmetrical bell-shaped distribution having half of the scores above and half below the mean

**FIGURE 8-16** Normal curve (distribution) of intelligence test scores. This curve has been very useful to psychologists as well as to researchers in other disciplines. Although the curve is derived from theoretical mathematics, researchers found that many psychological and biological variables are distributed in the general population in a manner that fits the curve. As you can see, the majority of the population obtains IQ scores that are close to the mean of 100; scores further away from the mean occur less often.

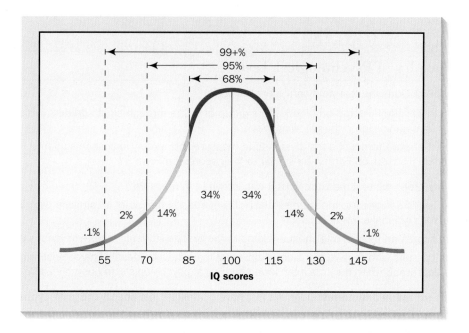

(American Psychiatric Association, 2000). The diagnosis of mental retardation requires that the condition begin before age 18. In many cases, deficits that occur after age 18 are the result of brain damage from automobile accidents or other forms of trauma to the head and brain.

**Exceptional Children.** Public Law 94-142 (Individuals with Disabilities Education Act, IDEA), includes provisions for educating all children with handicaps. This law brought the nature and needs of handicapped children to the attention of educators and the general public. Because the education of all children was affected, the term *handicapped* was changed to *exceptional*. Exceptional children may be classified into five major categories: those with learning disabilities, behavior and emotional disorders (Jensen, 2005), sensory disabilities, communication disorders, and intellectual deviations (gifted, talented, and mental retardation). Table 8-5 lists some of the major categories of exceptional individuals.

Standard intelligence tests such as the WISC-III are frequently used in the evaluation of children who are perceived as exceptional. Because there are many forms of exceptionality, however, psychologists have developed other assessment instruments in addition to direct observation of behavior (Jensen, 2005). For example, observation of classroom behaviors by teachers is an important component of the assessment of children with behavior disorders.

Exceptional children often require special attention and services, but there is no standard approach to dealing with their needs. For example, the verbal and physical aggression that may characterize children with emotional disturbances requires interventions that differ from those appropriate for children with mental retardation. School psychologists typically work with classroom teachers and special education teachers to develop an *individualized educational plan* (IEP) for each child (Eggen & Kauchak, 2001). By law, students with disabilities must be provided educational opportunities in the *least restrictive environment:* To the maximum extent that is appropriate, these children are to be educated with students who do not have disabilities and in the most normal type of educational settings (Jensen, 2005).

People with IQ scores of about 140 and above may be identified as *gifted*. There are quite a number of myths and misconceptions about gifted people, but fortunately there are data to address these myths and misconceptions. Using teacher recommendations and IQ tests, Lewis Terman identified 1,500 gifted children to track over a lifetime (the study is projected to run until 2010). This study of people who became affectionately

## TABLE 8-5

# Categories and Characteristics of Exceptional Individuals

These categories represent deviations from the average in some aspect of intellectual functioning; both impaired intellectual functioning and superior abilities are represented. Many children who are identified as falling into one of these categories of exceptionality receive some form of special education. Traditional intelligence tests or tests specially developed for use with certain populations, such as the deaf, are often used to collect information that is helpful in identifying cases of exceptionality.

### Mental Retardation

| Level of Mental Retardation | IQ | Percentage of Total Group | Characteristics |
|---|---|---|---|
| Mild | 50–55 to approximately 70 | 85% | * Often not distinguishable from other children until they begin school<br>* Able to develop social and language skills and can acquire academic skills up to about the sixth-grade level<br>* Usually live in the community or in a supervised group home |
| Moderate | 30–40 to 50–55 | 10% | * Can learn to communicate during preschool years but are not likely to proceed past second-grade-level academic skills<br>* Usually go through vocational training and may work in sheltered workshops |
| Severe | 20–25 to 35–40 | 3–4% | * Poor motor development and poor communication skills<br>* May learn to read "survival" words like *men, women,* and *stop*<br>* Need a protective living situation such as a group home |
| Profound | IQ below 20 | 1–2% | * Language and comprehension limited to simple requests and commands<br>* Majority have some brain abnormality<br>* Need constant supervision |

### Learning Disability

Group of disorders manifested by significant difficulties in the acquisition and use of listening, speaking, reading, writing, reasoning, or mathematical abilities. About 4% of individuals between the ages of 6 and 21 have learning disabilities.

### Gifted and Talented

The term *gifted* was first used to describe children whose scores on intelligence tests were well above average. The definition has been expanded to include *talented* individuals who display superlative skills in a specific area, as evidenced by outstanding performance or products. These talents are typically not assessed by intelligence tests. The prevalence of the gifted and talented is difficult to determine because the definitions vary greatly.

### Savant Syndrome

Designation for mentally retarded individuals who manifest at least one remarkable ability such as handling mathematical calculations quickly and without paper and pencil or calculators. This rare syndrome tends to occur more often among males and those diagnosed as autistic.

**Sources:** American Psychiatric Association (2000); Haring, McCormick, and Haring (1994).

Richard Wawro (b. 1952) is a Scottish artist who has earned widespread acclaim for his drawings. Although he experienced visual difficulties from birth (he is legally blind) and is autistic, he uses wax oil crayons to create detailed images of intense depth and color. His work has been exhibited throughout the world. A documentary film about him, *With Eyes Wide Open,* won several international awards. The film was viewed by Dustin Hoffman during his preparation for playing an autistic man in the film *Rain Man.* You can view some of Richard's works of art at www.wawro.net.

**savant syndrome**
Condition of a mentally retarded person who displays exceptional ability in a specific area

known as "Termites" enabled him to put to rest some myths about gifted people. For example, these gifted individuals equaled or surpassed an unselected sample of people in terms of physique and athletic ability. Not surprisingly, they did better academically, and Terman and his team found evidence of the following:

- They were healthier.
- They had more hobbies.
- They read more books.
- They were better adjusted as adults.
- They were better achievers and learned more easily.

**Savant Syndrome.**    In an 1887 lecture, J. Langdon Down (1828–1896) described a group of mentally retarded children who exhibited special abilities (Treffert, 1989). Down eventually became known for his description of *Down syndrome*, but in the 1887 lecture he offered a description of savant syndrome.

**Savant syndrome** occurs in people who are severely handicapped in overall intelligence yet demonstrate exceptional ability in a specific area such as art, calculation, memory, or music (Miller, 1999). For example, despite having very low scores on tests of intelligence (usually between 40 and 70) (Treffert & Wallace, 2002), some savants can report calendar dates from hundreds of years ago (calendrical calculation; O'Connor, Cowan, & Samella, 2000). Most cases of savant syndrome involve remarkable memory with little understanding of what is being described (Treffert & Wallace, 2002). The essence of the savant syndrome is captured in the following case (Treffert, 1989):

> Tom, a blind boy, had a vocabulary of less than 100 words. Yet he could play over 5,000 musical pieces from memory, including Bach, Beethoven, Chopin, and Rossini. At age 11, he played for the president of the United States. Some musicians felt that Tom had tricked the president and the public. They tested him: Tom was asked to listen to two unfamiliar musical pieces, of 13 and 20 pages each; he then played them perfectly from memory.

Most savants are male; the syndrome occurs in approximately one in 2,000 people with brain damage or mental retardation and about 1 in 10 people with autism (Treffert & Wallace, 2002). Autism is a rare mental disorder that typically begins during infancy or early childhood. It is characterized by failure to respond to people in socially appropriate ways; by serious deficits in speech, language, and communication; by abnormal relationships to objects and events; and by abnormal responses to sensory stimulation (Jensen, 2004). Some researchers believe that autism (or at least autistic traits) and savant skills are inextricably linked (Heaton & Wallace, 2004). Accumulating evidence suggests that people with savant syndrome have suffered damage to the left hemisphere, which apparently results in some form of compensation by the right hemisphere. In fact, all of the abilities exhibited by people with this syndrome are associated with the right hemisphere (see Chapter 2). Savant syndrome proves a fascinating puzzle for psychologists and other scientists who study the brain and intelligence. What's more, "No model of brain function will be complete until it can explain this rare condition" (Treffert & Wallace, 2002, p. 85). Although the cause of savant syndrome is largely a mystery, its existence prompts us to reconsider the concept of general intelligence.

## Kinds of Intelligence

We can divide theorists who study intelligence into two groups: "lumpers" and "splitters." Lumpers view intelligence as an overall ability to acquire knowledge, to reason, and to solve problems. As noted earlier, Sir Francis Galton is credited with originating the concept of intelligence. He could be considered a lumper. Most of the intelligence tests that were developed after his pioneering work yield a single number, which may lead us to oversimplify the nature of intelligence. Splitters view intelligence as a collection of abilities that reflect a diversity of individual strengths and weaknesses. They have developed several theories suggesting that there is more than one kind of intelligence.

**Spearman's Model.**    Charles Spearman (1863–1945), a British psychologist, believed that there are two types of intelligence, one called *g* for *general intelligence* and the other, representing a number of specific abilities, called *s*. Spearman observed that people who perform well on one type of intelligence task tend to do well on most other tasks, although their scores on these tasks are seldom the same. He proposed that any given task reflects both types of intelligence. General intelligence cuts across specific kinds of items and accounts for similar levels of performance on a variety of items. By contrast, specific intelligence is related to the particular task and thus is responsible for the fact that each person does better on some tasks than on others.

In part because there is no universal agreement on the precise definition of intelligence and the way in which it should be measured, theorists differ in how they conceptualize intelligence. Let's say that you view intelligence not as a single overall ability (the kind represented by Spearman's *g*) but as a collection of abilities. It follows, then, that any single number on an intelligence test will provide, at best, an inadequate account of a person's ability (Sternberg, Grigorenko, & Bundy, 2001). "Intelligence is plural, not singular," according to Stephen Ceci (2001, p. 49).

**Sternberg's Model.**    The kinds of intelligence that are rewarded in school may have little to do with success in life outside of school. Robert Sternberg (1988, 1997) believes that there are several ways to be adaptive or effective. He therefore proposed a new model of intelligence called the *triarchic theory of intelligence*. This model comprises (a) *analytical intelligence*, or the ability to break down a problem or situation into its components (the type of intelligence assessed by most current intelligence tests); (b) *creative intelligence*, or the ability to cope with novelty and to solve problems in new and unusual ways; and (c) *practical intelligence*, which is also known as *common sense* or "street smarts." The third type of intelligence is one that the public understands and values, yet it is missing in standard intelligence tests (Sternberg, Wagner, Williams, & Horvath, 1995).

Sternberg believes that most intelligence tests place a premium on speed, which is not relevant in most decisions we must make. This hurried approach to testing can discriminate against children who are not used to it—especially poor, minority, or immigrant children.

The triarchic theory of intelligence is the basis of efforts to match instruction to the strengths students exhibit in analytical, creative, or practical intelligence. Although these efforts are still in the early stage of development, they hold promise for increasing students' success. Students' strengths in one of the three components of the model are assessed; then students receive instruction that emphasizes their strength. At the end of the course, the students are evaluated; however, the focus of the evaluation is consistent with the component of the model that had been emphasized (Sternberg, Ferrari, Clinkenbeard, & Brigorenki, 1996). See Table 8-6 for examples of the types of questions that different disciplines might use to assess each of the triarchic components. The early results demonstrate some "interesting trends; for example, students who were identified as creative, and were subsequently taught in a section emphasizing creative performance, outperformed the other two groups when assessed for creativity related to the course work" (Sternberg, 1997, p. 358).

The triarchic theory on intelligence emphasizes the *processes* of intelligence. Next, we turn to a theory of intelligence that focuses on what could be called the *domains* of intelligence.

**Gardner's Multiple Intelligences.**    Tests of intelligence predict academic achievement because that is what they were designed to do. Had they been developed by artists, salespeople, or politicians, they might be different. To account for the broad range of achievements in modern society, Howard Gardner (2003) proposes the existence of "a number of relatively autonomous intellectual capacities or potentials" he calls *multiple intelligences* (p. 47). According to Gardner (1993, 1999), there is more to intelligence

**TABLE 8-6**

## Questions Based on Sternberg's Triarchic Theory of Intelligence

The triarchic theory can be applied to teaching and the evaluation of students. These sample questions are based on the three components of the model.

| Discipline | Analytic | Creative | Practical |
|---|---|---|---|
| Psychology | Compare Sigmund Freud's theory of dreaming to Calvin Hall's. | Design an experiment to test a theory of dreaming. | How does Sigmund Freud's theory of dreaming apply to your life? |
| Biology | Evaluate the validity of the bacterial theory of ulcers. | Design an experiment to test the bacterial theory of ulcers. | How would the bacterial theory of ulcers change conventional treatment approaches? |
| History | How did events in post–World War I Germany lead to the rise of Nazism? | How might President Truman have encouraged the surrender of Japan without dropping nuclear bombs on Hiroshima and Nagasaki? | What lessons does Nazism hold for events in the Middle East today? |

**Source:** Adapted from Sternberg (1997).

than the verbal and mathematical abilities measured by current intelligence tests. Each person may have different strengths and weaknesses and thus may manifest intelligence in various ways.

1. *Verbal/Linguistic:* Mastery, love, and ability to use language and words (in spoken and written forms); found in poets, lawyers, speakers, writers, and rap singers

2. *Musical:* Ability to hear, recognize, and manipulate patterns in music. High level of competence in composing and performing; sensitivity to pitch and tone; evident in composers, singers, and musicians

Howard Gardner suggests that there is more to intelligence than scores on current intelligence tests. People can manifest intelligence in many ways that are not tapped by such tests. Oprah Winfrey's high level of interpersonal intelligence is evident to anyone who has seen her show. These soccer players exhibit the characteristics of movement or bodily kinesthetic intelligence. Bono and U2 are known around the world for their music.

## MULTIPLE INTELLIGENCES FOR THE 21ST CENTURY

PROGRAMMING A VCR SO IT DOES NOT FLASH 12-12-12

RECALLING THE LOCATION OF THE REMOTE CONTROL

DRIVING AND SPEAKING ON A CELLULAR PHONE

**Source:** Reprinted with the permission of Psi Chi, The National Honor Society in Psychology.

3. *Logical/Mathematical:* Ability to detect patterns, think logically, reason deductively, and carry out mathematical operations. Used in solving mathematics problems and in logical thinking—for instance, in science and mathematics, especially highly advanced mathematics

4. *Visual/Spatial:* Ability to represent the spatial world (both wide spaces and confined spaces); likely to be found in pilots, navigators, sculptors, architects, and championship chess players

5. *Movement or Bodily Kinesthetic:* Ability to use and control parts (hands, fingers, arms) or the whole body and to handle objects skillfully; found in dancers, surgeons, athletes, and craftspeople

6. *Interpersonal Intelligence:* Sensitivity to people, ability to understand what motivates them and ability to recognize their intentions, understanding how to work effectively with people and how to lead and to follow; may be found in people involved in sales, teaching, counseling, or politics

7. *Intrapersonal Intelligence:* Understanding one's emotions and being able to draw on them to guide one's behavior to understand oneself and use that information to regulate one's own life

8. *Existential:* Ability to pose and ponder questions about life, death, and ultimate realities

9. *Naturalist:* Ability to discriminate among living things (plants, animals) and sensitivity to other features of the natural world (clouds, rock configurations). Values our evolutionary past as hunters, gatherers, and farmers; likely to be found in roles such as botanist, chef, and landscaping

Although Sternberg's and Gardner's perspectives seem to be alternatives to traditional views of intelligence, they are in many ways complementary in their emphasis on different aspects of intelligence. For example, you can think analytically, creatively, or practically in a particular domain (linguistic, for example). You can analyze a work of literature (analytic), write a poem (creative), or discuss the relevance of the travails of a literary character for one's own life (practical).

Sternberg and Gardner both suggest that people should be evaluated on the basis of factors other than their scores on tests of verbal and mathematical ability. Relying exclusively on these scores may cause us to overlook a person's other strengths, such as musical or athletic ability.

**STUDY TIP**

Describe the theories of intelligence. When appropriate, give examples (e.g., for the nine aspects of Howard Gardner's multiple intelligences).

## Misuse of Intelligence Tests

Although current intelligence tests provide reliable scores, those tests and scores have been at the center of controversy. What do intelligence scores mean? The high reliability coefficients that characterize most intelligence tests should not lead to the incorrect conclusion that assessments based on such tests are always accurate (valid). Psychological

**heritability**

Percentage of differences among a group of people in a characteristic, such as intelligence, that is believed to be due to inherited factors

testing has the potential for abuse when the scores are applied without a full understanding of their meaning. The following examples show the misuse of psychological testing.

Earlier in this chapter we learned that Galton believed that intelligence was determined by heredity. Based on this belief, he proposed that the general intelligence of an entire nation could be increased if only the more intelligent citizens were allowed to have children. This movement, known as *eugenics*, was popularized by Galton and brought to the United States, where sterilization laws in more than 30 states barred people of low intelligence from having children. In the early and mid-20th century, more than 60,000 mentally ill, retarded, and disabled people were sterilized without their consent (Brookes, 2004; Gould, 1981).

In what has been called "one of the saddest chapters in the history of the testing of intelligence" (R. J. Sternberg, 1998, p. 7), intelligence test scores were used to prevent some European immigrants from entering the United States (Kamin, 1982). The tests were usually administered in crowded conditions, and the items required a knowledge of U.S. culture that the foreign arrivals lacked. For example, one item asked examinees to look at a geometric figure and then use a pencil to copy it on a piece of paper. This item seems easy to us, but many of the immigrants had never seen, let alone used, a pencil. Nevertheless, the results were used to classify some immigrants as feebleminded (Gould, 1981; Zenderland, 1998).

## Hereditary and Environmental Determinants of Intelligence

The people responsible for testing immigrants' intelligence earlier in the 20th century believed that the test scores reflected the operation of heredity rather than environmental influences. The question of how heredity (nature) and environment (nurture) determine intelligence has sometimes mistakenly been posed as if one factor or the other alone accounted for intelligence. A more appropriate way to ask the question is "To what degree is intelligence influenced by heredity, environment, and a combination of the two?"

**Hereditary Determinants.**     One way researchers estimate the influence of heredity on intelligence is to use a mathematical measure called **heritability,** which can range from 0% to 100% (Petrill, 2003). A characteristic that has a heritability of 0% is not influenced by inherited factors at all. When heritability is 100%, inherited factors are completely responsible for that characteristic. Height has a heritability of 90%, which means that 90% of the differences in height among people are accounted for by variation in genetics; only 10% are due to environmental factors such as diet (Horgan, 1993). Although some estimates of the heritability of intelligence are as high as 80% (Jensen, 1969), most are in the range of 50 to 60% (Plomin, DeFries, McClearn, & Rutter, 1997; Snyderman & Rothman, 1987). Robert Plomin and his colleagues (Plomin et al., 1997) state, "The evidence for a strong genetic contribution to general cognitive ability (*g*) is clearer than for any other area of psychology" (p. 153). What's more, research identifying the specific genes responsible for a number of forms of mental retardation, reading disability, and late-onset Alzheimer's disease raise the possibility that in the near future breakthroughs will occur in the identification of genes responsible for general cognitive ability (Plomin et al., 1997; Plomin & DeFries, 1998; Plomin & Petrill, 1997).

Earlier in the 20th century, intelligence tests were used to restrict U.S. immigration. This was done without a proper understanding of the influence of environmental conditions on test scores.

Although we know the most about the heritability of intelligence at younger ages, evidence suggests that genetic factors can affect intelligence in older age populations. What's more, heritability estimates are not constant across the lifespan; rather, they change with age ranges (McClearn et al., 1997; Petrill et al.,

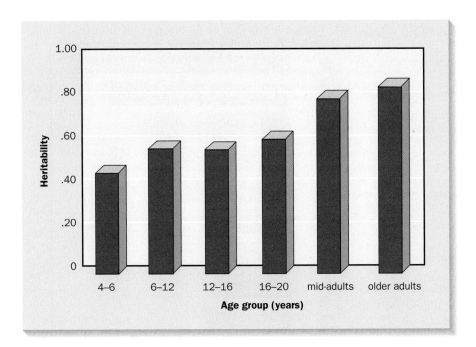

**FIGURE 8-17**  Influence of genetic factors across the lifespan. The heritability of intelligence tends to increase with age. In other words, the older we are, the greater the effect of genetic factors.

**Source:** Plomin and Petrill (1997).

1998). Researchers located a sample of twins from the Swedish Twin Registry; they were interested in twins who were 80 years of age or older and able to take part in a 1.5-hour testing period. The estimate of the heritability of general cognitive ability—based on an overall intelligence test—was quite high. As you can see from Figure 8-17, estimates of the heritability of intelligence actually tend to *increase* with age.

Even highly heritable characteristics can be influenced by environmental factors. For example, about 1 of every 10,000 American children is born with an inherited metabolic disorder called *phenylketonuria* (*PKU*), which was first described in 1934 by a Norwegian physician, Asbjorn Folling (Christ, 2003; Plomin et al., 1997). People with PKU are unable to produce the enzyme that breaks down phenylalanine, an amino acid found in many foods, especially meat. Undigested phenylalanine accumulates in the body, causes damage to the nervous system (including the brain), and leads to mental retardation and motor problems (Christ, 2003; Luciana, Sulliven, & Nelson, 2001). The IQ scores of people with PKU who are left untreated are often below 50 (Plomin et al., 1997).

A diagnostic test performed shortly after birth can determine whether a baby has PKU. Babies found to have PKU are put on a low-phenylalanine diet (some phenylalanine is essential for the body). The recommendation is to continue the special diet at least through the adolescent years (Plomin et al., 1997). In fact, the majority of treatment centers in the United States and Canada recommend that people with PKU continue their restricted diet throughout life (Fisch, Matalon, Weisberg, & Michaels, 1997). Although PKU has a heritability of 100%, it can be modified by changing the environment (in this case, diet). In short, heredity is not necessarily destiny.

### Psychological Detective

PKU occurs relatively rarely, so it does not tell us a great deal about how heredity influences intelligence in most people. What other evidence could shed light on the way heredity influences intelligence? Give this question some thought, and write down your answer before reading further.

Another way in which researchers estimate the degree to which intelligence is affected by inherited factors is by examining correlations between the intelligence test scores of family members (Bouchard & McGue, 1981). If intelligence runs in families,

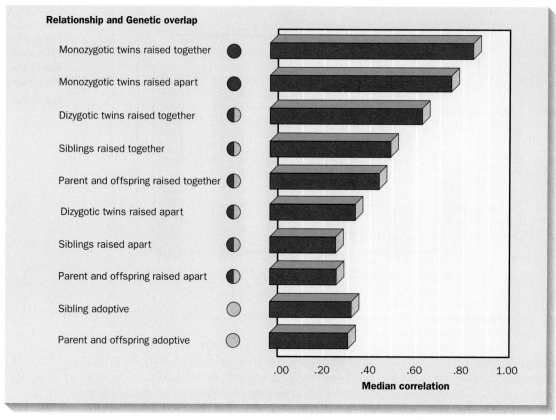

**Relationship and Genetic overlap**

- Monozygotic twins raised together
- Monozygotic twins raised apart
- Dizygotic twins raised together
- Siblings raised together
- Parent and offspring raised together
- Dizygotic twins raised apart
- Siblings raised apart
- Parent and offspring raised apart
- Sibling adoptive
- Parent and offspring adoptive

.00   .20   .40   .60   .80   1.00
**Median correlation**

**FIGURE 8-18** Median correlations between intelligence scores of family members. The degree of genetic overlap ranges from 100% for monozygotic (identical) twins, whether they are raised together or apart, to 0% for adopted siblings—unrelated children adopted by the same family. The correlations in this table provide evidence for the effects of *both* heredity and the environment.

**Source:** Plomin and Petrill (1997).

the intelligence scores of family members should be correlated. The study of twins also plays a key role in investigating the influence of heredity and environment on characteristics such as intelligence. **Identical twins** (also known as *monozygotic twins*) have exactly the same genes and therefore are always of the same sex. **Fraternal twins** (also known as *dizygotic twins*) are no more similar than two siblings in the same family. They were born together but have only 50% of their genes in common. As you can see in Figure 8-18, the correlation between the intelligence scores of twins is quite high; the scores of less closely related people exhibit lower correlations. These statistics seem to provide evidence for inherited influences on intelligence. In fact, "No plausible alternative to genetic influence exists to explain the IQ similarity in monozygotic twins reared apart" (Bouchard, 1997, p. 153).

Family members also share very similar environments, however, making it possible that the correlations among their test scores are due to environmental factors. Yet when twins are raised in separate environments, the correlation between their intelligence scores is still high. So it is unclear whether heredity or environment has a stronger influence on intelligence.

To disentangle the effects of similar environments and heredity, researchers have studied the intelligence test scores of adopted children. Figure 8-18 shows that the correlation between the scores of adoptive parents and their adopted children is approximately .30. What's more, the intelligence scores of adopted children tend to correlate more highly with those of their biological parents than with those of their adoptive parents. In fact, the biological parent's IQ is a better predictor of a child's IQ than is the IQ of the adopting parent, even when the adoption occurs virtually at birth (Hunt, 1995).

**identical twins**
Twins who develop from one ovum fertilized by one sperm; genetically identical to each other

**fraternal twins**
Twins who develop from two ova fertilized by two different sperm; genetically related as siblings

What do these results tell us? Do they make a strong case for the influence of heredity on intelligence? Are there any problems with the conduct of such studies that could influence the results?

Several lines of evidence point to a significant influence of the environment on intelligence (Scarr, 1998). Typically, research that investigates the intelligence of adopted children does not tell us whether the environments in which the children were raised were similar to those that their biological parents would or could provide. Sandra Scarr and Richard Weinberg (1986) reported a study of several hundred children in Minnesota who had been placed in adoptive homes. In this case the children were either African-American or of mixed racial background. Some of the adoptive parents were African-American, but many were white, and most were college graduates with professional occupations. The intelligence scores of these adopted children were similar to those of other children brought up in the same homes. A follow-up of these children in their adolescent years indicated that being reared in a middle- or upper-middle-class environment that represents the culture of the test and schools has a significant effect on adoptees' IQ scores (Weinberg, Scarr, & Waldman, 1992). These findings suggest that the social environment plays a dominant role in determining the IQ of African-American and interracial children and that both social and genetic variables contribute to individual variations among them (Weinberg et al., 1992). Thus studies of adopted children suggest that the environment plays a role in intelligence. Next, we discuss a number of these environmental influences.

**Environmental Determinants of Intelligence.**   A variety of environmental factors can affect intelligence. For example, exposure to lead is strongly linked to intellectual deficits (Needleman & Gatsonis, 1990). In Taiwan, children who had been exposed prenatally to polychlorinated biphenyls (PCBs; chemicals used to insulate electrical equipment) had small but detectable intellectual deficits that did not decrease with age (Y.-C. J., Chen et al., 1992).

In the 1930s, Howard Skeels decided that tender, loving care and stimulation could be beneficial for two children in an Iowa orphanage (Skeels & Dye, 1939). Skeels placed these quiet, slow, unresponsive sisters in a home for mentally retarded adolescents. On his return several months later, he was surprised to find that the sisters' intelligence test scores had increased and that they appeared alert and active. The attention and stimulation provided by the mentally retarded adolescents and the staff of the institution had made a difference. This finding encouraged Skeels to provide a similar level of stimulation for a larger group of children; again the procedure was successful (Skeels, 1966). Skeels's success provided evidence that early stimulation could influence intelligence.

Since the 1930s there has been a slow but steady rise in performance on IQ tests. This increase in IQ scores over time has been found in industrialized countries (especially urban areas) as well as developing (and rural) countries (Daley, Whaley, Sigman, Espinosa, & Neumann, 2003; Flynn, 1998). The average number of correct responses in samples from 20 countries has risen by about 3 points per decade, or 15 points in 50 years. This effect may be due to environmental factors, such as improved education, or perhaps it is the result of some glitch in the tests (Flynn, 1998; Holloway, 1998). However, although performance has improved, the average test score has remained essentially the same. Why is this true? The answer is that IQ scores are a relative rather than an absolute measure; your score is compared with everyone else's. In other words, as the raw scores improve, the standard on which the IQ scores are based also rises. If everyone else is improving, your relative score will not change much (Hunt, 1995). Put another way, a raw score that yielded an IQ of 100 in the 1930s would be equal to an 85 today.

What do you think happens if some children start school with weaker skills than other children? Can anything be done to increase their chances of success? One purpose of preschool programs such as Head Start is to provide these children with educational skills, social skills, and health care before they begin their formal schooling. Head Start is aimed at children around 4 years of age, especially those in low-income and minority populations.

Early evaluations of Head Start were not encouraging; the improvements reported in verbal abilities, emotional maturity, and motivation generally lasted only 3 to 4 years into elementary school—a fairly common phenomenon known as fadeout. On the other hand, some research on various forms of early childhood education, including Head Start, indicated that after participation in these programs, fewer of the children were placed in special education classes and fewer were held back in school (Consortium for Longitudinal Studies, 1983).

In retrospect, it seems that initial expectations for Head Start were too optimistic. Efforts to influence intellectual ability cannot overcome all other environmental influences (Lee, Brooks-Gunn, Schnur, & Liaw, 1990), and early intervention does not guarantee success in life: "Early intervention simply cannot overpower the effects of poor living conditions, inadequate nutrition and health care, negative role models, and substandard schools" (Zigler & Styfco, 1994, p. 129). What's more, many Head Start teachers did not have adequate training, and parents were not as involved as they should have been. In addition, the quality of programs varied quite a bit. In the better programs, whose purpose was in part to enhance school readiness, the children often become better achievers by the time they left the program.

Despite its shortcomings, Head Start has widespread public and political support (Takanishi & De Leon, 1994; Zigler & Styfco, 1994). Programs such as the Carolina Abecedarian Project, however, have had greater success. This project, begun between 1972 and 1977, was created to prevent lower intellectual functioning in children thought to be at risk (Campbell & Ramey, 1994; Ramey & Campbell, 1981). A sample of 111 low-income pregnant women with low educational achievement and low IQ scores was selected. Once their infants were born, approximately half were assigned to a treatment group and half to a control group. The treatment consisted of an early education program provided in a child-care center that was open 8 hours a day, 5 days a week, 50 weeks per year. These infants began attending the child-care facility at an average age of 4 months. The child-care facility maintained a low ratio of children to teachers and used a curriculum that emphasized cognitive, language, perceptual-motor, and social development. The researchers conducted a longitudinal evaluation of 104 of the original 111 children in the program; the results can be found in Figure 8-19. At each point of evaluation with intelligence tests (a similar pattern was found with reading

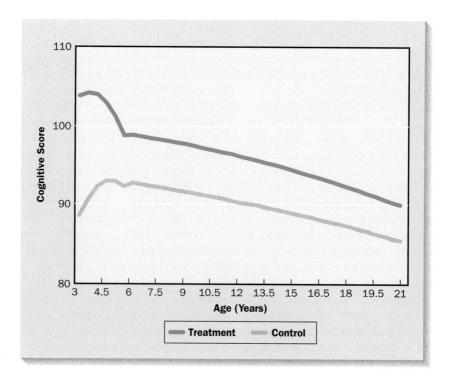

**FIGURE 8-19** The Abecedarian Project was an early educational intervention program for poor minority children. Two decades after the program began, follow-up research indicated that participants had higher cognitive scores (IQ) than a control group.

**Source:** Campbell et al. (2001).

and math achievement measures) the scores of the treatment group exceeded those of the control group. The researchers concluded, "This study indicates that intensive early childhood education can have long-lasting effects on cognitive and academic development. . . . The persistence into adulthood of the Abecedarian treatment effects on cognitive development is in contrast to the erosion of treatment-control test scores" in other programs (Campbell, Pungello, Miller-Johnson, Burchinal, & Ramey, 2001, p. 238).

## Myth or Science

For almost 30 years, the idea that birth order is related to intelligence scores has been the subject of articles and advice from professionals and nonprofessionals. Some articles had provocative (and, in retrospect, distressing) titles like "Dumber by the Dozen" (Zajonc, 1975). Here is advice from columnist Dr. Joyce Brothers (in answer to a question from a mother of four who asked if she should consider having another baby): "Studies have shown that children reared in small families are brighter, more creative, and more vigorous than those from large families" (Brothers, 1981). But was the advice based on solid evidence? Let's take a look.

One explanation offered to account for the apparent relationship between birth order and intelligence was Robert Zajonc's *confluence model*. This model says that family structure (birth order, family size, and child spacing) influences intellectual development in children. The model was used to explain evidence that average IQ declines with birth order. In other words, the average fifth-born child had a lower IQ than the average third-born child. The pattern was clear, but patterns can deceive us.

Joseph Lee Rodgers and his colleagues (2000, 2001) reported on the relation between birth order and intelligence. The observed decline in intelligence with birth order is based on what psychologists call *cross-sectional* research. In other words, researchers take all first-born, then all second-born, all third-born children, and so on in their sample and average intelligence scores in each group. The pattern is indeed one of declining intelligence scores with birth order, leading some to recommend keeping families small. But is it an accurate picture?

Using data from the National Longitudinal Survey of Youth, Rodgers and his colleagues looked at the data within families of a given size (all two-child families, then all three-child families, etc.). The results indicate that low-IQ parents tend to have larger families and thus are inconsistent with the belief that large families make low IQ children. "Parents with lower IQs in the modern United States on average have larger families and have been having larger families for some time" (Rodgers et al., 2000, p. 610). When researchers use birth order to compare across families, it confounds socioeconomic status, educational level, nutritional quality, maternal age, and other variables. The apparent decline in intelligence with birth order is due primarily to the fact that lower-IQ parents have larger families and these families differ from the rest of the population in variables that are correlated with intelligence.

"There are many good reasons why parents might consider limiting their family sizes. However, the belief that, for a particular set of parents in a modern country like the United States, a larger family will lead to children with lower IQs appears to be, simply, wrong" (Rodgers et al., 2000, p. 611). Simply put, there is no *causal* role for family size in IQ (Ceci, 2001).

## Psychological Detective

Look at the correlations in Figure 8-18. What evidence in those correlations points to the effects of the environment on intelligence? Why? Give this question some thought, and write down your answer before reading further.

People with above-average intelligence tend to have smaller families, but having a small family does not make people smart. Family size is correlated with variables such as socioeconomic status and educational opportunities than can impact measured intelligence.

A close look at the correlations in Figure 8-18 led some researchers to conclude that both heredity and environment strongly influence the development of intelligence (Plomin, 1989). Where is the support for the influence of the environment among those correlations? If two unrelated children are raised together, will their intelligence scores be similar? If heredity controls intelligence, the correlation between the intelligence scores of unrelated children should reflect their lack of family relationships—that is, it should be 0. Yet the correlation between the intelligence test scores of unrelated children raised together is greater than .30. Now look at the correlations for identical twins raised apart and raised together. The difference between those correlations also indicates that environmental factors have an effect on intelligence.

In most studies of intelligence (and other characteristics) of twins, researchers often assume that the twins (especially identical twins) are treated quite similarly. Researchers are increasingly finding, however, that twins and siblings in general are not treated as similarly as was once assumed. In fact, researchers have begun to use the terms *shared environment* and *nonshared environment* to describe the common and unique elements of the environment. They have found—sometimes to their surprise— that siblings tend to grow up in environments that are more different than similar. These differences in the environment—the nonshared environment—play a major role in accounting for differences among siblings in intelligence and in personality (Chapter 11). Earlier we described a study of the similarity of intelligence scores in twins aged 80 years and older. The major finding of that study was a high estimated heritability. From an environmental perspective, however, what is important is that the nonshared environment accounted for 27% of the differences in intelligence among older people. Thus, even in old age, differences in environment can play a role in shaping intelligence.

**Explaining Differences in Intelligence Scores.** The controversy surrounding intelligence testing continues today. Much of it concerns differences in the average intelligence scores attained by members of various racial and ethnic groups. For example, the average intelligence scores obtained by African Americans are lower than those of white Americans (MacKenzie, 1984). These group differences should not obscure the fact that there is a high degree of overlap in the distribution of intelligence scores for all groups.

Although individual differences in intelligence are due in part to heredity, the existence of group differences in IQ scores does not necessarily suggest that there are innate differences in intelligence among groups. Even characteristics that are affected by heredity can vary in response to environmental factors. Consider the analogy proposed by Richard Lewontin (1976): If we take a bag of seeds and sow half in fertile soil and the other half in barren soil, the plants that grow in barren soil will be shorter on average than the plants that grow in fertile soil. Even seeds with the genetic code for tallness are not likely to grow to their full potential if they are planted in barren soil. The differences among the plants within each group may be due to heredity, but the average difference between the two groups reflects environmental factors—in this case, the quality of the soil. In the same way, differences in IQ scores among groups can reflect such environmental factors as academic background, quality of education, and the availability of resources such as books and educational toys.

For this reason, critics of intelligence tests argue that we must take a closer look at the tests themselves. These tests are designed to measure a quality known as *intelligence*, but this quality can be difficult to define, let alone measure. Intelligence tests have moderately good predictive validity; that is, they effectively predict the performance of children in school. Success in school, however, can reflect many influences besides intelligence. Therefore critics warn against drawing conclusions concerning students' mental abilities based on their test performance.

Group differences in test scores might reflect certain characteristics of the tests themselves. Intelligence tests reflect white, middle-class values and therefore are innately biased against members of other cultural groups. For example, test writers assume that standard (white) English is best, so the tests are written in standard English. Similarly, some test questions are based on the assumption that the basic social unit is the nuclear family, which consists of a mother, a father, and their children. Thus children from groups that have a high rate of nonnuclear families are placed at a disadvantage in answering those questions.

Claude Steele of Stanford University has proposed that students' attitudes and approach to standardized tests can also affect their performance (Steele & Aronson, 1995; Steele, Spencer, & Aronson, 2002). According to Steele, African-American students face additional pressures in that a poor performance can be interpreted as confirming negative stereotypes about African Americans as a group. Thus African-American students carry an extra burden that Steele calls *stereotype vulnerability*. To test this hypothesis, Steele and Joshua Aronson gave African-American and white students a test composed of difficult verbal items from the Graduate Record Examination (GRE). Half of the students were told that the purpose of the exercise was to study "psychological factors involved in solving verbal problems." The remaining students were told that the exam was "a genuine test of your verbal abilities and limitations."

The results revealed that African-American students who thought they were simply solving problems performed as well as white students (who performed equally well in both situations). By contrast, the African-American students who had been told that the test measured their intellectual potential performed worse than all the other students. Significantly, all students had been asked to write down their race before taking the test. Thus African-American students who felt they were being evaluated as a group tried to deal with stereotype vulnerability by increasing their efforts, which led them to work inefficiently and inaccurately. Steele and Aronson (1995) concluded that they have uncovered "an underappreciated source of classic deficits in standardized test performance" (p. 810). Some attempts to reduce the impact of stereotype threat on test performance (such as telling test takers to view intelligence as a trait that is subject to change) have led to increases in test performance (Aronson, Fried, & Good, 2002).

The debate over differences in test scores is not merely an intellectual exercise; it has scientific, political, and social implications. Consider, for example, the controversy surrounding the publication of *The Bell Curve* (1994) by Richard Herrnstein and Charles Murray. Herrnstein and Murray assert that there are genetically based differences in intelligence among socioeconomic, racial, and ethnic groups. They further argue that intelligence as measured by IQ scores determines such attributes and behaviors as employment, income, welfare dependence, and quality of parental behavior. Thus low IQ is the best explanation of why some people never get off welfare, why crime is rampant in the inner cities, and why so many teenage girls get pregnant. This argument has profound implications for political and social policy: It suggests that educational and social welfare programs will have limited effectiveness because heredity, rather than environment, is primarily responsible for the problems of low-income groups.

A number of researchers (for example, Ceci, 2001; Gottfredson, 1997) have in fact pointed out that intelligence does matter; for example, intelligence scores are related to job training and performance. Critics note, however, that Herrnstein and Murray fail to distinguish between correlation and causation (see Chapter 1) and thus draw inappropriate conclusions (Hunt, 1995; Kamin, 1995). It is true that people living below the poverty line are likely to have lower IQs and poorer health and to come from families of lower socioeconomic status. Although all of these behaviors are correlated, we do not know whether any cause-and-effect relations exist among them (Hunt, 1995). For example, these behaviors could result from such environmental factors as inadequate schooling and lack of financial resources.

The controversy over how to interpret IQ scores will likely be with us for a long time. Although the issue is complex, the evidence suggests that performance on standardized tests reflects the interaction of genetic and environmental factors. Drawing conclusions about group differences based solely on test scores can be misleading and counterproductive. What's more, as we have seen, there is a great deal of overlap among all groups in test scores.

# R E V I E W   S U M M A R Y

**1.** Francis Galton initiated the intelligence testing movement by developing tests based on the assumption that level of intelligence is related to sensory abilities.

**2.** Alfred Binet and Theodore Simon developed an intelligence test to evaluate French schoolchildren. They proposed the concept of **mental age,** which compared a child's performance with the average performance of children at a particular age. The **intelligence quotient (IQ)** is the ratio of mental age divided by chronological age and multiplied by 100.

**3.** Binet's tests became the widely used Stanford-Binet test. Another set of tests, the Wechsler Scales, yield verbal and performance appraisals of intelligence.

**4.** The three characteristics of a good psychological test are reliability, validity, and standardization. **Reliability** refers to the consistency of scores obtained on repeated administrations of the test. **Validity** refers to a test's ability to measure what it was designed to measure. **Standardization** refers to uniformity in testing procedures and test scoring. **Norms** provide the distribution of scores of a large sample of people who have previously taken a test.

**5.** Intelligence test scores are distributed in the shape of a **normal curve.** The majority of the scores are clustered around the middle, with fewer scores found at either extreme.

**6.** According to Charles Spearman, we all possess general intelligence (*g*) along with specific abilities (*s*). Robert Sternberg

and Howard Gardner propose that we have several types of intelligence, most of which are not measured by current intelligence tests.

**7.** Intelligence tests have been used to deny entry into the United States. The *eugenics* movement proposed that the intelligence of an entire nation could be increased if only the more intelligent citizens had children.

**8.** The **heritability** of intelligence is an estimate of the influence of heredity in accounting for differences among people. Yet, even clearly inherited conditions, such as PKU, can be modified by altering a person's environment.

**9.** Correlations between the IQ scores of identical twins suggest that intelligence is strongly influenced by heredity. The closer the family relationship, the higher the correlation between the intelligence scores of family members. Studies of adopted children suggest that environmental factors also have an effect on intelligence.

**10.** Claude Steele has offered evidence that when taking standardized tests, African Americans may experience *stereotype vulnerability.* This notion suggests that something as simple as a question about one's race may have more significant meaning to African Americans than to other people.

# ✓ CHECK YOUR PROGRESS

**1.** Imagine that you are taken back in time to visit Galton's Anthropometric Laboratory. Which of these measurements would be of greatest interest to Galton?

a. visual imagery
b. short-term memory
c. ability to distinguish two objects by weight
d. speed with which you could run 100 yards

**2.** Distinguish between mental age and chronological age.

**3.** You have just completed your sophomore year in college, and you have no idea what you want to do when you graduate. Last week you took a test that was supposed to identify the things you enjoy doing. The results of the test strongly suggested that you should pursue a career in journalism, but you absolutely despise writing! What does the test apparently lack?

**4.** What do we mean when we say that intelligence scores are distributed like a normal curve? What does this interpretation tell us about extreme scores?

**5.** An expert on genetic influences on physical and psychological characteristics has been invited to campus to give a presentation. This expert has just finished a review of the evidence on genetics, heritability, and the public's knowledge of such concepts. Which of the following would be the best title for the presentation?

a. "Heritability Does Not Equal Destiny"
b. "Genetic Factors: How We Have Overstated Their Influence"
c. "All in the Genes: Location of the Genes Responsible for Various Facets of Intelligence"
d. "Genes Don't Influence Environmental Factors, and Environmental Factors Don't Influence Genes"

**6.** Your professor has given you an assignment to determine the estimates of the heritability of PKU, height, and intelligence. You are to turn in a list of these characteristics ranked from the one with the highest heritability to the one with the lowest. Of the following lists, which will you hand in?

a. PKU, height, intelligence
b. height, PKU, intelligence
c. intelligence, PKU, height
d. intelligence, height, PKU

**7.** What evidence supports the idea that intelligence is determined by heredity? What evidence supports the idea that intelligence results from environmental influences?

**8.** What is Claude Steele's stereotype vulnerability hypothesis?

**9.** What has happened to measures of intelligence over the past several decades?

a. Absolute intelligence has declined dramatically from generation to generation.
b. IQ scores adjusted for changes in level of education have not changed significantly.
c. It now takes more correct items to obtain an average intelligence score than it did in the past.
d. The range of acceptable responses has been expanded, so such comparisons cannot be made.

**10.** Which person is part of the age group that has the highest heritability for intelligence?

a. Alice, a newborn
b. Ted, a 14-year-old
c. Rob, a 22-year-old
d. Sonia, a 75-year-old

**ANSWERS: 1.** c **2.** Chronological age is simply how old a person is; mental age is how a child's intellectual development compares to other children's intellectual development. **3.** validity **4.** A normal curve tells us that most people obtain scores in the middle of a distribution, with fewer scores as we move away from the middle of the distribution. **5.** a **6.** a **7.** The high correlation between intelligence scores of close relatives and especially the high correlation between identical twins separated at birth support the idea that intelligence is determined by heredity. Research on environmental factors such as lead, and programs such as Head Start, suggests that intelligence is influenced by environmental factors. **8.** Claude Steele has proposed that when African-American students take standardized tests, they are subject to the effects of stereotype vulnerability. In addition to the pressures that occur for many students who take such tests, African-American students may feel pressure related to the possibility that poor performance on the test might be interpreted as confirming negative stereotypes about their race. **9.** c **10.** d

---

**ANSWERS** To Problems in Figures

## FIGURE 8-2, PAGE 326

The attribute that defines the concept is the geometric figure contains the letters to spell the name of the figure (1 is SQUARE, 4 is CIRCLE).

## PIGS IN PEN PROBLEM, PAGE 330

Place nine pigs into each of three pens. Then place all three pens inside one large pen.

**FIGURE 8-4,
PAGE 330**

**FIGURE 8-5,
PAGE 330**

**A.** Remove the matches at the top, bottom, and right.

**B.** Turn the book upside down.

**C.** The obvious answer is six and a half. Less obvious answers are:
- halving 13 gives 1 and 3 (1/3)
- halving the word thirteen gives 4 letters on each side
- converting 13 to roman numerals and halving it gives 11 and 2 (XI/II)
- halving it a different way gives 8 (X̶I̶I̶I̶)

**FIGURE 8-7,
PAGE 331**

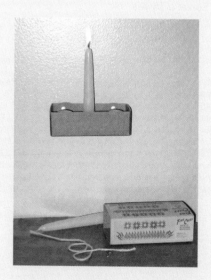

**FIGURE 8-8,
PAGE 333**

A Hare-Brained Scheme:

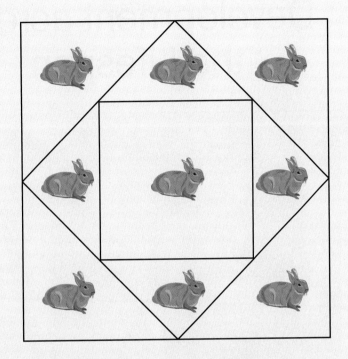

Six Drinking Glasses: Numbering the glasses from left to right, pour the contents of glass 2 into glass 5.

Six Pennies: Coins 1, 2, 4, and 6 are already in place, so move coins 3 and 5.

Ten Bowling Pins:

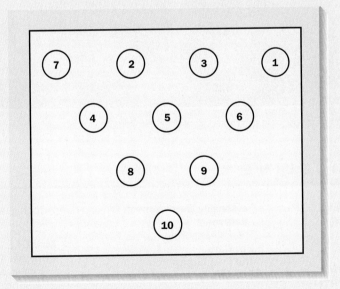

**FIGURE 8-12,
PAGE 341**

Row 1
a. Just under the wire
b. Balanced budget
c. Standing ovation
d. Shot in the dark
e. Space invaders

Row 2
a. Bottom of the ninth
b. Sitting on top of the world
c. All hands on deck
d. Skinny-dipping
e. Love at first sight

Row 3
a. Canceled check
b. Dashed hopes
c. Splitting headache
d. Three square meals a day
e. Open sesame

## CHAPTER 9

# Development across the Lifespan

## CHAPTER OUTLINE

So far we have established a biological basis for psychology, examined our sensory and perceptual processes, looked at emotions and states of consciousness, seen how learning takes place and how memories are stored, and considered cognitive processes. Keep in mind that all of these processes take place in the context of a developing organism. In this chapter we discuss the physical, intellectual, social, and psychological changes that occur throughout the lifespan (from conception through old age). As we bring the developmental cycle to its inevitable conclusion, we examine the area of death and dying and our reactions to such losses. As telecommunications and improved travel capabilities increase our knowledge of other cultures, it is important that we understand and appreciate that differences in birthing, child-rearing, and parenting practices—and in attitudes toward the elderly and death—can differ dramatically from one culture to another. Such differences can occur within large segments of the culture in the United States.

From the moment of conception until the moment of death, we change physically, cognitively, and psychosocially. **Lifespan developmental psychology** is concerned with the systematic physical, cognitive, and psychosocial processes that lead to these changes that occur throughout life. The various periods of growth across the life span are shown in Table 9-1.

When we think of human development, we probably think first about physical changes that can be *quantified*, or measured. Many of us have watched our younger brothers and sisters or our own children "grow like weeds." We also develop in *qualitative* ways that are not as easily measured as height, weight, and strength. Some of these qualitative changes involve cognitive processes and social interactions. As we grow older and add more information to long-term memory, our views on diverse topics such as pollution, love, and religion may change. We think in different and more complex ways about ourselves, our friends, and our environment.

**lifespan developmental psychology**
Study of physical, cognitive, and psychosocial changes throughout the lifespan, from conception until death

**TABLE 9-1**

## Approximate Periods of Growth and Development across the Lifespan

| | |
|---|---|
| Zygote | Conception to 2 weeks |
| Embryo | 2 to 9 weeks |
| Fetus | 9 weeks to birth |
| Infancy | Birth to age 1 year |
| Toddler | 1 to 3 years |
| Preschool period | 3 to 6 years |
| Middle childhood | 6 to 12 years |
| Adolescence | 12 to 20 years |
| Young adulthood | 20 to 40 years |
| Middle adulthood | 40 to 65 years |
| Late adulthood | 65 years to death |

**nature**
Theory that holds that physical and cognitive development is genetically determined

**nurture**
Theory that holds that physical and cognitive development is determined by environmental factors

**behavior genetics**
A new field, combining psychology and biology, that studies the influences of heredity and environment on behavior

# BASIC ISSUES IN DEVELOPMENTAL PSYCHOLOGY

John B. Watson (1924) boldly proclaimed that "there is no such thing as an inheritance of capacity, talent, temperament, mental constitution, and characteristics. These things depend on training that goes on mainly in the cradle" (pp. 74–75). Watson was so convinced of the impact of the environment on development that he declared that he could train any child to be a doctor, lawyer, artist, merchant, or even beggar or thief if he could control the child's environment (Watson, 1928). *Was Watson correct? Do all of our abilities develop as a result of environmental influences?*

## Nature and Nurture

Watson held strong views about the power of the environment to influence development, but many parents, as well as most present-day psychologists, would disagree. According to Robert Plomin (1990a), "Parents are environmentalists [that is, they stress nurture] until they have more than one child. With one child, it seems possible to explain anything that happens. However, when their second child turns out to be different in many ways from the first child, parents realize that they did not treat the two children differently enough to account for the behavioral differences that are so apparent between them" (p. 8). The contrast between these two views illustrates a significant issue in developmental psychology: To what degree does development result from **nature** (heredity) and to what extent is it a product of **nurture** (environmental factors)? In **behavior genetics,** a relatively new field that combines psychology and biology, researchers seek to provide answers to the nature-or-nurture question. Because of new technologies, such as bioinformatics and genetic engineering, researchers are now able "to measure, analyze, and manipulate genetic material rapidly and easily" (Benson, 2004, p. 42). The new technologies and their promises of valuable new findings have attracted numerous researchers.

### Psychological Detective

To grasp how behavior geneticists examine how people behave, take a moment to consider some of the differences you see in such characteristics as musical ability, athletic ability, shyness, or activity level in your friends and relatives. To what extent are these characteristics genetically determined, and to what extent are they environmentally determined? Write down some of your observations before reading further.

Some of the people you describe may have exceptional musical talent, whereas others may describe themselves as tone-deaf. A few of your friends and relatives are outgoing; others are painfully shy. Why do these people differ in these ways? Environmental factors probably play a critical role in enabling people to develop their individual capabilities. But are some of the differences we observe the result of factors other than environmental influences?

Behavior geneticists have found that heredity plays a significant role in intelligence, personality, and several patterns of abnormal behavior (Audrain-McGovern, Lerman, Wileyto, Rodriguez, & Shields, 2004). Yet "the same data that point to significant genetic influences provide the best available evidence for the importance of nongenetic factors" (Plomin, 1990a, p. 179). One of the most significant discoveries of behavior genetics is that environmental factors are experienced differently by children in the same family (see Chapter 11). Consider, for example, identical twins, who share the exact same genetic makeup. The fact that they do not have identical personalities points to the influence of environmental factors. Both nature and nurture play significant roles in development. If we are to understand the development of human thoughts, behaviors, motives, and emotions, we must learn to distinguish the influences of nature from those of nurture. Hence developmental psychologists are careful to use certain special research methods.

## Research Methods

Psychologists conducting research on developmental processes face some unique challenges. First, psychologists cannot isolate their human participants in cages like laboratory animals, allowing them to emerge only when it is time for their daily experimental sessions. What's more, ethical considerations prevent researchers from investigating some developmental processes. What is permissible? Is it acceptable to expose children to violent television programs to determine whether they will become violent or aggressive as a result? How does a researcher teach these children that their newly acquired aggressive behavior is wrong?

**Longitudinal versus Cross-Sectional Studies.** Research in human development may take longer than research in other areas of psychology. Developmental research may take months, years, or even decades. Long-term research projects in which the same participants are observed or tested repeatedly are called **longitudinal studies.** Studies that involve observing or testing participants of different ages at *one moment in time* are called **cross-sectional studies.** In other words, longitudinal projects study the same people over a period of time; cross-sectional studies cut across a section of the ages and types of people available at one moment in time (see Figure 9-1).

Longitudinal studies allow the researcher to see behavioral trends that develop over time, whereas cross-sectional studies allow the researcher to answer a specific question at a particular point in time. However, longitudinal studies can be very time-consuming and costly. Even though they are less time-consuming and costly, cross-sectional studies do not tell the researcher about behavioral trends over time.

Groups composed of participants born in the same year are called **cohorts** or *cohort groups*. In a *cohort design*, we compare the responses of different cohorts. For example, by looking at differences among cohorts, we determine the effects on shyness of being born

**longitudinal study**
Research technique in which the same participants are tested or observed repeatedly over a period of time

**cross-sectional study**
Research technique in which participants, often of different ages, are tested or observed during a limited time span or only once

**cohort**
Group of individuals born in the same period

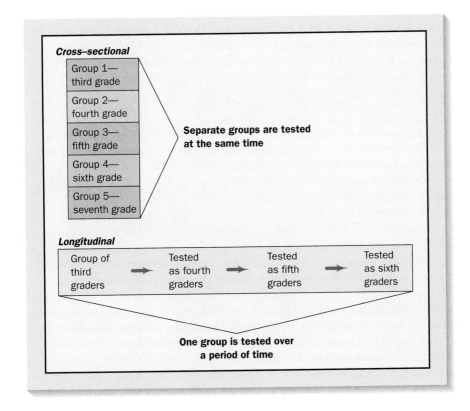

**FIGURE 9-1** Comparison of cross-sectional and longitudinal research designs. Because they are the same age, the children in this grade school class constitute a cohort.

Because they are the same age, the children in this grade school class constitute a cohort.

**zygote**
One-celled organism formed by the union of a sperm and an ovum

**mitosis**
Process of cell division in which each cell contains the same genetic information as other cells

in different decades from 1950 to 1990. The cohort design is also used in cross-cultural research in which same-age groups from different countries can be compared. The validity of a research finding is increased if it is verified across cultural groups as well as across age groups.

# DEVELOPMENT FROM CONCEPTION TO BIRTH

**Bob and Liz are thinking about having a baby, but they are concerned about the possibility that their child will have chromosomal abnormalities. Bob's brother, who is 22, has Down syndrome and lives in a group home with six men and women who also have Down syndrome. Some birth defects may be inherited, so Bob and Liz want to know what their chances are of having a baby with Down syndrome. *What can be done to provide Bob and Liz with information about their chances of having a child with Down syndrome?***

Fertilization occurs when the sperm penetrates the much larger ovum.

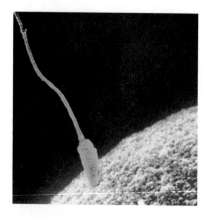

Great oaks grow from tiny acorns; a human grows from a cell that is smaller than the tip of a pin. Our lives can be traced to the union of our father's *sperm* (from the Greek word for "seed") and our mother's *ovum* (egg). In a single ejaculation, a man releases approximately 360 million sperm (Berk, 1998). The sperm immediately begin a journey from the woman's vagina to her fallopian tubes, where they may meet and penetrate an ovum, which is many times larger than the sperm. (One of the smallest cells in the body, the sperm is approximately 1/600th of an inch from head to tail.) On the way to the fallopian tubes, most sperm fall victim to acidic vaginal secretions; some are caught in recesses, and others are attacked as foreign substances by the woman's white blood cells. In fact, it is remarkable that any sperm survive the journey to penetrate an ovum. A healthy couple having intercourse regularly without contraception has only a 25 to 30% chance of beginning a pregnancy in any given menstrual cycle. Most conceptions occur on the day of ovulation or during the 2 days that precede it (Wilcox, Weinberg, & Baird, 1995). The union of the sperm and ovum forms a one-cell structure called a **zygote.**

The zygote moves from the fallopian tubes to the uterus (womb), a fist-sized, pear-shaped organ, and attaches itself to its inner wall. Through a process of cell division called **mitosis,** the zygote reproduces itself: One cell divides to become two, then four, and so on; after just 5 days, the zygote contains about 100 cells. During the next 9 months, cell division continues at a furious pace, eventually producing an individual with billions of cells, all of which contain identical genetic information.

From the 2nd to 9th weeks after fertilization, when the major organ systems are formed, the developing human is called an **embryo.** Not all zygotes become embryos, however; nearly one-third of implanted zygotes are rejected from the uterus through miscarriage (spontaneous abortion). The zygotes of most of these early miscarriages are defective in some way.

## Heredity

As noted earlier, fertilization occurs when the sperm and ovum fuse, providing the zygote with the inherited (genetic) material that will influence its development. This material is arranged in structures called **chromosomes** located in the cell nuclei. All human cells except the sperm and ovum contain 46 chromosomes, arranged in 23 pairs, with one member of each pair contributed by each parent. The chromosomes carry **genes,** which are the basic units of inheritance and the genetic blueprints for development.

The general chemical name for genetic material is **deoxyribonucleic acid,** or **DNA.** Chromosomes are actually large segments of DNA. The unique genetic blueprint for your development is contained in the chromosomes located in the nucleus of each cell (see Figure 9-2).

Our understanding of the mechanisms of heredity can be traced to the work of a monk, Gregor Mendel (1822–1884), who conducted a series of experiments using garden peas. Through these studies he unraveled the key principles of hereditary transmission; those principles are still relevant today.

During Mendel's time, people believed that a child's traits were a blend of the parents' traits; thus the child would have some intermediate or average value of a trait such as eye color. When Mendel bred peas having white flowers with peas having purple flowers, however, the offspring had purple flowers rather than pink ones. This surprising finding led him to conclude that the offspring plant's traits were not merely blends of the parent plants' traits.

Mendel also concluded that each adult plant carries hereditary factors that govern the inheritance of a trait. As you just saw, we call these factors *genes*, and they are carried on *chromosomes*. The hereditary factors of the mother and father separate before the formation of their offspring. Thus each parent contributes only *half* of the genetic material to the trait in question.

Finally, Mendel suggested that hereditary factors could be either dominant or recessive. When a *dominant gene* and a recessive gene are present in a pea plant, the dominant gene expresses itself. A *recessive gene* can express itself only in the absence of a dominant gene.

An example of this phenomenon in humans is the inheritance of sickle-cell anemia, which occurs when a person's blood contains too many abnormal hemoglobin molecules. Normal hemoglobin gives blood its red color and carries oxygen to body tissues. Too much abnormal hemoglobin causes the amount of oxygen in the blood to drop. The resulting low oxygen level causes cells to become crescent- or sickle-shaped. An attack of sickle-cell anemia is accompanied by high fever, severe pain, and potential injury to body parts and tissue (Sullivan, 1987).

Sickle-cell anemia occurs in people who have two recessive genes for that trait. People who have one dominant gene and one recessive gene for sickle-cell anemia are called *carriers* (see Figure 9-3, page 383) because they can pass the recessive gene on to their children, even though they do not have symptoms of the disease themselves. The children of two carriers have a one-in-four chance of having normal hemoglobin, a one-in-two chance of being a carrier, and a one-in-four chance of having sickle-cell anemia. Because of a relatively low rate of interracial marriage and because they are more likely to carry the recessive gene, African Americans have a higher incidence of sickle-cell anemia than people of other races. Likewise, persons from families of Eastern European Jewish origin are more

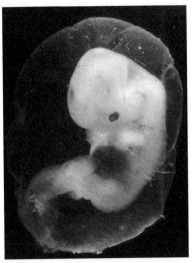

Between 2 weeks and 9 weeks following conception, the developing child is known as an embryo.

**9.1**

**embryo**
A developing organism during the stage when the major organ systems are formed

**chromosomes**
Segments of genetic material located in the nucleus of each cell; human cells have 23 pairs of chromosomes (numbered according to size), one of each pair being inherited from each parent

**genes**
Units of hereditary material that line the chromosomes and provide information concerning the form and function of each cell

**deoxyribonucleic acid (DNA)**
Chemical name for the genetic material located in the nucleus of each cell

**FIGURE 9-2**
Cells–chromosomes–genes–DNA.
Genetic material is contained in
chromosomes. The chromosomes
carry the genes, which are the
basic units of heredity. The genes
are composed of DNA.

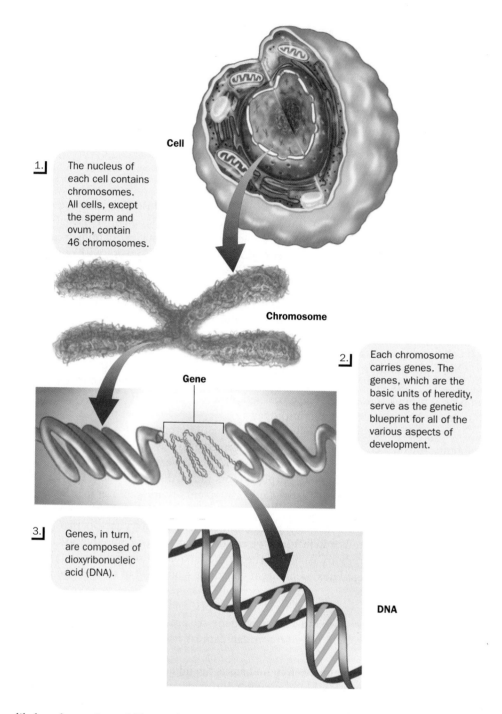

**1.** The nucleus of
each cell contains
chromosomes.
All cells, except
the sperm and
ovum, contain
46 chromosomes.

Cell

Chromosome

Gene

**2.** Each chromosome
carries genes. The
genes, which are the
basic units of heredity,
serve as the genetic
blueprint for all of the
various aspects of
development.

**3.** Genes, in turn,
are composed of
dioxyribonucleic
acid (DNA).

DNA

likely to be carriers of Tay-Sachs disease (Berkow, 1997). Tay-Sachs disease is caused by an enzyme deficiency that progressively leads to retarded development, paralysis, blindness, and death by age 5.

**Polygenic Heredity.**    Most human traits are controlled by a number of different genes, a phenomenon termed **polygenic inheritance.** For example, skin color, intelligence, and temperament are examples of polygenic inheritance.

Fraternal (*dizygotic*) twins develop from two ova fertilized by two different sperm. These children have no more resemblance to each other than do other children of the same parents. Identical (*monozygotic*) twins develop from one ovum fertilized by one sperm. The resulting cell immediately divides into two zygotes, each containing identical genetic material. Identical twins raised apart offer researchers the unique ability to study the relation of heredity and environment. Because the twins share the same genetic mate-

**polygenic inheritance**
Principle of heredity whereby
complex traits, such as intelligence
and personality, are determined by
many genes

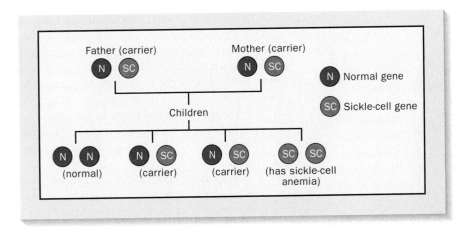

**FIGURE 9-3** Parents who have a recessive gene for sickle-cell anemia are carriers of this disease. One-fourth of their children will be normal, one-half will be carriers, and one-fourth will have the disease.

rial, shared traits would reflect genetic influences, whereas differences would reflect environmental causes.

**Determination of Sex.** Although many societies have deemed a woman's failure to produce male offspring to be a basis for divorce, the sex of a child is actually determined by the father, not the mother. To understand this process, we need to examine the 23rd pair of chromosomes, the sex chromosomes.

In females, both sex chromosomes are the same; they are labeled XX. After *meiosis* (a type of cell division that results in a reduced amount of genetic material in the cells), the ovum *always* contributes an X chromosome toward determining the child's sex. In males, the pair of sex chromosomes consists of a large chromosome and a smaller chromosome, which are labeled X and Y, respectively (the labels reflect the shapes of these chromosomes). The sperm may carry either an X or a Y sex chromosome. When the sperm contributes an X chromosome, the pair of sex chromosomes will be XX, and the baby will be female. If the sperm contributes a Y chromosome, the pair of sex chromosomes will be XY, and the baby will be male.

Because they developed from a single ovum that was fertilized by one sperm, these sisters are identical (monozygotic) twins.

**Sex-Linked Traits.** A gene located on a sex chromosome (X or Y) is called a *sex-linked gene*. The X chromosome is much larger than the Y chromosome and carries more genes. As a result, males are more vulnerable than females to some inherited disorders. In females, a recessive gene carrying a defect can be dominated by a gene on the other X chromosome; in males, however, the Y chromosome may not have the dominant gene, and the trait may appear. Such traits are called *sex-linked traits*.

Red–green color-blindness (see Chapter 3) is a sex-linked trait that occurs in about 8 of every 100 males in the United States. This most common form of color blindness is controlled by genes on the X chromosome. A female may carry a gene for color blindness on one X chromosome and a gene for normal vision, which is dominant, on the other X chromosome; she will have normal color vision. A male with a recessive gene for color blindness, however, has no dominant gene for normal color vision on the Y chromosome, so he will be color-blind. Other sex-linked disorders include hemophilia (the inability of the blood to clot), baldness, and some allergies.

## Prenatal Development

Let's return to our exploration of embryonic development. As we discussed, major organ systems are formed during the 2nd to 9th weeks after fertilization, when the developing human is called an embryo. Testes develop in the embryo 6 to 8 weeks after

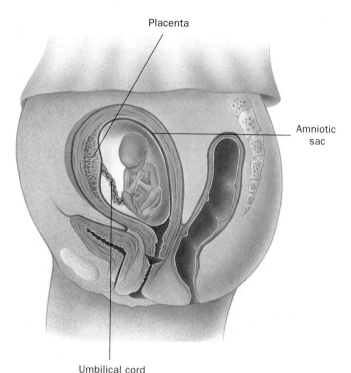

Placenta

Amniotic sac

Umbilical cord

**FIGURE 9-4** During gestation, the developing baby (fetus) is suspended in the fluid-filled amniotic sac. The fetus is connected to the placenta by the umbilical cord.

**fetus**
The developing baby from about the 9th week after conception until birth

**placenta**
Organ that develops in the uterus during pregnancy; it produces hormones that maintain pregnancy, transmits nourishment to the fetus, and filters out certain harmful substances

**teratogen**
Any biological, chemical, or physical agent capable of causing birth defects

**critical period**
A specific time during development when damage may occur or certain processes should take place

conception. If they start secreting testosterone (see Chapter 2), the developing baby will have male external genitals. The absence of testosterone leads to the development of a female.

From the 9th week until birth, the developing child is called a **fetus.** By the end of the 3rd month in the womb, the fetus is about 3 inches long and weighs about 1 ounce. Arms, legs, hands, and feet are visible and move in response to stimulation; the respiratory and digestive systems are functional. At the end of 6 months, the fetus is about 14 inches long and weighs 2 pounds.

The fetus is suspended in a fluid-filled *amniotic sac* that cushions it against sudden movements or blows to the mother. Although it is immersed in amniotic fluid (which is 98 to 99% water), the fetus begins to move as early as the end of the 3rd month of pregnancy (Moore & Persaud, 1993). The mother begins to feel movement toward the middle of her pregnancy, when the fetus is large enough to be felt through the abdominal wall (Maurer & Maurer, 1988).

The **placenta** (a Latin word meaning "flat cake") is an organ that develops even more rapidly than the fetus during the early months of pregnancy. The placenta allows an exchange of nutrients from the mother to the developing child and an exchange of waste products from the developing child to the mother. The mother's blood vessels intertwine with those that lead to the child through the umbilical cord (see Figure 9-4). Because the blood vessels of the mother are separated by a membrane from those that lead to the child, however, not all substances pass from one to the other. Nutrients in the mother's blood are released into the placenta (Rixxo, Metzger, Dooley, & Cho, 1997), where the fetus's blood takes them up and carries them, via the umbilical cord, to the fetus's body. Waste from the fetus goes in the opposite direction.

**Barriers to Prenatal Development.** If a pregnant woman's diet is inadequate, the baby is more likely to be born prematurely (at or before 37 weeks) or to have a low birth weight (less than 5.5 pounds). Low-birth-weight infants are 40 times more likely than normal-weight babies to die before their first birthday. However, it has been shown (Field, 2001) that low-weight newborns who received three 15-minute sessions of massage therapy for 5–10 days showed a 31 to 47% weight gain.

Countries that have high numbers of low-birth-weight infants include Canada, Germany, Iran, Japan, China, and Norway. Compared with other industrialized countries, the United States has a relatively high infant mortality rate; in fact, 40 countries rank higher than the United States in the rate of infants who survive to their first birthday (Central Intelligence Agency, 2004). The most important factor in causing this high rate of infant mortality is the lack of adequate prenatal care due to lack of adequate financial resources (Rice, 2001). Adequate prenatal care also means avoiding stress. Stressing the body during pregnancy may result in psychopathology (see Chapter 12) later in life (Dingfelder, 2004).

**Teratogens.** A wide variety of factors, including drugs, alcohol, and viruses, can affect the developing fetus. A **teratogen** (from the Greek word for "monster") is any biological, chemical, or physical agent that can lead to birth defects. For example, the virus that causes *rubella* (German measles) can cross the placenta to the fetus. If a pregnant woman contracts rubella before the 11th week of pregnancy, the baby is almost certain to have birth defects such as deafness or heart problems. If the mother contracts rubella after 16 weeks, the chances of birth defects are near zero (Miller, Cradock-Watson, & Pollock, 1982).

We draw attention to the period during which rubella exerts its effects to introduce the concept of the critical period. A **critical period** is a specific time during development when certain processes should occur or when damage to normal development can take place. For example, most teratogens exert their most damaging effects during the first 8 weeks of development. A baby may also contract AIDS (acquired immunodeficiency syndrome) if the mother has the disease (Grant, 1995). The virus that causes AIDS may pass through the placenta, or the baby may be exposed to the mother's infected blood during delivery (Weber, Redfield, & Lemon, 1986). Most infants live for only a short time (5 to 8 months) after AIDS symptoms appear (Chamberlain, Nichols, & Chase, 1991). Some researchers are now using fetal movements as a diagnostic tool to study possible effects of teratogens (Visser, 2003).

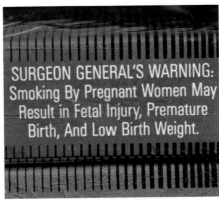

As few as five cigarettes a day can retard fetal growth.

**Drugs.** Almost all drugs cross the placenta freely (Feldman, 2005); among those that are harmful to the fetus are antibiotics (such as tetracycline), barbiturates, large doses of vitamins A and $B_6$, and an acne preparation (Accutane). Even aspirin and caffeine are suspected of causing harm to the fetus. Babies born to mothers who are addicted to heroin are also addicted to this drug and undergo a painful withdrawal process. For example, babies born to cocaine-addicted mothers may exhibit such behaviors as tremors, irritability, hypertension, rigidity, and poor sleep–wake schedules (Rice, 2001).

**Smoking.** *Fetal tobacco syndrome*, a condition characterized by retarded fetal growth resulting in lower birth weight and hyperactivity, can occur if a mother smokes as few as five cigarettes per day during pregnancy (Cnattingius, 2004). Maternal smoking (of cigarettes and marijuana; Iverson, 2000) increases the level of carbon dioxide in the blood of the fetus and is also related to higher rates of infant death (U.S. Department of Health and Human Services, 1989). The number of fetal and infant deaths in the United States could be reduced by about 5,600 each year if all pregnant women stopped smoking (Drews, Murphy, Yeargin-Allsopp, & Decoufle, 1996).

**Alcohol.** Scientists have been aware for many years that children of alcoholic parents exhibit learning and developmental problems like low birth weight, small head size, and mental retardation. Physicians discovered that the mother's drinking behaviors could significantly affect her newborn's health. The identification of the **fetal alcohol syndrome (FAS)** awakened the scientific community to the dangers of alcohol use during pregnancy (Jones & Smith, 1973; Sokol, Delaney-Black, Nordstrom, 2003). The signs of FAS include small head, flat midface, hearing loss, heart defects, and low intelligence (Aase, 1994; Day, 1992). Maternal alcohol use is also associated with adolescent and adult handicaps such as intellectual deficiencies, poor concentration, motor difficulties, and learning problems (Lee, Mattson, & Riley, 2004).

**Checking the Health of the Fetus.** Technological advances have greatly enhanced our ability to detect defects in the developing fetus (Moore & Persuad, 1993). Among the techniques available for this purpose are ultrasound and amniocentesis.

**Ultrasound.** The **ultrasound procedure** involves directing high-pitched sound waves (more than 20,000 cycles per second) toward the fetus. The sounds pass through the body and bounce back like the sonar waves used by submarines. A computer converts these echoed sound waves into a **sonogram,** an outline image of the fetus, uterus, and placenta. The sonogram determines if growth is normal or if there are any malformations.

**Amniocentesis.** The mother's age (especially if she is over 35), a family history of genetic defects, or detection of gross abnormalities by ultrasound may suggest the need for more precise testing by amniocentesis. **Amniocentesis** involves inserting a needle into the amniotic sac to withdraw about an ounce of amniotic fluid. The procedure can be done about 14 to 16 weeks after conception, when a sufficient amount of amniotic fluid is present. Amniocentesis tests done earlier may result in an increase in fetal loss and foot deformity (Schreck, 1998). Fetal cells floating in the amniotic fluid are then analyzed. Amniocentesis is not risk-free. There is a small risk of a miscarriage and the possibility of introducing an infection into the uterus (Robinson & Henry, 1985).

**fetal alcohol syndrome (FAS)**
Condition found in some children born to mothers who drank during pregnancy, characterized by lower birth weight, small head circumference, and mental retardation

**ultrasound procedure**
Projection of sound waves onto the fetus, uterus, and placenta to construct a sonogram

**sonogram**
Outline picture constructed through use of the ultrasound procedure

**amniocentesis**
Withdrawal and analysis of amniotic fluid to detect genetic abnormalities in the fetus

Analysis of chromosomes can reveal the sex of the fetus as well as the presence of chromosomal abnormalities such as Down syndrome, which occurs in about 1 in 800 births. In 95% of Down syndrome cases, the individual has three rather than two chromosomes in pair number 21 (Feldman, 2005). Children with Down syndrome are often in the mild-to-moderate range of mental retardation (see Chapter 8) and also may display such behavior disorders as depression and obsessive-compulsive disorder (see Chapter 12; Pary, 2004). Heart defects and malformations of the digestive tract put them at risk for premature death (relative to normal children) unless these malformations are recognized and corrected. Depending on the number and type of chromosomes that are present, several other sex-linked chromosomal abnormalities may occur. Among these abnormalities are Kleinfelter's, Fragile X, and Turner's syndromes. These abnormalities may result in physical abnormalities and mental retardation.

Returning to Bob and Liz, who are worried about having a Down syndrome baby because Bob's brother has the syndrome, amniocentesis will provide the answers they seek. However, the fact that Bob's brother has Down syndrome does not by itself mean that Bob and Liz are at risk. Liz's age is the most important risk factor. If she is well under the age of 40, her chances of having a Down syndrome child are greatly reduced.

## Birth

Unless the baby is premature, birth occurs approximately 266 days after fertilization, or 280 days after the last menstrual period. Birth may occur several days or even weeks before or after the "due date."

The first stage of the birth process, *labor*, begins when the pituitary gland and uterus release a hormone, oxytocin, that stimulates contractions of the uterus (Mittendorf, Williams, Berkley, & Cotton, 1990). Often the mother becomes aware of the onset of labor when her "water breaks," which refers to a sudden release of amniotic fluid through the widening *cervix* (the narrow, constricted portion of the uterus). Labor may last for a period ranging from a few hours to days; it is usually longer for a first birth than for later births. The second stage of the process is *delivery*, the actual birth of the baby. At birth, the average newborn in the United States weighs 7.5 pounds and is approximately 20 inches long. Delivery places tremendous force on the child's body, especially the head. Fortunately, the baby's skull is pliable enough so that it can squeeze through the birth canal.

Most of the drugs used to reduce the pain of labor and delivery cross the placenta and are associated with a number of adverse short- and long-term effects on infants. As a result, "the use of medication in labor and delivery is a complicated and sensitive issue, because fetal risk, maternal pain, and physician need are at constant odds" (Bornstein & Lamb, 1992, p. 124). Concern about the effects of pain-reducing drugs has led some physicians to use drugs more cautiously and in lower dosages than they did a few decades ago. Because it takes some time for drugs to cross the placenta, the longer the administration of drugs can be delayed, the better it is for the unborn child.

During the birth process, some babies experience **anoxia**, or lack of oxygen. Anoxia occurs for several reasons: The contractions may compress the umbilical cord, the baby may squeeze the cord, or the cord may be wrapped around the baby. Medication given to the mother usually crosses the placenta and may interfere with the baby's breathing, thus depriving the baby of even more oxygen. Severe anoxia can cause cerebral palsy, a motor disability affecting the arms, head, and legs.

## DEVELOPMENT IN INFANCY

You are at the hospital visiting a friend who has just had a baby. You have visited her several times and have seen her baby sleeping, crying, and just lying quietly in the crib. How utterly helpless and unable to interact with her environment she seems to be. *To what degree can newborns perceive and interact with their environment?*

Newborn infants (called *neonates*) may be quite different from those depicted in advertisements for baby products, which often use 3- or 4-month-old babies. The narrowness of the birth canal causes most newborns to emerge red and with facial bruises. The head is misshapen, and the baby is covered with a substance resembling cheese. This "bundle of joy" is apparently capable of little more than crying, sleeping, and excreting.

Just after birth, a baby's motor behavior appears to be uncoordinated and purposeless; however, newborns enter the world equipped with several reflexes (see Chapter 2). The precise functions of some reflexes remain a mystery, but others, such as blinking or sucking, clearly offer protection or promote survival (Berne, 2003). Lightly stroke a baby's cheek and the baby turns toward the touch; this is the **rooting reflex,** which aids the newborn in finding the mother's nipple to obtain nourishment. Lightly press a finger in a baby's palm and it grasps with more force than you might imagine. In fact, the **palmar or grasp reflex** is so strong that you can lift an infant by its hands. Sudden noise or the sensation of being dropped elicits the **Moro reflex:** The startled infant flings out its arms and then brings them toward its body as if to hug something. When the bottom of a newborn's foot is stroked, the toes fan upward. This response, the **Babinski reflex,** is routinely used to test the functioning of the central nervous system.

**rooting reflex**
Reflex in which the infant turns its head in the direction of a touch on its face

**palmar or grasp reflex**
Reflex consisting of a very strong hold on any object placed in the palm

**Moro reflex**
Startle reflex in response to a loud noise or the sensation of being dropped

**Babinski reflex**
Reflex in which the infant's toes fan upward when the bottom of the foot is stroked

## Sensory Abilities

Unable to do more than move reflexively, a baby may look like the picture of psychological incompetence. A closer look at newborns, however, reveals that they are remarkably competent.

**Voice Recognition.**   Very young infants can recognize their mother's voice just hours after birth. That recognition ability may actually develop before birth, while the baby is in the uterus. Psychologists Anthony De Casper and Melanie Spence (1986) asked 12 women to read a Dr. Seuss story aloud twice a day during the last 5 to 6 weeks of pregnancy. Three days after birth, their babies varied the way they sucked on a pacifier according to whether they heard that story or another one through a loudspeaker. The babies sucked more actively in response to the story they had heard while in the womb compared with a new story.

**Vision.**   Although estimates of the newborn's visual acuity range from 20/300 to 20/800, visual acuity improves to about 20/20 by 6 to 12 months (Cavallini et al., 2002). Despite having less than perfect vision, newborns can focus on objects that are about 8 to 10 inches away—the distance between the baby and the face of its caregiver during nursing or bottle feeding or when being held. Infants are attracted to and fascinated by faces, whether they are presented in two or three dimensions, in the flesh, or on film. Six-month-old babies prefer to look at attractive faces, even though they lack prior experience with cultural standards of beauty (Langlois, Ritter, Roggman, & Vaughn, 1991) and can also recognize their mother's face (DeHann & Nelson, 1997).

**Taste and Smell.**   Taste and smell receptors are present and probably functioning by the 4th month of prenatal development. Premature infants are capable of smell, suggesting that the fetus is capable of smell (Hughes & Noppe, 1991). Infant smell sensitivity seems to be present at birth for gross odor differences and rapidly increases during the first few weeks after birth (Porter, Makin, Davis, & Christensen, 1992). Likewise, newborns can discriminate between bitter and sour tastes and between sweet and nonsweet tastes.

## How Newborns Learn

As we have seen, newborns are quite adept at perceiving the world around them. Moreover, research on newborns in the United States has shown that they are also quite capable of learning (Adolph, 2000; Marcus, 2000) through classical conditioning, operant conditioning, and imitation.

**maturation**
Biological unfolding of the genetic plan for an individual's development

**Classical Conditioning.** We saw in Chapter 5 that John Watson and Rosalie Rayner were able to classically condition fear in an older infant, Albert. Carolyn Rovee-Collier and Lewis Lipsitt (1982) demonstrated that newborn infants can also be classically conditioned.

### Psychological Detective

How might you demonstrate classical conditioning in a newborn? First, you must select a behavior that occurs frequently and automatically when appropriate stimulation is presented. What is such a behavior called? Then there are other components to be considered. Try to recall the name of each element. A review of Chapter 5 will assist you. Write down your answers before reading further.

Sucking is a frequent and automatic response that can serve as the unconditioned response (UCR). A nipple placed in a baby's mouth elicits the sucking reflex, so the presence of the nipple in the mouth is an unconditioned stimulus (UCS). The sound of a particular phrase, such as "Are you hungry, baby?," spoken by the mother just before the baby begins to suck, could be the conditioned stimulus (CS). Each time the baby loses the nipple and stops sucking, the mother could repeat the question. Then one day, when the baby has just been put down for a nap but is a little fussy, the mother says, "Are you hungry, baby?," and the baby starts sucking (conditioned response, CR), leading her mistakenly to think that the baby really is still hungry. Try diagramming this arrangement of CS, UCS, UCR, and CR as we did in Chapter 5.

**Operant Conditioning.** Carolyn Rovee-Collier (1993) demonstrated that as early as 2 months after birth, an infant can learn to make a kick response when it is reinforced by movement of a mobile suspended over the crib. Moreover, this research has shown that the memory of this learning session may be retained for several days after the conditioning session.

**FIGURE 9-5** Young children are capable of imitating the behavior of an adult. This young child imitates his grandfather's shaving behavior.

**Source:** Kathleen Davis.

**Imitating Others.** Andrew Meltzoff and M. Keith Moore (1992) studied 40 babies less than 72 hours old to determine whether the newborns could imitate two behaviors modeled by an adult: protruding the tongue and moving the head. According to the authors, "The results show that infants systematically matched the adult display shown to them" (p. 966) (Figure 9-5). Sticking your tongue out and moving your head to imitate another person may not seem like much of an accomplishment, but think about the elements of the task that must be performed by a 3-day-old baby. First, the baby must be able to see the model's behavior well enough to discriminate between tongue protrusion and head movement. Then the baby must transform the perception of these behaviors into a behavioral imitation and store this sequence of perceptual discrimination and responding in memory in anticipation of the next occurrence of the situation. The next step is to generalize the imitation behavior from one situation to another (Leavenworth, Lamberth, & Rovee-Collier, 2004). By the time children are 12 months old, they are capable of observing and understanding goal-directed behaviors, such as putting a toy in a box (Woodward & Sommerville, 2000).

## Maturation

**Maturation** is the biological unfolding of an organism according to the plan stored in its genes. In humans it refers primarily to the development of the motor and nervous systems. In the nervous system, myelin sheaths (see Chapter 2) begin to cover more axons after birth (Lipsitt, 1986), but myelination may not be complete until young adulthood. The sequence of myelination parallels that of the maturation of the entire nervous system. The lack of myelin explains why

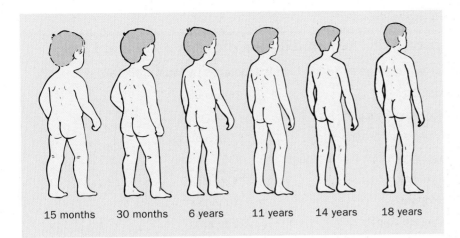

**FIGURE 9-6** Body proportions at various ages.

**Source:** Adapted from Bayley (1969).

15 months  30 months  6 years  11 years  14 years  18 years

a child cannot jump or stand on one leg at a young age. As myelin sheaths cover more motor axons, children gain voluntary control over their behavior; at the same time, reflexes like rooting drop out of their repertoire.

**Development of the Brain.** Before birth, the brain develops at an amazing rate, adding up to 250,000 new nerve cells each minute (Bornstein & Lamb, 1992). A spurt in cell development just before birth gives the newborn most, but not all, of its brain cells. The lower brain centers responsible for reflexes, breathing, digestion, and heartbeat are almost fully developed; cells in the cortex are numerous but not yet fully connected. The connections among these cells develop rapidly but are susceptible to environmental influences that include exposure to pollutants (such as dioxin, the industrial chemical PCB, and lead), toxoplasma (a parasite found in the fecal matter of cats), and heat (15 minutes in a hot tub containing water at 102°F can damage the central nervous system of the fetus).

**Physical Development.** The rate of physical development immediately after birth is not equaled during the rest of a person's life. By the first birthday, height has increased from 20 to 30 inches and weight has tripled, from an average of 7.5 to over 22 pounds (Watson & Lowney, 1967). Figure 9-6 shows different body proportions at different ages.

As you might expect from our discussion of nature and nurture, inherited characteristics and the environment interact to determine the course of growth (Mott, 1991; Scarr, 1992). Whether you will stand 42 inches tall and weigh 38 pounds by age 3 is determined by your genetic potential to attain this height and weight and the availability of a diet that allows you to realize that potential.

Table 9-2 lists several physical skills that develop during the first 2 years of life and the approximate age at which they are mastered by children in the United States. Some babies and toddlers perform motor behaviors at younger ages than those shown in Table 9-2. Such individuals are **precocious;** that is, they develop motor and cognitive abilities at an early age. Other children take longer than average to develop. Precocious development is frequently a source of pleasure and pride for parents, but slower motor development is not necessarily a cause for concern or alarm. Children develop motor behaviors at widely varying ages.

When a baby's development is seriously delayed, remedial steps can be taken. To determine whether such steps are required, a psychologist or pediatrician may administer the Bayley Scales of Infant Development (Bayley, 1969; Kaplan-Estrin, Jacobson, & Jacobson, 1994). These scales provide indications of average, below-average, and above-average responses for a range of behaviors and stages of intellectual development for children between the ages of 2 months and 2.5 years. Maturation is not an automatic process; cultural practices in infant rearing also can play an important role in physical development. For example, during the 1970s, "more than 75

**precocious**
Developing motor and cognitive abilities at an early age

Carlos is an active 2-year-old whose physical development owes a lot to the frequent use of his T-ball set.

## TABLE 9-2

### Physical Skills Acquired during the First 2 Years of Life

**Approximate Age at Which Skill Is Mastered by Most Children**

| | |
|---|---|
| Rolling over | 5.5 months |
| Sitting without support | 7 months |
| Standing while holding on | 8.5 months |
| Grasping with thumb and fingers | 10.5 months |
| Standing alone | 14 months |
| Walking well | 15 months |
| Walking up steps | 22 months |
| Kicking a ball forward | 23.5 months |

**Source:** Adapted from Frankenburg et al. (1992).

percent of American infants were bottle fed" (Berk, 1998, p. 124). Recently, along with an increase in the number of natural births, there has been renewed interest in breast-feeding. In addition to being emotionally satisfying for both mother and infant, breast-feeding offers some proven health advantages, especially in poverty-stricken countries.

The physical development that occurs during infancy and childhood is impressive. As we see in the next sections, psychosocial and cognitive development also occur at an impressive rate.

## R E V I E W   S U M M A R Y

**1. Developmental psychologists** are interested in the quantitative and qualitative changes that take place from conception until death. Both kinds of changes result from the interaction of hereditary **(nature)** and environmental **(nurture)** influences.

**2. Longitudinal studies** are conducted to evaluate changes over a period of time. **Cross-sectional studies** are used to obtain information at a particular point in time. A **cohort** study involves comparing individuals of the same age who were born in different generations.

**3.** Conception occurs when a sperm and an ovum unite. The child inherits half of its genetic makeup from each parent. A **zygote** is produced by the union of a sperm and an egg. The zygote embeds itself in the wall of the uterus and develops into an **embryo,** which at 9 weeks is considered a **fetus.** At birth, which occurs approximately 266 days after fertilization, the average baby weighs 7.5 pounds and is 20 inches long.

**4.** Despite the protection of the mother's body, the baby's development may be influenced by the mother's diet, her physical condition, and any drugs she may use, including tobacco and alcohol.

**5.** Both the **ultrasound procedure,** in which a sound-generated picture of the fetus (a **sonogram)** is produced, and **amniocentesis,** in which the genetic nature of fetal cells is analyzed, are used to determine the sex of the unborn child and whether any genetic defects are present.

**6.** Newborn infants are able to recognize voices (audition) and faces (vision), to make appropriate facial reactions to taste and smell, and even to learn.

**7.** When a particular spoken phrase (CS) is paired with the presence of a nipple in the mouth (UCS), the infant can be classically conditioned to elicit a sucking response (CR) when just the phrase is spoken. Infants have also been operantly conditioned to change their rate of sucking in response to a stimulus they like (positive reinforcer), such as their mother's voice.

**8.** The biological development of a person according to his or her genetic makeup is termed **maturation.** The rate of physical development right after birth is the highest it will be at any point.

**9.** The interaction of genetic makeup and environmental factors determines the specific growth pattern for each individual. Some **precocious** babies develop physical and cognitive abilities at an early age; others are slower to develop.

**10.** Psychologists may use the Bayley Scales of Infant Development to determine whether an infant is average, above average, or below average in behavioral and intellectual development.

# ✓ CHECK YOUR PROGRESS

**1.** Explain the concept of polygenic inheritance.

**2.** The one-celled structure formed when a sperm and an ovum unite is known as a(n)

  **a.** fetus.
  **b.** blastula.
  **c.** zygote.
  **d.** embryo.

**3.** The process by which a cell transmits its genetic information to other cells is

  **a.** mitosis.
  **b.** development.
  **c.** differentiation.
  **d.** RNA fragmentation.

**4.** Which chemical secreted by the testes causes a developing organism to become a male?

  **a.** dopamine
  **b.** estrogen
  **c.** estradiol
  **d.** testosterone

**5.** In the classical conditioning study of infants, identify the role played by the nipple, the spoken phrase, and sucking, respectively.

**6.** What types of responses did researchers find babies can learn to make through imitation?

  **a.** uttering sounds
  **b.** waving their arms
  **c.** kicking their legs
  **d.** sticking out their tongue

**7.** The biological unfolding of an individual according to a genetic plan is known as

  **a.** maturation.
  **b.** development.
  **c.** genetic inheritance.
  **d.** biological determinism.

**8.** What term describes babies who develop motor or cognitive activities at an early age?

  **a.** gifted
  **b.** precocious
  **c.** developmentally advanced
  **d.** motor capable

**9.** Where are the least developed brain cells located at birth?

  **a.** in the cortex
  **b.** in the hypothalamus
  **c.** in the breathing control center
  **d.** in the heart rate control center

**ANSWERS: 1.** Human traits are controlled by a number of different genes. **2.** c **3.** a **4.** d **5.** The UCS, CS, and UCR, respectively. **6.** d **7.** a **8.** b **9.** a

# PSYCHOSOCIAL DEVELOPMENT IN CHILDHOOD

Christiana is a single parent who works to support her 2-year-old daughter, Jerrie. The growing numbers of dual-career and single-parent families are increasingly relying on nonparental care for their children. Waiting lists at day-care centers are growing. Parents who cannot afford private day care may have to wait as long as 2 years for an opening at a subsidized day-care center. Despite the great demand for day care, little is known about the impact it may have on the development of young children. *What are the effects of day care on a child's development?*

The effects of day care are just one of the many topics studied by psychologists interested in the psychosocial development of young children. If you break the word *psychosocial* down into its two components, *psycho* and *social*, you have a good idea of what this section covers. We consider the development of the individual's unique personality (psycho) as well as factors that influence the ability to interact with other people (social). Such abilities may be present at birth; for example, newborns prefer human faces to other visual stimuli. Social behaviors clearly begin to emerge by the time a child is a year old (Moore & Corkum, 1994).

**psychosocial crisis**
Developmental problem or obstacle that is created when a psychological need conflicts with the demands of society

# Temperament

Physicians Alexander Thomas and Stella Chess (1980) were struck by the differences they observed in their own children; those differences were apparent even during the first weeks of life. They were also impressed by the low correlations between environmental influences, such as parental attitudes and practices, and the child's psychological development. They decided to study the causes and consequences of differences in temperament. *Temperament* is the "how" of behavior: its quickness, ease of approach to new situations, intensity, and mood. Thomas and Chess examined a cohort of children and identified three types of temperament:

1. *Easy children* (40%) behaved in consistent ways, had a positive approach to new situations, and were highly adaptable to change. Their mood was mild to moderate and predominantly positive.
2. *Slow-to-warm-up children* (15%) displayed a combination of intense, negative responses to new stimuli with slow adaptability even after repeated contact.
3. *Difficult children* (10%) did not behave in consistent ways, were nonadaptable, and usually were characterized by an intense negative mood.

As you can see from the percentages, not all children fit easily into one of these three groups. Although heredity seems to play an appreciable role in determining temperament (DiLalla, Kagan, & Reznick, 1994; Emde et al., 1992), the mother's child-rearing attitudes also can influence adolescent temperament (Katainen, Raikkonen, & Keltikanjas-Jarbinen, 1998).

# Personality Development

Both Sigmund Freud and Erik Erikson proposed theories of personality development based on the idea that childhood experiences leave lasting marks on the individual's personality. Whereas both theorists believed that personality develops in a series of orderly stages and that childhood experiences are important, they differed in their emphasis. Freud stressed the individual's biological makeup, whereas Erikson stressed social interactions.

**Sigmund Freud.**    During the late 1800s and early 1900s, Sigmund Freud radically influenced the way psychologists viewed the development of personality. Freud was the first person to propose that the early years of life are crucial to personality development. His theory was concerned with the manner in which children resolve conflicts between their biological urges (primarily sexual) and the demands of society, particularly those of the parents. Freud viewed these conflicts as a series of developmental stages determined largely by the child's age. These developmental stages, along with their unique characteristics and demands, are described more fully in Chapter 11. Freud, the first person to propose a stage theory of personality development, believed that each stage had the potential to affect the personality of the developing child.

**Erik Erikson.**    Erik Erikson (1902–1994) also proposed a stage theory of personality development. Unlike Freud, however, Erikson did not stress the need to resolve conflicts created by biological needs. According to Erikson, our personality is molded by the way we deal with a series of psychosocial crises that occur as we grow older. A **psychosocial crisis** occurs when a psychological need conflicts with societal pressures and demands. Different cultures present different obstacles to the resolution of these psychosocial crises. Hence certain developmental paths will be more appropriate in one culture than in others. For example, the child may have a psychological need to achieve independence. If this child grows up in a Western society that values independence, everything is fine. However, if this child grows up in a collectivist society that does not value independence, the child will develop more group-related activities and behaviors.

Erik Erikson proposed a stage theory of development that stressed the importance of psychosocial crises.

Babies experience two psychosocial crises. The first occurs from birth until about 1.5 years of age, when the infant is establishing a pattern of **basic trust versus basic mistrust.** Put another way, can infants trust their environment? Will food be there when they are hungry? Will their diapers be changed? Will other sources of pain and discomfort be alleviated? The person who usually attends to the child's needs, the primary caregiver, plays a major role in the development of basic trust or mistrust. Consistent, loving caregivers facilitate the development of a sense of trust. Having trust in one's caregivers and one's environment is important for developing trust in oneself.

Between the ages of about 1.5 and 3, children deal with a second psychosocial crisis, **autonomy versus shame and doubt.** *Autonomy* is the feeling that we can act independently and that we are in control of our own actions. Children start on the road to either autonomy or shame and doubt by developing a sense of how their behavior is controlled or determined. If children feel that their behavior is not under their control but is determined by other people or external forces, they develop an external sense of control. Doubt and shame concerning one's ability to function frequently accompany an external sense of control. For example, if the parents always insist on feeding a child, the child may begin to doubt his or her ability to perform this important activity.

If children develop a sense of being in charge of what happens to them, they have developed an *internal* sense of control, or **autonomy.** The relation between sense of control and autonomy is straightforward: The greater a child's internal sense of control, the greater the independence he or she will feel and exhibit.

The developing sense of independence allows children to begin doing things on their own. They decide what, when, and with whom they will play. This developing independence is the hallmark of the "terrible twos" and often brings children into conflict with their parents over such issues as what to eat and when to go to bed.

The child's growing sense of morality forms the basis for Erikson's third psychosocial crisis, **initiative versus guilt** (approximately ages 3 to 7). A developing sense of right and wrong leads children to evaluate the consequences of the behaviors in which they might engage. Some behaviors, such as playing by the rules and obeying one's parents, can produce desirable consequences; others, such as cheating or not obeying one's parents, produce undesired consequences. To resolve this conflict, children must take the initiative to adopt behaviors and goals that they enjoy *and* that society values. To do otherwise leaves the child (and later the adult) feeling guilty and fearful because his or her behaviors may not be appropriate or valued.

The importance of developing a sense of competence also underlies Erikson's fourth psychosocial crisis, **industry versus inferiority** (approximately ages 7 to 10). Once children have developed basic trust, autonomy, and initiative, it is time to learn the skills and acquire the knowledge that will allow them to become productive members of society. The acquisition of such skills and knowledge reflects the development of industry. If a child is to become a productive member of society, the lessons taught in school must be learned well.

Although critics point out that Erikson's theory lacks precision, supporters note that it captures the reality of the changes that occur as we grow and develop throughout the lifespan. In addition, it is generally conceded that Erikson's theory is far more optimistic than Freud's. For a summary of all of Erikson's stages, see the Summary Chart on page 425 later in this chapter.

If you read the sections about Freud and Erikson carefully, you noticed that personality develops in the context of significant other people, usually the parents. The attachments children form to their parents play a major role in shaping their developing personality.

## Attachment

**Attachment** refers to an intense reciprocal relationship occurring between two people, usually a child and an adult (Hays, 1998; Insel, 2000; Pietromonaco & Barrett, 2000). The first experimental studies on the effects of attachment were reported by

**basic trust versus basic mistrust**
Erikson's first psychosocial crisis (birth to 1.5 years), in which children learn through contact with their primary caregiver whether their environment can be trusted

**autonomy versus shame and doubt**
Erikson's second psychosocial crisis (1.5 to 3 years), in which children develop a sense of whether their behavior is under their own control or under the control of external forces

**autonomy**
The feeling of being able to act independently and having personal control over one's actions

**initiative versus guilt**
Erikson's third psychosocial crisis (3 to 7 years), in which children begin to evaluate the consequences of their behavior

**industry versus inferiority**
Erikson's fourth psychosocial crisis (7 to 10 years), in which children begin to acquire the knowledge and skills that will enable them to become productive members of society

**attachment**
Intense reciprocal relationship formed by two people, usually a child and an adult

**FIGURE 9-7** The wire and terrycloth surrogate mothers used by Harry and Marguerite Harlow in their research on the development of attachment in infant monkeys.

psychologists Harry and Marguerite Harlow (Harlow & Harlow, 1962). Approximately 8 hours after birth, baby monkeys were separated from their mothers. The baby monkeys were raised in experimental chambers, where they were exposed to an inanimate object that served as a surrogate (substitute) mother. Some of the surrogate mothers were plain wire cylinders; others were covered with soft terrycloth (see Figure 9-7). Some of the infant monkeys were allowed to come into contact with both types of objects. When a bottle was attached, the baby monkey could be "fed" by the wire or cloth-covered "mother."

The Harlows found that the infant monkeys showed a definite preference for the soft, cloth-covered mother. For example, when confronted by a strange and frightening situation, they ran to the cloth-covered mother for safety and security. The monkeys showed this preference even when they were fed by the plain wire mother; apparently, the **contact comfort,** or warmth provided by the soft terrycloth, was a more important determinant of attachment than the provision of nourishment.

In addition to demonstrating the importance of contact comfort, the Harlows found that raising baby monkeys in isolation in the laboratory had a detrimental effect on the animals' social behavior (Suomi & Harlow, 1972; Suomi & Ripp, 1983). When the laboratory testing was complete, the juvenile monkeys were returned to a colony with other monkeys. The experimental monkeys, however, did not adapt well in the colony. They avoided contact, fled from touch, curled up and rocked, or tried to attack the biggest, most dominant monkey in the group (often getting seriously injured in the process). Thus a major conclusion of the Harlows' research was that even though attachment was important, it did not ensure normal social development. Environmental contact (nurture) with members of one's own species is needed for this kind of development.

**Ethological Theory.** John Bowlby's **ethological theory of attachment** (1969; Ainsworth & Bowlby, 1991) stresses the adaptiveness of attachment. Bowlby believes attachment evolved because of its adaptive value; infants are protected when parents or caregivers are near.

For Bowlby, attachment progresses through four stages:

*Stage 1. Preattachment* (birth to 6 weeks). Babies emit behaviors, such as smiling and crying, that bring them into close contact with humans. Attachment has not occurred because infants do not mind being left with unfamiliar adults.

*Stage 2. Beginnings of Attachment* (6 weeks to approximately 7 months). Infants begin to respond differentially to familiar adults but do not protest when separated.

**contact comfort**
Preference for holding or clinging to objects, such as blankets or teddy bears, that yield physical comfort and warmth

**ethological theory of attachment**
Theory stating that attachment evolved because of its adaptive value to the infant

*Stage 3. Attachment* (approximately 7 months to approximately 21 months). Attachment to the familiar caregiver is evident. Babies show distress when the primary caregiver leaves. Such separation anxiety appears to begin at approximately 6 to 7 months and increases until 15 months in cultures around the world (Kagan, Kearsley, & Zelazo, 1978).

*Stage 4. Reciprocal Relationships* (approximately 21 months). As language develops, separation anxiety decreases and the child understands that the caregiver will return. Language allows the child to make requests of and bargain with the caregiver.

Bowlby (1980) believes that the experiences of these four stages result in the child's unique understanding of the parent–child bond. This understanding sets the stage for future close relationships (Pederson, Gleason, Moran, & Bento, 1998; Van den Bloom, 1997). Moreover, in support of Bowlby's theory, Hazan and Diamond (2000) have shown that attachment can, and does, have an impact on mate selection.

**The Strange Situation Test.** At birth, infants are equipped with behaviors such as crying that promote closeness to a caregiver and operate to activate caregiving behaviors. "At first," Ainsworth (1989) notes, "these attachment behaviors are simply emitted, rather than directed toward any specific person, but gradually the baby begins to discriminate one person from another and to direct attachment behavior differentially" (p. 710).

Once attachment occurs, it can take several forms. One way to determine the kind of attachment a baby has developed is to observe the baby's reaction to being put in a *strange situation*, such as an unfamiliar playroom and the departure of the familiar caregiver (McCartney, Owen, Booth, Clarke-Stewart, & Vandell, 2004). When Mary Salter Ainsworth (1913–1999) and her colleagues (Ainsworth, Blehar, Waters, & Wall, 1978) did just that, they found that most babies (66%) were *securely attached*. When their mother was present to provide attention and support, securely attached babies explored their environment. A smaller group (20%) of babies did not want to be held; they also did not want to be put down. They ignored their mother or greeted her casually on her return. In fact, they seemed to interact with a stranger the same way they did with their mother. Such babies are termed *avoidant*. A third group, the *resistant* babies, sought closeness with the mother before she left. When she returned, these babies displayed angry, resistive behaviors. A fourth group, *anxious-ambivalent* babies, became almost panic-stricken when their mother left. This panic reaction actually began before the mother left. When the mother returned, the baby actively sought, but at the same time actively resisted, contact and comfort.

The percentages of different types of attachment may vary from culture to culture (Van Ijzendoorn & Kroonenberg, 1988). For example, more German infants than infants in the United States, Israel, or Japan are anxiously attached. Cultural practices such as German parents' stressing autonomy at an earlier age may produce such differences; they are not interpreted as deficiencies. However, sleeping out of the home in communal arrangements, such as those found in Israeli kibbutzim, may lead to an increase in anxious-ambivalent attachments (Sagi, Van Ijzendoorn, Aviezer, & Donnell, 1994).

Infants' attachment styles are well documented, and the type of attachment (secure or insecure) with teachers influences the complexity of play or social competence of preschoolers (Flouhouse, Schorsch, & Vandermaas-Peeler, 2004); securely attached preschoolers displayed more complexity of play and social competence. However, not much is known about how these styles may influence individuals' behaviors as adults. Psychologists found a relation between the attachment style reported by the parents of college students and the students' preferred type of interpersonal relationship as adults (Feeney & Noller, 1990). For both men and women, there was a link between reported infant attachment style and preferred type of adult relationship (Cassidy, 2000; Fraley & Shaver, 2000). For example, securely attached babies grew into adults who had trusting attitudes toward others. A longitudinal study of German children indicates that the lasting effects of attachment style occur in other cultures (Rothbaum, Weisz, Pott, Miyake, & Morelli, 2000).

Children in an Israeli kibbutz Live in a communal arrangement.

Both mothers and fathers form
attachments with their children.

## The Father's Role

We have repeatedly described the attachment established between an infant and its mother. What about the father (Grossmann et al., 2002)? Do fathers form attachments with their children? There is some basis for the emphasis placed on the mother–infant attachment. Most fathers work away from the home and are gone quite a bit of the time. Despite this father-absent pattern, infants do establish attachments with their fathers at about the same age they form attachments with their mothers (Fox, Kimmerly, & Schafer, 1991). The types of interactions displayed by fathers with their infants may differ from those shown by mothers. Fathers are more likely to invest their time in playing with their children than in cleaning or feeding them (Hossain & Roopnarine, 1994). It appears, however, that delaying having children until the father is older (that is, age 35 and over) results in the father's spending more time with the child, having higher expectations for the child, and being more nurturant (Heath, 1994). However, Rothbaum et al. (2000) report that attachment may not occur according to a universal pattern; there are cultural differences that need to be illuminated by continued research.

The father-absent pattern does not occur in all cultures. For example, in the Chinese patriarchal (father-dominated) family, the most important relationship is between a father and his sons. Other cross-cultural research has found that infants in all cultures become attached to their parents despite widely varying child-rearing practices (Sagi, 1990).

## Day Care

In contemporary American society, "maternal employment is a reality. The issue today, therefore, is not whether infants should be in day care but how to make their experiences there and at home supportive of their development and of their parents' peace of mind" (Clarke-Stewart, 1989, p. 271). For example, some parents might be concerned that day care could weaken or change their child's attachment (Belsky, 1986). Comparisons of the attachment of infants who attended day-care centers with that of infants who were cared for at home by their mothers in the United States reveal that infants who attended day-care centers did not differ from infants who were raised at home. Thus concern that full-time day care results in more anxious and more insecure children still continues but seems unfounded (Azar, 2000). In fact, one study conducted in Switzerland reported that day-care variables were more important than parental variables (Pierrehumbert, Ramstein, Karmaniola, Miljkovitch, & Halfon, 2002).

Children may derive some benefits from good day care (Vernon-Feagans, Emanuel, & Blood, 1997), which may be more important for children from disadvantaged homes.

"Good quality child care can enhance development of children from disadvantaged, stressed, and dysfunctional homes" (Scarr & Eisenberg, 1993, p. 618). What constitutes a good day-care center? The Committee on Children, Youth and Families (1994) of the American Psychological Association proposed the following criteria for good day care:

- Is the number of providers sufficient? A ratio of three or four infants for each provider is desirable.
- Are activities done in small groups? A maximum of eight infants in a group is recommended.
- Do the providers genuinely like their job and enjoy caring for the infants during the day? They should not see this job as simply a way to earn money.
- Are the facilities safe and clean? Is the equipment in good repair?
- Do the providers have appropriate training and knowledge of infant care and development?
- Is the day-care center happy and cheerful?

In short, a good day-care center should function as much like a good parent as possible. The social and cognitive foundations established in a high-quality day-care center carry over to the kindergarten and preschool experiences that mark the end of early childhood (Feagans & Farran, 1994). These experiences set the stage for the beginning of formal education in middle childhood.

## The Peer Group

Typically composed of classmates, selected friends, or other children in the neighborhood, the **peer group** offers children many opportunities for feedback concerning their abilities, intelligence, and values as they grow into young adults. Lessons about how to get along in a group may also be learned. Social skills are initially learned from parents; then, as interactions with other children become more frequent, newly acquired behaviors may be tested on the parents. Thus the peer group can foster the development of self-esteem and a sense of autonomy. Peer group influences can be negative, however. A youth may start to shoplift, smoke, and drink alcoholic beverages because of pressure from peer group members. For children with low prestige in the peer group, it will be nearly impossible to say no; to do so would surely mean the loss of what little status and popularity they might have and likely encourage hostility and aggressive retribution (Henry, Cartland, Ruchross, & Monahan, 2004). Even though the peer group exerts a *tremendous* influence on young children, so do parents. For example, Taylor, Clayton, and Rowley (2004) have shown that "parental attitudes and practices provide the foundation for children's development of schemas [see Chapter 7] about school performance and then are critical determinants of children's early school experiences" (p. 163). Moreover, Evans (2004) has shown that children from low-income families may be at a greater disadvantage. Such children are read to less often, have less access to books and computers, and watch more TV. These children also experience more family violence, more instability, and less social support than do their more affluent counterparts. Parental attitudes in such an atmosphere do not always support school-related achievement.

## Television

Does television really exert as great an influence on children as researchers and the media have led us to believe? The first step toward answering this question is to determine how much television children actually watch. According to Rice (2001), children "spend more time watching television than engaging in any other activity (including playing and eating) except sleeping" (p. 264).

Although there is continuing debate over whether exposure to media violence (e.g., movies, television, and song lyrics; Palmer, 2003) leads to violence, 50 years of research indicates that the link between media violence and aggression is substantial and has

**peer group**
Group of neighborhood children, classmates, or selected friends of the same age

grown stronger (Bushman & Anderson, 2001). Moreover, it appears that exposure to violence on television may predict aggressive behavior in adulthood (Dittman, 2003). What about the media rating systems—don't they help curb this problem? For children up to age 8, the answer is yes; however, by age 11 they have an enticement effect and are not effective (Bushman & Cantor, 2003). Another influence of television is firmly established; the stark reality of adult life portrayed on television has, to a great extent, removed the innocence from childhood (Rossler & Brosius, 2001). So strong is the impact of television that some observers believe that television role models have undermined parents' ability to act effectively in this capacity (Friedrich-Cofer & Huston, 1986).

### Psychological Detective

Are the critics right? Has television assumed a major portion of the parenting role? Do you want the television set to be a surrogate parent for your children in the same way that the wire and cloth forms were surrogate parents for the Harlows' monkeys? What could (or should) be done to correct the situation? Give these questions some thought, and write down your views before reading further.

You could restrict the amount of television that your children watch. This option is effective, and many parents impose such restrictions. What about the quality of the television programs viewed by children? It needs to be improved. Calls for television reform have led legislators to introduce several bills in Congress that are designed to regulate the amount of time allocated for commercials during children's programming and require that stations provide educational programming for children. Although such legislation would be helpful, parents are still ultimately responsible for the type and amount of television their children watch. Too much television can take time away from other desired activities, such as reading and interacting with others (Singer & Singer, 1990). Interestingly, the same sorts of criticisms have been leveled against children's overuse of the Internet. It appears that use of the Internet at home does not have any adverse effects on social or psychological development; it does have positive effects on academic outcomes (Jackson, Van Eye, & Biocca, 2003).

## COGNITIVE DEVELOPMENT IN CHILDHOOD

In 1992, the American Psychological Association celebrated its 100th anniversary. As part of this celebration, a traveling psychology exhibit made stops in major cities. Many aspects of psychology were put on public display. Joe took his two daughters to see the exhibit. The children were fascinated by one of the exhibits, which consisted of two partially filled flasks. The flasks were very wide at the bottom and narrow at the top. They were mounted on a wall in such a way that they could be turned with the top up or down. When the flasks were turned bottom up, the children thought they were fuller than when they were turned bottom down. *What can this unusual display tell us about cognitive development in children?*

**cognitive development**
Changes that occur in our thought processes throughout life

**Cognitive development** refers to the changes that occur in our thought processes as we pass through life. Cognitive development and intelligence go hand in hand. As we saw in Chapter 8, psychologists have measured intelligence since 1905, when Alfred Binet developed a test to measure the intelligence of French schoolchildren. However, measuring the intelligence of babies and young children has been particularly difficult. Babies will not sit still for very long, and their ability to answer questions is limited. Despite such obstacles, the Swiss scientist Jean Piaget (1896–1980) spent his professional career studying the cognitive development of young children.

# Piaget's Theory

Early in his career, Piaget worked in Binet's laboratory translating tests. As Piaget tried out test items on French children, he grew curious about the children's incorrect answers. Children of the same age tended to give the same wrong answers, suggesting that they shared a common way of thinking. Piaget interviewed and observed numerous children (including his own) over the course of many years, concluding that a child's mind is not a miniature version of an adult's mind. Rather, children proceed through a series of *qualitative stages* of cognitive development.

Through his research Piaget identified the processes by which children gain new knowledge. Suppose a child has never seen a cow. The child tries to understand this new element or stimulus by using existing thought patterns or *schemas* (see Chapter 7). Being familiar with dogs, the child tries to understand the cow by using the schema for a dog. To use Piaget's terminology, the child assimilates the cow into the dog schema. **Assimilation** is the process by which we incorporate new information into our accustomed way of thinking. **Accommodation** is the process of altering our ways of thinking (schemas) so that we can include new information that does not fit into existing ways of thinking. For example, you probably found it difficult to include penguins in your schema for birds. Your schema had to be changed to include the fact that some birds do not fly. The processes of assimilation and accommodation operate throughout life.

Piaget proposed that all human beings proceed through a series of orderly and predictable stages of cognitive development at about the same ages. What's more, he claimed that a prior stage must be completed before progression to the next stage. Children proceed from concrete to more abstract thoughts as they grow older.

**The Sensorimotor Stage.**     During the **sensorimotor stage** (birth to age 2), infants learn to coordinate their senses and their motor behavior. For example, infants learn about a rattle by seeing and hearing it; they also learn about the rattle by grasping, shaking, and sucking it. They experience the world in a direct manner and learn basic lessons before proceeding to more complex thoughts. They do not yet use symbols or images to represent objects in the external world, so their world revolves around what they experience directly—the noise of a rattle, the sound of their mother's voice, the movement of a mobile hung over the crib.

Before symbolic communication is possible, infants must learn the principle of object permanence. **Object permanence** refers to the fact that a person or object does not cease to exist when it is not directly perceived. If a 4-month-old reaches for a small toy and you cover it with a cloth, the baby stops reaching and starts looking at something else. Lift the cloth, and the baby will be surprised to see the toy.

Contrast this response with the reaction of a 1-year-old. At this age, the child continues to reach for the cloth-covered toy and is not surprised to find it still there, but would

Jean Piaget spent much of his professional career studying cognitive development in young children.

**assimilation**
Piaget's term for the process of incorporating information into existing schemas

**accommodation**
Alteration of existing schemas to understand new information

**sensorimotor stage**
Piaget's first stage of cognitive development, in which children learn about their environment through direct sensory contact and motor activities

**object permanence**
Recognition that objects continue to exist even though they cannot be directly sensed

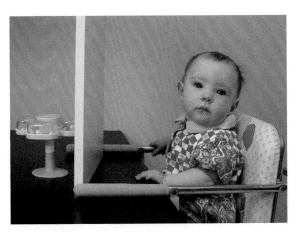

Because this young child does not look for the toy when it is hidden, object permanence has not been attained.

**mental representation**
An internal representation of an object or event that is not present

**preoperational stage**
Piaget's second stage of cognitive development, in which the child begins to think about objects that are not physically present

**symbolic representation**
Using a mental thought or activity as a substitute for an actual object

**egocentrism**
Inability to see a situation or event from another person's point of view

**concrete operational stage**
Piaget's third stage of cognitive development, in which the child is able to use mental representations to think about current objects and events but is not yet capable of abstract thought

be surprised or upset if you had secretly removed it. At this age, cognitive development centers on the ability to use **mental representation**. In other words, once the child begins to think about objects that are not physically present, the principle of object permanence has been established.

**The Preoperational Stage.**     According to Piaget, the child is in the **preoperational stage** of cognitive development from ages 2 to 7. During this stage, children become better able to represent events mentally; therefore they are less dependent on physical stimuli and physical reactions to guide their behavior. They begin to engage in pretend play, letting a doll represent a real baby or a toy car represent a real car. They use language (a symbol system) to ask for a drink rather than walking to the sink and pointing. In other words, the preoperational child is able to use **symbolic representation,** which occurs when a symbol is used to represent an actual object. If a toddler in the sensorimotor stage accidentally pushed a baby buggy against the wall, she might take a step back and thrust the buggy forward again and again, failing to reason out why her forward progress had been halted and what she could do to fix it. By contrast, a child in the preoperational stage would step back, look around, and think. Then she would aim the buggy toward an open doorway.

Children of this age should not, however, be given more credit than they are due. Their abilities have definite limitations. For example, the preoperational child's thought is characterized by **egocentrism,** or inability to see a situation or event from another person's point of view. Suppose a 3-year-old is talking on the phone to his grandfather. Grandpa asks, "Did you go to the circus yesterday?" The child nods his head silently. The child has failed to consider that Grandpa cannot see his head move. That is, he has failed to take Grandpa's point of view into account. Because preoperational children are not capable of reversible thinking, they frequently explain things by linking events together. This linking of often disconnected facts is called *transductive reasoning*. For example, when asked "Why does it rain?" a preoperational child might reply "Because we have an umbrella." Preoperational thinkers are often defined by their inability to reason logically. The concrete operations stage focuses on the child's changing abilities in this area.

**The Concrete Operational Stage.**     Children in the **concrete operational stage** are able to represent objects mentally and engage in logical reasoning about the world around them through the use of these mental representations, but they are not yet able to think abstractly. During this stage, thought becomes more logical. For example, at this stage, a child would be able to arrive at the conclusion that if she traded five baseball cards for one card, she would have fewer cards after the trade than before it. Baseball cards are things she is familiar with. Mental representations of such objects can be manipulated; objects can be added or subtracted. Likewise, the same child would deal with a question such as "What can be done to end world hunger?" by saying, "Drop food from parachutes" or "Grow more food."

Recall our description of the traveling psychology exhibit at the beginning of this section. What can the partially filled flasks tell us about the cognitive development of children? Piaget demonstrated that preoperational children do not grasp the principle of **conservation,** the understanding that a change in the size or shape of a substance does not change the amount of that substance. Consider Stacey, a 4-year-old who does not like carrots. Stacey's mother cuts the two carrots on Stacey's plate into several smaller pieces. Stacey bursts into tears and complains bitterly, "Before I only had two carrots; now I've got lots!"

Look at Figure 9-8. The two glasses contain exactly the same amount of water. To a 4-year-old boy who has not acquired the principle of conservation, however, the tall glass has more water than the short one. He will say this even after seeing the water being poured from the short glass into the tall glass. Now think of the flasks at

**9.2**

**conservation**
Recognition that a physical change in a substance does not change the amount of that substance

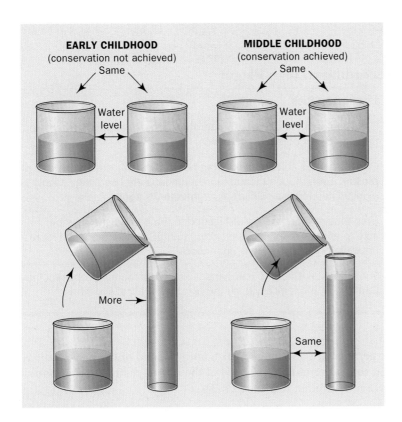

**FIGURE 9-8** An example of the acquisition of conservation. During early childhood, children are typically unable to tell that the tall glass and the short glass contain the same amount of water. By middle childhood, the child has acquired the principle of conservation and will be able to tell that the two glasses contain the same amount of water.

the psychology exhibit. When the flasks are turned base down, the fluid does not rise as high in the container. When the flasks are turned base up, the same fluid rises higher in the container, and the young child will say that there is more fluid. Until a child reaches the concrete operational stage and understands conservation, he or she will believe that changes in the shapes and sizes of objects indicate changes in quantity. Piaget's stages of cognitive development are summarized in the Study Chart on page 402.

**Challenges to Piaget's Theory.** Despite its impact and importance, Piaget's theory has not gone unchallenged. For example, the Russian psychologist Lev Vygotsky (1935/1978) stressed the social context in which a child learns (Berk, 2000). Whereas Piaget's theory deals with internal development, Vygotsky's theory emphasizes external factors such as society and culture. According to this researcher, the social interaction experienced by children facilitates learning and performing skills that are beyond their current capabilities. Because different cultures stress different types of social interactions, children may differ in their ability to solve various types of problems (Wahi & Johri, 1994). In this context, Vygotsky introduced the term *zone of proximal development* to describe tasks that are too difficult for the child to master alone. The zone is the distance between the actual ability level the child has reached on his or her own and the level of potential development that can be reached with guidance or supervision. The role of the teacher or adult is to provide help or assistance (known as *scaffolding*) during a teaching session. As the child learns, the teacher changes or adapts the scaffolding to reflect the newly acquired skills (Berk & Spuhl, 1995); the child gradually assumes more responsibility for the task.

The ages at which the cognitive changes proposed by Piaget occur have also been challenged. For example, psychologist Renee Baillargeon reports that infants display object permanence much earlier than Piaget proposed; she has found this ability in infants as young as 10 weeks old (Baillargeon, 1993, 1994; Overby, 1999). Piaget's belief

**STUDY TIP**

Write a summary of Piaget's stages of cognitive development in children. Underline or highlight important terms.

## Study CHART

### Stages of Cognitive Development, According to Jean Piaget

| Stage | Age | Characteristics |
| --- | --- | --- |
| Sensorimotor | Birth to 2 years | Child explores the environment through sensory and motor behavior. Develops the concept of object permanence. |
| Preoperational | 2 to 7 years | Child becomes able to think about people and objects that are not physically present. Even though mental representations are used, they cannot be manipulated logically. Child's thought reflects egocentrism. |
| Concrete operational | 7 to 11 years | Even though thoughts are still limited to the immediate situation, the child is able to engage in logical reasoning through the use of mental representations. Principle of conservation is understood. |
| Formal operational | Adolescence and adulthood | The individual is able to use symbolic representations in abstract thought. Can create and logically think through hypothetical situations. |

that object permanence does not stabilize until the end of the first year may be due to the fact that the motor task he required of the infants did not appear until later in development (Flavell, Miller, & Miller, 1993).

## Moral Development

In addition to developing in the physical, cognitive, and linguistic realms, children develop a sense of right and wrong. Consider the following example. Billy was told not to go into the dining room, but he wanted to help his mother set the table, so he entered the room, accidentally bumping into a tray of cups and breaking eight of them. Tommy had been told he could not go to the movies, so he was mad at his mother. He went into the dining room and deliberately broke a cup. Who is naughtier?

Lawrence Kohlberg (1973) proposed that there are three primary levels of moral development: the preconventional level, the level of conventional role conformity, and the level of autonomous moral principles. Each of these levels has two stages associated with it; thus the individual progresses through a total of six stages of morality as the three major levels are mastered.

At the **preconventional level** (ages 4 to 10), the child observes external conventions or standards set by others in order to avoid punishment (Stage 1) or receive reinforcement (Stage 2). If a road sign says STOP, the child expects you to stop immediately. Parents frequently hear their 5- or 6-year-old children reprimanding them for not stopping completely at a stop sign or for driving faster than the speed limit. Consider our example of Billy and Tommy in the dining room. To a preconventional child, Billy is naughtier because he broke eight cups, whereas Tommy broke only one. At this level of moral development, intentionality is not as relevant as level of damage.

Level 2, **conventional role conformity** (ages 10 to 13), involves greater internalization of standards and values. *Internalization* occurs when we make external standards and values part of our own set of values and standards. Children at this level are still controlled by external rules, but they now want to behave well to please important people in their lives. Charlie wants to "be good" to please his grandfather because that is what his grandfather expects (Stage 3). At Stage 4 we find children adhering to the rules of their peer group because they have promised to do so. The commitment is still to an external rule, but the promise to obey such rules has become even more internalized.

**preconventional level**
Kohlberg's first stage of moral development (ages 4 to 10), in which standards set by others are observed in order to receive reinforcement or avoid punishment

**conventional role conformity**
Kohlberg's second stage of moral development (ages 10 to 13), in which rules and standards are internalized and behaviors are performed in order to please others

Kohlberg's third major level of moral development, **autonomous moral principles,** involves true morality. At the earliest, this level may be reached by age 13. Some people reach it in young adulthood; others never achieve it. The attainment of true morality involves complete internalization of control over moral conduct. At Stage 5 we find the adolescent or young adult following, say, the rules of her sorority because it benefits the group. Although these rules may not apply in all situations, in the long run it is better to follow them. At Stage 6 the person decides whether a particular behavior is good or bad, regardless of what others think or of any legal restrictions that exist. For example, one may adopt the belief that life is sacred and may feel that killing is to be avoided at any cost.

Despite its popularity, Kohlberg's theory of moral development has had its share of problems and critics. Prominent among the critics is Carol Gilligan (1982; Gilligan, Lyons, & Hanmer, 1990), who argues that Kohlberg's theory was developed only with male participants but has been applied to women as well. The assumption is that men and women view moral situations in the same manner; Gilligan argues that they do not (Mitchell, 2002). According to Gilligan, men tend to have a more absolute view of morality and are more concerned about not interfering with the rights of others. By contrast, women are more concerned with the context in which a behavior occurs and the relationships involved.

Gilligan is not arguing that there are absolute differences between men and women in moral behavior; there is some degree of overlap. She believes, however, that a complete theory of moral development should stress both viewpoints. What's more, as men and women enter adulthood, their patterns of moral reasoning may become more similar (Gilligan, Murphy, & Tappan, 1990). The complexity of life's experiences causes adults to view morality in a more relative and changeable manner than children do.

Cross-cultural research presents another challenge to Kohlberg's stage theory of moral development. For example, Fuchs and colleagues (1986) reported that more Israeli children raised in kibbutzim, in which they received training in the governmental structure and laws of the kibbutz, reached Stages 4 and 5 sooner than did American children. Hence training in cultural laws influences the level of moral development that a person reaches. In a study of moral development in India, Vasudev and Hummel (1987) found that even though children may pass through the stages proposed by Kohlberg, their culture may dictate how they choose to deal with moral issues. For example, the resolution of moral dilemmas may be seen as a problem for the entire society (a collectivist view), not as an individual problem. Cross-cultural research also presents some obstacles for Gilligan's theory. For example, Shimizu (2001) reported that male and female Japanese adolescents did not differ as Gilligan predicts in terms of moral conflicts and decision making. Clearly, a comprehensive theory of morality remains elusive.

**autonomous moral principles**
Kohlberg's third stage of moral development (age 13 or later, if at all), in which control over moral conduct is completely internalized

# REVIEW SUMMARY

**1.** Three types of temperament in young children—easy, slow to warm up, and difficult—have been identified.

**2.** Sigmund Freud believed that the personality develops as a child deals with conflicts between biological urges and the demands of society.

**3. Psychosocial crises,** or conflicts between psychological needs and societal demands, were proposed as the main determinants of personality by Erik Erikson. Erikson's psychosocial crises include

**basic trust versus basic mistrust** (birth to age 1.5 years), **autonomy versus shame and doubt** (1.5 to 3 years), **initiative versus guilt** (3 to 7 years), and **industry versus inferiority** (7 to 10 years).

**4.** Studies of young monkeys conducted by Harry and Marguerite Harlow indicated that **attachment** was determined by contact comfort rather than by the presence of food. Attachment to an inanimate object, however, is not sufficient for normal social development.

**5.** Infants form attachments with their caregivers. Mary Salter Ainsworth reports four main types of attachment: securely attached, avoidant, resistant, and anxious-ambivalent. The baby's style of attachment can influence relationships established during adulthood and may even persist through several generations. Infants form attachments with both the mother and the father. The characteristics of the caregiver may also influence the type of attachment that develops.

**6.** Day-care centers have become more accepted as the demand for their services has grown. Good day care that is sensitive and responsive to each child's needs may be beneficial to the child's emotional development.

**7.** **Peer groups,** television, and growing up in troubled areas all influence psychosocial development during middle childhood (ages 6 to 12).

**8.** Jean Piaget proposed that cognitive development progresses through a series of qualitative stages. During the **sensorimotor stage,** infants and young children learn about their world through their senses and acquire the principle of **object permanence,** the recognition that objects do not cease to exist when we no longer have direct contact with them. The acquisition of object permanence is related to the nature of the object that is tested and the method of testing. During the **preoperational stage,** the child gains the ability to use **symbolic representations** for objects and events that are not physically present. This stage is also characterized by **egocentrism,** the inability to see situations from another person's point of view.

**9.** Children continue to use mental representations but are not yet able to think abstractly during the **concrete operational stage.** The principle of **conservation**—the recognition that changes in size or shape do not change the amount of a substance—is acquired during this stage.

**10.** Piaget's theory has been challenged on the basis of lack of supportive cross-cultural data and major deviations from the proposed time lines.

**11.** A stage theory of moral development was proposed by Lawrence Kohlberg. The three major levels of morality are preconventional (adherence to standards to avoid punishment or receive reinforcement), conventional role conformity (internalization of standards and values), and autonomous moral principles (complete internalization of control over moral conduct).

# ✓ CHECK YOUR PROGRESS

**1.** Freud believed that personality is formed by resolving conflicts that occur as a series of _____ determined largely by the child's age.

  **a.** evolutionary goals
  **b.** developmental paths
  **c.** psychosocial crises
  **d.** developmental stages

**2.** According to Erikson, children who can choose behaviors and goals they enjoy and societal values have achieved

  **a.** trust.
  **b.** industry.
  **c.** autonomy.
  **d.** initiative.

**3.** What were the major findings of the Harlows' studies of attachment behavior in infant monkeys?

**4.** When Harlow and his colleagues completed their research with baby monkeys raised in isolation, they returned them to the monkey colony. What did they find?

  **a.** The monkeys immediately fit in socially.
  **b.** After some initial isolation, the monkeys adapted socially.
  **c.** The monkeys did not fit in socially at all.
  **d.** The monkeys eventually became social leaders.

**5.** Identify four main types of human attachment.

**6.** Your little sister picks up objects, feels every part of them, and then puts them in her mouth. What stage of Piaget's model of cognitive development does this behavior suggest?

  **a.** sensorimotor
  **b.** preoperational
  **c.** formal operational
  **d.** concrete operational

**7.** A child's inability to see a situation from another person's point of view is known as

  **a.** self-view.
  **b.** narcissism.
  **c.** egocentrism.
  **d.** perceptual reversal.

**8.** Lev Vygotsky believed children's cognitive development depends on their

  **a.** age.
  **b.** heredity.
  **c.** memory ability.
  **d.** social interactions.

**ANSWERS: 1.** d  **2.** c  **3.** Warmth and contact comfort were important determinants of attachment. Social ability was harmed by raising the monkeys in isolation in the laboratory.  **4.** c  **5.** Securely attached, avoidant, anxious-ambivalent, and resistant.  **6.** a  **7.** c  **8.** d

# ADOLESCENCE

Some boys climb to the top of a tall platform; then they attach some vines around their ankles. Then they jump off the platform. This event is dangerous and scary; some of the boys will not survive the jump—the vines may break or be too long. *What can a phenomenon like bungee jumping tell us about developmental psychology?*

To answer this question, you need to know that the survivors will be honored by their village. You can think of these events as graduation ceremonies that mark the start of adulthood (see Figure 9-9).

In most modern societies, no single event or ceremony marks the passage from childhood to adulthood. Rather, we experience an extended transition period that links childhood and adulthood. That period is known as adolescence.

## Physical Changes

Many adults remember **adolescence**—the years between approximately ages 12 and 20—as a period filled with trouble and turmoil. Whether these perceptions of troubles and turmoil are accurate, adolescence is characterized by major physical, intellectual, psychological, and social changes. The hormonal changes and differences in brain functioning associated with adolescence appear to be part of the cause of this trouble and turmoil (DeAngelis, 2004).

**Pubescence** is the period (approximately 2 years long) that ends in the achievement of full sexual maturity, or **puberty.** During pubescence the sex organs mature and secondary sex characteristics appear. The dramatic physical maturation observed during pubescence, called the *growth spurt*, is second only to the one that occurs during infancy. Look at the picture of fifth graders in Figure 9-10. One feature of the growth spurt is apparent: Not all children enter pubescence at the same time.

Sex is among the most important factors determining the onset of pubescence. Girls begin pubescence, and therefore achieve sexual maturity, earlier than boys. The age range for girls entering pubesence is from 8 to 14; the typical girl begins at age 10 or 11. The age range for boys entering pubescence is from 10 to 16, with the typical boy beginning at 12 or 13. Thus a person who has reached puberty is still considered an

**adolescence**
The years between approximately age 12 and age 20

**pubescence**
Period of rapid growth, maturation of sexual organs, and appearance of secondary sex characteristics that precedes puberty

**puberty**
The time at which an individual achieves full sexual maturity

**FIGURE 9-9** These boys are not jumping for the thrill of it. This is a rite of passage into adulthood. If the boys survive this jump, they will have become men.

**FIGURE 9-10** The differences between these fifth graders indicate that children enter pubescence at different times.

**secular trend**
Tendency of members of one generation to begin puberty at an earlier age than their parents

**primary sex characteristics**
Characteristics directly related to reproduction

**menarche**
Beginning of menstruation

**secondary sex characteristics**
Sex-related characteristics that develop during adolescence and are not directly related to reproduction

adolescent. Interestingly, the higher a family's standard of living, the earlier children in succeeding generations reach puberty. This effect, referred to as a **secular trend,** is due to better nutrition and health care. In the late 1980s this trend appeared to level off in Europe and North America (Hopwood et al., 1990).

Although both boys and girls experience a growth spurt during pubescence, there are differences in the nature of that growth. In boys the shoulders broaden; in girls the hips broaden. Boys experience more large-muscle growth, giving them a strength advantage over girls for the first time in their lives. In other respects, growth is similar: Adolescents of both sexes may look gangly when their hands and feet grow more rapidly than their arms and legs. In addition, the lips, nose, and ears grow more quickly than the head. Complex hormonal changes underlie the development seen during pubescence. For example, increased secretions of *growth hormone* and *thyroxine* produce the growth spurt. Sexual development is controlled by the secretion of the male and female sex hormones, *androgens* and *estrogen*, respectively.

Primary and secondary sex characteristics and capabilities develop to full maturity during pubescence. **Primary sex characteristics** are directly related to reproduction. The maturation of these characteristics in girls includes development of the ovaries, uterus, and vagina. The occurrence of **menarche** (the first menstrual period) signals that puberty has been reached. The maturation of primary sex characteristics in boys includes development of the testes, penis, seminal vesicles, and prostate gland. The ability to ejaculate semen, often in *nocturnal emissions,* or "wet dreams," signals that a boy has reached puberty.

You can think of **secondary sex characteristics** as signals or signs not directly related to reproduction that sexual maturity has been achieved. The secondary sex characteristics found in both girls and boys include the growth of axillary (underarm) hair and pubic hair and changes in the skin, which becomes coarser and oilier, sometimes resulting in complexion problems.

The maturational differences we have mentioned can lead to adjustment problems. Early-maturing girls and late-maturing boys face the most difficult adjustments. Early-maturing girls are taller and show the developmental aspects of pubescence more obviously than their classmates. For example, their large feet and developing breasts often provoke teasing. In the United States, early-maturing girls may also feel social pressure to begin dating and associating with older adolescents. In countries such as India, where many marriages are arranged, early maturation does not create such problems.

The late-maturing boy presents a different picture. First, he sees himself physically outdistanced by the girls in his class, and then he is passed by most of the other boys.

*Is Jeremy a late-maturing boy?*

His lack of physical development becomes a source of scorn and shame. As a result, late-developing boys are sometimes less poised and less relaxed than their peers.

Adolescence ends when the individual becomes an adult; however, the exact point at which a person enters adulthood varies considerably from society to society. As we saw in the opening vignette, a ritual, such as jumping off a platform, may mark the passage to adulthood. In some countries, such as the United States, the definition is arbitrary and based on age. Despite such variability, almost all countries have a developmental period that intervenes between childhood and adulthood.

These student robotics inventors have likely progressed to Piaget's formal operations stage of cognitive development.

## Cognitive and Intellectual Changes

By the time they reach adolescence, many individuals have entered Piaget's final stage of intellectual development, the **formal operational stage.** This stage is characterized by abstract thinking—the ability to think in terms of possibilities as opposed to concrete reality. At this stage of cognitive development, the individual is able to think about an issue in general terms and then deduce specific outcomes from these general considerations (Inhelder & Piaget, 1958). For example, a high school student may read about the problem of noise pollution and then design and conduct an experiment to determine the effects of exposure to loud noises.

Although age may have something to do with entering this stage of development, merely having reached a certain age does not guarantee that a person will be capable of formal operations. Many adults remain at the level of concrete operations unless they are provided with appropriate educational opportunities and stimulation (Piaget, 1972).

**Adolescent Thought Patterns.** Although many adolescents can think and solve problems in an adult manner, much of their thought and behavior continues to be somewhat childish and contradictory. In his book *All Grown Up and No Place to Go*, David Elkind (1984) describes some of the thought patterns that characterize the adolescent years. Adolescent egocentric thought also leads to the belief that "I am invulnerable; it will never happen to me." This view of not being subject to the same rules as others is called the **personal fable** (Elkind, 1984). For example, although adolescents may think about death in the abstract, they frequently engage in high-risk behaviors, like taking drugs, driving fast, or being members of gangs.

According to Elkind, adolescents can envision ideal people, situations, and societies. Once such ideals are envisioned, the real world, with all its flaws and problems, becomes a target for criticism. Thus criticizing and finding fault are characteristic of adolescent thought. For example, Elkind (1984) indicates that "a boy who never washed, changed his shirt, or used a fork without a battle becomes a connoisseur of manners, dress, and behavior. Out of the blue, as it were, parents are told that they do not know how to walk, how to talk, how to dress, how to eat" (p. 30). If a better world can be envisioned, why has it not been created? When adolescents discuss such issues with adults, arguments may develop. Parents can turn this *argumentativeness* into a growth experience for the adolescent. Rather than seeing them as a time for combat, parents should view these arguments as opportunities to help adolescents develop and extend their reasoning powers.

In contrast to such lofty ideals, adults often find a great deal of *apparent hypocrisy* among adolescents. For example, adolescents may join a peace movement during a war. Their vocal demonstrations may lead to violent confrontations with people who support the war. How can the adolescent espouse peace and engage in violent behavior at the same time? Adolescent thought also becomes *self-centered* and *self-conscious*. Adolescents tend to create an **imaginary audience** that is constantly observing each and every one of their behaviors. David Elkind (1984) describes the imaginary audience in the following manner:

> Because teenagers are caught up with the transformations they are undergoing—in their bodies, in their facial structure, in their feelings and emotions, and in their thinking powers—they become self-centered. They assume that

**formal operational stage**
Piaget's final stage of intellectual development, characterized by abstract thinking; achieved during adolescence or adulthood

**personal fable**
Feeling shared by many adolescents that one is not subject to the same rules as other people

**imaginary audience**
The adolescent's assumption that everyone else is concerned with his or her appearance and behavior

everyone around them is concerned about the same thing they are concerned with, namely, themselves. I call this assumption the imaginary audience. It is the imaginary audience that accounts for the teenager's extreme self-consciousness. Teenagers feel that they are always on stage and that everyone around them is as aware and concerned about their appearance and behavior as they themselves are. (p. 33)

Through continuing interactions in which they become aware that other people have different, equally valid views and that their self-consciousness is greatly exaggerated, adolescents begin to establish the kind of understanding and empathy that form the basis for mature adult relationships. An increase in self-disclosure to others (Finkenauer, Engles, Branjie, & Meeus, 2004; see Chapter 15) and the keeping of a diary in which adolescents express their thoughts, feelings, and emotions (Burt, 1994) may be important components of this maturing process.

## Personality and Social Changes

Throughout the lifespan, social change appears to be the rule rather than the exception. How we react to such changes and challenges may affect our personality.

Erikson's fifth psychosocial crisis deals with **identity versus identity confusion.** For the adolescent who is experiencing a major growth spurt and developing signs of adulthood, the search for an identity and a place in society is most important (Erikson, 1975). This search can also be extremely frustrating. For some individuals, the search for an identity may not end for years; for others, it never ends.

The development of a strong sense of personal identity and intimacy may, however, take different courses for boys and girls. Susan Basow (1992) observes that, according to Erikson's lifespan perspective, "the sexes diverge during adolescence: boys generally establish a strong autonomous identity before establishing an intimate relationship, whereas girls frequently establish an intimate relationship first and may never establish a strong autonomous identity" (p. 120).

The new roles open to the adolescent also are influenced by ethnic and racial background, geographic locale, family values, and societal values. It is quite unlikely that a 15-year-old girl from rural Nebraska will see her place in society in the same way as a 15-year-old girl from Los Angeles. Being raised on a farm in a small town in the Midwest gives one a different view of possible societal roles than does being raised in a major metropolitan area. Although both adolescents search for a place in society, their perceived options are quite different. The same could be said for the comparison of adolescents in the United States with adolescents in other countries. For example, in the United States, young people tend to choose an occupation, whereas many adolescents in other cultures do not have a say in what their occupation will be. In some countries, such as Italy, the parents' occupation will likely become that of their children.

**Possible Outcomes of Identity Formation.**    In individualistic cultures such as the United States, adolescents who have explored the alternatives and adopted a well-chosen set of values and goals have reached **identity achievement** (Marcia, 1980). These adolescents have a good sense of psychological well-being. They know where they are headed and what it takes to get there (Tseung & Schott, 2004).

In other instances, the frustrations of this stage of development may cause adolescents to accept uncritically the values and desires of their parents. In this situation, called **foreclosure,** the adolescent's unique identity is not allowed to develop (Capps, 2003). Consider Willard, a successful but frustrated surgeon. Willard grew up in a small town in southwestern Oklahoma. As a boy, he enjoyed electronics and building radios. He could easily have become an electronics engineer. However, he became a doctor because that was the occupation his family chose for him; nobody asked him what he wanted to do with his life. Remember, however, that in many societies, lack of choice may be the norm with regard to occupation, family, and role according to birth order; it does not have the same stigma that it does in the United States.

---

**identity versus identity confusion**
Erikson's fifth psychosocial crisis, in which the adolescent faces the task of determining his or her identity and role in society

**identity achievement**
Adoption of a set of well-chosen values and goals

**foreclosure**
Uncritical acceptance of parental values and desires; hampers the development of a unique identity

Some adolescents find the identity expected of them unacceptable but are unable to replace it with an acceptable alternative. In such situations, the adolescent may develop a **negative identity** by adopting behaviors opposite to those that are expected (Hillier & Harrison, 2004). For example, Ken's family always expected that he would become a lawyer. After a rebellious college career and a frustrating semester of law school, Ken dropped out of school; he now drives a cab to support his real passion, building computers. **Identity diffusion** occurs when the adolescent has few goals and is generally apathetic about schoolwork, friends, and the future (Makros & McCabe, 2001). The individual lacks an identity and is not motivated to find one.

Finally, some adolescents may go through a period in which they try out several identities without intending to settle on a specific one. It is as if a **moratorium** had been called on actually selecting an identity. The years spent in college may be viewed as a moratorium. A student may sample several different subject areas before settling on a major and choosing a career.

The adolescent peer group promotes a sense of identity.

**Adolescent Peer Groups.**   During adolescence the peer group promotes a sense of identity and defends against identity confusion. The peer group can have a pronounced influence on an adolescent's attitudes, values, and behaviors. Belonging to groups such as the French club, the hiking club, or an athletic team may have a positive influence. Close friendships also can ease the adjustment many students have when they begin middle school (Dittmann, 2004). Not all adolescent groups, however, help develop a strong and productive sense of identity and an appropriate adjustment to society. For example, the prevalence of teenage gangs has added to the crime and violence in the nation's cities. John Coleman (1980) highlighted three functions that make peer groups so important to the adolescent:

1. Through the process of experimentation, adolescents find out which behaviors and personality characteristics will be accepted and praised and which ones will be rejected. Peer groups provide the all-important feedback.

2. The peer group serves as a support group of contemporaries who are also experiencing the same social and physical changes.

3. Because adolescence is a period of questioning the behavior, standards, and authority of adults, it is hard for adolescents to seek help and advice from their parents. The peer group serves this important function.

Any peer group can serve these three functions. Hence it is important for adolescents to be associated with a positive peer group if they are to become contributing members of society.

**Family Influences.**   The importance of the adolescent's peer groups should not lead you to believe that the family has ceased to have an influence (Jambori & Sallay, 2003). For example, Kenneth Felkers and Cathie Stivers (1994) found that family attitudes play a major role in determining whether adolescents, especially girls, develop eating problems such as anorexia nervosa and bulimia. Family relations are also an important variable in predicting juvenile delinquency and other instances of adolescent distress; parenting is the most powerful and "effective way to reduce adolescent problem behaviors" (Kumpfer & Alvarado, 2003, p. 457). A study of Norweigan adolescents indicated that good family relations were important in producing good mental health and reducing depression in adolescents (Pedersen, 1994); a study of Canadian adolescents has also shown the importance of family perceptions of adolescents in protecting them against depression (McFarlane, Bellissimo, Norman, & Lange, 1994).

**Making a Commitment.**   Adolescence is the stage of life in which most individuals begin to make sustained personal commitments. Such commitments may be to another person, a religious cause, career preparation, or a social program. Commitments help the adolescent develop a sense of identity and accomplishment.

The decision to become sexually active represents a major personal commitment that has important consequences. Nowhere is the importance of this decision more

**negative identity**
Adoption of behaviors that are the opposite of what is expected

**identity diffusion**
Failure to develop an identity because of lack of goals and general apathy

**moratorium**
Period during which an adolescent may try several identities without intending to settle on a specific one

clearly seen than in the case of teenage pregnancy in the United States (Henshaw, 1998). The teenage pregnancy rate in the United States is more than 90 pregnancies per 1,000 girls, and that rate is over double the rate for Great Britain, Canada, France, Australia, and Sweden (United Nations, 1991). Additionally, a high teenage abortion rate (approximately 40%) and a high percentage of births to unwed teenage mothers (approximately 70%; Children's Defense Fund, 1997) are associated issues that must be addressed. However, when adolescent abortion is viewed in an international context, a variety of issues not encountered in the United States are raised (Adler, Ozer, & Tschann, 2003). For example, parental involvement laws differ considerably, and the legal status of abortion varies from country to country, as does the age at which young women can marry and are considered adults. When careers and educational opportunities seem out of reach, many teenagers appear to turn to parenthood as a way of entering adulthood.

Effective procedures for encouraging teenagers not to be sexually active include teaching teenagers to understand the problems of sexual activity, stressing the importance of using contraceptives, and simulating the responsibility that raising an infant involves (Barnett & Hurst, 2004). For example, the adolescent role-plays various situations involving pressure to be sexually active and learns to say no. Role-playing helps adolescents find it easier to say no when the actual situation accurs. It also has been shown that successful programs to deal with teenage pregnancies (and other teenage problems, such as substance abuse and violence) require interventions and consensus at the community level (Wanderman & Florin, 2003). However, is also is clear that the particular cultural context will influence the type of prevention program that works best. For example, a prevention program that works well in the United States might not work as well in Mexico, where contraception was illegal until 1972 and sex education in schools is still controversial (Pick et al., 2003).

# EARLY ADULTHOOD

**Sam and Ann were married less than a year ago. They want to have children, but they are not sure that they want to start their family right away.** *What are some of the advantages of having children when you are in your mid- to late twenties? Are there any advantages to becoming a parent at an earlier age?*

**Early adulthood** lasts roughly 20 years, from approximately age 20 until age 40. During this period most people embark on careers, marry and have children, and become established members of society.

## Physical Changes

Early adulthood is usually characterized by good health. It is also the time at which we reach the peak of physical and sensory fitness. In our early twenties we possess our maximum strength and our greatest sensitivity in both vision and hearing.

Nowhere are the physical and sensory abilities of young adults more evident than in professional athletes. By the time athletes are in their mid-thirties or early forties, most are considered old-timers on the threshold of retiring. At about age 30, there is a *gradual* decline in muscular strength, vision, and hearing. The decline in visual and auditory sensitivity may not be noticeable until middle adulthood; it may be of some comfort to know that your sensitivity to tastes, odors, and temperatures does not begin to decline until your late forties or early fifties.

As we will see in Chapter 14, good health, a good diet, and exercise help us cope with stress. Engaging in these healthy practices during early adulthood has a major impact on health later in life. The way you treat your body during early adulthood directly affects your health during middle adulthood and old age. If you don't smoke, your lungs will be less susceptible to cancer; if you exercise, your risk of heart disease is decreased.

**early adulthood**
Period from approximately age 20 to age 40

The physical abilities of young adults are seen in their sports and leisure activities.

# Cognitive and Intellectual Changes

If our physical abilities begin to decline during early adulthood, it seems likely that our intellectual abilities may also decline as we grow older. But whether intellectual abilities decline during adulthood is a subject of debate.

## Psychological Detective

How would you investigate the prediction that intellectual abilities decline with age? What type of research would you conduct? Give this question some thought and write down some answers before reading further.

One possibility is to administer an intelligence test to a number of people in several age groups and compare the scores obtained by those groups (a cross-sectional approach). Will this procedure give us a valid answer to our question? No. The cohort effect that we discussed earlier has not been taken into account. For example, people who are currently 80 to 90 years old are fairly unlikely to have finished high school, but today's 40-year-olds are likely to have received at least that much education. Therefore, when we compare present-day 40- and 80-year-olds, they differ in terms of both aging and educational experience. Consequently we cannot be sure whether any differences we observe are due to the different ages of our participants or to differences in their past experiences. We should be looking at changes in intelligence in the same individuals (a cohort) over a specified period.

K. Warner Schaie (1983, 1990) recognized the problems involved in conducting cross-sectional studies and conducted his own cohort studies to determine whether intelligence actually declines with age. His results indicated that most people actually improve in basic mental ability during adulthood. To avoid the possibilities that the improvement he observed was due to familiarity with the test and the testing procedure and that only the most physically and mentally fit individuals returned for repeated testing, Schaie also tested a new group of individuals in each age category whenever he tested his original cohorts. After taking these possible problems into account, Schaie (1990) concluded that intelligence increases until the late thirties or early forties, remains stable until the mid-fifties or early sixties, and may not show any significant decline until the early seventies.

**Types of Intelligence.** Even though Schaie does not believe that a decline begins until late adulthood, others disagree and suggest that intellectual abilities continually decline as a person grows older. John Horn and his colleagues (Horn & Donaldson,

**fluid intelligence**
Intelligence involving the ability to see new relationships, solve new problems, form new concepts, and use new information

**crystallized intelligence**
Intelligence involving the ability to retrieve and use information that has been learned and stored

**intimacy versus isolation**
Erikson's sixth psychosocial crisis, in which the young adult faces the task of establishing a strong commitment to others (intimacy) or having to deal with isolation

1976; Horn & Hofer, 1992) believe that the answer to the question of whether intelligence declines with age is yes and no; it depends on the type of intelligence that is measured. There may well be a decline in **fluid intelligence,** which involves the ability to see new relations, solve new problems, form new concepts, and use new information. Putting together a jigsaw puzzle falls into this category of intelligence. The best puzzle solvers can visualize what a particular piece must look like if it is going to fit into a certain spot in the puzzle. Likewise, creative solutions are required to solve environmental problems, such as the need to recycle (see Chapter 8). The ability to see new relations reflects fluid intelligence in action. The decline in fluid intelligence appears to begin during young adulthood (approximately age 30) and continues gradually throughout the remainder of the individual's life.

A second type of intelligence, crystallized intelligence, appears to increase throughout life. **Crystallized intelligence** involves the ability to retrieve and use information that has been learned and stored. Solving a crossword puzzle is an example of the use of crystallized intelligence. Here are some examples from a crossword puzzle (the answers are given at the end of the chapter):

1. Acid found in apples (five letters)
2. Chinese temple (six letters)
3. Egg-shaped (five letters)
4. Hambletonian gait (four letters)

The best crossword puzzle solvers are those with the greatest usable store of knowledge. This type of intelligence favors older individuals who have been using their store of knowledge for years. The ability to remember words and meanings that most people have never heard of reflects crystallized intelligence. Figure 9-11 depicts the relation between changes in fluid and crystallized intelligence over the lifespan (Horn & Donaldson, 1980). The large number of politicians and judges who are over 65 demonstrates the importance of crystallized intelligence.

## Personality and Social Changes

Along with the physical and intellectual changes that characterize adulthood come important personality and social changes. In the United States and other individualistic cultures, the world is the adults' oyster; they can make of it what they want. For many persons, career and lifestyle choices are almost unlimited; *diversity* is a key word for the adult. Remember, however, that in collectivist cultures family responsibilities, group membership, and obligations to others may be the norm.

**Intimacy versus Isolation.** It may be difficult to believe that one can experience a psychosocial crisis when one is in the best of health and at the height of one's physical and intellectual powers. Yet this is exactly what Erikson suggests. He believes that young adults experience the crisis of **intimacy versus isolation.** *Intimacy* refers to the ability to

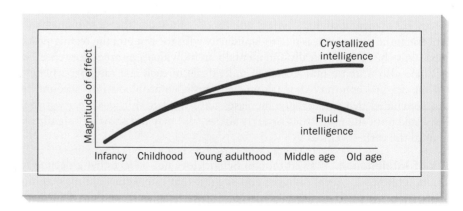

**FIGURE 9-11** As we grow older, fluid intelligence gradually declines, but crystallized intelligence continues to increase gradually.

**Source:** Horn and Donaldson (1980).

make a strong commitment to other people. An individual who cannot establish intimate relationships becomes isolated. Adolescents who have developed a strong sense of personal identity and worth are better prepared to make the compromises and sacrifices required in a successful relationship. When they become young adults, such adolescents are more likely to establish close and satisfying relationships in the workplace when a career takes precedence over marriage and family (Weiland, 1993). Those who lack a strong personal identity are likely to feel insecure and to avoid close relationships.

**Marriage.**   A young adult who is able to establish intimate relationships faces a number of important decisions. Among those decisions are whether to marry or cohabit. Research on such topics as cohabitation has yielded some interesting results (Horwitz & White, 1998). Data from a sample of 180 college students indicated that the willingness to cohabit was shown by older students who had lower levels of religiosity, more liberal attitudes toward sexual behavior, and less traditional views of marriage and sex roles (Huffman, Chang, Rausch, & Schaffer, 1994).

Both marriage and cohabitation have benefits and costs. For example, married people are healthier and tend to be happier than unmarried people. With nearly a million divorces granted each year in the United States, however, it is clear that marriage is difficult (Killan & Verkerk, 2004). According to Feldman (2000), "A look back at the television shows of the 1950s (such as *Ozzie and Harriet* and *Leave It to Beaver*) finds a world of families portrayed in a way that today seems oddly old-fashioned and quaint: mothers and fathers, married for years, and their good-looking children making their way in a world that seems to have few, if any, serious problems" (p. 205). Currently, we live in an era during which the number of single-parent families has grown dramatically, a large number of people live in nonfamily housing, and an adolescent gives birth every minute (Feldman, 2000). The divorce rate in the United States is the highest in the world. It is almost double that of Sweden, the country that ranks second (Berk, 1998). Although people who have divorced are likely to remarry, the rate of redivorce also has increased.

**Children.**   As you saw with the discussion between Sam and Ann (p. 410), whether and when to have children is another major issue of young adulthood that has both costs and benefits. Statistics show that the average age at which women have their first child has been rising since the 1960s (Rice, 2001).

If you wait until you are in your mid- to late twenties or older to have children, you will have greater earning power, and you will be able to provide a better lifestyle and education for your children. Your career goals will be more fully developed. Your role and responsibilities as a parent will be clearer, and you are likely to have more time to enjoy your children.

Most of the advantages of having children when one is younger are related to the effects of aging. Younger parents are likely to be more active and energetic than older parents; hence, they may be able to deal with the demands of caring for a baby more effectively than older parents. Health is another age-related factor. As the age of childbearing during young adulthood increases, the health risks to both mother and child increase (Feldman, 2005). Recall that the risk of having a child with Down syndrome increases as the age of the mother increases. Age is not the only factor that affects the decision to have children, however; career aspirations may also play a major role.

Consider the case of Nancy and Charles. Nancy aspires to become an electrical engineer, and Charles is planning a career in advertising. As partners in a dual-career marriage, they have been forced to make compromises; sometimes their schedules conflict and create tension between them.

But there are also several potential benefits. The sharing of child-care responsibilities can result in a closer relationship between a father and his children. Compared with wives who do not work outside the home, the wife in a dual-career couple has additional opportunities to develop her skills and build identity and self-esteem outside of her parenting role. Because neither partner dominates the family in terms of responsibility and earning power, dual careers can lead to a more egalitarian relationship. Dual careers can also result in a variety of problems, however, such as rivalry between husband and wife, conflicts between family and work roles, insufficient time to meet children's needs, and changes in family decision-making processes (Hoffman & Youngblade, 1998). On a more positive note, it is becoming more common to have *equally shared parenting* where the conventional images and stereotypes are replaced by a more equitable distribution of responsibilities (Deutsch, 2001).

**Parenting Styles.** Whether to place their children in a day-care center is only one of the many decisions parents face. How much television will the children be allowed to watch? Should children be spanked when they misbehave? How important to a child's diet are vitamins, vegetables, and milk? Such decisions reflect prevailing child-rearing practices and parenting styles as well as the personalities and preferences of individual parents.

On the basis of extensive observations and interviews, Diana Baumrind (1971) concluded that 77% of the families studied would fit into one of three parenting styles:

1. *Authoritarian.* Parents shape and control their children's behavior according to a set standard; they emphasize the importance of obedience and use punitive measures to reduce misbehavior.

2. *Authoritative.* Parents know that they have more knowledge, skill, control, resources, and physical power than their children, yet they believe that the rights of parents and children are reciprocal. They explain rules and decisions and are willing to listen to the child's point of view, although they do not always accept it. They are less likely to use physical punishment and less likely to stress obedience.

3. *Permissive.* Parents demonstrate less control than either authoritarian or authoritative parents because they believe children must learn how to behave through their own experience or because they do not take the time to discipline their children. They give children considerable leeway to set schedules and choose activities. They demand less achievement and are more willing to tolerate immature behavior.

Each parenting style is associated with a different set of habits and behaviors. Children of authoritarian parents tend to be less sociable and friendly and more withdrawn than other children. Children of permissive parents are more likely to be immature, moody, and dependent. Moreover, these children tend to be spoiled and place great demands on their parents (Gibbs, 2001). It appears that the number of these children is currently increasing in our society. Children of authoritative parents have good social skills and are well liked, independent, and cooperative. Moreover, these parenting styles influence children's behavior even after they have left home. For example, Trice (2002) found that the types and number of e-mails that college students sent home were related to the type of parenting they had experienced. Students from authoritative families made more contacts but did not seek as much academic and social advice. Students from authoritarian families made the most requests for advice. Students from permissive families made the fewest contacts and sought little advice.

Different cultures may emphasize different parenting styles (Bornstein, Tal, & Tamis-Lemonda, 1991). For example, the parenting styles of the Chinese are demanding and emphasize strict discipline and respect for elders (Chao, 1994). In turn, having been raised with a particular parenting style may assist one's adaptation to a particular culture. For example, children raised by authoritarian parents function well in a more regimented, authoritarian culture, whereas children raised in an individualistic culture would not function well in an authoritarian culture.

**The Feminization of Poverty.** If someone asks you to think about poverty, what image comes to mind? We asked a number of people, and the typical response was "minority people." That view is far from accurate. Because women, regardless of age, make up the majority of poverty-status adults, the term *feminization of poverty* is appropriate (Myers & Gill, 2004). What's more, this situation is not limited to any specific ethnic group(s). The poverty differential between men and women becomes even greater in cases of divorce or separation in families with children. Because children typically remain with the mother, she is faced with significant added responsibilities and demands. Given the high rate of divorce in the United States, it should not surprise you that the feminization of poverty in the United States is ahead of that in other industrialized societies.

This sex difference in poverty is not limited to the United States and other industrialized nations; it is a global problem (63% of the world's illiterate are women). According to a United Nations (1995) report, fewer than 50% of women in South Asia, sub-Saharan Africa, the Middle East, and North Africa are literate. The same situation does not exist for men. Illiteracy sets a vicious cycle into motion: Illiterate women marry at an early age, take poor-paying jobs, have large families, are likely to experience divorce, and are faced with severe poverty. The cycle repeats itself for the daughters of these women.

One step toward solving these problems is simple: Decrease illiteracy among women. In addition to benefiting individuals, such education has a positive impact on the entire country.

**Career Development.**     Career development is one of the major tasks young adults face. Moreover, it is important to avoid conflict between career development and family values (Perrewe & Hochwarter, 2001). If career development and family values conflict, then both job and life dissatisfaction are likely to result. Until fairly recently, a discussion of career development would have dealt exclusively with men. The dramatic increase in the number of women entering previously male-dominated professions has changed this situation, however. For example, in 1997, 62% of all married women over the age of 16 and 64% of all married women whose youngest child was under 6 years of age were in the workforce (U.S. Bureau of the Census, 1997). Despite the dramatic increase in the number of women in the workforce, however, women continue to encounter barriers, such as lack of equity in salaries. Even though they perform the same job as men, women are paid less in virtually all occupations (U.S. Bureau of Labor Statistics, 1998). Unfortunately, those who do succeed in male-dominated careers are often viewed negatively by both male and female coworkers (Dingfelder, 2004).

During young adulthood the main focus is on developing a well-paying, satisfying career.

# MIDDLE ADULTHOOD

Consider the case of John, a successful business executive. For years, his daily routine never varied, and most people saw him as dull. Then, at age 46, he made a dramatic change in his lifestyle. His gray and blue business suits and white dress shirts were replaced with brightly colored, trendy clothes. He traded the family sedan for a small sports car. John's new car and flashy clothes suggest that he is undergoing a midlife crisis. *Is it possible that he is trying to deny his advancing age by adopting symbols of youth? How satisfying and productive has his life really been?*

**Middle adulthood** encompasses the period from approximately age 40 to age 65. Many of the changes of middle adulthood are in the form of a decline; hence adjustments are made, and coping strategies are adopted.

## Physical Changes

The physical changes that began during early adulthood become more noticeable during middle adulthood. Changing sensory abilities may require new ways of adapting to the environment. Many people now need reading glasses to adjust to **presbyopia,** the farsightedness that often accompanies aging (Mordi & Ciuffreda, 2004). Presbyopia occurs because of a stiffening of the lens of the eye, resulting in difficulty in focusing on near objects (Lemme, 1995). The most pronounced hearing deficit, **presbycusis,** is

**middle adulthood**
Period from approximately age 40 to age 65

**presbyopia**
Farsightedness that normally develops during middle adulthood; stiffening of the lens results in difficulty in focusing on near objects

**presbycusis**
Middle adulthood hearing disorder involving reduced ability to distinguish sounds at higher frequencies

This woman's posture suggests that she may be suffering from osteoporosis. This condition, in which the bones become thinner and are prone to fractures, occurs in 25% of American women after menopause.

reduced ability to hear sounds at higher frequencies (see Chapter 3). Because these frequencies are not crucial to everyday behavior, such losses are often not noticed until they begin to interfere with speech perception. A detectable loss of sensitivity in other senses, such as taste and smell, does not occur until at least age 50.

The gradual decline that began in early adulthood eventually results in a reduction of more than 10% in physical strength. For individuals who rarely exert themselves fully, this decline in strength may not be detected. As we grow older, reaction time slows (Birren, Woods, & Williams, 1980) and may be more noticeable than the decline in strength; for example, it may take longer to step on the brakes when driving.

Middle adulthood also brings with it a change in reproductive ability. During the late forties or early fifties, a woman's body undergoes a series of hormonal changes, known as **menopause,** that lead to the cessation of ovulation and menstrual periods. Menopause may result in important psychological reactions. Some women mourn the loss of their reproductive capacity (even if they have not given birth in many years); others rejoice in their freedom from worry about pregnancy and the discomfort of monthly periods. The physical changes during menopause include a decrease in the level of estrogen, a hormone that plays a central role in the development of primary and secondary sex characteristics and the sexual drive. Unless preventive measures are begun before menopause, the decrease in estrogen can lead to **osteoporosis,** a condition in which the bones become thinner and are prone to fractures (Larkey, Day, Houtkooper, & Renger, 2003).

Osteoporosis occurs in approximately 25% of American women after menopause. It can be prevented if calcium intake is high enough so that the bones do not lose strength. Calcium supplements and weight-bearing exercise are the most popular treatments.

The reproductive changes of middle adulthood are not as dramatic or obvious in men as they are in women. Men in their late fifties may experience fluctuations in hormone production (Whitbourne, 1985), as well as impotence and depression. The symptoms associated with this period, often called the *male climacteric,* vary considerably from one person to another. For example, there is a decrease in the amount of semen and sperm (Murray & Meacham, 1993), and an increasing number of men age 60 and older suffer episodes of impotence (Whitbourne, 1996).

## Cognitive and Intellectual Changes

If changes in intelligence are inevitable with aging, then we might expect the gradual decline in fluid intelligence and the gradual increase in crystallized intelligence that began in early adulthood to continue during middle adulthood. During this period, a person may not be able to answer as many questions concerning new facts and knowledge as a younger person, yet people in their forties and fifties are better at solving problems that require the use of a store of practical knowledge. When middle adulthood is reached, considerable information concerning everyday problems and ways to solve them has been accumulated. For example, a seasoned politician can draw on years of experience to help resolve a political issue.

## Personality and Social Changes

During middle adulthood, one's occupation takes on added significance. Because prestige, productivity, and earning power may never be greater, these are the "golden years" for many people. The importance of one's job during this stage has been revealed in two different types of research. One set of studies of middle adulthood investigates what people feel they would do if they suddenly became millionaires. In one study, 80% of participants said they would keep working (Harpaz, 1985). The other type of research

**menopause**
Cessation of ovulation and menstruation; these changes mark the end of the childbearing years

**osteoporosis**
Condition in which the bones become thinner and more prone to fractures and breaks; typically appears in postmenopausal women

related to this stage of life deals with the effects of unemployment. Workers who have been laid off report feelings of depression, emptiness, and being lost (Kelvin & Jarrett, 1985). In short, according to Clay (2003), "midlife adults experience more 'overload' stressors—basically juggling too many activities at one time" (p. 38).

**Midlife Crisis.** Recall the description of John that opened this section. For some men in Western countries such as the United States, middle adulthood brings with it the well-known midlife crisis. The **midlife crisis** is a potentially stressful period that typically occurs during the mid-forties and is brought on when a person comes to grips with mortality issues and begins to review his or her life and accomplishments (Lachman, 2003). Dissatisfaction with one's life may be accompanied by the feeling that rapid action is needed to correct the situation or regain one's youth. It is therefore not uncommon for persons who experience such a crisis to make radical changes in their jobs or lifestyles.

Although some experts feel that few men can avoid the midlife crisis (for example, Levinson, 1986), other research does not paint as bleak a picture. The percentage who experience the classic midlife crisis may be quite low (less than 15%), and a sizable proportion (over 30%) report a satisfying adjustment to midlife (Farrell & Rosenberg, 1981). Thus only a small percentage of people change their lifestyle drastically.

Research on midlife changes in women has revealed a different pattern (Reinke, Ellicott, Harris, & Hancock, 1985). For women, age-related stress tends to occur later, in the late forties and early fifties, when parenting responsibilities have decreased and there is time to cope with other issues (Helson & Roberts, 1994). As more women return to college and enter the labor force, however, the likelihood of a midlife crisis appears to be decreasing. College training and job satisfaction, in conjunction with women's family roles, provide important buffers against midlife difficulties.

Erikson was not directly addressing the midlife crisis when he described the psychosocial crisis of middle adulthood, yet many of the same issues are involved. Erikson believes that during our early forties we face the crisis of **generativity versus stagnation.** To be generative is to have concern for the next generation and for the perpetuation of life. Because teaching, coaching, and parenting reflect an obvious desire to share one's talents and knowledge, this concern is frequently expressed through such activities.

**Other Stresses during Middle Adulthood.** As their children grow older and leave home to begin their own careers, middle-aged American parents must confront another challenge (Rosen, Ackerman, & Zosky, 2002). During the hustle and bustle of the child-rearing years, communication between the parents may have diminished and in some cases faded entirely. Now that there are no children at home, the parents must become reacquainted. This adjustment is called the **empty nest syndrome.**

## Psychological Detective

Many individuals report an improvement in marital satisfaction after their children have left home. What are some possible reasons for this increased satisfaction? Write down your answers before reading further.

Several factors appear to be responsible for the increase in marital satisfaction after the departure of children. First, the family's financial situation usually improves, and there are fewer worries about financial matters. Second, the goal of raising a family has been achieved. Once the children have left home, many of the anxieties associated with this goal are reduced. Finally, there is more time for the husband and wife to do things together (Clay, 2003).

Despite the benefits of having raised independent children, aging parents of middle-aged Americans may require additional care and attention, thus adding another source of stress (Ganong, Coleman, McDaniel, & Killian, 1998). The stress of attending to the needs of elderly parents is heightened when the parents live with their

**midlife crisis**
Potentially stressful period that occurs during the mid-forties and is triggered by reevaluation of one's accomplishments

**generativity versus stagnation**
Erikson's seventh psychosocial crisis, which occurs during middle adulthood and reflects concern, or lack thereof, for the next generation

**empty nest syndrome**
Period of adjustment for parents after all children have left home

children. Such strains can, and do, lead to violence. As many as 1.5 million cases of elder abuse may occur in the United States each year (Baron & Welty, 1996). The magnitude of this problem and the stress it creates have led to the development of counseling and support groups for people who care for the elderly.

Another source of stress that may be reintroduced after the empty nest adjustment period is the return of the birds to the nest. In times of economic hardship, many young couples are forced to return home to live with their parents. Similarly, a daughter and her young children may return to live with her parents after a divorce. These returning offspring are known as *boomerang children* (Mogelonsky, 1996). For middle-aged parents who have adjusted to the empty nest, the interactions and demands of this newly *refilled* nest may be stressful. Routines must be changed, and the needs and desires of additional family members must be addressed.

# REVIEW SUMMARY

**1.** In contemporary U.S. society, no single event marks the passage from childhood to adulthood. Children experience an extended period of **adolescence,** which lasts roughly from age 12 to age 20.

**2.** During **pubescence,** which takes approximately 2 years, adolescents experience a major growth spurt and the development of **primary** and **secondary sex characteristics. Puberty,** the achievement of full sexual maturity, marks the end of pubescence.

**3.** According to Piaget, if adolescents are given appropriate educational opportunities and stimulation, they will enter the **formal operational stage** of cognitive development and be capable of abstract thought.

**4.** Adolescents experience major psychological and social changes. Erik Erikson proposes that as adolescents struggle to determine what their roles in society will be, they experience the psychosocial crisis of **identity versus identity confusion.** The adolescent peer group provides feedback and helps adolescents achieve a sense of identity and belonging. Some peer groups, however, may interfere with satisfactory adaptation to society.

**5.** The establishment of a sustained personal commitment may provide adolescents with feedback concerning their identities and potential roles. Such commitments may involve major decisions, such as whether to be sexually active or use drugs.

**6.** According to Erikson, early adulthood is characterized by the psychosocial crisis of **intimacy versus isolation.** If individuals are not able to make the sacrifices and compromises needed to establish strong commitments, they will be isolated from others.

**7.** Diana Baumrind has found that over 77% of parents use one of three basic parenting styles: authoritarian, authoritative, or permissive. The particular parenting style has a major impact on the child's development of self-esteem and behavior.

**8.** Physical changes during **middle adulthood** are characterized by a gradual decline. Visual and auditory sensitivity declines, muscle strength decreases about 10%, and reaction time is noticeably slower. Women undergo a series of hormonal changes, known as **menopause,** that mark the end of childbearing. The decrease in estrogen production that accompanies menopause may result in **osteoporosis,** a condition in which the bones become thinner and prone to fractures.

**9. Fluid intelligence** (the ability to solve new problems and form new concepts) may begin a gradual decline at about age 30. **Crystallized intelligence,** the ability to retrieve and use stored information, shows a gradual increase throughout adulthood.

**10.** As people review their lives and achievements, they may experience a **midlife crisis,** which leads them to engage in radical behavior changes aimed at regaining youth.

**11.** The psychosocial crisis of middle adulthood, **generativity versus stagnation,** centers on concern for the well-being of future generations.

**12.** When their last child leaves home, parents may need to learn how to communicate and live as a couple once again. This adjustment is known as the **empty nest syndrome.** Other adjustments of middle adulthood include having to provide care for elderly parents.

# ✓ CHECK YOUR PROGRESS

**1.** What is the effect of the secular trend on puberty?
   **a.** The higher the family's standard of living, the earlier children reach puberty.
   **b.** The lower the family's standard of living, the earlier children reach puberty.
   **c.** Girls reach puberty before boys.
   **d.** Boys reach puberty before girls.

**2.** Identify each of the following as a primary or secondary sex characteristic.
   **a.** growth of axillary hair
   **b.** development of the uterus
   **c.** development of seminal vesicles
   **d.** coarser and oilier skin
   **e.** growth of pubic hair

**3.** Who has the most difficult adjustments to puberty?

   **a.** late-maturing girls and late-maturing boys
   **b.** early-maturing girls and late-maturing boys
   **c.** late-maturing girls and early-maturing boys
   **d.** early-maturing girls and early-maturing boys

**4.** All of the following are true of menopause except:

   **a.** Estrogen levels increase.
   **b.** It occurs during one's late forties and early fifties.
   **c.** Women may react favorably or unfavorably to it.
   **d.** Osteoporosis may result from changing estrogen levels.

**5.** Anita is in her late fifties. Recently, she suffered from several fractures in her arms and legs. The cause of these fractures is unknown. What condition may Anita be suffering from? How could she have avoided developing this condition?

**6.** Katie declares an art major, then decides this is impractical and switches to accounting. She does not enjoy accounting, so she transfers to psychology. According to one theory, she is experiencing

   **a.** moratorium.
   **b.** foreclosure.
   **c.** fragmentation.
   **d.** identity diffusion.

**7.** The uncritical acceptance of parental values and desires is termed

   **a.** moratorium.
   **b.** foreclosure.
   **c.** negative identity.
   **d.** identity diffusion.

**8.** An adolescent is likely to be in which of Piaget's stages of cognitive development?

   **a.** sensorimotor
   **b.** preoperational

   **c.** formal operational
   **d.** concrete operational

**9.** What type of intelligence is characterized by the ability to see new relationships, solve new problems, form new concepts, and use new information?

   **a.** fluid
   **b.** native
   **c.** intuitive
   **d.** crystallized

**10.** You observe a parent who emphasizes obedience through guidelines and punishment. According to Baumrind, such a parent would be termed

   **a.** permissive.
   **b.** rigid.
   **c.** authoritative.
   **d.** authoritarian.

**11.** Garland, a man in his forties, changed his appearance and image overnight! He now has a new hairstyle (and hair color), a new wardrobe, a new sports car with a sensational sound system, and new friends who are much younger than he is. What may Garland be experiencing?

**12.** At what point do most individuals begin to make sustained personal commitments?

   **a.** adolescence
   **b.** late adulthood
   **c.** early childhood
   **d.** middle adulthood

**13.** In Erikson's view, the sense that a person is making significant contributions to the next generation is known as achieving

   **a.** moratorium.
   **b.** stagnation.
   **c.** significance.
   **d.** generativity.

**ANSWERS: 1.** a  **2. a.** Growth of axillary hair—secondary sex characteristic  **b.** Development of uterus—primary sex characteristic  **c.** Development of seminal vesicles—primary sex characteristic  **d.** Coarser and oilier skin—secondary sex characteristic  **e.** Growth of pubic hair—secondary sex characteristic  **3.** b  **4.** a  **5.** Osteoporosis. She could have maintained a sufficiently high level of calcium intake over time.  **6.** a  **7.** b  **8.** c  **9.** a  **10.** d  **11.** Midlife crisis.  **12.** a  **13.** d

# LATE ADULTHOOD

Lex and Dana have been retired for several years. Their friends frequently comment on how mentally sharp they are. Lex and Dana just laugh and say that it's due to their enjoyment of playing games such as Scrabble several times each week. *Can playing games such as Scrabble really have an impact on a person's intellectual ability?*

Whether you agree with the theory that we grow old because of wear and tear on the body or the theory that we are genetically programmed to grow old, aging is an inevitable part of the developmental cycle. At approximately age 65 we enter the final period of adulthood—**late adulthood,** or old age.

**late adulthood**
Period from approximately age 65 until death

# Physical Changes

## Psychological Detective

The following statements will help you think about old age and put it in perspective. Mark each one as true or false before reading further.

- All five senses decline in old age.
- Physical strength tends to decline with age.
- Older workers cannot perform as effectively as younger workers.
- At least 25% of elderly citizens are living in institutions such as nursing homes, mental hospitals, and extended-care facilities.
- Medical practitioners tend to give low priority to senior citizens.

**cataracts**
Clouding of the lens of the eye

We will respond to these statements throughout the rest of this chapter, but let's focus first on those that are related to physical changes. Despite the physical changes that occur in late adulthood, keep in mind that chronological age may not be a good predictor of ability or performance in elderly people. Hence researchers (such as Neugarten & Neugarten, 1987) distinguish between the *young-old* and the *old-old*. The young-old appear physically young for their advanced years, whereas the old-old show definite signs of decline. A person who is 85 or older could be classified as young-old, whereas a person in his late 60s might be classified as old-old.

Despite the young-old and old-old distinction, predictable physical changes come with advancing age. For example, many older people must contend with impaired vision and hearing. For many, the middle-adulthood problem of farsightedness is replaced by the development of more serious problems, such as **cataracts** (clouding of the lens of the eye), that may require corrective surgery. Cataracts are currently the world's leading cause of blindness (Congdon, Friedman, & Lietman, 2003). The need for hearing aids increases as hearing ability decreases; however, many people refuse to use them because they are a visible sign of advancing age (Olsho, Harkins, & Lenhardt, 1985).

The *gradual* decline in sensitivity to taste and smell that began in middle adulthood continues until the late seventies; after that, the majority of people experience a very sharp drop in olfactory ability (Doty, 1984). Many older people do not enjoy eating as much as they once did because their food does not taste as good as it used to. Why? In Chapter 3 we saw that taste and olfaction influence each other. If we cannot smell our food, it does not taste as good, or as we expect it to taste, and so we may not eat as much as we should. Consequently, malnourishment may become a problem for some elderly people.

Playing tennis is only one of the many ways that older people can remain active. Continual activity is important to staying physically fit.

The ability to regulate body temperature also declines noticeably during old age. When you visit your older relatives or friends in the winter, you may find their homes very hot. Remember that it is hot for you but comfortable for them.

Although older people do not possess the physical strength that characterizes young adulthood, this decline does not render them unable to perform such activities as taking care of their houses, doing yard work, and playing tennis (Marsiske, Klumb, & Baltes, 1997). Most of these tasks and activities can still be carried out effectively and enjoyably, although they may take longer than previously. Such activities, even aerobic dancing (Hopkins, Murrah, Hoeger, & Rhodes, 1990), are important in helping elderly people stay physically fit (Rosengren, McAuley, & Mihalko, 1998).

The slowness of old age is reflected in longer reaction times and an increase in the time required to process information. Thus older people are increasingly likely to be involved in traffic accidents. This increase occurs because older individuals are unable to process information from traffic signals, such as stop signs and turn signals, as quickly or as well as they did when they were younger (AARP, 2000a).

Physical appearance also changes with advancing age. People actually shrink as they grow older (Whitbourne, 1985). The shrinking results from compression of the disks between the vertebrae of the spinal column (see Chapter 2). What's more, older people tend to stoop when they stand, which increases the perception of shortness.

Elderly people also experience changes in their sleep patterns. As noted in Chapter 4, their sleep becomes less efficient; that is, they spend less of their time in bed actually sleeping. Their sleep is punctuated by more frequent awakenings, which results from a reduction of Stage 4 sleep and an increase in the light sleep of Stage 1. Older individuals may counteract the loss of deep sleep during the night by napping during the day.

Most of the systems of the body become more susceptible to disease during old age. For example, heart disease is the most frequent cause of death for people over 65. Other prominent causes include cancer, stroke, diabetes, and kidney disease.

Increasing susceptibility to disease is frequently accompanied by an increase in the amount or number of medications taken. In some cases these drugs may combine or interact with one another in unintended, and potentially deadly, ways. Drugs may be prescribed in larger doses than necessary or may be prescribed by different physicians who are not aware that any other drugs have been prescribed.

Most medical practitioners give low priority to the aged population. Forgetfulness and declining abilities make many elderly people difficult to work with. Limited resources make them potential financial risks. Hence many elderly people receive less than adequate attention and care.

## Hands On

### Experiencing Old Age

Have you ever wondered what it's like to be old? Here's an easy and quick exercise that simulates some of the problems old age may bring that you and one or more friends can do just about anywhere. You will need the following supplies: plastic wrap, cotton, and masking tape. To simulate blurred vision owing to cataracts, cover your eyes (but not your nose or mouth!) with several layers of plastic wrap. Tape the wrap in place so that it will not fall off. Place cotton in your ears to simulate hearing loss, and put masking tape around your knuckles to simulate arthritis. Now try navigating around your dorm room, house, or apartment (try outdoors if you are really daring). Be sure someone is around to monitor your behavior. Once you have experienced this simulated old age, trade places with your friends. Once your entire group has had the "old-age experience," here are some questions you should try to answer (group collaboration is encouraged). What did it feel like to be old? Of all your senses, which would be worst to lose? Which is the second worst? Can you now relate better to old people? If so, how?

**Alzheimer's Disease.** **Dementia** is a condition of general intellectual decline involving loss of memory and disorientation (Erkinjuntti, Ostbye, Steenhuis, & Hachinski, 1997). Sometimes dementia is caused by a blood clot that prevents an adequate supply of blood from reaching the brain. This problem can be corrected, and many people who have experienced dementia are able to resume normal functioning. Others are not as fortunate. Unfortunately, the number of people predicted to suffer from dementia is increasing. For example, Wancata, Musalek, Alexandrowicz, and Krautgartner (2003) predict that the incidence of dementia in Europe will increase from 7.1 million in 2000 to 16.2 million by 2050.

One form of dementia, **Alzheimer's disease,** is irreversible, and there is no long-term treatment at present. (Some drugs, such as Tacrine and Aricept, *inhibit* an enzyme that breaks down the neurotransmitter acetylcholine, thus allowing acetylcholine to be active longer. Such drug treatment shows promise, as these drugs alleviate symptoms in some patients.) Alzheimer's disease is a degenerative brain condition, which means that victims of this disorder show progressive loss of intelligence, memory, and general awareness (Nash,

**dementia**
General intellectual decline associated with old age; may be reversible when caused by medication or blood clots

**Alzheimer's disease**
Degenerative brain disorder that results in progressive loss of intelligence and awareness

2000). Because Alzheimer's disease may affect nearly one-third of all people who live to be 85 or older, it is receiving considerable attention from caregivers and researchers.

Autopsies show that the brains of Alzheimer's disease patients have changed or deteriorated. For example, many of the axons of neurons in the brain (see Chapter 2) are abnormally twisted and tangled; there may even be loss of complete cells (Roth, Wischik, Evans, & Mountjoy, 1985). Under such conditions, the brain could hardly be expected to function well.

What causes Alzheimer's disease? To answer this question, we need to consider two variants of the disease. One type, which occurs at a somewhat earlier age (during middle adulthood), is thought to be caused by a genetic defect (Hendrie, 2001). If the gene responsible for the disorder could be identified and isolated, we might be able to find a cure for this form of the disease. A second type of Alzheimer's disease (the more common form) usually occurs after age 65. It may be caused by immune system deficiency, concentrations of aluminum in the brain (Cohen, 1987), or infection.

Only continued research will provide a clear picture of this disease and how to combat it. An interesting research project conducted by University of Kentucky researcher David Snowdon has provided some intriguing possibilities. Snowdon has studied 678 School Sisters of Notre Dame in an attempt to determine the factors that led some of the nuns to develop Alzheimer's disease, whereas other nuns did not develop the disease (Lemonick & Park, 2001). Several of these nuns have lived into their nineties without any sign of Alzheimer's disease; others have not fared nearly as well. Why the difference? Among the factors that may help prevent Alzheimer's disease are avoiding head trauma, including folic acid in your diet, expressing positive emotions (for example, love, hope, gratitude, and happiness) instead of negative emotions (for example, sadness, fear, and shame), and staying mentally active. Cross-cultural studies (Hendrie, 2001) support these views and suggest that differences in rates of Alzheimer's disease likely are attributable to the combined effects of genetics and environmental (especially diet) factors. Research showing that low levels of vitamin $B_{12}$ are associated with poor memory in a large sample of people over 75 highlights the importance of dietary factors (Adelson, 2004).

**Culture and Life Expectancy.**    Even with the physical problems associated with old age, the average life expectancy in the United States has increased at a steady rate (Aaron, 2000; Ervin, 2000). Better medical care and improved nutrition have extended the number of active years before illness or disability really begins. Moreover, it appears that people who provide emotional support and do things for others live

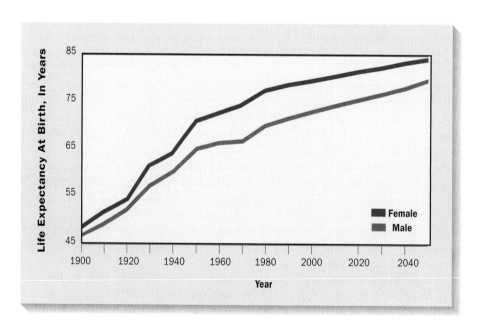

**FIGURE 9-12**   If increases in life expectancy continue, people may commonly live to be 100 by the next century.

**Source:** U.S. Bureau of the Census (1997).

longer (Greengrass, 2003). This increase in life expectancy has resulted in rapid growth of the elderly population. As Figure 9-12 shows, the number of elderly persons is projected to continue through the year 2040 (U.S. Bureau of the Census, 1997). What's more, women have longer life expectancies than men. The disparity, which was small at the start of the 1900s, has grown over the years.

Although longer life expectancies are a relatively new phenomenon in the United States, some areas of the world—Peru, Pakistan, the former Soviet Union, Japan, and Iceland—are famous for the longevity of their inhabitants. What is it about the cultural groups in which these people live that has produced longer average life expectancies? These people seem to share four characteristics: (a) Their diets are high in fruits and vegetables and low in meat and fat, (b) both relaxation and exercise are part of their daily routine, (c) they work throughout their lives, and (d) family and community activities are important to them (Pitskhelauri, 1982).

*"Look you're 103 years old, you've got to start taking better care of yourself."*

## Cognitive and Intellectual Changes

The increase in the proportion of older people (see Figure 9-13) has been accompanied by an increase in research on the intelligence and personality of senior citizens and the social aspects of old age. As we have seen, fluid intelligence begins a gradual decline toward the end of young adulthood, whereas crystallized intelligence continues to increase gradually. Why does the decline in fluid intelligence occur? Does the brain simply wear out? If there is some general deterioration, it seems reasonable to predict a decrease in both types of intelligence. As this decrease does not occur for both, we must look for another explanation.

Recall our discussion of the encoding, storage, and retrieval of memory in Chapter 7. The decline in fluid intelligence may be related to a problem with one of these memory processes. Consider the alternatives. The excellent crystallized memory shown during late adulthood indicates that storage problems can be ruled out. Obviously, already stored memories are not being lost. What about encoding? It may be that, as we grow older, we begin to experience difficulties in successfully encoding new material. If encoding problems are the cause of the decline in fluid intelligence, it might be possible to increase memory abilities in the elderly by teaching them techniques that aid encoding. Providing elderly individuals with encoding strategies such as arranging names alphabetically resulted in a level of retention similar to that shown by much younger persons (Jacobs, Rakitin, Zubin, Ventura, & Stern, 2001).

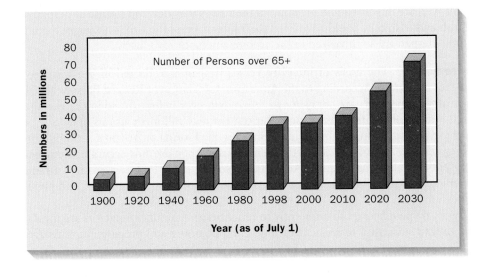

**FIGURE 9-13** Population of the United States aged 65 and older, 1900–2030.

**Source:** American Association of Retired Persons (1992); based on data from U.S. Bureau of the Census.

Continuing to be intellectually active may help prevent a decline in mental activities in old age.

**STUDY TIP**

Create a timeline showing Erik Erikson's stage theory of personality development. Use different colors, or draw icons, to represent the different stages.

**ageism**
The tendency to view the elderly in a negative manner

**integrity versus despair**
Erikson's eighth psychosocial crisis, which occurs during late adulthood; integrity reflects a feeling that one's life has been worthwhile; despair reflects a desire to relive one's life

What about retrieval? Do the elderly have difficulty with this process also? The results of a study in which elderly individuals were provided with memory prompts (Craik, Byrd, & Swanson, 1987) indicate that the answer is yes. When cues or prompts were presented, recall for words from a list improved significantly, as did performance on other verbal tasks. These results suggest that the memories had been encoded and stored but the participants had trouble retrieving them. This study also led to another interesting discovery: Not all of the elderly participants showed a loss in fluid intelligence. In fact, the memory abilities of elderly individuals who had been intellectually active and resourceful throughout their lives were comparable to those of undergraduate students. Results like these point to the advantage of continuing to be intellectually active throughout life. It is possible for older people to learn new things! Because they play board games such as Scrabble, Lex and Dana, whom we met at the beginning of this section, have continued to be intellectually active and mentally sharp.

Unfortunately, many people do not hold this view. What images flash through your mind when you see or hear such terms as *senior citizens, older Americans,* or *elderly persons?* Do these phrases bring to mind positive or negative scenes? Perhaps you responded with images of feeble individuals hobbling with canes and not understanding what is said to them. The tendency to view the elderly in a negative manner is termed **ageism.** It seems to be triggered by common words, such as *old* (Palmore, 2004). Although the use of such adjectives may be unintentional, it can lead to discrimination.

In many instances, ageism leads to isolation of elderly citizens and keeps them from making valuable contributions to society. A person who sits in a retirement apartment watching television contributes less than someone who has a part-time job or is active in other ways. As the number of elderly people in our society increases and research findings help psychologists and others view them more realistically and positively, perhaps we will see a decrease in ageism (Perdue & Gurtman, 1990). Such isolation may be the product of our more affluent society; in less developed countries, where there are no pension plans or Social Security, older adults do not officially retire. Therefore they do not become as isolated and are afforded greater social status as "wise elders."

## Personality and Social Changes

Erikson's final personality crisis, **integrity versus despair,** occurs during late adulthood. To accept one's impending death, one must be able to put one's life in perspective and attach meaning to it. Achieving this goal results in a sense of wholeness or integrity. People who are unable to find meaning in their lives may develop a sense of despair and anguish and wish they could have lived their lives differently. Erikson's stages throughout the lifespan are summarized in the accompanying Study Chart.

**Retirement.** The crisis of integrity versus despair is reflected in the way people adapt to retirement. According to the American Association of Retired Persons (2004b), more older Americans are choosing to retire than ever before. In addition, the age at which individuals retire is decreasing. Retirement may call forth visions of elderly people enjoying a vacation-like life in ideal climates like Florida or Arizona. Although these images sell condominiums and retirement houses, they are not accurate. Retirement represents a major adjustment (AARP, 2004). Some people look forward to retirement and enjoy it greatly. For others, retirement is a time of frustration, anger, and possibly depression.

Why do people react so differently to retirement? A number of factors are involved. The keys to successful retirement include good planning and preparation, satisfaction

## *Study* CHART

### Crises of Psychosocial Development, as Proposed by Erik Erikson

| Crisis | Approximate Age | Characteristics |
| --- | --- | --- |
| Basic trust versus basic mistrust | Birth to 1.5 years | Child learns whether to trust the environment. Ability to trust the environment is important for the development of trust in oneself. |
| Autonomy versus shame and doubt | 1.5 to 3 years | Child develops a sense of control. The sense that control is internal (autonomy) helps the child develop independence. The sense that control is external fosters shame and doubt and hinders the growth of independence. |
| Initiative versus guilt | 3 to 7 years | Child experiences conflict between the behaviors he or she wants to engage in and a growing sense of morality and begins to question whether certain behavior is right or good. |
| Industry versus inferiority | 7 to 10 years | To become a productive member of society, the child must master certain skills and acquire a basic amount of knowledge. Successful learning and skill acquisition lead to the development of a sense of competence. |
| Identity versus identity confusion | Adolescence | The individual asks, "Who am I?" Adolescents seek to establish their sexual, career, and ethnic identities during this period. If these identities are not established, the individual will be confused about the roles he or she plays in the future. |
| Intimacy versus isolation | Early adulthood | Patterns of intimacy, companionship, and love are established during this period. Failure to develop such patterns results in an individual who lives in isolation from others. |
| Generativity versus stagnation | Middle adulthood | The individual's career and productivity reach a peak during this period. Families are formed, and children are raised. Failure to accomplish these objectives results in inactivity and stagnation. |
| Integrity versus despair | Late adulthood | One's life and its meaning are put in perspective. Individuals who feel that their lives lack meaning experience despair over unattained goals and unresolved problems. |

**Source:** Erikson (1963).

with one's accomplishments, good health, and freedom from financial worries. Individuals who begin to attend to these issues during middle adulthood make the transition to retirement much more easily than those who do not. According to Benson (2003), recent research shows that negative emotions gradually decrease in older people. This finding, combined with an increase in positive memory bias, suggests that retirement and old age can be one of the most enjoyable times in a person's life.

Over 90% of elderly U.S. citizens live in a community, rather than in an institution such as a nursing home. Most elderly people prefer to live in their own homes or apartments and maintain their independence as long as possible. With some careful planning, it is often possible to achieve this objective. Consider the case of Peggy, now 91, whose husband died 10 years ago. She continues to live in her own house, as she has for over 40 years. During the day, a nurse assists her with meals and provides companionship, but Peggy is as independent as possible.

Owing to physical or financial limitations, however, not all elderly people are able to live in their own homes in this style. However, this situation is changing because of the cooperation of psychology and the technology of home design (Rogers & Fisk, 2004). New home construction has included an increasing number of "aware houses"—

**STUDY TIP**

After reading the section on late adulthood, write down each of the statistical and/or scientific facts that are part of late adulthood today. Briefly describe each fact's effects.

houses that contain state-of-the-art electronic monitoring systems that help facilitate independent living. However, in many cultures such responsibilities are handled by the extended family. In the United States, assisted living or extended care facilities, retirement villages, and cooperative housing arrangements, in which elderly people share a house, enable them to live in residential neighborhoods. As the average lifespan increases, we can expect to see additional arrangements of this nature.

# DEATH, DYING, AND BEREAVEMENT

Galen and Shandra lost their daughter in a car accident over a year ago. You saw them at the funeral. Your studies have kept you busy, however, and you haven't seen them since then. When you had dinner with them last week, all they could talk about was their daughter. After dinner, the conversation continued as you spent the rest of the evening watching home videos featuring their daughter. Their inability to take their minds off their loss struck you as morbid. *Is it typical for bereaved parents to dwell on the memory of their child for such a long time?*

For some people, death is seen as the final event in a person's lifespan. Although it marks the conclusion of a particular individual's developmental history, other people continue to be influenced by their memories of that person. In this section we examine attitudes toward death and the process of bereavement. We see that different attitudes toward death are associated with different stages of development.

## Attitudes toward Death

**Childhood.** Children do not have an accurate conception of death until they attain the ability to perform concrete operations. They believe that death is reversible—that a dead friend or pet can return to life. Before about age 6, children do not realize that all living things ultimately die and that all functions cease at the time of death. They believe death can be avoided.

**Adolescence.** Although adolescents understand the nature of death (Rask, Kaunonen, & Paunonen-Ilmonen, 2002), they do not have a healthy respect for its implications. They focus on how one lives, not on how long. Death may be glamorized and associated with daring deeds and heroic individuals. For example, James Bond, the international spy created by Ian Fleming, is depicted as an individual whose daring deeds repeatedly bring him to the brink of death; Bond, however, never seems concerned. Adolescents frequently idolize individuals who express such feelings; hence death may not be regarded as an event to be feared.

For some adolescents, death may seem the only way out of an intolerable situation. Their self-centered and self-conscious thoughts place a premium on how they lead their lives and who their friends are. Inability to lead one's life in a desired manner may be a major cause of teenage suicide. Having the right car, dating the right people, and being popular in school are important to adolescents. Perhaps as a result of the increased pressures of our complex society, the number of teenage suicides has risen during recent years. Approximately 1 in every 10,000 adolescents commits suicide each year. Warning signs such as a sudden decrease in school attendance, social withdrawal, a breakup in a romantic relationship, previous suicide attempts, and publicized suicides by other adolescents should be taken seriously (Votta & Manion, 2004).

Recall the egocentric thoughts and *personal fable* that we discussed earlier. Because they believe they are invulnerable, death is not considered a possibility by many adolescents.

**Young Adulthood.** Young adults are at the peak of their physical and sensory abilities and believe that the future has much to offer them. They rarely think of their own

Adolescents who idolize a seemingly indestructible hero may not see death as a feared event.

death. Consequently, the occurrence of a life-threatening illness usually provokes extreme anger and rage. Young adults with a terminal illness are typically poor hospital patients; they feel death is unfair and they are being robbed of their future.

**Middle Adulthood.**    During middle adulthood noticeable physical changes, coupled with the death of one's own parents, bring the realization that death is inevitable. This realization often results in changes in lifestyle. These changes may take one of two forms: The individual may adopt behaviors that are characteristic of an earlier developmental period, as in the reaction to a midlife crisis, or the individual may improve his or her dietary and exercise habits to become more physically fit and live as long as possible.

**Late Adulthood.**    Although death may be imminent, the elderly are more understanding and accepting of this eventuality than younger adults (Reker, Peacock, & Wong, 1987). Elderly people have put their lives in perspective and understand that death is a normal component of the developmental cycle. They have reached the developmental stage of integrity.

Research on terminally ill patients conducted by Elisabeth Kübler-Ross indicates that people may go through five stages in dealing with the approach of death.

## Confronting Death

Ultimately, we must all face our impending death. How will we react? According to Elisabeth Kübler-Ross (1926–2004), terminally ill patients typically go through five stages in dealing with and understanding death (Kübler-Ross, 1969, 1975): denial, anger, bargaining for extra time, depression, and acceptance (see Table 9-3).

Although a person is likely to experience each of these stages at one time or another, he or she will not necessarily proceed through them in an orderly manner (Kastenbaum, 1995). Individuals may experience these stages in different orders, and it is not uncommon to alternate between stages or to experience the emotions of two

**TABLE 9-3**

### Stages of Confronting Death

| Stage | Description |
|---|---|
| Denial | The typical reaction is "This can't happen to me." Because friends and family members may also deny the reality of death, the patient feels isolated and has no one with whom to talk. |
| Anger | Once the reality has been confronted, the "Not me" attitude changes to an angry "Why me?" complaint. Young and healthy individuals are envied. To move beyond this stage, patients must express their anger and rage. |
| Bargaining | Once rage and anger have been expressed, the terminally ill person bargains for additional time. Such bargains often take the form of prayers, such as "I will lead a better life if I can only live until. . . ." |
| Depression | Depression often follows the bargaining stage. Like anger, depression should not be hidden. Only by directly confronting and experiencing the normal feelings of sadness and grief will the person be able to progress to the stage of acceptance. |
| Acceptance | This stage is characterized by a feeling of being at peace with oneself. Unfinished business, such as setting one's finances in order and seeing old friends for a final time, has been taken care of, and the person accepts the fact that "the time is near." Research on terminally ill patients conducted by Elisabeth Kübler-Ross indicates that people may go through five stages in dealing with the approach of death. |

The emotional and role changes that follow a death are called bereavement. People whose emotions and roles change are the bereaved.

stages simultaneously. The nature of the disease leading to death also influences those emotions and the times when they are experienced. For example, a person suffering from a disease characterized by periods of remission may experience denial several times rather than once.

Cultural attitudes toward death differ significantly and influence the reactions to it. For example, in several Native American cultures, death is met with stoic self-control and a belief in the circular relation between life and death (Lewis, 1990). Buddhism also fosters acceptance of death (Truitner & Truitner, 1993).

## Bereavement, Grief, and Support

Death brings numerous changes and adjustments for those who are left behind. Roles change—a wife becomes a widow, a husband a widower, a child an orphan. In addition to adjusting to living alone, widows and widowers must assume the responsibilities of the deceased spouse. Orphans must adjust to a totally new living environment. The emotional and role changes that follow a death are called **bereavement,** and the people whose emotions and roles change are known as the *bereaved*.

**Grief,** encompassing the emotional changes associated with bereavement, is a normal part of this process and seems to progress through four stages (Kalish, 1985): shock and denial, intense concern, despair and depression, and recovery. First, the bereaved person expresses *shock and denial*. These reactions serve to protect the individual from pain. This stage may last as long as 2 or 3 months. Stroebe, Stroebe, and Schut (2001) report that the grief is greater for widowers than widows. Moreover, psychologists who specialize in grief and bereavement counseling have found that these reactions may vary greatly from person to person and that careful, thorough assessments and individualized counseling are very important (Kersting, 2004).

But what about Galen and Shandra, who were still grieving over the death of their daughter a year later? Is it typical to continue to dwell on the memory of a dead child for such a long time? The second phase of grief, which may last for 6 months to a year, is characterized by *intense concern* for perpetuating the memory of the dead person. The majority of the bereaved person's thoughts concern the person who has died. Thus the behaviors Galen and Shandra are displaying are entirely normal.

The third stage, *despair and depression*, is often characterized by confused thinking and anger. Irrational behaviors, such as suddenly selling one's house and moving to an area where one has no friends, may also occur during this phase. **Mourning** involves the behavioral changes associated with bereavement. Untimely deaths, such as the death of Galen and Shandra's daughter, may prolong or intensify the second and third phases, as compared with the natural death of an elderly parent who had been ill for a long time. When the bereaved person shows renewed interest in normal daily activities, he or she has reached the final stage—*recovery*—and the grief is resolved.

Social support is a key ingredient in successful coping with death and bereavement. In Western nations the hospice movement has taken the lead in the delivery of such support services. The **hospice** is more a philosophy of treatment than a set of buildings and equipment. In addition to providing normal medical services for the terminally ill, hospice physicians and staff are trained to give more personalized care and more time to terminally ill patients and their families. This philosophy of warm, personal concern and care is not confined to hospitals; it can be implemented just as effectively in the home (National Hospice and Pallatial Care Organization, 2004). The attitudes and adjustments of hospice patients and their families are superior to those of comparable patients receiving traditional hospital care.

**bereavement**
Emotional and role changes that follow death

**grief**
The emotional changes associated with bereavement

**mourning**
The behavioral changes associated with bereavement

**hospice**
Institution where terminally ill patients and their families are given warm, friendly, personalized care

# REVIEW SUMMARY

**1.** The physical decline experienced during early and middle adulthood continues during **late adulthood.** Vision and hearing are affected most adversely.

**2.** Late adulthood is accompanied by an increase in susceptibility to disease. Nearly one-third of individuals age 85 or older may suffer from **Alzheimer's disease,** a degenerative brain disease.

**3.** If the elderly are taught strategies to enhance encoding and are provided with retrieval cues, their memory capability may not differ from that of young adults. If people remain intellectually active, fluid intelligence may not decline.

**4.** The psychosocial crisis of **integrity versus despair** occurs during late adulthood. People who are unable to put their life in perspective may experience anger, bitterness, and despair.

**5.** Death brings the individual's developmental history to its conclusion. Attitudes toward death change with age. Young children believe that death is reversible; adolescents emphasize how one lives, not how long. The threat of death angers young adults and may cause substantial changes in the lifestyle of middle-aged individuals. The elderly are generally more understanding and accepting of the inevitability of death.

**6.** Elisabeth Kübler-Ross has identified five stages that an individual may go through in confronting death: denial, anger, bargaining for extra time, depression, and acceptance.

**7.** Role and status changes following a death constitute the process of **bereavement. Grief,** which is a normal part of bereavement, progresses through four stages: shock and denial, efforts to perpetuate the memory of the deceased, despair, and recovery.

# ✔ CHECK YOUR PROGRESS

**1.** A degenerative and irreversible brain disease that results in loss of intelligence, memory, and general awareness is

  **a.** dementia.
  **b.** dyslexia.
  **c.** narcolepsy.
  **d.** cerebral palsy.

**2.** Which of these individuals is part of the fastest-growing age group in our society?

  **a.** Jim, who is 65 and recently retired
  **b.** Dan, who is 33 and works in a factory
  **c.** Juan, a 14-year-old who lives on a farm
  **d.** Andrea, who is 22 and just graduated from college

**3.** Children do not have an accurate conception of death before they attain the cognitive stage Piaget labeled

  **a.** sensorimotor.
  **b.** preoperational.

  **c.** formal operations.
  **d.** concrete operations.

**4.** Describe the stages of confronting death outlined by Kübler-Ross.

**5.** The emotional and role changes that follow a death are called

  **a.** sorrow.
  **b.** despair.
  **c.** burnout.
  **d.** bereavement.

**6.** Allowing a person to die with dignity, away from a cold and impersonal institution, is the goal of

  **a.** hospices.
  **b.** nursing homes.
  **c.** moral hospitals.
  **d.** holistic hospitals.

**ANSWERS: 1.** a **2.** a **3.** d **4.** *Denial*—"This can't happen to me!" *Anger*—"Why me?" *Bargaining for extra time*—attempts to make bargains and gain extra time. *Depression*—feelings of sadness and guilt. *Acceptance*—feelings of being at peace with oneself. **5.** d **6.** a

---

**ANSWERS** To Crossword Puzzle Clues

**PAGE 412**

1. Malic

2. Pagoda

3. Ovoid

4. Trot

# Sex and Gender

To this point we have discussed a number of basic processes, such as learning, as well as the typical development of human beings across the lifespan. We now turn our attention to the study of how an individual's biological sex and a culture's gender expectations affect development. Although the biology of sex is the same throughout the world, culture can affect how individuals react to their biological sex by declaring certain behaviors and roles to be more consistent with one sex than with the other. As we will see, topics related to sex and gender have implications, ranging from what people view as appropriate occupations to the type of education they receive to how they are treated on the job.

In this chapter we discuss the biology of sex, sexual behavior, and the development of gender roles. Many people have opinions concerning similarities and differences between men and women; we focus our discussion on research investigating the cognitive and social behavior of males and females. Then we turn our attention to the influence of gender on education, work, and family responsibilities.

## SEX AND GENDER: AN INTRODUCTION

Several friends in a cafeteria are speculating about people sitting nearby. Jake decides that the workout clothes and muscular forearms of the young man at the next table indicate that he is an athlete. To Jessica, the unusual clothing worn by a young woman seated a few tables away indicates that she must be an art major. Everyone nods in agreement. Then a person at the far end of the cafeteria catches their attention. Clothing, haircut, and mannerisms offer no hints to suggest whether this person is male or female. After a while, the person of unknown sex is joined by a friend, and they leave the cafeteria, walking past the group of observers. Each member of the group listens to their conversation for clues to the mystery person's sex, but there are none. *Why is it so important to know whether a person is male or female?*

When we meet or observe people in passing, we often rely on physical features such as their sex and race to categorize them. Of all the possible personal characteristics, we are most likely to notice whether people are male or female (Aronson, Wilson, & Akert, 2002; Stangor, Lynch, Duan, & Glass, 1992). Why? If the only information you have about people is their sex, can you make more accurate predictions about them than if you did not have that information? Is a particular person likely to be an airline pilot? Do friends perceive the person to be warm and nurturing? Does this person enjoy "off-color" humor? Answers to these questions may be based on expectations about how males and females should act. In this chapter we discuss the biological factors that determine whether we are male or female, as well as sexual behavior. We look at how beliefs about what behaviors are deemed appropriate for males and females influence our perception of others as well as our own behaviors.

The word **sex** refers to a biological classification based on genetic composition, anatomy, and hormones. The term *gender* recognizes that culture influences the raw material of biological sex through beliefs and expectations about what it means to be masculine and feminine. Thus the word *sex* refers to biological categories of male and

**sex**
A category based on biological differences in anatomy, hormones, and genetic composition

**gender**
Social and psychological phenomena associated with being "feminine" or "masculine" as these concepts are defined in a given culture

female, categories that are distinguished by genes, chromosomes, and hormones (Helgeson, 2005). Of course, the word *sex* also has a second meaning; we use it to refer to intimate acts that involve pleasure and express affection and love, as we will see later in this chapter. By contrast, **gender** refers to the psychological and social phenomena associated with being *feminine* or *masculine* as these concepts are defined in a given culture.

Here is one way to illustrate this distinction: The primary sex characteristics—a vagina or a penis—represent sex; a baby's pink or blue clothing or blankets represent gender. Why? The colors of the hats or blankets encourage us to treat an infant as a boy or a girl rather than as a generic human. The difference between these words may appear subtle, but they are nonetheless very important.

Imagine that you and your spouse are the parents of a newborn child. Your relatives live 2,000 miles away, so you call them to announce the fantastic news: "The baby was born two hours ago." The first question family members and friends ask when new parents announce the birth of child is "Is it a boy or a girl?" (Intons-Peterson & Reddel, 1984). When Sigmund Freud claimed that "anatomy is destiny," he was suggesting that our biological makeup is the major determinant of our behavior. In other words, men and women behave differently because they differ in their genetic and hormonal makeup.

But consider the following: Most people who study art and music are women, yet can you name one famous female artist or composer? In fact, most orchestras are made up largely of men. Women are said to be good at fine and delicate tasks performed with the hands, such as embroidery and weaving. Yet very few neurosurgeons in the United States are female, although this profession requires the skills just described. Do biological factors account for these phenomena?

Individual and cultural expectations about feminine and masculine roles are significant influences on our behavior. For example, suppose a friend tells you that one of her parents is a dentist. Would you assume it was your friend's mother or her father?

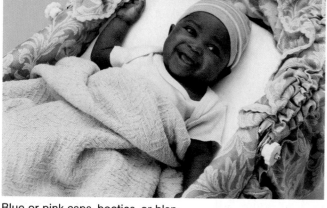

Blue or pink caps, booties, or blankets signal observers to react to children in different ways.

Chances are that you would assume your friend's father was the dentist. Your answer, however, could depend on where you live. Most dentists in Sweden and Russia are women; most dentists in the United States are men. The skills needed to be a dentist are *not* inherently male- or female-related, but different societies label them as such (Basow, 1992).

A classic study shows how beliefs about masculinity and femininity affect our perceptions. Parents of newborns interviewed on the days their children were born rated their sons as stronger, better coordinated, and more alert than their daughters. Newborn girls were rated as more delicate, smaller, and softer than newborn boys (Rubin, Provenzano, & Luria, 1974). Actual physical differences between infant girls and boys might have accounted for these different perceptions and reactions. The newborn boys and girls, however, did not differ in height, weight, or other physical characteristics at birth. Thus, merely changing the label of "boy" or "girl" can lead to differences in perceptions (Yoder, 2003). As noted in Chapter 3, our expectations can have powerful effects on our perceptions.

In this chapter we use the word *sex* when we are discussing biological factors primarily. When we refer to expectations about feminine and masculine ways of behaving, we use the term *gender*. Use of the term *gender* acknowledges that a particular difference between males and females is not an inevitable consequence of biological sex.

## The Biology of Sex

What determines biological sex? Although most people are unmistakably male or female, a human embryo has the potential to develop as either male or female.

Consequently, beginning at the embryonic stage, errors in sexual development can and do occur. In fact, some people—called *intersexes*—are born with mixtures of male and female biological characteristics (Witten, 2003). Some combination of male and female internal and external sexual characteristics occurs in approximately 1 to 2 out of every 1,000 births (Blackless et al., 2000). **Hermaphrodites** have a combination of female and male internal and external genitalia, including one testis and one ovary. (The term *hermaphrodite* is derived from the name of the offspring of the mythological Greek gods Hermes, messenger of the gods, and Aphrodite, the goddess of love and beauty.) **Pseudohermaphrodites** have two gonads (testes or ovaries) of the same kind, along with the usual male or female chromosomal makeup, but their external genitalia and secondary sex characteristics (see Chapter 9) do not match their chromosomal makeup (Fausto-Sterling, 1993).

**The Genetics of Sex.** Genetic factors are the first and most basic determinants of whether a person is male or female. The genetic blueprint that directs a person's development is established at fertilization by genes contained in the chromosomes of the ovum and sperm. As we saw in Chapter 9, the ovum and sperm each contribute 23 chromosomes to the *zygote*. One of the chromosomes is a sex chromosome. The ovum always contributes an X chromosome toward determining the child's sex, but the sperm may contribute either an X or a Y chromosome.

If the father contributes an X chromosome to the embryo at conception, the baby will be a girl (XX). If the father contributes a Y chromosome, the baby will be a boy (XY). Thus, the primary determinant of a person's sex is the chromosome contributed by the father's sperm cell (Hyde & DeLamater, 1999), although other factors, including hormones, also play a role (Paludi, 2002). The composition of our chromosomes is called our *genetic sex*.

Early in development, human embryos have an *undifferentiated*, or all-purpose, gonad (sex gland) that can become either a testis or an ovary. Approximately 7 weeks after fertilization, genes located on the Y chromosome are responsible for the production of a protein called *H-Y antigen* (the "testis-determining factor") that plays a role in molding the undifferentiated gonadal tissue into a testis (Yoder, 2003). These genes are also responsible for breaking down in males the embryonic structure that would lead to internal female organs. When no Y chromosome is present, the gonad develops as an ovary during the 13th week after fertilization.

**Genetic Abnormalities.** Genetic abnormalities that occur at conception can have major implications for later development (see Chapter 9). Some genetic abnormalities involve the sex chromosomes. For example, if the father's Y chromosome combines with an ovum carrying two X chromosomes, the result is an XXY chromosomal pattern known as *Klinefelter's syndrome*, which occurs in 1 in 1,000 births (Blackless et al., 2000). The key features of this syndrome are smaller than normal male genitals, enlarged breasts, poor muscular development, and possible mental retardation. In *Turner syndrome*, the child has one X chromosome instead of two (a pattern referred to as XO); the second X chromosome is either defective or missing (McCauley, Feuillan, Kushner, & Ross, 2001; Rovet, 2004). These individuals are usually characterized by short stature, a webbed neck, eyelid folds, and a shieldlike chest (Powell & Schulte, 1999). Although they may have a normal verbal IQ, they often have deficits in visual memory, perceptual skills, and visual-motor integration (Molko et al., 2004; Rovet, 2004). Compared to individuals without this condition, they are more likely to meet the diagnostic criteria for attention-deficit hyperactivity disorder (McCauley et al., 2001). Their ovaries never function properly, so they do not produce estrogen. Consequently, they do not menstruate, nor do they develop breasts without hormonal treatment.

Sometimes a single X chromosome from the mother unites with two Y chromosomes from the father (XYY). The resulting individual is male, usually tall, and likely to have below-average intelligence. Initial reports of an association between the XYY pattern and a tendency to commit violent crimes were not supported by subsequent

**hermaphrodite**
Individual who has both ovarian and testicular tissue

**pseudohermaphrodite**
Individual who possesses two gonads of the same kind along with the usual male or female chromosomal makeup, but has external genitalia and secondary sex characteristics that do not match his or her chromosomal makeup

research (Witkin et al., 1976). Compared with other criminals, those with the XYY pattern may be more likely to be caught, perhaps owing to their below-average intelligence. Less than 1% of the general population has the XYY chromosomal pattern, but the percentage of XYY individuals in prison is higher. This chromosomal pattern, however, is not related to a significant amount of crime.

As mentioned in Chapter 9, some genetic disorders, such as color blindness, are sex-linked, which means they are more likely to occur in one sex (usually males) than in the other. Because the Y chromosome is small compared with the X chromosome, it does not carry as many genes as the X chromosome. As a result, disorders or diseases carried on the X chromosome may not be countered by normal genes on the Y chromosome.

**Male Vulnerability.**     More boys than girls are conceived (approximately 125 boys for every 100 girls), but at birth the ratio narrows to 106 boys for every 100 girls because more male embryos are miscarried (Stillion, 1995). Longer maternal labor for boys than for girls is associated with problems such as mental retardation, which occurs at a higher rate among males than among females. The incidence of enuresis (bedwetting), sudden infant death syndrome (SIDS), stuttering, learning disabilities, autism, and hyperactivity is higher in males than in females. Although the death rate for infant boys is higher than for infant girls, males constitute slightly more than 50% of the population prior to age 40. Males constitute *less* than 50% of the population beginning with the age interval 30 to 39 (see Figure 10-1). Females outnumber males by approximately 3 to 1 among individuals aged 90 to 99 and by almost 5 to 1 among individuals 100 years old and over (U.S. Bureau of the Census, 2005). The death rate among males is higher than that among females throughout the lifespan, and men are more likely than women to die from 9 of the 10 leading causes of death in the United States (Hegelson, 2005).

Males have a greater chance of experiencing developmental difficulties such as reading problems and delayed speech, environmental health problems (such as cancer resulting from exposure to a toxic substance), and physical diseases (Jacklin, 1989). Compared with men, women have more disability days, physician visits, and surgical procedures. They are also more likely to be admitted to hospitals and to use more days of hospital care; only part of this difference is due to labor and delivery. Women are more likely to be treated for metabolic disorders; they are also prone to *osteoporosis*, which is an important factor in fractures (Travis, 1993). Although women are ill more frequently than men, they are more likely to suffer from serious but *not* life-threatening problems. Men tend to develop more critical illnesses; they have higher rates of chronic diseases, such as heart disease, which are among the leading causes of death in the

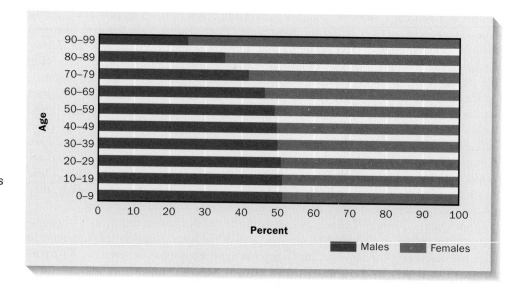

**FIGURE 10-1** Percentages of females and males across age groups. Although males and females constitute approximately half of the population at younger ages, the percentages begin to diverge with people in their 30s. Females make up an increasing percentage of the population as age increases.

United States (see Chapter 14). Part of this increased vulnerability is due to risks associated with smoking, alcohol consumption, and job-related hazards that can lead to deaths from accidents, homicides, suicide (see Chapter 12), and AIDS (Helgeson, 2005). As we noted, however, males' heightened vulnerability begins early in life and may be, in part, genetically based.

That "females appear to have some biological or environmental advantage over males that makes them less vulnerable to major contemporary life-threatening physical disorders as well as accidents and suicides" seems well established (Strickland, 1988, p. 382). For example, in most industrialized countries, the rate of heart disease is lower for females than for males. The leading cause of death among men and women is heart disease, but women tend to suffer heart disease deaths at a later age than men.

What causes these differences? Among the possible causes are biological factors, social roles, differing stressors men and women face, gender differences in behavioral risk factors, and gender differences in personality. An interesting question is "Are there differences within each gender that affect mortality?" To answer this question, researchers studied a sample of men and women from Lewis Terman's gifted children study (see Chapter 8; Lippa, Martin, & Friedman, 2000). One of the tests they had taken over many years was the Strong Vocational Interest Blank, which yields scores on a Masculinity-Femininity (M-F) scale and is scored so that high scores for men are labeled masculine and high scores for women are labeled feminine. A Gender Diagnosticity (GD) measure indicated how male- or female-typical an individual's occupation preferences were. For each sex separately, both measures (Strong M-F scores and GD) significantly predicted mortality risk. "For both men and women, individuals who were more male-typical in their occupational preferences tended to show higher mortality rates than did individuals who were more female-typical. These associations were not due to specific cause of death" (p. 1566). Put another way, masculine men and masculine women were more likely to die. The effects of these personality differences remained after the researchers controlled for actual health behaviors. The strength of this relation was comparable in magnitude to that associated with systolic blood pressure and cholesterol levels in the blood. The evidence suggests that masculinity and femininity have stronger effects on health than may have been thought to be the case.

## Sexual Behavior

As noted earlier, sexual differentiation does not begin until approximately the 7th week of embryonic development, when internal reproductive organs (testes or ovaries) develop in response to either the presence or the absence of genes carried on the Y chromosome. At that time, the testes produce hormones called *androgens* (of which the most important is testosterone), which direct development of the male genitals. If the male hormone is absent, the baby develops female genitals (ovaries, uterus, and vagina), regardless of the chromosomal makeup. The action of hormones during the embryonic and fetal stages as well as during adolescence gives rise to what is termed *anatomical sex*. In males an increase in the level of testosterone at puberty is responsible for the development and growth of the penis and testes as well as the secondary sex characteristics. In females an increase in estrogen at puberty is responsible for the growth of the uterus and the vagina and the development of the secondary sex characteristics. Development during puberty (see Chapter 9) consists of changes that occur in a range of physical attributes, from height and weight to changes associated with sexual maturation that make sexual reproduction possible. The most basic change in boys is growth of the penis and scrotum. In girls, menarche—the first menstrual period—is an indication of sexual maturity. Although the variety of sexual and nonsexual changes that characterize puberty do not occur at the same rate in a given individual, on average girls develop earlier than boys; therefore, they reach sexual maturity (ability to reproduce) before boys.

**STUDY TIP**

Create a visual organizer containing and describing the information outlined in the section on The Biology of Sex, including the topics of the genetics of sex, genetic abnormalities, and male vulnerability.

**adrenogenital syndrome**
Condition caused by exposure to excessive amounts of androgens during the fetal period; can result in a female with genitals resembling those of males

**androgen insensitivity syndrome**
Failure by a male embryo to respond to male hormones

The foregoing analysis of sex differentiation seems straightforward. As noted earlier, however, just as chromosomal problems can occur, other difficulties can occur during the embryonic stage as a result of the effects of hormones during early development, or later during puberty (Paludi, 2002). The hormonal environment of the womb, rather than the chromosomes, directly determines the sex of the fetus. For example, the mother may have ingested a drug that changes her hormone levels at a sensitive time for sex differentiation. In the 1950s, some pregnant women were prescribed a synthetic steroid that exposed their female fetuses to androgens; these genetic females (XX) were born with genitals resembling those of males. This condition, known as **adrenogenital syndrome,** often requires surgical correction. Individuals with this syndrome tend to exhibit more rough-and-tumble play, are more aggressive, and opt for more typically masculine toys than their unaffected sisters (Baxter, 1994).

A male embryo may fail to respond to male hormones, a condition called **androgen insensitivity syndrome,** which occurs in 1 in 13,000 births (Blackless et al., 2000). The XY fetus will develop testes that produce testosterone; however, the rest of the body acts as if the hormones were not there, and the genetically male (XY) fetus heads down a mostly female track of development. Genital tissue is shaped into a clitoris and labia, so the child looks like a girl at birth. The only sign of a difference is the presence of testes, which can be missed without a close physical examination (Pool, 1994).

**Sexual Orientation.** There is an old adage that says that if you randomly ask a class of college students "What was on your mind just now?" the most common response will have something to do with sex. In reality, the adage is an exaggeration; however, it does focus attention on the importance of sex in our lives. To be sure, unlike motives such as hunger and thirst, we do not need sex to survive, although, of course, the species requires sexual behavior to continue (see Chapter 6). There is little doubt that sex is a significant focus in the lives of most people. We think about it often, and we are surrounded by it in advertisements, movies, and newspapers. For many people, sexual performance is even linked to their self-esteem. No wonder psychologists have focused so much research on sexual behavior; and they have found a receptive audience for their findings.

For many years, researchers have used animals as models for studying the behavior of human beings. Sexual behavior in animals is controlled by genetically programmed factors, especially the levels of hormones that circulate in the bloodstream (see Chapters 2 and 6). Therefore female animals are receptive to sexual overtures only at certain biologically determined times, when they are said to be "in heat" (in estrus).

## Psychological Detective

In what ways is sexual arousal in human beings different from sexual arousal in animals? What are the consequences of these differences in arousal? Give these questions some thought and write down your answers before reading further.

Human sexual behavior—in contrast to that of many other living organisms—is a function of the complex interplay of genetic, prenatal, and environmental factors; thus human beings are not slaves to their hormone levels (Miracle, Miracle, & Baumeister, 2003). They can become sexually aroused by a range of stimuli, from smells to sights to fantasies. This observation accounts for some unusual sexual behaviors and arousal patterns that can be seen in humans but not in lower animals; some of these are described in Chapter 12.

Many people believe that men and women have entirely different sex hormones. In fact, both men and women have measurable quantities of the hormones estrogen, progesterone, and testosterone. The amounts of these hormones, however, differ in men and women.

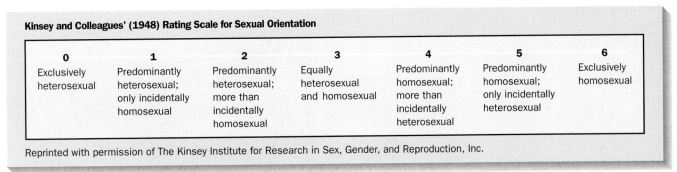

**Kinsey and Colleagues' (1948) Rating Scale for Sexual Orientation**

| 0 | 1 | 2 | 3 | 4 | 5 | 6 |
|---|---|---|---|---|---|---|
| Exclusively heterosexual | Predominantly heterosexual; only incidentally homosexual | Predominantly heterosexual; more than incidentally homosexual | Equally heterosexual and homosexual | Predominantly homosexual; more than incidentally heterosexual | Predominantly homosexual; only incidentally heterosexual | Exclusively homosexual |

Reprinted with permission of The Kinsey Institute for Research in Sex, Gender, and Reproduction, Inc.

**FIGURE 10-2** Sexual orientation can be viewed by degrees, ranging from exclusively heterosexual to exclusively homosexual. This notion was first developed by Kinsey for his pioneering studies of sexual behavior.

As we described in Chapter 6, *sexual orientation* is the tendency for a person to be attracted to members of the same sex, the other sex, or both sexes. Surveys of sexual practices have revealed that the majority of the population describes themselves as *heterosexual*, although the surveys also reveal that sexual orientation is, to some extent, a matter of degree (see Figure 10-2). For example, approximately 15% of adolescent boys and girls report having had emotional and sexual attractions to a member of their own sex (D'Augelli, 1996). In most cases, these experiences are part of a process of experimentation that is common among adolescents.

The Kinsey surveys put the percentage of the population of white men who were exclusively homosexual at 4%; among women, 1% to 3% were predominantly or exclusively homosexual. More recent surveys report lower percentages. What's more, surveys reveal that the homosexual population is not evenly distributed across geographical locations, but instead is concentrated in urban locales (Laumann, Gagnon, Michael, & Michaels, 1994). In part, this concentration may be due to the greater ease in finding companions and also as a means of dealing with homophobia. The term *homophobia* (from the Greek word *phobia*, meaning "fear") was coined in 1967 to describe an irrational fear of homosexuality often manifested in prejudice and hate crimes (*gay bashing*) against gay men and lesbians (Friedman & Downey, 1994; Strickland, 1995).

Growing evidence suggests that biological factors play an important role in the development of sexual orientation. What's more, same-sex sexual encounters have been observed in more than 450 species of animals (Bagemihl, 1999). A tiny portion of the hypothalamus is twice as large in men as in women and two to three times larger in heterosexual than in homosexual men (LeVay & Hamer, 1994). Neuron growth in this region may be related to levels of androgens such as testosterone: The higher the level of androgens, the greater the number of neurons that survive, and hence the larger the region. Thus, androgen levels may be unusually low in the fetuses of males who become gay and unusually high in the fetuses of females who become lesbian.

*"Multiple? Are you kidding? It wasn't even fractional!"*

As we discussed in Chapter 6, twins research suggests a genetic component for homosexuality. Several studies have led to the conclusion that there is "little doubt of a biological contribution to sexual orientation" (King, 2005, p. 278). Although the data are consistent with a genetic influence, they do not exclude environmental influences (Yoder, 2003). In general, research on sexual orientation is still evolving and we have much more to learn. At this point, however, the following points relevant to homosexuality seem well established (Kail & Cavanaugh, 2004):

- Sons do not become gay when raised by a domineering mother and a weak father.
- Girls do not become lesbians when their father is their primary role model.

**FIGURE 10-3**  Male sexual anatomy.

**Source:** Miracle et al. (2003).

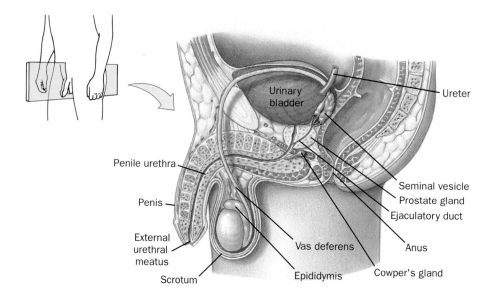

- Children raised by gay and lesbian parents typically do not adopt their parents' sexual orientation.

- Gay and lesbian adults were not seduced as children by an older person of their sex.

**Differences in Sexual Attitudes and Practices.**    The testes are the primary sex organs in males; they are located in the scrotum, which is a sac-like structure beneath the penis (see Figure 10-3). The testes manufacture sperm cells, which are contained in a fluid called *semen*. Semen is ejaculated through the penis, which also serves to rid the body of urine. The shaft of the penis is composed primarily of erectile tissue, which fills with blood during an erection.

The vagina is an elastic muscular tube that extends between a woman's cervix and her external genitalia (see Figure 10-4). The vagina serves several purposes: (a) it provides a passageway to eliminate menstrual fluids; (b) it receives the penis during sexual intercourse and holds the sperm before their passage to the uterus; and (c) during childbirth, it forms the lower portion of the birth canal. The two ovaries produce ova (or eggs) and also secrete the hormones estrogen and progesterone.

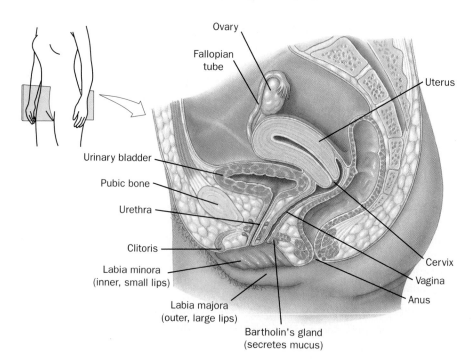

**FIGURE 10-4**  Female sexual anatomy.

**Source:** Miracle et al. (2003).

As we described in Chapter 6, the human sexual response cycle moves through several stages: excitement, plateau, orgasm, and resolution. Unlike lower animals, humans can become sexually aroused by a range of stimuli (odors, pictures, physical touch, sound), including a wide range of fantasies. In comparison to lower animals, human sexual behavior is not as controlled by purely biological factors such as hormones. Once a person's sexual interest has been piqued, two significant physiological changes occur. *Vasocongestion* is characterized by the engorgement (filling) of tissue with blood; in *myotonia* there is an energy buildup in the nerves and muscles, which results eventually in involuntary contractions.

Table 10-1 describes some of the differences in the sexual response cycle experienced by men and women. One of the most interesting findings relates to the experience of an

## TABLE 10-1

## Description of Sex Differences in the Stages of Sexual Response Cycle

### Excitement

*Men:* The first sign of arousal, erection of the penis, results from engorgement of blood. This vasocongestive response occurs when arteries carrying blood to the penis become dilated. Because erection of the penis is a reflex, men with spinal injuries may still be able to have an erection, although they cannot perceive the changes that occur. Among the other changes that occur are increased heart rate, increased blood pressure, myotonia (muscle tension), thickening of the scrotum, and movement of the testicles toward the body.

*Women:* The vaginal walls become engorged with blood and they secrete drops of fluid (resulting in vaginal lubrication). This vaginal lubrication may occur within 10–30 seconds after the start of sexual stimulation. The labia flatten and move apart, and other changes make the vagina ready to accommodate a penis. The clitoris becomes engorged with blood and the nipples become erect.

### Plateau

*Men:* The diameter of the penis increases further, and the testicles may increase in size from 50 to 100%.

*Women:* The tissue of the outer third of the vagina become engorged with blood, which actually narrows the vaginal opening by 30 to 50%. Blood flow to the skin changes, resulting in a rashlike appearance (called a *sex-tension flash*), which may appear on the chest or breasts. The clitoris actually pulls back and disappears beneath outer tissue.

### Orgasm

*Men:* The key to orgasm is rhythmic, muscular contractions. In addition, the sphincter muscles close off the urethra, preventing urine flow. Then there is an ejaculation of semen.

*Women:* Rhythmic, muscular contractions occur, especially in the outer third of the vagina, the uterus, and the anal sphincter muscles.

### Resolution

*Men:* The erection is lost, testicle size is reduced, and the testicles move away from the body. During a refractory period (which varies from individual to individual), another orgasm is not possible. This period may last a few minutes in adolescents or much longer in older men.

*Women:* Physiological responses drop below the plateau level and eventually to a nonaroused state; however, more women (compared to men) are capable of multiple orgasms.

**Source:** King (2005); Miracle et al. (2003).

**TABLE 10-2**

## Most Frequent Sexual Fantasies of College Men and Women

| Men | Women |
|---|---|
| 1. touching and/or kissing sensuously | 1. touching and/or kissing sensuously |
| 2. being sensuously touched | 2. being sensuously touched |
| 3. oral-genital sex | 3. naked caressing |
| 4. naked caressing | 4. walking hand in hand |
| 5. watching partner undress | 5. oral-genital sex |
| 6. seducing partner | 6. seducing partner |
| 7. intercourse in unusual positions | 7. watching partner undress |
| 8. masturbating your partner | 8. intercourse in unusual positions |
| 9. walking hand in hand | 9. sex in unusual locations |
| 10. sex that lasts for hours | 10. getting married |

**Source:** Adapted from Hsu (1994).

orgasm. Based on physiological research as well as analysis of individuals' descriptions of orgasms, it appears that the descriptions of orgasm are quite similar in men and women (King, 2005).

Young people are bombarded by messages focusing on sexual activity. Whether in CDs, advertisements, magazines, or movies, images of sexual behavior are highly prevalent. Consequently, it is not surprising that daydreaming about sexual activity (for example, petting or intercourse) is quite common (see Table 10-2). With the onset of puberty and sexual maturity, masturbation becomes a common sexual outlet. Although masturbation occurs in adolescents of both sexes, the rate is higher among boys.

Surveys of sexual activity among adolescents reveal several trends over past decades: earlier initiation of intercourse, increased premarital intercourse, a greater number of partners, and ineffective and inconsistent use of contraceptives. For example, the median age for the first intercourse is 15.5 among boys and 14.75 among girls (Seifert, Hoffnung, & Hoffnung, 2000). The difference in the median age may, in part, reflect differing ages at which boys and girls reach sexual maturity. Biological maturity does not necessarily impart social maturity; many adolescents do not seriously consider the potential consequences of their actions. Each year in the United States, approximately 1 million teenage girls become pregnant. In fact, the birth rate among teens in the United States is higher than that of most other industrial countries (Guttmacher Institute, 2005). What's more, ineffective and inconsistent use of contraceptives makes teenagers vulnerable to sexually transmitted diseases, including syphilis, gonorrhea, genital warts, genital herpes, and AIDS (see Table 10-3). Of the 20 million cases of sexually transmitted diseases reported each year in the United States, 50% occur among teenagers and young adults under age 25 (Seifert et al., 2000). Although young people have an especially elevated risk of contracting sexually transmitted diseases, the behaviors that put people at risk for such diseases are not confined to young people.

When it comes to sexual attitudes and behavior, some sex differences have been found repeatedly in surveys. Men are more sexually promiscuous and more likely to enjoy sex without emotional commitment (Laumann et al., 1994). Analysis of sexual attitudes and sexual behaviors reveal that men are more liberal in their overall attitude toward sex, including premarital sex, especially when it is casual. Men are also more accepting of extramarital sex, more likely to have had extramarital sex, and more likely to have had a larger number of sexual partners. Although researchers found a small difference in attitudes toward masturbation, there was a large difference in the incidence of masturbation; it is higher among males. In addition, men are more likely to fantasize about having sex with multiple partners at once (Leitenberg & Henning, 1995). On the other side, researchers noted no differences between males and females in incidence of kissing and incidence of oral sex (Oliver & Hyde, 1993).

## TABLE 10-3

## Sexually Transmitted Diseases

**Bacterial vaginosis** BV is a condition in women in which the normal balance of bacteria in the vagina is disrupted and replaced by an overgrowth of certain bacteria. It is sometimes accompanied by an abnormal vaginal discharge, (fishlike) odor, pain, itching around the outside of the vagina, and burning during urination. BV is the most common vaginal infection in women of childbearing age.

**Chlamydia** Chlamydia is a very common sexually transmitted disease caused by the bacterium *Chlamydia trachomatis*. Most people with *Chlamydia* are not aware of their infections and do not seek testing. In women, the bacterium initially infects the cervix and the urethra (urine canal). Women who have symptoms may have an abnormal vaginal discharge or a burning sensation when urinating. When the infection spreads to the fallopian tubes, women may have lower abdominal pain, low back pain, nausea, fever, and pain during intercourse. Men have a discharge from the penis or a burning sensation when urinating.

**Genital herpes** Genital herpes is a sexually transmitted disease caused by the herpes simplex viruses type 1 (HSV-1) and type 2 (HSV-2). Most genital herpes is caused by HSV-2. Most people with genital herpes have no signs or symptoms. When signs do occur, they typically appear as one or more blisters on or around the genitals or rectum. The blisters break, leaving tender ulcers (sores) that may take 2 to 4 weeks to heal the first time they occur. Typically, another outbreak can appear weeks or months after the first one, but it is almost always less severe and shorter than the first outbreak. The infection can stay in the body indefinitely, although the number of outbreaks tends to decrease over a period of years.

**Gonorrhea** Gonorrhea is a sexually transmitted disease caused by *Neisseria gonorrhoeae*, a bacterium that can grow and multiply rapidly in the warm, moist areas of the reproductive tract. It can also grow in the mouth, throat, eyes, and anus. Many men with gonorrhea may have no symptoms. Symptoms can take as long as 30 days to appear and include a burning sensation when urinating or a white, yellow, or green discharge from the penis. In women, the symptoms are often mild, but most women who are infected have no symptoms. Even when a woman has symptoms, they can be mistaken for bladder or vaginal infection. The initial symptoms include a painful or burning sensation when urinating, increased vaginal discharge, or vaginal bleeding between periods.

**Syphilis** Syphilis is caused by the bacterium *Treponema pallidum*. It is often called the "great imitator" because many of the signs and symptoms are indistinguishable from those of other diseases. Most people with syphilis have no symptoms for years, yet they remain at risk for late complications if they are not treated. The primary stage is marked by the appearance of a single sore (called a *chancre*), but there can be multiple sores. In the secondary stage, there is a skin rash and mucous membrane lesions. In the later stages the secondary symptoms disappear. Without treatment, the infected person will continue to have syphilis even though there are no signs. In the final stage, damage can occur to internal organs including the brain, nerves, eyes, heart, blood vessels, liver, bones, and joints. The damage may be serious enough to cause death.

**Source:** Centers for Disease Control and Prevention (2005).

Although the mass media tend to focus on high rates of sexual activity, survey research indicates that there is quite a bit of variability in sexual activity in the United States (Laumann et al., 1994). For example, about one-third of adults report having sex with a partner a few times a year or not at all, another one-third have sex once or several times a month, and the remaining one-third have sex with a partner two or more times a week. According to the same survey, most—but not all—people are generally satisfied with their sexual activity (see Figure 10-5), as we will see in the next section.

**Sexual Dysfunctions.** A *sexual dysfunction* is a persistent impairment of sexual interest or response that causes interpersonal difficulties or personal distress (American

**FIGURE 10-5** Sexual satisfaction in self-reported primary partnerships during the previous year.

**Source:** Laumann et al. (1994).

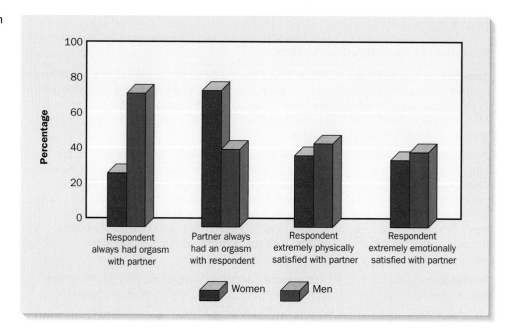

Psychiatric Association, 2000) that can occur at any stage of the sexual response cycle. These impairments can occur as a result of other psychological disorders or physical conditions; in other cases, sexual dysfunctions are independent of psychological and physical conditions. Among the common causes are developmental upbringing, personality factors, lack of information about sexual behavior, and sexual trauma. Sexual dysfunctions can be exacerbated by a variety of conditions ranging from stress, to anxiety, to depression, to the use of alcohol and other drugs.

How frequently do such disorders occur in the general population (see Figure 10-6)? As discussed in Chapter 6, 43% of women at some point in their lives had experienced a sexual dysfunction for several months. For men, the comparable figure was 31%. Among women, the most common problem was lack of interest, with about a third saying that they regularly did not want sex. Twenty-six percent of women said that they regularly did not have orgasms, and 23% said sex was not pleasurable. About a third of men had problems climaxing too early, 14% said they had no interest

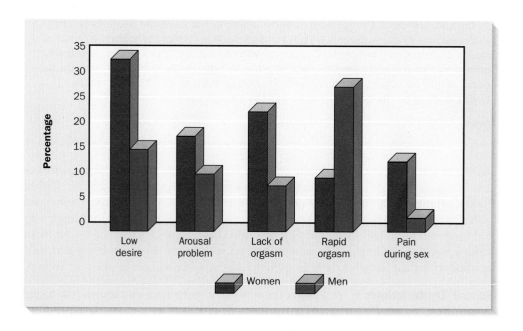

**FIGURE 10-6** Prevalence of sexual dysfunctions. More women than men experience sexual dysfunctions.

**Source:** Laumann et al. (1999).

## TABLE 10-4

## Major Types of Sexual Dysfunction

| | |
|---|---|
| **Hypoactive sexual desire disorder** | Persistently or recurrently deficient (or absent) sexual fantasies and desire for sexual activity |
| **Sexual aversion disorder** | Persistent or recurrent extreme aversion to and active avoidance of genital sexual contact with a sexual partner |
| **Female sexual arousal disorder** | Persistent or recurrent inability to attain, or to maintain until completion of the sexual activity, an adequate lubrication-swelling response of sexual excitement |
| **Male erectile disorder** | Persistent or recurrent inability to attain, or to maintain until completion of the sexual activity, an adequate erection |
| **Orgasmic disorder** | In women, the persistent or recurrent delay or absence of orgasm following a normal arousal phase; in men, the persistent or recurrent delay in, or absence of, orgasm following a normal arousal phase |
| **Premature ejaculation** | Persistent or recurrent onset of orgasm and ejaculation with minimal sexual simulation before or shortly after penetration and before the person wishes it |
| **Dyspareunia** | Genital pain associated with sexual intercourse, experienced by a man or woman |
| **Vaginismus** | Persistent or recurrent involuntary contraction of muscles surrounding the outer third of the vagina and when penetration is attempted |

**Source:** American Psychiatric Association (2000).

in sex, and 8% said they consistently derived no pleasure from sex (Laumann, Paik, & Rosen, 1999).

See Table 10-4 for a listing of sexual dysfunctions.

**Hypoactive Sexual Desire.**    People with hypoactive sexual desire have a "deficient" or abnormally low level of interest in sexual activity (American Psychiatric Association, 2000), although the meaning of *deficient* is not specified. Nevertheless, those who would receive this diagnosis typically do not seek out actual sexual relationships, nor do they imagine them. In many ways, sexual activity is not on their radar screens. Although some of them may not be concerned about their low level of sexual interest, it can have a negative impact on their relationships. In many cases, the disorder occurs as a result of a variety of factors including depression, prior sexual trauma, poor body image, or low self-esteem.

**Sexual Aversion Disorder.**    People with sexual aversion disorder have an active dislike and avoidance of genital contact with sexual partners (American Psychiatric Association, 2000). As a result, they experience personal distress or interpersonal problems. Although they may be interested in sex and may fantasize about sexual activity, they tend to be repulsed by the notion of actual sexual activity and contact. Some people with this disorder avoid *all* forms of sexual activity, including behaviors that are not strictly sexual such as kissing and hugging. In other cases, the aversion is more specific and may involve an aversion to penile penetration.

**gender roles**
Behaviors considered appropriate for males and females in a given culture

**Male Erectile Disorder.**    Men with erectile disorder have recurrent partial or complete failure to attain or maintain an erection during sexual activity (American Psychiatric Association, 2000). As a result, they become distressed and are likely to experience interpersonal problems. The term *impotence* was used in the past to describe this condition, but it is no longer used. A number of medical conditions can lead to male erectile disorder: diabetes, multiple sclerosis, and kidney failure. Male erectile disorder is the sexual dysfunction treated with drugs such as Viagra.

Seemingly the opposite disorder, *premature ejaculation*, occurs when a man reaches orgasm in a sexual encounter long before he or his partner wishes it to occur. In some cases, the ejaculation occurs even prior to penetration. As a result, he and his partner are likely to feel little or no sexual satisfaction. Premature ejaculation is not an uncommon occurrence during a man's first sexual encounter. Beyond that first encounter, it may be associated with anxiety over being caught "in the act."

**Sexual Pain Disorders.**    Two dysfunctions involve the reporting and experience of pain associated with sexual activity. *Dyspareunia* (from the Latin words meaning "painful mating") involves recurrent or persistent genital pain before, during, or after sexual intercourse. Although dyspareunia occurs in both sexes, it is much more common in women and is associated with inadequate lubrication. *Vaginismus* affects only females and involves recurrent or persistent involuntary spasms of the outer muscles of the vagina, which makes intercourse either difficult or impossible. Although pain occasionally occurs during intercourse, vaginismus probably occurs in less than 1% of all women.

The disorders described here and listed in Table 10-4 are often treated with a variety of techniques, ranging from psychotherapy, to behavioral treatments, to medical treatments. Many of the treatments were pioneered by Masters and Johnson (see Chapter 6) and are still in use today.

As you have seen, human sexual behavior can be quite complex; not surprisingly, a variety of attitudes and behaviors are expressed on the topic. We now turn to the development of what are termed *gender roles*.

# The Development of Gender Roles

Most children between the ages of 2 and 3 can label themselves as boys or girls; they can also classify other people as members of the same or the other sex. By age 3, most American children know the traditional expectations for males and females. Over and over they have heard that "boys don't play with dolls," "girls grow up to be nurses," and "it's okay if a boy gets dirty, but a girl should be dainty." They learn how these **gender roles,** or behaviors considered appropriate for males and females in a given culture, relate to clothing, games, tools, and toys (Biernat, 1991).

Children's letters to Santa Claus reveal that they have clear notions of which toys are considered appropriate for boys and girls (Richardson & Simpson, 1982). Their requests mirror gender-related participation in career and domestic activities. For example, at an early age boys ask for guns and race cars and girls ask for dolls. A study of children's letters to Santa (Freeman, Sims, Kutsch, & Marcon, 1995) found that some, but not all, toy preferences have changed over the years. For example, girls are now as likely as boys to enjoy riding bicycles and engaging in sports (see Table 10-5). Boys are as likely as girls to enjoy arts-and-crafts activities.

Between the ages of 4 and 5, children are aware that some occupations are "reserved" for men and others for women (Biernat, 1991). Children also learn that desires for autonomy and power are considered inappropriate for females and that feelings of vulnerability and dependency are considered inappropriate for males. For example, adults rarely notice or point out how strong a little girl may be or how nurturing a little boy is becoming, yet they readily note these attributes in the "appropriate" sex (Bem, 1993).

We label these differences *gender roles* because expectations seem to play a significant role in their development. How can we explain the development of gender roles in

Gender stereotypes influence children's choices of toys at an early age.

**TABLE 10-5**

## Types of Christmas Gifts Requested by 824 Boys and Girls

| Gifts Requested | Boys (%) | Girls (%) |
| --- | --- | --- |
| **Items not associated with gender** | | |
| Real vehicles | 29.7 | 28.7 |
| Sports equipment | 16.1 | 15.5 |
| Communication items | 12.2 | 14.3 |
| Musical instruments | 7.4 | 7.0 |
| **Items requested more by boys** | | |
| Games | 41.6 | 25.7 |
| Toy vehicles | 19.3 | 6.2 |
| Dolls (humanoid) | 17.8 | 7.4 |
| Military toys | 6.2 | 0.4 |
| **Items requested more by girls** | | |
| Dolls (baby) | 1.4 | 24.4 |
| Dolls (female) | 0.8 | 21.9 |
| Clothing accessories | 5.1 | 15.5 |
| Stuffed animals | 2.0 | 10.2 |

**Source:** Freeman et al. (1995).

children? Four theories, each with a slightly different focus, have been proposed to explain the development of gender roles: psychodynamic theory, observational theory, cognitive developmental theory, and gender-schema theory.

**Psychodynamic Theory.**    According to Freud's psychodynamic theory, young boys develop a sexual attraction to their mother and young girls develop a similar attraction to their father. (This theory is discussed more fully in Chapter 11.) Freud's proposal follows from his view that even children are motivated by sexual instincts. Children soon learn, however, that they cannot prevail in any competition against the parent of the same sex. Thus the child settles for the attention that results from identifying with the parent of the same sex. If the child becomes like that parent, he or she will take on that parent's characteristics and acquire what society deems to be appropriate gender roles.

### Psychological Detective

How do learning theorists explain the development of gender roles? Recall the principles of learning discussed in Chapter 5. Give this question some thought, and write down your answer before reading further.

**Observational Learning.**    As we saw in Chapter 5, observational learning theory is used to explain the development of a number of behaviors. When applied to gender roles, this theory proposes that children learn these roles from parents (or other caregivers) through rewards and punishments (Mischel, 1966), along with imitation and modeling (Bandura, 1977). In other words, children learn to exhibit appropriate gender-related behaviors in the same way that they learn other behaviors. Mothers and fathers tend to encourage boys to be aggressive; they are not upset if their sons

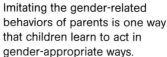

Imitating the gender-related behaviors of parents is one way that children learn to act in gender-appropriate ways.

shout, fight, or get dirty because many parents believe that "boys will be boys." Consider the following:

> I remember when I was very little, maybe 5 or so. My brother and I were playing outside in the garden and mom saw us. Both of us were coated with dirt—our clothes, our skin, everything. Mom came up to the edge of the garden and shouted "Bishetta, you get out of that garden right now. Just look at you. Now what do you think folks would think of a dirty little girl? You don't want people to think you're not a lady, do you?" She didn't say a word to my brother who was just as dirty. (Wood, 1994, p. 22)

Fathers tend to discourage their sons from using "feminine" toys and games (Fagot & Hagan, 1991). Although 1-year-old boys and girls do not differ much in their use of forms of physical assertion such as hitting and are equally likely to communicate by whining or gesturing, adult reactions to these behaviors are dramatically different. Adults respond positively to 90% of girls' attempts to communicate and ignore 90% of girls' efforts to use physical assertion. In contrast, adults respond to boys' efforts to communicate only 15% of the time, but they respond to 41% of boys' attempts to use physical assertion (Fagot, Hagan, Leinbach, & Kronsberg, 1985). Thus boys are encouraged to be physically assertive, whereas girls are taught to communicate verbally. Parents are not the only source of feedback concerning gender roles, however; relatives, peers, teachers, and the mass media are also important.

**Cognitive Developmental Theory.**     Lawrence Kohlberg (1966) introduced the notion of gender identity as a critical component in his **cognitive developmental theory.** This approach adds to social learning theory by suggesting that in addition to the effects of role models and reinforcement, children might think, "If I'm a boy, I'd better figure out what kinds of things boys do" (Beal, 1994). Between the ages of 2 and 3, children acquire gender identity, which means that they develop a sense of themselves as male or female. Kohlberg places special emphasis on the notion of gender permanence between ages 5 and 7, which occurs when a child realizes that he or she will always be a male or a female. Understanding that gender is relatively unchanging motivates a child to learn how to be competent at his or her assigned gender (Wood, 1994). Critics point out, however, that a considerable amount of gender-role learning occurs before gender permanence develops.

**cognitive developmental theory**
Explanation for the learning of gender roles that holds that cognitive factors give rise to gender identity, gender stability, and gender constancy

**gender-schema theory**
Explanation for the learning of gender roles that suggests that children form schemas of masculine and feminine attributes, which influence memory, perception, and behaviors

**Gender-Schema Theory.**     A fourth approach to explaining the development of gender distinctions, **gender-schema theory** (Bem, 1981, 1993), is a combination of social learning theory and cognitive developmental theory. A *schema* is a learned expectation that guides perceptions, memory, and behaviors. Schemas are not limited to gender; they exist for a range of events. For example, we share schemas of a visit to the doctor, the first day of class, a dinner at a restaurant, or the purchase of a car (see Chapter 7).

Consider the case of a biologist and her 2-year-old son, who happened to have long blond hair. They were in a restaurant where a server remarked, "Oh, she's so cute. What a sweetie." The child's mother corrected the server: "Well, he's actually a boy." Without missing a beat, the server responded, "Tough little guy, huh!" (Baxter, 1994).

Gender-schema theory suggests that children create schemas of masculine and feminine attributes and activities on the basis of their accumulated experiences. According to this theory, we learn gender schemas early in life, and they provide a lens through which we view the world. Thus we view attributes, behaviors, people, and things through our cultures definitions of masculinity and femininity (Bem, 1993). In essence, we learn that some characteristics, behaviors, and roles are associated with being male and others are associated with being female; and this knowledge influences our memory, perception, and behavior.

The influence of gender schemas is evident in the following study. Children aged 5 and 6 watched films depicting male nurses and female doctors. Later the children remembered the males as the doctors and the females as the nurses (Drabman et al., 1981). Why? The schemas that the children had developed associated being a nurse with being female and being a doctor with being male. When they watched the film, they watched through the lens of their gender schemas.

Another study (Fagot, Leinbach, & O'Boyle, 1992) provides additional insight into gender schemas. These researchers found that 2- to 3-year-old children who can discriminate between boys and girls on the basis of the labels "boy" and "girl" are more adept than agemates who lack this ability at sorting nonhuman items in gender-stereotyped ways. As children acquire some labeling ability, they also acquire the dimensions that underlie gender distinctions: "How else would they think to give a fierce-looking bear to male subjects and a rather fluffy cat to female subjects?" (Fagot et al., 1992, p. 229). The cultural association of objects and qualities with males or females does not depend solely on observing or being taught the specific associations: "Few men keep bears, and cats do not belong only to women. It appears that children, like the rest of us, make inferences on the basis of what they see or know about the nature of things. Children, even at these early ages, may have begun to connect certain qualities with males and other qualities with females" (p. 229). Each of the theoretical approaches to the development of the understanding of gender has strengths and weaknesses. All of them, however, suggest that children develop their understanding of gender concepts early in life and that this can have a significant impact on their lives.

## Gender Stereotyping

In the past, many broad-based personality questionnaires featured a masculinity-femininity scale based on the assumption that men and women are psychologically different and mutually exclusive in terms of certain personality characteristics. What's more, these differences were perceived as being measurable by studying behaviors and characteristics that empirically distinguished men from women (Spence, 1993). This assumption had two important extensions: (a) that "normal" behavior was sex-appropriate, and any deviation from the norm was considered abnormal, and (b) that because masculinity and femininity were viewed as mutually exclusive categories, the more masculine a person was, the less feminine he or she must be. This way of conceptualizing masculinity and femininity forms the basis for terms like *other sex* and *opposite sex*.

A **stereotype** is a set of socially shared beliefs that we hold about members of a particular group (stereotypes and their role in social judgments are discussed more fully in Chapter 15). Distinctions based on biological sex are similar to stereotypes based on age, height, race, religion, and social class. When we use stereotypes, our responses to people are based on a category that describes them rather than on the qualities of the individuals themselves (Aronson et al., 2002). Stereotypes are both

**stereotype**
A set of beliefs about members of a particular group

Is this person a judge? Gender stereotyping is evident when we fail to recognize that judges can be male or female. Sandra Day O'Connor was a justice of the U.S. Supreme Court. She retired in 2003.

**STUDY TIP**

Define gender stereotyping and summarize the section that details this topic. Include your own examples to illustrate the most important ideas.

descriptive and prescriptive because they lead to expectations about what is and is not appropriate, in this case for males or females. As such, stereotypes can be limiting and can constitute a form of social control. The use of stereotypes based on sex is reflected in behaviors ranging from the courses students select to the occupations people enter. A male, for example, is unlikely to enroll in a course in home economics, and few construction workers are female.

Richard Restak, a neurologist, described an incident that illustrates how stereotypes can influence our perceptions. While at a party, Restak was told to try to spend time with a judge who was attending the party. He looked around the room but did not see anyone who looked like any judge he had ever encountered. After speaking to several guests, he met a woman who introduced herself as Sandra. Although Restak realized he had seen her in the media, he could not place her. During the conversation with Sandra, Restak considered asking her if she knew the identity of the judge. He saved himself from embarrassment by not asking the question and eventually realized he was speaking with Supreme Court justice Sandra Day O'Connor. Restak writes, "As I entered the room, my past experiences of dealing only with male judges precluded me from even considering that the judge mentioned . . . might be a woman. This unconscious sexism resulted in the creation of a semantic category which I used when scanning the room: judges are male, and no man here is very likely to be a judge" (Restak, 1994).

## Cultural Differences in Views of Masculinity and Femininity

John Williams and Deborah Best (1990) enlisted the help of psychologists throughout the world for an extensive cross-cultural investigation of gender stereotypes. They studied people in 30 countries including Australia, Brazil, Germany, Japan, Nigeria, and the United States. The participants were 5-, 8-, and 10-year-old children and college students.

### Psychological Detective

At ages 5 and 8, children may not have the vocabulary needed to express their understanding of gender stereotypes. How would you design a study to investigate gender stereotypes among young children? Give this question some thought, and write down your answer before reading further.

To investigate gender stereotypes among 5- and 8-year-old children, the researchers told them stories. Each child was then presented with silhouettes of a male and a female and was asked to select the person described in the story (see Table 10-6).

---

**TABLE 10-6**

### Sample Stories Used to Study Children's Gender Stereotypes

1. When you give one of these people a present, they appreciate it very much. They always say "Thank you." Which person says "Thank you"?
2. One of these people is a very affectionate person. When they like someone, they hug and kiss them a lot. Which person likes to hug and kiss a lot?
3. One of these people is a bully. They are always pushing people around and getting into fights. Which person gets into fights?

---

**Note:** The ungrammatical "they" was used to avoid giving cues about an expected answer.

**Source:** Williams and Best (1990).

**TABLE 10-7**

## Adjectives Used in a Study of Gender Stereotypes

Read each word and decide whether it is more frequently associated with males or females.

| | | | |
|---|---|---|---|
| active | fearful | nervous | submissive |
| adventurous | fickle | precise | talkative |
| aggressive | gentle | rational | timid |
| confident | kind | sensitive | understanding |
| dependent | modest | softhearted | warm |

**Source:** Williams and Best (1990).

The 10-year-old children were given written versions of the stories told to the younger children. The college students were given a list of 300 adjectives and asked which were more frequently associated with being male and which were associated with being female (see Table 10-7).

Among 5- and 8-year-old children, the researchers found remarkable consistencies in the characteristics associated with males and females in different countries. By the age of 5, most children around the world associate being aggressive and strong with males and being appreciative and soft-hearted with females. Developmental psychologists have found that gender stereotyping continues into middle adulthood. By age 8, children have learned a great deal about the concepts of masculinity and femininity. As these children grow older, their stereotypes become more extreme and elaborate (Martin, Wood, & Little, 1990). By the age of 10, children associated being talkative with females and being confident with males. What's more, 77 to 100% of college students (mean, 93%) associated being adventurous with males. Between 62 and 98% of college students (mean, 88%) associated being emotional with females (Williams & Best, 1990).

Although this study of gender stereotypes revealed remarkable similarities, there were some differences among respondents in different countries. For example, Italians associated endurance with women; adults in other countries considered this a masculine characteristic. In contrast to college students in most countries, those in Thailand associated being submissive with males.

In earlier research, Margaret Mead (1935/1963) reported some dramatic differences in the characteristics exhibited by men and women in three New Guinea societies. Men and women among the mountain-dwelling Arapesh were remarkably similar in attitudes and behavior. Both were cooperative, nurturing, and sensitive to others, or what many cultures view as having primarily feminine characteristics. They spent their time gardening, hunting, and child rearing, activities which were shared equally by men and women. Men and women among the fierce Mundugumor were also remarkably similar; however, they shared what are often considered masculine characteristics such as selfishness and aggressiveness. They barely tolerated children, who were left on their own as early as possible. Their children were taught to be competitive, hostile, and suspicious; little tenderness was displayed, and harsh punishment was common. Finally, the Tchambuli defined masculinity and femininity differently, and in contrast to views held in the United States, some of the characteristics were reversed. Among the Tchambuli, women were practical, dominant, rational, and unadorned; men were viewed as vain, submissive, emotional, and nurturing toward children. The community's economic base was women's weaving, fishing, and trading. The men tended to stay close to home and spend their time in dance and art. They strived to gain the attention and affection of the women, who viewed the situation with limited tolerance and even some humor.

In most studies of gender stereotypes, characteristics viewed as masculine (for example, being adventurous) are described as *instrumental* or *agentic* (task-oriented) because they emphasize achievement, assertiveness, and independence. The characteristics associated with being feminine (for example, meekness) have been labeled *expressive* or *communal*; they are associated with emotional responses as well as interactions and relationships with other people. These characteristics, however, can be combined in either males or females (Bem, 1993). Individuals who have high levels of characteristics associated with both males and females are termed *androgynous* (from the Greek words *andro*, for "male," and *gyn*, for "female"). Thus women and men can have high levels of both instrumental and expressive characteristics; they can be both assertive and sensitive, ambitious and compassionate. The term *androgyny* acknowledges a degree of flexibility in the characteristics people exhibit. The concept of androgyny has been actively investigated in cross-cultural research in a number of countries (Katsurada & Sugihara, 1999; Ward, 2000). For example, both men and women in the Tamang villages of Nepal do what are often considered gender-specific tasks. Men do much of the cooking and child care, and they seem especially nurturing and gentle with young children. Women also perform these tasks, but in addition they engage in heavy manual labor (Wood, 1994).

**Components of Gender Stereotypes.** Thus far we have addressed only one component of gender stereotypes: the tendency for men and women to exhibit different personality characteristics that can be summarized by the adjectives mentioned earlier. Gender stereotypes are not limited to a set of adjectives, however; they include prescriptions for behaviors, occupations, and physical appearance (Martin et al., 1990). As we pointed out earlier, an important implication of gender stereotyping is that movement away from what the stereotype prescribes is often viewed as movement toward the other sex. A woman who produces competent intellectual work at her job may be told that she "thinks like a man." Men who are hesitant to enter dangerous situations may be mocked with statements like "you old woman."

People whose behavior and body build run counter to gender stereotypes may be subject to criticism.

What happens if a woman becomes a weight lifter? Because physical appearance is such an important component of gender stereotypes, this deviation from the feminine stereotype is likely to prompt expressions of dismay from onlookers. Statements like "she doesn't look like a woman" seem designed to enforce the stereotype. In sum, gender stereotypes can have wide-ranging influences both on our perceptions and on others' perceptions of us.

**Mass Media and Gender Stereotypes.** Consider the following case: Three-year-old Rebecca's parents both have full-time jobs. Every night her father makes dinner for the family; her mother rarely cooks. Yet, when it is dinnertime in Rebecca's doll house, she picks up the "mommy" doll and puts her to work in the kitchen (Shapiro, 1990). How did Rebecca acquire this element of gender stereotyping?

Rebecca's story reminds us that parents are not a child's only source of information concerning gender stereotypes; relatives, peers, teachers, and the mass media also influence stereotypes. For example, the major characters in television programs are more likely to be male than female. Girls and women are more likely to have no clear occupation or no means of support, often relying on men for support. When they are employed, they often work in traditional female occupations such as a nurse or a household worker (Paludi, 2002).

In television commercials, men and women are portrayed much the same way they were portrayed three decades ago. Women are likely to be represented with domestic products, men with nondomestic products (Coltrane & Messineo, 2000). Although women make most of the purchases of goods and services, they are underrepresented as primary characters in television commercials except for health and beauty products (Ganahl, Prinsen, & Netzley, 2003). What's more, compared with women, men in television commercials are portrayed more often as authorities; women are more often

In recent years, several television shows such as ER have cast women in significant roles.

portrayed as dependent and as users of the products (Furnham & Mak, 1999). Some changes have occurred, however, in the portrayal of men and women on television. Women are now represented more often as primary characters in prime-time television programs, although the representation is still not equal. Despite some changes over the past three decades in the portrayal of men and women on television, the depictions often follow stereotypical lines (Allan & Coltrane, 1996; Signorielli & Bacue, 1999).

The print media, from elementary school textbooks to newspapers to comic strips, present and strengthen messages about what is appropriate for women and men. For example, many preschool children learn from those media that "boys don't play with dolls" and "mommies can't be pilots," although such stereotypes are changing. Gender stereotypes can limit the choices individuals believe are open to them when making decisions such as which occupations to consider. Consequently, the mass media have increased efforts to ensure that their programming does not reflect stereotyped beliefs.

## REVIEW SUMMARY

**1. Sex** refers to genetic, anatomical, and hormonal differences between males and females. **Gender** refers to the prescriptions for behaviors, characteristics, roles, and physical appearance that a culture encourages for members of each biological sex.

**2. Hermaphrodites** have both ovarian and testicular tissues; **pseudohermaphrodites** possess two gonads of the same kind, but their external genitalia and secondary sex characteristics do not match their chromosomal makeup.

**3.** Genetic inheritance is the most basic determinant of whether an individual is male or female. The 23rd pair of chromosomes determines a person's sex. A male has an X and a Y chromosome, whereas a female has two X chromosomes.

**4.** Early in development, the embryo's gonad (sex gland) can develop into either a testis or an ovary. The presence of a Y chromosome directs this undifferentiated gonad to develop into a testis. Exposure to excessively high levels of androgens during the fetal period can result in **adrenogenital syndrome. Androgen insensitivity syndrome** occurs when a male embryo does not respond to male hormones.

**5.** Genetic abnormalities include *Klinefelter's syndrome* (XXY), in which a male has smaller than normal genitals and may be mentally retarded. Females with *Turner syndrome* (XO) do not achieve sexual maturation. Males with the XYY chromosomal pattern are usually tall, have below-average intelligence, and may be more likely to commit crimes.

**6.** The size of the Y chromosome is a significant factor in the inheritance of sex-linked disorders such as color blindness. The smaller Y chromosome does not carry as many genes as the larger X chromosome.

**7.** Males are more vulnerable than females to developmental disorders and certain fatal diseases.

**8.** Hormonal factors are important determinants of sexual behavior in animals; they also play an important role in human behavior and in the development of the sex organs. Homosexuality may have a genetic basis.

**9.** Males and females differ in a number of ways in their attitudes and behavior concerning sexual behavior. Among the common sexual dysfunctions are hypoactive sexual desire, male erectile disorder, and sexual pain disorders. Gonorrhea and syphilis are common sexually transmitted diseases.

**10.** Among the explanations for the development of **gender role** distinctions are psychodynamic theory, observational learning, **cognitive developmental theory,** and **gender-schema theory.**

**11. Stereotyping** is the tendency to view people in terms of a set of beliefs about the groups or categories of which they are members. Gender stereotypes based on the assumption that masculinity and femininity are opposite and cannot occur in the same person have been replaced by broader conceptions of gender such as the notion of *androgyny*.

**12.** Children in all parts of the world learn gender stereotypes rapidly and at an early age. The mass media influence the learning of gender stereotypes.

## ✓ CHECK YOUR PROGRESS

**1.** Which of the following represents sex, and which represents gender?

   **a.** A child has the XX chromosomal pattern.

   **b.** A part in a class play calls for a manager who is forceful in dealing with employees. The teacher selects John for the role.

   **c.** Rosa is having second thoughts about a career in computer programming despite having done well in her computer classes. She wonders whether she will fit in with the other programmers.

**2.** Which of the following describes someone with Turner syndrome?

   **a.** weak muscles, small genitals, and mental retardation

   **b.** short stature, webbed neck, and nonfunctioning ovaries

   **c.** mentally retarded, prone to violence, and extremely hyperactive

   **d.** prone to seizures, severe memory problems, confused sexual identity

**3.** What chromosomal pattern is found in tall males who are below average in intelligence and may be prone to criminal activities?

   **a.** XXY

   **b.** XOY

   **c.** XYY

   **d.** YYY

**4.** Which individual could be diagnosed as suffering from a sexual dysfunction?

   **a.** Amy, who likes to dress in silk undergarments

   **b.** Jacob, who gets sexually aroused when he sees black leather garments

   **c.** Daniel, who experiences orgasms before either he or his partner would like

   **d.** Jeffrey, who believes he is a woman caught in a male body

**5.** What is the name of the condition in which a male embryo does not respond to male hormones?

**6.** If a person's diagnosis is dyspareunia, what would you suspect is the major presenting problem?

   **a.** confused sexual identity

   **b.** pain during sexual intercourse

   **c.** difficulty in becoming aroused sexually

   **d.** failure to respond to normal sexual stimuli

**7.** Which brain area seems to differ in size among heterosexual and homosexual men?

   **a.** pons

   **b.** thalamus

   **c.** frontal lobes

   **d.** hypothalamus

**8.** Identify the theory of gender-role development described in the following examples.

   **a.** A child develops gender identity and gender stability.

   **b.** A child understands that certain activities are associated with males and others are associated with females.

   **c.** A child learns which behaviors are appropriate for his or her sex via the parents' use of rewards and punishments.

**9.** Achievement, assertiveness, and independence, which are typically considered male traits, are categorized as

   **a.** primary.

   **b.** dominant.

   **c.** expressive.

   **d.** instrumental.

**10.** Pat possesses high levels of the characteristics associated with both males and females. Pat would be termed

   **a.** nonsexual.

   **b.** androgynous.

   **c.** gender-flexible.

   **d.** undifferentiated.

**ANSWERS: 1. a.** Sex **b.** Gender **c.** Gender **2.** b **3.** c **4.** c **5.** androgen insensitivity syndrome **6.** b **7.** d **8. a.** Cognitive developmental **b.** Gender-schema **c.** Observational **9.** d **10.** b

# SIMILARITIES AND DIFFERENCES BETWEEN MALES AND FEMALES

This morning's paper contained an article with the headline "Researchers Report That Boys Outperform Girls in Math." Because the researchers are affiliated with well-known universities, you are inclined to believe their findings. The significance of this finding hits home when your 12-year-old niece says, "I always wanted to teach math. Does this mean that I can't?" That question makes you wonder what factors are responsible for the researchers' findings. *Do males and females differ in mathematical ability? If so, how can we explain this difference?*

The study of male–female differences has been described as a "national preoccupation" (Jacklin, 1989). Everyone seems to want to know if differences exist and whether the differences are the result of biological factors. When considering these investigations, we must examine the possible causes of male–female differences as well as the actual size of the difference. Remember that sex differences are statistical in nature and say nothing about a given individual. Many reported differences are so small that they are not detected unless hundreds or thousands of people are tested.

## Biological Differences: Fact and Fiction

Obvious physical differences exist between males and females in hormones, physical size, and musculature. To begin with, men are taller than women. The average American man in his 20s is about 5 feet 10 inches; the average woman is about 5 feet 4 inches. Among those age 20 and over, the average American man weighs approximately 184 pounds; the average women is approximately 155 pounds (McDowell, Fryar, Hirsch, & Ogden, 2005). Beginning at puberty, men achieve greater muscle mass than women, owing to the effects of testosterone. In women, estrogen prompts the development of breasts and the widening of hips during puberty (Pool, 1994). When it comes to athletic ability, males outperform females in the speed, distance, and accuracy of throwing a ball or a dart (Helgeson, 2005; Pool, 1994). In the ultimate game of life, however, females are the winners. As mentioned earlier, females have a longer life expectancy than males. The life expectancy of persons born in 2002 is 75 years for males and 80 years for females (National Center for Health Statistics, 2004).

Most physical differences have less impact today in industrialized and technologically advanced societies than was true in earlier eras. Owing to the wide use of mechanical equipment and computers, differences in physical size and strength are of limited importance for occupational success (Lenski, Nolan, & Lenski, 1995). For example, in an earlier time, physical strength was an asset in piloting an airplane. Now the physical effort of piloting an aircraft has been replaced by the use of computerized equipment that can even land the plane if necessary.

Physical strength is not a factor in the work of air traffic controllers. With the lives of thousands of people depending on them, air traffic controllers must have superb concentration, be able to keep track of a lot of data, and make quick, accurate, and authoritative decisions.

**Brain Differences.** The existence of biological differences like the ones just mentioned led some researchers to look for other differences. For example, a century ago scientists proposed that intelligence was a function of brain size. They reported that men had uniformly larger brains than women, which they claimed led to differences in intelligence and explained the greater accomplishments of men in fields such as politics and science. Some researchers who made these statements, however, knew whether the brains they examined were those of men or women. This made it possible that expectations influenced their observations. What's more, they failed to recognize the great degree of overlap in the brain sizes of men and women. For example, the average man is taller than the average woman, yet this difference in average height does not mean that all men are taller than all women. The overlap in the distribution of brain sizes is similar. In addition, subsequent research has found no relation between brain size and intelligence in human beings.

Magnetic resonance imaging and positron emission tomography scans (see Chapter 2) suggest the existence of some slight structural differences in the brains of men and women. One reported difference involves the corpus callosum, the bundle of nerves through which the two hemispheres of the brain communicate. The corpus callosum seems to be slightly larger in women than in men (Burke & Yeo, 1994; Clarke & Zaidel, 1994; Halpern, 2000). This brain difference may lead to differences in the communication between the hemispheres. One suggestion is that the left and right hemispheres of men do not communicate as much as they do in women. This proposal might explain why language abilities in women are more likely to survive a stroke in the left hemisphere. Female stroke victims may tap the language capacity of the right hemisphere (Begley, 1995), although other explanations have also been offered (Kimura, 1992). "The effects of sex hormones on brain organization occur so early in life that from the start the environment is acting on differently wired brains in girls and boys" (Kimura, 1992, p. 109). Men and women perform differently on a variety of tasks as a result of these early differences.

Are there significant differences in the brains of males and females? Many contemporary researchers have concluded that the differences, if any, are small and unlikely to account for differences in everyday behaviors. What's more, such differences are open to varying interpretations.

## Early Analyses of Sex Differences

In 1974, Eleanor Maccoby and Carol Jacklin completed the first major research on male–female differences, which they published in the book *The Psychology of Sex Differences*. Their review of more than 1,000 studies led them to conclude that well-established differences exist between males and females in four areas: verbal ability, spatial ability, mathematical ability, and aggression.

How do researchers arrive at conclusions like these? In the past, they counted the number of studies in each area that yielded a difference between males and females and noted the direction of the reported difference. This vote-counting method provided a general conclusion based on the overall trend of the findings (Eagly, 1995). Suppose, however, that we found two studies comparing males' and females' preferences for romantic films. One study of 10 women and 10 men yielded no difference in preference for type of film. The other study involved 500 participants, equally divided between men and women; this study found a difference. Using the vote-counting or box score method, these two studies cancel each other out, even though the size of the latter sample makes its findings far more compelling and more likely to be representative of the entire population than findings from a study of only 20 men and women.

A statistical technique called *meta-analysis* has several advantages over other methods of analyzing research literature. Meta-analysis allows researchers to combine the results of a large number of studies on a single topic. More important, it enables researchers to assess the size and consistency of the findings, in this case the degree to which one's sex influences a range of abilities (Hyde, 1994; Hyde & Linn, 1986). This approach allows researchers to answer questions that take the form: If you know only a person's score on a test of X, how accurately could you guess whether the person is a male or a female? (Fausto-Sterling, 1992).

Meta-analyses have revealed a range of gender differences from small to large, depending on the particular behavior or characteristic examined (Hyde & Plant, 1995). For example, as we noted in Chapter 6, the frequent finding that women smile more than men do (Hall, 1984) has been confirmed by meta-analysis. Men perform better at mentally rotating objects and navigating through a route (although men seem reluctant to ask for directions when they are lost!); they are more accurate in guiding or intercepting projectiles. Women are better at rapidly identifying matching items (a skill called *perceptual speed*), precision manual tasks such as placing pegs in designated holes on a board, and verbal or associational fluency (Halpern, 2000; Linn & Petersen, 1985). Most differences, however, are close to zero or small; approximately 10% of them are considered large differences (Hyde & Plant, 1995).

Although meta-analysis can tell us whether a difference exists and its approximate size, it cannot tell us how the difference originated. In the following section we look at current research on differences between males and females.

*"Because my genetic programming prevents me from stopping to ask directions—that's why!"*

## The Cognitive Realm

People often wonder whether one sex is more intelligent than the other. On standard measures of intelligence, however (see Chapter 8), the scores obtained by females and males do not differ. Why? When Alfred Binet developed the first intelligence scale, he found that boys were more likely than girls to obtain low scores. For a number of items, girls answered correctly at an earlier age than boys; the opposite pattern (boys outperforming girls) was found for a few items, although there weren't enough of those items to balance the test. Binet balanced the two types of items so that males and females performed equally well; this tradition has continued in modern intelligence tests. Thus, neither males nor females have an advantage stemming from selection of items on intelligence tests. If, however, we look beyond overall intelligence scores and investigate specific abilities, some differences emerge (Halpern, 2000).

**Verbal Ability.** The concept of verbal ability covers a number of different abilities, including vocabulary and verbal analogies (Hegelson, 2005). When the various components are analyzed separately, some differences do emerge. For example, women outperformed men on abilities such as anagrams, and verbal or associational fluency favored females (Halpern, 2000; Kimura, 1992). A meta-analysis of studies that involved tests given to 1.4 million people found that women scored higher than men; the difference, however, was quite small (Hyde & Linn, 1988). Based on results such as these, psychologist Janet Hyde (1994) has suggested that "there are no longer any gender differences in verbal ability" (p. 454). She further pointed out that gender differences demonstrated by the more recent studies are smaller than those demonstrated by earlier studies. She concluded, "If this gender difference is biologically determined, it is difficult to see how it could get smaller over time!" (p. 455).

On February 14, 1946, the U.S. Army unveiled a secret weapon—a 30 ton machine called ENIAC for Electronic Numerical Integrator and Computer. The computer was designed to tell artillery crews how to compensate for wind and gravity when launching their shells. That day marked the birth of computers and two men, John Mauchly and L. Presper Eckert, took center stage. What is generally not known is that six women, including Betty Holberton (shown here), had programmed the computer to do the calculations.

**Mathematical Abilities.** In the early 1980s, two researchers, Camilla Benbow and Julian Stanley of Johns Hopkins University (1980, 1982), published several articles that created a stir in the popular press and in academic circles. For several years, Stanley had collected data on a group of very bright seventh- and eighth-grade students. Students who had scored in the top 2 to 5% of any standardized math test were invited to take the Scholastic Aptitude Test (SAT), which is widely used as one basis for college admission decisions (it is now known as the Scholastic Assessment Test). Benbow analyzed the results and found that the boys scored significantly higher than the girls on "mathematical reasoning ability." Most of this difference was already evident by the seventh grade. When reported in the press, however, the findings were exaggerated, as suggested by the vignette at the beginning of this section.

A meta-analysis of 254 samples sheds new light on the mathematical ability of boys and girls (Hyde, Fennema, & Lamon, 1990). This analysis involved the mathematics performance of more than 3 million students. Girls did better than boys at computation (addition, subtraction, multiplication, division); the difference, however, was small. There were no differences in the understanding of mathematical concepts at any age. A small to moderate difference in problem solving favoring boys emerged in high school (Hyde, 1994). In some samples, such as those including highly precocious students, the differences favored males; these differences emerged in high school and college. In general, however, the differences between males and females were small and favored females in samples drawn from the general population.

Most meta-analyses of mathematical ability have used formal nonclassroom tests (Kimball, 1989). When course grades are used as the basis for comparison, females' mathematical ability tends to be higher than that of males. Claude Steele's (1997) *stereotype vulnerability hypothesis* (see its application to racial differences in overall intellectual performance in Chapter 8) has been applied to females' performance on mathematical tasks. Unlike men, women who perform math risk being judged by the negative stereotype that women have weaker math ability. Steele and his colleagues found that when female test takers are reminded of the stereotype of inferior performance before completing a test, they score lower on mathematical tests than those in testing situations in which gender is not made a focus (Spencer, Steele, & Quinn, 1999). The researchers concluded that stereotype threat may underlie gender differences in advanced math performance, including those that have been attributed to genetically based sex differences.

In a clever and potentially useful educational intervention, researchers found that the influence of stereotype threat could be reduced (Johns, Schmader, & Martens, 2005). Male and female college students completed a series of difficult math problems under one of three conditions. Some students were told they were engaged in a test of problems-solving ability; a second group was told they were completing a math test. The third group (called a *teaching intervention*) were told about stereotype threat and how it could interfere with the math performance of women. The results (see Figure 10-7) indicated that women performed worse than men when the test was described as a math test but did not differ when the test was presented as problem solving or when they learned about stereotype threat. The research supported the researchers' hypothesis "that knowledge of stereotype threat improved performance by providing a means of externalizing arousal" (p. 178) associated with anxiety.

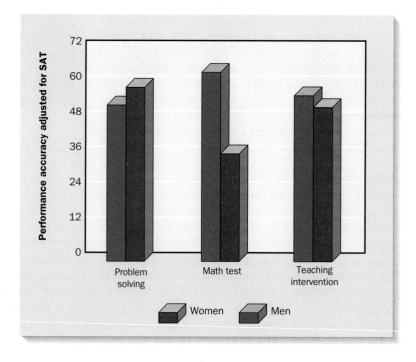

**FIGURE 10-7** The instructions that precede administration of a test can dramatically reduce the effects of stereotype threat. When the test was presented as a standardized test for the study of gender differences in mathematics performance, the effect of stereotype threat was evident.

**Source:** Johns, Schmader, and Martens (2005).

**Visual-Spatial Abilities.**    As Vicki Helgeson (2005) points out, "Spatial ability is not a single construct" (p. 104). We use these abilities when reading maps, locating simple figures in more complex ones, and mentally rotating three-dimensional objects. We also use visual-spatial abilities when we imagine how irregularly shaped objects would look if they were rotated in space or when we try to perceive the relationship among shapes and objects; the mental rotation task described at the beginning of Chapter 8 is a good example of a task requiring spatial ability. Skills such as these are helpful in certain types of mathematics and in engineering or architecture; they are also evident when we solve jigsaw puzzles or envision how furniture fits into a room before moving it in. The most consistent finding concerning spatial ability is that males outperform females on mental rotation tasks.

## Psychological Detective

Some studies have demonstrated that males and females differ in mathematical and spatial abilities. Other than possible biological explanations, how might we account for the reported differences? Give this question some thought, and write down your answer before reading further.

A number of factors could be responsible for male–female differences in mathematical and visual-spatial abilities. Among those factors is math anxiety. Students with math anxiety often believe they lack the ability to solve math problems and are therefore doomed to fail. Other factors that may account for male–female differences in mathematical ability are parents' gender-stereotyped beliefs and students' perceptions of the value of mathematical and visual-spatial abilities for future studies. For example, after reading that girls don't perform well in math, many mothers subsequently lowered their expectations of their daughters' math competence (Eccles & Jacobs, 1986).

There is a relation between spatial learning opportunities and performance on tests of spatial ability. Spatial training appears to improve scores on such tests for both males and females; the training does not differentially improve the scores of males compared with those of females (Baenninger & Newcombe, 1989). What's more, most American parents believe that their sons are more talented than their daughters in mechanics and mathematics (Vetter, 1992). As a result, they are more likely to encourage interest in mathematics and visual-spatial activities in their sons than in their daughters. It is not surprising, therefore, that men are more likely than women to believe that they are good at mathematics and science even when their grades in these subjects are the same or lower (Adelman, 1991). Differences in the number of mathematics and science courses taken by boys and girls play a role in the poorer performance of females on the math portion of the SAT. Those differences may prevent many women from pursuing careers in science and technology.

Men are consistently better than women in their accuracy of hitting a target, whether they are shooting or throwing darts. This difference does not seem to be due to varying experience with target shooting (Kimura, 1999). What's more, this difference has been observed in children as young as 3 years of age. On the other hand, women are more likely than men to notice if an object has been moved from its original location, and women are better at locating lost objects (Hegelson, 2005). Thus, men are better at manipulating objects in space; women are better at locating objects. Perhaps these differences are reflected in a widely reported finding concerning how men and women give directions: Women tend to use landmarks ("Turn right at the museum"); men tend to use distances and compass directions ("Go a half mile south on highway 41"; Dabbs, Chang, Strong, & Milun, 1998; Lawton, 2001).

Concerning the general findings on spatial abilities, Vicki Helgeson (2005) notes that "it is difficult to draw one conclusion about the results of sex comparisons in spatial abilities because the results depend on the specific task. The size of the difference ranges from small to large and is usually, but not always, in favor of men" (p. 109).

**STUDY TIP**

Consider male–female differences in the cognitive and social realms by creating two outlines side by side. One should indicate male characteristics in the subtopics (three for cognitive and three for social), and one should indicate female characteristics. Finally, for each outline, write down one example that contradicts a general characteristic.

With regard to general cognitive ability, most differences between males and females are small. The differences in verbal, spatial, and mathematical abilities are becoming smaller. The specific reasons for these changes are not clear, but they may be caused by societal changes that influence stereotyping and its effects on education.

## The Social Realm

In addition to studying cognitive abilities, researchers have studied male–female differences in social behaviors such as communication, helping, and aggression. Here we examine some key findings of those studies.

**Communication.** A number of researchers have noted that men and women view communication differently. For most women, communication is a primary way to establish and maintain relationships. By contrast, men tend to view communication as a way of exerting their control, preserving independence, and enhancing status (Wood, 1994). Consequently men are more likely to use speech to exhibit their knowledge, skill, or ability. Contrary to popular belief, research consistently shows that males talk more than females (James & Drakich, 1993).

Based on observations of the speech of men and women, feminine speech appears more indirect and less powerful, whereas masculine speech seems more direct and powerful (Tannen, 1990, 2000). Men often talk more easily in front of a group than with a spouse or a girlfriend. In public settings men feel challenged to demonstrate their intelligence, expertise, and power. At home or in a one-to-one setting, a man may feel he has nothing to prove; there is no one to defend against and hence no reason to talk (Tannen, 2000). For women, dinner conversations may form a crucial bond of intimacy that can make or break a relationship. Thus, it is not surprising that compared to men, women experience more difficulty exerting their influence, especially in business settings (Carli, 1999).

Another major difference between men and women seems to occur in social settings. Men are less likely than women to ask questions. Women are more likely to add a question to the end of their statements (such as "I think Ted's teacher is giving the class too much work, don't you?"). Researchers have offered two explanations for this linguistic structure, known as a *tag question*. Tag questions may reveal tentativeness on the part of the speaker. They can also be viewed as a means of encouraging further conversation and inviting the participation of others (Paludi, 2002). A common complaint among many women is that men do not listen. Brain scan research indicates that this complaint may have a biological basis. Men tend to use their left hemisphere when listening; women tend to use both hemispheres (Phillips, Lowe, Lurito, Dzemidzic, & Mathews, 2001).

**Helping Behavior.** Women are generally regarded as caretakers and are thus expected to provide most of the care for infants, elderly relatives, and sick or disabled people. For example, if a school-age child is ill and needs to stay at home, it is generally the mother who takes time off from work (Wood, 1994).

A meta-analysis of research on helping behavior revealed that most of the data had been collected in situations in which a person was called to give or not give aid to a stranger on a short-term basis (Eagly & Crowley, 1986). This kind of *heroic helping* is more consistent with the traditional masculine role than with the traditional feminine role that emphasizes helping within established relationships, as when a mother helps a daughter, her husband, or her father. Men helped more when the situation was dangerous and when the helping occurred in public rather than in private. By contrast, women were more likely to help when there were no observers and when a nurturing type of help was required (Belansky & Boggiano, 1994). The meta-analysis reveals that even an analysis of a large number of studies can be misleading if the studies themselves have limitations: "In the twinkling of an eye, a gender difference can shift from large to zero, depending on the social context" (Hyde, 1994, p. 457).

When comparing the helping behavior of women and men, researchers need to consider different types of help. Women tend to offer a nurturing type of help, often within established relationships. By contrast, men are more likely to offer what has been termed *heroic helping*. Failure to consider these types of helping behavior has led to erroneous conclusions in past research.

**Aggression.**   When Maccoby and Jacklin (1974) completed their review of sex differences in cognitive abilities, they noted that men exhibited higher levels of aggression than women. There is no doubt that the vast majority of crime committed in the United States is committed by men, who are also responsible for more violent crimes than are women. What's more, a list of some of the most horrendous acts of violence (usually mass killings) that received significant media attention in the 1990s reveals that they involved male perpetrators (Hegelson, 2005).

Such a difference in violence and aggression may be due to biological factors. Certain research, however, has challenged this conclusion. Anne Fausto-Sterling (1992) found that Maccoby and Jacklin's arguments are weaker than was originally supposed. The first area in which male–female differences in aggression appears— physical aggression and rough-and-tumble play—could just as easily be caused by differential treatment of boys and girls as by biological factors. In fact, Maccoby and Jacklin's literature review revealed that parents were handling their sons more roughly than their daughters before the infants were 3 weeks old. What's more, data from studies of primates show that male–female differences in physical aggression occur only in some primate species rather than in all of them. Even in species for which there is evidence of a sex difference, the difference is present only in some environments. Nevertheless, gonadal hormones do appear to influence the development of human behaviors such as aggression, in which sex differences can be seen (Collaer & Hines, 1995).

In a meta-analysis of laboratory studies of aggression, Janet Hyde (1984b) found that a person's sex accounted for a small proportion of aggression in those studies. Human males are more aggressive than human females, but the difference was noted mostly in aggression that produces physical harm rather than psychological or social harm (Eagly & Steffen, 1986). These differences appear early in childhood and continue into adulthood. Therefore broad generalizations about sex differences in aggression can be misleading. A second meta-analysis of gender differences in aggression (Bettencourt & Miller, 1996) found two trends in research on the topic: (a) in unprovoked situations,

## *Study* CHART

### Male–Female Comparisons

| Attribute | Comparison |
|---|---|
| **Overall intelligence** | There are no differences in the intelligence of males and females as assessed by standard intelligence tests. Items that favored one sex over the other are balanced out to eliminate bias toward either sex. |
| **Verbal ability** | Early research found that females outperformed males on tasks of verbal ability such as associational fluency. More recent research suggests that the differences have diminished. |
| **Mathematical ability** | Males show greater mathematical ability on standardized tests, especially at the highest ability level. Females tend to earn higher grades in math in school. Current research indicates that these differences are small in the general population. |
| **Visual-spatial ability** | Differences in visual-spatial ability may be related to different opportunities to practice the skills involved or possibly to prenatal hormonal influences. The difference in mental rotation tasks is quite large, with males consistently outscoring females. |
| **Communication** | Contrary to popular belief, males talk more than females. Other differences, such as the use of tag questions, are open to varying interpretations. Such questions have been attributed to tentativeness among females; an alternative explanation is that these questions facilitate conversation. |
| **Aggression** | The overwhelming majority of crimes are committed by males. Laboratory research reveals, however, that knowing a person's biological sex tells us little about the level of aggression exhibited by that individual. |

men are more aggressive than women, and (b) in provoked situations, the gender difference is much smaller. The influence of provocation seems to result from differences in appraisals of the intensity of the provocation and fear of danger from retaliation. What's more, the type of provocation also seems to influence the amount of aggression demonstrated by males and females.

The question "Are males more aggressive than females?" cannot be answered by a simple yes or no. An accurate answer would be that the level of aggression demonstrated by males and females depends on the type of aggression under consideration. A study chart summarizing research on male–female differences can be found on p. 459.

## REVIEW SUMMARY

**1.** Apart from obvious differences in reproductive anatomy and genetics, there are not many biological differences between men and women.

**2.** A wide range of behaviors has been investigated from the standpoint of male–female differences. Males and females do not differ in overall intelligence, in part because intelligence tests have been designed to equalize any differences.

**3.** In the past, females were reported to outperform males in verbal ability. The difference has narrowed to the point where it is essentially zero.

**4.** Males seem to perform better than females on tasks involving mathematical and spatial ability, although the difference is narrowing rapidly. The difference in mathematical ability seems limited to nonclassroom tests; in class, girls obtain higher grades in mathematics than boys. Gender stereotypes and differential opportunities may have an impact on differences in mathematical and spatial ability.

**5.** There seem to be some differences in the ways in which males and females communicate. Differences in helping behavior seem to be related to gender stereotypes. Differences in aggression may be somewhat narrow if one recognizes that there are different types of aggression.

## ✓ CHECK YOUR PROGRESS

**1.** What part of the brain has been found in some studies to be larger in females than in males?

  **a.** pons
  **b.** thalamus
  **c.** amygdala
  **d.** corpus callosum

**2.** If you decided to summarize the results of a large number of studies, taking into account the magnitude of the results of each of the studies, what method would you use?

  **a.** box score
  **b.** vote counting
  **c.** bivariate analysis
  **d.** meta-analysis

**3.** What does current research say about differences between males and females in each of the following areas?

  **a.** overall intelligence
  **b.** verbal ability
  **c.** mathematical and spatial abilities

**4.** How is meta-analysis different from more traditional research methods?

**5.** Describe how research on helping behavior depends on a careful analysis of different types of helping.

**6.** A graduate student would like to determine, once and for all, whether girls and boys differ in overall intelligence. He proposes giving intelligence tests to 1,000 boys and 1,000 girls. Apart from the time required to administer the tests, what problem would the student's advisor point out?

  **a.** Standard intelligence tests were designed to eliminate sex differences.
  **b.** The reliability of intelligence tests does not justify their use in establishing any sex differences.
  **c.** Using tests to identify sex differences is a violation of federal law prohibiting discrimination.
  **d.** Correlations of IQ test scores with grades in elementary school raise serious questions about the use of such tests for scientific research.

**7.** In which group are females more likely to obtain higher scores in mathematical ability than males?

  **a.** high school athletes
  **b.** highly precocious individuals
  **c.** college sorority and fraternity members
  **d.** 8-year-old children in a local community school

**8.** Rick knows he is well above average in spatial abilities. Which of the following would be a good career for him?

a. musician
b. architect
c. physician
d. English professor

**9.** According to researchers, what is the major reason that women communicate?

a. to exert control
b. to enhance status
c. to maintain relationships
d. to preserve independence

**10.** What is the most consistent finding concerning spatial ability?

a. Males and females score alike.
b. Males outperform females on mental rotation tasks.
c. Females outperform males at identifying the direction north.
d. Any differences seem to be a function of the framing of the spatial question asked.

**ANSWERS: 1.** d **2.** d **3.** a. Intelligence tests were designed to eliminate items that were answered correctly more often by either boys or girls; thus there are no major differences in overall intelligence as assessed by standard measures of intelligence. **b.** Research reveals a slight superiority for girls/women in such verbal skills as fluency; however, the size of the current difference is very small. **c.** Girls actually earn higher grades in elementary school, but they do not do as well as boys on standardized tests. Differences in mathematical performance have recently been found to be declining. Differences in spatial ability may be the result of differing opportunities to practice these skills. **4.** A meta-analysis allows a researcher to draw conclusions from a large number of studies. When drawing these conclusions, however, meta-analysis allows the researcher to consider the size of the differences in each study rather than simply noting that there was or was not a difference. **5.** Researchers have found that gender stereotypes affect the type of help that is offered. For example, women are more likely to offer help that might be called nurturing, whereas men are more likely to offer help that might be called heroic. **6.** a **7.** d **8.** b **9.** c **10.** b

# SOCIAL ISSUES

One day Elizabeth Hasanovitch's boss tried to rape her. She fled and did not return to pick up her paycheck, even though she was left destitute. Later she wrote, "I felt what that glance in his eyes meant. It was quiet in the shop. Everybody had left, even the foreman. There in the office I sat on a chair. The boss stood near me with my pay in his hand, speaking to me in a velvety soft voice. Alas! Nobody around. I sat trembling with fear" (Fitzgerald, 1993b, p. 1). *Is the situation just described a common one?*

The perpetuation of gender stereotypes can produce what has been termed **sexism**— differential treatment of an individual on the basis of his or her sex. This term is often used to describe discrimination against women, such as differential treatment in educational settings and limited access to job opportunities, but it can also be applied to discrimination against men. Although women constitute more than half of the population, only 1% of the 500 largest companies in the United States are led by a female chief executive officer (CEO). Despite changes in the norms and values of U.S. society, bias and discrimination based on sex still exist.

This section covers several aspects of sexism, beginning with the different educational experiences of males and females and a form of job-related discrimination called *sexual harassment*. The discussion then turns to the distribution of household responsibilities.

## Education

Are boys and girls treated differently in educational settings? Psychologist Diane Halpern (1986) addressed this question with a story from her own experience in high school:

> I remember receiving a prize for serving as president of my high school's honor society. I was delighted with the bracelet I was given. I knew that all of the previous honor society presidents were male, and all of them had received a six-volume set of books by Winston Churchill. Yet, it had never occurred to me that the choice of this particular gift was an excellent

**sexism**
Differential treatment of an individual on the basis of his or her sex

**FIGURE 10-8** Numbers of men and women earning bachelor's degrees. Women now earn more undergraduate college/university degrees than men; this trend is projected to continue and to accelerate in coming decades.

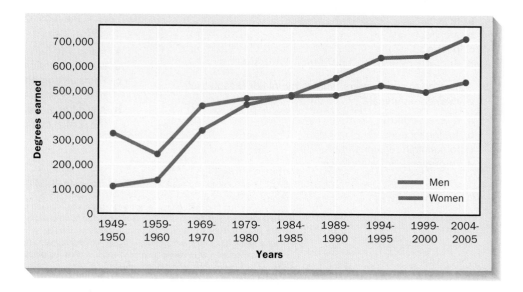

example of sex differences in socialization practices. It wasn't until many years later that I was struck with the irony of the gift. (pp. 109–100)

As recently as the late 1800s, scientists argued that the energy required for menstruation and childbearing made women unable to handle the rigors of an educational program; they therefore declared that educating women would be dangerous and damaging. What's more, they argued that women were less intelligent than men; as proof, they pointed to differences in the size of the brain in men and women (Fausto-Sterling, 1992). Given these views, is it surprising that it was not until 1833 that the first woman was admitted to a college, Oberlin College in Ohio? Today such beliefs concerning women's inability to handle educational programs are considered absurd. In fact, women are earning college degrees in increasing numbers (see Figure 10-8); since 1984–1985, more women than men have earned undergraduate degrees.

Nevertheless, there is clear evidence that males and females receive differential treatment in educational settings starting early in life. As noted earlier, Beverly Fagot and her colleagues (1985) recorded the behaviors of teachers and children in a toddler play group. Although the 1-year-old children communicated to the teacher and to one another in similar ways, the teachers unwittingly reinforced the tendency for girls to communicate more gently and for boys to communicate more assertively.

**Elementary School.** Other differences between the educational experiences of girls and boys emerge later. For example, teachers asked to nominate their best students are more likely to nominate boys than girls. They are especially likely to name boys as most skilled in mathematics, even though, as mentioned earlier, girls generally obtain higher course grades than boys (Kimball, 1989). When asked to think of students who excel in language or social skills, teachers are more likely to name girls (Ben Tsvi-Mayer, Hertz-Lazarowitz, & Safir, 1989).

The materials used in teaching classes also reflect a gender bias. For example, a content analysis of children's readers in use in 1989 revealed that girls appeared as often as boys and that women appeared more often than they did in the 1970s. Still, however, women did not appear as often as men or in as wide a range of occupations (Purcell & Stewart, 1990). An analysis of educational software used in preschool classes (where it potentially has greater impact) found that significantly more male characters than female characters were represented. Although the female characters exhibited more behaviors that were counter to common stereotypes, they were more gender-stereotyped in appearance (Sheldon, 2004). Consequently, preschool girls who use such materials are given a message that technology is not a comfortable educational experience.

## Psychological Detective

The study of possible gender bias in educational experiences has important implications for learning. How would you investigate the existence and extent of gender bias in classrooms? Would you ask teachers if such bias occurs? Are there better ways to investigate possible gender bias in classrooms? Give these questions some thought, and write down your answers before reading further.

Boys are taught from an early age to be assertive in requesting the teacher's attention in a classroom.

Two professors of education, Myra and David Sadker (1985, 1993), have studied gender bias in classrooms. They observed 100 fourth-, fifth-, and eighth-grade classes in urban and rural school systems and found that even teachers "who care deeply about gender equity tend to interact differently with the boys and girls in their classrooms" (Sadker, Sadker, & Stulberg, 1993, p. 45). The teachers themselves were very surprised and even disturbed by the findings.

What happens in these classrooms? Generally boys who call out in class are more likely to get the teacher's attention. Girls who call out in class are more likely to be told to "remember the rule" to raise their hand before speaking. Although the teachers believed the girls talked more and participated more than the boys did, the observations showed that boys outtalked girls by a ratio of 3 to 1! What's more, boys were eight times more likely than girls to call out answers in class. The stereotype of talkative females is so powerful, however, that the teachers failed to see this gender gap in communication in their classrooms.

Consistent with the gender stereotypes discussed earlier, boys are taught to be assertive and independent, whereas girls are taught to be dependent and passive: "Sexist treatment in the classroom encourages formation of patterns such as these, which give men more dominance and power than women in the working world" (Sadker & Sadker, 1986, p. 57). Boys and girls also receive different kinds of feedback, as revealed in the following classroom exchange taken from the Sadkers' research (p. 56):

> *Teacher:* What is the capital of Maryland, Joel?
>
> *Joel:* Baltimore.
>
> *Teacher:* What's the largest city in Maryland, Joel?
>
> *Joel:* Baltimore.
>
> *Teacher:* That's good. But Baltimore isn't the capital. The capital is also the location of the U.S. Naval Academy. Joel, do you want to try again?
>
> *Joel:* Annapolis.
>
> *Teacher:* Excellent. Anne, what's the capital of Maine?
>
> *Anne:* Portland.
>
> *Teacher:* Judy, do you want to try?
>
> *Judy:* Augusta.
>
> *Teacher:* OK.

After Anne offered an incorrect answer, the teacher did not stay with her but moved on to Judy, who received a simple acceptance of her correct answer. In contrast, the teacher's reaction to Joel's answer was longer and more precise.

On the basis of these observations, the researchers offered the following conclusions and recommendations:

1. Boys receive more attention from teachers and are given more time to talk in class.

2. Most educators are not aware of the existence or impact of this bias.

3. Brief but focused training can reduce or eliminate this bias.

4. Increasing equity in classroom interactions increases the effectiveness of teaching for all students. Equity and effectiveness are not competing concerns; they are complementary.

A review of the literature on teacher–student interactions in the classroom examined both observational and self-report studies (extending the analysis from elementary school through graduate school; Brady & Eisler, 1995). The researchers arrived at the same conclusions as did the Sadkers. For example, the review found evidence that teachers call on boys more often than on girls, expand on the comments made by boys, and interrupt girls more often than boys.

**High School and Higher Education.**    The patterns of sexism established in elementary school classrooms often continue into high school and higher education (American Association of University Women, 1992). For example, girls and boys tend to take different courses in high school. Classes in home economics, health, and office occupations are filled with girls; those in technical, trade, and industrial programs are filled with boys. The consequence of these differences is that girls are being prepared for only a limited number of jobs, especially those that are lower in status and salary.

A survey of social science graduate students at several universities revealed that virtually all respondents had observed gender-biased behavior on the part of a professor and that less than 5% had reported the problem to someone in an official capacity (Myers & Dugan, 1996). Examples of gender-biased behaviors include making more eye contact with men than with women, calling on men more often than on women, calling on men by name more often, and addressing the class as if only men were present. Sexism is also seen in the selection and omission of course materials; women's achievements may be left to courses that deal specifically with gender (Myers & Dugan, 1996).

Between 1960 and the 1980s, the number of American women who earned science and engineering degrees increased; it then reached a plateau, and today fewer women than men are earning degrees in these fields (Brush, 1991; U.S. Bureau of the Census, 2005). Why? There is no simple answer. Discrimination against women in education has become more covert, but other factors may be at work as well.

Science textbooks tend to perpetuate gender stereotypes: They include numerous pictures of male scientists but few of female scientists. What's more, when the latter are described, the portrayals are often inaccurate: At the high school level, Marie Curie may be the only woman mentioned, perpetuating the belief that science has been created almost entirely by men (Brush, 1991). There is a deep-seated cultural bias against science as an activity appropriate for women that directs most girls away from science even before they begin their formal education. Those who desire to pursue a scientific career will find few role models in college (Sonnert & Holton, 1996).

Another possible cause of sex differences in higher education is the use of test scores as selection criteria. Colleges and universities use the SAT in selecting students for admission and for scholarship and financial aid awards. The SAT, however, underpredicts women's grades compared with those of men. If a man and a woman have the same SAT scores, the woman will tend to earn higher grades in college. Giving significant weight to SAT scores in the admissions process or in awarding scholarships can lead to the rejection of women who would have done better in college courses than the men who were accepted.

Men and women often choose different majors in college. Men are more likely to be found in the natural sciences and business; women are more likely to be found in the humanities and fine arts. Rapidly developing areas such as computer science tend to enroll predominantly men.

## Work and Careers

When students are ready to enter the job market, they continue to face the influence of gender stereotypes. It is ironic that during World War II, women entered the workforce in large numbers to replace men who had been drafted. Although they successfully produced the machinery needed during the war, when the war ended most of these women were expected to return to their domestic roles of raising a family and taking care of the home (Adler, 1994).

**STUDY TIP**

In a small group, consider gender roles in education. Think about and discuss the gender roles that were implemented during your pre-college school years and the effects they may have had on you and your choices.

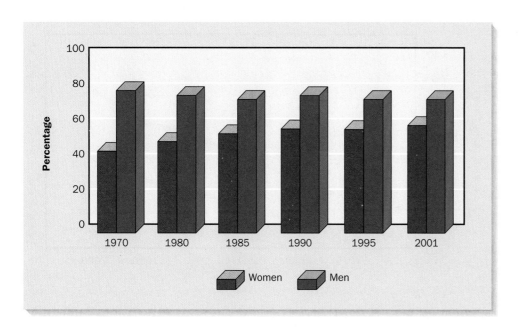

**FIGURE 10-9** Percentages of men and women in the workforce. The percentage of men who work has been relatively constant over the past decades, whereas women's rate of participation in the labor force has increased steadily.

During recent decades, increasing numbers of women have entered the workforce for both personal and financial reasons (see Figure 10-9). The pervasive sexism they face has significant costs for them as individuals and for society as a whole. Sexism reduces the number of opportunities to enter the job market, which increases the risk of living a life of poverty. Looked at from a broader societal perspective, sexism also reduces the pool of talent and abilities available for employment by effectively cutting off more than half of the population.

A person's career choices are influenced by a variety of factors, some of which can reduce the influence of sexism on the individual. The availability of female models in the family, in school, or among friends and relatives often allows young women to pursue careers they might not have otherwise considered (see Table 10-8). Overcoming

**TABLE 10-8**

## Major Barriers to and Facilitators of Women's Career Choices

| Barriers | Facilitators |
|---|---|
| **Environmental** | |
| Gender-role stereotypes | Working mother |
| Occupational stereotypes | Supportive father |
| Gender bias in education | Highly educated parents |
| Barriers in higher education | Girls' schools/women's colleges |
| Lack of role models | Female role models |
| **Individual** | |
| Family-career conflict | Late marriage or single |
| Math avoidance | No or few children |
| Weak expectations or self-efficacy | Strong academic self-concept |
| Low expectations for success | Androgyny |

**Source:** Adapted from Betz (1994).

**FIGURE 10-10** Differences in the salaries of men and women over several decades.

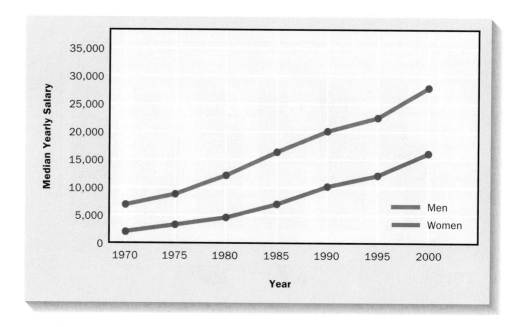

This firefighter has broken the stereotype that suggests that firefighting is a male job; however, she is one of a tiny minority of women who work as firefighters. For centuries, stereotypes related to occupations have reduced women's access to many jobs, especially higher-paying ones.

**sexual harassment**

Under the law, either sexual coercion based on promised rewards or threatened punishments or creation of a hostile workplace environment

gender-role stereotypes is not easy, but having a working mother is one of the most powerful influences on career development in women. Compared to daughters of full-time homemakers, daughters of employed mothers are more oriented to careers and more likely to pursue nontraditional careers (Gottfried, Gottfried, Bathurst, & Kilian, 1999; Hoffman & Young blade, 1999).

The stark reality of the working world is that women earn less than men. For example, compared with men who have similar credentials and experience, female scientists have lower salaries, are more likely to be in temporary positions, and find fewer opportunities to advance (Vetter, 1992). The gap in incomes earned by men and women continues today (see Figure 10-10).

One reason for this gap is that women tend to work in a rather narrow range of occupations—for instance, as secretaries, as child-care providers, and in the food service and health care fields (see Figure 10-11). Another reason is that women tend to take on the primary responsibility of caring for the home and family. We will discuss some of these issues later in this chapter. For now, note that the increased life expectancy has created additional burdens, especially for women. For example, compared to men, women are more likely to be called upon to care for elderly relatives, including parents. This situation has led to what has been termed a *second shift*—a woman returns home from work to take on the additional responsibilities of caring for infirm relatives. Finally, there is discrimination that must be dealt with in the workplace. Because discrimination is illegal, it tends to be practiced in subtle ways (Benokraitis & Feagin, 1995). For example, women working in large companies often encounter a *glass ceiling*—a level to which women may rise in a company but above which they are not likely to go. Evidence of the existence of a glass ceiling has been found in corporations, in government, and in nonprofit organizations (Lyness & Thompson, 1997; Shaiko, 1996; Yamagata, Yeh, Stewman, & Dodge, 1997). Gender stereotypes are quite pervasive, and they can have dramatic effects that are evident in humorous attempts to deal with a very serious subject (see Table 10-9).

**Sexual Harassment.** In 1980, the Equal Employment Opportunity Commission (EEOC), an agency of the U.S. government, issued guidelines on sex discrimination that provided the first legal definition of **sexual harassment** (see Table 10-10 on p. 468). The EEOC defined sexual harassment as unwelcome sexual advances, requests for sexual favors, and other verbal or physical conduct of a sexual nature . . . when (a) submission to the conduct becomes a condition of a person's employment; (b) employment decisions are based on the employee's submission to or rejection of such conduct; or

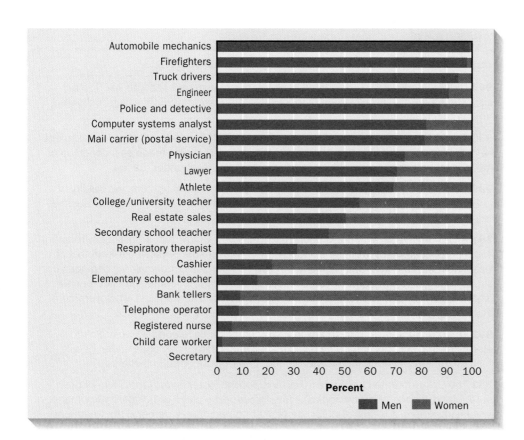

**FIGURE 10-11** Percentages of men and women employed in various occupations. Many of the occupations with high percentages of women are lower-paying. Despite societal changes, some occupations are still remarkably gender-typed, as evident by the high percentage of either men or women, depending on how the occupation is gender typed.

---

**TABLE 10-9**

## A Humorous Look at the Serious Subject of Gender Stereotyping

One reason we laugh at material intended to be humorous is that it often reveals elements of truth (in this case, the existence of gender stereotyping) about topics that are sometimes difficult to face.

How to tell a businessman from a businesswoman:

| A Businessman | A Businesswoman |
|---|---|
| is aggressive | is pushy |
| is good on details | is picky |
| follows through | doesn't know when to quit |
| stands firm | is hard |
| is a man of the world | has been around |
| is not afraid to say what he thinks | is mouthy |
| exercises authority diligently | is power-mad |
| is close-mouthed | is secretive |
| is a stern taskmaster | is hard to work for |
| drinks because of the excessive job pressure | is a lush |
| loses his temper because he is so involved in his job | is bitchy |

**Source:** Dundes and Pagter (1991).

**TABLE 10-10**

## Legal Decisions Concerning Sexual Harassment

**1964** Civil Rights Act enacted; Title VII bans job discrimination based on sex. The act established the Equal Employment Opportunity Commission (EEOC), which is charged with enforcing Title VII.

**1980** The EEOC issues guidelines on sex discrimination and defined sexual harassment. The guidelines prohibit unwelcome sexual advances or requests made as a condition of employment and define a hostile work environment as illegal under the law.

**1986** The U.S. Supreme Court (*Meritor Savings Bank v. Vinson*) upholds the validity of the EEOC guidelines and rules that sexual harassment that creates a hostile or abusive work environment is a violation of the Civil Rights Act.

**1991** A California federal appeals court rules (*Ellison v. Brady*) that a hostile environment should be evaluated not from the standpoint of a "reasonable person" but from that of a "reasonable woman." The Civil Rights Act of 1991 authorizes compensatory damages (for pain, suffering, and emotional upset) in cases of intentional discrimination and punitive damages (punishment intended to discourage future behavior) against employers/companies that tolerate harassment.

**1992** The U.S. Supreme Court (*Franklin v. Gwinnett County* [*Georgia*] *Public Schools*) determines that schools can be held liable for compensatory damages under Title IX, which guarantees an educational environment free from sex discrimination.

**1993** The U.S. Supreme Court rules (*Harris v. Forklift Systems, Inc.*) that Title VII does not require evidence of psychological injury to support a claim of hostile-environment sexual harassment. It is sufficient for the plaintiff to reasonably perceive the treatment as abusive.

**1998** The U.S. Supreme Court rules (*Gebser v. Lago Vista Independent School District*) that a school district cannot be held liable for damages resulting from sexual harassment of students by teachers unless a school official had been notified of the misconduct and was deliberately indifferent to that misconduct.

**Note:** Every state and many cities and towns have civil rights laws that deal with sexual harassment in the workplace.

Barbara Davis, a former New Jersey deputy attorney general, talked to reporters in front of the courthouse in Trenton, New Jersey, after a jury found that her former boss (a state deputy attorney general) had sexually harassed her. The jury awarded Davis back wages and compensation for emotional distress.

(c) the conduct substantially interferes with a person's work performance or creates an environment that is intimidating, hostile, or offensive.

According to this definition, incidents of sexual harassment can take two forms: (a) *quid pro quo* (Latin for "this for that"), in which a sexual proposition is tied to either a direct threat such as loss of a job or a direct offer such as a promotion, and (b) a hostile work (or educational) environment. A hostile environment is one pervaded by degrading, intimidating, or offensive behavior; explicit benefits, however, are not directly linked to sexual cooperation. In quid pro quo harassment, harassers use their power over the victims' employment to try to extort submission. Quid pro quo harassment can therefore only occur between a superior and a subordinate, and it can be based on a single incident (Conte, 1997). The hostile-environment form of sexual harassment can be based on the conduct of co-workers as well as supervisors. Thus sexual harassment involves a range of behaviors: verbal comments about a person's anatomy; posting sexually suggestive or demeaning cartoons, drawings, or photographs in the workplace and e-mail messages or the installation of pornographic software on company computers; touching someone in a sexually suggestive way; and rape, whether attempted or actual (Levy & Paludi, 1997).

In 1990, the EEOC declared that a person who claims to be the victim of a hostile environment must show that there was a pattern of offensive behavior. The agency advocates using the "reasonable person" standard to determine whether a work environment is hostile. A federal circuit court, however, determined that a "reasonable woman" standard should be used in place of the sex-blind reasonable person approach. The court concluded that conduct that men might find acceptable may be objectionable to women (Watts, 1996). According to this standard, if a reasonable woman would have felt harassed in a given situation, the environment was hostile. In 1993, the Supreme Court ruled (*Harris v. Forklift Systems, Inc.*) that a person alleging sexual harassment does not have to prove that the conduct affected his or her psychological well-being.

**Frequency of Sexual Harassment.**    Over several decades, surveys have revealed that sexual harassment in the workplace is widespread (Hordes, 2000). For example, in 1981 the Merit Systems Protection Board (MSPB) surveyed more than 20,000 government employees to determine the prevalence of sexual harassment. Among its findings were the following:

1. Forty-two percent of the federal government's female employees reported experiencing some form of sexual harassment during the 2 years preceding the survey.

2. Thirty-three percent of the women had experienced unwanted sexual remarks; 28% reported suggestive looks; and 26% reported being deliberately touched in a sexual manner. One percent of the sample had experienced actual or attempted rape or assault.

3. Many incidents of sexual harassment were repeated over extended periods of time, were of long duration, and cost the government an estimated $189 million over the 2-year period of the project.

Several years later another survey was conducted, with virtually the same results (Jackson & Newman, 2004: Merit Systems Protection Board, 1987).

Other surveys of the frequency of sexual harassment converge on the conclusion that approximately one out of every two U.S. women has been harassed during her working life (Gutek & Done, 2000; Hesson-McInnis & Fitzgerald, 1997). Sexual harassment of men is rare (Stockdale, Visio, & Batra, 1999); however, reports of harassment of men tend to receive significant media attention when they result in legal proceedings. The frequency and types of harassment in Canada and European countries are similar to those in the United States. A review of data on workplace sexual harassment in a number of countries led to the conclusion that it is a "relatively widespread phenomenon" (Barak, 1997). In Scandinavian countries, however, rates of harassment appear to be lower than those of the United States. One possible explanation is that women in Scandinavian countries have high rates of participation in the labor force and greater income parity; there is a greater degree of gender equity there than in other parts of the world (Gruber, 1997).

Females of all ages, races, and marital statuses have been harassed in the workplace and in educational settings from elementary school to medical school (Fineran & Bennett, 1999; Levy & Paludi, 1997; Murnen & Smolak, 2000; Recupero, Heru, Price, & Alves, 2004). The incidence of sexual harassment may be higher in workplaces where women have traditionally been underrepresented (Fitzgerald, 1993b), such as the trades, transit operations, and firefighting (Rosell, Miller, & Barber, 1995). Women are more likely to report receipt of unwanted sexual attention as the ratio of male co-workers increases (Jackson & Newman, 2004). The frequency of sexual harassment in the military has been described as "extraordinary" (Harris & Firestone, 1997). A recent focus of attention is on same-sex peer sexual harassment in schools (Fineran, 2002). Here is how a 14-year-old girl described her experiences of sexual harassment at and on her way to school:

> I started being sexually harassed constantly by a group of guys on my bus. It was horrible. They would grab my breasts, thighs, and other places, and make rude comments and sexual gestures toward me. When I finally yelled at them to stop, hit them, or moved away, the bus driver would yell at me. I felt helpless because my parents worked and couldn't drive me to school. Finally I got the courage to do something about it: I told my principal what was happening. He was skeptical about the whole thing, and he didn't do much about it. (Stein, 1995, pp. 19–20)

Such peer-to-peer harassment, which is common in elementary and secondary schools, includes flipping up a girl's skirt; nasty, personalized graffiti on bathroom walls; physical assault; and attempted rape. Quite often such behavior is tolerated "as a true-blooded, healthy American phenomenon, a normal stage of adolescent development" (Stein, 1995, p. 21) that is often perceived as "flirting." Yet one-third of college students asked to report on incidents of inappropriate behavior during their high school careers acknowledged the existence of dating relationships between students and teachers, and many reported other examples of sexual harassment (Corbett, Gentry, & Pearson, 1993). Although sexual harassment seems to occur throughout school, regardless of grade (Murnen & Smolak, 2000), female graduate students are an especially high-risk group (Kelley & Parsons, 2000).

The gender roles of the predominant group in a workplace influence expectations not only for the job but also for the treatment of women. Lois Robinson's experiences as a shipyard worker in Jacksonville, Florida, illustrate this influence. The atmosphere at the shipyard was distinctly male; men controlled social acceptance *and* tangible rewards. Outnumbered and perceived to be out of place, women were powerless. Men used several methods to maintain control: practical jokes, off-color jokes, visual displays of women in states of undress, vulgar graffiti, and use of demeaning nicknames (such as "Honey" and "Babe"). These incidents occurred all day and every day throughout the shipyard (Fiske, 1993; Fiske & Stevens, 1993).

Most victims of sexual harassment try to ignore the offensive behavior; consequently, they do not file complaints, often fearing retaliation or believing the organization will not respond to their complaint (Dansky & Kilpatrick, 1997). In fact, only about 13,000 complaints were filed with the EEOC in 2004, approximately the same number that were filed in 2003. Fifteen percent of the complaints were filed by males (U.S. Equal Employment Opportunity Commission, 2005). Victims of sexual harassment experience several work-related consequences such as declines in job performance and increased absenteeism (Paludi, 2002). Some victims have been fired after filing a complaint; others feel they must quit their jobs. Sexual harassment has a range of psychological effects, including anger, guilt, social withdrawal, decreased self-esteem, and depression (Fitzgerald, 2003; Harned, Ormerod, Palmieri, Collinsworth, & Reed, 2002; Paludi, 2002). Physical complaints include fatigue, headaches, nausea, and sleep and appetite disturbances (Fitzgerald, 2003; Paludi, 2002).

**Perceiving Sexual Harassment.**　　In several workplace and school surveys, significant numbers of women have described incidents that would qualify as instances of sexual harassment, yet only about 5% of them have reported these incidents to someone in authority, such as a work supervisor (Fitzgerald et al., 1988a; Fitzgerald, Weitzman, Gold, & Omerod, 1988b). Women who do file complaints that result in court proceedings are likely to find that the process of "litigation is deeply flawed, costing the plaintiff far more in anguish and humiliation that it ever awards in damages" (Fitzgerald, 2003, p. 917). What's more, the low rate of complaints seems, in part, the result of the fact that many women who tell researchers about such incidents do not perceive the incidents as sexual harassment. In addition, many examples of behavior that would meet the legal definition (for example, repeated sexual jokes, offensive comments about body parts) occur with such high frequency that they are not perceived as sexual harassment (Gutek & Done, 2000).

General stereotypes are not left behind when men and women go to work each day. Women are typically seen as dependent, helpful, nurturing, and sexual, whereas men are perceived as aggressive, dominant, and independent: "Gender stereotypes imply that men should be sexually aggressive and women should be ready and willing to be sex objects. Sexual harassment may occur when these gender stereotypes spill over into the workplace" (Levy & Paludi, 1997, p. 52).

Men and women do not differ in their perceptions of sexual harassment in explicitly coercive situations (for example, fondling a student) (Baker, Terpstra, & Larntz, 1990; Fitzgerald & Ormerod, 1991). Men, however, tend to view less explicit instances (such as suggestive jokes or comments about a women's body) as trivial or innocuous (Fitzgerald & Ormerod, 1991). Many men view this kind of "so-called harassment" as part of the normal interaction between men and women (Reilly, Lott, Caldwell, & De Luca, 1992).

The way men and women perceive interpersonal behaviors, especially women's friendliness, may be a key to understanding some incidents of sexual harassment (Stockdale, 1993). For example, college students were asked to observe a discussion group and then evaluate the participants. Compared with females' perception of males, males perceived more sexuality in the behavior of female participants (Saal, Johnson, & Weber, 1989).

In one study, college-age men and women watched a videotape of a female training manager discussing a training program with a male sales manager (Stockdale, Dewey, & Saal, 1992). The interaction was staged to be friendly and professional. Viewers rated how flirtatious, seductive, and sexy they considered the female actor's behavior. Men were more likely than women to rate the female actor as trying to behave sexually. In another study, viewers watched a videotape of actors portraying a male professor and a female student (Stockdale & Saal, 1990). Half of the viewers watched a portrayal of a friendly, nonharassing professor; the other half watched a portrayal of a harassing professor. The viewers who tended to misperceive the encounters were less repulsed by the harassing behavior than the accurate perceivers were.

The circumstances surrounding an event are also important in determining whether that event constitutes sexual harassment. A key factor is abuse of power. For example, a student who repeatedly asks another student for a date may be considered annoying or a pest. By contrast, a professor who pressures a student for a date is likely to be viewed as a threat, and the professor's persistence is therefore perceived as harassment.

Several programs have been developed to train people to recognize and deal with incidents of sexual harassment. There have been, however, limited attempts to evaluate the effectiveness of such programs (Fitzgerald & Shullman, 1993). One study involving college student participants found that brief sexual harassment training could eliminate the common gender difference in the perception of incidents of sexual harassment (Moyer & Nath, 1998). It remains to be seen whether these results can be replicated and impact the rate and reporting of sexual harassment.

**Gender Stereotyping on the Job.**    Psychological research on gender stereotyping can have a practical impact. Ann Hopkins, a manager at the accounting firm Price Waterhouse, had brought the firm $25 million worth of business. Her clients praised her work, and her supporters at the firm described her as aggressive and hardworking. When she applied for partnership, the firm put her "on hold" for a year, despite the fact that she had generated more billable hours than any other candidate. The next year the firm did not recommend her for partnership. She claimed the reason was sex discrimination and noted that only 7 of the firm's 662 partners were women. The firm countered that Hopkins had deficiencies in interpersonal skills: She was assertive, forceful, and had been described as "macho" and in need of a "course at charm school." A colleague offered her advice to improve her chances of becoming a partner: Walk, talk, and dress more femininely, wear makeup, and wear jewelry (Fiske, 1993; Fiske & Stevens, 1993).

Hopkins declined the advice and sued Price Waterhouse for violating her civil rights, protected under Title VII of the 1964 Civil Rights Act, which prohibits sex discrimination. Susan Fiske, a psychologist who investigates gender stereotypes, assisted in the lawsuit as an expert witness (Fiske, Bersoff, Borgida, Deaux, & Heilman, 1991). Research showed that stereotyping of behavior is more likely to occur when the targeted person is isolated or somehow stands out in a homogeneous environment. Stereotyping is also more likely when there is a perceived lack of fit between a person's category and the occupation in question. For example, managers are expected to be aggressive and tough; however, these are not attributes typically expected of women. Hopkins's detractors perceived her as aggressive (a desirable attribute); her failure to conform to the gender stereotype, however, led them to conclude that she was therefore

Unwanted sexual advances are one example of sexual harassment. Recognition of the frequency of sexual harassment has led to the establishment of policies to reduce harassment and to provide victims with a means of having their complaints heard.

abrasive. Yet her supporters and clients saw her as a determined go-getter. In fact, experimental research reveals that women are penalized in hiring decisions if their forcefulness is not tempered with a degree of niceness that is consistent with the female stereotype (Rudman & Glick, 2001). Finally, stereotyping is more likely when ambiguous criteria are used to evaluate persons. The accounting firm used subjective judgments of Hopkins's interpersonal skills rather than objective criteria such as the amount of business she had generated (Fiske, 1993).

The judge ruled in Hopkins's favor, asserting that "Price Waterhouse refused to make Ann Hopkins a partner. Gender-based stereotyping played a role in this decision" (*Hopkins v. Price Waterhouse*, 1990, p. 1). The company appealed this decision to the U.S. Supreme Court, which upheld it. Hopkins was awarded both the partnership that she had been denied and monetary damages.

Margaret C. Whitman is the President and Chief Executive Officer of Ebay; she has served in this capacity since 1998. This company—valued at approximately $57 billion—provides an online trading platform for buyers and sellers of a wide variety of items and operates in more than 23 countries.

**Women as Leaders.** The main issue in the case of Ann Hopkins was straightforward: Are women in leadership positions evaluated differently from men in such positions? To answer this question, Alice Eagly and her colleagues (1992) conducted a meta-analysis of studies that evaluated men and women in leadership roles. Those studies revealed a slight tendency for female leaders to be evaluated less highly than men in the same positions; women did not, however, receive lower evaluations in all situations. Instead the devaluation of female leaders was selective; it occurred when they occupied previously male-dominated roles and when the evaluators were men. What's more, women were evaluated less highly when they adopted more masculine styles of leadership, such as autocratic and nonparticipative management styles. A review of the effectiveness of men and women in the role of leaders or managers found that men and women were equally effective (Eagly, Karau, & Makhijani, 1995).

Gender has the potential to influence evaluations of managers, even though there may be no general tendency to devalue the managerial contributions of all women (Eagly, Makhijani, & Klonsky, 1992). How should a woman behave so as to avoid this devaluation? If women act like stereotypical males, their male colleagues may accuse them of not being feminine enough, yet if they behave in a stereotypically feminine manner, male colleagues are likely to accuse them of not being masculine enough (Tavris, 1991). Women are more likely to prosper if they are encouraged to use their people-oriented skills instead of adapting male "command and control" styles of leadership (Loden & Rosener, 1990).

Why is it so hard to overcome gender stereotypes in the workplace and elsewhere? One reason is that people often "fence off" individuals who do not fit their stereotypes. A person who disconfirms a stereotype is placed in a subtype, which serves to perpetuate the original stereotype. Women are not seen simply as doctors or professors but as *female professors* or *lady doctors* who are exceptions to the rule, thereby reinforcing gender stereotypes (Basow, 1992; Fiske & Stevens, 1993).

An investigation of the social categories of "woman" and "man," as well as others such as "Republican" and "Democrat," revealed that the general category of "woman" was evaluated quite favorably; in fact, it was evaluated more favorably than "man" (Eagly, Mladinic, & Otto, 1991). How can we reconcile these findings with those of studies like the ones investigating the evaluation of women in the workplace? Recent societal changes in the status of women may cause people to evaluate women more favorably than they did when the first studies of gender stereotypes were conducted. But a more important question is this: If people have such positive evaluations of women as a social category, why do data on wages and promotions indicate that women are at a disadvantage? The answer is that although qualities such as being understanding and gentle are positive attributes, these qualities are valued more in close relationships than in the more highly paid sectors of the workforce. Compared with men, female managers tend to be more open, more democratic, and more likely to allow employees a voice in decision making.

Many women face workplace obstacles such as gender stereotyping that can have detrimental effects on their chances for advancement. In recent years, more women have been hired and promoted into management-level positions. Changes in the sharing of family responsibilities, however, are slow in occurring.

## Family Responsibilities

"What do you do?" Perhaps you or your parents have been asked this question many times, and the answer most likely involved a statement about occupation. Many women are asked questions like "Do you work?" or "What does your husband do?" Such questions ignore the fact that more than half of all women in the United States now work outside the home. Many women, however, have two jobs—one outside the home and one at home, where they are usually responsible for cooking, cleaning, and caring for children. Even in dual-career families, mothers continue to have the primary responsibility for child care. The tasks that men engage in at home tend to be sporadic, variable, and adjustable in terms of timing, such as repairing appliances and mowing the lawn. Women tend to engage in tasks that are repetitive, routine, and constrained by deadlines. Although labor-saving devices have made the work less arduous, new tasks (for example, transporting children to music lessons and soccer practice) have taken the place of old ones (Crawford & Unger, 2000).

Monica Biernat and Camille Wortman (1991) conducted a longitudinal study of 139 married female professionals who had preschool children between the ages of 1 and 5. Most of the women and their husbands were in their 30s. All of these women worked at least 30 hours a week in high-status occupations (accounting, banking, higher education, law) that were equal in status to their husbands' occupations. The wives and their husbands evaluated their participation in 8 different child-care tasks (for example, caring for children's physical needs and getting up with them during the night) and 12 household activities (such as cooking and making repairs). They also rated their satisfaction with their role and their spouse's role in home labor. With the more enjoyable tasks (such as playing with children), there was greater equality. Unpleasant tasks, such as getting up in the middle of the night to care for a child, remained primarily the mother's responsibility. These data revealed that couples were more likely to share household chores than child care. Wives were more likely to be responsible for finances, cleaning, and cooking; husbands handled some household chores related to laundry and repairs. Nevertheless, researchers concluded that although there was equality outside the home, substantial inequity existed in the home, particularly in the distribution of child-care tasks (Biernat & Wortman, 1991)

Over the course of three decades, the difference in household labor and child care has decreased. The decrease seems to be due to two factors: (a) women are spending less time on such activities and (b) men are spending more time on such activities. Yet, as you will see in Figure 10-12, there is still a large difference in the number of hours men and women

When both wife and husband work outside the home, the majority of housework and child-care tasks remain the responsibility of the wife.

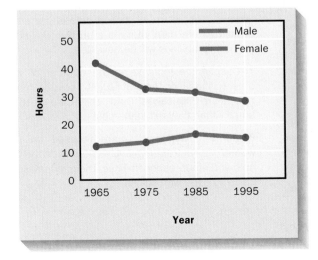

**FIGURE 10-12** Differences in amount of time devoted to household chores and child care by wives and husbands across several decades.

**Source:** Robinson and Godbey (1999).

spend on household chores and child care. Part of the reduction in hours women spend working on household tasks is accounted for by increased rates of employment outside the house (Robinson & Godbey, 1999). This situation has the effect of producing a "second shift" of work at home for women around the world (Hochschild, 1989; Mednick, 1993).

**Juggling.** Many psychologists who have studied stress have focused on stressors affecting men, particularly stressors in the workplace. They have tended to view the home as a benign environment in which one recuperates from the rigors of working—a picture drawn from a traditional male perspective (Hare-Mustin & Marecek, 1990a). This type of research does not recognize that women are more concentrated in lower-paying jobs than are men, have less upward mobility, have less control over their more tedious jobs, and experience sexual discrimination. For them, the home is a further source of stress as they struggle to perform household tasks after a difficult day at work.

Many married women may have hoped that when they entered the workplace, their husbands would take on more of the responsibility for caring for the children and the home. For many, however, this hope has not been realized. Instead of the envisioned role redefinition for men and women, the resulting situation has created a role expansion for women (Crosby & Jaskar, 1993). Faye Crosby (1991) uses the term *jugglers* to describe women who perform both job and family roles.

What are the consequences of these multiple roles for women? Contrary to expectations, Crosby (1991) found no evidence that role jugglers experience more stress than homemakers or other women with fewer roles. In fact, their multiple roles appear to insulate these women (and men also) against depression (Crosby & Jaskar, 1993). One likely reason for this effect is that multiple roles provide variety, change, and exposure to many viewpoints. These factors can buffer individuals against the impact of reversals and dissatisfactions in their daily lives (Crosby & Jaskar, 1993), thus serving as buffers for the psychological distress associated with caregiving (Pavalko & Woodbury, 2000). Women in multiple roles do not wallow in self-pity; instead they "take pride in how well they cope" (Crosby & Jaskar, 1993, p. 162).

We have seen how gender stereotypes exert a powerful influence on a wide range of behaviors. Although biological aspects of sex are difficult to change, gender stereotypes and their influence on behavior can change. As they change, more opportunities become open to people of both sexes.

# REVIEW SUMMARY

**1.** Continued reliance on gender stereotypes can result in **sexism**—differential treatment of individuals based on their sex.

**2.** Sexism has been noted in adults' interactions with toddlers in preschool settings. Observations of elementary school classrooms have found evidence that sexism pervades those settings as well. In schools boys tend to be reinforced for assertiveness; girls are reinforced for politeness. These differences can also be seen in high school and college classrooms.

**3. Sexual harassment** has been defined as (a) coercion of sexual favors by means of promised rewards or threatened punishments (quid pro quo) or (b) creation of a hostile environment.

**4.** More than half of working women have experienced some form of sexual harassment. Men and women differ in their interpretation of events as instances of sexual harassment.

**5.** Psychologists have applied what they have learned about gender stereotyping to claims of sex discrimination.

**6.** Women in leadership positions receive lower evaluations than men, although the difference is not large. There is evidence, however, that when evaluation criteria are ambiguous and the evaluators are men, there is a greater likelihood that women's leadership abilities will be devalued.

**7.** Despite the increase in the number of women who have entered the labor force in recent decades, men and women do not share household and child-care responsibilities more equally than they did in the past.

**8.** Some psychologists have focused on the benefits that women derive from *juggling* work outside the home with household and other responsibilities. These benefits include increased ability to cope with stress.

# ✓CHECK YOUR PROGRESS

1. What are the major findings of observations of gender stereotyping in elementary school classrooms?

2. Which type of sexual harassment involves coerced sexual behavior in exchange for rewards or avoiding punishments?
   a. pro bono
   b. quid pro quo
   c. sexual exchange
   d. negotiated rape

3. A survey of 10,000 women contained questions designed to determine whether the women had ever been sexually harassed. Based on past research, how many of these women are likely to give answers suggesting that they had been victims of sexual harassment?
   a. 100
   b. 1,000
   c. 2,500
   d. 5,000

4. Which of these would make a good title for the results of observations of teachers' interactions with boys and girls in elementary school classrooms?
   a. "Few Differences Noted"
   b. "Talkative Girls; Silent Boys"
   c. "Paying Attention to the Boys; Ignoring the Girls"
   d. "Smarter Girls Get More Than Their Share of the Teachers' Attention"

5. How does the number of men and women earning undergraduate degrees compare?
   a. More men than women earn degrees.
   b. More women than men earn degrees.
   c. Equal numbers of men and women earn degrees.
   d. Whether men or women earn more degrees changes each year, with no apparent trend over time.

6. In what ways do men and women differ in their perceptions of sexual harassment?

7. Which of the following is one of the most powerful influences on career development in girls and young women?
   a. having a working mother
   b. being the only child in the family
   c. having a younger sibling in need of assistance
   d. attending schools that enroll both boys and girls

8. In what ways do the typical household tasks done by husbands and wives differ?

9. A judge is about to instruct a jury that is deciding a trial involving alleged sexual harassment. The plaintiff alleges that she was subjected to a hostile environment. How will the judge instruct the jury?
   a. "You are to use your common sense and experience in deciding this case."
   b. "In deciding this case, you are to view it as a 'reasonable woman' would view the events."
   c. "This case is no different than any other; you must use your own backgrounds in deciding it."
   d. "You are to view the events as most of your friends and relatives would view the events had they occurred to you."

10. What did researchers find when they asked people to evaluate the social categories of *man* and *woman*?
    a. *Woman* and *man* were evaluated equally.
    b. *Man* was evaluated more favorably than *woman*.
    c. *Woman* was evaluated more favorably than *man*.
    d. People relied on memories of their parents when offering their evaluations.

**ANSWERS: 1.** Compared with girls, boys in elementary classrooms receive more attention and detailed feedback from teachers. **2.** b **3.** d **4.** c **5.** b **6.** Men and women do not differ in their perception of the more serious forms of sexual harassment; men, however, tend to view less serious forms as examples of the normal relationships among men and women at work. **7.** a **8.** Women are more active on all child-care tasks. On the more enjoyable tasks such as playing with children, there is greater equality. Generally, wives are more responsible for tasks such as cleaning, and cooking; husbands are more responsible for tasks such as making repairs. **9.** b **10.** c

# Personality

## CHAPTER OUTLINE

To this point we have covered several basic processes, starting with how our nerves transmit information, how we sense and then understand information from our environment, and how we learn and remember information. We have also looked at how we develop physically and socially, and we briefly considered how personality develops. In this chapter we present an overview of the major theories of personality. The concept of personality is familiar because our language contains many words that describe how our friends, relatives, and strangers differ from one another in the ways they act and react to events. Psychologists have devised a number of methods to quantify such personality differences. How these differences occur is one of the key questions posed by psychologists. In previous chapters we have seen how biological factors such as heredity influence many basic processes. In this chapter we will see that heredity has important influences on personality. Next, we will look more closely at Freud's model for personality development. We will also consider the perspective of psychologists who have proposed that the basic processes of learning can account for some personality differences. Finally, we will see how social and cognitive factors influence what and how we learn and how these differences create what we call *personality*.

# ANALYZING PERSONALITY

**Nancy and her friends were intrigued by a site on the Internet that advertised "Personality Analysis by Computer." She completed a test called the Generalized Personality Analysis (GPA), which was a series of true-or-false questions (see Table 11-1). Although she thought some of the items were unusual, she was pleased with the analysis she received. After reviewing the analysis with her friends, however, Nancy began wondering whether it was really accurate. *How could a computer generate a personality description based on a series of true-or-false questions?***

How would you describe a friend or relative without referring to his or her physical attributes? You might begin by saying that your friend has "a good personality." This statement usually means that a person has made a positive impression on you and exhibits characteristics that you find desirable. In contrast, when we say that someone has "no personality," we usually mean we consider his or her characteristics bland or disagreeable.

## Defining Personality

The word *personality* is derived from the Latin word *persona*, which means "mask." In ancient Greece and Rome, actors wore masks to convey the personality characteristics of the roles they were playing. The masks made it easier for the small number of actors who played all the parts to portray their diverse roles.

To psychologists, **personality** refers to a relatively stable pattern of thinking, feeling, and behaving that distinguishes one person from another. This definition has two important components. First, each person's pattern of thinking, feeling, and behaving makes him or her distinctive. Thus each of us wears a mask that is different from those worn by others. The second defining component is the notion that an individual's

**personality**
A relatively stable pattern of behaving, feeling, and thinking that distinguishes one person from another

| TABLE 11-1 |
| --- |

## The Generalized Personality Analysis (GPA) Questionnaire

This personality questionnaire contains a series of statements. Read each one, decide how you feel about it, and mark your answer to the item. If you agree with the statement or feel it is true about you, answer "true." If you disagree with the statement or feel it is not true about you, answer "false."

1. Cats are antisocial.
2. Some roads never end.
3. Fast walkers are slow thinkers.
4. I get into the tub with my right foot first.
5. A circle is a square that has rounded edges.
6. Oak trees seem friendlier than pine trees.
7. The majority of right-thinking people are wrong.
8. There is more air in a loaf of bread than in a balloon.
9. Snow can turn to rain faster than rain can turn to snow.
10. Being able to flick a light switch gives me a feeling of power and strength.

**Source:** Palladino and Schell (1980).

*"I don't know why everyone says
I don't have a personality."*

personality is relatively consistent. Psychologists have long debated and studied the issues of consistency across situations and stability over time, as we will see later in the chapter.

## Assessing Personality

The methods psychologists use to examine personality include case studies, interviews, naturalistic observations, laboratory investigations, and psychological tests. To be useful, a psychological test must have three characteristics: reliability, validity, and standardization (see Chapter 8). Many of the tests published in popular magazines and newspapers or found on the Internet lack all three characteristics; therefore, you should be skeptical of the supposed meaning attached to such tests.

**Self-Report Inventories.** Some of the best-known and most widely used personality measures are **self-report inventories** that require individuals to respond to statements about themselves (for example, "I am nervous when I speak to a large group of people") in the form of yes-no or true-false answers. This limited range of possible answers means that little, if any, judgment is required to score these tests. Two of the most frequently used self-report personality inventories are the Minnesota Multiphasic Personality Inventory (MMPI) and the California Psychological Inventory (CPI).

**The Minnesota Multiphasic Personality Inventory.** The most widely used self-report personality inventory, the MMPI (Butcher, Lim, & Nezami, 1998), was developed and first published in 1943 by Starke Hathaway and J. C. McKinley, both of the University of Minnesota. The test's long history of application is supported by evidence from thousands of studies, and its users have accumulated a great deal of experience (Caldwell, 2004). The purpose of the MMPI is to help diagnose psychological disorders such as depression and schizophrenia (see Chapter 12). Hathaway and McKinley began by collecting a large pool of items (for example, "I wish I could be as happy as other

**self-report inventory**
Psychological test in which individuals answer questions about themselves, usually by responding yes or no or true or false

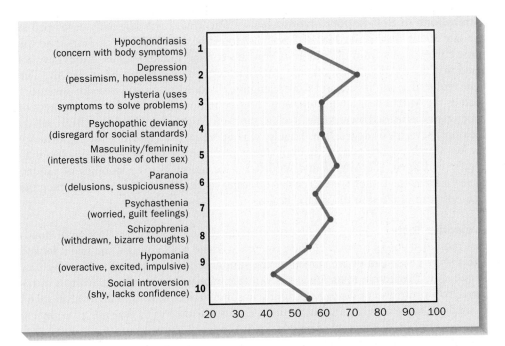

**FIGURE 11-1** MMPI profile of a 40-year-old male. This profile reveals a mild to moderate level of depression and anxiety that suggests ambivalence, indecisiveness, and low self-confidence. Energy and activity levels are likely to be below average. Getting started on new tasks presents difficulty; after tasks are started, there is often self-blame over minor deficiencies in performance.

**Sources:** Friedman, Webb, and Lewak (1989); Graham (1990); Greene (1991).

people") that could be answered "true" or "false." They retained items that were answered differently by normal people and those suffering from any of several psychological disorders. Most of the items deal with a range of psychological and physical symptoms.

A revision of the MMPI, the MMPI-2, has 567 items and 10 clinical dimensions or scales (see Figure 11-1) that were designed to assess characteristic symptoms associated with several of the major psychological disorders. Four validity scales were designed to detect the tendency of test takers to present themselves in a favorable light (such as answering "false" to "I do not read every editorial in the newspaper every day") or to assess other unusual ways of responding (Munley, Germain, Tovar-Murray, & Borgman, 2004).

The MMPI has been adapted for use in at least 22 languages and in many nations and cultures (Cheung, 2004). Test developers follow a series of procedures when adapting the test for use outside of the United States. The elimination of objectionable items during the MMPI-2 revision enhanced acceptability of the test by people in other cultures. The issue of item content, however, still must be addressed each time the test is adapted. For example, items referring to sex might be considered inappropriate by people taking the test in Arabic (Soliman, 1996). In addition to issues related to content, the items themselves must be translated; this process consists of several steps. First, items are translated from English. During this step, translators must take special care with words such as *frequently, sometimes,* and *usually,* as well as slang or colloquial expressions such as *muscle twitching and jumping.* To ensure that the translation retains the original meaning, the translated version is translated back into English (a *back translation*). Any failures to convey the original meaning of the items are identified in this back-and-forth process.

**The California Psychological Inventory.** The MMPI has served as the basis for the development of other personality inventories, including the California Psychological Inventory (CPI), which was designed for use with normal adolescents and adults. The 20 CPI scales, such as dominance, responsibility, and sociability, have been used to predict academic achievement, to understand leadership, to study individuals in various occupations (Sandal & Endresen, 2002), and to study the personalities of drug users (Song, Zhu, Yin, & Zhang, 2002). The CPI is widely used and has been translated into 29 languages (Paunonen & Ashton, 1998).

**projective test**
Psychological test that involves the use of unstructured or ambiguous stimuli in an effort to assess personality

**Limitations of Self-Report Inventories.** The MMPI was originally developed in the late 1940s. When the MMPI-2 was developed in the 1980s, the authors used the same clinical scales from the MMPI (Oltmanns & Emery, 2001). Thus, critics have argued that the MMPI-2 is based on outdated concepts that may not be applicable. The time required to administer and score a lengthy, all-encompassing personality inventory such as the MMPI is another limitation. This limitation has led to the development of shorter, more focused inventories, such as the Beck Depression Inventory (BDI), which measures severity of depression. Finally, self-report inventories offer the opportunity for less than honest responses. To evaluate the possibility of the patient's being less than honest and open, the MMPI and MMPI-2 have incorporated a number of validity scales, such as the L (lie) Scale. If scores on scales such as the L Scale are valid, then the examiner can proceed to the clinical scales.

**Projective Tests.** Have you ever stared at the sky and noticed a collection of clouds that reminded you of a crown? When you told a friend what you saw, she said it looked like a dog. Those clouds are similar to the stimuli used in projective tests to evaluate personality. **Projective tests** are assessment techniques that require individuals to respond to *unstructured* or *ambiguous* stimuli. In some projective tests, individuals respond to inkblots, make up stories about pictures, express themselves by drawing, or complete sentences such as "I think other people . . ."

Because there are no correct or best answers, proponents of projective tests believe test takers will find it difficult to fake their responses. The assumption underlying projective tests is that people project their personality characteristics onto the ambiguous stimuli. These responses are thought to reflect unconscious aspects of personality that are not likely to be revealed in answers to more obvious self-report inventory items. One projective test, the Thematic Apperception Test (TAT), has been used to measure achievement motivation (see Chapter 6) and to make predictions of future achievement-related behaviors (McClelland, Koestner, & Weinberger, 1989). The 20 TAT cards contain vague black-and-white pictures (one card is blank). When administering the test, the psychologist asks the participant to make up a story to fit what is happening in the card and what the character is thinking and feeling, and to give the outcome.

One of the most widely used projective tests is the Rorschach Inkblot Test (Lubin, Larsen, Matarazzo, & Seever, 1985), which was published in 1921 by a Swiss psychiatrist, Hermann Rorschach. Rorschach dropped ink onto a piece of paper and then folded the paper in half, thus creating a symmetrical pattern (see Figure 11-2). Five of the cards in the test are black, white, and gray; the remaining five cards include various colors.

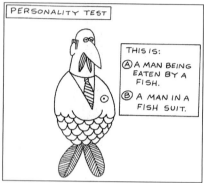

There are several steps in the administration of the Rorschach. First, the examiner displays the cards one at a time and asks the client to report what he or she sees in each card. The psychologist writes down the client's description of each card and then asks for the aspects of each card that influenced the responses. Finally, the psychologist may code the responses on the basis of characteristics such as the part of the card used (for example, whole blot or small details), the use of color, and the content of responses (for example, humans or sex). Users of the Rorschach test believe that these aspects of the responses yield information about an individual's personality. For example, heavy reliance on color might indicate impulsive behavior, and depressed people may use few, if any, colors in their responses.

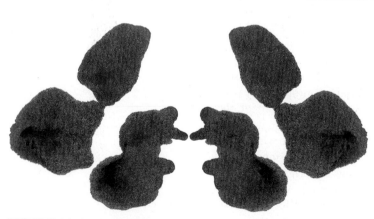

**FIGURE 11-2** A card similar to those presented in the Rorschach inkblot test. Projective tests use unstructured or ambiguous stimuli (without obvious meaning or interpretation) like this inkblot, which require test takers to make sense of stimuli that do not have any specific meaning.

**Limitations of Projective Tests.** Administering and interpreting projective tests requires extensive training. The degree of subjective judgment required to interpret them has led some psychologists to conclude that projective tests do not meet the same

## TABLE 11-2

### Nancy's Computer-Generated Personality Analysis

You have a great need for other people to like and admire you. You have a tendency to be critical of yourself. You have a great deal of unused capacity that you have not turned to your advantage. Although you have some personality weaknesses, you are generally able to compensate for them. Your sexual adjustment has presented problems for you. Disciplined and self-controlled outside, you tend to be worrisome and insecure inside. At times you have serious doubts as to whether you have made the right decision or done the right thing. You prefer a certain amount of change and variety and become dissatisfied when hemmed in by restrictions and limitations. You pride yourself as an independent thinker and do not accept others' statements without satisfactory proof. You have found it unwise to be too frank in revealing yourself to others. At times you are extroverted, affable, sociable, while at other times you are introverted, wary, reserved. Some of your aspirations tend to be pretty unrealistic. Security is one of your major goals in life.

**Source:** Forer (1949, p. 120).

objective standards as many self-report inventories. To address these concerns, more recent approaches to the interpretation of the Rorschach test place greater emphasis on the quantification of Rorschach responses and comparisons to norms describing the responses (McGrath, 2003). Although greater quantification and standardization of testing conditions are steps forward, critics still have concerns about validity and reliability (Allen & Dana, 2004) and the possibility that the behavior of the examiner may influence the client's responses.

**The Barnum Effect.** The assortment of methods used to analyze personality is fascinating. Consider Nancy's computer-generated personality analysis (Table 11-2). She believed that a computer had analyzed her answers to the GPA to produce an analysis just for her. She was not aware, however, that the items on the GPA are not typical of self-report inventories; they were selected by researchers who wanted to determine if people would accept general personality feedback they thought was based on unusual items. Thus her responses to those items revealed little about her personality.

The computer-generated personality description that Nancy received has much in common with those produced by several nonscientific methods of analyzing personality, such as handwriting analyses and horoscopes (Glick, Gottesman, & Jolton, 1989; McKelvie, 1990). Horoscopes contain statements that are similar to those found in Nancy's personality analysis; the statements in Table 11-2 were collected from an astrology book (Forer, 1949). Although repeated evaluations have demonstrated that astrology has no scientific basis (Crowe, 1990), many people consult their horoscopes every day.

### Psychological Detective

Can you provide reasons for people's acceptance of feedback from sources such as horoscopes or the GPA? Why would the statements in Table 11-2 lead an individual to report that his or her personality had been assessed accurately? Think about this question, and write down your answers before reading further.

In study after study, most people rate the personality statements in Table 11-2 as "good" or "excellent" descriptions of themselves (Forer, 1949). Why? Let's examine the first statement in the personality analysis: "You have a great need for other people to like and admire you." Does this statement describe any of your friends? How many? Read

Fortune-tellers rely on the Barnum effect; they often use favorable descriptions that apply to most people. They frequently phrase their statements as questions in order to elicit additional information from their clients.

**Barnum effect**
The tendency to accept generalized personality descriptions as accurate descriptions of oneself

the other statements and ask yourself the same questions. How many friends does each statement describe? In almost every case, the answer is "quite a few." These statements describe a considerable percentage of the population, and they are quite favorable (Emery & Lilienfeld, 2004). According to Paul Meehl (1956), these personality descriptions have something for everyone. He coined the term **Barnum effect** to describe them (after P. T. Barnum, the showman who said that a good circus has a "little something for everybody").

The statements in Nancy's personality analysis are similar to those found in analyses offered by fortune tellers. How do fortune tellers succeed in providing personality analyses their clients accept? In addition to relying on the Barnum effect, they use a method called *cold reading* to collect information from strangers. Fortune tellers do not ask for information directly (Hyman, 1989; Randi, 1995) but use clues such as clothing, physical features, speech, gestures, and eye contact.

**Other Measures.** As we noted at the beginning of this section, there are numerous ways to evaluate personality; self-report inventories and projective techniques are only two of these procedures. Other procedures include direct interviews, often conducted by a trained clinical psychologist, and direct observation of behavior. Developmental psychologists, who believe that childhood experiences are important in shaping personality, frequently use direct observations. For example, they may want to observe the interactions of children at a child-care center or family interactions.

## Is Behavior Consistent?

As we have seen, one of the elements of the definition of personality is consistency in behavior. Are you consistent from day to day? Is the behavior of your family members and friends consistent from day to day?

**Challenges to the Idea of Consistency.** Walter Mischel had the job of predicting how successful Peace Corps volunteers would be. After analyzing reports, Mischel (1968) concluded that "highly generalized behavioral consistencies have not been

One reason we believe that personality is stable is that we observe stability in a variety of characteristics, including physical appearance, over time. These two pictures show the same people.

demonstrated" (p. 140). He therefore advised psychologists to turn their attention from the search for traits to the study of *how situations influence behaviors* (Wright & Mischel, 1987). For example, when you are out with your friends, your behavior with them may be quite different from your behavior during a dinner with relatives. An observer might find it hard to believe you are the same person in the two situations. That is Mischel's point: Behavior is a function of situations, not traits.

**In Defense of Consistency.**     Although the idea of consistency of behavior was dealt some devastating blows by Mischel (1968), belief in this idea persisted. Darryl Bem and Andrea Allen (1974) offered several reasons for believing there is consistency in behavior. One reason is that we rely on preconceived notions of how behaviors are related and may jump to conclusions that are consistent with those preconceived notions. For example, if you expect friendly people to be honest, you may conclude that a friendly person is honest even when you have no evidence to support such a conclusion.

Some characteristics, such as intelligence, emotional reactions, and physical appearance, are consistent over time. For example, Carroll Izard and colleagues (1993) found that tendencies to exhibit certain emotional reactions (for example, anger or enjoyment) are stable across several years. What's more, after early childhood, scores on intelligence tests are quite stable into adulthood.

Although a number of studies have failed to demonstrate consistency of behavior across situations, there may be limitations in the methods used to study consistency (Bem & Allen, 1974). One problem can be illustrated by the following situation. Suppose your instructor decides that final grades for a course will be based on a single multiple-choice item. What do you think of this idea? We can hear the moans and groans. Let's examine the reasons for your objections. Your logic probably goes like this: "One multiple-choice item is not a good indicator of how much I have learned. What if I was sick the day the material in that item was covered in class? What if the item covers a topic that I found difficult?" Thus you have concluded that a single multiple-choice item is not a good indicator of your knowledge of the course material. Following the same logic, Lewis Goldberg (1992) notes that arguments against the consistency of behaviors are often based on the false premise that "scientists in the field of personality seek to predict a single response of a particular individual in a completely novel situation" (p. 93).

## Psychological Detective

Suppose we have developed a self-report inventory to measure altruism. We could find out how many people volunteered to work for a charity last year and then see whether volunteer work was related to scores on our altruism measure. There may be problems with this indicator of altruism, however. How could we provide more convincing evidence that this inventory measured altruism? Does volunteering to work for a charity provide evidence of the consistency of altruism over time? Give these questions some thought, and write down your answer before reading further.

We begin by separating a large group of individuals into two smaller groups on the basis of their altruism scores (a group of high scorers and a group of low scorers). When we ask the individuals in each group if they volunteered to help a charity last year, we find few differences between the two groups. We can also ask, however, how many of them donated money to the poor, how many gave clothing to charitable organizations, and how many signed petitions requesting funds to build homeless shelters.

There may be few differences between the two groups of individuals on any one of the behaviors just mentioned. When we look at several behaviors together, however, a pattern emerges. A single behavior is a weak indicator of altruism, just as a single test item is a weak indicator of your knowledge of course material. When the behaviors are added together (like the items on that test), patterns become discernible.

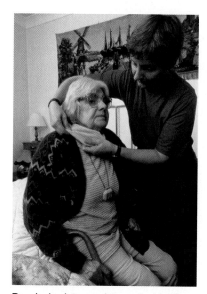

Psychologists are interested in the kind of helping behavior illustrated in this photograph. They avoid, however, relying on only one incident as an indicator of an individual's level of altruism.

Because a single example of any behavior is a weak indicator, Seymour Epstein (1979, 1980) suggests that researchers use the method of *aggregation*, in which they collect evidence of several behaviors, as we did in the example of altruism. The concept of aggregation is not new (Zuckerman, 1991). For example, psychologists who study operant conditioning do not study a single bar press in a Skinner box; instead they examine cumulative curves that are aggregations of a series of behaviors over time (Warner et al., 2004; see Chapter 5). Similarly, when we aggregate behaviors across situations, we can determine whether those behaviors are consistent over time.

**Evidence of Consistency Based on Multiple Measures.** Epstein (1983) notes that proponents of both views in this debate believe they are correct and that consequently the other side must be wrong. Each side offers evidence to support its position, but a paradox exists here. Consider the following statements:

1. Behavior is specific to a situation.
2. People exhibit broad, stable tendencies to respond in certain ways across situations.

Behavior depends on the situation, but there are consistent behavioral tendencies across situations. Can we resolve this paradox? The situation also influences the likelihood that a person will exhibit a specific behavior. For example, because there are clear norms for acceptable behavior at a funeral, few people laugh at those events. If we were interested in studying sense of humor and limited our observations to funerals, we might conclude that people with a high sense of humor were inconsistent. We need, however, to acknowledge the role of the situation. If we expanded our observations to other situations, it is likely that a pattern of consistency would emerge. People who are high in humor would laugh a lot (in the appropriate situations).

Having discussed the various techniques used to analyze or measure personality and whether personality is consistent, we now turn our attention to the various theoretical views of personality that psychologists have developed.

# TRAIT APPROACHES

We begin this section with a hands-on activity. Complete the following survey. We will have more to say about the "Big Five" shortly.

## Hands On

### The "Big Five" Test

Using the numbers on the scale from 1 to 5, indicate how true each of the following terms is in describing you.

1. = Not at all true of me: I am never this way.

2. = Mostly not true of me: I am rarely this way.

3. = Neither true nor untrue of me, or I can't decide.

4. = Somewhat true of me: I am sometimes this way.

5. = Very true of me: I am very often this way.

Instructions for scoring your answers to the "Big Five" Test can be found at the end of the chapter.

**Source:** Brody and Ehrlichman (1998).

We chose to start with trait theories because you use them, probably every day, to describe yourself as well as your friends and relatives. Also, from a historical perspective, the concept of traits may date to the first use of language. What's more, most approaches to personality make use of the concept of traits; where they differ is primarily in how they explain the development of individual differences. Indeed, trait theory has become very popular (McCrae, 2004).

When we asked you to describe a friend or relative, you probably used a number of words expressive of traits, such as *shy* or *friendly*, in your description. **Traits** are summary terms that describe tendencies to respond in particular ways that account for differences among people.

Some people exhibit high levels of a given trait; others exhibit low levels of the same trait. Most people, however, exhibit a moderate degree of a given trait, which is distributed according to the normal curve (see Chapter 8). Keep in mind that Barnum-type statements do not provide information about how much of a trait is exhibited (review the statements in Table 11-2). By contrast, most self-report inventories designed to measure a trait provide norms that allow us to determine the level of the trait that was assessed.

Psychologist Gordon Allport (1897–1967) set out to compose a list of traits, which he described as the building blocks of personality (1961). To do this, he examined everyday language because it seems likely that we would encode the most important individual differences in human transactions as single terms in our language (McCrae, 2004). Trait words are pervasive in our language; we use them to describe people and read them in advertisements that extol the virtues of various products (*dependable*, *exciting*).

After eliminating words that referred to temporary moods (*frantic*), social evaluations (*worthy*), or physical attributes (*lean*), Allport found that 4,500 words remained (Allport & Odbert, 1936). The key question raised by these results is, Which trait terms are the most important? The large number of terms seemed to be more than were needed to describe a person's personality.

Traits are summary terms that describe tendencies to respond in particular ways that account for differences among people. What traits do you associate with this person?

## Factors of Personality: Raymond B. Cattell

For some time, personality psychologists have been searching for the key personality traits. Raymond B. Cattell (1990) decided that he would identify and measure the most important traits. Cattell's approach is to administer a wide variety of personality measures to many people and to use the results to identify the key personality traits. Cattell used data from a number of sources, including objective tests, records of his participants' lives (for example, school and work records), and observations of their behaviors when placed in contrived situations. He then used a computer program to correlate the data. These correlations indicated that certain bits of information tended to cluster together. Cattell called these clusters *surface traits* because they were easy to identify from the correlations. What's more, Cattell assumed that these surface traits were in turn directed by a smaller number of traits called *source traits*.

Cattell's Sixteen Personality Factors Questionnaire (16PF) (Cattell, Eber, & Tatsuoka, 1970) provides an assessment of the levels of a person's source traits (see Figure 11-3); the latest version of this questionnaire is the 16PF5 (Conn & Rieke, 1994).

According to Cattell, the same 16 traits can be used to describe each of us; the levels of those traits, however, vary from person to person, which accounts for our distinctiveness as individuals.

## Categorization of Traits: Hans Eysenck

Psychologist Hans Eysenck was always interested in how traits are organized. He concluded that one way to deal with the large number of traits is to organize them first into narrowly defined categories, which are in turn placed into broader categories (Eysenck & Eysenck, 1985; see Figure 11-4).

**trait**
A summary term that describes the tendency to behave, feel, and think in ways that are consistent across different situations

**FIGURE 11-3** 16PF profiles of airline pilots, artists, and musicians.

**Source:** Cattell, Eber, and Tatsuoka (1970).

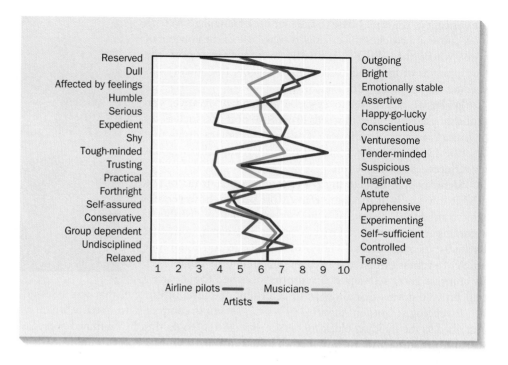

At the broadest level of abstraction, Eysenck said, we can describe personality as consisting of three basic traits: extraversion, neuroticism, and psychoticism. Neuroticism, or emotional instability, consists of traits such as anxiety, guilt feelings, low self-esteem, and shyness. Psychoticism consists of traits such as aggressiveness, impulsivity, and a lack of empathy. We will focus our attention on the trait of extraversion, which can be represented as a continuum from extreme extrovert to extreme introvert. People we label as *extroverts* are more outgoing than *introverts*, who are oriented toward internal stimuli such as their own thoughts and moods. Because this trait is a continuum, however, many people have scores that would put them in the middle of the distribution.

Extroverts and introverts differ in a number of ways and in a variety of settings. For example, Dewar and Whittington (2000) found that extroverts have a relatively short attention span and prefer to work in large groups. However, Elskamp and Broida (2004) reported that extroverted students preferred face-to-face interaction in the classroom; they did not differ from introverted students in their comfort level with computers in a class that used computers for quizzes, discussions, and e-mails.

## The "Big Five" Traits

Despite the work of Cattell and Eysenck, there is a growing consensus that personality traits can be reduced to five basic ones, although there is some disagreement about the precise labels for the five (Goldberg, 1995). The most common names for the "Big

**FIGURE 11-4** Eysenck's research focused on three major traits. A trait such as extraversion encompasses several other traits, as illustrated here.

**Source:** Eysenck and Eysenck (1985).

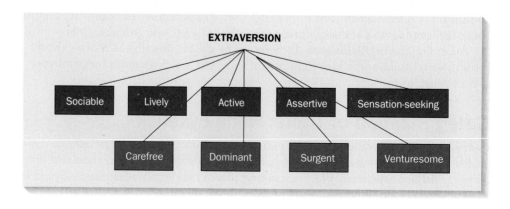

## TABLE 11-3

## Names and Descriptions of the "Big Five" Traits

**Major Trait Description of Personality**

| Major Trait | Description of Personality |
|---|---|
| Extraversion | People who score high are described as talkative and expressive, as indicated by facial expressions and gestures. They are also assertive, gregarious, highly active, and have good skills in using humor. They like excitement and stimulation and tend to be energetic, optimistic, and upbeat. People with low scores tend to be described as solitary, quiet, having low energy, and reserved. |
| Agreeableness | People who score high are described as fundamentally altruistic. They are likely to yield in interactions with others. Others view them as sympathetic, straightforward, warm, and considerate. People who score low are described as antagonistic, unkind, suspicious, and unsympathetic. |
| Conscientiousness | People who score high are described as well organized, dependable, competent, and responsible. They are likely to get things done, able to delay gratification, exhibit highly ethical behavior, and have a high level of aspiration. People who score low are described as disorganized, careless, inefficient, and undependable. |
| Neuroticism | People who score high are described as self-defeating, basically anxious, and concerned about personal adequacy. They are subject to mood fluctuations and negative emotions, such as anger, guilt, and disgust. They are also prone to irrational ideas, are not always able to control impulses, and are less effective than others at coping with stress. People who score low are described as unemotional, calm, even-tempered, self-satisfied, and comfortable with themselves. |
| Openness to Experience | People who score high exhibit a preference for new and unfamiliar experiences reflected in appreciation of knowledge, various art forms, and nontraditional values as opposed to tradition and the status quo. They are considered highly introspective, attentive to inner feelings and fantasies, intellectual, and creative. People who score low are described as down-to-earth, conventional, preferring routine, and not intellectually oriented. |

**Sources:** Adapted from Costa and McCrae (1992b); Formy-Duval et al. (1995); McCrae and John (1992).

Five" are (1) *openness to experience*, (2) *conscientiousness*, (3) *extraversion*, (4) *agreeableness*, and (5) *neuroticism* (Costa & McCrae, 1992a; Goldberg, 1995; McCrae & John, 1992). Table 11-3 lists and describes these five traits. Note that the names of the Big Five form the acronym OCEAN. Although not all psychologists are enamored of the Big Five approach, many others (for example, Fleeson & Baltes, 1998; Hall, Lindzey, & Campbell, 1998; Loehlin, McCrae, Costa, & John, 1998) consider it one of the most important developments in recent personality research.

There are several reasons for concluding that these five traits represent basic dimensions of personality (Costa & McCrae, 1992c). These traits appear when peers provided ratings of Air Force officers, fraternity brothers, Peace Corps trainees, and spouses (McRae & Costa, 1987). They also appear in studies of individuals of different ages, in both men and women, in different races, in different language groups, and across cultures (Worrell & Cross, 2004). On the other hand, not all researchers agree on the specific names for the Big Five traits, and there is some disagreement on the meaning of the traits, especially the one called *openness to experience*.

Advances in the technology of genetics and neuroscience have led to an increase in the ability to detect genetic and neurological bases of complex behavior (Turkheimer, 1998). This ability, combined with the interest in the Big Five, has led to the exploration of trait heritabilities. According to Loehlin et al. (1998), recent assessments of the heritability of the Big Five have concluded that all five traits are moderately and equally heritable. Using three alternative models of genetic and environmental influences, Loehlin et al. found that "51% to 58% of individual difference variation among the Big Five dimensions is genetic in origin" (p. 447). Other researchers, such as Turkheimer (1998), caution that discovering heritability is not necessarily a guarantee of finding specific genetic causes. At this point in time, scientists should use such discoveries as useful cues for continued research.

One aspect of research on the five major traits, namely an investigation of their stability, is especially relevant to the definition of personality. Do the levels of these traits in an individual change over time, or do they remain similar through the adult years? Scores on a self-report inventory and personality ratings completed by spouses tended to remain stable into adulthood (Costa & McCrae, 1988). In fact, a growing body of research suggests that personality traits have considerable long-term stability (McCrae & Costa, 1990). Another area of research has involved the use of the Big Five traits in personnel selection.

**STUDY TIP**

Make a mind map, graphic, or other visual representation depicting the Big Five traits of personality. Develop five icons, or pictures, to associate with the five traits; incorporate those icons into your visual representation.

**The Big Five and Job Performance.**   The Big Five factors have been used in research on personnel selection. However, which personality factors are related to job performance?

Gregory Hurtz and John Donovan (2000) completed an extensive search for research that investigated the relation between measures of the Big Five factors and job or training performance. Their search yielded 26 studies, with most of them describing a number of correlations for each of the Big Five dimensions.

Their results showed that *conscientiousness* had the highest correlation across occupations with job performance criteria ($r = 0.14$), which was low to moderate but stable across studies. In addition, they noted:

> Emotional Stability [Neuroticism] showed a rather stable influence on performance throughout nearly all of our analyses. It appears that being calm, secure, and well adjusted and low in anxiety has a small but consistent impact on job performance. Agreeableness also gains importance for those jobs that require interpersonal interactions, so that being likeable, cooperative, and good-natured has a small but consistent impact on performance. Finally, being Extraverted appears to influence sales and managerial jobs, and Openness to Experience appears to affect performance in customer service jobs. (p. 876)

Thus it appears that several of the Big Five dimensions of personality are related to job performance (Judge, Heller, & Mount, 2002; Rose, Murphy, Byard, & Nikzad, 2002).

## Alternatives to the Big Five

A great deal of attention has focused on the development of the five-factor model of personality. However, not everyone views the five factors as capturing the essence of personality. Drew Westen and Jonathan Shedler (1999) are psychotherapists and research psychologists who don't think questionnaire items address the deeper organizing principles of personality. What's more, the use of complex mathematical procedures, such as factor analysis, to identify the supposed key traits rests on the assumption that everyone has the same interpretation when reading the adjectives in such questionnaires. For example, is a disagreeable person someone who is hostile or someone who tends to pry into others' business? According to these psychologists, if we use questionnaires to provide a glimpse of personality, what we get is a description on a selection of traits that are just statistical entities and only skim the personality's surface.

Westen and Shedler believe that clinicians can use their expertise to get at underlying personality dynamics, especially those dynamics of significance in understanding personality disorders. Experienced clinicians listen to clients tell stories about their lives and watch their actual interactions, which provide rich sources of information for assessing personality.

Their method relies on clinical judgment: Clinicians rate personality-related statements as describing a patient on a scale of 0 to 7. Among the sample statements are "tends to feel empty or bored" or "tries to manipulate others' emotions to get what he/she wants." Then they use a statistical sorting technique, which has identified the dimensions of personality. These proposed dimensions are shown in Table 11-4. Note that these dimensions involve characteristics not tapped by the Big Five factors, and they have direct relevance to understanding personality disorders. Westen and Shedler believe that using their assessment system will help psychotherapists develop better treatment plans for clients (especially clients with personality disorders) in the future.

Based on his own research, Mayer (2003) has proposed a structural model that is related to the different types of processing areas in the brain. Mayer's model, called the *Primary Four*, identifies four central processing areas:

1. *Pleasant affect–depression.* This area encompasses both motivation and emotion.
2. *High versus low intelligence.* This processing area includes knowledge and general intelligence. "It is divisible into facets of verbal, spatial, and other specific intelligences" (p. 397).
3. *Social competency–incompetency.* This processing area is devoted to the ability to carry out social tasks. Mayer believes that "Its facets might include a blend of tact, politeness, acting ability, and similar competencies" (p. 397).
4. *Organized versus diffused awareness.* This processing area deals with general organized awareness. Good functioning in this area would be reflected via "general openness, mindfulness, and self-regulation," whereas poor functioning would result in "diffusion, dyscontrol, and constriction of awareness" (p. 397).

**TABLE 11-4**

## Dimensions of Personality Produced by Clinical Judgment and Clinical Sorting

| Dimension | Description |
| --- | --- |
| Psychological health | Ability to love others, find meaning in life, and gain personal insights |
| Psychopathy | Lack of remorse, presence of impulsiveness, and tendency to abuse drugs |
| Hostility | Deep-seated ill will |
| Narcissism | Self-importance, grandiose assumptions about oneself, and tendency to treat others as an audience to provide admiration |
| Emotional dysregulation | Intense and uncontrolled emotional reactions |
| Dysphoria | Depression, shame, humiliation, and lack of any pleasurable experiences |
| Schizoid orientation | Constricted emotions, inability to understand abstract concepts such as metaphors, and few or no friends |
| Obsessionality | Absorption in details, stinginess, and fear of dirt and contamination |
| Thought disorder | Believing that one has magical powers over others or can directly read their minds, for example |
| Oedipal conflict | Adult pursuit of romantic partners who are already involved with others, inappropriate seductiveness, and intense sexual jealousy |
| Dissociated consciousness | Fragmenting of thought and perception often related to past sexual abuse |
| Sexual conflict | Anxieties and fears regarding sexual intimacy |

**Source:** Westen and Shedler (1999).

Mayer is quick to add that there may be some supplementary traits; thus, his model actually is a Primary Four Plus model. It will be interesting to see how well this new model fares under research scrutiny in the coming years.

## REVIEW SUMMARY

1. Psychologists define **personality** as a stable pattern of thinking, feeling, and behaving that distinguishes one person from another. Two important components of this definition are distinctiveness and relative consistency.

2. Among the widely used **self-report inventories** of personality are the Minnesota Multiphasic Personality Inventory (MMPI) and the California Psychological Inventory (CPI). The MMPI was designed to help diagnose psychological disorders; the CPI is used to assess personality in the normal population.

3. **Projective tests** use ambiguous stimuli and require a great deal of interpretation by the test administrator. The most frequently used projective test is the Rorschach inkblot test.

4. The **Barnum effect** is the acceptance of generalized personality descriptions; it results from the use of favorable personality descriptions that apply to many people.

5. Critics of the concept of consistency in behavior argue that behavior is controlled by situations. In defense of the idea of

consistency, some researchers note that there are some problems with the methods used and the assumptions made in this research. Seymour Epstein proposes that both sides of the consistency issue are correct: Situations control behavior in a given instance, and broad consistencies do exist. Consistencies become visible when we add behaviors together, an approach termed *aggregation*.

6. **Traits** are summary terms that describe tendencies to act and interact in particular ways that are consistent across situations. Gordon Allport developed a list of trait terms.

7. Raymond Cattell proposed 16 source traits to describe personality and make predictions of future behaviors.

8. Hans Eysenck proposed the existence of three major traits. Extraversion has been associated with a number of differences in everyday behavior.

9. Current research offers a model of five major traits that seem to be relatively stable across the life span and across cultures.

## ✓ CHECK YOUR PROGRESS

1. Which psychological test might be used in each of the following circumstances?
   a. A hospital needs to determine the most likely diagnosis of mental patients.
   b. A company wants to use a self-report inventory to select new salespeople.
   c. A psychologist is interested in assessing a person's unconscious thought processes but has no direct access to those processes.

2. What term do psychologists use to describe a stable pattern of thinking, feeling, and behaving that distinguishes one person from another?
   a. ego
   b. psyche
   c. self-image
   d. personality

3. Fortune tellers use cues about people such as their clothing, speech, and gestures to persuade clients that

they know a great deal about them. This process is known as

a. cold reading.
b. aggregation.
c. standardization.
d. projective testing.

4. Which assessment technique requires individuals to respond to unstructured or ambiguous stimuli?

a. dynamic
b. objective
c. projective
d. predictive

5. Which of the following Big Five traits has been shown to be related to measures of job performance for several occupations?

a. neuroticism
b. agreeableness
c. conscientiousness
d. openness to experience

6. Personality descriptions that have something for everyone fit the

a. Barnum effect.
b. base-rate fallacy.
c. self-fulfilling prophesy.
d. social-desirability bias.

**ANSWERS: 1.** a. MMPI **b.** CPI **c.** Rorschach inkblot test or TAT  **2.** d  **3.** a  **4.** c  **5.** c  **6.** a

# BIOLOGICAL FACTORS IN PERSONALITY

The identical twins who live down the street—Kelly and Sharin—often dress alike. Family members, neighbors, and friends are amazed at how similar they are in their everyday behaviors. They are both on the high school basketball team, love to swim, and play in the school orchestra. Both sisters are outgoing and make friends easily. You wonder whether their similarities are due to the way they were raised (*nurture*) or to hereditary influences (*nature*). *To what extent are our personalities influenced by nurture (factors in our environment) or nature (hereditary factors)?*

There is little doubt that people differ in the personality traits they exhibit. But why? Are differences a result of early child-rearing experiences? Does heredity influence differences in personality? If heredity plays a role in personality traits, can those traits change over time?

## Early Biological Approaches

As you can see from the Myth or Science feature below, the idea that physical and biological factors hold a key to personality has a long history. From the perspective of modern science, however, some of the earliest attempts to relate personality to biological factors appear primitive. The research tools were too crude and the hypotheses too broad; nevertheless, those efforts started a search that continues to this day.

### Myth or Science

### Trepanation

Trephining (see Chapter 13), involves the opening of a hole in the skull, leaving the membranes surrounding the brain intact (Feilding, 1978). Trepanation, which involves operating on the skull but not on the brain, is one of the oldest medical procedures (Kabillo, 1998). Stone-age cave paintings suggest that primitive people used trepanation as a cure for seizures caused by epilepsy (McGrew, 1985) and as a treatment for mental disorders.

Trepanation did not cease as civilization progressed. It still generates interest and has some advocates today. (For example, a Google search yielded 2,800 hits for

A phrenology bust showing the numerous brain areas that the phrenologists thought they had identified by studying the bumps on the head.

Drag-race champion Eddie Hill was the first person to go 1/4-mile from a standing start in less than 5 seconds. Drag racing is a high-risk occupation that probably attracts people with high scores on the Sensation-Seeking Scale.

*trephining*.) The main concept of the modern trepanation movement lies in the word *brainbloodvolume* (the amount of blood supplied to the brain; Kabillo, 1998). Trepanation supposedly allows greater flow of blood in the capillaries of the brain. The increased amount of blood in the capillaries results in the brain cells having a larger source of energy. Therefore, they function at a higher level, accelerating brain metabolism and expanding consciousness. In short, trepanation may have a pronounced effect on a person's personality.

Most researchers and physicians do not have a high opinion of the supposed benefits of trepanation. Trepanation is illegal in the United States and Europe. Among the conditions it produces are blood clots, brain injuries, and infections leading to meningitis or death (Colton, 1998). Obviously, a great deal more research is needed before we can distinguish between myth and science with regard to trepanation. You can learn more about it, admittedly from the proponents' point of view, at http://www.trepan.com.

**Humors and Bumps.** Hippocrates (460–377 B.C.E.), a Greek philosopher and physician, believed that the human body contained four bodily "humors" or fluids: black bile, blood, phlegm, and yellow bile. The humor that predominated in a person was believed to determine that person's characteristics. For example, a predominance of black bile was thought to make a person depressed. Although we now know that the body is not filled with humors, interest in the role of biological factors in personality has continued.

In the 1800s, phrenologists (*phrenology* was an attempt to study a person by analyzing bumps and indentations on the skull; see Chapter 2) attempted to link personality with features of the brain. Franz Joseph Gall (1758–1828) compared the brain to a muscle and tried to locate various characteristics by looking for well-developed parts of the brain. Bumps on the skull might signify the development of underlying brain tissue, which in turn should reflect higher levels of characteristics such as benevolence. Eventually it became clear that any bumps on the skull had no connection to personal characteristics, and interest in phrenology faded. Still, phrenology played an important role in encouraging the study of brain functions.

**Body Types.** William Sheldon (1899–1977), a psychologist with medical training, suggested that the shape of one's body determines one's personality (Sheldon & Stevens, 1942; Sheldon, Stevens, & Tucker, 1940). He developed a scheme consisting of three body types: *Endomorphs* are round, *mesomorphs* are rectangular, and *ectomorphs* are thin. Sheldon also collected information about the personalities of people representing each of the body types and reported high correlations between body type and personality characteristics. According to Sheldon, endomorphs love comfort and are outgoing, mesomorphs are assertive and energetic, and ectomorphs are restrained and lonely. When other researchers could not replicate these correlations, they suspected that preconceptions about the relationship of body type to personality (for example, the stereotype of fat people as outgoing) had influenced Sheldon's results.

Although there is little convincing evidence that body type is related to personality, researchers are investigating the role of other biological factors in personality. Among those factors is the person's general level of neural arousal.

**Sensation Seeking.** Organisms appear to seek an optimal level of arousal or stimulation that varies by individual. Stimulation that is too far above or below that level is perceived as unpleasant. Is it possible to measure a person's need for stimulation? Psychologist Marvin Zuckerman has developed a self-report inventory to measure what he calls *sensation seeking* (see Chapter 6), defined as a general tendency to seek stimulation from a variety of sources. Sensation seeking is related to the broad trait of extraversion (review Figure 11-4) as well as to conscientiousness (Zuckerman, 1994).

Sensation seeking can be divided into several related components. *Disinhibition* is the tendency to seek sensation through social activities such as parties; *thrill seeking* is the desire to engage in physically risky activities; *experience seeking* is the tendency to seek novel experiences through the mind and the senses; and *boredom susceptibility* is an intolerance for repetitive experience.

## Hands On

## Sensation Seeking Scale

You will be able to estimate where your score falls on the Sensation Seeking Scale by completing the following items. The full scale consists of 40 items; we have reproduced 13 of them here so that you can get a feel for the types of items used to measure sensation seeking.

The Sensation Seeking Scale was designed to measure differences among individuals seeking stimulation from a variety of sources. For each of the following items, select the alternative that best indicates your preference. Then check your choices against the scoring key at the end of the chapter.

1. a. I would like a job that requires a lot of travel.
   b. I would prefer a job in one location.
2. a. I am invigorated by a brisk, cold day.
   b. I can't wait to get indoors on a cold day.
3. a. I get bored seeing the same old faces.
   b. I like the comfortable familiarity of everyday friends.
4. a. I would prefer living in an ideal society in which everyone is safe, secure, and happy.
   b. I would have preferred living in the unsettled days of our history.
5. a. I sometimes like to do things that are a little frightening.
   b. A sensible person avoids activities that are dangerous.
6. a. I would not like to be hypnotized.
   b. I would like to have the experience of being hypnotized.
7. a. The most important goal in life is to live it to the fullest and experience as much as possible.
   b. The most important goal in life is to find peace and happiness.
8. a. I would like to try parachute-jumping.
   b. I would never want to try jumping out of a plane, with or without a parachute.
9. a. I enter cold water gradually, giving myself time to get used to it.
   b. I like to dive or jump right into the ocean or a cold pool.
10. a. When I go on vacation, I prefer the comfort of a good room and bed.
    b. When I go on a vacation, I prefer the change of camping out.
11. a. I prefer people who are emotionally expressive even if they are a bit unstable.
    b. I prefer people who are calm and even-tempered.
12. a. A good painting should shock or jolt the senses.
    b. A good painting should give one a feeling of peace and security.
13. a. People who ride motorcycles must have some kind of unconscious need to hurt themselves.
    b. I would like to drive or ride a motorcycle.

**Source:** Zuckerman (1994).

Research on sensation seeking reveals that high sensation seekers enjoy spicy, sour, and crunchy foods more than low sensation seekers. This preference is probably due to the varied experiences such foods can provide. High sensation seekers tend to use more drugs and alcohol than low sensation seekers (Flory, Lynam, Milich, Leukefeld, & Clayton, 2004). Predictably, people in certain high-risk occupations—such as firefighters, race-car drivers, riot-squad police officers, and emergency-room nurses—tend to score rather high on this scale. Sports and recreation reveal similar expected differences: Scores of skydivers soar above those of golfers and aerobics participants. Likewise, gambling is positively related to sensation seeking (McDaniel & Zuckerman, 2003). A report by Hoffrage, Weber, Hertwig, & Chase (2003) indicated that it is important to identify risk takers early in life. They found that children who were high risk takers made more dangerous street crossings and were more likely to cause (hypothetical) accidents.

Biological differences may be at the root of differences in behavior related to sensation seeking, and these differences may have a genetic basis (Fulker, Eysenck, & Zuckerman, 1980; Tellegen et al., 1988). The enzyme monoamine oxidase (MAO) breaks down the neurotransmitter norepinephrine (see Chapter 2). Drugs that inhibit MAO increase levels of norepinephrine and cause individuals to be euphoric, impulsive, and aggressive. A negative correlation between MAO levels and sensation-seeking behavior (Longato-Stadler, Klinteberg, Garpenstrand, Oreland, & Hallman, 2002) indicates that low levels of MAO (and hence high levels of norepinephrine) are associated with high sensation-seeking scores. For example, gamblers who are well known for their impulsiveness and risk taking exhibit low levels of MAO (Carrasco et al., 1994). Lest we forget, a correlation between a biological variable and a personality variable does not prove causation; nevertheless, the findings are intriguing.

A growing body of research points to the importance of biological factors in several personality characteristics. Is it possible that some of these personality characteristics are inherited? The study of twins can shed light on questions concerning the heritability of personality characteristics.

## Twin Studies

Jim Springer and Jim Lewis had been adopted into separate working-class Ohio families in infancy. While in school, they both liked math but not spelling. Both had law enforcement training and worked part time as deputy sheriffs. They both vacationed in Florida, drove Chevrolets, and had dogs named Toy. Both had married and divorced women named Linda; their second marriages were to women named Betty. Both of them chew their fingernails and suffer late-afternoon headaches (Holden, 1980, 1987a).

This story depicts remarkable similarities in twins who were separated at birth. Since 1979, the University of Minnesota Study of Twins Reared Apart has been recruiting twin

**STUDY TIP**

Take the Big Five test on p. 484 and the Sensation Seeking Scale test on p. 493. Write a paragraph or two describing what you have learned about yourself using the terminology you have been introduced to in this chapter. In your description, note at least one finding that was a surprise to you, and discuss why.

The twins shown here are among those studied at the University of Minnesota. Many of those twins reported remarkable similarities across a range of experiences and behaviors.

pairs like those just described. Friends, relatives, or the twins themselves bring separated twin pairs to the attention of the researchers. Almost 1,000 twin pairs have agreed to participate in the research (Mann, 1994); most of them complete many hours of medical and psychological assessments.

## Psychological Detective

How can we explain the similarities in the behavior of twins who were separated early in life? Do these similarities convince you that they are due to inherited factors? What other evidence could be gathered from these twins that would help us understand genetic influences on personality? Give these questions some thought, and write down your answers before reading further.

The story of the Jim twins is dramatic, but we should ask whether the remarkable similarities might be coincidences. The participants had many opportunities during the lengthy testing they underwent to discover similarities in their behaviors. Is there other evidence of similar personalities in identical twins who were separated early in life that cannot be explained as a series of coincidences?

Recall from Chapter 9 that fraternal twins are no more similar to each other than you are to your brother or sister; in contrast, identical twins have the same genes. Because identical twins share the same genes, we would expect their personalities to be similar. A problem often arises, however, in conducting research on twins: Identical twins may be treated more similarly than fraternal twins. Thus we cannot be sure whether similarities between identical twins are due to their identical heredity or to the similarity of their environments. The study of twins who were separated early in life allows researchers to isolate the effects of nature (heredity) from those of nurture (environment).

The University of Minnesota research team reported the results of a study of 44 pairs of identical twins who were separated early in life (Tellegen et al., 1988). The twins completed the Multidimensional Personality Questionnaire, a self-report inventory that yields 11 scales. As you can see from Figure 11-5, the difference between the

 **11.1**

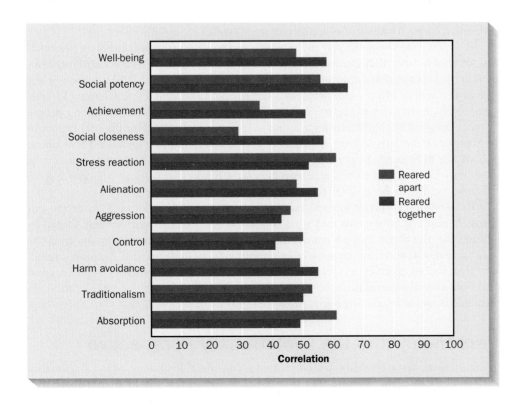

**FIGURE 11-5** Correlations of personality characteristics for identical twins reared apart and identical twins reared together. The small differences suggest that environmental factors play a small role in determining these personality characteristics.

**Source:** Tellegen et al. (1988).

**TABLE 11-5**

### Similarity in Identical and Fraternal Twins in Personality Assessed Using the Big Five Traits

| Big Five Trait | Self-Report Correlation | | Peer-Rating Correlation | |
|---|---|---|---|---|
| | Identical | Fraternal | Identical | Fraternal |
| Extraversion | .56 | .28 | .40 | .17 |
| **Neuroticism** | .53 | .13 | .43 | .03 |
| **Agreeableness** | .42 | .19 | .32 | .18 |
| **Conscientiousness** | .54 | .18 | .43 | .18 |
| **Openness to experience*** | .54 | .35 | .48 | .31 |

*Referred to as *culture* by these researchers.

**Source:** Angleitner, Riemann, and Strelau (1995).

correlations for identical twins reared apart and for those reared together are very small. The correlations are similar whether the identical twins were reared apart or together.

Let's turn to research focused on possible genetic influences on the Big Five traits we discussed earlier. Almost 1,000 twins took part in a study conducted in Germany and Poland. Each twin's personality was assessed by two different raters using the Big Five traits. A correlation of .63 between the raters demonstrated strong agreement in the assessments of the personalities by peers. The averaged peer ratings correlated .55 with the twins' self-report ratings. The correlations across identical twins were consistently higher than the correlations for fraternal twins, suggesting a genetic influence on personality (see Table 11-5).

The researchers concluded that personality measured either by self-ratings or peer ratings shows a genetic influence, with no evidence for a shared environmental influence (Angleitner, Riemann, & Strelau, 1995). Similar results were obtained in a study of twins in Canada and Germany, which the researchers interpreted as support for genetic influences on personality traits across cultures (Jang et al., 1998).

Before we are swept away by the research on the hereditary influences on personality, we should note that although heredity plays a substantial role in behavior, nongenetic factors are also important (Plomin, Owen, & McGuffin, 1994). Although the size of the genetic effect—estimated by what is called *heritability* (see Chapter 8)—can be 51–58%, most cases are between 20 and 50%. Therefore differences among people in most personality characteristics are due at least as much to environmental factors as to heredity (Horowitz, Videon, Schmitz, & Davis, 2003). Even in identical twins, about half of the differences in personality traits are not shared and hence are not due to hereditary factors. What's more, researchers have found that siblings who grow up in the same family can be very different (Dunn & Plomin, 1990).

In trying to explain differences among siblings, researchers focused on differences across families. It now seems that what is important is not the environment shared by siblings but the nonshared environment. That is, each child experiences the environment differently, and these nonshared environmental factors appear to be more important than shared experiences (Plomin et al., 1994). For example, surveys of parents and children, as well as naturalistic observations in the home, suggest that parents may not treat each child alike, despite social pressure to do so.

## Personality and the Evolutionary Perspective

We have seen, through the twin studies, that a considerable amount of our personality may be determined genetically. The evolutionary perspective would predict that those aspects of our personality that help us adapt to environmental demands are passed along to subsequent generations. Although it is one thing to *suggest* that personality characteristics might be transmitted genetically, it is a much more demanding task to offer scientifically acceptable evidence. (Remember that determining if a knowledge claim is based on scientific evidence is one of the guidelines for the psychological detective that we discussed in Chapter 1.)

Researchers have generated considerable data in support of the theory of psychologist David Buss (1987, 1989) that evolution has had an impact on the type of people that men and women choose as dates and mates. Specifically, Buss predicts that women will choose men who have good resources (food, shelter, and protection). He indicates that, "In humans, resources can take many forms . . . income, occupational and social status, possessions, networks of alliance, and family background. Personality characteristics such as hard-working, ambitious, energetic, industrious, and persevering also appear to be correlated with achievement potential" (Buss, 1987, p. 340). Buss believes that women will reject dates and sexual overtures from men who do not satisfy most or all of these criteria. What about men? Buss indicates that, "According to this evolutionary argument, males should come to value and view as attractive those physical and behavioral cues in potential mates that correlate with female reproductive capacity" (p. 341).

To understand these differing predictions, remember that perpetuation of a person's genes via his or her offspring is a key underlying principle. Because women produce only a limited number of offspring, it is important that each offspring receive optimal care in order to increase the chances of survival; hence, women seek men who have resources. Men, on the other hand, perpetuate their genes by (1) seeking a number of temporary mates or (2) seeking a single long-term mate. In either case, reproductive ability is the dominant characteristic that men seek, and Buss believes that age and health are two important indicators of this characteristic.

In a study that exemplifies the research support for Buss's theory, Driggers and Helms (2000) tested "the role of salary in date selection by men and women" (p. 76). They predicted that willingness to date would increase as salary increased and that salary would be more important to women because it was an indicator of greater resources. Male and female participants in three groups rated opposite-sex pictures in terms of willingness to date (15 not willing, 75 extremely willing). Scores were smallest (least willingness to date) in the lowest salary group and increased significantly at the next two salary levels. At the highest salary level, the women showed significantly more willingness to date; salary was indeed more important for them.

Clearly, genetic factors present at birth can have important influences on the development of our personality. Next, we turn to a very different approach to understanding personality. Sigmund Freud thought that our early experiences set the stage for personality throughout life; his focus, however, was on how unconscious factors could determine our personality.

## REVIEW SUMMARY

1. Efforts to connect personality to biological factors can be traced to Hippocrates's theory of humors and later to phrenology.

2. William Sheldon suggested a relationship between body type and personality. Subsequent research demonstrated that his findings were influenced by his preconceptions.

3. Additional support for the belief that biological factors influence personality is found in the negative correlation between sensation-seeking scores and levels of the enzyme MAO.

4. The study of identical twins reared apart allows researchers to identify the effects of heredity independently of the influence of environmental factors. Evidence from such studies indicates that heredity plays a role in a wide range of personality characteristics, as evidenced by heritability estimates between 20 and 50%.

5. Recent evidence suggests that nonshared experiences exert a major influence on the personality of siblings.

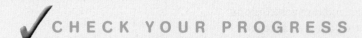

## ✓ CHECK YOUR PROGRESS

1. Who was the Greek philosopher who proposed that body fluids influenced personality? What name did he give those fluids?

2. Sheldon believed that personality was related to

   a. body type.
   b. bodily humors.
   c. facial features.
   d. bumps on the skull.

3. Why are identical twins reared apart so important in research designed to determine the influence of nature and nurture on personality?

4. The strongest evidence for a genetic role in personality is found in similar personality characteristics between

   a. identical twins reared apart.
   b. fraternal twins reared apart.

   c. identical twins reared together.
   d. fratenal twins reared together.

5. Researchers find that Ted's body has low levels of the enzyme MAO. Based on this finding, you conclude that Ted is likely to obtain a high score on a test designed to measure

   a. openness.
   b. achievement.
   c. sensation seeking.
   d. emotional stability.

6. What factor has been found to explain both differences in personality among siblings and personality change?

   a. shared heredity
   b. shared environment
   c. nonshared heredity
   d. nonshared environment

**ANSWERS: 1.** Hippocrates, humors **2.** a **3.** High correlations between identical twins reared together could be the result of similarities in the environment. When the twins are reared separately, the high correlations reflect hereditary influences on personality. **4.** a **5.** c **6.** d

# THE PSYCHODYNAMIC PERSPECTIVE

One morning, in Donna's philosophy class, the professor referred to the ideas of Sigmund Freud. Later in the day, the professor in a literature class used Freud's ideas to explain hidden meanings in a poem about dreams. Then a sociology professor used Freud's ideas to explain aggressive behavior in some members of society. *Why have Freud's ideas been influential in so many disciplines?*

Sigmund Freud, a neurologist, developed both a theory of personality that emphasized unconscious factors and a therapy for patients exhibiting abnormal behaviors.

Sigmund Freud (1856–1939), a neurologist, developed both a theory of personality (psychodynamic theory) that emphasized unconscious factors and a therapy (psychoanalytic therapy) for patients exhibiting abnormal behaviors (see Chapter 13). Today almost everyone knows the name Sigmund Freud. Have you ever heard or used the terms *Freudian slip*, *unconscious*, or *repression*? If you have, you should recognize Freud's impact. As we saw in the case of Sally's classes, Freud's views and theories have found their way into several academic disciplines as well as into everyday speech.

To understand Freud, it is important to understand the times in which he lived. Freud was born to Jewish parents in Austria in 1856 and grew up in Vienna. He lived during the Victorian era, a time notorious for its repressive views of sexuality. The prevailing social norms prohibited the discussion of sex. The time was also marked by extreme anti-Semitism (prejudice against Jews), which blocked Freud from pursuing a career as a scientist. His future looked bleak, and he needed money to get married, so he reluctantly went into private practice as a neurologist.

Most of Freud's patients were women who suffered from hysterical disorders. (As described in Chapter 12, these disorders involve physical symptoms such as blindness or paralysis that have no known physical cause.) Freud proposed that these disorders resulted from psychological conflicts, especially sexual ones. During therapy sessions, his patients related stories of sexual contact with an older male. At first Freud believed that these events had actually occurred, but later he changed his mind and concluded that they were fantasies. He believed his patients could not differentiate their sexual desires from what had actually happened earlier in their lives. Some critics believe Freud had uncovered evidence of sexual abuse of children, which he was either unwilling to report or unable to accept as true (Masson, 1985).

Freud believed that his patients were not consciously aware of these sexual conflicts. If these conflicts were not brought to conscious awareness, they would continue to exert an influence in the form of physical and psychological symptoms. To deal with these symptoms and to bring the conflicts to the conscious level, Freud developed a therapeutic approach called *psychoanalysis* or *psychoanalytic therapy* (see Chapter 13).

## Basic Concepts

Three concepts form the backbone of Freud's theory: psychic determinism, instincts, and levels of consciousness. Let's look at each of these concepts.

**Psychic Determinism.**    **Psychic determinism** refers to the influence of the past on the present. Freud believed that much of our behavior, feeling, and thinking is determined by events that occurred earlier in our lives. For example, sexual conflicts occurring in childhood can bring on physical symptoms in adulthood.

### Psychological Detective

What does the term *Freudian slip* mean to you? What, if anything, do you think a Freudian slip reveals about a person? Give these questions some thought, and write down your answer before reading further.

A Freudian slip is one example of the concept of psychic determinism. According to Freud, these errors in reading, speaking, or writing reveal something about our "inner" thoughts or "real" intent. Imagine attending an extremely boring party, which drags on for more hours than you can count. After several hours, you decide to leave and typically intend to say something like "I'm sorry I have to leave now." Your true feelings, however, may be revealed in words such as "I'm glad I have to leave now."

**Instincts.**    What inner forces might lead to these Freudian slips? Freud believed we are driven by the energy of certain instincts in much the same way that a car is propelled by the energy contained in gasoline. He described two key instincts: *eros* for life-giving and pleasure-producing activities, including sex, and *thanatos* for aggression or destruction.

**The Unconscious.**    The third major concept in psychodynamic theory is Freud's proposal that there are various levels of consciousness. In Chapter 4 we defined *consciousness* as personal awareness of internal and external events. Freud described three levels of consciousness (see Figure 11-6). The *conscious* level refers to the thoughts, wishes, and emotions you are aware of at this moment. The level just below consciousness is called the *preconscious;* its contents are waiting to be pulled into consciousness like fish from a pond.

The third – and in Freud's theory the most important – level of consciousness (or awareness) is below the preconscious and is called the **unconscious.** The unconscious consists of thoughts, wishes, and feelings that exist beyond our awareness; we can gain access to them only with great effort. The techniques of psychodynamic therapy are designed to gain access to the contents of the unconscious (see Chapter 13). Freud believed that much of our behavior is caused by unconscious forces and that the contents of conscious thought are only a small portion of our inner life.

**psychic determinism**
The psychodynamic assumption that all behaviors result from early childhood experiences, especially conflicts related to sexual instincts

**unconscious**
Part of the personality that lies outside of awareness yet is believed to be a crucial determinant of behavior

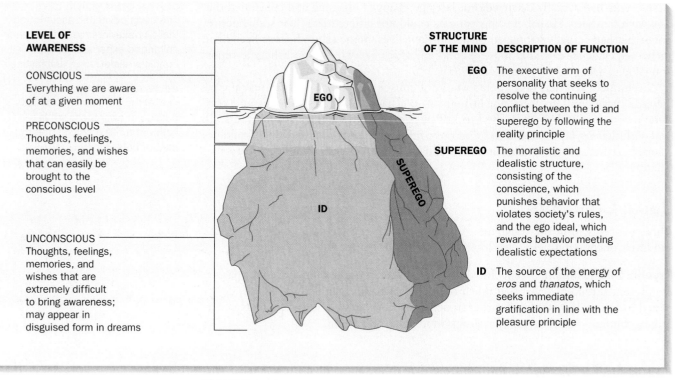

CONSCIOUS
Everything we are aware
of at a given moment

PRECONSCIOUS
Thoughts, feelings,
memories, and wishes
that can easily be
brought to the
conscious level

UNCONSCIOUS
Thoughts, feelings,
memories, and
wishes that are
extremely difficult
to bring awareness;
may appear in
disguised form in dreams

STRUCTURE
OF THE MIND | DESCRIPTION OF FUNCTION

EGO — The executive arm of
personality that seeks to
resolve the continuing
conflict between the id and
superego by following the
reality principle

SUPEREGO — The moralistic and
idealistic structure,
consisting of the
conscience, which
punishes behavior that
violates society's rules,
and the ego ideal, which
rewards behavior meeting
idealistic expectations

ID — The source of the energy of
*eros* and *thanatos*, which
seeks immediate
gratification in line with the
pleasure principle

**FIGURE 11-6** Relation of conscious, preconscious, and unconscious thought in Freudian theory. In this iceberg model, most of the contents of the mind are below the consciousness threshold and therefore are unavailable to our conscious thoughts.

## The Structure of the Mind

According to Freud's comprehensive theory, the mind consists of three separate but interacting elements: the id, the ego, and the superego. (Note that he was not describing actual parts of the brain but hypothetical concepts.) This model compares the mind to an iceberg (see Figure 11-6). Just as most of an iceberg lies beneath the surface of the water, much of what is truly significant in psychodynamic theory lies below conscious awareness. Figure 11-6 also depicts the relation of the three components of the mind to the levels of consciousness discussed earlier. The next sections examine that relationship.

**The Id.**   The **id** represents the primitive biological side of our personality. This reservoir of pleasure-seeking and aggressive instinctual energy aims to reduce tension that builds up when our wishes are thwarted. Moreover, the id is extremely selfish and has no concern for the needs or desires of others or for what society may want. As you can see in Figure 11-6, the id is entirely unconscious. Operating on the *pleasure principle*, it impulsively seeks immediate gratification of wishes through the ego.

**The Ego.**   As time passes, the id's relentless demands for instant gratification are reined in by a new structure, the ego. The **ego** is sometimes called the executive of the personality because it has a realistic plan for obtaining what the id wants; therefore it is said to operate on the *reality principle*. Seldom, however, do our surroundings provide immediate gratification of our needs, so the ego must tolerate some delay and occasional frustration.

**The Superego.**   The third element of the mind, the **superego,** has two components: the *conscience* and the *ego ideal*. Imagine yourself slightly exceeding the speed limit while

**id**
In psychodynamic theory, the most basic element of the personality; it is the source of the instincts and operates on the pleasure principle

**ego**
In psychodynamic theory, the element of the mind that operates according to the reality principle and serves to satisfy the id and the superego

**superego**
In psychodynamic theory, the element of the mind that incorporates parental and societal standards in what is commonly referred to as the conscience as well as the idealistic ego ideal

driving down a highway. Suddenly the red lights of a state police cruiser are reflected in your rear-view mirror. An anxious feeling spreads throughout your body, your heart beats rapidly, and you start to sweat as you wonder if the trooper is after you. When the cruiser zips by on its way to apprehend a "real" speeder, your heartbeat returns to normal. You reacted the way you did because you felt you had done something wrong and were about to be punished. This feeling stemmed from your conscience. This moral part of the superego is like a little voice that tells us when we have violated our parents' and society's rules. For many (but not all) of us, the conscience exacts punishment for even the possibility of violating those rules.

The second component of the superego, the ego ideal, represents the superego's positive side—the things that make us proud. Achieve excellent grades in school and the ego ideal "pats you on the back" in recognition of your accomplishment. The ego ideal aims for what is right, correct, and ideal; it motivates us to strive for perfection.

**Interaction of Id, Ego, and Superego.**     The relation among the id, ego, and superego is like a car with some special features. Suppose that this car—call it IES (for id, ego, superego)—is designed to pull both to the left and to the right sides of the road, often at the same time. The left and right wheels represent the id and the superego, and they often try to turn in opposite directions. The id tries to satisfy basic biological drives; the superego strives to impose highly perfectionistic and moralistic goals in their place. Thus the id and the superego are unrealistic and irrational in separate but competing ways. The driver represents the ego and is responsible for making adjustments as the id and superego struggle against each other. The ego tries to find an acceptable middle road between these two divergent forces.

# Defense Mechanisms

The ego is engaged in an ongoing battle to deal with the competing demands of the id and the superego. If you recall the iceberg model of the mind (Figure 11-6), you will realize that much of this conflict lies beneath the surface in the unconscious.

### Psychological Detective

Imagine that the id, ego, and superego are in conflict. How does a person know that this battle is happening? What does a person do when this conflict develops? Give these questions some thought, and write down your answers before reading further.

Freud proposes that there is a never-ending battle between two irrational forces (the id and the superego), with a mediator (the ego) in the middle. Much of this conflict is unconscious, but when it becomes serious, an alarm goes off. In psychodynamic theory, anxiety or guilt is a warning to the ego that conflict is occurring.

When the anxiety or guilt alarm rings, the ego defends itself through unconscious efforts referred to as **defense mechanisms** (Freud, 1958) that tend to deny or distort reality (see Table 11-6). The effect of defense mechanisms is to reduce anxiety or guilt. The use of defense mechanisms, however, can be helpful or harmful, depending on how much a person relies on them.

# Stages of Psychosexual Development

Freud proposed that an individual's personality develops through a series of five stages stretching from infancy to adulthood. These stages are called *psychosexual stages*

**defense mechanism**
Psychodynamic term used to describe primarily unconscious methods of reducing anxiety or guilt that results from conflicts among the id, ego, and superego

**TABLE 11-6**

# Defense Mechanisms

Defense mechanisms protect the ego from anxiety by distorting or otherwise altering reality. Although everyone uses defense mechanisms, excessive use of them is considered a sign of abnormality.

| Defense Mechanism | Descriptions | Examples |
|---|---|---|
| Denial | Refusing to acknowledge an undesirable experience, memory, or internal need that is anxiety-arousing and behaving as if it did not exist | A physician tells a parent that her son has terminal cancer. Despite overwhelming evidence that the cancer is not treatable, the parent remains convinced that the child will recover. |
| Displacement | Shifting feelings from one object to a substitute that is not as gratifying but is less anxiety-arousing | You want to retaliate against your boss for something she said to you during a performance evaluation. The ego, being relatively wise and in contact with reality, recognizes that such a course of action would be ill-advised. Later in the day, you find yourself yelling at the grocery clerk, cutting off other drivers on the way home, and hanging up on callers soliciting funds for a local charity. Each of these innocent bystanders is a safer outlet for aggression than your boss and hence is less threatening to the ego. |
| Projection | Attributing to others unwanted feelings, thoughts, or behaviors | A person who is having difficulty making it to work on time because of procrastination and failure to meet deadlines says, "It's not my fault. My bosses are just too demanding, and my coworkers are uncooperative." |
| Rationalization | Proposing socially acceptable feelings or reasons in place of actual, unacceptable feelings or reasons for a behavior | You did not do well on an exam in your economics course. You could admit that you found the material impossible to comprehend, but perhaps this admission would lead to additional anxiety. So you may tell yourself, and anyone else who is listening, that you "don't want to be an economist anyway." |
| Reaction formation | Defending against unacceptable feelings and behavior by exhibiting the opposite of one's true wishes or impulses | A person may be attracted to pornographic material (id) yet be repulsed by the thought of such material (superego). Such a person may become involved in a censorship campaign that places him or her in the position of having to review pornographic material. |
| Regression | Returning to forms of behavior that are indicative of an earlier level of development such as childhood (usually in response to an overwhelming stressor) | An adult has a temper tantrum (a common behavior of 3- or 4-year-olds). |
| Sublimation | A form of displacement in which a sexual or aggressive impulse is moved from an unacceptable object to one that is acceptable and ultimately has value to society | A typical example of sublimation involves the direction of sexual energy toward the creation of works of art. Another example involves turning aggressive energy toward socially desirable goals such as performing surgery to save lives rather than harming others. |

because each is characterized by efforts to obtain pleasure centered on one of several parts of the body called *erogenous zones*. (The term *psychosexual stages* might remind you of Erikson's stages of *psychosocial* development that we covered in Chapter 9. Although they sound similar, Freud's psychosexual stages were developed first; it is likely that Erikson used Freud's theory as a pattern for his own stage theory.) According to

Freud, the five stages of psychosexual development are the oral, anal, phallic, latency, and genital stages.

**The Oral Stage.** Pleasure-seeking behavior in the **oral stage** focuses on the baby's mouth. Infants and toddlers can often be seen biting, sucking, or placing objects in their mouths. Freud hypothesized that if oral needs such as the need for food are delayed, the child's personality may become arrested or fixated. A person whose development is arrested will display behaviors as an adult that are associated with the time of life during which the **fixation** occurred. For example, fixation at the oral stage may be manifest in behaviors such as chewing on pencils or overeating and in personality characteristics such as excessive dependency, optimism, and gullibility.

**The Anal Stage.** From about 18 months until about 3 years of age, the child is in the **anal stage.** As the child gains muscular control, the erogenous zone shifts to the anus, and the child derives pleasure from the expulsion and retention of feces. The key to this stage is toilet training. The way parents approach toilet training can have lasting effects on their children. Early in the anal stage the child gains pleasure from the expulsion of feces. A person who is fixated at this stage is referred to as *anal-expulsive.* As adults these people are overly generous. If the parents are strict and demanding, the child may rebel, and the result will be fixation at this stage. Individuals who are fixated at this stage may be overly rigid and orderly as adults and are referred to as *anal-retentive.*

**The Phallic Stage.** The **phallic stage,** which begins at about age 4 to 5, is ushered in by another shift in the erogenous zone and the child's pleasure-seeking behavior. During this stage, children derive pleasure from fondling their genitals. The phallic stage is also the time when the **Oedipal complex** (in boys) or the **Electra complex** (in girls) occurs.

Freud believed that young boys develop a sexual interest in their mothers, see their fathers as competitors for the mothers' affection, and therefore wish to get rid of their fathers. The name of this complex is derived from Oedipus, a character in an ancient Greek tragedy who had unwittingly killed his father and married his mother; when he discovered the truth, he gouged out his eyes and spent the rest of his life as a homeless wanderer.

The young boy fears his father's retaliation for these forbidden sexual and aggressive impulses. He fantasizes that the father's retaliation would involve injury to his genitals; as a result, he experiences what is called *castration anxiety.* To reduce the fear, the boy represses his sexual desire for his mother and begins to identify with his father, which means that he tries to be like Dad in his behavior, values, attitudes, and sexual orientation. Successful resolution of the Oedipal complex, according to Freud, leads to acquisition of the male sex role (see Chapter 10).

The Electra complex is named for a character in another Greek tragedy who conspired to kill her mother to avenge her father's death. Young girls become aware that they do not have penises, which Freud believed they both value and desire. Thus girls experience *penis envy,* which leads to anger directed at their mothers and sexual attraction toward their fathers. A girl's attraction to her father is rooted in a fantasy that seducing him will provide her with a penis. She also fantasizes about having a baby as another means of gaining the valued organ. Resolution of this complex occurs when the girl represses her sexual desires and begins to identify with her mother.

Freud believed that the male superego receives an intense unconscious push from Oedipal castration fears and that the female superego ends up weaker than that of the male. This belief, however, like a number of Freudian ideas, has not been supported by research (Bower, 1991).

**The Latency and Genital Stages.** At about age 6, children enter a period when their sexual interests are suppressed. This period, which lasts until the beginning of

The first stage of Freud's psychosexual stages—the oral stage—consists of attaining pleasure via the mouth.

**oral stage**
The first stage of psychosexual development in which the mouth is the focus of pleasure-seeking activity
The first stage of Freud's psychosexual stages—the oral stage—consists of attaining pleasure via the mouth

**fixation**
Cessation of further development, resulting in behaviors that are characteristic of the stage of development in which the fixation occurred

**anal stage**
Second stage of psychosexual development, during which the focus of pleasure is the anus and conflict often occurs as efforts are made to toilet-train the child

**phallic stage**
The third stage of psychosexual development, in which the genital organs become the focus of pleasure-seeking behavior

**Oedipal complex**
Process that occurs during the phallic stage in which a boy wishes to possess his mother sexually and fears retaliation by his father

**Electra complex**
Process that occurs during the phallic stage in which a girl wishes to possess her father sexually

## Study CHART

### Freud's Stages of Psychosexual Development

| Stage | Approximate Ages | Erogenous Zones | Major Characteristics |
|---|---|---|---|
| Oral | Birth to about 18 months | Mouth | Focus on oral gratification from sucking, chewing, eating, and biting |
| Anal | End of oral stage to 3 years | Anus | Gratification from holding and expelling feces at the time when these desires for gratification must meet societal demands to control the bladder and bowels (toilet training) |
| Phallic | End of anal stage to about 6 years | Genitals | Gratification focused on manipulation of genitals; development of sexual interest in the parent of the opposite biological sex |
| Latency | End of phallic stage to onset of puberty | None | Sexual desires not of paramount importance |
| Genital | Adolescence to adulthood | Genitals | Resurgence of sexual interests; focus on mature sexual adult relationships |

**latency stage**
Stage of psychosexual development that extends from about age 6 until the onset of puberty and is characterized by a low level of sexual interest

**genital stage**
Stage of psychosexual development that begins at puberty and usually leads to normal adult sexual development

**STUDY TIP**

Write an outline on the topic of Sigmund Freud. Include basic facts, his theories, and their influence on modern psychology.

adolescence, is called the **latency stage.** Sexual interests are reawakened at puberty and become stronger during the **genital stage.** In this stage, sexual pleasure is derived from heterosexual relationships. At the beginning of the genital stage, most adolescents have difficulty developing true affection and caring for others; they still experience the selfish qualities of earlier stages of development. As they mature, they develop greater ability to establish such relationships, thus setting the foundation for adult relationships. Freud's stages of psychosexual development are summarized in the accompanying Study Chart.

## Freud in Perspective

Freud attracted both supporters and critics. Some of his most outspoken critics were formerly his greatest admirers who once espoused his views, but for a variety of reasons they developed new perspectives that nonetheless fit the psychodynamic mold. For example, they did not accept Freud's emphasis on the id and the role of sexual motives; instead they emphasized the ego and its role in the development of personality, as well as the social aspects of personality. These individuals are frequently referred to as *neo-Freudians.*

## The Neo-Freudians

One of the best-known neo-Freudians, Carl Jung (1875–1961), split from Freud on more than one issue and developed his own psychodynamic viewpoint. For example, Jung did not want to place as much emphasis on sexuality as did Freud. Jung stressed a more generalized life force, emphasized the future, and placed even more emphasis on the unconscious than did Freud.

Jung suggested that a *collective unconscious* contains images shared by *all* people. Jung's name for these images is *archetypes*. These archetypes are passed along genetically and cause us to respond to events in our environment in particular ways. Among the archetypes that Jung proposed are *persona* (a mask of our true personality), *anima* and *animus* (exhibition of both feminine and masculine characteristics, respectively), *shadow* (the animal instinct or "dark" side of our personality), and *self* (the part of our personality that provides unity and stability and attempts to integrate the different aspects of the personality).

Jung proposed the concepts of *introversion* and *extraversion* to reflect the direction of the person's life force. The life force of an introvert is turned inward, whereas the life force of an extravert is turned outward. He also developed the word association test for use as a personality assessment device. The longer a person took to respond to a word, or if a word produced changes in breathing rate, then Jung believed that an unconscious emotional problem might exist.

Karen Horney (1885–1952), an early disciple of Freudian thinking, rejected several Freudian notions and added several of her own. She viewed personality disturbances not as resulting from instinctual strivings to satisfy sexual and aggressive urges but as stemming from the basic anxiety that all people share. We all feel anxiety because we find ourselves isolated and sometimes helpless in an unfriendly world. Anxiety is an unpleasant state that we seek to reduce.

In order to reduce anxiety, Horney believes that all people use three basic adjustment patterns: *moving toward people* (a person seeks affection and approval), *moving against people* (uses power to control and exploit other people), and *moving away from people* (withdraws from a situation). The choice of which behavior pattern a person uses should depend on the type of situation that is producing the anxiety. A person's behavior becomes abnormal (see Chapter 12) when he or she uses only one adjustment pattern in all situations.

Alfred Adler (1870–1937) was a Freudian disciple who was ejected from the Vienna Psychoanalytic Society in 1911 because of his disagreements with Freud. Adler believed that Freud overemphasized the sexual drive in explaining personality. He argued that the primary drive is social rather than sexual.

According to Adler, the young child is inevitably weak when compared to adults. This comparison has the effect that, throughout the rest of the child's life, he or she strives to overcome the inferiority feelings that these early experiences create. This striving for superiority is innate; people develop different lifestyles to achieve it; they are motivated to develop new skills and abilities that lead to a sense of superiority. Thus Adler shifted the emphasis in personality theory from the id to the ego, which strives to gain control over others. He noted that we spend much of our lives striving to compensate for our perceived shortcomings. For example, the Greek philosopher Demosthenes was embarrassed by his stuttering as a child, so he spent years practicing speaking clearly and eventually became a great orator.

Adler can be considered the first *self* theorist due to the emphasis he placed on this concept. For him the self was the most important part of the personality. It is constantly striving for unity. In this context, Adler postulated the *creative power of the self*—the notion that we are able to mold our own destinies (that is, we possess free will). Also, Adler was the first theorist to stress the importance of birth order as a determinant of personality. Although he had a great impact on psychoanalysis and personality theory, his system lacks hard data and replicability; it is largely based on anecdotes.

**Evaluation of Freudian Theory.** When Freud first published his ideas in the early 1900s, they met with strong negative reactions, especially his notions of sexuality in children. Most people were repulsed by the idea of viewing children as sexual beings. When Freud published his classic book on dreams, about 300 copies were sold.

Eventually Freud's ideas caught on, and they have had a lasting impact. Some researchers report that many of Freud's proposals, such as unconscious influences on emotional responses, social behavior, and habitual behavior, are supported by research (Westen, 1990). Research also has begun to link psychoanalytic concepts and neural pathways in the brain (Gelyana & Garfield, 2003). Nevertheless, there are a great number of critics who note that it is difficult to conduct research on psychodynamic concepts (Hergenhahn & Olson, 1999). For example, it is almost impossible to examine the effect of parenting practices on fixations because Freud did not specify the conditions that might lead to fixations. Even when such concepts can be tested, the tests have had mixed results.

Significantly, Freud's theory is based on the study of a small number of disturbed people, who may not provide the basis for generalizations applicable to most people. What's more, many of the patients that Freud treated were women, yet he developed a theory that dealt primarily with male sexuality; this inconsistency makes generalizations quite difficult. His method of data collection was a source of dismay for researchers. During his treatment sessions, Freud sat behind the patient, who was comfortably relaxing on a couch. Freud listened attentively to what the patient was saying. Only after the session was over did Freud write down anything pertaining to what the patient had said. How much information did he forget? How many changes did he make in trying to recall what was said? This subjectivity did not ensure confidence in many critics. Additionally, the validity of Freud's entire system is questionable because he never verified the information that his patients revealed to him during psychoanalysis. This information was used to construct his theory. Finally, Sundberg, Winebarger, and Taplin (2002) indicate that "Many psychologists have criticized Freud for his views of women, especially the notion that they suffer from 'penis envy'" (p. 205).

On the other side of the coin, Freud drew attention to the potential importance of early childhood experiences; he was the first to outline a stage theory of development and to identify key influences operating at each stage. Freud is also credited with drawing attention to the impact of sexuality on human behavior. It undoubtedly took courage for him to offer his ideas at a time when the public wanted to keep sexuality hidden and repressed. He noted the importance of unconscious factors in determining behavior. We are often unaware of the motivations and rationales that underlie our behavior. Some observers therefore view the concept of the unconscious as one of the enduring contributions of psychodynamic theory (Westen, 1998).

Freud's work also popularized counseling and psychotherapy in the United States and around the world. His ideas have been applied to the development of the form of psychotherapy called *psychoanalysis*, which strives to bring unconscious conflicts to the surface so that an individual can deal with them more effectively.

Still, critics note that Freud developed a theory that focused on concern for one's own desires, irresponsibility, and the denigration of women. For example, Freud saw women as more vain than men and having little sense of justice, along with a perpetual sense of inferiority owing to the lack of a penis. What's more, Freud's belief in unconscious instinctual drives may well have overstated the case for such influences.

Historically, a number of psychological perspectives developed, in part, in opposition to psychodynamic theory. Compared with Freud and his followers, the proponents of these perspectives had very different views on the development of personality. We next turn our attention to personality as viewed from the cognitive-learning and humanistic perspectives.

# REVIEW SUMMARY

**1.** Freud suggested that behaviors, feelings, and thoughts result from past events. Because this **psychic determinism** occurs at an unconscious level, we are often unaware of the true reasons for our behavior.

**2.** Freud compared the mind to an iceberg, with three levels of consciousness (*conscious, preconscious,* and *unconscious*) and three structures (**id, ego,** and **superego**). Conflicts among the structures of the mind occur beneath the level of conscious awareness.

**3.** Severe unconscious conflict produces anxiety or guilt that warn the ego. The ego uses **defense mechanisms** to protect itself from being overwhelmed by anxiety or guilt.

**4.** According to Freud, at different stages of development the id centers its pleasure-seeking behavior on different parts of the body, called *erogenous zones*. The resulting psychosexual stages begin with the **oral stage** and continue through the **anal** and **phallic stages.** The **Oedipal** and **Electra complexes** occur during the phallic stage. This stage is followed by the **latency stage** and then by the **genital stage** and the emergence of adult sexual desires.

5. The neo-Freudians—including Jung, Horney, and Adler—disagreed with a number of Freud's views (for example, those emphasizing the sexual and unconscious roots of behavior).

6. Freud is credited with pointing out the influence of early childhood experiences and with developing a stage theory of development. In addition, he noted the potential importance of unconscious experiences and the influence of sexuality on human behavior.

7. Critics of psychodynamic theory note that Freud based his ideas on small, unrepresentative samples of disturbed individuals. Additionally, many of his concepts and principles are not directly testable; hence, there is little scientific evidence to support his theory. His subjective method of data collection and views about women also have attracted criticism.

## ✓ CHECK YOUR PROGRESS

1. Consider each of the following situations, and determine whether the conflict involves the id, ego, and/or superego.

   a. You have not studied for an exam and are afraid that you will fail it. Your neighbor's paper is within sight, and you begin to think about "borrowing" some of her answers.

   b. You are late for an appointment on the other side of town. You are afraid that you will miss an important opportunity if you don't get there soon. While driving to your appointment, you spot a police cruiser just ahead of you.

2. Identify the stage of psychosexual development (oral, anal, phallic, latency, genital) described in each of the following statements:

   a. The Oedipus and Electra complexes occur during this stage.

   b. A child enjoys biting and chewing on almost any object.

   c. This period is relatively calm as far as sexual interests are concerned.

3. Which term describes the influence of the past on the present?

   a. instincts
   b. unconscious
   c. psychoanalysis
   d. psychic determinism

4. An individual operating on the reality principle seeks

   a. immediate gratification.
   b. the perfect accomplishment.
   c. to reveal his or her unconscious motivations.
   d. rational means for obtaining gratification.

5. What is the warning that signals when there is conflict involving the id and superego?

   a. fear
   b. stress
   c. anxiety
   d. delusion

6. The neo-Freudian, Carl Jung, suggested the existence of a collective unconscious that contained images shared by all people called

   a. schemas.
   b. paradigms.
   c. archetypes.
   d. prototypes.

ANSWERS: 1. a. Id and superego b. Id, ego, and superego  2. a. Phallic  b. Oral  c. Latency  3. d  4. d  5. c  6. c

# THE SOCIAL-COGNITIVE PERSPECTIVE

A major exam is scheduled for next week. Alice and Gil overhear several students predicting that they will fail; others say that they expect to "ace" the test. These differing expectations seem puzzling because everyone will take the same exam. Later that day, Alice and Gil talk about trying to stop smoking. Alice is certain she will succeed, but Gil doubts he will be able to quit. After realizing that they sound like the students who talked about the exam, they begin wondering why some people are sure they will ace an exam or quit smoking, whereas others are unsure. *What role do beliefs have in our understanding of personality?*

# Learning and Cognitive Perspectives

As we noted in Chapter 1, John B. Watson tried to rid psychology of terms like *thinking* and urged psychologists to avoid speculating about inner, unobservable processes. Later, B. F. Skinner suggested that the same principles that applied to rats and pigeons in his laboratory could be applied to humans (see Chapter 5). Hence, he believed that personality developed in the same manner as did any other learned behavior; it was influenced by reinforcers and punishers (see Chapter 5).

According to Skinner, we can explain the distinctiveness of individual personalities without using terms such as *traits*. Each person's behavior is distinctive because each one experiences different histories of reinforcement and punishment. Skinner focused attention on the environmental factors that initiate and maintain behaviors that ultimately distinguish one person from another. For example, John acts aggressively because he was probably reinforced for past aggressive behaviors. According to behavioral or learning psychologists, there is no need to use a concept such as traits in explaining John's aggressiveness or Natasha's sense of humor.

Few psychologists would dismiss the importance of environmental influences like reinforcement. Even studies of the heritability of personality tell us that the environment plays a role; learning can influence personality. Some psychologists such as Julian Rotter, however, say that there is more to understanding personality than a person's learning experiences might suggest. Although they do not deny the importance of reinforcement and punishment, these psychologists draw our attention to the effects these processes may have on our *thoughts and cognitive processes*. Because of our unique histories of reinforcement and punishment, each person comes to see his or her environment differently.

**Rotter's Social Learning Theory.** Julian Rotter notes that reinforcement does not automatically stamp in a behavior. Rotter continued Skinner's emphasis on the importance of learning; he carried it further, however, by recognizing that past learning affects not just behaviors but also *expectancies* about whether certain behaviors lead to desired outcomes. Most of the reinforcers we strive to obtain are social (for example, hugs, attention, praise), and most learning occurs in social situations (Rotter, 1990). Rotter combined these observations in his **social learning theory** of personality, which incorporated cognitive factors. He acknowledges the role of cognitive factors in understanding human behavior, noting that behavior is often a function of expectancies.

The concept of *expectancy* is one of the most important elements of Rotter's theory. When you take an exam, apply for a job, or ask someone out on a date, you have some notion of the likelihood of success or failure. Generalized expectancies operate across a wide variety of situations; specific expectancies are limited to particular situations. What's more, people differ in their tendencies to view themselves as capable of influencing reinforcers or being subject to fate (Zuckerman, Knee, Kieffer, & Gagne, 2004). Some people, called *internals*, believe that they can influence their reinforcers via their skill and ability. Others, called *externals*, believe that whether they attain a desired outcome is due primarily to chance or fate (Rotter, 1990).

Rotter (1966) devised the Internal-External (I-E) Scale to measure individuals' *locus of control* (internal or external); since then, **locus of control** has become one of the most studied concepts in psychology. Each of the 23 items on the I-E Scale offers a choice between an external alternative and an internal one.

Why does one person score in the external direction, whereas another obtains a score indicating an internal locus of control? One factor that accounts for differences in locus of control is the individual's learning history. Cultural factors also seem to influence locus-of-control scores. For example, people in Western countries tend to have more internal scores than people in Far Eastern countries, especially Japan (Marsh & Hau, 2004). Low socioeconomic status tends to be linked with external locus of control. These cultural differences influence our sense of self.

**social learning theory**
Theory that learning occurs through watching and imitating the behaviors of others

**locus of control**
Whether the person sees his or her behavior as controlled by external factors (external locus) or internal forces (internal locus)

Suppose we asked you to "describe yourself briefly." What would you write? American responses to this simple question tend to be more confident and elaborated. Japanese responses tend to be more tentative and more concerned with the responses of others (Markus & Kitayama, 1998). What's more, most American respondents focus on ways that make them unique in comparisons to others. This way of responding is characteristic of what has been called an *individualist* (independent) conception of the self. In contrast, people in Asian cultures emphasize what has been called a *collectivist* (or interdependent) conception of the self.

How do such differences in the evaluation of self develop? They reflect differences in socialization. Asian cultures tend to emphasize modesty and self-restraint, whereas American children are taught that "the squeaky wheel gets the oil." Conversely, Japanese children are taught that "The nail that stands out gets pounded down." These differences in socialization and their effects on behavior should serve as a reminder that when we speak of personality, we need to keep in mind the cultural context in which we ask questions concerning personality.

The concept of locus of control has a wide range of uses and applications (Kidwell & Jewell, 2003). For example, during the 1960s, researchers discovered that internals were more likely than externals to attend civil rights rallies, sign petitions, or participate in a freedom ride to challenge racial segregation in the South. Locus of control is related to measures of school achievement: Internals tend to outperform externals on standardized measures of achievement (Musher-Eizenman, Nesselroade, & Schmitz, 2002).

Locus of control is also related to health behaviors (see Chapter 15). Internals are more likely to interpret threatening events as challenges. They are more likely to reduce their stress by solving problems that are threatening; by contrast, externals focus on their own emotional responses rather than on the threats. Consequently, internals' reactions to stress are less negative, and externals experience greater anxiety, especially in the workplace (Muhonen & Torkelson, 2004).

**Bandura's Social Cognitive Theory.**   Albert Bandura is well known for his research on observational learning or modeling of aggressive behavior and for using modeling to overcome phobias (see Chapter 5). A fundamental question that personality psychologists ask is, Why do people act as they do? According to Bandura (1986), the answer is that a combination of factors, including an individual's cognitions and the environment, interact to produce a particular behavior. These factors are not independent; they work together and influence one another (Bandura, 1986). This notion, known as **reciprocal determinism,** tells us that the person, environment, and behavior influence one another (see Figure 11-7).

The behavioral/learning approaches focus on how environments (situations) influence behaviors (libraries are conducive to studying). An individual's personality also influences behavior, however, as the trait perspective has emphasized. Reciprocal

Albert Bandura added a concern for cognitive factors to the learning theorists' emphasis on external causes.

**reciprocal determinism**
Contention that person variables, situation variables, and behavior constantly interact

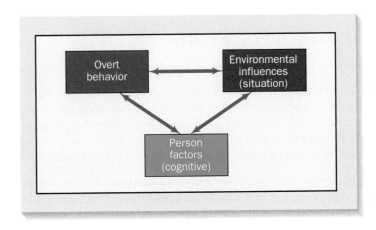

**FIGURE 11-7**  Bandura's model of reciprocal determinism.

**Source:** Bandura (1986).

**self-efficacy**

A person's expectancy concerning his or her ability to engage in effective behaviors; such expectancies differ from one behavior to another

**STUDY TIP**

Pair up with another student. One student should "play" Julian Rotter; the other, Albert Bandura. Each student, as that particular person, should explain his theory (for Rotter, social learning; for Bandura, social cognitive) to the other and invite questions and discussion.

determinism goes beyond these simple explanations of behavior as the result of either situations or personality by suggesting that our behavior can change the environment (studying instead of spending time with friends reduces social pressures or invitations to go out). Thus the environment is not only a cause of behavior, but it is also an effect of behavior. For example, one way personality influences situations is that we select situations differently, depending on our personalities. Achievement-oriented students are likely to spend their time in the library; extraverted people are likely to attend parties and other social gatherings. A complete understanding of personality requires recognition of the mutual influences among the person, the situation (environment), and behavior (Cloninger, 1996).

Another key concept in Bandura's theory is **self-efficacy,** a person's beliefs about his or her skills and ability to perform certain behaviors. The greater a person's sense of self-efficacy, the more confidence that person has in his or her ability to deal with life's challenges. A person's sense of self-efficacy has a powerful effect on his or her behavior, yet self-efficacy is not considered a trait. Why? Self-efficacy can be understood only in relation to specific behaviors and in specific situations. Unlike locus of control, it is not generalized across situations.

Four sources of information can influence self-efficacy. The first is *past performance* (successes or failures). The second is *watching others in similar situations and noting the consequences they experience.* The effect of observing others depends on factors such as one's similarity to the observed person. Third, *verbal persuasion* can affect levels of self-efficacy; its effect depends on the persuader's trustworthiness and level of expertise. Finally, self-efficacy can be related to *physiological arousal.* For example, we may associate aversive emotional states with poor performance, perceived incompetence, or perceived failure (Johnstone & Page, 2004).

The concept of self-efficacy has been applied to a range of outcomes. For example, measures of self-efficacy predict final course grades among high school and college students (Robbins et al., 2004). Self-efficacy also predicts the ability to resist relapse after treatment for alcohol problems (Blomqvist, Harnandez-Avila, Burleson, Ashraf, & Kranzler, 2003). It is also related to a career outcome such as career exploration (Solberg, 1998) and to how people attempt computer-related tasks (Brosnan, 1998).

Closely related to self-efficacy is the personality trait known as *perfectionism.* Although researchers continue to disagree about the definition of perfectionism and whether striving to be perfect is adaptive, it is clear that perfectionism can be linked to psychopathology (see Chapter 12). For example, when society demands perfection, it can create a feeling of helplessness because no matter how hard a person tries to be perfect, there are always expectations to do better and be more perfect (Fleet & Hewitt, 2002). This feeling of helplessness can lead to depression. What can the perfectionist do to deal with this feeling of helplessness? O'Connor and O'Connor (2003) report that perfectionists who have positive coping styles (they do not cope by avoiding) are no more depressed than the average person.

# THE HUMANISTIC PERSPECTIVE

One of Randy's favorite quotes from his introductory psychology course is:

> I have little sympathy with the rather prevalent concept that man is basically irrational, and that his impulses, if not controlled, will lead to the destruction of others and self. Man's behavior is exquisitely rational, moving with subtle and ordered complexity towards the goals his organism is endeavoring to achieve. (Rogers, 1961, pp. 194–195)

Certainly this view of human personality and behavior differs drastically from the learning-theory model and Freud's stages of psychosexual development. *What type of psychologist proposed this different viewpoint?*

As Randy found out in his introductory psychology course, not all psychologists believe that our behavior is determined by early childhood experiences, biological drives, or even learning histories. Some psychologists believe that to understand human behavior, we must look at unique human aspects and qualities. What sets us apart from lower animals is not objective reality but rather our ability to make choices and our individual perspectives on the world.

A group of theorists called **humanistic psychologists** oppose the basic beliefs of both psychodynamic theory and behaviorism. They focus on the present and the healthy personality. What's more, they view the individual's perceptions of events as more significant than the learning theorist's or therapist's perceptions. For these reasons, they are often called *phenomenological psychologists.* (Phenomenology is the study of experience just as it occurs.) The two most notable representatives of this humanistic or phenomenological perspective are Abraham Maslow and Carl Rogers.

**Abraham Maslow.**  Abraham Maslow (1908–1970) described humanistic psychology as the "third force" in American psychology because it offered an alternative to psychodynamic theory and behaviorism. He viewed those perspectives as incomplete because they emphasized early childhood experience or viewed people as captives of their environments. In addition, he did not believe that the study of laboratory animals or individuals suffering from psychological disorders provided a proper foundation for understanding human behavior.

**Basic Needs.**  According to Maslow, human beings have a set of needs that are organized in a hierarchy (see Chapter 6). These needs begin with physiological needs and move on to needs for safety, love and belongingness, and self-esteem. These basic needs exert a powerful pull on our behavior. Once you satisfy physiological needs, you can turn to the need for safety or to be loved by others. The basic biological needs exert a great deal of influence on our behavior, so much so that most people never reach the top level of the hierarchy.

**Self-Actualization.**  Self-actualization involves making "the full use and exploitation of talents, capacities, potentialities" (Maslow, 1970, p. 150). In other words, it is the need to develop one's full potential. Maslow believed that this need exists in everyone but is often thwarted by the environment. When our basic needs are met, energy is available for use in striving for greater understanding of ourselves and our surroundings. To illustrate these concepts, Maslow looked for healthy, self-actualized individuals who were doing the best that they were capable of doing.

Maslow's list of self-actualized people included Abraham Lincoln, Thomas Jefferson, Eleanor Roosevelt, and Albert Einstein. Because a number of them were deceased, he relied on historical documents to study them. The details of his analysis of these self-actualized individuals are sketchy, but he arrived at several general conclusions about their characteristics (see Table 11-7). For example, he found that these individuals tended to have accurate perceptions of their environments and were comfortable with those perceptions. Keep in mind that Maslow's selection process is subject to the same criticism that was directed at Freud's psychodynamic theory: The list of self-actualized individuals is not representative of the general population.

Maslow tried to move the study of personality away from the concern with pathology that was evident in Freud's work. He held a distinctly positive view of human nature. Many of his concepts, however, such as self-actualization, are difficult to test empirically.

**Carl Rogers.**  Carl Rogers (1902–1987) shared Maslow's belief that people are innately good and are directed toward growth, development, and personal fulfillment. What's more, he believed there is an "inherent tendency of the organism to develop all its capabilities in ways which serve to maintain or enhance the person" (Rogers, 1959, p. 196). Unfortunately, his clinical experience told him that people are frequently derailed from their quests for fulfillment.

A number of the people Maslow identified as self-actualized were historical figures who he analyzed by studying historical documents. Although she is now dead, there is a great deal of evidence to suggest that Mother Teresa would fit Maslow's description of self-actualization.

**humanistic psychology**
General approach to psychology, associated with Abraham Maslow and Carl Rogers, that emphasizes individuals' control of their behavior

**self-actualization**
Need to develop one's full potential

**TABLE 11-7**

## Characteristics of Maslow's Sample of Self-Actualized Individuals

Accept their own natures

Are spontaneous and natural

Are deeply democratic in nature

Like privacy and tend to be detached

Focus on problems outside themselves

Exhibit a strong ethical and moral sense

Have close but limited number of friendships

Are independent of their cultural and social environment

Prefer a philosophical rather than a hostile type of humor

Have efficient perceptions of reality and are comfortable with those perceptions

**Source:** Maslow (1970).

As we develop, our concept of self emerges. The self is our sense of "I" or "me"; it is generally conscious and accessible and is a central concept in Rogers's theory. The self-concept is our perception of our abilities, behaviors, and characteristics. Rogers believed that we act in accordance with our self-concept. If we have a positive self-concept, we tend to act in positive ways; if we have a negative self-concept, we often act in negative ways.

Maslow and Rogers agreed that people have a strong need to be loved, to experience affection. Sometimes, however, people experience affection that is *conditional*—given only if they engage in behaviors that are approved by others. Rogers contrasted this conditional regard with what he called *unconditional positive regard*, in which a person is accepted for what he or she is, not for what others would like the person to be. According to Rogers, if you grow up believing affection is conditional, you will distort your own experiences in order to feel worthy of acceptance from a wider range of people. For example, children may be told that they are incapable of doing something or that they are stupid, nasty, or disobedient. This may lead them to understand that conditions are placed on their self-worth; as a result, they may begin to question themselves. This conditional positive regard, in which love and praise are not given unless

Conditional positive regard can have a negative impact on a child's developing self-concept.

## Study CHART

### Overview of the Major Perspectives on Personality

| Perspective | Key Figures | Strengths | Weaknesses |
|---|---|---|---|
| Trait | Gordon Allport, Raymond Cattell, Hans Eysenck | Describes the major dimensions on which individuals differ from one another | Sometimes emphasizes different traits as key ones; may not provide an explanation of the development of traits |
| Biological | William Sheldon, University of Minnesota Twins Reared Apart Project | Focuses on biological aspects of individuals' differences with a special emphasis on genetic influences | May misinterpret research to conclude that environmental factors are not important or that personality cannot change |
| Psychodynamic | Sigmund Freud, neo-Freudians | Uses case studies to provide in-depth assessment of individuals; focuses on the importance of unconscious processes and conflict as key factors in the development of personality | Uses concepts that are difficult to define and to study; overemphasizes the importance of early development |
| Social-cognitive | Julian Rotter, Albert Bandura | Adds a cognitive focus to learning-theory explanations of personality | Does not appear to account for broad consistencies in behavior; does not account for genetic influences on personality |
| Humanistic | Carl Rogers, Abraham Maslow | Focuses on conscious influences on behavior and on the more positive aspects of human nature | Uses concepts, such as *self-actualization,* that are difficult to define and to measure; takes an overly optimistic view of human nature |

the child conforms to the expectations of others, can have negative effects on the child's self-concept.

Think of the self as two sides of a coin. One side is the self as it really is, a product of our experiences; this is called the *real self.* The other side is the *ideal self,* the self we would like to be. Maladjustment results when there is a discrepancy between the real self and the ideal self—when the two sides of the coin do not match up.

The major theoretical perspectives on personality we have covered in this chapter are summarized for you in the accompanying Study Chart. You should review it now.

## REVIEW SUMMARY

1. Behavioral and learning psychologists avoid commonly used terms such as *traits.* They explain the distinctiveness of a person's behavior as resulting from a unique learning history.

2. While acknowledging the importance of learning, Julian Rotter and Albert Bandura incorporated cognitive factors into their theories of personality.

3. Rotter's **social learning theory** recognizes that most reinforcers are social and that most learning takes place in social situations. Expectancy about obtaining a reinforcer in a given situation is an important cognitive variable. Individuals differ in the degree to which they see themselves or chance ("fate") as responsible for their successes and failures.

4. Measures of generalized expectancy, known as **locus of control,** are related to a variety of outcomes, including academic and health behaviors.

5. According to Albert Bandura, individuals not only are affected by the environment but also can influence it. What's more, cognitive factors can influence the person's behavior and his or her environment. This combination of cognitive, behavioral, and environmental effects is called **reciprocal determinism.**

6. **Self-efficacy** is a person's judgment about his or her ability to succeed in a given situation. Unlike a trait, self-efficacy is specific to the situation and can change over time.

**7.** Humanistic approaches evolved in opposition to the behavioral and psychodynamic perspectives. They propose that human beings are basically good and are directed toward development and growth.

**8.** Abraham Maslow's hierarchy of needs begins with deficiency needs and leads to **self-actualization** at the top. The power of deficiency needs keeps most people from reaching the level of self-actualization, which Maslow defines as doing the best that an individual is capable of doing.

**9.** On the basis of his work with disturbed people, Carl Rogers concluded that efforts to achieve personal fulfillment were being stifled. He proposed that people's self-concepts become distorted by conditions of worth imposed from the outside. In his theory, healthy individuals have a real self-concept that is consistent with their ideal self-concept.

 CHECK YOUR PROGRESS

**1.** B. F. Skinner explained the distinctiveness of individual personalities through different

a. genetic patterns.
b. thinking patterns.
c. individual traits.
d. histories of reinforcement and punishment.

**2.** Identify each of the following terms:

a. Rotter's term for generalized expectancies
b. In Rotter's social learning theory, a person who believes he or she can influence events
c. Bandura's term for the relation among person, behavior, and environment
d. In Bandura's theory, a person's belief that he or she has the skills to succeed in a given situation

**3.** If Woody believes he must have gotten his latest speeding ticket because the police have it out for him, he may be exhibiting

a. optimism.
b. pessimism.

c. an internal locus of control.
d. an external locus of control.

**4.** How did Carl Rogers use correlation coefficients to assess the similarity between real and ideal self-concepts? What type of correlation coefficient would suggest a high degree of similarity?

**5.** In Carl Rogers's theory, our perception of our abilities, behaviors, and characteristics is known as

a. personality.
b. self-regard.
c. self-esteem.
d. self-concept.

**6.** According to Carl Rogers, maladjustment occurs when

a. the individual has low self-esteem.
b. there is congruence between the real self and ideal self.
c. there is a discrepancy between the real self and ideal self.
d. the individual receives too much unconditional positive regard.

**ANSWERS: 1.** d **2. a.** Locus of control **b.** Internal **c.** Reciprocal determinism **d.** Self-efficacy **3.** d **4.** Rogers used the Q-sort to assess a person's actual and ideal self-concepts. High correlations between the two indicated good convergence and hence an accepting and healthy personality. **5.** d **6.** c

**SCORING** The "Big Five" Test

**PAGE 484**

To compute your score for each of the five scales, simply add your scores for the items that contribute to each of the scales.

Openness to Experience: 1, 6, 11, 16, 21
Conscientiousness: 2, 7, 12, 17, 22
Extraversion: 3, 8, 13, 18, 23
Agreeableness: 4, 9, 14, 19, 24
Neuroticism: 5, 10, 15, 20, 25

Mean scores for men and women on each of the scales are listed below:

|  | Men | Women |
|---|---|---|
| Openness to Experience | 20.3 | 19.4 |
| Conscientiousness | 18.8 | 20.2 |
| Extraversion | 18.8 | 19.0 |
| Agreeableness | 18.8 | 22.2 |
| Neuroticism | 16.3 | 18.5 |

**Source:** Brody & Erlichman (1998).

## SCORING Keys

**Source:** Zuckerman (1978).

**PAGE 493**

Add one point to your score for each of the following answers.

1. a
2. a
3. a
4. b
5. a
6. b
7. a
8. a
9. b
10. b
11. a
12. a
13. b

Use the following guidelines to compare your scores with others who have taken this questionnaire.

Score
0–3 Very low
4–5 Low
6–9 Average
10–11 High
12–13 Very high

# Psychological Disorders

## CHAPTER OUTLINE

For many students, the most intriguing behaviors are those labeled *abnormal*. Perhaps they see symptoms in themselves and wonder what causes such abnormal behaviors. We begin our discussion by describing how we decide which behaviors to label abnormal. The disorders we will describe span a wide range, including those that seem close to home—who has not felt anxiety at some time? Mood disorders are extreme examples of feelings and behaviors we experience and observe in others. Disorders like *schizophrenia*, involving symptoms such as delusions and hallucinations, are more difficult to understand because they are unlike anything many of us have encountered.

Our discussion of biological processes will help us understand some unusual forms of behavior. We will also see that learning plays a role in the development of some forms of abnormal behavior. The types of abnormal behavior we describe, however, often have no simple explanations; they result from a combination of factors within and outside the person.

# ABNORMAL BEHAVIOR

**Above the din of traffic on a downtown Chicago street, a voice filled with rage screams. A disheveled woman paces furiously back and forth, her shopping bag swinging as if to punctuate every angry word. When a passerby approaches, offering to help, the woman stops, stares intently, and then yells, "Get away. Leave me alone." Later she is taken to a mental hospital because city officials claim she was exhibiting abnormal behavior.** *What criteria are used to distinguish between "normal" and "abnormal" behaviors?*

What do we mean when we label a behavior "abnormal"? This is an important question. As we will see, the criteria we use to define abnormal behaviors influence the way we perceive and respond to other people. Thus the way we define abnormality is an important issue with serious consequences.

## Criteria of Abnormality

Over time, several criteria have been used to distinguish between normal and abnormal behaviors. Sometimes one criterion will do; at other times we rely on more than one. The most commonly used criteria for distinguishing between normal and abnormal behaviors are statistical rarity, interference with normal functioning, personal distress, and deviance from social norms.

**Statistical Rarity.**   A common way to define abnormal behavior is to determine how often the behavior occurs in the population. Abnormal literally means "away from the norm." Thus a behavior that is abnormal does not occur very often. A neighbor who checks the stove 26 times to be sure it has been turned off would be viewed as abnormal because such behavior is rare. Typing 125 words per minute is also rare and hence, by definition, is also abnormal. Some rare (and therefore statistically abnormal) behaviors, however, such as earning straight A's or writing a best-selling novel, are acceptable and desirable. By itself, statistical rarity is clearly not a consistently useful indicator of what we should label abnormal.

**dysfunctional**
Term used to describe behaviors that adversely affect an individual's day-to-day functioning

**abnormal**
Term used to describe behavior that is rare or dysfunctional, causes personal distress, or deviates from social norms

**Interference with Normal Functioning.**    Behavior is said to be **dysfunctional** when it interferes with a person's ability to function on a daily basis. Everyone probably experiences some degree of anxiety every day, but imagine a level of anxiety that renders you unable to speak in the presence of others or unable to leave your home. That degree of anxiety is dysfunctional because it interferes with daily activities and affects others who depend on you. Behavior that is dysfunctional is generally considered abnormal.

**Distress.**    People may be diagnosed as suffering from a psychological disorder if their behavior is upsetting, distracting, or confusing to themselves. The distress criterion is useful in cases in which the psychological disorder is accompanied by discomfort. Imagine the distress felt by someone who believes other people are "out to get" him or by a depressed person who sees suicide as "the only solution." Personal distress does not always accompany abnormal behavior, however. The woman screaming at unseen adversaries on a Chicago street was not distressed by her behavior; she wanted to be left alone. Her behavior would not be considered abnormal according to the criterion of personal distress; however, applying the criterion of statistical rarity would lead us to judge her behavior as abnormal.

**Deviance from Social Norms.**    All social groups, ranging from your neighborhood to an entire society, decide which behaviors are acceptable for group members. The resulting guidelines, called *social norms*, distinguish acceptable behaviors from unacceptable or deviant ones. Norms may be recorded as laws, like those that prohibit writing bad checks. Many social norms do not exist in written form; however, they still guide our behavior and influence opinions about the behavior of others. For example, there are no written laws dictating that people should use polite language such as "Excuse me" or "Thank you," but many people consider these phrases an essential part of interacting with others.

How do social norms relate to the definition of abnormal behavior? Depending on the context—that is, when and where they occur—certain behaviors are considered unacceptable. In other words, they are "against the norm," or abnormal. Norms differ from group to group and also change over time. For example, some groups view body piercing as self-mutilation; other groups see it as a valued expression of group solidarity or rebellion against conformity imposed from outside the group.

Difficulty in functioning on a daily basis and personal distress are two criteria used to identify abnormal behaviors.

## A Working Definition

Each of the criteria of abnormality we have discussed has advantages and disadvantages. We often use several criteria simultaneously in making judgments about particular behaviors; therefore we can define behaviors as **abnormal** when they are statistically unusual, are not socially approved, and cause distress to the person or interfere with his or her ability to function. Because different cultural groups have different social norms, definitions of abnormality using this criterion are culturally variable.

Keep the following points in mind when making such judgments. First, normality and abnormality are degrees of difference on a continuum; the point at which normal behavior becomes abnormal depends on how you define normality. When we perceive a behavior as abnormal, we make a value judgment about the appropriateness of that behavior. Second, the person whose behavior is judged may not accept your perspective. (Recall the woman on the street of Chicago described at the beginning of this section.) Finally, these judgments vary with social or cultural standards, which may change over time.

On March 30, 1981, radio and television stations flashed a news bulletin: John Hinckley, Jr., had shot and wounded President Ronald Reagan and three other people. On June 20, 2001, Andrea Yates drowned her five young children (6 months to 7 years old) and then called her husband at work, asking him to come home. For several years,

We use several criteria to judge whether people are exhibiting abnormal behavior. By some standards, the dress and behavior of these football fans would be judged abnormal. Many of the people in the stands, however, would judge these enthusiastic fans to be normal and perhaps even models to be imitated.

Yates had been under the care of a psychiatrist. She suffered from postpartum depression—a serious disorder that sometimes follows childbirth.

At the time Hinckley came to trial, federal law required prosecutors to prove that a defendant was sane. Hinckley's lawyers argued that their client had tried to kill the president to attract the attention of an actress. Experts testified that Hinckley suffered from a psychological disorder, but they disagreed about its severity. After deliberating on the conflicting testimony, the jury returned a verdict of not guilty by reason of **insanity,** the legal ruling that a person accused of a crime is not responsible for it. In the Yates trial, there was testimony concerning her mental illness but disagreement over whether she was insane under Texas law. The jury decided she was sane at the time she committed the crime. Although the prosecution had asked for the death penalty, the jury recommended life in prison. (On January 6, 2005, the First Texas Court of Appeals overturned the conviction and ordered a new trial. The court noted that an expert witness had made a false statement, which influenced the way the prosecution presented the case to the jury.)

**insanity**
Legal ruling that a person accused of a crime is not held responsible for that act; defined in most states as the inability to tell the difference between right and wrong at the time the crime is committed

The jury's determination that John Hinckley, Jr., was not guilty by reason of insanity led to changes in the application of the insanity plea across the country.

## The Concept of Insanity

The key to understanding the Hinckley and Yates decisions is the distinction between describing actions (Hinckley fired the shots, Yates drowned her children) and holding someone responsible for those actions (Hinckley was responsible for firing the shots and should be punished; Yates was responsible for the drownings and should be punished). Suppose a 4-year-old child found the keys to the family car, managed to start and drive it, and hit and seriously injured a neighbor. Everyone agrees on the description, but would we hold the child responsible for the consequences? Because we believe a 4-year-old child is not capable of understanding a wrongful and deliberate act, our legal system would not punish the child.

Even before the Hinckley trial focused attention on the insanity plea, many people held strong opinions about it. What do you think most people believe about the frequency of use and success of the insanity plea? What are the primary sources of the information that lead to these opinions?

In March 2002 a jury found Andrea Yates guilty of killing her five children (ages 6 months to 7 years) and sentenced her to life in prison. When a police officer arrived at her home, Yates said she had "just killed my children." At the trial, the defense argued that she suffered from postpartum depression and that her treatment had been inadequate. In 2005 the First Texas Court of Appeals threw out the conviction, citing false testimony by the state's expert psychiatric witness. The Court of Appeals ordered a new trial. Yates has pled "not guilty by reason of insanity."

The Hinckley and Yates cases showed the media to be powerful sources of information about the insanity defense. Millions of Americans saw newspaper and television coverage of the attempted assassination, which seemed to suggest that people with psychological disorders are dangerous. They saw extensive coverage of the deaths of the five children and scenes of the trial of Yates. As many as 86% of newspaper stories that deal with former mental patients focus on a violent crime, usually murder (Shain & Phillips, 1991). Media portrayals tend to focus on lurid crimes, often evoking images of defendants like Jeffrey Dahmer (Rogers & Shuman, 2000). Relying on such portrayals, many of us believe that defendants use the insanity plea as a loophole in an effort to escape punishment for illegal acts: The public thinks that 37% of felony indictments involve an insanity plea and that 44% of those pleas result in acquittal (Silver, Cirincione, & Steadman, 1994). Yet, the public as well as members of the legal profession are frequently uniformed about the facts of the insanity plea (Hooper & McLearen, 2002; Lymburner & Roesch, 1999). By stark contrast, an analysis of approximately 1 million felony indictments found that insanity pleas were used in less than 1% of the cases, and only 25% of those pleas were successful (Callahan, Steadman, McGreevy, & Robbins, 1991). In other words, out of every 10,000 felony indictments, 100 defendants will plead "not guilty by reason of insanity" and 25 will succeed (25% of the 1% that used this plea). These figures are a far cry from public perceptions of the insanity plea.

How did the concept of an insanity plea develop? In 1843, an Englishman, Daniel M'Naughton, attempted to assassinate the British prime minister but killed the minister's secretary instead. Convincing testimony supported the defense's contention that M'Naughton believed the prime minister and others were conspiring against him. When the prosecution could not refute that testimony, the jury found M'Naughton "not guilty by reason of insanity." Queen Victoria was understandably angry at this verdict; this was the fifth attempt to assassinate either British royalty or the British prime minister since 1800. She demanded that a panel of judges review the issue. The panel, including the judge that presided over the M'Naughton trial, developed what became known as the *M'Naughton standard*—an accused person is not held legally responsible if he or she was unable to tell the difference between right and wrong at the time of the crime (Rogers & Shuman, 2000). As much U.S. law is based on English law, this standard was adopted here, albeit with some modifications, depending on the state.

Following the Hinckley trial, most states revised their insanity laws, making it more difficult to plead insanity successfully. Today in most states and the District of Columbia (five have abolished the plea), the basis for determining insanity is the M'Naughton or "right-wrong" standard (Hooper & McLearen, 2002; Moran, 2002; Steadman et al., 1993): M'Naughton fired the gun in the belief that he was defending himself against people who were plotting to kill him. The determination of insanity is a legal decision (decided by a judge or a jury), rather than a psychological or psychiatric one, although psychologists and psychiatrists often offer testimony to the court in insanity cases.

Only 15% of insanity verdicts occur in murder cases; assault is the most frequent crime for which defendants plead "not guilty by reason of insanity" (Callahan et al., 1991). Most defendants who are ruled insane have a history of serious psychological disorders with prior hospitalizations (Callahan et al., 1991; Warren, Murrie, Chauhan, Dietz, & Morris, 2004). Release procedures are quite strict, so defendants who are judged insane spend as much or more time in confinement as people convicted of similar crimes. Thus these data contradict the widespread belief that the insanity plea is a legal loophole used by defendants to escape punishment.

# Models of Abnormal Behavior

Hundreds of years ago, many people believed that abnormal behaviors occurred when a person was "possessed" by demons. People who behaved in a bizarre fashion were often subjected to brutal treatments designed to drive the demons out. The belief in supernatural phenomena provided one way to understand disorders and also suggested possible treatments.

In their efforts to identify and explain abnormal behaviors, psychologists often adopt models, or general views of what causes those behaviors. Models help by pointing out which symptoms are most important, directing attention to their likely causes, and suggesting possible treatments. We can organize the models under two general headings: the medical model and psychological models.

**The Medical Model.** Near the end of the 18th century, physicians began to document their patients' symptoms and to note which ones occurred together. The occurrence of groups of symptoms, called *syndromes*, helped physicians identify underlying diseases and develop treatments. Approaching abnormal behaviors just as one would approach medical illnesses is known as the **medical model.**

Psychiatrist Thomas Szasz (1993) argues for limiting the medical model to conditions resulting from actual brain dysfunctions. In his opinion, this model has been expanded to cover behaviors that are perhaps annoying or inappropriate but do not constitute diseases of the brain. For example, the list of proposed or recognized diseases includes shoplifting, pathological gambling, and nicotine dependence. According to Szasz, applying the medical model to such behaviors does not advance our understanding of the causes of the problems and allows people to avoid taking responsibility for their problems by attributing them to a disease.

Accumulating evidence shows that a number of psychological disorders are related to elevated or reduced levels of certain neurotransmitters or structural abnormalities in the brain. What's more, evidence is increasing that heredity plays a significant role in the development of a number of psychological disorders.

**Psychological Models.** In contrast to the medical model, *psychological models* emphasize the importance of mental functioning, social experiences, and learning histories in trying to explain the causes of abnormal behaviors. Sigmund Freud's **psychodynamic model** focuses on unconscious conflicts involving the id, ego, and superego or fixations at an early stage of psychosexual development. For example, anxiety is seen as a warning that the ego is about to be overwhelmed by conflict. The **behavioral model,** by contrast, focuses on environmental factors that mold human and animal behaviors. Behavioral theorists such as John B. Watson and B. F. Skinner propose that we learn both normal and abnormal behaviors through the principles of classical conditioning, operant conditioning, and modeling (see Chapter 5). In contrast to the behavioral model, the **cognitive model** focuses on understanding the content and processes of human thought. Cognitive psychologists claim that to understand human behavior, we must look beyond actual events to understand how people interpret those events.

**Culture and Disorders.** The **sociocultural model** emphasizes the role of social and cultural influences on the frequency, diagnosis, and conception of psychological disorders. Factors such as poverty and discrimination may promote a climate that increases the likelihood that psychological disorders will develop. Poverty is related to the prevalence of psychological disorders, and rates of psychological disorders are influenced by socioeconomic status (Bruce, Takeuchi, & Leaf, 1991; Dohrenwend et al., 1992).

Some sets of symptoms, called *culture-bound syndromes*, tend to be limited to specific cultures. In Japan the syndrome called *taijin kyofusho* involves the intense fear that one's

**medical model**
The view that mental disorders are like physical illnesses and have underlying organic causes

**psychodynamic model**
The view that psychological disorders result from unconscious conflicts related to sex or aggression

**behavioral model**
The view that psychological disorders are learned behaviors that follow the principles of classical and operant conditioning or modeling

**cognitive model**
The view that emphasizes thinking as the key element in causing psychological disorders

**sociocultural model**
The view that emphasizes the importance of society and culture in causing psychological disorders

body or its functions are offensive to other people (American Psychiatric Association, 2000). This syndrome shares similarities with social phobias, which are concerns related to public scrutiny or possible embarrassment (Kleinknecht, Dinnel, Kleinknecht, Hiruma, & Harada, 1997). The focus of *taijin kyofusho*, however, is on offending others rather than on the self; the difference in the focus of these related disorders is consistent with conceptions of the self as independent or interdependent in the two cultures (see Chapter 11). In some Native American cultures, individuals may believe they can hear the voice of a dead person calling them as the spirit travels to the afterworld (Lu, Lim, & Mezzich, 1995). *Ataque de nervios* (attacks of nerves) is particularly prominent among Spanish-speaking people from the Caribbean but also occurs among other Hispanic groups, most frequently in women (Guarnaccia, Canino, Rubio-Stipec, & Bravo, 1993; Oquendo, 1995). This brief-duration syndrome involves a variety of symptoms: shouting uncontrollably, bursting into tears, trembling, heat in the chest rising into the head, verbal or physical aggression, and seizure-like or fainting episodes. The symptoms typically follow family-related stressful events, such as news of the death of a close relative or witnessing an accident involving a family member (American Psychiatric Association, 2000). Although this "culturally condoned expression of distress" shares symptoms with several disorders (Guarnaccia et al., 1993; Oquendo, 1995), someone unfamiliar with the cultures in which it developed would find it difficult to understand.

Do these models of abnormal behavior appear to conflict with one another? There is a growing recognition that many disorders have multiple causes; thus the simultaneous use of several models is likely to advance our understanding. This emphasis on multiple causation is evident in the *biopsychosocial* model, which incorporates *biological* (medical-model) factors along with psychological and sociocultural (social) factors. Some people may have inherited a tendency to exhibit strong autonomic reactions, which may predispose them to develop a number of disorders. But will they actually develop any of them? Whether a disorder develops may depend on an interaction of psychological and social factors with an inherited predisposition. For example, exposure to repeated stressful experiences that bring out strong autonomic reactions may lead certain people to begin questioning their ability to cope. Growing up in a family that typically reacts to stressful situations by presenting physical symptoms can lead an individual to report similar symptoms. Thus any one model of abnormal behavior may be an oversimplification.

# CLASSIFYING AND COUNTING PSYCHOLOGICAL DISORDERS

**You walk into a mental hospital and report that you heard a voice say "empty," "hollow," and "thud." You have no history of any psychological disorder, and except for giving the false report about hearing voices, you answer all questions truthfully. Will you be recognized as a fraud, or will you be diagnosed with a psychological disorder and treated for hearing voices in your head?** *Can we tell the difference between normal and disturbed people?*

Suppose someone tells you that your cousin has suffered a "nervous breakdown." You know something is wrong, but you also have a number of unanswered questions. What are the symptoms? How serious are they? Are any treatments available? When you ask these questions, you are asking whether there is a **diagnosis**—the process of recognizing the presence of a disorder and naming it by using an existing classification system.

A major purpose of diagnosis is to make predictions. Given a particular diagnosis, what is the likely course of the disorder? Will the disorder respond to treatment? Which treatment? Success in making such predictions depends on the availability of a diagnostic system that can be used to classify disorders in a reliable fashion.

**diagnosis**

The process of deciding whether a person has symptoms that meet established criteria of an existing classification system

# DSM-IV-TR

One reason for revising the diagnostic manual is that diagnoses based on the categories listed in earlier editions were not sufficiently reliable. At times, different mental health professionals who interviewed the same patient failed to agree on the diagnosis. To remedy this problem, the developers of the revised diagnostic manual added rules for making diagnoses. The manual spells out the number, severity, and duration of symptoms that define each diagnosis. These detailed rules have had the desired effect: Although the reliability of diagnoses has improved, critics question the very act of making a diagnosis.

The most frequently used system for classifying psychological disorders is the American Psychiatric Association's *Diagnostic and Statistical Manual of Mental Disorders, 4th Edition, Text Revision* (*DSM-IV-TR*). More than 200 psychological disorders are listed in the current manual (2000). The major *DSM-IV* categories and examples of each category are listed in Table 12-1.

**STUDY TIP**

In a group of three, quiz one another on the major categories of disorders listed in the *DSM-IV-TR*. Make a set of flash cards that list the disorder type on one side and an example of the disorder on the other. Randomly alternate the sides you use. If one student calls out a disorder type, another student should name an example. If a student calls out a disorder example, another student should name the disorder type. In either case, the third student should then offer a description of the disorder type.

---

**TABLE 12-1**

## Descriptions and Examples of Major Categories of Disorders Listed in *DSM-IV-TR*

| Disorder Type | Descriptions and Examples |
|---|---|
| Disorders usually first diagnosed in infancy, childhood, or adolescence | These disorders begin before adulthood and include mental retardation, attention-deficit hyperactivity disorder (ADHD), autistic disorder, and separation anxiety. |
| Delirium, dementia, and amnestic disorders | Disorders characterized by a significant deficit in cognition resulting from a medical condition or substance use. Delirium is a confused state of consciousness; dementia is characterized by multiple deficits in intellectual functioning, including memory deficits. Amnestic disorders affect memory but not other functioning. |
| Substance-related disorders | Disorders resulting from excessive and persistent use of mind-altering substances such as alcohol, amphetamines, or cocaine. |
| Schizophrenia and other psychotic disorders | Schizophrenia involves symptoms such as delusions, hallucinations, and deterioration from a previous level of functioning that last for at least six months (examples include catatonic schizophrenia and paranoid schizophrenia). |
| Mood disorders | Disorders that involve extremes in mood that cause people to feel inappropriately sad or highly elated or to swing between these extremes; category includes major depressive episode and bipolar disorder (formerly called manic depression). |
| Anxiety disorders | Anxiety is manifested in phobias, generalized anxiety disorder, panic disorder, obsessive–compulsive disorder, or posttraumatic stress disorder. |
| Somatoform disorders | Physical symptoms such as paralysis cause significant distress or impairment but do not have a medical explanation; examples include somatization disorder and hypochondriasis. |
| Dissociative disorders | Disorders characterized by a sudden change in the usually integrated functions of consciousness, memory, identity, or perception; they include dissociative amnesia, dissociative fugue, and dissociative identity disorder (multiple personality). |
| Sexual and gender identity disorders | Disorders include the paraphilias, characterized by arousal involving unusual objects, activities, or situations, and sexual dysfunctions such as inhibition of orgasms; category also includes gender identity disorder. |
| Personality disorders | Pervasive, inflexible patterns of inner experience and behavior beginning in adolescence or early adulthood that are stable over time, resistant to treatment, and lead to distress or impairment; category includes antisocial personality disorder and paranoid personality disorder. |

## The Labeling Issue

Recall the vignette at the beginning of this section, in which we put you in the position of someone who walked into a mental hospital and reported hearing a voice say "empty," "hollow," and "thud." Do you believe the hospital staff could tell the difference between a normal person and a disturbed one?

Psychologist David Rosenhan (1973) and seven colleagues carried out this research. They entered mental hospitals and reported hearing voices. Except for giving false names, they answered all questions truthfully. Most of these "pseudopatients" were admitted to the hospital with the diagnosis of *schizophrenia*, a serious psychological disorder. Although they stopped reporting the symptom immediately after admission, they were hospitalized for an average of 19 days and were given a combined total of more than 2,000 pills (which they did not swallow).

Not surprisingly, Rosenhan's research generated controversy. Critics pointed out that patients do not walk into hospitals and fake symptoms, and hence the study was invalid on its face. Nevertheless, the pseudopatients' experiences reveal how labels such as "schizophrenia" can influence our perceptions of behavior. Once the label "schizophrenic" had been applied to the pseudopatients, it influenced the staff's perceptions of them. Some normal behaviors were perceived as abnormal when filtered through that diagnostic label. For example, while in the hospital, the pseudopatients wrote notes describing their experiences. The hospital staff viewed the writing as a symptom of schizophrenia. Several real patients, however, recognized the pseudopatients as normal people who were collecting information about life in a mental hospital. The reactions of staff members were quite different. For example, a pseudopatient might say, "Pardon me, Dr. X. Could you tell me when I am eligible for grounds privileges?" The response would be "Good morning, Dave. How are you today?" Then the staff member would simply walk off (Rosenhan, 1973). Ironically, a recent attempt to replicate Rosenhan's study involving seven people with active symptoms of schizophrenia had a very different result. Six of the seven people were denied treatment, perhaps as a result of limitations on mental health treatment due to budget reductions and managed care (Scribner, 2001).

Rosenhan's pseudopatients could not escape the label, even when they were released from the hospital; they were given the diagnosis of "schizophrenia in remission." These results suggest that the use of diagnostic labels can be a double-edged sword. Diagnosis can help advance our knowledge about the causes of disorders and aid in making treatment decisions, but diagnostic labels may also create a stigma that can be difficult to overcome when looking for housing or a job or simply interacting with other people. Labels inevitably affect how we perceive and respond to others; our responses to those persons labeled as having a psychological disorder are often different from our responses to other people.

The setting and the labels we use influence our perceptions. Some of the people in this photograph are staff members and others are patients in a mental health treatment setting. Can you tell which people are staff members and which are patients? Would your perceptions of these people be affected if we identified the individuals who had the diagnosis of schizophrenia?

# The Prevalence of Psychological Disorders

*Epidemiologists* study the distribution and factors associated with accidents, diseases, and psychological disorders. The data they collect are our best estimates of the numbers of people who suffer from various ailments and disorders. The information is also used to identify subgroups (such as adolescents and the elderly) that are susceptible to particular disorders, to plan and evaluate treatments, and to determine the need for additional health care services. Just as it is problematic to define abnormal behavior, it is also difficult to collect accurate information about the number of people who experience psychological disorders. Many people who suffer from these disorders do not seek treatment; others seek help from family physicians rather than mental health professionals, and thus are not readily identified and counted among those who have psychological disorders. Nevertheless, several major surveys provide estimates of the frequency of these disorders in the general population.

Epidemiologists are interested in the **prevalence** of disorders—the percentage of a population or the number of persons experiencing a given disorder during some specified period. For example, if 500 people in a population of 10,000 had the flu during the past 6 months, the 6-month prevalence for flu would be 5% (500/10,000). Questions like "Did you have the flu at any time during your life?" yield lifetime prevalence figures. The **incidence** of a disorder is the rate (or number) of new cases reported during a given period. If there were 100 newly diagnosed cases this year, the incidence of flu in our population of 10,000 would be 1%.

One useful method for estimating the number of people who have psychological disorders is the face-to-face survey (see Chapter 1). This method was used in two surveys of more than 27,000 respondents: the Epidemiologic Catchment Area Study (Robins & Regier, 1991) and the National Comorbidity Survey (Kessler et al., 1994). Trained interviewers asked questions designed to elicit information that would establish the presence of psychological disorders. A reanalysis of data from these two surveys reported 1-year prevalence estimates of several disorders for cases in which the symptoms reached a level of clinical significance. In other words, these estimates represent the percentage of the population (18 years of age or older) whose symptoms interfere with their functioning (Narrow, Rae, Robin, & Regier, 2002). Twenty percent of respondents reported clinically significant psychological disorders within the 12 months before the interview. The most frequent diagnoses were phobias, alcohol and drug abuse or dependence (see Chapter 4), and major depressive disorder (see Figure 12-1).

These and other psychological disorders often occur with other disorders. Figure 12-2 illustrates the frequency of these concurrent or *comorbid* diagnoses in the same people (Kessler et al., 1994). Approximately 50% of all people with psychological disorders

**prevalence**
Number or percentage of people in a population that ever had a particular disorder during a specified time period

**incidence**
Number or percentage of newly diagnosed cases of a particular disorder in a given population

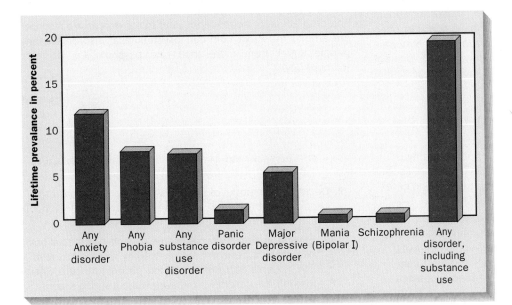

**FIGURE 12-1** One-year prevalence estimates for selected psychological disorders based on combined data from the Epidemiologic Catchment Area Study and the National Comorbidity Survey. These estimates represent the percentage of the population (age 18 or older) whose symptoms were associated with a "clinically significant" effect on their lives. The estimates are the average from the two surveys or they represent only one survey because the surveys did not include the same set of disorders.

**Source:** Narrow et al. (2002).

**FIGURE 12-2** Comorbid psychological disorders. Many people who have one psychological disorder experience other disorders at the same time. The simultaneous occurrence of disorders, or comorbidity, makes it more difficult to make appropriate diagnoses and to develop effective treatment plans.

**Source:** Kessler et al. (1994).

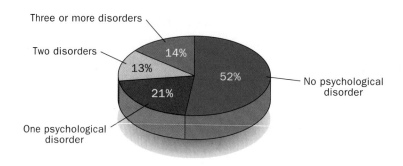

have more than one disorder; comorbidity is even higher in samples of people drawn from those who seek treatment (Clark, Watson, & Reynolds, 1995). The existence of several disorders in a person has implications for treatment planning. Compared to those with a single diagnosis, individuals with comorbid diagnoses have a more chronic history of disorders, report more physical health problems, and experience greater overall impairment (Newman, Moffitt, Caspi, & Silva, 1998).

Most people with psychological disorders do not receive treatment (Kessler et al., 2005). Yet psychological disorders are associated with significant disability, as measured by the number of days individuals are unable to carry out their usual activities or experience restrictions in their social or occupational roles (Ormel et al., 1994).

## REVIEW SUMMARY

**1.** By the standard of statistical rarity, behavior is abnormal when it is infrequent. **Dysfunctional** behavior interferes with a person's ability to function in day-to-day life. The criterion of personal distress is frequently used in identifying the presence of a psychological disorder. Departures from *social norms* are used to define deviant, and therefore **abnormal,** behaviors; social norms, however, can change over time and vary across cultures.

**2. Insanity** is a legal ruling that an accused individual is not responsible for a crime. Contrary to the public's understanding of the insanity plea, such pleas are infrequently used and rarely successful.

**3.** The **medical model** views abnormal behaviors as no different from illnesses and seeks to identify symptoms and prescribe medical treatments. The **psychodynamic model** considers abnormal behavior as the result of unconscious conflicts, often dating from childhood. The **behavioral model** views abnormal behaviors as learned through classical conditioning, operant conditioning, and modeling. The **cognitive model** suggests that

our interpretation of events and our beliefs influence our behavior. The **sociocultural model** emphasizes the importance of social and cultural factors in the frequency, **diagnosis,** and conception of disorders.

**4.** The American Psychiatric Association's *Diagnostic and Statistical Manual of Mental Disorders, 4th Edition, Text Revision (DSM-IV-TR)* provides rules for diagnosing psychological disorders that have increased reliability.

**5.** Rosenhan's pseudopatient study raises questions about our ability to distinguish normal and abnormal behaviors and shows how labels affect the perception of behavior.

**6.** *Epidemiologists* study the **prevalence** and **incidence** of accidents, diseases, and psychological disorders. Phobias, alcohol and drug abuse or dependence, and major depressive disorder are among the most common psychological disorders. Many people suffer from more than one psychological disorder (comorbidity).

## ✓ CHECK YOUR PROGRESS

**1.** Decide which criterion of abnormality—statistical rarity, dysfunction, personal distress, and/or deviance from social norms—could be used to judge each of the following cases. (More than one criterion may be applicable.)

 **a.** Sally spends much of her time daydreaming about "nothing in particular." Her work has suffered, and she has been put on probation because of her declining productivity.

 **b.** Tim spent most of his money on beer and has been neglecting his appearance. When a friend suggested

that he seek help, Tim responded, "Mind your business. I'm not bothering anyone."

**2.** Decide which model of abnormal behavior—medical, psychodynamic, behavioral, cognitive, or sociocultural—is most useful in understanding each of the following cases.

 **a.** Several students observed some patients at a mental hospital, including one who announced he was the "Creator." The students paid attention to this patient for hours; when they left, the patient walked away without saying a word.

**b.** After Cara got a D on an exam, she concluded that the low grade "proves that I'm stupid." She ignored the fact that a bout of flu had prevented her from studying.

**3.** A judge is about to instruct a jury that will begin deliberating in a case in which the defendant is pleading "not guilty by reason of insanity." Which of the following instructions is the judge most likely to give to the jury before they deliberate?

   **a.** "The defendant is not guilty by reason of insanity if he had a mental disorder at the time he committed the crime."

   **b.** "The defendant is not guilty if at the time of the crime he could not tell the difference between right and wrong."

   **c.** "If the defendant had an IQ that is lower than average, he should be found not guilty by reason of insanity."

   **d.** "If the defendant's mental state was influenced by drugs, including alcohol, he should be found not guilty by reason of insanity."

**4.** Which of these are among the most common disorders identified in surveys of the prevalence of disorders in the general population?

   **a.** depression and antisocial personality disorder

   **b.** schizophrenia and major depressive disorder

   **c.** bipolar disorder and panic disorder

   **d.** major depression and phobias

**5.** Of 1,000 felony cases in a nearby county, how many are likely to involve a plea of "not guilty by reason of insanity"?

   **a.** 1

   **b.** 10

   **c.** 25

   **d.** 50

**6.** Your roommate, a psychology major, is completing an internship at the mental health center. Today he told you about a client who was described during a case conference as *comorbid*. You do not want to reveal your ignorance, so

you look up the word later. What will you learn from the dictionary entry?

   **a.** More than one disorder has been diagnosed in this client.

   **b.** Some of the same symptoms have been reported by family members of the client.

   **c.** The client was suffering from a serious condition that is life-threatening.

   **d.** The word appears to be made up and probably is used by someone suffering a psychotic disorder.

**7.** Rosenhan and his colleagues presented themselves as patients with just one symptom—hearing a voice say "empty," "hollow," and "thud." What diagnosis were these pseudopatients given? What is the implication of Rosenhan's pseudopatient study?

**8.** In a survey conducted in a city of 20,000 people, researchers found that 200 of them had been diagnosed with ulcers during the past year. A total of 1,000 people reported having had an ulcer at some time during their life.

   **a.** What is the incidence of ulcers in this city?

   **b.** What is the lifetime prevalence of ulcers?

**9.** What is the most common crime for which a defendant pleads "not guilty by reason of insanity"?

   **a.** rape

   **b.** murder

   **c.** assault

   **d.** bank robbery

**10.** Which symptoms are most likely to be found in someone with *ataque de nervios*?

   **a.** crying, trembling, and fainting

   **b.** delusions, hallucinations, and insomnia

   **c.** chest pain, memory loss, and profuse sweating

   **d.** rapid heartbeat, amnesia, and loss of appetite

**ANSWERS: 1. a.** Dysfunctional or personal distress  **b.** Deviance from social norms  **2. a.** Behavioral  **b.** Cognitive  **3.** b  **4.** d  **5.** b  **6.** a  **7.** Schizophrenia. Labels can influence our perceptions of behavior.  **8. a.** 200 cases in a year  **b.** 1,000 is the lifetime prevalence (5%)  **9.** c  **10.** a

# ANXIETY, SOMATOFORM, AND DISSOCIATIVE DISORDERS

One day while driving home, Deb realized that her heart had suddenly begun racing; she was dizzy, short of breath, and sweating profusely. Afraid that she might pass out, she rolled down the car window to let cold air rush across her face. Over the next several months, these attacks occurred more frequently—at the laundromat, the grocery store, the bank, almost everywhere. She opted to drive on side streets to and from work out of fear that she might be caught in traffic during an attack. Deb began to think she was "going crazy" or was about to die. As she read the obituaries in the newspaper, she thought the deceased were lucky because "they didn't have to go on anymore." Eventually she was unable to leave home; she was even afraid to walk across the backyard

**anxiety**
General feeling of apprehension characterized by behavioral, cognitive, or physiological symptoms

**phobia**
Irrational fear of an activity, object, or situation that is out of proportion to the actual danger

**agoraphobia**
Avoidance of public places or situations in which escape may be difficult should the individual develop incapacitating or embarrassing symptoms of panic

**social phobia**
A fear related to being seen or observed by others

**specific phobia**
Any phobia other than agoraphobia or the social phobias, including the fear of specific animals, of elements of the natural environment, and of such things as blood, injections, or injury

Fear of animals is the most common specific phobia

to her neighbor's house. *Could symptoms like a racing heart and profuse sweating indicate a psychological disorder?*

In this and the following sections, we focus on specific types or categories of psychological disorders. In doing so, we might list some symptoms you may see in yourself. Like medical students who sometimes believe they have the diseases covered in their textbooks and courses, you may conclude that you have one or more of the disorders discussed in this chapter. Be aware of this tendency to diagnose yourself, and don't conjure up unnecessary worries. If you have troubling symptoms, however, do not hesitate to discuss them with a teacher, a counselor, or a therapist. These professionals can help you evaluate the severity of your symptoms and determine whether you need treatment.

The disorders described in the first part of this section are related to anxiety. People with anxiety disorders maintain good contact with reality, are not grossly disturbed, and usually are not hospitalized. Their symptoms, however, can be disturbing and may interfere with day-to-day living. After discussing the anxiety disorders, we will turn to the somatoform and dissociative disorders.

## Anxiety Disorders

Giving a speech in class, waiting to take an exam, interviewing for a job: What do these experiences have in common? Perhaps you feel apprehensive and uncomfortable. Does the word *anxious* come to mind? At moderate levels, anxiety is normal; it can provide the motivation needed to give an outstanding speech, "ace" an exam, or get a good job. High levels of **anxiety** or a general feeling of apprehension, however, are distressing and interfere with effective functioning. Severe anxiety that disrupts a person's life indicates the presence of an *anxiety disorder*. According to one survey, 19% of men and 31% of women have had at least one anxiety disorder at some time in their lives (Kessler et al., 1994).

But how do we recognize anxiety? There are three categories of indicators: behavioral, cognitive, and physiological. The behavioral indicators include shakiness and stuttering. Physiological signs like a rapid heart rate and dry mouth reflect sympathetic nervous system activation (see Chapter 2). Cognitive signs include difficulty concentrating and thoughts or beliefs that can fuel the anxiety (such as "I'll make a fool of myself when I give my speech").

**Phobias.** As we saw in Chapter 5, a **phobia** is an intense, excessive fear of an activity, object, or situation. The fear in a phobia is out of proportion to the real danger, and it is difficult to overcome. If your concern about facing fear-arousing stimuli leads to efforts to avoid those stimuli, you may have a phobia. Imagine a blood phobia so severe that a figure of speech like "cut it out" makes you faint. A fear of cats is so crippling that you send your daughter (now age 21) into a store to scout around and sound the all-clear before you can enter. Your daughter has been the "cat scout" since age 5 (Kluger, 2001). The *DSM-IV-TR* organizes phobias into three categories: *agoraphobia*, *social phobia*, and *specific phobia*.

**Agoraphobia** (literally "fear of the marketplace") is the most common phobia treated in mental health clinics. Most people with agoraphobia are women who avoid public places or situations from which it would be difficult to escape if they develop embarrassing or incapacitating symptoms such as dizziness or vomiting. They prefer the safety of a private place, quite often their home.

Different phobias tend to develop at different ages. Agoraphobia usually begins in one's 20s; **social phobias,** such as fear of speaking in front of a group, usually emerge between 15 and 25 years of age (Schneier & Johnson, 1992). **Specific phobias**—fears of particular objects or situations—often begin between ages 5 and 9 (Ost, 1987). Figure 12-3 depicts the prevalence rates of some social and specific phobias. Examples of specific phobias are fear of fire (*pyrophobia*) and fear of heights (*acrophobia*) (see Table 12-2 on p. 530). Specific phobias are among the most treatable of the anxiety disorders, although people with these disorders rarely seek treatment (Antony & Barlow, 2002).

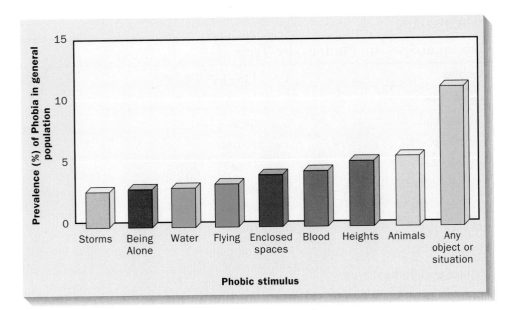

**FIGURE 12-3** Specific phobias are not uncommon. In one survey, the lifetime prevalence for specific phobias was 11%, with fears of animals being the most common specific phobia.

**Source:** Curtis, Magee, Eaton, Wittchan, and Kessler, (1998).

More than 50% of people with a *blood-injection-injury* phobia report a history of fainting. In contrast to the typical phobic reaction, their blood pressure *drops* dramatically when they are unable to avoid situations such as having blood drawn, coming across an accident scene, or seeing a syringe (Saul, 2001). Many victims of a blood phobia share the fear with a close family member, which may result from similar or common stressful experiences or genetic factors that predispose them to faint (Ost, 1992). These phobias are the only ones associated with fainting.

How do phobias develop? On the basis of their study of Little Albert (see Chapter 5), John B. Watson and Rosalie Rayner (1920) proposed that phobias are learned through classical conditioning. A phobia may result when a formerly neutral stimulus (such as a white rat) becomes associated with a fear-producing stimulus (such as a loud noise). Through this association, the neutral stimulus becomes a feared stimulus; that is, it is now the conditioned stimulus or phobic stimulus.

During World War II, London was subjected to heavy aerial bombardment. Despite the frequent occurrence of unconditioned stimuli (loud explosions), few Londoners developed phobias. The situation in London is one example of our tendency to develop phobias to some stimuli more readily than to others. According to the concept of *preparedness* (see Chapter 5), we are more likely to learn to fear stimuli that our ancestors had reason to fear, such as snakes, than nonharmful objects like flowers or stimuli that did not exist in our ancestors' time—for instance, aerial bombardments.

Phobias may also develop by observing (modeling) the behaviors and emotional reactions of others; this indirect form of learning is often called *vicarious conditioning*. Few people who fear mice or snakes have actually had adverse encounters with such creatures. They may have seen other people react fearfully in the presence of these stimuli, however, or perhaps they have heard discussions of the awful things such animals might do to humans. This type of modeling can be beneficial when it enables us to learn reasonable fears without directly encountering dangerous objects; still, it can lead us to fear stimuli simply because we have been exposed to the fears of others.

**Panic Disorder.** At the beginning of the section we met Deb, who experienced symptoms such as a racing

*"I'm facing my fears in alphabetical order. How about you?"*

**TABLE 12-2**

## Common Specific Phobias, by Type

| Phobias | Focus of the Fear |
| --- | --- |
| **Animal type** | |
| Ailurophobia | Cats |
| Arachnophobia | Spiders |
| Cynophobia | Dogs |
| Entomophobia | Insects |
| Equinophobia | Horses |
| Musophobia | Mice |
| Ranidaphobia | Frogs |
| **Natural environment type** | |
| Brontophobia | Thunder, thunderstorms |
| Frigophobia | Cold weather |
| Heliophobia | Sun |
| Nephophobia | Clouds |
| Phonophobia | Loud noises |
| Photophobia | Light |
| Xylophobia | Forests |
| **Blood-injection-injury type** | |
| Belonophobia | Pins and needles |
| Dermatophobia | Skin lesions |
| Epistaxiophobia | Nosebleeds |
| Hemophobia | Blood |
| Odynephobia | Pain |
| Parasitophobia | Parasites |
| Poinephobia | Punishment |
| **Situation type** | |
| Cainophobia | Novelty |
| Claustrophobia | Closed spaces |
| Ochlophobia | Crowds |
| Scotophobia | Being looked at |
| Gephyrophobia | Crossing bridges |
| **Other** | |
| Catoptrophobia | Mirrors |
| Coulrophobia | Clowns |
| Kakorrhaphiophobia | Failure |
| Logophobia | Words |
| Triskaidekaphobia | Number 13 |

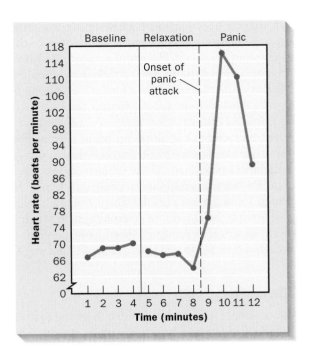

**FIGURE 12-4** Rapid increase in heart rate during a panic attack. In the midst of a diagnostic evaluation at a clinic, a 33-year-old woman experienced a panic attack a few minutes after she had been asked to relax her whole body. The sudden and intense physiological changes of a panic attack were also evident in increased levels of muscle tension in her forehead.

**Source:** Cohen, Barlow, and Blanchard (1985).

heart, profuse sweating, and difficulty breathing while driving home. Do these symptoms suggest she is suffering from a psychological disorder?

Deb had several panic attacks, which are intense physiological reactions that occur even in the absence of an emergency. Within seconds the heart rate of a person with this disorder can accelerate by 50 or more beats per minute (see Figure 12-4). In addition to rapid heartbeat, victims also report sweating, dizziness, shortness of breath, and shaking. An episode of panic typically lasts for 5 to 20 minutes, although victims perceive the duration of the attack to be endless (Rachman, 1998). Many victims believe they are "going crazy," losing control, or having a heart attack, yet there is no medical evidence of a heart condition. Panic attack victims seem frightened by the physical symptoms of their fear; thus, panic attacks probably represent a "fear of fear" (Craske & Barlow, 2001). Frequent panic attacks are diagnosed as **panic disorder,** the most severe anxiety disorder. The rate among women is more than twice that of men (Eaton, Kessler, Wittchen, & Magee, 1994), with some differences in reported symptoms: Women are more likely to report respiration-related difficulties (Sheikh, Leskin, & Klein, 2002). Panic disorder is often comorbid with other anxiety disorders, depression, substance abuse, and personality disorders (Craske & Barlow, 2001; Knowles & Weissman, 1995).

About 50% of the people who suffer from panic attacks also experience agoraphobia (Eaton et al., 1994), which is what happened to Deb. Thus it is possible that some cases of agoraphobia develop out of the experience of panic attacks (Barlow et al., 1985; White & Barlow, 2002). Most people with phobias can avoid the stimuli they fear, but victims of panic disorder are not so fortunate. Panic attacks can strike "out of the blue," so victims cannot hide. Perhaps this is why many victims of agoraphobia prefer to remain in "safe" locations like their homes, where they will not be embarrassed if they experience panic symptoms.

**panic disorder**
The most severe anxiety disorder, characterized by intense physiological arousal not related to a specific stimulus

*"Looks like your fears of people, speaking, computers, and all forms of transportation might limit your career opportunities."*

**Source:** Reprinted with the permission of Psi Chi, The National Honor Society in Psychology.

What causes such attacks? In patients with a history of panic attacks, the symptoms can be induced by an injection of sodium lactate (the amount of this chemical in the body increases after vigorous exercise). The sodium lactate leads to increased physiological arousal like that occurring during a panic attack. Two other findings also support a biological cause: (a) Panic disorder occurs at a higher rate among family members of victims than in the general population, and (b) victims respond well to antidepressant drugs. What's more, a number of tests called *biological challenges* have revealed that certain biologically related phenomena can bring on panic attacks. For example, people with a history of panic attacks experience panic attacks if they hyperventilate, inhale carbon dioxide, or breathe into a paper bag. These procedures raise carbon dioxide levels in the blood and brain. People who are prone to panic attacks may be especially sensitive even to a small increase in carbon dioxide, which the brain registers as the threat of suffocation, thus triggering the autonomic nervous system into a full fight-or-flight response—often interpreted as a heart attack. Victims of panic disorder may have a highly sensitive suffocation monitor that signals a lack of useful air (Klein, 1993).

### Psychological Detective

Between 15 and 30% of people surveyed report experiencing at least one panic attack (Eaton et al., 1994). If so many people experience panic attacks, why do only some of these people develop chronic panic disorder? According to cognitive psychologists, a key factor is the way people interpret their symptoms. What kinds of interpretations could lead an individual to develop panic disorder?

According to cognitive psychologists, panic attacks occur when the bodily sensations of anxiety are misinterpreted as signs of impending disaster. For example, people suffering from panic disorder and those without this diagnosis were given ambiguous written scenarios that could be interpreted as threatening or not threatening. For example, they might read a scenario in which they carried our routine activities, some of which involved mild exertion that was associated with a faster heart rate. Although most people attributed the increased heart rate to the physical exertion, individuals with panic disorder tended to think of a heart attack or the like (Barlow, 2002; Clark et al., 1997). Rather than attributing symptoms to physical exertion or stressors in their lives, victims of panic disorder interpret them as indicators of serious physical problems (McNally, Hornig, & Donnell, 1995). This interpretation increases their arousal during and after an attack and makes them more vigilant about physical signs in the future.

**Generalized Anxiety Disorder.** Chronic worriers may suffer **generalized anxiety disorder (GAD)**, a condition that typically begins in one's 20s or 30s. Their low tolerance for uncertainty and ambiguity plays havoc with decision making; they exhibit a continuous need for more evidence before rendering a decision (Ladouceur, Talbot, & Dugas, 1997). Like a car on cruise control, they are set to worry, albeit uncontrollably, about missing an appointment, losing a job, having an accident, family problems, and so on. The worry may extend to the unlikely or irrelevant—a character in a Woody Allen film was troubled by the thought that the universe is expanding! Spend hour upon hour worrying and the body pays a price in symptoms such as racing heart, dry mouth, upset stomach, and tension. A consistent finding from epidemiological research is that GAD occurs twice as often in women as in men (Brown, O'Leary, & Barlow, 2001). The anxiety characterizing this disorder is "free-floating" because it is not brought on by a specific stimulus. GAD is a highly comorbid condition that may increase the vulnerability to other disorders, such as depression, as well as increasing the use of health care services (Brown et al., 2001).

GAD, along with some other anxiety disorders, may result from low levels of the inhibitory neurotransmitter gamma-aminobutyric acid (GABA; see Chapter 2). Anxiety often occurs when there is a high level of nerve impulses in brain circuits related to fear

**generalized anxiety disorder (GAD)**

Chronically high level of anxiety that is not attached to a specific stimulus

and vigilance. Elevated levels of GABA block this neurological activity; low levels allow it to occur, and the result can be what we term anxiety.

**Obsessive–Compulsive Disorder.** "Did I turn off the stove?" "Are the windows closed?" Do thoughts like these run through your mind occasionally? If so, you are like most people. But some people are dominated by thoughts of this kind or worse. Intrusive recurrent thoughts, impulses, or images that are unwanted, inappropriate, and appear "out of the blue" are *obsessions* (from the Latin word meaning "to besiege"). The "battle in the mind" (Osborn, 1998) created by obsessions can cause unbearable anxiety that leads some people to feel they must do something to get rid of or reduce their occurrence. These people may check the stove or windows over and over each day. For example, a clerk spent up to 2 hours a day checking electrical appliances, doors, and windows in her house before she was able to leave (Rachman, 1998). These repeated, irresistible behaviors (such as hand washing) or mental acts (such as silent counting or repetition of words) that often follow obsessions are called *compulsions*. Performing these so-called rituals, however, provides only temporary relief; not performing them leads to a significant increase in anxiety. Although the specific content of the obsessions and associated rituals tend to be similar across cultures, culture and religion can influence the presentation of OCD. For example, some obsessive fears are quite culturally specific, such as the fear of leprosy in Africa. Historical shifts also occur in the focus of obsessive fears of disease. Twenty years ago, contamination fears focused on sexually transmitted diseases like syphilis; today, such fears focus on AIDS (Steketee & Barlow, 2002). Although obsessions and compulsions may occur separately, most people with **obsessive–compulsive disorder (OCD)** have both of them (Foa & Kozak, 1995). Table 12-3 lists some common obsessions and compulsions.

Mental health professionals use the words *obsession* and *compulsion* differently from the way we use them in everyday conversation. You may think that a friend who watches dozens of basketball games is "obsessed." To a basketball fan, however, his behavior is

**obsessive–compulsive disorder (OCD)**
An anxiety disorder characterized by repetitive, irrational, intrusive thoughts, impulses, or images (obsessions) and irresistible, repetitive acts (compulsions) such as checking that doors are locked or washing hands

---

**TABLE 12-3**

## Common Obsessions and Compulsions

The most common obsessions involve contamination and the fear of harming oneself or others. The most common compulsions involve checking objects (such as light switches or locks) and cleaning or washing.

### Obsessions

- A young woman's recurrent impulse to strangle children and domestic animals was followed by the thought that she might actually have committed this horrible act.
- A young man had recurrent intrusive images of violently attacking his elderly parents with an ax. The subsequent thought that he might have actually attacked them included images of the bloody victims.
- A young woman's recurrent, intrusive impulse to burn her eyes with a lighted cigarette was accompanied by images of the act.

### Compulsions

- A young woman repeatedly washed her hands to rid herself of contamination by germs. On every occasion, she washed six times without soap and six times with soap.
- A man opened letters he had written and sealed to make sure that he had written the correct things. He would rip open the envelope, reread the letter, and put it into a new envelope several times before mailing it.
- A woman in her 40s complained that every time she entered a room, she had to touch the four corners in a left-to-right sequence.

**Sources:** De Silva and Rachman (1992); *Harvard Mental Health Letter* (1998).

OCD Clinic

Knock 3 times,
wait 2.3 seconds,
knock 3 times,
wait 2.5 seconds,
grab handle,
turn 47.5
degrees to right.

**Source:** Reprinted with the permission of Psi Chi, The National Honor Society in Psychology.

desirable and enjoyable. People with OCD do not want or enjoy their obsessive thoughts or time-consuming compulsions; they perceive them as excessive and feel that they interfere with daily functioning. What's more, compulsive gambling and compulsive eating are often associated with some degree of pleasure. By contrast, the compulsions in OCD are irrational and do not give rise to pleasure.

The lifetime prevalence of OCD is about 2% (Narrow et al., 2002); the typical period of onset is from late adolescence to the early 20s. Among children and adolescents, the rate is higher among boys than girls; among adults, the disorder is more common among women. Across the entire lifespan, however, there is little difference in the rates of OCD among males and females (Steketee & Barlow, 2002). The disorder is sometimes accompanied by depression, eating disorders, substance abuse, Tourette's syndrome, or other anxiety disorders (Regier, Rae, & Narrow, 1998; Wonderlich & Mitchell, 1997). Consider this case of one adolescent's struggle with OCD:

> For years, 14-year-old Charles has spent hours in the shower removing a sticky substance from his body. His mother knew the washing was crazy, but she joined her son's rituals because he would be miserable otherwise. She scrubbed household objects with alcohol. Charles and his mother heard about a treatment program, but he was wary of the required EEG test because a sticky paste would be used to attach the electrodes. "Stickiness is terrible. It is some kind of disease," he said. (Rapoport, 1989, p. 86)

Behavioral psychologists view compulsions as learned habits that reduce anxiety. That is, the compulsive behavior has been associated with anxiety reduction through operant conditioning.

### Psychological Detective

Charles showered repeatedly in an effort to remove a sticky substance from his body. After each shower, his anxiety was reduced. The reduction in anxiety is an example of an operant conditioning principle (see Chapter 5). Before reading further, identify that principle. Then identify the specific reinforcer involved and the behavior that is being reinforced.

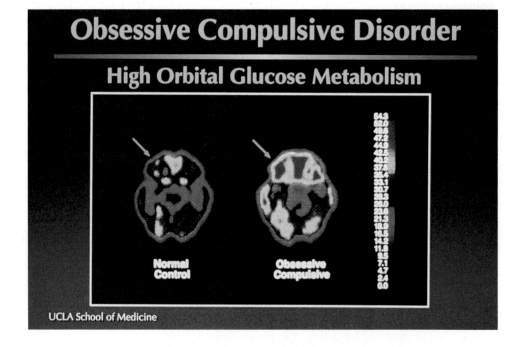

**FIGURE 12-5** Brain scans of a normal person and one with OCD. The greater frequency of reds and yellows in the brain scan of a person with OCD, indicates greater brain activity, especially in the frontal lobes.

Charles engaged in the behavior of showering, which led to a reduction of his anxiety. This sequence is an example of negative reinforcement: Showering behavior was reinforced by anxiety reduction (see Chapter 5). As a result, Charles is more likely to take showers in the future.

OCD runs in families; identical twins are more likely than fraternal twins to share the disorder. These findings point to an inherited biological predisposition (Andreasen & Black, 1995), which may involve abnormal levels of a neurotransmitter or abnormal functioning of certain parts of the brain. The neurotransmitter serotonin has been implicated in OCD because antidepressant drugs that affect this neurotransmitter are useful treatments (Penzel, 2000). OCD may involve elevated levels of activity in the frontal lobes and the basal ganglia (see Figure 12-5). This increased activity may account for the obsessions or merely reflect them; recall from Chapter 2 that the frontal lobes are involved in planning and thinking, an important component of obsessive–compulsive behavior. The basal ganglia play a role in motor movement and thus may be implicated in compulsions (Andreasen & Black, 1995).

The Study Chart below should provide a helpful summary and review of the anxiety disorders.

## Study CHART

### Anxiety Disorders

| | |
|---|---|
| **Agoraphobia** | Fear of being in places such as shopping malls or public transportation, where it might be difficult to escape if embarrassing symptoms occur suddenly. Sometimes occurs along with panic disorder. |
| **Social phobia** | Fears related to being in situations in which one might be subject to scrutiny. |
| **Specific phobia** | A large category of phobias other than those listed as agoraphobia or social phobia. These include phobias related to animals, the natural environment (storms, water), and blood-injection-injury. |
| **Panic disorder** | Recurrent panic attacks, which are intense physiological reactions in the absence of an emergency. There is also apprehension about the possibility of future attacks and concern about the seriousness of the attacks, which are often viewed as similar to heart attacks. |
| **Generalized anxiety disorder (GAD)** | A high level of anxiety not tied to a specific stimulus. Symptoms include excessive worry about a number of events or activities. |
| **Obsessive–compulsive disorder (OCD)** | Typically a combination of disturbing, persistent thoughts, impulses, or images (obsessions) followed by irresistible behaviors (compulsions) that tend to reduce the anxiety. |

## Somatoform Disorders

**Somatoform disorders** involve complaints of bodily symptoms (*soma* means "body") that do not have a known medical cause; instead psychological factors are involved. Do not confuse somatoform disorders with *psychophysiological disorders*, which have a medical basis; in the case of migraine headaches, for example, blood vessels in the head become so dilated that they cause pain. These disorders generally occur in parts of the body controlled by the autonomic nervous system, such as the digestive tract; by contrast, somatoform disorders usually affect body parts that are controlled by the central nervous system, such as the sensory organs or the limbs. Among the somatoform disorders listed in the *DSM-IV-TR* are hypochondriasis, somatization disorder, and conversion disorder.

**Hypochondriasis.** Hypochondriasis is a preoccupation with physical symptoms believed to indicate a serious illness; it occurs equally in men and women (American

**somatoform disorders**
Disorders involving physical complaints that do not have a known medical cause but are related to psychological factors

**hypochondriasis**
Somatoform disorder in which a person believes that he or she has a serious disease despite repeated medical findings to the contrary

**Source:** Reprinted by permission of Sidney Harris.

"IGNORE HIM. HE'S A HYPOCHONDRIAC."

Psychiatric Association, 2000). People with hypochondriasis detect aches, pains, or bodily changes that many of us would ignore; they interpret these signs as proof that they are suffering from some dire though undiagnosed disorder. People with this diagnosis (as well as those with somatization disorder) tend to agree with statements such as "Bodily complaints are always a sign of disease" and "Red blotches on the skin are a threatening sign of skin cancer" (Rief, Hiller, & Margraf, 1998). Their beliefs are genuine; they do not voluntarily produce their symptoms. Despite repeated assurances of having good health, they are never convinced and continually consult one physician after another.

**Somatization Disorder.** People with **somatization disorder** present vague but complicated and dramatic medical histories, usually beginning in their teenage years. In contrast to hypochondriasis, which centers on some specific disease, somatization disorder involves a large number of symptoms (for example, gastrointestinal, neurological, pain, and sexual complaints) (American Psychiatric Association, 2000). The symptoms cause significant distress that leads victims to consult physicians who inevitably fail to find a medical basis for the physical complaints. The disorder occurs more frequently in women than in men, although physicians may be less likely to recognize it in men.

**Conversion Disorder.** In contrast to hypochondriasis and somatization disorder, **conversion disorder** involves mainly sensory and motor functions that are normally under voluntary control. Consequently, symptoms can be dramatic and include apparent blindness, deafness, paralysis, and seizures (Conversion Disorder, 2005). For example, a patient who reports paralysis of the wrist may still be able to move the fingers, even though the fingers and wrist are on the same nerve pathway. The symptoms are real to these individuals, who do not feel that they produce them voluntarily. Nevertheless, there is no obvious medical explanation for the symptoms and the disability they produce. Consider the following case:

> After collapsing at home, a woman is brought to the hospital, apparently paralyzed and numb on her right side. A physician notes that her reflexes are normal and sensation is lost only in her right arm and right leg, which is not the usual pattern for a stroke. Although she staggers when she walks,

**somatization disorder**
Somatoform disorder involving multiple physical complaints that do not have a medical explanation and do not suggest a specific known disease

**conversion disorder**
Somatoform disorder in which a person presents sensory or motor symptoms that do not have a medical explanation

she engages in conversation with fellow patients and hospital staff as though the symptoms do not trouble her. The paralysis and numbness developed while the patient was watching her husband and adolescent son argue. The husband had already thrown two older sons out of the house after arguments about their behavior. The patient seemed determined that this would not happen to her third and favorite son. As the fight began, she felt weakness on her right side. When they saw her collapse, the men stopped arguing and brought her to the hospital, where they visit her every day. (Conversion disorder, 2005, p. 1)

This rare disorder is often a response to stressful situations such as family problems, war, or the death of a loved one. For example, a group of Cambodian women all had unexplained blindness. When they were interviewed, they related horrifying tales of having been forced to watch relatives being tortured and killed during political conflicts in their native country (Cooke, 1991).

The term *conversion* suggests that anxiety over a conflict or other difficult situation is converted into a physical manifestation. In the case above, the woman felt powerless to stop the arguments based on a history in which two other sons had been thrown out of the house. The response of others, called a *secondary gain*, tends to increase use of the symptoms; the *primary gain* is the avoidance of the anxiety associated with the conflict.

Modeling may occur in some cases of conversion disorder (Mucha & Reinhardt, 1970). Naval aviators who developed conversion disorders during their stressful training were likely to have parents who had physical problems in the same body parts in which the aviators developed symptoms.

How can we explain the development of somatoform disorders? First, the symptoms may be a defense against the distress of difficult situations. Second, when we have physical problems, relatives and friends often offer attention and sympathy, and these reactions can act as reinforcers for continued presentation of the symptoms. For example, conversion reactions often disappear without treatment in hours or days, sometimes in response to changes in the availability of attention and sympathy.

## Dissociative Disorders

**Dissociative disorders** involve a disruption in a particular function of the mind, such as memory or self-awareness, usually in response to extreme stress. These rare disorders are dramatic and have been the basis of plots for movies, books, and television shows, yet most of us have temporary and mild dissociative experiences at some time, such as when we daydream. Dissociative disorders include dissociative amnesia, dissociative fugue, and dissociative identity disorder (multiple personality).

**Dissociative Amnesia and Dissociative Fugue.** An individual with **dissociative amnesia** is unable to recall important personal information. The memory impairment is too extensive to be due to normal forgetting; it may involve a specific traumatic event, most of the person's life, or a stretch of time ending in the present. Dissociative amnesia occurs suddenly, does not affect storage of new information, and frequently ends abruptly, usually after a few weeks or months.

### Psychological Detective

When Ed took his friends for a ride, he drove too fast on a hairpin turn, and the car flipped over. Rescue crews found three dead passengers; Ed survived, sustaining several broken bones and chest injuries. After he recovered from his injuries, he had no memory of the accident. The memory loss was too profound to be attributed to ordinary forgetfulness. How can we explain Ed's failure to recall the events? Use the medical and psychodynamic models to explain Ed's failure to recall the events surrounding the car accident.

**dissociative disorders**
Disorders affecting a function of the mind, such as memory for events, knowledge of one's identity, or consciousness

**dissociative amnesia**
Dissociative disorder that involves a sudden inability to recall important personal information; often occurs in response to trauma or extreme stress

**dissociative fugue**
Dissociative disorder involving amnesia and flight from the workplace or home; may involve establishing a new identity in a new location

**dissociative identity disorder (multiple personality)**
Dissociative disorder in which a person has two or more separate personalities, which usually alternate

According to the medical model, amnesia results from physical causes such as a head injury or ingestion of large quantities of alcohol. Memory loss in these forms of amnesia is often permanent. Ed did not suffer a head injury and had no alcohol in his body, so we must consider another explanation. The psychodynamic explanation tells us that amnesia may occur as a defense against or escape from the anxiety caused by a traumatic event. In Ed's case, it appears that his recall failure was caused by the trauma of seeing his friends killed and feeling responsible for their deaths.

When amnesia is accompanied by travel, the person is suffering from **dissociative fugue.** People with this disorder may leave a stressful environment and take up residence in a distant city, with a new identity and no memory of their past life. Recovery is often sudden, and the victim's recall of the episode is no better than a dream. Cases of dissociative fugue are fascinating but extremely rare; more typical cases, although still infrequent, involve wandering away from a natural disaster.

**Dissociative Identity Disorder.**     The presence of more than one personality in a single individual, **dissociative identity disorder (multiple personality),** is the most dramatic dissociative disorder. Although it was once considered to be extremely rare, mental health professionals report significant numbers of cases of dissociative identity disorder, which they argue indicates that the disorder is not rare but underdiagnosed. There has been a clear increase in the number of cases of dissociative identity disorder reported during the past decade (Coons, 1998). On the other hand, some psychologists are cautious and note that this increase in diagnoses coincides with the recovered-memory movement, which has been implicated in a number of false reports of abuse (see Chapter 7) (Ofshe & Watters, 1994). Most cases of dissociative identity disorder are associated with an early childhood history of sexual or physical abuse (Gleaves, 1996; Lowenstein, 1994). Children are ill-equipped to cope with the trauma of abuse and may split off new personalities in an attempt to deal with it, in much the same way that some children invent imaginary playmates. "Dissociation is a way for abused children to deny their hatred and fear of adults. They begin to tell themselves that it is all happening to another person who can tolerate it, and eventually to isolate their catastrophic experiences in personality fragments" (Falling apart: Dissociation and its disorders, 2005, p. 2).

There are usually three or four personalities or *alters* (short for *alternate identities*), although more than 100 have been reported in a single individual. The alters in dissociative identity disorder often contrast sharply with one another and have very different personal histories, behavior patterns, friends, beliefs, habits, values, and even voices and facial expressions (Falling apart: Dissociation and its disorders, 2005). For example, in the classic case described in *The Three Faces of Eve* (Thigpen & Cleckley, 1957), Eve

Seventeen-year-old Cheryl Ann Barnes was reunited with her family after she disappeared from her Florida home in 1996; she was found a month later in a New York hospital, where she was listed as Jane Doe. Although quite rare, cases of dissociative fugue often receive widespread media attention.

White was shy and inhibited. At one point during psychotherapy, she put her hands on her temples and pressed hard, as if she was experiencing a severe headache. She then dropped her hands, smiled, and said in an unfamiliar voice, "Hi, there, Doc!" A few minutes later she introduced herself as Eve Black. In a subsequent publication by Chris Sizemore (Eve's real name), she revealed that she actually had 22 different personalities. These personalities always occurred in groups of three, always included a wife/mother image, a party girl, and a more normal intellectual personality (Sizemore & Pittillo, 1977). Here is her description of the different personalities:

> Among these twenty-two alters, ten were poets, seven were artists, and one had taught tailoring. Today, I paint and write, but I cannot sew. Yet these alters were not moods or the result of role-playing. They were entities that were separate from the personality I was born to be, and am today. They were so different that their tones of voice changed. What's more, their facial expressions, appetites, tastes in clothes, handwriting, skills, and IQ were all different too. (Sizemore, 1989, p. 9)

In most instances, 6 to 12 years elapse between the first occasion on which a person seeks treatment and the eventual diagnosis of dissociative identity disorder (Lowenstein, 1994). During that time several diagnoses may be suggested; the most common ones are depression, schizophrenia, and alcohol or drug abuse (Gleaves, 1996).

Psychodynamic theorists describe multiple personality as resulting from early traumas such as sexual assault or physical punishment. They regard patients with this disorder as victims of unconscious processes that suddenly take over when the individual faces a stressor. An alternative explanation suggests that presentation of multiple personalities is a learned role (Spanos, Weekes, & Bertrand, 1985). Movies, television shows, and books like *The Three Faces of Eve* provide vivid descriptions of people who have suffered from this disorder. People with dissociative identity disorder may have been reinforced for revealing those personalities. For example, some therapists are so intrigued with the symptoms of this disorder that they may inadvertently reinforce their clients for revelations concerning other personalities. Some researchers have found that many of the symptoms of the disorder occur for the first time during the course of treatment (Ofshe & Watters, 1994). What's more, using hypnosis in treatment may create a situation in which suggestible individuals turn the therapist's questions about other possible personalities into a belief in their existence. On the other hand, dissociative identity disorder is also viewed as an underrecognized and underdiagnosed response pattern that has similarities to posttraumatic stress disorder (Gleaves, 1996).

Ken Bianchi, the "Hillside Strangler" (there were actually two) presented symptoms that suggested dissociative identity disorder. Bianchi presented the symptoms while supposedly hypnotized; tape recordings indicated the hypnotist had suggested the presence of other personalities. Prosecutors demonstrated that his symptoms were faked, and he was convicted of multiple murders.

**STUDY TIP**

Develop a chart to summarize anxiety, somatoform, and dissociative disorders. Include a definition of each type of disorder as well as any other information you find important.

## *Study* CHART

### Somatoform and Dissociative Disorders

**Somatoform Disorders**

| | |
|---|---|
| **Hypochondriasis** | Preoccupation with physical symptoms that are believed to indicate a serious illness despite repeated medical evaluations that find no evidence of a disease |
| **Somatization disorder** | Presentation of a large number of gastrointestinal, pain, sexual, and/or neurological symptoms that do not suggest a recognized disease |
| **Conversion disorder** | A loss or impairment of motor function (for example, paralysis) or sensory function (for example, blindness) that does not coincide with the organization of the nervous system, with symptoms that may constitute a response to a very stressful situation |

**Dissociative Disorders**

| | |
|---|---|
| **Dissociative amnesia** | An inability to recall important personal information that is often related to a traumatic event and is too extensive to be the result of normal forgetting |
| **Dissociative fugue** | A rare disorder that combines amnesia with travel away from a stressful environment |
| **Dissociative identity disorder (multiple personality)** | The presence of two or more distinct personalities that often contrast sharply, associated with a history of sexual and physical abuse |

The Study Chart above should prove helpful; consult it frequently.

The disorders we have discussed so far rarely lead to hospitalization, although the symptoms can interfere with daily living. Other psychological disorders, which we discuss in the next sections, have more serious consequences.

## REVIEW SUMMARY

1. **Anxiety** involves behavioral, cognitive, and physiological elements. **Phobias** are excessive, irrational fears of activities, objects, or situations. The most frequently diagnosed phobia is **agoraphobia**. The *DSM-IV-TR* also lists **social phobia** and **specific phobia**. Classical conditioning and modeling have been offered as explanations for the development of phobias.

2. Frequent panic attacks (which resemble heart attacks) are the main symptom of **panic disorder**. Biological and cognitive explanations for this disorder have been proposed. A person with a chronically high level of anxiety may suffer from **generalized anxiety disorder (GAD).**

3. Most people who have the diagnosis of **obsessive–compulsive disorder (OCD)** have both obsessions and compulsions. Obses-

sions are senseless thoughts, images, or impulses that occur repeatedly; they are often accompanied by compulsions, which are irresistible, repetitive acts.

4. **Somatoform disorders** involve the presentation of physical symptoms that have no known medical causes, but psychological factors are involved. Among these disorders are **hypochondriasis, somatization disorder,** and **conversion disorder.**

5. **Dissociative disorders** involve disruptions in some function of the mind. In **dissociative amnesia,** memories cannot be recalled; in **dissociative fugue,** memory loss is accompanied by travel. **Dissociative identity disorder (multiple personality)** is characterized by the presence of two or more personalities in the same individual.

## ✓ CHECK YOUR PROGRESS

1. Identify the most likely diagnosis for each of the following conditions.

   a. Every day Brad thinks about hurting a family member. These thoughts are so repulsive that he begins counting backward from 1,000.

   b. Maria's 12 physical symptoms don't reflect any disease her physician has ever seen, and she is angry when the physician advises her to make an appointment to see a psychologist.

c. A week after reporting for military duty, Dean cannot use his arm to fire a gun. Medical causes have been ruled out.

d. Andrea reports symptoms such as a racing heart and difficulty breathing that last for 10–15 minutes several times a week. She thinks she is having a heart attack.

e. Nick always seems to be on edge, is often restless, and just can't relax. His mind always seems to be focused on some new worry.

2. What is the difference between an obsession and a compulsion?

3. Psychophysiological disorders are likely to affect parts of the body controlled by the _____ nervous system; somatoform disorders are likely to be found in parts of the body controlled by the _____ nervous system.

   a. autonomic, central
   b. central, autonomic
   c. parasympathetic, central
   d. somatic, sympathetic

4. Which neurotransmitter has been implicated in the development of OCD?

   a. Ach
   b. GABA
   c. dopamine
   d. serotonin

5. Angela is given an assignment to report back on the diagnosis of hypochondriasis with a focus on the rate of diagnosis in men and women. When she has completed her report, what will she find?

   a. Women are diagnosed with the disorder more often.
   b. Men are diagnosed with the disorder more often.
   c. The diagnosis is made equally often in men and women.
   d. Among children, girls receive the diagnosis more often; among adults men receive the diagnosis more often.

6. Researchers at the medical center are using sophisticated brain scanning devices to study the brains of people with OCD. Which areas of the brain would they expect to be especially active in this group of patients?

   a. cerebellum and temporal lobes
   b. basal ganglia and frontal lobes
   c. corpus callosum and thalamus
   d. thalamus and hypothalamus

7. While watching a talk show, you hear the announcer describe today's guests as suffering from multiple personality. What is the current name for this disorder? It takes several years before a proper diagnosis is made; give examples of typical diagnoses made in the meantime.

8. Which individual is suffering from the most common phobia treated in mental health centers?

   a. Dan, who suffers from zoophobia
   b. Alice, who suffers from agoraphobia
   c. Ben, who suffers from a social phobia
   d. Darla, who suffers from belonophobia

9. Ted is sitting in class when he is suddenly overcome by an intense fear that he has never experienced before. His heart is "racing out of control," and he wonders if he is having a heart attack. Which disorder is most consistent with Ted's symptoms?

   a. fugue
   b. panic disorder
   c. bipolar disorder
   d. depersonalization

10. The Psychiatric Research Center seeks volunteers for research involving a "biological challenge." Because the center is willing to pay volunteers, you are interested but would like to know what is involved. When you call for more information, what will they tell you about the procedure?

   a. You may be asked to breathe into a paper bag as part of research on the cause of panic disorder.
   b. The research involves electrical stimulation of parts of the brain to determine which areas house repressed memories.
   c. A series of increasingly difficult physical tasks will be presented as a way of mimicking the stress that can cause heart attacks.
   d. You may be asked to sit still for long periods of time during which bursts of light will be flashed. This method is used to determine how the brain responds to fearful stimuli.

**ANSWERS: 1. a.** OCD **b.** Somatization disorder **c.** Conversion disorder **d.** Panic disorder **e.** GAD **2.** An obsession is a recurrent, intrusive thought, impulse, or image that is unwanted and inappropriate; a compulsion is a repeated, irresistible behavior or mental act that often follows obsessions. **3.** a **4.** d **5.** c **6.** b **7.** Dissociative identity disorder; schizophrenia, depression, and alcohol or drug abuse **8.** b **9.** b **10.** a

# MOOD DISORDERS

Two years ago, Jim, a 62-year-old mechanic, tried to commit suicide by hanging himself; a neighbor found him just in time. Last week he told a co-worker, "There's no reason to live. I can't take it anymore. I've got a gun, and I'm going to use it." Jim has lived alone since his wife died 3 years ago; his two daughters live in another state. Fellow workers often detected signs that Jim had been drinking. One co-worker sought the advice of others, who seemed confident, saying, "Don't worry. He is all talk. People who talk about suicide don't do it." *Do people who commit suicide give advance warning of their plans?*

Mood is like a brush that paints a wide swath across all facets of our lives. Minor changes in our mood are normal and add variety to life. One day we feel fine; the next we feel blue. These feelings are insignificant, however, compared with the depths of despair experienced by seriously depressed people or the wild elation of those who suffer mania. Mood disorders occur at both ends of a continuum ranging from severe depression to excessive euphoria. In this section we discuss (unipolar) depression and bipolar (manic-depressive) disorder, disorders that involve extremes of mood.

## Depression

A lack of understanding of depression and the failure to recognize and treat this disorder costs $43 billion a year for treatment, absenteeism, lost productivity, and premature death (Hirschfeld et al., 1997). Clinical forms of depression are more severe than what we might call "the blues," so how do we recognize depression, and how common is it?

**Symptoms.** The symptoms of depression fall into four broad categories: emotional, cognitive, motivational, and somatic/behavioral (see Table 12-4). The most obvious symp-

**TABLE 12-4**

### Symptoms of Depression

**Emotional**

Tearfulness and/or episodes of crying

Increased irritability, jumpiness, or loss of temper

Persistent periods of feeling down, depressed, sad (dysphoric), or blue

**Cognitive**

Excessive or inappropriate guilt

Negative thoughts about oneself and the future

Lack of self-esteem, feelings of inadequacy or worthlessness

Recurrent thoughts of death or suicide (and actual suicide attempts)

Difficulty concentrating, remembering information, and making decisions

**Motivational**

Reduced interest in sex

Fatigue and reduced energy level

Feeling unmotivated, or having difficulty getting started in the morning or even getting out of bed

Reduced interest in social participation or pleasure in activities that were once perceived as pleasurable

**Somatic and Behavioral**

Gaining or losing weight

Psychomotor agitation or retardation

Changes in sleep habits (insomnia or hypersomnia)

Functioning less effectively than usual at work or in school

Chronic aches and pains that are not caused by physical illness or injury

toms of **depression** are sadness (dysphoria), lack of interest in previously pleasurable activities, and reduced energy. Depressed people often describe themselves in unflattering terms such as inferior and unattractive. They do not see themselves as capable of completing intellectually demanding tasks. This negative self-evaluation extends to their views of the world and the future. Time holds depressed people in a vicelike grip: On the one hand, they are tortured by guilt over what they see as past failures and inadequacies; when the time pendulum switches to future tense, they see no hope for any improvement in their lot. What's more, they may blame themselves for negative events, including ones that have no connection to them, yet they rarely credit themselves for any achievements. Their sense of worthlessness and hopelessness makes them vulnerable to thoughts of suicide. The essence of depression is captured in the following quotation: "I am now the most miserable man living. If what I feel were equally distributed to the whole human family, there would not be one cheerful face on earth. Whether I shall ever be better, I cannot tell; I awfully forebode I shall not. To remain as I am is impossible. I must die or be better" (Oats, 1977, p. 62).

Abraham Lincoln exhibited numerous symptoms of depression.

**Source:** Reprinted courtesy of the Library of Congress.

Other symptoms of depression can occur in different and even opposite ways. Two forms of insomnia are frequently associated with depression: difficulty falling asleep (*sleep-onset insomnia*) and awakening early in the morning with an inability to return to sleep (see Chapter 4). Conversely, about 10 to 20% of depressed people greatly extend their sleep, perhaps to provide temporary refuge (Kupfer & Reynolds, 1992). Most people who are depressed lose their appetite (anorexia) and consequently lose weight; a few people eat excessively and gain weight. Depression is typically evident in *psychomotor retardation*: a slowed rate of speaking (in extreme cases, the person may stop speaking altogether), slow walking, and stooped posture. Symptoms such as wringing of the hands, pacing, and bemoaning one's fate, called *agitated depression*, can also be present.

Depression occurs in all cultures; the similarities in depression across culture are more apparent than the differences. Nevertheless, some differences are noteworthy. For example, depressed people in Western countries report guilt more often than people in non-Western countries (Marsella, Sartorius, Jablensky, & Fenton, 1985). Another common difference is the manifestation of the symptoms. Although "feelings" may be important in our culture, depressed people in cultures such as China do not necessarily feel depressed, but they tend to report more somatic symptoms. One explanation for this finding is that some cultures have few words to convey emotions such as sadness (see the discussion in Chapter 8 of the linguistic relativity hypothesis). In addition, different cultures locate feeling states in different parts of the body, which may explain why some cultural groups emphasize somatic symptoms in the expression of depression (Matsumoto, 1996).

**Prevalence and Course.**     Depression strikes rich and poor, young and old, men and women, the famous (the quote above is from Abraham Lincoln) and the unknown. Major depression is the fourth leading cause of worldwide disease and is responsible for more disability than heart disease (Murray & Lopez, 1996). Major depression is one of the most commonly identified psychological disorders in the United States (Kessler et al., 1994) (see Figure 12-6). The onset of the first episode of a major depressive disorder often occurs in the late 20s (Judd, 1997). A milder, yet chronic form of depression (*dysthymic disorder*) is so common that it is known as the "common cold of psychological disorders." Major depressive disorder and dysthymic disorder may occur together in what has been called *double depression* (Hammen, 1997; McCullough et al., 2000). Affected people are chronically dysthymic and then occasionally experience a major depressive episode. As the episode passes, they return to their chronic level of dysthymia (moderate depression) rather than to a normal mood.

Depression does not strike adults alone. Data from U.S. samples indicate that 1% of preschoolers suffer major depressive disorder. The rate is 2% among school-age children and 5 to 8% among adolescents. Diagnosing depression in children poses special difficulties because they are not adept at expressing sadness verbally (Son & Kirchener, 2000). What's more, some typical signs of depression in adults (for example, appetite loss) are less common in children and adolescents. The symptoms of depression also change with age. For example, depressed adolescents may be angry rather than sad. Therefore, depression

**depression**
Mood disorder characterized by sadness; a feeling of guilt; changes in sleep, appetite, and motor behavior; and sometimes thoughts of suicide

The rate of depression is higher among women than men, and mothers of young children are especially vulnerable

**FIGURE 12-6** Prevalence of major depressive episodes in the United States by gender. Major depressive episodes tend to occur about twice as often in women as in men.

**Source:** Nevid (2006).

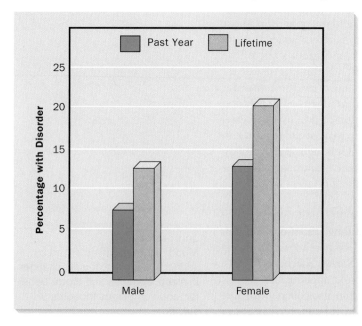

is usually inferred from behaviors such as apathy, withdrawal, delay or regression of developmental milestones, and failure to thrive that has no organic basis. Although school-age children are able to internalize environmental stressors such as family conflict (often associated with depression), their inner turmoil tends to be expressed through somatic symptoms such as headaches and stomachaches as well as irritability (temper tantrums).

In many cultures the rate of depression is twice as high among women as among men (Nolen-Hoeksema, 2001); however, accumulating evidence suggests that this sex difference occurs in developed countries rather than in developing countries, where the male: female ratio is closer to 1:1 (Culbertson, 1997). The disparity in developed countries begins at around puberty and continues throughout life (Weissman & Olfson, 1995). In children there is no sex difference in depression, but by about age 13, the rate of depression among girls begins to increase sharply; the rate among boys remains low. By late adolescence, the rate of depression among girls is twice that among boys, where it remains (Nolen-Hoeksema, 2001). There are several points that explain the higher rate of depression among women. Depression occurs more frequently when a person engages in passive and dependent behaviors and focuses on the depressed feelings (rumination) instead of acting to overcome the depression (Nolen-Hoeksema, 2001). Given the traditional gender roles in most societies, women are more likely to assume a passive role. Sexual abuse and physical abuse are other factors that put women at risk for depression. Although marriage may create a protective buffer against depression, the advantage is greater for men than it is for women. Mothers of young children are especially vulnerable to depression. Finally, poverty is a path to depression, and the rate of poverty is especially high among women and children.

The rate of depression has risen dramatically over the past century. Surveys of people in the United States, Western Europe, the Middle East, and Asia yielded two major findings: (a) rates of depression have risen steadily for each successive generation since 1915, and (b) depression begins at an earlier age with each successive generation (Cross-National Collaborative Group, 1992).

What accounts for this "epidemic" of depression? Close family and community ties are important in preventing depression. For example, the Amish people have maintained their customs in rural farming communities for generations. Their supportive families and community provide comfort and aid in times of need. When an Amish family loses a barn to a fire, neighbors join together to rebuild it. Depression occurs among the Amish at about one-fifth to one-tenth the rate that it does among people in, say, the city of Baltimore (Seligman, 1989).

Although depression usually diminishes with time (typically within 6 months), episodes tend to recur. Most people who experience one episode of major depression will experience another one (Judd, 1997). Compared to patients with chronic medical illnesses such as heart disease, people with depression report more physical pain, feel less well, and experience more social limitations. Depression tends to be comorbid with anxiety disorders, substance abuse, and eating disorders (Cicchetti & Toth, 1998). Comorbidity is associated with poorer functioning and a longer course of the disorder than what is termed "pure" depression (Hammen, 1997).

The symptoms of depression are somewhat more likely to occur at certain times during the year. Although a majority of people notice mood changes related to the seasons, some are so susceptible to these changes that they develop a form of depression called *seasonal affective disorder* (*SAD*). SAD typically occurs during the fall and winter months (October through February) and remits in the spring (Saeed & Bruce, 1998). This "winter depression" is associated with increased sleep, increased appetite, weight gain, fatigue, and social withdrawal. SAD occurs more often among women and is more likely to occur among people who live in northern latitudes (it is not likely to occur in Florida but is likely to occur in Maine and Canada) (Rosenthal, 1998). The symptoms may be related to levels of the hormone melatonin. In animals, melatonin seems to regulate hibernation. As the hours of light decrease with the approach of winter, the animal's body secretes more melatonin, which slows bodily processes in preparation for hibernation. Like hibernating animals, some humans also slow down as melatonin levels increase. People who suffer from this disorder can be helped by being exposed to greater amounts of bright light during winter, a treatment known as *phototherapy*.

**Suicide.** The most serious complication of severe depression is the possibility of suicide. Consider the following statistics:

- In the United States, someone commits suicide every 17 minutes (approximately 31,600 deaths per year); 1.3% of all deaths are suicides (National Center for Health Statistics, 2004).

- High rates of suicide are found in Belarus, Croatia, Estonia, Hungary, Lithuania, and the Ukraine. Low rates of suicide are found in Brazil, Greece, Mexico, Paraguay, the Philippines, and Portugal (see Figure 12-7). Compared with other countries, the U.S. suicide rate is moderate (World Health Organization, 2004).

- In the United States, more people die by suicide than from murder: The number of suicides is 79% higher than the number of homicides (U.S. Bureau of the Census, 2005).

- Suicide rates vary significantly with sex and race; white men have the highest suicide rate. The overall suicide rate also tends to rise with age (National Center for Health Statistics, 2004); however, the rise is due to one group—white men over age 50 (see Figure 12-8, on p. 547). They comprise 10% of the population but account for 30% of the suicides (Confronting suicide—Part I, 2003).

- Single men are twice as suicide-prone as married men; single women are more likely to commit suicide than married women but only up to age 45. Divorced and widowed men have high rates of suicide at all ages. Divorced women have high rates of suicide at all ages, but only young widows are more vulnerable than average (Confronting suicide: Part I, 2003).

- In 2002, suicide was the third leading cause of death in the 15–24 age range, second among people aged 25 to 34, and fourth among people aged 35 to 44 (Centers for Disease Control, 2005).

- The majority of suicide victims were suffering from depression, alcohol abuse/dependence, or schizophrenia (*Harvard Mental Health Letter*, 1996).

Phototherapy involves the use of fluorescent lamps (incandescent lights may damage the retina), which are 10 to 20 times brighter than ordinary indoor light. Patients suffering from SAD have daily 30- to 45-minute therapy sessions from fall into the spring that typically lead to a reduction in the depression within 2 to 4 days. Tanning beds, where the eyes are generally covered and the skin is exposed to light, have no effect on the symptoms of SAD.

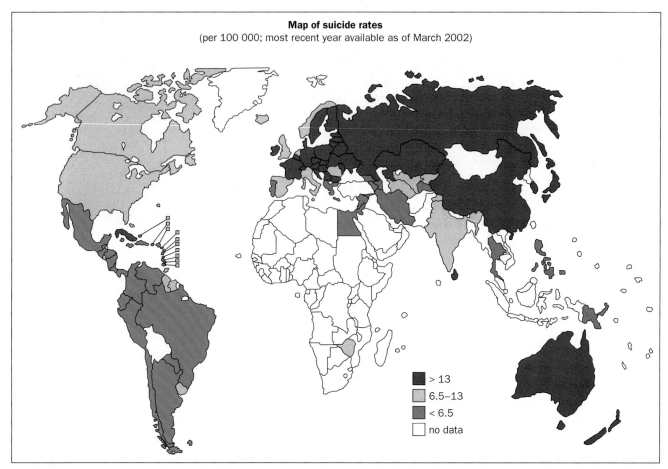

**Map of suicide rates**
(per 100 000; most recent year available as of March 2002)

> 13
6.5–13
< 6.5
no data

**FIGURE 12-7** High rates of suicide are found throughout much of Europe and parts of the former Soviet Union. Low rates of suicide are found in Mexico, South America, Greece, and Portugal. The rate of suicide in the United States is considered moderate.

**Source:** World Health Organization (2004).

• In most Western countries, women attempt suicide more frequently than men, but men succeed more often because they tend to use more lethal methods. A psychiatrist's chillingly blunt words make this point: "You can pump pills out of someone's stomach, you can't pump buckshot out of someone's brain."

## Myth or Science

Recall that Jim, the mechanic whom we met at the beginning of this section, described his suicide plan to a co-worker. The co-worker sought guidance and was told not to worry because "people who talk about suicide don't do it." Was this guidance correct, or should talk of suicide be taken seriously? Contrary to common belief, suicide is often preceded by a warning. About 80% of suicide victims give direct warnings like "I'm going to end it all" or indirect clues such as giving prized possessions to friends and relatives (*Harvard Mental Health Letter*, 1996). Statements about hopelessness and helplessness are especially common signs of suicidal thinking (Rudestam, 1971; Wrobleski, 1989). Unfortunately, people who hear or see evidence of suicidal potential often overlook or deny its significance.

Suicide researchers and prevention centers have accumulated information to assess an individual's suicidal potential. Jim closely matches the profile of the likely suicide victim: an older white man suffering from depression who has made a prior suicide attempt and now has a plan, has recently experienced stressful life events, abuses alcohol, and has few sources of social support. You can see that Jim is at high risk for committing suicide.

**A**

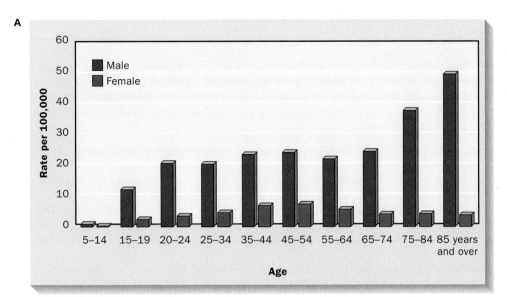

**B**

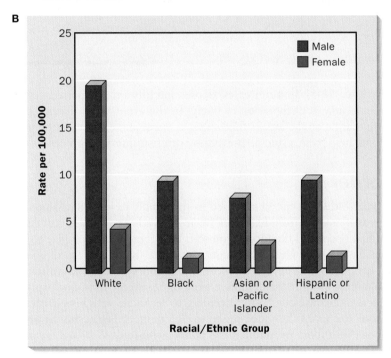

**FIGURE 12-8** (A) Rates of suicide per 100,000 for men and women at different ages. (B) Suicide rates also differ by race. Overall, the rate of suicide tends to increase with age.

What should you do if you suspect that someone you know might attempt suicide? You should not be afraid to ask, "Are you thinking about suicide?" Asking this question will not put the idea of suicide into anyone's mind. If someone asked you that question, your likely response might be, "Are you nuts?" What should you do if your depressed friend's response is "yes" or a halfhearted "no"? "People who talk about or attempt suicide need immediate medical and psychological help" (Wrobleski, 1989, p. 45). Most suicidal people are ambivalent about committing suicide; they are experiencing pain, helplessness, and hopelessness. Help them understand that their current stressors make it difficult for them to think clearly.

Time is an important ally in the effort to prevent a suicide because people do not usually remain seriously suicidal for long. In some cases, suicide may be less likely when individuals are in the depths of depression. Helplessness and passivity sap motivation and energy so much that depressed people are unlikely to carry out their suicide plans. Yet, some depressed people are so focused on committing suicide that they succumb to the depths of their depression, and there may be little that can be done to prevent their

**TABLE 12-5**

Most suicide attempts are described as "cries for help"—desperate attempts to let someone (often a relative or close friend) know how much pain the victim is experiencing. Cases of drug overdoses or slashing of wrists may fall into this category, as chances of survival are good if the victim is found soon enough. After such an attempt, some victims seek out others to obtain assistance or to take them to an emergency room. On the other hand, there appear to be cases in which the victim's depression and hopelessness are so deep that they want to die and thus take actions that virtually guarantee their demise. These genuinely suicidal people are not likely to contact suicide hotlines or other crisis services.

- A man wedged a large knife into an old radiator and then charged the knife repeatedly, butting the point with his head until the blade pierced his skull and killed him.
- Some victims of suicide have raised the hydraulic tailgate or lowered the beds of dump trucks onto their necks and heads, or they have driven into the lowered tailgate.
- An attorney shot himself in the head; his secretary could not reach him because he had locked the door from the inside. The police found the man alive and with a gun in his hand. The man died a few hours later in the hospital of five wounds to the head. He had put the gun in his mouth. Two bullets exited from the side of his face, two exited from the top of his skull, and the fifth remained in his brain.
- A college instructor taped a beer can opener and another metal object to his arm. He wrapped the objects with the frayed, bare ends of an electrical cord and plugged the cord into an appliance timer that he set for 4 A.M. The man took a large dose of sleeping pills. Apparently, he slept soundly and never awakened. When the timer went on, it completed the circuit, resulting in death by electrocution.

**Source:** Maples and Browning (1994).

ultimate demise (see Table 12-5). In other cases, depression lifts and the person seems to feel better, so suicide may actually be more likely. In the event that a friend talks about suicide, be sure that he or she knows that someone cares and encourage the person to seek professional help from a suicide prevention or crisis intervention center.

## Bipolar Disorder

Two weeks ago, 20-year-old Will's mood switched from friendly to irritable. When he thought some money was missing from his room, he accused a friend of taking it. After determining that he had misplaced the money himself, Will refused to apologize to his friend. Although he had no knowledge of music, he impulsively purchased a very expensive guitar. As his need for sleep decreased, he spent hours making long-distance calls to friends and planning to write the definitive work on "existentialism, divine providence, and the collective unconscious." After deciding to reconcile with his girlfriend, he knocked on her door at 2 A.M. When she refused to let him in, he began shouting and pounding on the door. Neighbors telephoned the police, who took Will to a hospital emergency room. While he was there, his speech was rapid, he shifted topics abruptly, and he was restless. A few weeks after his release from the hospital, he was extremely depressed (Andreasen, 1984).

Will experienced an episode of poor judgment, excessive activity, accelerated speech, and extreme euphoria known as **mania** (see Table 12-6). Manic symptoms can result from cocaine or amphetamine use or hyperthyroidism; therefore these possibilities must be considered when making a diagnosis and planning treatment (Werder, 1995). The knowledge that mood disorders run in families is helpful: Will's mother had been treated for depression, and an uncle was hospitalized several times for mania and depression. Will experienced mania followed by depression, and the diagnosis was **bipolar disorder** (occurrence of episodes at both ends of the mood spectrum). *Cyclothymic disorder* is a less severe, yet chronic, form of bipolar disorder; it is associated with a moderate level of mania called *hypomania* (American Psychiatric Association, 2000). Table 12-7 (p. 550) offers a glimpse of the experience the mood changes that occur in bipolar disorder in the words of those who have experienced it.

The depression and mania in bipolar disorder may occur simultaneously, but they usually alternate—often separated by periods of relative normalcy. During a manic

**mania**
Excessive activity, accelerated speech, poor judgment, elevated self-esteem, and euphoria that occur in bipolar disorder

**bipolar disorder**
Mood disorder in which a person experiences episodes of mania and depression, which usually alternate

| TABLE 12-6 |
| --- |

## Symptoms of Mania

**Emotional**

High level of humor

Lack of shame or guilt

Persistently elevated, euphoric, or irritable mood

**Cognitive**

Poor judgment

Inflated self-esteem or grandiosity

Distractibility, inability to concentrate

Racing thoughts and talking fast, jumping from one idea to another

**Motivational**

Increased sexual drive

Increased energy, activity, and restlessness

More talkative than usual or pressure to keep talking

Increase in goal-directed activity or psychomotor agitation

Excessive involvement in pleasurable activities that have a high potential for painful consequences

**Somatic and Behavioral**

Spending sprees

Decreased need for sleep (hyposomnia)

Provocative, intrusive, or aggressive behavior

Abuse of drugs, particularly cocaine, alcohol, and sleeping medications

episode, boundless energy replaces the fatigue of depression; sadness and despair give way to euphoria and elevated self-esteem. Depression often reduces the desire for sex; mania often brings uncharacteristic promiscuity (reflecting increased sexual drive or libido). During an episode of mania, people become highly sociable, although irritability lurks beneath the surface should anyone question their plans. They ignore painful or harmful consequences of their behavior and may incur huge debts or make unwise business and personal decisions. Fortunately, bipolar disorder responds quite effectively to treatment with lithium (see Chapter 13), which was the treatment prescribed for Will.

Bipolar disorder is less prevalent than depression; it affects about 1% of the population, with equal frequency in men and women (Leibenluft, 1996; Sadock & Sadock, 2003). The symptoms usually begin in the early 20s (Werder, 1995), as they did for Will. An episode of depression usually occurs first; a manic episode may not occur until several years later (*Harvard Mental Health Letter*, 2001). Like many other disorders, bipolar disorder often occurs with other disorders, including substance abuse and/or dependence, anxiety disorders, eating disorders, and personality disorders (Miklowitz, 2001).

## Causes of Mood Disorders

**Biological Explanations.** For several reasons, experts believe that biological factors play a role in the development of mood disorders. First, as noted earlier, the symptoms of depression tend to be similar across cultures, suggesting a common

Patty Duke, the actress, seeks to educate the public about bipolar disorder and its treatment. Before she was correctly diagnosed and treated with lithium, she attempted suicide several times, usually with pills. She also used alcohol and drugs to suppress her manic highs.

### TABLE 12-7

## Descriptions of Various Mood States

These descriptions were offered by people who have experienced various mood states. Their words offer some insights and how they were affected by the mood changes.

**Depression:** I doubt completely my ability to do anything well. It seems as though my mind has slowed down and burned out to the point of being virtually useless. . . . [I am] haunt[ed] . . . with the total, the desperate hopelessness of it all . . . . Others say, "It's only temporary, it will pass, you will get over it," but of course, they haven't any idea of how I feel, although they are certain they do. If I can't feel, move, or think, or care, then what on earth is the point?

**Hypomania:** At first when I'm high, it's tremendous . . . ideas are fast . . . like shooting stars you follow until brighter ones appear. . . . All shyness disappears, the right words and gestures are suddenly there . . ., things become intensely interesting. Sensuality is pervasive, the desire to seduce and be seduced is irresistible. Your marrow is infused with unbelievable feelings of ease, power, well-being, omnipotence, euphoria . . . you can do anything, but, somewhere this changes.

**Mania:** The fast ideas become too fast and there are far too many . . . overwhelming confusion replaces clarity . . . you stop keeping up with it—memory goes. Infectious humor ceases to amuse. Your friends become frightened . . . everything is now against the grain. . . you are irritable, angry, frightened, uncontrollable, and trapped.

**Source:** National Institute of Mental Health (2001).

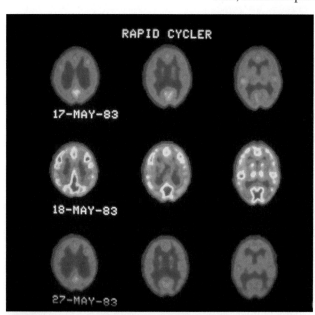

**FIGURE 12-9** PET scans of the brain of a person who cycled from depression to mania reveal remarkably different patterns of activity associated with the two mood states. Activity levels are indicated by a spectrum ranging from blue (low) through green to yellow and red (high). It is not clear if the brain activity levels associated with depression and mania cause the mood disorders or reflect underlying changes in mood (in which case they may be correlated with the mood).

**Source:** Nemeroff (1998).

underlying biological cause. Second, drugs such as Elavil and Prozac reduce depression; mania responds to lithium treatment. The effects of neurotransmitters seem to be reflected in the dramatic differences in the activity levels of the brains of people during depressive and manic episodes (see Figure 12-9). Third, mood disorders tend to run in families, which suggests genetic transmission. Nevertheless, researchers agree that rising rates of depression during recent decades are unlikely to have resulted from genetic factors; psychological and social factors also must be considered.

One way researchers study possible genetic influences on mood disorders is to compare the prevalence of these disorders in families with and without a family member with a mood disorder. Mood disorders occur more often in the first-degree relatives (parents, children, siblings) of family members with a mood disorder compared to relatives of individuals who do not have such disorders (Gershon & Nurnberger, 1995). Compared with relatives of patients with unipolar disorder, relatives of bipolar patients exhibit a higher rate of bipolar disorder but about the same rate of unipolar depression (see Figure 12-10). The evidence for genetic transmission is stronger for bipolar disorder than for unipolar depression.

In their efforts to understand the role of genetic factors in mood disorders, researchers also study identical and fraternal twins. They begin by identifying a twin who has a mood disorder, called an *index case*. Then they determine whether the second twin in each pair (the co-twin) also has a mood disorder. A twin pair is said to be *concordant* when both twins have mood disorders. The **concordance rate** is the percentage of twin pairs in which both twins have the disorder. The concordance rate for mood disorders among identical twins is approximately 65%; the rate among fraternal twins is about 14% (Andreasen & Black,

1995). As mentioned, there is strong evidence for a genetic component to bipolar disorder. The concordance rate for bipolar disorder among identical twins is in the range of 60–80%; it is 20% for fraternal twins. If both parents have bipolar disorder, their child's chance of developing the disorder is approximately 75% (*Harvard Mental Health Letter*, 2001).

These findings strengthen the belief that genetic factors are involved in depression. Investigators point to the involvement of multiple genes rather than a single gene in the transmission of bipolar disorder (Hyman, 1999; NIMH Genetics Workshop, 1998). But what exactly is inherited? To answer that question, we need to know that two neurotransmitters, norepinephrine and serotonin, seem to play significant roles in depression (Nemeroff, 1998). Antidepressant drugs increase the availability of norepinephrine or serotonin at synapses in the brain. The increased availability of these neurotransmitters alters neural transmission and can lead to increased activity and a lifting of the depression. These neurotransmitters may also be involved in altering levels of certain hormones, which could lead to depression.

Explaining mood disorders as the result of abnormal levels of certain neurotransmitters seems to be simple and straightforward. This theory cannot account for an intriguing finding, however: Antidepressant drugs alter neurotransmitter levels almost immediately, yet depression may take as long as 2 weeks to lift after the start of drug treatment. What's more, the levels of certain neurotransmitters could change in response to environmental factors such as the disappointment after a major personal failure or after the death of a loved one. Thus, although people with mood disorders may inherit a tendency to develop these disorders, other factors need to be understood to complete the picture.

**The Psychodynamic Explanation.** The psychodynamic model emphasizes early childhood experiences as the foundation of adult behavior and emotional reactions. An infant depends on its caregiver, usually its mother. As its needs are met, the infant feels supported and loved, and attachment develops (see Chapter 9). The mother, however, must leave at times, temporarily or perhaps permanently. When this happens, the child may experience rage at being abandoned yet be ambivalent (feeling both love and rage) because the mother was also a source of comfort and love. The rage is turned against a more convenient and acceptable target—the child itself. According to Freud, this inwardly directed anger can cause depression. Later in life, depression may reappear when losses such as the death of a loved one or the loss of a job reactivate the earlier experiences of loss.

**Cognitive and Behavioral Explanations.** Suppose you have been looking for a job for over a year, to no avail. Some job seekers might decide that they simply cannot get a

*"More lithium."*

**concordance rate**
Percentage of twin pairs in which both twins have a disorder that is of interest to an investigator

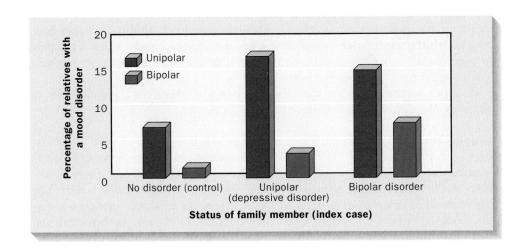

**FIGURE 12-10** Prevalence of unipolar depression and bipolar disorder in families at different levels of risk. Being born into a family with a member who has a mood disorder raises the risk of having a mood disorder.

**Source:** Gershon and Nurnberger (1995), p. 407.

Source: Reprinted with the permission of Psi Chi, The National Honor Society in Psychology.

job. They give up because they believe that no amount of searching will succeed. In short, if nothing they do makes a difference, why do anything at all? Under such circumstances, a psychological state known as **learned helplessness** may develop (Seligman, 1975/1992). Learned helplessness occurs when you believe you have no control over the reinforcements in your life, such as finding a job or getting a good grade on an exam. The result is often reduced efforts to attain those reinforcers. This model of depression explains the lethargy and lack of motivation seen in depressed individuals; one problem with this model, however, is that even in research situations designed to render people helpless, some individuals do not succumb. Hence there must be another variable that influences the development of depression.

A reformulation of the learned helplessness model, called the *hopelessness model*, focuses on people's beliefs about the situations in which they find themselves. Some people become depressed not because they lack control over a situation but because of the way they explain the situation. We differ in explanatory style—that is, the habitual way we explain good and bad events (see Chapter 13). Explanatory style is much more powerful than just the words a person uses. From the time we develop our explanatory style in childhood or adolescence, it serves as the mediator of whether we will suffer greatly from helplessness and possibly depression.

Explanatory style consists of three dimensions: permanent versus temporary, universal versus specific, and internal versus external. When bad events happen, we may view them as permanent or temporary. If you think about bad things in terms of "always," you have a permanent pessimistic style. Explanations may also be specific to the situation or universal, applying to all situations. People who rely on universal explanations for their failures often give up on everything when a failure strikes in one area. Finally, explanations may be either internal (we blame ourselves) or external (we believe outside forces are at work); people who use internal explanations find that their self-esteem is lowered significantly.

One combination of the dimensions of explanatory style is especially self-defeating: permanent, universal, and internal. People with this very pessimistic style who encounter bad events are more likely to become depressed, whereas those who have the opposite optimistic style and experience bad events will tend to resist depression. Suppose you got back an exam with a big red F on it. How would you explain that F? Research suggests that depression may be related to the tendency to use permanent, universal, and internal explanations for negative events (Sweeney, Anderson, & Bailey, 1986).

The hopelessness model has much in common with the cognitively oriented theories of researchers who view depression as stemming from problems in the way people think. Aaron Beck (1979), for example, concluded that depression results from the way people think about themselves and about what happens to them. They often blame themselves for events, so they focus on the negative. Depressed people hold negative views of themselves, their current experiences, and the future. They find themselves in this predicament because they are prone to commit errors in logic, which perpetuate their negative views. For example, depressed people may decide that no one likes them because no one spoke to them on the bus on the way to work. In this case, they have drawn an **arbitrary inference**—a conclusion based on insufficient evidence. They may also overgeneralize, like the student who decides that she will never get a good grade because she earned a C on her first exam.

Beck has devised a therapy that deals directly with these cognitive elements of depression. We discuss Beck's cognitive therapy in Chapter 13.

**Multiple Causes.**     To sum up, it appears that genetic factors play a role in mood disorders; clearly, however, they are not the only factors. As we have seen, factors such as explanatory style are also important components of depression. The levels of neurotransmitters may be influenced by a style of explaining negative events. One lesson is clear: The study of mood disorders leads us to recognize that there are no simple answers to questions about the causes of disorders; more often than not, biological, psychological, and social factors interact to affect the development and course of disorders. For example,

**learned helplessness**
Belief that one cannot control outcomes through one's actions; usually leads to passivity and reduced motivation and may cause depression

**arbitrary inference**
Conclusion drawn in the absence of supporting information

researchers have suspected that stressful life events have been linked to the incidence of depression. Clarifications of this link, however, suggest that only some forms of depression are strongly related to stressful events (Brown, Harris, & Hepworth, 1994; Frank et al., 1994). What's more, stressful life events may also play a role in the frequency and timing of future episodes of bipolar disorder (Johnson & Roberts, 1995).

## REVIEW SUMMARY

1. The symptoms of **depression** include sadness, reduced pleasure and energy levels, feelings of guilt, sleep disturbances, and suicidal thinking. The lifetime prevalence of depression is twice as high among women as among men; prevalence rates around the world are increasing.

2. Suicide, which is often associated with depression, is one of the leading causes of death in the United States. The risk factors for suicide include being a white male, being unmarried, and being depressed.

3. **Bipolar disorder** involves swings between depression and **mania.** The symptoms of mania include euphoria, increased energy, poor judgment, decreased sleep, and elevated self-esteem.

4. Mood disorders tend to run in families, which suggests genetic transmission. Researchers can use **concordance rates** to indicate the degree to which twins (fraternal and identical) share a given disorder. Higher concordance rates among identical than fraternal twins suggest a significant role for genetics in the etiology of bipolar disorder. Depression may involve low levels of norepinephrine or serotonin.

5. According to the **learned helplessness** model, depression can also be brought on when people believe that they cannot control outcomes. A refinement of this model, the *hopelessness model,* suggests that typical ways of explaining negative events may be at the root of depression. Cognitive explanations focus on how errors in logic contribute to the development of depression. Among the errors they are prone to make is **arbitrary inference,** which is a tendency to draw conclusions based on insufficient evidence.

## CHECK YOUR PROGRESS

1. What have epidemiological surveys revealed about the rate of depression around the world?

2. Identify the symptoms of depression in each of the following areas:
   a. appetite
   b. sleep
   c. self-descriptions

3. Certain demographic characteristics are related to the probability of suicide. State the major predictor of suicide in each of the following demographic categories:
   a. sex
   b. age
   c. marital status
   d. psychological disorders

4. A psychologist who reported on research to determine the extent of genetic influences on mood disorders, said, "Fifty percent of twin pairs shared mood disorders." What term describes this figure?
   a. bipolarity rate
   b. shared incidence
   c. prevalence rate
   d. concordance rate

5. Which neurotransmitters have been implicated in the development of depression?
   a. dopamine and GABA
   b. GABA and epinephrine
   c. norepinephrine and serotonin
   d. acetylcholine and norepinephrine

6. For weeks, Rod was unable to sleep more than an hour a night, yet he was energetic. He was developing plans for his own "Las Vegas on the Ohio River." When a friend asked about his plans, Rod berated him and physically attacked him. The police were called and took Rod to an emergency room, where a physician suspected bipolar disorder. The physician ran tests, however, to rule out physical causes such as
   a. angina.
   b. hyperthyroidism.
   c. Alzheimer's disease.
   d. barbiturate overdose.

7. Buddy graduated from college 3 months ago. His grades were generally good, in the B range, and he is well liked. His efforts to find a job have been unsuccessful, yet he is optimistic. Using the explanatory model, write a universal-internal-permanent explanation of his situation.

8. A patient's records indicate that she is suffering from dysthymic disorder. Which of these descriptions is most consistent with this diagnosis?
   a. The patient has a chronic form of moderate depression.
   b. The patient experiences swings in mood from depression to mania.
   c. The periods of upbeat mood are more frequent than the periods of depression.
   d. A series of medical problems are masking an underlying depressive mood disorder.

**9.** Depressed people may jump to conclusions based on insufficient evidence. This flaw in thinking is called

   **a.** maximization.
   **b.** inexact labeling.
   **c.** base-rate fallacy.
   **d.** arbitrary inference.

**10.** If Sally is diagnosed as suffering from a form of mood disorder called SAD, which of the following might her psychiatrist say to her when discussing treatments?

   **a.** "You need to increase your calcium intake."
   **b.** "Exposure to very bright light should reduce your symptoms."
   **c.** "Large doses of aspirin should reduce the symptoms."
   **d.** "An increase in total number of calories is highly recommended."

**ANSWERS: 1.** The rate of depression around the world is increasing, and people are experiencing the first episode at a younger age. **2. a.** Either increased appetite or loss of appetite (anorexia) **b.** Increased sleep (hypersomnia) or insomnia **c.** Depressed people often see themselves as unattractive and incapable of completing intellectually demanding tasks **3. a.** The rate of suicide is higher among men. **b.** The rate of suicide tends to increase with age. **c.** Divorced people have a higher rate of suicide than married people. **d.** The rate of suicide is highest among people suffering from depression or alcohol abuse/dependence **4. d 5. c 6. b 7.** Universal: "I am able to deal successfully with difficult situations." Internal: "My success in dealing with difficult situations is due to my ability to stay calm and assess each situation accurately." Permanent: "My ability to handle situations does not vary from one course or challenge to another." **8. a 9. d 10. b**

# SCHIZOPHRENIA

Although he was sometimes mischievous and moody, George usually appeared to be normal until the end of high school. At that time muffled sounds seemed to insult him, sudden movements were viewed as physical threats, and he saw a stove become "the Devil alive." After graduating from high school, George enlisted in the navy, where the symptoms continued. He thought the cook was Satan and food was poisoned. His babbling was difficult to understand: "Got one to seven—see, the life in the drain—it's all butaco." After George wandered away from a marching formation, an officer took him to the hospital, where he was diagnosed as suffering from schizophrenia (Heston, 1992). *What are the symptoms of schizophrenia?*

The Swiss psychiatrist Eugen Bleuler coined the terms *schizophrenia*, which literally means "splitting of the mind." **Schizophrenia** is a psychotic disorder that is characterized by positive symptoms (excesses) or negative symptoms (deficits). **Psychosis** is a general term for disorders in which severely disturbed people lose contact with reality and may require hospitalization.

Schizophrenia has been called "the cruelest and most devastating of the various mental illnesses" (Andreasen, 2001, p. 193). It strikes at a relatively early age (usually around 20), although deficiencies in attention and emotional responses are often noted in childhood. The symptoms frequently lead to significant social and occupational impairment at an estimated cost for treatment, lost wages, productivity losses, and disability benefits of over $100 billion a year (Andreasen & Black, 1995). Approximately 1% of the U.S. adult population has had the disorder (Andreasen, 2001); although some recent research suggests that the figure is actually somewhat lower (Saha, Chant, Welham, & McGrath, 2005). Although the rate of schizophrenia is approximately equal in men and women (Saha et al., 2005), it strikes men earlier and with greater severity (Beratis, Gabriel, & Hoidas, 1994). The overall death rate among victims of schizophrenia is higher than the expected rate, in part, as a result of increased rates of suicide (Meltzer, 1998).

Schizophrenia is often confused with dissociative identity disorder. The "split" in schizophrenia, however, is not among different personalities; it is a split from reality as well as a split between thoughts and emotions. As we discuss this disorder in detail, keep these two points in mind: Schizophrenia is not dissociative identity disorder, and it is far more prevalent.

**schizophrenia**
Psychotic disorder characterized by positive symptoms (excesses) such as delusions, hallucinations, and fluent but disorganized speech or negative symptoms (deficits) such as flat or blunted affect

**psychosis**
Any disorder in which a severely disturbed individual loses contact with reality

# Symptoms of Schizophrenia

Schizophrenia involves a wide range of symptoms, none of which is present in all cases. There may be disturbances in perception, language, thinking, and emotional expression. How do we make sense of this array of symptoms? One approach to classifying symptoms holds promise; it is based on two types of symptoms: positive and negative.

**delusion**
An obviously false belief that is extremely difficult to change

**Positive Symptoms.** The *positive symptoms* of schizophrenia are distortions or excesses of normal functions, such as fluent but disorganized speech, delusions, and hallucinations. While listening to the speech of a patient with schizophrenia, you may struggle to follow his or her pattern of thought; the disorganized speech is thought to reflect disturbances in the underlying thought processes (Barch & Berenbaum, 1996). The following excerpt from an interview illustrates an extreme form of disorganized speech:

> *Interviewer:* Have you been nervous or tense lately?
>
> *Patient:* No, I got a head of lettuce.
>
> *Interviewer:* You got a head of lettuce? I don't understand.
>
> *Patient:* Well, it's just a head of lettuce.
>
> *Interviewer:* Tell me about lettuce. What do you mean?
>
> *Patient:* Well . . . lettuce is a transformation of a dead cougar that suffered on the lion's toe. And he swallowed the lion and something happened. The . . . see, the . . . Gloria and Tommy, they're two heads and they're not whales. But they escaped with herds of vomit, and things like that. (Neale & Oltmanns, 1980, p. 102)

The ideas expressed by a person with schizophrenia can be like a train that has slipped off its track onto another track; this pattern of speech is called *loose associations*. As a result, it is difficult if not impossible to determine what the patient means, despite the fact that the words are recognizable and generally in grammatical form. Consider the following:

> I have a real yen for chocolate. The Japanese have all the yen and have taken all our money and marked it. You know, you have to be careful of the Marxists because they are friends with the Swiss and they have all the cheese and all the watches and that means they have taken all the time. The worst thing about Swiss cheese is all the holes. People have to be careful about falling into holes. (Stuart & Laraia, 2005, p. 391)

To complicate matters even further, some patients use *neologisms*, common words used in uncommon ways ("I wrote the letter with my writing toy") or newly created words ("I wrote the letter with my zemps"). Words may be strung together in ways that seem to follow grammatical rules, yet the words form an incoherent collection called a *word salad*. A simple question like "What brought you here?" can give rise to an odd response like "The, my, not, rode, for, new, cold, it, what, may, so" (Othmer & Othmer, 1989). Speech may also be characterized by *clang associations*, word connections dictated by sound similarity, not by logic or meaning. For example, one patient, when asked what he was doing, responded, "Eating wires and lighting fires" (Spitzer, Gibbon, Skodol, Williams, & First, 1994). Can you make sense of the following?

> "I got a new shirt but the buttons became loose. Do you suppose Lucifer's buttons become lucent or are they lucid like Lucy's lucky ducky."
>
> "I want to sing ping pong that song wong kong long today hey way." (Stuart & Laraia, 2005, p. 391)

Among the most frequently observed positive symptoms are **delusions,** or false beliefs that cannot be corrected despite strong evidence to the contrary. Delusions can appear in numerous forms. One university student wrote a letter to her professor (one of your authors) in which she stated that she frequently experienced 100 orgasms a day!

The life story of John Nash (1928–) is presented in the film *A Beautiful Mind.* As a 21-year-old Princeton University graduate student this mathematical genius made a significant breakthrough in understanding game theory, which was recognized in 1994 by a Nobel Prize in economics. The road to that Nobel Prize, however, was bumpy. He claimed that foreign governments communicated with him through *The New York Times,* and he turned down a position at the University of Chicago because he said he was about to become emperor of Antarctica. His wife had him committed to a mental hospital, where he was diagnosed with paranoid schizophrenia. Beginning in the 1980s, the symptoms of schizophrenia began to taper off.

**hallucinations**
Sensory experiences that are not caused by stimulation of the relevant sensory organ; may occur in any of the senses

She also took pride in her efforts to bring a major auto manufacturer to the region. Later, it was determined that the student had been diagnosed as suffering from schizophrenia. Individuals with *persecutory delusions* (most common) believe that others are tormenting, following, or ridiculing them. Some delusions are bizarre, as is evident in the case of a patient who said she was "persecuted by a secret insect from the District Office" (Spitzer et al., 1994). A *delusion of grandeur* is a person's belief that he or she has special powers or abilities; for example, a computer programmer imagined that the end of the world was coming, and *he* determined which of his colleagues would survive in the afterlife by the keys he pressed on his keyboard. *Thought broadcasting* is the idea that one's thoughts are being broadcast to others. Imagine walking down the street and believing that every thought you have is shared with every person you pass.

Delusions are real to the people who experience them, so it is difficult to convince patients that they are false. What's more, if you believe others are persecuting or controlling you, you may feel a need to protect yourself. Delusions have led some persons to take action against people or institutions perceived to be intent on causing them harm or interfering with their lives. Cultural factors influence the content of delusions. For example, delusions of being controlled often involve reports of ghosts and witches in underdeveloped countries and nonindustrial areas; the mechanism of control in developed countries is more likely to be X-rays and lasers (Maher & Spitzer, 1993).

Schizophrenia often alters perceptions of the world. Objects take on unusual dimensions, and sensations seem to materialize from thin air. A frequent perceptual symptom is the hallucination (from a Latin word meaning "to wander mentally"). **Hallucinations** are perceptions that are not caused by stimulation of the relevant sensory receptors. They can occur in any of the senses, although *auditory hallucinations* are the most common. The person may hear voices that give orders, criticize, or offer ongoing commentary. *Visual* hallucinations, such as George's seeing a stove turn into a devil, are less common. Hallucinations seem real to the person experiencing them and can be quite frightening, as they were to George.

**Negative Symptoms.** Negative symptoms are reductions or losses of function. These behavior deficits or defects include *poverty of speech* as well as disturbances in affect and volition (will). These symptoms are associated with more cognitive impairment and poorer prognoses than positive symptoms.

The speech of people with schizophrenia may be adequate in amount yet convey little information: Language that is vague, too abstract, too concrete, or repetitive is termed *poverty of content*. A restriction in the amount of spontaneous speech that is evident in brief and unelaborated replies to questions is called *poverty of speech*. Interviewers frequently find it necessary to prompt the person for additional information (Andreasen & Black, 1995).

Failure to experience any emotion is called *flat affect*; an inability to experience the typical range of emotions is called *blunted affect*. Disturbances in affect are evident in rigid facial expressions, few expressive gestures, poor eye contact, and a lack of vocal inflection. *Avolition* (difficulty making decisions) and *apathy* are characterized by a lack of energy and drive such that a person is unable to initiate or persist in tasks. Unlike the lack of energy in depression, however, the apathy associated with schizophrenia is not accompanied by sadness. A number of disturbances in motor movements and a lack of self-care also characterize some forms of schizophrenia.

## Subtypes of Schizophrenia

The *DSM-IV-TR* describes five subtypes of schizophrenia: catatonic, disorganized, paranoid, residual, and undifferentiated (see Table 12-8). Although the prevalence of schizophrenia is similar around the world, rates of diagnosis of the subtypes differ. For example, disorganized schizophrenia accounts for about 50% of the diagnoses of schizophrenia in Japan but only about 10% in other countries (Nakane, Ohta, & Radford, 1992). Catatonic schizophrenia is more common in Asia, Africa, and developing countries (Shives, 2005). Such differences may be due to diagnostic, social, or cultural factors.

Catatonic schizophrenia. The unusual postures seen here are common in this subtype of schizophrenia.

**TABLE 12-8**

## Subtypes of Schizophrenia

| Subtype | Key Symptoms |
|---|---|
| Catatonic | Unusual motor symptoms ranging from rigidity to wild hyperactivity and occasional alterations between inactivity and excitement. Less common today because drug treatments reduce or eliminate the symptoms. |
| Disorganized | Incoherent speech with highly unusual verbal associations along with flat or inappropriate affect (emotional expressions that are often the opposite of expected reactions). Patients often seem silly and childlike and may grimace, giggle inappropriately, and appear absorbed in thought. The onset of symptoms usually occurs during adolescence—the earliest onset of the subtypes. The symptoms do not seem to be reactions to stressful life events. The continuous nature of the disorder leads to a downhill progression that often results in long-term institutionalization. |
| Paranoid | Delusions of grandeur or persecution with possible auditory hallucinations. Has the latest age of onset of the subtypes. Develops in individuals who often have demonstrated good functioning before the relatively acute onset of symptoms. Has a generally good outcome and good recovery rates. |
| Residual | Delusions, hallucinations, and incoherent language are absent, but continuation of the disorder is evident in social withdrawal or odd beliefs. |
| Undifferentiated | Symptoms may include prominent delusions, hallucinations, and disorganized speech that do not fit other subtypes. Long-term outcomes of this subtype are highly variable. |

Each subtype of schizophrenia is characterized by a different set of symptoms, although distinctions among the types are not always clear-cut and there is significant overlap in symptoms. Indeed, the undifferentiated subtype is a category for cases that do not fit into other subtypes. A patient may exhibit the symptoms of different subtypes of schizophrenia at different times during the course of the disorder.

## Causes of Schizophrenia

The search for what causes schizophrenia is difficult because there are no physical tests for the disorder. What's more, researchers are not sure if schizophrenia results from a single process or several processes. There have been many false leads and potential breakthroughs.

After decades of searching for the cause or causes of schizophrenia, certain trends are beginning to emerge. First, people with schizophrenia perform poorly on a wide variety of cognitive tests, both simple and complex. They exhibit weaknesses in perception, motor speed, coordination, memory, reasoning, problem solving, planning, and initiation of action (Javitt & Coyle, 2004; see Figure 12-11). In fact, failure on such tasks could indicate an elevated risk for schizophrenia. Researchers administered a battery of neuropsychological tests to three groups: individuals diagnosed with schizophrenia, siblings without the diagnosis, and controls (no diagnosis) matched for age, sex, and education. Compared to the contols, the siblings (relatives of individuals with schizophrenia) showed impaired performance (Thompson, Watson, Steinhauer, Goldstein, & Pogue-Geile, 2005). Any explanation for schizophrenia should account for the extensive weaknesses people with schizophrenia exhibit on a variety of tasks. Currently considered to be among the possible causes are genetic factors, brain abnormalities, altered neurotransmitter levels, and environmental factors.

**STUDY TIP**

Develop visual representations—pictures or icons—that will help you remember each of the five types of schizophrenia. Use them in your class notes.

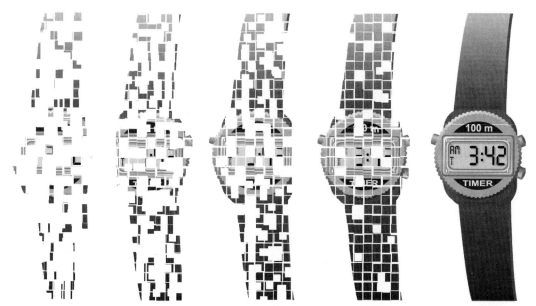

**FIGURE 12-11**   People with schizophrenia exhibit widespread dysfunction ranging from basic sensory processes to the more complex aspects of cognitive functioning. When you look at the series of fragments shown here (from left to right), most of you will quickly perceive the object to be a watch. By contrast, people who suffer from schizophrenia take longer to perceive these pieces as part of a whole object.

**Genetic Factors.**   When Beth was 3 years old, her father died in a mental hospital, where he was being treated for schizophrenia. Beth, who is expecting a baby, wants to know whether her family history means that her child is at risk for developing schizophrenia. To help answer Beth's question, let's suppose that we randomly selected a person from the general population. What are the chances that this person will develop schizophrenia? Suppose that we randomly select another person from a family with a member who has been diagnosed as suffering from schizophrenia. Does the risk change?

We noted earlier that approximately 1% of the population develops schizophrenia, so the answer to the first question is about 1%. Because schizophrenia runs in families, the odds that it will occur in a person selected from a family with a member who has the diagnosis are greater than 1%. How much greater depends on the person's relationship to the family member with schizophrenia. Figure 12-12 lists the risk (odds) of developing schizophrenia for various family members. The risk increases with the degree of genetic relatedness (Gottesman, 1991). Thus having a brother or sister with schizophrenia raises the risk to 9%; the risk spirals to 46% for children of two parents with the disorder. Beth's baby has about a 5% chance of developing schizophrenia because her grandfather (Beth's father) had the disorder. The concordance rates (both twins diagnosed with schizophrenia) across several reports are 48% for identical twins and 17% for fraternal twins (Gottesman, 1991). This 3:1 ratio in the concordance rates for identical to fraternal twins strongly implicates genetic factors. In sum, this research has produced evidence suggesting that risk for developing schizophrenia may be transmitted genetically.

We need to be cautious in interpreting these results because they may not be as clear-cut as we presume. When children are reared by parents diagnosed with schizophrenia, we cannot separate genetic factors from the effects of being raised by parents with the disorder (environmental factors). For this reason, psychologists rely on studies of adopted children to distinguish the effects of genetics (nature) from those of the environment (nurture). In a study of children with at least one biological parent diagnosed with schizophrenia, rates of the disorder among the children were similar, regardless of whether they were raised by the biological parents or adopted parents (Wender, Rosenthal, Kety, Schulsinger, & Welner, 1974). These results suggest that nature does play a more

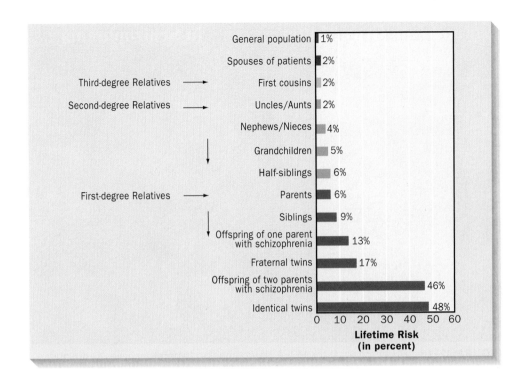

**FIGURE 12-12** Degree of genetic relation and average risk for developing schizophrenia. The risk varies as a function of genetic relatedness to a person afflicted with the disorder compared with the risk in the general population. The highest risk occurs among co-twins of identical (monozygotic) twins who suffer from schizophrenia, which suggests that genetic factors play a role in schizophrenia. The fact that the risk is not 100% for identical twins, however, suggests that nongenetic (environmental) factors also play a role.

**Source:** Gottesman (1991).

significant role than nurture in the development of schizophrenia. In fact, "Well-replicated findings from family, twin, and adoption studies indicate that there is a substantial genetic component to the predisposition for schizophrenia" (Conklin & Iacono, 2002, p. 33).

## Psychological Detective

Is schizophrenia a genetically transmitted disorder? Can you identify reasons that genetic factors may not be the entire story? Twins are often reared in similar environments, raising the issue of nature versus nurture. What's more, if one twin has schizophrenia, the other (co-twin) twin does not always develop the disorder. If schizophrenia were transmitted entirely by genes, what concordance rate would you expect to find in identical twins? Why?

If genetic factors provided a complete answer to the cause of schizophrenia, we would expect a concordance rate of 100% among identical twins because such twins share all their genetic material (Conklin & Iacono, 2002). The less than 100% concordance rate for identical twins suggests a role for nongenetic factors (Moldin & Gottesman, 1997).

**Brain Abnormalities.** A promising area of research on the causes of schizophrenia is the study of brain abnormalities. Evidence indicates that there is widespread atrophy (wasting away) of the cerebral cortex in patients with schizophrenia. What's more, blood flow in the brains of people with schizophrenia is often abnormal, with increases in some parts of the brain and decreases in other parts (Javitt & Coyle, 2004; On the trail of schizophrenia, 2005).

The extensive nature of this atrophy is clearly visible in high-resolution MRI scans of 12 adolescents with schizophrenia who were compared to 12 matched healthy controls. Over the course of 5 years, these 24 individuals had repeated MRI scans of their brains; the results were averaged for each group to create the very revealing comparison you can see in Figure 12-13. The diagnosis of those with schizophrenia was childhood-onset schizophrenia, which occurs in children under age 13. This form of schizophrenia

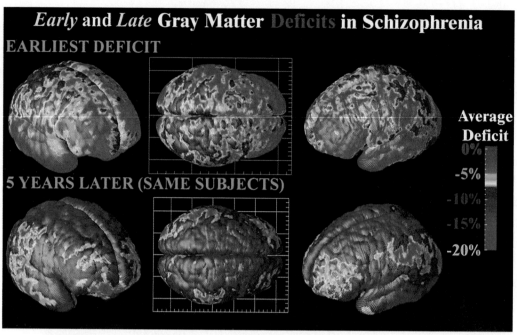

**FIGURE 12-13** Researchers at the UCLA Neuro Imaging Laboratory have used high-resolution MRI scans to study the brains of people with schizophrenia. Across a 5-year span, the brains of 12 people with schizophrenia were compared to the brains of 12 matched healthy controls. A severe loss of gray matter in the brains of those diagnosed with schizophrenia is indicated by the red and pink colors; more stable regions are in blue. The individuals with schizophrenia suffered from childhood-onset schizophrenia (which occurs in approximately 1 in 40,000 people). This form of schizophrenia is often more aggressive than forms of schizophrenia that occur later in life (late adolescence or early adulthood). It is hoped that insights into the process that leads to schizophrenia will be provided by studying this aggressive form of schizophrenia.
**Source:** Thompson et al. (2001).

is considered especially aggressive, as the extensive loss of gray matter in the brain seems to attest (Thompson et al., 2001). Such extensive loss of brain tissue would seem to impact functioning on a wide range of tasks.

Several studies have also demonstrated that patients with schizophrenia have significantly larger cerebral ventricles—fluid-filled chambers in the brain—than nonschizophrenic people and therefore have smaller brain areas (Lickey & Gordon, 1991; Suddath, Christison, Torrey, Casanova, & Weinberger, 1990). In fact, ventricular enlargement (with its accompanying reduction in brain volume) is found in the majority of patients with schizophrenia (Vita et al., 2000). The enlarged ventricles seem to reduce other brain areas as well. For example, limbic-area brain structures such as the hippocampus are smaller in some people with schizophrenia (Cannon & Marco, 1994), and the thalamus is also smaller (Gaser, Nenadic, Buchsbaum, Hazlett, & Buchsbaum, 2004). The limbic system plays a role in emotional response, memory, and other functions (see Chapter 2), and the thalamus is an integrative center for sending sensory inputs to their proper destinations within the brain. Reductions in these areas would seem to have significant effects on the ability to process and make sense of sensory inputs, to remember, and to monitor feelings and respond emotionally.

Are brain abnormalities associated with schizophrenia genetically transmitted? MRI scans of the brains of discordant twin pairs—in which one twin had schizophrenia and the other did not—have revealed clear differences in their brains. The ventricles in the twin with schizophrenia were larger than those in the normal twin (see Figure 12-14). A difference in ventricle size in identical twins could *not* result from genetic factors and thus provides further evidence that genetic factors are not the sole cause of schizophrenia. Both men and women diagnosed with schizophrenia show this pattern of ventricle

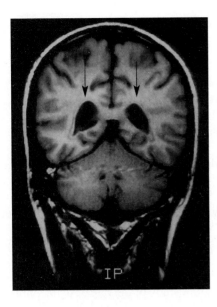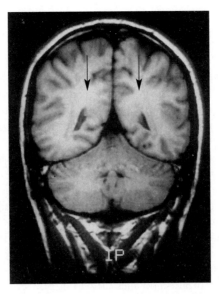

**FIGURE 12-14** MRI scans of the brains of identical twins, one with schizophrenia (left) and the other normal. The arrows indicate the ventricles (fluid-filled spaces in the brain). Note the difference in the size of the ventricles in these identical twins. One theory proposed to account for such a difference is the existence of a virus that infected one twin but not the other.

**Source:** Suddath et al. (1990).

enlargement; ventricle enlargement in men, however, is greater and may account for the common finding that the symptoms of schizophrenia are more severe in men than in women (Nopoulos, Flaum, & Andreasen, 1997).

The exact cause of the differing size of the ventricles has not been identified; one proposed cause is viral infection very early in life (Torrey, 1991). An association of viral infections with schizophrenia was demonstrated in a follow-up of children born in 1966 in northern Finland. There was a strong association between the risk of developing schizophrenia and infections. According to the data, however, less than 6% of those in the sample with a diagnosis of schizophrenia had experienced infection. This finding suggests that viral infections may be one of many factors that could lead to the development of schizophrenia (Rantakallio, Peter, Moring, & Von Wendt, 1997).

**Neurotransmitters.**    Another focus of research is the role of neurotransmitters. Not long ago, patients could be seen roaming the halls of mental hospitals, behaving in erratic, sometimes violent ways, because available therapies were ineffective in controlling their behavior. Many patients were confined in straitjackets to prevent them from harming themselves and others. In the 1950s, antipsychotic drugs were developed (see Chapter 13); these drugs made most patients more cooperative and easier for the hospital staff to manage. The effectiveness of these drugs suggested another possible cause: biochemical abnormalities.

Available evidence suggests that the neurotransmitter dopamine plays a role in schizophrenia. Drugs such as amphetamines and cocaine can induce some symptoms of schizophrenia, and these drugs are known to increase dopamine levels in the brain. The brains of people with schizophrenia may have more dopamine receptors, or their dopamine receptors may be more sensitive than those of a person not suffering from the disorder. What's more, levels of dopamine activity may differ in different parts of the brain, and this could account for some of the variations in the symptoms of schizophrenia (Conklin & Iacono, 2002; Javitt & Coyle, 2004). In some areas, there is increased dopamine activity, whereas in other areas there is reduced activity. Thus, the simple equation of "High levels of dopamine = schizophrenia" does not capture the complexity of this disorder. Researchers now suspect that brain circuits involving glutamate may be involved in schizophrenia. This neurotransmitter operates in areas that connect the executive control centers of the prefrontal cortex with the emotion and memory centers in the limbic system including the hippocampus. Disruptions in this connection may help to explain the widespread dysfunction people with schizophrenia exhibit on many measures of cognitive functioning (Javitt & Cole, 2004).

Of course, genetic factors may influence either dopamine levels or sensitivity to dopamine. The evidence, however, does not prove that schizophrenia is caused by biochemical factors alone.

**Environmental Causes.** Genetic and various biological factors are not the only possible causes of schizophrenia. Consider the following: Schizophrenia runs in families, and identical twins are concordant for schizophrenia more often than fraternal twins. Yet 89% of all people with schizophrenia do not have a parent who suffers from schizophrenia (Gottesman, 1991).

The failure of genetic factors to provide a full explanation of why some people develop schizophrenia has fueled interest in environmental, including psychological, explanations. Stressful events and conditions have been shown to play a role in schizophrenia (Dohrenwend & Ergi, 1981). Schizophrenia is diagnosed more frequently among people in lower socioeconomic classes than among those in higher classes (see Figure 12-15). Low-income people experience many stressors, including inadequate housing, substandard medical care, and poor diet. What's more, schizophrenia is more prevalent in urban areas than in rural ones—a tendency not attributed to differences in hospitalization policies (Torrey & Bowler, 1990). A study of the rate of schizophrenia in the Netherlands near the end of World War II suggests that prenatal nutritional deficiencies may play a role in the origin of some cases. Residents of the Netherlands endured severe famine as a result of the Nazi blockade of ports and other supply routes. Compared with people conceived at other times during the study period, individuals conceived at the height of the famine exhibited twice the rate of schizophrenia (Susser et al., 1996).

A series of studies demonstrates a relation between home environment and the risk of relapse for patients with schizophrenia. These studies have focused on *expressed emotion (EE)*, the degree to which family members' spontaneous talk about the patient is described as critical, hostile, or overinvolved. EE levels are assessed by interviewing family members and examining the content and vocal qualities of speech. A meta-analysis of 27 studies found that EE was a significant predictor of relapse among patients with schizophrenia and an even stronger predictor of relapse among patients with mood disorders and eating disorders (Butzlaff & Hooley, 1998). EE, however, is a controversial topic because it can be viewed as blaming family members for the disorder and its relapses. What's more, the direction of the effect is not clear: The family's emotional climate may be a reaction to the patient's symptoms rather than a result of those symptoms. For example, patients from families with high levels of EE are more likely to display odd and disruptive behavior within the family than patients from low-EE families (Rosenfarb, Goldstein, Mintz, & Neuchterlain, 1995).

Can stressors like poverty, urban life, or family conflict actually cause schizophrenia? Thousands of people have gone off to wars, suffered in major natural disasters, or been victims of violent crimes; few of them have developed schizophrenia. Researchers now believe that schizophrenia may result from several causes rather than a single cause.

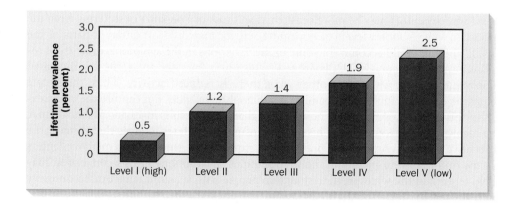

**FIGURE 12-15** Socioeconomic status and prevalence of schizophrenia. (Socioeconomic status decreases from left to right.)

**Source:** Robins and Regier (1991).

**Multiple Causes.**    April 14, 1930, was a special day for one family in a small midwestern town—they were thrilled by the birth of four identical baby girls. The joy of that day eventually turned to anguish. Known as the Genain quadruplets (not their real name), the sisters would experience a turbulent family life. By the time they reached the age of 25, all four had been hospitalized with the diagnosis of schizophrenia. The probability of identical quadruplets all developing schizophrenia is estimated to be 1 in 1.5 billion births. Such a rare occurrence attracted the attention of the National Institute of Mental Health, where staff members identified the sisters by the nicknames Nora, Iris, Myra, and Hester (N-I-M-H), which also represented their order of birth.

Over several decades, the Genain sisters were studied extensively by mental health experts, who attributed their common disorder to the interaction of several factors, including genetics and dysfunctional family life (Mirsky & Quinn, 1988; Mirsky, Quinn, De Lisi, Schwerdt, & Buchsbaum, 1987). For example, their father was irritable, abusive, intrusive, and suspicious; he exhibited EEG abnormalities and reportedly suffered seizures. Their mother probably suffered from paranoid schizophrenia. Given this family background, it is not surprising that some of the sisters would develop problems. What struck researchers, however, were the variations in the onset and severity of their illnesses. For example, Hester (last born and smallest) probably suffered the greatest brain insult at birth. She showed signs of schizophrenia as early as age 11 and was never able to function independently outside the home or institution. By contrast, Myra worked as a secretary for most of her life; she was married and had two sons and lives in her own home today.

Psychologists have studied the Genain quadruplets for more than three decades in an attempt to unravel the mystery of schizophrenia. All of the sisters were diagnosed as suffering from schizophrenia, although their level of adjustment and length of hospitalization varied.

She did not show signs of schizophrenia until age 24. Hester's treatment by her parents reflected their view that she was the "moron type," whereas their treatment of Myra was much better. As the sisters approached their 66th birthday, they were studied once again, perhaps for the last time. The researchers concluded: "Although the genetic endowment of the Genians is presumed to be identical, the . . . expression of the disorder is relatively unique in each of the sisters. The outcome and life course of the Genain quadruplets remind us that any genetic model that could account for such diversity must include the participation of environmental factors, such as . . . brain injury at birth, differential expectations of and treatment by parents, and, most likely, the operation of chance factors" (Mirsky et al., 2000, p. 706).

In sum, it appears that no one inherits the specific symptoms of schizophrenia, although genetic factors play a role in a person's chances of developing the disorder. Despite past reports isolating a specific gene related to schizophrenia, the consensus of researchers suggests that multiple genes are involved in the disorder's development (Moldin & Gottesman, 1997). Researchers are beginning to converge on what they have called a *neurodevelopmental model*, which suggests that schizophrenia results from a combination of a genetic predisposition along with other factors. Irving Gottesman (1991) suggests that "what is inherited is a predisposition toward developing the disorder—a loading of nature's dice that increases the risk of developing schizophrenia" (p. 91). The child of a parent with schizophrenia is at higher risk for developing the disorder than the cousin of an individual with schizophrenia. The model suggests that schizophrenia is due to a disruption in forebrain development that occurs prior to or at birth in a person who has the genetic predisposition to develop schizophrenia. A brain lesion that occurs early in life remains dormant until around adolescence, when the signs of schizophrenia are likely to become evident. However, the model suggests that the loading of nature's dice provided by genetic factors is not enough to cause schizophrenia; there are other factors involved. Among the likely factors are birth complications and viral infections (Conklin & Iacono, 2002).

# REVIEW SUMMARY

1. **Schizophrenia** affects approximately 1% of the population. Although it is often confused with dissociative identity disorder, the two disorders are different. Schizophrenia is characterized by a split between thoughts and emotions and a separation from reality.

2. The symptoms of schizophrenia are classified as *positive* (distortions or excesses) or *negative* (reductions or losses). Positive symptoms include fluent but disorganized speech, **delusions,** and **hallucinations.** *Negative* symptoms include poverty of speech and disturbances in emotional expression such as flat affect.

3. The *DSM-IV-TR* lists five subtypes of schizophrenia: catatonic, disorganized, paranoid, residual, and undifferentiated.

4. Schizophrenia tends to run in families; the risk of developing the disorder increases with the degree of genetic relatedness between an individual and a family member who has schizophrenia.

5. Evidence of various brain abnormalities, including larger ventricles, in people with schizophrenia suggests a possible biological cause. The neurotransmitter, dopamine, seems to be involved in the development of schizophrenia.

6. Environmental influences on schizophrenia include stress and hostile family communication. A predisposition to schizophrenia may be inherited, with the actual development of the disorder requiring the presence of other factors.

# ✓ CHECK YOUR PROGRESS

1. Identify the following symptoms of schizophrenia as either positive or negative.

   a. The patient hears voices in an empty house.
   b. The patient believes others are controlling his thoughts.
   c. The patient rarely smiles, does not change her tone of voice, and does not maintain eye contact.

2. On the basis of the following symptoms, identify the most likely subtype of schizophrenia.

   a. The patient grimaces and assumes unusual postures.
   b. The patient is suspicious and has delusions of persecution.
   c. There are no prominent symptoms, but the patient is withdrawn.

3. A sample of 1,000 people was randomly selected from the population. Which of the following represents the most likely number who have ever been diagnosed as suffering from schizophrenia?

   a. 1
   b. 5
   c. 10
   d. 25

4. If schizophrenia were entirely a genetic disorder, what concordance rate would you expect to find among identical twins?

5. What is the most common type of hallucination reported by people diagnosed as suffering from schizophrenia?

   a. visual
   b. tactile
   c. auditory
   d. gustatory

6. Which neurotransmitter has been most often implicated in the development of schizophrenia?

   a. ACh
   b. GABA
   c. serotonin
   d. dopamine

7. What evidence suggests that schizophrenia is not entirely genetically based?

8. During an interview, a patient says that he has frequently seen a hand come out of the bathroom sink to grab a bar of soap. The psychologist who is conducting the interview most likely writes that the patient presents evidence of

   a. delusions.
   b. hallucinations.
   c. negative symptoms.
   d. loose associations.

9. What is the approximate risk of developing schizophrenia if both parents have schizophrenia?

   a. 1%
   b. 15%
   c. 20%
   d. 50%

10. What family variable is linked to relapse risk in people with schizophrenia who live with their families?

   a. poverty
   b. EE
   c. number of children
   d. sublimated emotion

# PERSONALITY AND SEXUAL DISORDERS

When he was younger, Chuck spent plenty of time in the principal's office for fighting. One night during Christmas vacation, Chuck left his house and stole decorations from neighbors' homes. Footprints in the freshly fallen snow led the police to Chuck, who nonetheless denied knowledge of the incident. When he was 14, Chuck vandalized cars; when he was 18, he was arrested for dangling an acquaintance from a bridge. When asked why he committed such acts, he said that he was bored and wanted to "stir up some excitement." *Does Chuck's long-standing pattern of deviant behavior indicate that he exhibits a psychological disorder?*

## Personality Disorders

**Personality disorders** are long-standing patterns of maladaptive behavior that are usually evident during the adolescent years and are resistant to treatment, which is seldom sought. Approximately 10% of the adult population may have one or more personality disorders. The high rate of comorbidity of personality disorders with other psychological disorders and medical conditions complicates diagnosis and treatment (Oldham, 1994; Personality disorders—Part I, 2000). Two-thirds of people with one personality disorder have another and in some cases, several personality disorders (Personality disorders—Part I, 2000). Most people with personality disorders are convinced that if a problem exists, it lies not in them but in other people's reactions to their behaviors. For example, the key feature of *narcissistic personality disorder* is an inflated sense of self-importance and superiority. Narcissistic individuals are preoccupied with fantasies of success, power, beauty, or ideal love. They are sure that other people recognize their special qualities and are therefore envious. Expectations of attention, admiration, and compliance with their wishes are frequently expressed. Yet a lack of empathy leaves them unable to understand others' reactions to their behavior.

The *DSM-IV-TR* describes 10 personality disorders divided into three clusters (see Table 12-9). Personality disorders have been criticized for low reliability and questionable validity, especially in comparison to other psychological disorders. The definitions of the disorders have been described as ambiguous and overlapping, and the boundaries between normal personality and characteristics that would lead to a diagnosis are not clear. For example, how indecisive does someone have to be before being diagnosed with OCD? What's more, most of these disorders are relatively new to the diagnostic system. Since the first diagnostic manual was published in 1952, only three personality disorders (paranoid, schizoid, and antisocial) have remained essentially unchanged (Personality disorders—Part I, 2000). Although there are 10 personality disorders, more attention has been focused on antisocial personality disorder than the others. About 5 to 6% of adult men and 1% of adult women meet the criteria for this diagnosis (Kessler et al., 1994). Consider Chuck, whom we described at the beginning of the section. Is his long-standing pattern of deviant behavior characteristic of a psychological disorder?

Chuck was eventually diagnosed as exhibiting **antisocial personality disorder;** in the past, he would have been called a *psychopath* or a *sociopath*. People exhibiting this disorder are often selfish, reckless, deceitful, impulsive, and remorseless. Robert Hare (1993), who has spent his career investigating these individuals, concluded that "lying, deceiving, and manipulation are natural talents" for them (p. 46). For example, one antisocial individual spotted a couple admiring a sailboat that had a For Sale sign on it. He introduced himself as the owner and invited them aboard for a closer look. They liked what they saw and handed him a deposit of $1,500. That was the last time they saw their money and the man who was not the owner of the boat (Hare, 1993).

The signs of disturbance seen in other disorders—anxiety, depression, delusions, or hallucinations—are absent in antisocial personality disorder.

**personality disorders**
Disorders characterized by long-standing, difficult-to-treat, dysfunctional behaviors that are typically first observed in adolescence

**antisocial personality disorder**
Personality disorder characterized by deceitful, impulsive, reckless actions that violate social norms for which the individual feels no remorse

Ted Bundy was an American serial killer and rapist who confessed to over 30 murders during the 1970s. His behavior seems consistent with the diagnosis of antisocial personality disorder. This educated, handsome, and charming man was capable of very brutal crimes. He was executed in the electric chair by the State of Florida in 1989

**TABLE 12-9**

## Personality Disorders and Their Characteristics

| | **Odd or Eccentric Behavior** |
|---|---|
| Paranoid | Tense, guarded, suspicious, tends to hold grudges and believes that others are untrustworthy. |
| Schizoid | Detached from social relationships, with a restricted range of expression of emotions, indifferent to both praise and criticism. |
| Schizotypal | Marked by peculiarities of speech, perceptions, appearance, and behavior that are often disconcerting to others; emotionally detached, socially isolated, and suspicious. |
| | **Dramatic, Emotional, or Erratic Behavior** |
| Antisocial | Manipulative, reckless, dishonest, impulsive, lacks guilt, habitually breaks social rules, childhood history of such behavior, often in trouble with the law as an adult. |
| Borderline | Cannot stand to be alone; intense, unstable moods and personal relationships; chronic, inappropriate anger, drug and alcohol abuse, suicide attempts. |
| Histrionic | Highly dramatic, seductive behavior, needs immediate gratification and constant reassurance, rapidly changing moods, shallow emotions. |
| Narcissistic | Self-absorbed, expects special treatment and adulation, envious of the attention others receive. |
| | **Anxious or Fearful Behavior** |
| Avoidant | Socially inhibited, easily hurt and embarrassed, few close friends, sticks to routines to avoid new and possibly stressful experiences. |
| Dependent | Wants others to make decisions, excessive need to be taken care of, leading to submissive and clinging behavior, needs constant advice and reassurance, fears being abandoned. |
| Obsessive–compulsive | Preoccupied with rules and details, perfectionistic at the expense of flexibility; indecisive, stiff, unable to express affection. |

**Source:** American Psychiatric Association (2000).

Individuals with this disorder rarely seek professional help unless their goal is to obtain an excuse to be absent from work, to acquire drugs, or to avoid prison by submitting to court-ordered treatment. They can appear so normal that psychiatrist Hervey Cleckley (1976) titled his classic book about them *The Mask of Sanity*.

Because antisocial individuals do not experience the warning signals of anxiety, they are prone to act impulsively, without regard for the feelings or well-being of others. They want immediate gratification, fail to develop emotional attachments, and have no remorse for their actions: "They leave in their wakes a huge amount of human suffering. The pain [these individuals] wreak on other human beings can be physical, or it can be the mental anguish often felt by those who try to form relationships" with them (Magid & McKelvey, 1987, p. 4). Yet these individuals can be charming and ingratiating when it is to their advantage. Serial killer Ted Bundy used his charm to lure dozens of young women to accompany him to isolated places; only one of them was ever seen alive again.

Many antisocial people do not come into contact with law enforcement agencies. These con men, unethical business leaders, and crooked politicians are less dramatic but more numerous than the Ted Bundy type of killer. Nevertheless, our understanding of this disorder is based largely on studies of the unlucky or unsuccessful antisocial individuals found in prisons.

Cathy Spatz Widom (1977) devised a clever plan to identify antisocial people who are not in prison. She placed the following advertisement in newspapers: "Are you adventurous? Psychologist studying adventurous carefree people who've led exciting impulsive lives" (p. 675). A number of respondents to the advertisement met the criteria for antisocial personality disorder. Almost 50% of them had a history of heavy drinking and considerable experience with other drugs. Many had been arrested but had spent little time in jail, preferring court-ordered psychotherapy. Widom concluded that many people outside of prisons could be diagnosed as exhibiting antisocial personality disorder.

The childhood and adolescent years of people diagnosed with antisocial personality disorder as adults are marked by hyperactivity, impulsivity, attention problems, and neuropsychological impairment (Lynam, 1998). Nevertheless, many of them tend to engage in fewer criminal activities after age 40 (Hare, McPherson, & Forth, 1988). The specific reasons for this decrease are not clear. Perhaps they continue their antisocial activities but have developed better strategies for staying out of prison.

Because people with antisocial personalities do not conform to social norms, researchers have turned their attention to the socializing agent that is primarily responsible for instilling social norms in the young: the family. They have found that during childhood, many antisocial people were subjected to inconsistent discipline or no discipline at all. As in Chuck's case, their future course was evident in early episodes of fighting, lying, stealing, and vandalism. Many children who are raised with little or no discipline, however, do not develop antisocial tendencies. Thus it appears that lack of discipline during childhood is not a complete explanation of the emergence of antisocial tendencies.

## Psychological Detective

Over the years, researchers have found that antisocial individuals have a low level of physiological arousal, a condition that is so uncomfortable that they will do almost anything to change it. As Chuck said, he was just trying to "stir up some excitement." How could researchers determine that an individual has a low level of arousal? How could they determine whether level of arousal is related to antisocial activity? Before reading further, design a study to gather evidence that might show that physiological arousal is or is not related to antisocial behavior.

Just such a study was conducted by Adrian Raine and his colleagues (Rainee, Venables, & Williams, 1990). They recruited 101 teenagers between ages 14 and 16 to take part in a program to measure heart rate and brain waves, which served as indicators of arousal. Assessing the relationship of physiological arousal to antisocial behavior required a longitudinal research design. The criminal records of these young men were checked when they reached age 24. The men with a criminal record at that age were more likely to have had low arousal levels when they were teenagers than were the men with no criminal record. Using only the indicators of physiological arousal, the researchers correctly classified 75% of the men as criminal or noncriminal.

The physiological dysfunction in people with antisocial personality disorder may be more complex than was once thought. To address this issue, researchers (Raine, Lencz, Bihrle, LaCasse, & Colletti, 2000) studied three groups: 21 community volunteers with antisocial personality disorder (71% had a history of being arrested), 34 healthy control participants, and 26 individuals with substance dependence problems. All participants were asked to spend 2 minutes preparing a speech about their faults. Then they spent 2 minutes giving the speech to the experimenter while being videotaped. During this social stressor, all participants had their galvanic skin response and heart rate measured. Consistent with previous research, the antisocial group had lower heart rate and skin conductance levels than the other two groups (see Figure 12-16). What's more, results of MRI scans revealed that they also had less volume in the prefrontal cortex (11% less compared to the control group). In a related study, adolescents who were prone to antisocial behavior showed lower levels of anticipatory galvanic skin response; in other words, they did not respond with the same level of autonomic activation as most people. Such activation plays a key role in learning, especially in developing fear reactions (Fung et al., 2005).

Taken together, these results paint a picture of antisocial persons as individuals who do not develop conditioned fear responses readily. The reduced volume in the prefrontal lobes may leave them subject to whim, as they seem to lack the inhibitory control of a properly functioning prefrontal cortex. One of the functions of the prefrontal lobes is to serve as a check in assessing risk and reining in our impulses. Reduced autonomic activation makes them less likely to develop fear at the same time that reduced prefrontal lobes leave them less able to assess risk properly and more likely to act impulsively—a combination that invites trouble.

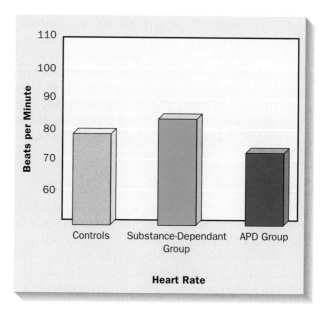

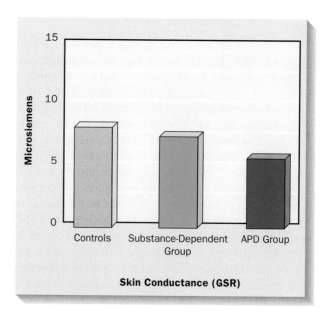

**FIGURE 12-16** Three groups of males (controls, those with substance-dependence problems, and those exhibiting antisocial personality disorder) were compared after delivering a short speech to researchers. The antisocial personality disorder group had lower heart rates and lower levels of skin conductance (GSR). Both findings suggest that autonomic nervous system deficits may play a role in this disorder. What's more, the antisocial group also had a reduced volume of both gray and white matter in the prefrontal cortex, which is responsible for judgment, among other abilities.

**Source:** Raine et al. (2000).

# Sexual Disorders

The *DSM-IV-TR* divides sexual disorders into several categories: gender identity disorder (transsexualism), the paraphilias, and sexual dysfunctions. In this section we discuss the first two categories.

**Gender Identity Disorder.**    Are you a male or a female? Although this seems to be a silly question, for some people it is a serious matter. Beginning in childhood, some people believe that their anatomical sex does not match their gender identity. Many cases of **gender identity disorder (transsexualism)** in childhood cease by the time the individual reaches adolescence, but some cases progress to transsexualism.

Transsexualism is a disorder in which a person is uncomfortable with his or her anatomical sex, views it as inappropriate, and wants to be a member of the other sex. This rare disorder occurs in 1 in 30,000 biological males and 1 in 100,000 biological females (American Psychiatric Association, 2000). One treatment, sex-reassignment surgery, involves surgically creating external sex organs that are characteristic of the other biological sex. Mental health professionals screen candidates for sex reassignment surgery to ensure that disorders like schizophrenia are not present. Once a patient is considered eligible for the surgery, hormone therapy can begin. This therapy develops the secondary sex characteristics and must be continued for life. For males wanting to be female, estrogen and drugs to inhibit testosterone production promote breast growth, soften the skin, reduce body and facial hair, and reduce muscle mass. Females wishing to be male are given testosterone to increase body and facial hair, deepen the voice, suppress menstruation, and reduce breast tissue. The next step is a "real life test" in which the individual lives as a member of the other sex for a year or more prior to the surgery (Miracle, Miracle, & Baumeister, 2003). Although evidence suggests that transsexuals who have undergone the operation are generally quite satisfied (Pauly, 1990), controversy surrounds the treatment because it is radical and irreversible.

**Paraphilias.**    **Paraphilia** literally means "love beyond the usual." People with paraphilias are sexually aroused by objects or situations that are considered unusual or bizarre by most people, ranging from animals to dressing in the clothes of the other sex. Most of these individuals are men; their unusual activity is typically harmless or involves consenting others. Some of these people, however, can be dangerous and may come into contact with legal authorities. Table 12-10 lists some of the more common paraphilias.

**Fetishism.**    Derived from a French word for a magical charm, a *fetish* is an object that arouses sexual passion in some people. **Fetishism** is a sexual disorder in which an object or body part becomes associated with sexual arousal. A variety of objects may serve as fetishes: shoes, boots, fur, women's underwear, and rubber or leather products (Junginger, 1997; Mason, 1997). Some of these objects are associated with sexual activity; others are rarely associated with sexual excitement by most people. Fetishists may kiss, taste, or smell the fetish and masturbate while fondling it. Most fetishists pose no danger to others and pursue use of the fetish in private (Miracle et al., 2003).

Consider the case of a 32-year-old man who was sexually excited at a young age by pictures of women wearing panties. At the age of 12, he ejaculated for the first time while fantasizing about panties. Thereafter he began to steal panties from his sister and her friends. His preferred pattern of sexual excitement involved panties, which he used while masturbating. Dating made him uncomfortable because he feared that if he and his date became intimate, she would not understand his sexual practices (Spitzer et al., 1994).

Psychodynamic theorists see paraphilias as associated with early childhood experiences or, in some cases, as alternatives that arouse less anxiety than sexual encounters with adult partners. Behavioral psychologists, in contrast, believe that most fetishes, and probably many of the paraphilias, develop through classical conditioning. Perhaps the

Lauraine (bottom), a 28-year-old blonde, and her younger half-sister Lenette, 22, were once half brothers, Cary and Burt, from a small Minnesota town. Sex reassignment surgery was performed on the older sibling, Cary, at the University of Minnesota when he was 21. When he turned 21, Burt also had the surgery performed. Following surgery, court proceedings made their sex reassignments legal.

**STUDY TIP**

Write a two-paragraph summary of the material on personality and sexual disorders—one paragraph for each category.

**gender identity disorder (transsexualism)**
Sexual disorder characterized by a person's belief that he or she was born with the wrong biological sex organs

**paraphilia**
Sexual arousal by objects or situations not considered sexual by most people

**fetishism**
Paraphilia involving sexual arousal by unusual objects or body parts

People who exhibit one of the paraphilias are sexually aroused by objects or situations that most people consider bizarre or unusual. Unlike lower animals, humans can be sexually aroused by a wide range of objects and situations. Some businesses cater to the needs of paraphiliacs by providing objects used in their sexual activities. The man pictured here is standing outside a shop that sells leather dominatrix costumes, often used by people practicing sexual masochism and sexual sadism.

**Masochism Clinic**

Knock with forehead.

**Source:** Reprinted with the permission of Psi Chi, The National Honor Society in Psychology.

## TABLE 12-10

## Paraphilias

**Autopedophilia:** Sexual arousal by imagining oneself as a child or being treated as a child.

**Autoscopophilia:** Sexual gratification from looking at one's own body, particularly the genitals.

**Avoniepiphilia:** Sexual arousal from wearing diapers.

**Exhibitionism (indecent exposure, flashing):** Repeated exposure of genitals to unsuspecting strangers, usually women and children. The exhibitionist may masturbate while exposing his genitals but usually does not pursue further sexual activity. Exhibitionists seem to desire surprise or shock in victims but are usually not physically dangerous to them.

**Fetishism:** Sexual arousal associated with nonliving objects, called *fetishes*, such as stockings, shoes, or boots. The fetishist often masturbates while fondling the desired object.

**Formicophilia:** Sexual arousal associated with bugs or other crawling creatures.

**Frotteurism:** Sexual arousal as a result of rubbing against or touching a nonconsenting person. The behavior usually occurs in crowded places like busy sidewalks or on public transportation. Victims may not protest at first because they cannot believe that such provocative acts are occurring in a public place.

**Klismaphilia:** Sexual arousal resulting from receiving or giving an enema.

**Mysophilia:** Sexual arousal that involves the presence of or use of filthy or soiled objects.

**Narratophilia:** Sexual arousal from listening to erotic stories.

**Necrophilia:** Sexual pleasure from viewing or having sexual contact with a corpse.

**Partialism:** Intense sexual attraction to specific body parts (most often legs or feet, and excluding genitals, breasts, and buttocks).

**Pedophilia:** Sexual activity with a child who has not reached puberty. Attraction to girls is twice as common as attraction to boys.

**Pictophilia:** The need for sexual pictures for sexual response.

**Sexual masochism:** Sexual arousal that involves being humiliated, beaten, bound, or made to suffer in other ways.

**Sexual sadism:** Sexual arousal associated with the physical or psychological suffering of victims.

**Transvestic fetishism:** Sexual arousal associated with cross-dressing, that is, dressing in the clothes of the opposite sex.

**Voyeurism (peeping):** Sexual arousal as a result of observing unsuspecting individuals, most often strangers, who are either naked, in the process of undressing, or engaging in sexual activity. The voyeur usually does not seek any sexual liaison with the observed person.

**Zoophilia:** Sexual activity with animals.

**Sources:** American Psychiatric Association (2000); Miracle et al. (2003); Money (1984).

object that becomes a fetish was accidentally paired with sexual arousal and thus acquired the power to elicit arousal later in life. In laboratory experiments, psychologists have paired pictures of boots with slides of nudes (Rachman, 1966). The participant's level of sexual arousal was measured by a device placed on the penis. The results showed that the arousal caused by the nudes was transferred to the boots.

# REVIEW SUMMARY

**1. Personality disorders** are long-standing dysfunctional patterns of behavior. Persons with **antisocial personality disorder** display few of the signs usually associated with psychological disorders, such as anxiety. They are often described as deceitful, impulsive, and remorseless. Low levels of arousal may play a role in the development of this disorder.

**2. Gender identity disorder (transsexualism)** is a sexual disorder in which a person believes that he or she should have been a member of the opposite sex.

**3. Paraphilias** are disorders involving sexual arousal in unusual situations or in response to unusual objects. **Fetishism** is a paraphilia in which a person is sexually aroused by objects such as boots. One of the explanations for fetishism and perhaps other paraphilias is classical conditioning.

 CHECK YOUR PROGRESS

**1.** Of 100 randomly selected people, approximately how many are likely to meet the diagnostic criteria for one of the personality disorders?

   **a.** 1
   **b.** 3
   **c.** 5
   **d.** 10

**2.** What are the key symptoms of antisocial personality disorder? In what ways do antisocial individuals appear to be quite normal?

**3.** What are the key symptoms of transsexualism?

**4.** Give the name of each of the following sexual disorders.

   **a.** sexual activity with a child
   **b.** sexual contact with animals
   **c.** sexual contact with dead bodies
   **d.** sexual arousal from rubbing against a person
   **e.** sexual arousal from receiving or giving an enema
   **f.** sexual arousal related to boots or fur

**ANSWERS: 1.** d **2.** The individual with antisocial personality disorder is described as irresponsible, deceitful, manipulative, and remorseless. People with this disorder do not, however, exhibit anxiety, depression, hallucinations, or delusions. **3.** A transsexual is a person who has no genetic abnormality yet believes he or she has the sex organs of the wrong sex. **4. a.** Pedophilia **b.** Zoophilia **c.** Necrophilia **d.** Frotteurism **e.** Klismaphilia **f.** Fetishism

# 13

# Therapy

## CHAPTER OUTLINE

By now you have seen that our earlier discussions of basic processes such as learning provide the background necessary to understand more complex topics such as the causes and treatment of psychological disorders. We can now appreciate the role biological mechanisms play in shaping both normal and abnormal behaviors. In addition, our growing awareness of human diversity helps us recognize how ethnicity and culture affect both our choice of treatment and the effectiveness of the therapies we choose. As we shall see, even biomedical treatments can be influenced by these factors.

The psychological disorders discussed in Chapter 12 sometimes become so distressing that the people who experience them seek treatment or therapy. Where do these people seek help? What kinds of therapies are available? Do current therapies reduce or eliminate the patients' symptoms? In this chapter we attempt to answer these questions. As we do so, keep in mind that our beliefs about the nature and origins of psychological disorders often determine which therapies we deem appropriate and useful.

## THERAPY THROUGH THE AGES

The morning sun radiates across the sky; the birds greet the new day with a chorus of song. A young man, Oag, rises from sleeping quarters he shares with others. Although all the adults in the community are attending to their chores, the young man wanders off. On a typical day he sits and stares for long periods; then suddenly he seems propelled into a frenzied state. His behavior is unpredictable, and everyone is afraid of him. The elders decide the time has come to deal with his strange behavior. *How did our earliest ancestors treat abnormal behaviors?*

### The History of Therapy

Thousands of years ago, our ancestors attributed earthquakes, lightning, and thunder to evil spirits or demons. A successful hunt might have been viewed as the work of good spirits. Similarly, a person's bizarre behavior was often viewed as the work of a demon (bad spirit) that had "possessed" or taken command of the person's body. Techniques such as exorcism or *trephining* (chipping a hole in the skull to let the demon out; Sarason & Sarason, 2002) were used to rid the body of demons. The elders used exorcism to treat Oag. Such beliefs are evident today in our use of language, as when we ask someone who has engaged in unusual behavior, "What got into you?" This question suggests earlier notions of demon possession.

The Greek philosopher and physician Hippocrates (460–377 B.C.) proposed that physical and psychological disorders have natural causes. He suggested that some disorders result from imbalances among four *humors* (liquids) in the body: black bile, blood, phlegm, and yellow bile (see Chapter 11). For example, elevated levels of black bile were thought to lead to *melancholia*, a term we use today to denote an especially severe form of depression (Nevid & Greene, 2001). The Greek emphasis on naturalistic explanations continued in ancient Rome, where people received treatments such as baths, exercise, and massage.

**Asylums and Hospitals.** During the 16th and 17th centuries, some people whose only "crimes" may have been that they suffered from psychological disorders were

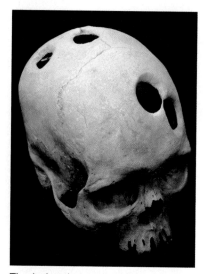

The holes that were chipped in this *trephined* skull to release the evil spirits can be seen clearly.

St. Mary of Bethlehem Hospital in London. Visitors amused themselves by watching patients. Can you see how the word "bedlam" (a contraction of Bethlehem) got its meaning?

Tranquilizer chair. Benjamin Rush, recognized as the "Father of American Psychiatry," recommended use of the tranquilizer chair for patients suffering from mania. He also used bloodletting to treat the symptoms of mania; some of his patients died when he removed too much blood.

accused of being witches. The body of an accused witch might be examined for marks, which were considered evidence of a pact with Satan. The "witch" was often brutally tortured and was frequently killed.

Not all mentally ill people were tortured or put to death. Some were housed in institutions like St. Mary of Bethlehem Hospital in London, where patients were often kept in chains and slept on straw beds. On weekends, visitors could pay a penny to amuse themselves by watching these patients. The hospital was known for its disorganization, unsanitary conditions, and inhumane treatment of patients. The word *bedlam*, a contraction of *Bethlehem*, came into the language to describe such conditions (Sarason & Sarason, 2002).

**Moral Therapy.** In the 18th century, mentally ill people in Paris were often chained to walls. The attendants, or "keepers" as they were called, rarely showed compassion and even administered punishment when they deemed it necessary. A physician, Philippe Pinel (1745–1826), argued that these patients needed humane care and treatment. His ideas, however, ran counter to the prevailing notion that mental hospitals should function to protect society from the insane. Many of Pinel's ideas were derived from the work of Jean-Baptiste Pussin, a former patient at a hospital in which Pinel worked. After he was discharged, Pussin was given a job at a hospital in Paris. When he became superintendent of a ward for incurable mental patients, he insisted that the staff should be kind and gentle, dismissed those who mistreated patients, and removed the patients' chains.

After being named chief physician at another hospital, Pinel followed in the footsteps of Pussin and removed the patients' chains, directed the staff to treat the patients kindly, and stopped the use of bloodletting and punishment. Pinel's efforts led to a treatment philosophy called *moral management* or *moral therapy*. The term did not suggest any moralistic content of the treatment; rather, it reflected the belief that providing a humane and relaxed environment could produce positive changes in a person's behavior.

Benjamin Rush (1745–1813) introduced moral therapy at Philadelphia's Pennsylvania Hospital, the first general hospital in the United States with a separate unit for the mentally ill (Talbott, 1994). Rush expected staff members to be friends to the patients.

Yet he restrained manic patients in his tranquilizer chair, which he thought was more humane than other restraints used at the time (Gamwell & Tomes, 1995).

### State Mental Hospitals.

In the mid-19th century, Dorothea Dix (1802–1887), a former teacher, became concerned about the plight of homeless and disturbed people. Her survey of Massachusetts institutions that housed the mentally ill yielded numerous examples of misery and horror. Armed with knowledge and determination, Dix insisted that the states had an obligation to provide care for the mentally ill. She convinced legislatures in 20 states to establish or enlarge mental hospitals (Grob, 1994).

As the states assumed more responsibility for custodial care of the mentally ill, economics dictated that they build larger institutions to handle more patients. As the institutions expanded, conditions deteriorated and the use of restraining devices increased. Clifford W. Beers provides an example of the use of such restraints in his 1908 book *A Mind That Found Itself.* This book is based on Beers's own experiences in an early institution for the mentally ill.

> To guard me at night my hands were imprisoned in what is known as a 'muff.' A muff, innocent enough to the eyes of those who have never worn one, is in reality a relic of the Inquisition. The muff I wore was made of canvas, and differed in construction from a muff designed for the hands of fashion only in the inner partition, also of canvas, which separated my hands, but allowed them to overlap. At either end was a strap which buckled tightly around the wrist and was locked.
>
> The putting on of the muff was the most humiliating incident of my life. I resisted weakly, and, after the muff was adjusted and locked, for the first time since my mental collapse I wept. (Beers, 1908/1937, pp. 46–48)

The early institutions were more like warehouses for patients who were less likely to recover.

### New Forms of Treatment.

Franz Anton Mesmer and his notion of animal magnetism offered a very different view of psychological disorders and their treatment (see Chapter 4). Mesmer believed he could harness this magnetism as a form of therapy to treat patients. With modifications, his techniques evolved into hypnotism. Sigmund Freud, an early advocate of hypnotism as a therapeutic technique, developed the notion that psychological disorders result from unconscious feelings and conflicts, which required a different approach to therapy. At first he believed that hypnosis was an appropriate way to deal with these feelings and conflicts, but he later turned to other techniques when hypnosis proved less effective than he had hoped.

While Freud was exploring the unconscious for clues to the causes and treatment of psychological disorders, others were exploring the biological roots of such

The determined efforts of Dorothea Dix convinced many states to build institutions to treat people suffering from mental disorders. When she agreed to teach a religious class in a Massachusetts jail, she observed mentally ill persons confined in facilities with criminals. She spent more than a year traveling throughout Massachusetts inspecting places where mentally ill patients were housed. Her observations became part of a petition to the legislature to expand the Worcester Hospital and to build other facilities. She followed a similar strategy in other states, where she would gather data and then present her findings to the legislature.

**Source:** Grob, 1994.

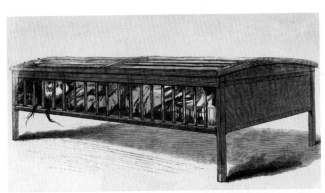

As institutions for the mentally ill became larger and more crowded, staff members resorted to restraint devices like this criblike enclosure from the 1800s. The use of restraints declined dramatically with the development of antipsychotic drugs.

**deinstitutionalization**
The policy of discharging mentally ill patients from institutions on the assumption that they can be cared for in their communities; the policy also led to the closing of part or all of these institutions

disorders. Early in the 20th century, the disorder known as *general paresis*, which included symptoms such as paralysis and memory difficulties, was found to result from syphilis. This finding stimulated the search for biological causes of other psychological disorders, as well as the development of biomedical treatments such as psychosurgery and electroconvulsive (shock) therapy, which are described later in this chapter.

**Deinstitutionalization.**    Despite the availability of new treatments, many seriously disturbed patients continued to be housed in overcrowded and understaffed mental hospitals. Beginning in the 1950s, the populations of these hospitals began to decline. One reason for this decline was the use of drugs, which made it possible to control many serious symptoms (Sundberg, Winebarger, & Taplin, 2002). At the same time, there was a growing belief that community care was more effective than hospitalization. What's more, during the 1960s, courts restricted the grounds for committing people to hospitals: states could involuntarily commit patients only if they were judged to be dangerous to themselves or others or in need of treatment. The courts also insisted that institutionalized patients had rights to minimum levels of treatment and care. These factors led to **deinstitutionalization,** a policy of discharging large numbers of patients from mental hospitals and then closing part or all of those hospitals. As a result of deinstitutionalization, the population of mental hospitals decreased from more than 500,000 in the 1950s to less than 100,000 in 1995, despite a substantial increase in the overall population and the number of people suffering from psychological disorders (Torrey, 1997). If we consider the rate of increase in the overall population and the associated increase in the number of people with disorders, an estimated 90% of the people who would have been institutionalized in the 1950s are now living outside of institutions.

**The Community Mental Health Movement.**    In 1963, Congress passed the Community Mental Health Centers Act. This law provided funds for the establishment of community mental health centers in which patients would be treated on an outpatient basis.

In addition, the 1963 law helped finance community-based programs to prevent mental illness. Thus mental health professionals placed more emphasis on preventing as well as treating psychological disorders (Sundberg et al., 2002). Psychologists recognize three forms of prevention: primary, secondary, and tertiary. *Primary prevention*

The policy of deinstitutionalization has added to the number of people who are homeless. The rates of schizophrenia and alcohol/drug abuse among the homeless tend to be higher than in the general population.

is designed to prevent disorders from occurring. Such efforts might include workshops on stress reduction or community recreation programs. *Secondary prevention* is designed to detect existing disorders and provide treatment at early stages. A crisis telephone line for individuals experiencing extreme stress is an example. The goal of *tertiary prevention* is to reduce the damage caused by disorders for both the patients and society. An after-care program for former patients of psychiatric hospitals is an example of tertiary prevention.

Decades after the passage of the Community Mental Health Centers Act, many of the reformers' goals have not been achieved. Reflecting the need for continued mental health reform, in July 2003 President Bush's New Commission on Mental Health set six broad-based goals for mental health in the future (Holloway, 2003):

1. Americans need to understand that mental health is essential to overall health.
2. Mental health should be more consumer and family driven.
3. Disparities in mental health services ought to be eliminated.
4. Early mental health screening, assessment, and referral to services should become common practice.
5. Providers need to deliver excellent mental health care, and research needs to be accelerated.
6. Technology—such as telehealth and integrated electronic health records—ought to be used to access mental health care information.

This poster is intended to prevent a substance abuse problem from developing. It is an example of primary prevention.

In addition to these goals, the mental health needs of several specific groups will need attention in the future. For example, the mental health needs of children and youth are escalating; for example, "one in five children and teens suffers from mental health problems, and the number is growing" (DeAngelis, 2004, p. 38). The number of college students with mental health problems also is climbing (O'Connor, 2001). Moreover, the prescribing of psychotropic drugs for children is on the rise, even though complete data on drug safety and long-term effects may be lacking (Kennedy, 2003). Demographic changes in the United States clearly point to additional pressing mental health needs. For example, there is genuine need for Hispanic psychologists to work with the rapidly expanding Hispanic population (Winerman, 2005). Similarly, there continues to be a long-standing need for psychologists in rural areas (Benson, 2003). Unfortunately, it is difficult to lure professionals from the urban centers to the more rural environments. The six goals established by the New Commission on Mental Health in 2003, in conjunction with these specific needs, will determine, to a large extent, the nature of mental health services in the United States in the coming decades.

**STUDY TIP**

Construct a timeline of the history of therapy from ancient Greek times through the present. Briefly describe each era in your timeline.

## Therapy and Therapists

Not everyone who seeks therapy suffers from a psychological disorder. Some people need help to cope with such lifestyle events as the loss of a job, school-related difficulties, or family disagreements. During a 1-year period, 28.1% of U.S. adults (about 50 million) would qualify for a diagnosis of some psychological disorder, and 14.7% received some mental health service (Bourdon et al., 1994). Of those people who had a disorder, however, only about 30% sought treatment (Figure 13-1). Of the people who sought treatment, 55% were suffering from a disorder. The remainder did not meet the diagnostic criteria for any psychological disorder during the year, although many had a previous disorder during their lifetimes. In any case, actual mental health services provided fall short of the potential need (Regier et al., 1998a,b).

What factors influence the decision to seek (or not to seek) mental health treatment? One key factor is the nature of the disorder. For example, the use of mental health services is high among people diagnosed with schizophrenia (64%), bipolar

**FIGURE 13-1** The annual prevalence of psychological disorders and treatment seeking. Only a small percentage of adults who had a psychological disorder sought some form of treatment; many people who sought mental health treatment did not have a psychological disorder.

**Source:** Bourdon et al. (1994).

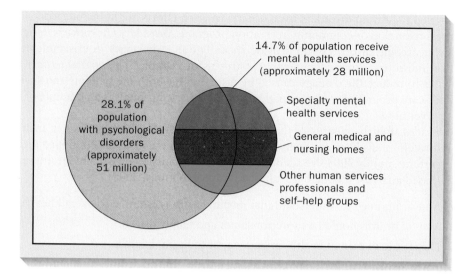

28.1% of population with psychological disorders (approximately 51 million)

14.7% of population receive mental health services (approximately 28 million)

Specialty mental health services

General medical and nursing homes

Other human services professionals and self–help groups

disorder (61%), and panic disorder (59%). By contrast, only 24% of individuals with a substance-use disorder seek help. In addition, people with multiple disorders are more likely to seek treatment (Regier et al., 1998a,b).

Where do people go to receive treatment? Most receive outpatient rather than inpatient treatment: 5% of patients receive inpatient care only, 10% receive a combination of inpatient (usually hospital) and outpatient treatment, and 85% are exclusively outpatients (Melton et al., 1997).

There are more than 400 different treatments for psychological disorders. These treatments can be divided into two broad categories: **biomedical therapies** and **psychological therapies.** The biomedical therapies use psychotropic drugs (drugs that affect the brain), electroconvulsive therapy, and psychosurgery to alter brain functioning and thus reduce symptoms. Psychological therapies range from "talk therapies" to treatments based on the principles of learning.

**Psychotherapy** is a general term that describes psychological treatments designed to help people resolve behavioral, emotional, and interpersonal problems and improve the quality of their lives (Prochaska & Norcross, 1999). The primary means of achieving these goals is for a therapist to engage a client in discussions and interactions. Some of these forms of therapy, often called *behavior therapy*, are based on the principles of classical conditioning, operant conditioning, and modeling (see Chapter 5).

**Types of Therapists.**     Members of several professions as well as paraprofessionals provide psychotherapeutic services. The term *therapist* encompasses a diverse group of people with different backgrounds. Included here are people with a master's or doctoral degree in psychology and people with a medical degree and special training in psychiatry, as well as self-designated psychotherapists (Nevid & Greene, 2001). Among the most common types of licensed psychotherapists are clinical and counseling psychologists, psychiatric nurses, psychiatrists, and social workers. Table 13-1 describes the qualifications and roles of these and other mental health professionals.

Although states regulate many mental health professions, they do not regulate practitioners like *psychotherapists* or *counselors.* Consequently, some practitioners who offer psychotherapeutic services may have little or no training. In addition, a state license does not guarantee that a therapist will have qualities such as empathy. Licensed therapists, however, are accountable to a professional licensing board for maintaining professional standards and keeping up with advances in knowledge through continuing education. Most health insurance policies that pay for psychotherapy require the services to be provided by licensed professionals (Erskine, 1998).

**biomedical therapies**
A set of treatments for mental illness that include drugs, psychosurgery, and electroconvulsive therapy

**psychological therapies**
Treatments for psychological disorders such as psychotherapy or therapies based on classical or operant conditioning principles

**psychotherapy**
A special relationship between a distressed person and a trained therapist in which the therapist aids the client in developing awareness and changing his or her thinking, feeling, and behavior

**TABLE 13-1**

## Types of Therapists and Their Training

| | |
|---|---|
| **Clinical psychologists** | Have earned a doctoral degree (Ph.D., Psy.D., or Ed.D.), which usually takes 4 or more years after an undergraduate degree. Their training includes completion of a dissertation based on research and a 1-year internship in a mental hospital or community mental health center. During their schooling, they take courses on the diagnosis and treatment of psychological disorders. They must meet state certification or licensing requirements that typically require doctoral training, an internship, a number of hours of supervised clinical work in addition to the internship, and a national licensing examination. |
| **Counselors** | Have a range of educational backgrounds, from a bachelor's degree to a doctorate. They may be members of the clergy (pastoral counselors) or professional educators; some counselors are trained to work with specific populations such as drug and alcohol abusers. Some people who identify themselves as counselors, however, have little formal training in providing psychotherapeutic services. |
| **Marriage and family therapists** | Usually, but not always, complete a 2-year master's program. Their training focuses on therapy with couples and families and is typically followed by 2 or more years of supervised work. These therapists are specially trained to deal with marital problems and child–parent conflicts. Some states license marriage and family therapists. |
| **Psychiatric nurses** | Are registered nurses who usually have earned a master's degree from a psychiatric nursing program, which usually takes about 2 years. Psychiatric nurses are especially proficient in evaluating the effects of a person's environment and physical functioning on his or her mental health status. |
| **Psychiatrists** | Are medical doctors (holders of an M.D.) who have completed a 3-year residency in psychiatry, usually in a psychiatric hospital or community mental health center. As physicians, they can prescribe drugs and hospitalize patients. They treat problems ranging from mild emotional problems to severe psychotic disorders. In addition to drug and other medical treatments, they can use a full range of individual and group psychotherapies; some psychiatrists also use behavior therapy. |
| **Psychoanalysts** | Often (but not always) hold an M.D. and have additional training in the psychoanalytic tradition of therapy developed by Sigmund Freud. A person without an M.D. can qualify as a psychoanalyst by completing the required training and undergoing psychoanalysis, a costly and time-consuming process. |
| **Social workers** | Constitute the largest group of professionals in the mental health field. Most have earned a master's degree in social work (M.S.W.), which usually takes 2 years of full-time study; a few social workers have earned a doctorate. Their course work includes practical experience (called *field placement*) in social work agencies or mental health facilities. As part of their training, they learn to use the services of agencies and groups to meet their clients' needs. They may direct clinics or have private practices. Licensing requirements vary from state to state. Psychiatric social workers specialize in treating mentally ill patients. |

# REVIEW SUMMARY

1. Throughout history, prevailing views of the causes of psychological disorders have influenced treatments. Some people believed in "possession" by evil spirits, so they used treatments such as exorcism. The ancient Greeks proposed natural causes and treatments.

2. Belief in demon possession was common during the 16th and 17th centuries. Some accused witches may have suffered from psychological disorders. Asylums and hospitals did not always provide a humane refuge for afflicted people.

3. Jean-Baptiste Pussin removed the chains from mental patients in France. Philippe Pinel and Benjamin Rush advocated kind treatment (moral therapy) of individuals with psychological disorders.

4. Dorothea Dix spearheaded a movement that led to state-operated custodial institutions. As state mental hospitals grew larger, however, their effectiveness declined.

5. The community mental health movement recommended community-based treatment and emphasized prevention. Use of drugs coupled with growing awareness of the ineffectiveness of large institutions led to a policy of **deinstitutionalization,** the release of patients from mental hospitals.

6. Many people who seek mental health treatment do not have a psychological disorder. About 30% of individuals with a psychological disorder seek treatment. Those with schizophrenia, bipolar disorder, or panic disorder are more likely to seek treatment than individuals with substance-use disorders.

**7.** There are two treatment categories for psychological disorders: **biomedical** and **psychological therapies. Psychotherapy** is a general term for psychological treatments designed to help people resolve behavioral, emotional, and interpersonal problems. Among the licensed practitioners who provide therapy for psychological disorders are clinical psychologists and psychiatrists.

## ✓ CHECK YOUR PROGRESS

**1.** How did the ancient Greeks view psychological disorders?

   **a.** They focused on the influence of the weather.

   **b.** Disorders in ancient Greece were viewed as punishment from the gods.

   **c.** They offered naturalistic explanations for the disorders.

   **d.** Disorders in ancient Greece were viewed as failures to live a life consistent with sound philosophical principles.

**2.** A student was asked to describe the treatment approach called *moral management*. Which of the following would be the best brief description?

   **a.** Provide a humane and relaxed environment, and patients will recover.

   **b.** Focus on a person's failure to live a moral and ethical life.

   **c.** Strict discipline from morning to night is the path to a sound mind.

   **d.** Patients need to accept a set of philosophical principles for any treatment to be successful.

**3.** A group of students is asked to develop a vignette about the life and accomplishments of Dorothea Dix. Which of the following is likely to be included in that vignette?

   **a.** She is ministering to those she believes are possessed by demons.

   **b.** She meets with state legislators to convince them to approve funds for mental hospitals.

   **c.** She is shown removing chains from patients housed in hospitals throughout the United States.

   **d.** She is being interviewed for a newspaper article focused on her beliefs about the genetic causes of mental illness.

**4.** What factors led to significant reductions in the number of hospitalized mental patients beginning in the 1950s?

**5.** What factor began the policy of deinstitutionalization in the United States?

   **a.** psychoanalysis

   **b.** drug treatments

   **c.** electroshock treatment

   **d.** new forms of psychotherapy

**6.** Identify the type of therapist (clinical psychologist, psychiatrist, social worker, counselor, marriage and family therapist, psychoanalyst) described in each of the following:

   **a.** Prescribes drugs for the symptoms of anxiety

   **b.** Has undergone personal therapy and strives to uncover unconscious conflicts that are believed to cause distress

   **c.** Completed an internship at a community mental health center, earned a Ph.D., and currently maintains a private practice

**7.** The community mental health movement placed the greatest emphasis on

   **a.** preventing mental illness.

   **b.** training competent therapists.

   **c.** finding suitable locations for mental hospitals.

   **d.** reducing crime as an indirect means of treating mental illness.

**8.** A group of women who have been victims of rape establish a crisis line for rape victims. What type of prevention program does this crisis line represent?

   **a.** primary

   **b.** tertiary

   **c.** secondary

   **d.** fundamental

**9.** Which mental health professional would have a medical degree?

   **a.** psychiatrist

   **b.** psychiatric nurse

   **c.** clinical psychologist

   **d.** psychiatric social worker

**ANSWERS: 1.** c **2.** a **3.** b **4.** The availability of new drug therapies made it possible to reduce the symptoms experienced by some patients and allow them to leave hospitals. **5.** b **6.** a. psychiatrist **b.** psychoanalyst **c.** clinical psychologist **7.** a **8.** c **9.** a

# PSYCHOLOGICALLY BASED THERAPIES

Curita is overwhelmed with doubt, does not sleep well, cannot relax, and feels isolated from friends and co-workers. For more than a year, she has realized that something has been "wrong." After deciding to see a psychotherapist, she begins to wonder what therapy will be like. She recalls the bewildering array of therapies discussed in the psychology course she took 3 years ago. *What are the common forms of psychotherapy?*

Some forms of psychotherapy focus on individuals; others focus on groups. In some forms of therapy the therapist is quite active; in others the therapist is more passive. Some psychotherapies try to help clients develop insight into their troubling behavior; others aim squarely at changing the client's distressing behaviors. Although it is convenient to distinguish among various forms of psychotherapy, clinical psychologists are increasingly using elements of different therapeutic approaches in treating their clients (see Figure 13-2). The use of components from several therapies is called an *eclectic* or *integrative* approach. Because of the complexities of each client and his or her unique problems, the integrative approach has gained popularity (Corey, 2001). Managed care and insurance companies have recently impacted therapy because these agencies can determine the kind(s) of therapy and the number of sessions that a client receives (West et al., 2003). Most forms of psychotherapy have two key characteristics. First, psychotherapy is a special relationship between a distressed person and a trained therapist. The relationship is special because the therapist tries to create an atmosphere in which the distressed person feels comfortable expressing important and often confidential information. Second, therapists help their clients develop awareness and bring about changes in their behavior, feeling, and thinking (Prochaska & Norcross, 1999).

## Psychoanalytic Therapy

Several of the forms of psychotherapy used in the United States can be traced to Sigmund Freud, who developed **psychoanalytic therapy** near the end of the 19th century. As we saw in Chapter 11, Freud contended that the symptoms of psychological disorders are due to unconscious feelings and conflicts, especially those involving sexual or aggressive urges that conflict with societal prohibitions. This view of psychological disorders called for a new treatment approach that could uncover unconscious feelings and conflicts that were protected by defense mechanisms (Sundberg et al., 2002). Freud searched for ways to probe beneath the surface of a patient's conscious feelings and thoughts. This probing not only proved to be time-consuming and painstaking, but it also required the development of special therapeutic techniques and processes that are the hallmarks of psychoanalytic therapy. We discuss four of these processes: free association, dream interpretation, resistance, and transference.

**Free Association.** After Freud graduated from medical school, he became interested in using hypnosis as a technique for treating his patients. While treating a patient suffering from a conversion disorder (see Chapter 12) who could not be hypnotized, he found that free association could be used to recall the repressed memories he believed to be at the heart of the disorder. In **free association**, patients are asked to relate thoughts, feelings, or images without modifying them in any way. Psychoanalysts believe that in freely discussing their feelings, patients will reveal unconscious thoughts, fears, and desires.

The operation of various defense mechanisms makes it difficult to see connections between a patient's current problems and what is revealed during free association. However, free association provides clues that psychoanalysts use to help their patients identify hidden conflicts. As the clues are revealed, the therapist asks questions or offers suggestions that are designed to help the patient gain insight into these unconscious conflicts.

**Dream Interpretation.** Freud called dreams "the royal road to the unconscious" and distinguished between two forms of dream content: manifest and latent (see Chapter 4). *Manifest content* is the dream you recall when you awaken; *latent content* is the underlying meaning of that dream. The manifest content is a disguised version of the latent content of the dream. The psychoanalyst's task is to interpret dreams by discovering the latent content. Consider a man's dream of riding in the back seat of a car

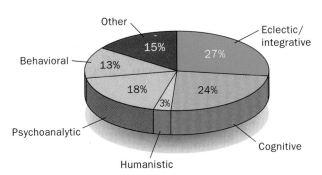

**FIGURE 13-2** The primary theoretical orientations of clinical psychologists. More therapists now use elements from different therapeutic approaches in their work.

**Source:** Adapted from Norcross, Karg-Bray, and Prochaska (1995).

**psychoanalytic therapy**
Treatment of maladaptive behavior developed by Sigmund Freud; its goal is to uncover unconscious conflicts and feelings and bring them to the conscious level

**free association**
A psychoanalytic technique in which the patient is asked to say whatever comes to mind without censoring anything

The setting of psychoanalytic therapy was conceived to foster free association. Note how the therapist sits out of the patient's line of vision.

discovering the latent content. Consider a man's dream of riding in the back seat of a car driven by another man; this is the manifest content. Like an archaeologist, the psychoanalyst tries to uncover the deeper (latent) meaning of the dream. One possible interpretation of this dream is that the man wants someone (most likely his father) to stop running his life.

**Resistance.** Freud used free association to ask patients to report whatever came to mind without censoring anything. An uninterrupted flow of words, thoughts, and images spilled forth, but often the flow was halted. Why? Freud believed that the patient was coming closer to significant information that needed to be uncovered if the therapy was to succeed. **Resistance** occurs during free association when the patient's flow of words and thoughts stops. The cessation of associations might indicate that the defense mechanism of repression is operating to protect the ego from the anxiety generated by the thoughts and feelings revealed through the associations.

**Transference.** People undergoing psychoanalytic therapy often reveal highly confidential and emotionally wrenching information to someone who just a short time earlier was a complete stranger. The bond that often develops between the patient and the therapist can foster strong feelings. Sometimes during psychoanalysis a patient transfers feelings about a significant person (such as a parent or sibling) to the psychoanalyst. The psychoanalyst thus becomes a screen onto which a patient projects feelings about other people. The psychoanalyst searches for the meaning of this **transference** because it is one more clue to the conflicts in a person's life. In *countertransference* the psychoanalyst transfers feelings to the client. This transfer is based on the psychoanalyst's responses to significant persons in his or her life.

**Evaluation of Psychoanalysis.** One problem that researchers of psychoanalytic therapy face is the difficulty of defining the essential elements of the treatment and knowing when they are present. For example, how does a researcher investigate whether a patient has gained insight into unconscious conflicts? If the therapist interprets a statement by the patient, does the patient's acceptance of that interpretation constitute support for the effectiveness of psychoanalytic therapy? Suppose the patient rejects the psychoanalyst's interpretation. Does this mean that the therapy is not working or the patient is resisting the analysis?

The psychoanalytic approach assumes that if a symptom is addressed before the patient can deal with it effectively, new symptoms will appear in its place because the basic underlying conflict or feeling was not resolved. Despite this belief, the evidence suggests that *symptom substitution* does not typically occur.

Although traditional psychoanalytic therapy is costly and may require therapy sessions 5 days a week, sometimes for years, a newer form, *brief psychodynamic therapy*, only requires between 4 and 25 sessions (Peretz, 2004). Thus psychoanalytic therapy seems to be more suited to clients with less serious problems, especially those who have been described as *yavis*—young, attractive, verbal, intelligent, and successful. Psychoanalytic therapy is not effective with patients who have lost contact with reality, as in schizophrenia.

## Humanistic Therapies

In contrast to psychoanalytic therapies, **humanistic therapies** emphasize the here and now, the subjective interpretation of experience, and the human capacity for self-determination (Oltmanns & Emery, 2001). Humanistic therapies seek to reduce blocks to growth that can create a poor self-concept. Humanistic therapists believe that clients who are more accepting will be better able to solve their own problems.

**Client-Centered Therapy.** Early in his career, Carl Rogers (1902–1987) practiced psychoanalysis, but his growing dissatisfaction with that form of therapy led him to

**resistance**
A stage of psychoanalysis in which blocking of free association occurs because critical unconscious material is close to conscious awareness

**transference**
In psychoanalysis, the patient's positive or negative reaction to the therapist, which is believed to reflect the patient's relationship to a significant person outside of therapy

**humanistic therapies**
Therapies that emphasize the present and the ability of clients to solve their own problems once they are able to accept themselves

create a radically different approach. Rather than delving into unconscious conflicts, Rogers's **client-centered therapy** focuses on the conscious level.

According to Rogers, personal problems can develop when a person's ideal self differs from his or her real self (see Chapter 11). These discrepancies can occur if a person trusts other people's evaluations rather than his or her own. Rogers steadfastly believed in the innate goodness of human beings and saw people as capable of curing themselves, provided that they were in the right environment—one that was caring and accepting. The goal of client-centered therapy is to provide just such an environment (Rogers, 1957).

Client-centered therapists are guided by several assumptions (Patterson, 1985):

1. People are basically good and possess an innate drive toward self-actualization.

2. Clients can assume responsibility for themselves. Therapists do not initiate therapy, ask questions, give advice, or encourage clients to make certain choices. They respond to the client, and this responsiveness helps the client develop self-understanding. Consequently, this form of therapy is often called *nondirective therapy.*

3. Clients can resolve their own problems within a facilitating relationship.

4. The therapist's basic attitude is deep respect for the client as a person of worth. This is known as *unconditional positive regard.*

The key to successful client-centered therapy is the therapist's ability to create an environment in which the client feels accepted and able to find solutions to his or her problems. Client-centered therapists create such an environment by demonstrating unconditional positive regard, empathy, and genuineness in their sessions.

Therapists show unconditional positive regard by not evaluating, judging, or criticizing. They listen to the client without interrupting. Sitting back, listening, and not offering advice may be difficult for some therapists; however, the act of offering advice conveys the message that the client cannot solve problems without outside help. Client-centered therapists also show *empathy*—sensing how the client feels at every moment. Finally, the therapist must be *genuine* and not put on airs or try to be something he or she is not.

The following dialogue demonstrates how client-centered therapy proceeds. Note how the therapist reflects the message and emotion heard from the client and does not direct the flow of the conversation or ask questions.

> *Client:* I'm feeling lousy today.
>
> *Therapist:* You're feeling pretty bad.
>
> *Client:* Yeah. I'm really ticked about something, and that made me feel bad. But I can't do much about it; I think I've got to live with it.
>
> *Therapist:* You're angry and feel like there's nothing you can safely do with your feelings.
>
> *Client:* Uh-huh. If I yell at my boss, he yells back even louder. If I don't speak up, he continues to get on my case.
>
> *Therapist:* You feel like you're between a rock and a hard place. No matter what, you end up feeling bad.

**Gestalt Therapy.** The psychoanalyst Fritz Perls (1893–1970) made revisions in psychoanalytic therapy that developed into **Gestalt therapy,** which focuses on emotions and feelings. Perls believed that psychological difficulties can develop when people are unwilling to accept or express themselves because they are avoiding their real selves. This lack of self-awareness, coupled with a fear of other people's judgments, causes people to behave defensively. The primary goal of therapy is therefore to increase awareness and self-acceptance. Like client-centered therapy, Gestalt therapy focuses on

Carl Rogers developed client-centered therapy, which is designed to establish an environment in which individuals can solve their own problems. To create this environment the therapist demonstrates unconditional positive regard for clients, is genuine, and demonstrates empathy.

MOB PSYCHOLOGIST

"*So, while extortion, racketeering, and murder may be bad acts, they don't make you a bad person.*"

Could this therapist be expressing unconditional positive regard?

**client-centered therapy**
Therapy designed to create an environment in which the client is able to find solutions to his or her problems

**Gestalt therapy**
A humanistic form of therapy developed by Fritz Perls in which therapists may frustrate and challenge clients to lead them toward self-acceptance

the present. Unlike client-centered therapists, however, Gestalt therapists will confront, frustrate, or challenge their clients' beliefs and feelings. They offer opinions or hunches about what a client is experiencing while also providing support as the client discovers what he or she feels and needs (Oltmanns & Emery, 2001). Gestalt therapists look for nonverbal clues that may reveal hidden feelings and then dramatize the clients' feelings by having them sit in different chairs to play various "parts" of themselves, such as a guilty conscience or a resentful but submissive child. By making these parts obvious, the therapist helps the client bring them into harmony.

Although their methodologies differ in some ways, client-centered therapy and Gestalt therapy share the common goal of helping clients develop greater personal insights. The number of therapists who practice either of these forms of humanistic therapy is small (Norcross, Karg-Bray, & Prochaska, 1995). As we shall see, however, client-centered therapy has made a major contribution in identifying some of the conditions conducive to effective therapy.

## Cognitive Therapies

Gayle is so upset with her therapist that she storms into the office of the director of the community mental health center. "All she does is question me and make me feel stupid," she complains. "I didn't come here to be made to feel like a fool." The director explains that the therapist is using one of the **cognitive therapies,** called *rational-emotive behavior therapy*, which is quite different from other therapies and is clearly different from Gayle's expectations. In these therapies, cognitions (thoughts and beliefs) hold the keys to understanding psychological disorders; these therapies have been quite effective in treating phobias and depression and in helping patients cope with medical procedures.

The goal of cognitive therapy is to change distorted cognitions in order to eliminate maladaptive behaviors. The cognitive therapist's targets are the client's thoughts and beliefs, which are more accessible than the unconscious feelings and conflicts that psychoanalysts seek to uncover. Compared with the methods used by client-centered therapists, a cognitive therapist's techniques are quite directive. Although the targets of cognitive therapy are closer to the surface, clients may not recognize these things until they are asked to confront their thought patterns.

**Rational-Emotive Behavior Therapy.** A basic assumption of **rational-emotive behavior therapy** is that our emotional responses are an outgrowth of our cognitions (Ellis & Tafrate, 1997). This principle is not new. It was proposed centuries ago by the Greek philosopher Epictetus, who said, "What disturbs people's minds is not events but their judgments of events." Shakespeare made the point in *Hamlet:* "There's nothing either good or bad but thinking makes it so."

The pioneer of rational-emotive behavior therapy, Albert Ellis (1987), describes the basis for this therapy: "I have stubbornly held the near-pollyannaish position that humans largely disturb themselves" (p. 364). To illustrate, suppose you see a job advertised in the newspaper and become excited because you feel it is the perfect job for you. With great anticipation, you apply for the job. You expect the phone to ring, but 3 weeks later, a letter arrives announcing that your perfect job was offered to someone else. You are devastated.

Ellis argues that failing to get that job should not in itself make you unhappy or depressed. If, however, you interpret the situation as being due to lack of ability on your part, you are on your way to inappropriate negative consequences. You could recognize that there were hundreds of applicants for the job and that not getting it is not a reflection on your ability. What's more, the employer will not have the benefit of your hard work. Now you may feel very different about the same event.

Rational-emotive behavior therapy is understood best in terms of what Ellis calls the *ABC framework* (see Figure 13-3). *A* represents an *activating* event related to an important desire, goal, or preference (getting the job, in our example); *B* is the *belief*, usually related to failure to attain the goal, that follows the activating event ("I'm no

**cognitive therapies**
Therapies designed to change cognitions in order to eliminate maladaptive behaviors

**rational-emotive behavior therapy**
A cognitive therapy in which the therapist challenges and questions the client's irrational ideas

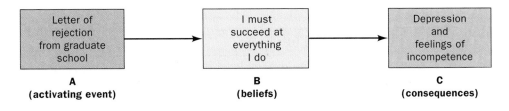

**A**
(activating event)

**B**
(beliefs)

**C**
(consequences)

**FIGURE 13-3** The ABC framework, the cornerstone of rational-emotive behavior therapy practice.

good because I didn't get the job"). That belief determines *C, consequences*, such as feelings of anger, anxiety, and depression.

According to Ellis, we hold a large number of irrational beliefs that interfere with our ability to perceive events clearly and often lead to negative feelings. Irrational beliefs often take the form of dogmatic *shoulds, oughts, musts, commands,* and *demands:* "If you understand how you upset yourself by slipping into irrational shoulds, oughts, demands, and commands, unconsciously sneaking them into your thinking, you can just about always stop disturbing yourself about anything" (Ellis, 1990, p. 17). Several irrational beliefs that Ellis identified on the basis of his clinical experience are listed in Table 13-2.

Rational-emotive behavior therapy is a very active, directive form of psychotherapy. A glimpse of it is captured in the following dialogue taken from one of Ellis's sessions:

> *Client:* I don't know! I'm not thinking clearly at the moment. I'm too nervous!
>
> *Ellis:* Well, but you can think clearly. Are you saying, "It's hopeless! I can't think clearly"? You see you're blaming yourself.
>
> *Client:* (*visibly upset, can't seem to say anything and then nods*)
>
> *Ellis:* No! You'll never get better unless you think. And you're saying, "Can't we do something magical to get me better?" And the answer is No! (Ellis, 1973, p. 186)

**Beck's Cognitive Therapy.** Aaron Beck has devoted a lifetime to treating psychological disorders, especially depression. Beck notes that depressed people have negative views of their world, themselves, and their future—called the *cognitive triad.* They often interpret events in ways that lead to self-blame, and they also rely on cognitive distortions that can maintain their negative views. These distorted interpretations and errors are fueled by automatic thoughts (negative sentences repeated to oneself) that occur despite their being contrary to objective reality (Beck, 1979).

## TABLE 13-2

### Examples of Irrational Beliefs Described by Albert Ellis

| Focus | Irrational Belief |
|---|---|
| **Competence and success** | "Because I strongly desire to perform important tasks competently and successfully, I absolutely must perform them well (and am an inadequate, incompetent person if I don't)." |
| **Love and approval** | "Because I strongly desire to be approved of by people I find significant, I absolutely must have their approval (and am an unlovable and worthless person if I do not)." |
| **Fair treatment** | "Because I strongly desire people to treat me considerately and fairly, they absolutely must do so (and they are evil, damnable people who deserve to be severely condemned and punished when they don't)." |
| **Safety and comfort** | "Because I strongly desire to have a safe, comfortable, and satisfying life, the conditions under which I live absolutely must be easy, convenient, and gratifying (and it is awful, I can't bear it, and can't be happy at all when they are unsafe and frustrating)." |

**Source:** Ellis (1987).

## TABLE 13-3

### Typical Cognitive Distortions Treated with Cognitive Therapies

| Distortion | Definition | Example |
|---|---|---|
| Arbitrary inference | Drawing an erroneous conclusion without sufficient evidence | When your hairdresser suggests you try a new hairstyle, you assume he or she believes you are becoming older-looking and unattractive. |
| Selective abstraction | Taking a detail out of context and using it to misrepresent the entire experience | A politician gives a rousing speech at a rally but mispronounces one word in the 30-minute talk. She concludes, "There's proof that I'm not cut out to be a political leader." |
| Overgeneralization | Drawing a general conclusion on the basis of a single incident | A student fails the first quiz of his college career and concludes that "I'm just not college material." |
| Magnification and minimization | Altering the significance of specific events in a way that yields negative interpretations | The significance of a success may be minimized (a good grade is considered trivial because the exam was easy), and the significance of a failure is maximized (losing a tennis match is seen as evidence that you will never succeed at anything). |

**Sources:** Andreasen and Black (1995).

*Automatic thoughts* arise quickly and are perceived as plausible. Although they are frequently followed by unpleasant emotions, we are generally not aware of their influence on our emotional reactions (Beck, 1991). After their attention was directed to such thoughts, Beck's clients reported a variety of automatic thoughts, such as "I'm not capable of having any friends," that can intervene between outside events and a person's emotional reactions. These thoughts are repeated so often that they become part of the way the person thinks.

Other cognitive distortions include *selective abstraction* and *overgeneralization* (see Table 13-3). Someone who focuses only on the negative aspects of an event and ignores the positive details is relying on selective abstraction. For example, a student who becomes depressed because he focuses on a single error in an otherwise excellent term paper is using selective abstraction. Overgeneralization occurs when a person makes a generalization based on limited information.

### Psychological Detective

Take a moment to reflect on a situation that is probably close to home. Throughout your years in school, you have taken a number of tests. Think about an example of overgeneralization that might follow your receipt of a poor grade on an exam.

After receiving a poor grade, you may conclude, "I am just not college material" and "There is no use trying; I'm going to fail at everything I do." If your conclusions are similar to these, then your thought processes reveal overgeneralization. You have taken a single incident and exaggerated its significance for your life.

Beck's goal is to have the depressed person consider these automatic thoughts and cognitive distortions from a more scientific perspective. The following dialogue (adapted from Young, Beck, & Weinberger, 1993, pp. 263–264) provides a glimpse of this form of therapy:

> **Therapist:** Let's do an experiment and see if you can respond to the automatic thought and then let's see what happens to your feeling. See if responding rationally makes you feel worse or makes you feel better. Okay, why didn't I answer that question right?

*Client:* Why didn't I answer that question right? Because I thought for a second that that was what I was supposed to say, and then when I heard the question over again, then I realized that was not what I heard. I didn't hear the question right, that's why I didn't answer it right.

*Therapist:* Okay, so that is the situation. And so is the situation that you look dumb or you just didn't hear the question right?

*Client:* I didn't hear the question right.

*Therapist:* Or is it possible that I didn't say the question in such a way that it was clear? I'm not perfect, so it's very possible that I didn't express the question properly.

*Client:* But instead of saying you made a mistake, I would still say I made a mistake.

*Therapist:* We'll have to watch the video and see. Whichever. Does it mean if I didn't express the question, if I made a mistake, does it make me dumb?

*Client:* No.

*Therapist:* And if you made the mistake, does it make you dumb?

*Client:* No, not really.

*Therapist:* But you felt dumb?

*Client:* But I did, yeah.

*Therapist:* Do you feel dumb still?

*Client:* No.

Psychologists Steven Hollon, Richard Shelton, and Peter Loosen (1991) reviewed research comparing cognitive therapy to drug therapy for depression. They concluded that cognitive therapy is at least as effective as antidepressant drugs. What's more, cognitive therapy may prevent the return of depression after the completion of treatment if it helps clients learn new coping skills that can be useful in warding off the return of symptoms.

## Hands On

### Assertiveness Questionnaire

This questionnaire can be used to assess your level of assertiveness. Psychologists use such scales to screen people for possible instruction in assertiveness training. Many people experience difficulty in handling interpersonal situations requiring them to assert themselves in some way—for example, turning down a request, asking a favor, giving someone a compliment, expressing disapproval or approval. Lack of assertiveness is a common problem that is treated with the cognitive and behavioral therapies we are discussing. Use the following scale to indicate your degree of discomfort or anxiety in the space provided for each situation listed below. When you are finished, you might want to compare your score with the class average.

1 = none     2 = a little     3 = a fair amount     4 = much     5 = very much

1. Turn down a request to borrow your car        _____
2. Compliment a friend        _____
3. Ask a favor of someone        _____
4. Resist sales pressure        _____
5. Apologize when you are at fault        _____
6. Turn down a request for a meeting or date        _____
7. Admit fear and request consideration        _____

8. Tell a person you are intimately involved with, when he/she says or does something that bothers you _____

9. Ask for a raise _____

10. Admit ignorance in some areas _____

11. Turn down a request to borrow money _____

12. Ask personal questions _____

13. Turn off a talkative friend _____

14. Ask for a constructive criticism _____

15. Initiate a conversation with a stranger _____

16. Compliment a person you are romantically involved with or interested in _____

17. Request a meeting or a date with a person _____

18. Your initial request for a meeting is turned down and you ask the person again at a later time _____

19. Admit confusion about a point under discussion and ask for clarification _____

20. Apply for a job _____

21. Ask whether you have offended someone _____

22. Tell someone that you like them _____

23. Request expected service when such is not forthcoming (for example, in a restaurant) _____

24. Discuss openly with the person his/her criticism of your behavior _____

25. Return defective items (for example, store or restaurant) _____

26. Express an opinion that differs from that of the person you are talking to _____

27. Resist sexual overtures when you are not interested _____

28. Tell the person when you feel he/she has done something that is unfair to you _____

29. Accept a date _____

30. Tell someone good news about yourself _____

31. Resist pressure to drink _____

32. Resist a significant person's unfair demands _____

33. Quit a job _____

34. Resist pressure to use drugs _____

35. Discuss openly with a person his/her criticism of your work _____

36. Request the return of a borrowed item _____

37. Receive compliments _____

38. Continue to converse with someone who disagrees with you _____

39. Tell a friend or someone with whom you work when he/she says or does something that bothers you _____

40. Ask a person who is annoying you in a public situation to stop _____

**Source:** Gambrill and Richey (1975).

**STUDY TIP**

Gather in an even-numbered group and designate pairs. Write on same-sized, folded pieces of paper the following therapies:

• Psychoanalytic therapy

• Client-centered therapy

• Gestalt therapy

• Rational-emotive behavior therapy

• Beck's cognitive therapy

• Stress inoculation training

Each pair should choose one or two slips of paper and keep the contents hidden from the other pairs. Pairs should take ten minutes to huddle and create a short skit to demonstrate the therapy or therapies that they have chosen—one person acts as a therapist, the other as a client. Pairs then take turns performing their skits to the others who are challenged to guess what therapy is being portrayed and say what about the skit represents that particular therapy.

# Behavior Therapies

Behavior therapists do not delve into unconscious conflicts derived from early experiences; instead they focus on current factors such as reinforcers that are maintaining maladaptive behaviors. The terms *behavior modification* and *behavior therapy* are sometimes used interchangeably to describe techniques based on the principles of classical conditioning, operant conditioning, and modeling. Behavior modification is the broader of the two; it covers the application of behavioral techniques to behaviors in nonclinical settings. For example, behavior modification might include programs to reduce littering or increase the use of seat belts. Behavior therapy involves application of behavioral principles to change maladaptive behaviors, often in clinical settings.

Most behavioral techniques derive from the work of well-known psychologists such as John B. Watson and B. F. Skinner. Among the most frequently used behavioral techniques are systematic desensitization, aversion therapy, modeling, extinction, punishment, and the token economy.

**Systematic Desensitization.**   John B. Watson and Rosalie Rayner (1920) used the case of Little Albert, described in Chapter 5, to demonstrate how classical conditioning principles could be used to create an emotional response (phobia). Mary Cover Jones (1924) used a technique called *counterconditioning* to reduce a young child's fear of a rabbit. Jones presented the child, Peter, with his favorite food. Then she slowly inched a caged rabbit closer to the child. Eventually the pleasant feelings evoked by the food became associated with the rabbit, and the child's fear diminished. Today counterconditioning of phobias has been replaced by techniques such as **systematic desensitization,** which was developed by the psychiatrist Joseph Wolpe in the 1950s.

The first step in systematic desensitization is to find a procedure that counters the anxiety people experience when they confront feared objects such as snakes. Hypnosis, biofeedback, and even drugs have been used to counter the anxiety, but the most popular choice is progressive relaxation (see Chapter 14). Instruction in progressive relaxation during the first few therapy sessions, accompanied by practice outside of the sessions, enables most people to reach a state of calm that they may not have known they could achieve.

There are two versions of systematic desensitization: *in vivo* (real-life) *graduated exposure* to the feared stimuli and *imaginal graduated exposure*. In either case, the client and therapist work together to construct a list of scenes related to the phobic object or situation. An example of a scene related to ophidiophobia (fear of snakes) is looking up the word *snake* in a dictionary and reading the definition. Here's another possible scene: walking into a room with a dozen snakes on the floor and hearing the door lock behind you. The scenes are arranged in a hierarchy, starting with one that arouses no fear and progressing to one that causes great fear (see Table 13-4).

## Psychological Detective

How could psychologists combine progressive relaxation with scenes related to a particular phobia to reduce the fear? Give this question some thought, and write down a procedure that you think might work.

In imaginal graduated exposure the relaxed client is asked to imagine one scene at a time, starting with the scene that arouses no anxiety. Then the client moves through the hierarchy to scenes that create more and more anxiety (see Figure 13-4). During systematic desensitization, it is quite likely that the client will experience some degree of anxiety as the scenes are imagined. When this happens, the therapist returns to the instructions for relaxation to ensure that the client is completely relaxed before proceeding. The client does not proceed to the next scene in the hierarchy until he or she is able to maintain a relaxed state while imagining the current one. Thus the client slowly learns to

**systematic desensitization**
A behavioral technique, based on classical conditioning, that is used to treat phobias; the technique usually combines training in relaxation with exposure to imagined scenes related to a phobia

**aversion therapy**
Classical conditioning technique for reducing or eliminating behavior by pairing the behavior with an unpleasant (aversive) stimulus

---

**TABLE 13-4**

## Systematic Desensitization Hierarchy Used in Treating the Fear of Flying

The scenes are listed in order, starting with the one that causes the least fear and ending with the one that causes the greatest fear.

The plane has landed and stopped at the terminal.

A trip has been planned, and I have decided to travel by plane.

I call a travel agent for times and flight numbers.

I pack my suitcase the day before the trip.

On the day of the flight, I am leaving home. I lock the door, put the bags in the car, and check my tickets.

As I drive to the airport, I am aware of many planes.

With my bags in hand, I enter the terminal.

I walk to the counter, wait in line, and have the agent check my ticket and bags.

I am waiting in the lounge for my flight to be called over the intercom.

After hearing my flight number called, I proceed to the security checkpoint.

I walk down the ramp leading to the plane and enter the door of the plane.

I walk down the aisle and sit down in my assigned seat.

The plane is in flight, and I decide to walk to the restroom.

I notice that the seat belt signs are illuminated and the pilot announces that we are preparing to land.

The plane is descending to the runway for a landing.

**Source:** Adapted from Martin and Pear (1996, p. 341).

---

**FIGURE 13-4** The components of systematic desensitization. Individuals with a phobia are often very anxious when they think about or are near the feared object (1). The purpose of systematic desensitization is to replace the symptoms of anxiety with a relaxed state while the individuals contemplate scenes that have caused significant anxiety (2, 3). After treatment, many individuals can approach the previously feared stimulus (4).

associate relaxation with scenes related to the phobias as he or she proceeds through the list to the scene that arouses the greatest fear. Eventually the fear is markedly reduced or completely eliminated and is replaced with more relaxed feelings.

In conducting systematic desensitization, therapists now rely more on real objects than on imagined scenes because greater fear reduction is achieved with real objects (Sarason & Sarason, 2002). Although there is debate about the theoretical explanation of the success of systematic desensitization, there is little doubt that it is very effective in reducing a number of phobias.

**Aversion Therapy.** Aversion therapy uses unpleasant or painful stimuli such as electrical shock, nausea-inducing drugs, or repugnant tastes or smells to decrease unwanted behavior. Aversion therapy is based on classical conditioning principles; it involves the repeated pairing of a problem behavior with an aversive stimulus. For example, in treating alcoholism, a person is given a drug, Antabuse (disulfiram), that will induce nausea. Just before the drug takes effect, the person is given a sip of an alcoholic beverage (see Figure 13-5). Thus the sight, smell, and taste of the drink are followed by nausea. This pairing of alcohol with the nausea-inducing drug is repeated over several sessions. Eventually the alcohol itself elicits nausea, which may cause the person to avoid alcohol in the future. One problem with this treatment occurs when unsupervised clients fail to take the Antabuse, thus reducing the chances for successful treatment. One form of aversion therapy, *covert sensitization*, involves having clients visualize or imagine adverse consequences that might accompany unwanted behavior.

Aversion therapy has been used to reduce and sometimes eliminate cigarette smoking, overeating, alcoholism, and sexual deviations such as exhibitionism. Because this procedure involves aversive stimulation, only qualified personnel should carry it out to guard against potential side effects (Martin & Pear, 2003).

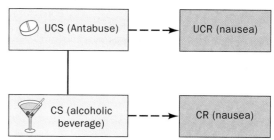

**FIGURE 13-5** Aversion therapy for alcoholics. The repeated pairing of an alcoholic drink with the nausea induced by the drug Antabuse may reduce the desire to continue drinking. Some courts have sentenced convicted drunk drivers who have a serious problem with alcohol to undergo this form of treatment.

**Modeling.** One of the most effective techniques for treating phobias is *modeling*, or observational learning (see Chapter 5). Modeling is so common in our everyday behavior that we may miss its potential as a therapeutic technique. In this procedure a person—live or on videotape—demonstrates gradual contact with the feared object under controlled or protected circumstances. The client observes these behaviors and is given the opportunity to engage in similar behaviors. In one version, called *participant modeling*, a therapist model encourages and guides the client in taking a progressively more active role in interacting with the anxiety-provoking stimuli. Albert Bandura (1977) has explained the success of this therapy as the result of providing experiences that enhance perceptions of self-efficacy.

**Extinction.** Recall from Chapter 5 that *extinction* occurs when reinforcers that maintained an undesired behavior no longer follow that behavior. Under these circumstances, the frequency of the behavior is likely to drop to zero. The speed with which a behavior is extinguished, however, depends on the schedule of reinforcement and the amount of reinforcement that maintained the behavior in the past. As noted in Chapter 5, intermittent or partial reinforcement schedules and larger reinforcements result in greater resistance to extinction.

Richard Foxx (1982) described the use of extinction in the case of Bruce, an institutionalized, severely retarded adolescent who constantly demanded his instructors' attention. Bruce did almost anything to gain their attention, including exposing himself.

## Psychological Detective

Suppose you are one of Bruce's instructors. What would you and your fellow instructors do to extinguish this inappropriate behavior?

To extinguish a behavior, you must know what reinforcer is maintaining it. Bruce's instructors were convinced that their attention maintained this behavior. Before making any efforts to extinguish the behavior, they recorded the frequency of the behavior for 1 week and found that Bruce engaged in the behavior about 14 times a day. Then they agreed that they would not look at or speak to Bruce when he exposed himself. Instead they guided him in raising his pants without speaking to or looking at him directly. On the first day of extinction training Bruce exposed himself 30 times; on the second day he began having temper tantrums, likely due to frustration; on the third day he exposed himself 40 times. Nevertheless, the instructors continued their extinction efforts; 2 1/2 weeks later, Bruce stopped exposing himself.

**Punishment.** Another procedure used by behavior therapists is punishment, which can be either the withdrawal of a positive stimulus (such as candy) or event or the presentation of a negative stimulus or event (such as an electric shock). As noted in Chapter 5, when used as a technique for altering maladaptive behaviors, punishment can have serious shortcomings and is not always effective. What's more, ethical and legal considerations mandate that less distressing forms of treatment be tried before punishment is

**token economy**

A technique that reinforces desirable behaviors with tokens (secondary reinforcers), which can be redeemed for other reinforcers, especially primary reinforcers

considered. Nevertheless, some serious maladaptive behaviors are so resistant to change that punishment may be used as a last resort. Consider the following case:

> Susan, a profoundly retarded child, hit her face with her fist four or five times a minute, 3,000 times a day. Drug treatment reduced the hitting, but when Susan began to cry frequently, the neurologist reduced the medication. The hitting increased, and the crying remained. Increased doses and trials of other drugs did not alter the behavior. When psychologists found that various behavioral techniques such as extinction had been tried and failed, they wired Susan's legs so she would receive electrical shocks when she hit herself. On the first day, Susan hit herself 45 times compared to the usual 3,000 times. The rate of hitting dropped to 6 hits a day, and the apparatus was removed. During the next 5 years, Susan hit herself 250 times compared to the 5 million hits she might have delivered. (Prochaska & Norcross, 1999, pp. 284–285)

In Chapter 5 we discussed several factors that influence the effectiveness of punishment in reducing behaviors. One of these factors was evident in this case: delivery of the punishment *each* time Susan hit herself. Susan did not find hitting herself to be aversive, but when control of a punisher was in the therapist's hands, it became aversive.

**Token Economy.**    A number of patients in mental hospitals, especially the larger and more impersonal ones, tend to lose their social skills. Everyday social skills such as knowing how to greet another person and respond when spoken to are necessary for getting along outside the hospital. Psychologists have found that it is important to reward patients for displaying such skills immediately after the desired behaviors occur. To do so, they have used a method known as the **token economy,** a behavior therapy system in which desired behaviors are reinforced with tokens, that is, the patients "earn" the tokens by engaging in appropriate social behaviors. Once the tokens are earned, the patients can exchange them for a desired reinforcer, such as food. Almost any object—poker chips, gold stars, or check marks on a graph—can be called a token (Baldwin & Baldwin, 2001).

### Psychological Detective

Awarding poker chips may seem an unlikely way to alter maladaptive behaviors. Such tokens have little or no intrinsic value, yet they are a key ingredient in the success of this method. What are the advantages of using tokens to alter behaviors? How could tokens be used so that they do have value? In answering these questions, recall our discussion of secondary reinforcers in Chapter 5. Give these questions some thought, and write down your answers before reading further.

There are three major steps in establishing a token economy (Oltmanns & Emery, 2001). First, the psychologist must identify the target behaviors; then the contingencies for each target must be established (for example, how many tokens are presented for each of the target behaviors). Tokens (or points) are usually awarded as soon as they are earned to facilitate rapid learning (Wolfe, Dattilo, & Gast, 2003). Finally, the developer of the token economy must set the exchange rules for using the tokens.

Patients can use tokens as a medium of exchange to acquire desired reinforcers such as candy, television time, and grounds privileges. The tokens are used in the same way that money is used outside the hospital. They are *secondary* reinforcers that can be exchanged for other reinforcers, especially *primary* reinforcers such as candy. If psychologists used primary reinforcers to reward each occurrence of a desired behavior, patients might grow tired of them; they would then lose their reinforcing value. As learned or secondary reinforcers, however, tokens are less likely to lose their value because patients can accumulate them and exchange them later for the primary reinforcers they desire.

The following Study Chart summarizes the behavior therapy techniques.

**STUDY TIP**

Create visuals that help you remember the six major behavior therapy techniques—draw cartoons, use particular colors, make a collage with photographs from the media, or design icons.

## *Study* CHART

### Behavior Therapy Techniques

| Technique | Description |
|-----------|-------------|
| Systematic desensitization | Treatment for phobias that combines relaxation training with graduated exposure to the feared stimuli |
| Aversion therapy | A technique based on classical conditioning that associates an undesired behavior with aversive (unpleasant) stimuli such as shock or nausea-inducing drugs |
| Modeling | A form of learning—also known as *observational learning*—that occurs by observing and imitating a model; it is an effective treatment for phobias |
| Extinction | A technique used to eliminate an undesirable behavior, consisting of withholding reinforcers that had maintained a behavior |
| Punishment | Either the removal of a positive stimulus or event (such as candy) or the presentation of a negative stimulus or event (such as a shock) |
| Token economy | Application of positive reinforcement using tokens (secondary reinforcers) that can be exchanged for other reinforcers |

## Group Therapies

Most forms of psychotherapy and behavior therapy involve interactions between a therapist and a client. Therapy sessions may not, however, reflect life outside the therapist's office (Moursund & Kenny, 2002). Clients are not likely to have a psychoanalyst available to offer interpretations of their actions; a behavior therapist will not be available to reinforce appropriate behaviors, nor will a client-centered therapist be present to offer unconditional positive regard. Problems that bring clients to therapists do not occur in a vacuum; often those problems reflect the clients' difficulties in interacting with family, friends, co-workers, and even strangers.

**Group therapy** can be a primary form of treatment or an adjunct to individual sessions; its different forms depend on the individuals who compose the groups, the problems or disorders they are confronting, the role the group leader takes, and the therapeutic goals that have been established (Brown, 2003). Group therapy can be very valuable in treating a number of psychological disorders such as depression, phobias, and alcohol or drug abuse. It is useful in reducing problems related to stress and anger, as well as resolving difficulties in social behavior that can also cause distress.

As you can see from Table 13-5, group therapies share several common features. Such features give group therapy several definite advantages. Clients can try out new behaviors in the group setting and receive feedback from other people who may be very different from the therapist, thus facilitating the generalization of behaviors to everyday situations. In comparison to individual therapy sessions, group sessions are also cost-effective because several people are treated at the same time. Moreover, group therapy can be used by different types of therapists, such as psychodynamic, humanistic, cognitive, and behavioral therapists (Beck & Lewis, 2000).

**Marital and Family Therapy.** Two forms of group therapy—marital and family therapy—are based on the assumption that problems presented for treatment should be addressed within the context of a larger family unit.

**group therapy**
Therapy in which clients discuss problems in groups that may include individuals with similar problems

Some of the advantages of group therapy are social support and opportunities to practice coping skills and to receive feedback.

**TABLE 13-5**

## The Most Common Features of Group Therapy

1. *Self-disclosure*—the opportunity to tell the group about one's personal problems and concerns.
2. *Acceptance and support*—feeling a sense of belongingness and being valued by the other group members.
3. *Norm clarification*—learning that one's problems are neither unique nor more serious than those of other group members.
4. *Social learning*—being able to relate constructively and adaptively within the group.
5. *Vicarious learning*—learning about oneself through the observation of other group members, including the therapist.
6. *Self-understanding*—finding out about one's behavior in the group setting and the motivations contributing to the behavior.

**Source:** Sarason and Sarason (2002).

These therapies are among the most common forms of treatment; therapists from all mental health professions use them to treat a variety of problems (Johnson & Lebow, 2000). *Marital therapy* typically attempts to stabilize and improve the relationship of two individuals who regard themselves as marital partners. In contemporary society, this form of therapy has expanded from clients who are husband and wife to unmarried or homosexual couples who are cohabiting, in which case the therapy is often called *couples therapy* (Sarason & Sarason, 2002).

*Family therapy* focuses on the larger family unit: a parent and a child at a minimum, or both parents, stepparents, or grandparents, depending on the environment in which the child lives. Quite often a child is brought in for therapy for a specific problem, such as school difficulties, delinquency, or aggressive behavior, and the therapist finds that the problems exist in the context of the family setting, especially in the ways parents and children interact. Returning the child to the family without changing those interaction patterns does not alleviate the problems. Therefore parents, spouses, and children should play a role in therapy for the client's problems. Moreover, a growing number of psychologists believe that incorporating spirituality into family therapy is beneficial to the treatment process (Kersting, 2003).

The Study Chart on page 595 summarizes the major types of psychological therapies.

## Self-Help

A person who feels overwhelmed by life's problems may turn to friends, relatives, or perhaps teachers for guidance and support. Professional therapists are not the only source of assistance for people in need of help. In fact, professional therapists alone could not meet the need for mental health services. Paraprofessionals are another source of assistance; they can be found in a variety of roles, such as staffing telephone crisis lines. An additional source of help, the self-help group, provides assistance to an estimated 7 to 15 million people (Christensen & Jacobson, 1994).

Most self-help groups are developed and run by laypersons, although some invite professional therapists to help with unusual cases (Richards, 2004). A guiding principle is that compassion and understanding do not require advanced degrees. People in these groups pool their knowledge, share their experiences with common problems, and help one another. What's more, self-help groups have the potential to prevent more serious problems by providing social support during a time of need and by helping people develop coping skills (Oltmanns & Emery, 2001).

## *Study* CHART

### Major Types of Psychological Therapies

| Therapy Type | Description |
|---|---|
| **Psychoanalytic therapy** | A form of therapy developed by Sigmund Freud that is intended to bring unconscious influences on behavior to the conscious level. Key techniques and processes include free association, resistance, dream interpretation, and transference. This therapy is costly and often requires a significant time commitment. Most of the individuals who seek this form of therapy are articulate and suffer from relatively minor problems. |
| **Humanistic therapies** | Therapies that emphasize the present and are based on the assumption that people can solve their own problems after they develop self-awareness. Client-centered therapy aims to develop self-awareness in a nondirective manner; Gestalt therapy relies on more active elements, including confronting and frustrating clients. |
| **Cognitive therapies** | A related series of therapies that focus on clients' thinking about problems they encounter, especially logical errors that might be made. Cognitive therapies are quite effective in treating anxiety disorders, depression, and stress-related problems. |
| **Group therapy** | A form of therapy that may be used alone or in combination with individual therapy. It provides opportunities to obtain both social support and feedback while developing new skills for dealing with problem behaviors. Marital and family therapy is based on the assumption that problem behaviors are best treated in the context of the couple or the family. |

There are many kinds of self-help groups. Some of the best known are designed for people suffering from specific medical conditions, for people facing acute crises, and for individuals coping with mental illness. For example, the typical member of the National Alliance for the Mentally Ill is the parent of an adult child with schizophrenia. The oldest and largest self-help group is Alcoholics Anonymous, with over 1.5 million members worldwide (Wallace, 1999).

Two rapidly expanding sources of self-help are telephone- and Internet-based groups (Humphreys, Marcus, Stewart, & Oliva, 2004). The electronic communications of online groups focus on requests for information and provision of emotional support. A major advantage of Internet self-help groups is that they are available at times when traditional sources of support have limited or no availability, such as at night (Winzelberg, 1997). Users of telephone self-help programs comment favorably on the programs' flexibility, accessibility, and the autonomy afforded by telephone-based guidance for problems such as binge eating (Wells et al., 1997). Table 13-6 lists contact data for some self-help groups.

"*No one understands me. So as a last resort, my shrink referred me to you.*"

**Source:** Reprinted with the permission of Harley Schwadron.

The health care reforms of the 1970s brought with them a system that sought to control health care costs: managed health care. Managed care of mental health services has generated considerable debate, especially about the quality of care (Sanchez & Turner, 2003). This debate now includes the Internet because more managed care companies *and* consumers of mental health services are going online. Why? For consumers, using their home PC is easy, convenient, and anonymous. "Managed-care firms see the Internet as a means to improve their bottom line" (Rabasca, 2000, p. 28). However, consumers need to be *especially good* psychological detectives when they use the Internet for mental health services. How valid are the questionnaires you take on the Internet? Who is making the recommendations you are receiving? What are their credentials? Consumers need to be very cautious about services they can receive on the Internet.

Mental health services on the Internet aren't the only new forms of mental health service to come under close scrutiny. Some forms of therapy, especially those involving

**TABLE 13-6**

## Some Self-Help Groups

Most of these national organizations maintain files of local self-help groups. They also can provide literature on the problem that is their focus.

| Group | Phone Number | Web Site |
| --- | --- | --- |
| OC Foundation (for obsessive–compulsive disorder) | (800) 540-4000 | www.ocdhelp.org |
| Alcoholics Anonymous | (212) 870-3400 | www.alcoholics-anonymous.org |
| Anxiety Disorders Association of America | (301) 231-9350 | www.adaa.org |
| Cocaine Anonymous | (800) 347-8998 | www.ca.org |
| National Alliance for the Mentally Ill (families of mentally ill) | (800) 950-NAMI | www.nami.org |
| National Association of Anorexia Nervosa and Associated Disorders | (800) 424-3410 | www.anad.org |
| National Depressive and Manic-Depressive Association | (312) 642-0049 | www.ndmda.org |
| SIDS Alliance (sudden infant death syndrome) | (800) 221-7437 | www.sidsalliance.org |
| Suicide Awareness Voices of Education (SAVE) | (612) 946-7998 | www.save.org |
| Widowed Persons Services | (202) 434-2260 | www.aarp.org |

self-help, have been sensationalized, and their presentation by the media may even strain our credibility. For some critics, using pets to reduce psychological problems ("pet therapy") falls into this category. According to Allen (2003), "In recent years the popular media have publicized widely the idea of the 'healing power of pets.' Ubiquitous advertisements featuring winsome puppies and kittens suggest that having a pet can cure everything from loneliness and alienation to hypertension and heart disease" (p. 236).

Because her previous research had shown that, during a stressful situation, the presence of pet dogs kept blood pressure from rising, whereas the presence of the person's best friend resulted in an increase in blood pressure, Allen (2003) was "inspired to learn more about social factors and blood pressure" (p. 237). According to Allen, because "marriage involves the closest of relationships, we reasoned that a person's soul mate would be perceived positively and have a calming effect. We wondered about the relative influence of a pet. Once again, however, people experiencing a stressor in the presence of other people (however supportive and friendly they tried to appear) exhibited dramatically large increases in blood pressure" (p. 237). Those participants who had only their pet present showed only very slight increases.

Allen (2003) indicates that she and her colleagues have taken their research one step further: "To test if a pet effect would occur among people who had not acquired pets on their own, we conducted a study in which half the participants were randomly selected to adopt a pet cat or dog from an animal shelter" (p. 236). Their participants were stockbrokers with high blood pressure. They described their work as being very stressful. None of the participants had owned a pet during the previous 5 years. The participants were scheduled to begin drug therapy with Lisinopril (a drug that is successful in reducing resting blood pressure but not reducing responses to stress).

According to Allen (2003):

> Results of the study provide strong evidence for the role of pets in providing social support. As predicted, Lisinopril lowered the resting blood pressure of all participants. While under stress, however, the individuals who acquired pets had blood pressure increases that were less than half the increases of their counterparts without pets. Interestingly, we also found that people who reported the fewest social contacts and friends benefited the most from the companionship of their pets. [Thus], we demonstrated that resting blood

pressure and blood pressure reactions to stress are influenced by independent mechanisms. That is, resting blood pressure can be influenced by a drug, but adding a pet to the environment can alter stress responses. In conclusion, existing evidence about how pets influence people's blood pressure suggests that for people who enjoy animals, and especially for those with few social contacts, pets can be a healthy pleasure. (pp. 238–239)

Perhaps pet therapy deserves more serious consideration and evaluation from the scientific community.

# REVIEW SUMMARY

1. **Psychotherapy** involves a special relationship between a distressed person and a therapist in which the therapist helps the client make changes in his or her thinking, feeling, and behavior.

2. **Psychoanalytic therapy** aims to help the patient develop insight into unconscious feelings and conflicts by using **free association, dream interpretation,** and interpretation of **resistance** and transference.

3. **Humanistic therapies** emphasize the ability of each person to solve his or her problems. **Client-centered therapy** seeks to develop an accepting environment for the client. **Gestalt therapy** helps clients develop self-acceptance, but Gestalt therapists are more directive than client-centered therapists.

4. **Cognitive therapies** are designed to change the way the client thinks. Albert Ellis, the founder of **rational-emotive behavior therapy,** assumes that people are disturbed by the way they interpret events. Therefore, the role of the therapist is to challenge the client's irrational beliefs. Aaron Beck's cognitive therapy has been applied to depression with promising results.

5. Behavior therapists view maladaptive behaviors as learned and rely on classical and operant conditioning and modeling to teach the client new behaviors.

6. **Systematic desensitization** is an effective treatment for phobias in which clients are taught relaxation techniques and then asked to imagine or approach feared situations gradually. Modeling is also an effective treatment for phobias. **Aversion therapy** reduces undesirable behaviors by pairing them with an aversive (unpleasant) stimulus.

7. **Extinction** is an operant conditioning technique used to reduce the occurrence of maladaptive behaviors. Reinforcers are withheld after the maladaptive behavior has occurred.

8. Ethical and legal concerns restrict the use of punishment to cases in which a maladaptive behavior is highly resistant to other forms of therapy.

9. **Token economies** are used to provide secondary reinforcement of desired behaviors. The tokens can be exchanged for primary reinforcers.

10. **Group therapy** is based on the assumptions that behavior does not occur in a vacuum and that behaviors learned in group settings are more likely to generalize to everyday situations. Marital therapy and family therapy are two forms of group therapy.

11. A significant number of people find support and comfort in self-help groups.

# ✓ CHECK YOUR PROGRESS

1. Identify the form of psychotherapy described in each of the following statements:
   a. The therapist seeks to uncover the patient's unconscious conflicts.
   b. The therapist reflects the emotional content of the client's statements.
   c. Therapists use a scientific approach to help clients assess the validity of statements made during sessions.
   d. Staff members at a mental hospital ignore patients when they use odd words.
   e. The therapist works with the client to develop self-talk to deal with stressful situations.

2. According to client-centered therapists, what are the major characteristics that a therapist should demonstrate to create the type of environment that leads to success in therapy?

3. Using Ellis's ABC framework, suggest two contrasting interpretations of the following situation: You tried out for the class play but were not selected. What consequences is each interpretation likely to have?

4. What is the *primary* goal of psychoanalytic therapy?
   a. to develop the patient's self-concept
   b. to improve the patient's use of regression
   c. to make the patient a fully functioning member of society
   d. to help patients develop insight into their behaviors

5. According to humanistic therapists, what types of clients are better able to resolve their own problems?
   a. clients who are more accepting
   b. clients who have above-average intelligence
   c. clients who are able to communicate one-on-one
   d. clients who are motivated to change their behavior

**6.** Judy's therapist listens to her without interrupting, never evaluating or judging her. This therapist is demonstrating

  **a.** empathy.
  **b.** genuineness.
  **c.** unconditional positive regard.
  **d.** nondirective countertransference.

**7.** Which therapy is based on the assumption that our emotional responses are an outgrowth of our cognitions?

  **a.** behavior
  **b.** psychoanalytic

  **c.** client-centered
  **d.** rational-emotive

**8.** Beck's cognitive therapy is used primarily to treat

  **a.** mania.
  **b.** depression.
  **c.** schizophrenia.
  **d.** dissociative identity disorder.

**ANSWERS: 1. a.** psychoanalytic therapy **b.** client-centered therapy **c.** rational-emotive behavior therapy **d.** behavioral (extinction) **e.** stress inoculation therapy **2.** unconditioned positive regard, genuineness, empathy **3.** You could interpret the failure to be selected as evidence that you have no ability at all, and consequently you may feel depressed. On the other hand, you might recognize that there were many qualified actors who have more experience than you and that you have skills that are apparent in other areas besides acting. **4.** d **5.** a **6.** c **7.** d **8.** b

# THE EFFECTIVENESS OF PSYCHOTHERAPY

Tim has been having some difficulties adjusting to college and getting along with his roommates. He also has trouble making decisions and often feels lonely. At times Tim feels that "life is one big vacuum waiting to suck me up." His level of distress is rising daily, and he wants to do something about it, but he wonders whether psychotherapy is worth the time and effort. *Is psychotherapy an effective treatment for psychological disorders?*

Does therapy work, and if so, why? Is one form of therapy superior to another? These questions are not easy to answer for several reasons. First, it is difficult to define clearly what we mean by "success" in psychotherapy. Some therapies, such as psychoanalytic therapy, define success as the development of insight. It is difficult, however, to determine when a person has developed insight. Second, therapies are used in treating a wide variety of problems that may have little in common. When people seek therapy, they have made a decision to change some important aspect of their lives—an aspect that may differ greatly from one individual to another. Third, there is the ever-present *placebo effect.* Clients may improve during therapy because they expect to improve, regardless of any specific aspects of the therapy.

A British psychologist, Hans Eysenck, published the first major study of the effectiveness of psychotherapy in 1952. Eysenck examined 24 studies involving more than 8,000 clients who had moderately severe disorders and received either psychoanalytic therapy, eclectic therapy, or no psychotherapy. Eysenck (1952) reported that the results "show that roughly two-thirds of a group of . . . patients will recover, whether they are treated by means of psychotherapy or not" (p. 322). The publication of Eysenck's report caused a furor among psychotherapists, and his review was subjected to numerous appraisals. Critics noted that the therapists who had published the studies Eysenck reviewed had different goals and orientations in evaluating therapy and probably used different criteria when judging success (Garfield, 1980). Also, it appeared that Eysenck had overestimated the rate of spontaneous remission in the studies he reviewed.

One way to answer questions about the effectiveness of psychotherapy is to combine the results of a large number of different studies, using *meta-analysis* (see Chapter 11). The results of several meta-analyses have been reported and support the conclusion that "psychotherapy is generally effective," although "we are uncertain as to why" (Kopta, Howard, Lowry, & Beuther, 1994, p. 1010).

Keep in mind that these conclusions about the effectiveness of psychotherapy are limited to therapies that have been formally evaluated (Lambert & Bergin, 1994). The new therapies that are touted on a regular basis are often inadequately tested. Their effectiveness is often supported by testimonials from satisfied clients, which should give us pause (see "Guidelines for the Psychological Detective" in Chapter 1).

## Characteristics of Effective Psychotherapy

Which form of psychotherapy works best? This question has been asked repeatedly. Meta-analysis supports the idea that there is little difference among various psychotherapy treatments.

Certain characteristics of therapy may contribute to improvement, regardless of the form of therapy we are considering. For example, the therapist's ability to communicate empathy to clients is important (Moursund & Kenny, 2002). A therapeutic relationship characterized by warmth, acceptance, and trust facilitates psychotherapy. Even when therapists use the same techniques (based on a treatment manual) and are monitored and supervised throughout the course of treatment, some have significantly better outcomes than others. We cannot escape the fact that some people are simply better than others at establishing a caring relationship and instilling hope.

The evidence also suggests that particular therapies are effective in alleviating certain problem behaviors. For example, behavioral therapies such as systematic desensitization are the treatment of choice for phobias, especially the specific phobias.

## Psychotherapy and the Needs of Diversity

Culture, ethnicity, and sex have significant effects on our behavior, values, and attitudes; therefore it is not surprising that they influence psychotherapy in significant ways (Kottler & Brown, 2000). For example, Nai-Kan ("look within at oneself"), a therapy practiced in Japan, is designed to discover how a client has been ungrateful and troublesome to people who have extended themselves, such as parents and teachers. The therapy's primary goal is to find ways for the client to demonstrate gratitude to and alliance with these people (Foulks, Bland, & Shervington, 1995). We cannot fully understand this therapy unless we have some knowledge of Japanese culture, in which the focus is on the group rather than the individual, as is the case in the United States.

There is a growing appreciation that the United States is a multicultural nation with a diversity of ethnic and cultural backgrounds. This reality affects patterns of therapy. In

Clients are often more comfortable with a therapist of the same sex or ethnic background.

**TABLE 13-7**

## Clinical Psychologists and the U.S. Population Compared

| Characteristic | Clinical Psychologists (%) | U.S. Population (%) |
| --- | --- | --- |
| **Sex** | | |
| Female | 30 | 51 |
| Male | 70 | 49 |
| **Race or ethnicity** | | |
| Caucasian | 93 | 83 |
| Other | 7 | 17 |

**Sources:** Norcross, Karg-Bray, and Prochaska (1995); U.S. Bureau of the Census (1997).

general, ethnic minority group members in the United States neither use nor provide psychotherapy in anything like their proportion in the population (see Table 13-7). Do not, however, confuse this pattern of use with the need for help for emotional problems. Several minority groups experience a higher proportion of poverty and social stressors that can contribute to psychological disorders. Mental health services for U.S. minority groups are generally inadequate (Moursund & Kenny, 2002). For example, African Americans, Native Americans, Asian Americans, and Latinos terminate psychotherapy earlier and also average fewer sessions than whites (Parham, White, & Ajamu, 1999). Between 42 and 55% of minority clients failed to return after a single session, compared with a 30% dropout rate for white clients.

Psychotherapy requires intimate conversations between socially distant individuals. Clients typically desire communication patterns that are similar to their own and respectful of their values (Dyche & Zayas, 2001). Many ethnic groups and cultures reserve such intimate conversations for family members. Formal and polite but nonrevealing patterns of communication are used with outsiders. For example, Latino clients tend to use Spanish at home and English in psychotherapy, even when the therapist is bilingual. The formality of the therapy situation and the therapist's customary use of English may lead clients to see the relationship as similar to previous formal relationships that minimized self-disclosure.

Language discrepancies between therapists and clients whose native language is not English can affect treatment in a number of ways (Corey, Corey, & Callahan, 1998). For example, identification with the therapist is an important factor in the way the client and therapist relate. Language is an important factor in establishing the existence of common cultural experiences that enable clients to feel comfortable and develop a therapeutic alliance. Clients may seek therapists of the same ethnic group, race, and sex because they anticipate a feeling of shared values and understanding that will make them more comfortable in revealing intimate details of their lives (Cohen & Cohen, 1999).

Among the reasons ethnic clients terminate psychotherapy so early are a lack of bilingual therapists and therapists' stereotypes about ethnic clients. The single most important reason may be that therapists do not provide culturally responsive forms of therapy. They may be unaware of values and customs within a culture that would help them in understanding and treating certain behaviors. Consider the case of a young Latino who went through assertiveness training at the suggestion of his therapist. When the young man went home and asserted himself with his father, he encountered a very negative reaction. Therapy should be undertaken with an understanding of cultural values, which in this case included properly respectful behavior toward one's father (Yamamoto et al., 1993).

To counter the high rate of early termination of treatment by minority clients, some psychologists have suggested that therapists develop greater cultural understanding and knowledge. In addition, therapists from diverse ethnic backgrounds and ethnic-specific therapeutic services are needed. There is also a need for more bilingual and bicultural personnel who could work more effectively with clients from different cultures and those for whom English is a second language. Does responsiveness to cultural factors work? Sue and his colleagues (1991) analyzed the services, length of treatment, and outcomes of therapy for several ethnic groups in Los Angeles. Ethnic match (in which client and therapist were members of the same ethnic group) was related to the length and success of treatment among Mexican Americans. Among clients for whom English was not their first language, when the therapist had the same ethnic background and spoke the same language as the client, treatment tended to last longer and was more likely to be successful. Thus matching is important because it is related to length of treatment (Sue et al., 1991).

Growing appreciation of the ethnic and racial diversity of the U.S. population has led therapists to consider these factors in providing various forms of treatment (Canino & Spurlock, 2000). For example, Fassinger (2000) advocates the use of the humanistic approach, which provides a safe, open, and caring relationship, with gay and lesbian clients. Moursund and Kenny (2002) believe that such considerations are not trivial. Likewise, therapists need to be sensitive to the physical limitations of their elderly clients (Kottler & Brown, 2000).

## When to Begin Psychotherapy and What to Expect

How does someone like Tim, described at the beginning of this section, decide whether to enter psychotherapy? The answer to this question should be based on a range of considerations. People may decide to enter psychotherapy for shyness, anxiety, depression, an inner conflict, a traumatic or stressful event, or a marital or family problem. Others may find that they continually develop self-destructive relationships or that their strong need to control others creates problems. Still others may have physical symptoms that are caused by emotional problems.

In *The Consumer's Guide to Psychotherapy*, Jack Engler and Daniel Goleman (1992) suggest three key issues to consider when deciding to enter psychotherapy:

**1.** Is your distress level intense enough that you want to do something about it now?

**2.** Are you no longer able to handle your problems on your own? Do you feel the need for more support?

**3.** Is your distress affecting your personal life, family, or work?

If the answer to any or all of these questions is yes, you may want to consider entering psychotherapy. One of the best ways to start is to seek recommendations from friends, relatives, or other professionals. Another good starting point is to call the community mental health center in your area.

Having decided on psychotherapy, what can you expect? Most clients do not anticipate lengthy treatment and easily become disenchanted with its slow progress. Long-term psychotherapy offers little to patients who are in the middle of crises that require immediate intervention. One response to these concerns has been short-term psychotherapy, which is carried out in fewer sessions. At the beginning of therapy the therapist states that there will be a fixed number of sessions—usually no more than 25 and often fewer. Short-term psychotherapy focuses on a few goals, such as removal or reduction of the client's most troubling symptoms. The new short-term forms of psychotherapy are quite active; clients should be prepared to listen to suggestions for changes in their behavior. Because time is limited, the therapist is likely to give the client homework assignments such as analyzing emotional reactions or practicing relaxation techniques. These assignments enable the client and therapist to make maximum use of their limited time together. The image of the client stretched out on a couch has become outdated as therapies have become shorter and more active. But just how short are the more modern forms of psychotherapy? Most psychotherapy treatment programs involve 12 or fewer sessions (Hersen & Biaggio, 2000).

Finally, we live in a culture that urges us to make changes in our lives. Flick on the television and you see no end to the talk shows touting new forms of therapy for old and newly discovered problems. When considering how to make changes in some aspect of your life, it would be helpful to know the likelihood that change is possible. Some problem behaviors are easier to change than others. Some behaviors are very difficult to change because "our biology can make changing despite our efforts almost impossible" (Seligman, 1993). Having this kind of information helps you assess your situation; perhaps you will decide that you like yourself the way you are. Such a decision can save you from the self-reproach and remorse that often accompany failed efforts to alter problem behaviors. Here is a partial list of various problems and the likelihood of improvement:

> Curable: panic
> Almost curable: specific phobias
> Moderate or mild relief: agoraphobia, depression, obsessive–compulsive disorder
> Marginal relief: posttraumatic stress disorder
> Temporary change: overweight
> Unchangeable: sexual orientation (Seligman, 1993)

A final concern about beginning and continuing therapy deals with stigma. "Many people who would benefit from mental health services opt not to pursue them or fail to fully participate once they have begun" (Corrigan, 2004, p. 614). In short, these people are avoiding the perceived stigma that is attached to the label *mental illness*. The first of the six goals set by the New Commission on Mental Health in 2003 (see page 577) calls for an understanding that mental health is essential for good physical health. Hopefully, antistigma programs will be developed that will enable everyone who is in need of professional mental health services to benefit from them without fear. Only under these circumstances will our country be able to achieve this mental health goal.

## REVIEW SUMMARY

**1.** After Eysenck concluded that psychotherapy clients are just as likely to improve without it, psychotherapists sought to provide better information about the success of therapy.

**2.** Meta-analysis allows researchers to combine the results of a number of studies. Using this technique, researchers have found that therapy does lead to greater improvement than no treatment and that differences among the various forms of therapy are not great.

**3.** The search for the keys to successful therapy has led researchers to focus on factors such as the therapist's ability to communicate empathy, which can lead to improvement in distressed individuals.

**4.** Therapists are becoming increasingly aware of the influence of ethnic and cultural factors on psychotherapy. Members of many ethnic groups drop out early from psychotherapy, in part because there is a dearth of therapists who share their native language as well as a failure to provide appropriate forms of therapy.

**5.** The decision to enter psychotherapy should involve asking questions about the degree of distress one is experiencing; one's ability to cope with that distress; and the effect of the symptoms on oneself, one's family, and one's work. Current forms of psychotherapy are offered in fewer sessions than in the past. Many symptoms, especially distress symptoms, respond quickly to treatment. There is also a growing recognition that there are limits to what aspects of our behavior can be changed.

## ✓ CHECK YOUR PROGRESS

**1.** What conclusions did Eysenck draw from his study of the effectiveness of psychotherapy? What was the impact of his research?

**2.** What term describes the tendency for improvement in problems without therapy?

    **a.** double blind
    **b.** biased response

    **c.** spontaneous remission
    **d.** extinction

**3.** What statistical technique combines the results of a large number of different studies?

    **a.** meta-analysis
    **b.** path analysis
    **c.** inclusive analysis
    **d.** analysis of variance

**4.** One characteristic of therapy that research suggests contributes to improvement regardless of other factors is the

  **a.** form of therapy.
  **b.** client's verbal ability.
  **c.** simultaneous use of drug therapy.
  **d.** therapist's ability to communicate empathy.

**5.** Which form of therapy is the preferred treatment for phobias?

  **a.** Gestalt
  **b.** behavioral

  **c.** psychoanalytic
  **d.** client-centered

**6.** Many clients have become disenchanted with psychotherapy. One response to this concern has been to

  **a.** use short-term, more focused forms of therapy.
  **b.** ask for more feedback from clients during treatment.
  **c.** encourage therapists to become more eclectic in their approach.
  **d.** pay more attention to creating a warm and inviting therapeutic environment.

# BIOMEDICAL THERAPIES

While walking through a mall, Alice decides to stop in the bookstore, where she pauses at the magazine section. The cover story in major magazines is touting the latest "wonder drugs" for treating psychological disorders. Alice wonders if the drugs really work and whether they are safe. *What are the benefits and the costs associated with drug therapies for psychological disorders?*

The brain plays a crucial role in every breath you take, every word you utter—every experience of each day of your life. Thus the proposal that altering the brain may be useful in treating psychological disorders is not radical. Although some past efforts to alter brain functioning appear drastic, more recent efforts, primarily the use of psychotropic drugs, have been hailed as breakthroughs in treating psychological disorders. Even drug therapies, however, are not without problems—namely, harmful side effects. In this section we describe several biomedical therapies for psychological disorders.

## Drug Therapy

As we saw in Chapters 2 and 4, neurotransmitters have powerful effects on behavior, emotions, and thinking. Most drugs affect neurotransmitter levels and thus can play a prominent role in treating psychological disorders. As of 2004, two states, New Mexico and Louisiana, have passed laws that "give specially trained psychologists authorization to prescribe certain drugs related to the diagnosis and treatment of mental health disorders" (Holloway, 2004, p. 20). In this section we examine the drugs most frequently prescribed to treat psychological disorders.

**Antianxiety Drugs.** Anxiety is the primary symptom in several of the disorders discussed in Chapter 12. Although opinions vary on what causes anxiety disorders, **antianxiety drugs** can reduce the severity of many symptoms, especially physiological ones like increased heart rate. Antianxiety drugs are frequently prescribed to treat generalized anxiety disorder; they are also used to treat agitation, alcohol withdrawal, insomnia, and muscle spasms (Sarason & Sarason, 2002).

The major class of antianxiety drugs (also known as *minor tranquilizers*) are the *benzodiazepines*, such as Valium, Librium, and Xanax (Rybacki, 1997). These drugs increase the ability of gamma-aminobutyric acid (GABA), an inhibitory neurotransmitter, to bind to receptor sites at synapses in the brain. The resulting increase in the firing of inhibitory neurons lowers the level of the neurological activity that produces anxiety.

**antianxiety drugs**
Minor tranquilizers, such as the benzodiazepines, used to reduce anxiety, usually by increasing the ability of the neurotransmitter GABA to bind at synapses

Antianxiety drugs are relatively safe because a lethal overdose requires a very large amount of the drug. Combining antianxiety drugs with alcohol or other drugs, however, can produce severe depression and can sometimes lead to suicide. The most common side effects of antianxiety drugs—drowsiness and impaired ability to acquire or store information—are usually temporary. Some patients develop a tolerance for these drugs, which means they need larger doses to maintain the initial effect. Most patients who take antianxiety drugs every day for 3 months or longer run the risk of developing dependence, which will be followed by withdrawal symptoms if they stop taking the drugs (Nevid & Greene, 2001).

**Antidepressant Drugs.** Significant strides have been made in the treatment of depression since the era when bloodletting was a common treatment. Antidepressant drugs are the most frequently prescribed psychotropic drugs in the United States, having recently surpassed antianxiety drugs (Pincus et al., 1998). This increase is, in part, a result of the increasing number of disorders for which antidepressant drugs are prescribed (eating disorders, obsessive–compulsive disorder). There are three classes of antidepressant drugs: tricyclic antidepressants, monoamine oxidase (MAO) inhibitors, and selective serotonin reuptake inhibitors.

The chemical structure of *tricyclic antidepressants* resembles three connected circles, hence the name. Drugs in this class, such as Elavil, reduce the reuptake of serotonin and norepinephrine, thus making more of these chemical messengers available at synapses. Although these changes at the synapse occur immediately, 10 to 14 days usually pass before there is a reduction in the symptoms of depression. The side effects of antidepressants include constipation, dizziness, and dry mouth.

The enzyme MAO breaks down the neurotransmitters norepinephrine and serotonin before they can be repackaged for future use. When MAO is blocked, the levels of these neurotransmitters increase at the synapse. A second class of drugs used to treat depression, MAO *inhibitors*, prevent MAO from breaking down norepinephrine and serotonin and thus increase their levels in the brain. Patients who do not respond to tricyclic antidepressants may be switched to one of the MAO inhibitors. Although the side effects of MAO inhibitors are similar to those of the tricyclic antidepressants, they tend to be more serious. For example, MAO inhibitors can produce a dangerous rise in blood pressure if taken at the same time as tyramine, a substance found in alcoholic beverages (beer and red wine), aged cheese, beans, liver, salami, pepperoni, and yogurt (Amsterdam, 2003).

As we have seen, many drugs have side effects that range from annoying to life-threatening. Many of the side effects of tricyclic antidepressants result from their effects on the neurotransmitter norepinephrine. The third group of drugs used to treat depression, however, the *selective serotonin reuptake inhibitors* (SSRIs), have little, if any, effect on norepinephrine. The best-known drug in this class, Prozac (fluoxetine), is the most widely prescribed drug for the treatment of depression. One reason for its popularity is a low rate of short-term side effects. Despite this popularity, it is not certain that Prozac is actually superior to other drugs used to treat depression (Levkovitz, Caftori, Avital, & Richter-Levin, 2002). Nevertheless, Prozac (as well as other SSRIs) is prescribed for a growing number of problems, including anorexia nervosa, bulimia nervosa, obsessive–compulsive disorder, and panic disorder (Greene, 2001).

**Mood Stabilizers.** Drugs used to treat bipolar disorder (reduce mania and raise the depressive mood) are called *mood stabilizers* (Young, 2004). The most widely used mood stabilizer is lithium.

The natural mineral salt, *lithium*, is the drug of choice for treating the manic episodes of bipolar disorder; it also tends to reduce the wild mood swings associated with this disorder (Oltmanns & Emery, 2001). About 70 to 80% of patients respond to lithium treatment, usually within 5 to 14 days (Hopkins & Gelenberg, 1994). Bipolar patients often continue taking lithium even when they no longer display

Prozac, an antidepressant drug (selective serotonin reuptake inhibitor), has been hailed as a breakthrough. It is the most frequently used drug in the treatment of depression.

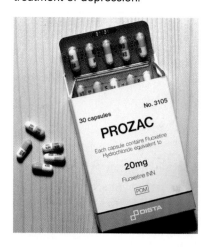

symptoms of mania or depression to prevent a recurrence. However, not all bipolar patients respond to lithium treatment; as many as 50% do not improve significantly (Mendlewicz, Souery, & Rivelli, 1999).

Lithium has a narrow margin of safe use. The level of lithium in the blood required for effective treatment is close to the toxic level that can result in symptoms such as vomiting, nausea, and even death. Therefore patients must have periodic blood tests to check lithium levels and to adjust the dosage (Rybacki, 1997). Therapeutic levels of lithium are associated with side effects such as hand tremor, excessive thirst, and urination.

A number of mechanisms have been proposed to explain how lithium reduces mood swings. For example, lithium influences the passage of ions into and out of cell membranes (see Chapter 2); it may also regulate levels of norepinephrine (and perhaps other neurotransmitters).

Because some patients do not respond adequately to lithium therapy, the search continues for other treatments (Silverstone & Silverstone, 2004). Among the alternative treatments are anticonvulsant drugs (Advokat, Dixon, Schneider, & Comaty, 2004), which are especially effective for the rapid cycling form of bipolar disorder (four or more episodes of disturbed mood in 1 year).

**Antipsychotic Drugs.** The first antipsychotic drug was discovered in France in 1952 when a surgeon, Henri Laborit, observed that a new anesthetic calmed his patients without loss of consciousness. He persuaded several psychiatrists to try the drug on patients with schizophrenia. The drug, Thorazine (chlorpromazine), was soon widely adopted for treating schizophrenia, although it has now been replaced by more potent drugs. The discovery of **antipsychotic drugs** was a major factor in the deinstitutionalization of patients; these drugs became the principal method for treating schizophrenia (Shen, 1999).

Antipsychotic drugs seem to work by occupying receptor sites in neurons that respond to dopamine, a neurotransmitter that has been implicated in the development of schizophrenia (see Chapter 12). When these receptor sites are occupied, nerve conduction is reduced. Antipsychotic drugs are very effective at decreasing positive symptoms such as delusions and hallucinations; they are less effective at reducing negative symptoms such as apathy. Although antipsychotic drugs do not cure schizophrenia and other psychotic disorders, they are effective in controlling many of the symptoms.

The development of antipsychotic drugs was a major change in the treatment of mentally ill patients, but their use is not without problems. Movement disorders such as restlessness, tremors, and shuffling gait are major reasons that many patients stop taking their medications. The long-term use of antipsychotic drugs can lead to **tardive dyskinesia** ("late-appearing movement disorder"), which is characterized by symptoms such as persistent, involuntary chewing movements, lip smacking, and rolling movements of the tongue. This chronic and sometimes irreversible effect of antipsychotic drugs is a serious problem. Elderly patients and persons with brain damage or diabetes have an elevated risk of developing tardive dyskinesia. The symptoms tend to develop gradually, so this condition can be recognized in its early stages, and treatment can be altered. The changes in treatment include reducing the dose of the antipsychotic drug to the lowest effective level or adding vitamin E to the treatment (Zhang et al., 2004).

An estimated 30 to 40% of patients with schizophrenia do not respond adequately to typical antipsychotic drugs. Some of these patients, however, respond to the atypical antipsychotic clozapine, which was introduced in 1990 (several more *atypical antipsychotic drugs* have been developed since that time). In addition to its effectiveness in some patients who do not respond to other antipsychotic drugs, clozapine produces low rates of tardive dyskinesia (Iqbal et al., 2003). One reason for this low rate of motor effects is that clozapine affects serotonin as well as the dopamine receptors affected by most antipsychotic drugs. Clozapine, however, can seriously impair the ability of the bone

**antipsychotic drugs**
Drugs that reduce the symptoms of schizophrenia by blocking dopamine receptors in the brain; the typical antipsychotic drugs work by blocking dopamine, whereas the atypical drugs (such as Clozapine) also block serotonin

**tardive dyskinesia**
A serious adverse effect of antipsychotic drugs characterized by involuntary motor symptoms such as lip smacking

marrow to produce white blood cells, which leaves individuals highly vulnerable to infections (Rybacki, 1997). This problem occurs in about 1% of patients, and is potentially life-threatening; therefore patients who take Clozapine must have weekly blood tests to determine if their white blood count is within normal limits (Haber et al., 1997). Although clozapine does not lead to tardive dyskinesia, it is associated with side effects such as dizziness, drowsiness, and seizures that have led some psychiatrists to describe it as "not a user-friendly medication" (Pies, 1998, p. 52). Clozapine is recommended for use only in patients who have not responded adequately to two or more typical antipsychotic drugs (Pies, 1998). The history of antipsychotic drugs shows us that no drug is absolutely free of risk.

**Variations in Drug Response Related to Ethnicity and Sex.** Ethnic groups differ in their susceptibility to certain physical disorders such as Tay-Sachs disease and sickle-cell anemia; men and women also differ in their susceptibility to certain diseases. Given these general findings, we may also find differences in the response to psychotropic drugs.

Ethnicity and culture can interact in a complex manner to affect a person's response to drug treatment (Yamamoto & Lin, 1995). When Keh-Ming Lin arrived in the United States from Taiwan in 1974 for a residency in psychiatry, he noted that Caucasian patients with schizophrenia were given drug dosages 10 times higher than those given in Taiwan. Lin and his colleagues have been investigating ethnic differences in response to drug treatment for psychological disorders. Accumulating evidence reveals the existence of some pharmacokinetic differences among ethnic groups; these are group differences in the concentration of a drug in the blood after taking similar doses. Such ethnic differences may be a significant cause of the different response to drug therapies. For example, East Asian patients suffering from schizophrenia require lower doses of Haldol (haloperidol) to produce an optimal response. What's more, the side effects of antipsychotic drugs become evident in East Asian patients at lower doses than in Caucasian patients (Lin et al., 1989). The differential response to Haldol does not seem to result from lifestyle factors; similar responses were found in American- and foreign-born East Asians living in the United States (Lin et al., 1988). East Asian men also seem to be more sensitive to the drug Xanax (alprazolam, a benzodiazepine), which is used to treat anxiety and panic symptoms. Levels of Xanax and Haldol reach significantly higher concentrations in East Asian patients and remain in the body longer than they do in Caucasian patients after both oral and intravenous administration (Chien, 1993).

These results suggest that East Asians may require lower doses than Caucasians to achieve comparable results. Moreover, there is evidence that Asians require lower doses of tricyclic antidepressants and lithium to yield the same effects (Yamamoto & Lin, 1995).

What accounts for such differences in the drug response among ethnic groups? There may be differences in the number or type of drug receptors in the brain, in the effects of enzymes in the body, or in the way the body metabolizes (breaks down) drugs (Smith & Lin, 1996). Regardless of the actual causes of the differences, remember that the ultimate goal of this research is not to stereotype any individual or group; rather, it is to provide more appropriate treatment for all individuals suffering from psychological disorders.

Can a person's biological sex affect his or her response to psychotropic drug therapy? The answer is important in making treatment decisions; however, the question is not easy to answer. The Food and Drug Administration's (FDA) 1977 guidelines prohibited inclusion of "women of childbearing potential" in drug studies until the drugs had been tested on animals and been shown to be effective in men or older women. In 1993, the FDA replaced the earlier guidelines with new ones requesting the study of possible sex differences (Sherman, Temple, & Merkatz, 1995).

Drugs taken by the usual oral route are metabolized by the digestive tract; most of the drug travels to the liver, where it is metabolized and excreted, and some is eliminated through the kidneys. As little as 10% of a psychotropic drug remains to reach the brain. Differences between women and men may arise at any of these steps (Yonkers & Hamilton, 1995a).

Given the same dose, women generally have higher levels of a drug in their bloodstreams because they tend to weigh less than men. Complicating the picture, however, are the hormones estrogen and progesterone because they slow down the emptying time of the stomach, which can lower the amount of a drug that reaches the brain. Thus women can require higher doses of some drugs than men do. Conversely, women secrete less stomach acid than men do, and tricyclic antidepressants, benzodiazepines, and certain antipsychotic drugs are more likely to be absorbed by the body before they are neutralized by stomach acid. Thus women often require lower doses of these drugs (Yonkers & Hamilton, 1995a,b).

In sum, sex differences are difficult to categorize; sometimes women require higher levels of drugs than men do, and sometimes they require lower levels. The FDA guidelines will make more information available about sex differences in determining the appropriate levels of specific drugs.

## Drug Therapy

Table 13-8 (page 608) summarizes the drugs commonly used to treat psychological disorders. Proponents of drug therapy believe that the increased use and effectiveness of drugs heralded a new era in treating psychological disorders. In *Mind, Mood, and Medicine* (1981), Paul Wender and Donald Klein call the use of drugs a "virtual revolution." They suggest that drugs are used more frequently and more quickly than psychotherapy because of their greater availability.

Drugs can make some patients more manageable for therapists and hospital staff, reduce patients' anxiety levels, lift a depressed mood, and eliminate some delusions. But they cannot replace lost social skills or teach patients how to interact with family members and other people. Therapy programs that combine drug therapy with efforts to enhance patients' social skills and to assist family members in dealing with former patients have shown promise (Hogarty et al., 1991).

As we have indicated, many psychotropic drugs reduce the symptoms of various psychological disorders; however, they are also often associated with side effects. As we have discussed, for example, antipsychotic drugs can lead to adverse effects such as tardive dyskinesia. But withdrawing the drug can lead to a worsening of the symptoms or a relapse (return of symptoms). One study of the use of antipsychotic drugs found that about half of the patients with schizophrenia who were taking such drugs suffered a relapse when the drugs were withdrawn. Because about half of the patients did not suffer a relapse, researchers suggest a program of slowly tapering the dosage to the lowest effective dosage that controls the symptoms, which may be zero (Gilbert et al., 1995).

## Electroconvulsive Therapy

In 1938, the police in Rome found a man who suffered from schizophrenia wandering through a train station. They sent him to two psychiatrists, Ugo Cerletti and Lucio Bini, who had been experimenting with a new procedure to induce seizures. Seizures were thought to be beneficial in treating schizophrenia. The psychiatrists applied an electrical current to the man's head; the current triggered a seizure that jolted his body. After the third shock-induced seizure, the man appeared to recover from his schizophrenia (Valenstein, 1986). Cerletti and Bini's technique became known as **electroconvulsive therapy (ECT),** but it is also called *shock therapy*.

When ECT was first used, the seizures it induced were so violent that some patients suffered broken bones and a few even died. Consequently, it has been stigmatized by past misapplications and overuse (Sarason & Sarason, 2002). Today, repeated evaluations of ECT indicate that it is a successful treatment for severe depression, especially in cases that have not responded to antidepressant drugs (Berry, 2003). ECT is

**electroconvulsive therapy (ECT)** A biomedical treatment in which an electric current is passed through the brain to induce a seizure; most often used to treat severe depression

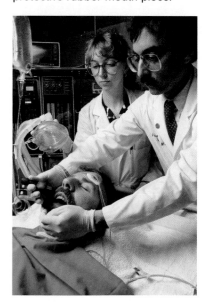
This patient is about to receive ECT treatment. The doctor is inserting a protective rubber mouth piece.

**TABLE 13-8**

## Major Categories of Drugs Used to Treat Psychological Disorders

| Type of Drug | Chemical Group | Generic Name | Brand Name | Side Effects | Mode of Action |
|---|---|---|---|---|---|
| Antianxiety drugs | Benzodiazepines | alprazolam chlordiazepoxide diazepam | Xanax Librium Valium | Dizziness, drowsiness, unsteadiness, impaired memory and concentration | Enhances the action of inhibitory neurotransmitter GABA, which in turn reduces arousal of higher brain centers |
| Antidepressants | Tricyclics | amitriptyline clomipramine imipramine | Elavil Anafranil Tofranil | Drowsiness, dry mouth, blurred vision, constipation, weight gain | Increase availability of the neurotransmitters norepinephrine and serotonin by blocking their reuptake |
| | Selective serotonin reuptake inhibitors (SSRIs) | fluoxetine paroxetine sertraline | Prozac Paxil Zoloft | Gastrointestinal side effects (nausea, vomiting, and diarrhea), dizziness, dry mouth, sexual dysfunctions (e.g., decreased libido, erectile dysfunction) | Enhance the activity of serotonin by preventing its uptake |
| | Monoamine oxidase (MAO) inhibitors | isocarboxazid phenelzine | Marplan Nardil | Excessive thirst, increased frequency of urination, altered blood pressure | Block the action of the enzyme MAO, which breaks down norepinephrine |
| Mood stablizers | | lithium | Eskalith | Increased thirst and urination, drowsiness, dizziness, tremors, weight gain, nausea, vomiting | Lithium has diverse actions on several neurotransmitters and may alter neuronal function through effects on ion distribution. |
| | Anticonvulsants | carbamazepine valproic acid | Tegretol Depakote | Increased thirst and urination, drowsiness, dizziness, tremors, weight gain, nausea, vomiting | Valproic acid may increase levels of GABA; carbamazepine may have widespread effects on neural function via its blocking of sodium channels. |
| Antipsychotic drugs | Typical | chlorpromazine fluphenazine haloperidol | Thorazine Prolixin Haldol | Drowsiness, dizziness, dry mouth, tardive dyskinesia, restlessness | Generally block dopamine receptors in the brain |
| | Atypical | clozapine risperidone | Clozaril Riserdal | Dizziness, drowsiness, weight gain, loss of capacity of the bone marrow to make white blood cells, seizures | Atypical antipsychotic drugs affect serotonin and dopamine receptors |

**Sources:** Bhatia and Bhatia (1997); Pies (1998).

**TABLE 13-9**

## Improvements in ECT That Have Increased Its Safety

1. *Length of electrical charge*—reduced from one second to one twenty-fifth of a second.
2. *Intensity of electrical charge*—reduced greatly.
3. *Timing of sessions*—reduced from as often as every day or even two or three a day to no more than three times a week.
4. *Length of treatment*—formerly up to 20 sessions or more; now typically 10 or fewer.
5. *Use of anesthetics and muscle relaxants*—formerly no anesthetics or muscle relaxants; now both are used.
6. *Monitoring*—both brain waves and the electrical functioning of the heart and now monitored through EEG and EKG [see Chapter 2]
7. *Placement of electrodes*—formerly on both sides of the head; now on the nondominant side only or on the right and left sides of the forehead.

**Source:** Sarason and Sarason (2002).

frequently used when there is a great risk of suicide because it works faster than drug therapies (Tondo, Isacsson, & Baldessarini, 2003).

Beginning in the 1950s, ECT was modified to reduce the more serious side effects. The improvements in ECT that have increased its safety are shown in Table 13-9.

After the patient is prepared for the treatment, electrodes are attached to the patient's head. In bilateral ECT the electrodes are attached to each of the patient's temples; in unilateral ECT they are attached to one side of the head. The electrodes deliver a current of electricity about equal to that required to light a 20-watt bulb for 2 seconds (Andreasen & Black, 1995). The equipment now in use delivers shorter bursts of electricity than that used before the 1950s. The current causes the patient to experience a convulsion, which should last at least 25 seconds to be effective. The recommended procedure is 3 treatments per week, for a total of 8 to 12 treatments.

### Psychological Detective

What effects do you think ECT would have on a patient immediately after the treatment? What psychological processes would be affected? Give these questions some thought and write down your answers before reading further.

After undergoing ECT, patients are confused, do not remember what happened during the treatment, and may experience memory impairment for about an hour (Fink, 2000). These effects occur because administration of the electrical shock disrupts the process of consolidation, which is crucial to the formation of long-term memories (see Chapter 7). The use of unilateral ECT may reduce the memory impairment because the treatment is usually not administered to the brain hemisphere that is responsible for language. There is concern, however, that unilateral ECT may not be as effective as bilateral treatment (Carney et al., 2003).

### Myth or Science

The application of electrodes to a person's skull to induce a seizure as a form of therapy has been controversial. Critics question the treatment because it looks like punishment; they also wonder if ECT damages the brain. Earlier research could not provide definitive answers to questions about the effects of ECT on the brain because researchers often did not have data on the condition of the patient's brain before ECT

**psychosurgery**
The alteration of brain tissue in an attempt to alleviate psychological disorders

was administered. They now have obtained magnetic resonance images (MRIs) before and after administration of bilateral ECT. Comparison of these images reveals no evidence of changes in the brain a few days or 6 months after the treatment (Coffey et al., 1991). Although this finding is encouraging, it cannot tell us whether ECT causes subtle changes that are not detectable by the MRI.

The reason for the effectiveness of ECT is still not known (Kellner et al., 1997). It has been suggested (but not proven) that ECT increases the levels of several neurotransmitters, such as norepinephrine, in the brain. These biochemical changes are thought to reverse processes that occur during depression and are similar to the changes that occur with drug treatments. ECT, however, has other effects on the central nervous system and hormone levels that might be responsible for lifting the depression (Fink, 1999).

## Psychosurgery

In *Great and Desperate Cures*, Elliot Valenstein (1986) describes a procedure from the 1930s: "After drilling two or more holes in a patient's skull, a surgeon inserted into the brain any of various instruments—some resembling an apple corer, a butter spreader, or an ice pick—and, often without being able to see what he was cutting, destroyed parts of the brain" (p. 3). This depiction is neither science fiction nor fiendish torture. Valenstein was describing an early version of **psychosurgery,** surgical alteration of brain tissue.

In 1935, Egas Moniz, a Portuguese neurologist, suggested that psychological problems might result from what he termed "reverberating circuits" in the brain. To break these circuits, Moniz proposed a simple surgical procedure that involved cutting nerve fibers of the brain's frontal lobes (see Chapter 2). Moniz coined the term *psychosurgery*, and his procedure became known as a *prefrontal lobotomy*. Psychosurgery found its way to the United States as a treatment for significantly impaired patients when Walter Freeman, a neurosurgeon, read an article by Moniz and decided to try the procedure in 1936. Despite the fact that Moniz won a Nobel Prize for his work in 1949 (Pressman, 1998), "there was nothing compelling about any of his arguments that should have persuaded a prudent man to attempt psychosurgery" (Valenstein, 1986, p. 100).

Why was such a radical and irreversible treatment used on thousands of patients? (The full number of patients operated on will never be known.) For one reason, there were no alternative treatments available for the thousands of chronically ill patients in increasingly overcrowded hospitals. In addition, these procedures were evaluated by surgeons whose enthusiasm may have overridden their objectivity. Dramatic changes in a few patients were widely reported; some patients who were given local anesthesia reported almost immediate symptom relief (Swayze, 1995). According to Robyn Dawes (1994), "Without doing anything even remotely close to a scientific examination of the procedure, the doctors performing it advocated its widespread use" (p. 48). Eventually, more objective and long-term evaluations were conducted. These studies were less enthusiastic about psychosurgery and noted possible severe complications such as hemorrhage, seizures, and major personality changes (Nevid & Greene, 2001). The development of drug treatments beginning in the 1950s provided a less drastic alternative to psychosurgery.

Present-day psychosurgical procedures are more refined than the earlier, crude operations; nevertheless, they are rarely performed, and then only as a last resort. Some cases of obsessive–compulsive disorder are so serious and unresponsive to drug or behavioral treatments that patients seek a surgical alternative (Persaud et al., 2003). In an operation called a *cingulotomy*, the surgeon cuts a bundle of nerve fibers that play a role in the obsessions and compulsions (Sachdev & Hay, 1996). Although this surgical procedure has reduced symptom severity in some cases, most patients exhibit little, if any, change as a result of this surgery.

This patient is undergoing psychosurgery.

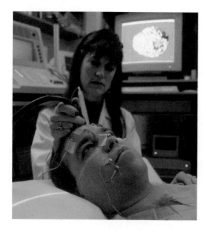

# REVIEW SUMMARY

**1.** The major category of **antianxiety drugs,** the *benzodiazepines*, affect the ability of the inhibitory neurotransmitter GABA to bind to receptor sites in the brain.

**2.** Three categories of drugs are used to treat depression: tricyclic antidepressants, MAO inhibitors, and SSRIs. Tricyclic antidepressants prevent reuptake of norepinephrine and serotonin. MAO inhibitors prevent an enzyme from breaking down norepinephrine and serotonin. Drugs such as Prozac reduce the reuptake of serotonin. Lithium and anticonvulsant drugs are treatments for mania.

**3.** **Antipsychotic drugs** occupy dopamine receptor sites in the brain. These drugs are more effective at reducing the positive symptoms of schizophrenia than the negative ones. The use of antipsychotic drugs can lead to **tardive dyskinesia,** a serious adverse reaction involving involuntary motor movements.

**4.** There are some significant ethnic differences in responses to some drugs used to treat psychological disorders. The FDA has issued new guidelines for the study of possible sex differences in responses to drugs.

**5.** **Electroconvulsive therapy (ECT)** is effective for major depression. Modified procedures for administering ECT, such as use of muscle relaxants, have reduced the severity of side effects. The most prominent side effect is memory disturbance immediately following ECT administration.

**6.** In 1935, Egas Moniz devised the first **psychosurgery,** the prefrontal lobotomy. The few psychosurgical operations done today involve alteration of much smaller areas of brain tissue.

## ✓ CHECK YOUR PROGRESS

**1.** Identify the categories of drugs that are most likely to be prescribed for each of the following disorders.

  **a.** mania

  **b.** schizophrenia

  **c.** major depression

**2.** Identify the neurotransmitter that is affected by each of the following categories of drugs.

  **a.** antipsychotic drugs

  **b.** benzodiazepines

  **c.** tricyclic antidepressants

**3.** What is the major class of antianxiety drugs such as Valium?

  **a.** tricyclics

  **b.** lithium family

  **c.** phenothiazines

  **d.** benzodiazepines

**4.** What is the most serious side effect of treatment with clozapine?

  **a.** insomnia

  **b.** memory impairment

  **c.** inability to manufacture white blood cells

  **d.** behavioral changes such as increased aggression

**5.** Gary takes antipsychotic drugs to control the symptoms of schizophrenia. After taking the drug for some time, he begins exhibiting symptoms such as smacking his lips and flailing his limbs. Gary is showing signs of

  **a.** tardive dyskinesia.

  **b.** a clozapine overdose.

  **c.** inoperative movements.

  **d.** neuroleptic malignant syndrome.

**6.** A psychiatrist prescribed a drug for your uncle's psychological disorder. As part of the treatment regimen, the psychiatrist periodically checks the level of the drug in your uncle's blood. Based on your knowledge of drug therapy, you conclude the prescribed drug is

  **a.** lithium.

  **b.** Valium.

  **c.** Elavil.

  **d.** Haldol.

**7.** ECT was originally developed to treat

  **a.** depression.

  **b.** schizophrenia.

  **c.** anxiety disorders.

  **d.** dissociative identity disorder.

**8.** The first psychosurgery involved severing nerve tracts in the

  **a.** occipital lobes.

  **b.** thalamus.

  **c.** frontal lobes.

  **d.** corpus callosum.

**9.** What is one of the common side effects of psychosurgery?

  **a.** fevers

  **b.** extreme weight gain

  **c.** susceptibility to colds

  **d.** major personality changes

**ANSWERS: 1. a.** mood stabilizers (especially lithium but also anticonvulsants) **b.** antipsychotic **c.** tricyclic antidepressant drugs, MAO inhibitors, or SSRIs **2. a.** dopamine; atypical antipsychotic drugs also affect serotonin **b.** GABA **c.** norepinephrine and serotonin **3.** d **4.** c **5.** a **6.** a **7.** b **8.** c **9.** d

# Health Psychology

## CHAPTER OUTLINE

We now turn our attention from psychological disorders to those affecting our physical health. Progress during recent decades has altered the threats to our health. Many of the current causes of illness and death are related to our behaviors, such as eating and exercise. As awareness of our personal vulnerability to illnesses increases, we try to determine what we can do to reduce our risk and maintain good health. In this chapter we explore some of the issues surrounding disease and health.

# HEALTH PSYCHOLOGY: AN OVERVIEW

**Outside a small town just before the turn of the 19th century, a family struggles for survival. Pitted against the forces of nature, family members try to grow the food they need, as they hope to be spared the illnesses that have affected other people in the town. For example, an epidemic of influenza swept through the community last year and took a heavy toll.** *How have the diseases experienced by Americans changed over the years?*

Dramatic changes in the causes of death in the United States over the past century have led to a focus on how emotional reactions, social influences, and overt behaviors affect our health. In 1900, the major causes of death were contagious diseases, such as influenza, pneumonia, and tuberculosis. By about 1950, changes in sanitation and mass vaccinations had enabled Americans to avoid or at least to recover from many of these diseases. Today the leading causes of death—cardiovascular disease (heart disease and stroke) and cancer (U.S. National Center for Health Statistics, 2001)—are noncontagious diseases that are linked to our behaviors or lifestyle. Our behavior has a powerful influence on our health; behavior changes might have prevented half the deaths in the United States in 1990 (see Table 14-1; Holloway, 2004). Although noncontagious diseases are now responsible for most deaths, deaths owing to infectious diseases have increased. Much of this increase is the result of *acquired immunodeficiency syndrome (AIDS)*, in which certain behaviors put individuals at risk for a disease caused by a virus (Temoshok, 1998).

**Health psychology** is a relatively new scientific discipline; the Division of Health Psychology of the American Psychological Association was formed in 1978 (Belar, 2001), and the first issue of the journal *Health Psychology* was published in 1982 (Friedman, 2002). Health psychology is the subfield of psychology devoted to understanding how psychological and social variables affect health and how we respond when we become ill. Health psychologists focus on how emotions, such as anger and anxiety (Suinn, 2001), social factors (such as the tendency for men not to manage their health care especially well (Hewlett, 2001), and behavior influence health and illness (McCarthy, 2000; Rogers, 2000). They also develop programs to reduce the levels of risk factors related to diseases. For example, health psychologists have developed school-based programs to strengthen students' ability to resist social pressures to start smoking cigarettes (Botvin et al., 1992).

We are still subject to attacks from bacteria and viruses, such as the virus that causes AIDS. In our modern world, however, the "new germs" are more often personal habits like smoking, a sedentary lifestyle, excessive intake of dietary fat, and strong emotional reactions to life events such as job loss or divorce that can produce the affliction we call stress (Ursin & Eriksen, 2004). Behavior and lifestyle affect our health (Carpenter, 2001), and culture affects our behavior and lifestyle; consequently, there are major cultural

**health psychology**
Subfield of psychology that is concerned with how psychological and social variables affect health and illness

## TABLE 14-1

### Deaths from Preventable Causes in the United States, 1990

A significant number of deaths could be prevented each year by changes in behaviors that are related to our risk of disease and death.

| Cause | Estimated Deaths | Percentage of Total Deaths |
|---|---|---|
| Smoking tobacco | 400,000 | 19 |
| Dietary factors and physical inactivity | 300,000 | 14 |
| Use of alcohol | 100,000 | 5 |
| Microbial agents | 90,000 | 4 |
| Toxic agents | 60,000 | 3 |
| Firearms | 35,000 | 2 |
| High-risk sexual behavior | 30,000 | 1 |
| Motor vehicle injuries | 25,000 | 1 |
| Illicit use of drugs | 20,000 | less than 1 |
| Total | 1,060,000 | 50 |

**Source:** McGinnis and Foege (1993).

differences in health and disease around the world. In previous chapters, we have pointed several times to the importance of the cultural concepts of collectivism and individualism. Whether a culture is described as collectivistic or individualistic can influence the types and prevalence of diseases. For example, individualistic cultures such as the United States have lower rates of infectious and parasitic diseases compared to collectivistic cultures. On the other hand, individualistic cultures have higher rates of various types of cancer (Matsumoto, 1996).

Joseph Matarazzo (1984), a health psychologist, has offered a list of behaviors that are related to good health (see Table 14-2). These health-promoting behaviors should

## TABLE 14-2

### Behaviors That Have a Positive Influence on Health

- Do not smoke.
- Engage in 30 minutes of physical activity almost every day.
- Eat breakfast every day.
- Get your weight to a normal level.
- Learn and follow a healthful diet.
- If you drink alcohol, do so in moderation.
- Get the amount of sleep that your body needs.
- Use seat belts every time you are in a vehicle.
- Do not drive at excessive speeds.
- Women, do a regular breast exam; men, get a regular prostate exam.
- Find a physician with whom you can communicate openly and effectively.

**Source:** Adapted from Matarazzo (1984).

not surprise you. Although initiating them seems difficult, they can easily become part of your daily routine. Begin each day by eating breakfast, and you will be less likely to eat snack foods to tide you over until lunch. Likewise, once you start buckling your seat belt, it becomes as automatic as putting the key in the ignition. All of these behaviors are components of a healthy lifestyle.

## STRESS AND ILLNESS

**Almost every day, Beth relates another story about school and job pressures. Her courses this semester are especially difficult. A reduction in the size of the sales force at work means she is on the go from the time she arrives until closing. According to the newspaper, a virus is spreading through the area. Yesterday Beth sensed that she was developing a cold and wondered if the stress she is experiencing has left her more vulnerable to that virus.** *Can stress make us more vulnerable to illness?*

Just about every day we hear or use the word *stress* in conversations, yet the term did not come into widespread use until 1936, when a Canadian endocrinologist, Hans Selye (1907–1982), published a book titled *The Stress of Life* (1978). While he was in medical school, Selye noticed that many patients had similar symptoms—fatigue, loss of appetite, fever—regardless of the particular disease that was diagnosed.

Selye's experiments with rats led him to conclude that regardless of the external or internal stressful event, the body (whether of a rat or a human being) responds in comparable ways, which he described as a *stress syndrome*. He defined **stress** as the nonspecific response of the body to any demand or unexpected event in the environment that requires an adjustment. **Stressors** are the environmental events that cause an organism to adjust and display this nonspecific stress response.

## The General Adaptation Syndrome

Selye outlined a series of biological responses, called the **general adaptation syndrome (GAS),** that occur as the body deals with stressors. The nervous and endocrine systems orchestrate this series of responses or stages: the alarm stage, the resistance stage, and the exhaustion stage.

**Alarm Stage.** The *alarm* stage of the GAS is equivalent to the well-known fight-or-flight response (see Chapter 2). During this "call to arms," the hypothalamus signals the sympathetic nervous system and the pituitary.

The combination of the activation of the sympathetic nervous system and an outpouring of stress hormones prepares the body for a brief period of physical action in response to a threat. One consequence of the release of these hormones is easily recognized—your heart races. You may also experience "butterflies" in your stomach because digestion slows and blood is redirected to the muscles in preparation for action. The body burns more energy, which may provide physical strength we did not believe we possessed.

The fight-or-flight response prepared our ancestors exceptionally well for physical actions such as fleeing from a dangerous woolly mammoth, but this response is not always useful today. Modern stressors like mammoth traffic jams do not call for physical responses; nevertheless, our biological equipment and responses to stressors are the same as those of our ancestors (Mohlman et al., 2004).

**Resistance Stage.** When a stressor continues past the alarm stage, the body moves to the second stage of the general adaptation syndrome, *resistance* (see Figure 14-1). The body maintains a moderate level of arousal, which enhances our ability to withstand the original stressor. If new stressors are introduced, however, the ability to resist

**stress**
Nonspecific response of the body to any demand made on it

**stressor**
Anything that causes an organism to adjust and display the nonspecific stress response

**general adaptation syndrome (GAS)**
Typical series of responses to stressful situations that includes the alarm, resistance, and exhaustion stages

 **14.1**

FIGHT OR FLIGHT

**FIGURE 14-1** Hans Selye's general adaptation syndrome (GAS). He outlined three phases of the typical biological response to stressors: alarm, resistance, exhaustion.

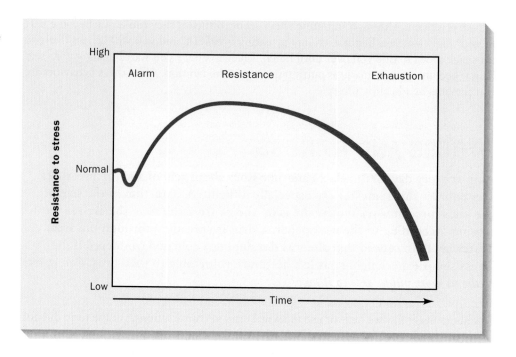

the demands of all these stressors decreases. For example, a laboratory animal in the resistance stage may have greater ability to resist extreme cold, but it becomes more vulnerable to bacterial infections.

## Myth or Science

Have you wondered if feeling overwhelmed by a set of circumstances—term papers, exams, job searching—could make you more vulnerable to a virus that can cause a cold? Such circumstances, such as problems with a roommate, can affect your ability to resist new stressors, and they may also reduce the ability of your immune system to fight a virus. Sheldon Cohen and his colleagues (1991) intentionally exposed students (with their informed consent) to one of several types of respiratory viruses. Did all the students develop colds after being infected? No. Students who were experiencing high levels of stressors were more likely to develop colds than students who were experiencing low levels of stressors. A similar finding in a second study reinforces these findings (Cohen, Tyrrell, & Smith, 1993). Thus the belief that stress makes us more vulnerable to colds is not a myth: High levels of stressors can make us more vulnerable to a virus.

**Exhaustion Stage.**   When demands for adjustment exceed the body's ability to respond, the body enters the third stage of the GAS, *exhaustion*. At this point the stress response has lost its adaptive quality and actually contributes to pathological changes that result in disease. For example, continued high levels of heart rate and blood pressure raise the risk of heart disease. In fact, the stress response actually suppresses the body's immune system, which leaves us more vulnerable to diseases (Segerstrom & Miller, 2004). When the body has reached the limits of its ability to adapt to stress, various physical disorders known as *psychophysiological disorders* (formerly called *psychosomatic disorders*) may develop. A wide range of diseases has been linked to stress, including asthma, herpes, and hypertension (high blood pressure). In short, certain diseases are influenced by our inability to adapt to excessive stress.

Stress is not, however, something that needs to be—or even can be—avoided. Stress can impair your performance on exams and papers, but it can also provide the energy and zest to propel you to a first-rate performance. Consider an example. Chantel prepares to ride what has been described as the "most thrilling, spine-tingling roller coaster on the planet." Her friends watch as the ride takes her up, down, and even upside down. They can hear her scream at the top of her lungs; nevertheless, when the ride stops, Chantel sprints past you to line up for another go!

When Chantel experiences the fight-or-flight response during the roller coaster ride, the stress is positive, and the physiological arousal is pleasant and exciting. Under some conditions, this arousal can lead to emotional or intellectual growth and development. Selye called this pleasant, positive kind of stress *eustress* (from the Greek *eu*, meaning "good," as in *euphoria*); the damaging form of stress is called *distress*. Thus we should not seek to avoid stress altogether; instead we should find ways to channel the physiological arousal of the stress response more effectively. Some stressful events, however, are easier to avoid or channel than others.

**STUDY TIP**

Create a visual representation of the entire general adaptation syndrome (GAS).

## Sources of Stress

Although in modern times we are not likely to have to flee from wild animals, we are at the mercy of sudden, unpredictable catastrophes, such as fires and hurricanes, and we may experience major changes in our lives: We move our homes, change jobs, get married, raise children. In addition, every day we encounter minor irritations: The toaster doesn't work, a careless driver backs into our car and dents it, and so on. Such minor annoyances can affect our sense of well-being and our health.

**Catastrophes.**    Catastrophes test our ability to adapt. Natural disasters like earthquakes, hurricanes, and tornados can cause devastation over vast areas. To this list of natural disasters we add a growing number of disasters caused by human error, such as toxic spills, nuclear accidents, and transportation accidents.

**Major Life Events.**    Dave, a 44-year-old laborer, has rarely experienced any illnesses. The past 6 months, however, have been "unbearable." He lost his job, the family home was damaged by a tornado, and his daughter was killed in an automobile accident. After he started experiencing insomnia, dizziness, and loss of appetite, Dave decided to see his physician. He wondered whether his symptoms were caused by the major life events he had recently experienced.

*Major life events* require significant adjustments in almost all aspects of our lives; therefore they can be powerful stressors. Thomas Holmes and Richard Rahe (1967) wished to determine how much adjustment such events require. To accomplish their goal, they developed the 43-item Social Readjustment Rating Scale, which is often printed in magazines, newspapers, and textbooks. A number expressed in life change units (LCUs) indicates the amount of adjustment each item requires. Holmes and Rahe determined the LCUs by asking groups of people to compare the amount of adjustment required by each item to the amount of adjustment that occurs when a person is married. (The amount of adjustment required by marriage was set at 50 LCUs.)

Holmes and Rahe administered the Social Readjustment Rating Scale to many people, who were also asked to report their illnesses across some span of time, usually 1 year. Those persons with high scores reported more illnesses than persons with low scores. This dramatic finding seemed to support the notion that too much change really is bad for us.

The excitement generated by these findings turned to skepticism when subsequent investigators could not replicate the original strong relations. The relation between major life events and illness still existed, but it was not as strong as was originally reported.

A wide range of events can affect our psychological and physical health. These potential stressors range from unpredictable catastrophes such as fires to everyday hassles such as having to wait in lines.

## Psychological Detective

Not everyone who is exposed to numerous major life events develops physical or psychological symptoms. Think of reasons that might explain why people differ in their responses to similar sets of life events. Here is a hint: Imagine that both you and your roommate have exams next week. If you both rated the degree of stress the exams cause, would you give similar ratings? Write down your answer before reading further.

Does everyone interpret major life events in the same way? Probably not. The circumstances of a divorce, for example, often determine whether it is viewed positively or negatively. Culture also seems to play a role in how people interpret and react to major life events. Compared with Americans and Japanese, Europeans gave lower ratings (indicating less change) to divorce (Ornstein & Sobel, 1987). What's more, some events on the Social Readjustment Rating Scale could be viewed as positive and therefore are not necessarily troublesome or disturbing. Starting a new job and moving to a new city can signify exciting opportunities that are likely sources of eustress, not distress. Also, events that do *not* occur can be just as stressful as—perhaps more so than—events that do occur. To take just one example, imagine being jilted at the altar. Despite these concerns and criticisms, research (Owen et al., 2004) has shown that the number and magnitude of life change events can influence the recovery rate of some medical patients. There appears to be something of scientific merit here to be investigated.

As we see later in the chapter, people differ in the way they interpret and respond to change. Some individuals are able to call friends and relatives for support in times of need; others may be more vulnerable to stressors because they must bear the full weight of major life changes with no support from others.

**Acculturative Stress.**  With travel to and from foreign countries a commonplace occurrence, it is not surprising to find people from different cultures living abroad. The United States, with its large number of refugees and immigrants, is a prime example. **Acculturative stress,** the stress of adapting to a new culture, can be quite traumatic; there may be an entirely new language to master, new values and customs to evaluate, and new styles of dress to consider.

Consider how stressful it would be for an American, who was raised in the individualistic society of the United States, to emigrate to a country, such as Japan, that has a collectivist society.

What is the best way to deal with acculturative stress? Many researchers (for example, Ward & Rana-Deuba, 1999) suggest that accepting the values and customs of the new culture as fully as possible results in the best adaptation. There may be some stress involved in adopting new values and customs; however, the experts argue that this stress is less than the stress of trying to deny the new culture.

**Posttraumatic Stress Disorder.**  Some events are so far beyond our usual experience that they would deeply disturb almost anyone who encountered them. Events like being raped or observing a violent death are not included in the Social Readjustment Rating Scale, yet their impact can be so great that they may result in **posttraumatic stress disorder (PTSD).** The primary symptom of PTSD is experiencing intense fear while reliving a shocking event in dreams, flashbacks, or intrusive thoughts. Victims of PTSD are often anxious and irritable, find it difficult to concentrate, suffer from sleep disturbances, and experience guilt. (This disorder is classified as an anxiety disorder; the other anxiety disorders were discussed in Chapter 12.) Consider the following case, and imagine how you might react if you were Ed:

A man was standing on his tiptoes on the curb so Ed slowed the bus as he approached. Just before the bus reached the corner, the man flung himself against the windshield and was killed. For weeks after, Ed cried and could not

**acculturative stress**
The stress of adapting to a new culture

**posttraumatic stress disorder (PTSD)**
Set of symptoms that may follow deeply disturbing events; symptoms include reliving the event, difficulty in concentrating, sleep disturbances, anxiety, and guilt

function on the job; eventually he was admitted to a hospital with the diagnosis of posttraumatic stress disorder. He said, "I felt like somebody put a gun in my hand, pointed it at his head, and pulled the trigger." (Miller et al., 1988, p. 43)

The effects of traumas can last long after the original event. Many victims of PTSD exhibit sympathetic nervous system and hormonal changes (Ford et al., 2004). Victims of PTSD often become highly sensitive; events that would not have evoked a response in the past now evoke cognitive and physical responses as if the original trauma was being experienced again. For example, war veterans with PTSD were found to exhibit an exaggerated startle response to sound, which did not occur in veterans or civilians without PTSD (Morgan, Grillon, Southwick, Davis, & Charney, 1996).

PTSD occurs in about 5 men and 13 women per 1,000 American adults. What about the other people who are confronted by loss and trauma and do not develop PTSD; what happens to them? Bonanno (2004) presents data indicating that many people who are exposed to potentially traumatic events "show only minor and transient disruptions in their ability to function" (p. 20). Because researchers have given much attention to PTSD sufferers, little is known about persons who are resilient in the face of such traumatic events. Hopefully, continued research will clarify this issue.

**Everyday Hassles.** Hassles are minor everyday occurrences that are distressing, frustrating, and irritating; they include slow-moving traffic, long lines at the supermarket, and lost keys. Each hassle may elicit a minor alarm reaction; thus we can say that some people have their alarms going off continuously! Although such minor alarms may not seem capable of producing major consequences, psychologist Richard Lazarus and his colleagues have found that hassles can accumulate and become associated with physical and psychological problems. In one investigation, researchers found a correlation between the occurrence of daily hassles and the presence of current and subsequent health problems such as flu, headaches, and sore throats (Cassidy, 2000). Likewise, Suinn (2001) reported that anxiety and anger can increase vulnerability to illness, increase cholesterol levels, and increase the risk of death from cardiovascular disease. Certainly anxiety and anger qualify as daily hassles!

How could such minor annoyances have significant health consequences? Apparently the effect of several minor daily annoyances can accumulate and raise the levels of your body's stress hormones, which are released early in the GAS. How can you reduce such daily hassles? One way is to maintain a positive emotional style. People with a positive emotional style do not have as much illness as people with negative emotional styles (Palmer, 2003).

There is growing awareness that the symptoms of PTSD can strike not only immediate victims of disasters such as the World Trade Center attack; but also their rescuers. At a moment's notice, rescue workers can be summoned to the scene of a horrible disaster. The social support they provide to one another is often a major factor in helping them to deal with the human tragedies they observe firsthand.

## What Makes Events Stressful?

Consider the following real-life event: Your younger brother arrives home breathless and with a bit of apprehension recounts how "another car hit mine." You quickly determine that it was *your* car, driven by your brother, that hit the other car. How do you react? You examine the damage and imagine $100 bills exiting your wallet. The alarm reaction has kicked into gear. Your interpretation of this event, however, can dramatically influence your physical reaction to it. If you focus on damage, costs, and inconvenience, anger builds within and is fueled by the actions of the sympathetic nervous system and the release of stress hormones. Now imagine that you take a moment to reevaluate the situation. No one was hurt (which is important), cars can be repaired, and the inconvenience will not be excessive. If you adopt this approach, your physical response to the same event will be quite different.

Richard Lazarus and Susan Folkman (1984) believe that the way we deal with potential stressors begins with our appraisal of the event. When faced with a potential stressor like the one we just described, our first task is to determine whether the event

**FIGURE 14-2** The two-stage process of primary and secondary appraisal helps us determine whether an event is stressful and, if so, how we can cope.

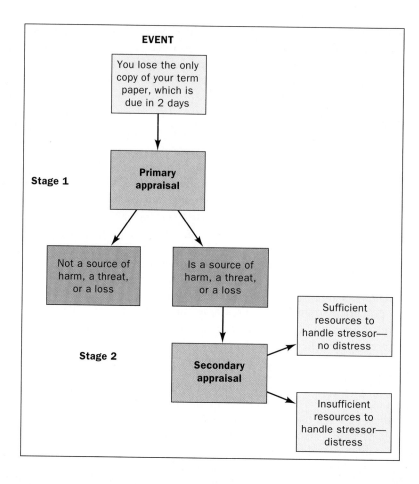

or situation is stressful. In other words, should we be upset? This evaluation, called **primary appraisal,** can result in several conclusions. We may determine that an event or situation is irrelevant because it is of little or no consequence to us. In other cases, we may determine that an event is actually beneficial (a form of eustress). Finally, we may determine that an event or situation is stressful, is potentially harmful, or creates a loss such as illness or injury. Potentially harmful events such as living in a violent neighborhood or facing a difficult exam involve an expectation of future physical or psychological harm. When we decide that an event is a stressor, we must determine how we will deal with it—a process called **secondary appraisal** (see Figure 14-2).

Jobs that demand a great deal of responsibility but do not permit workers to control their time are more likely to lead to stress-induced illnesses. Air traffic controllers at large airports, medical interns, police officers, and secretaries experience high levels of stress for these reasons. Race-car drivers may not be bothered by speeds that reach more than 200 miles per hour, but they tense up when they pull off the track and turn over control of their car to their pit crew. The same is true of employees whose companies are being acquired by other firms. Their sense of control is lost for a time, and as a result they may experience a variety of stress symptoms.

## How Stress and Disease May Be Related

The immune system can be described as a sense organ because its job is to "sense" cells and substances that don't belong in our body. Thus the **immune system** is the body's major defense against foreign invaders like bacteria or viruses. The specialized cells and organs that make up this complex system are located throughout the bloodstream and the lymphatic system. To do its job properly, the immune system must first distinguish between cells that are part of the organism and those that are not. If the immune system fails to make this distinction, it can become too active and attack harmless cells, thereby

**primary appraisal**
The first step in coping with stress; consists of determining whether an event is a threat

**secondary appraisal**
The second step in coping with stress; consists of deciding how to deal with the stress-producing situation

**immune system**
System that protects the body against foreign substances such as viruses and bacteria

aggravating conditions such as allergies and arthritis. In some cases the immune system may be so impaired that a person can become vulnerable to a range of diseases.

The immune system recognizes foreign invaders and then deactivates them and removes them from the body (Kang, 2003). The substances that trigger an immune response are called **antigens;** these include bacteria, fungi, parasites, and viruses. The task of ridding the body of these substances falls to a variety of specialized cells, including two forms of white blood cells: *lymphocytes*, small white cells produced in the bone marrow or the thymus, and *phagocytes* (literally, "eater cells"), large white cells that engulf foreign matter, such as viruses. When they are activated, cells in the immune system also release proteins, called *cytokines*, which activate brain areas and alert us concerning this immune activity (Maier & Watkins, 2000).

**Psychoneuroimmunology.**    A new science called *psychoneuroimmunology* focuses on how the body defends itself against foreign substances and how psychological and physiological factors influence the immune system. The term focuses attention on the interactions of the brain, endocrine system, and immune system (Azar, 2001).

How can stress affect the immune system? We know that stress leads to activity in the sympathetic nervous system and the release of the hormones cortisol, epinephrine, and norepinephrine. These hormones help us resist stress, but in the long run they reduce the effectiveness of the immune system. A variety of stressful events—loss of a spouse, divorce, depression, exams—have been found to suppress the functioning of the immune system and make people more susceptible to disease (Gomez-Merino, Chennaoui, Burnat, Drogou, & Guezennec, 2003; Senior, 2001). Long-term stressors are also associated with lowered immune system functioning. For example, Janice Kiecolt-Glaser and her colleagues (1991) studied the health status of caregivers who had been providing daily care for spouses suffering from Alzheimer's disease for an average of 5 years. Compared with a group of people with similar demographic characteristics who were not caring for such patients, the caregivers had lowered immune system functioning and reported more days of infectious illnesses. In a literature review, researchers concluded that in the relation between stress levels and immune system functioning, there were "relatively strong and consistent associations" (Herbert & Cohen, 1993). Kiecolt-Glaser and Glaser (2001) have also found that the detrimental effects of stress on the immune system increase with age; that is, older adults show even greater immune system problems when they are confronted with stress.

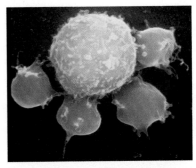

The specialized cells and organs that make up the immune system serve to recognize and destroy foreign substances called antigens. Among the specialized cells are lymphocytes that are shown here attacking bacteria.

**antigens**

Foreign substances such as bacteria that trigger an immune response

Dear Mom and Dad,

    I'm sorry for not writing but hope you will understand. First, sit down before you read further.
    I'm doing much better now after recovering from the concussion and the broken leg I received when I jumped from the window of my dorm after it caught fire last month. I can almost see and walk normally thanks to the loving care of the wonderful man who risked his life to save me. He more than saved me; he has become my whole family. You see, I have been living with him since the fire, and we are planning to get married. We haven't set a date yet but plan to have one soon, before my pregnancy starts to show.

Love always,

*Mary*

P.S.: There was no fire, I am perfectly healthy, and I'm not pregnant. In fact, I do not even have a boyfriend. However I did get a D in German, a D- in physics, and an F in algebra. I wanted you to keep this all in perspective.

The writer of this letter is absolutely correct. The perspective or context can dramatically change how stressful the same event can be.

# REVIEW SUMMARY

1. **Health psychology** is a subfield that is concerned with the social and psychological factors that influence health and illness.

2. Hans Selye developed the concept of **stress,** the nonspecific response of the body to demands to adjust to a wide range of changes.

3. **Stressors** are demands that give rise to the **general adaptation syndrome (GAS),** which consists of three stages: *alarm, resistance,* and *exhaustion.*

4. Among the circumstances that could lead to stress are catastrophes, major life changes such as divorce, **acculturative stress,** traumatic events such as criminal victimization, and hassles. They have been associated with physiological responses such as increased levels of stress hormones.

5. Researchers found that high levels of life change were associated with illness. Subsequent investigation showed that the relation between major life events and illness is not as strong as was originally reported. One explanation is that a person's interpretation of events is an important determinant of the event's impact.

6. **Posttraumatic stress disorder (PTSD)** occurs in the aftermath of deeply disturbing experiences such as rape and combat. Victims of PTSD often relive the traumatic event in dreams, flashbacks, or intrusive thoughts.

7. Everyday minor annoyances can accumulate and become associated with subsequent health problems.

8. Interpretation or appraisal of an event often determines whether that event is stressful. **Primary appraisal** occurs when we determine whether an event is a threat; in **secondary appraisal** we decide how to deal with the threat.

9. The **immune system** is the body's major defense against bacteria and viruses. *Psychoneuroimmunology* is the study of how psychological and physiological factors interact to influence the immune system. A wide variety of stressful events can affect immune system functioning.

# ✓ CHECK YOUR PROGRESS

1. Your interest in health psychology has been piqued, so you decide to find the causes of death for family members. At the beginning of the 20th century, your family members were likely to die as a result of _____; at the end of the 20th century, the cause of death was more likely to be

   a. accidents, cancer
   b. cancer, heart disease
   c. influenza, heart disease
   d. heart disease, accidents

2. What is the nonspecific response of the body to any demand?

   a. stress
   b. the defensive reaction
   c. general adaptation syndrome
   d. the syndrome of "being sick"

3. A researcher for the National Institutes of Health is asked to review the causes of death in the United States and report on the potential for efforts to reduce the deaths. She is asked to write a report to Congress. Which of the following would make the best title for that report?

   a. "Leading Cause of Death: Environmental Pollution"
   b. "Toxins Are Taking a Greater Toll Than Was Suspected"
   c. "Growing Influence of Genetic Factors on Death Rates"
   d. "Focus on Behavior: Half of Deaths Could Be Prevented"

4. Identify the GAS stage described in each of the following situations:

   a. A motorist cuts you off on the interstate, and you must slam on the brakes to avoid a collision. Your heart rate accelerates, your muscles tense, and your mouth is dry.

   b. Your uncle has had a series of significant financial and social setbacks in the past 2 years. His physician just told him that he has hypertension and ulcers.
   c. For several weeks Jane was fighting a "flu bug." She seemed to be succeeding, but then her husband asked for a divorce and she lost her job. Shortly afterward she came down with the flu.

5. You have avoided going sky diving with your friends for a number of months, After you have finally done it, you want to go right back and do it again. What type of stress have you experienced?

   a. eustress
   b. distress
   c. ego stress
   d. constructive stress

6. Describe the effects of the fight-or-flight response (alarm stage) on each of the following: heart rate, blood flow, breathing, hormones, and muscles.

7. Minor everyday occurrences that can be distressing, frustrating, and irritating are termed

   a. hassles.
   b. annoyers.
   c. life events.
   d. mini-stressors.

8. After a stressful event has occurred, which part of the brain sends a chemical signal to the adrenal gland to tell it to release its hormones?

   a. thalamus
   b. pituitary
   c. amygdala
   d. hippocampus

**9.** Answer the following questions.

    **a.** A person who is deciding whether an event is stressful is engaged in what process?

    **b.** Jill decides that she will be able to complete the papers that are due next week because her friends can give her some advice and she has learned how to use her new computer. Jill's thinking can be described as what process?

**10.** What are the key symptoms of PTSD? What types of situations seem most likely to lead to it?

**ANSWERS: 1.** c **2.** a **3.** d **4. a.** Alarm **b.** Exhaustion **c.** Resistance **5.** a **6.** Heart and blood pressure increase, breathing becomes deeper, most muscles are engorged with blood, epinephrine and norepinephrine are released to power these changes. **7.** a **8.** b **9. a.** Primary appraisal **b.** Secondary appraisal **10.** The symptoms of PTSD include anxiety, irritability, difficulty in concentrating, sleep disturbances, guilt, and reliving the shocking event in dreams or flashbacks. Among men, the most common circumstances leading to PTSD are being in combat and seeing someone hurt or die; physical attacks, especially rape, are the most common circumstances leading to PTSD among women.

# LIFESTYLE INFLUENCES ON DISEASE RISK

Rich, 60, has been smoking for as long as he can remember. He knows the health risks associated with smoking because he has heard them "a million times." Yet he is hesitant to stop his 15-cigarette-a-day habit out of fear that he will gain weight. "Why stop smoking if all I'll do is gain weight and trade one risk factor for another?" *Do people usually gain weight when they stop smoking?*

An illness or accident can occur at any time. In some cases it results primarily from chance or genetic factors, which we really can't control. Our decisions to engage in certain behaviors, however, can have a profound effect on our health. *Lifestyle* refers to our daily voluntary decisions about how to act that can affect our risk of developing health problems (McFarland & Sanders, 2003). As you have seen in Table 14-1, deaths in the United States due to lifestyle factors have risen significantly. We now look closely at several behaviors that can influence our risk of developing certain diseases. This section focuses on smoking, the development of heart disease, and AIDS. Recall that we discussed the effects of nutrition and eating behaviors in Chapter 6.

## Smoking

Smoking-related illnesses continue to be the single most preventable cause of death and illness in the United States. The fact that over 430,000 smoking-related deaths are reported each year (Carpenter, 2001) reflects its significant role as a lifestyle factor. The current concern about the hazards of smoking was foreshadowed decades ago. Beginning in 1893, several states outlawed the sale, manufacture, advertising, or use of cigarettes (Tate, 1989).

A single puff of a cigarette sends the stimulant nicotine on a 10-second journey to your brain, where it causes a release of norepinephrine that increases your heart rate and blood pressure. Over time, the damage resulting from this nicotine-induced heart acceleration coupled with the effects of components of cigarette smoke such as tar can help bring on cancer, heart disease, and pulmonary diseases (Orlando, Tucker, Ellickson, & Klein, 2004). Smoking is considered extremely addictive; few people who have smoked regularly for a year or more find it easy to quit (Schelling, 1992). Even nonsmokers suffer some consequences of smoking. Passive (secondhand or involuntary) smoking is a potential cause of lung cancer (Environmental Protection Agency, 1990) and also reduces the blood's ability to deliver oxygen to the heart. In this section we discuss the risks associated with smoking and describe efforts to reduce the number of Americans who smoke.

Because the smoking habit often begins in adolescence, more effort is being directed toward preventing smoking by people in this age group.

**Who Smokes and Why?** Despite repeated warnings about the risks associated with smoking, about one in four U.S. adults continues to smoke. (Despite the fact that the number of smokers has been declining, "about 4,000 American adolescents begin smoking cigarettes each day" [Friedman, 2002, p. 257]). The decline has not been equal among all groups; however, the rate of decline is greater for men than it is for women.

The rate of smoking among Americans with less education is declining at a slower rate than among those with more education. Although the number of smokers is declining in the United States, other countries report significant increases. For example, China's rate of cigarette production is increasing 11% per year to keep up with the demand (Bartecchi, MacKenzie, & Schrier, 1995).

Smoking typically begins in the adolescent years. About 90% of smokers smoked their first cigarette before age 18. The majority of first-time smokers are between 11 and 13 years of age; almost no regular smoking begins after the age of 20 (Goldberg, 2003). Peer-group identification has a strong effect on the probability that children and adolescents will begin smoking (Goodrow, Seier, & Stewart, 2003). What's more, in the past the tobacco industry targeted adolescents with promotional activities and advertising designed to entice them to begin smoking (Taylor & Bonner, 2003). Such promotional activities and advertising aimed at adolescents are now banned as part of the tobacco settlement between the federal government and the tobacco industry. However, tobacco promotion is heavy in bars and clubs, and this promotion has targeted young adults as potential consumers (Biener & Albers, 2004).

The recent increase in smoking and tobacco use by youth in the United States has spurred an increase in research on tobacco knowledge and smoking cessation among teens and college students (Carpenter, 2001). Biasco and Hartnett (2002) reported that the majority of their sample of 810 college students believed that smoking was harmful and that people should not be harmed by another person's smoking. However, these same students did not want further legal restrictions to control smoking; they indicated that education was a better choice. The results of a study by Easley and Range (2004) suggest that this view may be accurate. These researchers found that nonsmoking college students had better tobacco knowledge. However, even though the educational approach may work well for college students, it may not work as well for younger adolescents. Shadel, Niaura, and Abrams (2001) have shown that different types of advertising work better with different adolescent ages. For example, early adolescents are more likely to be influenced by peripheral cues, such as source expertise and attractiveness (see Chapter 15), than are middle adolescents, who are more motivated to process and understand the message being presented. Clearly, different strategies are needed for different ages.

**Quitting the Smoking Habit.** Mark Twain said, "Quitting smoking is easy; I've done it a thousand times." Although Twain's comment is an exaggeration, most people stop and resume smoking several times before they quit for good (Shiffman et al., 1996). People who finally quit often proceed through several steps during which they collect information and become attuned to quitting. The process continues until a trigger such as the death of a close friend or family member or strong social pressure makes the smoker especially sensitive to the drawbacks of smoking. Although a variety of aids and programs are available to help people stop smoking, about 90% of ex-smokers quit on their own (U.S. Department of Health and Human Services, 1989). Group or individual counseling, multiple contacts with clinicians, and treatments focused on coping skills and stress management, however, can increase cessation rates (Mendez & Warner, 2004).

One reason often cited by smokers for their reluctance to quit is the fear of gaining weight. At the beginning of this section, we met Rich, who has been smoking for years and knows the risks. He would like to quit but is afraid he will gain weight if he does. Weight gain after quitting smoking is fact, not folklore. On average, men gain about 6 pounds and women about 8 pounds after quitting; 10% of men and 13% of women gain more than 28 pounds. The risk of gaining weight is greater for those who smoke 15 or more cigarettes a day (Williamson et al., 1991). Why do people gain weight? The

**TABLE 14-3**

## Fagerstrom Test for Nicotine Dependence

| | 0 | 1 | 2 | 3 |
|---|---|---|---|---|
| 1. How soon after you wake up do you smoke your first cigarette? | More than 1 hour | 1/2 to 1 hour | 6 to 30 minutes | 5 minutes or less |
| 2. Do you find it difficult to refrain from smoking in places where it is forbidden (in church, at the library, in a movie theater)? | No | Yes | | |
| 3. Which cigarette (i.e., morning, evening) would you hate to give up the most? | Any other | The first one in the morning | | |
| 4. How many cigarettes do you smoke per day? | 10 or fewer | 11 to 20 | 21 to 30 | More than 31 |
| 5. Do you smoke more frequently during the first hours after waking than during the rest of the day? | No | Yes | | |
| 6. Do you smoke if you are so ill that you are in bed most of the day? | No | Yes | | |

*Scoring:* Add all of your scores. A score of 7 or greater indicates a high degree of dependence, possibly more severe withdrawal symptoms, greater difficulty quitting, and possibly the need for higher doses of nicotine supplements.

**Source:** Heatherton et al. (1991), as adapted by Danis and Seaton (1997).

primary reason is that smoking increases the number of calories burned, which in turn suppresses weight gain (Talcott et al., 1995). After people stop smoking, they burn fewer calories. If ex-smokers increase their physical activity, however, they will burn more calories; limiting the intake of foods that are high in fat and sugar is also helpful.

Another reason that many people are reluctant to quit smoking is *nicotine dependence*, which is considered a mental disorder (American Psychiatric Association, 2000). The degree of nicotine dependence, which is related to the amount and duration of smoking, can be assessed by using questionnaires such as the one in Table 14-3.

The sudden cessation of smoking and the elimination of nicotine from the body can lead to a variety of withdrawal symptoms: depressed mood, insomnia, headaches, irritability, anxiety, concentration difficulties, and increased appetite that can lead to the weight gain already mentioned. People who are heavily dependent on nicotine can reduce the symptoms of withdrawal by using one of several methods of supplementing nicotine while they are quitting. The currently available methods are a nicotine gum, a nicotine patch, nicotine nasal spray, and nicotine tablets. There is sufficient evidence on the effectiveness of nicotine gum and the nicotine patch to show that they both increase cessation rates (Wetter et al., 1998).

## Heart Disease

According to the American Heart Association, "Cardiovascular diseases account for about 950,000 deaths annually (about 41 percent of total mortality from all causes). These diseases as a whole represent the number one cause of death in the United States" (2002). Although most of the research on heart disease has been done on men, it is important to realize that both men and women are susceptible to heart disease. The fact that men experience heart attacks earlier in life than do women leads to a strong association between men and heart attacks, which sometimes makes it difficult to recognize the signs of heart disease when they occur early in women. The risk of heart disease also varies with race (see Figure 14-3).

One of the risk factors for heart disease, hypertension (high blood pressure), occurs at a higher rate among African Americans than among other Americans and Africans. What's

**FIGURE 14-3** Death rates from heart disease. Both sex and race have significant effects on the rate of death owing to heart disease.

**Source:** National Center for Health Statistics (1993).

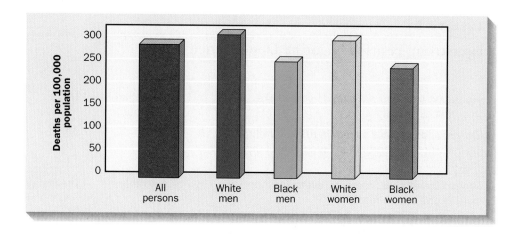

more, the difference in hypertension is most pronounced between urban African Americans and rural Nigerians, which suggests that the disease is primarily one of modern life (Ewing, Schmid, Killingsworth, Zlot, & Raudenbusch, 2003). Taking a global perspective, the rate of heart disease is much lower in Japan compared to the United States (U.S. Bureau of the Census, 2000). What accounts for such differences? One clue comes from research conducted on Japanese Americans. Those who were described as "traditionally Japanese" (those who spoke Japanese at home and retained traditional values and behaviors) had lower rates of heart disease that were comparable to those of Japanese people living in Japan. The group that was "least" Japanese had a three to five times greater incidence of heart disease (Matsumoto, 1996). Many of these deaths could be prevented because several risk factors for heart disease can be modified (see Table 14-4).

One of the processes that leads to heart disease is *atherosclerosis*, in which a fatty substance called *cholesterol* lines the walls of arteries near the heart, eventually choking off the supply of blood to the heart. This process often begins in childhood (Hajjar & Nicholson, 1995). The current soaring rates of childhood obesity prompted a special Institute of Medicine committee to call for measures to counter this trend (Greer, 2004). Unfortunately, our fast-food culture and its stress on "supersizing" portions make this task quite difficult (DeAngelis, 2004). Susan Bennett, a registered dietician with the Texas Department of Health, put the seriousness of child obesity in bold

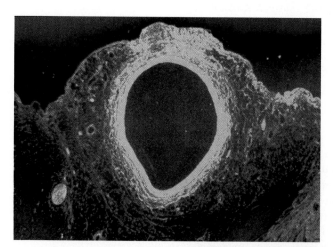

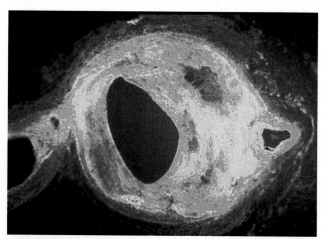

*Left*: Blood can flow easily through the opening of a normal artery (red center area). *Right*: Over the course of many years, cholesterol deposited along the inner wall of an artery can harden and restrict the passage of blood ("hardening of the arteries"). Note the difference in the size of the opening in the two arteries. The blockage can severely impair the flow of blood to the heart and result in cardiac arrest (heart attack), during which some of the heart muscle dies.

## TABLE 14-4

## Major Risk Factors for Heart Disease

### Risk Factors That Cannot Be Modified

**Heredity**   The tendency to develop heart disease seems to be inherited.

**Gender**   Men are at greater risk for heart disease and are likely to have heart attacks earlier in life than women.

**Increasing age**   More than half of all heart attack victims are 65 or older. The increase in heart disease with age seems to be due, however, to the longer time available for other risk factors to have an impact rather than being an inevitable part of aging.

### Risk Factors That Can Be Modified

**Cigarette smoking**   A smoker's risk of heart disease is twice that of a nonsmoker. What's more, after cardiac arrest, smokers are more likely to die within an hour than nonsmokers. How rapidly smoking cessation reduces the risk of heart disease is a matter of controversy.

**High blood pressure (hypertension)**   Elevated blood pressure increases the heart's workload and causes the heart to weaken over time. High blood pressure in combination with obesity, smoking, high cholesterol, or diabetes raises the risk of heart disease.

**Blood cholesterol levels**   The risk of heart disease rises as blood cholesterol levels increase. A growing focus of attention is levels of HDL (high-density lipoprotein) and LDL (low-density lipoprotein), also known as "good cholesterol" and "bad cholesterol," respectively. Higher HDL levels are associated with lower rates of heart disease. Cholesterol levels are affected by age, sex, heredity, and diet.

**Obesity**   Although some studies show an increasing risk of heart disease with increased weight, study findings are inconsistent. Certain population subgroups, however, seem to be at greater risk than others. For example, those with male-type (apple-shape) obesity are at higher risk than those with female-type (pear-shape) obesity, in which excess fat is distributed more evenly. What's more, obesity is related to other risk factors such as high blood pressure, cholesterol levels, and physical inactivity.

**Physical inactivity**   When combined with overeating, physical inactivity can lead to excess weight and higher cholesterol levels.

**Stress**   Although life would be impossible without some stress, how we react to stressors can put us at increased risk for heart disease, either directly or by influencing other risk factors.

**Sources:** American Heart Association (1993); Smith and Leon (1992).

perspective by saying that "If an answer to this obesity epidemic is not found soon, for the first time this century the present generation of children will not live as long as their parents" (Ellis, 2004, p. 1).

To move through the blood, cholesterol molecules attach to special transport systems called *lipoproteins* (Hajjar & Nicholson, 1995). About two-thirds of the cholesterol in our blood is carried on *low-density lipoproteins* (LDL), which are most responsible for atherosclerosis. The cholesterol carried on *high-density lipoproteins* (HDL) tends to be carried to the liver, where it is disposed of in the form of bile; hence HDL is often called "good cholesterol." In contrast, LDL is called "bad cholesterol" because it is more likely to clog our arteries and thus increase our risk for heart disease.

The influence of blood cholesterol levels on heart disease was studied in a group of more than 1,000 individuals (average age, 22 years) who were followed for more than 30 years. These individuals' cholesterol levels were strongly associated with their incidence of heart disease, deaths owing to heart disease, and deaths from all causes (Klag et al., 1993).

One source of the cholesterol in our blood is dietary fat. The chance of developing atherosclerosis is a function, in part, of our intake of animal fats, but our behavior also plays a role. Some people frequently interpret events in ways that lead to anger and hostility, which invokes the fight-or-flight response and puts them at greater risk for developing heart disease. How? Fat deposited in the blood for the purposes of fueling the fight-or-flight response can harden and build up in the arteries.

Two cardiologists, Meyer Friedman and Ray Rosenman (1974), found that many new cases of heart disease could not be predicted from known medical risk factors. They concluded that there must be another piece to the puzzle of heart disease; our thoughts, emotions, and behaviors could play a role in its development. They labeled this piece of the heart-disease puzzle *Type A behavior*. **Type A behavior** is a collection of personality characteristics and behaviors that includes aggressiveness, competitiveness, impatience, and the inability to relax. By contrast, a more easygoing and relaxed person is called a *Type B* person.

**The Toxic Component of Type A Behavior.** The inconsistent results of the various Type A studies led some researchers to consider that perhaps some of the characteristics that make up Type A behavior are related to heart disease but others are not. The focus of research on Type A behavior thus switched to identifying the "toxic" component of this behavior. The prime candidates seem to be hostility and anxiety, which have been related to early death, especially from heart disease (Clay, 2001; Suinn, 2001). Hostile individuals tend to perceive the behavior of others as intended to provoke or harm them; consequently they often interact with others in an antagonistic manner. They react quickly and strongly to potential threats; not surprisingly, they secrete greater amounts of the stress hormone cortisol during the day (Pope & Smith, 1991). The hostile person is like a powder keg waiting to explode. Here is an example of such an explosion:

It is likely that many Type A people who are high in hostility also display road rage.

> A medical writer was riding with a very hostile Type A surgeon. When the surgeon was slow to step on the gas pedal after a traffic light turned green, the driver behind him honked. The surgeon's temper flared; he bolted from his car, walked to the car behind his, grabbed the keys from the ignition, and threw them into a snowbank. (Adapted from Friedman & Ulmer, 1984, p. 35.)

Imagine the surgeon's internal reactions as he grabbed the keys and tossed them into the snow.

### Hands On

### Are You a Hostile Person?

Each of the following questions describes a specific or general situation that you have probably encountered. If you haven't encountered it, imagine as vividly as you can how you would react in the situation. After each description you are presented with two responses, A or B, describing how that situation might affect you or how you might behave under those circumstances. In some instances neither response may seem to fit, or both may appear equally desirable. This is normal; go ahead and answer anyway, choosing the single response that is more likely for you in that situation.

1. The person who cuts my hair trims off more than I wanted.
    A. I tell this person what a lousy job he or she did.
    B. I figure it'll grow back, and I resolve to give my instructions more forcefully next time.

**Type A behavior**
Behavioral and personality characteristics that include competitiveness, aggressiveness, achievement drive, and inability to relax

2. I am in the express checkout line at the supermarket, where a sign reads "No more than 10 items, please!"
   A. I pick up a magazine to pass the time.
   B. I glance ahead to see if anyone has more than 10 items.

3. I am stuck in a traffic jam.
   A. I usually am not particularly upset.
   B. I quickly start to feel irritated and annoyed.

4. Another driver cuts in ahead of me in traffic.
   A. I usually flash my lights or honk my horn.
   B. I stay farther back behind such a driver.

5. Someone treats me unfairly.
   A. I usually forget it rather quickly.
   B. I am likely to keep thinking about it for hours.

6. I am caught in a slow-moving bank or supermarket line.
   A. I usually start to fume at people who dawdle ahead of me.
   B. I seldom notice the wait.

7. Someone is being rude or annoying.
   A. I am apt to avoid him or her in the future.
   B. I might have to get rough with him or her.

8. An elevator stops too long on a floor above where I am waiting.
   A. I soon start to feel irritated and annoyed.
   B. I start planning the rest of my day.

9. I am riding as a passenger in the front seat of a car.
   A. I take the opportunity to enjoy the scenery.
   B. I try to stay alert for obstacles ahead.

10. Someone is speaking very slowly during a conversation.
    A. I am likely to finish his or her sentence.
    B. I am likely to listen until he or she finishes.

11. I am requesting a seat assignment for an airline flight.
    A. I usually request a seat in a specific area of the plane.
    B. I generally leave the choice to the agent.

12. I recall something that angered me previously.
    A. I feel angry all over again.
    B. The memory doesn't bother me nearly as much as the actual event did.

13. I see people walking around in shopping malls.
    A. Many of them are either shopping or exercising.
    B. Many are wasting time.

14. Someone is hogging the conversation at a party.
    A. I look for an opportunity to put him or her down.
    B. I soon move to another group.

15. Slow-moving lines can often be found in banks and supermarkets.
    A. They are an unavoidable part of modern life.
    B. They are often due to someone's incompetence.

*Scoring:* Give yourself one point each time your answer agrees with the letter in parentheses after each item number. 1 (A), 2 (B), 3 (B), 4 (A), 5 (B), 6 (A), 7 (B), 8 (A), 9 (B), 10 (A), 11 (A), 12 (A), 13 (B), 14 (A), 15 (B).

**Source:** Adapted from Williams and Williams (1993).

**Reducing the Risk of Heart Disease.**   Can the behavior of a Type A person be changed to decrease the risk of a heart attack? Meyer Friedman and his colleagues (1984) attempted to do just that in the Recurrent Coronary Prevention Project. This program

**STUDY TIP**

Define the basic components of the four lifestyle influences on disease risk—their characteristics, their effects, and significant related facts. Comparing the influences, briefly discuss which you believe creates the most significant disease risk; support your idea with examples.

**FIGURE 14-4** Reductions in recurring heart attacks. Efforts to change Type A behaviors reduced the rate of recurrent heart attacks as compared with the rate among heart attack victims who received the typical counseling given to all heart attack patients.

**Source:** Friedman and Ulmer (1984).

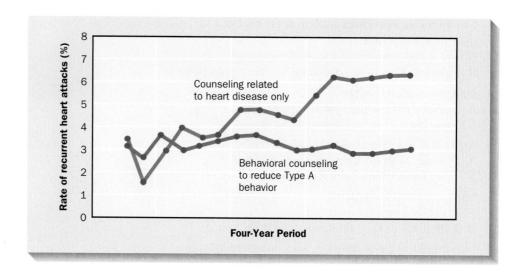

involved a group of individuals who should be highly motivated to reduce their risk: people who had suffered heart attacks. Friedman and his colleagues assigned 270 patients to counseling sessions designed to increase their compliance with physician-prescribed drug, dietary, and exercise programs. Another group of 592 patients received standard counseling plus training to reduce Type A behaviors. The training included practice in relaxation along with instruction in recognizing and altering emotional reactions. At the end of 3 years, 44% of the patients who received the combined treatment had reduced their Type A behavior; they were also less likely to experience recurrent heart attacks as patients in the group that received only counseling (see Figure 14-4).

The researchers concluded that Type A behavior can be changed in many heart attack victims. For example, Type A people can reduce their risk by becoming aware of their cynical, hostile, and mistrustful thoughts, perhaps by keeping a daily log of such thoughts. Then they can apply the lessons we learned in our earlier discussion of the appraisal of potential stressors. They can reason with themselves about these thoughts. If that sounds silly, think about the following: Do you really believe the people two floors up are holding the elevator to spite you? That really sounds silly! Perhaps once we can laugh at the folly of our own stressful thoughts and emotions, we are on the way toward reducing hostility (Coon, Thompson, Steffen, Sorocco, & Gallagher-Thompson, 2003).

**Source:** Reprinted by permission of Tribune Media Services.

## Environmental Factors

So far we have considered research evidence showing that our lifestyle can lead to health risks, such as smoking and heart disease (see pages 623–627). Unfortunately, there are equally devastating health threats lurking in our environment that our lifestyle may bring us in contact with. Methylmercury is one of these health-threatening agents. Research interest in methylmercury dates back to April 1956, when a number of children in Minamata, a fishing village in southern Japan, were hospitalized with the same complaints: Suddenly they could not walk, their speech was incoherent, and they were delirious. According to Newland and Rasmussen (2003):

> This was the beginning of a major industrial disaster caused by tons of mercury that were being dumped into Minamata Bay. Adults became blind, and children were born with cerebral palsy and mental retardation.

By 1993, 2,256 children were diagnosed with Minamata disease in the fishing village that gave methylmercury poisoning its name (Harada, 1995). Methylmercury-contaminated fish were identified as the cause of the disease. (p. 212)

Even though all the evidence pointed directly to methylmercury as the agent that was responsible for the disease, researchers could not reach definite conclusions because they were not able to conduct controlled experiments using human participants.

Currently, researchers are using rats as test subjects to evaluate the effects of methylmercury exposure. In most studies, the rats are exposed to methylmercury in utero (before birth). One such study (Newland & Rasmussen, 2000) showed that rats exposed to methylmercury only during gestation, unlike normal rats, suffered learning/performance deficits when they were old.

According to Newland and Rasmussen (2003):

> The episode at Minamata showed not only that methylmercury is a hazard, but also that it is found in fish. It is now known that fish is the major source, close to the only source, of human methylmercury exposure worldwide. Therefore, advice about consuming methylmercury will influence the consumption of fish, an excellent source of nutrients important to neural development and cardiovascular health. It is crucial to understand how methylmercury acts, and at what doses, to ensure that advisories are not drawn so cautiously that they reduce fish consumption inappropriately. (p. 216)

The message from this line of research should be clear; methylmercury can be very dangerous, especially to the fetus. Modifying your lifestyle to avoid this environmental contaminant may be an important behavior. Certainly, moderation in what you consume is a key behavior.

## Acquired Immunodeficiency Syndrome (AIDS)

On June 5, 1981, the U.S. Centers for Disease Control reported that five gay men in Los Angeles had lost their ability to fight infections; they had acquired an immune deficiency of unknown origin. Two years later, scientists isolated the **human immunodeficiency virus (HIV)** that causes **acquired immunodeficiency syndrome (AIDS)**. A test developed in 1985 detects antibodies produced by the immune system to fight the virus (Newton, 1992). A person infected with HIV, as indicated by the test, is designated as HIV+ (positive).

**HIV: A Global Perspective.**   AIDS is the 10th leading cause of death in the United States. Most of its victims are young adults and members of minority groups. In 1997 AIDS was the leading cause of death for men between the ages of 25 and 44 and the fifth-leading cause for women in this age range (U.S. Bureau of the Census, 2000).

The year 1996 was a watershed in the history of AIDS in the United States: After more than a decade of increases, deaths from AIDS declined, and similar reductions in AIDS-related deaths were noted in France and Great Britain (Mann & Tarantola, 1998). A major reason for this drop in deaths and disease was the introduction of several powerful drugs that retard the activity of HIV (Mann & Tarantola, 1998), with special importance attached to the increasing use of therapies that combine several drugs (Palella et al., 1998).

The picture of the HIV epidemic is not as encouraging in other parts of the world. Consider the following statistics from the British research group AVERT (2002):

- Almost 22 million people have died (leaving at least 13 million orphans) since the early 1980s.
- In 2001, 5 million people were infected with HIV.
- In 2001, 3 million people died from AIDS infection.
- As of December 2001, 40 million people were living with HIV/AIDS.

**human immunodeficiency virus (HIV)**
A virus that is usually contracted through the transfer of semen, blood, or vaginal secretions and is the cause of AIDS

**acquired immunodeficiency syndrome (AIDS)**
Viral disease transmitted via bodily fluids such as blood and semen, usually during sexual relations or by sharing needles used by a person infected with the human immunodeficiency virus (HIV); the virus attacks the body's immune system, resulting in vulnerability to infections and diseases, which eventually cause death

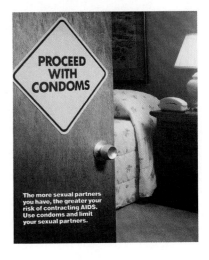

These pamphlets encourage sexually active people to take precautions to prevent being infected by the AIDS virus.

HIV infection is spreading most rapidly in sub-Saharan Africa and parts of Asia, especially in India and Thailand (Benatar, 2004). Two-thirds of all the world's HIV-infected children live in the regions below the Sahara. In Botswana, Swaziland, and several provinces of South Africa, one in four adults is afflicted with HIV. Unprotected heterosexual sex accounts for most of the cases of HIV in sub-Saharan Africa (Mann & Tarantola, 1998) and is a significant factor in India (Shrotri et al., 2003). Most of the countries experiencing a rapid spread of HIV infection do not have funds for the expensive new drug therapies (estimated to be $10,000 to $12,000 per person per year) or the infrastructure to deliver the drugs if they had the money (Mann & Tarantola, 1998).

The percentage of all AIDS cases among adolescent girls and women "more than tripled from 7 percent in 1985 to 25 percent in 1999" (Crawford, 2003, p. 85). African-American and Hispanic women account for 75% of the reported cases of AIDS among women, yet they constitute less than 25% of all women in the United States. Even more sobering is the report from the Centers for Disease Control that the rate of AIDS infection in teenage girls rose 117% between 1994 and 1998 (Crawford, 2003). The development of effective HIV prevention programs is a must to help women cope effectively.

How accurate is your information about AIDS? Health educators trying to reduce the incidence of HIV have found that the public has a great deal of misinformation. A wide variety of educational programs have been developed to provide accurate information that can be used to make prudent choices. The following statements set the record straight on a number of topics related to HIV and AIDS:

- AIDS is caused by a virus.
- AIDS is a fatal disease for which there is currently no cure.
- You can contract AIDS by sharing a needle with a drug user who has the disease.
- You can contract AIDS by having sex with someone who has AIDS.
- Using a condom during sex can lower the risk of getting AIDS.
- HIV is not spread by using someone's personal belongings, such as a comb or a hairbrush.

HIV is actually a fragile virus that does not survive well outside of the body: It does not survive in the air, on plates or cups, on the skin, on door knobs, on toilet seats, or in drinking water. Thus HIV cannot be transmitted by casual social contact like shaking hands, hugging, or being in the same room with an infected person (Newton, 1992). HIV can be transmitted only by direct contact with bodily fluids that contain HIV-infected cells. The most common means of transmitting the virus are contact with semen or vaginal secretions and sharing hypodermic needles (Figure 14-5). The risk of HIV infection from blood transfusions is very small because all blood is now screened by a sensitive test for the presence of HIV (U.S. Department of Health and Human Services, 2001).

Once HIV infects a person, it sets up a mammoth struggle between the immune system and the virus, which destroys white blood cells called *T lymphocytes*. Shortly after a person is infected, HIV replicates rapidly and can cause symptoms resembling the flu (Fackelmann, 1995). The immune system fights back and gains the upper hand, and the victim may then enjoy years of relatively good health. The immune system continues fighting valiantly, generally for 8 to 10 years, until HIV replicates so rapidly that it destroys too many T cells (Ullrich, Lutgendorf, Stapleton, & Horowitz, 2004).

**FIGURE 14-5** Number and percentages of American adolescents and adults with AIDS through June 2001 and mode of exposure to HIV. The number of AIDS cases among men is substantially higher than the number of cases among women. Men and women differ in their likelihood of being exposed to infection with HIV.

**Source:** U.S. Department of Health and Human Services (2000).

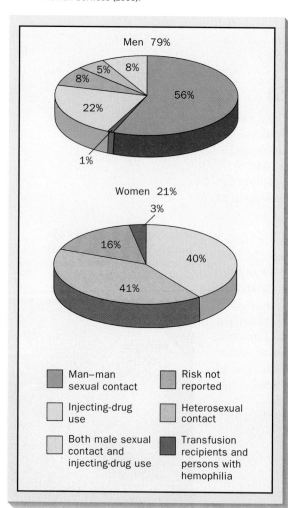

Men 79%
5% 8%
8%
22%
56%
1%

Women 21%
3%
16%
40%
41%

- Man–man sexual contact
- Risk not reported
- Injecting-drug use
- Heterosexual contact
- Both male sexual contact and injecting-drug use
- Transfusion recipients and persons with hemophilia

Why does HIV defeat the immune system? A major reason is that HIV mutates (alters its genetic material) continuously into a vast number of different forms that overwhelm the immune system. Thus a disease that would not be a threat to a healthy person can become a serious concern for someone with HIV. Once the immune system becomes compromised, infected individuals are subject to *opportunistic infections* such as pneumonia (Goedert, Fung, Felton, Battjes, & Engels, 2001). Whether HIV develops into AIDS slowly or quickly depends on a number of factors, including the level of stress in a person's life. As we have seen, stress can reduce the functioning of the immune system. Combining stress, which weakens the immune system, with HIV, which attacks it directly, can hasten the onset of AIDS.

**burnout**
Emotional and physical exhaustion that interferes with job performance

## Stress in the Workplace

Our lifestyle also includes the type of work environment we choose; some occupations are more stressful than others. As you can see in Figure 14-6, occupational stress can lead to greater illness, injury, and negative psychological reactions to the job.

**Burnout.**    For 20 years, Jim, a clinical psychologist, has helped people solve emotional and psychological problems. He is quite good at his job and has become one of the most popular therapists at the mental health center. Lately, however, his work has been less satisfying. He is tired and discouraged all the time and does not feel that he is doing a good job. He is seriously thinking about leaving this line of work. What caused this change in his feelings about his job, and what can be done to improve his attitude?

For some people, employment may be characterized by high levels of stress and frustration, eventually creating a condition known as burnout. **Burnout** is a feeling of emotional and physical exhaustion that interferes with job performance and can lead to reduced self-esteem and, eventually, depression. This condition is one of the hazards of high-stress occupations with long hours, such as medicine, police work, air traffic control, psychological counseling,

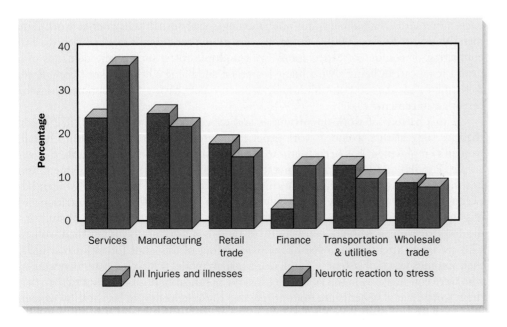

**FIGURE 14-6** Industries with the most cases of occupational stress.
**Source:** U.S. Department of Labor (1999).

teaching, and legal practice. For example, clinical psychologists who feel they are no longer able to help their clients often experience burnout (Hannigan, Edwards, & Burnard, 2004).

Many students enter the field of psychology with the goal of becoming clinical psychologists. Although this occupation can be very rewarding, the typical day of a clinical psychologist at a mental health center may be very stressful. The psychologist will see at least four or five clients for psychotherapy. Conducting psychotherapy sessions is a draining experience. In addition, there will be at least one meeting pertaining to the operation of the mental health center. Each of the numerous phone calls from patients will require 10 to 15 minutes of the psychologist's time. If student interns are studying at the center, the psychologist may be asked to supervise them. At some point during the day, the psychologist will have to find time to write up therapy notes and prepare complete written reports on each patient for use by the mental health center, the consulting psychiatrist, or the local judge. In short, there is too much to accomplish and not enough time in which to accomplish it. Is it any wonder that there is a high rate of burnout among clinical psychologists?

What can be done to prevent or alleviate burnout? Many experts suggest that taking vacations and breaks from the job can help. Sophia Kahill (1986) suggests that adopting realistic expectations about one's job, developing outside interests, establishing a social support system, and having a hobby can also help counteract burnout.

**Stress and Women in the Workplace.** Women have been a vital component of the workforce for decades, and their presence in the work environment outside the home continues to grow. In accordance with U.S. Bureau of Labor and Statistics (2000) projections, women will comprise over 47% of the civilian labor force by the year 2008. Women's representation in employment settings was one of the most dramatic work changes of the 20th century. Today women are employed in just about every industry and hold nearly every kind of job (see Chapter 10).

The presence of women in the labor force cannot be denied; however, the nature of women's work is often quite different from men's work. Although women are working in a variety of occupations, some vocations are still overwhelmingly represented by men (for example, construction, the military, politics, and law enforcement). What's more, women are overrepresented in clerical, nursing, and child-care occupations (Collins et al., 2000) and underrepresented in manufacturing and resource generation.

Furthermore, men and women have different work expectations. Women experience more sexual harassment and nonharassing social-sexual behaviors at work than men (Nelson & Burke, 2000). Women also are more prone to *role overload* as a result of competing or conflicting expectations from multiple roles, such as the demands of a professional career, being a wife, being a mother, and being a homemaker (Allen, Reid, & Riemenschneider, 2004). Additionally, women report having fewer opportunities for career advancement.

Is this pattern of work opportunities and expectations related to health? Several theories suggest that women's work experiences are related to their health. Overall, women's employment has been found to have a positive effect on their health. For example, Pavalko and Smith (1999) investigated women's patterns of employment and health in a longitudinal study. Their sample consisted of more than 5,000 women between the ages of 30 and 44 when initially selected in 1967. By 1989, due to attrition and missing data, the sample size was reduced to 2,763 women. The results of their study indicated that women who are consistently in the labor force are healthier than women who are intermittently employed or consistently out of the labor force. Furthermore, their findings were consistent with the work-benefit model, which indicates that women who were continuously in the labor force had the best health. It is important to note that these work-related benefits are not entirely due to the selection of less healthy women out of the labor force. Overall, the results indicate that employment is advantageous for both physical and emotional health.

The type of organization a person works for also has an impact on the amount of occupational stress. Licht (2000) and Licht and Solomon (2001) surveyed women who worked for nonprofit and for-profit organizations. Their respondents completed the Job Stress Survey (Spielberger & Reheiser, 1994). The results of both studies indicated that women who worked at nonprofit organizations perceived more job-related stress than did women who work at for-profit organizations.

## Psychological Detective

How would you account for this difference between stress levels at the two types of organizations? Give this question some thought, and write down some reasons before reading further.

According to Licht and Solomon (2000), "Inspection of items found most stressful by nonprofit employees suggested that they do not feel adequately compensated for the amount and type of work they are faced with on a daily basis" (p. 17).

## REVIEW SUMMARY

1. Smoking-related illnesses are the most preventable cause of death in the United States. The number of smokers is declining, but people with less education are more likely to smoke than people with more education. Most smokers tried their first cigarette before age 18. Peer pressure is a major factor leading individuals to start smoking.

2. Although there are many programs to help people stop smoking, most people who quit do so on their own, usually after several unsuccessful attempts. Anticipated weight gain after quitting is often cited as a reason for continuing to smoke.

3. **Type A behavior** has been considered a risk factor in the development of heart disease. Type A individuals tend to be aggressive, competitive, impatient, and have difficulty relaxing.

4. The Western Collaborative Group Study indicated that a Type A individual was twice as likely to develop heart disease as the more relaxed and easygoing Type B person. Subsequent studies did not replicate this finding, and it became apparent that not all the components of Type A behavior impart risk. Current research focuses on hostility as the toxic component of Type A behavior.

5. The workplace can be a significant source of stress. Some people in high-stress occupations experience **burnout.** Women who are consistently in the workforce are in better health.

## ✓ CHECK YOUR PROGRESS

1. Describe several factors that have been associated with the decline in the number of smokers in the United States in the past two decades.

2. Some people who want to stop smoking are afraid they will put on weight if they quit. What information and advice would you give them about the relation between quitting smoking and gaining weight?

3. What is one of the effects of passive smoking?
   a. causes bone cancer
   b. raises the risk of obesity
   c. alters body temperature
   d. reduces the body's ability to deliver oxygen to the heart

4. What is the strongest influence on the probability that children will begin smoking?

   a. tobacco advertisements
   b. peer group identification
   c. the known risk for contracting cancer
   d. health warnings from the Surgeon General

5. The immune system seems capable of fighting off HIV infection for 8 to 10 years or more. Why does the virus eventually destroy the effectiveness of the immune system?
   a. Unprotected sex causes localized infections.
   b. The virus invades brain areas responsible for breathing.
   c. Reduced appetite caused by the virus saps energy reserves needed to fight the virus.
   d. Genetically altered forms of the virus are too much for the immune system to fight.

**6.** The new employee arrives today; the manager has described him as a Type A. Because you are not sure what this means, you ask a fellow worker. She tells you to expect the new employee to be

   **a.** shy and asocial.
   **b.** sociable and responsible.
   **c.** humorless and unassertive.
   **d.** aggressive and competitive.

**7.** A feeling of emotional and physical exhaustion that interferes with job performance is called

   **a.** burnout.
   **b.** job panic.
   **c.** habituation.
   **d.** job-related stress.

**ANSWERS: 1.** Among the factors that have been associated with the decline in the number of smokers are growing awareness of the dangers of smoking and decreases in the number of places where smoking is permitted. **2.** People who stop smoking do gain weight, but the amount of weight gain is not great in most cases. Increases in exercise can control this weight gain.    **3.** d   **4.** b   **5.** d   **6.** d   **7.** a

# COPING WITH STRESS

The news conference is about to begin. The grim faces around the small room suggest that the company will be downsizing during the next 6 months. Nevertheless, employees throughout the facility are listening to the live news feed, hoping against hope. The initial reaction, as expected, is shock. Several weeks later, some of the employees are weathering the storm much better than others. Some continue to be just as devastated as they were on the day the cutbacks were announced. *What factors predict the different reactions of people facing stressors such as the loss of a job?*

Some people seem to crumble after catastrophes, major life events, traumatic occurrences, or hassles; others "roll with the punches." As we have seen, the concept of control is important in determining what we perceive as stressful. Let's extend that concept by noting that one way to control stress is to control our emotional reactions, alter our interpretations of events, and engage in behaviors such as physical activity that reduce the effects of stress. These various cognitive and behavioral efforts to control stress are called **coping.** However, all coping strategies are not equally beneficial (Creswell & Chalder, 2001). *Negative* strategies, such as avoidant coping (that is, simply avoiding the stress-producing problem), can result in poorer emotional and physical health (Davis, Zautra, & Reich, 2001; Packenham, 2001). Men tend to use avoidant coping strategies more than women. In this section we take a closer look at some of the positive ways people cope with stress.

## Psychological Moderators of Stress

Many people benefit from certain psychological and social characteristics that reduce their vulnerability to the harmful effects of stress. Among them are hardiness, explanatory style, distraction, social support, and a sense of humor.

**Hardiness.** To explain why some people cope with stress better than other people, psychologist Suzanne Kobasa (1982; Maddi & Kobasa, 1984) focuses on a characteristic she calls **hardiness.** For example, when the Illinois Bell Telephone Company was undergoing a major reorganization, the employees were very uncertain about their jobs. Kobasa and her colleagues studied Illinois Bell executives and found that some of them had frequent bouts of illness, whereas others, who were subjected to the same stressors, did not become ill. Demographic variables could not explain the different responses of the two groups. What was the key?

Kobasa found that the executives who had few or no illnesses during the period of uncertainty could be characterized as hardy individuals. Hardiness is a psychological

**coping**
Cognitive and behavioral efforts that are used to reduce the effects of stress

**hardiness**
A psychological characteristic that can reduce the impact of stressors; it consists of commitment, belief in a sense of control, and viewing change as a challenge

characteristic composed of three elements: *commitment* to self, work, and family; belief in a sense of *control* over one's life, no matter what may happen; and a view of change as a normal process and as a *challenge* that offers opportunities rather than threats. These three Cs—*commitment*, *control*, and *challenge*—seemed to make the hardy executives more resistant to the negative effects of stressors. They experienced the same events as others, yet they saw them in a different light and consequently reacted in a healthier manner.

**Explanatory Style.**    Hardy executives faced the future with some optimism even when confronting a serious stressor such as job loss. Accumulating research suggests that the influence of optimism is not wishful thinking. Martin Seligman writes, "Laboratories around the world have produced a steady flow of scientific evidence that psychological traits, particularly optimism, can produce good health" (1990, p. 1,992). A person's perspective on current and future events can also influence health status in both the short and long terms. For example, the tendency to use pessimistic explanations for bad events has been associated with poorer health than an optimistic style.

Although the precise mechanism for findings such as these is not known, we know that optimists do not become depressed easily when they fail. They are more likely to stick to medical regimens and to seek medical advice, and they tend to have their major life events buffered by higher levels of social support than pessimists (Seligman, 1990).

**Distraction.**    One way to deal with stressful situations is to ignore them: Go to a movie, take a ride, wander through a shopping mall. Getting away may not eliminate stressful events, but the distraction or diversion can make difficult situations more tolerable, at least for a while. A recently widowed individual who volunteers at a community service center may find that this activity reduces the frequency of memories of the deceased spouse.

**Social Support.**    Where do you turn when you need help, want a shoulder to cry on, need a favor, or are looking for advice? The answer may be your spouse or significant other, a close relative, or a friend—someone who can provide support in time of need. **Social support** is the availability of comfort, information, recognition, companionship, approval, advice, money, and encouragement from others (Rodriguez & Cohen, 1998). Women typically use social support as a coping technique more frequently than men (Mullis & Chapman, 2000; Porter, Marco, et al., 2000).

Social support can play a role in reducing the possible negative side effects of major life events, and it can also play a role in reducing the influence of daily hassles. Anita De Longis and her colleagues (1988) found that individuals with social support experienced fewer detrimental effects from daily hassles. Likewise, "supportive relationships may also significantly protect individuals from various causes of mortality, including cardiovascular disease" (Uchino, Uno, & Holt-Lunstad, 1999, p. 145). Longitudinal research designs involving thousands of people reveal that those with the fewest social ties had the highest death rates, whereas those with the most social ties had the lowest rates. Such research demonstrates the "enormous role sociocultural factors may play in the maintenance of physical health and illness" (Matsumoto, 1996, p. 224).

But social support is not a bed of roses. Although research emphasizes the positive value of supportive friends, relatives, and co-workers, there may be some drawbacks as well. Well-intentioned friends or relatives can sometimes be annoying, irritating, or overly involved and can actually become additional sources of stress.

**Sense of Humor.**    The belief that humor can enhance health is not new. The Bible tells us, "A merry heart doeth good like a medicine; but a broken spirit drieth the bones" (Proverbs 17:22). Norman Cousins (1979) drew attention to the potential of humor to reduce stress in *Anatomy of an Illness as Perceived by the Patient*. Cousins had contracted a connective tissue disease that leads to spinal deterioration and paralysis. After learning that his chances for recovery were 1 in 500, Cousins devised a regimen that included viewing comedy films and reading humorous materials. A few minutes of laughter gave

Social support in the form of comfort, information, recognition, companionship, approval, and even financial assistance can have an important impact on the development and reduction of stress symptoms.

**social support**
Availability of comfort, recognition, approval, advice, money, or encouragement from others; social support in the form of comfort, information, recognition, companionship, approval, and even financial assistance can have an important impact on the development and reduction of stress symptoms

**FIGURE 14-7** Relation between sense of humor and depression. If a sense of humor serves as a buffer against stress, persons with little sense of humor will have higher levels of depression in response to negative life events.

**Source:** Nezu, Nezu and Blissett (1988).

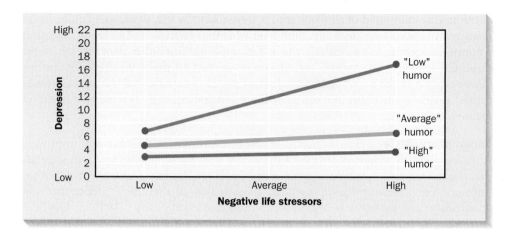

**STUDY TIP**

Gather in a group of three to six. Each student should be assigned one or two of the six psychological moderators of stress (depending on how many are in the group). Then, as a group, brainstorm a short list of stressful situations. Considering each situation individually, each student should develop an idea about improving that situation using his or her particular psychological moderator(s). Finally, each student should present his or her idea(s) to the group for discussion.

him an hour or more of pain-free sleep, and he eventually recovered from the illness (Cousins, 1989). When writing about his experience, he was careful to point out that he did not regard the use of laughter as a substitute for traditional medical care.

Several lines of research seem to support the notion that humor and laughter can have positive psychological and physical benefits. Arthur Nezu, Christine Nezu, and Sonia Blissett (1988) found that undergraduate students with an average or high sense of humor reported few increases in depression over time (see Figure 14-7). In contrast, students with a low sense of humor were more likely to become depressed in response to negative life events. Thus it appears that a sense of humor may function to reduce the impact of some stressful events.

**Religion and Spirituality.**    Researchers have shown that there is a positive correlation between measures of religion and spirituality and health (Hill & Pargament, 2003). Although the exact reasons for this relation are unclear, research data appear to link religiosity/spirituality to biological processes, such as cardiovascular, neuroendocrine, and immune system functioning (Seeman, Dubin, & Seeman, 2003). The greater a person's religiosity/spirituality, the better his or her health. Clearly, research on spirituality, religion, and health is both warranted and clinically relevant (Miller & Thorensen, 2003).

## Reducing Arousal with Relaxation and Physical Activity

Stressful situations can quickly elicit the alarm reaction of the GAS; however, many people have difficulty activating the parasympathetic nervous system to counter heightened arousal and thereby cope more effectively. As one psychologist has noted, "The fight-or-flight response . . . is not an appropriate method for coping with traffic jams . . . and interpersonal conflict. If humans still inhabit the earth a million years from now, they very well may develop a natural relaxation response to daily frustrations and hassles" (Kleinke, 1991, p. 32). There is no need to wait to learn to relax and cope more effectively with stressful situations. Several approaches that reduce arousal are available now. They include relaxation techniques, biofeedback, and exercise.

**Relaxation Techniques.**    Imagine this scene: You are sitting in class when the instructor strolls in, armed with a stack of exams. Your heart begins to race, your muscles tense, and you start to perspire. You try relaxing, but to no avail. As your tension escalates, you silently admit you do not know how to relax.

Few ways of reducing stress reactions are as powerful and widely applicable as relaxation techniques. These techniques differ in complexity but have similar effects on the body. Like any skill, relaxation techniques require practice. How do you select the relaxation technique that is right for you? Try it and see how it feels.

Edmund Jacobson (1888–1983), a psychologist and physician, developed a method for learning to reduce muscle tension. Psychiatrist Joseph Wolpe modified Jacobson's techniques in order to reduce the training time (Bernstein & Carlson, 1993). The resulting series of exercises is called **progressive relaxation.** To become relaxed, you repeatedly tense and then relax each major muscle group one by one, such as the shoulders, thighs, and legs, for a total of about 20 minutes. After several sessions, most people find that they reach levels of relaxation they have never experienced before.

Some individuals have turned to various forms of **relaxation responses** called *meditation* to reduce their arousal levels. In one popular form, called *transcendental meditation* (*TM*), an individual silently repeats a sound (*om*), a word (*one*), a phrase (*may I be peaceful*), or a prayer, called a *mantra*, over and over. The use of this mantra in rhythm with inhaling or exhaling is intended to divert attention from one's surroundings and to keep one from thinking about anything that could be arousing. Many meditators report that they feel refreshed after meditating and that it reduces their arousal.

Several physiological changes result from relaxation. The brain's electrical activity changes to include more alpha waves (see Chapter 2), breathing slows, the heart rate slows, and blood pressure decreases. Using techniques like relaxation can lead to lower levels of sympathetic nervous system arousal during stressful situations.

A number of biological changes, such as increased muscle tension, occur in reaction to stressors. The technique of **biofeedback** involves attaching electronic sensors (electrodes) to a person's body to detect these changes. The information detected is then fed to an electronic device that selects the appropriate signals and amplifies them for feedback to the person, usually in the form of sound or digital readouts (see Figure 14-8). The feedback is helpful in guiding bodily changes that typically lead to a greater degree of relaxation.

Several types of biofeedback equipment that detect different biological responses are available. For example, the *electromyograph* (*EMG*) provides feedback on the electrical activity of the muscles as they contract and relax. Placing electrodes on the skin surface of the head provides biofeedback that can be used to treat muscle-tension headaches. Temperature biofeedback involves the use of temperature-sensitive sensors that reflect constriction and dilation of the blood vessels. This form of biofeedback has been used to treat migraine headaches.

Exactly how people use biofeedback is not clear (Astin, 2004). We know that some forms of biofeedback, such as that provided about muscle tension in tension headaches, can be quite valuable. Other forms of biofeedback, such as information about alpha brain waves, add little to a person's ability to enhance relaxation.

**Physical Activity.** The tempo of everyday life and the rate of change have accelerated in recent decades. We move our households more times, change jobs more frequently, and travel at greater speeds than did previous generations. Yet we live a more sedentary life than our grandparents and thus spend less time engaging in physical activity. However, the recommended amount of physical exercise is only 30 minutes, total, per day.

Why engage in physical activity? Consider this information as you reach for the remote control: A sedentary lifestyle can lower your life expectancy and contribute to the development of chronic diseases (Konno, Katsumata, Arai, & Tamashiro, 2004). The benefits of physical activity are evident in a study of 17,000 Harvard University graduates. Those who walked 9 miles or more per week had a 21% lower risk of death than those who walked less than 3 miles per week. Those who burned less than 2,000 calories per week in physical activity had a 38% higher risk of death than those who burned more than 2,000 calories per week (Paffenbarger et al., 1986). See Figure 14-9 for more evidence on the benefits of physical fitness.

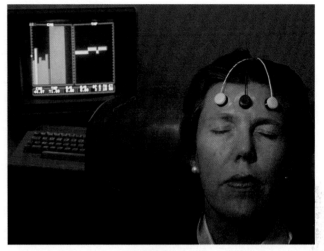

**FIGURE 14-8** Electrodes (sensors) gather information about changes in the levels of biological processes such as muscle tension (in the forehead in this example) or temperature. This information is filtered and amplified before it is returned to the client in the form of auditory or visual feedback that can be used to alter these indicators of level of relaxation.

**progressive relaxation**
Series of exercises consisting of alternately tightening and relaxing major muscle groups

**relaxation response**
Relaxation technique that involves the use of a mental device

**biofeedback**
Providing information about some ongoing biological process such as muscle tension in the hope that a person will learn to adjust the process

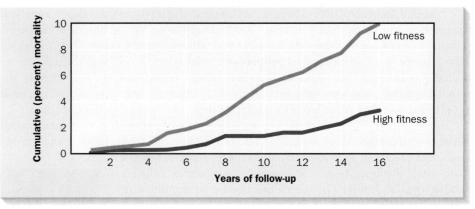

**FIGURE 14-9** Relation of high and low levels of physical fitness to deaths from all causes. A sample of men had their levels of physical fitness evaluated. The men in the top 25% had a high level of physical fitness; the bottom 25% of the sample had a low level of physical fitness. The cumulative mortality percentages (an indication of the number who died over time) is strongly related to these individuals' levels of fitness.

**STUDY TIP**

After reading the chapter, write a brief evaluation of your own mind–body connection. What behaviors of yours have positive effects on your health? Negative effects? How do you cope with stress? What behaviors might you change to improve your health? Use the vocabulary you have learned in the chapter.

Despite the apparent benefits of physical activity (see Table 14-5), "Diet and inactivity result in 250,000 preventable deaths in the U.S. each year. It [poor diet and inactivity] is second only to smoking" (American Heart Association, 2002). Only one out of five adults in the United States engages in physical activity at a level sufficient to attain these benefits.

Why don't more people engage in physical activity? One reason is that most of us believe that to attain benefits, we must engage in rigorous, continuous exercise. Think of exercise as planned, structured, and repetitive body movements done to improve or maintain physical fitness. You don't have to go to the gym to accumulate 30 minutes of physical activity. If you are not physically active now and want to boost your activity level, here are some suggestions:

1. Build physical activity into your daily routine. The average adult watches 30 hours of television a week, yet many who do not engage in physical activity cite a lack of time. Use the stairs instead of an elevator. Park your car at the far end of the lot at school or the shopping mall so that you'll have some exercise both coming and going.

**TABLE 14-5**

## Some Effects of Physical Activity on Physical and Psychological Well-Being

1. Helps reduce weight by burning calories.
2. Produces endorphins, the body's opiate-like painkillers.
3. Strengthens the heart muscle so that it works more efficiently.
4. Improves the sense of well-being; reduces anxiety, depression, and anger.
5. Improves the functioning of the heart and lungs and reduces blood pressure.
6. Burns stress-produced epinephrine, which provides quicker recovery from acute stress.
7. Increases levels of HDL and reduces LDL in the blood.

**Sources:** Czajkowski et al. (1990); Plante and Rodin (1990).

The benefits of exercise include stress reduction and weight control.

**2.** Set realistic goals to set yourself up for success. You will not be ready to run a marathon after 1 week of physical activity! Go slowly at first, and select activities that are enjoyable and within your current ability. For example, walking is the most popular form of physical activity in America, and nature has provided just about everything you need to get started.

**3.** Add variety to your program. Among the pleasures of a physically active lifestyle are the experiences you would have missed otherwise. Vary your route if you are walking or running, and enjoy the sights.

**4.** Adopt an activity that fits your social needs. People who need time to think by themselves may find a solitary jog to their liking; others may benefit from the support and encouragement of a group of joggers, especially when motivation wanes, as it inevitably does.

**5.** Depend on physical activity as a replacement for unhealthy habits, such as smoking, overeating, excessive television watching, or other behaviors you wish to change. This strategy can compound the benefit and satisfaction derived from the time spent exercising.

Physical activity can have positive benefits for the heart because the heart responds to exercise as do other muscles—it gets stronger. As a result of activity, the heart beats at a slower rate, yet it can pump more blood with each beat. In other words, physical activity makes the heart a more efficient pump.

**Does Physical Activity Reduce Stress?**     Some research suggests that exercise helps reduce the negative effects of stress. For example, individuals who are physically fit have lower cardiovascular and subjective responses to psychological stress than individuals who are not physically fit.

## Myth or Science

## Will Crying Make You Feel Better and Be Healthier?

How often have you heard or been told that crying will make you feel better? Is this advice true? Vingerhoets, Cornelius, Van Heck, and Becht (2000) reviewed the literature on crying and came to several conclusions. First, there do not appear to be any relevant physiological differences (such as heart rate, promotion of homeostasis, or removal of toxic waste products) between criers and noncriers. Second, studies investigating the prediction that people who cry should feel better and be in better health have not found a consistent pattern. In view of these results, does crying do anything beneficial? It would appear that the answer is no. On the other hand, "active inhibition of any emotional response (including crying) may be accompanied by increased sympathetic arousal, in the long-term resulting in adverse health changes" (Vingerhoets et al., 2000, p. 370). Thus, even though crying may not make you feel better and be healthier, not crying can have undesired effects.

# REVIEW SUMMARY

1. A number of psychological factors have been shown to modify stress reactions. **Hardiness** is a psychological characteristic composed of commitment, a sense of control, and a tendency to view change as a challenge. Hardy individuals react differently to stressful events and experience fewer illnesses than less hardy individuals.

2. Distraction has been used to reduce the side effects of chemotherapy in pediatric cancer patients. Experimental research reveals that distraction has benefits in dealing with other stressful situations.

3. **Social support** is the availability of approval, advice, money, or encouragement from others. Social support may reduce the negative effects of stressful events.

4. There is growing support for the notion that humor and laughter can reduce mood disturbances, buffer the effects of life events, and aid in dealing with pain.

5. Many people have never developed the skill of relaxing. Among the techniques used to produce relaxation are **progressive relaxation,** the **relaxation response,** and **biofeedback.** Relaxation activates the parasympathetic nervous system and is helpful in reducing stress reactions.

6. Physical activity is associated with increased longevity and positive effects on physical and psychological health. Current recommendations call for at least 30 minutes of physical activity per day, which can be accumulated in short bouts throughout the day.

# ✓ CHECK YOUR PROGRESS

1. Efforts we make to control the effects of stress are called

    a. coping.
    b. resistors.
    c. subsistence.
    d. survival tactics.

2. Kobasa studied executives whose companies were undergoing reorganization. Compared to those executives who became ill because of stress, the executives who did not become ill exhibited high levels of

    a. hardiness.
    b. distraction.
    c. sense of humor.
    d. social support.

3. What evidence supports the notion that a good sense of humor has positive benefits for health?

4. Identify the technique for inducing relaxation, described in each of the following.

    a. You tense and then relax each of the major muscle groups in your body.
    b. A technician connects a small device to your forehead. A wire from that device is connected to a box with a digital display.
    c. You find a quiet spot and repeat a sound silently again and again.

5. What division of the nervous system is activated to relax and reduce stress?

    a. sensory
    b. central
    c. sympathetic
    d. parasympathetic

6. Andrew is trying to relax by repeating a mantra to divert his attention from his surroundings. He is practicing

    a. biofeedback.
    b. alpha relaxation.
    c. progressive relaxation.
    d. transcendental mediation.

**7.** What technique induces relaxation through the use of electronic equipment?

  **a.** biofeedback
  **b.** consciousness
  **c.** physiomonitoring
  **d.** classical conditioning

**8.** What is the current recommendation for the amount of physical activity that will lead to health benefits?

  **a.** Anything short of a full exercise program is a waste of time.
  **b.** Exercise rigorously to raise the heartbeat to 150 beats per minute.
  **c.** Accumulate 30 minutes of physical activity in short bouts throughout the day.
  **d.** Only a physical trainer can determine the amount of exercise required for benefits.

**ANSWERS: 1.** a **2.** a **3.** Case studies initially pointed to the benefits of a sense of humor. Now both longitudinal and experimental studies have provided evidence of the benefits of humor and laughter in reducing depression. **4. a.** Progressive relaxation **b.** Biofeedback **c.** Relaxation response **5.** d **6.** d **7.** a **8.** c

CHAPTER 15

# Social Psychology: The Individual in Society

## CHAPTER OUTLINE

**SOCIAL PSYCHOLOGY AND CULTURE**

**HOW WE VIEW OTHERS AND THEIR BEHAVIOR**

Impression Formation

Social Judgments: Attributing Causes to Behavior

Attitudes

**INTERPERSONAL RELATIONS**

Attraction

Friendship

Love

Prosocial Behavior: Helping Others

Aggression

**SOCIAL INFLUENCES ON BEHAVIOR**

Persuasion

Obedience

Conformity and Compliance

**THE INDIVIDUAL AS PART OF A SOCIAL GROUP**

Social Facilitation

Social Loafing

Audiences and Coactors

Group Interactions and Group Decisions

Prejudice and Discrimination

So far we have considered the behavior of individuals independently of the groups to which they belong. In this chapter our focus expands to the individual as a member of various groups, including society as a whole; we describe the domain of social psychology. We examine the ways we view others and their behavior; interpersonal relations such as attraction, friendship, love, helping others, and aggression; social influences on behavior; and how the individual functions as part of a social group. As you read this chapter, you will encounter familiar terms and concepts from previous chapters. In a very real sense, social psychology is psychology in action. It applies what you have already learned to real-life behaviors in social settings.

## SOCIAL PSYCHOLOGY AND CULTURE

**Several students in your psychology class are discussing a new research finding. The results are exciting and seem to add considerably to our understanding of patterns of human interaction. You find the research particularly interesting because it was conducted in a foreign country. After further discussion, one of your classmates suggests that the results are presented in an ethnocentric manner. What does the term *ethnocentric* mean?**

The study of social psychology is nearly as old as scientific psychology itself. The results of the first social-psychological experiment were published in 1898, just 19 years after Wilhelm Wundt founded the science of psychology (see Chapter 1). In that experiment, Norman Triplett (1898) found that the presence of other people could enhance or facilitate the performance of a behavior requiring skill, such as bicycle racing. This effect, known as *social facilitation*, is still being studied by social psychologists. Social psychologists also study aspects of human interaction such as the formation of impressions, the development of attitudes, the effects of group pressure, the bases of interpersonal attraction, and the causes of prejudice and discrimination. Thus **social psychology** may be defined as the study of the causes, types, and consequences of human interaction.

As you read this chapter, keep in mind that the human interactions we are discussing do not occur in isolation; they occur in a specific cultural context. As you are aware, cultures can be very different; hence it should not surprise you to find that the results of a research project conducted in one culture may not be the same when the project is conducted in a different culture. Unfortunately, researchers are sometimes guilty of **ethnocentrism;** they disregard cultural differences and see other cultures as an extension of their own "superior" culture. As Smith and Davis (2004) point out, such researchers "interpret research results in accord with the values, attitudes, and behaviors that define their own culture and assume that these findings are applicable in other cultures as well" (p. 149). Because culture can influence the type of research problem we choose to investigate, the nature of our research hypothesis, and the selection of the variables we choose to manipulate (the independent variable; see Chapter 1) and record (the dependent variable), researchers must guard against ethnocentrism (Sharma, 2004).

Consider the issue of individualism and collectivism. **Individualism** is defined as placing one's own goals over those of the group, whereas **collectivism** is defined as placing group goals above individual goals. The degree of individualism or collectivism in a

**social psychology**
Study of the causes, types, and consequences of human interaction

**ethnocentrism**
Belief that one's own country or culture is superior to all other countries and cultures

**individualism**
Placing one's own goals above those of the group

**collectivism**
Placing group goals above individual goals

Social facilitation occurs when the presence of other people enhances an individual's performance.

culture can influence many aspects of behavior, such as interpersonal relations, self-concept, parenting practices, self-esteem, and emotional expression (Triandis, 1995).

Because cultures vary so widely, social psychologists need to conduct cross-cultural studies to determine whether the results of research conducted in one culture can be *generalized* to other cultures (Sharma, 2004). Even with cross-cultural studies, however, you must learn to be a good psychological detective. In addition to ascertaining the effects of culture, you need to ask about the conditions under which the research was conducted and even the nature of the research participants. For example, many psychologists rely on college students as participants because they constitute a convenient population for drawing a sample. What about a study from another culture that used college students as participants? Are college students in Iran or South Africa comparable to those in the United States? (Closer to home, we can ask if college students in different parts of the United States are comparable to one another. Remember, the United States is composed of different subcultures.) Questions such as these are difficult to answer. Yet they must be addressed if we are truly committed to developing a general body of knowledge.

# HOW WE VIEW OTHERS AND THEIR BEHAVIOR

Last week you attended a party and made several new acquaintances, including Antonio and Roberto. Something about Antonio attracted other people to him immediately; he was the life of the party. By contrast, Roberto blended into the background; you hardly knew he was there. You left the party with very definite but different views of each of your new acquaintances. *What factors influenced your impressions of Antonio and Roberto?*

**Impression formation** is the process of developing an opinion about another person. In addition to forming impressions of others, we also make judgments, called *attributions*, about the reasons for or causes of this person's behavior. In this section we discuss these two processes and their effects, as well as the larger category, *attitudes*, that includes both impressions and judgments.

## Impression Formation

The process of impression formation requires an actor and a perceiver. As the perceiver, you form an impression about the actor. The views and thoughts of the perceiver and the appearance and behaviors of the actor influence the impressions that are formed. Let us take a closer look at each of these dimensions of impression formation.

**Aspects of the Perceiver.**  Have you ever made a snap judgment about someone you just met? We do not enter into interpersonal relationships with a completely blank mind; we bring preconceived ideas or stereotypes to every situation. A **stereotype** is a set of beliefs about members of a particular group (Aronson, Wilson, & Akert, 2002). Stereotypes can be either negative or positive. Examples of negative stereotypes are "Jocks are dumb" and "Film stars are temperamental." "Beautiful people are good people" is an example of a positive stereotype (Ramsey & Langlois, 2002).

It is important to distinguish between *in-group* and *out-group* stereotypes. In-group stereotypes refer to the stereotypes that we have about people who are in the same group(s) we belong to; they typically are positive stereotypes. For example, in the aftermath of the 9/11 terrorist attack, "many Americans did something that they had never done before: they displayed an American flag" (Prentice & Miller, 2002, p. 352). These flags were positive signs to the American public (the in-group) that Americans were unified and patriotic (the stereotype). Such a stereotype that develops from within the

**impression formation**
The process of forming an opinion about another person

**stereotype**
Set of beliefs about members of a particular group

If we view beautiful people as good, the "beautiful is good" stereotype may be influencing our attitudes.

group is known as a *homegrown stereotype*. Out-group stereotypes tend to be negative and describe others in such terms as "them" or "those people."

Why do we form stereotypes? In Chapter 3 we saw that the nervous system is not capable of processing all the sensory information to which we are exposed at any given time. To reduce this *information overload*, we create perceptual categories, such as "red objects," "square objects," "sweet objects," and "loud objects." The same logic applies to the formation of stereotypes. If you put people into categories, you have fewer items of information to deal with—you can think about a small number of categories rather than a large number of individuals (Kaplan, Wanshula, & Zanna, 1992). Those categories are stereotypes.

Obviously, a lot of information about an individual is lost when he or she is viewed as part of a category. Take the "beautiful is good" stereotype as an example. When we meet an attractive person, we may unconsciously put him or her in the beautiful-is-good category and assume that he or she possesses all the positive characteristics associated with that stereotype; this process of assuming that a person possesses all the characteristics of a category is known as *assimilation* (Biernat, 2003).

## Psychological Detective

Continued interactions with people should demonstrate that individuals in a given category do not necessarily share the same personality traits. Yet stereotypes persist, often in the face of contradictory evidence. Why do we continue to hold stereotypes? Write down at least one reason before reading further.

There are two reasons for the persistence of stereotypes. First, if we believe that a group of people (such as community leaders) possesses certain characteristics, we may selectively note behaviors that are consistent with those characteristics (such as volunteering to serve in the chamber of commerce) and fail to notice behaviors that are inconsistent (such as driving under the influence of alcohol). The second reason that stereotypes are durable involves the effects of our own reactions and behaviors on the individuals in question. Do you treat attractive people and unattractive people differently? Perhaps you treat individuals in ways that elicit behaviors consistent with your stereotype. For example, grade school teachers who are told that the children in their classes are slow learners treat those children differently from the children they are told are gifted

**self-fulfilling prophecy**
Phenomenon whereby our expectations elicit behaviors in others that confirm those expectations

**self-disclosure**
An individual's decision to share personal information

(Rosenthal & Jacobson, 1968; Smith, Jussim, & Eccles, 1999). These different instructor reactions result in different behaviors on the part of the students, even if the students are not different in any appreciable manner. When your behaviors influence others to respond the way you expect, a **self-fulfilling prophecy** is at work (McNatt, 2000).

Clearly the perceiver can and does play an active role in the process of impression formation. Certain characteristics of the actor, however, also play a prominent role in this process.

**Aspects of the Actor.** Four features of the actor have been shown to influence impression formation. Those features are (1) physical appearance, (2) style and content of speech, (3) nonverbal mannerisms and nonverbal communication, and (4) the perceiver's prior information about the actor.

**Appearance.** The "beautiful is good" stereotype assumes that attractive people have positive characteristics—they are witty and intelligent and have pleasing personalities. Therefore attractive people can be expected to make better impressions. Research has shown that these expectations are borne out in reality (Dion & Stein, 1978); our first impressions of attractive people are more favorable than those of less attractive individuals. Despite the prevalence of this "beautiful" stereotype, however, research has shown that people also find *average* facial features to be quite attractive. In fact, research participants routinely rate a composite (average) face created by a computer blending other faces as more attractive than the individual faces that contributed to the composite (Halberstadt & Rhodes, 2000). What's more, the attractiveness of a face can be increased or decreased by changing its amount of correspondence with the average face (Rhodes, Sumich, & Byatt, 1999).

**Speech.** *How* you do things makes a difference. With regard to impression formation, an actor's style of speech is important. Among the aspects of speech that are influential are speed, volume, and inflections (variations). For example, a New Yorker's rapid, clipped speech may not appeal to a native of Atlanta, whose slower style may make the New Yorker impatient. When we meet someone with a foreign accent, we tend to talk more slowly and more loudly. In addition, straightforward, clear speech is more appealing than speech that contains numerous qualifiers and hesitations, such as *like, maybe, kinda, I guess,* and *you know.*

The content of speech is also important. Research on **self-disclosure,** the amount of personal information a person is willing to share with others, indicates that the more a person reveals, the more positive the impression others form. Although self-disclosure by one individual prompts self-disclosure by another, too much self-disclosure early in a relationship can create a negative impression. How have you reacted when people whom you have just met told you highly personal information? Your reaction was probably unfavorable because you were unwilling to disclose the same kind of information about yourself. Most people are not willing to share intimate experiences and feelings with others whom they know only casually. As the relationship develops, they are more likely to reveal private information. Whereas self-disclosure is valued in Western industrialized cultures like the United States that stress individualism (especially on radio and television talk shows), it is not as highly valued in Asian cultures like Japan that stress collectivism.

Favorable impressions are also created by people who respond appropriately to what has just been said to them. Suppose you have just told a new acquaintance what your major is. How would you react if the response to this self-disclosure was silence or a comment on an unrelated topic? Would your impression be different if the other person had said something positive about your choice of a major?

Nonverbal communication can tell us a lot about other people.

**Nonverbal Communication.** Instructors often say that the first class session in a course is the most important one. As a student, your initial impression of the teacher may greatly influence your enjoyment of that first class. The instructor's nonverbal communication plays an important role in determining this initial impression. Which course would you rather take: one in which the instructor never makes eye contact with students and has unusual mannerisms (such as blinking rapidly, a behavior associated with anxiety) or one in which the instructor looks each student in the eye, smiles frequently, and has an easygoing, relaxed manner?

Mark Snyder and his colleagues (Snyder & Gangestad, 1986) have developed the Self-Monitoring Scale to measure the degree to which individuals manipulate the nonverbal signals they send to others in social situations and how well they are able to adjust their behaviors to fit the specific situation. The Self-Monitoring Scale is reproduced below; see how you score on this dimension.

## Hands On

## Self-Monitoring Scale

The following statements concern your personal reactions to a number of situations. No two statements are exactly alike, so consider each statement carefully before answering. If a statement is true or mostly true as applied to you, mark T as your answer. If a statement is false or not usually true as applied to you, mark F as your answer. It is important that you answer frankly and honestly. Scoring instructions and interpretive comments are found at the end of the chapter.

1. I find it hard to imitate the behavior of other people.
2. My behavior is usually an expression of my true inner feelings, attitudes, and beliefs.
3. At parties and social gatherings I do not attempt to do or say things that others will like.
4. I can only argue for ideas I already believe.
5. I can make impromptu speeches even on topics about which I have almost no information.
6. I guess I put on a show to impress or entertain people.
7. When I am uncertain how to act in a social situation, I look to the behavior of others for cues.
8. I would probably make a good actor.
9. I rarely need the advice of my friends to choose movies, books, or music.
10. I sometimes appear to others to be experiencing deeper emotions than I actually am.
11. I laugh more when I watch a comedy with others than when alone.
12. In a group of people, I am rarely the center of attention.
13. In different situations and with different people, I often act like very different persons.
14. I am not particularly good at making other people like me.
15. Even if I am not enjoying myself, I often pretend to be having a good time.
16. I'm not always the person I appear to be.
17. I would not change my opinions (or the way I do things) in order to please someone else or to win his or her favor.
18. I have considered being an entertainer.
19. In order to get along and be liked, I tend to be what people expect me to be rather than anything else.
20. I have never been good at games like charades or improvisational acting.
21. I have trouble changing my behavior to suit different people and different situations.
22. At a party I let others keep the jokes and stories going.
23. I feel a bit awkward in company and do not show up quite so well as I should.

**attribution**

The process of assigning causes to events and behaviors

24. I can look anyone in the eye and tell a lie with a straight face (if for a right end).

25. I may deceive people by being friendly when I really dislike them.

**Source:** Snyder and Gangestad (1986).

**Prior Information.**     Information that is available to you before you meet someone can affect your impression of that person. For example, if a label is applied to an individual, it may stick, regardless of its accuracy. A classic study by the psychologist Harold Kelley (1950) illustrates this point. The students in a class were told that they would be hearing a visiting lecturer. Half of the students received a written description that portrayed the lecturer as "warm." The rest received a description that portrayed the lecturer as "cold." After the lecture, the students who had read the "warm" description had a more favorable impression of the speaker than the students who had read the "cold" description. Likewise, the context you find yourself in can activate stereotypes (Castelli, Macrae, Zogmaister, & Arcuri, 2004).

**Stereotype Activation.**     Although researchers have gathered considerable information about the nature, content, and origin of stereotypes, they know relatively little about the effects of stereotypes (Spencer, Steele, & Quinn, 1999). What reactions do people have when they are the target of a stereotype that has been activated? The answer to this question depends on whether the stereotype is negative or positive. The activation of a negative stereotype can cause the target person's performance to decrease. For example, increasing the awareness of minority or low socioeconomic status resulted in minority students and students with low socioeconomic status (Croziet & Claire, 1998) scoring lower on standardized tests (see Chapter 8). Because of the undesirable outcomes, the term *stereotype threat* is often used to describe such effects (Croziet & Claire, 1998). On the other hand, Shih, Pittinsky, and Ambady (1999) found that the activation of a positive stereotype can *enhance* performance. They activated the stereotype of Asian-American mathematics excellence and found that the test performance of Asian-American students increased significantly when compared to a group of Asian-American students who did not have this stereotype activated. Research of this nature appears to offer answers to behavioral differences in numerous situations, such as group testing, where stereotypes can be activated.

# Social Judgments: Attributing Causes to Behaviors

In addition to forming impressions of others, we seek to discern the causes of their behavior. **Attribution** is the process by which we decide why certain events occurred or why a particular person acted in a certain manner (Ross, 1998). Several factors influence our attributions. Among them are internal versus external causes, distinctiveness, consistency, consensus, and our role as actor or perceiver in the situation.

**Internal versus External Causes.**     In attempting to determine the cause of a particular event or behavior, we first decide whether it was due to internal factors, such as personality traits (see Chapter 11), or to external situational factors, such as the stressors a person is experiencing. Because the determinants of many social events and behaviors are unclear, these attributions are not always automatic or trivial.

### Psychological Detective

Consider each of the following events:

1. Your best friend made an excellent grade on her midterm exam.

2. An automobile was stolen from the parking lot of a fancy restaurant.

3. An anonymous benefactor made a large donation to the local hospital.

Write a likely explanation (attribution) for each event before reading further.

What causes did you assign to each of these situations? Here are some possibilities:

1. Your best friend earned an excellent grade on her midterm exam. Was her grade due to effort (internal cause) or an easy test (external cause)?

2. An automobile was stolen from the parking lot of a fancy restaurant. Did the theft result from a premeditated plan (internal cause) or peer pressure (external cause)?

3. An anonymous benefactor made a large donation to the local hospital. Was the donation prompted by the desire to help sick people (internal cause) or by the need to have a large tax deduction (external cause)?

Deciding whether the cause of an event or behavior is internal or external has a major impact on the attributional process. If we decide that the behavior has an internal cause, we attribute it to the individual in question; if the behavior has an external cause, we attribute it to the environment. According to Harold Kelley (1967, 1971; Gilbert, 1998), factors such as *distinctiveness, consistency,* and *consensus* influence our decisions about internal or external causes.

**Distinctiveness.** *Distinctiveness* refers to the extent to which a person's responses vary from situation to situation (for example, Roman likes this modern painting but not that one). The greater the variability, the higher the distinctiveness.

**Consistency.** Has this behavior occurred before? Our confidence in making attributions regarding internal or external causes is greatest when the behaviors we observe are *consistent.*

**Consensus.** Have others also observed this behavior? *Consensus* refers to the reactions of other people to the external object or behavior in question. When consensus is high and everyone views the behavior or object in the same manner, we tend to make external attributions; when it is low and no one agrees about the behavior or object in question, we tend to make internal attributions.

The percentage of internal attributions in an individualistic society such as the United States increases dramatically starting at about age 11, whereas internal attributions increase only slightly in a collectivist society such as India (Miller, 1984). The converse pattern is true for external attributions.

**Attributional Biases.** We are not as objective as we might think when we make attributions about the causes of behaviors, events, and situations. Various biases can and do influence our attributions. Some of those biases are described in the following pages.

## Myth or Science

One of the most prominent myths in our society concerns the belief that individuals can control chance. Dice players believe that throwing the dice in a certain manner results in a high number, whereas throwing the dice in a different manner results in a low number. In one study, college students believed that once a particular number had been rolled with the dice, the person who rolled could roll that number again (Fleming & Darley, 1990). This feeling of control is not limited to dice; it has also been shown for picking lottery numbers (Langer, 1977) and flipping a coin. Despite such widespread belief in one's ability to beat the odds, such behavior is only an illusion of control. In the long run, an unbiased coin always averages half heads and half tails. Fair dice yield high and low numbers regardless of how they are thrown. A particular selection of lottery numbers has no bearing on those actually selected. Why does this illusion persist? Every once in a while a person is reinforced with an appropriate number on a roll of the dice, a lottery ticket pays off, or a coin toss ends as predicted. Behavior does not change the odds. As we saw in Chapter 5, partial reinforcement can cause people to repeat a behavior for a long time.

**The Fundamental Attribution Error.** Fritz Heider (1958) pointed out that people tend to pay more attention to the behavior and characteristics of an actor than to the

**fundamental attribution error**
The tendency to attribute behaviors to internal causes

**STUDY TIP**

Pair up to illustrate the actor–perceiver bias. Each student in the pair should develop two situations (using the sample situations on p. 652 as a guide). Then the pair should consider each of the four situations, with one student arriving at an interpretation appropriate for the actor, and the other student taking the part of the perceiver (switch off for each situation).

The self-serving bias suggests that we are quick to accept credit for our successes but tend to blame our failures on factors beyond our control.

situation in which the behavior occurs. This tendency biases them toward making internal attributions. Think back to the Psychological Detective on page 650. When you wrote explanations about your friend's midterm grade, the automobile that was stolen from the parking lot, and the anonymous benefactor, did you focus on the individuals more than on the situations? This internal attribution bias, which occurs even when strong situational determinants are not present, is termed the **fundamental attribution error.** It becomes especially pronounced when the actor's behavior is unclear and ambiguous (Vonk, 1999).

Imagine that you have volunteered to participate in a psychology experiment. You arrive at the designated testing room and find it decorated like a television studio. As you enter the room, you are randomly designated as either a contestant or a quizmaster. The quizmasters prepare several general questions, which the contestants try to answer. Without fail, the contestants find themselves unable to answer the questions. When the quiz is over, the intelligence of the quizmasters and contestants is rated. Quizmasters are always rated as smarter than contestants.

## Psychological Detective

Is this internal attribution accurate, or are there situational factors that have not been taken into account? If there are such factors, what are they and why were they overlooked? Jot down some possibilities before reading further.

Recall that the participants were randomly assigned to either the quizmaster or the contestant role at the beginning of the experiment. The two groups should therefore have been comparable. What occurred next? The quizmasters created the questions that the contestants attempted to answer. This arrangement may have created a problem for the contestants. Who chose the categories of the questions? The quizmasters did. Why might this have created a problem? The contestants were forced to answer questions derived from the quizmasters' areas of greatest knowledge. Because the contestants' areas of greatest knowledge were different, they were placed at a disadvantage. (If you are an expert on sports trivia, it should not be surprising to find that your questions stump people who are not sports enthusiasts.) Yet in making their attributions, both the contestants and the quizmasters overlooked this aspect of the situation. The quizmasters repeatedly stumped the contestants, so they were seen as more intelligent; that is, an internal attribution was made. This experiment (Ross, Amabile, & Steinmetz, 1977) provides a clear example of the fundamental attribution error.

**The Actor-Perceiver Bias.**   Any behavior that is observed by others can have two attributions—the attribution of the person who performed the behavior (the actor) and that of someone who witnessed the behavior (a perceiver). Are these two attributions likely to be the same?

Consider the following situations, first from the standpoint of the perceiver and then from that of the actor:

**1.** A person stumbles and falls down a flight of stairs.

**2.** A middle-aged man is stopped for speeding.

If you adopt the role of the perceiver and then that of the actor in each of these situations, you should find a difference in your attributions. Perceivers are more likely to make internal attributions: The person stumbled because he or she is clumsy; the driver was stopped for speeding because he did not believe traffic laws applied to him. In the role of the actor, you are more likely to make an external attribution: I fell down the stairs because the heel of my shoe came off; I was speeding because my speedometer is not accurate. Thus the fundamental attribution error may be committed more frequently by perceivers than by actors.

**Self-Serving Bias.** Attributional differences between actors and perceivers lead to the prediction that perceivers make more internal attributions than actors. Another bias, however, may influence the attributions of the actors. So far, we have not considered the impact of success and failure on a person's attributions.

### Psychological Detective

Will an actor's attributions be different for successful experiences than for failures? Put yourself in each of the following situations:

1. Your short story has just been accepted for publication in a regional literary magazine.
2. Your psychology exam was just returned with a D on it.

Write down the attribution you would make in each situation before reading further.

Who was responsible for the *success* of the short story, and who is to *blame* for the D on the exam? Generally, we are quick to accept credit for our successes and equally quick to blame our failures on factors beyond our control. In short, we tend to make internal attributions when our behaviors are successful and external attributions when we fail (Sedikides et al., 1998). This attributional pattern is called the **self-serving bias.** The self-serving bias occurs more often in individualistic societies, such as the United States, but less often in collectivist societies, such as Japan, that stress interdependence, not independence (Kudo & Numazaki, 2003).

Another aspect of the self-serving bias involves the **just world belief.** According to this view, we see ourselves as decent and capable human beings (Chasteen & Madey, 2003). Because we are good people, only good things happen to us; bad things happen to bad people. The just world belief leads to an attribution called *blaming the victim* (Richards, Reid, & Watt, 2003). Because of their misfortunes, victims must be bad people who caused their own fate. For example, there is a tendency to blame rape victims. It is easy to focus on just internal and external issues and lose sight of contextual and cultural factors when considering the process of attribution. Such judgments always take place within a specific context or cultural background, and researchers have shown that these factors can influence the attribution process as much as—if not more than—specific internal or external factors that are attended to (Branscombe et al., 1997). These researchers showed that the degree to which individuals identify themselves with the particular culture that is present affects the attribution process. Likewise, the operation of the fundamental attribution error has been shown in several individualistic Western societies (Gilbert & Malone, 1995) but not in the more collectivist culture of India.

**self-serving bias**
The tendency to make internal attributions when we are successful and external attributions when we fail

**just world belief**
The belief that bad things happen to bad people and good things happen to good people

**attitudes**
Evaluative judgments about objects, people, and thoughts that include affective, knowledge, and behavioral components

## Attitudes

Earlier in the chapter we saw that impression formation involves the judgment of an actor's character by a perceiver. Because impressions are evaluative judgments, they could also be included in the larger category that we call *attitudes*. **Attitudes** are evaluative judgments, but they are not limited to judgments about people. We form attitudes about objects, people, and thoughts (Petty & Wegener, 1998). What is your attitude about AIDS, religion, soccer, abortion, opera, politicians, crossword puzzles, plastic surgery, and the death penalty? As these examples suggest, attitudes can be positive, negative, or neutral; they can also vary greatly in intensity. For example, some people feel very strongly about abortion; others do not. Some people are passionate about soccer; others find the game boring. Attitudes influence many of your thoughts, behaviors, and interactions. For example, intense political attitudes influence our thoughts about society, our behavior toward others with dissimilar views, and the people whom we call our friends.

Live! psych 15.1

**Components of Attitudes: Affect, Cognition, and Behavior.** Let's say you love rollerblading. Just the thought of strapping on your "blades" brings a smile to your face.

You also know that rollerblading is excellent exercise and a great way to stay in shape. You have a positive attitude about it.

This description of rollerblading illustrates the three components of an attitude: affect, cognition, and behavior. You love the activity; it's great fun. These feelings highlight the *affective* or *emotional* component. The knowledge we have about the object or the focus of our attitude (in this case, rollerblading) constitutes the second, or *cognitive*, component of an attitude. You understand the health benefits that the activity can bring. Finally, attitudes have a *behavioral* component (Tesser & Martin, 1996). Our attitudes prompt us to do or say something. You strap on the "blades" and go outside to enjoy rollerblading.

Now, we don't want to leave you with the impression that these three components always work together perfectly. They don't; sometimes they clash. For example, let's say that you love pizza (affective component); however, you have high cholesterol and understand (knowledge component) that eating pizza may be bad for your health. Which behavior will your attitude result in, eating pizza or avoiding it? The answer depends on which component happens to be stronger. If you are walking past a pizza restaurant at lunchtime, your emotions and feelings probably will be stronger than your knowledge that pizza may not be the best food for your health. In that instance, you have pizza for lunch. If you are at home trying to decide where to go for dinner, however, the knowledge component may be stronger, and you decide to go where you can eat a healthier meal.

**Functions of Attitudes.**  Although it is easy to see that we all have attitudes, it is more difficult to understand why we have them and what their purpose is. Attitudes serve several distinct functions (Olson & Fazio, 2004): ego defense, adjustment, and knowledge.

**Ego Defense.**  Attitudes protect us from threats to the self or ego. If a person makes statements that we perceive as threatening, we might say, "He makes comments like that because he's a dumb jock (writer, bookworm, musician)." Attributing threatening statements to the type of individual making them allows us to avoid confronting the possibility that the statements are accurate.

**Adjustment.**  Attitudes can maximize reinforcements and minimize punishments from the environment. People and behaviors that yield reinforcement are viewed positively; those that yield unpleasant effects are viewed negatively. For example, an individual who is being reinforced on a new job would be likely to say, "I am very impressed with the supervisors on my new job. They are friendly, fair, and understanding people."

**Knowledge.**  Attitudes can help bring order and meaning to one's world. For example, the following attitudes may help a person who is trying to understand an apparently unjust situation: "Most football players have skills that others lack. That's why they are paid such incredibly high salaries."

**Measuring Attitudes.**  Theoretically, it should be simple to measure attitudes—just ask individuals to tell you their attitudes. Self-reports are often used to measure attitudes, but this method is far from simple. The types of questions asked, as well as the way they are asked, can influence the responses. For example, some people may try to hide their true feelings about sensitive topics such as AIDS, abortion, or the death penalty. Therefore psychologists have developed several other measurement techniques. Among them are Likert scales and behavioral measures.

**Likert Scales.**  **Likert scales** are questionnaires that require participants to indicate the extent to which they agree or disagree with particular statements. As with other types of self-report, honesty of responses can't really be ascertained with these scales. See Figure 15-1 for examples of Likert scale items.

The advantage of Likert scales is that they are easily quantified, which enables investigators to make comparisons among different groups of individuals. In addition,

**STUDY TIP**

Create a mnemonic device to help you remember the components and functions of attitudes—make up an acronym, poem, or song.

**Likert scale**

Questionnaire that requires individuals to indicate their degree of agreement or disagreement with a set of statements

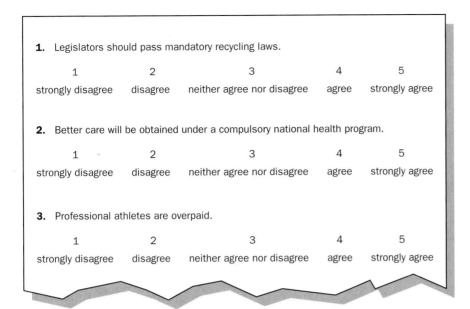

1. Legislators should pass mandatory recycling laws.

| 1 | 2 | 3 | 4 | 5 |
|---|---|---|---|---|
| strongly disagree | disagree | neither agree nor disagree | agree | strongly agree |

2. Better care will be obtained under a compulsory national health program.

| 1 | 2 | 3 | 4 | 5 |
|---|---|---|---|---|
| strongly disagree | disagree | neither agree nor disagree | agree | strongly agree |

3. Professional athletes are overpaid.

| 1 | 2 | 3 | 4 | 5 |
|---|---|---|---|---|
| strongly disagree | disagree | neither agree nor disagree | agree | strongly agree |

**FIGURE 15-1** Examples of Likert scale items.

several items can be combined to form an attitude scale. For example, the question about recycling could be used in a scale that measured attitudes toward various aspects of environmental protection. Such scales can be developed to measure attitudes toward literally any topic.

**Behavioral Measures.** The saying "Actions speak louder than words" indicates that we place considerable value on the behavioral component of attitudes. For example, if we tell others that energy conservation is a good cause, we are expected to be willing to invest time and effort in conservation activities, such as planting trees or stuffing envelopes to raise funds for conservation.

The attitudes we express to others may not, however, coincide with our actual behaviors. For example, in a study of academic dishonesty (cheating), Stephen Davis and his colleagues (1992) found that over 90% of their college-student respondents felt that cheating is wrong. However, between 40 and 60% of the same participants reported that they had cheated on at least one exam (Davis & Ludvigson, 1995). Clearly, these participants' expressed attitudes did not coincide with their behaviors. Because expressed attitudes do not always coincide with behaviors, it is important to observe the behavior of participants in addition to obtaining self-reports of their attitudes.

**How Are Attitudes Formed?** The process of attitude formation has been of interest to social psychologists for many years. *If* we understood this process, we could apply it in numerous real-life situations. For example, we could create favorable attitudes about particular politicians, toothpastes, and automobiles. In turn, those attitudes might lead to behaviors that would be financially rewarding to us. Because of the attitudes we had created, people would now be purchasing the toothpaste and automobiles that we manufactured and electing politicians who shared our views.

**Learning.** Attitudes can be acquired through the process of classical conditioning (see Chapter 5), in which a conditioned stimulus (CS) comes to elicit a conditioned response (CR). When classical conditioning takes place, we also develop an attitude toward the CS; we either like it or dislike it. For example, assume that the sight of food (CS) has been paired with a mild electric shock (unconditioned stimulus, UCS). After this procedure has been repeated several times with several different types of food, what is your attitude toward the sight of food? It should be rather negative. This procedure is used in weight-reduction programs in cases of extreme obesity.

Operant conditioning can also serve as a basis for the establishment of attitudes. Behaviors that result in reinforcement produce positive attitudes, whereas behaviors

**cognitive dissonance**
Aversive state produced when an individual has two incompatible thoughts or cognitions simultaneously

that result in punishment produce negative attitudes. For example, children whose schoolwork is praised develop positive attitudes toward school; children whose schoolwork is continually criticized develop negative attitudes toward school.

**Cognitive Dissonance.**    In 1957, Leon Festinger proposed that a condition known as **cognitive dissonance** occurs when a person experiences an inconsistency between thoughts and behaviors. Because cognitive dissonance is an unpleasant or aversive state, we seek to reduce it and instead create *cognitive consonance*—the state in which behaviors and thoughts are compatible. Recall the example of the person who was concerned about cholesterol and high-fat foods but who loved to eat pizza. Here we have dissonant thoughts and behaviors. The dissonance in this situation could be resolved by finding reasons to distrust the medical advice about cholesterol or by finding new reasons to avoid eating pizza. In either instance, the individual would strengthen an attitude about an object or event in his or her environment. Thus the formation of new attitudes is involved in the reduction of cognitive dissonance. Dissonance appears to be a common phenomenon that occurs in both individualistic and collectivist societies in most parts of the world (Sakai, 1999).

Attitudes are at the core of *interpersonal relations*. We consider this topic in the next section.

## REVIEW SUMMARY

**1. Social psychology** examines the causes, types, and consequences of human interaction.

**2.** Cultural differences, such as **individualism** (in which the individual's goals are most important) versus **collectivism** (in which group goals are most important), can influence the results of social-psychological research. Researchers need to avoid **ethnocentrism** (viewing other cultures as inferior extensions of their own).

**3. Impression formation** requires an actor and a perceiver. The views of the perceiver, as well as the appearance and behaviors of the actor, influence the impression of the actor that is formed by the perceiver.

**4. Stereotypes** are negative or positive sets of beliefs about members of particular groups. They reduce the amount of information that must be processed and are very resistant to change because we tend selectively to notice behaviors that confirm our stereotypes. What's more, our treatment of other people as prompted by our stereotypes often brings forth the very behaviors that we associate with our stereotypes of those people.

**5.** Some **self-disclosure** fosters a positive impression, but excessive self-disclosure early in a relationship may result in a negative first impression.

**6.** The process of **attribution** involves deciding why certain events occurred and why certain people behaved as they did. With internal attributions, behavior is seen as being caused by factors that reside within a person. With external attributions, the causes of behavior are viewed as residing outside an individual. We are more confident in our attributions when behaviors are consistent and have also been witnessed by others. The **fundamental attribution error** occurs when internal factors are emphasized to the exclusion of external or situational factors.

**7.** Perceivers may be biased toward internal attributions, whereas actors are biased toward external attributions, especially when failure is involved.

**8. Attitudes** are evaluative judgments (negative, positive, or neutral) that are formed about people, places, and things. Affect, cognition, and behavior are the three components of an attitude.

**9.** Attitudes can serve ego-defensive, adjustment, and knowledge functions. They can be measured by **Likert scales** and evaluation of observed behaviors. Learning (classical and operant conditioning) and reduction of **cognitive dissonance** lead to the formation of attitudes.

## ✓ CHECK YOUR PROGRESS

1. What factor makes social psychology different from other areas of psychology?

2. Viewing other cultures as inferior extensions of one's own culture describes

   a. ethnocentrism.
   b. cultural bias.

   c. nationalism.
   d. the just world stereotype.

3. Placing the goals of the group above one's own goals is called

   a. collectivism.
   b. individualism.

    **c.** ethnocentrism.

    **d.** impression formation.

**4.** When your behaviors influence others to respond the way you expect them to respond, what has occurred?

    **a.** a stereotype

    **b.** an expectation

    **c.** a self-fulfilling prophecy

    **d.** a behavioral-outcome prediction

**5.** You spend a few minutes talking with a new acquaintance after class. He tells you several interesting things about himself, and you form a favorable impression of him. What process has facilitated impression formation in this case?

**6.** The process of deciding why certain events occurred or why a particular person acted in a certain manner is called

    **a.** ascribing.

    **b.** attribution.

    **c.** stereotyping.

    **d.** causality analysis.

**7.** The tendency to make internal attributions about others, even when strong situational determinants are present, is known as the

    **a.** stereotyping effect.

    **b.** attribution illusion.

    **c.** internal attribution bias.

    **d.** fundamental attribution error.

**8.** Evaluative judgments about people, objects, or things are known as

    **a.** stereotypes.

    **b.** cognitions.

    **c.** attitudes.

    **d.** attributions.

**9.** The tendency to make internal attributions when we succeed and external attributions when we fail is called the

    **a.** self-serving bias.

    **b.** actor-observer bias.

    **c.** self-attribution error.

    **d.** fundamental attribution error.

**10.** A telemarketer calls and asks, "The JP45 is the best car on the road. Would you say you strongly agree, agree, disagree, disagree strongly, or are neutral?" What is this telephone surveyor doing?

    **a.** reducing cognitive dissonance

    **b.** inquiring about your level of knowledge

    **c.** using a Likert scale to survey attitudes

    **d.** relying on behavioral measures to identify stereotyping

**ANSWERS: 1.** Social psychology studies the individual as part of a group, whereas other areas tend to study individuals in isolation. **2.** a **3.** a **4.** c **5.** Self-disclosure **6.** b **7.** d **8.** c **9.** a **10.** c

# INTERPERSONAL RELATIONS

Whenever Bonny has a problem that she cannot solve, she calls her best friend, Kathleen. Kathleen does the same. These two friends originally met over 25 years ago. Since then Bonny and her family have moved several times; they now live thousands of miles from Kathleen. Despite the distance and infrequent visits, their friendship remains as strong as ever. *What factors or behaviors serve to maintain friendships?*

During their lives, people form several kinds of interpersonal relationships. Some individuals become close friends; others remain casual acquaintances. The establishment of good interpersonal relationships is one key to a successful adjustment to society (Berscheid & Reis, 1998). In this section we examine the factors that cause us to be attracted to others (interpersonal attraction), as well as those that lead us to help or hurt others.

## Attraction

**Attraction** refers to the extent to which we like or dislike other people. In this instance, our attitudes deal exclusively with others. How often do you find yourself saying, "I was naturally attracted to that person"? If someone asked you exactly what you meant by that statement, what would you say? What are the factors that attract us to others?

**Proximity.** Proximity to others is positively related to the establishment of friendships; people who live or work near us tend to become our friends (Berscheid & Reis, 1998). For

**attraction**
The extent to which we like or dislike other people

**FIGURE 15-2** People who live in apartment buildings tend to have friends who live in nearby apartments.

**Source:** Adapted from Nahemow and Lawton (1975).

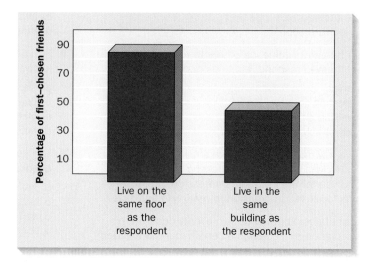

**FIGURE 15-2** People who live in apartment buildings tend to have friends who live in nearby apartments.

example, apartment dwellers are often attracted to individuals who live in nearby apartments (Nahemow & Lawton, 1975; see Figure 15-2). Likewise, police trainees who were assigned alphabetically to seats in a class reported having friends whose last names started with the same letter as theirs or with the adjacent letters (Segal, 1974).

Proximity is an important determinant of attraction because it encourages interaction and repeated exposure. The more frequent the contact, the greater the positive attraction; repeated contact turns a stranger into a familiar individual. (Just to make the picture complete, keep in mind that frequent contact can also intensify negative feelings. For example, repeated interaction with an annoying co-worker may increase dislike for that person.) Possibly you are a step ahead of us and you have already wondered about Internet relationships where there is considerable interaction and repeated exposure (Aronson et al., 2002). It remains for research to determine if online relationships will survive face-to-face meetings.

**Affect and Emotions.** "Laugh, and the world laughs with you," wrote the poet Ella Wheeler Wilcox. Research supports her observation—a person's affect or emotional state can influence attraction (Herbst, Gaertner, & Insko, 2003). We are attracted to people who arouse positive feeling in us; we avoid individuals who arouse negative feelings. For example, what are you likely to do when you hear someone laugh? Most people join in the laughter, even if they don't know why they are laughing (see Chapter 6). The converse can be said for the effect of sad moods.

In addition to our emotional state, the nature of our social interaction is an important ingredient in creating affect. For example, the type of opening line that is used in speaking to a stranger can determine attraction. Consider the following: You are sitting next to a stranger in the local laundromat waiting for your clothes to finish washing. Which of the following lines would elicit a positive response from you (Kleinke, Meeker, & Staneski, 1986): "Want to have a cup of coffee while we're waiting?" or "Those are some nice undies you have there"? Generally, direct opening lines are rated as more likable (positive) than cute or flippant opening lines (Kleinke & Dean, 1990).

Why are emotions and affect important to attraction? The principle of reinforcement (see Chapter 5) gives us a clue.

**Reinforcement.** Let's say that you're having a conversation with a new acquaintance. If that person pays you several compliments that make you feel good (positive reinforcers), you are more likely to be attracted to that person. Similarly, positive *affects*, such as laughing and smiling, also make us feel good. We like people who reward us and tend to dislike or avoid those who do not (Reisbult, 1980).

**Similarity.** We are also attracted to and make friends with people who are similar to ourselves (Drwecki, Przygodski, & Horton, 2004). In addition to such observable characteristics as race, age, and sex, similarity of attitudes, beliefs, and values is very important in the development of attraction. For example, Theodore Newcomb (1961) found that attitude similarity played a major role in the development of friendships among transfer students living in a boardinghouse at the University of Michigan. Research has shown, however, that similarity may not be such a powerful determinant of attraction in all cultures. For example, because the Japanese culture recognizes and values status more highly than our equality-oriented American culture does, the Japanese are more attracted to individuals of superior status (Nakao, 1987).

Our feelings toward another person can affect our perceptions of similarity. In general, the more we like an individual, the more we perceive that person as being similar to us. For example, men overestimate the similarity between themselves and a woman in whom they have a romantic interest (Dryer & Horowitz, 1997).

Similarity can have positive benefits in a relationship. For example, the more similar a husband and wife are, the lower the likelihood that they will divorce and the less their personalities will change over time.

As we have suggested, being positively attracted to someone can lead to the development of a friendship. How does friendship differ from attraction?

## Friendship

Unlike a casual relationship or chance attraction, a **friendship** is an interpersonal attraction that involves a set of rules, often informal, that must be followed if the friendship is to survive. Michael Argyle and Monica Henderson (1984) identified nine such rules:

**1.** Show emotional support.

**2.** Volunteer help in time of need.

**3.** Strive to make a friend happy when in each other's company.

**4.** Trust and confide in each other.

**5.** Share news of success with a friend.

**6.** Stand up for a friend in his or her absence.

**7.** Don't nag a friend.

**8.** Be tolerant of (other) friends.

**9.** Repay debts and favors.

Friendships do not simply happen. Certain factors are important in the development of a friendship. In addition to the factors such as proximity, affect and emotions, reinforcement, and similarity that are important in establishing the attraction that underlies a friendship, self-disclosure is an important factor.

**Self-disclosure.** We saw earlier that self-disclosure influences the process of impression formation; it also influences the formation of friendships. We are more likely to form friendships with people who are willing to disclose information about themselves. Our level of self-disclosure evolves through several stages as a friendship develops. In the initial stage, we disclose relatively unimportant information. If these self-disclosures are reciprocated, subsequent disclosures will be more personal. Through this process the self-disclosures become progressively more personal, and the friendship becomes stronger. If the level of self-disclosure does not become more intimate or personal, the friendship stagnates. This is why we tend to have a group of casual friends who are in the category of "speaking acquaintances;" our level of self-disclosure with these individuals probably will not increase.

## Love

Although most of us would agree that there is a difference between friendship and love, defining love is difficult. Is love the emotion that accompanies sexual attraction? Is it a

**friendship**
Form of interpersonal attraction that is governed by an implicit set of rules

**passionate love**
Transitory form of love that involves strong emotional reactions, sexual desires, and fantasies

**companionate love**
Long-lasting form of love that involves commitment

stronger form of friendship that we reserve for our children, our parents, and other family members? Theorists have proposed that there are actually several types of love (Berscheid & Meyers, 1997). For example, a distinction is often made between passionate and companionate love. **Passionate love** is a transitory form of love characterized by strong emotional reactions and arousal, sexual desires, and fantasies (Regan & Berscheid, 1999). Passionate love is another area in which researchers have found cultural differences. For example, German and American students place a higher value on romantic love than Japanese students do (Simmons, vom Kolke, & Shimizu, 1986). This difference may be due to the fact that Japanese women assume a more dependent role than American and German women or to the fact that love does not have as positive a connotation in Japan as in the other two countries. Similarly, American couples place a higher value on passionate love than do Chinese couples, who value companionate love (Ting-Toomey & Chun, 1996).

**Companionate love** is characterized by a long-term relationship and commitment. Even though most relationships begin with passionate love, companionate love must develop if the relationship is to survive.

The passionate-companionate distinction is not the only psychological model of love. For example, Clyde and Susan Hendrick (1992) propose the existence of six different types of love, giving them names derived from their ancient Greek equivalents:

*eros*—romantic, passionate love

*ludus* (loo'dus)—game-playing love

*storge* (stor'gay)—friendship love

*mania*—possessive, dependent love

*pragma*—logical, "shopping list" love

*agape* (ah'gah-pay)—all-giving, selfless love

Despite the complexity of love relationships and the difficulty of defining them, researchers have identified a number of factors that influence love relationships. These factors include sex roles, the presence of children, and the degree of dependence of each partner on the other.

**Sex Roles.** As shown in Chapter 10, boys and girls learn to engage in different patterns of behavior. These childhood sex roles influence their behavior as adults. The sex roles of men and women often reflect the stereotypes of maleness and femaleness prevailing in the culture in which they were raised. For example, some men perceive the dating behaviors of women more sexually than women perceive those of men; friendliness on a woman's part is seen as reflecting a desire for sex. What's more, men in our society traditionally have been expected to initiate sexual activity, and women are expected to react to their advances (Impett & Peplau, 2002). Research has verified this predicted pattern: Men made sexual advances, and women resisted. Although such sex role stereotypes are still prevalent, other research indicates that they are changing. For example, Robin Kowalski (1993) has shown that men who have accepted the changing roles of women in our society do not misperceive the dating behaviors of women.

**Marital Satisfaction and Dissatisfaction.** A longitudinal view of the love relationship is provided through the study of marital satisfaction. Typically, marital satisfaction is described as a U-shaped function; satisfaction is high during the early years of marriage, decreases during the middle years, and increases during the later years. The decrease in satisfaction during the middle years of marriage is associated with having and raising children; the responsibilities of raising children can take a significant toll on a marriage (Cohan & Bradbury, 1997). Predictably, the increase in marital satisfaction during the later years is linked to the fact that the children have grown up and left home, thus enabling the partners to rediscover that which brought them together initially.

Unfortunately, some marriages go beyond mere dissatisfaction. In fact, nearly 15% of all marriages in the United States are characterized by persistent, severe physical violence (Holtzworth-Munroe, 1995).

## Psychological Detective

Glenda is a battered spouse. For the past 7 years her marriage has been a nightmare. More often than not, she goes to work with several black-and-blue marks. It is difficult to cover the signs of the abuse she receives. Several of her friends have pleaded with her to leave her husband, but for some reason she cannot bring herself to make the break. Why does Glenda continue to stay in an abusive marriage? Write down some possible reasons before you continue reading.

Social psychologists have provided some insight into why such abusive relationships persist. **Interdependence theory** (Thibault & Kelley, 1959) takes into account the costs and rewards involved in a relationship, as well as the available alternatives. Here's how the theory works. Each person develops a **comparison level** (CL); this CL is the general outcome you expect from a relationship. Your CL is based on your past experiences and the experiences of others (such as your parents and friends) in similar situations. You are satisfied with a relationship when the outcomes are equal to or above your CL. You become dissatisfied when the outcomes fall below your CL. The more the outcomes in a relationship fall below your CL, the more dissatisfied you become. It is important to remember that different individuals may have very different CLs. We cannot assume that everyone sees the world exactly as we do.

When do you leave a relationship? It is predictable that we would leave a relationship when the outcomes fall below our CL. Surprisingly, this action seldom occurs; we continue to find ourselves in relationships that are not satisfying. Why? According to interdependence theory, we also develop a CL for alternative relationships. Given this information, we can say that we will leave a relationship when the outcomes for that relationship fall below our CL for relationships in general and our CL for alternative relationships.

Why does Glenda continue to stay in an abusive marriage? Although we would expect that the outcomes of this relationship are below her CL, the alternatives are even worse: Glenda has no family, her self-esteem is low, and her educational training prepared her only for jobs that pay the minimum wage. There also may be cultural imperatives that place a premium on the intact family unit and view divorce as unacceptable. Thus the outcomes for the current relationship do not fall below Glenda's CL for the alternative relationships she perceives as available to her. To test your understanding of interdependence theory, try turning the tables and ask the question, "Why does Glenda's husband continue to batter?" What factors keep this behavior above his CL for other relationships?

## Prosocial Behavior: Helping Others

Behavior that benefits society or helps others is called **prosocial behavior.** One of the most widely studied forms of prosocial behavior is altruism, or helping behavior that is performed voluntarily for the benefit of another person, with no anticipation of reward (Aronson et al., 2002). Examples of altruistic behaviors abound. Individuals have faced great danger to save others from situations such as drowning or being hurt in an automobile accident, burned in a fire, or injured in combat.

True instances of **altruism** are rare and difficult to document, because it is difficult to prove that an altruistic person is not rewarded in some way for his or her actions. Some theorists, such as Robert Cialdini and his colleagues (1987), feel that altruistic behavior always involves a reward of some kind. The reward may be extrinsic (money or praise) or intrinsic (a boost to the ego). Because it cannot be shown that intrinsic rewards are lacking, Cialdini and his colleagues question the existence of true altruism.

By contrast, Daniel Batson and his colleagues (1988; Batson, 1998; Batson & Moran, 1999) contend that altruism is a genuine phenomenon. The defining characteristics of altruism are empathy (an emotional reaction to the suffering of another person that produces the desire to help) and exceptionally small and uncertain rewards. When

**interdependence theory**
Theory of interpersonal relationships that stresses the costs and rewards involved

**comparison level**
General outcome expected from a particular relationship

**prosocial behavior**
Behavior that benefits society or helps others

**altruism**
Helping behavior performed voluntarily with no anticipation of reward

Sights like this underscore the concept of altruism.

these characteristics are not present, Batson agrees with Cialdini that some selfish motive is involved and that true altruism is not being shown. Thus soldiers who cover an exploding grenade with their own bodies to protect their comrades are showing altruism, whereas a person who donates blood, wears a sticker announcing this fact, and receives the admiration of friends may not be altruistic.

Regardless of whether a reinforcer or a selfish motive is involved, individuals who display high levels of prosocial behavior have certain characteristics. For example, a study of female Japanese undergraduate students indicated that higher levels of prosocial behavior are positively correlated with empathy, social skills, and extraversion. The positive influence of empathy on prosocial behavior has also been shown in research on children (Bengtson & Johnson, 1992) and may even be related to parenting style. These positive characteristics also are shown by individuals who have accepted the care of a spouse who is suffering from a long-term chronic illness and by Japanese individuals who are asked to make a sacrifice for other persons (Suzuki & Greenfield, 2002). Notice that we are using cross-cultural research to reach a generalized conclusion; prosocial people may be similar across cultures.

**Situational and Personal Influences on Helping Behavior.** Most of us do not demonstrate prosocial behavior whenever an opportunity presents itself. We are reluctant to stop for hitchhikers on the highway; we give the cold shoulder to people asking for handouts on street corners; appeals from the Big Brothers and Big Sisters fall on deaf ears. Why? Research has shown that situational and personal influences may determine whether we are willing to help.

Much of the research on the factors influencing helping behavior has focused on the so-called bystander effect. We all hope that someone will come to our aid if we are in trouble—say, if we are being robbed. Unfortunately, this does not always happen. In a famous incident that occurred in 1964 in the borough of Queens in New York City, a young woman named Kitty Genovese was stabbed to death. An especially horrifying aspect of her murder was the fact that the killer attacked the woman three separate times over the course of half an hour, during which time at least 38 people saw the attacks or heard the woman's screams. The killer was frightened off twice when people turned on their lights or called from their windows. On both occasions, however, he resumed his attack. None of the people who witnessed the attack came to the victim's aid, and no one called the police while she was being attacked. Why?

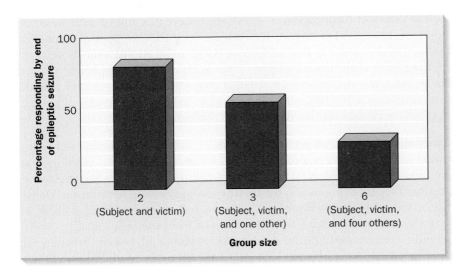

**FIGURE 15-3** Effect of group size on the likelihood of helping the victim of an apparent epileptic seizure. As group size increased, the likelihood of helping decreased.

**Source:** Darley and Latané (1968).

Two social psychologists, John Darley and Bibb Latané, provided some of the answers. Their laboratory studies demonstrated that individuals are more likely to give assistance when they are alone than when other people are present (Darley & Latané, 1968). As you can see in Figure 15-3, a person who appeared to be having an epileptic seizure was very likely to receive assistance when the person providing the assistance was alone. The finding that groups of bystanders are less likely than individuals to aid a person in trouble is known as the **bystander effect.**

Among the factors that determine the bystander effect are degree of danger, embarrassment, not knowing how to help, and diffusion of responsibility. Certainly there was a potential for great danger in the Kitty Genovese situation; the involved risks prevented many of the bystanders from coming to her aid. Likewise, it would be difficult to know how to help in such a situation.

Similarly, research has shown that people are less likely to help when the situation is perceived as serious. Most of us are not competent to help seriously injured people; we could do more harm than good. Likewise, most people are more reluctant to offer assistance in a foreign country. They fear that they will do something wrong. Such factors, however, should not prevent us from calling 911 for assistance.

Finally, when other people are present, the responsibility for acting is shared. Therefore the responsibility of each member of the group is lower than it would be for an individual. As a result of this diffusion of responsibility, each person is less likely to help the person in distress. This diffusion of responsibility is quite pervasive and is prevalent even on the Internet. In fact, one researcher (Markey, 2000) found that members of a chat group were less likely to assist each other as the size of the group increased.

## Aggression

The converse of prosocial behavior is aggression. **Aggression** is any physical or psychological behavior that is performed with the intent of harming someone or something. This definition indicates that aggressive behavior is intentional; there is a deliberate intent to do harm. Deliberately hitting someone and yelling at an annoying driver are both aggressive behaviors.

Researchers have identified at least two major types of aggression (Buss, 1961). **Hostile aggression** occurs when a person is angry or annoyed with someone else; the goal is to harm the other person (Berkowitz, 1994). Most murders tend to be impulsive, emotional acts of hostile aggression. **Instrumental aggression** is performed to achieve a goal. For example, a robber may attack a victim to steal something, not because the robber is angry with the victim but because the aggressive behavior is instrumental in achieving the intended goal.

**bystander effect**
The tendency for a group of bystanders to be less likely than an individual to provide assistance to a person in trouble

**aggression**
Physical or psychological behavior that is performed with the intent of doing harm

**hostile aggression**
Aggressive behavior that is performed with the specific intent of harming another person

**instrumental aggression**
Aggression that causes harm in the process of achieving another goal

A hot summer day can encourage the display of hostile aggression.

**frustration-aggression hypothesis**
The hypothesis that aggression is likely to occur when a person is frustrated

**Biological Views of Aggression.**    *Ethologists* believe that at least some forms of aggression are inherited. Most territorial disputes among animals, however, do not result in physical damage or death. Konrad Lorenz (1966) believed that animals instinctively refrain from using their natural weapons, such as claws, horns, and fangs, to kill their opponents in aggressive conflicts. The conflict ends when the loser acknowledges defeat by displaying submissive behavior. Modern wars, in which thousands of people are killed, demonstrate that humans do not have a comparable instinct.

**Environmental Conditions and Aggression.**    Although ethologists and biological psychologists argue that aggression is part of human nature, other psychologists stress the importance of environmental factors in producing aggressive behavior. Among the explanations they have proposed is the **frustration-aggression hypothesis** (Dollard et al., 1939). According to this hypothesis, an individual, when frustrated, is likely to act aggressively. *Frustration* is defined as being blocked from attaining a goal.

Consider an example. The decision to take a summer job as a construction worker seemed like a great idea at the time. The pay was reasonably good, and the physical labor would keep you in shape. After 2 days on the job, you are questioning your sanity. Your body aches, the heat is unbearable, and you feel as though you are about to die of thirst. Finally, it's time for a break. You head for the water cooler stored in your car, only to find that you forgot to refill it this morning. No problem; a cool soft drink will do just as well. But after three tries, you find that the vending machine is still returning your money. How will you respond?

The chances are quite good that you will direct some aggressive responses toward the machine. Some of those responses may be verbal; others, such as shoves, kicks, and hits, may be physical. Your frustration has led to aggression.

Since its publication in 1939, the frustration-aggression hypothesis has generated considerable research. Much of this research indicates that aggression results from a variety of frustrating conditions.

## Psychological Detective

Put yourself in the following situation. You have been waiting in line for a long time to purchase concert tickets; you are now second in line. Your turn is next, but someone cuts in ahead of you. Is this frustrating? Will you act aggressively? Would you be less aggressive if you were 12th in line when someone cut in? Write down your answers to these questions before reading further.

Mary Harris (1974) conducted this experiment in theater and grocery store lines. She found that cutting in front of the 2nd person in line resulted in more aggression than cutting in front of the 12th person. In other words, the closer you are to your goal, the more frustrated you become when you are blocked from attaining it. Harris concluded that aggressiveness is directly related to level of frustration: The greater the frustration, the greater the aggression.

After several decades of research on the frustration-aggression hypothesis, it became apparent that a third factor must be involved. Why does frustration lead to aggression in some instances but not in others? Anger seems to be the answer. If the frustrating event does not result in anger, the probability that aggressive behavior will be displayed is reduced.

Leonard Berkowitz (1984) contends that in addition to frustration and anger, cues for aggressive responding must be present. Those cues elicit an aggressive response when frustration has caused anger. What are those cues? Visual images that suggest aggression may be one such cue. For example, video game images may be these cues. Anderson and Dill (2000) reported that playing violent video games was positively correlated with violence and delinquency in children. Likewise, studies have shown that there is a relation between viewing violence on television and engaging in violent behavior.

**International Terrorism.**   The destruction of the World Trade Center in New York on September 11, 2001, brought a frightening aspect of contemporary society into bold relief; international terrorism took center stage. Without question, terrorist activities fall within the realm of aggression. Davis (2002) indicated that

> [t]he fact that terrorism is on the rise globally and is an increasing threat to all civilized countries means that now is the time for psychologists to pay more attention to it and to improve public understanding of the problem and its possible solutions. (p. 4.13)

What exactly is terrorism? Although researchers have proposed numerous definitions, Moghaddam's (2005) view that terrorism is "politically motivated violence, perpetrated by individuals, groups or state-sponsored agents, intended to instill feelings of terror and helplessness in a population in order to influence decision making and to change behavior" (p. 161) is appropriate and suited to the needs of this discussion.

However, having a definition is not sufficient for our purposes; in order to combat terrorism, we also will need to know who the terrorists are and why they became terrorists. Sageman (2004), after analyzing the biographical data on over 400 Islamic terrorists, has found that they are *not* brainwashed, poor, or disenfranchised. On the contrary, the typical al Queda–type terrorist is in his late 20s, upper middle class, married, and educated.

Why would people in this preferred stratum of society become terrorists? In presenting his answer, Moghaddam (2005) adopted a staircase model. According to this model, the hypothetical staircase is quite wide on the ground floor; however, it narrows and offers fewer behavioral alternatives as a person climbs to the five higher floors. The bulk of the population occupies the ground floor. It is at this level that people evaluate their "perceptions of fairness and feelings of relative deprivation" (Moghaddam, 2005, p. 162). In recent years, international mass media have spread "images of affluence and democratic lifestyles" (p. 163) around the world. These images of Western countries, especially the United States, have caused the expectations of many people, especially people in Africa, Asia, and some areas of Eastern Europe, to rise drastically. Because they are not able to attain such levels of affluence and democratic lifestyles, many people who occupy the ground floor are frustrated and angry. Moghaddam believes that some of these frustrated and angry people will seek solutions and ultimately climb the staircase to the first floor. If these frustrated individuals who have climbed to the first floor have any sort of participation in the decision-making processes (that is, a democratic government), the problems of terrorism likely would end at this point. Unfortunately, Moghaddam believes that these individuals have virtually no opportunity for personal expression.

Their continued frustration encourages them to continue up the staircase to the second floor, where they are exposed to the idea of displacing their aggression. It is at this level that out-groups begin to take a more clear and distinct shape. Individuals who are ready to displace their aggression onto the perceived out-groups may climb the staircase to the third floor. Here the person climbing the staircase will directly encounter the parallel or shadow world of terrorism and its parallel morality that believes that the use of any means possible is justified to achieve the ideal society. It is on this third floor that "Recruits are persuaded to become committed to the morality of the terrorist organization through a number of tactics, the most important of which are isolation, affiliation, secrecy, and fear. . . . [E]ven when terrorists continue to live their 'normal' lives as members of communities, their goal is to develop their parallel lives in complete isolation and secrecy. Recruits are trained to keep their parallel lives a secret even from their wives, parents, and closest friends" (Moghaddam, 2005, p. 165).

Once recruits have accepted and adopted the shadow life and morality of terrorism, they have ascended the staircase to the fourth floor. Their fate has been sealed; there is little likelihood that they can or will leave the parallel life they have chosen. On this level, a recruit becomes a member of a terrorist cell. Such cells typically consist of four or five members; they are small to help limit antiterrorist infiltration. The original members of a cell are responsible for recruiting the persons who will actually carry out such terrorist attacks as suicide bombings. This recruitment frequently involves friends coercing and encouraging their friends to join the group. Once in the group, the new recruits are convinced quickly of the legitimacy of the parallel morality of terrorism and the "us versus them" view of the world. In short, the new recruits become socialized into their new in-group.

At some point, these new recruits will ascend the staircase to the fifth and final floor—the terrorist act. Because they have been trained that the *enemy* includes *everyone*, including civilians, outside the cell, the killing of civilians does not disturb them and they commit the terrorist act.

Based on his staircase model, Moghaddam (2005) indicates that "Ultimately, terrorism is a moral problem with psychological underpinnings; the challenge is to prevent disaffected youth and others from becoming engaged in the morality of terrorist organizations. Over at least the last few decades, policies for ending terrorism have tended to be short-term, often driven by immediate political demands rather than by scientific understanding" (p. 168). Moghaddam offers four suggestions for countering terrorism:

1. *Prevention must come first.* Basically, this involves eliminating the conditions that result in the perceptions of unfairness and unjustness on the ground floor. Removing these perceptions is the only procedure that will keep potential terrorists from beginning their climb up the staircase.

2. *Support the development of democracies.* Efforts to establish democracies that involve everyone, including women and minorities, must be undertaken.

3. *Educate against us-versus-them thinking.* If the millions of people on the ground floor do not learn to see the world in us-versus-them categories, it will be much more difficult for people to climb the staircase of terrorism. If "them" does not exist, who would terrorist acts be directed against?

4. *Promote interobjectivity and justice.* Moghaddam (2005) indicates that "Greater international dialogue and improved intercultural understanding must come about as part of a long-term solution" (p. 168).

Davis (2002) also addressed the topic of combating terrorism and suggested that international psychology, "the social psychology of international relations" (Holtzman, 2001, p. 781), could (and should) play a role in countering terrorism. Davis (2002) made four specific recommendations:

1. *Train more psychologists worldwide.* Currently there is an information gap concerning terrorism and dealing with individuals from different cultures. More international psychologists are needed to close this gap.

2. *Increase psychological research and information sharing worldwide.* Only a few terrorism databases are currently available in English, the language used by the majority of psychologists worldwide. This situation needs to be rectified.

3. *Further utilize the international organizations of psychology.* The international organizations of psychology, such as the International Union of Psychological Science, can help by developing and providing translation services and promoting cross-cultural understanding.

4. *Educate the public.* The key to making any other measures work is to have the support of the average citizens of many nations. Hence, educating the public about terrorism is a mandatory objective.

Clearly, there is a lot of work and research yet to be done on the topic of terrorism. Hopefully, psychological science will be a major component of the efforts to understand and combat this aggressive plague of the 21st century.

**Workplace Violence.**     Because a considerable amount of violence occurs in the workplace, psychologists have given this topic careful scrutiny and research attention.

LeBlanc and Barling (2004) indicate clearly the extreme to which workplace aggression can go with their description of Michael McDermott:

> December 26, 2000, Wakefield, MA: Michael McDermott, a 42-year-old employee of Edgewater Technology, shot dead seven of his coworkers; five of his victims worked in the accounting department. McDermott was apparently upset because the accounting department, at the request of the Internal Revenue Service, was preparing to garnish a portion of his wages. (p. 216)

The sensational nature of this attack notwithstanding, LeBlanc and Barling indicate that Michael McDermott is not a typical workplace killer; the vast majority of workplace aggression is perpetrated by members of the public or by organizational outsiders.

One of the key factors in workplace aggression is the assailant's relationship to the victim. LeBlanc and Barling (2004) propose four types of workplace aggression based on this relationship:

> In the first type (Type I), the perpetrator has no legitimate relationship with the targeted organization or its employees and enters the work environment to commit a criminal act (e.g., robbery). More employees in America are murdered each year as a result of Type I aggression than from the other three types combined. Individuals who interact and exchange money with the public (e.g., taxicab drivers) are at highest risk of being victims of this type of workplace aggression. In the second type (Type II), the assailant has a legitimate relationship with the organization and commits an act of violence while being served by the organization. Although perpetrators of Type II aggression rarely kill their victims, they are responsible for an estimated 60% of all nonfatal assaults at work. Employees who provide service, care, advice, or education (e.g., nurses, social workers, teachers) are at increased risk for Type II aggression, especially if their clients, customers, or patients are experiencing frustration, insecurity, or stress. In the third type of workplace aggression (Type III), the offender is typically a current or former employee of the organization (i.e., an insider) who targets a coworker or supervisor for perceived wrongdoing. Unlike Type I and Type II aggression, Type III aggression does not appear to be more associated with certain occupations or industries than with others. Rather, insider-initiated aggression has been linked to both individual (e.g., alcohol consumption) and organizational (e.g., perceived injustice) factors. In the fourth type of workplace aggression (Type IV), the perpetrator has an ongoing or previous legitimate relationship with an employee of the organization. This category includes violence by an intimate partner that takes place at work. In the United States in 1997, 5% of homicides on the job were the result of Type IV aggression.

**Sexual Aggression.**    As discussed earlier, many marriages are characterized by abuse and aggression, which is most often directed toward the wife. The dramatic increase in the incidence of rape indicates that such aggression and abuse are not limited to marital relationships (Ullman & Filipas, 2001). The extent of this problem is staggering. For example, crime reports from the Federal Bureau of Investigation indicate that in 2000, rapes occurred at the rate of one every 6 minutes. These are the known cases of rape; many others go unreported (Bachman, 1994).

Motivated by both scientific and social concerns, psychologists have investigated sexual aggression. What have they learned? What factors contribute to the increasing number of rapes?

The increased availability and tolerance of pornography, especially pornography depicting violence and domination, are correlated with the increase in sexual assaults. For example, one study found that sales of sexually explicit magazines were positively correlated with the rape rate in all 50 states; a Canadian investigation (Marshall, 1989) found that rapists and child molesters viewed pornographic materials more often than non–sex offenders. Because pornography supports the myth that women enjoy sexual abuse and aggression, these findings should not be surprising.

Many unreported rapes fall into the category of date or acquaintance rape (Viki, Abrams, & Masser, 2004). In many instances date rape may be a result of misperceptions, especially on the part of the man. For example, research conducted by Tracy Bostwick and Janice De Lucia (1992) investigated the perceived desire for sex. They presented their participants with several dating scenarios. Except for varying the party who asked for the date and the party who paid for it, the scenarios were the same. Even though there is no proven relation between these behaviors and the desire for sex, when the woman asked for the date and paid the bill, she was perceived as having a greater desire for sex than when the man asked and paid the bill. Likewise, men believed that sexual aggression was more justified when the man had paid all of the date's expenses. In short, some women may be trapped in the dating relationship: If a woman asks and pays for the date, she is assumed to desire sex; if the man pays for the date, he may feel that he has the right to demand sex. Moreover, "no" is frequently misunderstood to mean "yes" (Osman, 2003).

There are additional factors that contribute to the prevalence of date rape. The length of the steady dating relationship is positively related to men's perception of the acceptability of date rape: The longer the dating relationship, the more acceptable date rape is perceived to be. Heavy alcohol consumption is another factor that often leads to date rape on college campuses (Abbey, 1991). Again, the explanations for this joint occurrence of alcohol consumption and date rape suggest that men often misinterpret the sexual desires of women and that men frequently use the supposed liberating effects of alcohol as a justification for sexual behavior (see Chapter 4).

To help college women deal with the threat of date or acquaintance rape, some authorities (Cummings, 1992) have advocated courses in defense training. Other authorities (Lenihan, Rawlins, & Eberly, 1992) have explored the effectiveness of a date or acquaintance rape education program. Although such a program was effective in raising women's sensitivity to potentially dangerous situations, it had no influence on the men's attitudes. More effective solutions for this problem are needed.

Having looked at interpersonal relations, we next examine the effects of social influences on our behaviors. Have you ever bought something, only to get home and wonder why you made that purchase? We will find out what makes a good salesperson in the next section.

# REVIEW SUMMARY

1. **Attraction** is the extent to which we like or dislike other people. Attraction is determined by proximity, affect and emotions, reinforcement, and similarity.

2. **Friendship** is a form of interpersonal attraction that involves a set of unwritten rules.

3. **Passionate love** is characterized by strong emotional reactions, sexual desire, and fantasies. **Companionate love** is characterized by a long-term relationship and commitment. Several other types of love have been proposed. Sex roles can influence the love relationship.

4. **Interdependence theory** takes into account the costs and rewards in a relationship. Each person develops a **comparison level** (CL), or expected outcome, for the relationship. Dissatisfaction occurs when the outcomes of the relationship fall below the CL. People leave a relationship when the outcomes fall below their CLs for other relationships.

5. **Prosocial behavior** benefits society or helps others. **Altruism** occurs when a person helps others with no thought of reward. Because it is difficult to prove that no reward is present when a person behaves altruistically, the genuineness of this behavior has been questioned.

6. The **bystander effect** refers to the fact that people are less likely to provide assistance in an emergency when others are present than when they are alone. The bystander effect is attributable to potential embarrassment, fear of failure, and diffusion of responsibility.

7. **Aggression** is any behavior that is performed with the intent of doing harm. **Hostile aggression** occurs when the goal is specifically to harm another individual. **Instrumental aggression** occurs when someone hurts another person in the pursuit of another goal—for example, during a robbery. Biological views stress the inherited nature of aggressive behaviors.

**8.** The **frustration-aggression hypothesis** predicts that frustration, or being blocked from attaining a goal, results in aggression. In addition to frustration, the presence of anger and certain cues may be necessary for aggression to occur.

**9.** Physical and verbal attacks, as well as adverse environmental conditions, may also elicit aggressive behavior. A high level of general arousal can facilitate aggressive responding.

**10.** Current statistics underestimate the prevalence of sexual aggression directed toward women. Viewing of pornography is positively related to sexual aggression.

**11.** Terrorism has plagued numerous nations in recent times. Moghaddam (2005) has proposed a staircase model for the development of terrorists. Moghaddam (2005) and Davis (2002) have proposed measures for counteracting terrorism..

**12.** Many incidents of rape can be classified as date or acquaintance rape. Date rape appears to result from misperceptions, especially on the part of men, about the acceptability of sexual relations in certain situations.

# ✓ CHECK YOUR PROGRESS

**1.** What is attraction? Explain the factors that influence or determine whether we will be attracted to another person.

**2.** The interpersonal attraction that involves a set of rules, often informal, that must be followed if the relationship is to persist is called

  **a.** altruism.
  **b.** friendship.
  **c.** love.
  **d.** admiration.

**3.** Hendrick and Hendrick proposed six different types of love. Which name and description are mismatched?

  **a.** *ludus*–game-playing love
  **b.** *storge*–logical, "shopping-list" love
  **c.** *mania*–possessive, dependent love
  **d.** *agape*–all-giving, selfless love

**4.** What term refers to helping behavior that is performed voluntarily for the benefit of another person, with no anticipation of reward?

  **a.** altruism
  **b.** munificence
  **c.** interdependence
  **d.** humanitarianism

**5.** Your anger at your upstairs neighbor, who plays loud music at 3 A.M., has finally hit the boiling point; you are on your way upstairs to punch him in the jaw. This is an example of what type of aggression? The statement "Only a few people will be hurt in the accomplishment of this objective" is an example of what type of aggression?

**6.** In a busy shopping mall, a young man faints and falls to the ground. Several shoppers stare, but no one helps the man. This situation is an example of

  **a.** reactance.
  **b.** deindividuation.
  **c.** comparison level.
  **d.** the bystander effect.

**7.** What third variable often determines the nature and strength of the relation between frustration and aggression?

  **a.** anger
  **b.** experience
  **c.** familiarity
  **d.** interpretation

**8.** All of the following factors contribute to date rape except

  **a.** men paying expenses.
  **b.** alcohol consumption.
  **c.** males' misinterpretation of females' desires.
  **d.** brief dating relationships.

**ANSWERS: 1.** Attraction is the extent to which we like or dislike other people. The features that influence attraction are *proximity* (nearness if positively related to attraction), *affect and emotions* (we are attracted to people who arouse positive emotions in us), *reinforcement* (we are attracted to those who reinforce us), and *similarity* (we like those who are similar to us). **2.** b **3.** b **4.** a **5.** Hostile, instrumental **6.** d **7.** d **8.** d

# SOCIAL INFLUENCES ON BEHAVIOR

It's Saturday morning, time for your weekly trip to the local discount store. A large crowd has gathered around a display case. A handsome young man in a neatly pressed business suit and tie is encouraging the crowd to buy the brand-new Ronco Veg-O-Matic. "No more hassles with carrots, radishes, peppers, beets, or tomatoes—a perfect salad every time!" You listen to the sales pitch and even watch the salesman perform wonders with the Veg-O-Matic. You

**persuasion**
The use of social influence to cause people to change attitudes or behavior

decide not to take advantage of his "wonderful introductory offer," however. There is something about him that just doesn't seem right. *Why was the salesman unsuccessful in his attempt to persuade you to take a chance on his product?*

Other people are constantly trying to influence us. Sales pitches are just one example of the numerous social influences and pressures on our behavior. In this section we examine three kinds of social influences: those designed to persuade us to change our attitudes and behaviors, to produce obedience, and to induce conformity.

# Persuasion

**Persuasion** is the use of social influence to cause other people to change their attitudes and behaviors (Aronson et al., 2002). We are bombarded with hundreds of persuasive messages every day: Buy this car, join that group, support our cause, vote for this political candidate, give to that charitable organization. Some persuasive messages are effective; others are not. Social psychologists have identified four main factors that influence persuasion: source, message, channel, and audience. Let's take a closer look at each.

**Source Factors.** Certainly the source of a persuasive message plays a role in determining whether the message changes our attitudes and behaviors. What is it about the source that is important in facilitating persuasion? Among the characteristics of sources that have been found to increase the impact of persuasive messages are expertise, attractiveness, and trustworthiness.

**Expertise.** The greater the perceived expertise of the source of a message, the more persuasive the message (Chen & Chaiken, 1999). To demonstrate the importance of expertise, the following experiment has been conducted numerous times. First, participants are randomly assigned to one of two groups, and an initial appraisal of their attitudes on a particular subject, such as the dependability of American-made cars, is made. Then both groups read a message designed to change their attitudes. The only difference is that the message for one group is attributed to a recognized expert (for example, *Road and Track*), whereas the message for the other group is attributed to a questionable source (for example, *Better Homes and Gardens*). After the message has been read, the participants' attitudes are measured again. The results indicate that the message from the recognized authority has produced significantly more attitude change. Assuming that the attitudes of the two groups were comparable on the first measurement, any differences that appear in the second must reflect the influence of the perceived expertise of the source.

**Attractiveness.** The source's attractiveness also influences the likelihood of persuasion; the more attractive the source, the more effective the message. The same physical factors that influence impression formation also influence persuasion (Dion & Stein, 1978). That is, the better your impression of the source, the more likely you are to be persuaded.

## Psychological Detective

How would you conduct a research project to evaluate the influence of attractiveness on persuasion? Would it be possible to use the same research strategy that has been used to evaluate expertise? As you think about this research project, you might want to diagram your proposed study on a sheet of paper. Be sure to take all the important possibilities into account. When you are satisfied with your research design, continue reading.

To evaluate the influence of attractiveness, we would start with two randomly formed groups of participants and measure their attitudes. Then both groups would be given the same persuasive message, but the message would be delivered by individuals

**TABLE 15-1**

## Design of an Experiment to Determine the Influence of Attractiveness on Persuasion

|  | Step 1 | Step 2 | Step 3 | Results |
|---|---|---|---|---|
| Group 1 (attractive source) | Evaluate the attitude in question | Message presented by the attractive source | Reevaluate the attitude in question | Greater persuasion for attractive source |
| Group 2 (unattractive source) | Evaluate the attitude in question | Message presented by same source but unattractive | Reevaluate the attitude in question | Less persuasion for unattractive source |

who differed in attractiveness. What other major influences must be controlled if our conclusions are to be valid? What about the level of expertise of the individuals who deliver the message? If we wish to measure only attractiveness, the degree of perceived expertise must be the same for both groups. What's more, the individuals delivering the message should be of the same sex. The ideal condition would be for the same individual to present the message to both groups. With a change of clothes, a pair of last year's running shoes, and mussed hair, the attractive expert would become less attractive. This research strategy is shown in Table 15-1.

**Trustworthiness.** A persuasive message may fail to produce a change in attitude even if it is presented by an attractive expert. It takes more than an attractive expert to persuade us; the source of the persuasive message must also be trustworthy (Priester & Petty, 2003). Most individuals are very conscious of the prevalence and intent of persuasive communications and are skeptical of the vast array of claims they are exposed to. To be persuaded, they must trust the source of the message.

One of the major factors contributing to trustworthiness is the listener's perception of whether the speaker stands to gain from acceptance of the message. When speakers do not have anything to gain from presenting a particular message, they are more likely to be perceived as trustworthy. For example, suppose a series of TV commercials features a famous athlete urging you to buy a certain type of running shoe. Is this a trustworthy

Would this salesperson be successful in convincing you to buy one of his used cars?

**sleeper effect**
Occurs when the message and its source become detached; messages from sources low in expertise, attractiveness, and trustworthiness may increase in effectiveness

source? Probably not. The more shoes that are sold, the more high-paying commercials the athlete will be hired to make. But what if the same athlete appears in a series of public-service announcements about AIDS? In the latter instance the athlete's credibility may be enhanced; in this role the athlete does not stand to gain from urging listeners to practice safe sex.

Recall the Veg-O-Matic salesman described at the beginning of this section. Why was he unable to persuade you to take a chance on his product? He was attractive; that's a point in his favor. What about his level of expertise? World-class chefs do not usually demonstrate products in local discount stores; thus the salesman's level of expertise is questionable. How trustworthy is the salesman? Because his only reason for being in the store is to sell as many Veg-O-Matics as possible, you immediately question his claims. His apparent lack of expertise and trustworthiness has greatly reduced his persuasiveness.

If a *sleeper effect* occurs, however, his message may be more effective than we have led you to believe. The **sleeper effect** occurs when the message becomes detached from its source. For example, over time an audience member may forget which person presented which message. In such instances, messages from sources low in expertise, attractiveness, or trustworthiness increase in effectiveness and result in potentially flawed decision making. Thankfully, the sleeper effect does not appear to play a major role in everyday life (Pratkanis et al., 1988).

**Message Factors.**     Features of the message itself also influence whether we are persuaded. Those factors include attention, drawing conclusions, and message acceptance.

**Attention.**     To be persuaded by a message, you must pay attention to it. This simple fact has led to the development of numerous procedures designed to attract attention, such as printing signs upside down or backwards, using vivid colors, using unusual music and sounds, and featuring sexually arousing stimuli. Unless the sights and sounds are the message, however, the story does not end here. The audience must attend to the message that accompanies these attention-getters.

Advertisers use bright colors, unusual scenes, and unusual shapes to attract attention.

**Drawing Conclusions.**     Messages are designed to change our attitudes and thereby cause us to reach a particular conclusion. A basic research question concerns who draws

the conclusion, the person delivering the message or the individuals receiving it. Should conclusions be part of the message, or should members of the audience be allowed to draw their own conclusions? The answer depends on the involvement of the audience. If the audience simply receives the message without being actively involved in processing it, explicitly drawn conclusions are more effective (Papavassiliou & Mentzas, 2003). This situation fits the majority of television commercials. Conversely, when people are actively involved in processing persuasive messages, greater persuasion is achieved by allowing them to draw their own conclusions. For example, individuals who were in the market for compact disc players were influenced more by magazine ads that presented relevant facts and allowed readers to draw their own conclusions than by ads that presented the same facts and then stated conclusions (Petty & Cacioppo, 1996).

**Message Acceptance.**     The fact that someone attends to a message does not ensure that it will be persuasive. How many times have you heard a televised speech and said something like "That's absolute nonsense"? For a message to be persuasive, it should not differ drastically from the attitudes of the audience. Thus, during a recession, when people are losing their jobs, television commercials urging us to buy imported goods are less likely to be persuasive. Messages that do not differ from our beliefs too much appear to result in the greatest amount of attitude change (Petty & Wegener, 1998).

Reactance advertising tries to make consumers believe that their freedom to purchase goods and pay low prices is limited; hence, you buy their products so you will not feel that you have missed an opportunity.

Reactance is another means by which message acceptance is manipulated. **Reactance** theory states that individuals tend to react rather strongly in the opposite direction to a persuasive appeal that has the potential to restrict their freedom (Brehm, 1972; Engs & Hanson, 1989). For example, most people are unlikely to react favorably to a proposal to raise taxes, regardless of the need for added revenue, because the resulting loss of income would limit their financial freedom. It should be evident that reactance is another name for what is popularly known as "reverse psychology."

### Psychological Detective

Consider the ads we encounter every day on television, in newspapers and magazines, online, and in stores. Do those ads use the reactance principle to encourage us to make purchases? As you answer this question, try to think of as many specific examples as possible, and write them down before reading further.

We encounter reactance advertising every day in the form of proclamations such as "Sale! Everything Must Go," "Prices Will Never Be Lower," and "Limited Edition." Ads like these are designed to make us believe that our freedom to pay such low prices or purchase scarce merchandise is being restricted. It is expected that you will react to the threat of such restrictions by attending the sale or purchasing the scarce product.

**Primacy and Recency Effects.**    We noted in Chapter 7 that items that are presented first (*primacy effect*) or last (*recency effect*) are remembered best. If your audience receives two persuasive messages that oppose each other, would you prefer to have your message delivered first or last? The answer to this question depends on when the audience is required to act. If there is a delay between the presentation of the message and the required action, the first message is typically more effective (primacy). If action is required immediately after the message has been delivered, however, the last message has the advantage (recency). For example, suppose that you are the campaign manager for a political candidate. Your candidate and the opposing candidate are scheduled to debate the issues. Should your candidate speak first or last? If the election is a couple of weeks away, your candidate should speak first. If the election is tomorrow, your candidate should speak last.

**Channel Factors.**    Persuasive messages are presented through a variety of channels—printed words, spoken words, pictures, movies, and videos. The term *channel* can

**reactance**
The tendency to react in the opposite direction to a persuasive message when compliance might place limits on personal freedom

refer to any means by which a message is presented to the audience. Often two or more channels are used simultaneously (Devos-Comby & Salovey, 2003). For example, television is popular with advertisers because it combines visual and auditory channels (French & Richards, 1996). Some channels, such as radio, television, newspapers, and electronic media, make it possible to present messages to large audiences.

### Psychological Detective

Are persuasive messages more effective when they are delivered to a group or when they are delivered on a personal (one-to-one) basis? If a message can be delivered as effectively to a group as to an individual, much time and effort can be saved by delivering it to a large number of people simultaneously. Recall several situations in which you were the recipient of a persuasive message. Was the message more effective when you were by yourself or when others were present? Write down your answers to these questions before reading further.

Time and again, researchers have demonstrated that the person-to-person approach is more effective than appealing to a larger group (Maccoby & Alexander, 1980). Why? The same message is received in both cases. What factor of the one-on-one situation is lacking in a group presentation? When we are in a one-on-one situation, questions can be asked and answers given. In addition, the person who is presenting the message can extract a commitment from the receiver on the spot. This approach is known as the *foot-in-the-door* technique. We say more about this phenomenon later in this chapter.

The persuasive supremacy of one-on-one communication accounts for the recent growth of telemarketing, or direct telephone solicitation. The next time your phone rings and you find yourself being asked to subscribe to a magazine, switch your long-distance telephone service, or purchase credit card insurance, see how many features of effective persuasion are present in the message you are receiving.

**Audience Factors.**     So far we have discussed the nature of the source, message, and channel factors that influence persuasion. The nature of the audience also influences persuasion.

The knowledge and past experiences of the receiver of a persuasive message are important. If the audience is naive and unaware that the message is intended to persuade— as in the case of young children watching Saturday morning television programs—the message is more likely to persuade. This effect is seen in the attempts of children to get their parents to buy the toys and foods they see advertised on TV. In general, the most persuasive messages differ only moderately from the attitudes of the audience.

Research has shown that audiences can defend themselves against persuasion. The most frequently used procedure is analogous to vaccination—giving people a mild case of a disease (such as measles) to inoculate them against that disease. With this method, the audience is exposed to a mild form of the persuasive message before the main or real message is presented. For example, exposing teenagers to a mild form of peer pressure to smoke, in anticipation of the pressure they will encounter later, has been shown to reduce the likelihood that they will smoke (Chassin, Presson, & Sherman, 1990). Inoculation effects work best when the audience is encouraged to develop counterarguments to the message being presented.

### What We Attend To: The Central and Peripheral Routes of Persuasion.     What
do you attend to when you are exposed to a persuasive message—the content of the message or the attributes of the person presenting the message? The answer to this question involves the nature of the message and the motivation to attend to the

message (Chen & Chaiken, 1999; Petty & Wegener, 1999). If the message is relevant to you, then you are more likely to attend to the content. Additionally, because some people enjoy thinking about the content of a persuasive message, they are more likely to be motivated to attend to the message; these people are high in the *need for cognition*. When you pay attention to the content of the message, the *central route* of persuasion is being used. If you find that the persuasive message is not especially relevant to you and you do not enjoy thinking about its content, then you are more likely to attend to the attributes of the presenter (for example, credibility or attractiveness). When you pay attention to these attributes, persuasion is following the *secondary route* (Petty & Cacioppo, 1986).

**STUDY TIP** 👁

Create a mind map or think link for the section on persuasion. Use different colors for the different factors (source, message, channel, audience) illustrated in your visual organizer.

## Obedience

In Chapter 1 we met Keith, who was learning in his history class about the atrocities of war. He left the class wondering whether his psychology class would provide any answers to the question of why people commit such terrible acts. The psychology instructor asked the students, "How much electric shock, from 0 to 450 volts, would you administer to someone as part of a psychology experiment?" This question refers to one of the most famous series of studies in the history of social psychology: a study of obedience to authority conducted by Stanley Milgram in the 1960s.

More than 800 townspeople in New Haven, Connecticut, served as the participants in these experiments. Upon arrival at the laboratory, each participant was greeted by two people—a rather serious-looking scientist (the experimenter) wearing a white laboratory coat and a middle-aged man who was actually a confederate of the experimenter. The scientist informed the participant and the confederate that they were about to participate in a study of teaching and learning, and that one of them would play the role of the teacher. The confederate assumed the role of the learner; the real participant was the teacher.

The teacher read a list of pairs of words, then gave the learner the first word of a pair and asked the learner to identify the second word from among four words. Each time the learner gave an incorrect answer, the teacher was instructed to administer an electric shock to him. Before the session began, each teacher experienced a mild (45-volt) shock to appreciate what the learner would feel. Then the questioning began. As the session progressed and the learner began to make mistakes, the scientist (experimenter) demanded that the intensity of the shock be increased. The teachers followed these instructions until the learner had received a large number of what *appeared* to be very painful shocks. After the initial "shocks" were administered by the teacher, the learner protested and also indicated that he had a heart condition. In many instances the teachers became tense and faced a real conflict. They wanted to stop, but felt they could not. The stress they faced raised ethical issues about the conduct of this experiment.

When behavior is initiated or changed in response to the direct command of a person with authority, **obedience** has occurred. In the experiment just described, no electric shocks were actually administered to the learners, but the teachers were unaware that this was the case. All the teachers obeyed the instructions of the experimenter until the 300-volt shock level was reached. (The electric current in your house is 110 to 120 volts.) In one experiment, 65% of the teachers obeyed the experimenter's commands all the way to the 450-volt level (see Figure 15-4).

Why did the teachers repeatedly administer shocks to the learners? "Because they were told to" seems to be the best answer to this question. Before you say, "I'd never do that," bear in mind that Milgram's research involved more than 800 participants. Equal numbers of men and women continued to administer shocks up to the 450-volt level. The same logic may apply in the case of prisoner abuse. Why did some U.S. military personnel abuse Iraqi prisoners at Abu Ghraib Prison? Just as in Milgram's research, the

**obedience**
Initiating or changing a behavior in response to a direct command of an authority

**FIGURE 15-4** The teachers (participants) in the Milgram experiment believed they were administering electric shocks to the learners when incorrect answers were given. (A) The machine that "controlled" the shock intensity. (B) Preparing the "learner" for the experiment. (C) The experimenter directs the "teacher" to administer the shock. (D) The "teacher" checks on the status of the "learner."

**Source:** © 1965 Stanley Milgram. From the film "Obedience," distributed by Pennsylvania State University, Media Sales.

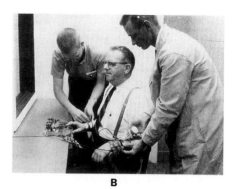
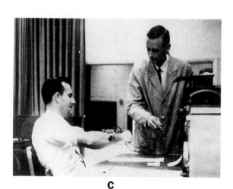
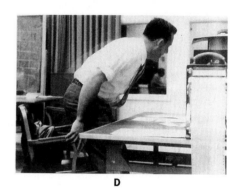

situation may have placed these personnel under great pressure to obey authority and conform to peer pressure (Dittmann, 2004; Staub, 2004).

Now consider an even more horrifying situation. In 1978, hundreds of people in Jonestown, Guyana, poisoned their own children with cyanide-laced Kool-Aid and then poisoned themselves. Why did this tragedy occur? The most plausible answer is that a charismatic leader, Jim Jones, gave commands that were obeyed (see Chapter 2). Tragic events like this one underscore the power of social psychological research findings and the need to use them wisely (Dittmann, 2003).

Research like Milgram's and events like the Jonestown tragedy lead us to conclude that people can be too obedient. Several factors, including proximity to the victim, proximity to the authority figure, and assumption of responsibility, influence how obedient we are. The closer the victim is to the participant, the lower the percentage of participants who obey a command to harm the victim. This factor is known as *victim proximity*. In the Milgram studies, fewer shocks were administered when the learner was in the same room with the teacher. Likewise, the closer the person commanding obedience (*authority proximity*), the more obedient participants are (Blass, 1996). In the Milgram studies, obedience was greater if the experimenter was in the same room as the teacher but decreased greatly if the experimenter telephoned the commands from another room.

Responsibility is also directly related to level of obedience. If the experimenter assumes responsibility for any harm that befalls the victim, as was the case in the Milgram studies, obedience is high. When responsibility is shifted to the participant, however, the likelihood of obedience drops dramatically. Similarly, if one of the experimenter's assistants defies the experimenter, the obedience of the teachers is reduced appreciably.

## Conformity and Compliance

Imagine that you are a participant in an experiment. You and seven other students are seated around a table. You have been told that the experiment is on visual judgments.

Your task is to determine which of three lines is the same length as a fourth line, the standard (see Figure 15-5). The person at the far end of the table answers first. Looking down the row, you see that you will be the next to last to answer. You think to yourself, "This is a piece of cake—the answer is obvious." Then something astonishing happens. All the students give the wrong answer; no one picks the line that matches the standard. Now it's your turn.

In the case of obedience, the *commands* to change behavior are clear, and the authority issuing the commands is obvious. In the case of **conformity**, there are *pressures*, often indirect, to change behavior and thoughts. The nature of the authority behind pressures for conformity is not as obvious as it is in commands for obedience. Think about the study just described. What would your response be under its conditions?

As with the obedience studies, many of us say that we would choose the correct line. However, Solomon Asch (1956), who conducted these influential studies, found that participants conformed to the rest of the group—that is, chose the wrong line— 30% of the time. In case you have not already guessed, there was only one real participant in each group: the next-to-last person to answer. All the other students in the group were confederates of the experimenters. Asch (1955) also varied the number of confederates who were present; he found that as few as three people giving the wrong answer was sufficient to produce conformity. It was important that the confederates be *unanimous* in their wrong answers. If one of the confederates gave the correct answer, there was a significant decrease in the rate of conformity by the real participants. Having only one other person support you can wipe out most of the effects of group influence.

Asch's classic studies soon gave rise to other research dealing with the effects of groups on judgments. Although group pressures do result in conformity, James Stoner (1961) showed that decisions reached by a group may be riskier than the independent decisions reached by individual members of the group. In many of the research projects conducted in this area, individuals were asked to read an account of a situation in which the central character faced a potentially risky decision, such as conducting a lengthy and time-consuming research project to enhance a career. For a time, the results of such studies tended to support the notion of a **risky-shift phenomenon:** Groups make riskier decisions than individuals. This general conclusion was soon questioned, however.

Imagine changing the situation just mentioned. Instead of simply expending time and effort on an experiment that may enhance a career, the central character faces the decision of whether to sell a life insurance policy to invest in a risky but potentially very high-paying stock. What is your reaction to this situation? Most people would advise against selling the life insurance policy to play the stock market. What will the group decision be? Contrary to the risky-shift prediction, the group decision will be more strongly opposed to selling the life insurance policy than the individual opinions.

Findings like these prompted some researchers, such as Serge Moscovici and Marisa Zavalloni (1969), to propose that a group's influence is to strengthen or intensify preexisting attitudes, not simply to produce riskier decisions. In the case of the life insurance policy, the initial attitude was not to sell the policy; group discussion served to intensify this non–risk-taking attitude. In the case of expending time and effort on an experiment that may enhance one's career, the initial attitude might be favorable because there is nothing to lose. A group discussion would further enhance this preexisting attitude and lead to greater risk-taking. The effect of group discussion enhancing preexisting attitudes is known as **group polarization** (Pascarella & Terenzini, 1991).

As a group's cohesiveness or shared values increase, so does conformity on the part of its members. For example, as sorority members grow closer, they are more likely to share such behaviors as binge eating (Crandall, 1988). Yet the presence of just one person who resists the pressure to conform can reduce conformity by others. For example,

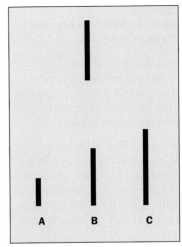

**FIGURE 15-5**  An example of the lines used in Asch's experiments. Although selecting the matching line might seem simple, approximately one-third of the participants chose the wrong answer to conform with the group.

  **15.2**

**conformity**
Initiating or changing a behavior in response to indirect social pressures

**risky-shift phenomenon**
The finding that groups make riskier decisions than individuals

**group polarization**
Phenomenon in which group decision making enhances or amplifies the original opinions of the group's members

**compliance**
Initiating or changing a behavior in response to a request

**foot-in-the-door effect**
Phenomenon in which a person who has agreed to a small request is more likely to comply with a subsequent larger request

**door-in-the-face technique**
People are first presented with an extremely large request, which they likely will refuse, and then they are presented with a more reasonable request that they are more likely to accept

**reciprocity**
Tactic for increasing compliance that involves doing something for others to create a feeling of obligation on their part

the presence of a nonjaywalking confederate reduced jaywalking to 17%; when the confederate jaywalked, the percentage of jaywalkers rose to 44% (Mullen, Copper, & Driskell, 1990).

Culture also influences the likelihood that a person will conform. For example, when Asch's line-judging experiment was replicated, similar rates were found in cultures that have comparable views of conformity, such as those of industrialized Europe. However, in cultures that value conformity more highly, the rate of conformity rose appreciably (Whittaker & Meade, 1967). In all cultures, as the spirit of individualism increases, the rate of conformity decreases (Alwin, 1990; Remley, 1988).

When we conform, we yield to group pressures in the absence of direct requests to change behavior. Obedience involves a direct request to change behavior, but the request is in the form of an order. **Compliance** refers to behavior that is initiated or changed in response to a request, but the request is not a command or direct order. Compliance may seem rather simple: Requests are made, and behaviors result. It is actually more complicated than that, however; social psychologists have studied—and salespeople have exploited—numerous strategies designed to increase compliance. It is common lore among salespeople that if they are successful in getting a customer to comply with a small request, the chances of compliance with a larger request (a sale) are greatly increased. For example, if you can be talked into taking a test ride in a new car, the chances of your buying the car increase. This phenomenon is known as the **foot-in-the-door effect.** The converse procedure also is effective in securing compliance. In this condition, known as the **door-in-the-face technique,** the chances for compliance are increased by first asking for an exceptionally large response, such as a $1,000 donation to a charitable cause. This request is purposely so large that it will make most people want to slam their door (Cialdini & Trost, 1998). The refusal of the exceptionally large request allows the proposal of a smaller, more reasonable request, such as $10, that the person is more likely to agree to.

Compliance also may be influenced by what another person has done for you. Consider the following situation. Suppose that a computer salesperson has come to your apartment to discuss a new computer system. She arrives with details about several systems based on your current and projected needs. How will you respond when she asks which configuration you want to invest in? With all the work that went into preparing these proposals for you, don't you feel obligated to purchase one of the packages she has prepared? This tactic for increasing compliance is known as **reciprocity.** With reciprocity, the person seeking compliance does something for you to make you feel obligated when he or she makes a request.

One of the most common examples of reciprocity occurs in supermarkets. Suppose that while doing your grocery shopping you see a person handing out free samples of

A man hands out free samples to shoppers in hopes that they will reciprocate by buying some of this product.

chips and cheese dip. It is late in the afternoon, and a bite to eat would taste good; you accept the sample. How will you respond to a request to buy some chips and dip? The salesperson anticipates that your acceptance of the free samples will put pressure on you to make a purchase.

In sum, we have seen how social influences affect persuasion, obedience, conformity, and compliance in individuals. In the next section we examine the effects of group membership.

# THE INDIVIDUAL AS PART OF A SOCIAL GROUP

**Many college students pride themselves on their ability to play pool. Pool balls can be heard being racked and shot at all hours in the student center. Perhaps you are a campus pool shark. It is Friday afternoon, and you and a friend are playing a casual game of pool. Halfway through the game, some friends from your dorm drop by and decide to watch the rest of the game. It is your turn to shoot. *Will the presence of your friends help or hinder your game?***

Most people have a strong need for affiliation; they enjoy being with others. Hence people frequently join and interact in groups like the group of friends just described. Being a member of a social group implies that there are membership criteria, responsibilities, privileges, and statuses. You are aware of your group memberships and responsibilities, as well as who does and does not belong to your group. The extent to which the members share the values of the group is known as *cohesion*. When there is high cohesion, group values are shared by all members. Low cohesion indicates that group values are not shared by all members and that conflict is likely.

In this section we examine group influences on individual behavior. We begin by looking at the effects of the simple presence of other people on the behavior of individuals.

## Social Facilitation

Robert Zajonc (1965) proposed that the presence of other people increases arousal (general physiological or psychological excitement). Greater arousal increases the likelihood that the most dominant response for a particular behavior will be shown. If you have performed a task many times in the past, the correct response dominates, and the increased arousal causes you to perform even better when other people are present. As noted at the beginning of this section, the increase in performance that occurs when others are present is called **social facilitation** (Platania & Moran, 2001). If, however, the task has not been practiced or learned very well and the correct response is not dominant, the presence of others tends to reduce the level of performance. This effect can be seen in the performance of children in a piano recital: Those who have practiced carefully perform as if inspired, whereas those who have devoted as little time as possible to practicing are plagued by wrong notes and memory lapses.

In the example at the beginning of the section, will the presence of your friends help or hinder your game of pool? As you now know, the answer to this question is "it depends." It depends on how good a pool player you are. If you are an above-average player, your performance should improve when others are present. If you are a below-average player, your performance should decline when others are present. As you can see from Figure 15-6, a study conducted by James Michaels and his colleagues (1982) verified this prediction. The accuracy of above-average players increased from making their shots 71% of the time when they were not watched closely to making their shots

**social facilitation**
An increase in performance that occurs when other people are present

**FIGURE 15-6** The presence of others can improve your game of pool if you are a good player. This effect is known as *social facilitation*. If you are a poor player, the presence of others may hurt your game.

**Source:** Michaels et al. (1982).

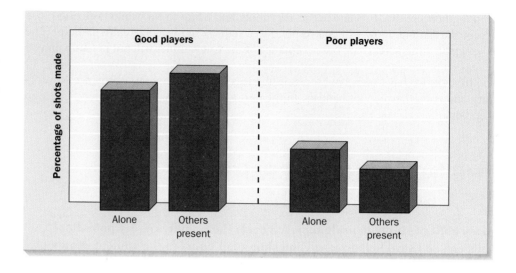

80% of the time when friends were nearby. By contrast, the accuracy of below-average players fell from 36% to 25% when their friends were watching.

Social facilitation does not always occur, however. If the pressure is too great, even professional athletes falter in front of their fans. For example, major league baseball players have lower batting averages in critical situations.

## Social Loafing

The presence of others does not automatically guarantee that performance will improve. When one's individual efforts are being evaluated, social facilitation can be predicted to occur. When a group collectively works toward a common goal and individual efforts are not monitored or evaluated, however, social loafing is likely to occur.

**Social loafing** is the tendency to exert less effort when working on a group task if individual contributions are not evaluated. A French engineer, Max Ringlemann (1913), initially studied this phenomenon in the late 1880s. He found that when a group of men pulled a rope, each man exerted less effort than when he pulled alone. Laboratory research has shown that people clap and cheer louder when they believe they are alone (Shepperd & Taylor, 1999). Social loafing has also been shown in more complex tasks such as relay swimming performance (Everett, Smith, & Williams, 1992). What's more, Karu and Williams (1993) reported that men engage in more social loafing than do women, and that people in Western cultures are more likely to engage in social loafing than people in Asian cultures.

Social loafing can be reduced by making the task more involving, challenging, appealing, or competitive (Heuze & Brunel, 2003). The coach of a good athletic team is well aware of social loafing and uses pep talks to counteract it. These motivational speeches are designed to challenge the team members to become more involved in the competition.

**social loafing**
The tendency to exert less effort when working on a group task that does not involve evaluation of individual participants

**coactors**
Other people who are present and are engaging in the same behaviors as an individual at the same time

## Audiences and Coactors

So far we have seen that the presence of other people may cause an individual to perform better at a task or to "goof off," depending on the situation. We need to add a clarification, however, about the other people who are present. In discussing social facilitation, we assumed that the "others" constituted an audience. Sometimes the other people present are doing the same thing you are doing. In these instances they are called **coactors.** What happens when there are many coactors and few, if any, people in the audience? The answer is that the process known as *deindividuation* is likely to occur.

**Deindividuation.**    When everyone is doing the same thing (that is, when there are many coactors) and no one is watching (there is no audience), **deindividuation,** or a loss of personal identity and a decrease of responsibility in the presence of a group, frequently occurs (Aronson et al., 2002). Deindividuation is the feeling of being lost in a crowd. Students at very large universities who complain about being a number instead of a name are experiencing deindividuation. Deindividuation often leads to uninhibited behavior. In some instances this behavior is positive, but the most frequent outcome is destructive or unauthorized behavior. The wild and destructive behavior of crowds after a major victory by the hometown sports team is an example of such behavior. Extra police and security guards must be hired to control the crowds.

Deindividuation has a powerful influence on the behavior of both adults and children. Some more extreme examples of deindividuation include the behavior of Ku Klux Klan members (they wear white sheets), military training (it is easier to kill an unseen, unnamed enemy), and mob behavior (most destruction and looting take place at night).

Fathali Moghaddam (1998) has proposed an alternate interpretation of the effects of deindividuation. Rather than losing themselves or experiencing diffusion of responsibility in such situations (Postmes & Spears, 1998), "deindividuated" individuals, Moghaddam suggests, have not abandoned all group norms and social controls; they simply have adopted new antisocial norms and values. This view is supported by research on street gangs in which members, who might be seen as deindividuated, now obey a new code of behavior (Sheldon, Tracy, & Brown, 1997).

The sheets and masks of the Ku Klux Klan hide personal identities and promote deindividuation.

# Group Interactions and Group Decisions

There are many instances in which cooperation among group members is required. Families could not function, juries could not reach verdicts, and teams could not win games without interaction and cooperation among members. As we have seen, the presence of groups may result in riskier decisions or the strengthening of preexisting attitudes. The rest of this section explores several of the dynamics and processes of group interaction.

**Group Formation and Effectiveness.**    When a group of unacquainted individuals is formed, certain predictable behaviors occur. First, the group will need a leader if it is to function effectively. Robert F. Bales (1950) found that two types of leaders emerge in a group. One leader is task-oriented; the business of the group is of primary importance to that individual. Another leader is socially oriented; he or she is more likely to show concern for the feelings and emotions of group members. What else do we know about people who emerge as leaders of groups? The individuals who become leaders typically talk more, talk first, and sit at the head of the table (Chemers, Watson, & May, 2000). Studies of leadership in India, Iran, and Taiwan have also emphasized the importance of task and social leadership (Smith & Tayeb, 1989).

**Brainstorming.**    In some situations group leaders may defer their leadership role in an attempt to involve all the members of the group. Because of the different viewpoints and experiences that a group's members bring to a situation, it is reasonable to predict that groups should be more effective than individuals in solving problems (Kelly & Karu, 1999). Most research on this topic has dealt with the effects of a technique known as brainstorming. **Brainstorming** is a problem-solving technique involving the free expression of ideas by group members (Faure, 2004). Once ideas have been expressed, they lead to the generation of other, related ideas. Ultimately, the collection of ideas is

**deindividuation**
Phenomenon in which the presence of a group results in a loss of personal identity and a decrease in responsibility

**brainstorming**
Free expression of ideas by members of a group to solve a problem

In this brainstorming session, company executives pool their ideas concerning how to increase productivity.

pooled and a solution is achieved. For free expression of ideas to occur, it is important that brainstorming be conducted in an uncritical atmosphere. No ideas may be labeled as "dumb" or "stupid."

### Psychological Detective

Brainstorming sounds impressive: Several individuals working together should be able to solve problems very effectively. This prediction has not proved to be true, however. Researchers have shown that the same number of individuals working independently actually generate more ideas than a brainstorming group (Madsen & Finger, 1978). Imagine yourself in a brainstorming session, and then imagine yourself trying to solve a problem by yourself. What is there about the brainstorming session that actually decreases the number of ideas generated? Write down some possibilities before reading further.

In a brainstorming situation everyone is encouraged to express opinions in an uncritical atmosphere. Problems may arise, however, when several people are ready to express their ideas. In a group, only one person can talk at a time, whereas many ideas can be generated simultaneously by individuals working alone. The presentation of ideas in the group setting may have a second unwanted effect as well. When one's train of thought is interrupted, it may be impossible to return to an idea that came to mind earlier. This situation often happens in groups but not when people work alone. Clearly brainstorming is not always the best way to generate ideas.

**Groupthink.**   Are there any other factors that might cause a group to be less effective than individuals? Yes—when maintaining harmony among group members becomes more important than carefully analyzing the problem at hand, the group's effectiveness decreases. The process of making decisions that tend to promote the harmony of the group is known as **groupthink** (Janis, 1972, 1982). Groupthink occurs most often in very cohesive groups that are insulated from other opinions and groups, feel that they are invulnerable, have a respected and directive leader, and are placed under time con-

**groupthink**
The tendency to make decisions intended primarily to promote the harmony of the group

straints to reach a decision concerning a threat to the group (Kerr & Tindale, 2004). In these circumstances groups tend to make premature and poorly considered decisions (Esser, 1998). The first suggestion proposed by the leader is usually adopted, especially if there is little hope of finding a better solution. For example, analyses of the decisions to cross the 38th parallel during the Korean War, to invade Cuba at the Bay of Pigs in 1961, and to escalate the Vietnam War in the mid-1960s have concluded that these were poor decisions prompted by groupthink (Janis, 1972). The activities of the Ku Klux Klan and lynch mobs also reflect groupthink in action.

What can be done to avoid groupthink? Group members and leaders can take several steps to help avoid being snared into the groupthink trap. First, the leader should strive to remain impartial and nondirective. Second, opinions should be gathered from people outside the group. Finally, the group should use secret ballots when making decisions in order to ensure that group members express their true feelings (Zimbardo & Andersen, 1993).

## Prejudice and Discrimination

Membership in a group such as a volleyball league team or a political action committee is usually voluntary. Some forms of group identification, however, are beyond our control. Most people are members of a variety of social categories of this type; they may be students, teachers, bricklayers, Italians, actors, rock musicians, alcoholics, Jews, or Catholics. When membership in such groups or categories determines how other people feel about us and act toward us, we are dealing with prejudice and discrimination. These are important aspects of interpersonal relationships and deserve a closer look.

**Prejudice.**    Think about the country you live in. Now think about several other countries. The chances are good that your feelings were more positive when you thought about your own country than when you thought about others. This occurs because the group to which we belong is the ideal against which other groups are compared and evaluated. Other groups naturally fall short of ours. When we make such comparisons between our nation or culture and others, we are being ethnocentric. Ethnocentrism is a form of prejudice.

Because the majority of psychological research is conducted in the United States, many of the results have been seen through ethnocentric eyes—that is, it has been assumed that the results produced in our culture are characteristic of other cultures. The results of cross-cultural studies are helping us remove these blinders. *Social loafing* provides a clear example of the influence of culture. We presented research results (see p. 680) that support the contention that people do not work as hard in groups as they do individually. These results, however, appear to be valid in *individualist* cultures where individual performance is valued. In *collectivist* cultures, such as China and Japan, where contributing to the group and group performance are valued, just the opposite is observed; research participants perform better in groups than individually (Gabrenya, Wang, & Latané, 1985).

Often our judgments of other individuals are based on only one characteristic—their social category or group membership. We do not need to know anything about the individual in question; all that matters is the category. Several examples of such group memberships were mentioned earlier; others are young, old, rich, poor, and intellectual. Judgments based solely on such characteristics are examples of **prejudice.** Ethnocentrism is an example of positive prejudice. Our thoughts about other countries and cultures probably reflect negative prejudice.

### Psychological Detective

As we have described it, the negative or positive evaluation that is at the heart of prejudice is quite general. Still, we all know that prejudices can be very specific. They enable us to describe exactly why a certain person is desirable or undesirable. If

**prejudice**
Judging a person on the basis of stereotypes about the group to which the person belongs

**discrimination**
Behaviors that adversely affect members of a particular group

prejudice creates a general negative appraisal, where do the specifics come from? Give this question some thought, and write down your answer and your reasons for selecting it before reading further. Here's a hint: The answer involves a topic discussed earlier in this chapter.

If you agree that these specifics are a set of beliefs concerning the members of a particular group, you already know the answer: We are dealing with stereotypes. Recall the examples at the beginning of this chapter: All actors are temperamental; all jocks are dumb. These general views can be directed toward individuals: The softball player in your history class is seen as a dumb jock; your friend the theater major is regarded as temperamental by the algebra instructor. Stereotypes are a major component of prejudice.

**Discrimination.**    The experience of prejudice frequently results in behaviors that adversely affect members of the targeted group; such behaviors are known as **discrimination**. In turn, prejudice can result in the belief that discrimination is acceptable; hence a vicious cycle is created (Bowser & Hunt, 1996). Discrimination can occur along many dimensions, including age, sex, religion, race, and political views. For example, for all the faculty members at a certain college to be men, despite the fact that many qualified women had applied for faculty positions, would be an instance of sex discrimination.

**Sources and Functions of Prejudice.**    Prejudice serves several functions and springs from a variety of sources. Here we examine both social and emotional sources and functions of prejudice.

**Social Function.**    Prejudice frequently justifies social standing or maintains self-esteem. For example, by holding a negative, degrading prejudice toward certain groups, individuals can rationalize mistreatment of (discrimination against) members of those groups. Consider the treatment of slaves, women, racial minorities, and people of different religions. Such discrimination implies the existence of two groups: "us" and "them," or *in-group* and *out-group* (Brewer & Brown, 1998). Members of the in-group share common values, goals, and beliefs, whereas members of the out-group are seen as different from members of the in-group. The perception of in-groups and out-groups is relative, however; your in-group may be our out-group, and vice versa. What's more, the size of the in-group influences the strength of members' feelings toward that group; smaller in-groups result in stronger favorable attitudes toward other members of the group. An example of the effect of in-group size is frequently experienced when a small group of fans travels to a neighboring school for an athletic contest. Each member's ties to the group seem closer and stronger in the face of the large home crowd ("them").

**Emotional Function.**    Earlier in this chapter we saw that frustration can lead to aggression. When we are frustrated, who becomes the target of our aggression? Who can serve this function better than the objects of prejudice and discrimination, especially if they are competing with us for scarce resources? Are there prejudices and discrimination in the business world? What happens when there is a union strike and nonunion employees are hired? What would happen if a professor announced that there would be only four A grades in a class of 20 students? Which groups would be the targets of prejudice and discrimination in these situations?

When the city commissioned several different gangs to paint these murals, cooperation in this activity led to a decrease in prejudice and violence among the gangs.

Because it makes us feel superior, prejudice can also satisfy our emotional need for status. In fact, an increase in the feeling of insecurity often results in our judging others more harshly. For example, students who wrote a short essay about dying (designed to increase the feeling of insecurity) showed stronger prejudice against members of out-groups (Greenberg et al., 1990). Prejudice is prevalent and can have quite negative effects. Can it be reduced?

**How to Reduce Prejudice.** Prejudice and its outward manifestation, discrimination, are common occurrences that almost everyone has experienced in one form or another. Nearly five decades ago, Gordon Allport (1954/1979) proposed that "equal status contact between majority and minority groups in the pursuit of common goals" (p. 281) would reduce prejudice. His hypothesis predicts that close and extensive contact between group members will result in greater understanding because such contact shows that stereotypes are inaccurate. Before this hypothesis becomes workable, however, several additional qualifications are needed; otherwise, people may dismiss the inaccurate examples and actually strengthen their existing stereotypes (Kunda & Oleson, 1997). First, for contact to be effective in reducing prejudice, the parties in both groups must be of equal status. The importance of this factor is shown in the problems encountered in attempting to integrate public schools and urban neighborhoods. When one group is perceived as having lower social or economic status than another, it is difficult to overcome prejudice.

Second, contact is more effective in breaking down stereotypes and reducing prejudices when both groups are united in the pursuit of a common goal. For example, in the classic piece of research in this area, Muzafer Sherif and his colleagues (1961) demonstrated that competition between groups at a summer boys' camp resulted in strong prejudice and discrimination. But when the groups were forced to cooperate to achieve a common goal (starting the water-tank truck on which the camp's water supply depended), prejudice and discrimination decreased. In sum, cooperation that is successful in achieving a goal generally leads to reduced prejudice and discrimination.

 **15.3**

**STUDY TIP**

Make flash cards for the marginal definitions in this chapter—write the word or phrase on one side, and definition on the other. Then, sort the cards into groups according to whatever system of categories you think is applicable. Use this grouping technique to help you better recall the terms and definitions.

# R E V I E W   S U M M A R Y

**1.** The use of social influence to cause other people to change their attitudes and behaviors defines **persuasion.** The expertise, attractiveness, and trustworthiness of the source of a message are important determinants of persuasion.

**2.** The most persuasive messages are those that attract attention, draw conclusions (if the audience is passively involved), differ only moderately from the attitudes of the audience, are the last message heard (if action is required immediately), and are presented on a one-to-one basis.

**3.** Naive audiences that are unaware of the intent of persuasive messages are more likely to be influenced by these messages. If the audience has previously been exposed to a mild form of the persuasive message, persuasion will be more difficult.

**4.** The cognitive approach to persuasion seeks to determine the thought processes that occur during persuasion.

**5.** **Obedience** is the initiating or changing of behavior in response to a direct command. In cases in which obedience will result in harm to another person, obedience increases with prox-

imity to the source of the commands but decreases with proximity to the victim. If the source of the commands takes responsibility for any harm resulting from obedience to those commands, the likelihood of obedience is high.

**6.** **Conformity** results from indirect pressure on an individual to change his or her behaviors and thoughts. The authority behind these pressures is less obvious than in cases of obedience.

**7.** The decisions of a group may be riskier than those of individuals. This **risky-shift phenomenon** is attributable to the **group polarization effect,** in which the original attitudes of the group's members are enhanced during group discussions.

**8.** **Compliance** refers to behavior that is initiated or changed as a result of a request. The compliance technique known as **reciprocity** involves doing something for someone else to make that person feel obligated to do something in return.

**9.** The presence of other people increases arousal, which may result in enhanced ability to perform a desired response. This effect is known as **social facilitation.**

10. **Social loafing** occurs when people working on a group task that lacks individual evaluation perform at a lower level than they would if they worked alone.

11. When there is no audience and only **coactors** are present, **deindividuation** may occur. Deindividuation is the feeling of being lost in a crowd; it may lead to uninhibited behavior that is often unauthorized and destructive.

12. Two types of leaders emerge in a group. One leader is concerned with the tasks confronting the group; the other is concerned with the interpersonal needs of the group's members.

13. **Brainstorming,** or free expression of ideas by the members of a group, is often not as effective in solving problems as the generation of ideas by individuals.

14. The process of making group decisions that promote group harmony is known as **groupthink.** Groupthink may hinder effective solution of problems.

15. **Prejudice** is judging others solely on the basis of their group membership. Stereotypes about the members of certain groups are an integral part of prejudice. Prejudice may be reduced through contact among members of different groups. Such contact is most effective where status is equal and common goals are being pursued.

16. **Discrimination** consists of behaviors directed at members of a particular group that affect them adversely.

## ✓ CHECK YOUR PROGRESS

1. "The use of social influences to cause other people to change their attitudes and behaviors" is a definition of
   a. obedience.
   b. persuasion.
   c. brainstorming.
   d. discrimination.

2. Companies advertising motor oil often use race-car drivers as spokespersons because they are
   a. perceived as experts.
   b. perceived as trustworthy.
   c. attractive sources.
   d. able to attract listeners' attention.

3. What is the relationship between attractiveness and persuasion?

4. Attention, acceptance, primacy, and recency all pertain to which factor of persuasion?
   a. source
   b. channel
   c. audience
   d. message

5. What is the term for what we call "reverse psychology" in everyday life?
   a. reactance
   b. persuasion
   c. reaction formation
   d. unconscious motivation

6. The _____ occurs when the source of a message is forgotten and the effectiveness of the message increases.
   a. dissociation effect
   b. sleeper effect
   c. channel effect
   d. audience effect

7. Which term do psychologists use to describe situations in which behavior is initiated or changed because of a direct command of a person with authority?
   a. obedience
   b. compliance
   c. conformity
   d. persuasion

8. Giving in to indirect pressure to change your behavior and thoughts is called
   a. obedience.
   b. persuasion.
   c. compliance.
   d. conformity.

9. The extent to which members share the values of a group is known as
   a. cohesion.
   b. solidarity.
   c. belongingness.
   d. group identity.

10. An increase in performance caused by greater arousal is called
   a. social loafing.
   b. social idleness.
   c. social facilitation.
   d. social productivity.

11. All of the following would help reduce prejudice except
   a. heightened group awareness.
   b. equal-status groups.
   c. pursuit of common goals.
   d. close and extensive contact.

**ANSWERS: 1.** b **2.** a **3.** The more attractive the source, the more persuasive the message. **4.** d **5.** a **6.** b **7.** a **8.** c **9.** d **10.** c **11.** a.

## SCORING | For Self-Monitoring Scale

**PAGES 649–650**

Give yourself 1 point for every answer that corresponds to the following key:

1. F
2. F
3. F
4. F
5. T
6. T
7. T
8. T
9. F
10. T
11. T
12. F
13. T
14. F
15. T
16. T
17. F
18. T
19. T
20. F
21. F
22. F
23. F
24. T
25. T

High self-monitoring scores range from 15 to 22, whereas intermediate scores range from 9 to 14. Scores of 0 to 8 are in the low range. Individuals with high scores are sensitive to situational cues, can detect deception on the part of others, and know how to influence other people's emotions.

# Industrial, Organizational, and Other Applications of Psychology

Psychology is not a stagnant discipline residing only in textbooks. Many of the theories, techniques, methods, and research results we have discussed are applied daily in the real world. Psychology has come a long way from its somewhat humble beginnings in search of the elements of consciousness. The theories and research findings that have developed over more than a century have been put to good use. Today, we can say that there are few, if any, human endeavors that do not interest psychologists and have not benefited from psychological research. For example, the cereal you purchase may have been influenced by research completed by a consumer psychologist. The packaging used to sell that product may have been influenced by additional research by psychologists. Using psychology to improve the safety of pedestrians is another area that is actively pursued by psychologists. For example, asking residents of a college community to sign a promise card to yield to pedestrians increased the behavior, which remained high a year after the program (Boyce & Geller, 2000).

**Industrial and organizational (I/O) psychology** is the scientific study and application of psychology to the workplace. I/O psychologists examine all aspects of the worker, the organization, and the work itself. One challenge I/O psychologists face today is the rapid change occurring in the workplace, including a more diverse labor force, the effects of new technologies, and globalization (Riggio, 2003). More and more minorities, women, and people with disabilities in America are entering the workforce. In the future, employers will face a "skills gap" — there will not be enough qualified applicants to fill positions requiring high-level skills (Offermann & Gowing, 1990). What's more, workplace violence affecting more than 2 million U.S. residents a year has led to a concern for identifying violence-prone employees and for defusing incidents that could escalate to violence (LeBlanc & Kalloway, 2002). Workplace violence results in the deaths of several hundred employees each year; it also increases stress levels for employees and has significant associated legal costs (Harley et al., 2002; Tebo, 2001). I/O psychologists confront a daunting task: to increase compatibility between employees and jobs at a time when the composition of the labor force and the workplace is rapidly changing in a competitive and global marketplace. Like the other psychologists you have read about previously, I/O psychologists actively conduct research using many of the methods we have already discussed. However, because they often conduct research in the workplace, they use different methods.

# RESEARCH METHODS IN INDUSTRIAL/ ORGANIZATIONAL PSYCHOLOGY

The I/O psychologist, like many other psychological researchers, uses a variety of research methods, such as the experimental method, correlational methods, the case study method (see Chapter 1), and meta-analysis (see Chapter 10). Additionally, because I/O researchers often study on-the-job behavior(s) of employees, they frequently use direct observation–either *obtrusive* (where the researcher is visible) or *unobtrusive* (where the researcher is not visible) (Riggio, 2003). The I/O psychologist also uses a variety of self-report techniques (such as surveys) to measure such attributes as workers' attitudes toward their jobs, occupational interests, management style, performance evaluation, and personality characteristics. Because these methods typically involve some type of measurement and statistical analysis, they are called **quantitative research methods**.

**industrial and organizational (I/O) psychology**
The scientific study and application of psychology to the workplace

**quantitative research methods**
Research methods that typically involve some type of numerical measurement and statistical analysis

**qualitative research methods**
Research conducted in a natural setting that seeks to understand complex humans by developing a complete narrative description of their behavior

A growing number of researchers are using qualitative research methods to answer I/O research questions. **Qualitative research methods** are "an inquiry process of understanding a social or human problem, based on building a complex, holistic picture, formed with words, reporting detailed views of informants, and conducted in a natural setting" (Cresswell, 1994, p. 2). Certainly, a qualitative approach seems appropriate for I/O research. What conditions or circumstances would lead a researcher to use this approach? Bachiochi and Weiner (2002) have listed four guidelines for the use of qualitative procedures. They are:

1. *Is the context central to the research question?*   Because qualitative research methods produce a report that is specific to a certain situation or industry, they do not generalize widely. However, if the researcher is interested in a specific industry or a particular company, then a qualitative approach may be the best choice.

2. *Is the participant's interpretation central to the research question(s)?*   If the participant's own view of a situation, such as reasons for leaving a job, is important, then a qualitative research approach may be the best way to answer the research question.

3. *Is depth/richness of data important?*   When greater detail is needed, qualitative approaches, such as case studies, interviews, and focus groups, may be best suited to provide these details.

4. *Is the research exploratory?*   For problems that are new and questions that may be threatening (such as a discussion of downsizing), a qualitative research procedure may provide a level of insight that other techniques, such as a structured survey, easily might miss.

The focus group is a frequently used qualitative research technique. In this procedure, the researcher selects 8 to 10 participants for the group. The group is kept small and the participants are heterogeneous in order to facilitate interaction (Bachiochi & Weiner, 2002). The facilitator, who is in charge of the group sessions, has a prepared guide that will help the sessions to stay focused on the topic of interest. Sessions are recorded by either audio or video and transcribed at a later time. Once these transcripts (the researcher's data) are prepared, they are ready for content analysis. Just as with experimental research procedures, the qualitative researcher uses rigorous and systematic data analytic procedures. For example, with content analysis, researchers frequently seek to achieve meaning condensation and categorization (that is, finding common

Newspaper advertisements such as these are often the beginning of the process of selecting employees. For many companies, the advertisements represent a significant amount of effort to identify the knowledge, skills, abilities, and other characteristics needed to perform the job.

themes that run throughout the session and putting them into appropriate categories). Frequently these procedures are guided by a theoretical model. Additionally, qualitative researchers frequently use more than one rater in order to achieve a measure on **interrater reliability**—how well the two raters agree about the meaning and categorization of the data they are independently evaluating. The end result of the focus group process is an in-depth and detailed analysis of the topic that was discussed.

In addition to using several diverse research methods, I/O psychology includes a variety of areas that can be explored in relation to the workplace, including job satisfaction, performance appraisal, training, personnel selection, and work-related law. For our purposes, we divide the field into three broad subcategories: human resources, organizational psychology, and human-factors psychology.

# HUMAN RESOURCES PSYCHOLOGY

**The year is 1917, and the United States has just entered World War I. The Secretary of War assigns you the task of identifying, classifying, and selecting Army recruits based on the area in which they could best be used (for example, infantry, officers, artillery, medical personnel). To complicate your job, many of the recruits are either illiterate or do not speak English. *How would you go about fulfilling your commissioned duties?***

This scenario represents one of the key steps in the development of I/O psychology. Although I/O psychology had been developing since the turn of the 20th century, it was not used on a large scale until World War I (Goodwin, 2005). For example, Walter Dill Scott headed a committee for the War Department that developed a rating scale for selecting officers. Based on their reported success, Scott took on the job of assigning the "right man to the right job" in the army. The Committee on Classification of Personnel in the Army was headed by Robert M. Yerkes, who was assisted by two other psychologists, Walter Bingham and Edward Thorndike. Their task was to work on the problem of identifying and eliminating the "mentally unfit" from service in the U.S. Army. By 1919 1,175,000 men had been tested using the first large-scale group intelligence test, *Army Alpha*, developed by the committee and the nonlanguage version, *Army Beta*, for illiterate and non–English-speaking soldiers (Leahey, 2000). After the war, psychologists began to develop other tests for the selection of civilian personnel.

**Human resources psychology** is the study and analysis of individual differences in relation to jobs and the development and maintenance of an organization's human resources (its workers). A key responsibility of human resources psychologists (formerly called *personnel psychologists*) is determining the basic knowledge, skills, abilities, and other characteristics (KSAOs) needed to perform a given job. To this end, personnel psychologists may develop a *functional job analysis*, which begins by examining what gets done in the order in which the elements are completed. Functional job analyses have been helpful in developing the U.S. Department of Labor's *Dictionary of Occupational Titles* (U.S. Department of Labor, 1991) of over 40,000 different jobs (see Table 16-1 for the entry for an Industrial-Organizational Psychologist).

Once KSAOs are established, human resources psychologists try to match the right employee to the right job, often by using personality, cognitive (intelligence), and motor/sensory ability tests (see Chapters 8 and 11). Additionally, it is important to take steps to maintain a mentally healthy workforce. "For example, at Bank One—now J.P. Morgan Chase—employees' mental health issues from 2000–2002 accounted for the second leading cause of short-term disability and were second in total of days absent from work—behind only pregnancy" (Dittmann, 2005, p. 36). Such features as team-building interventions that lead to better communication and employee satisfaction, working-parent programs, and flexible work schedules are important in this regard (Dittmann, 2005).

**interrater reliability**
Degree of agreement among observers

**human resources psychology**
The study and analysis of individual differences in relation to jobs and the development and maintenance of an organization's human resources (its workers)

| TABLE 16-1 |
| --- |

### Sample Entry from the Dictionary of Occupational Titles (DOT)

**Job: 045.107–030 Psychologist, Industrial-Organizational**

Develops and applies psychological techniques to personnel administration, management, and marketing problems: Observes details of work and interviews workers and supervisors to establish physical, mental, educational, and other job requirements. Develops interview techniques, rating scales, and psychological tests to assess skills, abilities, aptitudes, and interests as aids in selection, placement, and promotion. Organizes training programs, applying principles of learning and individual differences, and evaluates and measures effectiveness of training methods by statistical analysis of production rate, reduction of accidents, absenteeism, and turnover. Counsels workers to improve job and personal adjustments. Conducts research studies of organizational structure, communication systems, group interactions, and motivational systems, and recommends changes to improve efficiency and effectiveness of individuals, organizational limits, and organization. Investigates problems related to physical environment of work, such as illumination, noise, temperature, and ventilation, and recommends changes to increase efficiency and decrease accident rate. Conducts surveys and research studies to ascertain nature of effective supervision and leadership and to analyze factors affecting morale and motivation. . . . May adapt machinery, equipment, workspace, and environment to human use. . . .

**How to Interpret the DOT Code**

The first three digits indicate the occupational code, title, and industry designations. The next three digits represent the job's typical interaction with data, people, and things. The final three digits denote an alphabetical ordering of jobs within the same occupational grouping.

**Source:** U.S. Department of Labor, *Dictionary of Occupational Titles*, rev. 6th ed. (Washington, DC: U.S. Government Printing Office, 1991).

Human resources psychologists must also be knowledgeable about employment law, which affects their work in a variety of ways (Riggio, 2000). Table 16-2 summarizes some of the most important laws and their impact on the field.

## Personnel Selection

Under existing laws, the tools used in selecting, promoting, and terminating employees *must* be nondiscriminatory and unbiased. The Equal Employment Opportunity Commission (EEOC) requires test users to provide evidence that a test is related to meaningful aspects of job performance before it can be used to select employees. Consequently, human resources psychologists devote a great deal of time to ensuring that their tools meet these legal requirements. If the tools used to make employment decisions work to the disadvantage of members of a group protected under the law, they exhibit an *adverse impact*. An employer using a selection tool (for example, a test) that exhibits an adverse impact must demonstrate that the test is related to the job. If the employer fails to do so, it must stop using the test. For example, suppose that as part of a selection procedure a city requires applicants for the position of firefighter to do 50 pushups in 2 minutes. Under the law, the city must demonstrate that this requirement is related to the job. If firefighters who can do 50 pushups demonstrate higher levels of job performance than those who cannot do 50 pushups, the test may be used for selection (Arthur & Benjamin, 1999).

Another issue that concerns human resources psychologists is affirmative action—a social policy developed to reduce the effects of decades of prior discrimination (Muchinsky, 2000). Although affirmative action is not a requirement under the Civil

**TABLE 16-2**

## U.S. Laws and Their Effects on Human Resources Psychology

| Law | Effect |
|---|---|
| U.S. Constitution | Fifth Amendment requires "due process"; it gives individuals the right to a legal hearing and covers employment law. |
| | Thirteenth Amendment abolished slavery and involuntary servitude. It has been interpreted to include issues of racial discrimination in the workplace that can be legally viewed as a form of slavery. |
| | Fourteenth Amendment requires that all people be given equal and fair treatment under state laws in terms of both liabilities and privileges. |
| Equal Pay Act of 1963 | Passed as an amendment to an earlier act, this law prohibits sex discrimination in wages. Equal jobs require equal pay, regardless of gender. |
| Civil Rights Act of 1964 | This landmark antidiscrimination law is composed of sections or titles, each of which deals with a different aspect of discrimination. Title VII, which focuses on employment-related issues, prohibits discrimination based on race, color, religion, sex, or national origin. To enforce these mandates, the act created the Equal Employment Opportunity Commission (EEOC). The Equal Employment Opportunity Act of 1972 amended Title VII by granting the EEOC the power to initiate lawsuits against employers accused of practicing discrimination. Title VII now applies to virtually all employers with 15 or more employees, including state and local governments and educational institutions. |
| Age Discrimination in Employment Act of 1967 | This act, later amended in 1986, extended discrimination protection on the basis of age for workers over the age of 40. Companies can present arguments that age is a factor if they can show that older people cannot successfully perform the job. Employers, however, must pass a rigorous legal test to prove their case. The objective was to prevent companies from singling out older employees (with higher salaries) and terminating them or replacing them with younger workers to save money. |
| Americans with Disabilities Act of 1990 | Passed to protect the estimated 43 million Americans with disabilities, this law prohibits discrimination against qualified job applicants with disabilities and requires employers to make "reasonable accommodations" for disabled workers. It requires new businesses to be accessible to the disabled and existing businesses to make improvements where possible. |
| Civil Rights Act of 1991 | The most current civil rights legislation altered a variety of employment practices. For example, results of employment tests used in personnel selection cannot be adjusted on the basis of race ("race-norming") or gender to compensate for racial and gender differences in testing. The law also changed the way "adverse impact" (employment policies that negatively affect minority groups) is interpreted in the courtroom. |

Rights Act, it is included in the EEOC guidelines. There are four goals of affirmative action: (1) to correct present inequities in job and educational opportunities; (2) to compensate for past inequities (even if current practices are not discriminatory, past discrimination may put members of a minority group at a disadvantage); (3) to provide role models by increasing the number of minority group members in various positions; and (4) to promote diversity (Campbell, 1996).

As part of the personnel selection process the I/O psychologist will expend considerable time and effort on a job analysis. **Job analysis** is a thorough description of the responsibilities of a job and the qualities and abilities needed to perform that job (Riggio, 2003). During the preparation of the job analysis, several important products are produced: (1) a *job description* that includes the responsibilities, equipment used, and expected outcomes or products; (2) a description of *job specifications* that lists the characteristics and abilities that are needed to perform the job; and (3) a *job evaluation* that reflects the value of the job to the organization and recommends an appropriate wage.

The basic goal of any selection system is to predict the success of job candidates before offering them a job (or turning them down). Some of the recognized procedures

**job analysis**
A thorough description of the responsibilities of a job and the qualities and abilities needed to perform that job

include interviews, work samples, applications, letters of recommendation, tests, and situational exercises. We discuss the interview in some depth.

### Psychological Detective

Interviews are the most commonly used selection procedure, yet research shows that they have poor validity (little ability to predict which job candidates become good workers). Yet, employers continue using interviews to select workers. What are some reasons that employers continue using such a poor selection device? Consider this question from a company recruiter's perspective. Write your reasons before proceeding further.

Selection procedures vary in terms of their reliability, validity, fairness, applicability, time requirements, and cost (Muchinsky, 2000). For example, job application forms have good validity and reliability (when verified), fairness, applicability, little time, and low cost. Consequently, application forms are a standard part of job selection. By contrast, interviews are less valid owing to their more subjective nature unless the interview is *structured* (all candidates are asked the same questions in the same format) and contain situational questions (hypothetical situations requiring respondents to "think on their feet" to answer). Yet *unstructured* interviews continue to be a mainstay in business because many employers are reluctant to hire people without first meeting them face to face and assessing their "personality" (Blackman, 2002). In addition, most interviewers (and the public) believe they can "size people up" through an interview and accurately determine whether they will be good employees. Interviews are also relatively cost- and time-efficient.

Selection interviews are so well established that they are difficult to abandon, yet these interviews are frequently criticized for their limited reliability and validity. The reliability and validity of interviews, however, can be improved by following research-based guidelines (Campion, Palmer, & Campion, 1998). For example, questions should be based on a job analysis, which is required by professional and legal guidelines. This approach should raise validity by increasing the job relatedness of interview questions and reducing the amount of irrelevant (non–job-related) information collected during the interview. Second, the same questions (structured interview) should be asked of each job candidate in order to standardize the sample of behavior used to judge each interviewee.

The interview is the most frequently used selection procedure despite its shortcomings; its ability to predict which applicants will be successful is rather low. In recent years, researchers have found that the validity of the interview can be improved by using a standard set of questions (structured interview) and situational questions.

Third, questions can be improved by using more hypothetical situations, questions that require answers related to past behaviors, and questions concerning the candidate's background. Finally, there should be several interviewers, and the same interviewers should interview each candidate. The use of multiple interviewers should average out random errors across interviewers. One advantage of these guidelines is that employers who follow them would be in a better position to defend their selection procedures against allegations of discrimination in the hiring process (Williamson et al., 1997).

*Testing* is another common practice, and human resources psychologists have a variety of tests available. Descriptions of some commonly used tests can be found in Table 16-3, and sample questions from some of these tests can be found in Figure 16-1. Recall from Chapter 8 that successful tests must be reliable, valid, and standardized. These requirements extend to personnel tests as well. Tests that lack reliability and validity could be considered unfair or discriminatory and therefore illegal.

After falling out of favor for some time, personality testing for selection has made a comeback. With the exception of the interview, the most frequently used selection measure in the past has been cognitive tests. Because cognitive tests inevitably result in adverse impact, employers have searched for alternative selection measures. The recent development of the five-factor model (see Chapter 11) provided a useful way to organize personality traits and apply them to job performance (Hogan & Roberts, 2001). Ultimately, a human resources psychologist must decide which methods will yield the best predictions. By combining the most applicable methods, human resources psychologists can determine which applicants should be hired. We examine this process in more detail in the next section.

---

### TABLE 16-3

## Types and Examples of Commonly Used Tests That Are Used for Employee Selection

**Cognitive Ability Tests**

*Wonderlic Personnel Test*: This 50-item paper-and-pencil test measures level of mental ability.

**Mechanical Ability Tests**

*Bennett Mechanical Comprehension Test*: This is a 68-item paper-and-pencil test of the ability to understand physical and mechanical principles in practical situations. Can be administered to groups.

**Motor and Sensory Ability Tests**

*Hand-Tool Dexterity Test*: Using a wooden frame, wrenches, and screwdrivers, the test taker takes apart 12 bolts in a prescribed sequence and reassembles them in another position. This test of speed measures manipulative skills that are important in factory jobs and in jobs servicing mechanical equipment and automobiles.

**Job Skills and Knowledge Tests**

*Minnesota Clerical Assessment Battery (MCAB)*: A self-administered battery of six subtests measuring the skills and knowledge necessary for clerical and secretarial work (typing, proofreading, filing, business vocabulary, business math, and clerical knowledge). Testing is completely computer-administered.

**Personality Tests**

*Revised NEO Personality Inventory (NEO-PI-R)*: An increasingly popular personality inventory based on the Big five factors that is used in employee screening and selection.

**Source:** Adapted from Riggio (2003).

**FIGURE 16-1** Sample items from several tests commonly used in job selection. Psychologists have a wide variety of tests that could be used as part of the selection process. Employers are required to demonstrate that the test is related to meaningful aspects of job performance.

**Source:** Sample items from the Bennett Mechanical Comprehension test. Copyright 1942, 1967, 1970, 1980 by the Psychological Corporation. Reproduced by permission. All rights reserved. Sample items from the Minnesota Clerical Test. Copyright 1933, renewed 1961 by The Psychological Corporation. Reproduced by permission. All rights reserved.

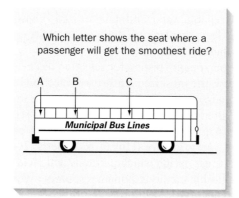

When the two numbers or names in a pair are exactly the same, make a check mark on the line between them.

66273894 _____ 66273984
527384578 _____ 527384578
New York World _____ New York World
Cargill Grain Co. _____ Cargil Grain Co.

Which letter shows the seat where a passenger will get the smoothest ride?

*Municipal Bus Lines*

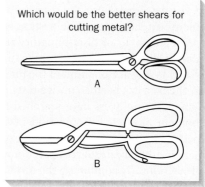

Which would be the better shears for cutting metal?

**Using Personality Tests in Selecting Police Officers.** The selection of law enforcement officers is a major societal concern. Could psychological tests play a role in these selections? In the past, psychological tests such as the MMPI and the MMPI-2 (see Chapter 11) were used to screen out applicants for consideration (Detrick, Chibnall, & Rosso, 2001). These tests could not be used, however, to select applicants who had qualities that would make them good officers because there was no evidence that the test scores were related to job performance.

Psychologists interested in investigating personality tests as potential measures for selecting police officers studied police cadets who were selected for training without the use of any psychological test (Hargrave & Hiatt, 1989). While at the police academy, these cadets completed the California Psychological Inventory (CPI) (see Chapter 11). At the end of training, their instructors rated each cadet's suitability for work in law enforcement. The 13% of cadets who were rated as "psychologically unsuited" differed from suitable cadets on nine scales of the CPI.

These researchers also studied officers (not cadets) who had experienced serious job problems such as physical confrontations with other officers. These officers also differed from other officers on several CPI scales, leading the researchers to conclude that the "CPI has potential value as a selection instrument" (Hargrave & Hiatt, 1989, p. 276). The CPI is used as a component in the selection of officers in the United States, Canada, and Australia (James, 1993).

The five-factor model of personality has proven useful in personnel selection. For example, compared to individuals with low self-ratings, those who rate themselves as more conscientious (dependable, reliable, and responsible) are less likely to have accidents (Arthur & Benjamin, 1999). This type of information can be useful to employers concerned with reducing the rate of accidents among employees, especially those in high-risk occupations. Psychologists have also developed what they have termed *criterion-focused occupational personality scales* including drug and alcohol scales, stress tolerance scales, and customer service scales. These scales have proven to be related to job performance in specific occupations, and all have been found to tap some of the Big Five factors (Ones & Viswesvaran, 2001).

Based on a review of the use of personality tests as predictors of job performance in several occupational groups, researchers caution that there must be a clear basis for using a particular personality characteristic in the selection process. Administering a psychological test in the hope that it will yield information useful in selecting future employees can be inefficient and illegal.

Psychologists have also investigated drug testing and genetic screening as predictors of future work performance. One study found that employees who tested positive for illegal drugs had a job absenteeism rate almost 60% greater than that of those testing negative, and the turnover rate (as evidenced by employees quitting or being fired) was 47% greater for drug users as compared with nondrug users (Normand, Salyards, & Mahoney, 1990). The successful application of a drug-testing system can save a company millions of dollars. Critics argue that it violates a person's right to privacy and that such tests are not sufficiently accurate. Nevertheless, surveys over the past two decades indicate an increase in the prevalence of drug testing by employers as well as an increasingly favorable attitude toward testing among employees.

Once an applicant has been selected, the next step for the new recruit is to be placed into a job and trained.

## Training

**training**
The deliberate and planned process by which employees are exposed to learning experiences designed to teach new skills and improve job performance

**Training** is the deliberate and planned process by which employees are exposed to learning experiences designed to teach new skills and improve job performance. Training typically follows personnel selection because new employees need to be trained in company procedures, policies, and equipment. One of the newest employment areas in which psychologists are making major contributions is the job of federal flight deck officer (Winerman, 2004). This job was created shortly after the September 11, 2001, terrorist attacks. Federal flight deck officers have jurisdiction *only* on the airplane flight deck (cockpit) and act as a last line of defense against possible terrorism. I/O psychologists were involved in the development of an effective screening program and the training of officers once they were selected. Clearly, selection and training go together.

*On-the-job training* may be sufficient for some jobs; more complex jobs may require weeks or even months of intensive training. Technical fields, such as computer systems, involve continuous training because knowledge becomes obsolete in a short time period. Thus training is not just for new recruits; experienced personnel also benefit from new training programs and refresher courses.

A comprehensive training program involves several steps. The first step, a *needs assessment* (McMahon, Rye, & Ward, 1996), is equivalent to a job analysis in personnel selection. The needs assessment determines who needs to be trained, what training program to use, and what is to be taught. Unfortunately, many companies do not conduct a needs assessment to determine their training requirements. Once a needs assessment is completed, the company establishes the training objectives. At this point trainers select the training methods (see Table 16-4) and design the training program.

Training programs often combine several methods, and most involve a mix of learning principles (see Chapter 5). The last step, after the actual training program has been implemented, is to evaluate the training program. Four types of measures are used in evaluating a training program (Kirkpatrick, 1976):

- *Reaction measures* indicate whether participants enjoyed the training program, valued it, and felt they had learned.
- *Learning measures* test retention of new skills and knowledge from the training program.
- *Behavior measures* determine the extent to which the training transferred to the job environment (in other words, can the trainee now perform satisfactorily in the real work situation?).
- *Results measures* show whether certain predetermined organizational goals (for example, increased productivity, increased sales figures, improved quality of work) were attained.

**TABLE 16-4**

## Training Methods

| | |
|---|---|
| **On-the-job training (OJT)** | The trainee mimics the behavior of other employees, who instruct the trainee on the correct behaviors while working on the job. |
| **Lectures** | The trainer addresses a group of trainees by speaking to them. |
| **Vestibule training** | Common in production line work, vestibule training involves a smaller version of the production line that employees can practice on without affecting the real production line. |
| **Audiovisual material** | The trainee may be exposed to films, slides, videotapes, audiotapes, transparencies on an overhead projector, or computer presentations as a training technique. The trainee may also be videotaped, which provides a basis for feedback. |
| **Job rotation** | Similar to OJT, job rotation involves having the trainee learn by performing several different jobs over an extended time period, thereby gaining a "bigger picture" of the overall process. |
| **Conferences (discussion method)** | Multiple trainers and trainees interact as if in a conference room or discussion group. A variation of this method is the training group (or T-group), often incorporating role-playing or sensitivity training to accomplish the training goals. |
| **Apprentice training** | A trainee is paired up with a more experienced worker and serves as the worker's apprentice. In white-collar jobs, this approach is called mentoring. Typically, the one-to-one relationship is maintained over an extended period of time until the job has been mastered. |
| **Programmed instruction** | The older version of this technique involved booklets (like study guides); newer versions usually use computers (called computer-assisted instruction). The trainee proceeds through a series of stages of self-teaching, using the booklets or the computer. Answering a battery of questions at each stage determines advancement to the next stage. |
| **Simulation** | Simulations involve a modeled version of a "real life" scenario that the trainee can practice with or without actually being exposed to the consequences. Flight simulators for pilots are an excellent example. Games can be used to simulate situations in financial or business environments. Military simulators are common in training soldiers for the battlefield. Much of this technology is now employed in video and arcade games available to the public. |

Unfortunately, few companies evaluate their training programs, and those that do often merely evaluate trainees' *attitudes*—reaction measures—about the training program rather than the program's effectiveness.

Finally, keep in mind that there are several types of employee training and education. For example, there is *new employee training*, where newly hired persons are oriented to the company and trained for their specific job. Second, because many skills become obsolete during a worker's career, more and more companies are instituting *retraining programs* to bring workers' skills up-to-date. Likewise, many companies now offer their employees *retirement planning training* and programs. A fourth type of

**Source:** From Eye on Psi Chi (Winter 1998).

employee training program that is becoming very popular with a number of organizations is *career development training* for their employees.

The ultimate purpose of recruiting, selecting, and training workers is to enable them to perform satisfactorily on the job; however, the hiring institution cannot take this for granted. Management must invest the time to determine that employees are performing as desired.

## Performance Appraisal

If you have ever held a job, you have experienced a performance evaluation or appraisal. **Performance appraisal** is the evaluation of a person's functioning on job-related tasks; it usually includes some formal assessment and feedback. Typically, the evaluation involves ratings across a series of performance dimensions or criteria. Accurate performance appraisals are important because they can affect decisions about promotions, raises, and layoffs. One of the greatest challenges in appraisal is to make the evaluations fair and systematic (Arvey & Murphy, 1998). For example, supervisors may give ratings that are inconsistent with employees' actual performance. In the worst cases, they may give a favorable rating to get a troublesome employee transferred to another department or a poor evaluation to punish an employee. One way to increase interrater agreement in performance appraisals is to provide explicit instructions and standards on which employee performance rating is based.

There are two types of performance appraisal criteria: objective and subjective. *Objective* or *hard criteria* consist of variables that can be measured numerically, such as the number of sales made, the number of televisions made, or the speed of data entry. Objective criteria are easily observed and totaled, so different raters should arrive at the same numeric rating. For example, if two production managers watch a worker assemble radios, both should determine accurately the number of radios assembled by counting the number of radios produced at the end of the day. By contrast, *subjective* or *soft criteria* are personal evaluations, as when a rater makes a judgment of the quality of work performed. Subjective criteria are more variable than objective criteria. In our radio assembly example, managers may arrive at different estimates of the *quality* of a worker's performance in assembling the radios. The actual performance appraisal instrument used to record subjective ratings is also highly variable in the sense that it can be affected by a range of personal styles.

There are two main methods for rating performance: comparative methods and individual methods. The *comparative methods* involve comparing a worker's performance with the performance of other workers. These methods include (1) *ranking* workers on one or more performance dimensions; (2) *forced distributions*, in which a supervisor assigns workers to performance categories that range from superior to poor, with a fixed percentage of workers required for each category; and (3) *paired comparisons*, in which a worker is individually compared with every other worker on a variety of performance criteria and one of each pair is selected as better. The *individual methods* are more common and involve evaluating each employee alone. Even though the employee is rated individually, comparisons with other employees are frequently made. According to Riggio (2003, p. 134), "The vast majority of performance appraisals use graphic rating scales which offer predetermined scales to rate the worker on a number of important aspects of the job, such as quality of work, dependability, and ability to get along with coworkers." An example of an item from a graphic rating scale might be

Dependability

High                        Low
7      6    5    4    3    2     1

Graphic rating scales typically evaluate 7 to 12 performance dimensions. The best graphic rating scales are those that define the performance dimensions and rating categories clearly, precisely, and carefully. The *narrative* is another form of individual performance rating. This technique involves a written account of the worker's

**STUDY TIP**

Create icons or other visual representations for the various training methods described in Table 16-4.

performance. The better narratives include specific examples in support of the rater's commentary.

Performance ratings can be influenced by a number of errors and biases (Arvey & Murphy, 1998).

- *Leniency error* occurs when a rater gives only favorable, above-average marks to all ratees. The opposite of this is *severity error*, in which the rater systematically gives only unfavorable, below-average ratings to almost all employees.

- *Central tendency error* occurs when raters consistently rank all employees in the middle of the rating scale.

- *Halo error* involves rating a person favorably on all performance dimensions because the rater has a favorable overall impression of the person or because the worker did an outstanding job on a particular task. A "reverse" halo effect (*rusty halo*) occurs when an overall negative evaluation is given on the basis of one instance of failure or one negative characteristic.

- *Recency effects* reflect the tendency of evaluators to assign more weight to more recent performance and less weight to earlier performance. To avoid this error, it is important that performance appraisals are made as soon after completion of the job as possible.

- As we saw in Chapter 15, *attribution errors* include the *causal attribution error* and the *actor-observer bias*. These effect are frequently found in performance appraisals—for example, when the supervisor believes that personal effort is involved. Superior performance will be rated more highly and inferior performance will be rated more harshly; these are causal attribution errors. Moreover, it has been shown that supervisors attribute more weight to the actions of the employee, whereas employees attribute more weight to the situation (these errors reflect actor-observer bias).

- Evaluators also must take *cross-cultural issues* into account. Supervisors/evaluators must keep in mind that individual appraisal represents a typically Western view of evaluation. Moreover, there are culturally dependent ways of providing assessment feedback to employees (Fletcher & Perry, 2001).

Some biases are unconscious on the part of the rater and thus can be difficult to detect. I/O psychologists have devised a number of ways to reduce these errors; these approaches include improving the rating instruments by clearly specifying the meaning associated with each numeric rating.

Next, we turn our attention to how I/O psychologists work to improve the effectiveness of the entire organization.

# ORGANIZATIONAL PSYCHOLOGY

**Organizational psychology** is the scientific study of organizations and their social processes. Thus it blends work-related psychology, social psychology, human relations, and business. Organizational psychology developed during the 1960s from the study of social conditions in the workplace. This subfield of I/O psychology is concerned primarily with the organization itself and issues like organizational structure and culture, leadership, and motivation. Two key issues of organizational psychology that merit further discussion are motivation and job satisfaction.

## Motivation

Every year thousands of motivation seminars are held around the world to convey the secrets to motivating people. Why? Most people believe that a motivated workforce performs better. The secret to motivating people, however, is more complex than many seminars convey. *Work motivation* is an internal state that activates and energizes job

**organizational psychology**
The scientific study of organizations and their social processes

behavior such that it is directed and sustained toward a job or organizational goal. Many of the concepts discussed in Chapter 6 on motivation and in Chapter 5 on learning can be applied to work motivation. For example, several behavior modification programs in manufacturing plants use reinforcement to increase performance and enhance productivity. Some common workplace reinforcers are bonuses, promotions, more vacation time, and new equipment.

Setting goals, a widely accepted technique for increasing work motivation, is often coupled with reinforcement. *Goal-setting theory* proposes that managers should establish specific difficult-but-attainable goals for employees to enhance performance. If the workers take part in setting these goals, the motivation to achieve them will be even higher. What's more, such goals are more effective than easy but vague suggestions to "do the best you can."

To be effective, employees must be committed to achieving the work goals. This outcome can be accomplished in several ways: (1) providing employees with feedback on their work performance; (2) allowing employees to participate in the goal-setting process; and (3) rewarding employees for attaining goals.

*Equity theory*, a cognitive theory of motivation, suggests that motivation involves comparing what we invest in work with what we get out of it (Adams, 1965). We mentally weigh our inputs, such as education, time, experience, and skills, against our work outputs: job satisfaction, pay, and recognition. If our outputs are equal to or exceed our perceived inputs—if the situation seems to provide equity—our motivation is likely to remain constant. If, however, our inputs exceed our outputs (inequity), we are likely to be motivated in a different direction. Thus we might demand a raise, decrease our effort, alter our perception of the situation, or look for another job. Equity theory also states that in addition to analyzing our own situation cognitively, we compare our input–output ratio to other workers' ratios. If we perceive others as having more favorable ratios, we may be motivated to increase our own performance so as to gain the rewards they have.

The *expectancy (VIE) theory* is another cognitive theory of motivation. According to Riggio (2003, p. 204), "the three core components of expectancy theory are *valence* [V], which refers to the desirability (or undesirability) of a particular outcome to an individual; *instrumentality* [I], which is the perceived relationship between the performance of a particular behavior and the likelihood that a certain outcome will result—in other words, the link between one outcome (the worker's behavior) and another outcome (obtaining recognition or a pay raise, for example); *expectancy* [E], which is the perceived relationship between the individual's effort and performance of the behavior." Expectancy theory indicates that the motivation to perform a specific behavior depends on the strength and interaction of the three factors (VIE). This theory is well suited to explain individual differences in motivation. For example, what is important to one worker (positive valence) may be unimportant to another worker (neutral valence); these differences would lead to different levels of motivation.

Ultimately, motivating workers is a tricky proposition because motivation is a highly individualized phenomenon: What motivates Employee A may have little effect on Employee B. What's more, motivation can be sustained only for short periods of time because it causes physiological arousal. As we saw in Chapter 14, extensive arousal can be stressful to the body. This finding might explain why people who attend motivational seminars often come out of them energized, but 3 months later they have noticed little change in their work behaviors.

## Job Satisfaction

The most widely researched work attitude in organizational psychology is job satisfaction, which is linked to productivity, turnover, and absenteeism. *Job satisfaction* is defined as relatively stable positive feeling toward one's job. Ultimately, job satisfaction is a measure of the discrepancy between expected levels of satisfaction and the actual satisfaction an employee feels. High levels of job satisfaction are likely when adequate resources are provided, when the work is interesting and challenging, when good working relationships

**STUDY TIP**

From memory, write brief descriptions of the four types of training program evaluation measures. Then, write a description of a work training program you have experienced. Finally, using the four measures, write an evaluation of the success of your training.

exist with supervisors and co-workers, when opportunities exist for advancement and recognition, and when the job offers security and a perception of equitable pay.

The Minnesota Satisfaction Questionnaire (MSQ; Weiss, Dawis, England, & Lofquist, 1967) and the Job Descriptive Index (JDI; Smith, Kendall, & Hulin, 1969) are two surveys that psychologists frequently use to measure job satisfaction. The MSQ has employees rate their satisfaction (dissatisfaction) on 20 aspects of the job (for example, compensation, responsibility, opportunity for advancement, working conditions). The JDI is a briefer survey that only measures five job-related aspects: satisfaction with the job, supervision, promotion, co-workers, and pay. The JDI yields five separate satisfaction scores and is the most widely used measure of job satisfaction.

Although common sense suggests that satisfied workers are productive workers, research does not consistently support this assumption. In one study researchers found a correlation of only .12 between job satisfaction and productivity (Muchinsky, 1987). This relatively low correlation suggests that satisfaction is not a key ingredient in employee productivity. The relationship between job satisfaction and absenteeism is not particularly strong either (Tuten & Neidermeyer, 2004). So what does job satisfaction lead to? Job satisfaction may have stronger ties to personal health; job dissatisfaction has been linked with elevated stress and poorer health. What's more, satisfied workers are more likely than dissatisfied workers to help co-workers, to improve their own skills, and to provide constructive criticism for the betterment of the company. The relationship between job satisfaction and productivity increases substantially when the organization has an effective reward system. Sustaining satisfied employees is desirable but often can be maintained only when compensation systems reflect actual productivity. Some researchers have been moving toward an integrated theory of job satisfaction that encompasses several theories to help explain how satisfaction should be measured and what correlates are related to high and low satisfaction.

One avenue of research suggests that certain people may be genetically predisposed to be more or less satisfied with their lives and jobs. Termed *positive* and *negative affectivity*, these personality dimensions have been found to be measurable and correlated with satisfaction (James, Brodersen, & Jacob, 2004). Someone with negative affectivity is predisposed to have lower job satisfaction levels, whereas a person with positive affectivity is genetically inclined toward high job satisfaction levels. A study of identical twins found that as much as 30% of job satisfaction could be traced to a genetic predisposition to be satisfied (Arvey et al., 1989). Further research in this area is needed, but perhaps tests for positive and negative affectivity may find their way into the personnel selection process.

# HUMAN-FACTORS PSYCHOLOGY

*Computers, robots,* and other technological innovations are changing the way we work. One division within psychology focuses on the interactions among people, machines, and the work environment; it is called *human-factors psychology.* Also known as *ergonomics* or *engineering psychology,* **human-factors psychology** is the science of engineering and designing equipment and machines for human use and modifying human behavior so that workers can operate machines more efficiently. British psychologists use the term *ergonomics,* which means "laws of work." The primary functions of human-factors psychology are reducing stress in workers confronted with new technology and making machines safer, more efficient, and more comfortable to use. Human-factors psychology is a combination of industrial engineering and applied psychology.

Human-factors psychology began developing during World War II. Previously, people had to adapt to a machine no matter how unsafe, inefficient, or uncomfortable it was. Even when the machines functioned properly and the people were highly skilled, costly errors occurred. With the coming of the war, human–machine interactions had to be better coordinated. Over time, physicians, physiologists, and psychologists joined military engineers in redesigning tank and submarine stations, military uniforms, and aircraft cockpits.

**human-factors psychology**
The science of engineering and designing equipment and machines for human use and modifying human behavior so that workers can operate machines more efficiently (also known as *engineering psychology* and *ergonomics*)

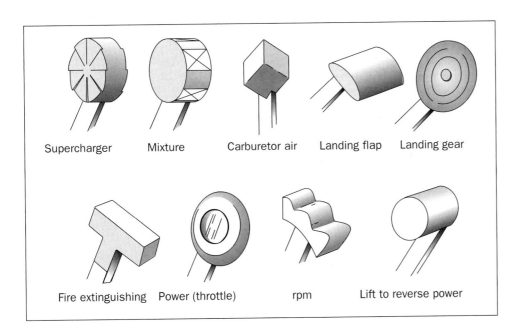

Supercharger    Mixture    Carburetor air    Landing flap    Landing gear

Fire extinguishing    Power (throttle)    rpm    Lift to reverse power

**FIGURE 16-2** Control devices and the types of information they transmit best.

At the beginning of the war, different aircraft had different cockpit arrangements. This situation is analogous to trying to drive different cars in which the brakes, gas pedal, and clutch are rearranged; a safe response in one may lead to death in another. Today the military uses a uniform and more efficient system of cockpit controls for aircraft (see Figure 16-2).

Human-factors psychology has helped redesign cars, computers, work cubicles, chairs, nuclear power plant control rooms, and products as simple as the potato peeler (Petroski, 2001). Despite this progress, however, we have a long way to go. We don't use all the features on our digital cameras or computers, some doors push and others pull, and many people have trouble figuring out how to turn on the water in a hotel shower.

## Human-Machine System

The combination of a machine and the person operating it is referred to as a *human-machine system* (or *person-machine system*). Examples of human-machine systems are a person typing on a computer keyboard, a construction worker driving a bulldozer, and a factory worker using a drill press machine. Ideally, the integration of the person and the machine should follow the *principle of compatibility*: If the machines follow certain guidelines that are compatible with our expectations, we will be able to use them efficiently, effectively, and safely. For example, red lights universally mean "stop" or "danger." Using a green light on a control panel to show danger would cause problems because it violates our expectations. Similarly, we are accustomed to turning knobs and screwdrivers clockwise (to the right). Machines or tools that require the reverse, a counterclockwise turn (to the left), would be problematic.

By now you have probably determined that many human-factors designs involve display systems (speedometer, computer screen) or control systems (knobs, buttons). There are several criteria for the good design of these systems. First, each control should have *only one function*. For example, separate controls in showers and sinks for hot and cold water were converted to a single control that adjusts hot and cold water simultaneously to reduce the likelihood of being scalded or frozen. The second criterion is *immediate feedback*. The control or display should immediately signal us when an action is being or has been performed. In other words, when you push a button, a light should come on or a buzzer should sound. Modern automated teller machines (ATMs) are good examples; in response to any button you press, a message appears on the screen giving you more choices from which to select. The ultimate feedback to show that you

At times, most of us deal with machines that were not constructed according to the principles of good design. For example, this ATM would be much easier to use if each button has only one function and if the machine provides immediate feedback so users know if they are on the right track.

**FIGURE 16-3** Engineering redesign of a stove.

**Source:** Adapted from Sanders and McCormick (1987).

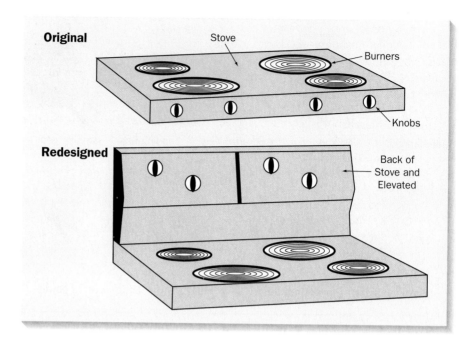

did everything right is obtaining your money from the ATM. The last criterion for good design is *visibility*: Systems should be easily understood through visual clues. A light switch provides just an on-off position and requires no extensive labels or instructions. As controls get more complicated, they may still possess good visibility if they are well designed.

Imagine that you had to redesign a stovetop to make it more useful. How might you redesign burner control knobs using visual cues? You can apply another principle called *proximity*. As shown in Figure 16-3, the knobs should be positioned in a staggered, square pattern corresponding to the pattern of the burners on the stovetop as opposed to being in a straight line. Many accidents blamed on human error may actually be due to poor machine design (Norman, 1995).

## Workplace Design

In some cases, human–machine interaction can be improved by redesigning a single knob or control. In other cases, the entire workplace needs to be revised. Workplace design should adhere to several key principles:

1. All tools, materials, equipment, and supplies should be positioned in order of use so that employees' movements are continuous from beginning to end. Items should be positioned so that they are accessible and placed within a comfortable reaching distance from any work position so that there is minimal need to change positions.

2. The most important operations or functions should be positioned in a central location. Any crucial displays or controls on the workstation should be located in the middle, directly in front of the worker.

3. Workstations that are used most frequently should be centrally located to reduce the amount of travel necessary to reach them.

4. Work areas should be grouped according to the similarity of their function. Similar stations or controls and displays should be near one another.

Consider the poor design of the U.S. Army's M-1 Abrams tank, which was built in the mid-1980s without using human-engineering research. When the tank's turret blowers and engine were operating, approximately 50% of the tank crews reported that they could not hear one another over the noise. The work consoles for each crew member created visibility problems. The front fenders were so badly designed that they did not protect the tank commander or driver from mud, rocks, and other debris kicked up by the treads when riding in an open hatch. Finally, from their position in the tank, drivers were able to see the ground only about 25 feet in front of the tank. This huge blind spot made negotiating obstacles very difficult. The design of the tank's workspace area would have benefited from a subfield of engineering psychology known as *anthropometry*.

**Engineering anthropometry,** a subset of human-factors psychology and engineering, involves measurement of human physical characteristics and development of machines and equipment to fit those characteristics. When designing equipment and workstations, engineers must consider people's height, weight, eye level, reaching distance, and so forth. A common use of engineering anthropometry is in the development of chairs. The clothing and shoe industries also make use of anthropometry because they need to know the most common shapes and sizes of the human body. An indispensable source for such information is the handbook *The Measure of Man and Woman: Human Factors in Design* (Tilley & H. Dreyfuss Associates, 1993). The charts in this handbook show the normal range of dimensions of parts of the human body that must be accommodated when designing everything from computer keyboards to potato peelers. The difficulty in designing products even with this information at hand can be understood by focusing on one of the charts in this handbook. The average adult male is 69.1 inches tall, with 62.6 inches being the 1st percentile and 75.6 being the 99th percentile. In other words, when designing a chair, designers must deal with the fact that there is more than a 1-foot range in the height of men; the design difficulties become even greater when the range of height among women is added to the design consideration (Petroski, 2001).

**Safety.**    Safety is a major concern for human-factors psychologists. Equipment and machines must be designed so that our bodies are not subjected to undue stress or physical damage. The design and setup of equipment is a major factor in the potential for injury. For example, poor setup of computer equipment can lead to neck, shoulder, and wrist problems (Sarkis, 2000). Work-related musculoskeletal disorders, collectively referred to as *cumulative trauma disorders* (*CTDs*), involve damage to joints, muscles, and tendons. One of the most common and widely publicized CTDs is *carpal tunnel syndrome*, a very painful condition of the wrist and hand resulting from compression of the nerve that controls movements of the thumb and some of the fingers. The disorder is more common among women and is especially associated with repetitive work such as keyboard entry (Butler & Liao, 2002). Approximately 200,000 cases of carpal tunnel syndrome are reported each year in the United States. On a broader scale, approximately 7 workers per 100 experience an occupational injury or illness each year. There were more than 6,000 deaths due to occupational injuries in 1996, and in 1997 there were 125,000,000 days lost from work due to injuries. The total cost of work-related deaths and injuries in 1997 was $128 billion, which includes wage and productivity losses, medical costs, and administrative expenses (National Safety Council, 1998).

Human-factors psychologists (sometimes referred to as *safety psychologists*) use several approaches to make work environments safer. One approach is to distinguish accidents caused by unsafe conditions from those caused by unsafe acts. *Unsafe conditions* can be any degraded or deteriorating environmental state, such as a chemical spill or faulty equipment. Human-factors psychologists can prevent unsafe conditions by redesigning tools, machines, or the workplace environment. This approach is called the *ergonomic approach* to accident reduction.

By contrast, unsafe acts are caused by human error. As many as 50 to 80% of all accidents may fall into this category. For example, aircraft have become more reliable over time, yet accidents continue to occur. Human error has played a progressively more

**STUDY TIP**

Gather in a small group. Each student should briefly describe one job that he or she has held. Using the terminology in the section on organizational psychology, the group should ask questions to evaluate the level of motivation and job satisfaction that the student experienced on that job.

**engineering anthropometry**
The measurement of human physical characteristics and development of machines and equipment to fit those characteristics

The goal of human-factors psychologists is to design equipment so it can be used efficiently and safely. This *ergonomic keyboard* was designed for maximum comfort; it is shaped in a way that makes typing more natural, and thus reduces the risk of injury such as carpal tunnel syndrome.

important role in aviation accidents (Wiegmann & Shappell, 2001). Psychologists have proposed two strategies for reducing these types of accidents. According to the *personnel selection approach*, companies can prevent workplace accidents through the use of psychological assessment to hire only people who possess a safety-conscious personality (Forcier et al., 2001). Several dimensions of personality (for example, thrill seeking) are significantly related to the occurrence of accidents owing to risky driving. That is, people who scored high on these personality traits had significantly higher rates of automobile accidents than those who scored low. Insurance companies have long been aware that single males under the age of 25 are more likely to be involved in driving accidents than any other demographic group. The accident rate decreases, however, if the young, single male driver has a good GPA, is a nonsmoker, and has graduated from a driver education class. Although driving style does not necessarily conform to workplace practices, many of the same personality dimensions may account for workplace accidents. Hence companies may want to screen applicants for traits and habits that reflect an accident-prone or risk-taking personality.

The second strategy for accident reduction is to train workers to be more safety-conscious. This *personnel training approach* rewards employees for engaging in safe behaviors. Common characteristics of good safety programs are active management and better selection and retention of quality employees.

Psychologists have been involved in a number of efforts to increase safety in the workplace. One intriguing example involves efforts to increase the use of seat belts and use of turn signals by pizza delivery drivers. The intervention consisted of a range of efforts, including radio and newspaper promotions and coupons to patrons who asked the dispatcher to remind the driver to buckle up when delivering the pizza. Use of seat belts increased 32% and turn signal use increased 41% over the period before the interventions began. These increases were maintained for 24 weeks after the intervention, suggesting that the changes in driver behavior had some staying power. Drivers at a control site did not exhibit any increases in safe driving behaviors (Ludwig & Geller, 2000).

# REVIEW SUMMARY

1. **Industrial and organizational (I/O) psychology** is the application of scientific principles to all aspects of work, including personnel selection and training.

2. When they conduct research, I/O psychologists use a variety of **quantitative research methods**, which involve gathering numerical data and conducting statistical analyses. Many I/O psychologists also conduct **qualitative research,** which is research conducted in a natural setting that seeks to understand a complex human by developing a complete narrative description of that behavior.

3. **Human resources psychology** focuses on the ways to recruit, select, train, and evaluate workers. Several selection instruments, such as the interview and tests, are available to assist psychologists. Human resources psychologists must also know employment law.

4. The planned process of systematically teaching employees new skills to enhance job performance is called **training.** Training should begin with a needs assessment and end with an evaluation of the program.

5. **Performance appraisal** is the evaluation of how well employees perform on the job. Job performance may be rated according to objective or subjective criteria. Raters are prone to a variety of rating errors, including *leniency error* and *halo error.*

6. **Organizational psychology** emphasizes an organization's social processes. *Work motivation* involves internal states that activate and direct behavior toward a goal. Two prominent work motivation theories are *goal-setting* and *equity.* A pleasant attitude toward one's work indicates *job satisfaction.* Many work factors correlate with job satisfaction, but it is a complex attitude.

7. **Human-factors psychology** is the science of designing human–machine interactions to be safer and more efficient. The development of new technology and equipment should follow principles such as compatibility. The design of workplaces is especially important to prevent disastrous outcomes such as the U.S. Army's M-1 tank. **Engineering anthropometry** involves the measurement of human physical characteristics to determine the fit of equipment built for people to use.

8. Safety is a key concern of human-factors psychology. Statistics have shown that the workplace can be a dangerous environment. Safety specialists can select from the ergonomic approach, personnel selection approach, and personnel training approach to maximize worker safety.

# ✓ CHECK YOUR PROGRESS

1. For 8 years Alice has worked for a company that issues credit cards. Last year she was seriously injured in a boating accident. After several months she was able to return to work, although she is now disabled. Under the Americans with Disabilities Act, what is the company's legal responsibility to Alice?

   a. The company must offer her a schedule of days only.
   b. The company must make reasonable accommodations for her.
   c. In order to compete for other jobs within the company, she must be offered training.
   d. Although her pay may be adjusted to reflect her level of disability, the company must return her to her old job.

2. What changes could be made to interviews to improve their validity as selection procedures?

3. What term is used for the first step in the training process?

   a. ergonomics
   b. beta testing
   c. needs assessment
   d. behavioral measure

4. For years, a company with more than 500 employees has used a "personality test" to select employees. When they ask a psychologist to examine their human resources policies, what concern is she likely to raise in her report?

   a. The test may not be valid, and if so, its use is probably illegal.
   b. A projective test would be a better choice because personality tests tend to be transparent.
   c. A test that is used by only one company does not meet legal and professional guidelines for personnel selection.
   d. The Civil Rights Act of 1991 prohibits use of personality tests in the selection process of companies with more than 15 employees.

5. Classify each of these as either an objective or a subjective performance measure:

   a. number of days absent
   b. number of televisions sold
   c. supervisor's assessment of work quality
   d. supervisor's judgment of rapport a salesperson established with clients

6. How can we motivate employees according to goal-setting theory?

7. List the major factors that an engineering psychologist would have to keep in mind when designing even something as simple as an office desk.

8. Which personality dimension has been related to the occurrence of accidents?

   a. tolerance
   b. thrill seeking
   c. openness to experience
   d. achievement via conformance

9. An insurance company clerk is processing a claim for a person diagnosed with carpal tunnel syndrome. The space for including the person's occupation was left blank. Before calling to ask for the information, the clerk suspects that the employee is most likely employed as a

   a. teacher.
   b. lifeguard.
   c. salesperson.
   d. computer clerk.

10. What is one reason for increased interest in the use of personality tests in selecting personnel?

    a. New research has validated Freud's concepts.
    b. The Big Five factors have provided a convenient way to assess personality.
    c. Recent changes in laws have allowed employers to use such factors in selection.
    d. These tests provide a subtle way to ask questions that are forbidden under the law.

**ANSWERS: 1. b. 2.** Research suggests that the use of structured interviews and situational questions can improve the validity of interviews for job selection. **3.** c **4.** a **5. a.** objective **b.** objective **c.** subjective **d.** subjective **6.** We must provide them with difficult but attainable goals. The goals must also be specific (not ambiguous). Additionally, feedback, employee participation, and rewards for good performance should be used. **7.** Important factors: **a.** Everything should be positioned so that it is easily accessible, comfortable, in order, and requires little movement/effort to use. **b.** Important things should be located centrally and at a level easily viewed by the operator. **c.** The object itself should be centrally located in the room if used by all. **d.** Similar items or work areas should be grouped together. **8.** b **9.** d **10.** b

# OTHER APPLICATIONS OF PSYCHOLOGY IN THE REAL WORLD

Police in New Jersey received a report that a child-care worker was sexually abusing children. Such allegations are taken seriously, so the police devoted a great deal of time and effort to their investigation. They interviewed all of the children, often several times. What they found alarmed them. According to their reports, the children were sexually violated with a variety of objects. Despite the fact that most of the objects could not be located in the child-care facility and no adult witnesses had ever observed any abuse, the alleged abuser, Kelly Michaels, was tried and convicted. Police and prosecutors were convinced that children make good witnesses because they would not fabricate stories. *What role might a psychologist have in a case such as this in which children are the sole witnesses to alleged abuse?*

Although I/O psychology is perhaps the most visible application of psychology, it is not the only area in which psychologists have applied their theories and findings. In fact, almost any human activity is likely to be one in which psychology can make a contribution. Three of the emerging areas of application are forensic (legal) psychology, occupational health psychology, and sport psychology.

## Forensic Psychology

**Forensic psychologists** apply psychology to law and legal proceedings; as a result, they are involved in a variety of consulting activities involving police, attorneys, and the courts. The beginnings of psychology's interest in legal matters can be traced to the work of Hugo Munsterberg (1863–1916) and publication of his book *On the Witness Stand: Essays on Psychology and Crime* (1908/1927).

**Memory and the Law.** Almost singlehandedly, experimental psychologist Elizabeth Loftus established a new area of interest for psychologists—evaluation of eyewitness testimony. For several decades, Loftus has demonstrated repeatedly that eyewitness reports are not necessarily accurate. She has shown how investigators (for example, police) can intentionally or unintentionally lead witnesses to believe they observed events that never happened (see Chapter 7). What's more, individuals can come to believe that events, such as alleged abuse, occurred when they did not.

There are a variety of ways in which interviewers may suggest general and specific answers to their questions. For example, they may ask leading questions, make overt suggestions, or excessively repeat a question (Ceci, Bruck, & Battin, 2000). In the Kelly Michaels case, children were interviewed together, thus allowing them to hear others' answers and incorporate those responses into their own memories. In contrast to the opinions of many police officials and prosecutors, psychologists have concluded that "a scientifically prudent position is that young children are disproportionately more vulnerable to a host of suggestive techniques than are older children and adults" (Ceci et al., 2000, p. 197). Although Kelly Michaels was convicted, her conviction was overturned after several years, and the state of New Jersey finally decided against pursuing the case.

As a result of the work of Loftus as well as other psychologists, there is a recognition of the fallibility of eyewitnesses. "It is indisputable that people's memories can be affected by suggestions presented in various forms from various sources" (Tsai et al., 2000, p. 43). The witness who says, "I will never forget that face as long as I live" could be mistaken, with dire consequences. Eyewitness identification is a dramatic and powerful force in the courtroom, but it is far from infallible. Such identifications have been key sources of evidence in a number of cases in which innocent people have been convicted, only to be found innocent on the basis of DNA evidence, often years after the conviction (Scheck, Neufeld, & Dwyer, 2000). Partly as a result, researchers are turning their attention to indicators that are more reliable than the confidence of an eyewitness. One promising example is the speed with which an identification is made. Accuracy seems to be associated with quick identifications (less than 10 seconds). One advantage of this approach is that "Confidence is a self-report that is subject to distortion . . . , whereas decision time is a behavior that can be directly observed" (Wells, Olson, & Charman, 2002, p. 153). What's more, the Department of Justice has developed a series of guidelines for law enforcement to use when creating lineups for witnesses. The guidelines for creating photo lineups can be found in Table 16-5.

**TABLE 16-5**

## U.S. Department of Justice Recommended Procedures for Composing Photo Lineups for Eyewitness Identification

1. Include only *one* suspect in each identification procedure.
2. Select fillers who generally fit the witness's description of the perpetrator. When there is limited/inadequate description of the perpetrator provided by the witness, or when the description of the perpetrator differs significantly from the appearance of the suspect, fillers should resemble the suspect in significant features.
3. Include a *minimum* of five fillers (nonsuspects) per identification procedure.
4. Complete uniformity of features is not required. Avoid fillers who so closely resemble the suspect that a person familiar with the suspect might find it difficult to distinguish the suspect from the fillers.
5. Create a consistent appearance between the suspect and fillers with respect to unique or unusual features (for example, scars, tattoos) used to describe the perpetrator by artificially adding or concealing that feature.
6. Consider placing suspects in different positions in each lineup, both across cases and with multiple witnesses in the same case. Position the suspect randomly in the lineup.
7. When showing a new suspect, do not reuse fillers in lineups shown to the same witness.
8. View the spread, once completed, to ensure that the suspect does not stand out.
9. Preserve the presentation order of the photo lineup. The photos themselves should be preserved in their original condition.

**Source:** U.S. Department of Justice (1999).

**Insanity, Competence, and Civil Commitment.**    Psychologists are called upon to offer expert opinions on a number of legal issues beyond those involving witness memory; these cases range from those in which a defendant pleads "not guilty by reason of insanity" to custody matters (Otto & Heilbrun, 2002). As we pointed out in Chapter 12, the general public's perceptions of the incidence of the insanity plea does not match reality. Very few defendants offer this plea and only a small percentage of those who do are found to be insane. Nevertheless, when such decisions are before a court, expert witnesses (often including psychiatrists) provide information to the judge and jury. For example, in the state of Indiana, when a defendant pleads not guilty by reason of insanity, the judge is required to appoint at least two disinterested mental health professionals to provide expert opinions to the court. These experts have an especially difficult job because they are asked to offer opinions on a defendant's ability to differentiate right from wrong (the most common basis for determining insanity) at the time the crime was committed.

Psychologists are also asked to offer expert opinions on another matter: Is the defendant mentally competent to stand trial? Approximately 60,000 criminal defendants are evaluated each year for competence to stand trial (Otto & Heilbrun, 2002). Issues of competency to stand trial are actually raised much more frequently than the insanity defense (Roesch et al., 1999). Under our laws, only individuals who are mentally competent may be tried; defendants must be able to understand the charges against them as well as assist in their defense (Zapf & Roesch, 2001).

Psychologists have developed a number of instruments to assess individuals' competency, although interviews are still the most commonly used method. Despite the high rate of requests for competency evaluations, only about 20% of these defendants are found to be incompetent to stand trial (Roesch et al., 1999). What happens if a defendant is found not competent to stand trial? The individual is transferred to a mental health facility for treatment until such time that he or she is competent to stand trial.

Another area in which psychologists offer their expertise is *civil commitment*—a legal procedure by which a person can be forced into mental health treatment, often in a mental hospital. The state may ask a court to commit a person if he or she is in need of treatment, exhibits what is termed a *grave disability*, or is dangerous to the self or to others.

**occupational health psychologist**
A psychologist who is concerned with removing health hazards of all types from the workplace and preventing accidents

**safety climate**
The positive attitudes that workers have about encouraging safe work behaviors

The last criterion (dangerous to self) is controversial because predictions of dangerousness are subject to error (Buchanan, 1999), which can result in an unnecessary commitment. Most mentally ill people do not commit crimes at rates higher than those of the general population; however, a subset of mentally ill people do commit crimes at a higher rate. The mentally ill people who commit crimes are very likely to receive media attention; consequently, the public tends to believe that there is a strong association between psychological disorders and crime. In fact, the association between psychological disorders and the tendency to commit violent acts is actually small and is accounted for primarily by individuals with substance abuse and psychotic disorders (Monahan, 2001).

## Occupational Health Psychology

As we have seen already, I/O psychology is concerned with safety conditions in the workplace. **Occupational health psychology** is a closely related area that is concerned with removing health hazards of all types from the workplace and preventing accidents.

Frequently organizational health psychologists work with an organization to help achieve compliance with Occupational Safety and Health Administration (OSHA) guidelines and standards. The Occupational Safety and Health Act, passed by Congress in 1970, created OSHA to establish and enforce health and safety regulations, to enhance safety education and training, and to promote safety research. This administration inspects worksites and assesses fines and penalties against employers who violate safety regulations. It has also established standards, ranging from the correct height for fire extinguishers to the amount and density of particles in the air. The most difficult challenge for OSHA is enforcing its guidelines and standards. Critics charge that its budget is inadequate and its inspection force is overworked. Thus, despite the fact that OSHA can levy fines for violations, the workplace can still be very dangerous.

**Workplace Dangers.**    Workplace dangers typically stem from one of three sources: (1) workplace conditions, (2) errors in the design of the person-machine system, and (3) the workers themselves. The great diversity of *workplace conditions* can offer numerous dangers. For example, working under extremess in temperature, lighting conditions, and noise can be a health hazard. Pollution in the workplace can be another severe health hazard. Table 16-6 shows several of the diseases that workplace pollution has caused.

Occupational health psychologists frequently assist a company to establish a **safety climate**—the positive attitudes that workers have about encouraging safe work behaviors. Many of these programs involve setting safety goals and providing incentives for

**TABLE 16-6**

## Some Common Workplace Pollutants and the Diseases They Cause

| Disease | Causes | Symptoms | Occupational Victims |
|---|---|---|---|
| Angiosarcoma | Inhaling vinyl chloride | Liver or brain cancer | Plastics workers |
| Anthrax | Bacteria from animals | Fever, pneumonia | Agricultural workers, ranchers |
| Asbestosis | Inhaling asbestos | Lung irritation or cancer | Miners, workers exposed to asbestos insulation |
| Black lung disease | Inhaling coal dust | Lung irritation or cancer, emphysema | Coal miners |
| Byssinosis | Inhaling cotton dust | Bronchitis, emphysema | Textile workers |
| Lead poisoning | Exposure to lead | Kidney disease, anemia, birth defects | Metal workers |
| Radiation poisoning | Exposure to radiation | Thyroid, lung, or bone cancer; leukemia; genetic damage | Medical technicians, nuclear plant workers, uranium miners |
| Silicosis | Inhaling silica | Bronchitis, emphysema, pneumonia | Miners, quarry workers, glass workers |

**Source:** Pelletier (1984).

engaging in safe behaviors and avoiding accidents. Stressing positive actions, such as setting safety goals and providing incentives, has resulted in a significant increase in safety-related behaviors and a corresponding reduction in accidents.

**Preventing Disease and Promoting Good Health in the Workplace.** The occupational health psychologist also is concerned with preventing the spread of disease in the workplace. In order to achieve this goal, psychologists have helped companies establish *employee assistance programs* (EAPs). EAPs help workers deal with such issues as substance abuse problems and psychological problems that may interfere with job performance. Additionally, such programs deal with the spread of AIDS and the promotion of better attitudes toward workers who have AIDS (Herold, Davis, & Maslyn, 1998).

In addition to preventing the spread of disease in the workplace, more occupational health psychologists are becoming advocates for health promotion. The benefits to the company are significant; healthy, physically fit workers have less absenteeism, fewer job-related accidents, and higher productivity. The psychologist's involvement in this aspect of the organization often is visible via a *health promotion program*. These programs are typically presented in seminar style and feature such topics as good nutrition, smoking cessation, and the benefit of exercise. Additionally, many organizations have opened on-site fitness and exercise centers where workers can actively modify their lifestyles. The results of such programs and centers have been very positive (Adkins, 1999; Greer, 2004).

# Sport Psychology

During basketball practice, Ted is able to shoot free throws with amazing accuracy. When game time arrives, Ted's amazing accuracy evaporates. Out of desperation, his coach asks for the help of a sport psychologist who teaches in the university's psychology department. After several meetings with Ted, the psychologist suggests that Ted has an extreme form of *competitive anxiety* that interferes with his ability to focus on the task at hand; in more common language, he has a tendency to "choke" when he shoots free throws during a game. The psychologist suggests a number of techniques, and Ted agrees to try them. Beginning with some relaxation training, Ted feels more comfortable but the problem is not yet solved. The psychologist then suggests the use of imagery techniques (see Chapter 8). Ted conjures up images of failure and replaces them with thoughts and images of success. In the end, Ted's performance improves (based on Roberts & Treasure, 1999).

Although sport psychology (also known as *exercise and sport psychology*) is one of the newer applied areas of psychology, it does have a history, albeit a brief one. For example, Norman Triplett's research on the effects of the presence of others on bicycle riders is considered the first experiment in social psychology; it could also be considered the first sport psychology research (Gill, 2000). As you will recall from Chapter 15, the presence of others can facilitate the performance of behaviors such as bicycle riding. Although there have been occasional research reports and efforts to use psychology in sports in the past, a decision by the U.S. Olympic Committee in 1978 was a significant turning point in the history of sport psychology. The committee decided to employ the services of psychologists to enhance the performance of its athletes. One of the first psychologists to work with Olympic athletes was Richard Suinn (see Chapter 1), a clinical psychologist and former president of the American Psychological Association, who consulted with U.S. Olympic skiers. Today a growing number of individual athletes and teams (professional and collegiate) consult **sport psychologists** to help them improve their performance.

**Enhancing Athletic Performance.** Among the most common areas of consultation for sport psychologists are those that are similar to the recommendations made to Ted in the vignette that opened this section. As we saw, competitive anxiety can be an obstacle to high levels of sport performance. Although anxiety is an everyday occurrence, we must learn to deal with it or it can interfere with our functioning; the same is true for athletes. "Competition creates some anxiety in nearly everyone, and intense anxiety keeps some from

Safety is a major concern for all businesses. On-the-job injuries and deaths cost $128 billion in 1997. Safety psychologists use several approaches to make work environments safer for everyone.

**sport psychologist**
Psychologist who provides services to athletes and coaches based on psychological principles

The level of physiological arousal and cognitive activation called *competitive anxiety* can affect sport performance. Sport psychologists have developed several techniques for reducing competitive anxiety.

performing well or enjoying the activity. Most athletes must deal with intense anxiety at some time, and competitors may experience states ranging from relative calm to utter panic" (Gill, 2000, p. 159). It is important to recognize that anxiety is a sign of physiological arousal, which can energize performance, but this effect depends on the skill involved. Shooting free throws requires less arousal than tackling a fullback at the goal line.

Psychologists have developed several techniques to help athletes deal with competitive anxiety, including self-talk and imagery. Self-talk can serve as a form of self coaching and verbal persuasion ("I can do it," "Keep your head down"); it can also be used to correct bad habits, focus attention, modify levels of activation, build self-confidence, and increase self-efficacy (Gill, 2000).

Another common technique recommended by sport psychologists is imagery, which is widely used by elite athletes like Olympic diver Greg Louganis (see Chapter 8). A number of suggestions can enhance the effectiveness of imagery in improving athletic performance:

- Practice imagery regularly.
- Use all your senses to enhance the vividness of the imagery.
- Facilitate the imagery by using various relaxation techniques.
- Use imagery in practice as well as in competition (Gould & Damarjian, 1996).

**Coaching.** Sport psychologists have also contributed by investigating coaching behavior and using their findings to develop programs to enhance the effectiveness of coaches at all levels. One widely known and respected program is *Coach Effectiveness Training* (Smoll & Smith, 1997). Among the principles that form the foundation of this program is that winning is defined as giving maximum effort and improving. The program advocates a positive approach that makes liberal use of reinforcement, encouragement, and sound technical instruction. What's more, there is an emphasis on mutual support and involvement of the athletes. The program is presented in workshops that last approximately 3 hours and has been taken by a wide range of coaches.

**Fan Violence.** Although the development of sport psychology has focused primarily on enhancing sports performance, some sport psychologists have devoted attention to fan violence. Researchers have found, not surprisingly, that those who engage in riots at sporting events tend to be angry, high in sensation seeking, willing to take risks, and impulsive. By contrast, other people at sporting events at which violence breaks out serve as *peacemakers*. In fact, fans randomly stopped at sporting events are more likely to be peacemakers than those bent on violence. These peacemakers tend to be physically bigger than rioters, less angry, less impulsive, low on sensation seeking, and high in self-esteem (Wann, Melnick, Russell, & Pease, 2001).

Although there have been some ugly scenes of violence at sporting events in the United States, nothing compares to the *hooliganism* that has occurred at British and European soccer events. How can we explain this cross-cultural difference? Most of the stadiums used for British soccer were built at the end of the 19th century and thus have few amenities; most U.S. stadiums are modern, clean, and comfortable. Most of the fans attending soccer in Britain walk to the games because the stadiums are centrally located and the fans generally lack transportation. As a result, there are many opportunities to engage opposing fans on the way to the game. In the United States, most spectators arrive at games in small groups and generally do not come in contact with opposing fans until they are in the facility. Most European soccer fans stand, which is more conducive to developing camaraderie and unity; most U.S. spectators are seated. The timing of the events also makes a difference: British soccer games begin at around 3 P.M. on Saturday, which provides a substantial amount of time for drinking prior to the match; by contrast, most U.S. football and soccer games start at 1 P.M. (Wann et al., 2001).

Although fan violence in the United States typically does not reach the levels found among British and European soccer fans, fan violence does occur here. In fact, one of the first reported instances of fan violence occurred in 1897. A major league baseball crowd became violent; fans stormed the field and threw bricks at an umpire who had

**STUDY TIP**

Look at the basic outline of the chapter shown on the chapter opener page. Using that outline as a beginning structure, construct a more detailed outline of the chapter material to help you see the logic of the flow of information through the chapter.

ejected their favorite player (Wann, 1997). Daniel Wann has several suggestions for reducing such fan violence:

- Limit the sale of alcoholic beverages, especially late in the contest.
- Seat supporters of the opposing teams in different sections of the arena.
- Promote the idea that a team's effort is more important than a game's outcome.

The efforts of sport psychologists to develop ideas to reduce fan violence are an excellent example of how psychology responds to current needs. It is not likely that the founders of the discipline would have envisioned these applications. This example also illustrates how the various subfields in psychology begin to blend into one another. For example, many of the suggestions for dealing with fan violence follow some of the principles developed by environmental psychologists who focus on ways to design spaces for comfort, safety, and efficient use.

## REVIEW SUMMARY

1. Three of the newest areas of applied psychology are **forensic psychology, occupational health psychology**, and **sport psychology.**

2. **Forensic psychologists** have found that eyewitness testimony is not necessarily accurate; individuals can be influenced to "remember" events that never happened. Psychologists offer expert opinions on issues such as competency to stand trial. A person cannot be tried unless he or she understands the charges and can assist in his or her defense. Insanity is a legal judgment that a person is not legally responsible for a criminal act. Commitment is a determination that a person needs mental health treatment.

3. **Occupational health psychology** is a closely related area that is concerned with removing health hazards of all types from the workplace and preventing accidents.

4. A **safety climate** refers to the positive attitudes that workers have about encouraging safe work behaviors.

5. **Sport psychologists** offer techniques to improve athletic performance, including imagery and self-talk. They also consult on coaching effectiveness and on issues such as ways to reduce fan violence.

## ✓ CHECK YOUR PROGRESS

1. If a lawyer asks a judge for funds to assess his client's competency, which of the following is the likely focus of the lawyer's concern?
   a. the client's ability to pay fees
   b. the client's ability to assist in his defense
   c. existence of a prior history of criminal behavior
   d. the influence of genetic factors on the tendency to commit a crime

2. Elizabeth Loftus has been invited to give a public lecture on a topic related to forensic psychology. Which of the following would make the best title for her presentation?
   a. "The Insanity Plea: Sham and Shame"
   b. "The Genetics of Crime"
   c. "Witness Memories Can Be Altered"
   d. "Innocence and Children: They Tell the Truth"

3. Which event was the beginning of the modern era of sport psychology?
   a. Universities granted the first advanced degrees in sport psychology.

   b. Professional sports teams began hiring psychologists as consultants.
   c. The U.S. Olympic Committee asked psychologists to provide services to athletes.
   d. Television networks asked psychologists to assist in developing ways to attract more fans to watch sports.

4. Aimee has been escorted to court by a sheriff for a hearing to determine if she should be committed. What is one of the bases for such commitment?
   a. grave disability
   b. presence of a low IQ
   c. genetic abnormality
   d. presence of a psychotic disorder

5. What is the more technical term for "choking?"
   a. divided attention
   b. stimulative arousal
   c. dissociative attention
   d. competitive anxiety

6. What is one of the ways in which investigators may unwittingly implant memories in witnesses?

**ANSWERS: 1.** b **2.** c **3.** c **4.** a **5.** d **6.** Memories can be altered or implanted by asking leading questions, making overt suggestions, and asking particular questions repeatedly.

# Statistics and Psychology

**DESCRIPTIVE STATISTICS**
Measures of Central Tendency
Graphing Your Results
Measures of Variability
Correlation

**INFERENTIAL STATISTICS**
The *t* Test

In Chapter 1 you found that becoming a good psychological detective involved using and understanding statistics. We expand on that discussion here.

Let's begin with a definition of statistics. **Statistics** is a branch of mathematics that involves the collection, analysis, and interpretation of data. As we said in Chapter 1, you can and should use statistics to aid in the decision-making process about knowledge claims. The two main branches of statistics assist your decisions in different ways. **Descriptive statistics** are used to summarize any set of numbers so you can understand and talk about them more intelligibly. **Inferential statistics** are used to analyze data after an experiment is conducted to determine if an independent variable had a significant effect.

## DESCRIPTIVE STATISTICS

We use descriptive statistics when we want to summarize a set of numbers (often referred to as a *distribution*) so that their essential characteristics can be communicated. As we saw in Chapter 1, one of these essential characteristics is a measure of the typical score (called a measure of central tendency). The *mode, median,* and *mean* are the measures of central tendency used by psychologists. A second essential characteristic that we need to know about a distribution is how much variability or spread exists.

### Measures of Central Tendency

Measures such as the mode, median, and mean tell us about the typical score in a distribution.

**Mode.**  The **mode** is the number or event that occurs most frequently in a distribution. If students reported the following work hours

> 12, 15, 20, 20, 20

the mode would be 20.

> **Mode** = 20

**statistics**
Branch of mathematics that involves the collection, analysis, and interpretation of data

**descriptive statistics**
Procedures used to summarize any set of data

**inferential statistics**
Procedures used to analyze data after an experiment is completed; used to determine if the independent variable has a significant effect

**mode**
Score in a distribution that occurs most often

**Median.**    The **median** (mdn) is the number or score that divides the distribution into equal halves. To be able to calculate the median, you must first rank order the scores. Thus if you started with the scores

56, 15, 12, 20, 17

you would need to rank order them as

12, 15, 17, 20, 56

Now, it's an easy task to determine that 17 is the median.

**mdn** = 17

What if you have an even number of scores, as in the following distribution?

1, 2, 3, 4, 5, 6

In this case the median lies halfway between the two middle scores (3 and 4). Thus the median would be 3.5, halfway between 3 and 4.

**Mean.**    The **mean** is defined as the arithmetic average. To find the mean we add all the scores in the distribution and then divide by the number of scores we added. For example, we start with

12, 15, 18, 19, 16

We use the Greek letter sigma, $\Sigma$, to indicate the sum. If $X$ stands for the numbers in our distribution, then $\Sigma X = 80$. If $N$ stands for the number of scores in the distribution, the mean would equal $\Sigma X/N$. For the preceding example, $\Sigma X(80)/N(5) = 16$. The sum of these numbers is 80, and the mean is 16 (80/5). The mean is symbolized by $\overline{X}$ ($X$ bar). Thus

$\overline{X} = 16$

Which measure of central tendency should you choose? The answer depends on the type of information you seek. If you want to know which score occurred most often, then the mode is the choice. The mode may not, however, be very *representative* of the other scores in your distribution. Consider the following distribution:

1, 2, 3, 4, 5, 11, 11

The mode is 11. The other scores, however, are considerably smaller; therefore the mode does not accurately describe the typical score.

In this case the median may be a better choice to serve as the representative score because it takes all of the data in the distribution into account. There are drawbacks to this choice, however. The median treats all scores alike; differences in magnitude are not taken into account. Thus the median for *both* of the following distributions is 14. Other than rank ordering the numbers, the values of the other scores do not enter into our calculations.

*Distribution 1:* 11, 12, 13, 14, 15, 16, 17     mdn = 14

*Distribution 2:* 7, 8, 9, 14, 23, 24, 25     mdn = 14

When we calculate the mean, however, the value of each number is taken into account. Although the medians for the two preceding distributions are the same, the means are not.

*Distribution 1:* 11, 12, 13, 14, 15, 16, 17
$\Sigma X = 98$     $\overline{X} = 98/7$     $\overline{X} = 14.00$

*Distribution 2:* 7, 8, 9, 14, 23, 24, 25
$\Sigma X = 110$     $\overline{X} = 110/7$     $\overline{X} = 15.71$

The fact that the mean of Distribution 2 is larger than that of Distribution 1 indicates that the value of each individual score has been taken into account.

**psych**    A.1

**pie chart**
Diagram in which the percentage allocated to each alternative is graphically represented as a slice of a circular pie

**bar graph**
Presents the frequencies for each category as a vertical column or bar

Because the mean takes the value of each score into account, it usually is seen as providing a more accurate picture of the typical score and is favored by psychologists. The mean can be misleading, however. Consider the following distribution of charitable donations:

> *Charitable donations:* $1, 1, 1, 5, 10, 10, 100
> mode = $1.00
> mdn = $5.00
> mean = $128.00/7     $\overline{X}$ = $18.29

If you wanted to report the "typical" gift, would it be the mode? Probably not. Even though $1.00 is the most frequent donation, this amount is substantially smaller than any of the other donations, and more people made contributions larger than $1.00 than those who made the $1.00 contribution. What about the median? Five dollars appears to be more representative of the typical donation; there are equal numbers of higher and lower donations. Would the mean be better? In this example the mean is substantially inflated by one large ($100.00) donation; it is $18.29, although six of the seven donations are $10.00 and under. Reporting the mean in this case may look good on a report of giving, but it does not reflect the typical donation.

When you have only a limited number of scores in your distribution, the mean may be inflated (or deflated) by extremely large (or extremely small) scores. The median may be a better choice as your measure of central tendency in such instances. As the number of scores in your distribution increases, the effect of extremely large (or extremely small) scores decreases. Look what happens when we add two additional $5.00 donations:

> *Charitable donations:* $1, 1, 1, 5, 5, 5, 10, 10, 100
> mode = $1.00 and $5.00
> mdn = $5.00
> mean = $138.00/9     $\overline{X}$ = $15.33

Note that we now have two values for the mode ($1.00 and $5.00). The median stays the same ($5.00). The mean, however, has decreased to $15.33; the addition of only two scores moved it appreciably closer to the median.

**FIGURE A-1** A pie chart depicting TV preferences (percentages) for college men.

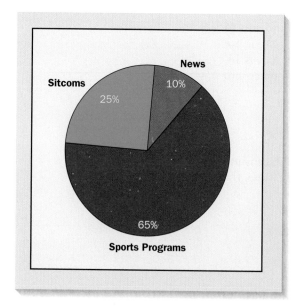

## Graphing Your Results

Once a measure of central tendency has been calculated, this information can be conveyed to others. If you have only one set of scores, the task is simple; you write down the values as part of your paper or report.

What if you are dealing with several groups or sets of numbers? The task becomes complicated, and the inclusion of several numbers in a paragraph of text might be confusing. In such cases a graph or figure can be used advantageously; a picture may be worth a thousand words. You may choose one of several types of graphs.

**Pie Chart.**    If you are dealing with percentages that total 100 percent, then the familiar **pie chart** may be a good choice. The pie chart depicts the percentage represented by each alternative as a slice of a circular pie. The larger the slice, the greater the percentage. A pie chart depicting TV preferences for college men is shown in Figure A-1.

**Bar Graph.**    We use the **bar graph** to present our data in terms of frequencies per category. For example, Figure A-2 shows the sports and fitness preferences of (1) men and boys and (2) women and girls who are frequent participants in such activities.

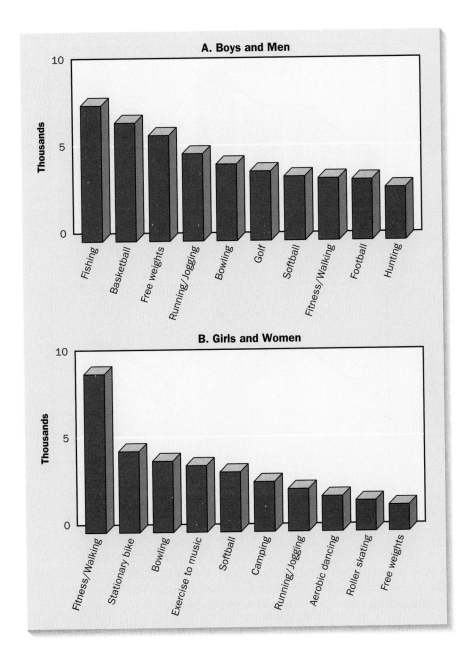

**FIGURE A-2**   A bar graph
depicting the sports and fitness
preferences of men and boys
(A) and women and girls (B) who
are frequent participants in such
activities.

**Source:** The American Enterprise,
September–October 1993.

You can see at a glance that the type of activities and number per category differ
drastically between the two groups. (If the sports and fitness categories in Figure A-2
could be quantified and arranged numerically, the columns depicting the frequencies
would touch each other and the figure would be known as a *histogram*.) How many
words would it take to write about these results rather than present them as a graph?

**Frequency Polygon.**   If we mark the middle of the cross-piece of each bar in a bar
graph, connect the dots, and remove the bars, we have constructed a **frequency
polygon** (see Figure A-3). The frequency polygon, like the histogram, displays the
frequency of each number or score.

**Line Graph.**   The results of psychological experiments are often presented as a line
graph. Let's examine the construction of the line graph. We start with two axes or
dimensions. The vertical or Y axis is known as the **ordinate;** the horizontal or X axis is

**frequency polygon**
Line graph that is used to represent
the frequencies for each category

**ordinate**
Vertical or Y axis of a graph

**FIGURE A-3** The frequency polygon is constructed by placing a dot in the center of each bar of a bar graph and connecting the dots (A) and removing the bars (B). The frequency polygon, like the bar graph, displays the frequency of each score or number.

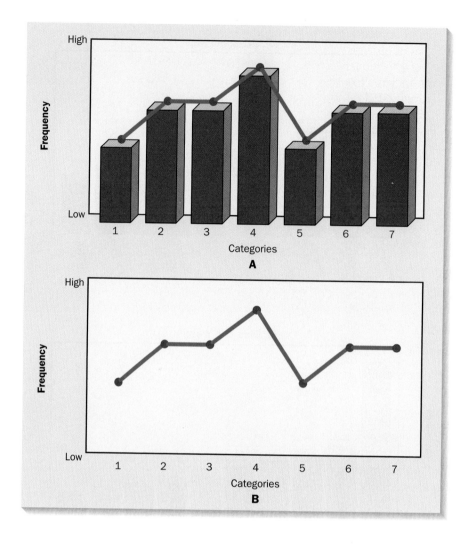

**FIGURE A-4** The ordinate, or *Y* axis, and abscissa, or *X* axis. The ordinate should be about two-thirds the size of the abscissa to portray the data as clearly as possible.

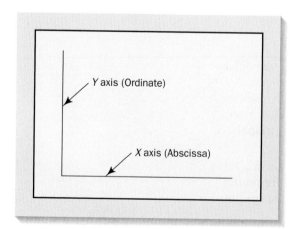

known as the **abscissa** (see Figure A-4). When we construct a line graph, our scores or data (the dependent variables) are plotted on the ordinate. The values of the variable we are manipulating (the independent variable) are plotted on the abscissa.

How tall should the *Y* axis be; how long should the *X* axis be? A good rule of thumb is for the *Y* axis to be approximately two-thirds as tall as the *X* axis is long (see Figures A-4 and A-5). Other configurations give a distorted picture of the data. For example, if the ordinate is considerably shorter, differences between groups or treatments are obscured (see Figure A-6A), whereas lengthening the ordinate tends to exaggerate differences (see Figure A-6B).

In Figure A-5 we have plotted the results of a hypothetical experiment in which the effects of different levels of stress on correct responding in air traffic controllers were evaluated. As stress increased, the number of correct responses increased.

Although measures of central tendency and graphs convey considerable information, we can learn still more about the numbers we have gathered. We also need to know about the variability in our data.

## Measures of Variability

**abscissa**
Horizontal or *X* axis of a graph

You have just got your last psychology test back; your score was 64. What does that number tell you? By itself it may not mean very much. You ask your professor for additional information and find that the class mean was 56. You feel better because you were above the mean. After a few moments of reflection, however, you realize that you still need more information. How were the other scores grouped? Were they all clustered close to the mean, or did they spread out considerably? The amount of variability or spread in the other scores has a bearing on the meaning of your score. If most of the other scores are very close to the mean, then your score is among the highest in the class. If the other scores are spread out widely around the mean, then your score is not one of the strongest. These situations are diagrammed in Figure A-7.

Obviously we need a measure of variability. The range and standard deviation are two measures of variability frequently reported by psychologists.

**Range.** The **range** is the easiest measure of variability to calculate; you rank order the scores in your distribution and then subtract the smallest score from the largest. Consider the following distribution:

1, 1, 1, 1, 5, 6, 6, 8, 25

When we subtract 1 (smallest score) from 25 (largest score), we find that the range is 24.

**range:** $25 - 1 = 24$

Other than telling us the difference between the largest and smallest scores, however, the range does not provide much information. Knowing that the range is 24 does not tell us about the distribution of the scores we just considered. Consider Figure A-8.

The range is the same for parts A and B; however, the spread of the scores differs drastically between these two distributions. Most of the scores are clustered in the center of the first distribution (Figure A-8A), whereas the scores are spread out more

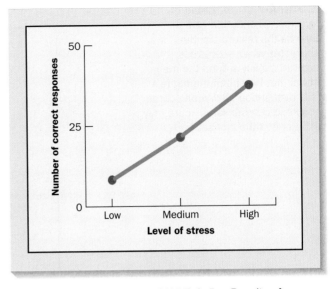

**FIGURE A-5**  Results of a hypothetical experiment investigating the effects of stress on correct responding in air traffic controllers.

**range**

Measure of variability that is computed by subtracting the smallest score from the largest score

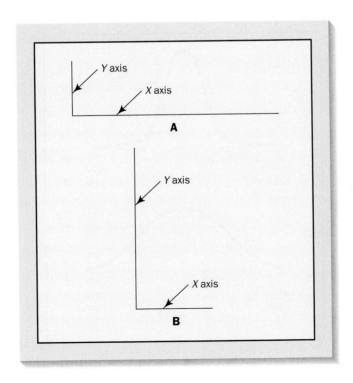

**FIGURE A-6**  Altering the $X$ (abscissa) or $Y$ (ordinate) axis can distort the results of an experiment. (A) If the ordinate is considerably shorter than the abscissa, significant effects can be obscured. (B) If the ordinate is considerably longer than the abscissa, very small effects can be exaggerated.

**FIGURE A-7** **FIGURE A-7** The spread of scores in a distribution can influence the relative standing of a score. (A) When scores are clustered closely around the mean, a score may be one of the highest in the distribution. (B) When scores are spread out, the same score may not be one of the highest.

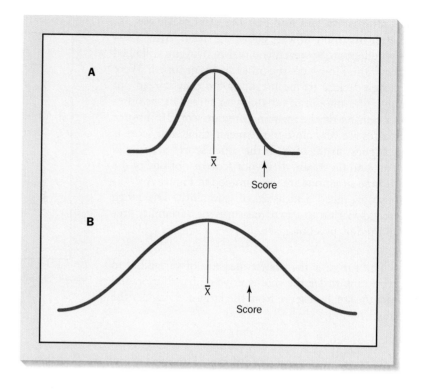

evenly in the second distribution (Figure A-8B). We must turn to another measure, the standard deviation, to provide this additional information.

**Variance and Standard Deviation.** To obtain the standard deviation, we must first calculate the **variance.** You can think of the variance as a single number that represents the total amount of variability in our distribution. The larger this number, the greater the spread of the scores. The variance and standard deviation are based on

**variance**

Single number that represents the total amount of variation in a distribution

**FIGURE A-8** The range does not provide much information about the distribution under consideration. Even though the range is the same, these two distributions differ drastically.

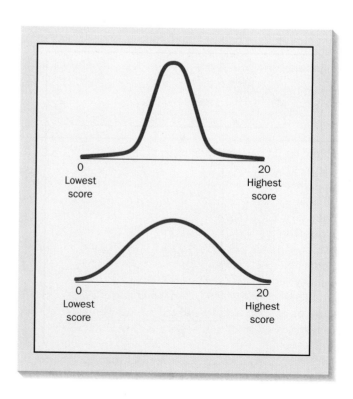

how much each score in the distribution deviates from the mean. To calculate the variance for the distribution we just considered:

**1.** Find the mean. Mean = 54/9 = 6.

$$\Sigma X = 54 \quad N = 9 \quad \overline{X} = \frac{\Sigma X}{N} \quad \overline{X} = 54/9 \quad \overline{X} = 6$$

**2.** Subtract the mean (column 2) from each score (column 1). This procedure yields a deviation score ($x$, column 3).

**3.** Square each deviation score ($x^2$, column 4).

| Score | − | Mean | = | DEVIATION Score ($x$) | $x^2$ |
|---|---|---|---|---|---|
| 1 | − | 6 | = | −5 | 25 |
| 1 | − | 6 | = | −5 | 25 |
| 1 | − | 6 | = | −5 | 25 |
| 1 | − | 6 | = | −5 | 25 |
| 5 | − | 6 | = | −1 | 1 |
| 6 | − | 6 | = | 0 | 0 |
| 6 | − | 6 | = | 0 | 0 |
| 8 | − | 6 | = | 2 | 4 |
| 25 | − | 6 | = | 19 | 361 |
| $\Sigma X = 54$ | | | | $\Sigma x = 0$ | $\Sigma x^2 = 466$ |

To calculate the variance, all we have to do is take the sum of the squared deviations and divide by the number of scores.

$$\text{variance} = \frac{\Sigma x^2}{N} = 466/9$$
$$= 51.78$$

To find the **standard deviation,** take the square root of the variance.

$$\text{standard deviation (SD)} = \sqrt{\text{variance}}$$
$$= \sqrt{51.78}$$
$$= 7.20$$

As with variance, the larger the standard deviation, the greater the variability or spread of scores.

Now that we have calculated the standard deviation, what does it tell us? To answer that question, we must consider the normal distribution (also called the *bell curve*). The concept of the **normal distribution** is based on the finding that as we increase the number of scores in our sample, many distributions of interest to psychologists become symmetrical or bell shaped. The majority of the scores are clustered around the measure of central tendency, with fewer and fewer scores occurring as we move away from it. As you can see from Figure A-9, the mean, median, and mode of a normal distribution have the same value.

Normal distributions also have some interesting relationships to the standard deviation. For example, distances from

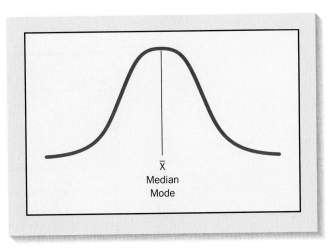

**FIGURE A-9**  A symmetrical or bell-shaped normal distribution. Note that the mean, median, and mode coincide in a normal distribution.

**FIGURE A-10** Relation of SDs and the normal distribution.

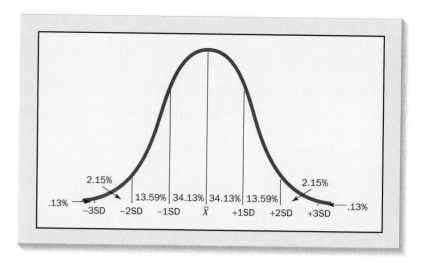

the mean of a normal distribution can be measured in standard deviation units. Consider a distribution with an $\overline{X}$ of 56 and SD of 4; a score of 60 can be described as falling one SD above the mean (+1 SD), whereas a score of 48 is two SDs (−2 SD) below the mean. As Figure A-10 shows, approximately 34 percent of all the scores in *all* normal distributions occur between the mean and one SD *above* the mean. Likewise, 34 percent of all the scores in all normal distributions occur between the mean and one SD *below* the mean. About another 13.5 percent of the scores occur between one and two SDs above the mean, whereas another 13.5 percent of the scores occur between one and two SDs below the mean. Thus about 95 percent of all the scores in a normal distribution occur between two SDs below the mean and two SDs above the mean. Approximately 2.5 percent of the scores occur beyond two SDs above the mean, and another 2.5 percent of the scores occur beyond two SDs below the mean. It is important to remember that these percentages hold true for *all* normal distributions.

Let's return to your test score of 64 (see p. 763). You know that the mean of the class is 56. What if the instructor tells you that the SD is 4; what would your reaction be? Your score of 64 would be two SDs above the mean; you should feel happy. Your score of 64 puts you in the top 2.5 percent of the class (50 percent of the scores below the mean plus 34 percent from the mean to one SD above the mean plus 13.5 percent that occur between one and two SDs above the mean; see Figure A-11A).

What if your instructor had told you that the SD was 20? Your score of 64 does not stand up as well as it did when the SD was 4. You are above the mean but a long way from being even one SD above it (see Figure A-11B).

Because the percentage of the scores that occurs from the mean to the various SD units is the same for all normal distributions, we can compare scores from different distributions by discussing them in terms of SDs above or below the mean. Consider the following scores:

| Test No. | Your Score | $\overline{X}$ | SD | Relationship of Your Score to $\overline{X}$ |
|---|---|---|---|---|
| 1 | 46 | 41 | 5 | One SD above |
| 2 | 72 | 63 | 4 | Over 2 SDs above |
| 3 | 43 | 71 | 10 | Over 2 SDs below |

Even though your scores, the means, and the SDs differ considerably, we can determine how many SD *units* away from the mean each of your scores is. In turn, these differences can be compared. When these comparisons are made, we find that your first two scores are consistently one SD or more above the mean; you are in at least the top 16 percent of the class. Test 3 is a different matter! By comparing scores from various

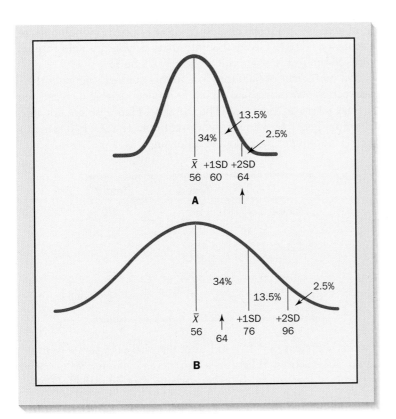

**FIGURE A-11**   (A) A score of 64 is exceptionally good when the mean is 56 and the SD is 4. (B) The same score is not as highly regarded when the SD is 20.

distributions in this manner, we are able to see patterns and possibly even make predictions about the nature of future scores.

# Correlation

We can also use descriptive statistics for predictive purposes. Prediction forms an important part of psychology. For example, you probably took a college entrance examination while you were in high school. Based on the results of this exam, a prediction about your grades in college might be made. Similarly, should you plan to go on for graduate training after you complete your undergraduate degree, you probably will take another entrance examination. Depending on your area of interest, you might take the Graduate Record Examination (GRE), the Law School Aptitude Test (LSAT), the Medical College Aptitude Test (MCAT), or some similar test.

Such predictions are based on the calculation of a correlation coefficient. A **correlation coefficient** is a single number that represents the degree of relationship ("co-relation") between *two* variables; it can range in value from −1.00 to +1.00.

A correlation coefficient of –1.00 indicates there is a *perfect negative relationship* between the two variables of interest. That is, whenever we see an increase of one unit in one variable, there is a proportional decrease in the other variable. Consider the following scores on Texts $X$ and $Y$:

**correlation coefficient**
Single number representing the degree of relationship between two variables

|  | Test *X* | Test *Y* |
|---|---|---|
| Student 1 | 49 | 63 |
| 2 | 50 | 61 |
| 3 | 51 | 59 |
| 4 | 52 | 57 |
| 5 | 53 | 55 |

For each unit of increase in a score on Test $X$, there is a corresponding decrease of two units in the score on Test $Y$. Given this information, you are able to predict that if Student 6 scores 54 on Test $X$, the score on Test $Y$ will be 53.

A correlation coefficient of 0.00 (or close to this number) indicates that there is *no relationship* between the two variables. As scores on one variable increase, scores on the other variable may increase, decrease, or be the same. Hence we are not able to predict how you will do on Test $Y$ by knowing your score on Test $X$. Two sets of scores that have a 0.00 correlation might look like the following:

|  | Test $X$ | Test $Y$ |
|---|---|---|
| Student 1 | 58 | 28 |
| 2 | 59 | 97 |
| 3 | 60 | 63 |
| 4 | 61 | 15 |
| 5 | 62 | 50 |

A correlation coefficient of $+1.00$ indicates that there is a *perfect positive relationship* between the two sets of scores. When we see an increase of one unit in one variable, we will see a proportional increase in the other variable. Consider the following scores on Texts $X$ and $Y$:

|  | Test $X$ | Test $Y$ |
|---|---|---|
| Student 1 | 25 | 40 |
| 2 | 26 | 41 |
| 3 | 27 | 42 |
| 4 | 28 | 43 |
| 5 | 29 | 44 |
|  | $\Sigma X = 135$ | $\Sigma Y = 210$ |
|  | $\overline{X} = 27$ | $\overline{Y} = 42$ |

In this example there is an increase of one unit in the score on Test $Y$ for every unit increase on Test $X$. The perfect positive correlation leads you to predict that if Student 6 scores 30 on Test $X$, then the score on Test $Y$ will be 45.

The most common correlation coefficient is the Pearson product moment correlation coefficient. To calculate a Pearson product moment correlation coefficient, we use the following formula:

$$r = \frac{\Sigma(X - \overline{X})(Y - \overline{Y})}{\sqrt{\Sigma(X - \overline{X})^2 \, \Sigma(Y - \overline{Y})^2}}$$

The steps involved in calculating the correlation coefficient ($r$) may be summarized as follows:

**Numerator**

1. Subtract $\overline{X}$ from each $X$ to get $(X - \overline{X})$.
2. Subtract $\overline{Y}$ from each $Y$ to get $(Y - \overline{Y})$.
3. For each pair, multiply $(X - \overline{X})$ by $(Y - \overline{Y})$ to get $(X - \overline{X})(Y - \overline{Y})$.
4. Add to get $\Sigma(X - \overline{X})(Y - \overline{Y})$.

## Denominator

1. Square each $(X - \overline{X})$ to get $(X - \overline{X})^2$.
2. Add all of the $(X - \overline{X})^2$s to get $\Sigma(X - \overline{X})^2$.
3. Square each $(Y - \overline{Y})$ to get $(Y - \overline{Y})^2$.
4. Add all of the $(Y - \overline{Y})^2$s to get $\Sigma(Y - \overline{Y})^2$.
5. Multiply $\Sigma(X - \overline{X})^2$ by $\Sigma(Y - \overline{Y})^2$.
6. Take the square root.

Then divide the numerator by the denominator to get $r$. Using the data from the preceding example, we can calculate the correlation where:

$$\Sigma X = 135 \qquad \overline{X} = 27 \qquad \Sigma Y = 210 \qquad \overline{Y} = 42$$

## Numerator

$(X - \overline{X})(Y - \overline{Y})$

$$(25 - 27)(40 - 42) = (-2)(-2) = 4$$
$$(26 - 27)(41 - 42) = (-1)(-1) = 1$$
$$(27 - 27)(42 - 42) = (0)(0) = 0$$
$$(28 - 27)(43 - 42) = (1)(1) = 1$$
$$(29 - 27)(44 - 42) = (2)(2) = 4$$
$$\Sigma(X - \overline{X})(Y - \overline{Y}) = 10$$

## Denominator

$(X - \overline{X})^2$

$$(25 - 27)^2 = (-2)^2 = 4$$
$$(26 - 27)^2 = (-1)^2 = 1$$
$$(27 - 27)^2 = (0)^2 = 0$$
$$(28 - 27)^2 = (1)^2 = 1$$
$$(29 - 27)^2 = (2)^2 = 4$$
$$\Sigma(X - \overline{X})^2 = 10$$

$(Y - \overline{Y})^2$

$$(40 - 42)^2 = (-2)^2 = 4$$
$$(41 - 42)^2 = (-1)^2 = 1$$
$$(42 - 42)^2 = (0)^2 = 0$$
$$(43 - 42)^2 = (1)^2 = 1$$
$$(44 - 42)^2 = (2)^2 = 4$$
$$\Sigma(Y - \overline{Y})^2 = 10$$

$$r = \frac{\Sigma(X - \overline{X})(Y - \overline{Y})}{\sqrt{\Sigma(X - \overline{X})^2 \; \Sigma(Y - \overline{Y})^2}}$$

$$r = \frac{10}{\sqrt{(10)(10)}} = \frac{10}{\sqrt{100}} = \frac{10}{10} = 1$$

In this case our correlation coefficient is 1.00, indicating a perfect positive relationship between these two variables. For every increase of one unit in a score on Test $X$, there is a corresponding increase of one unit in the Test $Y$ score. Our ability to predict a score on Test $Y$, knowing a corresponding score on Test $X$, is perfect. The following is an example in which the correlation is very high and positive, but not perfect.

|  | Test $X$ | Test $Y$ |
|---|---|---|
| Student 1 | 67 | 71 |
| 2 | 71 | 77 |
| 3 | 77 | 83 |
| 4 | 80 | 86 |
| 5 | 84 | 93 |
|  | $\Sigma X = 379$ | $\Sigma Y = 410$ |
|  | $\overline{X} = 75.8$ | $\overline{Y} = 82.0$ |

**Numerator**

$$(X = \overline{X})(Y = \overline{Y})$$

| | | |
|---|---|---|
| $(67 - 75.8)(71 - 82) = (-8.8)(-11) =$ | 96.8 |
| $(71 - 75.8)(77 - 82) = (-4.8)(-5) =$ | 24.0 |
| $(77 - 75.8)(83 - 82) = (1.2)(1.0) =$ | 1.2 |
| $(80 - 75.8)(86 - 82) = (4.2)(4.0) =$ | 16.8 |
| $(84 - 75.8)(93 - 82) = (8.2)(11.0) =$ | 90.2 |

$$\Sigma(X - \overline{X})(Y - \overline{Y}) = 229.0$$

**Denominator**

$$(X - \overline{X})^2$$

| | |
|---|---|
| $(67 - 75.8)^2 = (-8.8)^2 =$ | 77.44 |
| $(71 - 75.8)^2 = (-4.8)^2 =$ | 23.04 |
| $(77 - 75.8)^2 = (1.2)^2 =$ | 1.44 |
| $(80 - 75.8)^2 = (4.2)^2 =$ | 17.64 |
| $(84 - 75.8)^2 = (8.2)^2 =$ | 67.24 |

$$\Sigma(X - \overline{X})^2 = 186.80$$

$$(Y - \overline{Y})^2$$

| | |
|---|---|
| $(71 - 82)^2 = (-11)^2 = 121$ |
| $(77 - 82)^2 = (-5)^2 = 25$ |
| $(83 - 82)^2 = (1)^2 = 1$ |
| $(86 - 82)^2 = (4)^2 = 16$ |
| $(93 - 82)^2 = (11)^2 = 121$ |

$$\Sigma(Y - \overline{Y})^2 = 284.00$$

$$r = \frac{\Sigma(X - \overline{X})(Y - \overline{Y})}{\sqrt{\Sigma(X - \overline{X})^2 \, \Sigma(Y - \overline{Y})^2}}$$

$$r = \frac{229}{\sqrt{(186.80)(284.00)}} = \frac{229}{\sqrt{53051.20}} = \frac{229}{\sqrt{230.33}} = .99$$

**FIGURE A-12** Scatter diagram showing (A) perfect positive and perfect negative correlations, (B) positive and negative correlations, and (C) a 0.00 correlation.

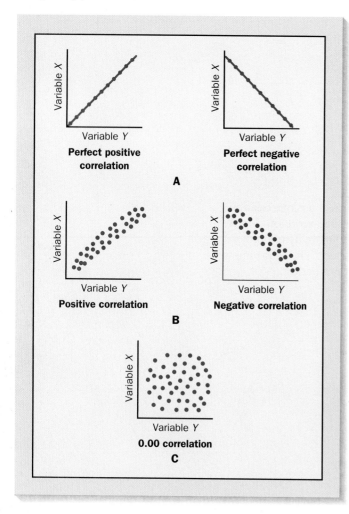

The scatter diagrams in Figure A-12 will help you visualize the various correlations we have discussed. Perfect positive and perfect negative correlations always fall on a straight line, whereas nonperfect correlations do not. For positive correlations the trend of the points is from lower left to upper right; the trend is from upper left to lower right for negative correlations. As you can see, there is no consistent pattern for a 0.00 correlation.

Although descriptive statistics can tell us much about the data we have collected, they cannot tell us everything. For example, if we have conducted an experiment, descriptive statistics cannot tell us if the independent variable we manipulated had a significant effect on the behavior of the participants we were testing or if the results we obtained would have occurred by chance. To make such determinations we must conduct an inferential statistical test.

# INFERENTIAL STATISTICS

The results of an inferential statistical test tell us whether our results would occur frequently or rarely by chance. If the results would occur often by chance, we say they are *not significant* and conclude that our independent variable did not affect the dependent variable. If, however, the results of our inferential statistical test would occur rarely by chance, then our result is *significant*, and we conclude that some factor besides chance is operative. If we have conducted our experiment properly and have exercised good control, then our significant statistical result gives us reason to believe that the independent variable we manipulated was effective.

For example, we might be interested in determining if a new method of studying will improve scores in introductory psychology. Twenty students are randomly selected from an introductory psychology class. In turn, these students are randomly assigned to one of two groups of ten students each. Because the groups are *randomly* formed at the start of the experiment, we assume that they are comparable.

The students in Group A use the new method of studying, whereas the students in Group B use the old method. All students take the same comprehensive final examination at the end of the course. We compare the scores of the two groups on this exam to see if the new method of studying was superior to the old. The scores for these two groups are

| Group A (New Study Method) | Group B (Old Study Method) |
|---|---|
| 63 | 58 |
| 71 | 64 |
| 74 | 68 |
| 77 | 71 |
| 85 | 71 |
| 88 | 73 |
| 88 | 73 |
| 91 | 74 |
| 94 | 78 |
| 97 | 86 |
| $\Sigma A = 828$ | $\Sigma B = 716$ |
| $\overline{X}_A = 82.8$ | $\overline{X}_B = 71.6$ |

Was the new study method effective? Just looking at the differences between the groups suggests that it might be; the mean score of Group A is higher than that of Group B. On the other hand, there is considerable overlap between the two groups; several of the students using the old method scored as well as or better than some students using the new method. Is the difference we obtained large enough to be genuine, or is it just a chance happening? Simply looking at the results will not answer that question. An inferential statistical test is needed to determine if our difference is significant or if it can be attributed to chance.

## The *t* Test

The *t* **test** is an inferential statistical test used to evaluate the difference between two means. The formula for the *t* test is

$$t = \frac{\overline{X}_A - \overline{X}_B}{\sqrt{\frac{(N_A - 1)V_A + (N_B - 1)V_B}{N_A + N_B - 2}\left(\frac{1}{N_A} + \frac{1}{N_B}\right)}}$$

Although this formula may look a bit intimidating, it really is easy. Just follow along, step by step.

**1.** Calculate the following:

  **a.** mean for each group

  $\overline{X}_A$ = mean Group A      $\overline{X}_B$ = mean Group B

      = 82.80               = 71.60

*t* **test**
Inferential statistical test used to evaluate the difference between two means

b. variance for each group

$$V_A = \text{variance for Group A} \qquad V_B = \text{variance for Group B}$$
$$= 121.73 \qquad\qquad\qquad = 57.16$$

**2.** Determine $N$ for each group

$$N_A = 10 \qquad\qquad\qquad N_B = 10$$

**3.** Plug the values you have calculated into the above formula.

$$t = \frac{82.80 - 71.60}{\sqrt{\dfrac{(10-1)121.73 + (10-1)57.16}{10 + 10 - 2}\left(\dfrac{1}{10} + \dfrac{1}{10}\right)}}$$

$$t = \frac{11.20}{\sqrt{\dfrac{1095.57 + 514.44}{18}\left(\dfrac{2}{10}\right)}} = \frac{11.20}{\sqrt{\dfrac{1610.01}{18}}(.20)}$$

$$t = \frac{11.20}{\sqrt{89.445(.20)}} = \frac{11.20}{\sqrt{17.889}} = \frac{11.20}{4.23} = 2.647$$

Once the $t$ value is calculated, you are ready to determine if it occurs frequently or *rarely by chance*.

When do we consider that an event occurs rarely by chance? Traditionally psychologists have said that any event that occurs by chance alone 5 times or fewer in 100 occasions is a rare event. Thus you will see frequent mention of the ".05 level of significance" in journal articles. This statement means that a result is considered significant if it would occur five or fewer times by chance in 100 replications of the experiment. The experimenter decides on the level of significance before the experiment is conducted.

If we say that a result occurs rarely by chance, what caused it? If we have conducted the experiment properly and exercised good control to rule out unwanted effects, we hope that the manipulation of the independent variable is responsible for the differences we have observed. Was the independent variable (type of study method) responsible for the differences we observed in the experiment just described? Recall that our $t$ value is 2.647. Once we have obtained our $t$ value, several steps must be followed to interpret its meaning:

**1.** Determine the degree of freedom ($df$) involved. For our study method problem

$$df = (N_A - 1) + (N_B - 1)$$
$$= (10 - 1) + (10 - 1)$$
$$= 18$$

**2.** The degrees of freedom are used to enter a $t$ table. The $t$ table contains values that occur by chance. We compare our $t$ value to these chance values. To be significant, the calculated $t$ must be equal to or larger than the one in the table. An example of a $t$ table follows.

| | LEVEL OF SIGNIFICANCE | | |
|---|---|---|---|
| *df* | .05 | .02 | .01 |
| 4 | 2.776 | 3.747 | 4.604 |
| 10 | 2.228 | 2.764 | 3.169 |
| 15 | 2.131 | 2.602 | 2.947 |
| 18 | 2.101 | 2.552 | 2.878 |
| 21 | 2.080 | 2.518 | 2.831 |

We enter the *t* table on the row for 18 degrees of freedom. Reading across this row, we find that a value of 2.101 occurs by chance 5 percent of the time (.05 level of significance). Because our value of 2.647 is larger than the value in the table, we can conclude that our result is significant. The type of study method had a significant effect on examination scores. This result is one that occurs 5 or fewer times in 100 by chance. Had we chosen a different level of significance (such as twice in 100 occurrences, .02, or once in 100 occurrences, .01), we would have used one of those columns to determine significance instead of the .05 column.

Clearly inferential statistics play an important role in the scientific process. They provide much of the confidence with which we make our decisions as consumers of psychological information. The *t* test is only one example of an inferential statistic. If you continue your coursework in psychology, you will encounter others.

# REFERENCES

Aaron, H. J. (2000, Spring). *The centenarian boom. Brookings Review*, 22–25.

Aase, J. M. (1994). Clinical recognition of FAS: Difficulties of detection and diagnosis. *Alcohol Health and Research World, 18*, 5–9.

Abbey, A. (1991). Acquaintance rape and alcohol consumption on college campuses: How are they linked? *Journal of American College Health, 39*, 165–169.

Abplanalp, J. M., Rose, R. D. M., Donnelly, A. F., & Livingston-Vaughan, L. (1979). Psychoneuroendocrinology of the menstrual cycle: 2. The relationship between enjoyment of activities, moods, and reproductive hormones. *Psychosomatic Medicine, 41*, 605–615.

Abrams, R. L., & Greenwald, A. G. (2000). Parts outweigh the whole (word) in unconscious analysis of meaning. *Psychological Science, 11*, 118–124.

Ackerman, D. (1990). *A natural history of the senses.* New York: Random House.

Ackerman, D. (2004). *An alchemy of mind: The marvel and mystery of the brain.* New York: Scribner.

Adams, J. S. (1965). Inequity in social exchange. In L. Berkowitz (Ed.), *Advances in experimental social psychology* (Vol. 2, pp. 267–299). New York: Academic Press.

Adelman, C. (1991). *Women at thirty-something: Paradoxes of attainment.* Washington, DC: U.S. Department of Education, Office of Educational Research and Development.

Adelson, R. (2003). Driven to distraction. *Monitor on Psychology, 34*(8), 24–25.

Adelson, R. (2004). Take your vitamins. *Monitor on Psychology, 35*(5), 24–25.

Ader, R., & Cohen, N. (1981). Conditioned immunopharmacologic responses. In R. Ader (Ed.), *Psychoneuroimmunology.* New York: Academic Press.

Ader, R., & Cohen, N. (1982). Behaviorally conditioned immunosuppression and murine systemic lupus erythematosus. *Science, 215*, 1534–1536.

Ader, R., & Cohen, N. (1985). CNS–immune system interactions: Conditioning phenomena. *Behavior and Brain Science, 8*, 379–394.

Adkins, J. A. (1999). Promoting organization health: The evolving practice of occupational health psychology. *Professional Psychology: Research and Practice, 30*, 129–137.

Adler, L. L. (1994). Women and gender roles. In L. L. Adler & U. P. Gielen (Eds.), *Cross-cultural topics in psychology* (pp. 89–101). Westport, CT: Praeger.

Adler, N. E., Ozer, E. J., & Tschann, J. (2003). Abortion among adolescents. *American Psychologist, 58*, 211–217.

Adolph, K. E. (2000). Specificity of learning: Why infants fall over a veritable cliff. *Psychological Science, 11*, 290–295.

Advokat, V., Dixon, D., Schneider, J., & Comaty, J. E., Jr. (2004). Comparison of risperidone and olanzapine as used under "real-world" conditions in a state psychiatric hospital. *Neuropsychopharmacology, 29*, 487–495.

Afifi, A. K., & Bergman, R. A. (2005). *Functional neuroanatomy: Text and atlas.* New York: Lange Medical Books/McGraw-Hill.

Ahn, W., Brewer, W. F., & Mooney, R. J. (1992). Schema acquisition from a single example. *Journal of Experimental Psychology: Learning, Memory, and Cognition, 18*, 391–412.

Ainsworth, M. D. S. (1989). Attachments beyond infancy. *American Psychologist, 44*, 709–716.

Ainsworth, M. D. S., Blehar, M. C., Waters, E., & Wall, S. (1978). *Patterns of attachment: A psychological study of the strange situation.* Hillsdale, NJ: Erlbaum.

Ainsworth, M. D. S., & Bowlby, J. (1991). An ethological approach to personality development. *American Psychologist, 46*, 331–341.

Akerstedt, T. (1991). Sleepiness at work: Effects of irregular work hours. In T. M. Monk (Ed.), *Sleep, sleepiness and performance* (pp. 129–152). New York: Wiley.

Akutsu, P. D., Sue, S., Zane, N. W. S., & Nakamura, C. Y. (1989). Ethnic differences in alcohol consumption among Asians and Caucasians in the United States: An investigation of cultural and physiological factors. *Journal of Studies on Alcohol, 50*, 261–267.

Alberti, R. E., & Emmons, M. L. (1990). *Your perfect right* (6th ed.). San Luis Obispo, CA: Impact.

Alcock, J. E. (1989). *Science and supernature: A critical appraisal of parapsychology.* Buffalo, NY: Prometheus.

Alexander, P. A. (2006). *Psychology in learning and instruction.* Upper Saddle River, NJ: Pearson Merrill Prentice Hall.

Allan, K., & Coltrane, S. (1996). Gender display in television commercials: A comparative study of television commercials in the 1950s and 1980s. *Sex Roles, 35*(3–4), 185–203.

Allen, J., & Dana, R. H. (2004). Methodological issues in cross-cultural and multicultural Rorschach research. *Journal of Personality Assessment, 82*, 189–206.

Allen, J. S., Bruss, J., & Damasio, H. (2004). The structure of the human brain. *American Scientist, 92*, 246–253.

Allen, K. (2003). Are pets a healthy pleasure? The influence of pets on blood pressure. *Current Directions in Psychological Science, 12*, 236–239.

Allen, L. S., Richey, M. F., Chai, Y. M., & Gorski, R. A. (1991). Sex differences in the corpus callosum of the living human being. *Journal of Neuroscience, 11*, 933–942.

Allen, M. W., Reid, M., & Riemenschneider, C. (2004). The role of laughter when discussing workplace barriers: Women in information technology jobs. *Sex Roles, 50*, 177–189.

Allen, R. P. (1997). The significance and interpretation of the polysomnogram. In M. R. Pressman & W. C. Orr (Eds.), *Understanding sleep: The evaluation and treatment of sleep disorders* (pp. 193–208). Washington, DC: American Psychological Association.

Allis, S. (1991, March 25). Kicking the nerd syndrome. *Time*, 64.

Allport, G. W. (1961). *Pattern and growth in personality.* Austin, TX: Holt, Rinehart & Winston.

Allport, G. W. (1979). *The nature of prejudice.* Reading, MA: Addison-Wesley. (Originally published in 1954).

Allport, G. W., & Odbert, H. S. (1936). Trait names: A psycho-lexical study. *Psychological Monographs, 47*(1, Whole No. 211).

Alwin, D. F. (1990). Historical changes in parental orientations to children. In N. Mandell (Ed.), *Sociological studies of child development* (Vol. 3). Greenwich, CT: JAI Press.

Amabile, T. M. (1982). Social psychology of creativity: A consensual assessment technique. *Journal of Personality and Social Psychology, 43*, 997–1013.

Amabile, T. M. (1988). A model of creativity and innovation in organizations. *Research in Organizational Behavior, 10*, 123–167.

Amabile, T. M. (1996). *Creativity in context.* Boulder, CO: Westview Press.

Amabile, T. M., Hennessey, B. A., & Grossman, B. S. (1986). Social influences on creativity: The effects of contracted-for reward. *Journal of Personality and Social Psychology, 50*, 14–23.

American Association of Retired Persons. (2000a). *AARP driver safety program, Edition 5.* Washington, DC: Author.

American Association of Retired Persons. (2000b). *A profile of older Americans.* Washington, DC: Author.

American Association of University Women. (1992). *How schools short-change girls.* Washington, DC: AAUW Educational Foundation.

American Heart Association. (1993). *1992 heart and stroke facts.* Dallas, TX: Author.

American Heart Association (2002). My fitness. Retrieved May 5, 2002, from http://www.justmove.org/myfitness.

American Heart Associaton. (2005). Physical activity calorie use chart. Retrieved July 16, 2005, from www.americanheart.org/presenter.jhtml?identifier-5756.

American Psychiatric Association. (2000). *Diagnostic and statistical manual of mental disorders* (4th ed. Text Revision). Washington, DC: Author.

American Psychological Association. (1992). Ethical principles of psychologists and code of conduct. *American Psychologist, 47*, 1597–1611.

American Psychological Association. (2002). Ethical principles of psychologists and code of conduct. *American Psychologist, 57*(12), 1060–1073.

Amoore, J. E. (1970). *Molecular basis of odor.* Springfield, IL: Charles C. Thomas.

Amsel, A. (1962). Frustrative nonreward in partial reinforcement and discrimination learning: Some recent history and a theoretical extension. *Psychological Review, 69*, 306–328.

Amsterdam, J. D. (2003). A double-blind, placebo-controlled trial of the safety and efficacy of selegiline transdermal system without dietary restrictions in patients with major depressive disorder. *Journal of Clinical Psychiatry, 64*, 208–214.

Anastasi, A., & Urbina, S. (1997). *Psychological testing* (7th ed.). Upper Saddle River, NJ: Prentice Hall.

Anch, A. M., Browman, C. P., Mitler, M. M., & Walsh, J. L. (1988). *Sleep: A scientific perspective.* Upper Saddle River, NJ: Prentice Hall.

Anderson, A. R., & Henry, C. S. (1994). Family system characteristics and parental behaviors as predictors of adolescent substance use. *Adolescence, 29*, 405–420.

Anderson, C. A., Berkowitz, L., Donnerstein, E., Huesmann, L. R., Johnson, J. D., Linz, D., et al. (2003). The influence of media violence on youth. *Psychological Science in the Public Interest, 4*(3), 81–110.

Anderson, C. A., & Bushman, B. J. (2001). Effects of violent video games on aggressive behavior, aggressive cognition, aggressive affect, physiological arousal, and prosocial behavior: A meta-analysis review of the scientific literature. *Psychological Science, 12*, 353–359.

Anderson, C. A., Carnagey, N. L., & Eubanks, J. (2003). Exposure to violent media: The effects of songs with violent lyrics on aggressive thoughts and feelings. *Journal of Personality and Social Psychology, 84*, 960–971.

Anderson, C. A., & Dill, K. E. (2000). Video games and aggressive thoughts, feelings, and behavior in the laboratory and in life. *Journal of Personality and Social Psychology, 78*, 772–790.

Anderson, J. R., & Bower, G. H. (1974). A propositional theory of recognition memory. *Memory and Cognition, 2*, 406–412.

Anderson, J. R., & Fincham, J. M. (1994). Acquisition of procedural skills from examples. *Journal of Experimental Psychology: Learning, Memory, and Cognition, 20*, 1322–1340.

Anderson, V. C., Burchiel, K. J., Hogarth, P., Favre, J., & Hammerstand, J. P. (2005). Pallidal vs subthalamic nucleus deep brain stimulation in Parkinson disease. *Archives of Neurology, 62*(4), 554–560.

Andreasen, N. C. (1984). *The broken brain: The biological revolution in psychiatry.* New York: HarperCollins.

Andreasen, N. C. (2001). *Brave new brain: Conquering mental illness in the era of the genome.* New York: Oxford University Press.

Andreasen, N. C., Flaum, M., Swayze, V. W., II, Tyrrell, G., & Arndt, S. (1990). Positive and negative symptoms in schizophrenia. *Archives of General Psychiatry, 47*, 615–621.

Angleitner, A., Riemann, R., & Strelau, J. (1995). *A study of twins using the self-report and peer-report NEO-FFI scales.* Paper presented at the seventh meeting of the International Society for the Study of Individual Differences, July 15–19. Warsaw, Poland.

Animal Behaviour. (2004). Guidelines for the treatment of animals in behavioural research and teaching. *Animal Behaviour, 67*, i–vi.

Anorexia Nervosa—Part I. (2003). *Harvard Mental Health Letter, 19*(8), 1–4.

Antony, M. M., & Barlow, D. H. (2002). Specific phobias. In D. H. Barlow (Ed.), *Anxiety and its disorders: The nature and treatment of anxiety and panic* (2nd ed., pp. 380–417). New York: Guilford Press.

Ap, D. (2004). I like myself but I don't know why: Enhancing implicit self-esteem by subliminal evaluative conditioning. *Journal of Personality and Social Psychology, 86*, 345–355.

Archer, D. (1997). Unspoken diversity: Cultural diversity in gestures. *Qualitative Sociology, 20*, 79–105.

Archer, D., & Akert, R. M. (1984). Nonverbal factors in person perception. In M. Cook (Ed.), *Issues in person perception* (pp. 114–144). New York: Methuen.

Archibold, R. C. (2001, August 22). Hospital details failures leading to M.R.I. fatality. *New York Times.*

Ardrey, R. (1966). *The territorial imperative.* New York: Atheneum.

Argyle, M., & Henderson, M. (1984). The rules of friendship. *Journal of Social and Personal Relationships, 1*, 211–237.

Arnett, P. A. (2003). Neuropsychological presentation and treatment of demyelinating disorders. In P. W. Halligan, U. Kischka, & J. C. Marshall (Eds.), *Handbook of neuropsychology* (pp. 528–543). Oxford: Oxford University Press.

Aronson, E., Wilson, T. D., & Akert, R. M. (2002). *Social psychology* (4th ed.). Upper Saddle River, NJ: Prentice Hall.

Aronson, J., Fried, C. B., & Good, C. (2002). Reducing the effects of stereotype threat on African American college students by shaping theories of intelligence. *Journal of Experimental Social Psychology, 38*, 113–125.

Arrigo, J. M., & Pezdek, K. (1997). Lessons from the study of psychogenic amnesia. *Current Directions in Psychological Science, 6*, 148–152.

Arthur, W., Jr., & Benjamin, L. T., Jr. (1999). Psychology applied to business. In A. M. Stec D. A. Bernstein (Eds.), *Psychology: Fields of application* (pp. 98–115). Boston: Houghton Mifflin.

Arvey, B. D., Bouchard, T. J., Segal, N. L., & Abraham, L. M. (1989). Job satisfaction: Environmental and genetic components. *Journal of Applied Psychology, 74*, 187–192.

Arvey, B. O., & Campion, J. E. (1982). The employment interview: A summary and review of recent research. *Journal of Applied Psychology, 39*, 281–322.

Arvey, R. D., & Murphy, K. R. (1998). Performance evaluation in work settings. In J. T. Spence, J. M. Darley, & D. J. Foss (Eds.), *Annual review of psychology, 49* (pp. 141–168). Palo Alto, CA: Annual Reviews.

Asch, S. E. (1955). Opinions and social pressure. *Scientific American, 193*, 31–35.

Asch, S. E. (1956). Studies of independence and conformity: A minority of one against a unanimous majority. *Psychological Monographs, 70* (9, Whole No. 416).

Aseltine, R. H., Jr. (2003). An evaluation of a school based suicide prevention program. *Adolescent and Family Health, 3*, 81–88.

Aserinsky, E., & Kleitman, N. (1953). Regularly occurring periods of eye motility and concomitant phenomena during sleep. *Science, 118*, 273–274.

Ash, M. G. (1995). *Gestalt psychology in German culture, 1890–1967: Holism and the quest for objectivity.* New York: Cambridge University Press.

Ashcraft, M. H. (1994). *Human memory and cognition* (2nd ed.). New York: HarperCollins.

Ashcraft, M. H. (2006). *Cognition* (4th ed.). Upper Saddle River, NJ: Pearson Prentice Hall.

Associated Press. (2000, December 10). Research reveals the flaws of memory: Eyewitness errors can doom innocent. *The Kansas City Star,* A14.

Astin, J. A. (2004). Mind-body therapies for the management of pain. *Clinical Journal of Pain, 20*, 27–32.

Atkinson, J. W. (1974). The mainsprings of achievement-oriented activity. In J. W. Atkinson & J. O. Raynot (Eds.), *Motivation and achievement.* New York: Wiley.

Atkinson, R. C., & Shiffrin, R. (1968). Human memory: A proposed system and its control processes. In

K. Spence & J. Spence (Eds.), *The psychology of learning and motivation: Advances in research and theory* (Vol. 2). New York: Academic Press.

Atkinson, R. C., & Shiffrin, R. M. (1971). The control of short-term memory. *Scientific American, 225*, 82–90.

Audrain-McGovern, J., Lerman, C., Wileyto, E. P., Rodriguez, D., & Shields, P. G. (2004). Interacting effects of genetic predisposition and depression on adolescent smoking progression. *American Journal of Psychiatry, 161*, 1224–1230.

Augurelle, A-S., Smith, A. M., Lejeune, T., & Thonnard, J-L. (2003). Importance of cutaneous feedback in maintaining a secure grip during manipulation of hand-held objects. *Journal of Neurophysiology, 89*, 665–671.

AVERT, British Research Group. Retrieved May 5, 2002, from http://www.avert.org.

Axelrod, S., & Apsche, J. (1983). *The effects of punishment on human behavior.* New York: Academic Press.

Ayers, M. S., & Reder, L. M. (1998). A theoretical review of the misinformation effect: Predictions from an activation-based memory model. *Psychonomic Bulletin & Review, 5*, 1–21.

Azar, B. (2000, March). The debate over child care isn't over yet . . . *Monitor on Psychology*, 32–34.

Azar, B. (2001). A new take on psychoneuroimmunology. *Monitor on Psychology, 32*(11), 34–36.

Azrin, N. H., & Holz, W. C. (1966). Punishment. In W. K. Honig (Ed.), *Operant behavior: Areas of application* (pp. 380–447). New York: Appleton-Century-Crofts.

Bach, A. K., Wincze, J. P., & Barlow, D. H. (2001). Sexual dysfunction. In D. H. Barlow (Ed.), *Clinical handbook of psychological disorders: A step-by-step treatment manual* (pp. 562–608). New York: Guilford Press.

Bachiochi, P. D., & Weiner, S. P. (2002). Qualitative data collection and analysis. In S. G. Rogelberg (Ed.), *Handbook of research methods in industrial and organizational psychology* (pp. 161–183). Malden, MA: Blackwell.

Bachman, J. G., Johnston, L. D., & O'Malley, P. M. (1990). Explaining the recent decline in cocaine use among young adults: Further evidence that perceived risks and disapproval lead to reduced drug use. *Journal of Health and Social Behavior, 31*, 173–184.

Bachman, R. (1994). *Violence against women: A National Crime Victimization Survey report.* Washington, DC: U.S. Department of Justice.

Baddeley, A. (1998). *Human memory.* Boston: Allyn & Bacon.

Baddeley, A. (2004). *Your memory: A user's guide.* Buffalo, NY: Firefly Books.

Baddeley, A. D. (1988). Cognitive psychology and human memory. *Trends in Neurosciences, 11*, 176–181.

Baddeley, A. D. (1992a). Is working memory working? *Quarterly Journal of Experimental Psychology, 44A*, 1–31.

Baddeley, A. D. (1992b). Working memory. *Science, 255*, 556–559.

Baddeley, A. D., Papagno, C., & Andrade, J. (1993). The sandwich effect: The role of attentional factors in serial recall. *Journal of Experimental Psychology: Learning, Memory, and Cognition, 19*, 862–870.

Badia, P. (1993). Learning. In M. A. Carskadon (Ed.), *Encyclopedia of sleep and dreaming* (pp. 327–328). New York: Macmillan.

Baenninger, M., & Newcombe, N. (1989). The role of experience in spatial test performance: A meta-analysis. *Sex Roles, 20*, 327–344.

Baer, L., Rauch, S. L., Ballantine, T., Martuza, R., Cosgrove, R., Cassem, E., et al. (1995). Cingulotomy for intractable obsessive-compulsive disorder. *Archives of General Psychiatry, 52*, 384–392.

Bagemihl, B. (1999). *Biological exuberance: Animal homosexuality and natural diversity.* New York: St. Martin's Press.

Bailey, D. S. (2004). Number of psychology PhDs declining. *Monitor on Psychology, 35*(2), 18–19.

Baillargeon, R. (1993). The object concept revisited: New directions in the investigation of infants' physical knowledge. In C. Granrud (Ed.), *Visual perception and cognition in infancy: Carnegie Mellon symposia on cognition* (pp. 265–315). Hillsdale, NJ: Erlbaum.

Baillargeon, R. (1994). How do infants learn about the physical world? *Current Directions in Psychological Science, 3*, 133–140.

Baker, D. D., Terpstra, D. E., & Larntz, K. (1990). The influence of individual characteristics and severity of harassing behavior on reactions to sexual harassment. *Sex Roles, 22*, 305–325.

Baker, R. A. (1990). *They call it hypnosis.* Buffalo, NY: Prometheus.

Baker, R. A. (1993). *The art of cold reading.* Lexington, KY: Author.

Baldwin, E. (1993). The case for animal research in psychology. *Journal of Social Issues, 49*, 121–131.

Baldwin, J. D., & Baldwin, J. I. (1998). *Behavior principles in everyday life* (3rd ed.). Upper Saddle River, NJ: Prentice Hall.

Baldwin, J. D., & Baldwin, J. I. (2001). *Behavior principles in everyday life* (4th ed.). Upper Saddle River, NJ: Pearson Prentice Hall.

Bales, R. F. (1950). *Interaction process analysis: A method for the study of small groups.* Reading, MA: Addison-Wesley.

Ballew, H., Brooks, S., & Annacelli, C. (2001, March). *Children with dyslexia have impaired low contrast visual acuity.* Paper presented at the annual meeting of the Southeastern Psychological Association, Atlanta, GA.

Ballie, R. (2001). Where are the new psychologists going? *Monitor on Psychology, 32*(1), 24–25.

Bandla, H., & Splaingard, M. (2004). Sleep problems in children with common medical conditions. *Pediatric Clinics of North America, 51*(1), 203–227.

Bandura, A. (1977a). Self-efficacy: Toward a unifying theory of behavior change. *Psychological Review, 84*, 191–215.

Bandura, A. (1977b). *Social learning theory.* New York: General Learning Press.

Bandura, A. (1986). *Social foundations of thought and action: A social-cognitive theory.* Upper Saddle River, NJ: Prentice Hall.

Bandura, A., Blanchard, E. B., & Ritter, B. (1969). Relative efficacy of desensitization and modeling approaches for inducing behavioral, affective, and attitudinal changes. *Journal of Personality and Social Psychology, 13*, 173–199.

Bandura, A., Ross, D., & Ross, S. (1963). Imitation of film-mediated aggressive models. *Journal of Abnormal and Social Psychology, 66*, 3–11.

Barak, A. (1997). Cross-cultural perspectives on sexual harassment. In W. O'Donohue (Ed.), *Sexual harassment: Theory, research, and treatment.* Boston: Allyn & Bacon.

Barch, D. M., & Berenbaum, H. (1996). Language production and thought disorder in schizophrenia. *Journal of Abnormal Psychology, 105*, 81–88.

Barker, L. M. (2001). *Learning and behavior: Biological, psychological, and sociocultural perspectives* (3rd ed.). Upper Saddle River, NJ: Prentical Hall.

Barlow, D. H. (2002). *Anxiety and its disorders: The nature and treatment of anxiety and panic* (2nd ed.). New York: Guilford Press.

Barlow, D. H., Vermilyea, J., Blanchard, E. B., Vermilyea, B. B., Di Nardo, P. A., & Cerny, J. A. (1985). The phenomenon of panic. *Journal of Abnormal Psychology, 94*, 320–328.

Barnett, J. E., & Hurst, C. S. (2004). Do adolescents take "baby think it over" seriously? *Adolescence, 39*, 65–75.

Barnlund, D. C. (1989). *Public and private self in Japan and the United States.* Tokyo: Intercultural Press.

Baron, L., & Straus, M. A. (1984). Sexual stratification, pornography, and rape in the United States. In N. M. Malamuth & E. Donnerstein (Eds.), *Pornography and sexual aggression.* San Diego, CA: Academic Press.

Baron, S., & Welty, A. (1996). Elder abuse. *Journal of Gerontological Social Work, 25*, 33–57.

Barrett, L. F., Lane, R. D., Sechrest, L., & Schwarz, G. E. (2000). Sex differences in emotional awareness. *Personality and Social Psychology Bulletin, 26*(9), 1027–1035.

Barrick, M. R., & Mount, M. K. (1993). Autonomy as a moderator of the relationships between the Big Five personality dimensions and job performance. *Journal of Applied Psychology, 78*, 111–118.

Barron, F. (1958). The psychology of imagination. *Scientific American, 199*, 150–166.

Barron, F. (1988). Putting creativity to work. In R. J. Sternberg (Ed.), *The nature of creativity* (pp. 76–98). New York: Cambridge University Press.

Barry, J. J. (2003). The recognition and management of mood disorders as a comorbidity of epilepsy. *Epilepsia, 44*(Suppl 4), 30–40.

Bartecchi, C. E., MacKenzie, T. D., & Schrier, R. W. (1995). The global tobacco epidemic. *Scientific American, 272*, 44–51.

Barth, D. S., & MacDonald, K. D. (1996). Thalamic modulation of high-frequency oscillating potentials in auditory cortex. *Nature, 383*, 78–81.

Bartlett, F. C. (1932). *Remembering: A study in experimental and social psychology.* Cambridge: Cambridge University Press.

Barton, A. (1992). Humanistic contributions to the field of psychotherapy: Appreciating the human and liberating the therapist. *Humanistic Psychologist, 20*, 332–348.

Bartoshuk, L. M. (1991). Taste, smell, and pleasure. In R. C. Bolles (Ed.), *The hedonics of taste* (pp. 15–28). Hillsdale, NJ: Erlbaum.

Bartram, D. (2004). Assessment in organisations. *Applied Psychology: An International Review, 53*, 237–259.

Basow, S. A. (1992). *Gender: Stereotypes and roles* (3rd ed.). Pacific Grove, CA: Brooks/Cole.

Basson, R. (2001). Human sex-response cycles. *Journal of Sex and Marital Therapy, 27*, 33–43.

Basson, R. (2002). A model of women's sexual arousal. *Journal of Sex and Marital Therapy, 28*, 1–10.

Batsell, W. R., Jr., & Best, M. R. (1992). Variations in the retention of taste aversion: Evidence for retrieval competition. *Animal Learning and Behavior, 20*, 146–159.

Batsell, W. R., Jr., & Best, M. R. (1993). One bottle too many? Method of testing determines the detection of overshadowing and retention of taste aversion. *Animal Learning and Behavior, 21*, 154–158.

Batson, C. D. (1998). Altruism and prosocial behavior. In D. T. Gilbert, S. T. Fiske, & G. Lindzey (Eds.), *The handbook of social psychology* (4th ed., Vol. 2, pp. 282–316). New York: McGraw-Hill.

Batson, C. D., Dyck, J. L., Brandt, J. R., Batson, J. G., Powell, A. L., McMaster, M. R., et al. (1988). Five studies testing two new egoistic alternatives to the empathy-altruism hypothesis. *Journal of Personality and Social Psychology, 55*, 52–77.

Batson, C. D., & Moran, T. (1999). Empathy-induced altruism in a prisoner's dilemma. *European Journal of Social Psychology, 29*, 909–924.

Baumrind, D. (1971). Harmonious parents and their preschool children. *Developmental Psychology, 41*, 92–102.

Baumrind, D. (1983). Rejoinder to Lewis reinterpretation of parental firm control affects: Are authoritative families rarely harmonious? *Psychological Bulletin, 94*, 132–142.

Baxter, S. (1994, March–April). Gender differences. *Psychology Today*, 50–53, 85–86.

Bayley, N. (1969). *Bayley Scales of Infant Development.* New York: Psychological Corporation.

Beal, C. (1994). *Boys and girls: The development of gender roles.* New York: McGraw-Hill.

Beatty, W. W., & Aupperle, R. L. (2002). Sex differences in cognitive impairment in multiple sclerosis. *Clinical Neurospsychologist, 16*(4), 472–480.

Beaumont, J. H. (1988). *Understanding neuropsychology.* New York: Blackwell.

Beck, A. P., & Lewis, C. M. (2000). *The process of group psychotherapy.* Washington, DC: American Psychological Association.

Beck, A. T. (1979a). *Cognitive therapy and the emotional disorders.* Cleveland, OH: Meridian.

Beck, A. T. (1979b). *Cognitive therapy of depression.* New York: Guilford Press.

Beck, A. T. (1991). Cognitive therapy: A 30-year retrospective. *American Psychologist, 46*, 369–375.

Beckman, M. (2004, August). A matter of taste. *Smithsonian*, 24–26.

Bee, H. (1989). *The developing child* (5th ed.). New York: Harper & Row.

Beers, C. W. (1908/1937). *A mind that found itself: An autobiography.* New York: Doubleday, Doran, & Company.

Begley, S. (1995, March 27). Gray matters. *Newsweek*, 48–54.

Beins, B. (1993, February). *The assumptions we make: Right or wrong.* Paper presented at the Fifth Southeastern Conference on the Teaching of Psychology. Kennesaw State College, Marietta, OK.

Bekesy, G., von. (1956). Current status of theories of hearing. *Science, 123*, 779–783.

Belansky, E. S., & Boggiano, A. K. (1994). Predicting helping behaviors: The role of gender and instrumental/expressive self-schemata. *Sex Roles, 30*, 647–661.

Belar, C. (2001). Education for health. *Monitor on Psychology, 32*(1), 50.

Belsky, J. (1984). Two waves of day-care research: Developmental effects and conditions of quality. In R. Ainslie (Ed.), *The child and the day-care setting.* New York: Praeger.

Belsky, J. (1986). Infant day care: A cause for concern? *Zero to Three, 6*, 1–9.

Belsky, J., Gilstrap, B., & Rovine, M. (1984). The Pennsylvania Infant and Family Development Project: 1. Stability and change in mother–infant and father–infant interaction in a family setting—1- to 3- to 9-months. *Child Development, 55*, 692–705.

Bem, D. J., & Allen, A. (1974). On predicting some of the people some of the time: The search for cross-situational consistencies in behavior. *Psychological Review, 81*, 506–520.

Bem, D. J., & Honorton, C. (1994). Does psi exist? Replicable evidence for an anomalous process of information transfer. *Psychological Bulletin, 115*, 4–18.

Bem, S. L. (1981). Gender schema theory: A cognitive account of sex typing. *Psychological Review, 88*, 354–364.

Bem, S. L. (1993). *The lenses of gender.* New Haven, CT: Yale University Press.

Ben Tsvi–Mayer, S., Hertz-Lazarowitz, R., & Safir, M. P. (1989). Teachers' selection of boys and girls as prominent pupils. *Sex Roles, 21*, 231–245.

Benatar, S. R. (2004). Health care reform and the crisis of HIV and AIDS in South Africa. *New England Journal of Medicine, 351*, 81–92.

Benbow, C. P., & Stanley, J. C. (1980). Sex differences in mathematical ability: Fact or artifact? *Science, 210*, 1262–1264.

Benbow, C. P., & Stanley, J. C. (1982). Consequences in high school and college of sex differences in mathematical reasoning ability: A longitudinal perspective. *American Educational Research Association Journal, 19*, 598–622.

Bengtson, H., & Johnson, L. (1992). Perspective taking, empathy, and pro-social behavior in late childhood. *Child Study Journal, 22*, 11–22.

Benoit, D., & Parker, K. C. H. (1994). Stability and transmission of attachment across three generations. *Child Development, 65*, 1444–1456.

Benokraitis, N., & Feagin, J. (1995). *Modern sexism: Blatant, subtle, and overt discrimination* (2nd ed.). Englewood Cliffs, NJ: Prentice Hall.

Benson, E. (2002, October). Pheromones, in context. *APA Monitor*, 46–48.

Benson, E. (2003a). Old and untroubled. *Monitor on Psychology, 34*(6), 24–25.

Benson, E. (2003b). Beyond "urbancentrism." *Monitor on Psychology, 34*(6), 54–55.

Benson, E. (2003c). The many faces of perfectionism. *Monitor on Psychology, 34*(10), 18–20.

Benson, E. S. (2004). Behavior genetics: Meet molecular biology. *Monitor on Psychology, 35*(4), 42–45.

Benson, H. (1975). *The relaxation response.* New York: Morrow.

Benson, H. (1984). *Beyond the relaxation response.* New York: Times Books.

Beratis, S., Gabriel, J., & Hoidas, S. (1994). Age at onset in subtypes of schizophrenia disorders. *Schizophrenia Bulletin, 20*, 287–296.

Berenbaum, H., & James, T. (1994). Correlates and retrospectively reported antecedents of alexithymia. *Psychosomatic Medicine, 56*, 353–359.

Berk, L. E. (2000). Development. In S. F. Davis & J. S. Halonen (Eds.), *The many faces of psychological research in the twenty-first century.* Washington, DC: American Psychological Association.

Berk, L. E., & Spuhl, S. T. (1995). Maternal interaction, private speech, and task performance in preschool children. *Early Childhood Research Quarterly, 10*, 145–169.

Berke, R. L. (2000, September 12). Democrats see, and smell, "rats" in GOP ad. *New York Times on the Web*, http://www.nytimes.com

Berkow, R. (Ed.) (1997). *The Merck manual of medical information* (Home ed.). Whitehouse Station, NJ: Merck Research Laboratories.

Berkowitz, L. (1965). The concept of aggressive drive: Some additional considerations. In L. Berkowitz (Ed.), *Advances in experimental social psychology* (Vol. 2). San Diego, CA: Academic Press.

Berkowitz, L. (1984). Some effects of thoughts on anti- and pro-social influences of media events: A cognitive neoassociation analysis. *Psychological Bulletin, 95*, 410–427.

Berkowitz, L. (1994). On the escalation of aggression. In M. Potegal & J. F. Knutson (Eds.), *The dynamics of aggression: Biological and social processes in dyads and groups* (pp. 33–41). Hillsdale, NJ: Erlbaum.

Berne, S. A. (2003). The primitive survival reflexes. *Journal of Optometric Vision Development, 34*, 83–85.

Bernstein, D. A., & Carlson, C. R. (1993). Progressive relaxation: Abbreviated methods. In P. M. Lehrer & R. L. Woolfolk (Eds.), *Principles and practice of stress management* (2nd ed., pp. 53–88). New York: Guilford Press.

Bernstein, I. L. (1978). Learned taste aversions in children receiving chemotherapy. *Science, 200*, 1302–1303.

Bernstein, I. L., & Webster, M. M. (1980). Learned taste aversions in humans. *Physiology and Behavior, 25*, 363–366.

Bernstein, I. L., & Webster, M. M. (1982). Food aversions in children receiving chemotherapy for cancer. *Cancer, 50*, 2961–2963.

Berntsen, D., & Thomsen, D. K. (2005). Personal memories for remote historical events: Accuracy and clarity of flashbulb memories related to World War II. *Journal of Experimental Psychology: General, 134*, 242–257.

Berscheid, E., & Meyers, S. A. (1997). The language of love: The difference a preposition makes. *Personality and Social Psychology Bulletin, 23*, 347–362.

Berscheid, E., & Reis, H. T. (1998). Attraction and close relationship. In D. T. Gilbert, S. T. Fiske, & G. Lindzey (Eds.), *The handbook of social psychology* (4th ed., Vol. 2, pp. 193–281). New York: McGraw-Hill.

Best, J. B. (1999). *Cognitive psychology.* Pacific Grove, CA: Brooks/Cole.

Bettencourt, B. A., & Miller, N. (1996). Gender differences in aggression as a function of provocation: A meta-analysis. *Psychological Bulletin, 119*, 422–447.

Betz, N. E. (1994). Basic issues and concepts in career counseling for women. In W. B. Walsh & S. H. Osipow (Eds.), *Career counseling for women* (pp. 1–41). Hillsdale, NJ: Erlbaum.

Biasco, F., & Hartnett, J. P. (2002). College students' attitudes toward smoking. *College Student Journal, 36*, 442–447.

Biener, L., & Albers, A. B. (2004). Young adults: Vulnerable new targets of tobacco marketing. *American Journal of Public Health, 94*, 326–330.

Biernat, M. (1991). Gender stereotypes and the relationship between masculinity and femininity: A developmental analysis. *Journal of Personality and Social Psychology, 61*, 351–365.

Biernat, M. (2003). Toward a broader view of social stereotyping. *American Psychologist, 58*, 1019–1027.

Biernat, M., & Wortman, C. (1991). Sharing of home responsibilities between professionally employed women and their husbands. *Journal of Personality and Social Psychology, 60*, 844–860.

Birren, J. E., Woods, A. M., & Williams, M. V. (1980). Behavioral slowing with age: Causes, organization and consequences. In L. W. Poon (Ed.), *Aging in the 80's: Psychological issues.* Washington, DC: American Psychological Association.

Bjarnason, G. A., Jordan, R.C., & Sothern, R. B. (1999). Circadian variation in the expression of cell-cycle proteins in human oral epithelium. *American Journal of Pathology, 154*, 613–622.

Björk, R. A. (1975). Short-term storage: The ordered output of a central processor. In F. Restle, R. M. Shiffrin, N. J. Castellad, H. R. Lindman, & D. B. Pisoni (Eds.), *Cognitive theory*, Vol. 1. Hillsdale, NJ: Erlbaum.

Blackless, M., Charuvastra, A., Derryck, A., Fausto-Sterling, A., Lauzanne, K., & Lee. E. (2000). How sexually dimorphic are we? Review and synthesis. *American Journal of Human Biology, 12*, 151–166.

Blackman, M. C. (2002). Personality judgment and the utility of the unstructured employment interview. *Basic and Applied Social Psychology, 24,* 241–250.

Blackmore, S. J. (1992). Psychic experiences: Psychic illusions. *Skeptical Inquirer, 16,* 367–376.

Blackmore, S. J. (1994). Psi in psychology. *Skeptical Inquirer, 18,* 351–355.

Blackmore, S. J., & Troscianko, T. (1985). Belief in the paranormal: Probability judgments, illusory control, and the "chance baseline shift." *British Journal of Psychology, 76,* 459–468.

Blass, E. M., Ganchrow, J. R., & Steiner, J. E. (1984). Classical conditioning in newborn infants 2–48 hours of age. *Infant Behavior and Development, 7,* 223–235.

Blass, T. (1996). Attribution of responsibility and trust in the Milgram obedience experiment. *Journal of Applied Social Psychology, 26,* 1529–1535.

Block, R. I., Farinpour, R., & Braverman, K. (1992). Acute effects of marijuana on cognition: Relationships to chronic effects and smoking techniques. *Pharmacology Bulletin, 43,* 907–917.

Block, R. I., & Ghoneim, M. M. (1993). Effects of chronic marijuana use on human cognition. *Psychopharmacology, 110,* 219–228.

Blomqvist, O., Harnandez-Avila, C. A., Burleson, J. A., Ashraf, A., & Kranzler, H. R. (2003). Self-efficacy as a predictor of relapse during treatment for alcohol dependence. *Addictive Disorders and Their Treatment, 2,* 135–145.

Blum, D. (1998). Face it! *Psychology Today, 31*(5), 32–39, 66–67, 69–70.

Blumenthal, J. A., Emery, C. F., Walsh, M. A., Cox, D. R., Kuhn, C. M., Williams, R. B., et al. (1988). Exercise training in healthy Type A middle-aged men: Effects on behavioral and cardiovascular responses. *Psychosomatic Medicine, 50,* 418–433.

Bohn, M. J., Babor, T. F., & Kranzler, H. R. (1995). The Alcohol Use Disorders Identification Test (AUDIT): Validation of a screening instrument for use in medical settings. *Journal of Studies on Alcohol, 56,* 423–432.

Bolles, R. C. (1979). *Learning theory* (2nd ed.). Austin, TX: Holt, Rinehart & Winston.

Bollinger, K., Bialozynski, C., Nietz, J., & Nietz, M. (2001). The importance of deleterious mutations of M pigment genes as a cause of color vision defects. *Color Research and Application, 26*(Suppl), S100–S105.

Bonanno, G. A. (2004). Loss, trauma, and human resilience: Have we underestimated the human capacity to thrive after extremely aversive events? *American Psychologist, 59,* 20–28.

Book, H. E. (Ed.) *How to practice brief psychodynamic psychotherapy: The core conflictual relationship theme method.* Washington, DC: American Psychological Association.

Booth-Kewley, S., & Friedman, H. S. (1987). Psychological predictors of heart disease: A quantitative review. *Psychological Bulletin, 101,* 343–362.

Bootzin, R. R., Epstein, D., & Wood, J. M. (1991). Stimulus control instructions. In P. J. Hauri (Ed.), *Case studies in insomnia* (pp. 19–28). New York: Plenum.

Bornstein, M. H., & Lamb, M. E. (1992). *Development in infancy* (3rd ed.). New York: McGraw-Hill.

Bornstein, M. H., Tal, J., & Tamis-Lemonda, C. S. (1991). Parenting in a cross-cultural perspective: The United States, France, and Japan. In M. H. Bornstein (Ed.), *Cultural approaches to parenting.* Hillsdale, NJ: Erlbaum.

Bornstein, R. F. (1992). Subliminal mere exposure effects. In R. F. Bornstein (Ed.), *Perception without awareness: Cognitive, clinical, and social perspectives* (pp. 191–210). New York: Guilford Press.

Boroditsky, L. (2001). Does language shape thought? Mandarin and English speakers' conceptions of time. *Cognitive Psychology, 43,* 1–22.

Bostwick, T. D., & De Lucia, J. L. (1992). Effects of gender and specific dating behaviors on perceptions of sex willingness and date rape. *Journal of Social and Clinical Psychology, 11,* 14–25.

Botvin, G. J., Dusenbury, L., Baker, E., James-Ortiz, S., Botvin, E. M., & Kerner, J. (1992). Smoking prevention among urban minority youth: Assessing effects on outcome and mediating variables. *Health Psychology, 11,* 290–299.

Bouchard, T. J., Jr. (1997). IQ similarity in twins reared apart: Findings and responses to critics. In R. J. Sternberg & E. Grigorenko (Eds.), *Intelligence, heredity, and environment* (pp. 126–160). New York: Cambridge University Press.

Bouchard, T. J., Jr., & McGue, M. (1981). Familial studies of intelligence. *Science, 212,* 1055–1059.

Bourdon, Rae, D. S., Narrow, W. E., Manderscheid, R. W., & Regier, D. A. (1994).

Bourne, L. E., Dominowski, R. L., Loftus, E. F., & Healy, A. F. (1986). *Cognitive processes.* Englewood Cliffs, NJ: Prentice Hall.

Bousfield, W. A. (1953). The occurrence of clustering in the recall of randomly arranged associates. *Journal of General Psychology, 49,* 229–240.

Bouton, M. E., & Brooks, D. C. (1993). Time and context effects on performance in a Pavlovian discrimination reversal. *Journal of Experimental Psychology, 19,* 165–179.

Bowd, A. D., & Shapiro, K. J. (1993). The case against laboratory animal research in psychology. *Journal of Social Issues, 49,* 133–142.

Bower, B. (1991). Oedipus wrecked. *Science News, 140,* 248–250.

Bower, B. (1993). Sudden recall: Adult memories of child abuse spark a heated debate. *Science News, 144,* 184–186.

Bower, G. H. (1981). Mood and memory. *American Psychologist, 36,* 129–148.

Bower, J. M., & Parsons, L. M. (2003, August). Rethinking the "lesser brain." *Scientific American,* 50–57.

Bowlby, J. (1969). *Attachment and loss: Vol. 1. Attachment,* New York: Basic Books.

Bowlby, J. (1980). *Attachment and loss: Vol. 3. Loss: Sadness and depression.* New York: Basic Books.

Bowser, B. P., & Hunt, R. G. (Eds.). (1996). *Impacts of racism on white Americans* (2nd ed.). Beverly Hills, CA: Sage.

Boyce, T. E., & Geller, G. E. (2000). A community-wide intervention to improve pedestrian safety: Guidelines for institutionalizing large-scale behavior change. *Environment & Behavior, 32,* 502–520.

Brackett, M. A., & Mayer, J. D. (2003). Convergent, discriminant, and incremental validity of competing measures of emotional intelligence. *Personality and Social Psychology, 29,* 1147–1158.

Bradshaw, C. M. (2003). Neuropsychopharmacology. In P. W. Halligan, U. Kischka, & J. C. Marshall (Eds.), *Handbook of neuropsychology* (pp. 447–469). Oxford: Oxford University Press.

Bradshaw, J. L., & Nettleton, N. C. (1981). The nature of hemispheric specialization in man. *Behavioral and Brain Sciences, 4,* 51–91.

Brady, K. L., & Eisler, R. M. (1995). Gender bias in the college classroom: A critical review of the literature and implications for future research. *Journal of Research and Development in Education, 29*(1), 9–19.

Branscombe, N. R., N'gbala, A., Kobrynowicz, D., & Wann, D. L. (1997). Self and group protection concerns influence attributions but they are not determinants of counterfactual mutation focus. *British Journal of Social Psychology, 36,* 387–404.

Bransford, J. D., & Stein, B. S. (1984). *The ideal problem solver.* New York: Freeman.

Brantley, P. J., Dietz, L. S., McKnight, G. T., Jones, G. N., & Tulley, R. (1988). Convergence between the Daily Stress Inventory and endocrine measures of stress. *Journal of Consulting and Clinical Psychology, 56,* 549–551.

Braun, S. (1996). *Buzz: The science and lore of alcohol and caffeine.* New York: Oxford University Press.

Bray, G. A. (2004). Classification and evaluation of the overweight patient. In G. A. Bray & C. Bouchard (Eds.), *Handbook of obesity: Clinical applications* (2nd ed., pp. 1–32). New York: Marcel Dekker.

Breer, H., & Boekhoff, I. (1992). Second messenger signaling in olfaction. *Current Opinion in Neurobiology, 2,* 439–443.

Brehm, J. W. (1956). Post-decision change in the desirability of alternatives. *Journal of Abnormal and Social Psychology, 52,* 384–389.

Brehm, J. W. (1972). *Responses to loss of freedom: A theory of psychological reactance.* Morristown, NJ: General Learning Press.

Breslau, N., Davis, G. C., Andreski, P., & Peterson, E. (1991). Traumatic events and posttraumatic stress disorder in an urban population of young adults. *Archives of General Psychiatry, 48,* 216–222.

Brewer, M. B., & Brown, R. J. (1998). Ingroup relations. In D. T. Gilbert, S. T. Fiske, & G. Lindzey (Eds.), *The handbook of social psychology* (4th ed., Vol. 2, pp. 554–594). New York: McGraw-Hill.

Bringmann, W. G., Bringmann, N. J., & Ungerer, G. A. (1980). The establishment of Wundt's laboratory: An archival and documentary study. In W. G. Bringmann & R. D. Tweney (Eds.), *Wundt studies: A centennial collection* (pp. 123–157). Toronto: C. J. Hogrefe.

Brink, S. (2000, October 16). Sleepless society. *U.S. News & World Report,* 63–72.

Brock, E. T., & Shucard, D. W. (1994). Sleep apnea. *American Family Physician, 49,* 385–394.

Brock, G. W., & Barnard, C. P. (1992). *Procedures in marriage and family therapy* (2nd ed.). Boston: Allyn & Bacon.

Brock, P., Fisher, R. P., & Cutler, B. L. (1999). Examining the cognitive interview in a double-test paradigm. *Psychology, Crime and Law, 5*(1–2), 29–45.

Brock, T. C., Green, M. C., & Reich, D. A. (1998). New evidence in the Consumer Reports study of psychotherapy. *American Psychologist, 53,* 62–63.

Brody, L. R., & Hall, J. A. (1993). Gender and emotion. In M. Lewis & J. M. Haviland (Eds.), *Handbook of emotions* (pp. 447–460). New York: Guilford Press.

Brody, N., & Ehrlichman, H. (1998). *Personality psychology: The science of individuality.* Upper Saddle River, NJ: Prentice Hall.

Brook, J. S., Whiteman, M., Gordon, A. S., & Brook, D. W. (1989). The role of older brothers in younger brothers' drug use viewed in the context of parent and peer influences. *Journal of Genetic Psychology, 151,* 59–75.

Brookes, M. (2004). *Extreme measures: The dark visions and bright ideas of Francis Galton.* New York: Bloomsbury Publishing.

Brothers, J. (1981, February). Large versus small families. *Good Housekeeping.*

Broughton, R. S. (1991). *Parapsychology: The controversial science.* New York: Ballantine.

Brown, G. W., Harris, T. O., & Hepworth, C. (1994). Life events and endogenous depression. *Archives of General Psychiatry, 51,* 525–534.

Brown, J. A. (1958). Some tests of the decay theory of immediate memory. *Quarterly Journal of Experimental Psychology, 10,* 12–21.

Brown, J. F., Spencer, K., & Stella, S. (2002). A parent training programme for chronic food refusal: A case study. *British Journal of Learning Disabilities, 30,* 118–121.

Brown, J. L. (1987). Hunger in the U.S. *Scientific American, 256,* 37–41.

Brown, N. W. (2003). Conceptualizing process. *International Journal of Group Psychotherapy, 53,* 225–244.

Brown, P. K., & Wald, G. (1964). Visual pigments in single rods and cones in the human retina. *Science, 144,* 45–52.

Brown, R., & McNeill, D. (1966). The "tip-of-the-tongue" phenomenon. *Journal of Verbal Learning and Verbal Behavior, 5,* 325–337.

Brown, T. A., Cash, T. F., & Lewis, R. L. (1989). Body-image disturbances in adolescent female binge-purgers: A brief report of the results of a national survey in the U.S.A. *Journal of Child Psychology and Psychiatry, 30,* 605–613.

Brown, T. A., O'Leary, T. A., & Barlow, D. H. (2001). Generalized anxiety disorder. In D. H. Barlow (Ed.), *Clinical handbook of psychological disorders: A step-by-step treatment manual* (3rd ed., pp. 154–208). New York: Guilford Press.

Brownlee, N. (2003). *The complete illustrated guide to cannabis.* London: Sanctuary Publishing.

Bruce, M. L., Takeuchi, D. T., & Leaf, P. J. (1991). Poverty and psychiatric status. *Archives of General Psychiatry, 48,* 470–474.

Bruck, M., Cavanagh, P., & Ceci, S. J. (1991). Fortysomething: Recognizing faces at one's 25th reunion. *Memory and Cognition, 19,* 221–228.

Bruck, M., & Ceci, S. J. (1997). The suggestibility of young children. *Current Directions in Psychological Science, 6*, 75–79.

Brush, S. G. (1991). Women in science and engineering. *American Scientist, 79*, 404–419.

Bryant, J., & Zillmann, D. (1979). The effect of the intensification of annoyance through residual excitation from unrelated prior stimulation on substantially delayed hostile behavior. *Journal of Experimental Social Psychology, 15*, 470–480.

Buchanan, A. (1999). Risk and dangerousness. *Psychological Medicine, 29*, 465–473.

Buck, L., & Axel, R. (1991). A novel multigene family may encode odorant receptors: A molecular basis for odor recognition. *Cell, 65*, 175–187.

Buckingham, R. W. (1983). Hospice care in the United States: The process begins. *Omega, 13*, 159–171.

Buckley, K. W. (1989). *Mechanical man: John Broadus Watson and the beginnings of behaviorism.* New York: Guilford Press.

Bukatko, D., & Daehler, M. W. (2004). *Child development* (5th ed.). Boston: Houghton Mifflin.

Bulike, C. M., Sullivan, P. F., & Kendler, K. S. (2003). Genetic and environmental contributions to obesity and binge eating. *International Journal of Eating Disorders, 33*(3), 293–298.

Burgess, A. P., Rehman, J., & Williams, J. D. (2003). Changes in neural complexity during the perception of 3D images using random dot stereograms. *International Journal of Psychophysiology, 48*, 35–42.

Burkard, J., Ruggiero, G. M., Edlund, B., Gomez-Perretta, C., Lang, F., Mohammadkhani, P., et al. (2002). *Psychotherapy & Psychsomatic, 71*, 54–61.

Burke, H. L., & Yeo, R. A. (1994). Systematic variations in callosal morphology: The effects of age, gender, hand preference, and anatomic asymmetry. *Neuropsychology, 8*, 563–571.

Burnett, D., Rudolph, L., & Clifford, K. O. (1998). *Academic integrity matters.* Washington, DC: National Association of Student Personnel Administrators.

Burns, B. D., & Corpus, B. (2004). Randomness and inductions from streaks: "Gambler's fallacy" versus "hot hand." *Psychonomic Bulletin and Review, 11*, 179–184.

Burt, C. D. B. (1994). An analysis of self-initiated coping behavior: Diary-keeping. *Child Study Journal, 24*, 171–189.

Bushman, B. J. (1996). Individual differences in the extent and development of aggressive cognitive-association networks. *Personality and Social Psychology Bulletin, 22*, 811–819.

Bushman, B. J., & Anderson, C. A. (2001). Media violence and the American public: Scientific facts versus media misinformation. *American Psychologist, 56*, 477–489.

Bushman, B. J., & Cantor, J. (2003). Media ratings for violence and sex: Implications for policymakers and parents. *American Psychologist, 58*, 130–141.

Buss, A. H. (1961). *The psychology of aggression.* New York: Wiley.

Buss, D. M. (1987). Sex differences in human mate selection criteria: An evolutionary perspective. In C. B. Crawford, M. Smith, & D. Krebs (Eds.), *Sociobiology and psychology: Ideas, issues and applications* (pp. 335–352). Hillsdale, NJ: Erlbaum.

Buss, D. M. (1989). Sex differences in human mate selection preferences: Evolutionary hypotheses tested in 37 cultures. *The Behavioral and Brain Sciences, 12*, 1–49.

Butler, R. A., & Harlow, H. F. (1954). Persistence of visual exploration in monkeys. *Journal of Comparative and Physiological Psychology, 47*, 258–263.

Butler, R. J., & Liao, H. (2002). Job performance failure and occupational carpal tunnel claims. *Journal of Occupational Rehabilitation, 12*, 1–12.

Butzlaff, R. L., & Hooley, J. M. (1998). Expressed emotion and psychiatric relapse: A meta-analysis. *Archives of General Psychiatry, 55*, 547–552.

Buxbaum, L. J., & Coslett, H. B. (1996). Deep dyslexic phenomena in a letter-by-letter reader. *Brain and Language, 54*, 136–167.

Cacioppo, J. T., Bush, L. K., & Tassinary, L. G. (1992). Microexpressive facial actions as a function of affective stimuli: Replication and extension. *Personality and Social Psychology Bulletin, 18*, 515–526.

Cacioppo, J. T., Klein, D. J., Berntson, G. G., & Hatfield, E. (1993). The psychophysiology of emotion. In M. Lewis & J. M. Haviland (Eds.), *Handbook of emotions* (pp. 119–142). New York: Guilford Press.

Cain, W. S. (1982). Odor identification by males and females: Predictions versus performance. *Chemical Senses, 7*, 129–142.

Caldwell, A. B. (2004). My love affair with an instrument. *Journal of Personality Assessment, 82*, 4–10.

Callahan, L. A., Steadman, H. J., McGreevy, M. A., & Robbins, P. C. (1991). The volume and characteristics of insanity defense pleas: An eight-state study. *Bulletin of the Academy of Psychiatry and the Law, 19*, 331–338.

Calle, E. E., Rodriquez, C., Walker-Thurmond, K., & Thun, M. J. (2003). Overweight, obesity, and mortality from cancer in a prospectively studied cohort of U.S. adults. *New England Journal of Medicine, 348*, 1625–1638.

Calmels, C., Berthoumieux, C., & d'Arippe-Longueville, F. (2004). Effects of an imagery training program on selective attention of national softball players. *Sport Psychologist, 18*(3), 272–296.

Campbell, F. A., & Ramey, C. T. (1994). Effects of early intervention on intellectual and academic achievement: A follow-up on children from low-income families. *Child Development, 65*, 684–698.

Campbell, F. A., Ramey, C. T., Pungello, E., Sparling, J., & Miller-Johnson, S. (2002). Early childhood education: Young adult outcomes from the Aecedarian Project. *Applied Developmental Science,6*(1), 42–57.

Campbell, J. P. (1996). Group differences and personnel decisions: Validity, fairness, and affirmative action. *Journal of Vocational Behavior, 49*, 122–158.

Campion, M. A., Palmer, D. K., & Campion, J. E. (1998). Structuring employment interviews to improve reliability, validity, and users' reactions. *Current Directions in Psychological Science, 7*, 77–82.

Canino, I. A., & Spurlock, J. (2000). *Culturally diverse children and adolescents* (2nd ed.). New York: Guilford Press.

Cannon, T. D., & Macro, E. (1994). Structural brain abnormalities as indicators of vulnerability to schizophrenia. *Schizophrenia Bulletin, 20*, 89–101.

Cannon, W. B. (1927). The James-Lange theory of emotions: A critical examination and an alternative. *American Journal of Physiology, 39*, 106–124.

Capaldi, E. D., & Sheffer, J. D. (1992). Contrast and reinforcement in consumption. *Learning and Motivation, 23*, 63–79.

Capelli, C. A., Nakagawa, N., & Madden, C. M. (1990). How children understand sarcasm: The role of context and intonation. *Child Development, 61*, 1824–1841.

Capps, D. (2003). John Nash's predelusional phase: A case of acute identity confusion. *Pastoral Psychology, 51*, 361–386.

Caramazza, A., & Miozzo, M. (1997). The relation between syntactic and phonological knowledge in lexical access: Evidence from the "tip-of-the-tongue" phenomenon. *Cognition, 64*, 309–343.

Carello, C., & Turvey, M. T. (2004). Physics and psychology of the muscle sense. *Current Directions in Psychological Science, 13.*

Carew, T. J., Walters, E. T., & Kandel, E. R. (1981). Classical conditioning in a simple withdrawal reflex in *Aplysia californica*. *Journal of Neuroscience, 1*, 1426–1437.

Carli, L. (1999). Gender, interpersonal power, and social influence. *Journal of Social Issues, 55*, 81–99.

Carmichael, L., Hogan, H. P., & Walter, A. A. (1932). An experimental study of the effect of language on the reproduction of visually perceived forms. *Journal of Experimental Psychology, 15*, 73–86.

Carney, S., Cowen, P., Geddes, J., Goodwin, G., Rogers, R., Dearness, K, et al. (2003). Efficacy and safety of electroconvulsive therapy in depressive disorders: A systematic review and meta-analysis. *Lancet, 361*, 799–808.

Carolson, N. R. (2001). *Psysiology of behavior* (7th ed.). Boston: Allyn & Bacon.

Carpenter, S. (2001). Research on teen smoking cessation gains momentum. *Monitor on Psychology, 32*(6), 54–55.

Carpenter, S. (2001). Stop ignoring the data. *Monitor on Psychology, 32*(8), 34–35.

Carpenter, S. (2000). Memory illusions wobble, but they don't fall down. *Monitor on Psychology, 31*(9), 38.

Carr, J. (1994). Long-term outcome for people with Down's syndrome. *Journal of Child Psychology and Psychiatry and Allied Disciplines, 35*, 425–439.

Carrasco, J. L., Saiz-Ruiz, J., Hollander, E., & Cesar, J. (1994). Low platelet monoamine oxidase activity in pathological gambling. *Acta Psychiatrica Scandinavica, 90*, 427–431.

Carskadon, M. A. (2002). Risk of driving while sleepy in adolescents and young adults. In M. A. Carskadon (Ed.), *Adolescent sleep patterns: Biological, social, and psychological influences* (pp. 148–158). New York: Cambridge University Press.

Carskadon, M. A., & Dement, W. C. (2005). Normal human sleep: An overview. In M. H. Kryger, T. Roth, & W. C. Dement (Eds.), *Principles and practice of sleep medicine* (4th ed., pp. 13–25). New York: Elsevier Saunders.

Carter, R. (1998). *Mapping the mind.* Berkeley: University of California Press.

Cartwright, R. D., & Lamberg, L. (1992). *Crisis dreaming: Using your dreams to solve your problems.* New York: HarperPerennial.

Cascio, W. F. (1995). *Managing human resources* (4th ed.). New York: McGraw-Hill.

Cassidy, J. (2000). Adult romantic attachments: A developmental perspective on individual differences. *Review of General Psychology, 4*, 111–131.

Cassidy, T. (2000). Stress, healthiness and health behaviours: An exploration of the role of life events, daily hassles, cognitive appraisal and the coping process. *Counseling Psychology Quarterly, 13*, 293–311.

Castelli, L., Macrae, C. N., Zogmaister, C., & Arcuri, L. (2004). A tale of two primes: Contextual limits on stereotype activation. *Social Cognition, 22*, 233–247.

Catania, A. C., & Reynolds, G. S. (1968). A quantitative analysis of the responding maintained by interval schedules of reinforcement. *Journal of the Experimental Analysis of Behavior, 11*, 327–383.

Cattell, R. B. (1990). Advances in Cattellian personality theory. In L. A. Pervin (Ed.), *Handbook of personality theory and research* (pp. 101–110). New York: Guilford Press.

Cattell, R. B., Eber, H. W., & Tatsuoka, M. M. (1970). *Handbook for the Sixteen Personality Factor Questionnaire (16PF).* Champaign, IL: Institute for Personality and Ability Testing.

Cavallero, C., Cicogna, P., Natale, V., & Occhionero, M. (1992). Slow wave sleep dreaming. *Sleep, 15*, 562–566.

Cavallini, A., Fazzi, E., Viviani, V., Astori, M. G., Zaviero, S., Bianchi, P. E., & Lanzi, G. (2002). Visual acuity in the first two years of life in healthy term newborns: An experience with the Teller Acuity Cards. *Functional Neurology: New Trends in Adaptive and Behavioral Disorders, 17*, 87–92.

Ceci, S. (2001, July–August). Intelligence: The surprising truth. *Psychology Today*, 46–53.

Ceci, S. J., & Loftus, E. F. (1994). "Memory work." A royal road to false memories. *Applied Cognitive Psychology, 8*, 351–364.

Ceci, S. J., Bruck, M., & Battin, D. B. (2000). The suggestibility of children's testimony. In D. J. Bjorklund (Ed.). *False-memory creation in children and adults: Theory, research, and implications* (pp. 169–201). Mahwah, NJ: Erlbaum.

Centers for Disease Control and Prevention. (1994a). AIDS among racial/ethnic minorities—United States, 1993. *Morbidity and Mortality Weekly Report, 43*, 644–647, 653–655.

Centers for Disease Control and Prevention. (1994b). Attitudes toward smoking policies in eight states—United States, 1993. *Morbidity and Mortality Weekly Report, 43*, 786–789.

Centers for Disease Control and Prevention. Retrieved August 12, 2005 from http://cdc.gov/std.

Centers for Disease Control, National Center for Health Statistics. (2004a). Prevalence of overweight and obesity among adults: United States, 1999–2002. Retrieved August 15, 2005, from http://www.cdc.gov/nchs/products/pubs/pubd/hestats/obese/obse99.htm.

Centers for Disease Control, National Center for Health Statistics. (2004b). Prevalence of overweight among children and adolescents: United States,

1999–2002. Retrieved August 15, 2005, from http://www.cdc.gov/nchs/products/pubs/pubd/hestats/overwght99.htm.

Central Intelligence Agency (1996). *The world fact book.* Washington, DC: U.S. Government Printing Office.

Central Intelligence Agency (2004). *The world fact book.* Washington, DC: U.S. Government Printing Office.

Challis, B. H. (1993). Spacing effects on cued-memory tests depend on level of processing. *Journal of Experimental Psychology: Learning, Memory, and Cognition, 19*, 389–396.

Challis, B. H., & Brodbeck, D. R. (1992). Level of processing affects priming in word fragment completion. *Journal of Experimental Psychology: Learning, Memory, and Cognition, 18*, 595–607.

Chamberlain, M. C., Nichols, S. L., & Chase, C. H. (1991). Pediatric AIDS: Comparative cranial MRI and CT scans. *Pedriatric Neurology, 7*, 357–362.

Chandra, S. (1973). The effects of group pressure in perception: A cross-cultural conformity study in Fiji. *International Journal of Psychology, 8*, 37–39.

Chao, R. K. (1994). Beyond parental control and authoritarian parenting style: Understanding Chinese parenting through the cultural notion of training. *Child Development, 65*, 1111–1119.

Chassin, L., Presson, C. G., & Sherman, S. J. (1990). Social psychological contributions to the understanding and prevention of adolescent cigarette smoking. *Personality and Social Psychology Bulletin, 16*, 133–151.

Chasteen, A. L., & Madey, S. F. (2003). Belief in a just world and the perceived injustice of dying young or old. *Omega: Journal of Death and Dying, 47*, 313–326.

Chemers, M. M., Watson, C. B., & May, S. T. (2000). Dispositional affect and leadership effectiveness: A comparison of self-esteem, optimism, and efficacy. *Personality and Social Psychology Bulletin, 26*, 267–277.

Chen, C., Kasof, J., Himsel, A. J., Greenberger, E., Dong, Q., & Xue, G. (2002). Creativity in drawings of geometric shapes: A cross-cultural examination with the consensual assessment technique. *Journal of Cross-Cultural Psychology, 33*(2), 171–187.

Chen, Y.-C. J., Guo, Y.-L., Hsu, C.-C., & Rogan, W. J. (1992). Cognitive development of yu-cheng ("oil disease") children prenatally exposed to heat-degraded PCBs. *Journal of the American Medical Association, 268*, 3213–3218.

Chermack, S. T., & Taylor, S. P. (1995). Alcohol and human physical aggression: Pharmacological versus expectancy effects. *Journal of Studies on Alcohol, 56*, 449–456.

Cherry, C. J., & Bowles, J. (1960). Contribution to the study of the cocktail-party phenomenon. *Journal of Acoustical Society of America, 32*, 884.

Cheung, F. M. (2004). Use of Western and indigenously developed personality tests in Asia. *Applied Psychology: An International Review, 53*, 173–191.

Chien, C.-P. (1993). Ethnopsychopharmacology. In A. C. Gaw (Ed.), *Culture, ethnicity, and mental illness* (pp. 413–430). Washington, DC: American Psychiatric Association.

Children's Defense Fund. (1997). *The state of America's children: Yearbook 1997.* Washington, DC: Author.

Chomsky, N. (1972). *Language and mind* (2nd ed.). San Diego, CA: Harcourt Brace.

Chorover, S., & Schiller, P. (1965). Short-term retrograde amnesia in rats. *Journal of Comparative and Physiological Psychology, 59*, 73–78.

Christ, S. E. (2003). Asbjorn Folling and the discovery of phenylketonuria. *Journal of the History of the Neurosciences, 12*(1), 44–54.

Christensen, A., & Jacobson, N. S. (1994). Who (or what) can do psychotherapy: The status and challenge of nonprofessional therapies. *Psychological Science, 5*, 8–14.

Christensen, D. (2003). Dietary dilemmas. *Science News, 163*, 88–90.

Cialdini, R. B., Schaller, M., Houlihan, D., Arps, K., Fultz, J., & Beaman, A. L. (1987). Empathy-based helping: Is it selflessly or selfishly motivated? *Journal of Personality and Social Psychology, 52*, 749–758.

Cialdini, R. B., & Trost, M. R. (1998). Social influence: Social norms, conformity, and compliance. In D. T. Gilbert, S. T. Fiske, & G. Lindzey (Eds.), *The handbook of social psychology* (4th ed., Vol. 2, pp. 151–192). New York: McGraw-Hill.

Cicchetti, D., & Toth, S. L. (1998). The development of depression in children and adolescents. *American Psychologist, 53*, 221–241.

Cincinnati Children's Hospital Medical Center. (2003). Talk it up! Language development starts early. Retrieved from www.cincinnatichildrens.org/health/yh/archives/ 2003/spring/speak/htm.

Ciuffreda, K. J., & Engber, K. (2002). Is one eye better than two when viewing pictorial art? *Journal of Optometric Vision Development, 33*, 172–177.

Clark, C. M. (1994). Clinical assessment of adolescents involved in satanism. *Adolescence, 29*, 461–468.

Clark, D. M., Salkovskis, P. M., Ost, L.-G., Breitholtz, E., Koehler, K. A., Wrestling, B. E, et al. (1997). Misinterpretation of body sensations in panic disorder. *Journal of Consulting and Clinical Psychology, 67*, 203–213.

Clark, L. A., Watson, D., & Reynolds, S. (1995). Diagnosis and classification of psychopathology: Challenges to the current system and future directions. *Annual Review of Psychology, 46*, 121–153.

Clark, W. C., & Clark, S. B. (1980). Pain responses in Nepalese porters. *Science, 209*, 410–412.

Clarke, J. M., & Zaidel, E. (1994). Anatomical-behavioral relationships: Corpus callosum morphometry and hemispheric specialization. *Behavioral Brain Research, 64*, 185–202.

Clarke, S., Assal, G., & deTribolet, N. (1993). Left hemisphere strategies in visual recognition, topographical orientation and time planning. *Neuropsychologia, 31*, 99–113.

Clarke-Stewart, K. A. (1989). Infant day care: Maligned or malignant? *American Psychologist, 44*, 266–273.

Clay, R. A. (2001). Research to the heart of the matter. *Monitor on Psychology, 32*(1), 42–45.

Clay, R. A. (2003). Researchers replace midlife myths with facts. *Monitor on Psychology, 34*(4), 38–39.

Cleckley, H. (1976). *The mask of sanity* (5th ed.). St. Louis: Mosby.

Clifford, B. R., & Gwyer, P. (1999). The effects of the cognitive interview and other methods of context reinstatement on identification. *Psychology, Crime, and Law, 5*, 61–80.

Clifford, J. S., Boufal, M. M., & Kurtz, J. E. (2004). Personality traits and critical thinking: Skills in college students' empirical tests of a two-factor theory. *Assessment, 11*, 169–176.

Cloninger, S. C. (1996). *Theories of personality: Understanding persons* (2nd ed.). Upper Saddle River, NJ: Prentice Hall.

Cnattingius, S. (2004). The epidemiology of smoking during pregnancy: Smoking prevalence, maternal characteristics, and pregnancy outcomes. *Nicotine and Tobacco Research, 6*(Suppl 2), S125–S140.

Coffey, C. E., Weiner, R. D., Djang, W. T., Figiel, G. S., Soady, S. A. R., Patterson, L. J., et al. (1991). Brain anatomic effects of electroconvulsive therapy: A prospective magnetic resonance imaging study. *Archives of General Psychiatry, 48*, 1013–1021.

Cogan, D., & Cogan, R. (1984). Classical salivary conditioning: An easy demonstration. *Teaching of Psychology, 11*, 170–171.

Cohan, C. L., & Bradbury, T. N. (1997). Negative life events, marital interaction, and the longitudinal study of newlywed marriage. *Journal of Personality and Social Psychology, 73*, 114–128.

Cohen, A. S., Barlow, D. H., & Blanchard, E. B. (1985). The psychophysiology of relaxation-associated panic attacks. *Journal of Abnormal Psychology, 94*, 96–101.

Cohen, D. B., & Wolfe, G. (1973). Dream recall and repression: Evidence for an alternative hypothesis. *Journal of Consulting and Clinical Psychology, 41*, 349–355.

Cohen, E., & Cohen, G. (1999). *The virtuous therapist: Ethical practice of counseling and psychotherapy.* Belmont, CA: Brooks/Cole.

Cohen, G. D. (1987). Alzheimer's disease. In G. L. Maddox (Ed.), *The encyclopedia of aging.* New York: Springer.

Cohen, J. D., Noll, D. C., & Schneider, W. (1993). Functional magnetic resonance imaging: Overview and methods for psychological research. *Behavioral Research Methods, Instruments, and Computers, 25*, 101–113.

Cohen, S., Kessler, R. C., & Gordon, L. U. (Eds.). (1997). *Measuring stress: A guide for health and social scientists.* New York: Oxford University Press.

Cohen, S., Tyrrell, D. A. J., & Smith, A. P. (1991). Psychological stress and susceptibility to the common cold. *New England Journal of Medicine, 325*, 606–612.

Cohen, S., Tyrrell, D. A. J., & Smith, A. P. (1993). Negative life events, perceived stress, negative affect, and susceptibility to the common cold. *Journal of Personality and Social Psychology, 64*, 131–140.

Coinklin, H. M., & Iacono, W. G. (2002). Schizophrenia: A neurodevelopmental perspective. *Current Directions in Psychological Science, 11*, 33–37.

Colangelo, A., Buchanan, L., & Westbury, C. (2004). Deep dyslexia and semantic errors: A test of the failure of inhibition hypothesis using a semantic blocking paradigm. *Brain and Cognition, 54*, 232–234.

Cole, C., & Rodman, H. (1987). When school-age children care for themselves: Issues for family life education and parents. *Family Relations, 36*, 92–96.

Coleman, J. C. (1980). Friendship and the peer group in adolescence. In J. Adelson (Ed.), *Handbook of adolescent psychology.* New York: Wiley.

Coleman, R. M. (1986). *Wide awake at 3:00 A.M.: By choice or by chance?* New York: Freeman.

Collaer, M. L., & Hines, M. (1995). Human behavioral sex differences: A role for gonadal hormones during early development. *Psychological Bulletin, 118*, 55–107.

Collins, A. M., & Loftus, E. F. (1975). A spreading activation theory of semantic processing. *Psychological Review, 82*, 407–428.

Collins, A. M., & Quillian, M. R. (1972). How to make a language user. In E. Tulving & W. Donaldson (Eds.), *Organization of memory* (pp. 383–415). San Diego, CA: Academic Press.

Collins, B. S., Hollander, R. B., Koffman, D. M., Reeve, R., & Seidler, S. (1997). Women, work and health: Issues and implications for worksite health promotion. *Women and Health, 25*(4), 3–38.

Collins, W. A., & Kuczaj, S. A., II. (1991). *Developmental psychology: Childhood and adolescence.* New York: Macmillan.

Colton, M. (1998, May 31). You need it like . . . a hole in the head? If you're looking for enlightenment, here's the drill. *Washington Post*, F01, F04.

Coltrane, S., & Messineo, M. (2000). The perpetuation of subtle prejudice: Race and gender imagery in 1990s television advertising. *Sex Roles, 42*, 363–389.

Colwell, K., Hiscock, C. K., & Memon, A. (2002). Interviewing techniques and the assessment of statement credibility. *Applied Cognitive Psychology, 16*(3), 287–300.

Committee on Children, Youth and Families. (1994). *When you need child day care.* Washington, DC: American Psychological Association.

Confronting suicide—Part I. (2003). *Harvard Mental Health Letter, 19*(11), 1–4.

Congdon, N. G., Friedman, D. S., & Lietman, T. (2003). Important causes of visual impairment in the world today. *Journal of the American Medical Association, 290*, 2057–2060.

Conn, S. R., & Rieke, M. L. (1994). *The 16PF fifth edition technical manual.* Champaign, IL: Institute for Personality and Ability Testing.

Consortium for Longitudinal Studies (1983). *As the twig is bent: Lasting effects of preschool programs.* Hillsdale, NJ: Erlbaum.

Conte, A. (1997). Legal theories of sexual harassment. In W. O'Donohue (Ed.), *Sexual harassment: Theory, research and treatment* (pp. 50–83). Boston: Allyn & Bacon.

Conversion disorder. (2005). *Harvard Mental Health Letter, 22*(2), 1–3.

Cook, M., Mineka, S., Wolkenstein, B., & Laitsch, K. (1985). Observational conditioning of snake fear in unrelated rhesus monkeys. *Journal of Abnormal Psychology, 94*, 591–610.

Cooke, P. (1991, June 23). They cried until they could not see. *New York Times Magazine*, pp. 24–25, 45–48.

Coon, D. J. (1993). Standardizing the subject: Experimental psychologists, introspection, and the quest for a technoscientific ideal. *Technology and Culture, 34*, 757–783.

Coon, D. W., Thompson, L., Steffen, A., Sorocco, K., & Gallagher-Thompson, D. (2003). Anger and depression management: Psychoeducational skill training interventions for women caregivers of a relative with dementia. *Gerontologist, 43*, 678–689.

Coons, P. M. (1998). The dissociative disorders: Rarely considered and underdiagnosed. *Psychiatric Clinics of North America, 21*(3), 637–648.

Coons, P. M., Bowman, E. S., & Milstein, V. (1988). Multiple personality disorder: A clinical investigation of 50 cases. *Journal of Nervous and Mental Disease, 176*, 519–527.

Cooper, R. K., & Sawaf, A. (1997). *Executive EQ: Emotional intelligence in leadership and organization.* New York: Grosset/Putnam.

Corbett, K., Gentry, C. S., & Pearson, W., Jr. (1993). Sexual harassment in high school. *Youth and Society, 25*, 93–103.

Coren, S. (1996). *Sleep thieves: An eye-opening exploration into the science and mysteries of sleep.* New York: Free Press.

Coren, S. (1999). Psychology applied to animal training. In A. Stec & D. Bernstein (Eds.), *Psychology: Fields of application.* Boston: Houghton Mifflin.

Corey, G. (2001). *Theory and practice of group counseling* (5th ed.). Belmont, CA: Wadsworth/Thompson Learning.

Cornelissen, P., Hansen, P., Hutton, J., Evangelinou, V., & Stein, J. (1998). Magnocellular visual function and children's single word reading. *Vision Research, 38*, 471–482.

Corrigan, P. (2004). How stigma interferes with mental health care. *American Psychologist, 59*, 614–625.

Corrigan, P. W. (1995). Use of token economy with seriously mentally ill patients: Criticisms and misconceptions. *Psychiatric Services, 46*, 1258–1263.

Costa, P. T., Jr., & McCrae, R. R. (1988). Personality in adulthood: A six-year longitudinal study of self-reports and spouse ratings on the NEO Personality Inventory. *Journal of Personality and Social Psychology, 54*, 853–863.

Costa, P. T., Jr., & McCrae, R. R. (1992a). Four ways five factors are basic. *Personality and Individual Differences, 13*, 653–665.

Costa, P. T., Jr., & McCrae, R. R. (1992b). *NEO-PI-R and NEO-FFI professional manual.* Odessa, FL: Psychological Assessment Resources.

Costa, P. T., Jr., & McCrae, R. R. (1992c). Trait psychology comes of age. In T. B. Sonderegger (Ed.), *Nebraska symposium on motivation: Psychology and aging* (pp. 169–204). Lincoln: University of Nebraska Press.

Costanzo, M., & Archer, D. (1989). Interpreting the expressive behavior of others: The Interpersonal Perception Task. *Journal of Nonverbal Behavior, 13*, 225–245.

Costanzo, M., & Archer, D. (1991). A method for teaching about verbal and nonverbal communication. *Teaching of Psychology, 18*, 223–226.

Cousins, N. (1979). *Anatomy of an illness as perceived by the patient.* New York: Norton.

Cousins, N. (1989). *Head first: The biology of hope.* New York: Dutton.

Coutts, L. M. (1991). The organizational psychologist. In B. Gifford (Ed.), *Applied psychology: Variety and opportunity* (pp. 273–299). Needham Heights, MA: Allyn & Bacon.

Cowley, G. (1997, February 3). Can marijuana be medicine? *Newsweek,* 22–23, 26–27.

Craik, F. I. M., Byrd, M., & Swanson, J. M. (1987). Patterns of memory loss in three elderly samples. *Psychology and Aging, 2*, 79–86.

Craik, F. I. M., & Lockhart, R. S. (1972). Levels of processing: A framework for memory research. *Journal of Verbal Learning and Verbal Behavior, 11*, 671–684.

Crandall, C. S. (1988). Social contagion of binge eating. *Journal of Personality and Social Psychology, 55*, 588–598.

Craske, M. G., & Barlow, D. H. (2001). Panic disorder and agoraphobia. In D. H. Barlow (Ed.), *Clinical handbook of psychological disorders: A step-by-step treatment manual* (3rd ed., pp. 1–59). New York: Guilford Press.

Crawford, M., & Unger, R. (2000). *Women and gender: A feminist psychology.* New York: McGraw-Hill.

Crawford, N. (2003). Helping women beat the odds. *Monitor on Psychology, 34*(10), 85–86.

Creswell, C., & Chalder, T. (2001). Defensive coping styles in chronic fatigue syndrome. *Journal of Psychosomatic Research, 51*, 607–610.

Creswell, J. W. (1994). *Research design: Qualitative and quantitative approaches.* Thousand Oaks, CA: Sage.

Crews, F. (1996). The verdict on Freud. *Psychological Science, 7*, 63–68.

Crichton-Browne, J. (1980). On the weight of the brain: Its component parts in the insane. *Brain, 2*, 42–67.

Crosby, F. J. (1991). *Juggling: The unexpected advantages of balancing a career and home for women and their families.* New York: Free Press.

Crosby, F. J., & Jaskar, K. L. (1993). Women and men at home and at work: Realities and illusions. In S. Oskamp & M. Costanzo (Eds.), *Gender issues in contemporary society* (pp. 143–171). Newbury Park, CA: Sage.

Crose, R. (1994). Family bonding and attachment patterns late in life. *Family Therapy, 21*, 217–221.

Cross-National Collaborative Group. (1992). The changing rate of major depression. *Journal of the American Medical Association, 268*, 3098–3105.

Crowe, L. C., & George, W. H. (1989). Alcohol and human sexuality: Review and integration. *Psychological Bulletin, 105*, 374–386.

Crowe, R. A. (1990). Astrology and the scientific method. *Psychological Reports, 67*, 163–191.

Croziet, J., & Claire, T. (1998). Extending the concept of stereotype threat to social class: The intellectual underperformance of students from low socioeconomic backgrounds. *Personality and Social Psychology Bulletin, 24*, 588–594.

Culbertson, F. M. (1997). Depression and gender: An international review. *American Psychologist, 52*, 25–31.

Culliton, B. (1987). Osteoporosis reexamined: Complexity of bone biology is a challenge. *Science, 235*, 833–834.

Cummings, N. (1992). Self-defense training for college women. *Journal of American College Health, 40*, 183–188.

Cunningham, S., Scerbo, M. W., & Freeman, F. G. (2000). The electrocortical correlates of daydreaming during vigilance tasks. *Journal of Mental Imagery, 24*(1), 61–72.

Curran, T., & Keele, S. W. (1993). Attentional and nonattentional forms of sequence learning. *Journal of Experimental Psychology: Learning, Memory, and Cognition, 19*, 189–202.

Curtis, G. C., Magee, W. J., Eaton, W. W., Wittchen, H-U, & Kessler, R. C. (1998). Specific fears and phobias: Epidemiology and classification. *British Journal of Psychiatry, 173*, 212–217.

Czajkowski, S. M., Hindelang, R. O., Dembrowski, T. M., Mayerson, S. E., Parks, E. B., & Holland, J. C. (1990). Aerobic fitness, psychological characteristics, and cardiovascular reactivity to stress. *Health Psychology, 9*, 676–692.

Czeisler, C. A., Allan, J. S., Strogatz, S. H., Ronda, J. M., Sanchez, R., Rios, C. D., et al. (1986). Bright light resets the human circadian pacemaker independent of the timing of the sleep–wake cycle. *Science, 233*, 667–671.

Czeisler, C. A., Buxton, O. M., & Khalsa, A. B. S. (2005). The human circadian timing system and sleep–wake regulation. In M. H. Kryger, T. Roth, & W. C. Dement (Eds.), *Principles and practice of sleep medicine* (4th ed., pp. 375–394). New York: Elsevier Saunders.

Czeisler, C. A., Duffy, J. F., Shanahan, T. L., Brown, E. N., Mitchell, J. F., Rimmer, D. W., et al. (1999). Stability, precision, and near-24-hour-period of the human pacemaker. *Science, 284*, 2177–2181.

Czeisler, C. A., Moore-Ede, M. C., & Coleman, R. M. (1982). Rotating shift work schedules that disrupt sleep are improved by applying circadian principles. *Science, 217*, 460–463.

Czeisler, C. A., Weitzman, E. D., Moore-Ede, M. C., Zimmerman, J. C., & Knauer, R. S. (1980). Human sleep: Its duration and organization depend on its circadian phase. *Science, 210*, 1264–1267.

Dabbs, J. M., Jr., Chang, E.-L., Strong, R. A., & Milun, R. (1998). Spatial ability, navigation strategy, and geographic knowledge among men and women. *Evolution and Human Behavior, 19*, 89–98.

Dabbs, J. M., & Dabbs, M. G. (2000). *Heroes, rogues, and lovers: Testosterone and behavior.* New York: McGraw-Hill.

Dabbs, J. M., Jr., & Morris, R. (1990). Testosterone and antisocial behavior in a sample of 4462 men. *Psychological Science, 1*, 209–211.

Dabbs, J. M., Jr., Riad, K. K., & Chance, S. E. (2001). Testosterone and ruthless homicide. *Personality and Individual Difference 31*(4), 599–603.

Dabbs, J. M., Jr., & Ruback, R. B. (1984). Vocal patterns in male and female groups. *Personality and Social Psychology Bulletin, 10*, 518–525.

Daley, T. C., Whaley, S. E., Sigman, M. D., Espinosa, M. P., & Neumann, C. (2003). IQ on the rise: The Flynn effect in rural Kenyan children. *Psychological Science, 14*, 215–219.

Damasio, A. R. (1994). *Descartes' error: Emotion, reason, and the human brain.* New York: Avon Books.

Damasio, H., Grabowski, T., Frank, R., Galaburda, A. M., & Damasio, A. R. (1994). The return of Phineas Gage: Clues about the brain from the skull of a famous patient. *Science, 264*, 1102–1105.

Dansky, B. S., & Kilpatrick, D. G. (1997). Effects of sexual harassment. In W. O'Donohue (Ed.), *Sexual harassment: Theory, research, and treatment* (pp. 152–174). Boston: Allyn & Bacon.

Darley, J. M., & Latané, B. (1968). Bystander intervention in emergencies: Diffusion of responsibility. *Journal of Personality and Social Psychology, 8*, 377–383.

Dartnall, H. J. A., Bowmaker, J. K., & Mollen, J. D. (1983). Human visual pigments: Micro-spectrophotometric results from the eyes of seven persons. *Proceedings of the Royal Society of London, B, 220*, 115–130.

Darwin, C. J., Turvey, M. T., & Crowder, R. G. (1972). An auditory analogue of the Sperling partial report procedure: Evidence for brief auditory storage. *Cognitive Psychology, 3*, 255–267.

Darwin, C. R. (1859). *The origin of species.* London: John Murray.

Darwin, C. R. (1965). *The expression of emotions in man and animals.* Chicago: University of Chicago Press. (Originally published in 1872).

Davidson, J., & Harlan, C. (1993, April 20). As Waco ends, Clinton's leadership comes under scrutiny. *Wall Street Journal,* pp. A1, A6.

Davidson, R. J. (1993). The neuropsychology of emotion and affective style. In M. Lewis & J. M. Haviland (Eds.), *Handbook of emotions* (pp. 143–154). New York: Guilford Press.

Davis, G. A. (1993). *A survey of adult aphasia and related language disorders.* Englewood Cliffs, NJ: Prentice Hall.

Davis, J. M. (2002). Countering international terrorism: Perspectives from international psychology. In C. E. Stout (Ed.), *The psychology of terrorism* (pp. 4.11–4.33). New York: Prager.

Davis, M. C., Zautra, A. J., & Reich, J. W. (2001). Vulnerability to stress among women in chronic pain from fibromyalgia and osteoarthritis. *Annals of Behavioral Medicine, 23*, 215–226.

Davis, S. F., & Ludvigson, H. W. (1995). Additional data on academic dishonesty and a proposal for remediation. *Teaching of Psychology, 22*, 119–122.

Davis, S. F., & Smith, R. A. (2005). *An introduction to statistics and research methods: Becoming a psychological detective.* Upper Saddle River, NJ: Prentice Hall.

Daw, J. (2001, June). The ritalin debate. *APA Monitor,* 64–65.

Dawes, R. M. (1994). *House of cards: Psychology and psychotherapy built on myth.* New York: Free Press.

Dawes, R. M. (1998). Behavioral decision making and judgment. In D. T. Gilbert & S. T. Fiske (Eds.), *The handbook of social psychology* (Vol. 2, 4th ed., pp. 481–492). Boston: McGraw-Hill.

Day, N. L. (1992). The effects of prenatal exposure to alcohol. *Alcohol Health and Research World, 16*, 238–244.

DeAngelis, T. (1992, April). Health psychology grows both in stature, influence. *APA Monitor,* pp. 10–11.

DeAngelis, T. (2004a). What's to blame for the surge in super-size Americans? *Monitor on Psychology, 35*(1), 46–49.

DeAngelis, T. (2004b). Research-based help for teens in jeopardy. *Monitor on Psychology, 35*(2), 40–43.

DeAngelis, T. (2004c). Taking action for children's mental health. *Monitor on Psychology, 35*(11), 38–41.

D'Augelli, A. R. (1996). Lesbian, gay, and bisexual development during adolescence and young adulthood. In R. P. Cabaj & T. S. Stein (Eds.), *Textbook of homosexuality and mental health* (pp. 267–288). Washington, DC: American Psychological Association.

DeCarvalho, R. J. (1991). *The founders of humanistic psychology*. New York: Praeger.

DeCarvalho, R. J. (1992). The institutionalization of humanistic psychology. *Humanistic Psychologist, 20,* 124–135.

De Casper, A. J., & Fifer, W. (1980). Newborns prefer their mothers' voices. *Science, 208,* 1174–1176.

De Casper, A. J., & Prescott, P. A. (1984). Human newborns' perception of male voices: Preference, discrimination, and reinforcing value. *Developmental Psychobiology, 17,* 481–491.

De Casper, A. J., & Spence, M. J. (1986). Prenatal maternal speech influences newborns' perception of speech sounds. *Infant Behavior and Development, 9,* 133–150.

DeHaan, N., & Nelson, C. A. (1997). Recognition of the mother's face by six-month-old infants: A neurobehavioral study. *Child Development, 68,* 187–210.

De Kruijk, J. R., Leffers, P., Menheere, P. P. C. A., Meerhoff, S., Rutten, J., & Twijnstra, A. (2003). Olfactory function after mild traumatic brain injury. *Brain Injury, 17,* 73–78.

De Longis, A., Folkman, S., & Lazrus, R. S. (1998). The impact of daily stress on health and mood: Psychological and social resources and medications. *Journal of Personality and Social Psychology, 54,* 486–495.

De Reamer, B. (1980). *Modern safety and health technology*. New York: Wiley.

De Silva, P., & Rachman, S. (1992). *Obsessive compulsive: The facts*. Oxford: Oxford University Press.

De Valois, R. L., & Jacobs, G. H. (1968). Primate color vision. *Science, 162,* 533–540.

Decety, J., & Ingvar, D. H. (1990). Brain structures participating in mental simulation of motor behavior: A neuropsychological interpretation. *Acta Psychologica, 73,* 13–34.

Delemater, A. R. (1995). Outcome-selective effects of intertrial reinforcement in a Pavlovian appetitive conditioning paradigm with rats. *Animal Learning and Behavior, 23,* 31–39.

Dement, W. C. (1978). *Some must watch while some must sleep*. New York: Norton.

Dement, W. C. (1986). Normal sleep, disturbed sleep, transient and persistent insomnia. *Acta Psychiatrica Scandinavica Supplement, 74,* 41–46.

Dement, W. C., & Vaughan, C. (1999). *The promise of sleep: A pioneer in sleep medicine explores the vital connection between health, happiness, and a good night's sleep* New York: Delacorte.

Dement, W., & Wolpert, E. A. (1958). The relation of eye movement, body motility, and external stimuli to dream content. *Journal of Experimental Psychology, 44,* 543–555.

Denton, G. C. (1980). The influence of visual patterns on perceived speed. *Perception, 9,* 393–402.

Denton, R. E., & Kampfe, C. M. (1994). The relationship between family variables and adolescent substance abuse: A literature review. *Adolescence, 29,* 475–495.

Derksen, J., Kramer, I., & Katzko, M. (2002). Does a self-report measure for emotional intelligence assess something different than general intelligence? *Personality and Individual Differences, 32,* 37–48.

Desantis, A. D. (2003). A couple of white guys sitting around talking: The collective rationalization of cigar smokers. *Journal of Contemporary Ethnography, 32*(4), 432–466.

Detrick, P., Chibnall, J. T., & Rosso, M. (2001). Minnesota Multiphasic Personality Inventory-2 in police officer selection: Normative data and relation to the Inwald Personality Inventory. *Professional Psychology: Research and Practice, 32,* 484–490.

Deutsch, F. M. (2001). Equally shared parenting. *Current Directions in Psychological Science, 10,* 25–28.

Devine, D. P., & Spanos, N. P. (1990). Effectiveness of maximally different strategies and expectancy in attenuation of reported pain. *Journal of Personality and Social Psychology, 58,* 672–678.

Devos-Comby, L., & Salovey, P. (2003). Applying persuasion strategies to alter HIV-relevant thoughts and behavior. *Review of General Psychology, 6,* 287–304.

Dewar, T., & Whittington, D. (2000). Online learners and their learning strategies. *Journal of Educational Computing Research, 23,* 385–403.

Dewhurst, S. A., & Conway, M. A. (1994). Pictures, images, and recollective experiences. *Journal of Experimental Psychology: Learning, Memory, and Cognition, 20,* 1088–1098.

Deyoung, Y., & Zigler, E. F. (1994). Machismo in two cultures: Relation to punative child-rearing practices. *American Journal of Orthopsychiatry, 64,* 386–395.

Diamond, R., White, R. F., Myers, R. H., & Mastromauro, C. (1992). Evidence of pre-symptomatic cognitive decline in Huntington's disease. *Journal of Clinical and Experimental Neuropsychology, 14,* 961–975.

Dick-Read, G. (1959). *Childbirth without fear*. New York: Harper & Row.

Di Clemente, R. J., Zorn, J., & Temoshok, L. (1986). Adolescents and AIDS: A survey of knowledge, attitudes and beliefs about AIDS in San Franscisco. *American Journal of Public Health, 76,* 1443–1445.

Diener, E. (1980). Deindividuation: The absence of self-awareness and self-regulation in group members. In P. B. Paulus (Ed.), *Psychology of group influence*. Hillsdale, NJ: Erlbaum.

Diener, E., Fraser, S. C., Beaman, A. L., & Kelem, R. T. (1976). Effects of deindividuation variable on stealing among Halloween trick-or-treaters. *Journal of Personality and Social Psychology, 33,* 178–183.

Diller, L. (1992). Introduction to the special section of neuropsychology and rehabilitation: The view from New York University. *Neuropsychology, 6,* 357–359.

Dingfelder, S. F. (2004a). Programmed for psychopathology? *Monitor on Psychology, 35*(2), 56–57.

Dingfelder, S. (2004b). Schizophrenia may be characterized by unique smell deficits. *Monitor on Psychology, 35*(6), 13.

Dingfelder, S. F. (2004c). Protecting participants. *Monitor on Psychology, 35*(10), 32–33.

Dion, K. K., & Stein, S. (1978). Physical attractiveness and interpersonal influence. *Journal of Experimental Social Psychology, 14,* 97–108.

Dittmann, M. (2003a). Childhood exposure to televised violence may predict aggressive behavior in adults. *Monitor on Psychology, 34*(5), 13.

Dittmann, M. (2003b). Lessons from Jonestown. *Monitor on Psychology, 34*(10), 36–38.

Dittmann, M. (2004a). Psychological science offers clues to Iraqi prisoner abuse. *Monitor on Psychology, 35*(7), 13.

Dittmann, M. (2004b). Friendships ease middle school adjustment. *Monitor on Psychology, 35*(7), 18.

Dittmann, M. (2005). Building a mentally healthy work force. *Monitor on Psychology, 36*(1), 36–37.

Dohrenwend, B. P., & Ergi, G. (1981). Recent stressful life events and episodes of schizophrenia. *Schizophrenia Bulletin, 7,* 12–23.

Dohrenwend, B. P., Levav, I., Shrout, P. E., Schwartz, S., Naveh, G., Link, B. G., et al. (1992). Socioeconomic status and psychiatric disorders: The causation-selection issue. *Science, 255,* 946–951.

Dolan, M., Anderson, I. M., & Deakin, J. F. W. (2001). Relationship between 5-HT and impulsivity and aggression in male offenders with personality disorders. *British Journal of Psychiatry, 178,* 352–359.

Dollard, J., Doob, L., Miller, N., Mowrer, O., & Sears, R. (1939). *Frustration and aggression*. New Haven, CT: Yale University Press.

Domhoff, G. W. (1996). *Finding meaning in dreams: A quantitative approach*. New York: Plenum.

Domino, G. (2000). *Psychological testing: An introduction*. Upper Saddle River, NJ: Prentice Hall.

Domjan, M., & Purdy, J. E. (1995). Animal research in psychology: More than meets the eye of the general psychology student. *American Psychologist, 50,* 496–503.

Dopkins, S., Pollatsek, A., & Nordlie, J. (1994). Role of an abstract order schema in conceptual judgment. *Journal of Experimental Psychology: Learning, Memory, and Cognition, 20,* 1283–1295.

Dosher, B. A., Han, S., & Lu, Z.-L. (2004). Parallel processing in visual search asymmetry. *Journal of Experimental Psychology: Human Perception and Performance, 30,* 3–27.

Dosher, B. A., & Ma, J. (1998). Output loss or rehearsal loop? *Journal of Experimental Psychology: Learning, Memory, and Cognition, 24,* 316–335.

Doty, R. L. (1984). Smell identification ability: Changes with age. *Science, 226,* 1441–1443.

Drabman, R., Robertson, S., Patterson, J., Jarvie, G., Hammer, D., & Cordua, G. (1981). Children's perceptions of media-portrayed sex roles. *Sex Roles, 7,* 379–389.

Drews, C. D., Murphy, C. C., Yeargin-Allsopp, M., & Decoufle, P. (1996). The relationship between idiopathic mental retardation and maternal smoking during pregnancy. *Pediatrics, 97,* 547–553.

Driggers, K. J., & Helms, T. (2000). The effects of salary on willingness to date. *Psi Chi Journal of Undergraduate Research, 5,* 76–80.

Driskell, J. E., Copper, C., & Moran, A. (1994). Does mental practice enhance performance? *Journal of Applied Psychology, 79,* 481–492.

Drubach, D. (2000). *The brain explained*. Upper Saddle River, NJ: Prentice Hall.

Drwecki, B. B., Przygodski, D. J., & Horton, R. S. (2004). Style and attraction: The power of attractiveness and similarity of attitudes. *Psi Chi Journal of Undergraduate Research, 9,* 105–113.

Dryer, D. C., & Horowitz, L. M. (1997). When do opposites attract? Interpersonal complementarity versus similarity. *Journal of Personality and Social Psychology, 72,* 592–603.

Duffy, J. F., Rimmer, D. W., & Czeisler, C. A. (2001). Association of intrinsic circadian period with morningness-eveningness, usual wake time, and circadian phase. *Behavioral Neuroscience, 2001, 115,* 895–899.

Dufour, M. C. (1995). Twenty-five years of alcohol epidemiology: Trends, techniques, and transitions. *Alcohol Health and Research World, 19,* 77–84.

Duncker, K. (1945). On problem-solving. *Psychological Monographs, 58*(5 Whole No. 270).

Dundes, A., & Pagter, C. R. (1991). *Never try to teach a pig to sing*. Detroit: Wayne State University.

Dunn, J., & Plomin R. (1990). *Separate lives: Why siblings are so different*. New York: Basic Books.

Durant, J. E. (1999). Evaluating the success of Sweden's corporal punishment ban. *Child Abuse and Neglect, 23,* 435–448.

Dyche, L., & Zayas, L. H. (2001). Cross-cultural empathy and training the contemporary psychotherapist. *Clinical Social Work Journal, 29,* 245–258.

D' Zmura, M. (1991). Color in visual search. *Vision Research, 31,* 951–966.

D' Zmura, M., Lennie, P., & Tiana, C. (1997). Color search and visual field segregation. *Perception and Psychophysics, 59,* 381–388.

Eagly, A. H. (1995). The science and politics of comparing women and men. *American Psychologist, 50,* 145–158.

Eagly, A. H., & Crowley, M. (1986). Gender and helping behavior: A meta-analytic review of the social psychology literature. *Psychological Bulletin, 100,* 283–308.

Eagly, A. H., Karau, S. J., & Makhijani, M. G. (1995). Gender and the effectiveness of leaders: A meta-analysis. *Psychological Bulletin, 117,* 125–145.

Eagly, A. H., Makhijani, M. G., & Klonsky, B. G. (1992). Gender and the evaluation of leaders: A meta-analysis. *Psychological Bulletin, 111,* 3–22.

Eagly, A. H., Mladinic, A., & Otto, S. (1991). Are women evaluated more favorably than men? *Psychology of Women Quarterly, 15,* 203–216.

Eagly, A. H., & Steffen, V. J. (1986). Gender and aggressive behavior: A meta-analytic review of the social psychological literature. *Psychological Bulletin, 100,* 309–330.

Easley, A. R., & Range, L. M. (2004). Tobacco knowledge among college students. *Psi Chi Journal of Undergraduate Research, 9,* 14–18.

Eastell, R. (1998). Treatment of postmenopausal osteoporosis. *New England Journal of Medicine, 338,* 736–746.

Eaton, W. W., Kessler, R. C., Wittchen, H. U., & Magee, W. J. (1994). Panic and panic disorder in the United States. *American Journal of Psychiatry, 151*, 413–420.

Ebbinghaus, H. (1885). *On memory.* Leipzig: Duncker & Humblot.

Eccles, J. S., & Jacobs, J. E. (1986). Social forces shape math attitudes and performance. *Signs, 11*, 367–380.

Eden, G., VanMeter, J., Rumsey, J., Maisog, J., Woods, R., & Zeffiro, T. (1996). Abnormal processing of visual motion in dyslexia revealed by functional brain imaging. *Nature, 382*, 66–69.

Edwards, K. (1998). The face of time: Temporal cues in facial expression of emotion. *Psychological Science, 9*, 270–276.

Eggen, P., & Kauchak, D. (2001). *Educational Psychology: Windows on classrooms* (5th ed.). Upper Saddle River, NJ: Prentice Hall.

Eidelberg, D., & Galaburda, A. M. (1982). Symmetry and asymmetry in the human posterior thalamus. *Archives of Neurology, 39*, 325–332.

Ekman, P. (1992). Facial expression of emotion: New findings, new questions. *Psychological Science, 3*, 34–38.

Ekman, P. (1993). Facial expressions and emotion. *American Psychologist, 48*, 384–392.

Ekman, P. (1994). Strong evidence for universals in facial expressions: A reply to Russell's mistaken critique. *Psychological Bulletin, 115*, 268–287.

Ekman, P. (2003). *Emotions revealed: Recognizing faces and feelings to improve communication and emotional life.* New York: Times Books.

Ekman, P., Davidson, R. J., & Friesen, W. V. (1990). The Duchenne smile: Emotional expression and brain physiology II. *Journal of Personality and Social Psychology, 58*, 342–353.

Ekman, P., & Friesen, W. V. (1971). Constants across cultures in the face and emotion. *Journal of Personality and Social Psychology, 17*, 124–129.

Ekman, P., Friesen, W. V., & Bear, J. (1984, May). The international language of gestures. *Psychology Today*, pp. 64–69.

Ekman, P., Friesen, W. V., & O'Sullivan, M. (1988). Smiles when lying. *Journal of Personality and Social Psychology, 54*, 414–420.

Ekman, P., Friesen, W. V., O'Sullivan, M., Chan, A., Diacoyanni-Tarlatzis, I., Heider, K., et al. (1987). Universals and cultural differences in the judgments of facial expressions of emotion. *Journal of Personality and Social Psychology, 53*, 712–717.

Ekman, P., Levenson, R. W., & Friesen, W. V. (1983). Autonomic nervous system activity distinguishes among emotions. *Science, 221*, 1208–1210.

Elfenbein, H. A., & Ambady, N. (2002). On the universality and cultural specificity of emotion recognition: A meta-analysis. *Psychological Bulletin, 128*, 203–235.

Elfenbein, H. A., Mandal, M. K., Ambady, N., Harizuka, S., & Kumar, S. (2002). Cross-cultural patterns in emotion recognition: Highlighting design and analytical techniques. *Emotion, 2*, 75–84.

Elkind, D. (1984). *All grown up and no place to go.* Reading, MA: Addison-Wesley.

Elliot, A. J., & Devine, P. G. (1994). On the motivational nature of cognitive dissonance: Dissonance as psychological discomfort. *Journal of Personality and Social Psychology, 67*, 283–294.

Ellis, A. (1973). *Humanistic psychotherapy: The rational-emotive approach.* New York: McGraw-Hill.

Ellis, A. (1977). The basic clinical theory of rational-emotive therapy. In A. Ellis and R. Grieger (Eds.), *Handbook of rational-emotive therapy* (pp. 3–34). New York: Springer.

Ellis, A. (1987). The impossibility of achieving consistently good mental health. *American Psychologist, 42*, 364–375.

Ellis, A. (1990). *How to stubbornly refuse to make yourself miserable about anything, yes anything!* New York: Lyle Stuart.

Ellis, A., & Tafrate, R. C. (1997). *How to control your anger before it controls you.* Secaucus, NJ: Carol Publishing Group.

Ellis, M. (2004). Answer to child obesity epidemic needed soon. *Tyler Morning Telegraph, 74*(162), 1A, 6A.

Ellsworth, P. (1994). Sense, culture, and sensability. In S. Kitayama & H. R. Markus (Eds.), *Emotion and culture: Empirical studies of mutual influence* (pp. 23–50). Washington, DC: American Psychological Association.

Elskamp, J. G., & Broida, J. P. (2004). Extroverted students have difficulties learning in courses that utilize computers. *Psi Chi Journal of Undergraduate Research, 9*, 25–28.

Emery, C. L., & Lilienfeld, S. O. (2004). The validity of childhood sexual abuse checklists in the popular psychology literature: A Barnum effect? *Professional Psychology: Research and Practice, 35*, 268–274.

Emmorey, K., Allen, J. S., Bruss, J., Schenker, N., & Damasio, H. (2003). A morphometric analysis of auditory brain regions in congenitally deaf adults. *Proceedings of the National Academy of Sciences of the U.S.A., 100*, 10049–10054.

Engle, R. W., Cantor, J., & Carullo, J. J. (1993). Individual differences in working memory and comprehension: A test of four hypotheses. *Journal of Experimental Psychology: Learning, Memory, and Cognition, 19*, 972–992.

Engler, J., & Goleman, D. (1992). *The consumer's guide to psychotherapy.* New York: Simon & Schuster.

Engs, R., & Hanson, D. J. (1989). Reactance theory: A test with collegiate drinking. *Psychological Reports, 64*, 1083–1086.

Environmental Protection Agency. (1990). *Health effects of passive smoking: Assessment of lung cancer in adults and respiratory disorders in children*, Washington, DC: Environmental Protection Agency.

Epstein, J. F., & Gfroerer, J. C. (1997). *Heroin abuse in the United States.* Rockville, MD: Substance Abuse and Mental Health Services Administration, Office of Applied Studies.

Epstein, R. (2000). *The big book of creativity games.* New York: McGraw-Hill.

Epstein, S. (1979). The stability of behavior: 1. On predicting most of the people much of the time. *Journal of Personality and Social Psychology, 37*, 1097–1126.

Epstein, S. (1980). The stability of behavior: 2. Implications for psychological research. *American Psychologist, 35*, 790–806.

Epstein, S. (1983). The stability of confusion: A reply to Mischel and Peake. *Psychological Review, 90*, 179–184.

Equal Employment Opportunity Commission. (1980). Discrimination because of sex under Title VII of the 1964 Civil Rights Act as amended: Adoption of interim guidelines—sexual harassment. *Federal Register, 45*, 25024–25025.

Erdelyi, M. (1994). Hypnotic hypermnesia: The empty set of hypermnesia. *International Journal of Clinical and Experimental Hypnosis, 42*, 379–390.

Erickson, R. P., DiLorenzo, P. M., & Woodbury, M. A. (1994). Classification of taste responses in brain stem: Membership in fuzzy sets. *Journal of Neurophysiology, 71*, 2139–2150.

Erikson, E. H. (1963). *Childhood and society* (2nd ed.). New York: Norton.

Erikson, E. H. (1975). *Life history and the historical movement.* New York: Norton.

Eriksson, P. S., Perfilieva, E., Bjork-Eriksson, T., Alborn, A. M., Nordborg, C., Peterson, D. A., et al. (1998). *Nature Medicine, 4*, 1313–1317.

Erkinjuntti, T., Ostbye, T., Steenhuis, R., & Hachinski, V. (1997). The effect of different diagnostic criteria on the prevalence of dementia. *New England Journal of Medicine, 337*, 1667–1674.

Ervin, S. L. (2000, November–December). Fourteen forecasts for an aging society. *The Futurist*, 24–28.

Eskenazi, B. (1993). Caffeine during pregnancy: Grounds for concern? *Journal of the American Medical Association, 270*, 2973–2974.

Esser, J. K. (1998). Alive and well after 25 years: A review of groupthink research. *Organizational Behavior and Human Decision Processes, 73*, 116–141.

Evans, G. W. (2004). The environment of childhood poverty. *American Psychologist, 59*, 77–92.

Evans, R. B. (2003). Georg von Bekesy: Visualization of hearing. *American Psychologist, 58*, 742–746.

Evans, W. A., Krippendorf, M., Yoon, J. H., Posluszny, P., & Thomas, S. (1990). Science on the prestige and national tabloid presses. *Social Science Quarterly, 71*, 105–117.

Everett, J. J., Smith, R. E., & Williams, K. D. (1992). Effects of team cohesion and identifiability on social loafing in relay swimming performance. *International Journal of Sport Psychology, 23*, 311–324.

Ewing, R., Schmid, T., Killingsworth, R., Zlot, A., & Raudenbusch, S. (2003). Relationship between urban sprawl and physical activity, obesity, and morbidity. *American Journal of Health Promotion, 18*, 47–57.

Eysenck, H. J. (1952). The effects of psychotherapy: An evaluation. *Journal of Consulting Psychology, 16*, 319–324.

Eysenck, H. J., & Eysenck, M. W. (1985). *Personality and individual differences.* New York: Plenum.

Ezzell, C. (2003). Why? The neuroscience of suicide. *Scientific American*, 45–51.

Fagan, T. K. (2000). Practicing school psychology: A turn of the century perspective. *American Psychologist, 55*, 754–757.

Fagot, B. I., & Hagan, R. (1991). Observations of parent reactions to sex-stereotyped behaviors: Age and sex effects. *Child Development, 62*, 617–628.

Fagot, B. I., Hagan, R., Leinbach, M. D., & Kronsberg, S. (1985). Differential reactions to assertive and communicative acts of toddler boys and girls. *Child Development, 56*, 1499–1505.

Fagot, B. I., Leinbach, M. D., & O'Boyle, C. (1992). Gender labeling, gender stereotyping, and parenting behaviors. *Developmental Psychology, 28*, 225–230.

Falling apart: Dissociation and its disorders. (2005). *Harvard Mental Health Letter, 21*(7), 1–4.

Fantz, R. L. (1964). Visual experience in infants: Decreased attention to familiar patterns relative to novel ones. *Science, 146*, 668–670.

Farquhar, J. W., & Spiller, G. A. (1990). *The last puff.* New York: Norton.

Farrell, M. P., & Rosenberg, S. D. (1981). *Men at midlife.* Westport, CT: Auburn House.

Farwell, L. A., & Donchin, E. (1988). Talking off the top of your head: Toward a mental prosthesis utilizing event-related brain potentials. *Electroencephalography and Clinical Neurophysiology, 70*, 510–523.

Fassinger, R. E. (2000). Applying counseling theories to lesbian, gay, and bisexual clients: Pitfalls and possibilities. In R. M. Perez, K. A. DeBord, & K. J. Bieschke (Eds.), *Handbook of counseling and psychotherapy with lesbian, gay, and bisexual clients* (pp. 107–131). White Plains, MD: Automated Graphic Systems.

Faure, C. (2004). Beyond brainstorming: Effects of different group procedures on selection of ideas and satisfaction with the process. *Journal of Creative Behavior, 38*, 13–34.

Fausto-Sterling, A. (1992). *Myths of gender: Biological theories about women and men* (2nd ed.). New York: Basic Books.

Fausto-Sterling, A. (1993, March-April). The five sexes: Why male and female are not enough. *Sciences*, pp. 20–25.

Feagans, L. V., & Farran, D. C. (1994). The effects of daycare intervention in the preschool years on the narrative skills of poverty children in kindergarten. *International Journal of Behavioral Development, 17*, 503–523.

Feather, N. T. (1961). The relationship of persistence on a task to expectation of success and achievement-oriented motives. *Journal of Abnormal and Social Psychology, 63*, 552–561.

Feeney, J. A., & Noller, P. (1990). Attachment style as a prediction of adult romantic relationships. *Journal of Personality and Social Psychology, 58*, 281–291.

Feilding, A. (1978). *Blood and consciousness.* New York: Clucocrazy.

Feldman, R. S. (2000). *Development across the life span* (2nd ed.). Upper Saddle River, NJ: Prentice Hall.

Feldman, R. S. (2005). *Development across the life span* (3rd ed.) (Media and Research Update). Upper Saddle River, NJ: Prentice Hall.

Felkers, K. & Stivers, C. (1994). The relationship of gender and family environment to eating disorder risk in adolescents. *Adolescence, 29*, 821–834.

Fernandez, E., & Turk, D. C. (1992). Sensory and affective components of pain: Separation and synthesis. *Psychological Bulletin, 112*, 205–217.

Festinger, L. (1957). *A theory of cognitive dissonance.* New York: HarperCollins.

Field, T. (2001). Massage therapy facilitates weight gain in preterm infants. *Current Directions in Psychological Science, 10*, 51–54.

Fields, R. D. (2004). The other half of the brain. *Scientific American*, 54–61.

Findlaw, (2005). DUI laws. Retrieved August 1, 2005 from http://dui.findlaw.com/dui/dui_overview/dui law.html.

Finernan, S. (2002). Sexual harassment between same-sex peers: Intersection of mental health, homophobia, and sexual violence in schools. *Social Work, 47,* 65–74.

Finernan, S., & Bennett, L. (1999). Gender and power issues of peer sexual harassment among teenagers. *Journal of Interpersonal Violence, 14,* 626–641.

Fink, M. (1993). Post-ECT delirium. *Convulsive Therapy, 9,* 326–330.

Fink, M. (1999). *Electroshock: Restoring the mind.* New York: Oxford University Press.

Fink, M. (2000). Electroshock revisited. *American Scientist, 88,* 162–167.

Finkenauer, C., Engels, R. C. M. E., Branje, S. J. T., & Meeus, W. (2004). Disclosure and relationship satisfaction in families. *Journal of Marriage and Family, 66,* 195–209.

Fisch, R. O., Matalon, R., Weisberg, S., & Michaels, K. (1997). Phenylketonuria: Current dietary treatment practices in the United States and Canada. *Journal of the American College of Nutrition, 16,* 147–151.

Fischbach, G. D. (1992). Mind and brain. *Science, 267,* 48–57.

Fischler, M. A., & Firschein, O. (1987). *Intelligence: The eye, the brain, and the computer.* Reading, MA: Addison-Wesley.

Fisher, R. P. (1995). Interviewing victims and witnesses of crime. *Psychology, Public Policy, and Law, 1,* 732–764.

Fisher, R. P., & Geiselman, R. E. (1992). *Memory-enhancing techniques for investigative interviewing: The cognitive interview.* Springfield, IL: Charles C. Thomas.

Fisher, S., & Greenberg, R. (1977). *The scientific credibility of Freud's theories and therapy.* New York: Basic Books.

Fisher, S., & Greenberg, R. (1996). *Freud scientifically appraised.* New York: Wiley.

Fisher, S., & Greenberg, R. P. (Eds.). (1989). *The limits of biological treatments for psychological distress.* Hillsdale, NJ: Erlbaum.

Fiske, S. T. (1993). Controlling other people: The impact of power on stereotyping. *American Psychologist, 48,* 621–628.

Fiske, S. T., Bersoff, D. N., Borgida, E., Deaux, K., & Heilman, M. E. (1991). Social science research on trial: The use of sex stereotyping research in *Price Waterhouse* v. *Hopkins. American Psychologist, 46,* 1049–1060.

Fiske, S. T., & Stevens, L. E. (1993). What's so special about sex? Gender stereotyping and discrimination. In S. Oskamp & M. Costanzo (Eds.), *Gender issues in contemporary society* (pp. 173–196). Newbury Park, CA: Sage.

Fitzgerald, L. F. (1993a, February). *The last great open secret: The sexual harassment of women in the workplace and academia.* Science and Public Policy Seminar address presented to the Federation of Behavioral, Psychological and Cognitive Sciences, Washington, DC.

Fitzgerald, L. F. (1993b). Sexual harassment: Violence against women in the workplace. *American Psychologist, 48,* 1070–1076.

Fitzgerald, L. F. (2003). Sexual harassment and social justice: Reflections on the distance yet to go. *American Psychologist, 58*(11), 915–924.

Fitzgerald, L. F., & Ormerod, A. J. (1991). Perceptions of sexual harassment: The influence of gender and academic context. *Psychology of Women Quarterly, 15,* 281–294.

Fitzgerald, L. F., & Shullman, S. L. (1993). Sexual harassment: A research analysis and agenda for the 1990s. *Journal of Vocational Behavior, 42,* 5–27.

Fitzgerald, L. F., Shullman, S. L., Bailey, N., Richards, M., Swecker, J., Gold, Y., et al. (1988). The incidence and dimensions of sexual harassment in academia and the workplace. *Journal of Vocational Behavior, 32,* 152–175.

Fitzgerald, L. F., Weitzman, L. M., Gold, Y., & Ormerod, M. (1988). Academic harassment: Sex and denial in scholarly garb. *Psychology of Women Quarterly, 12,* 329–340.

Flaks, D. K., Ficher, I., Masterpasqua, F., & Joseph, G. (1995). Lesbians choosing motherhood: A comparative study of lesbian and heterosexual parents and their children. *Developmental Psychology, 31,* 105–114.

Flavell, J. H., Miller, P. H., & Miller, S. A. (1993). *Cognitive development* (3rd ed.). Upper Saddle River, NJ: Prentice Hall.

Fleck, D. E., Berch, D. B., Shear, P. K., & Strakowski, S. M. (2001). Directed forgetting in explicit and implicit memory: The role of encoding and retrieval mechanisms. *The Psychological Record, 51,* 207–222.

Fleeson, W., & Baltes, P. B. (1998). Beyond present day personality assessment: An encouraging exploration of the measurement properties and predictive power of subjective lifetime personality. *Journal of Research in Personality, 32,* 411–430.

Fleischmann, J. (2002). *Phineas Gage: A gruesome but true story about brain science.* Boston: Houghton Mifflin.

Fleming, J. H., & Darley, J. M. (1990). The purposeful-action sequence and the "illusion of control": The effects of foreknowledge and target involvement on observers' judgments of others' control over random events. *Personality and Social Psychology Bulletin, 16,* 346–357.

Fletcher, C., & Perry, E. L. (2001). Performance appraisal and feedback: A consideration of national culture and a review of contemporary research and future trends. In N. Anderson, D. S. Ones, H. K. Sinangil, & C. Viswesvaran (Eds.), *Handbook of industrial, work, and organizational psychology* (pp. 127–144). London: Sage.

Flory, K., Lynam, D., Milich, R., Leukefeld, C., & Clayton, R. (2004). Early adolescent through young adult alcohol and marijuana use trajectories: Early predictors, young adult outcomes, and predictive utility. *Development and Psychopathology, 16,* 193–213.

Flouhouse, K., Schorsch, J., & Vandermaas-Peeler, M. (2004). Influence of teacher–child attachment on complexity of play and social competence. *Psi Chi Journal of Undergraduate Research, 9,* 39–44.

Flynn, J. R. (1998). IQ gains over time. Toward finding the causes. In U. Neisser (Ed.), *The rising curve: Long-term gains in IQ and related measures* (pp. 25–66). Washingotn, DC: American Psychological Association.

Foa, E. B., & Kozak, M. J. (1995). DSM-IV field trial: Obsessive-compulsive disorder. *American Journal of Psychiatry, 152,* 90–96.

Forcier, B. H., Walters, A. E., Brasher, E. E., & Jones, J. W. (2001). Creating a safer environment through psychological assessment: A review of a measure of safety consciousness. *Journal of Prevention and Intervention in the Community, 22,* 53–65.

Ford, J. P., Schnurr, P. P., Friedman, M. J., Green, B. L., Adams, G., & Jex, S. (2004). Posttraumatic stress disorder symptoms, physical health, and health care utilization 50 years after repeated exposure to a toxic gas. *Journal of Traumatic Stress, 17,* 185–194.

Forer, B. R. (1949). The fallacy of personal validation: A classroom demonstration of gullibility. *Journal of Abnormal and Social Psychology, 44,* 118–123.

Formy-Duval, D. L., Williams, J. E., Patterson, D. J., & Fogle, E. E. (1995). A "Big Five" scoring system for the item pool of the Adjective Check List. *Journal of Personality Assessment, 65,* 59–76.

Foster, R. G., & Kreitzman, L. (2004). *Rhythms of life: The biological clocks that control the daily lives of every living thing.* New Haven, CT: Yale University Press.

Foulkes, D. (1962). Dream reports from different states of sleep. *Journal of Abnormal and Social Psychology, 65,* 14–25.

Foulks, E. F., Bland, I., & Shervington, D. (1995). Psychotherapy across cultures. In J. M. Oldham & M. B. Riba (Eds.), *Review of psychiatry* (Vol. 14, pp. 511–528). Washington, DC: American Psychiatric Association.

Fowler, R. D. (1990). In memoriam: Burrhus Frederic Skinner, 1904–1990. *American Psychologist, 45,* 1203.

Fox, N. A., Kimmerly, N. L., & Schafer, W. D. (1991). Attachment to mother/attachment to father: A meta-analysis. *Child Development, 62,* 210–225.

Foxx, R. M. (1982). *Decreasing behaviors of severely retarded and autistic persons.* Champaign, IL: Research Press.

Fraley, R. C., & Shaver, P. R. (2000). Adult romantic attachment: Theoretical developments, emerging controversies, and unanswered questions. *Review of General Psychology, 4,* 132–154.

Frank, E., Anderson, B., Reynolds, C. F., III, Ritenour, A., & Kupfer, D. J. (1994). Life events and the research diagnostic criteria endogenous subtype. *Archives of General Psychiatry, 51,* 519–524.

Frank, M. G., & Ekman, P. (1993). Not all smiles are created equal. The differences between enjoyment and nonenjoyment smiles. *Humor: International Journal of Humor Research, 6,* 9–26.

Frank, M. G., & Gilovich, T. (1988). The dark side of self- and social perception: Black uniforms and aggression in professional sports. *Journal of Personality and Social Psychology, 54,* 74–85.

Franken, R. E. (1998). *Human motivation* (4th ed.). Pacific Grove, CA: Brooks/Cole.

Frankenburg, W. K., Dodds, J., Archer, P., Bresnick, B., et al. (1992). *DENVER II Training manual.* Denver: Denver Developmental Materials.

Franz, V. H., Gegenfurtner, K. R., Bulthoff, H. H., & Fahle, M. (2000). Grasping visual illusions: No evidence for a dissociation between perception and action. *Psychological Science, 11,* 20–25.

Freckelton, I. (2004). The closing of the coffin on forensic polygraph evidence for Australia. *Psychiatry, Psychology and Law, 11*(2), 359–366.

Fredrikson, M., & Gunnarsson, R. (1992). Psychobiology of stage fright: The effect of public performance on neuroendocrine, cardiovascular, and subjective reactions. *Biological Psychology, 22,* 51–61.

Freedman, D. H. (1992, June). The aggressive egg. *Discover,* pp. 61–65.

Freeman, G., Sims, T., Kutsch, K., & Marcon, R. A. (1995). *Linking gender-related toy preferences to social structure: Changes in children's letters to Santa since 1978.* Paper presented at the annual meeting of the Southeastern Psychological Association, Savannah, GA.

French, D., & Richards, M. (Eds.). (1996). *Contemporary television.* Thousand Oaks, CA: Sage.

Freud, A. (1958). *The ego and the mechanism of defense.* Madison, CT: International Universities Press.

Freud, S. (1965). *The psychopathology of everyday life* (A. Tyson, trans.). New York: Norton. (Originally published in 1901)

Friedman, A. F., Webb, J. T., & Lewak, R. (1989). *Psychological assessment with the MMPI.* Hillsdale, NJ: Erlbaum.

Friedman, H. S. (2002). *Health psychology* (2nd ed.). Upper Saddle River, NJ: Prentice Hall.

Friedman, M., & Rosenman, R. H. (1974). *Type A behavior and your heart.* New York: Knopf.

Friedman, M., & Ulmer, D. (1984). *Treating Type A behavior and your heart.* New York: Knopf.

Friedman, M., Thoresen, C. E., Gill, J. J., Powell, L. H., Ulmer, D., Thompson, L., et al. (1984). Alteration of Type A behavior and reduction in cardiac recurrences in postmyocardial infarction patients. *American Heart Journal, 108,* 237–248.

Friedman, M. I., & Stricker, E. M. (1976). The physiological psychology of hunger: A physiological perspective. *Psychological Review, 83,* 409–431.

Friedman, R. C., & Downey, J. I. (1994). Homosexuality. *New England Journal of Medicine, 331,* 923–930.

Friedrich-Cober, L., & Huston, A. C. (1986). Television violence and aggression: The debate continues. *Psychological Bulletin, 100,* 364–371.

Friman, P. C., & Warzak, W. J. (1990). Nocturnal enuresis: A prevalent, persistent, yet curable parasomnia. *Pediatrician, 1,* 38–45.

Fritz, R. (1993). *Sleep disorders: America's hidden nightmare.* Naperville, IL: National Sleep Alert.

Fuchs, I., Eisenberg, N., Hertz-Lazarowitz, R., & Sharabany, R. (1986). Kibbutz, Israeli city, and American children's moral reasoning about prosocial moral conflicts.

Fulker, D. W., Eysenck, S. B. G., & Zuckerman, M. (1980). A genetic and environmental analysis of sensation seeking. *Journal of Research in Personality, 14,* 261–281. 37–50.

Fullerton, C. S., & Ursano, R. J. (1997). The other side of chaos: Understanding the patterns of posttraumatic responses. In C. S. Fullerton & R. J. Ursano. (Eds.), *Posttraumatic stress disorder: Acute and long-term responses to trauma and disaster* (pp. 3–18). Washington, DC: American Psychiatric Association.

Funder, D. C. (1991). Global traits: A neo-Allportian approach to personality. *Psychological Science, 2,* 31–39.

Funder, D. C., & Colvin, C. R. (1991). Explorations in behavioral consistency: Properties of persons, situations, and behaviors. *Journal of Personality and Social Psychology, 60,* 773–794.

Fung, M. T., Raine, A., Loeber, R., Lynam, D. R., Steinhauer, S. R., Venables, P. H., et al. (2005). Reduced electrodermal activity in psychopathy-prone adolescents. *Journal of Abnormal Psychology, 114*(2), 187–196.

Furnham, A., & Mak, T. (1999). Sex-role stereotyping in television commercials: A review and comparison of fourteen studies done on five continents over 25 years. *Sex Roles, 41,* 413–437.

Furnham, A., McManus, C., & Scott, D. (2003). Personality, empathy and attitudes to animal welfare. *Anthrozoos, 16,* 135–146.

Furumoto, L. (1979). Mary Whiton Calkins (1863–1930): Fourteenth president of the American Psychological Association. *Journal of the History of the Behavioral Sciences, 15,* 346–356.

Furumoto, L. (1992). Joining separate spheres—Christine Ladd-Franklin, woman scientist (1847–1930). *American Psychologist, 47,* 175–182.

Gabrenya, W. K., Jr., Wang, Y.-E., & Latané, B. (1985). Social loafing on an optimizing task: Cross-cultural differences among Chinese and Americans. *Journal of Cross-Cultural Psychology, 16,* 223–242.

Gaffner, J. (2003, September 15). Are superior wine-tasting abilities all in the mind? *Wine Spectator,* 13.

Gahlinger, P. (2004). *Illegal drugs: A complete guide to their history, chemistry, use and abuse.* New York: Penguin.

Galati, D., Scherer. K. R., & Ricci-Bitti, P. E. (1997). Voluntary facial expression of emotion: Comparing congenitally blind with normally sighted encoders. *Journal of Personality and Social Psychology, 73,* 1363–1379.

Galler, J. R., Ramsey, C. F., Morely, D. S., Archer, E., & Salt, P. (1990). The long-term effects of early kwashiorkor compared with marasmus. IV. Performance on the National High School Entrance Examination. *Pediatric Research, 28,* 235–239.

Gallup, G. H., Jr., & Newport, F. (1991). Belief in paranormal phenomena among adult Americans. *Skeptical Inquirer, 15,* 137–146.

Galton, F. (1869). *Hereditary genius: An inquiry into its laws and consequences.* London: Macmillan.

Galvin, S. L., & Herzog, H. A., Jr. (1992). Ethical ideology, animal rights activism, and attitudes toward the treatment of animals. *Ethics and Behavior, 2,* 141–149.

Gambrill, E. D., & Richey, C. A. (1975). An assertion inventory for use in assessment and research. *Behavior therapy, 6,* 550–561.

Gamwell, L., & Tomes, N. (1995). *Madness in America: Cultural and medicinal perceptions of mental illness before 1914.* Ithaca, NY: Cornell University Press.

Ganahl, D. J., Prinsen, T. J., & Netzley, S. B. (2003). A content analysis of prime time commercials: A contextual framework of gender representation. *Sex Roles, 49*(9–10), 545–551.

Ganong, L., Coleman, M., McDaniel, A. K., & Killian, T. (1998). Attitudes regarding obligations to assist an older parent or stepparent following later-life remarriage. *Journal of Marriage and the Family, 60,* 595–610.

Garb, J. L., & Stunkard, A. J. (1974). Taste aversions in man. *American Journal of Psychiatry, 131,* 1204–1207.

Garcia, J., Ervin, F. R., & Koelling, R. A. (1966). Learning with prolonged delay of reinforcement. *Psychonomic Science, 5,* 121–122.

Garcia, J., & Koelling, R. A. (1966). Relation of cue to consequence in avoidance learning. *Psychonomic Science, 4,* 123–124.

Gardner, H. (1993). *Frames of mind: The theory of multiple intelligences.* New York: Basic Books.

Gardner, H. (1999a). *Intelligence reframed: Multiple intelligences for the 21st century.* New York: Basic Books.

Gardner, H. (1999b, November). The understanding pathway. *Educational Leadership, 57*(3), 12–17.

Gardner, H. (2003). Three distinct meanings of intelligence. In R. J. Sternberg, J. Lautrey, & T. I. Lubart (Eds.), *Models of intelligence: International perspectives* (pp. 43–54). Washington, DC: American Psychological Association.

Gardner, M. (1956). *Mathematics, magic and mystery.* New York: Dover.

Garfield, S. L. (1980). *Psychotherapy: An eclectic approach.* New York: Wiley.

Garry, M., & Polaschek, D. L. L. (2000). Imagination and memory. *Current Directions in Psychological Science, 9,* 6–10.

Gaser, C., Nenadic, I., Buchsbaum, B. R., Hazlett, E. A., & Buchsbaum, M. S. (2004). Ventricular enlargement in schizophrenia related to volume reduction of the thalamus, striatum, and superior temporal cortex. *American Journal of Psychiatry, 161*(10), 154–156.

Gastil, J. (1990). Generic pronouns and sexist language: The oxymoronic character of masculine generics. *Sex Roles, 11/12,* 629–643.

Gaulin, S. J. C., & McBurney, D. H. (2001). *Psychology: An evolutionary approach.* Upper Saddle River, NJ: Prentice Hall.

Gazzaniga, M. S. (1967). The split brain in man. *Scientific American, 217,* 24–29.

Gazzaniga, M. S., Ivry, R. B., & Mangun, G. R. (1998). *Cognitive neuroscience: The biology of the mind.* New York: Norton.

Geen, R. G. (1998). Aggression and antisocial behavior. In D. T. Gilbert, S. T. Fiske, & G. Lindzey (Eds.), *The handbook of social psychology* (4th ed., Vol. 2, pp. 317–356). New York: McGraw-Hill.

Geisler, W., & Chou, K. (1995). Separation of low-level and high-level factors in complex tasks: Visual search. *Psychological Review, 102,* 356–378.

Gelfand, T., & Kerr, J. (Eds.). (1992). *Freud and the history of psychoanalysis.* Hillsdale, NJ: Analytic Press.

Gelyana, D., & Garfield, D. (2003).The neuroscience of psychotherapy: Building and rebuilding the human brain. *Psychiatric Services, 54,* 1419–1420.

Gerrig, R. J., & McKoon, G. (2001). Memory processes and experiential continuity. *Psychological Science, 12,* 81–85.

Gershberg, F. B., & Shimamura, A. P. (1994). Serial position effects in implicit and explicit tests of memory. *Journal of Experimental Psychology: Learning, Memory, and Cognition, 20,* 1370–1378.

Gershoff , E. T. (2002). Corporal punishment by parents and associated child behaviors and experiences. A meta-analytic and theoretical review. *Psychological Bulletin, 128,* 539–570.

Gershon, E. S., & Nurnberger, J. I. (1995). Bipolar illness. In J. M. Oldham & M. B. Riba (Eds.), *Review of Psychiatry* (Vol. 14, pp. 405–424). Washington, DC: American Psychiatric Association.

Ghiselin, B. (Ed.). *The creative process.* New York: Mentor.

Giambra, L. M. (1999–2000). The temporal setting, emotions, and imagery of daydreams: Age changes and age differences from late adolescent to the old-old. Imagination, *Cognition and Personality, 19,* 367–413.

Giannelli, P. C. (1995). The admissibility of hypnotic evidence in U.S. courts. *International Journal of Clinical and Experimental Hypnosis, 43,* 212–233.

Gibbs, N. (2001, August 6). Who's in charge here? *Time,* 39–49.

Gibbs, W. W. (1998, November). Dogma overturned. *Scientific American,* 19–20.

Gibson, A. R., Smith, K., & Torres, A. (2000). Glancing behavior of participants using automated teller machines while bystanders approach. *Psi Chi Journal of Undergraduate Research, 5,* 148–151.

Gibson, E. J., & Walk, R. D. (1960). The "visual cliff." *Scientific American, 202,* 64–71.

Gilbert, B. (1990, December). Once a malcontent, Ruby has taken up brush and palette. *Smithsonian,* pp. 40–50.

Gilbert, D. T. (1998). Ordinary personology. In D. T. Gilbert, S. T. Fiske, & G. Lindzey (Eds.), *The handbook of social psychology* (4th ed., Vol. 2, pp. 89–150). New York: McGraw-Hill.

Gilbert, D. T., & Malone, P. S. (1995). The correspondence bias. *Psychological Bulletin, 117,* 21–38.

Gilbert, P. L., Harris, M. J., McAdams, L. A., & Jeste, D. V. (1995). Neuroleptic withdrawal in schizophrenic patients: A review of the literature. *Archives of General Psychiatry, 52,* 173–188.

Gilbertson, T. A., & Boughter, J. D., Jr. (2003). Taste transduction: Appetizing times in gustation.

*NeuroReport: For Rapid Communication of Neuroscience Research, 14,* 905–911.

Gill, D. L. (2000). *Psychological dynamics of sport and exercise* (2nd ed.). Champaign, IL: Human Kinetics.

Gilligan, C. (1982). *In a different voice: Psychological theory and women's development.* Cambridge, MA: Harvard University Press.

Gilligan, C., Lyons, N. P., & Hanmer, T. J. (Eds.). (1990). *Making connections: The relational worlds of adolescent girls at Emma Willard School.* Cambridge, MA: Harvard University Press.

Gilligan, C., Murphy, J. M., & Tappan, M. B. (1990). Moral development beyond adolescence. In C. N. Alexander & E. J. Langer (Eds.), *Higher stages of human development.* New York: Oxford University Press.

Ginsberg, M. D. (1995). Neuroprotection in brain ischemia: An update (part I). *The Neuroscientist, 1,* 95–103.

Giovino, G. A., Henningfield, J. E., Tomar, S. L., Escobedo, L. G., & Slade, J. (1995). Epidemiology of tobacco use and dependence. *Epidemiologic Reviews, 17,* 48–65.

Gleaves, D. H. (1996). The sociocognitive model of dissociative identity disorder: A reexamination of the evidence. *Psychological Bulletin, 126,* 42–59.

Gluck, J. P., & Bell, J. (2003). Ethical issues in the use of animals in biomedical and psychopharmacological research. *Psychopharmacology, 171,* 6–12.

Gobet, F. L., Peter, C. R., Croker, S., Cheng, P., Jones, G., Oliver, I., et al. (2001). Chunking mechanisms in human learning. *Trends in Cognitive Science, 5,* 236–243.

Goedert, J. J., Fung, M. W., Felton, S., Battjes, R. J., & Engels, E. A. (2001). Cause-specific mortality associated with HIV and HTLV-II infections among injecting drug users in the USA. *AIDS, 15,* 1295–1302.

Goldberg, A. M., & Frazier, J. M. (1989). Alternatives to animals in toxicity testing. *Scientific American, 261,* 24–30.

Goldberg, E. (2001). *The executive brain: Frontal lobes and the civilized mind.* New York: Oxford University Press.

Goldberg, L. R. (1992). The social psychology of personality. *Psychological Inquiry, 3,* 89–94.

Goldberg, L. R. (1995). What the hell took so long? Donald W. Fiske and the big-five factor structure. In P. E. Shrout & S. T. Fiske (Eds.), *Personality research, methods, and theory: A festschrift honoring Donald W. Fiske* (pp. 29–43). Hillsdale, NJ: Erlbaum.

Goldberg, M. E. (2003). Correlation, causation, and smoking initiation among youths. *Journal of Advertising Research, 43,* 431–440.

Goldberg, S., MacKay-Soroka, S., & Rochester, M. (1994). Affect, attachment, and maternal responsiveness. *Infant Behavior and Development, 17,* 335–339.

Golden, L. (2001, March). Flexible work schedules: What are we trading off to get them? *Monthly Labor Review,* 50–67.

Golden, L., & Jorgensen, H. (2001). *Time after time: Mandatory overtime in the U.S. economy.* Briefing paper. Washington, DC: Economic Policy Institute: Retrieved October 30, 2005, from http://epinet.org.

Goldringer, S. D. (1996). Words and voices: Episodic traces in spoken word identification and recognition memory. *Journal of Experimental Psychology: Learning, Memory, and Cognition, 22,* 1166–1183.

Goldsmith, H. H., & Campos, J. J. (1982). Toward a theory of infant temperament. In R. N. Emde & R. J. Harmon (Eds.), *The development of attachment and affiliative systems: Psychobiological aspects.* New York: Plenum.

Goleman, D. (1995). *Emotional intelligence: Why it can matter more than IQ.* New York: Bantam Books.

Gomez-Merino, D., Chennaoui, M., Burnat, P., Drogou, C., & Guezennec, C. Y. (2003). Immune and hormonal changes following intense military training. *Military Medicine, 168,* 1034–1038.

Gonzalez, F., Justo, M. S., Bermudez, M. A., & Perez, R. (2003). Sensitivity to horizontal and vertical disparity and orientation preference in areas V1 and V2 of the monkey. *Neuroreport: For Rapid Communication of Neuroscience Research, 14,* 829–832.

Goodenough, J., McGuire, B., & Wallace, R. A. (2005). *Biology of humans: Concepts, applications, and issues.* Upper Saddle River, NJ: Pearson Prentice Hall.

Goodman, J., Loftus, E. F., & Greene, E. (1990). Matters of money: Voir dire in civil cases. *Forensic Reports, 3,* 303–329.

Goodrow, B., Seier, E., & Stewart, K. (2003). Social influences and adolescent attitudes on smoking: Analysis of the 2000 Tennessee Youth Tobacco Survey. *Adolescent and Family Health, 3,* 89–94.

Goodwin, C. J. (1988). Selective attention with human earphones. *Teaching of Psychology, 15,* 104–105.

Goodwin, C. J. (2005). *A history of modern psychology* (2nd ed.). New York: Wiley.

Gordon, H. (1987). *Extrasensory deception: ESP, psychics, Shirley MacLaine, ghosts, UFOs . . .* Buffalo, NY: Prometheus.

Gottesman, I. I. (1991). *Schizophrenia genesis: The origins of madness.* New York: Freeman.

Gottfredson, L. S. (1997). Why g matters: The complexity of everyday life. *Intelligence, 24*(1), 79–132.

Gottfried, A., Gottfried, A., Bathurst, K., & Kilian, C. (1999). Maternal and dual-earner employment. Family environment, adaptations, and the developmental impingement perspective. In M. Lamb et al. (Eds.), *Parenting and child development in "nontraditional" families.* Mahwah, NJ: Erlbaum.

Gould, D., & Damarjian, N. (1996). Imagery training for peak performance. In J. L. Van Raalte & B. W. Brewer (Eds.), *Exploring sport and exercise psychology* (pp. 25–80). Washington, DC: American Psychological Association.

Gould, S. J. (1981). *The mismeasure of man.* New York: Norton.

Gould, S. J. (1994, November 28). Curveball. *New Yorker,* pp. 139–149.

Graham, J. W., Marks, G., & Hansen, W. B. (1991). Social influence processes affecting adolescent substance abuse. *Journal of Applied Psychology, 76,* 291–298.

Gram, L. F. (1994). Drug therapy: Fluoxetine. *New England Journal of Medicine, 331,* 1354–1361.

Grant, B. F., Dawson, D. A., Stinson, F. S., Chou, S. P., DuFour, M. C., & Pickering, R. P. (2004). The 12-month prevalence and trends in DSM-IV alcohol abuse and dependence: United States 1991–1992 and 2001–2002. *Drugs and Alcohol Dependence, 74,* 223–234.

Grant, J. P. (1995). *The state of the world's children 1995.* New York: Oxford University Press.

Grayson, G. (2003). *Talking with your hands, listening with your eyes: A complete photographic guide to American Sign Language.* Garden City Park, NY: Square One Publishers.

Gredler, M. E. (2001). *Learning and instruction: Theory into practice* (4th ed.) Upper Saddle River, NJ: Prentice Hall.

Green, J. P., Lynn, S. J., & Malinoski, P. (In press). Hypnotic pseudomemories: The effects of warnings and hidden observer instructions. *Applied Cognitive Psychology.*

Green, J. P., Lynn, S. J., & Malinoski, P. (1998). Hypnotic pseudomemories, prehypnotic warnings, and malleability of suggested memories. *Applied Cognitive Psychology, 12,* 431–444.

Greenberg, J., Pyszczynski, T., Solomon, S., Rosenblatt, A., Veeder, M., Kirkland, S., et al. (1990). Evidence for terror management theory: 2. The effects of mortality salience on reactions to those who threaten or bolster the cultural worldview. *Journal of Personality and Social Psychology, 58,* 308–318.

Greene, M. A. (2001). The effects of the introduction of medication on the psychoanalytic process: A case study. *Journal of the American Psychoanalytic Association, 49,* 607–627.

Greene, R. L. (1991). *The MMPI-2/MMPI: An interpretive manual.* Needham Heights, MA: Allyn & Bacon.

Greenfield, P. (1992, June). *Notes and references for developmental psychology.* Paper presented at the Conference on Making Basic Texts in Psychology More Culture-Inclusive and Culture-Sensitive. Western Washington University, Bellingham, WA.

Greengrass, M. (2003). Giving to others linked to longer life. *Monitor on Psychology, 34*(2), 17.

Greenhill, L. L. (2005). The science of stimulant abuse. *Psychiatric Annals, 35*(3), 210–214.

Greer, M. (2004a). People don't notice unexpected visual changes: Though they predict they will. *Monitor on Psychology, 35*(8), 10.

Greer, M. (2004b). Positive reinforcement helps children avoid junk food. *Monitor on Psychology, 35*(11), 10.

Greer, M. (2004c). A happier, healthier workplace. *Monitor on Psychology, 35*(11), 28–29.

Gregory, R. J. (2004). *Psychological testing: History, principles, and applications* (4th ed.). Boston: Allyn & Bacon.

Grewal, D., & Salovey, P. (2005). Feeling smart: The science of emotional intelligence. *American Scientist, 93,* 330–339.

Griffin, K. (1992, November-December). A whiff of things to come. *Health,* pp. 34–35.

Griffith, H. W. (2004). *Complete guide to prescription and nonprescription drugs, 2005 edition* (revised and updated by S. Moore). New York: Perigee.

Grilo, C. M., & Pogue-Geile, M. F. (1991). The nature of environmental influences on weight and obesity: A behavior genetic analysis. *Psychological Bulletin, 110,* 520–537.

Grinspoon, L., & Bakalar, J. B. (1993). *Marihuana, the forbidden medicine.* New Haven, CT: Yale University Press.

Grob, G. N. (1994). *The mad among us: A history of the care of America's mentally ill.* New York: Free Press.

Gross, J. J., & John, O. P. (1998). Mapping the domain of expressivity: Multimethod evidence for a hierarchical model. *Journal of Personality and Social Psychology, 74,* 170–191.

Grossman, M., & Wood, W. (1993). Sex differences in intensity of emotional experience: A social role interpretation. *Journal of Personality and Social Psychology, 65,* 1010–1022.

Grossmann, K., Grossmann, K. E., Fremmer-Bombik, E., Kindler, H., Scheuerer-Englisch, H., & Zimmerman, P. (2002). The uniqueness of the child-father attachment relationship: Fathers' sensitive and challenging play as a pivotal variable in a 16-year longitudinal study. *Social Development, 11,* 307–331.

Gruber, J. E. (1997). An epidemiology of sexual harassment: Evidence from North America and Europe. In W. O'Donohue (Ed.), *Sexual harassment: Theory, research, and treatment* (pp. 84–98). Boston: Allyn & Bacon.

Guarnaccia, P. J., Canino, G., Rubio-Stipec, M., & Bravo, M. (1993). The prevalence of ataques de nervios in the Puerto Rico Disaster Study: The role of culture in psychiatric epidemiology. *Journal of Nervous and Mental Disease, 181,* 157–163.

Guenther, R. K. (1998). *Human cognition.* Upper Saddle River, NJ: Prentice Hall.

Gulevich, G., Dement, W. C., & Johnson, L. (1966). Psychiatric and EEG observations on a case of prolonged (264 hours) wakefulness. *Archives of General Psychiatry, 15,* 29–35.

Gur, R. C., Mozley, L. H., Mozley, P. D., Resnick, S. M., Karp, J. S., Alavi, A., et al. (1995). Sex differences in regional glucose metabolism during a resting state. *Science, 267,* 528–531.

Gurian, B. G. (1993). What is old-old age? *Harvard Mental Health Letter, 11,* 8.

Gutek, B. A. (1985). *Sex and the workplace: The impact of sexual behavior and harassment on women, men, and organizations.* San Francisco: Jossey-Bass.

Guthrie, R. V. (1998). *Even the rat was white* (2nd ed.). Needham Heights, MA: Allyn & Bacon.

Guttmacher Institute. Retrieved November 9, 2005, from http://www.agi-usa.org/pubs/fb teen sex.html.

Haber, J., Krainovich-Miller, B., Leach McMahon, A. L., & Price-Hoskins, P. (1997). *Comprehensive psychiatric nursing* (5th ed.). St. Louis: Mosby.

Haber, R. N. (1958). Discrepancy from adaption level as a source of affect. *Journal of Experimental Psychology, 56,* 370–375.

Haber, R. N. (1969). Eidetic images. *Scientific American, 220*(4), 36–44.

Haber, R. N., & Haber, R. B. (1964). Eidetic imagery: I. Frequency. *Perceptual and Motor Skills, 19*(1), 131–138.

Hafer, C. I. (2000). Investment in long-term goals and commitment to just means drive the need to believe in a just world. *Personality and Social Psychology Bulletin, 26,* 1059–1073.

Hagenah, B. J., Heaps, C., Gilden, E., & Roberts, M. (2001). Human sex differences in aggression within an evolutionary model. *Psi Chi Journal of Undergraduate Research, 6,* 123–131.

Haines, V. J., Diekhoff, G. M., LaBeff, E. E., & Clark, R. E. (1986). College cheating: Immaturity, lack of commitment, and the neutralizing attitude. *Research in Higher Education, 25,* 342–354.

Haist, F., Shimamura, A. P., & Squire, L. R. (1992). On the relationship between recall and recognition. *Journal of Experimental Psychology: Learning, Memory, and Cognition, 18,* 691–702.

Hajjar, D. J., & Nicholson, A. C. (1995). Atherosclerosis. *American Scientist, 83,* 460–467.

Halberstadt, J., & Rhodes, G. (2000). The attractiveness of nonface averages: Implications for an evolutionary explanation of the attractiveness of average faces. *Psychological Science, 11,* 285–288.

Hales, D. (2001). *An invitation to fitness and wellness.* Belmont, CA: Wadsworth.

Hall, C. S. (1966). *The meaning of dreams.* New York: McGraw-Hill.

Hall, C. S., Lindzey, G., & Campbell, J. B. (1998). *Theories of personality* (4th ed.). New York: Wiley.

Hall, E. G., & Davies, S. (1991). Gender differences in perceived intensity and affect of pain between athletes and nonathletes. *Perceptual and Motor Skills, 73,* 779–786.

Hall, E. G., & Lee, A. M. (1984). Sex differences in motor performance of young children: Fact or fiction? *Sex Roles, 10,* 217–230.

Hall, E. T. (1966). *The hidden dimension.* New York: Doubleday.

Hall, J. A. (1978). Gender effects in decoding nonverbal cues. *Psychological Bulletin, 85,* 845–857.

Hall, J. A. (1984). *Nonverbal sex differences: Communication accuracy and expressive style.* Baltimore: Johns Hopkins University Press.

Halligan, P. W., Kischka, U., & Marshall, J. C. (Eds.). (2003). *Handbook of clinical neuropsychology.* Oxford: Oxford University Press.

Halpern, D. F. (1986). *Sex differences in cognitive abilities.* Hillsdale, NJ: Erlbaum.

Halpern, D. F. (1992). *Sex differences in cognitive abilities* (2nd ed.). Hillsdale, NJ: Erlbaum.

Halpern, D. F. (2000). *Sex differences in cognitive abilities* (3rd ed.). Mahwah, NJ: Erlbaum.

Hamann, S. B., & Squire, L. R. (1996). Level-of-processing effects in word-completion priming: A neuropsychological study. *Journal of Experimental Psychology: Learning, Memory, and Cognition, 22,* 933–947.

Hamilton, M. C. (1991). Masculine bias in the attribution of personhood. *Psychology of Women Quarterly, 15,* 393–402.

Hammen, C. (1997). *Depression.* East Sussex, U.K: Psychology Press.

Hannigan, B., Edwards, D., & Burnard, P. (2004). Stress and stress management in clinical psychology: Findings from a systematic review. *Journal of Mental Health (UK), 13,* 235–245.

Hanson, S., & Hanson, P. (1989, April). Mean spirits: Why the strange friendship of Harry Houdini and Sir Arthur Conan Doyle didn't have a ghost of a chance. *Los Angeles Times Magazine,* pp. 94–104.

Harada, M. (1995). Minamata disease: Methylmercury poisoning in Japan caused by environmental pollution. *Critical Reviews in Toxicology, 25,* 1–24.

Hardy, C. L., & Van Leeuwen, S. A. (2004). Interviewing young children: Effects of probe structures and focus of rapport-building talk on the qualities of young children's eyewitness statements. *Canadian Journal of Behavioural Science, 36,* 155–165.

Hare, R. D. (1993). *Without conscience: The disturbing world of the psychopaths among us.* New York: Basic Books.

Hare, R. D., McPherson, L. M., & Forth, A. E. (1988). Male psychopaths and their criminal careers. *Journal of Consulting and Clinical Psychology, 56,* 710–714.

Haring, N. G., McCormick, L., & Haring, T. G. (1994). *Exceptional children and youth* (6th ed.). Upper Saddle River, NJ: Prentice Hall.

Harley, D. A., Riggar, T. F., Jolivette, K., & Christie, C. A. (2002). Violence in work settings: Understanding risk and developing solutions. *Journal of Rehabilitation Administration, 26,* 111–122.

Harlow, H. F., & Harlow, M. K. (1962). The effect of rearing conditions on behavior. *Bulletin of Menninger Clinic, 26,* 213–224.

Harlow, H. F., Harlow, M. K., & Meyer, D. R. (1950). Learning motivated by a manipulation drive. *Journal of Experimental Psychology, 40,* 228–234.

Harlow, J. M. (1868). Recovery from the passage of an iron bar through the head. *Massachusetts Medical Society Publication, 2,* 329–347.

Harned, M., S., Ormerod, A. J., Palmieri, P. A., Collinsworth, L. L., & Reed, M. (2002). Sexual assault and other types of sexual harassment by workplace personnel: A comparison of antecedents and consequences. *Journal of Occupational Health Psychology, 7,* 174–188.

Harpaz, I. (1985). Meaning of working: Profiles of various occupational groups. *Journal of Vocational Behavior, 26,* 25–40.

Harris, M. B. (1974). Mediators between frustration and aggression in a field experiment. *Journal of Experimental Social Psychology, 10,* 561–571.

Harris, R. J., & Firestone, J. M. (1997). Subtle sexism in the U.S. military: Individual responses to sexual harassment. In N. V. Benokraitis (Ed.), *Subtle sexism: Current practice and prospects for change* (pp. 154–171). Thousand Oaks, CA: Sage.

Hartman, T. F., & Grant, D. A. (1960). Effect of intermittent reinforcement on acquisition, extinction, and spontaneous recovery of the conditioned eyelid response. *Journal of Experimental Psychology, 60,* 89–96.

Hartmann, E. (1987). *The sleep book: Understanding and preventing sleep problems in people over 50.* Glenview, IL: Scott, Foresman.

Haruki, Y., Ishii, Y., & Suzuji, M. (Eds.). (1996). *Comparative and psychological study on meditation.* Delft, the Netherlands: Eburon.

*Harvard Mental Health Letter.* (1996, November). Suicide—Part I, *13,* 1–5.

*Harvard Mental Health Letter.* (1998, August). Obsessive-compulsive disorder—Part I, *15*(4), 1–4.

*Harvard Mental Health Letter.* (2001, April). Bipolar disorder-Part I, *1,* 1–4.

*Harvard Mental Health Letter* (2001, October). Alzheimer's Disease: Recent Progress and Prospects—Part I, *18*(4), 1–4.

*Harvard Mental Health Letter* (2002, February). Depression in children—Part I, *18,* 1–3.

*Harvard Mental Health Letter.* (2003, June). Confronting suicide: Part II, *19*(12), 1–5.

*Harvard Mental Health Letter.* (2004). The addicted brain, *21*(1), 1–4.

Harvard Medical School. (2001). *Improving sleep: A guide to a good night's rest.* Boston: Harvard Health Publications. (2002, February).

Harwood, H. (2000). *Updating estimates of the economic costs of alcohol abuse in the United States: Estimates, update methods and data.* Report prepared by the Lewin Group for the National Institute on Alcohol Abuse and Alcoholism. Bethesda, MD: National Institute on Alcohol Abuse and Alcoholism.

Hatsukami, D. K., & Zeller, M. (2004). Tobacco harm reduction: The need for research to inform policy. *APA Online: Psychological Science Agenda, 18*(4).

Hauri, P. J. (1992). *Sleep disorders.* Kalamazoo, MI: Upjohn.

Hayashi, M., Watanabe, M., & Hori. T. (1999). The effects of a 20 min nap in the mid-afternoon on mood, performance and EEG activity. *Clinical Neurophysiology, 110,* 272–279.

Hazan, C., & Diamond, L. M. (2000). The place of attachment in human mating. *Review of General Psychology, 4,* 186–204.

Heath, A. C., Kendler, K. S., Eaves, I. J., & Martin, N. G. (1990). Evidence for genetic influences on sleep disturbance and sleep patterns in twins. *Sleep, 13,* 318–335.

Heath, T. D. (1994). The impact of delayed fatherhood on the father–child relationship. *Journal of Genetic Psychology, 155,* 511–530.

Heatherton, T. F., Kozlowski, L. T., Frecker, R. C., & Fagerstrom, K. O. (1991). The Fagerstrom test for nicotine dependence: A revision of the Fagerstrom tolerance questionnaire. *British Journal of Addictions, 86,* 119–127.

Heaton, P., & Wallace, G. L. (2004). Annotation: The savant syndrome. *Journal of Child Psychology and Psychiatry, 45*(5), 899–911.

Heider, F. (1958). *The psychology of interpersonal relationships.* New York: Wiley.

Hejmadi, A., Davidson, R. J., & Rozin, P. (2000). Exploring Hindu Indian emotion expressions: Evidence for accurate recognition by Americans and Indians. *Psychological Science, 11,* 183–187.

Helgeson, V. S. (2002). *The psychology of gender.* Upper Saddle River, NJ: Prentice Hall.

Helgeson, V. S. (2005a). The *psychology of gender* (2nd ed.). Upper Saddle River, NJ: Pearson Prentice Hall.

Helgeson, V. S. (2005b). *Sex and gender* (2nd ed.). Upper Saddle River, NJ: Pearson Prentice Hall.

Helms, J. E. (1992). Why is there no study of cultural equivalence in standardized cognitive ability testing? *American Psychologist, 47,* 1083–1101.

Helson, R., & Roberts, B. W. (1994). Ego development and personality change in adulthood. *Journal of Personality and Social Psychology, 66,* 911–920.

Helzer, J. E., Burnam, A., & McEvoy, L. T. (1991). Alcohol abuse and dependence. In L. N. Robins & D. A. Regier (Eds.), *Psychiatric disorders in America: The Epidemiologic Catchment Area Study* (pp. 81–115). New York: Free Press.

Helzer, J. E., Canino, G. J., Yeh, E.-K., Bland, R. C., Lee, C. K., Hwu, H.-G., et al. (1990). Alcoholism—North America and Asia. *Archives of General Psychiatry, 47,* 313–319.

Henderson, P. H., Clarke, J. E., & Woods, C. (1998). *Summary report 1996: Doctoral recipients from United States universities.* Washington, DC: National Academy Press.

Hendrick, C., & Hendrick, S. (1986). A theory and method of love. *Journal of Personality and Social Psychology, 50,* 392–402.

Hendrick, S. S., & Hendrick, C. (1992). *Liking, loving, and relating* (2nd ed.). Pacific Grove, CA: Brooks/Cole.

Hendrie, H. C. (2001). Exploration of environmental and genetic risk factors for Alzheimer's disease: The value of cross-cultural studies. *Current Directions in Psychological Science, 10,* 98–101.

Henley, N. M. (1989). Molehill or mountain? What we know and don't know about sex bias in language. In M. Crawford & M. Gentry (Eds.), *Gender and thought: Psychological perspectives* (pp. 59–78). New York: Springer-Verlag.

Hennager, K. (1993). Senoi dream theory. In M. A. Carsakadon (Ed.), *Encyclopedia of sleep and dreaming* (pp. 532–533). New York: Macmillan.

Henning, H. (1916). *Der Geruch.* Leipzig: Barth.

Henry, D. B., Cartland, J., Ruchross, H., & Monahan, K. (2004). A return potential measure of setting norms for aggression. *American Journal of Community Psychology, 33,* 131–149.

Henshaw, S. K. (1998). Unintended pregnancy in the United States. *Family Planning Perspectives, 30,* 24.

Herbert, T. B., & Cohen, S. (1993). Stress and immunity in humans: A meta-analytic review. *Psychosomatic Medicine, 55,* 364–379.

Herbst, K. C., Gaertner, L., & Insko, C. A. (2003). My head says yes but my heart says no: Cognitive and affective attraction as a function of similarity to the ideal self. *Journal of Personality and Social Psychology, 84,* 1206-1219.

Hergenhahn, B. R., & Olson, M. H. (1999). *An introduction to theories of learning* (5th ed.). Upper Saddle River, NJ: Prentice Hall.

Hergenhahn, B. R., & Olson, M. H. (2001). *An introduction to theories of learning* (6th ed.). Upper Saddle River, NJ: Prentice Hall.

Hergovich, A. (2004). The effect of pseudo-psychic demonstrations as dependent on belief in paranormal phenomena and suggestibility. *Personality and Individual Differences, 36,* 365–380.

Herold, D. M., Davis, W. D., & Maslyn, J. M. (1998). An investigation of workplace AIDS training with implications for occupational health promotion efforts. *Journal of Occupational Health Psychology, 3,* 276–286.

Herrnstein, R.J., & Murray, C. (1994). *The bell curve: Intelligence and class structure in American life.* New York: Free Press.

Hersen, M., & Biaggio, M. (Eds.). (2000). *Effective brief therapies: A clinician's guide.* Orlando, FL: Academic Press.

Herzog, H. A. (1990). Discussing animal rights and animal research in the classroom. *Teaching of Psychology, 17,* 90–94.

Hesson-McInnis, M. S., & Fitzgerald, L. F. (1997). Sexual harassment: A preliminary test of an integrative model. *Journal of Applied Social Psychology, 27,* 877–901.

Heston, L. L. (1992). *Mending minds: A guide to the new psychiatry of depression, anxiety, and other serious mental disorders.* New York: Freeman.

Hetherington, A. W., & Ranson, S. W. (1940). Hypothalamic lesions and adiposity in the rat. *Anatomical Record, 78,* 149–172.

Heuze, J.-P., & Brunel, P. C. (2003). Social loafing in a competitive context. *International Journal of Sport and Exercise Psychology, 1,* 246–263.

Hewlett, K. (2001). Has men's health become invisible? *Monitor on Psychology, 32*(11), 42–43.

Hewstone, M. (1988). Causal attribution: From cognitive processes to collective beliefs. *Psychologist, 8,* 323–327.

Heyes, C. M., Jaldow, E., & Dawson, G. R. (1993). Observational extinction: Observation of nonreinforced responding reduces resistance to extinction in rats. *Animal Learning and Behavior, 21,* 221–225.

Hickey, M. (2001). An application of Amabile's consensual assessment technique for rating the creativity of children's musical compositions. *Journal of Research in Music Education, 49*(3), 234–244.

Hickok, G., Bellugi, U., & Klima, E. S. (2001). Sign language in the brain. *Scientific American,* 57–65.

Higbee, K. L. (1993). *Your memory: How it works and how to improve it.* New York: Paragon House.

Hilgard, E. R. (1991). Suggestibility and suggestions as related to hypnosis. In J. F. Schumaker (Ed.), *Human suggestibility: Advances in theory, research, and application* (pp. 38–58). New York: Routledge.

Hill, K., & Pomeroy, C. (2001). Assessment of physical status of children and adolescents with eating disorders and obesity. In J. K. Thompson & L. Smolak (Eds.), *Body image, eating disorders, and obesity in youth: Assessment, prevention, and treatment* (pp. 171–191). Washington, DC.: American Psychological Association.

Hill, P. C., & Pargament, K. I. (2003). Advances in the conceptualization and measurement of spirituality. Implications for physical and mental health research. *American Psychologist, 58,* 64–74.

Hillier, L., & Harrison, L. (2004). Homophobia and the production of shame: Young people and same-sex attraction. *Culture, Health and Sexuality, 6,* 79–94.

Hilton, D. J., Smith, R. H., & Kin, S. H. (1995). Processes of causal explanation and dispositional attribution. *Journal of Personality and Social Psychology, 68,* 377–387.

Hirschfeld, R., Keller, M., Panico, S., Arons, B., Barlow, D., Davidoff, F., et al. (1997). The National Depressive and Manic-Depressive Association Consensus Statement on the Undertreatment of Depression. *Journal of the American Medial Association, 277,* 333–340.

Hirschman, E., Whelley, M. M., & Palij, M. (1989). An investigation of paradoxical memory effects. *Journal of Memory and Language, 28,* 594–609.

Hirshkowitz, M. (2002). Neuropsychiatric aspects of sleep and sleep disorders. In S. C. Yudofsky & R. E. Hales (Eds.), *The American psychiatric publishing textbook of neuropsychiatry and clinical neurosciences* (pp. 697–722). Washington, DC: American Psychiatric Association.

Hobson, J. A. (1989). *Sleep.* New York: Scientific American Library.

Hobson, J. A. (2005). *13 dreams Freud never had: The new mind science.* New York: Pi Press.

Hobson, J. A., & McCarley, R. W. (1977). The brain as a dream state generator: An activation-synthesis hypothesis of the dream process. *American Journal of Psychiatry, 134,* 1335–1348.

Hobson, J. A., & Silvestri, L. (1999, February). Parasomnias. *The Harvard Mental Health Letter,* 3–5.

Hochschild, A. (1989). *The second shift: Working parents and the revolution at home.* New York: Viking Penguin.

Hoffman, L. W., & Youngblade, L. M. (1998). Maternal employment, morale, and parenting style: Social class comparisons. *Journal of Applied Developmental Psychology, 19*, 389–413.

Hoffrage, U., Weber, A., Hertwig, R., & Chase, V. M. (2003). How to keep children safe in traffic: Find the daredevils early. *Journal of Experimental Psychology: Applied, 9*, 249–260.

Hogan, R. T., & Roberts, B. W. (2001). Introduction: Personality and industrial and organizational psychology. In B. W. Roberts & R. Hogan (Eds.), *Personality psychology in the workplace* (pp. 3–44). Washington, DC: American Psychological Association.

Hogarty, G. E., Anderson, C. M., Reiss, D. J., Kornblith, S. J., Greenwald, D. P., Ulrich, R. F., et al. (1991). Family psychoeducation, social skills training, and maintenance chemotherapy in the aftercare treatment of schizophrenia. *Archives of General Psychiatry, 48*, 340–347.

Holden, C. (1980). Identical twins reared apart. *Science, 207*, 1323–1328.

Holden, C. (1987a). The genetics of personality. *Science, 237*, 598–601.

Holden, C. (1987b). OTA cites financial disaster of Alzheimer's. *Science, 236*, 253.

Holden, C. (1990). Head Start enters adulthood. *Science, 247*, 1400–1402.

Holland, A., & Andre, T. (1994). The relationship of self-esteem to selected personal and environmental resources of adolescents. *Adolescence, 29*, 345–360.

Hollander, H. (1979). Historical review and clinical relevance of real-time observations of fetal movement. *Contributions to Gynecology and Obstetrics, 6*, 26–28.

Hollister, L. E. (1988). Marijuana and immunity. *Journal of Psychoactive Drugs, 20*, 3–8.

Hollon, S. D., Shelton, R. C., & Loosen, P. T. (1991). Cognitive therapy and pharmacotherapy for depression. *Journal of Consulting and Clinical Psychology, 59*, 88–99.

Holloway, J. D. (2003). U.S. mental health system needs less stigma, more consumer input. *Monitor on Psychology, 34*(8), 20–22.

Holloway, J. D. (2004a). Unhealthy behaviors cause approximately half of U.S. deaths. *Monitor on Psychology, 35*(5), 15.

Holloway, J. D. (2004b). Louisiana grants psychologists prescriptive authority. *Monitor on Psychology, 35*(6), 20–21.

Holloway, K. S., & Domjan, M. (1993). Sexual approach conditioning: Unconditional stimulus factors. *Journal of Experimental Psychology: Animal Behavior Processes, 19*, 38–46.

Holloway, M. (1999). Flynn's effect. *Scientific American, 280*, 37–38.

Holmes, D. S. (1994). Is there evidence for repression? Doubtful. *Harvard Mental Health Letter, 10*(12), 5–6.

Holmes, T. H., & Rahe, R. H. (1967). The Social Readjustment Rating Scale. *Journal of Psychosomatic Research, 11*, 213–218.

Holowchak, M. A. (2002). *Philosophy of sport: Critical readings, crucial issues.* Upper Saddle River, NJ: Prentice Hall.

Holtkamp, K., Hebeband, J., Mika, C., Grzella, I., Heer, M., Heussen, N., et al. (2003). The effects of therapeutically induced weight gain on plasma leptin levels in patients with anorexia nervosa. *Journal of Psychiatric Research, 37*, 165–169.

Holtzman, W. H. (2001). International psychology. In W. E. Craighead & C. D. Nemeroff (Eds.), *The Corsini encyclopedia of psychology and behavioral sciences* (3rd ed., Vol. 2, pp. 781–783). New York: Wiley.

Holtzworth-Munroe, A. (1995, August). Marital violence. *The Harvard Mental Health Letter*, pp. 4–6.

Honkalampi, K., Hintikka, J., Laukkanen, E., Lehtonen, J., & Viinamaki, H. (2001). Alexithymia and depression: A prospective study of patients with major depressive disorder. *Psychosomatics: Journal of Consultation Liaison Psychiatry, 42*, 229–234.

Honkalampi, K., Koivumaa-Honkanen, H., Tanskanen, A., Hintikka, J., Lehtonen, J., & Vinamaeki, H. (2001). Why do alexithymic features appear to be stable? *Psychotherapy and Psychosomatic, 70*, 247–253.

Honma, K., Haskimoto, S., Nakao, M., & Honma, S. (2003). Period and phase adjustments of human circadian rhythms in the real world. *Journal of Biological Rhythms, 18*(3), 261–270.

Honts, C. R., & Kircher, J. C. (1994). Mental and physical countermeasures reduce the accuracy of polygraph tests. *Journal of Applied Psychology, 79*(2), 252–259.

Hooper, J., & Teresi, D. (1987). *The 3-pound universe.* New York: Dell.

Hooper, J. F., & McLearen, A. M. (2002). Does the insanity defense have a legitimate role? *Psychiatric Times, XIX*(4).

Hopkins, B., & Westra, T. (1988). Maternal handling and motor development: An intracultural study. *Genetic, Social, and General Psychology Monographs, 14*, 377–420.

Hopkins, D. R., Murrah, B., Hoeger, W. W. K., & Rhodes, R. C. (1990). Effect of low-impact aerobic dance on the functional fitness of elderly women. *Gerontologist, 30*, 189–192.

Hopkins, H. S., & Gelenberg, A. J. (1994). Treatment for bipolar disorder: How far have we come? *Psychopharmacology Bulletin, 30*, 27–38.

Hoptman, M. J., & Davidson, R. J. (1994). How and why do the two hemispheres interact? *Psychological Bulletin, 116*, 195–219.

Hopwood, N. J., Kelch, R. P., Hale, P. M., Mendes, T. M., Foster, C. M., & Beitins, I. Z. (1990). The onset of human puberty: Biological and environmental factors. In J. Bancroft & J. M. Reinisch (Eds.), *Adolescence and puberty.* New York: Oxford University Press.

Hordes, D. (2000, August). *The workplace.* Paper presented at the meeting of the International Coalition Against Sexual Harassment. Washington, DC.

Horgan, J. (1993). Eugenics revisited. *Scientific American, 268*, 122–131.

Horn, J. L., & Donaldson, G. (1976). On the myth of intellectual decline in adulthood. *American Psychologist, 31*, 701–719.

Horn, J. L., & Donaldson, G. (1980). Cognitive development II: Adulthood development of human abilities. In O. G. Brian & J. Kagan (Eds.), *Constancy and change in human development.* Cambridge, MA: Harvard University Press.

Horn, J. L., & Hofer, S. M. (1992). Major abilities and development in the adult period. In R. J. Sternberg & C. A. Berg (Eds.), *Intellectual development.* New York: Cambridge University Press.

Hornstein, S. L., Brown, A. S., & Mulligan, N. W. (2003). Long-term flashbulb memory for learning of Princess Diana's death. *Memory, 11*(3), 293–306.

Horowitz, A. V., Videon, T. M., Schmitz, M. F., & Davis, D. (2003). Rethinking twins and environments: Possible social sources for assumed genetic influences in twin research. *Journal of Health and Social Behavior, 44*, 111–129.

Horwitz, A. B., & White, H. R. (1998). The relationship of cohabitation and mental health: A study of a young adult cohort. *Journal of Marriage and the Family, 60*, 505–514.

Hossain, Z., & Roopnarine, J. L. (1994). African-American fathers' involvement with infants: Relationship to their functioning style, support, education, and income. *Infant Behavior and Development, 17*, 175–184.

Houts, A. C. (1991). Nocturnal enuresis as a biobehavioral problem. *Behavior Therapy, 22*, 133–151.

Hovland, C. I., Janis, I. K., & Kelley, H. H. (1953). *Communication and persuasion.* New Haven, CT: Yale University Press.

Howard, K. I., Kopta, S. M., Krause, M. S., & Orlinsky, D. E. (1986). The dose-effect relationship in psychotherapy. *American Psychologist, 41*, 159–164.

Hoyenga, K. B., & Hoyenga, K. T. (1984) *Motivational explanations of behavior.* Belmont, CA: Brooks/Cole.

Hoyer, W. J., & Rybash, J. M. (1994). Characterizing adult cognitive development. *Journal of Adult Development, 1*, 7–12.

Hsu, B., Kling, A., Kessler, C., Knapke, K., Dienfenbach, P., & Elias, J. E. (1994). Gender differences in sexual fantasy and behavior in a college population: A ten-year replication. *Journal of Sex and Marital Therapy, 20*(2), 103–118.

Hsu, L. K. G. (1989). The gender gap in eating disorders: Why are the eating disorders more common among women? *Clinical Psychology Review, 9*, 393–407.

Hsu, L. K. G. (1990). *Eating disorders.* New York: Guilford Press.

Huesmann, L. R. (1986). Psychological processes promoting the relation between exposure to media violence and aggressive behavior by the viewer. *Journal of Social Issues, 42*, 125–139.

Huesmann, L. R., Moise-Titus, J., Podolski, C. L., & Eron, L. (2003). Longitudinal relations between children's exposure to TV violence and their aggressive and violent behavior in young adulthood: 1977–1992. *Developmental Psychology, 39*, 201–221.

Huettel, S. A., Song, A. W., & McCarthy, G. (2004). *Magnetic resonance imaging.* Sunderland, MA: Sinauer Associates.

Huffman, T., Chang, K., Rausch, P., & Schaffer, N. (1994). Gender differences and factors related to the disposition toward cohabitation. *Family Therapy, 21*, 171–184.

Hughes, F. P., & Noppe, L. D. (1991). *Human development across the life span.* New York: Macmillan.

Hughes, H. C., Nozawa, G., & Kitterle, F. (1996). Global precedence, spatial frequency channels, and the statistics of natural images. *Journal of Cognitive Neuroscience, 8*, 197–203.

Hughes, J., Smith, T. W., Kosterlitz, H. W., Fothergill, L. A., Morgan, B. A., & Morris, H. R. (1975). Identification of two related pentapeptides from the brain with the potent opiate agonist activity. *Nature, 258*, 577–579.

Hull, C. L. (1943). *Principles of behavior.* New York: Appleton-Century-Crofts.

Hull, C. L. (1952). *A behavior system.* New York: Appleton.

Humphreys, G. W., & Mueller, H. (2000). A search asymmetry reversed by figure-ground assignment. *Psychological Science, 11*, 196–201.

Humphreys, K., Marcus, S., Stewart, E., & Oliva, E. (2004). Expanding self-help group participation in culturally diverse urban areas: Media approaches to leveraging referent power. *Journal of Community Psychology, 32*, 413–424.

Hunt, E. (1995). The role of intelligence in modern society. *American Scientist, 83*, 356–368.

Hunt, E., & Agnoli, F. (1991). The Whorfian hypothesis. A cognitive psychology perspective. *Psychological Review, 98*, 377–389.

Hur, Y. M., Bouchard, T. J., Jr., & Lykken, D. T. (1998). Genetic and environmental influences on morningness-eveningness. *Personality and Individual Differences, 25*, 917–925.

Hurtz, G. M., & Donovan, J. J. (2000). Personality and job performance: The big five revisited. *Journal of Applied Psychology, 85*, 869–879.

Huston, A. C., Donnerstein, E., Fairchild, H., Feshbach, N. D., Katz, P. A., Murray, J. P., et al. (1992). *Big world, small screen: The role of television in American society.* Lincoln: University of Nebraska Press.

Hyde, J. S. (1984a). Children's understanding of sexist language. *Developmental Psychology, 20*, 697–706.

Hyde, J. S. (1984b). How large are gender differences in aggression? A developmental meta-analysis. *Developmental Psychology, 20*, 722–736.

Hyde, J. S. (1994). Can meta-analysis make feminist transformations in psychology? *Psychology of Women Quarterly, 18*, 451–462.

Hyde, J. S., & DeLamater, J. (1999). *Understanding human sexuality.* New York: McGraw-Hill.

Hyde, J. S., & Linn, M. C. (Eds.). (1986). *The psychology of gender: Advances through meta-analysis.* Baltimore: Johns Hopkins University Press.

Hyde, J. S., & Linn, M. C. (1988). Gender differences in verbal ability: A meta-analysis. *Psychological Bulletin, 104*, 53–69.

Hyde, J. S., Fennema, E., & Lamon, S. J. (1990). Gender differences in mathematics performance: A meta-analysis. *Psychological Bulletin, 107*, 139–155.

Hyde, J. S., & Plant, E. A. (1995). Magnitude of psychological gender differences: Another side to the story. *American Psychologist, 50*, 159–161.

Hyde, T. S., & Jenkins, J. J. (1969). Differential effects of incidental tasks on the organization of recall of a list of highly associated words. *Journal of Experimental Psychology, 82*, 472–481.

Hyman, R. (1989). *The elusive quarry: A scientific appraisal of psychical research.* Buffalo, NY: Prometheus.

Hyman, R. (1994). Anomaly or artifact? Comments on Ben and Honorton. *Psychological Bulletin, 115,* 19–24.

Hyman, S. E. (1999). Introduction to the complex genetics of mental disorders. *Biological Psychiatry, 45*(5), 518–521.

Iacono, W. G., & Lykken, D. T. (1997). The validity of the lie detector: Two surveys of scientific opinion. *Journal of Applied Psychology, 82.* 426–433.

IInhelder, B., & Piaget, J. (1958). *The growth of logical thinking from childhood to adolescence.* New York: Little, Brown.

Ilan, A. B., Smith, M. E., & Gevins, A. (2004). Effects of marijuana on neurophysiological signals of working and episodic memory. *Psychopharmacology, 176*(20), 214–222.

Impett, E. A., & Peplau, L. A. (2002). Why some women consent to unwanted sex with a dating partner: Insights from attachment theory. *Psychology of Women Quarterly, 26,* 360–370.

Ingram, V. (2003). Alzheimer's disease. *American Scientist, 91,* 312–321.

Insel, T. R. (2000). Toward a neurobiology of attachment. *Review of General Psychology, 4,* 176–185.

Institute for Women's Policy Research (1997, January). *The wage gap: Women's and men's earnings* (briefing paper). Washington, DC: Author.

Intons-Peterson, M. J., & Reddel, M. (1984). What do people ask about a neonate? *Developmental Psychology, 20,* 358–359.

Iqbal, M. M., Tahman, A. T., Husain, Z., Mahmud, S. Z., Ryan, W. G., & Feldman, J. M. (2003). Clozapine: A clinical review of adverse effects and management. *Annals of Clinical Psychiatry, 15,* 33–48.

Irle, E., et al. (1998). Obsessive-compulsive disorder and ventromedial frontal sessions: Clinical and neuropsychological findings. *American Journal of Psychiatry, 155,* 255–263.

Isaacs, W., Thomas, J., & Goldiamond, I. (1960). Application of operant conditioning to reinstate verbal behavior in psychotics. *Journal of Speech and Hearing Disorders, 25,* 8–12.

Isen, A. M., Daubman, K. A., & Nowicki, G. P. (1987). Positive affect facilitates creative problem solving. *Journal of Personality and Social Psychology, 52,* 1122–1131.

Iverson, L. L. (2000). *The science of marijuana.* Oxford: Oxford University Press.

Izard, C. E. (1990). Facial expression and the regulation of emotion. *Journal of Personality and Social Psychology, 58,* 487–498.

Izard, C. E. (1994). Innate and universal facial expressions: Evidence from developmental and cross-cultural research. *Psychological Bulletin, 115,* 288–299.

Izard, C. E., Libero, D. Z., Putnam, P., & Haynes, O. M. (1993). Stability of emotion experiences and their relations to traits of personality. *Journal of Personality and Social Psychology, 64,* 847–860.

Jacklin, C. N. (1989). Female or male: Issues of gender. *American Psychologist, 44,* 127–133.

Jackson, L. A., von Eye, A., & Biocca, F. (2003). Children and Internet use: Social, psychological and academic consequences for low-income children. *APA Online Psychological Science Agenda, 17*(2).

Jackson, R. A., & Newman, M. A. (2004). Sexual harassment in the federal workplace revisited: Influences on sexual harassment by gender. *Public Administration Review, 64*(6), 705–717.

Jacobs, D. M., Rakitin, B. C., Zubin, N. R., Ventura, P. R., & Stern, Y. (2001). Cognitive correlates of mnemonics usage and verbal recall memory in old age. *Neuropsychiatry, Neuropsychology, and Behavioral Neurology, 14,* 15–22.

Jambori, S., & Sallay, H. (2003). Parenting styles, aims, attitudes, and future orientation of adolescents and young adults. *Review of Psychology, 10,* 131–140.

James, D., & Drakich, J. (1993). Understanding gender differences in amount of talk: A critical review of research. In D. Tannen (Ed.), *Gender and conversational interaction* (pp. 281–312). New York: Oxford University Press.

James, K., Brodersen, M., & Jacob, E. (2004). Workplace affect and workplace creativity: A review and preliminary model. *Human Performance, 17,* 169–194.

James, S. P. (1993). Neglected images of policing: Looking beyond the rhetoric of performance assessment. *Policing and Society, 3,* 73–89.

Jamieson, K. M., & Flanagan, T. J. (1988). *Sourcebook of criminal justice statistics, 1988.* Washington, DC: U.S. Department of Justice, Bureau of Justice Statistics.

Jang, K. L., McCrae, R. R., Angleitner, A., Riemann, R., & Livesley, W. J. (1998). Heritability of facet-level traits in a cross-cultural twin sample: Support for a hierarchical model of personality. *Journal of Personality and Social Psychology, 74,* 1556–1565.

Janis, I. L. (1972). *Victims of groupthink.* Boston: Houghton Mifflin.

Janis, I. L. (1982). *Groupthink: Psychological studies of policy decisions and fiascoes* (2nd ed.). Boston: Houghton Mifflin.

Javitt, D. C., & Coyle, J. T. (2004). Decoding schizophrenia. *Scientific American,* 48–55.

Jefferson, D. J. (2005). America's most dangerous drug. *Newsweek* article retrieved August 1, 2005, from www.msnbc.msn.com/id/8770112/site/newsweek.

Jenike, M. A., (1998). Neurosurgical treatment of obsessive-compulsive disorder. *British Journal of psychiatry, 173*(Suppl 35), 79–90.

Jenkins, J. G., & Dallenbach, K. M. (1924). Obliviscence during sleeping and waking. *American Journal of Psychology, 35,* 605–612.

Jennison, K. M. (2004). The short-term effects and unintended long-term consequences of binge drinking in college: A 10-year follow-up study. *American Journal of Drug and Alcohol Abuse, 30*(3), 659–684.

Jensen, A. R. (1969). How much can we boost IQ and scholastic achievement? *Harvard Educational Review, 39,* 1–123.

Jensen, L. A., Arnett, J. J., Feldman, F. S., & Cauffman, E. (2002). It's wrong, but everybody does it: Academic dishonesty among high school and college students. *Contemporary Educational Psychology, 27*(2), 209–228.

Jensen, M. M. (2004). *Introduction to emotional and behavioral disorders: Recognizing and managing problems in the classroom.* Upper Saddle River, NJ: Pearson Merrill Prentice Hall.

John, O. P. (1990). The search for basic dimensions of personality. In P. McReynolds, J. C. Rosen, & G. J. Chelune (Eds.), *Advances in psychological assessment* (Vol. 7, pp. 1–37). New York: Plenum.

Johns, M., Schmader, T., & Martens, A. (2005). Knowing is half the battle: Teaching stereotype threat as a means of improving women's math performance. *Psychological Science, 16,* 175–179.

Johnson, L. D., O'Malley, P. M., Bachman, J. G., & Schulenberg, J. E. (2005). *Monitoring the Future national results on adolescent drug use: Overview of key findings, 2004* (NIH Publication No. 05-5726). Bethesda, MD: National Institute on Drug Abuse.

Johnson, S., & Lebow, J. (2000). The "Coming of Age" of couple therapy. *Journal of Marital and Family Therapy, 26,* 23–38.

Johnson, S. L., & Roberts, J. E. (1995). Life events and bipolar disorder: Implications from biological theories. *Psychological Bulletin, 117,* 434–449.

Johnston, J. C., & McClelland, J. L. (1973). Visual factors in word perception. *Perception and Psychophysics, 14,* 365–370.

Johnston, J. C., & McClelland, J. L. (1974). Perception of letters in words: Seek not and ye shall find. *Science, 184,* 1192–1194.

Johnston, L. D., O'Malley, P. M., & Bachman, J. G. (1996). *Natinal survey results on drug use from the Monitoring the Future study, 1975–1995* (NIH Publication No. 96–4139). Rockville, MD: National Institute of Health and Human Services.

Johnston, M. V. (2004). Clinical disorders of brain plasticity. *Brain & Development, 26*(2), 73–80.

Johnstone, K. A., & Page, A. C. (2004). Attention to phobic stimuli during exposure: The effect of distraction on anxiety reduction, self-efficacy and perceived control. *Behaviour Research and Therapy, 42,* 249–275.

Jones, K. L., & Smith, D. W. (1973). Recognition of the fetal alcohol syndrome in early infancy. *Lancet, 2,* 999–1001.

Jones, M. C. (1924). A laboratory study of fear: The case of Peter. *Journal of Genetic Psychology, 31,* 308–315.

Joy, J. E., Watson, S. J., Jr., & Benson, J. A. (Eds.). (1999). *Marijuana and medicine: Assessing the science base.* Washington, DC: National Academy Press.

Joyner, A. L., & Guillemot, F. (1994). Gene targeting and development of the nervous system. *Current Opinion in Neurobiology, 4,* 37–42.

Judd, L. L. (1997). The clinical course of unipolar major depressive disorders. *Archives of General Psychiatry, 54,* 989–991.

Judge, T. A., Heller, D., & Mount, M. K. (2002). Five-factor model of personality and job satisfaction: A meta-analysis. *Journal of Applied Psychology, 87,* 530–541.

Jung, J. (2001). *Psychology of alcohol and other drugs.* Thousand Oaks, CA: Sage.

Junginger, J. (1997). Fetishism. In D. R. Laws & W. T. O'Donohue (Eds.), *Handbook of sexual deviance: Theory and application.* New York: Guilford Press.

Kabillo, E. (Producer & Director). (1998). *A hole in the head* [film]. (Available from International Trepanation Advocacy Group, P.O. Box 65, Wernersville, PA 19565.

Kagan, J., Kearsley, R. B., & Zelazo, P. R. (1978). *Infancy: Its place in human development.* Cambridge, MA: Harvard University Press.

Kagan, J., Reznick, J. S., & Snidman, N. (1987). The physiology and psychology of behavioral inhibition in children. *Child Development, 58,* 1459–1473.

Kahill, S. (1986). Relationship of burnout among professional psychologists to professional expectations and social support. *Psychological Reports, 59,* 1043–1051.

Kahneman, D., & Tversky, A. (1973). On the psychology of prediction. *Psychological Review, 80,* 237–251.

Kahneman, D., & Tversky, A. (2000). *Choice, values, and frames.* New York: Cambridge University Press.

Kail, R. V. (2004). *Children and their development* (3rd ed.). Upper Saddle River, NJ: Pearson Prentice Hall.

Kail, R. V., & Cavanaugh, J. C. (2000). *Human development: A lifespan view* (2nd ed.). Belmont, CA: Wadsworth.

Kail, R. V., & Cavanaugh, J. C. (2004). *Human development: A lifespan view* (3rd ed.). Belmont, CA: Wadsworth/Thompson.

Kalat, J. W. (1995). *Biological psychology* (5th ed.). Pacific Grove, CA: Brooks/Cole.

Kalat, J. W. (2001). *Biological psychology* (7th ed.). Belmont, CA: Wadsworth.

Kalish, R. A. (1985). The social context of death and dying. In R. H. Binstock & E. Shanas (Eds.), *Handbook of aging in the social sciences.* New York: Van Nostrand Reinhold.

Kamin, L. J. (1969). Predictability, surprise, attention, and conditioning. In B. Campbill & R. Church (Eds.), *Punishment and aversive behavior.* New York: Appleton-Century-Crofts.

Kamin, L. J. (1982). Mental testing and immigration. *American Psychologist, 37*(1), 97–98.

Kamin, L. J. (1994). Behind the curve (book review of *The Bell Curve*). *Scientific American, 241,* 67–76.

Kamin, L. J. (1995). Behind the curve. *Scientific American, 272,* 99–103.

Kang, D-H. (2003). Psychoneuroimmunology in nursing research: A biobehavioral model. *Research in Nursing and Health, 26,* 421–423.

Kaplan, M. F., Wanshula, L. T., & Zanna, M. P. (1992). Time pressure and information integration in social judgment: The effect of the need for structure. In O. Svenson & J. Maule (Eds.), *Time pressure and stress in human judgment and decision making.* Cambridge: Cambridge University Press.

Kaplan-Estrin, M., Jacobson, S. W., & Jacobson, J. L. (1994). Alternative approaches to clustering and scoring the Bayley Infant Behavior Record. *Infant Behavior and Development, 17,* 149–157.

Karu, S. J., & Williams, K. D. (1993). Social loafing: A meta-analytic review and theoretical integration. *Journal of Personality and Social Psychology, 65,* 681–706.

Kassin, S. M., & Liechel. (1996). The social psychology of false confessions: Compliance, internalization, and confabulation. *Psychological Science, 7*(3), 125–128.

Kastenbaum, R. J. (1995). *Death, society, and human experience* (5th ed.). Boston: Allyn & Bacon.

Katainen, S., Raikkonen, K., & Keltikanjas-Jarbinen, L. (1998). Development of temperament, childhood temperament, and the mother's childrearing attitudes as predictors of adolescent temperament in a nine-year follow-up study. *Journal of Research on Adolescents, 8,* 485–509.

Katsurada, E., & Sugihara, Y. (1999). A preliminary validation of the Ben Sex Role Inventory in Japanese culture. *Journal of Cross-Cultural Psychology, 30,* 641–645.

Kazdin, A. E. (1989). *Behavior modification in applied settings* (4th ed.). Pacific Grove, CA: Brooks/Cole.

Kazdin, A. E., & Benjet, C. (2003). Spanking children: Evidence and issues. *Current Directions in Psychological Science, 12,* 99–103.

Kebbell, M. R., Milne, R., & Wagstaff, G. F. (1999). The cognitive interview: A survey of its forensic effectiveness. *Psychology, Public Policy, and Law, 5,* 101–115.

Keefauver, S. P., & Guilleminault, C. (1994). *Sleep terrors and sleepwalking.* In M. Kryger, T. Roth, & W. C. Dement (Eds.), *Principles and practices of sleep medicine* (2nd ed., pp. 567–573). Philadelphia: Saunders.

Keel, P. K. (2005). *Eating disorders.* Upper Saddle River, NJ: Pearson Prentice Hall.

Keel, P. K., & Klump, K. L. (2003). Are eating disorders culture-bound syndromes? Implications for conceptualizing their etiology. *Psychological Bulletin, 129,* 747–769.

Keeling, R. P. (1987). Effects of AIDS on young Americans. *Medical Aspects of Human Sexuality, 21,* 22–33.

Kelley, H. H. (1950). The warm-cold variable in first impressions of persons. *Journal of Personality, 18,* 431–439.

Kelley, H. H. (1967). Attribution theory in social psychology. In D. Levine (Ed.), *Nebraska symposium on motivation* (Vol. 15). Lincoln: University of Nebraska Press.

Kelley, H. H. (1971). *Attribution in social interaction.* Morristown, NJ: General Learning Press.

Kelley, M. L., & Parsons, B. (2000). Sexual harassment in the 1990s. *Journal of Higher Education, 71,* 548–568.

Kelly, J. R., & Karu, S. J. (1999). Group decision making: The effects of initial preferences and time pressure. *Personality and Social Psychology Bulletin, 25,* 1342–1354.

Keltner, D., & Haidt, J. (1999). Social functions of emotions at four levels of analysis. *Cognition and Emotion, 13,* 505–521.

Kelvin, P., & Jarrett, J. A. (1985). *Unemployment: Its social and psychological effects.* Cambridge: Cambridge University Press.

Kenchaiah, A., Evans, J. C., Levy, D., Wilson, P. W. F., Benjamin, E. J., Larson, M. G., et al. (2002). Obesity and the risk of heart failure. *New England Journal of Medicine, 347*(5), 305–313.

Kenneday, K., Nowak, S., Raghuraman, R., Thomas, J., & Davis, S. F. (2000). Academic dishonesty and distance learning: Student and faculty views. *College Student Journal, 34,* 309–314.

Kennedy, J. (2003). Psychotropic drug use in young patients is rising. *Monitor on Psychology, 34*(4), 13.

Kenrick, D. T., & Funder, D. C. (1990). Profiting from controversy: Lessons from the person–situation debate. *American Psychologist, 43,* 23–34.

Kerr, N. L., & Tindale, R. S. (2004). Group performance and decision making. *Annual Review of Psychology, 55,* 623–655.

Kersting, K. (2003). Religion and spirituality in the treatment room. *Monitor on Psychology, 34*(11), 40–42.

Kersting, K. (2004). A new approach to complicated grief. *Monitor on Psychology, 35*(10), 51–52.

Kessler, R. C., Demler, O., Frank, R. G., Olfson, M., Pincus, H. A., Walters, E. E., et al. (2005). Prevalence and treatment of mental disorders, 1990 to 2003. *New England Journal of Medicine, 352*(24), 2515–2523.

Kessler, R. C., McGonagle, K. A., Zhao, S., Nelson, C. B., Hughes, M., Eshleman, S., et al. (1994). Lifetime and 12-month prevalence of *DSM-III-R* psychiatric disorders in the United States. *Archives of General Psychiatry, 51,* 8–19.

Kidwell, B., & Jewell, R. D. (2003). The moderated influence of internal control: An examination across health-related behaviors. *Journal of Consumer Psychology, 13,* 377–386.

Kiecolt-Glaser, J. K., Dura, J. R., Speicher, C. E., Trask, O. J., & Glaser, R. (1991). Spousal caregivers of de-

mentia victims: Longitudinal changes in immunity and health. *Psychosomatic Medicine, 53,* 345–362.

Kiecolt-Glaser, J. K., & Glaser, R. (2001). Stress and immunity: Age enhances the risks. *Current Directions in Psychological Science, 10,* 18–20.

Kihlstrom, J. F. (1985). Hypnosis. *Annual Review of Psychology, 36,* 385–418.

Killan, K. D., & Verkerk, C. (2004). Inside the American couple: New thinking, new challenge. *Family Relations: Interdisciplinary Journal of Applied Family Studies, 53,* 118–119.

Kim, U., & Chun, M. B. J. (1994). Educational "success" of Asian Americans: An indigenous perspective. *Journal of Applied Developmental Psychology, 15,* 329–339.

Kim, Y. S. E. (2003). Understanding Asian American clients: Problems and possibilities for cross-cultural counseling with special reference to Korean Americans. *Journal of Ethnic and Cultural Diversity in Social Work, 12,* 91–114.

Kimball, C. T. (2000). *Workplace health and safety sourcebook.* Detroit: Omnigraphics.

Kimball, M. M. (1989). A new perspective on women's math achievement. *Psychological Bulletin, 105,* 198–214.

Kimura, D. (1992). Sex differences in the brain. *Scientific American, 267,* 118–125.

Kimura, D. (1999). *Sex and cognition.* Cambridge, MA: MIT Press.

King, B. M. (2002). *Human sexuality today* (4th ed.). Upper Saddle River, NJ: Prentice Hall.

King, B. M. (2005). *Human sexuality today* (5th ed.). Upper Saddle River, NJ: Pearson Prentice Hall.

King, D. L. (2001). Grouping and assimilation in perception, memory, and conditioning. *Review of General Psychology, 5,* 23–43.

Kinney, H. C., Filiano, J. J., Sleeper, L. A., Mandell, F., Valdes-Dapena, M., & White, W. F. (1995). Decreased muscarinic receptor binding in the arcuate nucleus in sudden infant death syndrome. *Science, 269,* 1446–1450.

Kinsey, A. C., Pomeroy, W. B., & Martin, C. E. (1948). *Sexual behavior in the human male.* Philadelphia: Saunders.

Kinsey, A. C., Pomeroy, W. B., & Martin, C. E. (1953). *Sexual behavior in the human female.* Phildelphia: Saunders.

Kirkpatrick, O. L. (1976). Evaluation of training. In B. L. Craig (Ed.), *Training and development handbook* (2nd ed., pp. 301–319). New York: McGraw-Hill.

Kixmiller, J. S., Wann, D. L., Weaver, K. A., Grover, C. A., & Davis, S. F. (1987). Effect of elaboration levels on content comprehension. *Bulletin of the Psychonomic Society, 26,* 32–33.

Klag, M. J., Ford, D. E., Mead, L. A., He, J., Whelton, P. K., Liang, K.-Y., et al. (1993). Serum cholesterol in young men and subsequent cardiovascular disease. *New England Journal of Medicine, 328,* 313–318.

Klare, R. (1990). Ghosts make news: How four newspapers report psychic phenomena. *Skeptical Inquirer, 14,* 363–370.

Klatsky, A. L. (2003). Drink to your health? *Scientific American, 291,* 75–81.

Kleinknecht, R. A., Dinnel, D. L., Kleinknecht, E. A., Hiruma, N., & Harada, N. (1997). Cultural factors in social anxiety: A comparison of social phobia symptoms and taijin kyofusho. *Journal of Anxiety Disorders, 11,* 157–177.

Kleim, J. A., Vij, K., Ballard, D. H., & Greenough, W. T. (1997). Learning-dependent synaptic modifications in the cerebellar cortex of the adult rat persist for at least four weeks. *Journal of Neuroscience, 17,* 717–721.

Klein, D. F. (1993). False suffocation alarms, spontaneous panics, and related conditions: An integrative hypothesis. *Archives of General Psychiatry, 50,* 306–317.

Klein, S. B. (2000). *Biological psychology.* Upper Saddle River, NJ: Prentice Hall.

Kleinke, C. L. (1986). *Meeting and understanding people.* New York: Freeman.

Kleinke, C. L. (1991). *Coping with life challenges.* Pacific Grove, CA: Brooks/Cole.

Kleinke, C. L., & Dean, G. D. (1990). Evaluation of men and women receiving positive and negative responses with various acquaintance strategies. *Journal of Social Behavior and Personality, 5,* 369–377.

Kleinke, C. L., Meeker, F. B., & Staneski, R. A. (1986). Preference for opening lines: Comparing ratings by men and women. *Sex Roles, 15,* 585–600.

Kleinman, J. C., Pierre, M. B., Jr., Madans, J. H., Land, G. H., & Schramm, W. F. (1988). The effects of maternal smoking on fetal and infant mortality. *American Journal of Epidemiology, 127,* 274–282.

Klerman, G. L., Weissman, M. M., Markowitz, J., Glick, I., Wilner, P. J., Mason, B., et al. (1994). Medication and psychotherapy. In A. E. Bergin & S. L. Garfield (Eds.), *Handbook of psychotherapy and behavior change* (4th ed., pp. 734–782). New York: Wiley.

Klinger, E. (1990). *Daydreaming: Using waking fantasy and imagery for self-knowledge and creativity.* Los Angeles: Tarcher.

Kluger, J. (2001, April 2). Fear not! *Time,* 52–62.

Knapp, M. L., & Hall, J. A. (1997). *Nonverbal communication in human interaction.* Orlando, FL: Harcourt Brace.

Knight, J. (2004). The truth about lying. *Nature, 428,* 692–694.

Knowles, J. A., & Weissman, M. M. (1995). Panic disorder and agoraphobia. In J. M. Oldham & M. B. Riba (Eds.), *Review of psychiatry* (Vol. 14, pp. 383–404). Washington, DC: American Psychiatric Association.

Kobasa, S. C. (1982). Commitment and coping in stress resistance among lawyers. *Journal of Personality and Social Psychology, 42,* 707–717.

Kohlberg, L. (1966). A cognitive-developmental analysis of children's sex role concepts and attitudes. In E. E. Maccoby (Ed.), *The development of sex differences* (pp. 82–173). Stanford, CA: Stanford University Press.

Kohlberg, L. (1973). Continuities in childhood and adult moral development revisited. In P. Baltes & K. W. Schaie (Eds.), *Life-span development psychology: Personality and socialization.* San Diego, CA: Academic Press.

Köhler, W. (1927). *The mentality of apes.* San Diego, CA: Harcourt Brace.

Kohnken, G., Milne, R., Memon, A., & Bull, R. (1999). The cognitive interview: A meta-analysis. *Psychology, Crime, and Law, 5,* 3–27.

Kolb, B., & Whishaw, J. Q. (1990). *Fundamentals of human neuropsychology* (3rd ed.). New York: Freeman.

Konno, K., Katsumata, Y., Arai, A., & Tamashiro, H. (2004). Functional status and active life expectancy among senior citizens in a small town in Japan. *Archives of Gerontology and Geriatrics, 38,* 153–166.

Kontos, S., Hsu, H., & Dunn, L. (1994). Children's cognitive and social competence in child-care centers and family day-care homes. *Journal of Applied Developmental Psychology, 15,* 387–411.

Kopta, S. M., Howard, K. I., Lowry, J. L., & Beuther, L. E. (1994). Patterns of symptomatic recovery in psychotherapy. *Journal of Counseling and Clinical Psychology, 62,* 1009–1016.

Korner, A., Zeanah, C., Lindin, J., Berkowitz, R., Krapmen, H., & Agras, W. (1985). The relation between neonatal and later activity and temperament. *Child Development, 56,* 38–42.

Kottler, J., & Brown, R. (2000). *Introduction to therapeutic counseling: Voices from the field* (4th ed.). Belmont, CA: Wadsworth.

Kowalski, R. M. (1993). Inferring sexual interest from behavioral cues: Effects of gender and sexually relevant attitudes. *Sex Roles, 29,* 13–36.

Kracke, W. H. (1993). Cultural aspects of dreaming. In M. A. Carsakadon (Ed.), *Encyclopedia of sleep and dreaming* (pp. 151–155). New York: Macmillan.

Kral, A., Hartman, R., Tillein, J., Heid, S., & Klinke, R. (2002). Hearing after congenital deafness: Central auditory plasticity and sensory deprivation. *Cerebral Cortex, 12,* 797–807.

Kribbs, N. B. (1993). Siesta. In M. A. Carsakadon (Ed.), *Encyclopedia of sleep and dreaming* (pp. 544–545). New York: Macmillan.

Kring, A. M., & Gordon, A. H. (1998). Sex differences in emotion: Expression, experience, and physiology. *Journal of Personality and Social Psychology, 74,* 686–703.

Kübler-Ross, E. (1969). *On death and dying.* New York: Macmillan.

Kübler-Ross, E. (1975). *Death: The final stage of growth.* Upper Saddle River, NJ: Prentice Hall.

Kudo, E., & Numazaki, M. (2003). Explicit and direct self-serving bias in Japan. Reexamination of self-serving bias for success and failure. *Journal of Cross-Cultural Psychology, 34,* 511–521.

Kuhn, C., Swartzwelder, S., & Wilson, W. (2003). *Buzzed: The straight facts about the most used and abused drugs from alcohol to Ecstasy* (rev. ed.). New York: Norton.

Kulik, J. A., & Mahler, H. I. M. (1987). Effects of preoperative roommate assignment on preoperative anxiety and recovery from coronary-prone surgery. *Health Psychology, 6,* 525–543.

Kumpfer, K. L., & Alvarado, R. (2003). Family-strengthening approaches for the prevention of youth problem behaviors. *American Psychologist, 58,* 457–465.

Kunda, Z., & Oleson, K. C. (1997). When exceptions prove the rule: How extremity of deviance determines the impact of deviant examples on stereotypes. *Journal of Personality and Social Psychology, 72,* 965–979.

Kupfer, D. J., & Reynolds, C. F., III. (1992). Sleep and affective disorders. In E. S. Paykel (Ed.), *Handbook of affective disorders* (2nd ed., pp. 311–323). New York: Guilford Press.

Kurtz, Mothers of invention: Women in technology. *Indiana Business Review, 78*(3).

Lacayo, R. (1993, May 3). In the grip of a psychopath. *Time,* pp. 34–35.

Lachman, M. E. (2003). Development in midlife. *Annual Review of Psychology, 55,* 305–331.

Lackritz, E. M., Satten, G. A., Aberle-Grasse, J., Dodd, R. Y., Raimondi, V. P., Janssen, R. S., et al. (1995). Estimated risk of transmission of the human immunodeficiency virus by screened blood in the United States. *New England Journal of Medicine, 333,* 1721–1725.

Ladouceur, R., Talbot, F., & Dugas, M. J. (1997). Behavioral expressions of intolerance of uncertainty in worry. *Behavior Modification, 21,* 355–371.

Laffaldano, M. T., & Muchiosky, P. M. (1985). Job satisfaction and job performance: A meta-analysis. *Psychological Bulletin, 97,* 251–273.

Lajunen, T., Hakkarainen, P., & Summala, H. (1996). The ergonomics of road signs: Explicit and embedded speed limits. *Ergonomics, 39,* 1069–1083.

Lamaze, F. (1958). *Painless childbirth.* London: Burke.

Lamb, M. E., Frodi, A. M., Frodi, M., & Hwang, C. P. (1982). Characteristics of maternal and paternal behavior in traditional and nontraditional Swedish families. *International Journal of Behavioral Development, 5,* 131–141.

Lamb, M. E., Pleck, J. H., Charnov, E. L., & Levine, J. A. (1987). A biosocial perspective on paternal behavior and involvement. In J. B. Lancaster, J. Altmann, A. Rossi, & L. R. Sherrod (Eds.), *Parenting across the lifespan: Biosocial perspectives.* Hawthorne, NY: Aldine de Gruyter.

Lamberg, L. (1984). *The American Medical Association guide to better sleep.* New York: Random House.

Lamberg, L. (1994). *The American Medical Association guide to better sleep.* New York: Random House.

Lambert, M. J., & Bergin, A. E. (1994). The effectiveness of psychotherapy. In A. E. Bergin & S. L. Garfield (Ed.), *Handbook of psychotherapy and behavior change* (4th ed., pp. 142–189). New York: Wiley.

Lamiell, J. T. (2000). A periodic table of personality elements? The "Big Five" and trait "psychology" in critical perspective. *Journal of Theoretical and Philosophical Psychology, 20,* 1–24.

Laming, D. (1992). Analysis of short-term retention: Models for Brown-Peterson experiments. *Journal of Experimental Psychology: Learning, Memory, and Cognition, 18,* 1342–1365.

Landrum, E., Davis, S. F., & Landrum T. A. (2000). *The psychology major: Career options and strategies for success.* Upper Saddle River, NJ: Prentice Hall.

Landrum, R. E., & Davis, S. F. (2004). *The psychology major: Career options and strategies for success* (2nd ed.). Upper Saddle River, NJ: Prentice Hall.

Lane, S. D., Cherek, D. R., Lieving, L.M., & Tcheremissine, O. V. (2005). Marijuana effects on human forgetting functions. *Journal of Experimental Analysis of Behavior, 83,* 67–83.

Langer, E. J. (1977). The psychology of chance. *Journal of the Theory of Social Behavior, 7,* 346–357.

Langlois, J. H., Ritter, J. M., Roggman, L. A., & Vaughn, L. S. (1991). Facial diversity and infant preferences for attractive faces. *Developmental Psychology, 27,* 79–84.

Lapointe, A. E., Askew, J. M., & Meade, N. A. (1992). *Learning mathematics.* Princeton, NJ: Educational Testing Service.

Larkey, L. K., Day, S. H., Houtkooper, L., & Renger, R. (2003). Osteoporosis prevention: Knowledge and behavior in a southwestern community. *Journal of Community Health: The Publication for Health Promotion and Disease Prevention, 28,* 377–388.

Lashley, K. (1938). The thalamus and emotion. *Psychological Review, 45,* 42–61.

Lauber, J. K., & Kayten, P. J. (1988). Sleepiness, circadian dysrhythmia, and fatigue in transportation system accidents. *Sleep, 11,* 503–512.

Laumann, E. O., Gagnon, J. H., Michael, R. T., & Michaels, S. (1994). *The social organization of sexuality.* Chicago: University of Chicago Press.

Laumann, E. O., Paik, A., & Rosen, R. C. (1999). Sexual dysfunction in the United States: Prevalence and predictors. *Journal of the American Medical Association, 281,* 537–544.

Lawton, C. A. (2001). Gender and regional differences in spatial referents used in direction giving. *Sex Roles, 44,* 321–337.

Lazarus, R. S. (1994). Universal antecedents of the emotions. In P. Ekman & R. J. Davidson (Eds.), *The nature of emotion: Fundamental questions* (pp. 163–171). New York: Oxford University Press.

Lazarus, R. S., & Folkman, S. (1984). *Stress, appraisal and coping.* New York: Springer.

Leahy, T. H. (2001). *A history of modern psychology* (3rd ed.). Upper Saddle River, NJ: Prentice Hall.

Leahy, T. H., & Harris, R. J. (2001). *Learning and cognition* (5th ed.). Upper Saddle River, NJ: Prentice Hall.

Leahey, T. H. (2004). *A history of psychology: Main currents in psychological thought.* Upper Saddle River, NJ: Prentice Hall.

Learmonth, A. E., Lamberth, R., & Rovee-Collier, C. (2004). Generalization of deferred imitation during the first year of life. *Journal of Experimental Child Psychology, 88,* 297–318.

Leary, M. R., Britt, T. W., Cutlip, W. D., II, & Templeton, J. L. (1992). Social blushing. *Psychological Bulletin, 112,* 446–460.

Leary, M. R., & Meadows, S. (1991). Predictors, elicitors, and concomitants of social blushing. *Journal of Personality and Social Psychology, 60,* 254–262.

Leavenworth, A. E., Lamberth, R., & Rovee-Collier, C. (2004). Generalization of deferred imitation during the first year of life. *Journal of Experimental Child Psychology, 88,* 297–318.

LeBlanc, M. M., & Barling, J. (2004). Workplace aggression. *Current Directions in Psychological Science, 13,* 215–218.

LeBlanc, M. M., & Kalloway, E. K. (2002). Predictors and outcomes of workplace violence and aggression. *Journal of Applied Psychology, 87,* 444–453.

Lederer, R. (1991). *The miracle of language.* New York: Pocket Books.

LeDoux, J. E. (1994). Emotion, memory and the brain. *Scientific American, 270,* 50–57.

LeDoux, J. (1996). *The emotional brain.* New York: Simon & Schuster.

Lee, K. T., Mattson, S. N., & Riley, E. P. (2004). Classifying children with heavy prenatal alcohol exposure using measures of attention. *Journal of the International Neuropsychological Society, 10,* 271–277.

Lee, V. E., Brooks-Gunn, J., Schnur, E., & Liaw, F. (1990). Are Head Start effects sustained? A longitudinal follow-up comparison of disadvantaged children attending Head Start, no preschool, and other preschool programs. *Child Development, 61,* 495–507.

Legerstee, M. (1994). The role of familiarity and sound in the development of person and object permanence. *British Journal of Developmental Psychology, 12,* 455–468.

Lehtonen, K., Korhonen, T., & Korvenranta, H. (1994). Temperament and sleeping patterns in colicky infants during the first year of life. *Journal of Developmental and Behavioral Pediatrics, 15,* 416–420.

Leibenfult, E. (1996). Women with bipolar illness: Clinical and research issues. *American Journal of Psychiatry, 153,* 163–173.

Leitenberg, H., & Henning, K. (1995). Sexual fantasy. *Psychological Bulletin, 117,* 469–496.

Lemme, B. H. (1995). *Development in adulthood.* Needham Heights, MA: Allyn & Bacon.

Lemonick, M. D., & Park, A. (2001). The nun story. *Time, 157*(19), 54–59, 62, 64.

Lenihan, G. O., Rawlins, M. E., & Eberly, C. G. (1992). Gender differences in rape supportive attitudes before and after a date rape education intervention. *Journal of College Student Development, 33,* 331–338.

Lenski, G., Nolan, P., & Lenski, J. (1995). *Human societies: An introduction to macrosociology* (7th ed.). New York: McGraw-Hill.

Lesch, M. F., & Pollatsek, A. (1993). Automatic access of semantic information by phonological codes in visual word recognition. *Journal of Experimental Psychology: Learning, Memory, and Cognition, 19,* 285–294.

Le Vay, S., & Hamer, D. H. (1994). Evidence for a biological influence in male homosexuality. *Scientific American, 272,* 44–49.

Levenson, R. W. (1992). Autonomic nervous system differences among emotions. *Psychological Science, 3,* 23–27.

Levenson, R. W. (1994). The search for autonomic specificity. In P. Ekman & R. J. Davidson (Eds.), *The nature of emotion: Fundamental questions* (pp. 252–257). New York: Oxford University Press.

Levenson, R. W. (1999). The intrapersonal functions of emotion. *Cognition and Emotion, 13,* 481–504.

Levenson, R. W., Ekman, P., & Friesen, W. V. (1990). Voluntary facial action generates emotion-specific autonomic nervous system activity. *Psychophysiology, 27,* 363–384.

Levenson, R. W., Ekman, P., Heider, K., & Friesen, W. V. (1992). Emotion and autonomic nervous system activity in the Minangkabau of West Sumatra. *Journal of Personality and Social Psychology, 62,* 972–988.

Levkovitz, Y., Caftori, R., Avital, A., & Richter-Levin, G. (2002). The SSRI drug fluoxetine, but not the noradrenergic tricyclic drug desipramine, improves memory performance during acute major depression. *Brain Research Bulletin, 58,* 345–350.

Levy, A., & Paludi, M. (1997). *Workplace sexual harassment.* Upper Saddle River, NJ: Prentice Hall.

Levy, B. A., Campsall, J., Browne, J., Cooper, D., Waterhouse, C., & Wilson, C. (1995). Reading fluency: Episodic integration across texts. *Journal of Experimental Psychology: Learning, Memory, and Cognition, 21,* 1169–1185.

Levy, J. (1983). Language, cognition, and the right hemisphere: A response to Gazzaniga. *American Psychologist, 38,* 538–541.

Lewin, K. *The conceptual representation and the measurement of psychological forces.* Durham, NC: Duke University Press.

Lewis, M. (1992). *Shame: The exposed self.* New York: Free Press.

Lewis, M. (1993a). The emergence of human emotions. In M. Lewis & J. M. Haviland (Eds.), *Handbook of emotions* (pp. 223–235). New York: Guilford Press.

Lewis, M. (1993b). Self-conscious emotions: Embarrassment, pride, shame, and guilt. In M. Lewis & J. M. Haviland (Eds.), *Handbook of emotions* (pp. 563–573). New York: Guilford Press.

Lewis, M. (1995). Self-conscious emotions. *American Scientist, 83,* 68–78.

Lewis, R. (1990). Death and dying among the American Indians. In J. K. Parry (Ed.), *Social work practice with the terminally ill: A transcultural perspective* (pp. 23–32). Springfield, IL: Charles C. Thomas.

Lewontin, R. C. (1976). Race and intelligence. In N. J. Block & G. Dworkin (Eds.), *The IQ controversy* (pp. 78–92). New York: Pantheon.

Liberman, R. P., Teigen, J., Patterson, R., & Baker, V. (1973). Reducing delusional speech in chronic paranoid schizophrenics. *Journal of Applied Behavior Analysis, 6,* 57–64.

Licht, C. (2000). Occupational stress as a function of type of organization and sex of employee. *Psi Chi Journal of Undergraduate Research, 5,* 46–55.

Licht, C., & Solomon, L. Z. (2001). Occupational stress as a function of type of organization and sex of employee: A reassessment. *Psi Chi Journal of Undergraduate Research, 6,* 14–20.

Lickey, M. E., & Gordon, B. (1991). *Medicine and mental illness: The use of drugs in psychiatry.* New York: Freeman.

Liebert, R. M., & Sprafkin, J. (1988). *The early window: Effects of television on children and youth.* New York: Pergamon.

Liebman, D. A. (1979). Behaviorism and the mind: A (limited) call for a return to introspection. *American Psychologist, 34,* 319–333.

Lin, K.-M., Poland, R. E., Lau, J. K., & Rubin, R. T. (1988). Haloperidol and prolactin concentrations in Asians and Caucasians. *Journal of Clinical Psychopharmacology, 8,* 195–201.

Lin, K.-M., Poland, R. E., Nuccio, I., Matsuda, K., Hathuc, N., Su, T.-P., et al. (1989). A longitudinal assessment of haloperidol doses and serum concentrations in Asian and Caucasian schizophrenic patients. *American Journal of Psychiatry, 146,* 1307–1311.

Linden, W., Wen, F., & Paulhus, D. L. (1995). Measuring alexithymia: Reliability, validity, and prevalence. In J. N. Butcher & C. D. Spielberger (Eds.), *Advances in personality assessment* (Vol. 10, pp. 51–95). Hillsdale, NJ: Erlbaum.

Lindsay, D. S., & Read, J. D. (1993). Psychotherapy and memories of childhood sexual abuse: A cognitive perspective. *Applied Cognitive Psychology, 8,* 281–338.

Lindsay, P. H., & Norman, D. A. (1977). *Human information processing.* San Diego, CA: Academic Press.

Lindsey, L. L., & Beach, S. (2002). *Sociology* (2nd ed.). Upper Saddle River, NJ: Prentice Hall.

Lindsey, L. L., & Beach, S. (2004). *Sociology* (3rd ed.). Upper Saddle River, NJ: Pearson Prentice Hall.

Linn, M. C., & Petersen, A. C. (1985). Emergence and characterization of sex differences in spatial ability: A meta-analysis. *Child Development, 56,* 1479–1498.

Lippa, R. A., Martin, L. R., & Friedman, H. S. (2000). Gender-related individual differences and mortality in the Terman Longitudinal Study: Is masculinity hazardous to your health? *Journal of Personality and Social Psychology Bulletin, 26,* 1560–1570.

Lipsitt, L. (1986). Learning in infancy: Cognitive development in babies. *Journal of Pediatrics, 109,* 172–182.

Liska, K. (2004). *Drugs and the human body with implications for society* (7th ed.). Upper Saddle River, NJ: Pearson Prentice Hall.

Littner, M., Johnson, S. F., McCall, W., McCall, W. V., Anderson, W. M., Davila, D., et al. (2001). Practice parameters for the treatment of narcolepsy. *Journal of Sleep and Sleep Disorders Research, 24,* 451–466.

Liu, Y. (1996). Interactions between memory scanning and visual scanning in display monitoring. *Ergonomics, 39,* 1038–1053.

Lockhead, G. R. (2004). Absolute judgements are relative: A reinterpretation of some psychophysical ideas. *Review of General Psychology, 8,* 265–272.

Loden, M., & Rosener, J. B. (1990). *Workforce America! Managing employee diversity as a vital resource.* Burr Ridge, IL: Irwin.

Loehlin, J. C., McCrae, R. R., Costa, P. T., Jr., & John, O. P. (1998). Heritabilities of common and measure-specific components of the Big Five personality factors. *Journal of Research in Personality, 32,* 431–453.

Loftus, E. F. (1975). Leading questions and the eyewitness report. *Cognitive Psychology, 7,* 560–572.

Loftus, E. F. (1979). *Eyewitness testimony.* Cambridge, MA: Harvard University Press.

Loftus, E. F. (1984, February). Eyewitness: Essential but unreliable. *Psychology Today,* pp. 22–27.

Loftus, E. F. (1991). *Witness for the defense.* New York: St. Martin's Press.

Loftus, E. F. (1993). The reality of repressed memories. *American Psychologist, 48,* 518–537.

Loftus, E. F. (1997a). Creating false memories. *Scientific American, 277,* 70–75.

Loftus, E. F. (1997b). Memory for a past that never was. *Current Directions in Psychological Science, 6,* 60–65.

Loftus, E. F., & Ketcham, K. (1994). *The myth of repressed memory: False memories and allegation of sexual abuse.* New York: St. Martin's Press.

Loftus, E. F., Miller, D. G., & Burns, H. J. (1978). Semantic integration of verbal information into a visual memory. *Journal of Experimental Psychology: Human Learning and Memory, 4,* 19–31.

Loftus, E. F., & Polage, D. C. (1999). Repressed memories: When are they real? How are they false? *The Psychiatric Clinics of North America, 22,* 61–71.

Logue, A. W., Ophir, I., & Strauss, K. E. (1981). The acquisition of taste aversions in humans. *Behaviour Research and Therapy, 19,* 319–333.

Long, H. B. (1980). Characteristics of senior citizens' educational tuition waiver in twenty-one states: A follow-up study. *Educational Gerontology, 5,* 139–149.

Long, J. W., & Rybacki, J. J. (1994). *The essential guide to prescription drugs, 1994 edition.* New York: Harper-Perennial.

Longato-Stadler, E., Klinteberg, B., Garpenstrand, H., Oreland, L., & Hallman, J. (2002). Personality traits and platelet monoamine oxidase activity in a Swedish male criminal population. *Neuropsychobiology, 46,* 202–208.

Lopes, P. N., Brackett, M. A., Nezlek, J., Schultz, A., Sellin, I., & Salovey, P. (2004). Emotional intelligence and social interaction. *Personality and Social Psychology Bulletin, 30,* 1018–1034.

Lorenz, K. (1966). *On aggression.* San Diego, CA: Harcourt Brace.

Lowenstein, R. J. (1994). Diagnosis, epidemiology, clinical course, treatment, and cost effectiveness of treatment for dissociative disorders and MPD: Report submitted to the Clinton Administration Task Force on Health Care Financing Reform. *Dissociation, 7,* 3–11.

Lu, F. G., Lim, R. F., & Mezzich, J. E. (1995). Issues in the assessment and diagnosis of culturally diverse individuals. In J. M. Oldham & M. B. Riba (Eds.), *Review of psychiatry* (Vol. 14, pp. 477–510). Washington, DC: American Psychiatric Association.

Lu, Z.-L., Williamson, S. J., & Kausfman, L. (1992). Behavioral lifetime of human auditory sensory memory predicted by physiological measures. *Science, 258,* 1668–1670.

Lubart, T. I. (1994). Creativity. In R. L. Sternberg (Ed.), *Thinking and problem solving* (pp. 289–332). San Diego, CA: Academic Press.

Lubart, T. I. (2003). In search of creative intelligence. In R. J. Sternberg, J. Lautrey, & T. I. Lubart (Eds.), *Models of intelligence: International perspectives* (pp. 279–292). Washington, DC: American Psychological Association.

Lubin, B., Larsen, R. M., Matarazzo, J. D., & Seever, M. (1985). Psychological test usage patterns in five professional settings. *American Psychologist, 40,* 857–861.

Luborsky, L., Chandler, M., Auerbach, A. H., Cohen, J., & Bachrach, H. M. (1971). Factors influencing the outcome of psychotherapy: A review of quantitative research. *Psychological Bulletin, 75,* 145–185.

Lubow, R., & Kaplan, O. (1997). Visual search as a function of prior experience with target and distractor. *Journal of Experimental Psychology: Human Perception and Performance, 23,* 14–24.

Luchins, A. S. (1942). Mechanization in problem solving: The effect of Einstellung. *Psychological Monographs, 54* (Whole No. 248).

Luchins, A. S. (1946). Classroom experiments on mental set. *American Journal of Psychology, 59,* 295–298.

Luciana, M., Sullivan, J., & Nelson, C. A. (2001). Associations between phenylalanine-to-tyrosine ratios and performance on tests of neuropsychological function in adolescents treated early and continuously for phenylketonuria. *Child Development, 72*(6), 1637–1652.

Ludwig, T. D., & Geller, E. S. (1999). Behavior change among agents of a community safety program: Pizza deliverers advocate comunity safety belt use. *Journal of Organizational Behavior Mangement, 19,* 3–24.

Lutz, W. (1990). *Doublespeak.* New York: HarperCollins.

Lykken, D. T. (1981). *A tremor in the blood.* New York: McGraw-Hill.

Lymburner, J. A., & Roesch, R. (1999). The insanity defense: Five years of research (1993–1997). *International Journal of Law and Psychiatry, 22*(3–4), 213–240.

Lynam, D. R. (1998). Early identification of the fledgling psychopath: Locating the psychopathic child in the current nomenclature. *Journal of Abnormal Psychology, 107,* 566–575.

Lyness, K. S., & Thompson, D. E. (1997). Above the glass ceiling? A comparison of matched samples of female and male executives. *Journal of Applied Psychology, 82,* 359–375.

Lynn, D. B. (1974). *The father: His role in child development.* Pacific Grove, CA: Brooks/Cole.

Lynn, S. J., Lock, T. G., Myers, B., & Payne, D. G. (1997). Recalling the unrecallable: Should hypnosis be used to recover memories in psychotherapy? *Current Directions in Psychological Science, 6,* 79–83.

Lynn, S. J., Myers, B., & Malinoski, P. (In press). Hypnosis, pseudomemories, and clinical guidelines: A sociocognitive perspective. In J. D. Read & D. S. Lindsay (Eds.), *Recollections of trauma: Scientific studies and clinical practice.* New York: Plenum Press.

Lynn, S. J., & Payne, D. G. (1997). Memory as the theater of the past: The psychology of false memories. *Current Directions in Psychological Science, 6,* 55.

Lynn, S. J., Rhue, J. W., & Weekes, J. R. (1989). Hypnosis and experienced nonvolition: A social-cognitive integrative model. In N. P. Spanos & J. F. Chaves (Eds.), *Hypnosis: The cognitive-behavioral perspective* (pp. 78–109). Buffalo, NY: Prometheus.

Maas, J. B. (1998). *Power sleep.* New York: Villard.

Maccoby, E. E., & Alexander, J. (1980). Use of media in lifestyle programs. In P. O. Davidson & S. M. Davidson (Eds.), *Behavioral medicine: Changing health lifestyles.* New York: Brunner/Mazel.

Maccoby, E. E., & Jacklin, C. N. (1974). *The psychology of sex differences.* Stanford, CA: Stanford University Press.

MacDonald, T. K., Zanna, M. P., & Fong, G. T. (1995). Decision making in altered states: Effects of alcohol on attitudes toward drinking and driving. *Journal of Personality and Social Psychology, 68,* 973–985.

MacKenzie, B. (1984). Explaining race differences in IQ: The logic, the methodology, and the evidence. *American Psychologist, 39,* 1214–1233.

MacKinnon, D. W. (1978). *In search of human effectiveness: Identifying and developing creativity.* Buffalo, NY: Creative Education Foundation.

Macmillian, M. (2000a). *An odd kind of fame: Stories of Phineas Gage.* Cambridge, MA: MIT Press.

Macmillian, M. (2000b). Restoring Phineas Gage: A 150th retrospective. *Journal of the History of the Neurosciences, 9*(1), 46–66.

MacPhee, G. J. A., & Steward, D. A. (2001). Parkinson's disease. *Reviews in Clinical Gerontology, 11*(1), 33–49.

Maddi, S. R., & Kobasa, S. C. (1984). *The hardy executive: Health under stress.* Belmont, CA: Dorsey/Wadsworth.

Mader, S. S. (2000). *Human biology* (6th ed.). Boston: McGraw-Hill.

Madigan, S., & O'Hara, R. (1992). Short-term memory at the turn of the century: Mary Whiton Calkins's memory research. *American Psychologist, 47,* 170–174.

Madsen, D. B., & Finger, J. R., Jr. (1978). Comparison of a written feedback procedure, group brainstorming, and individual brainstorming. *Journal of Applied Psychology, 63,* 120–123.

Magid, K., & McKelvey, C. A. (1987). *High risk: Children without a conscience.* New York: Bantam Books.

Maher, B. A., & Spitzer, M. (1993). Delusions. In C. G. Costello (Ed.), *Symptoms of schizophrenia* (pp. 92–120). New York: Wiley.

Mahowald, M. W., & Schenck, C. H. (2003). REM sleep behavior disorder—past, present, and future. *Schweizer Archiv für Neurologie und Psychiatrie, 154*(7), 363–368.

Maier, N. R. F. (1931). Reasoning in humans II: The solution of a problem and its appearance in consciousness. *Journal of Comparative Psychology, 12,* 181–194.

Maier, S. F., & Watkins, L. R. (2000). The immune system as a sensory system: Implications for psychology. *Current Directions in Psychological Science, 9,* 98–102.

Maio, G. R., & Olson, J. M. (1995). Relations between values, attitudes, and behavioral intentions: The moderating role of attitude function. *Journal of Experimental Social Psychology, 31,* 266–285.

Maki, W. S. (1986). Distinction between new and used traces: Different effects of electroconvulsive shock on memories for places present and places past. *Quarterly Journal of Experimental Psychology: Comparative and Physiological Psychology, 38,* 397–423.

Makros, J., & McCabe, M. P. (2001). Relationships between identity and self-representations during adolescence. *Journal of Youth and Adolescence, 30,* 623–639.

Maletzky, B. M., & Field, G. (2003). The biological treatment of dangerous sexual offenders: A review and preliminary report of the Oregon pilot Depo-Provera program. *Aggression and Violent Behavior, 8*(4), 391–412.

Malnic, B., Hirono, J., & Buck, L. B. (1999). Combinatorial receptor codes for odors. *Cell, 96,* 713.

Mann, C. C. (1994). Behavioral genetics in transition. *Science, 264,* 1686–1689.

Mann, J. J., Brent, D. A., & Arange, V. (2001). The neurology and genetics of suicide and attempted suicide: A focus on the serotonergic system. *Neuropsychopharmacology, 24*(5), 467–477.

Maples, W. R., & Browning, M. (1994). *Dead men do tell tales: The strange and fascinating tales of a forensic anthropologist.* New York: Doubleday.

Marcia, J. E. (1980). Identity in adolescents. In J. Adelson (Ed.), *Handbook of adolescent psychology* (pp. 159–187). New York: Wiley.

Marcus, G. F. (2000). Pabiku and Ga Ti Ga: Two mechanisms infants use to learn about the world. *Current Directions in Psychological Science, 9,* 145–147.

Mark, V. H., & Ervin, F. R. (1970). *Violence and the brain.* New York: HarperCollins.

Markey, P. M. (2000). Bystander intervention in computer-mediated communication. *Computers in Human Behavior, 16,* 183–188.

Marks, D., & Kammann, R. (1980). *The psychology of the psychic.* Buffalo, NY: Prometheus.

Markus, H. R., & Kitayama, S. (1998). The cultural psychology of personality. *Journal of Cross-Cultural Psychology, 29,* 63–87.

Marsella, A. J., Sartorius, N., Jablensky, A., & Fenton, F. R. (1985). Cross-cultural studies of depressive disorders: An overview. In A. Kleinman & B. Good (Eds.), *Culture and depression* (pp. 299–324). Berkeley: University of California Press.

Marsh, H. W., & Hau, K-T. (2004). Explaining paradoxical relations between academic self-concepts and achievements: Cross-cultural generalizability of the internal/external frame of reference predictions across 26 countries. *Journal of Educational Psychology, 96,* 56–67.

Marshall, W. L. (1989). Pornography and sex offenders. In D. Zillmann & J. Bryant (Eds.), *Pornography: Research advances and policy considerations.* Hillsdale, NJ: Erlbaum.

Marshuetz, C. (2005). Order information in working memory: An integrative review of evidence from brain and behavior. *Psychological Bulletin, 131,* 323–339.

Marsiske, K., Klumb, P., & Baltes, M. M. (1997). Everyday activity patterns and sensory functioning in old age. *Psychology and Aging, 12,* 444–457.

Martin, C. L., Wood, C. H., & Little, J. K. (1990). The development of gender stereotype components. *Child Development, 61,* 1891–1904.

Martin, G. L., & Pear, J. (1996). *Behavior modification: What it is and how to do it* (5th ed.). Upper Saddle River, NJ: Prentice Hall.

Martin, G. L., & Pear, J. (2003). *Behavior modification: What it is and how to do it* (7th ed.). Upper Saddle River, NJ: Prentice Hall.

Martin, L. L., Harlow, T. F., & Strack, F. (1992). The role of bodily sensations in the evaluation of social events. *Personality and Social Psychology Bulletin, 18,* 412–419.

Martin, P. (2002). *Counting sheep: The science and pleasures of sleep and dreams.* New York: Thomas Dunne (St. Martin's Press).

Martini, F. H. (1992). *Fundamentals of anatomy and physiology* (2nd ed.). Upper Saddle River, NJ: Prentice Hall.

Martini, R., & Bartholomew, E. (2000). *Essentials of anatomy and physiology.* Upper Saddle River, NJ: Pearson Prentice Hall.

Martinic, M., & Leigh, B. (2004). *Reasonable risk: Alcohol in perspective.* New York: Brunner-Routledge.

Maslow, A. H. (1970). *Motivation and personality* (2nd ed.). New York: HarperCollins.

Mason, F. L. (1997). Fetishism: Psychopathology and theory. In D. R. Laws & W. T. O'Donohue (Eds.), *Handbook of sexual deviance: Theory and application.* New York: Guilford Press.

Masson, J. M. (1985). *The assault on truth.* New York: Viking Penguin.

Masters, W. H., & Johnson, V. E. (1966). *Human sexual response.* Boston: Little, Brown.

Masters, W. H., Johnson, V. E., & Kolodny, R. C. (1994). *Heterosexuality.* New York: HarperCollins.

Masters, W. J., et al. (1994). *Heterosexuality.* New York: HarperCollins.

Matarazzo, J. D. (1984). Behavioral immunogens. In B. L. Hammonds & C. J. Scheirer (Eds.), *Psychology and health* (pp. 9–43). Washington, DC: American Psychological Association.

Mather, M., Henkel, L. A., & Johnson, M. K. (1997). Evaluating characteristics of false memories. Remember/know judgments and memory characteristics questionnaires compared. *Memory and Cognition, 25*(6), 826–837.

Mather, M., Henkel, L. A., & Johnson, M. K. (1999). Evaluating characteristics of false memories: Remember/know judgements and memory characteristics questionnaire compared. *Memory and Cognition, 25*(6), 826–837.

Matsumoto, D. (1992). More evidence for the universality of a contempt expression. *Motivation and Emotion, 16,* 363–368.

Matsumoto, D. (1996). *Culture and psychology.* Pacific Grove, CA: Brooks/Cole.

Matsumoto, D. (1997). *Culture and modern life.* Pacific Grove, CA: Brooks/Cole.

Matsumoto, D. (1998, March). *Culture, emotion, and the teaching of psychology.* Paper presented at the annual Great Plains Students' Psychology Convention, Lincoln, NE.

Matsumoto, D., & Ekman, P. (1989). American–Japanese cultural differences in intensity ratings of facial expressions of emotion. *Motivation and Emotion, 13,* 143–157.

Matsumoto, D., Kasri, F., & Kooken, K. (1999). American-Japanese cultural differences in judgements of expression intensity and subjective experience. *Cognition and Emotion, 13,* 201–218.

Matthews, G., & Deary, I. J. (1998). *Personality traits.* Cambridge: University Press.

Matthews, K. A. (1989). Interactive effects of behavior and reproductive hormones on sex differences in risk for coronary heart disease. *Health Psychology, 8,* 373–387.

Matz, D. C., & Wood, W. (2005). Cognitive dissonance in groups: The consequences of disagreement. *Journal of Personality and Social Psychology, 88,* 22–37.

Maurer, D., & Maurer, C. (1988). *The world of the newborn.* New York: Basic Books.

Mayer, J. D. (2003). Structural divisions of personality and the classification of traits. *Review of General Psychology, 7,* 381–401.

Mays, V. M., & Albee, G. W. (1992). Psychotherapy and ethnic minorities. In D. K. Freedheim (Ed.), *History of psychotherapy: A century of change* (pp. 552–570). Washington, DC: American Psychological Association.

Mazur, J. E. (2006). *Learning and behavior* (6th ed.). Upper Saddle River, NJ: Prentice Hall.

McBurney, D. H. (2002). *How to think like a psychologist: Critical thinking in psychology.* Upper Saddle River, NJ: Prentice Hall.

McCabe, D. L., Trevino, L. K., & Butterfield, K. D. (2001). Cheating in academic institutions: A decade of research. *Ethics and Behavior, 11*(3), 219.

McCarley, J. S., Kramer, A. F., Colcombe, A. M., & Scialfa, C. T. (2004a). Priming of pop-out in visual search: A comparison of young and old adults. *Aging, Neuropsychology, and Cognition, 11,* 80–88.

McCarley, J. S., Kramer, A. F., Wickens, C. D., Vidoni, E. D., & Boot, W. R. (2004b). Visual skills in airport-security screening. *Psychological Science, 15,* 302–306.

McCarroll, J. E., Ursano, R. J., & Fullerton, C. S. (1997). Exposure to traumatic death in disaster and war. In C. S. Fullerton & R. J. Ursano (Eds.), *Posttraumatic stress disorder: Acute and long-term responses to trauma and disaster* (pp. 37–58). Washington, DC: American Psychiatric Publishing.

McCarthy, L. (2000, November). What you must know about kids' headaches. *Family Life,* 30–32.

McCartney, K. (1984). Effect of quality of day care environment on children's language development. *Developmental Psychology, 20,* 244–260.

McCartney, K., Owen, M. T., Booth, C. L., Clarke-Stewart, A., & Vandell, D. L. (2004). Testing a maternal attachment model of behavior problems in early childhood. *Journal of Child Psychology and Psychiatry, 45,* 765–778.

McCauley, E., Feuillan, P., Kushner, H., & Ross, J. L. (2001). Psychosocial development in adolescents with Turner syndrome. *Journal of Developmental and Behavioral Pediatrics, 22,* 360–365.

McClearn, G. E., Johansson, B., Berg, S., Pedersen, N. L., Ahern, F., Petrill, S. A., et al. (1997). Substantial genetic influence on cognitive abilities in twins 80 or more years old. *Science, 276,* 1560–1563.

McClelland, D. C. (1958). Some social consequences of achievement motivation. In M. R. Jones (Ed.), *Nebraska symposium on motivation.* Lincoln: University of Nebraska Press.

McClelland, D. C. (1985). *Human motivation.* Glenview, IL: Scott, Foresman.

McClelland, D. C., Koestner, R., & Weinberger, J. (1989). How do self-attributed and implicit motives differ? *Psychological Review, 67,* 690–702.

McClintock, M. (1971). Menstrual synchrony and suppression. *Nature, 229,* 244–245.

McConnell, A. R., & Gavanski, I. (1994). *Women as "men" and "people": Occupation title suffixes as primes.* Paper presented at the annual meeting of the Midwestern Psychological Association, Chicago.

McConnell, J. B., Cutler, R. L., & McNeil, E. B. (1958). Subliminal stimulation: An overview. *American Psychologist, 13,* 229–239.

McConnell, J. V. (1990). Negative reinforcement and positive punishment. *Teaching of Psychology, 17,* 247–249.

McCrae, R. R. (2004). Human nature and culture: A trait perspective. *Journal of Research in Personality, 38,* 3–14.

McCrae, R. R., & Costa, P. T., Jr. (1987). Validation of the five-factor model of personality across instruments and observers. *Journal of Personality and Social Psychology, 52,* 81–90.

McCrae, R. R., & Costa, P. T., Jr. (1990). *Personality in adulthood.* New York: Guilford Press.

McCullough, J. P., Jr., Klein, D. N., Keller, M. B., Holzer, C. E., II, Davis, S. M., Kornstein, S. G., et al. (2000). Comparison of DSM-III-R chronic major depression and major depression superimposed on dysthymia (double depression): Validity of the distinction. *Journal of Abnormal Psychology, 109,* 419–427.

McDaniel, S. R., & Zuckerman, M. (2003). The relationship of impulsive sensation seeking and gender to interest and participation in gambling activities. *Personality and Individual Differences, 35,* 1385–1400.

McDonald, G., Nail, P. R., & Levy, D. A. (2004). Expanding the scope of the social response context model. *Basic and Applied Social Psychology, 26,* 77–92.

McDonald, P. W., & Prkachin, K. M. (1990). The expression and perception of facial emotion in alexithymia: A pilot study. *Psychosomatic Medicine, 52,* 199–210.

McDowell, M. A., Fryar, C. D., Hirsch, R., & Ogden, C. L. (2005). *Anthropometric reference data for children and adults: U.S. population, 1999–2002. Advance data from vital and health statistics, no. 362.* Hyattsville, MD: National Center for Health Statistics.

McFarland, D. (Ed.). (1991). *The Guinness book of world records, 1991.* New York: Bantam Books.

McFarland, P. L., & Sanders, S. (2003). A pilot study about the needs of older gays and lesbians: What social workers need to know. *Journal of Gerontological Social Work, 40,* 67–80.

McFarlane, A. H., Bellissimo, A., Norman, G. R., & Lange, P. (1994). Adolescent depression in a school-based community sample: Preliminary findings on contributing social factors. *Journal of Youth and Adolescence, 23,* 601–620.

McGilley, B. M., & Holmes, D. S. (1988). Aerobic fitness response to psychological stress. *Journal of Research in Personality, 22,* 129–139.

McGillicuddy–De Lisi, A. V., & Subramanian, S. (1994). Tanzanian and United States mothers' beliefs about parents' and teachers' roles in children's knowledge acquisition. *International Journal of Behavioral Development, 17*, 209–237.

McGrath, E., Puryear-Keita, G., Strickland, B. R., & Russo, N. F. (Eds.). (1990). *Women and depression: Risk factors and treatment issues.* Washington, DC: American Psychological Association.

McGrath, R. E. (2003). Enhancing accuracy in observational test scoring: The comprehensive system as a case example. *Journal of Personality Assessment, 81,* 104–110.

McGregor, L., Miller, H. R., Mayleben, M. A., Buzzanga, V. L., Davis, S. F., & Becker, A. H. (1991). Similarities and differences between "traditional" and "nontraditional" college students in selected personality characteristics. *Bulletin of the Psychonomic Society, 29*, 128–130.

McGrew, R. E. (1985). *Trepanation. Encyclopedia of medical history* (pp. 219, 321). New York: McGraw-Hill.

McGubbin, M. (1994). Deinstitutionalization: The illusion of disillusion. *Journal of Mind and Behavior, 15,* 35–54.

McGue, M., Bacon, S., & Lykken, D. T. (1992). Personality stability and change in early adulthood: A behavioral genetic analysis. *Developmental Psychology, 29,* 96–109.

McKee, J. K., Poirier, F. E., & McGraw, W. S. (2005). *Understanding human evolution* (5th ed.). Upper Saddle River, NJ: Pearson Prentice Hall.

McKelvie, S. J. (1990). Student acceptance of a generalized personality description: Forer's graphologist revisited. *Journal of Social Behavior and Personality, 5,* 91–95.

McKim, W. A. (1997). *Drugs and behavior: An introduction to behavioral pharmacology* (3rd ed.). Upper Saddle River, NJ: Prentice Hall.

McKinney, B. A., & McAndrew, F. T. (2000). Sexuality, gender, and sport: Does playing have a price? *Psi Chi Journal of Undergraduate Research, 5,* 152–158.

McKusick, V. A. (1986). *Mendelian inheritance in man* (7th ed.). Baltimore: Johns Hopkins University Press.

McKusick, V. A. (1995). *Mendelian inheritance in man: Catalogs of autosomal dominant, autosomal recessive, and X-linked phenotypes* (10th ed.). Baltimore: Johns Hopkins University Press.

McLaughlin, S., & Margolskee, R. F. (1994). The sense of taste. *American Scientist, 82,* 538–545.

McLean, L. D. (2005). Organizational culture's influence on creativity and innovation: A review of the literature and implications for human resource development. *Advances in Developing Human Resources, 7,* 226–246.

McNally, R. J., Hornig, C. D., & Donnell, C. D. (1995). Clinical versus nonclinical panic: A test of suffocation false alarm theory. *Behaviour Research and Therapy, 33,* 127–131.

McNatt, D. B. (2000). Ancient Pygmalion joins contemporary management: A meta-analysis of the result. *Journal of Applied Psychology, 85,* 314–322.

Mead, M. (1963). *Sex and temperament in three primitive societies.* New York: Morrow. (Originally published 1935).

Medin, D. L., Ross, B. H., & Markman, A. B. (2001). *Cognitive psychology* (3rd ed.). Dallas, TX: Harcourt Brace.

Mednick, A. (1993, May). World's women familiar with a day's double shift. *APA Monitor,* pp. 32–33.

Mednick, M. T. S., & Mednick, S. A. (1967). *Examiner's manual for the Remote Associations Test.*

Meehl, P. E. (1956). Wanted—a good cookbook. *American Psychologist, 11,* 263–272.

Meijer, J. H., & Rietveld, W. J. (1989). Neurophysiology of the suprachiasmatic circadian pacemaker in rodents. *Physiological Review, 69,* 671–707.

Melton, G. B., Petrila, J., Poythress, N. G., & Slobogin, C. (1997). *Psychological evaluations for the courts* (2nd ed.). New York: Guilford Press.

Meltzer, H. Y. (1998). Suicide in schizophrenia: Risk factors and clozapine treatment. *Journal of Clinical Psychiatry, 59*(Suppl. 3), 15–20.

Meltzoff, A. N., & Moore, M. K. (1992). Early imitation within a functional framework: The importance of person identity, movement, and development. *Infant Behavior and Development, 15,* 479–505.

Melzack, R., & Wall, P. D. (1965). Pain mechanisms: A new theory. *Science, 150,* 971–979.

Melzack, R., & Wall, P. D. (1982). *The challenge of pain.* Harmondsworth, England: Penguin.

Memon, A., & Higham, P. A. (1999). A review of the cognitive interview. *Psychology, Public Policy, and Law, 5,* 177–196.

Mendez, D., & Warner, K. E. (2004) Adult cigarette smoking prevalence: Declining as expected (not as desired). *American Journal of Public Health, 94,* 251–252.

Mendlewicz, J., Souery, D., & Rivelli, S. K. (1999). Short-term and long-term treatment for bipolar patients: Beyond the guidelines. *Journal of Affective Disorders, 55,* 79–85.

Meoli, A. L., Casey, K. R., Clark, R. W., Coleman, J. A., Fayle, R. W., Troell, R. J., et al. (2001). Hypopnea in sleep-disordered breathing in adults. *Journal of Sleep and Sleep Disorders, 24,* 469–470.

Merit Systems Protection Board. (1981). *Sexual harassment of federal workers: Is it a problem?* Washington, DC: U.S. Government Printing Office.

Merit Systems Protection Board. (1987). *Sexual harassment of federal workers: An update.* Washington, DC: U.S. Government Printing Office.

Merzenich, M., Jenkins, W., Johnston, P., Schreiner, C., Miller, S., & Tallal, P. (1996). Temporal processing deficits of language-learning children ameliorated by training. *Science, 271,* 77–81.

Mesquita, B., & Frijda, N. H. (1992). Cultural variations in emotions: A review. *Psychological Bulletin, 112,* 179–204.

Messer, W. S., & Griggs, R. A. (1989). Student belief and involvement in the paranormal and performance in introductory psychology. *Teaching of Psychology, 16,* 187–191.

Michaels, J. W., Blommel, J. M., Brocato, R. M., Linkous, R. A., & Rowe, J. S. (1982). Social facilitation and inhibition in a natural setting. *Replication in Social Psychology, 2,* 21–24.

Michalko, M. (1991). *Thinkertoys.* Berkeley, CA: Ten Speed Press.

Mignot, E. (2005) Narcolepsy: Pharmacology, pathophysiology, and genetics. In M. H. Kryger, T. Roth, & W. C. Dement (Eds.), *Principles and practice of sleep medicine* (4th ed., pp. 761–779). New York: Elsevier Saunders.

Miklowitz, D. J. (2001). Bipolar disorder. In D. H. Barlow (Ed.), *Clinical handbook of psychological disorders: A step-by-step treatment manual* (3rd ed., pp. 523–561). New York: Guilford Press.

Milgram, S. (1974). *Obedience to authority.* New York: HarperCollins.

Miller, A., Springen, K., Gordon, J., Murr, A., Cohn, B., Drew, L., et al. (1988, April 25). *Newsweek,* 40–45.

Miller, E., Cradock-Watson, J. E., & Pollock, T. M. (1982 October 9). Consequences of confirmed maternal rubella at successive stages of pregnancy. *The Lancet,* 781–784.

Miller, G. A. (1956). The magical number seven, plus or minus two: Some limits on our capacity for processing information. *Psychological Review, 63,* 81–97.

Miller, J. G. (1997). A cultural-psychology perspective on intelligence. In R. J. Sternberg & E. L. Grigorenko (Eds.), *Intelligence, heredity, and environment* (pp. 269–302). New York: Cambridge University Press.

Miller, K. (1994, March 17). Safety quiz: Insurance claims data don't show advantage of some auto devices. *Wall Street Journal,* pp. Al, A7.

Miller, L. B., & Bizzell, R. P. (1983). Long-term effects of four preschool programs: Sixth, seventh, and eighth graders. *Child Development, 54,* 727–741.

Miller, L. K. (1999). The savant syndrome: Intellectual impairment and exceptional skill. *Psychological Bulletin, 125*(1), 31–46.

Miller, M. C. (2005). What are the dangers of methamphetamine? *Harvard Mental Health Letter, 22,* 8.

Miller, N. E. (1985). The value of behavioral research on animals. *American Psychologist, 40,* 423–440.

Miller, W. R., & Thoresen, C. E. (2003). Spirituality, religion and health: An emerging research field. *American Psychologist, 58,* 24–35.

Minton, H. L. (2000). Psychology and gender at the turn of the century. *American Psychologist, 55,* 613–615.

Miracle, T. S., Miracle, A. W., & Bauermeister, R. F. (2003). *Human sexuality: Meeting your basic needs.* Upper Saddle River, NJ: Prentice Hall.

Mirsky, A. F., Bieliauskas, L. A., French, L. M., Van Kammen, D. P., Jonsson, E., & Sedvall, G. (2000). A 39-year followup of the Genain quadruplets. *Schizophrenia Bulletin, 26,* 699–708.

Mirsky, A. F., & Quinn, O. W. (1988). The Genain quadruplets. *Schizophrenia Bulletin, 14,* 595–612.

Mirsky, A. F., Quinn, O. W., De Lisi, L. E., Schwerdt, P., & Buchsbaum, M. S. (1987). The Genain quadruplets: A 25-year follow-up of four monozygous women discordant for the severity of schizophrenic illness. In N. E. Miller & G. D. Cohen (Eds.), *Schizophrenia and aging* (pp. 83–94). New York: Guilford Press.

Mischel, W. (1966). A social-learning view of sex differences in behaving. In E. E. Maccoby (Ed.), *The development of sex differences* (pp. 56–81). Stanford, CA: Stanford University Press.

Mischel, W. (1968). *Personality and assessment.* New York: Wiley.

Mitchell, K. (2002). Women's morality: A test of Carol Gilligan's theory. *Journal of Social Distress and the Homeless, 11,* 81–110.

Mittendorf, R., Williams, M. A., Berkley, C. S., & Cotton, P. F. (1990). The length of uncomplicated human gestation. *Obstetrics and Gynecology, 75,* 929–932.

Mlot, C. (1998). Probing the biology of emotion. *Science, 28,* 1005–1007.

Mogelonsky, M. (1996, May). The rocky road to adulthood. *American Demographics,* pp. 26–35, 56.

Moghaddam, F. M. (1990). Modulative and generative orientations in psychology: Implications for psychology in the three worlds. *Journal of Social Issues, 46,* 21–41.

Moghaddam, F. M. (1994). Ethnic segregation in a multicultural society: A review of recent trends in Montreal and Toronto and reconceptualization of "causal factors." In F. Frisken (Ed.), *The changing Canadian metropolis* (pp. 237–258). Berkeley, CA, and Toronto: University of California Press and Canadian Urban Studies Institute.

Moghaddam, F. M. (1998). *Social psychology: Exploring universals across cultures.* New York: W. H. Freeman.

Moghaddam, F. M. (2005). The staircase to terrorism: A psychological explanation. *American Psychologist, 60,* 161–169.

Mohlman, J., de Jesus, M., Gorenstein, E. E., Kleber, M., Gorman, J. M., & Papp, L. A. (2004). Distinguishing generalized anxiety disorder, panic disorder, and mixed anxiety states in older treatment-seeking adults. *Journal of Anxiety Disorders, 18,* 275–290.

Mohr, D. C., & Darcy, C. (2001). Multiple sclerosis: Empirical literature for the clinical health psychologist. *Journal of Clinical Psychology, 57,* 479–499.

Moldin, S. O., & Gottesman, I. I. (1997). At issue: Genes, experience, and chance in schizophrenia: Positioning for the 21st century. *Schizophrenia Bulletin, 23,* 547–561.

Molineuvo, J., Liado, A., & Rami, L. (2005). Memantine: Targeting glutamate excitotoxicity in Alzheimer's disease and other dementias. *American Journal of Alzheimer's Disease and Other Dementias, 20*(2), 77–85.

Molko, N., Cachia, A., Riviere, D., Mangin, J. F., Bruandet, M., LeBihan, D., et al. (2004). Brain anatomy in Turner syndrome: Evidence for impaired social and spatial networks. *Cerebral Cortex, 14*(8), 840–850.

Monahan, J. (2001). Major mental disorders and violence: Epidemiology and risk assessment. In G. F. Pinard & L. Pagani (Eds.), *Clinical assessment of dangerousness: Empirical contributions* (pp. 89–102). New York: Cambridge University Press.

Monahan, J. L., Murphy, S. T., & Zajonc, R. B. (2000). Subliminal mere exposure: Specific, general, and diffuse effects. *Psychological Science, 11,* 462–466.

Money, J. (1980). Endocrine influences and psychosexual status spanning the life cycle. In H. M. Van Praag, M. H. Lader, O. J. Rafaelsen, & E. H. Sachar (Eds.), *Handbook of biological psychiatry: Part 3. Brain mechanisms and abnormal behavior—genetics and neuroendocrinology.* New York: Dekker.

Money, J. (1984). Paraphilias: Phenomenology and classification. *American Journal of Psychotherapy, 38,* 164–179.

Montgomery, G. H., DuHamel, K. N., & Redd, W. H. (2000). A meta-analysis of hypnotically induced analgesia: How effective is hypnosis? *International Journal of Clinical and Experimental Hypnosis, 48,* 138–153.

Moorcraft, W. H. (1989) *Sleep, dreaming, and sleep disorders.* Lanham, MD: University Press of America.

Moorcroft, W. H. (1993). *Sleep, dreaming, and sleep disorders: An introduction* (2nd ed.). Lanham, MD: University Press.

Moore, B. N., & Parker, R. (1995). *Critical thinking* (4th ed.). Mayfield, CA: Mountain View.

Moore, C., & Corkum, V. (1994). Social understanding at the end of the first year of life. *Developmental Review, 14,* 349–372.

Moore, K. L., & Persaud, T. V. N. (1993). *Before we are born* (4th ed.). Philadelphia: Saunders.

Moore, T. E. (1982). Subliminal advertising: What you see is what you get. *Journal of Marketing, 46,* 38–47.

Moran, M. (2002). Insanity standards may vary, but plea rarely succeeds. *Psychiatric News, 37*(8), 24.

Moravcsik, J. E., & Healey, A. F. (1995). Effect of meaning on letter detection. *Journal of Experimental Psychology: Learning, Memory, and Cognition, 21,* 82–95.

Mordi, J. A., & Ciuffreda, K. J. (2004). Dynamic aspects of accommodation: Age and presbyopia. *Vision Research, 44,* 591–601.

Morgan, C. A., III, Grillon, C., Southwick, S. M., Davis, M., & Charney, D. S. (1996). Exaggerated acoustic startle reflex in Gulf War veterans with posttraumatic stress disorder. *American Journal of Psychiatry, 153,* 64–68.

Morganthau, T. (1994, October 24). IQ: Is it destiny? *Newsweek,* pp. 53–55.

Morreall, J. (1997). *Humor works.* Amherst, MA: HRD Press.

Morris, C. G., & Maisto, A. A. (2006). *Understanding psychology* (7th ed.). Upper Saddle River, NJ: Pearson Prentice Hall.

Morris, D. (1994). *Bodytalk: The meaning of human gestures.* New York: Crown.

Morris, R. W. (1989, January). Chronobiology and health part I: Basic principles. *Pharmindex,* 6–16.

Morrow, R. D. (1989). Southeast Asian child rearing practices: Implications for child and youth care workers. *Child and Youth Care Quarterly, 18,* 273–287.

Moscovici, S., & Zavalloni, M. (1969). The group as a polarizer of attitudes. *Journal of Personality and Social Psychology, 12,* 124–135.

Mount, M. K., Barrick, M. R., & Strauss, J. P. (1994). Validity of observer ratings of the Big Five personality factors. *Journal of Applied Psychology, 79,* 272–280.

Moursund, J., & Kenny, M. C. (2002). *The process of counseling and therapy* (4th ed.). Upper Saddle River, NJ: Prentice Hall.

Moyer, R. S., & Nath, A. (1998). Some effects of brief training interventions on perceptions of sexual harassment. *Journal of Applied Social Psychology, 28,* 333–356.

Mozel, M. M., Smith, B., Smith, P., Sullivan, R., & Swender, P. (1969). Nasal chemoreception in flavor identification. *Archives of Otolaryngology, 90,* 367–373.

Mucha, T. F., & Reinhardt, R. F. (1970). Conversion reactions in student aviators. *American Journal of Psychiatry, 127,* 493–497.

Muchinsky, P. M. (1987). *Psychology applied to work* (2nd ed.). Chicago: Dorsey.

Muchinsky, P. M. (2000). *Psychology applied to work: An introduction to industrial and organizational psychology* (6th ed.). Belmont, CA: Wadsworth.

Muhonen, T., & Torkelson, E. (2004). Work locus of control and its relationship to health and job satisfaction from a gender perspective. *Stress and Health: Journal of the International Society for the Investigation of Stress, 20,* 21–28.

Mukerjee, M. (1997, February). Trends in animal research. *Scientific American,* 86–93.

Mullen, B., Copper, C., & Driskell, J. E. (1990). Jaywalking as a function of model behavior. *Personality and Social Psychology Bulletin, 16,* 320–330.

Mullen, B., & Johnson, C. (1988). *The psychology of consumer behavior.* Hillsdale, NJ: Erlbaum.

Mullis, R., & Chapman, P. (2000). Age, gender, and self-esteem differences in adolescent coping styles. *Journal of Social Psychology, 140,* 539–542.

Munley, P. H., Germain, J. M., Tovar-Murray, D., & Borgman, A. L. (2004). MMPI-2 profile code types and measurement error. *Journal of Personality Assessment, 82,* 179–188.

Munsterberg, H. (1908/1927). On the witness stand. Available at Classics in the History of Psychology Web site.

Murnen, S. K., & Smolak, L. (2000). The experience of sexual harassment among grade-school students: Early socialization of female subordination. *Sex Roles, 43,* 1–17.

Murphy, C., Cain, W. S., & Bartoshuk, L. M. (1977). Mutual action of taste and olfaction. *Sensory Processes, 1,* 204–211.

Murphy, S. M. (1994). Imagery interventions in sport. *Medicine and Science in Sports and Exercise, 26,* 484–494.

Murray, B. (2000, March). From brain scan to plan. *APA Monitor,* 22–26.

Murray, B. (2001). Fast-food culture serves up supersize Americans. *Monitor on Psychology, 32*(11), 33.

Murray, C. J., & Lopez, A. D. (1996). *Global burden of disease.* Cambridge, MA: Harvard University Press.

Murray, M. J., & Meacham, R. B. (1993). The effect of age on male reproductive function. *World Journal of Urology, 11,* 137–140.

Murray, T. J. (2005). *Multiple sclerosis: The history of a disease.* New York: Demos.

Murstein, B. I., & Fontaine, P. A. (1993). The public's knowledge about psychologists and other mental health professionals. *American Psychologist, 48,* 839–845.

Murstein, B. L., Merighi, J. R., & Vyse, S. A. (1991). Love styles in the United States and France: A cross-cultural comparison. *Journal of Social and Clinical Psychology, 10,* 37–46.

Murtagh, D. R. R., & Greenwood, K. M. (1995). Identifying effective psychological treatments for insomnia: A meta-analysis. *Journal of Consulting and Clinical Psychology, 63,* 79–89.

Musen, G., & Squire, L. R. (1993). Implicit learning of color-word association using a Stroop paradigm. *Journal of Experimental Psychology: Learning, Memory, and Cognition, 19,* 789–798.

Musher-Eizenman, D. R., Nesselroade, J. R., & Schmitz, B. (2002). Perceived control and academic performance: A comparison of high- and low-performing children on within-person change patterns. *International Journal of Behavioral Development, 26,* 540–547.

Mussell, M. P., & Mitchell, J. E. (1998). Anorexia nervosa and bulimia nervosa. In H. S. Friedman (Ed.), *Encyclopedia of mental health.* (Vol. I, pp. 111–118). San Diego: Academic Press.

Myers, D. J., & Dugan, K. B. (1996). Sexism in graduate school classrooms: Consequences for students and faculty. *Gender and Society, 19,* 330–350.

Myers, J. E., & Gill, C. S. (2004). Poor, rural and female: Under-studied, under-counseled, more at-risk. *Journal of Mental Health Counseling, 26,* 225–242.

Myers, J. J., & Sperry, R. W. (1985). Interhemispheric communication after section of the forebrain commisures. *Cortex, 21,* 249–260.

Nahemow, L., & Lawton, M. P. (1975). Similarity and propinquity in friendship formation. *Journal of Personality and Social Psychology, 33,* 205–213.

Nairne, J. S. (2003). Sensory and working memory. In A. F. Healy & R. W. Proctor (Eds.), *Handbook of psychology: Experimental psychology* (Vol. 4, pp. 423–444). New York: Wiley.

Nakajima, S. (1993). Asymmetrical effect of a temporal gap between feature and target stimuli on Pavlovian feature-positive and feature-negative discrimination. *Learning and Motivation, 24,* 255–265.

Nakane, Y., Ohta, Y., & Radford, M. H. B. (1992). Epidemiological studies of schizophrenia in Japan. *Schizophrenia Bulletin, 18,* 75–84.

Nakao, K. (1987). Analyzing sociometric preferences: An example of Japanese and U.S. business groups. *Journal of Social Behavior and Personality, 2,* 523–534.

Narrow, W. E., Rae, D. S., Robin, L. N., & Regier, D. A. (2002). Revised prevalence estimates of mental disorders in the United States. *Archives of General Psychiatry, 59,* 115–123.

Nash, J. M. (2002, September). Cracking the fat riddle. *Time,* 46–55.

Nash, J. M. (2000, July 17). The new science of Alzheimer's. *Time,* 51–57.

Nash, M. R. (2001, July). The truth and the hype of hypnosis. *Scientific American,* 47–55.

National Center for Education Statistics. (1997). *Digest of education statistics.* Washington, DC: U.S. Department of Education.

National Center for Health Statistics. (1993). Advance report of final mortality statistics, 1990. *Monthly Vital Statistics Report, 41*(7).

National Center for Health Statistics. (2004a). *Health, United States, 2004.* Hyattsville, MD: Centers for Disease Control and Prevention.

National Center for Health Statistics. (2004b). *Health, United States, 2004: With chartbook on trends in the health of Americans.* Hyattsville, MD: U.S. Government Printing Office.

National Center for Injury Prevention and Control. (2001). *Injury fact book 2001–2002.* Atlanta, GA: Centers for Disease Control and Prevention.

National Commission on Sleep Disorders Research. (1993). *Report of the National Commission on Sleep Disorders Research.* Submitted to the secretary of the U.S. Department of Health and Human Services.

National Highway Traffic Safety Administration (2005a). Motor vehicle traffic crash fatalities and injuries: 2004 projections. Retrieved July 15, 2005, from www.nhtsa.gov.

National Highway Traffic Safety Administration. (2005b). traffic safety facts: 2004 traffic safety annual assessment—early results. Retrieved July 15, 2005, from www.nhtsa.gov.

National Highway Transportation Administration. (2005). 2004 projections: Motor vehicle traffic crash fatalities and injuries. National Center for Statistics and Analysis. Retrieved July 20, 2005, from www.nhtsa.gov.

National Hospice and Palliatial Care Organization. Hospice effective in delivering quality care to dying Americans according to current research. Retrieved September 15, 2004, from http://www.nhpco.org/i4a/pages/Index.cfm?pageid-54210.

National Institute of Child Health and Human Development. (2001). *Targeting sudden infant death syndrome (SIDS): A strategic plan.* Rockville, MD: Author.

National Institute of Mental Health. (2001). Bipolar disorder. Retrieved from www.nimh.nih.gov/publicat/bipolar.cfm.

National Institute of Neurological Disorders and Stroke. (2005a). NINDS Sleep apnea information page. Retrieved August 2, 2005, from sleep_apnea/sleep_apnea.htm.

National Institute of Neurological Disorders and Stroke. (2005b). NINDS narcolepsy information page. Retrieved July 15, 2005, from www.ninds.nih.gov/disorders/narcolepsy/narcolepsy.htm.

National Institute on Alcohol Abuse and Alcoholism. (1991, October). Alcoholism and co-occurring disorders. *Alcohol Alert, 14* (PH302).

National Institute on Alcohol Abuse and Alcoholism. (1997, October). Alcohol, violence, and aggression. *Alcohol Alert,* No. 38.

National Institute on Alcohol Abuse and Alcoholism. (2004). Alcohol—an important women's health issue. *Alcohol Alert, 62,* 1–6.

National Institute on Drug Abuse. (1997a). *Marijuana* (Capsule 12). Rockville, MD: U.S. Department of Health and Human Services.

National Institute on Drug Abuse. (1997b). *Mind over matter: The brain's response to steroids* (NIH Publication No. 00-3860). Rockville, MD: National Institute of Health.

National Institute on Drug Abuse. (2005). NIDA InfoFacts: MDMA (Ecstasy). Retrieved August 2, 2005, from www.nida.nih.gov/infofacts/ecstasy.html.

National Institutes of Health. (2005). National Institutes of Health state-of-the science conference statement: Manifestations and management of chronic insomnia in adults. Retrieved October 30, 2005, from consensus.nih.gov/2005/2005Insomnia-SOS26html.htm.

National Research Council. (2003). *The polygraph and lie detection.* Washington, DC: National Academies Press.

National Safety Council. (1998). *Accident facts.* Chicago: Author.

National Sleep Foundation. (2005a). Sleep Library/ Can't sleep? Learn about insomnia. Retrieved July 30, 2005, from www.sleepfoundation.org/sleeplibrary. index.

National Sleep Foundation. (2005b). Summary of findings: Sleep in America poll. Retrieved August 1, 2005, from www.sleepfoundation.org.

National Sleep Foundation. (2005c). 2005 Sleep in American poll. Retrieved November 13, 2005, from www.sleepfoundation.org.

National Transportation Safety Board. (2005, March 29). NTSB reports decrease in aviation accidents in 2004. NTSB Press Release.

Neale, J. M., & Oltmanns, T. F. (1980). *Schizophrenia.* New York: Wiley.

Needleman, H. L., & Gatsonis, C. A. (1990). Low-level lead exposure and the IQ of children. *Journal of the American Medical Association, 263,* 673–678.

Neimark, E. D. (1982). Cognitive development in adulthood: Using what you've got. In T. M. Field, A. Huston, H. C. Quay, L. Troll, & G. E. Finley (Eds.), *Review of human development.* New York: Wiley.

Neisser, U. (1967). *Cognitive psychology.* Upper Saddle River, NJ: Prentice Hall.

Neisser, U., Broodoo, G., Bouchard, T. J., Boykin, A. W., Brody, N., Ceci, S. J., et al. (1996). Intelligence: Knowns and unknowns. *American Psychologist, 51,* 77–101.

Nelson, D. L., & Burke, R. J. (2000). Women executives: Health, stress, and success. *The Academy of Management Executive, 14,* 107–121.

Nemeroff, C. B. (1998). The neurobiology of depression. *Scientific American, 278,* 42–49.

Nestler, E. J., & Malenka, R. C. (2004, March). The addicted brain. *Scientific American,* 78–85.

Neugarten, B., Havighurst, R., & Tobin, S. (1968). Personality and patterns of aging. In B. Neugarten (Ed.), *Middle age and aging.* Chicago: University of Chicago Press.

Neugarten, B., & Neugarten, D. (1987, May). The changing meanings of age. *Psychology Today, 21*(5), 29–33.

Neumann, K., Preibisch, C., Euler, H. A., von Gudenberg, A. W., Lanfermann, H., Gall et al. (2005). Cortical plasticity associated with stuttering therapy. *Journal of Fluency Disorders, 30*(1), 23–39.

Nevid, J. S., & Greene, B. (2001). *Essentials of abnormal psychology in a changing world.* Upper Saddle River, NJ: Prentice Hall.

Newcomb, T. M. (1961). *The acquaintance process.* Austin, TX: Holt, Rinehart & Winston.

Newland, M. C., & Rasmussen, E. B. (2000). Aging unmasks adverse effects of gestational exposure to methylmercury in rats. *Neurotoxicology and Teratology, 22,* 819–828.

Newland, M. C., & Rasmussen, E. B. (2003). Behavior in adulthood and during aging is affected by contaminant exposure in utero. *Current Direction in Psychological Science, 12,* 212–217.

Newman, A. W., & Thompson, J. W., Jr. (2001). The rise and fall of hypnosis in criminal investigation. *Journal of the American Academy of Psychiatry and Law, 29,* 75–84.

Newman, D. L., Moffitt, T. E., Caspi, A., & Silva, P. A. (1998). Comorbid mental disorders: Implications for treatment and sample selection. *Journal of Abnormal Psychology, 107,* 305–311.

Newton, D. E. (1992). *AIDS issues: A handbook.* Hillsdale, NJ: Enslow.

Nezu, A. M., Nezu, C. M., & Blissett, S. E. (1988). Sense of humor as a moderator of the relation between stressful events and psychological distress: A prospective analysis. *Journal of Personality and Social Psychology, 54,* 520–525.

Nicholas, S., Gyselinck, V., Murray, D. J., & Bandomir, C. A. (2002). French descriptions of Wundt's laboratory in Leipzig in 1886. *Psychological Research/Psychologische Forschung, 66,* 208–214.

Nicoll, R. A., & Alger, B.E. (2004, December). The brain's own marijuana. *Scientific American,* 69–75.

Nielsen Media Research. (1990). *Report on television.* Summarized in *American Enterprise,* July–August, 1990.

Nielsen Media Research. (1998). Report on television. *National Audience Demographic Report,* February 1997.

Nietzel, M. T., Bernstein, D. A., & Milich, R. (1994). *Clinical psychology* (4th ed.). Upper Saddle River, NJ: Prentice Hall.

NIMH Genetics Workshop. (1998). *Genetics and mental disorders.* NIH Publication No. 98-4268. Rockville, MD: National Institute of Mental Health.

Nolan-Hoeksema, S. (2001). Gender differences in drepression. *Current Directions in Psychological Science, 10,* 173–176.

Nopoulos, P., Flaum, M., & Andreasen, N. C. (1997). Sex differences in brain morphology in schizophrenia. *American Journal of Psychiatry, 154,* 1648–1654.

Norcross, J. C., Karg-Bray, R. S., & Prochaska, J. O. (1995). *Clinical psychologists in the 1990s.* Unpublished paper.

Nordin, S. M., & Cumming, J. (2005). More than meets the eye: Investigating imagery type, direction, and outcome. *Sport Psychologist, 19*(1), 1–17.

Norman, D. A. (1988). *The psychology of everyday things.* New York: Basic Books.

Norman, D. A. (1995). Designing the future. *Scientific American, 273,* 194–198.

Norman, K. A., & Schacter, D. L. (1997). False recognition in young and older adults: Exploring the characteristics of illusory memories. *Memory and Cognition, 25,* 838–848.

Norman, K. A., & Schachter, D. L. (In press). False recognition in younger and older adults: Exploring the characteristics of illusory memories. *Memory and Cognition.*

Normand, J., Salyards, S. D., & Mahoney, J. J. (1990). An evaluation of preemployment drug testing. *Journal of Applied Psychology, 75,* 629–639.

Nossiter, A. (1994, November 10). A daughter's death, a father's guilt. *New York Times,* p. A24.

Nothdurft, H. (1993). The role of features in preattentive vision: Comparison of orientation, motion, and color cues. *Vision Research, 33,* 1937–1958.

Nugent, J. K. (1991). Cultural and psychological influences on the father's role in infant development. *Journal of Marriage and the Family, 53,* 475–485.

Nyberg, L., & Tulving, E. (1996). Classifying human long-term memory: Evidence from converging dissociations. *European Journal of Cognitive Psychology, 8,* 163–183.

Oats, S. B. (1977). *With malice toward none.* New York: NAL Penguin.

O'Conner, P. G., & Schottenfeld, R. S. (1998). Patients with alcohol problems. *New England Journal of Medicine, 338,* 592–602.

O'Connor, E. M. (2001). Student mental health: Secondary education no more. *Monitor on Psychology, 32*(8), 44–47.

O'Connor, N., Cowan, R., & Samella, K. (2000). Calendrical calculation and intelligence. *Intelligence, 28*(1), 31–48.

Offermano, L. B., & Cowing, M. K. (1990). Organizations of the future. *American Psychologist, 45,* 95–108.

Ofshe R. & Watters, E. (1994). *Making monsters: False memories, psychotherapy, and sexual hysteria.* New York: Scribner.

Ohayon, M., & Zulley, J. (1999). Prevalence of naps in the general population. *Sleep and Hypnosis, 1,* 88–97.

Olanow, C. W., Goetz, C. G., Kordower, J. H., Stoessel, A. J., Sossi, V., Brin, M. F., et al. (2003). A doubleblind controlled trial of bilateral fetal nigral transplantation in Parkinson's disease. *Annals of Neurology, 54*(3), 403–414.

Oldham, J. M. (1994). Personality disorders: Current perspectives. *Journal of the American Medical Association, 272,* 1770–1776.

Olian, J. D. (1984). Genetic screening for employment purposes. *Personnel Psychology, 37,* 423–438.

Oliver, M. B., & Hyde, J. S. (1993). Gender differences in sexuality: A meta-analysis. *Psychological Bulletin 104,* 29–51.

Olsen, D. E., Harris, J. C., Capps, M. H., & Ansley, N. (1997). Computerized polygraph scoring system. *Journal of Forensic Sciences, 42,* 61–70.

Olsho, L. W., Harkins, S. W., & Lenhardt, M. L. (1985). Aging and the auditory system. In J. E. Bir-

ren & K. W. Schaie (Eds.), *Handbook of the psychology of aging.* New York: Van Nostrand Reinhold.

Olson, M. A., & Fazio, R. H. (2001). Implicit attitude formation through classical conditioning. *Psychological Science, 12,* 413–417.

Olson, M. A., & Fazio, R. H. (2004). Trait inferences as a function of automatically activated racial attitudes and motivation to control prejudiced reactions. *Basic and Applied Social Psychology, 26,* 1–11.

Oltmanns, T. F., & Emery, R. E. (2001). *Abnormal psychology* (3rd ed.). Upper Saddle River, NJ: Prentice Hall.

On the trail of schizophrenia. (2005). *Harvard Mental Health Letter, 21*(9), 1–4.

O'Neill, W. M. (1995). American behaviorism: A historical and critical analysis. *Theory and Psychology, 5,* 285–305.

Ones, D. S., & Viswesvaran, C. (2001). Personality at work: Criterion-focused occupational personality scales used in personnel selection. In B. W. Roberts & R. Hogan, (Eds.), *Personality psychology in the workplace* (pp. 6–92). Washington, DC: American Psychological Association.

Oquendo, M. A. (1995). Differential diagnosis of ataque de nervios. *American Journal of Orthopsychiatry, 65,* 60–65.

Orbach, I., Mikulincer, M., Sirota, P., & Giboa-Schechtman, E. (2003). Mental pain: A multidimensional operationalization and definition. *Suicide and Life-Threatening Behavior, 33,* 219–230.

Orlando, M., Tucker, J. S., Ellickson, P. L., & Klein, D. J. (2004). Developmental trajectories of cigarette smoking and their correlates from early adolescence to young adulthood. *Journal of Consulting and Clinical Psychology, 72,* 400–410.

Orleans, C. T., Schoenbach, V. J., Wagner, E. H., Quade, D., Salmon, M. A., Pearson, D. C., et al. Self-help quit smoking interventions: Effects of self-help materials, social support instructions, and telephone counseling. *Journal of Consulting and Clinical Psychology, 59,* 439–448.

Ormel, J., Von Korff, M., Ustun, B., Pini, S., Korten, A., & Oldehinkel, T. (1994). Common mental disorders and disability across cultures: Results from the WHO Collaborative Study on Psychological Problems in General Health Care. *Journal of the American Medical Association, 272,* 1741–1748.

Orwell, G. (1949). *1984.* New York: Signet.

Oscar-Berman, M., Shagrin, B., Evert, D. L., & Epstein, C. (1997). Impairments of brain and behavior: The neurological effects of alcohol. *Alcohol Health and Research World, 21*(1), 65–75.

Osman, S. L. (2003). Predicting men's rape perceptions based on the belief that "No" really means "Yes." *Journal of Applied Social Psychology, 33,* 683–692.

Ost, L.-G. (1987). Age of onset in different phobias. *Journal of Abnormal Psychology, 96,* 223–239.

Ost, L.-G. (1992). Blood and injection phobia: Background and cognitive, physiological, and behavioral variables. *Journal of Abnormal Psychology, 101,* 68–74.

Othmer, E., & Othmer, S. C. (1989). *The clinical interview: Using DSM-III-R.* Washington, DC: American Psychiatric Association.

Otto, R. K., & Heilbrun, K. (2002). The practice of forensic psychology: A look toward the future in light of the past. *American Psychologist, 57,* 5–18.

Overby, G. (1999, October). *Beyond Piaget: Symbol understanding in young children.* Paper presented at the Mid-America Conference for Teachers of Psychology, Evansville, IN.

Owen, D. M., Hastings, R. P., Noone, S. J., Chinn, J., Harman, K., Roberts, J., & Taylor, K. (2004). Life events as correlates of problem behavior and mental health in a residential population of adults with developmental disabilities. *Research in Developmental Disabilities, 25,* 309–320.

Owens, J., Capaldi, E. D., & Sheffer, J. D. (1993). An exposure effect opposes flavor-nutrient learning. *Animal Learning and Behavior, 21,* 196–202.

Packenham, K. I. (2001). Coping with multiple sclerosis: Development of a measure. *Psychology, Health, and Medicine, 6,* 411–428.

Paffenbarger, R. S., Hyde, R. T., Wing, A. L., & Hsieh, C. (1986). Physical activity, all-cause mortality, and longevity of college alumni. *New England Journal of Medicine, 314,* 605–613.

Page, R. M., Scanlan, A., & Deringer, N. (1994). Childhood loneliness and isolation: Implications for childhood educators. *Child Study Journal, 24,* 107–118.

Paivio, A. (1971). *Imagery and verbal processes.* Austin, TX: Holt, Rinehart & Winston.

Paivio, A. (1986). *Mental representations: A dual coding approach.* New York: Oxford University Press.

Palella, F. J., Jr., Delaney, K. M., Moorman, A. C., Loveless, M. O., Fuhrer, J., Satten, G. A., et al. (1998). Declining morbidity and mortality among patients with advanced human immunodeficiency virus infections. *New England Journal of Medicine, 338,* 853–860.

Palladino, J. J., & Schell, K. A. (1980, March). *Student acceptance of personality descriptions based on the BRPI.* Paper presented at the meeting of the Southeastern Psychological Association, Washington, DC.

Palmer, A. (2003a). Violent song lyrics may lead to violent behavior. *Monitor on Psychology, 34*(5), 15.

Palmer, A. (2003b). Positive emotion styles linked to the common cold. *Monitor on Psychology, 34*(10), 16.

Palmore, E. B. (2004). Research note: Ageism in Canada and the United States. *Journal of Cross-Cultural Gerontology, 19,* 41–46.

Paludi, M. A. (2002). *The psychology of women* (2nd ed.). Upper Saddle River, NJ: Prentice Hall.

Papavassiliou, G., & Mentzas, G. (2003). Knowledge modelling in weakly-structured business processes. *Journal of Knowledge Management, 7,* 18–33.

Paquier, P. F., & Marien, P. (2005). A synthesis of the role of the cerebellum in cognition. *Aphasiology, 19*(1), 3–19.

Parham, T., White, J., & Ajamu, A. (1999). *The psychology of blacks: An African centered perspective* (3rd ed.). Upper Saddle River, NJ: Prentice Hall.

Parker, J. D. A., Bauermann, T. M., & Smith, C. T. (2000). Alexithymia and impoverished dream content: Evidence from rapid eye movement sleep awakenings. *Psychosomatic Medicine, 62,* 486–491.

Parks, A. S., & Bruce, H. M. (1961). Olfactory stimuli in mammalian reproduction.

Pary, R. J. (2004). Behavioral and psychiatric disorders in children and adolescents with Down syndrome. *Mental Health Aspects of Developmental Disabilities, 7,* 69–76.

Pascarella, E. T., & Terenzini, P. T. (1991). *How college affects students: Findings and insights from twenty years of research.* San Francisco: Jossey-Bass.

Pascualy, R. A., & Soest, S. W. (2000). *Snoring and sleep apnea: Sleep well, feel better.* New York: Demos.

Patterson, C. H. (1985). *The therapeutic relationship: Foundations for an eclectic psychotherapy.* Monterey, CA: Brooks/Cole.

Patterson, D. R. (2004). Treating pain with hypnosis. *Current Directions in Psychological Science, 13,* 252–255.

Patterson, D. R., & Jensen, M. (2003). Hypnosis for clinical pain control. *Psychological Bulletin, 129,* 495–521.

Paulos, J. A. (1991). Coincidences. *Skeptical Inquirer, 15,* 382–385.

Pauly, I. B. (1990). Gender identity disorders: Evaluation and treatment. *Journal of Sex Education and Therapy, 16,* 2–24.

Paunonen, S. V., & Ashton, M. C. (1998). The structured assessment of personality across cultures. *Journal of Cross-Cultural Psychology, 29,* 150–170.

Pavalko, E. K., & Smith, B. (1999). The rhythm of work: Health effects of women's work dynamics. *Social Forces, 77,* 1141–1162.

Pavalko, E. K., & Woodbury, S. (2000). Social roles as process: Caregiving careers and women's health. *Journal of Health and Social Behavior, 41,* 91–105.

Pavlov, I. P. (1927). *Conditioned reflexes.* Oxford: Oxford University Press.

Pavlov, I. P. (1928). *Lectures on conditioned reflexes: The higher nervous activity of animals* (Vol. 1), H. Gantt (Trans.). London: Lawrence and Wishart.

Payne, B. R., & Cornwell, P. (2004). Greater sparing of visually guided orienting behavior after early unilateral occipital lesions: Insights from a comparison with the impact of bilateral lesions. *Behavioural Brain Research, 150,* 109–116.

Payne, D. G., Elie, C. J., Blackwell, J. M., & Neuschatz, J. S. (1996). Memory illusions: Recalling, recognizing, and recollecting events that never occurred. *Journal of Memory and Language, 35,* 261–285.

Payne, D. G., Neuschatz, J. S., Lampinen, J. M., & Lynn, S. J. (1997). Compelling memory illusions: The qualitative characteristics of false memories. *Current Directions in Psychological Science, 6,* 56–60.

Pedersen, F. A., Rubenstein, J. L., & Yarrow, L. J. (1979). Infant development in father-absent families. *Journal of Genetic Psychology, 135,* 51–61.

Pedersen, W. (1994). Parental relations, mental health, and delinquency in adolescents. *Adolescence, 29,* 975–990.

Pederson, B. R., Gleason, K. E., Moran, G., & Bento, S. (1998). Maternal attachment representations, maternal sensitivity, and the infant–mother attachment relationship. *Developmental Psychology, 34,* 925–933.

Pelayo, R., Chen, W., Monzon, S., & Guilleminault, C. (2004). Pediatric sleep pharmacology: You want to give my kid sleeping pills? *Pediatric Clinics of North America, 51*(1), 117–134.

Pelletier, K. R. (1984). *Healthy people in unhealthy places: Stress and fitness at work.* New York: Delacorte.

Penzel, F. (2000). *Obsessive-compulsive disorders: A complete guide to getting well and staying well.* New York: Oxford University Press.

Pepler, D. J., & Craig, W. M. (1995). A peek behind the fence: Naturalistic observatons of aggressive children with remote audiovisual recording. *Developmental Psychology, 31,* 548–553.

Peretz, J. R. (2004). Treating affect phobia: A manual for short-term dynamic psychotherapy. *Psychotherapy Research, 14,* 261–263.

Perrewe, P. L., & Hochwarter, W. A. (2001). Can we really have it all? The attainment of work and family values. *Current Directions in Psychological Science, 10,* 29–33.

Perry, S. (1998, May). A hole in the head. *Spin, 14,* 114–119.

Persaud, R., Crossley, D., Freeman, C., Cannon, M., McKenzie, K., & Sims, A. (2003). Should neurosurgery for mental disorder be allowed to die out? *British Journal of Psychiatry, 183,* 195–196.

Personality disorders—Part I. (2000). *Harvard Mental Health Letter, 16*(9), 1–5.

Pert, C. B. (2002). The wisdom of the receptors: Neuropeptides, the emotions, and the bodymind. *Advances in Mind-Body Medicine, 18*(10), 30–35.

Pert, C. B., & Snyder, S. H. (1973). The opiate receptor: Demonstration in nervous tissue. *Science, 179,* 1011–1014.

Pete, J. M., & De Santis, L. (1990). Sexual decision making in young black adolescent females. *Adolescence, 25,* 145–154.

Peterson, L. R., & Peterson, M. J. (1959). Short-term retention of individual items. *Journal of Experimental Psychology, 58,* 193–198.

Petrill, S. A. (2003). The development of intelligence: Behavioral genetic approaches. In R. J. Sternberg, J. Lautrey, & T. I. Lubart (Eds.), *Models of intelligence: International perspectives* (pp. 81–89). Washington, DC: American Psychological Association.

Petrill, S. A., Plomin, R., Berg, S., Johansson, B., Pedersen, N. L., Ahern, F., et al. (1998). The genetic and environmental relationship between general and specific cognitive abilities in twins age 80 and older. *Psychological Science, 9,* 183–189.

Petroski, H. (2001). Everyday design. *American Scientist, 89,* 495–499.

Petty, R. E., & Cacioppo, J. T. (1996). *Attitudes and persuasion: Classic and contemporary approaches.* Boulder, CO: Westview Press.

Pfaffmann, C. (1955). Gustatory nerve impulses in rat, cat, and rabbit. *Neurophysiology, 18,* 429–440.

Phillips, M. D., Lowe, M. J., Lurito, J. T., Dzemidzic, M., & Mathews, V. P. (2001). Temporal lobe activation demonstrates sex-based differences during passive listening. *Radiology, 220,* 202–207.

Piaget, J. (1972). Intellectual evolution from adolescence to adulthood. *Human Development, 15,* 1–12.

Piccinino, L. J., & Mosher, W. D. (1998). Trends in contraceptive use in the United States: 1982–1995. *Family Planning Perspectives, 30,* 4–10, 46.

Piccione, C., Hilgard, E. R., & Zimbardo, P. G. (1989). On the degree of stability of measured hypnotizability over a 25-year period. *Journal of Personality and Social Psychology, 56,* 289–295.

Pick, D., & Reid, S. (1995, October). *The red in trichromatic theory.* Paper presented at the Mid-America Conference for Teachers of Psychology, Evansville, IN.

Pierce, J. D., Jr., Cohen, A. B., & Ulrich, P. M. (2004). Responsivity to two odorants, androstenone and amyl acetate, and the affective impact of odors on interpersonal relationships. *Journal of Comparative Psychology, 118,* 14–19.

Piercey, M. F., Schroeder, L. A., Folkens, K., Xu, J. C., & Horig, J. (1981). Sensory and motor functions of spinal cord substance P. *Science, 187,* 1361–1363.

Pierrehumbert, B., Ramstein, T., Karmaniola, A., Miljkovitch, R., & Halfon, O. (2002). Quality of child care in the preschool years: A comparison of the influence of home care and day care characteristics on child outcome. *International Journal of Behavioral Development, 26,* 385–396.

Pietromonaco, P. R., & Barrett, L. F. (2000). Attachment theory as an organizing framework: A view from different levels of analysis. *Review of General Psychology, 4,* 107–110.

Piliavin, I. M., Rodin, J., & Piliavin, J. A. (1969). Good samaritanism: An underground phenomenon? *Journal of Personality and Social Psychology, 13,* 289–299.

Pincus, H. A., Tanielian, T. L., Marcus, S. C., Olfson, M., Zarin, D. A., Thompson, J., et al. (1998). Prescribing trends in psychotropic medications: Primary care, psychiatry, and other medical specialties. *Journal of the American Medical Association, 279,* 526–531.

Pine, D. S., Grun, J., Zarahn, E., Fyer, A., Koda, V., Li, W., et al. (2001). Cortical brain regions engaged by marked emotional faces in adolescents and adults: An fMRI study. *Emotion, 1,* 137–147.

Pinel, J. P. J. (2006). *Biopsychology* (6th ed.). Boston: Allyn & Bacon.

Pinker, S. (1994). *The language instinct: How the mind creates language.* New York: Morrow.

Pinner, R. W., Teutsch, S. M., Simonsen, L., Klug, L. A., Graber, J. M., Clarke, M. J., et al. (1996). Trends in infectious disease mortality in the United States. *Journal of the American Medical Association, 275,* 189–193.

Piomelli, D. (2004). The endogenous cannabinoid system and the treatment of marijuana dependence. *Neuropharmacology, 47,* 359–367.

Pitskhelauri, R. Z. (1982). *The long-living of Soviet Georgia.* New York: Human Sciences Press.

Pittam, J., & Scherer, K. R. (1993). Vocal expression and communication of emotion. In M. Lewis & J. M. Haviland (Eds.), *Handbook of emotions* (pp. 185–197). New York: Guilford Press.

Plante, T. G., & Rodin, J. (1990). Physical fitness and enhanced psychological health. *Current Psychology: Research and Reviews, 9,* 3–24.

Platania, J., & Moran, G. P. (2001). Social facilitation as a function of mere presence of others. *Journal of Social Psychology, 141,* 190–197.

Plomin, R. (1989). Environment and genes. *American Psychologist, 44,* 105–111.

Plomin, R. (1990). *Nature and nurture: An introduction to human behavioral genetics.* Pacific Grove, CA: Brooks/Cole.

Plomin, R., & DeFries, J. C. (1998). The genetics of cognitive abilities and disabilities. *Scientific American,* 62–69.

Plomin, R., De Fries, J. C., & McClearn, G. E. (1990). *Behavioral genetics: A primer.* New York: Freeman.

Plomin, R., Owen, M. J., & McGuffin, P. (1994). The genetic basis of complex human behaviors. *Science, 264,* 1733–1739.

Plomin, R., & Petrill, S. A. (1997). Genetics and intelligence: What's new. *Intelligence, 24,* 53–77.

Plutchik, R. (1980a). A general psychoevolutionary theory of emotion. In R. Plutchik & H. Kellerman (Eds.), *Emotion: Theory, research, and experience, Vol. 1: Theories of emotion* (pp. 3–33). New York: Academic Press.

Plutchik, R. (1980b). *Emotion: A psychoevolutionary synthesis.* New York: HarperCollins.

Plutchik, R. (1993). Emotions and their vicissitudes: Emotions and psychopathology. In M. Lewis & J. M. Haviland (Eds.), *Handbook of emotions* (pp. 53–66). New York: Guilford Press.

Plutchik, R. (2001). The nature of emotions. *American Scientist, 89,* 344–350.

Poldrack, R. A., & Cohen, N. J. (1998). Priming of new associations in reading time: What is learned? *Psychonomic Bulletin and Review, 4,* 398–402.

Pollak, S. D., & Tolley-Schell, S. (2003). Selective attention to facial emotion in physically abused children. *Journal of Abnormal Psychology, 112,* 323–338.

Ponsonby, A., Dwyer, T., Gibbons, L. E., Cochrane, J. A., & Wang, Y. (1993). Factors potentiating the risk of sudden infant death syndrome associated with the prone position. *New England Journal of Medicine, 329,* 377–382.

Pool, R. (1994). *Eve's rib: The biological roots of sex differences.* New York: Crown.

Pope, M. K., & Smith, T. W. (1991). Cortisol excretion in high and low cynically hostile men. *Psychosomatic Medicine, 53,* 386–392.

Porter, R. H., Makin, J. W., Davis, L. B., & Christensen, K. M. (1992). An assessment of the salient olfactory environment of formula-fed infants. *Physiology and Behavior, 50,* 907–911.

Porter, S. (2004). Forensic psychology. *Canadian Journal of Behavioural Science, 36,* 81–83.

Porter, S., Birt, A. R., Yuille, J. C., & Lehman, D. R. (2000). Negotiating false memories: Interviewer and rememberer characteristics relate to memory distortion. *Psychological Science, 11,* 507–510.

Porter, S., Marco, C., Schwartz, J., Neale, J., Shiffman, S., & Stone, A. (2000). Gender differences in coping: A comparison of trait and momentary assessments. *Journal of Social and Clinical Psychology, 19,* 480–498.

Postmes, T., & Spears, R. (1998). Deindividuation and antinormative behavior: A meta-analysis. *Psychological Bulletin, 123,* 238–259.

Poussaint, A. F. (1990). Introduction. In Cosby, B., *Fatherhood.* New York: Berkley.

Powell, D. H. (2004). Behavioral treatment of debilitating test anxiety among medical students. *Journal of Clinical Psychology, 60*(8), 853–865.

Powell, M., & Schulte, T. (1999). Turner syndrome. In S. Goldstein et al. (Eds.), *Handbook of neurodevelopmental and genetic disorders in children.* New York: Guilford Press.

Pratkanis, A. R., Greenwald, A. G., Leippe, M. R., & Baumgardner, M. H. (1988). In search of reliable persuasion effects: III. The sleeper effect is dead, long live the sleeper effect. *Journal of Personality and Social Psychology, 54,* 203–218.

Premack, D. (1965). Reinforcement theory. In D. Levine (Ed.), *Nebraska Symposium on Motivation* (Vol. 13, pp. 3–41). Lincoln: University of Nebraska Press.

Prentice, D. A., & Miller, D. T. (2002). The emergence of homegrown stereotypes. *American Psychologist, 57,* 352–359.

Pressman, J. D. (1998). *Last report: Psychosurgery and the limits of medicine.* New York: Cambridge University Press.

Price, D. D., & Barber, J. (1987). An analysis of factors that contribute to the efficacy of hypnotic analgesia. *Journal of Abnormal Psychology, 96,* 46–51.

Priester, J. R., & Petty, R. E. (2003). The influence of spokesperson trustworthiness on message elaboration, attitude strength, and advertising effectiveness. *Journal of Consumer Psychology, 13,* 408–421.

Prochaska, J. O. (1979). *Systems of psychotherapy: A transtheoretical analysis.* Belmont, CA: Dorsey/Wadsworth.

Prochaska, J. O., & Norcross, J. C. (1999). *Systems of psychotherapy* (4th ed.). Pacific Grove, CA: Brooks/Cole.

Proctor, R. W., & Capaldi, E. J. (2001). Improving the science education of psychology students: Better teaching of methodology. *Teaching of Psychology, 28,* 173–181.

Provine, R. R. (1997). Yawns, laughs, smiles, tickles, and talking: Naturalistic and laboratory studies of facial action and social communication. In J. A. Russell & J. M. Fernandez (Eds.), *The psychology of facial expression* (pp. 158–175). Cambridge: Cambridge University Press.

Provine, R. R. (2000). *Laughter: A scientific investigation.* New York: Viking.

Pulsifer, M. B., Brandt, J., Salorio, C. F., Vining, E. P. G., Benjamin, S., & Freeman, J. M. (2004). The cognitive outcome of hemispherectomy in 71 children. *Epilepsia, 45*(3), 243–254.

Purcell, P., & Stewart, L. (1990). Dick and Jane in 1989. *Sex Roles, 22,* 177–185.

Quinn, T. C. (1996). Global burden of the HIV pandemic. *Lancet, 348,* 99–106.

Rabasca, L. (2000). Self-help sites: A blessing or a bane? *Monitor on Psychology, 31*(4), 28–30.

Rachman, S. (1998). *Anxiety.* East Sussex, United Kingdom: Psychology Press.

Rachman, S. J. (1966). Sexual fetishism: An experimental analog. *Psychological Record, 18,* 25–27.

Rachman, S. J. (1990). *Fear and courage* (2nd ed.). New York: Freeman.

Rachman, S. J. (2000). Joseph Wolpe (1915–1997): Obituary. *American Psychologist, 55,* 431–432.

Rahman, Q., & Wilson, G. D. (2003). Born gay? The psychobiology of human sexual orientation. *Personality and Individual Differences, 34,* 1337–1382.

Raine, A., Lencz, T., Bihrle, S., LaCasse, L., & Colletti, P. (2000). Reduced prefrontal gray matter volume and reduced autonomic activity in antisocial personality disorder. *Archives of General Psychiatry, 57,* 119–127.

Raine, A., Venables, P. H., & Williams, M. (1990). Relationships between central and autonomic measures of arousal at age 15 years and criminality at age 24 years. *Archives of General Psychiatry, 47,* 1003–1007.

Rajaram, S., & Roediger, H. L., III. (1993). Direct comparison of four implicit memory tests. *Journal of Experimental Psychology: Learning, Memory, and Cognition, 19,* 765–776.

Ramey, C. T., & Campbell, F. A. (1981). Educational intervention for children at risk for mild retardation: A longitudinal analysis. In P. Mittler (Ed.), *Frontiers of knowledge in mental retardation:* Vol. 1: *Social, educational, and behavioral aspects* (pp. 47–57). Baltimore: University Park Press.

Raming, K., Krieger, J., Strotman, J., Boekhoff, I., Kubick, S., Baumstark, C., et al. (1993). Cloning and expression of odorant molecules. *Nature, 361,* 353–356.

Ramsey, J. L., & Langlois, J. H. (2002). Effects of the "beauty is good" stereotype on children's information processing. *Journal of Experimental Child Psychology, 81,* 320–340.

Randi, J. (1987). *Flim-flam: Psychics, ESP, unicorns, and other delusions.* Buffalo, NY: Prometheus.

Randi, J. (1995). *An encyclopedia of claims, frauds, and hoaxes of the occult and supernatural.* New York: St. Martin's Press.

Rantakallio, P., Peter, J., Moring, J., & Von Wendt, L. (1997). Association between central nervous system infections during childhood and adult onset schizophrenia and other psychoses: A 28-year follow-up. *International Journal of Epidemiology, 26,* 837–843.

Rapoport, J. L. (1989). *The boy who couldn't stop washing: The experience and treatment of obsessive-compulsive disorder.* New York: Dutton.

Rask, K., Kaunonen, M., & Paunonen-Ilmonen, M. (2002). Adolescent coping with grief after the death of a loved one. *International Journal of Nursing Practice, 8,* 137–142.

Reason, J., & Mycielska, K. (1982). *Absent-minded? The psychology of mental lapses and everyday errors.* Upper Saddle River, NJ: Prentice Hall.

Recarte, M. A., & Nunes, L. M. (2003). Mental workload while driving: Effects of visual search, discrimination, and decision making. *Journal of Experimental Psychology: Applied, 9,* 119–137.

Rechtschaffen, A. (1998). Current perspectives on the function of sleep. *Perspectives in Biology and Medicine, 41,* 359–390.

Records, R. E. (1979). Retina: Metabolism and photochemistry. In R. E. Records (Ed.), *Physiology of the human eye and visual system* (pp. 296–318). New York: HarperCollins.

Recupero, P. R., Heru, A. M., Price, M., & Alves, J. (2004). Sexual harassment in medical education: Liability and protection. *Academic Medicine, 79*(9), 817–824.

Redd, W. H., Jacobsen, P. B., Die-Trill, M., Dermatis, H., McEvoy, M., & Holland, J. C. (1987). Cognitive/attentional distraction in the control of conditioned nausea in pediatric cancer patients receiving chemotherapy. *Journal of Consulting and Clinical Psychology, 55,* 391–395.

Regan, P. C., & Berscheid, E. (1999). *Lust: What we know about human sexual desire.* Thousand Oaks, CA: Sage.

Regier, D. A., Kaelber, C. T., Rae, D. S., Farmer, M. E., Knauper, B., Kessler, R. C., et al. (1998a). Limitations of diagnostic criteria and assessment instruments for mental disorders. *Archives of general Psychology, 55,* 109–115.

Regier, D. A., Narrow, W. E., Rae, D. S., Manderscheid, R. W., Locke, B. Z., & Goodwin, F. K. (1993). The de facto U.S. mental and addictive disorders service system. *Archives of General Psychiatry, 50,* 85–94.

Regier, D. A., Rae, D. S., Narrow, W. E., Kaelber, C. T., & Schatzberg, A. F. (1998b). Prevalence of anxiety disorders and their comorbidity with mood and addictive disorders. *British Journal of Psychiatry, 173* (Suppl 34), 24–28.

Reichling, D. B., Kwait, G. C., & Basbaum, A. I. (1988). Anatomy, physiology, and pharmacology of the periaqueductal gray contribution to antinociceptive controls. In H. C. Fields & J. M. Benson (Eds.), *Progress in brain research* (pp. 31–46). Amsterdam: Elsevier.

Reifman, A. S., Larrick, R. P., & Fein, S. (1991). Temper and temperature on the diamond: The heat-aggression relationship in major league baseball. *Personality and Social Psychology Bulletin, 17,* 580–585.

Reilly, M. E., Lott, B., Caldwell, D., & De Luca, L. (1992). Tolerance for sexual harassment related to self-reported sexual victimization. *Journal of Social Issues, 38,* 99–110.

Reinke, B. J., Ellicott, A. M., Harris, R. L., & Hancock, E. (1985). Timing of psychosocial changes in women's lives. *Human Development, 28,* 259–280.

Reisbult, C. E. (1980). Commitment and satisfaction in romantic associations: A test of the investment model. *Journal of Experimental Social Psychology, 16,* 172–186.

Reker, G. T., Peacock, E. J., & Wong, P. T. P. (1987). Meaning and purpose in life and well-being: A life-span perspective. *Journal of Gerontology, 42,* 44–49.

Remley, A. (1988, October). From obedience to independence. *Psychology Today,* pp. 56–59.

*Report of the Presidential Commission on the Space Shuttle Challenger Accident.* (1986). Washington, DC: U.S. Government Printing Office.

Rescorla, R. A. (1968). Probability of shock in presence and absence of CS in fear conditioning. *Journal of Comparative and Physiological Psychology, 66,* 1–5.

Restak, R. (2000). *Mysteries of the mind.* Washington, DC: National Geographic Society.

Restak, R. M. (1988). *The mind.* New York: Bantam Books.

Restak, R. M. (1994). *The modular brain.* New York: Scribner's.

Rhodes, G., Sumich, A., & Byatt, G. (1999). Are average facial configurations attractive only because of their symmetry? *Psychological Science, 10,* 52–58.

Rice, F. P. (2001). *Human development: A life-span approach.* Upper Saddle River, NJ: Prentice Hall.

Rice, L. N., & Greenberg, L. S. (1992). Humanistic approaches to psychotherapy. In D. K. Freedheim (Ed.), *History of psychotherapy: A century of change.* Washington, DC: American Psychological Association.

Richards, D. (2004). Self-help: Empowering service users or aiding cash strapped mental health services? *Journal of Mental Health (UK), 13,* 117–123.

Richards, H., Reid, M., & Watt, G. (2003). Victim-blaming revisited: A qualitative study of beliefs about illness causation, and responses to chest pain. *Family Practice, 20,* 711–716.

Richardson, J. G., & Simpson, C. H. (1982). Children, gender, and social structure: An analysis of the contents of letters to Santa Claus. *Child Development, 53,* 429–436.

Richmond, V. P., & McCroskey, J. C. (1995). *Nonverbal behavior in interpersonal relations* (3rd ed.). Needham Heights, MA: Allyn & Bacon.

Richter, C. P. (Ed.). (1922). A behavioristic study of the activity of the rat. *Comparative Psychology Monographs, 1.*

Rideout, V. J., Vandewater, E. A., & Wartella, E. A. (2003). *Zero to six: Electronic media in the lives of infants, toddlers, and preschoolers.* Menlo Park, CA: Kaiser Family Foundation.

Rief, W., Hiller, W., & Margraf, J. (1998). Cognitive aspects of hypochondriasis and the somatization syndrome. *Journal of Abnormal Psychology, 107,* 587–595.

Riggio, R. E. (2003). *Introduction to industrial/organizational psychology* (4th ed.). Upper Saddle River, NJ: Prentice Hall.

Ringlemann, M. (1913). Recherches sur les moteurs animes: Travail de l'homme. *Annales de l'Institut National Agronomique*, Series 2, *12*, 1–40.

Rixxo, T. A., Metzger, B. E., Dooley, S. L., & Cho, N. H. (1997). Early malnutrition and child neurobehavioral development: Insights from the study of children and diabetic mothers. *Child Development, 68*, 26–38.

Robbins, S. B., Lauver, K., Le, H., Davis, D., Langley, R., & Carlstrom, A. (2004). Do psychosocial and study skill factors predict college outcomes? A meta-analysis. *Psychological Bulletin, 130*, 261–288.

Roberts, D. F., Foehr, U. G., Rideout, V. J., & Vrodie, M. (1999). *Kids & media in the new millennium.* Menlo Park, CA: Kaiser Family Foundation.

Roberts, G. C., & Treasure, D. C. (1999). Psychology applied to sport. In A. M. Stec & D. A. Bernstein (Eds.), *Psychology: Fields of application* (pp. 116–126). Boston: Houghton Mifflin.

Roberts, L. W., & Krystal, J. (2003). A time of promise, a time of promises: Ethical issues in advancing psychopharmacological research. *Psychopharmacology, 171*, 1–5.

Robins, L. N., & Regier, D. A. (Eds.). (1991). *Psychiatric disorders in America: The Epidemiologic Catchment Area Study.* New York: Free Press.

Robinson, A., & Henry, G. P. (1985). Prenatal diagnosis by amniocentesis. *Annual Review of Medicine, 36*, 13–26.

Robinson, J. P., & Godbey, G. (1999). *Time for life: The surprising ways American use their time.* University Park: Pennsylvania State University Press.

Rock, I., & Palmer, S. (1990). The legacy of Gestalt psychology. *Scientific American, 263*, 84–90.

Rodgers, J. L., Cleveland, H. H., van den Oord, E., & Rowe, D. C. (2000). Resolving the debate over birth order, family size, and intelligence. *American Psychologist, 55*(6), 599–612.

Rodgers, J. L., Cleveland, H. H., van den Ooord, E., & Rowe, D. C. ( 2001). Birth order and intelligence: Together again for the last time? *American Psychologist, 56*(6–7), 523–524.

Rodin, J. (1992). *Body traps.* New York: Morrow.

Rodriguez, M. S., & Cohen, S. (1998). Social support. In H. S. Friedman (Ed.), *Encyclopedia of mental health* (Vol. 3, pp. 535–544). San Diego, CA: Academic Press.

Roesch, R., Zapf, P. A., Golding, S. L., & Skeem, J. L. (1999). Defining and assessing competency to stand trial. In A. K. Hess & I. B. Weiner (Eds.), *The handbook of forensic psychology* (2nd ed., pp. 327–349). New York: Wiley.

Roffwarg, H. P., Muzio, J. N., & Dement, W. C. (1966). Ontogenetic development of the human sleep-dream cycle. *Science, 37*, 604–619.

Rogelberg, S. G. (Ed.). (2002). *Handbook of research methods in industrial and organizational psychology.* Maiden, MA: Blackwell.

Rogers, A., E., Aldrich, M. S., & Lin, X. (2001). A comparison of three different sleep schedules for reducing daytime sleepiness in narcolepsy. *Journal of Sleep and Sleep Disorders Research, 24*, 385–391.

Rogers, C. (1959). My philosophy of interpersonal relationships and how it grew. *Journal of Humanistic Psychology, 28*, 3–15.

Rogers, C. R. (1957). The necessary and sufficient conditions of therapeutic personality change. *Journal of Consulting Psychology, 21*, 95–103.

Rogers, C. R. (1991, October). Children in gangs. *UNESCO Courier*, pp. 19–21.

Rogers, J. (2000, March–April). Heart patients, stay calm. *Psychology Today, 33*, 22.

Rogers, R., & Shuman, D. W. (2000). *Conducting insanity evaluations* (2nd ed.). New York: Guilford Press.

Rogers, W., & Fisk, A. D. (2004). Psychological science and intelligent home technology: Supporting functional independence of older adults. *APA Online Psychological Science Agenda, 18*(2).

Rohrer, D., Wixted, J. T., Salmon, D. P., & Butters, N. (1995). Retrieval from semantic memory and its implications for Alzheimer's disease. *Journal of Experimental Psychology: Learning, Memory, and Cognition, 21*, 1127–1139.

Roid, G. (2003). *Stanford-Binet Intelligence Scales–Fifth Edition.* Itasca, IL: Riverside Publishing.

Rollin, B. E. (1985). The moral status of research animals in psychology. *American Psychologist, 40*, 920–926.

Rolls, B. J., Roe, L. S., Kral, T. V. E., Meengs, J. S., & Wall, D. E. (2004). Increasing the portion size of a packaged snack increases energy intake in men and women. *Appetite, 42*(1), 63–69.

Romero, K., & Silvestri, L. (1990). The role of mental practice in the acquisition and performance of motor skills. *Journal of Instructional Psychology, 17*, 218–221.

Rosch, E. H. (1975). Cognitive representations of semantic categories. *Journal of Experimental Psychology: General, 104*, 192–233.

Rose, C. L., Murphy, L. B., Byard, L., & Nikzad, K. (2002). The role of the Big Five personality factors in vigilance performance and workload. *European Journal of Personality, 16*, 185–200.

Rose, J. E., Brugge, J. F., Anderson, D. J., & Hind, J. E. (1967). Phase-locked response to low-frequency tones in single auditory nerve fibers of the squirrel monkey. *Journal of Neurophysiology, 30*, 769–793.

Rosebush, P. (1994). What is neuroleptic malignant syndrome and how is it treated? *Harvard Mental Health Letter, 11*(6), 8.

Rosell, E., Miller, K., & Barber, K. (1995). Firefighting women and sexual harassment. *Public Personnel Management, 24*, 339–350.

Roseman, I. J., Dhawan, N., Rettek, S. I., Naidu, R. K., & Thapa, K. (1995). Cultural differences and cross-cultural similarities in appraisals and emotional responses. *Journal of Cross-Cultural Psychology, 26*, 23–48.

Rosen, E., Ackerman, L., & Zosky, D. (2002). The sibling empty nest syndrome: The experience of sadness as siblings leave the family home. *Journal of Human Behavior in the Social Environment, 6*, 65–80.

Rosen, E., Anthony, D. L., Booker, K. M., Brown, T. L., Christian, E., Crews, R. C., et al. (1991). A comparison of eating disorder scores among African-American and white college students. *Bulletin of the Psychonomic Society, 29*, 65–66.

Rosenfarb, I. S., Goldstein, M. J., Mintz, J., & Neuchterlein, K. H. (1995). Expressed emotion and subclinical psychopathology observable within the transactions between schizophrenic patients and their family members. *Journal of Abnormal Psychology, 104*, 259–267.

Rosenfeld, A. (1985). *Prolongevity: 2. An updated report on the scientific prospectus for adding good years to life.* New York: Knopf.

Rosenfeld, J. P. (1995). Alternative views of Bashore and Rapp's (1993) alternatives to traditional polygraphy: A critique. *Psychological Bulletin, 117*, 159–166.

Rosenfeld, J. P., Soskins, M., Bosh, G., & Ryan, A. (2004). Simple, effective countermeasures to P300-based tests of detection of concealed information. *Psychophysiology, 41*(2), 205–219.

Rosengren, K. D., McAuley, E., & Mihalko, S. L. (1998). Gait adjustments in older adults: Activity and efficacy influences. *Psychology and Aging, 13*, 375–386.

Rosengren, K. S., & Hickling, A. K. (1994). Seeing is believing: Children's explanations of commonplace, magical, and extraordinary transformations. *Child Development, 65*, 1605–1626.

Rosenhan, D. L. (1973). On being sane in insane places. *Science, 179*, 250–258.

Rosenthal, N. E. (1998). *Winter blues: Seasonal affective disorder: What it is and how to overcome it* (rev. ed.). New York: Guilford Press.

Rosenthal, R. (2003). Covert communication in laboratories, classroom, and the truly real world. *Current Directions in Psychological Science, 12*, 151–154.

Rosenthal, R., & Jacobson, L. (1968). *Pygmalion in the classroom: Teacher expectation and intellectual development.* Austin, TX: Holt, Rinehart & Winston.

Rosenzweig, M. R. (1984). Experience, memory, and the brain. *American Psychologist, 39*, 365–376.

Rosenzweig, M. R. (1996). Aspects of the search for neural mechanisms of memory. *Annual Review of Psychology, 47*, 1–32.

Rosenzweig, M. R., Bennett, E. L., & Diamond, M. C. (1976). Brain changes in response to experience. *Progress in psychobiology.* New York: Freeman.

Ross, B. H., & Spalding, T. L. (1994). Concepts and categories. In R. J. Sternberg (Ed.), *Thinking and problem solving* (pp. 119–148). San Diego, CA: Academic Press.

Ross, L. (1998). Comment on Gilbert. In J. M. Darley & J. Cooper (Eds.), *Attribution and social interaction* (pp. 53–66). Washington, DC: American Psychological Association.

Ross, L., Amabile, T. M., & Steinmetz, J. L. (1977). Social roles, social control, and biases in social-perception processes. *Journal of Personality and Social Psychology, 35*, 485–494.

Rossler, P., & Brosius, H.-B. (2001). Do talk shows cultivate adolescents' views of the world? A prolonged-exposure experiment. *Journal of Communication, 51*, 143–163.

Roth, M., Wischik, C. M., Evans, N., & Mountjoy, C. (1985). Convergence and cohesion of recent neurobiological findings in relation to Alzheimer's disease and their bearing on its etiological basis. In M. Bergener, M. Ermini, & H. B. Stahelin (Eds.), *Thresholds in aging.* London: Academic Press.

Rothbaum, F., Weisz, J., Pott, M., Miyake, K., & Morelli, G. (2000). Attachment and culture: Security in the United States and Japan. *American Psychologist, 55*, 1093–1104.

Rotter, J. B. (1966). Generalized expectancies for internal versus external control of reinforcement. *Psychological Monographs, 80* (Whole No. 609).

Rotter, J. B. (1990). Internal versus external control of reinforcement. *American Psychologist, 45*, 489–493.

Rotton, J., & Kelly, I. W. (1985). Much ado about the full moon: A meta-analysis of lunar-lunacy research. *Psychological Bulletin, 97*, 286–306.

Roure, R., Collect, C., Deschaumes-Molinaro, C., Delhomme, G., Dittmar, A., & Vernet-Maury, E. (1999). Imagery quality estimated by autonomic response is correlated to sporting performance enhancement. *Physiology and Behavior, 66*(1), 63–72.

Rovee-Collier, C. (1993). The capacity for long-term memory in infancy. *Current Directions in Psychological Science, 2*, 130–135.

Rovee-Collier, C., & Lipsitt, L. (1982). Learning, adaptation, and memory in the newborn. In P. Stratton (Ed.), *Psychobiology of the human newborn.* New York: Wiley.

Rovet, J. (2004). Turner syndrome: A review of genetic and hormonal influences on neuropsychological functioning. *Child Neuropsychology, 10*(4), 262–279.

Rozin, P., Lowery, L., & Ebert, R. (1994). Varieties of disgust faces and the structure of disgust. *Journal of Personality and Social Psychology, 66*, 870–881.

Ru, B. L., & Makosso, J. P. M. (2001). Prey habitat location by the cassava mealybug predator *Exochomus flaiventris*: Olfactory responses to odor of plant, mealybug, plant-mealybug complex, and plant-mealybug-natural enemy complex. *Journal of Insect Behavior, 14*, 557–572.

Rubin, R. T., Provenzano, F. J., & Luria, Z. (1974). The eye of the beholder: Parents' views on sex of newborns. *American Journal of Orthopsychiatry, 43*, 720–731.

Ruchlis, H. (1990). *Clear thinking: A practical introduction.* Buffalo, NY: Prometheus.

Rudestam, K. E. (1971). Stockholm and Los Angeles: A cross-cultural study of the communication of suicidal intent. *Journal of Consulting and Clinical Psychology, 36*, 82–90.

Rudman, L. A., & Glick, P. (2001). Prescriptive gender stereotypes and backlash toward agentic women. *Journal of Social Issues, 57*, 743–762.

Russell, J. A. (1991). Culture and the categorization of emotions. *Psychological Bulletin, 110*, 426–450.

Russell, J. A., & Sato, K. (1995). Comparing emotion words between languages. *Journal of Cross-Cultural Psychology, 26*, 384–391.

Ruzgis, P., & Grigorenko, E. L. (1994). Cultural meaning systems, intelligence, and personality. In R. J. Sternberg & P. Ruzgis (Eds.), *Personality and intelligence* (pp. 248–270). New York: Cambridge University Press.

Saal, F. E., Johnson, C. B., & Weber, N. (1989). Friendly or sexy? It may depend on whom you ask. *Psychology of Women Quarterly, 13*, 263–276.

Saarijaervi, S., Salminen, J. K., & Toikka, T. B. (2001). Alexithymia and depression: A 1-year follow-up study in outpatients with major depression. *Journal of Psychosomatic Research, 51,* 729–733.

Sachdev, P., & Hay. P. (1996). Site and size of lesion and psychosurgical outcome in obsessive-compulsive disorder. A magnetic resonance imaging study. *Biological Psychiatry, 39,* 739–742.

Sacks, O. (1985). *The man who mistook his wife for a hat.* New York: Summit Books.

Sadker, M., & Sadker, D. (1985, March). Sexism in the schoolroom of the '80s. *Psychology Today,* pp. 54–57.

Sadker, M., & Sadker, D. (1986, March). Sexism in the classroom: From grade school to graduate school. *Phi Delta Kappan,* pp. 512–515.

Sadker, M., & Sadker, D. (1993). *Failing at fairness.* New York: Scribner.

Sadker, M., Sadker, D., & Stulberg, L. M. (1993, March). Fair and square? Creating a nonsexist classroom. *Instructor,* pp. 45–46, 67–68.

Sadock, B. J., & Sadock, V. A. (2003). *Kaplan and Sadock's synopsis of psychiatry: Behavioral sciences/clinical psychiatry* (9th ed.). Philadelphia: Lippincott Williams & Wilkins.

Sadoski, M., & Paivio, A. (2001). *Imagery and text: A dual coding theory of reading and writing.* Mahwah, NJ: Lawrence Erlbaum.

Saeed, S. A., & Bruce, T. J. (1998). Seasonal affective disorder. *American Family Physician, 57,* 1340–1346.

Sageman, M. (2004). *Understanding terror networks.* Philadelphia: University of Pennsylvania Press.

Sagi, A. (1990). Attachment theory and research from a cross-cultural perspective. *Human Development, 33,* 10–22.

Sagi, A., Van Ijzendoorn, M. H., Aviezer, O., & Donnell, F. (1994). Sleeping out of home in a kibbutz communal arrangement: It makes a difference for infant-mother attachment. *Child Development, 65,* 992–1004.

Saha, S., Chant, D., Welham, J., & McGrath, J. (2005). A systematic review of the prevalence of schizophrenia. *PLoS Medicine, 2*(5), 413–433. Accessed June 18, 2005, at www.plosmedicine.org

Sakai, H. (1999). A multiplicative power-function model of cognitive dissonance: Toward an integrated theory of cognition, emotion, and behavior after Leon Festinger. In E. Harmon-Jones & J. S. Mills (Eds.), *Cognitive dissonance: Process on a pivotal theory in social psychology.* Washington, DC: American Psychological Association.

Salminen, J.K., Saarijanvi, S., Aairela, E., & Tamminen, T. (1994) Alexithymia: State on trait? One–year follow–up study of general hospital psychiatric consultation outpatients. *Journal of Psychosomatic Research, 38,* 681–685.

Sam, M., Vora, S., Malnic, B., Ma, W., Novotny, M., & Buck, L. B. (2001). Odorants may arouse instinctive behaviours. *Nature, 412*(6843), 142.

Samovar, L. A., & Porter, R. E. (1991). *Communication between cultures.* Belmont, CA: Wadsworth.

Sams, M., Hari, R., Rif, J., & Knuutila, J. (1993). The human auditory memory trace persists about 10 sec: Neuromagnetic evidence. *Journal of Cognitive Neuroscience, 5,* 363–370.

Sanchez, L. M., & Turner, S. M. (2003). Practicing psychology in the era of managed care: Implications for practice and training. *American Psychologist, 58,* 116–129.

Sandal, G. M., & Endresen, I. M. (2002). The sensitivity of the CPI Good Impression scale for detecting "Faking Good" among Norwegian students and job applicants. *International Journal of Selection and Assessment, 10,* 304–311.

Sarason, I. G., & Sarason, B. R. (2002). *Abnormal psychology* (10th ed.). Upper Saddle River, NJ: Prentice Hall.

Sarkis, K. (2000, May). Computer workers at risk for stress injuries. *Occupational Hazards, 62,* 33.

Sarver, D. B. (2001). Plastic surgery in children and adolescents. In J. K. Thompson & L. Smolak. (Eds.), *Body image, eating disorders, and obesity in youth: Assessment, prevention, and treatment* (pp. 341–366.) Washington, DC: American Psychological Association.

Saternberg, R. J., & O'Hara, L. A. (1999). Creativity and intelligence. In R. J. Sternberg (Ed.), *Handbook of creativity* (pp. 251–272). New York: Cambridge University Press.

Saudino, K. J. (1997). Moving beyond the heritability question: New directions in behavioral genetic studies of personality. *Current Directions in Psychological Science, 6,* 86–90.

Saul, H. (2001). Phobias: Fighting the fear. In D. H. Barlow (Ed.), *Anxiety and its disorders: The nature and treatment of anxiety and panic* (2nd ed., pp. 516–550). New York: Guilford Press.

Saunders, J. B., Aasland, O. G., Babor, T. F., de la Fuente, J. R., & Grant, M. (1993). Development of the Alcohol Use Disorders Identification Test (AUDIT): WHO Collaborative Project on Early Detection of Persons with Harmful Alcohol Consumption–II. *Addiction, 88,* 791–804.

Savage, R. (2004). Motor skills, automaticity and developmental dyslexia: A review of the research literature. *Reading and Writing, 17,* 301–324.

Saxe, L. (1991). Lying: Thoughts of an applied social psychologist. *American Psychologist, 46,* 409–415.

Saxe, L. (1994). Detection of deception: Polygraph and integrity tests. *Current Directions in Psychological Science, 3*(3), 69–73.

Scarborough, E., & Furumoto, L. (1987). *Untold lives:The first generation of American women psychologists.* New York: Columbia University Press.

Scarr, S. (1992). Developmental theories for the 1990s: Development and individual differences. *Child Development, 63,* 1–19.

Scarr, S. (1998). How do families affect intelligence? Social environmental and behavior genetic prediction. In J. J. McArdle, R. W. Woodcock, et al. (Eds.), *Human cognitive abilities in theory and practice.* (pp. 113–136). Mahwah, NJ: Erlbaum.

Scarr, S., & Eisenberg, M. (1993). Child care research: Issues, perspectives, and results. *Annual Review of Psychology, 44,* 613–644.

Scarr, S., & Weinberg, R. A. (1986). The early childhood enterprise: Care and education of the young. *American Psychologist, 41,* 1140–1146.

Schaap, D., & Gerberg, M. (Eds.). (1992). *Joy in Mudville: The big book of baseball humor.* New York: Doubleday.

Schab, F. R. (1990). Odors and the remembrance of things past. *Journal of Experimental Psychology: Learning, Memory, and Cognition, 16,* 648–655.

Schachter, D. L. (1997). False recognition and the brain. *Current Directions in Psychological Science, 6,* 65–70.

Schacter, D. L., & Badgaiyan, R. D. (2001). Neuroimaging of priming: New perspectives on implicit and explicit memory. *Current Directions in Psychological Science, 10,* 1–4.

Schacter, D. L. (2001). *The seven sins of memory: How the mind forgets and remembers.* Boston: Houghton Mifflin.

Schachter, D. L., Curran, T., Galluccio, L., Milberg, W., & Bates, J. (1996). False recognition and the right frontal lobe: A case study. *Neuropsychologica, 34,* 793–808.

Schachter, S., & Singer, J. E. (1962). Cognitive, social, and physiological determinants of emotional state. *Psychological Review, 69,* 379–399.

Schacter, S., & Singer, J. E. (2001). Cognitive, social, and psychological determinants of emotional state. In G. W. Parrott (Ed.), *Emotions in social psychology: Essential readings* (pp. 76–93). Philadelphia: Psychology Press.

Schafer, M., & Crichlow, S. (1996). Antecedents of groupthink. *Journal of Conflict Resolution, 40,* 415–435.

Schaffer, R. (1977). *Mothering.* Cambridge, MA: Harvard University Press.

Schaie, K. W. (1977–1978). Toward a stage theory of adult cognitive development. *Journal of Aging and Human Development, 8,* 129–138.

Schaie, K. W. (1983). The Seattle longitudinal study: A twenty-one year investigation of psychometric intelligence. In K. W. Schaie (Ed.), *Longitudinal studies of adult psychological development.* New York: Guilford Press.

Schaie, K. W. (1990). Intellectual development in adulthood. In J. E. Birren & K. W. Schaie (Eds.), *Handbook of the psychology of aging.* San Diego, CA: Academic Press.

Scharff, L. V., & Ahumada, A. J. (2001). Predicting readability of transparent text on textured backgrounds. *Investigative Ophthalmology and Visual Science, 42,* S733.

Scharff, L. V., Hill, A. L., & Ahumada, A. J. (2000). Discriminability measures for predicting readability of text on textured backgrounds. *Optics Express, 6*(4), 81–91.

Scheck, G., Neufeld, P., & Dwyer, J. (2000). *Actual innocence.* New York, Random House.

Schelling, T. C. (1992). Addictive drugs: The cigarette experience. *Science, 255,* 430–433.

Schenck, C. H., Hurwitz, T. D., & Mahowald, M. W. (1993). REM sleep behaviour disorder: An update on a series of 96 patients and a review of the world literature. *Journal of Sleep Research, 2,* 224–231.

Scherer, K. R., & Wallbott, H. G. (1994). Evidence for universality and cultural variation of differential emotion response patterning. *Journal of Personality and Social Psychology, 66,* 310–328.

Schiffman, S. S. (1983). Taste and smell in disease. *New England Journal of Medicine, 308,* 1275–1279.

Schindler, L. W. (1991). *Understanding the immune system.* Rockville, MD: National Institutes of Health.

Schnedier, W. J., & Nevid, J. S. (1993). Overcoming math anxiety: A comparison of stress inoculation training and systematic desensitization. *Journal of College Student Development, 34,* 283–288.

Schneier, F. R., & Johnson, J. (1992). Social phobia: Comorbidity and morbidity in an epidemiological sample. *Archives of General Psychiatry, 49,* 282–288.

Schou, M. (1997). Forty years of lithium treatment. *Archives of General Psychiatry, 54,* 9–13.

Schousboe, K., Visscher, P. M., Erbas, B., Kyvik, K. O., Hopper, J. L., Henriksen, J. E., et al. (2004). Twin study of genetic and environmental influences on adult body size, shape, and composition. *International Journal of Obesity and Related Metabolic Disorders, 28*(1), 39–48.

Schrader, B. W., & Steiner, D. D. (1996). Common comparison standards: An approach to improving agreement between self and supervisory performance ratings. *Journal of Applied Psychology, 81,* 813–820.

Schreck, L. (1998). After early amniocentesis, chances of fetal loss and foot deformity rise. *Family Planning Perspectives, 30,* 249–250.

Schreurs, B. G. (1993). Long-term memory and extinction of the classically conditioned rabbit nictitating membrane response. *Learning and Motivation, 24,* 294–302.

Schutte, N. S., Malouff, J. M., Hall, L. E., Haggerty, D. J., Cooper, J. T., Golden, C. J., et al. (1998). Development and validation of a measure of emotional intelligence. *Personality and Individual Differences, 25,* 167–177.

Schweinberger, S. R. (1996). How Gorbachev primed Yeltsin: Analyses of associative priming in person recognition by means of reaction times and event-related brain potentials. *Journal of Experimental Psychology: Learning, Memory, and Cognition, 22,* 1383–1407.

Scott, A. J. (1994). Chronobiological considerations in shiftworker sleep and performance and shiftwork scheduling. *Human Performance, 7,* 207–233.

Scoville, W. B., & Milner, B. (1957). Loss of recent memory after bilateral hippocampal lesions. *Journal of Neurology, Neurosurgery, and Psychiatry, 20,* 11–19.

Scribner, C. M. (2001). Rosenhand revisted. Professional psychology: *Research and Practice, 12,* 215–216.

Sedikides, C., Campbell, W. K., Reeder, G. D., & Elliot, A. J. (1998). The self-serving bias in relational context. *Journal of Personality and Social Psychology, 74,* 378–386.

Seeman, T. E., Dubin, L. F., & Seeman, M. (2003). Religiosity/spirituality and health: A critical review of the evidence for biological pathways. *American Psychologist, 58,* 53–63.

Segal, M. W. (1974). Alphabet and attraction: An unobtrusive measure of the effect of propinquity in a field setting. *Journal of Personality and Social Psychology, 30,* 654–657.

Segerstrom, S. C., & Miller, G. E. (2004). Psychological stress and the human immune system: A meta-analytic study of 30 years of inquiry. *Psychological Bulletin, 130,* 601–630.

Seifert, K., Hoffnung, R., & Hoffnung, M. (2000). *Lifespan human development* (2nd ed.). Boston: Houghton Mifflin.

Seligman, M. E. P. (1970). On the generality of the laws of learning. *Psychological Review, 77,* 406–418.

Seligman, M. E. P. (1989). Research in clinical psychology: Why is there so much depression today? In I. S. Cohen (Ed.), *The G. Stanley Hall Lecture Series* (Vol. 9, pp. 75–96). Washington, DC: American Psychological Association.

Seligman, M. E. P. (1990). *Learned optimism: How to change your mind and your life.* New York: Pocket Books.

Seligman, M. E. P. (1992). *Helplessness: On depression, development and death.* New York: Freeman. (Originally published in 1975).

Seligman, M. E. P. (1993). *What you can change and what you can't.* New York: Knopf.

Seligman, M. E. P. (1995). The effectiveness of psychotherapy: The *Consumer Reports* study. *American Psychologist, 50,* 965–974.

Seligman, M. E. P. (1996). Long-term psychotherapy is highly effective: The *Consumer Reports* study. *Harvard Mental Health Letter,* 5–7.

Selling it. (1991, April). *Consumer Reports,* p. 295.

Selye, H. (1978). *The stress of life.* New York: McGraw-Hill.

Senior, K. (2001). Should stress carry a health warning? *Lancet, 357,* 126–127.

Seymour, T. L., Seifert, C. M., Shafto, M. G., & Mosmann, A. L. (2000). Using response time measures to assess "guilty knowledge." *Journal of Applied Psychology, 85,* 30–37.

Shadel, W. G., Niaura, A. H., & Abrams, D. B. (2001). How do adolescents process smoking and antismoking advertisements? A social cognitive analysis with implications for understanding smoking initiation. *Review of General Psychology, 5,* 429–444.

Shaiko, R. G. (1996). Female participation in public interest nonprofit governance: Yet another glass ceiling? *Nonprofit Management and Leadership, 8*(2), 121–139.

Shain, R., & Phillips, J. (1991). The stigma of mental illness: Labeling and stereotyping in the news. In L. Wilkins & P. Patterson (Eds.), *Risky business: Communicating issues of science, risk, and public policy* (pp. 61–74). Westport, CT: Greenwood Press.

Shapiro, B. E., & Danly, M. (1985). The role of the right hemisphere in the control of speech prosody in propositional and affective contexts. *Brain and Language, 25,* 19–36.

Shapiro, L. (1990, May 28). Guns and dolls. *Newsweek,* pp. 56–65.

Shapiro, L. (1998, June 15). Fat, fatter, But who's counting? *Newsweek,* p. 55.

Sharma, A., Lynch, M. A., & Irvine, M. L. (1994). The availability of advice regarding infant feeding to immigrants of Vietnamese origin: A survey of families and health visitors. *Child: Care, Health, and Development, 20,* 349–354.

Sharma, S. (2004). Psychology and the study of differences in human functioning: Some reflections. *Psychological Studies, 49,* 1–5.

Sharps, M. J., & Wertheimer, M. (2000). Gestalt perspectives on cognitive science and on experimental psychology. *Review of General Psychology, 4,* 315–336.

Shaw, J. I., Borough, H. W., & Fink, M. I. (1994). Perceived sexual orientation and helping behavior by males and females: The wrong number technique. *Journal of Psychology and Human Sexuality, 6,* 73–81.

Shean, G. (1978). *Schizophrenia: An introduction to research and theory.* Framingham, MA: Winthrop.

Shearn, D., Bergman, E., Hill, K., & Abel, A. (1990). Facial coloration and temperature responses in blushing. *Psychophysiology, 27,* 687–693.

Sheikh, J. I., Leskin, G. A., & Klein, D. F. (2002). Gender differences in panic disorder: Findings from the National Comorbidity Survey. *American Journal of Psychiatry, 159*(1), 55–58.

Sheldon, J. P. (2004). Gender stereotypes in educational software for young children. *Sex Roles, 51*(7–8), 433–444.

Sheldon, R. G., Tracy, S. K., & Brown, W. B. (1997). *Youth gangs in American society.* New York: Wadsworth.

Sheldon, S. H. (2004). Parasomnias in childhood. *Pediatric Clinics of North America, 51*(1), 69–88.

Sheldon, W. H., & Stevens, S. S. (1942). *The varieties of temperament: A psychology of constitutional differences.* New York: HarperCollins.

Sheldon, W. H., Stevens, S. S., & Tucker, W. B. (1940). *The varieties of human physique: An introduction to constitutional psychology.* New York: HarperCollins.

Shen W. E. W. (1999). A history of antipsychotic drug development. *Comprehensive Psychiatry, 40,* 407–417.

Shephard, R. N., & Cooper, L. A. (1982) *Mental images and their transformations.* Cambridge, MA: MIT Press.

Shepard, R. N., & Metzler, J. (1971). Mental rotation of three-dimensional objects. *Science, 171,* 701–703.

Shephard, R. N., & Metzler, J. (1994). Mental rotation of three-dimensional objects. In H. Gutfreund & G. Toulouse (Eds.), *Biology and computation: A physicist's choice* (pp. 180–182). River Edge, NJ: World Scientific Publishing.

Shepperd, J. A., & Taylor, K. M. (1999). Social loafing and expectancy-value theory. *Personality and Social Psychology Bulletin, 25,* 1147–1158.

Sherif, M., Harvey, O. J., White, B. J., Hood, W. E., & Sherif, C. W. (1961). *Intergroup conflict and cooperation: The Robber's Cave Experiment.* Norman, OK: Institute of Group Relations.

Sherman, L. A., Temple, R., & Merkatz, R. B. (1995). Women in clinical trials: An FDA perspective. *Science, 269,* 793–795.

Shiffman, S., Gnys, M., Richards, T. J., Paty, J. A., Hickcox, M., & Kassel, J. D. (1996). Temptations to smoke after quitting: A comparison of lapsers and maintainers. *Health Psychology, 15,* 455–461.

Shih, M., Pittinsky, T. L., & Ambady, N. (1999). Stereotype susceptibility: Identity salience and shifts in quantitative performance. *Psychological Science, 10,* 80–83.

Shimizu, H. (2001). Japanese adolescent boys' senses of empathy (*omoiyari*) and Carol Gilligan's perspectives on the morality of care: A phenomenological approach. *Culture and Psychology, 7,* 453–475.

Shives, L. R. (2005). *Basic concepts of psychiatric-mental health nursing* (6th ed.). Philadelphia: Lippincott Williams & Wilkins.

Shoho, A. R. (1994). A historical comparison of parental involvement of three generations of Japanese Americans (isseis, niseis, sanseis) in the education of their children. *Journal of Applied Developmental Psychology, 15,* 305–311.

Shrotri, A., Shankar, A. V., Sutar, S., Joshi, A., Suryawanshi, N., Pisal, H., et al. (2003). Awareness of HIV/AIDS and household environment of pregnant women in Pune, India. *International Journal of STD and AIDS, 14,* 835–839.

Shull, R. L., & Lawrence, P. S. (1998). Reinforcement: Schedule performance. In K. A. Lattal & M Perone (Eds.), *Handbook of research methods in human operant behavior* (pp. 95–121). New York: Plenum Press.

Siegel, J. M. (2000). Narcolepsy. *Scientific American, 282,* 77–81.

Siegel, J. M. (2001). The REM sleep-memory consolidation hypothesis. *Science, 294,* 1058–1063.

Siegel, J. M. (2003, November). Why we sleep. *Scientific American,* 92–97.

Siegel, J. M. (2005). REM sleep. In M. H. Kryger, T. Roth, & W. C. Dement (Eds.), *Principles and practice of sleep medicine* (4th ed., pp. 120–135). New York: Elsevier Saunders.

Siegel, R. K. (1989). *Intoxication: Life in pursuit of artificial paradise.* New York: Dutton.

Signorielli, N., & Bacue, A. (1999). Recognition and respect: A content analysis of prime-time television across three decades. *Sex Roles, 40*(7–8), 527–544.

Silver, E., Cirincione, C., & Steadman, H. J. (1994). Demythologizing inaccurate perceptions of the insanity defense. *Law and Human Behavior, 18,* 63–70.

Silverberg, S. B., Tennenbaum, D. L., & Jacob, T. (1992). Adolescence and family interaction. In V. B. Van Hasselt & M. Hersen (Eds.), *Handbook of social development: A life-span perspective.* New York: Plenum.

Silverstone, P. H., & Silverstone, T. (2004). A review of acute treatments for bipolar depression. *International Clinical Psychopharmacology, 19,* 113–124.

Simmons, C. H., vom Kolke, A., & Shimizu, H. (1986). Attitudes toward romantic love among American, German, and Japanese students. *Journal of Social Psychology, 126,* 327–336.

Simon, L. (Ed.) (1996). *William James remembered.* Lincoln: University of Nebraska Press.

Simonton, D. K. (2004). Psychology's status as a scientific discipline: Its empirical placement within an implicit hierarchy of the sciences. *Review of General Psychology, 8,* 59–67.

Singer, D. G., & Singer, J. L. (1990). *The house of make-believe.* Cambridge, MA: Harvard University Press.

Sizemore, C. C. (1989). *A mind of her own.* New York: Morrow.

Sizemore, C. C., & Pittillo, E. S. (1977). *I'm Eve.* New York: Doubleday.

Skeels, H. M. (1966). Adult status of children with contrasting early life experiences: A follow-up study. *Monographs of the Society in Child Development, 31* (Serial No. 105).

Skeels, H. M., & Dye, H. B. (1939). A study of the effects of differential stimulation on mentally retarded children. *Proceedings of the American Association for Mental Deficiency, 44,* 114–136.

Skinner, B. F. (1938). *The behavior of organisms: An experimental analysis.* Upper Saddle River, NJ: Prentice Hall.

Skinner, B. F. (1957). *Verbal behavior.* New York: Appleton-Century-Crofts.

Sleek, S. (1997, June). Can "emotional intelligence" be taught in today's schools? *APA Monitor,* 25.

Slotnick, R. S. (2002). Diogenes' new lamp. *American Scientist, 90*(2), 127–128.

Smith, A. E., Jussim, L., & Eccles, J. S. (1999). Do self-fulfilling prophecies accumulate, dissipate, or remain stable over time? *Journal of Peronality and Social Psychology, 77,* 548–565.

Smith, D., Holmes, P., Whitmore, L., Collins, D., & Davenport, T. (2001). The effect of theoretically-based imagery scripts on field hockey performance. *Journal of Sport Behavior, 24*(4), 408–419.

Smith, D. V., & Margolskee, R. F. (2001). Making sense of taste. *Scientific American,* March, 32–39.

Smith, E. E. (2000). Neural bases of human working memory. *Current Directions in Psychological Science, 9,* 45–49.

Smith, M., & Lin, K. M. (1996). Gender and ethnic differences in the pharmacogenetics of psychotropics. In M. F. Jensvold, U. Halbreich, & J. A. Hamilton (Eds.), *Psychopharmacology and women: Sex, gender, and hormones* (pp. 121–136). Washington, DC: American Psychiatric Association.

Smith, M. C., Coleman, S. R., & Gormezano, I. (1969). Classical conditioning of the rabbit's nictitating membrane response at backward, simultaneous, and forward CS-US intervals. *Journal of Comparative and Physiological Psychology, 69,* 226–231.

Smith, P. B., & Tayeb, M. (1989). Organizational structure and processes. In M. Bond (Ed.), *The cross-cultural challenge to social psychology.* Newbury Park, CA: Sage.

Smith, P. C., Kendall, L. M., & Hulin, C. L. (1969). *The measurement of satisfaction in work and retirement.* Chicago: Rand-McNally.

Smith, R. A., & Davis, S. F. (1996). *The psychologist as detective.* Upper Saddle River, NJ: Prentice Hall.

Smith, R. A., & Davis, S. F. (2001). *The psychologist as detective: An introduction to conducting research in psychology* (2nd ed.). Upper Saddle River, NJ: Prentice-Hall.

Smith, S. M., Brown, H. O., Toman, J. E. P., & Goodman, L. S. (1947). The lack of cerebral effects of d-tubocurarine. *Anesthesiology, 8,* 1–14.

Smith, T. W., & Leon, A. S. (1992). *Coronary heart disease: A behavioral perspective.* Champaign, IL: Research Press.

Smoll, F. L., & Smith, R. E. (1997). *Coaches who never lose: A 30-minute primer for coaching effectiveness.* Portola Valley, CA: Warde Publishers.

Snyder, M., & Gangestad, S. (1986). On the nature of self-monitoring: Matters of assessment, matters of validity. *Journal of Personality and Social Psychology, 51,* 125–139.

Snyderman, M., & Rothman, S. (1987). Survey of expert opinion on intelligence and aptitude testing. *American Psychologist, 42,* 137–144.

Sobal, J., & Stunkard, A. J., Jr. (1989). Socioeconomic status and obesity: A review of the literature. *Psychological Bulletin, 105,* 260–275.

Sokol, R. J., Jr., Delaney-Black, V., & Nordstrom, B. (2003). Fetal alcohol spectrum disorder. *Journal of the American Medical Association, 290,* 2996–2999.

Soliman, A. M. (1996). Development of an Arabic translation of the MMPI-2: With clinical applications. In J. N. Butcher (Ed.), *International adaptation of the MMPI-2* (pp. 463–486). Minneapolis: University of Minnesota Press.

Son, S. E., & Kirchener, J. T. (2000). Depression in children and adolescents. *American Family Physician, 62*(10), 2297–2308.

Song, Z., Zhu, H., Yin, S., & Zhang, F. (2002). A study on personality characteristics and personality types of drug users. *Chinese Journal of Clinical Psychology, 10,* 224–226.

Sonnert, G., & Holton, G. (1996). Career patterns of women and men in the sciences. *American Scientist, 84,* 63–71.

Soto, J. A., Levenson, R. W., & Ebling, R. (2005). Cultures of moderation and expression: Emotional experience, behavior, and physiology in Chinese Americans and Mexican Americans. *Emotion, 5,* 154–165.

Soussignan, R. (2002). Duchenne smile, emotional experience, and autonomic reactivity: A test of the facial feedback hypothesis. *Emotion, 2*(1), 52–74.

Spake, A. (2002, August 19). America's "supersize" diet is fatter and sweeter—and deadlier. *U.S. News & World Report,* 41–47.

Spanos, N. P. (1987–1988). Past-life hypnotic regression: A critical review. *Skeptical Inquirer, 12,* 174–180.

Spanos, N. P. (1991). Hypnosis, hypnotizability, and hypnotherapy. In C. R. Snyder & D. R. Forsyth (Eds.), *Handbook of social and clinical psychology* (pp. 644–663). New York: Pergamon.

Spanos, N. P., Menary, E., Gabora, N. J., Du Breuil, S. C., & Dewhirst, B. (1991). Secondary identity enactments during hypnotic past-life regression: A sociocognitive perspective. *Journal of Personality and Social Psychology, 61,* 308–320.

Spanos, N. P., Weekes, J. R., & Bertrand, L. D. (1985). Multiple personality: A social psychological perspective. *Journal of Abnormal Psychology, 94,* 362–376.

Spence, J. T. (1993). Women, men, and society: *Plus ça change, plus c'est la même chose.* In S. Oskamp & M. Costanzo (Eds.), *Gender issues in contemporary society* (pp. 3–17). Newbury Park, CA: Sage.

Spencer, S. J., Steele, C. M., & Quinn, D. M. (1999). Stereotype threat and women's math performance. *Journal of Experimental Social Psychology, 35,* 4–28.

Sperling, G. (1960). The information available in brief visual presentation. *Psychological Monographs, 74* (Whole No. 11).

Sperry, R. W. (1964). The great cerebral commissure. *Scientific American, 210,* 42–52.

Spiegel, D., & Scheflin, A. W. (1994). Dissociated or fabricated? Psychiatric aspects of repressed memory in criminal and civil cases. *International Journal of Clinical and Experimental Hypnosis, 42,* 411–432.

Spielberger, C. D., & Reheiser, E. C. (1994). The job stress survey: Measuring gender differences in occupational stress. *Journal of Social Behavior and Personality, 9,* 199–218.

Spitzer, R. L., Gibbon, M., Skodol, A. E., Williams, J. B. W., & First, M. B. (Eds.). (1994). *DSM-IV case book: A learning companion to the Diagnostic and Statistical Manual of Mental Disorders, Fourth Edition.* Washington, DC: American Psychiatric Association.

Springen, K. (2000, October 16). On spanking. *Newsweek,* 64.

Srivastava, A. K., & Misra, G. (1996). Changing perspectives on understanding intelligence: An appraisal. *Indian Psychological Abstract Review, 3,* 1–34.

Stangor, C., Lynch, L., Duan, C., & Glass, B. (1992). Categorization of individuals on the basis of multiple social features. *Journal of Personality and Social Psychology, 62,* 207–218.

Stapel, D. A., & Koomen, W. (1997). Social categorization and perceptual judgement of size: When perception is social. *Journal of Personality and Social Psychology, 73,* 1177–1190.

Staub, E. (2004). The route to prisoner abuse in Iraq. *Monitor on Psychology, 35*(7), 9.

Steadman, H. J., McGreevy, M. A., Morrissey, J. P., Callahan, L. A., Robbins, P. C., & Cirincione, C.

(1993). *Before and after Hinckley: Evaluating insanity defense reform.* New York: Guilford Press.

Steadman, H. J., Mulvey E. P., Monahan, J., Robbins, P. C., Applebaum, P. S., Grisso, T., et al. (1998). Violence by people discharged from acute psychiatric inpatient facilities and by others in the same neighborhoods. *Archives of General Psychiatry, 55,* 393–401.

Steblay, N., Mehrkens, N., & Bothwell, R. K. (1994). Evidence for hypnotically refreshed testimony: The view from the laboratory. *Law and Human Behavior, 18,* 635–651.

Steele, C. M. (1997). A threat in the air: How stereotypes shape intellectual identity and performance. *American Psychologist, 52,* 613–629.

Steele, C. M., & Josephs, R. A. (1990). Alcohol myopia: Its prized and dangerous effects. *American Psychologist, 45,* 921–933.

Steele, C. M., Spencer, S. J., & Aronson, J. (2002). Contending with group image: The psychology of stereotype and social identity threat. In M. Zanna (Ed.), *Advances in experimental social psychology* (Vol. 34, pp. 379–440). New York: Academic Press.

Stein, J., & Walsh, V. (1997). To see but not to read: The magnocellular theory of dyslexia. *Trends in Neuroscience, 20,* 147–152.

Stein, N. (1995). The definition of sexual harassment applies to schools. In K. L. Swisher (Ed.), *What is sexual harassment?* (pp. 19–24). San Diego: Greenhaven Press.

Steinbrook, R. The polygraph test: A flawed diagnostic method. *New England Journal of Medicine, 327,* 122–123.

Steiner, J. (1979). Human facial expressions in response to taste and smell stimulation. In H. Reese & L. P. Lipsitt (Eds.), *Advances in child development and behavior* (Vol. 13, pp. 257–295). San Diego, CA: Academic Press.

Steketee, G., & Barlow, D. H. (2002). Obsessive-compulsive disorder. In D. H. Barlow (Ed.), *Anxiety and its disorders: The nature and treatment of anxiety and panic* (2nd ed., pp. 516–550). New York: Guilford Press.

Sternberg, R. J. (1988). *The triarchic mind: A new theory of human intelligence.* New York: Viking Penguin.

Sternberg, R. J. (1997a). Educating intelligence: Infusing the Triarchic Theory into school instruction. In R. J. Sternberg & E. L. Grigorenko (Eds.), *Intelligence, heredity, and environment* (pp. 343–362). New York: Cambridge University Press.

Sternberg, R. J. (1997b). *Successful intelligence.* New York: Plume.

Sternberg, R. J., Conway, B. E., Ketron, J. L., & Bernstein, M. (1981). People's conceptions of intelligence. *Journal of Personality and Social Psychology, 41,* 37–55.

Sternberg, R. J., Ferrari, M., Clinkenbeard, P., & Brigorenki, E. L. (1996). Identification, instruction, and assessment of gifted children: A construct validation of a triachic model. *Gifted Child Quarterly, 40,* 129–137.

Sternberg, R. J., Forsythe, G. B., Hedlund, J., Horvath, J. A., Wagner, R. K., Williams, et al. (2000). *Practical intelligence in everyday life.* New York: Cambridge University Press.

Sternberg, R. J., Grigorenko, E. L., & Bundy, D. A. (2001). The predictive value of IQ. *Merrill-Palmer Quarterly, 47,* 1–41.

Sternberg, R. J., & Kaufman, J. C. (1998). Human abilities. In J. T. Spence, J. M. Darley, & D. J. Foss (Eds.), *Annual Review of Psychology* (Vol. 49, 479–502). Palo Alto, CA: Annual Reviews.

Sternberg, R. J., & Lubart, T. I. (1999). The concept of creativity: Prospects and paradigms. In R. J. Sternberg (Ed.), *Handbook of creativity* (pp. 3–15). Cambridge: Cambridge University Press.

Sternberg, R. J., Wagner, R. K., & Williams, W. M., Horvath, J. A. (1995). Testing common sense. *American Psychologist, 50,* 912–927.

Sternberg, S. (1966). High speed scanning in human memory. *Science, 153,* 652–654.

Sternberg, S. (1975). Memory scanning: New findings and current controversies. *Quarterly Journal Experimental Psychology, 27,* 1–32.

Stevens, P., & Smith, R. L. (2001). *Substance abuse counseling: Theory and Practice* (2nd ed.). Upper Saddle River, NJ: Prentice Hall.

Stevenson, H. W., Stigler, J. W., Lee, S. Y., Lucker, G. W., Kitamura, S., & Hsu, C. (1985). Cognitive performance and academic achievement of Japanese, Chinese, and American children. *Child Development, 56,* 718–734.

Stillion, J. M. (1995). Premature death among males. In D. Sabo & D. F. Gordon (Eds.), *Men's health and illness: Gender, power, and the body* (pp. 46–67). Thousand Oaks, CA: Sage.

Stillman, J. A. (2002). Gustation: Intersensory experience par excellence. *Perception, 31,* 1491–1500.

Stockdale, M. S. (1993). The role of sexual misperceptions of women's friendliness in an emerging theory of sexual harassment. *Journal of Vocational Behavior, 42,* 84–101.

Stockdale, M. S., Dewey, J. D., & Saal, F. E. (1992). *Evidence that misperception tendencies relate to a sexual harassment belief system.* Unpublished manuscript, Southern Illinois University, Carbondale.

Stockdale, M. S., & Saal, F. E. (1990, April). *The relationship between misperceiving friendly cues and condoning or tolerating sexual harassment.* Paper presented at the annual meeting of the Southeastern Psychological Association, Atlanta.

Stockdale. , M. S., Visio, M., & Batra, L. (1999). The sexual harassment of men: Evidence for a broader theory of sexual harassment and sex discrimination, *Psychology, Public Policy, and Law, 5,* 630–664.

Stone, T., & Darlington, G. (2000). *Pills, potions, and poisons: How drugs work.* New York: Oxford University Press.

Stoner, J. A. F. (1961). *A comparison of individual and group decisions* involving risk. Unpublished master's thesis, Massachusetts Institute of Technology, Cambridge.

Strack, F., Martin, L. L., & Stepper, S. (1988). Inhibiting and facilitating conditions of the human smile: A nonobtrusive test of the facial feedback hypothesis. *Journal of Personality and Social Psychology, 54,* 768–777.

Straus, M. A., Gelles, R. J., & Steinmetz, S. K. (2003). The marriage license as a hitting license. In M. Silberman (Ed.), *Violence and society: A reader.* Upper Saddle River, NJ: Prentice Hall.

Strawbridge, W. J., Wallhagen, M. I., & Sheman, S. J. (2000). New NHBLI clinical guidelines for obesity and overweight. Will they promote health? *American Journal of Public Health, 90,* 340–343.

Strayer, D. L., Drews, F. A., & Johnston, W. A. (2003). Cell phone–induced failures of visual attention during simulated driving. *Journal of Experimental Psychology: Applied, 9,* 23–32.

Streissguth, A. P. (1994). A long-term perspective of FAS. *Alcohol Health and Research World, 18,* 74–81.

Strickland, B. R. (1995). Research on sexual orientation and human development: A commentary. *Developmental Psychology, 31,* 137–140.

Stroebe, M., Stroebe, W., & Schut, H. (2001). Gender differences in adjustment to bereavement: An empirical and theoretical review. *Review of General Psychology, 5,* 62–83.

Strupp, H. H. (1986). Psychotherapy: Research, practice, and public policy (how to avoid dead ends). *American Psychologist, 41,* 120–130.

Stuart, G. W., & Laraia, M. T. (2005). *Principles and practice of psychiatric nursing* (8th ed.). St. Louis: Mosby.

Stunkard, A. J., Jr., Harris, J. R., Pedersen, N. L., & McClearn, G. E. (1990). The body-mass index of twins who have been reared apart. *New England Journal of Medicine, 322,* 1483–1487.

Substance Abuse and Mental Health Services Administration. (2004). *Overview of findings from the 2003 National Survey on Drug Use and Health* (Office of Applied Studies, NSDUH Series H-24, DHHS Publication No. SMA 04-3963). Rockville, MD: U.S. Department of Health and Human Services.

Suddath, R. L., Christison, G. W., Torrey, E. F., Casanova, M. F., & Weinberger, D. R. (1990). Anatomical abnormalities in the brains of monozygotic twins discordant for schizophrenia. *New England Journal of Medicine, 322,* 789–794.

Sue, S., Fujino, D. C., Hu, L., Takeuchi, D. T., & Zane, N. W. S. (1991). Community mental health services for ethnic minority groups: A test of the cultural responsiveness hypothesis. *Journal of Consulting and Clinical Psychology, 59,* 535–540.

Sue, S., & Okazaki, S. (1990). Asian-American educational achievements: A phenomenon in search of an explanation. *American Psychologist, 45,* 913–920.

Sufka, K. J., & Price, D. D. (2002). Gate control theory reconsidered. *Brain and Mind, 3,* 277–290.

Suinn, R. M. (2001). The terrible twos: Anger and anxiety. *American Psychologist, 56,* 27–36.

Sullivan, E. V., & Marsh, L. (2003). Hippocampal volume deficits in alcoholic Korsakoff's syndrome. *Neurology, 61,* 1716–1719

Sullivan, L. W. (1987). The risks of the sickle-cell trait: Caution and common sense. *New England Journal of Medicine, 317,* 830–831.

Sundberg, N. D., Winebarger, A. A., & Taplin, J. R. (2002). *Clinical psychology: Evolving theory, practice and research* (4th ed.). Upper Saddle River, NJ: Prentice Hall.

Suomi, S. J., & Harlow, H. (1972). Social rehabilitation of isolate-reared monkeys. *Developmental Psychology, 6,* 487–496.

Suomi, S. J., & Ripp, C. (1983). A history of motherless monkey mothering at the University of Wisconsin Primate Laboratory. In *Child abuse: The nonhuman primate data.* New York: Liss.

Super, C. M. (1981). Behavioral development in infancy. In R. H. Monroe, R. L. Monroe, & B. B. Whiting (Eds.), *Handbook of cross-cultural development* (pp. 181–270). New York: Garland.

Super, C. M., & Harkness, S. (1982). The infants' niche in rural Kenya and metropolitan America. In L. L. Adler (Ed.), *Cross-cultural research at issue* (pp. 47–55). New York: Academic Press.

Susser, E., Neugebauer, R., Hoek, H. W., Brown, A. S., Lin, S., Labovitz, D., et al. (1996). Schizophrenia after prenatal famine. *Archives of General Psychiatry, 53,* 25–31.

Suter, P. M., Schutz, Y., & Jequier, E. (1992). The effect of ethanol on fat storage in health subjects. *New England Journal of Medicine, 326,* 983–987.

Sutton, S., Teuting, P., Zubin, J., & John, E. R. (1967). Information delivery and the sensory evoked potentials. *Science, 155,* 1436–1439.

Suzuki, L. K., & Greenfield, P. M. (2002). The construction of everyday sacrifice in Asian Americans and European Americans: The roles of ethnicity and acculturation. *Cross-Cultural Research: The Journal of Comparative Social Science, 36,* 200–228.

Suzuki, S., & Peterson, M. A. (2000). Multiplicative effects of intention on the perception of bistable apparent motion. *Psychological Science, 11,* 202–209.

Suzuki, T. (1992). Some factors influencing prosocial behavior: Empathy, social skill and extraversion. *Japanese Journal of Experimental Social Psychology, 32,* 71–84.

Swayze, V. W., II. (1995). Frontal leukotomy and related psychosurgical procedures in the era before antipsychotics (1935–1954): A historical overview. *American Journal of Psychiatry, 152,* 505–515.

Sweeney, P. D., Anderson, K., & Bailey, S. (1986). Attributional style in depression: A meta-analytic review. *Journal of Personality and Social Psychology, 50,* 974–991.

Swerdlow, J. L. (1995, June). Quiet miracles of the brain. *National Geographic, 87*(6), 2–41.

Swets, J. A., Tanner, W. P., & Birdsall, T. G. (1961). Decision processes in perception. *Psychological Review, 68,* 301–340.

Swiller, H. I. (1988). Alexithymia: Treatment utilizing combined individual and group psychotherapy. *International Journal of Group Psychotherapy, 38*(1), 47–61.

Szasz, T. (1993). *A lexicon of lunacy: Metaphoric malady, moral responsibility, and psychiatry.* New Brunswick, NJ: Transaction.

Tajima, N., Hill, G. W., Willey, D. L., Asao, K., Uemura, K., & Firment, M. J. (1991, August). *A cross-cultural investigation of implicit concepts of intelligence.* Paper presented at the meeting of the American Psychological Association, San Francisco.

Takanishi, R., & De Leon, P. H. (1994). A head start for the 21st century. *American Psychologist, 499,* 120–122.

Talarico, J. M., & Rubin, D. C. (2003). Confidence, not consistency, characterizes flashbulb memories. *Psychological Science, 14,* 455–461.

Talbott, J. A. (1994). Fifty years of psychiatric services: Changes in treatment of chronically mentally ill patients. In J. M. Oldham & M. B. Riba (Eds.), *Review of Psychiatry* (Vol. 13, pp. 93–120).

Talcott, G. W., Fiedler, E. R., Pascale, R. W., Klesges, R. C., Peterson, A. L., & Johnson, R. S. (1995). Is weight gain after smoking cessation inevitable? *Journal of Consulting and Clinical Psychology, 63,* 313–316.

Tallal, P. (1980). Auditory temporal perception, phonics, and reading disabilities in children. *Brain and Language, 9,* 182–198.

Tannen, D. (1990). *You just don't understand: Women and men in conversation.* New York: Ballantine.

Tannen, D. (2000). Framing and reframing. In R. Lewicki et al. (Eds.), *Negotiation: Readings, exercises, and cases.* Boston: McGraw-Hill.

Tarsy, D. (2001). Deep brain stimulation and movement disorders. *Epilepsy and Behavior, 2*(3, Part 2), S45–S54.

Tate, C. (1989, July). In the 1800s, antismoking was a burning issue. *Smithsonian,* pp. 107–117.

Taub, E. (2004). Harnessing brain plasticity through behavioral techniques to produce new treatments in neurorehabilitation. *American Psychologist, 59,* 692–704.

Tavris, C. (1991). The mismeasure of women. In J. D. Goodchilds (Ed.), *Psychological perspectives on human diversity in America* (pp. 91–136). Washington, DC: American Psychological Association.

Taylor, C. R., & Bonner, P. G. (2003). Comment on "American media and the smoking-related behaviors of Asian adolescents." *Journal of Advertising Research, 43,* 419–430.

Taylor, L. C., Clayton, J. D., & Rowley, S. J. (2004). Academic socialization: Understanding parental influences on children's school-related development in the early years. *Review of General Psychology, 8,* 163–178.

Taylor, S. P., & Pasano, R. (1971). Physical aggression as a function of frustration and physical attack. *Journal of Social Psychology, 84,* 261–267.

Tebo, M. G. (2001, July). Rage. *ABA Journal, 59,* 28–33.

Teigen, K. H. (1986). Old truths or fresh insights? A study of students' evaluations of proverbs. *British Journal of Social Psychology, 25,* 43–49.

Tellegen, A., Lykken, D. T., Bouchard, T. J., Jr., Wilcox, K. J., Segal, N. L., & Rich, S. (1988). Personality similarity in twins reared apart and together. *Journal of Personality and Social Psychology, 54,* 1031–1039.

Temoshok, L. (1998). HIV/AIDS. In H. S. Friedman (Ed.), *Personality and disease* (pp. 203–225). New York: Wiley.

Tennant-Clark, C. M., Fritz, J. J., & Beauvais, F. (1989). Occult participation: Its impact upon adolescent development. *Adolescence, 96,* 757–772.

Tesser, A., & Martin, L. (1996). The psychology of evaluatiuon. In E. T. Higgins & A. W. Kruglanski (Eds.), *Social psychology: Handbook of basic principles* (pp. 400–432). New York: Guilford Press.

Tharp, W. (2003). *The creative habit: Learn it and use it for life.* New York: Simon & Schuster.

Thayer, R. E. (1987). Energy, tiredness, and tension effects of a sugar snack versus moderate exercise. *Journal of Personality and Social Psychology, 52,* 119–125.

Thibault, J. W., & Kelley, H. H. (1959). *The social psychology of groups.* New York: Wiley.

Thigpen, C. H., & Cleckley, H. M. (1957). *The three faces of Eve.* Augusta, GA: Authors.

Thomas, A., & Chess, S. (1980). *The dynamics of psychological development.* New York: Brunner/Mazel.

Thompson, J. K., & Smolak, L. (2001). Introduction: Body image, eating disorders, and obesity in youth—the future is now. In J. K. Thompson & L. Smolak (Eds.), *Body image, eating disorders, and obesity in youth: Assessment, prevention, and treatment* (pp. 1–18). Washington, DC: American Psychological Association.

Thompson, J. L., Watson, J. R., Steinhauer, S. R., Goldstein, G., & Pogue-Geile, M. F. (2005). Indicators of genetic liability to schizophrenia: A sibling study of neuropsychological performance. *Schizophrenia Bulletin, 31*(1), 85–96.

Thompson, P. J. (2003). Neuropsychological assessment and treatment of epilepsy. In P. W. Halgina, E. Kischka, & J. C. Marshall (Eds.), *Handbook of clinical psychology* (pp. 584–605). Oxford: Oxford University Press.

Thompson, P., Vidal, C., Giedd, J. N., Goodman, P., Blumenthal, J., Nicolson, R., Toga, A. W., & Rapoport, J. L. (2001). Mapping adolescent brain changes reveals dynamic wave of accelerated gray matter loss in very early-onset schizophrenia. *Proceedings of the National Academy of Sciences of the USA, 98*(20), 11650–11655.

Thorndike, E. L. (1898). Animal intelligences. An experimental study of the associative processes in animals. *Psychological Review Monograph Supplement, 2,* 8.

Thorndike, E. L. (1911). *Animal intelligence.* New York: Macmillan.

Thorndike, E. L. (1927). The law of effect. *American Journal of Psychology, 39,* 212–222.

Tilley, A. R., & H. Dreyfuss Associates. (1993). *The measure of man and woman: Human factors in design.* New York: Watson-Guptill.

Timiras, P. S. (1972). *Developmental physiology and aging.* New York: Macmillan.

Tinbergen, N. (1951). *The study of instinct.* Oxford: Claredon Press.

Ting-Toomey, S. (1991). Intimacy expressions in three cultures: France, Japan, and the United States. *International Journal of Intercultural Relations, 15,* 29–46.

Ting-Toomey, S., & Chun, L. (1996). Cross-cultural interpersonal communication: Theoretical trends and research directions. In W. B. Gudykunst, S. Ting-Toomey, & T. Nishida (Eds.), *Communication in personal relationships across cultures* (pp. 237–261). Thousand Oaks, CA: Sage.

Toates, F. (2001). *Biological psychology: An integrative approach.* Upper Saddle River, NJ: Prentice Hall.

Tolman, E. C., & Honzik, C. H. (1930). Introduction and removal of reward, and maze performance in rats. *University of California Publication in Psychology, 4,* 257–275.

Tondo, L., Isacsson, G., & Baldessarini, R. J. (2003). Suicidal behaviour in bipolar disorder: Risk and prevention. *CNS Drugs, 17,* 491–511.

Toppino, T. C. (2003). Reversible-figure perception: Mechanisms of intentional control. *Perception and Psychophysics, 65,* 1285–1295.

Toren, P., Eldar, S., Laor, N., Wolmer, L., Samuel, E., & Weizman, R. (2001). Fluvoxamine is ineffective in the treatment of enuresis in children and adolescents: An open-label pilot study. *Human Psychopharmacology: Clinical and Experimental, 16,* 327–332.

Torrey, E. F. (1991). A viral-anatomical explanation of schizophrenia. *Schizophrenia Bulletin, 17,* 15–18.

Torrey, E. F. (1997). *Out of the shadows: Confronting America's mental illness crisis.* New York: Wiley.

Torrey, E. F., & Bowler, A. (1990). Geographical distribution of insanity in America: Evidence for an urban factor. *Schizophrenia Bulletin, 16,* 591–604.

Tracy, J. L., & Robins, R. W. (2004). Show your pride: Evidence for a discrete emotion expression. *Psychological Science, 15*(3), 194–197.

Tran, T. X., Day, J. A., Eskin, T. A., Carney, P. R., & Maria, B. L. (2000). Rasmussen's syndrome: Aetiology, clinical features and treatment options. *CNS Drugs, 14*(5), 343–354.

Trappey, C. (1996). A meta-analysis of consumer choice and subliminal advertising. *Psychology and Marketing, 13,* 517–530.

Travis, C. B. (1993). Women and health. In F. L. Denmark & M. A. Paludi (Eds.), *Psychology of women: A handbook of issues and theories* (pp. 283–323). Westport, CT: Greenwood Press.

Treffert, D. A. (1989). *Extraordinary people: Understanding "idiot savants."* New York: HarperCollins.

Treffert, D. A., & Wallace, G. L. (2002). Islands of genius. *Scientific American,* 76–85.

Triandis, H. C. (1995). *Individualism and collectivism.* Boulder, CO: Westview Press.

Trice, A. (2002). First semester college students' email to parents: I. Frequency and content related to parenting style. *College Student Journal, 36,* 327–334.

Triplett, N. (1898). The dynamogenic factors in pacemaking competition. *American Journal of Psychology, 9,* 507–533.

Trosman, H. (1993). Freud's dream theory. In M. A. Carskadon (Ed.), *Encyclopedia of sleep and dreaming* (pp. 251–254). New York: Macmillan.

True, R. M. (1949). Experimental control in hypnotic age regression states. *Science, 110,* 583–584.

Truitner, K., & Truitner, N. (1993). Death and dying in Buddhism. In D. P. Irish, K. F. Lundquist, & V. J. Nelson (Eds.), *Ethnic variations in dying, death, and grief* (pp. 125–136). Washington, DC: Taylor & Francis.

Tsai, A., Loftus, E., & Polage, D. (2001). Current directions in false-memory research. In D. F. Bjorklund (Ed.), *False-memory creation in children and adults: Theory, research, and implications* (pp. 31–44). Mahwah, NJ: Erlbaum.

Tseung, C. N., & Schott, G. (2004). The quality of sibling relationship during late adolescence: Are there links with other significant relationships? *Psychological Studies, 49,* 20–30.

Tulving, E. (1983). *Elements of episodic memory.* Oxford: Oxford University Press.

Tulving, E., & Schachter, D. L. (1990). Priming and human memory systems. *Science, 247,* 301–306.

Turkheimer, E. (1998). Heritability and biological explanation. *Psychological Review, 105,* 782–791.

Turnbull, C. M. (1961). Some observations concerning the experiences and behavior of the BaMbuti Pygmies. *American Journal of Psychology, 74,* 304–308.

Tutati, C. (2004). Why faces are not special to newborns: An alternative account of the face preference. *Current Directions in Psychological Science, 13,* 67–70.

Tuten, T. L., & Neidermeyer, P. E. (2004). Performance, satisfaction and turnover in call centers: The effects of stress and optimism. *Journal of Business Research, 57,* 26–34.

Tversky, A., & Kahneman, D. (1981). The framing of decisions and the psychology of choice. *Science, 211,* 453–458.

Uchino, B. N., Uno, D., & Holt-Lunstad, J. (1999). Social support, physiological processes, and health. *Current Directions in Psychological Science, 8,* 145–148.

Ullman, S. E., & Filipas, H. H. (2001). Correlates of formal and informal support seeking in sexual assaults victims. *Journal of Interpersonal Violence, 16,* 1028–1047.

Ullrich, P. M., Lutgendorf, S. K., Stapleton, J. T., & Horowitz, M. (2004). Self regard and concealment of homosexuality as predictors of CD4+ cell count over time among HIV seropositive gay men. *Psychology and Health, 19,* 183–196.

Ulrich, R. E., & Azrin, N. H. (1962). Reflexive fighting in response to aversive stimulation. *Journal of the Experimental Analysis of Behavior, 5,* 511–520.

Underwood, J., & Szabo, A. (2003). Academic offences and e-learning: Individual propensities in cheating. *British Journal of Educational Technology, 34*(4), 467–477.

United Nations. (1991). *World population trends and policies: 1991 monitoring report.* New York: Author.

United Nations. (1995). *Women in a changing global economy.* New York: Author.

Ursano, R. J., & McCarroll, J. E. (1994). Exposure to traumatic death: The nature of the stress. In R. J. Ursano, B. G. McCaughey, & C. S. Fullerton (Eds.), *Individual and community responses to trauma and disaster: The structure of human chaos* (pp. 46–71). London.

Ursin, H., & Eriksen, H. R. (2004). The cognitive activation theory of stress. *Psychoneuroendocrinology, 29,* 567–592.

U.S. Bureau of Labor and Statistics. Retrieved September 24, 2000, from http://stats.bls.gov:80/news.release/ecopro.t05.htm.

U.S. Bureau of the Census. (1993). *Statistical abstract of the United States, 1993.* Washington, DC: U.S. Government Printing Office.

U.S. Bureau of the Census. (1996). *Statistical abstract of the United States* (117th ed.). Washington, DC: U.S. Government Printing Office.

U.S. Bureau of the Census. (1997). *Current population reports.* Washington, DC: U.S. Government Printing Office.

U.S. Bureau of the Census. (1997). *Statistical abstract of the United States, 1997* (118th ed.). Washington, DC: U.S. Department of Commerce.

U.S. Bureau of the Census. (1998). *Statistical abstract of the United States, 1998.* Washington, DC: U.S. Government Printing Office.

U.S. Bureau of the Census. (2001). *Statistical Abstract of the United States: 2000* (121st ed.). Washington, DC: U.S. Government Printing Office.

U.S. Bureau of the Census. (2005). *Statistical abstract of the United States: The national data book, 2004–2005* (124th ed.). Washington, DC: U.S. Government Printing Office.

U.S. Department of Health and Human Services. (1988). *The health consequences of smoking: Nicotine addiction.* Washington DC: U.S. Government Printing Office.

U.S. Department of Health and Human Services. (1989). *Reducing the health consequences of smoking: 25 years of progress.* Washington, DC: U.S. Government Printing Office.

U.S. Department of Health and Human Services. (1990). *Healthy people 2000: National health promotion and disease prevention objectives* (DHHS PHS Publication No. 91-50212). Washington, DC: U.S. Government Printing Office.

U.S. Department of Health and Human Services. (2001). *The Surgeon General's call to action to prevent and decrease overweight and obesity.* Rockville, MD: U.S. Department of Health and Human Services, Public Health Service, Office of the Surgeon General.

U.S. Department of Justice, Bureau of Justice Statistics (1995). *Criminal victimization in the United States, 1993,* NCJ-151657. Washington, DC: U.S. Department of Justice.

U.S. Department of Justice. (1999). *Eyewitness evidence: A guide for law enforcement.* Washington, DC: U.S. Government Printing Office.

U.S. Department of Labor. (1985). *Employed persons by major occupational groups and sex.* Washington, DC: U.S. Government Printing Office.

U.S. Department of Labor. (1991). *Dictionary of occupational titles* (6th ed.). Washington, DC: U.S. Government Printing Office.

U.S. Department of Labor, Women's Bureau. (1998). *The median wages of women as a proportion of the wages that men receive.* Washington, DC: U.S. Department of Labor.

U.S. Department of Labor. (1999). Industries with the most causes of occupational stress. Retrieved May 5, 2002, from http://www. bureauoflaborstatistics.

U.S. Equal Employment Opportunity Commission (2005). Sexual harassment. Retrieved August 10, 2005, from http://eeoc.gov/types/sexual harassment.html.

U.S. National Center for Health Statistics. (2001). *Vital statistics of the United States 1999.* Hyattsville, MD: Author.

U.S. Public Health Service. (1999). Achievements in public health, 1900–1999: Tobacco use: United States, 1900–1999. *Morbidity and Mortality Weekly Report, 48*(43), 986–993.

Valenstein, E. S. (1973). *Brain control.* New York: Wiley.

Valenstein, E. S. (1986). *Great and desperate cures: The rise and decline of psychosurgery and other radical treatments for mental illness.* New York: Basic Books.

Valera, E. M., & Berenbaum, H. (2001). A twin study of alexithymia. *Psychotherapy and Psychosomatics, 70,* 239–246.

Van den Bloom, D. C. (1997). Sensitivity and attachment: Next steps for developmentalists. *Child Development, 64,* 592–594.

Van Empeien, R., Jennekens-Schinkel, A., Buskens, E., Helders, P. J. M., & Van Nieuwenhuizen, O. (2004). Functional consequences of hemispherectomy. *Brain, 127*(9), 2071–2079.

Van Gundy, A. B. (1995). *Brain boosters for business advantage.* San Diego, CA: Pfeiffer.

Van IJzendoorn, M. H., & Kroonenberg, P. M. (1988). Cross-cultural patterns of attachment: A meta-analysis of the strange situation. *Child Development, 59,* 147–156.

Vasudev, J., & Hummel, R. C. (1987). Moral stage sequence and principled reasoning in an Indian sample. *Human Development, 30,* 103–118.

Ventis, W. L., Higbee, G., & Murdock, S. A. (2001). Using humor in systematic desensization to reduce fear. *Journal of General Psychology, 128,* 241–253.

Verhaeghe, R., Mak, R., Van Maele, G., Kornitzer, M., & De Backer, G. (2003). Job stress among middle-aged health care workers and its relation to sickness absence. *Stress and Health: Journal of the International Society for the Investigation of Stress, 19,* 265–274.

Vernon-Feagans, L., Emanuel, D. C., & Blood, I. (1997). The effects of otitis media and quality of day care on children's language development. *Journal of Applied Developmental Psychology, 18,* 395–409.

Vernoy, M. W. (1987). Demonstrating classical conditioning in introductory psychology: Needles don't always make balloons pop! *Teaching of Psychology, 14,* 176–177.

Verschuere, B., Crombez, G., De Clercq, A., & Koster, E. H. W. (2005). Psychopathic traits and autonomic responding to concealed information in a prison sample. *Psychophysiology, 42*(2), 239–245.

Vertosick, F. (1996). *When the air hits your brain: Tales of neurosurgery.* New York: Norton.

Vetter, B. (1992). Ferment: yes; progress: maybe; change: slow. *Mosaic, 23*(3), 34–41.

Vigliocco, G., Antonini, T., & Garrrett, M. F. (1997). Grammatical gender is on the tip of Italian tongues. *Psychological Sciences, 8,* 314–317.

Viken, R. J., Rose, R. J., Kaprio, J., & Koskenvuo, M. (1994). A developmental genetic analysis of adult personality: Extraversion and neuroticism from 18 to 59 years of age. *Journal of Personality and Social Psychology, 66,* 722–730.

Viki, G. T., Abrams, D., & Masser, B. (2004). Evaluating stranger and acquaintance rape: The role of benevolent sexism in perpetrator blame and recommended sentence length. *Law and Human Behavior, 28,* 295–303.

Vingerhoets, A. J. J. M., Cornelius, R. R., Van Heck, G. L., & Becht, M. C. (2000). Adult crying: A model and review of the literature. *Review of General Psychology, 4,* 354–377.

Visser, G. H. A. (2003). Fetal behavior: A commentary. *Neurobiology of Aging, 24*(Suppl 1), S47–S49.

Vita, A., Dieci, M., Silenzi, C., Tenconi, F., Giobbio, G. M., & Invernizzi, G. (2000). Cerebral ventricular enlargement as a generalized feature of schizophrenia: A distribution analysis of 502 subjects. *Schizophrenia Research, 44*(1), 25–34.

Volkmann, F. C., Riggs, C. A., & Moore, R. K. (1980). Eyeblinks and visual suppression. *Science, 207,* 1206–1208.

Vonk, R. (1999). Effects of outcome dependency on correspondence bias. *Personality and Social Psychology Bulletin, 25,* 382–389.

Vook, R. (1997). Animal rights, animal wrongs and the question of balance. *Psychological Science, 8,* 197–201.

Votta, E., & Manion, I. (2004). Suicide, high-risk behaviors, and coping style in homeless adolescent males' adjustment. *Journal of Adolescent Health, 34,* 237–243.

Vrij, A. (2001). Detecting the liars. *Psychologist, 14*(11), 596–598.

Vygotsky, L. S. (1978). *Mind in society: The development of higher psychological processes.* Cambridge, MA: Harvard University Press. (Original works published 1930, 1933, and 1935).

Vyse, S. A. (1997). *Believing in magic: The psychology of superstition.* New York: Oxford University Press.

Wade, N. J. (2003). The search for a sixth sense: The cases for vestibular, muscle, and temperature senses. *Journal of the History of the Neurosciences, 12,* 175–202.

Wahi, S., & Johri, R. (1994). Questioning a universal theory of mind: Mental–real distinctions made by Indian children. *Journal of Genetic Psychology, 155,* 503–510.

Wallace, B. (1993). Day persons, night persons, and variability in hypnotic susceptibility. *Journal of Personality and Social Psychology, 64,* 827–833.

Wallace, J. (1999). The twelve-step recovery approach. In P. J. Ott, R. E. Tarter, & R. T. Ammerman (Eds.), *Sourcebook on substance abuse: Etiology, epidemiology, assessment, and treatment* (pp. 293–302). Boston: Allyn & Bacon.

Wallen, K. (1990). Desire and ability: Hormones and the regulation of female sexual behavior. *Neuroscience and Biobehavioral Reviews, 14,* 233–241.

Wallin, M. T., Page, W. F., & Kurtzke, J. F. (2004). Multiple sclerosis in U.S. veterans of the Vietnam era and later military service: Race, sex and geography. *Annals of Neurology, 55*(1), 65–71.

Walsh, W. M. (1991). *Case studies in family therapy: An integrative approach.* Needham Heights, MA: Allyn & Bacon.

Walster, E., & Walster, G. W. (1978). *Love.* Reading, MA: Addison-Wesley.

Walster, E., Walster, G. W., & Berscheid, E. (1978). *Equity: Theory and research.* Needham Heights, MA: Allyn & Bacon.

Wancata, J., Musalek, M., Alexandrowicz, R., & Krautgartner, M. (2003). Number of dementia sufferers in Europe between the years 2000 and 2050. *European Psychiatry, 18,* 306–313.

Wandersman, A., & Florin, P. (2003). Community interventions and effective prevention. *American Psychologist, 58,* 441–448.

Wang, H.-W., Wysocki, C. J., & Gold, G. H. (1993). Induction of olfactory sensitivity in mice. *Science, 260,* 998–1000.

Wang, L., McCarthy, G., Song, A. W., & LaBar, K. S. (2005). Amygdala activation to sad pictures during high-field (4 Tesla) functional magnetic resonance imaging. *Emotion, 5,* 12–22.

Wang, Q., Cavanagh, P., & Green, M. (1994). Familiarity and pop-out in visual search. *Perception and Psychophysics, 56,* 495–500.

Wang, Q., Schoenlein, R. W., Peteanu, L. A., Mathies, R. A., & Shank, C. V. (1994). Vibrationally coherent photochemistry in the femtosecond primary event of vision. *Science, 266,* 422–424.

Wann, D. L. (1997). *Sport psychology.* Upper Saddle River, NJ: Prentice Hall.

Wann, D. L., Melnick, M. J., Russell, G. W., & Pease, D. G. (200). *Sports fans: The psychology and social impact of spectators.* New York: Routledge.

Warach, S. (1995). Mapping brain pathophysiology and higher cortical function with magnetic resonance imaging. *The Neuroscientist, 1,* 221–235.

Ward, A., & Mann, T. (2000, April). Don't mind if I do: Disinhibited eating under cognitive load. *Journal of Personality and Social Psychology, 78,* 753–763.

Ward, C., & Rana-Deuba, A. (1999). Acculturation and adaptation revisited. *Journal of Cross-Cultural Psychology, 30,* 422–442.

Ward, C. A. (2000). Models and measurements of psychological androgyny: A cross-cultural extension of theory and research. *Sex Roles, 43,* 529–552.

Warm, J. S., Dember, W. N., & Parasuraman, R. (1991). Effects of olfactory stimulation on performance and stress in a visual sustained attention task. *Journal of Society of Cosmetic Chemists, 42,* 199–210.

Warner, M. B., Morey, L. C., Finch, J. F., Gunderson, J. G., Skodol, A. E., Sanislow, C. A., et al. (2004). The longitudinal relationship of personality traits and disorders. *Journal of Abnormal Psychology, 113,* 217–227.

Warren, J. I., Murrie, D. C., Chauhan, P., Dietz, P. E., & Morris, J. (2004). Opinion formation in evaluating sanity at the time of the offense: An examination of 5175 pre-trial evaluations. *Behavioral Sciences and the Law, 22*(2), 171–186.

Warrington, E. K., & Weiskrantz, L. (1968). New method of testing long-term retention with special reference to amnesic patients. *Nature, 217,* 972–974.

Wartik, N. (1993, May). A question of abuse. *American Health,* pp. 62–67.

Wartner, U. G., Grossman, K., Fremmer-Bombik, E., & Suess, G. (1994). Attachment patterns at age six in south Germany: Predictability from infancy and implications for preschool behavior. *Child Development, 65,* 1014–1027.

Wason, P. C. (1960). On the failure to eliminate hypotheses in a conceptual task. *Quarterly Journal of Experimental Psychology, 12,* 129–140.

Wasserman, E. A., Young, M. E., & Cook, R. G. (2004). Variability discrimination in humans and animals: Implications for adaptive action. *American Psychologist, 59,* 879–890.

Waterhouse, J., Reilly, T., & Atkinson, G. (1997). Jetlag. *The Lancet, 350,* 1611–1616.

Watson, E. H., & Lowney, G. H. (1967). *Growth and development of children* (5th ed.). St. Louis: Mosby–Year Book.

Watson, J. B. (1924). *Behaviorism.* New York: Norton.

Watson, J. B. (1928). *Psychological care of infant and child.* New York: Norton.

Watson, J. B., & Rayner, R. (1920). Conditioned emotional responses. *Journal of Experimental Psychology, 3,* 1–14.

Watson, O. M. (1970). *Proxemic behavior: A cross-cultural study.* The Hague: Mouton.

Watson, R. I. (1962). The experimental tradition and clinical psychology. In A. J. Bachrach (Ed.), *Experimental foundations of clinical psychology.* New York: Basic Books.

Watts, B. (1996). Legal issues. In M. A. Pauludi (Ed.), *Sexual harassment on college campuses: Abusing the ivory tower* (pp. 1–24). Albany: State University of New York Press.

Weaver, K. A., & McNeill, A. N. (1992). Null effect of mood as a semantic prime. *Journal of General Psychology, 119,* 295–301.

Weaver, R. L., II. (1993). *Understanding interpersonal communication* (6th ed.). New York: HarperCollins.

Webb, W. B. (1992). *Sleep: The gentle tyrant* (2nd ed.). Bolton, MA: Anker.

Weber, D. J., Redfield, R. R., & Lemon, S. M. (1986). Acquired immunodeficiency syndrome: Epidemiology and significance for the obstetrician and gynecologist. *American Journal of Obstetrics and Gynecology, 155,* 235–239.

Wechsler, D. (1991). *Manual for the Wechsler Intelligence Test for Children-III.* New York: The Psychological Corporation.

Wechsler, D. (1992). *The Wechsler Preschool and Primary Scales of Intelligence-Revised.* San Antonio, TX: Psychological Corporation.

Wechsler, D. (1994). *The Wechsler Intelligence Scale for Children–Third Edition.* San Antonio, TX: Psychological Corporation.

Wechsler, D. (1997). *The Wechsler Adult Intelligence Scale–Third Edition.* San Antonio: TX: Psychological Corporation.

Wechsler, H., Davenport, A., Dowdall, G., Moeykens, B., & Castillo, S. (1994). Health and behavioral consequences of binge drinking in college: A national survey of students at 140 campuses. *Journal of the American Medical Association, 272,* 1672–1677.

Wechsler, H., & Wuethrich, B. (2002). *Dying to drink: Confronting binge drinking on college campuses.* Emmaus, PA: Rodale.

Weiland, S. (1993). Erik Erikson: Ages, stages, and stories. *Generations, 17*(2), 17–22.

Weinberg, R. A., Scarr, S., & Waldman, I. D. (1992). The Minnesota Transracial Adoption Study: A follow-up of IQ performance at adolescence. *Intelligence, 16,* 117–135.

Weiner, I. B., & Hess, A. K. (Eds.) (in press). *Handbook of forensic psychology* (2nd ed.). New York: Wiley.

Weiss, D. J., Dawis, R. V., England, G. W., & Lofquist, L. H. (1967). *Manual for the Minnesota Satisfaction Questionnaire.* Minnesota Studies on Vocational Rehabilitation (Vol. 22). Minneapolis: University of Minnesota Industrial Relations Center.

Weissman, M. M., & Olfson, M. (1995). Depression in women: Implications for health care research. *Science, 269,* 799–801.

Weller, A., & Weller, L. (1992). Menstrual synchrony in female couples. *Psychoneuroendocrinology, 17,* 171–177.

Wells, G. L., Malpass, R. S., Kindsay, R. C. L., Fisher, R. P., Turtle, J. W., & Fulero, S. M. (2000). From the lab to the police station: A successful application of eyewitness research. *American Psychologist, 55,* 581–598.

Wells, G. L. Olson, E. A., & Charman, S. D. (2002). The confidence of eyewitnesses in their identifica-

tions from lineups. *Current Directions in Psychological Science, 11,* 151–154.

Wender, P. H., & Klein, D. F. (1981). *Mind, mood and medicine: A guide to the new psychiatry.* New York: Farrar, Straus & Giroux.

Wender, P. H., Rosenthal, D., Kety, S. S., Schulsinger, F., & Welner, J. (1974). Cross-fostering: A research strategy for clarifying the role of genetic and experiential factors in the etiology of schizophrenia. *Archives of General Psychiatry, 30,* 121–128.

Werder, S. F. (1995). An update on the diagnosis and treatment of mania in bipolar disorder. *American Family Physician, 51,* 1126–1136.

West, J. C., Wilk, J. E., Rae, D. S., Narrow, W. E., Regier, D. A., & Sharfstein, S. S. (2003). Financial disincentives for the provision of psychotherapy. *Psychiatric Services, 54,* 1582–1583.

Westen, D. (1990). Psychoanalytic approaches to personality. In L. A. Pervin (Ed.), *Handbook of personality: Theory and research* (pp. 21–65). New York: Guilford Press.

Westen, D., & Shedler, J. (1999). Revising and assessing Axis II, Part II: Toward an empirically based and clinically useful classification of personality disorders. *American Journal of Psychiatry, 156,* 273–285.

Whalen, P. J., Shin, L. M., McInerney, S. C., Fischer, H., Wright, C. I., & Rauch, S. L. (2001). A functional MRI study of human amygdala responses to facial expressions of fear versus anger. *Emotion, 1,* 70–83.

Whitbourne, S. K. (1985). *The aging body.* New York: Springer-Verlag.

Whitbourne, S. K. (1996). *The aging individual: Physical and psychological perspectives.* New York: Springer.

White, K. S., & Barlow, D. H. (2002). Panic disorder and agoraphobia. In D. H. Barlow (Ed.), *Anxiety and its disorders: The nature and treatment of anxiety and panic* (2nd ed., pp. 328–379). New York: Guilford Press.

Whitley, B. E., Jr., & Keith-Spiegel, P. (2001). *Academic dishonesty: An educator's guide.* Mahwah, NJ: Erlbaum.

Whittaker, J. O., & Meade, R. D. (1967). Social pressure in the modification and distortion of judgment: A cross-cultural study. *International Journal of Psychology, 2,* 109–113.

Wickelgren, I. (1998). Obesity: How big a problem? *Science, 280,* 1364–1367.

Widom, C. S. (1977). A methodology for studying noninstitutionalized psychopaths. *Journal of Consulting and Clinical Psychology, 45,* 674–683.

Wiegmann, D. A., & Shappell, S. A. (2001). Human error perspectives in aviation. *International Journal of Aviation Psychology, 11,* 341–357.

Wilcox, A. J., Weinberg, C. R., & Baird, D. D. (1995). Timing of sexual intercourse in relation to ovulation: Effects on the probability of conception, survival of the pregnancy, and sex of the baby. *New England Journal of Medicine, 333,* 1517–1519.

Wilcoxin, H. C., Dragoin, W. B., & Kral, P. A. (1971). Illness-induced aversion in rat and quail: Relative salience of visual and gustatory cues. *Science, 171,* 826–828.

Williams, B. A. (1994). Blocking despite changes in reinforcer identity. *Animal Learning and Behavior, 22,* 442–457.

Williams, J. E., & Best, D. L. (1990). *Measuring sex stereotypes: A multination study* (Vol. 6, rev. ed.). Newbury Park, CA: Sage.

Williamson, D. F., Madams, J., Ada, R. F., Kleinman, J. C., Giovino, G. A., & Byers, T. (1991). Smoking cessation and severity of weight gain in a national cohort. *New England Journal of Medicine, 324,* 739–745.

Williamson, L. G., Campion, J. E., Malos, S. B., Roehling, M. V., & Campion, M. A. (1997). Employment interview on trial: Linking interview structure with litigation outcomes. *Journal of Applied Psychology, 82,* 900–912.

Wilson, B. J., Kunkel, D., Linz, D., Potter, J., Donnerstein, E., Smith, S. L., et al. (1997). Violence in television programming overall: University of California, Santa Barbara study. In M. Seawall (Ed.), *National television violence study* (Vol. 1, pp. 3–184). Thousand Oaks, CA: Sage.

Wilson, B. J., Smith, S. L., Potter, W. J., Kunkel, D., Linz, D., Colvin, C. M., & Donnerstein, E. (2002).

Violence in children's television programming: Assessing the risk. *Journal of Communication, 52,* 5–335.

Wilson, S. C., & Barber, T. X. (1983). The fantasy-prone personality: Implications for understanding imagery, hypnosis, and parapsychological phenomena. In A. A. Sheikh (Ed.), *Imagery: Current theory, research, and application.* New York: Wiley.

Winerman, L. (2004). Post-9/11 pilot training taps psychologists' expertise. *Monitor on Psychology, 35*(6), 40–41.

Winerman, L. (2005). Leading the way. *Monitor on Psychology, 36*(1), 64–67.

Winn, M. (1977). *The plug-in drug.* New York: Viking Penguin.

Winzelberg, A. (1997). The analysis of an electronic support group for individuals with eating disorders. *Computers in Human Behavior, 13,* 393–407.

Wiseman, R., Greening, E., & Smith, M. (2003). Belief in the paranormal and suggestion in the seance room. *British Journal of Psychology, 94,* 285–297.

Witkin, H. A., Mednick, S. A., Schulsinger, F., Bakkestrom, E., Christiansen, K. O., Goodenough, D. R., et al. (1976). Criminality in XYY and XXY men. *Science, 193,* 547–555.

Witten, T. M. (2003). Life course analysis—the courage to search for something more: Middle adulthood issues in the transgender and intersex community. *Journal of Human Behavior in the Social Environment, 8*(2–3), 189–224.

Wolfe, B. D., Dattilo, J., & Gast, D. L. (2003). Effects of a token economy system within the context of cooperative games on social behaviors of adolescents with emotional and behavioral disorders. *Therapeutic Recreation Journal, 37,* 124–141.

Wonderlich, S. A., & Mitchell, J. E. Eating disorders and comorbidity: Empirical, conceptual, and clinical implications. *Psychopharmacology Bulletin, 33*(3), 381–390.

Wood, J. T. (1994). *Gendered lives: Communication, gender, and culture.* Belmont, CA: Wadsworth.

Woods, C., & Oross, S. (1998, March). *Recognition of contrast and texture defined letters in individuals with developmental disabilities.* Paper presented at the Gatlinburg Conference on Research and the Theory in Mental Retardation and Developmental Disabilities, Charleston, SC.

Woods, C. B., & Krantz, J. H. (2000). Sensation and perception: A window into the brain and mind. In S. F. Davis & J. Halonen (Eds.), *The many faces of psychological research in the 21st century.* Washington, DC: American Psychological Association.

Woods, C. B., & Krantz, J. H. (2001). Sensation and perception: A window into the brain and mind. In J. S. Halonen & S. F. Davis (Eds.). *The many faces of psychological research in the Twenty-First Century.* Society for the Teaching of Psychology. http://teachpsych.lemoyne/teachpsych/faces.

Woods, S. C., Seeley, R. J., Porte, D., Jr., & Schwartz, M. W. (1998). Signals that regulate food intake and energy homeostasis. *Science, 280,* 1378–1382.

Woodward, A. L., & Sommerville, J. A. (2000). Twelve-month-old infants interpret action in context. *Psychological Science, 11,* 73–77.

Woodward, E. H. (2000). *Media in the home 2000: The fourth annual survey of parents and children (Survey Series No. 7).* Philadelphia, Annenberg Public Policy Center of the University of Pennsylvania.

Workman, J. E., & Johnson, K. K. P. (1994). Effects of conformity and noncomformity to gender-role expectations for dress: Teachers versus students. *Adolescence, 29,* 207–223.

World Health Organization (2004). Suicide rates (per 100,000), by country, year, and sex. Accessed August 8, 2005, at www.who.org.

World Health Organization. (2005). Obesity and overweight. Retrieved July 15, 2005, from http://who.int/dietphysicalactivity/publications/facts/obesity/en/print/html

Worrell, F. C., & Cross, W. E., Jr. (2004). The reliability and validity of Big Five inventory scores with African American college students. *Journal of Multicultural Counseling and Development, 32,* 18–32.

Wraga, M., Creem, S. H., & Proffitt, D. R. (2000). Perception—action dissociations of a walkable Muller-Lyer configuration. *Psychological Science, 11,* 239–243.

Wright, J. C., & Mischel, W. (1987). A conditional approach to dispositional constructs: The local predictability of social behavior. *Journal of Personality and Social Bheavior, 53,* 1159–1177.

Wrightsman, L. S., Nietzel, M. T., & Fortune, W. H. (1994). *Psychology and the legal system* (3rd ed.). Pacific Grove, CA: Brooks/Cole.

Wrobleski, A. (1989). *Suicide: Why? 85 questions and answers about suicide.* Minneapolis: Afterwords.

Wujec, T. (1995). *Five-star mind: Games and puzzles to stimulate your creativity and imagination.* New York: Doubleday.

Wyatt, R. J., Henter, I., Leary, M. C., & Taylor, E. (1991). An economic evaluation of schizophrenia—1991. *Social Psychiatry and Psychiatric Epidemiology, 30,* 196–205.

Yamagata, H., Yeh, K. S., Stewman, S., & Dodge, H. (1997, August). *Sex segregation and glass ceilings: A comparative statistics model of women's career opportunities in the federal government over a quarter of a century.* Paper presented at the annual meeting of the American Sociological Association, Toronto.

Yamamoto, J., & Lin, K.-M. (1995). Psychopharmacology, ethnicity, and culture. In J. M. Oldham & M. B. Riba (Eds.), *Review of psychiatry* (Vol. 14, pp. 529–541). Washington, DC: American Psychiatric Association.

Yamamoto, J., Silva, J. A., Justice, L. R., Chang, C. Y., & Leong, G. B. (1993). Cross-cultural psychotherapy. In A. C. Gaw (Ed.), *Culture, ethnicity, and mental illness* (pp. 101–124). Washington, DC: American Psychiatric Association.

Yang, S. Y., & Sternberg, R. J. (1997). Taiwanese conceptions of intelligence. In J. T. Spence, J. M. Darley, & D. J. Foss (Eds.), *Annual Review of Psychology* (Vol. 49, pp. 479–502). Palo Alto, CA: Annual Reviews.

Yapko, M. D. (1994). *Suggestions of abuse.* New York: Simon & Schuster.

Yoder, J. D. (2003). *Women and gender: Transforming psychology* (2nd ed.). Upper Saddle River, NJ: Pearson Prentice Hall.

Yonelinas, A. P., Hockley, W. E., & Murdock, B. B. (1992). Test of the list-strength effect in recognition memory. *Journal of Experimental Psychology: Learning, Memory, and Cognition, 18,* 345–355.

Yonkers, K. A., & Hamilton, J. A. (1995a). Do men and women need different doses of psychotropic drugs? *Harvard Mental Health Letter, 11*(11), 8.

Yonkers, K. A., & Hamilton, J. A. (1995b). Psychotropic medications. In J. M. Oldham & M. B. Riba (Eds.), *Review of psychiatry* (Vol. 14, pp. 307–332). Washington, DC: American Psychiatric Association.

Young, J. E., Beck, A. T., & Weinberger, A. (1993). Depression. In D. H. Barlow (Ed.), *Clinical handbook of psychological disorders: A step-by-step treatment manual* (2nd ed., pp. 240–277). New York: Guilford Press.

Young, L. T. (2004). What exactly is a mood stabilizer? *Journal of Psychiatry and Neuroscience, 29,* 87–88.

Young, M. W. (2000, March). The tick-tock of the biological clock. *Scientific American,* 64–71.

Young, T., Evans, L., Finn, L., & Palta, M. (1997). Estimation of the clinically diagnosed proportion of sleep apnea syndrome in middle-aged men and women. *Sleep, 20,* 705–706.

Zadra, A., & Donderi, D. C. (2000). Nightmares and bad dreams: Their prevalence and relationship to well-being. *Journal of Abnormal Psychology, 109,* 273–281.

Zajonc, R. B. (1965). Social facilitation. *Science, 149,* 269–274.

Zajonc, R. B. (1975, January). Dumber by the dozen. *Psychology Today,* 37–43.

Zajonc, R. B. (1980). Feeling and thinking; Preferences need no inference. *American Psychologist, 35,* 151–175.

Zakhari, A. (1997). Alcohol and the cardiovascular system: Molecular mechanisms for beneficial and harmful action. *Alcohol Health and Research World, 21,* 21–29.

Zapf, P. A., & Roesch, R. (2001). A comparison of Mac-Cat-CA and the FIT for making determinations of competency to stand trial. *International Journal of Law and Psychiatry, 24,* 81–92.

Zeki, S. (1993). *A vision of the brain.* London: Blackwell Scientific.

Zenderland, L. (1998). *Measuring minds: Henry Herbert Goddard and the origins of American intelligence testing.* Cambridge Studies in the History of Psychology. New York: Cambridge University Press.

Zepelin, H., Siegel, J. M., & Tobler, I. (2005). Mammalian sleep. In M. H. Kryger, T. Roth, & W. C. Dement (Eds.), *Principles and practice of sleep medicine* (4th ed., pp. 91–101). New York: Elsevier Saunders.

Zhang, X. Y., Zhou, D. F., Cao, L. Y., Xu, C. Q., Chen, D. C., & Wu, G. Y. (2004). The effect of vitamin E treatment on tardive dyskinesia and blood superoxide dismutase: A double-blind placebo-controlled trial. *Journal of Clinical Psychopharmacology, 24,* 83–86.

Zigler, E., & Styfeo S. J. (1994). Head Start: Criticism in a constructive context. *American Psychologist, 49,* 127–132.

Zillman, D. (1979). *Hostility and aggression.* Hillsdale, NJ: Erlbaum.

Zimbardo, P. G., & Andersen, S. (1993). Understanding mind control: Exotic and mundane mental manipulations. In M. D. Langone (Ed.), *Recovery from cults* (pp. 104–125). New York: Norton.

Zisapel, N. (2001). Circadian rhythm sleep disorders: Pathophysiology and potential approaches to management. *CNS Drugs, 15*(4), 311–328.

Zornetzer, S. F. (1985). Catecholamine system involvement in age-related memory dysfunction. *Annals of the New York Academy of Sciences, 44,* 242–254.

Zuckerman, B., Frank, D. A., Hingson, R., Amaro, H., Levenson, S. M., & Kayne, H. (1989). Effects of maternal marijuana and cocaine use on fetal growth. *New England Journal of Medicine, 320,* 762–768.

Zuckerman, M. (1978). The search for high sensation. *Psychology Today, 11*(8), 38–46.

Zuckerman, M. (1991). *Psychobiology of personality.* Cambridge: Cambridge University Press.

Zuckerman, M. (1994). *Behavioral expression and biosocial bases of sensation seeking.* Cambridge: Cambridge University Press.

Zuckerman, M., Knee, C. R., Kieffer, S. C., & Gagne, M. (2004). What individuals believe they can and cannot do: Explorations of realistic and unrealistic control beliefs. *Journal of Personality Assessment, 82,* 215–232.

SuperStock, Inc.; p. 455: (T) (c) The New Yorker Collection 1991 Donald Reilly from cartoonbank.com. All Rights Reserved. (B) Frances Miller, Getty Images/Time Life Pictures; p. 458: Penny Tweedie, Getty Images Inc.—Stone Allstock; p. 463: Suzanne Szasz, Photo Researchers, Inc.; p. 466: Ellis Herwig, Stock Boston; p. 468: AP Wide World Photos; p. 471: Willie Hill, Jr., The Image Works; p. 472: AP Wide World Photos; p. 473: Joananthan Nourok, PhotoEdit Inc.

**Chapter 11** Page 476: Jeff Greenberg, PhotoEdit Inc.; p. 478: Joseph Palladino; p. 480: (c) 2006 Charles Barsotti from cartoonbank.com. All; p. 482: (T) David Young-Wolff, PhotoEdit Inc. (B) Left: Arnold Michlin, PhotoEdit Inc. (B) Right: PhotoEdit Inc.; p. 484: Penny Tweedie, Getty Images Inc.—Stone Allstock; p. 485: (c) Gabe Palmer/CORBIS. All Rights Reserved; p. 490: (c) ZITS—ZITS PARTNERSHIP KING FEATURERS SYNDICATE; p. 492: (T) Brooks/Brown, Photo Researchers, Inc. (B) AP Wide World Photos; p. 494: T. K. Wanstal, The Image Works; p. 498: Image Works/Mary Evans Picture Library Ltd; p. 503: Nick Gunderson, Nick & Flavia Gunderson; p. 509: Linda A. Cicero/Stanford News Service; p. 511: (c) CORBIS SYGMA; p. 512: Ryan McVay, Getty Images, Inc.—Photodisc.

**Chapter 12** Page 516: Getty Images, Getty Images, Inc.; p. 518: Stockbyte; p. 519: (T) Catherine Karnow, Woodfin Camp & Associates (B) AP Wide World Photos; p. 520: Steve Ueckert, AP Wide World Photos; p. 524: Frank Siteman; p. 528: Myrleen Ferguson, PhotoEdit Inc.; p. 529: (c) The New Yorker Collection 1992,Victoria Roberts from cartoonbank.com. All Rights Reserved; p. 531: Joseph Palladino; p. 534: Lewis R. Baxter, Jr., M.D.; p. 536: Reprinted by permissin of Sidney Harris.; p. 538: AP Wide World Photos p. 539: (T) AP Wide World Photos (B) (c) Bettmann/CORBIS. All Rights Reserved; p. 543: Library of Congress; p. 544: Tony Freeman, PhotoEdit Inc.; p. 545: John Griffin, The Image Works; p. 549: Frank Edwards/Fotos International/Archive PhotosGetty Images Inc.—Hulton Archive Photos; p. 550: Lewis R. Baxter, Jr., M.D.; p. 551: (c) The New Yorker Collection 2007 Tom Cheney from cartoonbank.com. All Rights Reserved; p. 555: Ray Stubblebine/Reuters, Corbis/ Bettmann; p. 556: Will Hart, Will Hart; p. 560: "Courtesy, Dr. Arthur W. Toga, Laboratory of Neuro Imaging"; p. 561: (L&R) Courtesy of Drs. E. Fuller Torrey and Daniel R. Weinberger, National Institute of Mental Health; p. 563: Edna Morlok; p. 565: AP Wide World Photos; p. 569: AP Wide World Photos; p. 570: Jeff Greenberg, Stock Boston

**Chapter 13** Page 572: Will Hart, Will Hart; p. 574: (L) Katsuyoshi Tanaka, Woodfin Camp & Associates (R) Corbis/Bettmann (B) Corbis/Bettmann; p. 575: (T) Culver Pictures, Inc. (B) Corbis/Bettmann; p. 576: (c) Andrew Holbrooke/CORBIS. All Rights Reserved; p. 577: David Young-Wolff, PhotoEdit Inc.; p. 581: Bill Aron, PhotoEdit Inc.; p. 583: (T) Carl Rogers Memorial Library (B) (C) The New Yorker Collection 1991 Robert Mankoff from cartoonbank.com. All Rights Reserved; p. 593: Bob Daemmrich, Stock Boston; p. 595: Reprinted with the permission of Harley Schwadron.; p. 599: Michael Newman, PhotoEdit Inc.; p. 604: Damien Lovegrove/SPL, Photo Researchers, Inc.; p. 605: (c) 2006 David Sipress from cartoonbank.com. All Rights Reserved; p. 607: W & D McIntyre, Photo Researchers, Inc.; p. 610: Sam Ogden/Science Photo Library, Photo Researchers, Inc.

**Chapter 14** Page 612: Jack Affleck, SuperStock, Inc.; p. 614: (c) 2005 Mike Twohy from cartoonbank.com. All rights reserved; p. 615: AP Wide World Photos; p. 619: Shannon Stapleton, Corbis/Reuters America LLC; p. 621: Benjamin Koziner, Phototake NYC; p. 624: (c) 2005 G. Primo Gottman, www.universalcat.org; p. 626: (L&R) Custom Medical Stock Photo, Inc.; p. 628: (T) John Chase (B) ImageState/International Stock Photography Ltd.; p. 630: (c) 2003 Creators Syndicate. All Rights Reserved. Used with Permission; p. 631: Rhoda Sidney, Stock Boston; p. 633: (c) 2005 David Sipress from cartoonbank.com. All Rights Reserved; p. 637: Esbin-Anderson, The Image Works; p. 639: Dan McCoy, Rainbow; p. 641: Jochen Tack, Peter Arnold, Inc.

**Chapter 15** Page 644: Getty Images Inc.—Stone Allstock; p. 646: AP Wide World Photos; p. 647: Stockbyte Royalty Free Photos Superstock Royalty Free; p. 648: Bob Daemmrich, Stock Boston; p. 652: AP Wide World Photos; p. 662: AP Wide World Photos; p. 663: Bob Daemmrich, Stock Boston; p. 671: Bruce Laurance, Workbookstock.com; p. 672: AP Wide World Photos; p. 673: Ed Bohon, Corbis/Stock Market; p. 676: (a, b, c, d) Copyright 1965 Stanley Milgram. From the film "Obedience," distributed by Pennsylvania State University, Media Sales; p. 678: Spencer Grant, PhotoEdit Inc.; p. 679: Bob Daemmrich, Stock Boston; p. 680: Masterfile Corporation; p. 684: Alan Reininger, Woodfin Camp & Associates

**Chapter 16** Page 688: (c) ZEFA/Masterfile; p. 690: Jonathan Nourok, PhotoEdit Inc.; p. 694: Michael Newman, PhotoEdit Inc.; p. 695: Joseph Palladino; p. 703: Weinberg Clark, Getty Images Inc.—Image Bank; p. 704: Dion Ogust, The Image Works; p. 711: (T) David Austen, Stock Boston (B) AP Wide World Photos

# Text, Table, and Figure Credits

The publishers acknowledge the copyright owners for permission to reprint the following copyrighted materials:

*Study Tips:* Carter, Carol; Bishop, Joyce; Kravits, Sarah; Block, Judy, *Keys to Success in College, Career and Life, Brief, 3rd,* © 2003. Electronically reproduced by permission of Pearson Education, Inc., Upper Saddle River, New Jersey.

*Page 6, Table 1-2:* From "The Assumptions We Make: Right Can Be Wrong" by Dr. Barney Beins as presented at the fifth Southeastern Conference on the Teaching of Psychology. Reprinted by permission of Dr. Barney Beins.

*Page 14, Figure 1-2:* From McKinney BA, McAndrew, FT (2000). Sexuality, Gender, and Sports. *Psi Chi Undergrad Research 5,* 152–158.

*Page 29, Figure 1-5:* www.nsf.gov/sbe/srs

*Page 35, Table 1-5:* Landrum, R. Eric; Davis, Stephen F., *Psychology Major, The: Career Options and Strategies for Success, 2nd,* © 2003. Electronically reproduced by permission of Pearson Education, Inc., Upper Saddle River, New Jersey.

*Page 45, Figure 2-3:* Shaver, Kelly G.; Tarpy, Roger M., *Psychology, 1st,* © 1993. Electronically reproduced by permission of Pearson Education, Inc., Upper Saddle River, New Jersey.

*Page 45, Figure 2-5:* N/A

*Page 53, Figure 2-8:* Morris, Charles G.; Maisto, Albert A., *Psychology: An Introduction, 11th,* © 2002. Electronically reproduced by permission of Pearson Education, Inc., Upper Saddle River, New Jersey.

*Page 70, Figure 2-17:* Morris, Charles G.; Maisto, Albert A., *Psychology: An Introduction, 11th,* © 2002. Electronically reproduced by permission of Pearson Education, Inc., Upper Saddle River, New Jersey.

*Page 72, Figure 2-18:* Morris, Charles G.; Maisto, Albert A., *Psychology: An Introduction, 11th,* © 2002. Electronically reproduced by permission of Pearson Education, Inc., Upper Saddle River, New Jersey.

*Page 73, Figure 2-19:* Kassin, Saul, *Psychology, 3rd,* © 2001. Electronically reproduced by permission of Pearson Education, Inc., Upper Saddle River, New Jersey.

*Page 74, Figure 2-20:* Morris, Charles G.; Maisto, Albert A., *Psychology: An Introduction, 11th,* © 2002. Electronically reproduced by permission of Pearson Education, Inc., Upper Saddle River, New Jersey.

*Page 75, Figure 2-21:* (A) Kassin, Saul, *Psychology, 3rd,* © 2001. Electronically reproduced by permission of Pearson Education, Inc., Upper Saddle River, New Jersey.

*Page 79, Figure 2-22:* Klein, Stephen, *Biological Psychology, 1st,* © 2000. Electronically reproduced by permission of Pearson Education, Inc., Upper Saddle River, New Jersey.

*Page 80, Figure 2-23:* Morris, Charles G.; Maisto, Albert A., *Psychology: An Introduction, 11th,* © 2002. Electronically reproduced by permission of Pearson Education, Inc., Upper Saddle River, New Jersey.

*Page 94, Figure 3-3:* From *Biopsychology, 2/e,* by J. Pinel, p. 189, fig. 702. Copyright © 1993 Allyn and Bacon. Reprinted by permission.

*Page 95, Figure 3-4:* Morris, Charles G.; Maisto, Albert A., *Understanding Psychologoy, 6th,* © 2003. Electronically reproduced by permission of Pearson Education, Inc., Upper Saddle River, New Jersey.

*Page 103, Figure 3-11:* Morris, Charles G.; Maisto, Albert A., *Psychology: An Introduction, 11th,* © 2002. Electronically reproduced by permission of Pearson Education, Inc., Upper Saddle River, New Jersey.

*Page 108, Figure 3-13:* From *Human Anatomy and Physiology* by Gaudin, Jones, Cotanche & Jones. Copyright © 1989 by International Thomson Publishing. Reprinted with permission from Anthony J. Gaudin.

*Page 111, Figure 3-14:* Shaver, Kelly G.; Tarpy, Roger M., *Psychology, 1st,* © 1993. Electronically reproduced by permission of Pearson Education, Inc., Upper Saddle River, New Jersey.

*Page 121, Figure 3-19:* Morris, Charles G.; Maisto, Albert A., *Psychology: An Introduction, 11th,* © 2002. Electronically reproduced by permission of Pearson Education, Inc., Upper Saddle River, New Jersey.

*Page 124, Figure 3-22:* From *Psychology, 2nd* Edition, by John Seamon and Douglas Kenrick. Copyright © 1994 by Prentice Hall. Reprinted by permission of John Seamon.

*Page 126, Figure 3-23:* From Stapel, D. A. & Kooman, W. 1997. Social Categorization and Perceptual Judgement of Size: When Perception is Social. *Journal of Personality and Social Psychology, 73,* p. 1183.

# A

Abecedarian Project, 368–369

**Abnormal** Term used to describe behavior that is rare or dysfunctional, causes personal distress, or deviates from social norms, **518**

Abnormal behavior
concept of insanity, 519–521
criteria of, 517–518
defined, 518–519
models of, 521–522

**Absolute threshold** Minimum amount of energy required for conscious detection of a stimulus 50% of the time by participants, **89**–90

**Accommodation**
Alteration of existing schemas to understand new information, **399**
In focusing, action of the ciliary muscles to change the shape of the lens, **94**

**Acculturative stress** The stress of adapting to a new culture, **618**

Acetylcholine (ACh), 55, 56

**Achievement** Manipulation of the environment according to established rules to attain a desired goal, **252**
motivation and, 252–253

Ackerman, Diane, 107, 109

Acquired immunodeficiency syndrome. *See* AIDS

Acquisition, 191–192

**Acronyms** A word formed by the initial letter(s) of the items to be remembered, **316**

**Acrostic** A verse or saying in which the first letter(s) of each word stands for a bit of information, **316**

**Action potential** Reversal in electrical charge of a neuron that occurs when the neuron fires, **60**–61

**Activation-synthesis hypothesis**
Explanation of dreams that suggests that they result when the cortex seeks to explain the high level of neuronal activity occurring during REM sleep, **158**

Actor-perceiver bias, 652

**Adaptation** Loss of sensitivity to a stimulus by the receptors as a result of continued presentation of that stimulus, **88**

Adaptors, 274

Addiction, 168

Adjustment, attitudes and, 654

Adler, Alfred, 505

**Adolescence** The years between approximately age 12 and age 20, **405**
AIDS and, 632
antisocial personality disorder and, 565
attitudes toward death, 426

commitments in, 409–410
eating disorders in, 409
family influences, 409
identity in, 408–409
intellectual changes in, 407–408
peer groups, 409
physical changes in, 405–407
puberty, 405
social changes in, 408–410

Adoption studies, schizophrenia and, 559, 560

Adrenal cortex, 48

**Adrenal glands** Pair of glands located at the top of each of the kidneys; they release a range of hormones including epinephrine and norepinephrine, **48**

Adrenocorticotropic hormone (ACTH), 47

**Adrenogenital syndrome** Condition caused by exposure to excessive amounts of androgens during the fetal period; can result in a female with genitals resembling those of males, **436**

**Adulthood, early** Period from approximately age 20 to age 40, **410**
attitudes toward death, 426–427
career development, 415
intellectual changes in, 411–412
marriage and children, 413–414
physical changes in, 410
social changes in, 412–415

**Adulthood, late** Period from approximately age 65 until death, **419**
attitudes toward death, 427
intellectual changes in, 423–424
life expectancy, 422–423
physical changes, 420–423
retirement, 424–426
social changes in, 424–426

**Adulthood, middle** Period from approximately age 40 to age 65, **415**
attitudes toward death, 427
burnout, 633–634
intellectual changes in, 416
midlife crisis, 417
physical changes, 415–416
social changes in, 416–418
stress during, 417–418

Affect
attitudes and, 654
attraction and, 658

**Afferent (sensory) nerves** Nerves that carry information from the receptors to the spinal cord and brain, **42**

Affiliation, motivation and, 237

African Americans, in psychology, 28–29

Age, mental, 353

**Ageism** The tendency to view the elderly in a negative manner, **424**

Age regression, hypnosis and, 162–163

**Aggression** Physical or psychological behavior that is performed with the intent of doing harm, **663**
alcohol and, 173
biological views of, 664
environmental conditions and, 664
fan violence, 712–713
frustration-aggression hypothesis, 664
gender differences, 459–460
hostile, 663
instrumental, 663
media and impact on, 225–226
sexual, 667–668
terrorism, 665–666
workplace violence, 666–667

Agitated depression, 543

Agitated dysphoria, 179

**Agonists** Drug that enhances the effects of a particular neurotransmitter, **57**–58

**Agoraphobia** Avoidance of public places or situations in which escape may be difficult should the individual develop incapacitating or embarrassing symptoms of panic, **528**

Agreeableness, 487

**AIDS (acquired immunodeficiency syndrome)** Viral disease transmitted via bodily fluids such as blood and semen, usually during sexual relations or by sharing needles used by a person infected with the human immunodeficiency virus (HIV); the virus attacks the body's immune system, resulting in vulnerability to infections and diseases, which eventually cause death, **631**–633
prenatal development and, 385

Ainsworth, Mary Salter, 395

Alarm stage, 615

Alcock, James, 128

**Alcoholism/alcohol abuse** Depressant psychoactive substance, also known as ethyl alcohol or ethanol, **169**
cultural differences and, 175
effects of, 170–173
factors that influence the use of, 174–175
myopia, 173
prenatal development and, 385

Alcohol use disorders identification test (AUDIT), 171

Alexithymia, 262

**Algorithm** A systematic procedure that is guaranteed to furnish the correct answer to a problem if it is followed correctly because the procedure involves all possible solutions, **328**–329

Allen, Andrea, 483

Allen, K., 596–597

*All Grown Up and No Place to Go* (Elkind), 407